# WTO ACCESSIONS AND TRADE MULTILATERALISM

G000036875

What have WTO accessions contributed to the rules-based multilateral trading system? What demands have been made by original WTO members on acceding governments? How have the acceding governments fared? This volume of essays offers critical readings on how WTO accession negotiations have expanded the reach of the multilateral trading system not only geographically but also conceptually, clarifying disciplines and pointing the way to their further strengthening in future negotiations. Members who have acceded since the WTO was established now account for twenty per cent of total WTO membership. In the age of globalization there is an increased need for a universal system of trade rules. Accession negotiations have been used by governments as an instrument for domestic reforms, and one lesson from the accession process is that there are contexts which lead multilateral trade negotiations to successful outcomes even in the complex and multi-polar twenty-first-century economic environment. The contributions in this volume illuminate the pressing question regarding why some trade negotiations fail, some stall and others succeed.

URI DADUSH is Senior Associate in the International Economics Program at the Carnegie Endowment for International Peace in Washington, DC. He is also President and Founder of Economic Policy International, LLC. He was formerly Director of Trade at the World Bank, a department he founded in the run-up to the WTO Doha Ministerial Conference.

CHIEDU OSAKWE is Director of the WTO Accessions Division, having acted as director of various divisions within the WTO Secretariat for many years. Before joining the WTO Secretariat, he was a Nigerian diplomat, serving at the Permanent Missions of Nigeria to the United Nations in New York, Geneva and the GATT/WTO.

# WTO ACCESSIONS AND TRADE MULTILATERALISM

Case Studies and Lessons from the WTO at Twenty

Edited by

URI DADUSH AND CHIEDU OSAKWE

CAMBRIDGE
UNIVERSITY PRESS

# CAMBRIDGE
## UNIVERSITY PRESS

University Printing House, Cambridge CB2 8BS, United Kingdom

Cambridge University Press is part of the University of Cambridge.

It furthers the University's mission by disseminating knowledge in the pursuit of education, learning and research at the highest international levels of excellence.

www.cambridge.org
Information on this title: www.cambridge.org/9781107093362

© World Trade Organization 2015

First published 2015

Printed in the United Kingdom by TJ International Ltd. Padstow Cornwall

*A catalogue record for this publication is available from the British Library*

*Library of Congress Cataloguing in Publication data*
WTO accessions and trade multilateralism : case studies and lessons from the WTO at twenty / edited by Uri Dadush and Chiedu Osakwe.
pages   cm
ISBN 978-1-107-09336-2 (Hardback) – ISBN 978-1-107-47224-2 (Paperback)   1. World Trade Organization.   2. International economic relations.   3. International trade.   4. International economic relations–Case studies.   5. International trade–Case studies.   I. Dadush, Uri B.
II. Osakwe, Chiedu   I. (Chiedu Igwebuike)
HF1385.W7776 2015
382′.92–dc23   2015006506

ISBN 978-1-107-09336-2 Hardback
ISBN 978-1-107-47224-2 Paperback

# DISCLAIMER

The opinions, arguments and conclusions contained in this publication are the sole responsibility of the individual authors. This includes contributions prepared by individual staff of the Secretariat of the World Trade Organization. None of the chapters purports to reflect the opinions or views of WTO members or the Secretariat, directly or indirectly. Any citation of the chapters should ascribe authorship to the individuals who have written the contributions. This book should not be viewed as advancing any form of legal interpretation or any policy position, and no views or analysis in this publication should be attributed to the WTO, its Secretariat or its members.

# CONTENTS

vii

     Plates appear between pages 456 and 457

# CONTRIBUTORS

**Editors**

CHIEDU OSAKWE is the Director of the WTO Accessions Division.

URI DADUSH is Senior Associate in the International Economics Program at the Carnegie Endowment for International Peace in Washington, and President and Founder of Economic Policy International, LLC.

**Contributors**

RAJESH AGGARWAL is Chief of the Business and Trade Policy Section at the International Trade Centre.

RAFAT AL-AKHALI is a former researcher on accessions in the WTO Accessions Division of the WTO.

ROBERT D. ANDERSON is Counsellor and Team Leader for Government Procurement and Competition Policy in the Intellectual Property Division of the WTO.

JOAN LAKER APECU is an economic affairs officer at the Council and Trade Negotiations Committee Division of the WTO.

ROBERTO AZEVÊDO is the Director-General of the WTO.

PRAJWAL BARAL is an independent consultant, providing services on climate finance, climate adaptation, technology transfer, international trade and sustainable investment.

PETRA BESLAĆ is a legal affairs officer in the Accessions Division of the WTO.

ALEXANDRA BHATTACHARYA is a legal intern at the South Centre in charge of the Innovation and Access to Knowledge Programme.

EMIL P. BOLONGAITA is a Distinguished Service Professor of Public Policy and Management and Deputy Director of the Carnegie Mellon University (Australia).

DIMITAR BRATANOV works at the Secretary-General's Office of the European Free Trade Association.

ANTONIA CARZANIGA is a counsellor in the Trade in Services Division at the WTO and Secretary to the WTO Council for Trade in Services.

HUI CHEN is a former researcher on accessions in the Accessions Division of the WTO.

CHARLOTTA FALENIUS is an associate expert at the International Trade Centre and manages technical assistance programmes for least-developed countries' accessions of the WTO.

TING FANG is a former researcher on accessions in the Accessions Division of the WTO.

DANIJELA GAČEVIĆ is a senior advisor at the Directorate for Multilateral and Regional Trade Cooperation and Foreign Economic Relations, Ministry of Economy, and has worked for the Ministry since 2007.

CARLOS GIMENO VERDEJO is a policy coordinator at the WTO Unit of the European Commission's Directorate-General for Trade.

JULIE-ANN GUIVARRA is the Director of the Services and Trade Negotiations Section in the Department of Foreign Affairs, in the Australian Government.

MONA HADDAD is Sector Manager of the International Trade Department, World Bank.

BERNARD M. HOEKMAN is the Director of the research strand "Global Economics: Multilateral Cooperation and Policy Spillovers" at the European University Institute.

CLAIRE H. HOLLWEG is a consultant at the International Trade Department of the World Bank.

VALERIE HUGHES is the Director of Legal Affairs Division of the WTO.

STEFÁN H. JÓHANNESSON is the Secretary of State of Iceland for EU Negotiations and the Chief Negotiator for Iceland's accession to the European Union.

LIDET KEBEDE is a former researcher on accessions in the Accessions Division of the WTO.

ALEXEI KIREYEV is a senior economist at the International Monetary Fund and the former IMF representative to the WTO.

CECILIA KLEIN is Senior Director for WTO Accessions of the Office of WTO and Multilateral Affairs of the US Trade Representative.

CLYDE KULL is Deputy Permanent Representative of Estonia to the European Union.

JUNEYOUNG LEE is a legal affairs officer in the Accessions Division of the WTO.

AIK HOE LIM is the Director of the WTO Trade and Environment Division.

MARK LINSCOTT is the Assistant US Trade Representative for WTO and multilateral affairs.

XIANKUN LU is Chairman of the WTO's Import Licence Committee and a Counsellor, Head of Division at the Permanent Mission of China to the WTO.

DMITRY LYAKISHEV is Director of the International Cooperation Department in the Central Bank of the Russian Federation (Bank of Russia).

MAXIM MEDVEDKOV is Head of the Department for Trade Negotiations of the Ministry of Economic Development of the Russian Federation and is the Chief Negotiator of Russia at the WTO.

ANNA CAROLINE MÜLLER is a legal affairs officer in the government procurement team of the Intellectual Property Division of the WTO.

SAIDRAHMON NAZRIEV from Tajikistan is Deputy Minister of Economic Development and Trade of the Republic of Tajikistan.

AMARA OKENWA is a former researcher on accessions in the Accessions Division of the WTO.

MAIKA OSHIKAWA is Counsellor of the Accessions Division of the WTO.

JOSEFITA PARDO DE LEÓN is a legal affairs officer in the Accessions Division of the WTO.

THOMAS PEN-CHUNG TUNG served as Liaison Officer in the Representative Office in Geneva, Switzerland throughout Chinese Taipei's accession process during the 1990s.

KHEMMANI PHOLSENA is the Minister of Industry and Commerce of Lao PDR.

ALBERTO PORTUGAL-PEREZ is a senior economist in the International Trade Department at the World Bank.

CHAM PRASIDH is the Minister for Commerce and ASEAN Economic Minister for Cambodia.

VALERIY PYATNITSKIY is the Ukrainian Government's Commissioner for European Integration and an adviser of the Vice Prime Minister of Ukraine.

JOAKIM REITER is Deputy Secretary-General at UNCTAD and Chairman of the Working Party on the accession of Liberia.

JÜRGEN RICHTERING is Head of the Market Access Intelligence Section in the Economic Research and Statistics Division of the WTO.

GORAN ŠĆEPANOVIĆ is the Deputy Minister of the Economy for Multilateral and Regional Trade Cooperation and Foreign Economic Relations of Montenegro.

MUSTAPHA SEKKATE is an economic affairs officer in the Accessions Division of the WTO.

ERIC NG SHING is a statistical officer in the Market Access Intelligence Section in the Economic Research and Statistics Division of the WTO.

ANDREY SLEPNEV is Minister for Trade (Member of the Board) of the Eurasian Economic Commission.

STEFFEN SMIDT is Permanent Representative of Denmark to the United Nations Office and other international organizations in Geneva, and Chairperson of the Sub-Committee on Least-Developed Countries of the WTO.

SAADALDEEN ALI BIN TALIB is the Minister of Industry and Trade of Yemen.

GEORGE TEBAGANA is a former researcher on accessions in the Accessions Division of the WTO.

ANNA VARYANIK is a legal affairs officer in the Accessions Division of the WTO.

BUAVANH VILAVONG is the Deputy Director-General of the Department of Import and Export, Ministry of Industry and Commerce of Lao PDR.

DAYONG YU is a senior statistical officer in the Market Access Intelligence Section in the Economic Research and Statistics Division of the WTO.

SVITLANA ZAITSEVA is the Head of the WTO Division at the Ministry of Economic Development and Trade of Ukraine.

RUTA ZARNAUSKAITE is a policy officer and trade negotiator at the Directorate-General for Trade of the European Commission.

# FOREWORD

Welcoming new members to the WTO is a highlight of my position as Director-General. The tangible sense of pride that I have felt from acceding governments – and their expectations of what membership will mean for their citizens – is a reminder of the importance of the multilateral trading system. Thirty-three new members have joined the WTO since it was established in 1995. At the time of writing we have 161 members, covering 98 per cent of the global economy, and there are over twenty more countries in the process of joining.

Increasing the membership of the WTO has always been a priority for our organization – not as an end in itself, but as a means to extend the coverage of multilateral trade rules. When a new country goes through the process of integrating into the multilateral trading system, we see tariffs lowered, market access increased, and the principles of non-discrimination, transparency and predictability extended. In addition, in the WTO's dispute settlement system, new members have access to one of the most highly regarded bodies in international law to help them to resolve trade disputes in a fair and objective manner. The overall effect of increasing the membership is therefore to boost growth and increase stability in the global economy.

This book seeks to tell the story of WTO accessions and show the importance of our work in this area. Over fifty contributors from inside and outside the WTO assess the results of our efforts and how they have served the trading system. As a result, these pages contain a mix of analysis, experience and lessons for the future. They highlight the value of accessions in increasing market access, supporting domestic reforms and contributing to rule making in the WTO.

The contributors include chief negotiators of original members; chief negotiators of members which have acceded since 1995; highly regarded economists, lawyers and academics; and experts from the WTO, World Bank, International Monetary Fund and the International Trade Centre.

In considering our work on accessions we should recall the genesis of this organization. The WTO was first conceived as part of the post-war Bretton Woods framework of global economic governance, with the aim of achieving greater openness, prosperity and stability among nations. This remains central to my vision of the WTO today. By bringing an increasing number of countries together in an atmosphere of cooperation and shared rules, the multilateral trading system is a means not just to achieve growth and development, but also to support peace.

I congratulate everyone who has been involved in producing this important book – particularly the contributors and the co-editors. It is an excellent contribution to the debate on the work of the WTO during our twentieth anniversary year.

Roberto Azevêdo
WTO Director-General

# ACKNOWLEDGEMENTS

Beyond the institutions and their elaborate structures and protocols, there are the *individuals*. They are the negotiators, aid and trade policy experts, researchers in academia and think tanks who have toiled constantly to promote open and predictable trade as a means to expand global welfare, prosperity and security. These individuals inside and outside the WTO are part of an ongoing mission. They are countless. The authors of the chapters in this book are part of this family. As editors of this book, we express our profound appreciation to all the authors whose contributions feature in this volume. We are immensely grateful for the time, energy and intellect they have invested in this project. The range of perspectives represented in these chapters will help to improve understanding of how accession to the WTO has contributed to the multilateral trading system, supported domestic reforms and fostered international cooperation. We also believe that the contributions in this volume hold important lessons for the WTO as it adapts to a global economy at a time of rapid and dynamic transformation. Many colleagues were indispensable in the preparation of this book. We received inspiration, strong support and thoughtful reflections, at every stage, from WTO Deputy Director-General David Shark, Graça Andresen-Guimaraes, Senior Adviser in the Office of WTO Director-General Azevêdo and Tristan Bauswein, Director of Administration and General Services Division in the WTO. For their editorial work in preparing the manuscript and refining it through many stages, we are very grateful indeed to Nadia Ferdi Demierre, Samantha Evans, Serge Marin-Pache, Anthony Martin, Helen Swain and Souda Tandara-Stenier. We received excellent research assistance from Shimelse Ali, Bennett Stancil and Zaahira Wyne. Last but not least, we are grateful to Finola O'Sullivan at Cambridge University Press whose 'interest' in the idea of this book was the spur to move ahead with this book project.

# ABBREVIATIONS

| | |
|---|---|
| ACDB | accession commitments database |
| ACWL | Advisory Centre on WTO Law |
| AD | anti-dumping |
| ADB | Asian Development Bank |
| AFT | WTO Aid for Trade |
| AGST | agricultural supporting tables |
| AMS | aggregate measurement of support |
| AoA | Agreement on Agriculture |
| ASEAN | Association of Southeast Asian Nations |
| BIT | bilateral investment treaty |
| CEFTA | Central European Free Trade Agreement |
| CET | common external tariff |
| CPIA | country policy and institutional assessment |
| CRN | WTO Central Registry of Notifications |
| CU | Customs Union of Belarus, Kazakhstan and Russia |
| CVD | countervailing duties |
| DDA | Doha Development Agenda |
| DFQF | duty-free, quota-free |
| DPO | development policy operations |
| DSU | Dispute Settlement Understanding |
| EAEU | Eurasian Economic Union |
| EC | European Commission |
| EFTA | European Free Trade Association |
| EIF | Enhanced Integrated Framework |
| ESCAP | Economic and Social Commission for Asia and the Pacific |
| EU | European Union |
| EurAsEC/EAEC | Eurasian Economic Community |
| FAO | Food and Agriculture Organization of the United Nations |
| FBR | Federal Board of Revenue |
| FDI | foreign direct investment |
| FRY | Federal Republic of Yugoslavia |
| FTA | free trade agreement |

| G-20 | Group of Twenty – a mix of the world's largest advanced and emerging economies |
| GATS | General Agreement on Trade in Services |
| GATT | General Agreement on Tariffs and Trade |
| GDP | gross domestic product |
| GPA | Agreement on Government Procurement |
| GSP | Generalised System of Preferences |
| GVC | global value chains |
| IBR | International Bank for Reconstruction |
| ICRG | International Country Risk Guide |
| ICSID | International Centre for Settlement of Investment Disputes |
| ICTSD | International Centre for Trade and Sustainable Development |
| IDB | WTO Integrated Data Base |
| IEC | International Electrotechnical Commission |
| IEF | International Energy Forum |
| IGA | Informal Group on Accessions |
| ILO | International Labour Organization |
| IMF | International Monetary Fund |
| INRs | initial negotiating rights |
| IOM | International Organization for Migration |
| IP | intellectual property |
| IPPC | International Plant Protection Convention |
| ISPMs | International Standards for Phytosanitary Measures |
| ITA | Information Technology Agreement |
| ITC | International Trade Centre |
| LDC | least-developed country |
| MENA | Middle East and North Africa region |
| MFN | most-favoured nation |
| MFTR | Memorandum on the Foreign Trade Regime |
| MONSTAT | Statistical Office of Montenegro |
| MRL | maximum residue level |
| NAFTA | North American Free Trade Agreement |
| NAMA | non-agricultural market access |
| NAV | non-ad valorem |
| NDRC | National Development and Reform Commission |
| NGO | non-governmental organization |
| NME | non-market economy |
| NTM | non-tariff measures |
| ODCs | other duties or charges |
| OECD | Organisation for Economic Co-operation and Development |
| OIE | World Organisation for Animal Health |
| OPEC | Organization of Petroleum Exporting Countries |

| PTA | preferential trade agreement |
| RAMs | recently acceded members |
| RCEP | regional comprehensive economic partnership |
| RTA | regional trade agreement |
| S&D | special and differential treatment |
| SCM | subsidies and countervailing measures |
| SES | single economic space |
| SFRY | Socialist Federal Republic of Yugoslavia |
| SMEs | small and medium-sized enterprises |
| SNA | System of National Accounts |
| SOEs | state-owned enterprises |
| SPS | sanitary and phytosanitary measures |
| STEs | state trading enterprises |
| TBT | technical barriers to trade |
| TF | Trade Facilitation |
| TFEU | Treaty on the Functioning of the European Union |
| TISA | Trade in Services Agreement |
| TPP | Trans-Pacific Partnership |
| TPR | Trade Policy Review |
| TPRM | Trade Policy Review Mechanism |
| TRIMs | trade-related investment measures |
| TRIPs | trade-related aspects of intellectual property rights |
| TRQ | tariff rate quota |
| TTIP | Transatlantic Trade and Investment Partnership |
| UNCITRAL | United Nations Commission on International Trade Law |
| UNCPC | United Nations' Central Product Classification |
| UNCTAD | United Nations Conference on Trade and Development |
| UNECE | United Nations Economic Commission for Europe |
| UNIDO | United Nations Industrial Development Organization |
| UPOV | International Union for the Protection of New Varieties of Plants |
| USAID | United States Agency for International Development |
| VAT | value-added tax |
| VCLT | Vienna Convention on the Law of Treaties |
| WCO | World Customs Organization |
| WEF | World Economic Forum |
| WIPO | World Intellectual Property Organization |
| WP | working party |
| WPR | working party report |
| WTO | World Trade Organization |

# EDITORS' NOTE

The analyses in the chapters in this book were finalised at the end of December 2014. Since then the Republic of Seychelles acceded to the World Trade Organization (WTO) on 26 April 2015. This expanded total WTO membership from 160 to 161.

The chapters in this book are, however, based on the analysis of the results from the accession-specific commitments of the 32 Article XII members which had joined the WTO up to the end of 2014. The relevant chapters include a footnote to indicate this.

On the pace of the current accession negotiations work programme, the negotiations for the membership of the Republic of Kazakhstan should be concluded before the summer break of 2015. Kazakhstan should become the 162nd member of the WTO by the Tenth WTO Ministerial Conference in December 2015.

# PART I

WTO accessions, the trading system
and the global economy

# A reflection on accessions as the WTO turns twenty

URI DADUSH AND CHIEDU OSAKWE

## ABSTRACT

*As the WTO celebrates its twentieth year, it is appropriate to ask what WTO accessions have contributed to the rules-based multilateral trading system. What demands have been made by the original and incumbent WTO members on acceding governments? How have the acceding governments fared? This chapter finds that WTO accessions have expanded the reach of the trading system, not only geographically but conceptually, by clarifying disciplines and pointing the way to their further strengthening in future negotiations. Members who have acceded under Article XII of the General Agreement on Tariffs and Trade now account for 20 per cent of total membership of the WTO. Meanwhile, with globalisation, the increased prevalence, complexity and capillarity of international exchange has greatly increased the need for a universal system of trade rules. Crucially, accession negotiations have been used by governments as an instrument for wide-ranging domestic reforms, including by means of far-reaching new legislation that has effectively changed the business landscape. In several instances, the WTO accession negotiating platform has been used for the much broader purpose of facilitating new, closer, geopolitical relationships. As the negotiating arm of the WTO continuously adapts, the success of accession negotiations also points to the opportunities inherent in variable negotiating configurations, such as plurilaterals around specific issues. There is also considerable scope for improving the process of accession negotiations to ensure greater transparency, streamlining and fairness.*

The analyses in the chapters in this book were finalised at the end of December 2014. Since then the Republic of Seychelles acceded to the World Trade Organization (WTO) on 26 April 2015. This expanded total WTO membership from 160 to 161. Please see the editors' note.

Nations home to some two billion people have become integrated into the global trading system since the Berlin Wall fell in 1989. In the intervening period, despite the damage wrought in recent years by the Great Recession, the growth of developing countries has been rapid, absolute poverty has fallen sharply and trade and foreign investment – especially in developing countries – have outstripped the rate of advance of world gross domestic product (GDP) by a wide margin. Trade in intermediate products has grown even more rapidly than trade in final goods and services, causing trade and production to become increasingly and inextricably intertwined. As a share of world GDP, trade in goods and services has surged over the last twenty years, from about 30 to 50 per cent.

These broadly favourable outcomes can be attributed primarily to domestic reforms that have re-oriented economies towards the market – themselves the result of big political and ideological shifts – as well as to the application of transportation and communication technologies developed over many decades. In this long process, widespread trade liberalisation, supported by the ideas and mechanisms that underpin the WTO and its predecessor the General Agreement on Tariffs and Trade (GATT), have played a significant role. Most recently, accession to the WTO under Article XII in the Marrakash Agreement Establishing the World Trade Organization has provided an important framework to help effect the transition of twenty formerly planned economies to a market-based system as well as twelve others classified as developing countries by the World Bank. China, the largest Article XII member, now plays a locomotive role in world trade comparable to that of the United States. As a group, China together with the other developing countries as classified by the World Bank appear destined to hold by far the largest share of world trade within a generation. In 2015, WTO rules and disciplines extended the rule of trade law to 98 per cent of world trade between its 161[1] members, of which the 128 original members' share of world trade is 80.1 per cent and that of the thirty-three Article XII members is 17.6 per cent. Another twenty-two governments accounting for 2.1 per cent of world trade are in the process of accession. When their accession negotiations are concluded, only 0.1 per cent of world trade will be outside the rules-based global economy.

---

[1] The WTO General Council formally approved the Accession Package of Seychelles in December 2014. After parliamentary ratification by Seychelles of the formally approved package by the WTO General Council in December 2014, and twenty days after the deposit of the WTO instrument of accession of Seychelles, Seychelles became the 161st member of the WTO.

Unlike accession to the GATT, which included a large number of original members and countries that acceded, virtually automatically under colonial preferences, accession to the WTO is a hard and long-drawn-out process. Accession negotiations typically last about ten years and require far-reaching commitments by the acceding government (or separate customs territory), as well as the acceptance of disciplines and binding commitments which in several instances go beyond those applied to existing members, and occasionally even acquiescence to lesser rights – at least temporarily. This procedure has sometimes been characterised in the development and legal literature as 'unfair' to new members, as discriminatory, arbitrary and as possibly undermining the legitimacy of the WTO as a body of law.

Others, however, have argued that while core WTO principles and disciplines such as transparency and non-discrimination are constant, accession terms relating to the scope and extent of liberalisation can and should vary, as they do vary greatly for original members. All WTO commitments, under Article XII or otherwise arrived at, are the result of reciprocal and legally binding concessions in negotiations, under a 'Legal Single Undertaking', which are at the core of the way the WTO functions. In the case of Article XII economies, the argument goes, concessions must be measured against the prize of secure access to essentially the totality of their export markets – a big prize indeed.

Both sides of this ongoing argument are presented in this volume, as are ideas to improve the workings of accession. However, the main focus of the volume is on outcomes, not process. Specifically, has WTO accession helped to stimulate reforms, and increase trade, investment and economic growth in Article XII members? Did accession strengthen the multilateral trading system? A review of the most recent and volu-minous economic literature on this question, as well as of the writings presented here, spanning the views of negotiators as well as development practitioners and trade experts, strongly suggests that – even though accessions pose negotiating challenges and entail a drawn-out and difficult process of domestic institutional reform – the answer to both questions is in the affirmative.

A recurring theme among the authors of this volume is that countries that undertook the most far-reaching trade reforms in the course of accession negotiations – either because they were so inclined, or because more was demanded of them, or both – tended to perform better than those for which the process was much less demanding: Article XII members did better on various scores than the world average, and those

Article XII members that undertook the most far-reaching commitments did even better. Without claiming causality – which is difficult to establish given the impossibility of controlled experiments – it is nevertheless worth noting that Article XII members, including China, increased their share of world trade by 125 per cent between 1995 and 2013. Excluding China, the share increase was 42 per cent.

Improved governance and application of the rule of law most probably played a significant role in effecting these outcomes. The role played by governance in achieving poverty reduction and growth has long been recognised, but governance reforms are hard to make and must overcome opposition. It turns out that WTO accession can provide the political push as well as useful instruments for reform. Rules such as those on transparency, non-discrimination and the necessity of and adherence to international standards, based on science, make rent-seeking more difficult. WTO agreements such as on government procurement, which most acceding governments agree to join 'upon accession', help to address an area where rent-seeking or outright corruption is most prevalent.

The willingness of nations to embark on the protracted and costly process of accession and to persevere until it is concluded is a measure of the value they place on membership. After all, sovereign entities choose to join the WTO. In the words of Long Yongtu, the chief negotiator for China's WTO accession at the First China Round Table on LDC Accessions in Beijing in 2012, 'China used the WTO accession process to leverage and accelerate its domestic reforms. Acceding Governments should consider WTO accession as part and parcel of the national strategy to strengthen [their] development efforts and strengthen [their] external trade.' In this book, Chinese negotiator Xiankun Lu adds that 'countries choose to be part of the rules-based multilateral trading system for different reasons. But there is a common reason behind each and every accession: i.e., it is overwhelmingly in their interest to do so.' Even though they lament the difficulties of accession, negotiators from Article XII members who contributed to this volume uniformly recognise the value of the process, and not just of the outcome. They emphasise four aspects in particular: the importance of WTO accession-triggered reforms as a platform for their own domestic reforms, as a bulwark against back-tracking, as a means to secure market access for their exports and as a clear signal that their country is open for business and wants to become an attractive place to invest.

The numerous dispute settlement decisions which refer to Accession Protocols and related working party reports show that these documents, which sometimes run to thousands of pages, have become an integral part of WTO law. Article XII members appear as complainants in thirty-four disputes, while dozens of other countries appear as interested third parties. The more demanding conditions typically placed on these new members have also pushed out the frontier of WTO disciplines across a very broad front – ranging from the framework for making and enforcing trade and trade-related policies, to setting sanitary and phytosanitary (SPS) standards, to adopting disciplines in areas ranging from investment, energy, intellectual property and state (either owned, controlled, invested or trading) enterprises. Accession Protocols have thus strengthened the multilateral trading system not just by extending its geographic reach, but also by providing an important source of precedent for negotiations, promoting adherence to other WTO agreements, such as the plurilateral Agreement on Government Procurement (GPA) and pointing to the system's possible evolution. They have, moreover, provided many opportunities for clarifying and giving greater precision to the rules of the WTO.

We believe that an important contribution of this volume is to show that – even as the Doha negotiations continue to face strong headwinds, if not to stall – the multilateral trading system has advanced impressively: the achievement of near-universal coverage of WTO rules and disciplines has helped spur reforms among its Article XII members, has greatly enhanced the value of the institution to its original members and has also increased its gravitational pull on the relatively small number of countries that remain outside it. The increased importance of trade and foreign investment in economic activity, and the proliferation of closely integrated international production networks across many interdependent industries, made possible by a rules-based system, further reinforce the importance of the WTO as an arbitrator of disputes and raise the stakes on the adoption of new rules and disciplines in the future.

This volume aims to provide a comprehensive review of accession to the WTO and its implications for original members, Article XII members, acceding governments and for the global trade system. It is articulated in five parts. Part I reviews the global economic context and the trends in world trade within which the accession process occurs, as well as the impact of accession on macroeconomic policy and structural reforms. Part II examines some of the effects of accessions on WTO law and on the broader trading system. Part III provides the perspectives of accession negotiators, from the standpoint of Article XII members, original members and chairs of working groups. Part IV takes a horizontal cut across accessions, examining the salient features of accession commitments by subject matter, such as services or state enterprises. Part V concludes by examining the potential of accessions as building blocks for the multilateral trading system in the future. In the remainder of this introductory chapter, we summarise the book's findings on the effects of accession on Article XII members, as well as on the rules-based multilateral trading system.

## The effects of accession on Article XII members

The thirty-three Article XII members are a diverse group. Most were classified as developing countries by the World Bank at the time when their accession working parties were established. Saudi Arabia and Russia are now recognised as high-income oil exporters. At the other extreme, seven are least-developed countries (LDCs), some of the world's poorest countries. Twenty, including Russia, are formerly centrally planned economies, several of which have become European Union (EU) members, and another ten are middle-income and low-income developing countries which decided to embark on reform later than their peers – usually because of internal or international conflicts or an ideological bent in favour of self-sufficiency. The twenty-two countries currently in the process of accession constitute a diverse group of oil exporters, LDCs, formerly planned economies and countries that continue to struggle to resolve civil and/or cross-border conflicts.

Dating the time taken to accede requires a benchmark, since the formal process may be preceded by informal negotiations that can take years. The average time elapsed between establishment of the accession working party and actual accession approval by consensus in a General Council or Ministerial Meeting is ten years, varying from the shortest – three years in the case of Kyrgyz Republic – to the longest – twenty years, in the case of Seychelles. Other countries, for example, Algeria, whose working party was established under the GATT in 1987 and is still in progress, have been in negotiations for even longer.

Under the terms of accession, members demand of the acceding government WTO-consistency in its domestic laws and regulations. Moreover, members request that the acceding government take on specific obligations on rules as well as market access. The acceding government can request concessions which pertain largely to transitional periods for the elimination of WTO-inconsistent measures. They may also have 'red lines' for which they may seek differentiated treatment.

Their ability to win such concessions depends on the power of the arguments presented and on concrete evidence. An example would be limits on imports of alcoholic beverages in Muslim countries on religious grounds. In another instance, Russia obtained 'a transitional concession' for its WTO-inconsistent measures in the automobile sector. However, it is a fact that – as a general rule – the fundamentals of WTO *acquis* are taken as given and cannot be changed. Accession is by consensus of the membership which means that – at least in theory – objection by even one or a small number of members can delay or block the process. Since accession is a one-off event, and the stakes for the country acceding are large, it represents a unique opportunity for original members to make demands, which can range from pressing for a specific commercial interest to a desire to see the acceding government's regulatory system upgraded. Although there are acknowledged best practices and norms that guide negotiations, the negotiations are unequal, in the sense that demands on the acceding government can be made by any of the members, and there is no rulebook that places hard-and-fast limits on what can be demanded. The outcome is that typically the acceding government takes on more demanding obligations than original members, which did not have to go through the same process. These obligations can take the form of more stringent commitments within established areas such as tariff bindings, or they can be 'WTO+' (or WTO-plus), commitments in areas for which there is no precedent. Yet the fact remains that the results from this process have strengthened the WTO as a rules-based system and taken it further, with positive knock-on effects for the global economy. The latter are discussed more fully in the next part, which reviews the effect of Accession Protocols on the evolution of WTO disciplines.

The extent of commitments by Article XII members in established areas is best understood by comparing original and Article XII members with regard to their tariff concessions and specific commitments in Goods and Services Schedules. While original members bound about three-quarters of their tariff lines, Article XII members have agreed to bind nearly 100 per cent. Moreover, the average bound rate for original members is 45.5 per cent, whereas it is 13.8 per cent for Article XII members. Article XII members also committed to liberalise over twice as many service subsectors as original members. However, differences in applied tariffs were much smaller, 7.3 per cent on average for Article XII members versus 9.7 per cent for original members, suggesting that while Article XII members gave up much of their 'policy space', so-called, in protection on joining the WTO, the actual adjustment in their trade regimes was relatively modest, especially considering the fact that adjustment typically occurs over the course of a negotiation which takes many years.

Why were Article XII members willing to engage in protracted negotiations and undertake these commitments? The contributions by negotiators of Article XII members in this volume give considerable weight to the security afforded by the WTO membership on access to foreign markets, as might be expected. However, the overall picture that emerges is one that places even greater importance on the domestic transformation required by WTO membership. In the words of the Cambodian negotiator Cham Prasidh, '[b]eing a WTO member is one of the main pillars of Cambodia's successful economic performance. This does not mean, however, that membership automatically leads to trade-led economic development ... Post-accession policies in areas such as commercial legislation, supply-side development ... trade facilitation ... will ultimately determine the extent to which WTO membership triggers an acceleration'. The negotiators Khemmani Pholsena and Buavanh Vila-vong of Lao PDR, whose accession took fifteen years, write that 'Lao PDR used the WTO accession process as a very useful tool to implement its decision to establish a market economy ... accession ... allowed Lao PDR to apply international best practices ... [and] ... help[ed] create an enabling environment for business and trade in the country'. Thus, while the thirty-three Article XII members accepted approximately 1,361 specific obligations that, pursuant to the WTO Accession Protocol, are integral to the Marrakesh Agreement Establishing the World Trade Organization (WTO Agreement), they also enacted approximately 7,356 WTO-consistent laws and associated implementing regulations across the principal areas of the foreign trade regime.

Correspondingly, the negotiators of original members also place great emphasis on facilitating trade-supportive domestic reforms in new members, and not just on securing their own market access. Thus, EU negotiator Ruta Zarnauskaite refers to the WTO as a 'unique platform to anchor growth' targeting reforms and writes '[i]t is for these reasons that the European Union has been systematically engaged in consultations with acceding governments not only on the market access side ... but also, and with no less vigour, on the rules side'.

As discussed above, numerous commentators have been critical of WTO accession, as a process that – in their eyes – demands too much and takes too long, especially as the Article XII members are predominantly developing countries and even more especially as the group includes LDCs, with limited resources and capacity, and fragile economic structures with limited or non-existent safety nets. Some have even suggested that, in actual practice, WTO accession represents the opposite of what is intended by special and differential treatment, a form of discrimination that hits the poorest countries harder, and they point to instances of arbitrary treatment by members intent on gaining a particular trade advantage or bent on a political agenda.

Any reasonable assessment of these issues must in the end rest in part on an evaluation of the outcomes observed in the countries that have acceded. The analysis by World Bank economists in Chapter 4 suggests that – as a group, excluding and including China – Article XII members have done better in comparison with world averages with respect to exports, imports and foreign direct investment (FDI). They also saw improvements in credit ratings and various measures of policy and institutional strength. Key to understanding these outcomes is the fact that states and separate customs territories in the process of accession have fairly systematically embarked on more far-reaching domestic reforms – ranging from macroeconomic policy to structural reforms such as those that affect the business climate, banking system, education and health provision, labour markets and competition, and the freedom to import and to invest. Indeed, in the view of these analysts, '[a]pplying for WTO membership signals the willingness of a government to undertake deep reforms regardless ... when countries decide to join they are already thinking of a reform process that is wider than the WTO itself'.

Given the interplay of many factors, the correlation between WTO accession and favourable trade and investment outcomes hardly constitutes definitive scientific proof that WTO accession has boosted the performance of Article XII members. What can be said is that the correlation is consistent with the basic idea that making trade possible and predictable, and simultaneously embarking on domestic reforms that improve the business climate, will pay dividends in terms of increased productivity and living standards – an idea that provides the rationale for the existence of the WTO in the first place.

The World Bank findings are broadly consistent with the evolving consensus in the academic literature on the subject, also reviewed in Chapter 8. Initial research findings on the impact of GATT/WTO membership on trade outcomes had found no significant impact. Subsequent research has overturned this conclusion, using successively more refined metrics of what in shorthand can be described as 'membership'. For example, many former colonies participated in the GATT even though they were not formally members, biasing downward the estimates of the beneficial effect of formal membership. Subsequent analyses showed that those GATT/WTO members that undertook extensive obligations saw better trade performance than those that did not. For example, trade has grown relatively rapidly in industrial countries and in recently acceded developing countries and separate customs territories. These countries have committed to much greater tariff cuts than developing countries that joined the GATT with minimal commitments during the early days. Even more recent research has shown a strong correlation between the number and extent of WTO commitments and favourable outcomes. In the same vein, some recent studies identify a substantial growth dividend in the wake of WTO accession, lasting some five years or so, a dividend that is more pronounced in countries which undertook deeper reforms and more extensive WTO accession commitments.

### The effects of accessions on the world trading system

Accessions have expanded the reach of the multilateral trading system. But, as already mentioned, the process of accession is lengthy and costly, and questions have been raised about the legitimacy of some of the demands addressed to Article XII members. Moreover, when combined with an increasingly complex agenda, the 'larger' membership at the establishment of the WTO in 1995, and the addition of a further large number of 'new' Article XII members, with vastly diverse economic structures and levels of income, has introduced complexity to trade rounds. This is despite the fact that Article XII members have often espoused higher rather than lower levels of ambition in negotiations and expressed a preference for broader rather than narrower negotiating agendas.

As already shown, accessions have expanded market access and made it more predictable for both original and Article XII members. Original members have seen the coverage of WTO disciplines apply to an additional 20 per cent or so of their export markets, while Article XII members and separate customs territories have gained secure access for the near totality of their trade for the first time. All WTO members benefit from this 'network effect', making membership of the institution of greater value to all. This is a crucial beneficial effect of accessions but it is only a part of the story. Accessions have strengthened the multilateral trading system in three other quite distinct ways: by reinforcing the geopolitical underpinnings of a globally encompassing trading system; by embedding trade more firmly in reformed domestic laws in Article XII members; and by adding to WTO law, clarifying and deepening existing rules and disciplines and enabling 'WTO-plus' innovation in many areas to strengthen and advance the rules-based system.

The world trading system does not operate in a vacuum – like all other forms of international cooperation it is conditioned by the core values and the geopolitical interests of its members. Similarly, accession to the WTO is a 360 degree process, one that cannot be neatly compartmentalised into economic or legal aspects on the one hand and international relations on the other, but is motivated by and entails consideration of each of these dimensions. By facilitating the integration of economies with disparate economic systems at the end of the Cold War and accelerating the convergence of these systems, accessions have simultaneously helped improve the political understanding and orderly international relations that must underpin trade. Moreover, by establishing a common set of rules and providing an arbitration mechanism, the WTO has reduced the risk of commercial disputes between former adversaries escalating dangerously.

The systemic change of which accessions have been both an outcome and a driver will not be easy to reverse. As this volume shows, the domestic market-oriented reforms that have accompanied accessions have often been transformational; they are not typically only at the margin. The domestic reflection of accession-specific commitments can be found in the laws, as discussed and shown in Table 9.1. The security afforded by WTO disciplines and related market reforms has made investment in Article XII members more attractive, and has also had a beneficial effect on investment in original members. It should be recognised that once large numbers of enterprises become dependent on foreign markets and on imported inputs to serve both domestic and foreign markets – the integration of global production chains – domestic interests in favour of openness are strengthened. The resilience of the world trading system, its resistance to protectionism, depends not only on the international laws and regulations which govern its functioning, but also on the core values of the market economy, the acceptance of the rule of law and of good governance principles at home – in short, the support afforded to it by members' domestic legal and political systems.

Accession Protocols, and the Working Party Reports and Goods and Services Schedules which accompany them, typically run to thousands of pages. They result from multilateral, bilateral and plurilateral negotiations of the applicant with dozens of countries, and require a decision by consensus of the WTO membership. Although largely flying below the radar, accessions have thus come to constitute one of the most active and continuously ongoing negotiating agendas of world trade. The Accession Protocols are integral to the WTO Agreement, and have been cited in close to thirty disputes, of which close to twenty have proceeded to Panel stage. These disputes have included both original and Article XII members as complainants and defendants, as well as several interested parties in each instance. Panels have found, and the Appellate Body has upheld, that specific accession commitments in accession Working Party Reports are enforceable in WTO Dispute Settlement, and that the WTO Accession Protocol is an integral part of the WTO Agreement, signalling a major extension of the disciplines at the core of the global trading system.

In the process of negotiating accessions, many opportunities have arisen to apply, deepen and refine existing rules and disciplines, as well as to extend WTO rules and disciplines into new areas, so-called 'WTO-plus'. Several of these areas have been the object of negotiation under the Doha Development Agenda, with little progress. What follows are some salient examples, drawn mainly from the technical chapters in this volume, which do not constitute a comprehensive list.

## Trade in services

A striking feature of the services accession commitments has been the depth and range of domestic regulation-type disciplines which a number of Article XII members have undertaken. Out of thirty-three Article XII members, eleven have undertaken 'horizontal and sector-specific obligations' on policies affecting trade in services. These specific obligations go further than the existing provisions of the General Agreement on Trade in Services (GATS) Article VI (Domestic Regulation) as they require acceding members to ensure that their licensing procedures and conditions are transparent, reasonable, impartial and no more burdensome than necessary. The accession-specific obligations on the so-called 'necessity test' are an example of this. This is a powerful discipline which would allow WTO members to challenge other members on the trade-restrictiveness of their measures.

In heavily regulated sectors, such as financial services and telecommunication services, accession-specific services obligations have included, for example, a specific time frame for allowing foreign services providers; non-discriminatory treatment when regulatory changes occur; and the obligation of the acceding government to consult with members on new regulations in a specific sector.

## Market access

Accession market access negotiations have endeavoured to eliminate the frequent use of complex compound and specific duties, replacing them with *ad valorem* equivalent duties (AVEs). These AVEs have been confirmed at technical verification meetings of bilateral market access agreements between signatory members. The AVE is a transparency measure. Moreover, compared to the original members, Article XII members have a significantly higher coverage of tariff lines subject to restrictions that prevent breaching bound tariffs. In Goods Schedules, the use of initial negotiating rights (INRs) – a GATT creation – by members must meet a transparency test. The INR is a negotiating modality which allows for the 'right of a member' to request tariff negotiations and concessions, even if it is not a principal supplier with a substantial trade interest. This is a systemic right. In its evolution, consequent on accession negotiations, it has become a tool by which members limit the capacity of other members to arbitrarily, or without cause, seek an increase in their tariff bindings. Accession negotiations have consolidated transparency in the use of this mechanism and reinforced safeguards against market access instability in goods schedules.

## Agriculture

Most Article XII members with trade-distorting aggregate measurements of support (AMS) have had them bound, subject to reduction commitments. With the exception of one member, Article XII members have also committed to bind their export subsidies at zero upon accession. This is consistent with paragraph 20 of the Agreement on Agriculture and has been one of the central objectives of the Doha Round negotiations on agriculture. It is worth noting that recent studies show that membership of the GATT/WTO increased agricultural trade by 68 per cent, compared with 31 per cent for non-agricultural trade. The results from WTO accessions have contributed significantly to the market reform direction in the Agreement on Agriculture.

### SPS standards

SPS accession commitments undertaken by thirty-three Article XII WTO members have exercised a significant influence on WTO jurisprudence, clarifying and strengthening WTO law. Given the potential for hidden protection 'behind the border', special attention has been paid to SPS measures in accession negotiations, so that some ninety SPS accession-specific commitments have been undertaken by Article XII WTO members. The SPS chapters in working party reports are consistently the most voluminous and detailed, covering items such as shelf life and expiry dates, maximum residue levels, risk assessments, precautionary measures and international standards, audits, listing and de-listing of establishments, veterinary certificates, etc. The obligations accepted by Russia in this area were the most comprehensive to date, on import permits, transit requirements, veterinary certificates, establishment approval procedures and inspections. This reflected a desire by members to guard against the uncertainty caused by rapidly changing regulations in the Eurasian Economic Union between Armenia, Belarus, Kazakhstan, Kyrgyz Republic and Russia.

### Government procurement

Of the thirty-three Article XII members, twenty-three undertook GPA-related commitments, and seven subsequently completed accession to the GPA. Out of the ten WTO members that are currently seeking accession to the GPA, nine undertook commitments related to joining the GPA at the time of their WTO accessions, while five other Article XII WTO members that have not yet initiated their accession to the GPA have also undertaken commitments to eventually do so. Thus this is an example of WTO accession negotiations strengthening not only the main body of WTO disciplines but also adherence to this key plurilateral agreement.

### Energy

Although there are no specific rules on energy *per se* in WTO Agreements, all tradable energy goods and services are covered by the GATT and GATS respectively. Energy-specific commitments were first undertaken by Ukraine in 2008 in its Accession Protocol. The commitment confirmed guaranteed freedom of transit for energy. This guarantee was subsequently confirmed in the Accession Protocols of Montenegro, Russia and Tajikistan. These commitments have enhanced legal certainty and reinforced the provisions of GATT Article V. The obligations assumed by these Article XII members clarified that their laws, regulations and other measures governing the transit of goods included energy. Accession-specific commitments undertaken with regard to 'pipeline transportation' are of particularly notable geopolitical importance. Ukraine and Montenegro made commitments on transparency and non-discrimination for pipeline transportation of fuels. These energy-related accession-specific obligations go beyond those made by original members and could form the basis of future commitments by countries still in the process of accession and also provide a broader energy framework within the rules-based multilateral trading system.

Specific to energy trade, obligations on pricing policies were also undertaken by Saudi Arabia and Russia. These stipulated that they would operate on the basis of normal commercial considerations, based on recovery of costs and profit. The accession obligations on energy pricing did not eliminate price controls, but essentially brought price controls within the regulatory framework of the WTO, subjected them to commercial considerations and improved transparency by annexing to these binding commitments 'lists' specifically identifying the goods and services subject to price controls.

## Rule-making

Accession results show that the majority of Article XII members have undertaken commitments stating that sub-central or local government entities will have no autonomous authority regarding subsidies, taxation, trade policy or any other measures covered by WTO provisions. An even larger number committed to central government authorities eliminating or nullifying measures taken by sub-central or local authorities that were inconsistent with WTO provisions, and enforcing these provisions without requiring affected parties to petition through the courts or requiring formal legal proceedings. Nearly all Article XII members accepted specific obligations that the provisions of the WTO Agreement would be applied uniformly throughout the customs territory of the new member. It is worth noting, in contrast, that several original members have limitations on the uniform application of the WTO Agreement across the totality of their customs territories.

## Appeal

The Reports of Working Parties of twenty-six Article XII members recorded discussions on the right to appeal against administrative decisions, while several accepted commitments regarding the establishment of a system of appeal, judicial review or a system of commercial courts.

## Export duties

Although export duties have been prohibited in several free trade agreements (FTAs) and some bilateral trade agreements, the specific obligations in WTO Accession Protocols represent the best efforts, so far, to discipline the use of export duties, substantively and multilaterally. Nearly half of all Article XII members have accepted accession-specific obligations on the application of export duties. Specifically, these range from obligations to 'abide' by the provisions of the WTO Agreement; 'bind and/or fix' applied export duty rates; and 'reduce', 'eliminate' or 'foreclose' on the use of such duties. A precedent was set by the WTO accession commitments of Russia, whereby export duties were 'fixed' and bound on 704 tariff lines, of which 544 are subject to reduction commitments. The commitment by Montenegro stipulated that 'from the date of accession, Montenegro would neither apply nor reintroduce any export duty'. This commitment represents the strictest discipline on export duties to date in all Article XII accessions.

## State enterprises

The existing multilateral framework of rules remains fragmented and in some ways inadequate in establishing disciplines for state enterprises engaged in trade and participating in international production chains. In fact, there is ambiguity in the GATT definition of what constitutes a state enterprise. The accession process has provided a fertile testing ground for devising approaches to deal with practical issues related to state trading. Accessions have helped clarify the definition of 'state trading enterprise (STE)', broadening it to include state trading and production activities in both goods and services, as well as state investment in enterprises, and have also addressed the transparency deficit in this area. In the China accession, a supplementary obligation – not derived from the GATT – is added for 'state owned' enterprises, which stipulates that the government undertakes not to 'influence, directly or indirectly, commercial decisions . . ., including on the quantity, value or country of origin of any goods purchased or sold'. In some instances, Article XII members undertook obligations either to limit or phase out STEs. The accession process establishes a list of STEs, promoting transparency and assisting in the monitoring of post-accession implementation. The notification rate of Article XII members has been consistently higher than that of original members.

## Investment

While WTO Dispute Settlement applies, strictly, only to state-to-state disputes, a couple of Accession Protocols have reinforced the right of private investors' access to impartial binding procedures to settle investment-related disputes with host governments, through alternative arrangements. For example, some Article XII members have accepted explicit accession commitments to guarantee the right to alternative dispute settlement. For example, in the Georgia accession, it is stipulated that disputes between the state and a foreign investor could be settled in the courts of Georgia or other fora, including arbitration, such as the International Centre for Settlement of Investment Disputes (ICSID).

## Land

Foreign investment in land has often been marked by lack of information, transparency and uncertainty as to what is allowed and what is not. Moreover, purchases of land by foreigners have often triggered controversies and accusation of 'land grabs'. The investment-related entries on land in the GATS schedules of Article XII members offer transparency and predictability for services-related FDI in land. The vast majority of Article XII members have made commitments to streamline services-related FDI in land. These include putting in place clear and precise rules on ownership, leasing, duration and usage of land for FDI by foreign services providers.

## Transparency and privatisation

A large majority of Article XII members have committed to regularly 'notifying' their privatisation programmes to WTO members. These specific commitments are not explicitly linked to a notification requirement under any particular WTO Agreement, but are aimed at enhancing systemic transparency. Between 1995 and 2013, approximately 43,500

notifications and related information were entered in the Central Registry of Notifications. Almost one-fifth of these notifications (17 per cent)
were made by Article XII members. This number is significant because
many Article XII members completed their accessions only relatively
recently and, unlike original members, they have not been subject to
notification requirements since 1995. Article XII members have, on
average, been more active in fulfilling their notification requirements,
although scope for improvement remains.

## A brief word on reform implications

The fact that the accession process – accompanied by vigorous domestic
reforms – appears to both enhance development outcomes and
strengthen the world trading system does not mean that we cannot do
better. The review of accessions presented in this volume raises two
reform questions: can the WTO accession process be improved and, if
so, how? How should the institution improve its workings in the light of
its much expanded membership? On both these issues, numerous ideas
have been put forward by negotiators, professionals and academics.

On the process of accession, it has been argued that, at a minimum, the
WTO Secretariat should catalogue accession-specific commitments that
are so-called 'departures', and include them in an official index. The
objection raised against this proposal is that accession provisions are not
'departures', but form part of a WTO Single Legal Undertaking, and this
has been the case ever since the rules-based multilateral trading system
emerged in 1947. In this view, the system of rules is continuously evolving, whether through accessions, other negotiations, or deliberations
under dispute settlement. Rules and commitments agreed by members,
multilaterally, are not 'departures', but form part of the Single Legal
Undertaking. Other proposals include an evaluation of the acceding
government's trade regime by a panel of independent experts instead of
by interested parties, as well as the establishment of reference points for
commitments by suitable peer groups as a guideline for negotiators. The
counter is that the WTO is an intergovernmental institution. Proposals
have also been made to 'accelerate' and 'fast-track' the accession process
by, for example, allowing more flexibility in the application of commitments, instead of insisting on their implementation before accession is
agreed, and improving the coordination of aid to finance reforms. The
most ambitious proposals call for a new broad-ranging agreement on
accessions, which might include provisions limiting the extent to which

original members can ask for 'WTO-plus' commitments from acceding governments. But, since non-members could not be party to such an agreement by definition, it is not clear why original members would limit their policy space in the absence of any quid pro quo.

There are, in our view, three mutually reinforcing ways in which the accession process can be improved: there is scope for acceleration, there is also scope for greater transparency and, commensurate with its policy importance, the accession process should be guided by policy-makers at the highest levels in the conduct and management of trade policy. Although steps have been taken in recent years to remedy existing shortcomings, more can and should be done.

The drawbacks are not new. When the WTO was established as an international organisation in 1995 and the accession process was initiated, evolving from the GATT's protocol of provisional application, the transparency deficit was already evident, and there was clearly considerable scope for sharpening the negotiating process to make it analysis and fact based. Technical assistance and capacity-building for acceding governments was too general and untailored. There was insufficient evidence about the results of accession and its effect on growth, exports and domestic reform, and insufficient understanding of how the process could strengthen the international trading system for everyone. The leadership of the Secretariat, pulled in many directions, was not systematically engaged in removing roadblocks in negotiations, in encouraging members and the acceding government to look beyond the negotiating minutiae and see the big picture. In commissioning this study, Director-General Roberto Azevêdo has properly situated WTO accession as a strategic priority in trade policy that requires improved understanding.

There has been progress. To improve transparency, the Informal Group on Accessions (IGA) was expanded in 2009 and it became more representative of the whole membership. Since 2010, accession newsletters have been reporting on the substance of the negotiations. A 'Facilitation Mechanism' was established in 2010 to mediate 'blockages' in the LDC accessions of Yemen and Lao PDR. Directors-general became less tolerant of unreasonable blockages, and became more insistent on ensuring that the terms and conditions of membership safeguarded the rules-based system. The Secretariat conducts an annual outreach cycle of engagement with all WTO 'constituency groups' to address questions and concerns. An Accession Commitments Database (ACDB) was established in 2010 that created an inventory of all the accession-specific commitments contained in accession working party reports that are now integral to (part of) the WTO rule-book. Technical assistance has been more closely tailored to the requirements of acceding governments. The WTO Secretariat routinely suggests road maps to acceding governments to assist them in managing their accessions and bringing them to closure. In 2009 a reporting system was established with annual reports by directors-general *ex officio*, now in its seventh year. As observed in Chapter 9, the Secretariat and the broader membership recognise that 'it is in the nature of the process and substance of accession negotiations that they do not conclude, either naturally, or routinely. The "delivery of an accession has to be midwifed".'

More can be done to make the accession process faster, more transparent and more connected to strategic policy-making. While the Secretariat has work to do in all these dimensions, especially in the area of preparation, outreach and analysis, progress depends critically on the way in which original members and acceding governments interact and how the acceding government relates to its own domestic reforms and regulatory change. In many instances the speed of accession depends most critically on the capacity of the acceding government to acknowledge and understand the changes needed, which are often more far-reaching than it originally expected, to explain the changes to its domestic constituencies, and to orchestrate and implement the domestic regulatory reforms to become WTO compatible. The process of accession can be characterised without exaggeration as regime change, and for this reason should be supported at the highest levels, and be led by an individual able to handle the politics as well as to think strategically about the reforms required. On their part, original members, especially those directly engaged in the working party, need to focus on the most important changes required of the acceding government, not lose themselves in minutiae or make unreasonable demands unrelated to the economic and trade agenda that is at the heart of accession. They must push for their commercial interests but also see themselves as supporters of the domestic changes needed, understanding the constraints and limitations faced by the acceding government. In all this, it is difficult to overestimate the importance of analysis and outreach by all concerned to domestic constituencies, beginning with the acceding government supported by the WTO Secretariat. The international development community, including the multilateral development banks and the International Monetary Fund (IMF), also has a significant role to play in the provision of technical assistance and in the analysis of the impact of accession on specific sectors and the economy as a whole.

On the issue of how to conduct multilateral trade negotiations among a much expanded membership, there is a very valid concern that the WTO has become a victim of its own success. As its membership has become almost universal, and the negotiating agenda has simultaneously become broader and more complex, negotiations based on a single undertaking to be agreed by consensus of the whole membership have become increasingly unwieldy – some would say impossible.

As has often been argued, a powerful case exists for having members focus on a narrower agenda, placing greater focus on concluding plurilateral agreements under the auspices of the WTO. These may be more tractable, since they are sector or issue specific instead of being all encompassing, and can include a critical mass of the interested members instead of the whole membership. Plurilateral agreements can take two forms. The first form consists of an agreement between members on certain rules of the game whose obligations apply only to the contracting parties to the agreements but whose benefits are accorded to the whole membership, i.e. are on a most-favoured-nation basis. Examples include the 1997 Information Technology Agreement, as well as ongoing negotiations to extend it. These are the Annex-4-type agreements, which form part of the 'Covered Agreements' of the WTO Agreement. The downside of this type of plurilateral agreement is that it allows most members to free-ride, reducing the value of the deal for contracting parties, while at the same time creating an incentive not to participate. The other form of plurilateral agreement enables the signatories to conclude a deal between themselves without extending either the obligations or the benefits to the rest of the membership. Examples are the GPA and the Civil Aviation Agreement. As a matter of current practice – if not law – inclusion of these agreements under WTO auspices requires the consensus of the membership, which may or may not be forthcoming, because excluded members may consider that the agreement will put them at a disadvantage or create precedents that they disfavour.

Although overcoming the obstacles in the way of both types of plurilateral agreement is not easy, it should be possible to expand their use through a combination of so-called side payments to enlist the support of excluded members or reluctant participants, as well as by including provisions for well-designed, system-enhancing special and differential treatment to enlist the support of other members.

Indeed, the successful conclusion of thirty-three accession negotiations, requiring the consensus of the broad WTO membership, demonstrates that multilateral negotiations based on progressive layers of consultations around a well-defined issue can yield results even if large all-encompassing trade rounds – whose appeal is rapidly fading – may not. An important lesson from the accession process is that there are contexts and modalities which lead multilateral trade negotiations to successful outcomes, even in the complex and multi-polar twenty-first century economy.

# 2

# Developments in the global economy and trading system effects: the transformation of world trade

URI DADUSH

## ABSTRACT

*The Great Recession of 2008–2009 tested the resilience of economies across the world and placed enormous strain on the frameworks underpinning global cooperation. In no arena was the test more severe than in world trade, which, against a background of collapsing output and surging unemployment in the industrialised countries, fell about one-quarter in the first half of 2009, a rate of decline that exceeded the worst years of the Great Depression of the 1930s. Although the rate of recovery remains sluggish and the pace of trade liberalisation has slowed, a relapse into protectionism has been avoided and world trade volumes have surpassed the pre-crisis peak by some 25 per cent. The world trading system seems to have passed this most strenuous of tests. This chapter examines how two great changes in the global economic landscape, deepening trade integration (trade as a means of production as well as consumption), and the rising weight of developing countries, are changing trade and investment flows and creating new challenges for policy-makers.*

This chapter aims to examine the state of world trade as the effects of the Great Recession (2008–2009) dissipate and to identify some of the trends that are determining its mass and defining its contours. It will document how world trade is currently undergoing a profound transformation driven primarily by two fundamental forces: the progressive embedding of trade and foreign investment in domestic as well as international production and distribution chains, making the fabric of global and domestic production effectively inseparable; and the rise of developing countries as the main drivers of global demand as well as shapers of new patterns of comparative advantage.

Despite the difficulties confronting trade negotiations under the Doha Development Agenda and the many uncertainties surrounding the new mega-regional initiatives, such as the Trans-Pacific Partnership (TPP) and Transatlantic Trade and Investment Partnership (TTIP), the prospects for continued expansion of trade remain positive, due to a combination of technological, economic and domestic policy factors.

Progress could be much faster, however. Studies using gravity models have shown that world trade remains well below its theoretical maximum relative to world gross domestic product (GDP), even though it has come significantly closer to that benchmark over the last thirty years. Moreover, there are plenty of risks and pitfalls that could slow it again. In particular, despite the impressive expansion of the WTO to cover 97 per cent of world trade, the uneven progress achieved so far in integrating developing countries in the rules and disciplines of the global trade system represents the greatest challenge.

### Embedding of trade in domestic production and consumption

The simplest way to illustrate the rising importance of trade is to examine its trend relative to GDP. As Figure 2.1, borrowed from a comprehensive

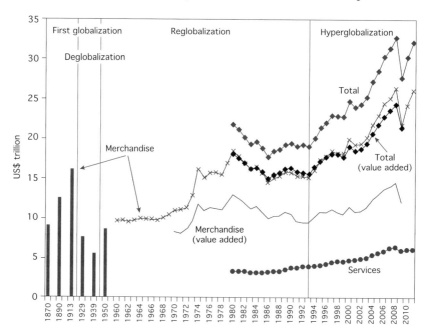

**Figure 2.1**   World exports, in current US$ trillion, 1870–2011 (Subramanian and Kessler (2013)).

review by Subramanian and Kessler (2013), shows, the advance has been dramatic and accelerated sharply around the mid to late 1980s, coinciding with accelerated reforms and growth in a large number of developing countries, including giant economies such as China and India. In the years that followed, a large number of countries ranging from the former planned economies in Eastern Europe to those in the Pacific Rim of Latin America and Asia undertook measures to open their economies and reorient them towards world markets. World merchandise exports, expressed in current US dollars and as a share of world GDP, had exceeded 15 per cent in the early twentieth century, hit a low of 5 per cent during the Great Depression, and recovered their earlier levels only around the time of the first oil shock in 1973. The mid to late 1980s saw the next big surge which continues to today (with the Great Recession effecting a massive but temporary shock), with merchandise exports rising to 25 per cent of world GDP. Meanwhile, exports of services also grew in importance and now represent an additional 10 per cent of world GDP. Impressive as these numbers are, they do not adequately convey the extent to which economies have become intertwined.

Trade can be examined through its mirror images, exports and imports. Taken together, exports and imports of goods and services now represent over 60 per cent of world GDP, about twice the ratio of forty years ago. Looking at trade from the perspective of exporters illustrates its importance for producers, while looking at imports illustrates their importance for final consumers as well as producers purchasing raw materials and machines. Even in very large and relatively self-sufficient economies, such as the United States, virtually every activity of the economy is directly or indirectly dependent on international trade either for its markets or for its inputs or both, and consumers have become accustomed to the enormous expansion of variety enabled by importing everything from out-of-season fruits to the latest hit TV series or game console. For example, the US Chamber of Commerce notes that about one-quarter of US jobs depend directly or indirectly on international trade.

Looking at trade figures in isolation does not adequately capture the increased reliance of producers and consumers on 'foreign' goods and services. One reason is that trade statistics do not reflect the sales of foreign affiliates of multinational corporations, which now greatly exceed world exports. Thus, a French consumer driving a Honda made in France using parts made in Japan is deriving benefit from the ability of Japanese engineers and workers to design and build cars, which is only very partially reflected in trade statistics. The same applies to, say, a US manufacturer employing special plastics purchased from BASF, a German chemical company that has invested in extensive manufacturing facilities in the United States. And, building on these two examples, both Honda and BASF are more dependent on selling in foreign markets than can be discerned from trade statistics. Trade statistics also obscure the fact that a large part of trade consists of parts and raw materials exchanged within a single firm rather than across firms, again underscoring the inseparability of domestic and foreign production. Thus, trade occurring between US multinational corporations and their majority-owned affiliates abroad amounted to about 40 per cent of total US trade over the past ten years.

Correspondingly, foreign direct investment (FDI), which finances the start-up or acquisition and expansion of foreign affiliates, has surged in recent years, and has advanced even more rapidly than trade. For example, the United Nations Conference on Trade and Development (UNCTAD) estimates that the stock of global FDI has increased from 10 per cent of global GDP in 1990 to some 30 per cent in recent years.

Imports also amplify domestic value added through the logistics and retail chains they require to reach final consumers. Expenditures on transportation, storage, insurance, retailing and the like as well as sales taxes reflect the large local value-added components associated with imports which are not reflected in trade statistics. For example, distribution margins (which include retail trade, wholesale trade, transportation costs and value-added taxes) in many advanced economies are about 20–25 per cent of the price to consumers. One example can be found in the import of an iPod Touch to the United States, where 30 per cent of the retail value is retained domestically through marketing and distribution. Another large chunk of the retail value of the iPod Touch consists of royalties for patents owned by inventors in the United States and in other parts of the world, which are again only partially reflected in trade statistics.

Lower trade barriers, reductions in transport costs, organisational innovations and progress in information and communication technologies have made the slicing up of the production process across countries cheaper and easier. Coordination costs have fallen, and different stages of production are now more frequently located in different countries. High labour costs and heavy regulations in rich countries have also helped to accelerate the shift through a wave of outsourcing and offshoring to developing countries.

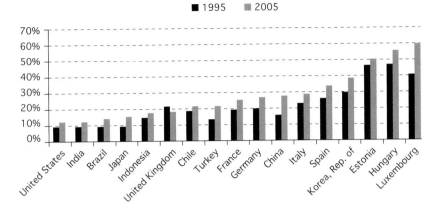

**Figure 2.2** Import content of exports (%) (OECD Input-Output database).

In this way, intermediate inputs have become a salient part of world trade, particularly as imports of these goods have increased sharply relative to their total use. Intermediate inputs now represent more than half of the goods imported by Organisation for Economic Co-operation and Development (OECD) economies and close to three-quarters of the imports of large developing economies, such as Brazil and China.

Imported intermediate inputs feed into goods destined domestically and for export. According to OECD estimates,[1] imported content accounts for about one-quarter of OECD economies' exports, and the European Central Bank estimates that import content accounted for about 44 per cent (or 20 per cent for extra-European Union (EU) imports) of EU exports in 2000, ranging from about 35 per cent in Italy to about 59 per cent in the Netherlands.[2] In the United States, a relatively self-sufficient economy, the import content of exports was about 10 per cent in 2005. Among emerging economies, exports are especially reliant on imported content in China – about 30 per cent, while in Brazil and India the share of imported content in exports is about half as large (Figure 2.2).

More recent estimates by UNCTAD indicate that in 2010 the share of foreign value added in total exports was 28 per cent, with the exports of advanced countries relying on foreign value added more than the exports of developing countries, 31 and 25 per cent respectively. Reliance on

---

[1] Dadush and Ali (2011).    [2] Ibid.

foreign value added also varies greatly by export sector, ranging from an average of around 40 per cent in sectors such as machinery to 5 per cent in exports of petroleum and 10 per cent in agriculture.

With globalisation, the use of imported intermediates for exports has been growing. According to the OECD, all but one of its member countries increased the import content of its exports over the period 1995–2005. The increase was particularly marked in small countries such as Israel and Luxembourg, which saw increases of about 20 percentage points, compared to 3 to 8 percentage points in the large countries, such as Germany, Japan and the United States. This is in keeping with the general trend of import content accounting for a larger share of exports in smaller economies. According to a report[3] to the 2014 G-20 summit in Sydney, Australia, between 30 per cent and 60 per cent of the exports of G-20 countries consist of imported intermediate goods and services, and all G-20 countries saw an increase in this share from 1995 to 2009.

The increased trade in intermediate goods – commonly exported several times before becoming embedded in a final product – helps account for the rapid growth of trade relative to GDP. This is shown, for example, by the fact that the sectors which have registered large export growth, such as machinery, are also the sectors where the most vertical specialisation has occurred.[4] The growth of trade in intermediate goods also helps account for the enormous share of exports in GDP in a few mega-traders, such as Singapore and Hong Kong, sometimes called entrepôt (or re-export) economies.[5]

Generally, intermediate imports appear to be more important for exports of manufactures than those of services. In Japan and the United States, the import content of manufactures exports – nearly 20 per cent – is four times that of services exports; in China, it is twice that of services exports. Although manufactures dominate world exports expressed in gross terms, it turns out that services are more important than manufactures when trade is measured in terms of domestic value added. According to UNCTAD (2013) while, measured in gross terms, manufactures account for 71 per cent of world exports and services 22 per cent, measured in terms of value added manufactures account for 43 per cent of world exports while services account for 46 per cent.[6] Not only does

---

[3] See OECD, WTO and World Bank Group (2014).    [4] Nordås (2003).
[5] O'Rourke (2009).
[6] The primary sector accounts for only 7 per cent of world exports in gross terms, but 11 per cent in value-added terms.

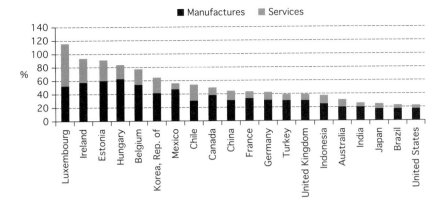

**Figure 2.3**  Import content of exports by industry (%, mid-2000s) (OECD Input-Output database).

one US dollar of services exports typically represent more domestic value added than one dollar of manufactured exports, but manufactured exports incorporate a large amount of services inputs that also represent domestic value added. This fact also underscores the dependence of many domestic activities apparently isolated from foreign markets – such as construction or the provision of local government public services – on international trade (Figure 2.3).

The extent to which trade has become part of the fabric of global production has been recently identified by UNCTAD, which estimated that 57 per cent of world exports are either composed of foreign value added or constitute an intermediate input into foreign production, with only 43 per cent of exports destined for final consumption. In this sense, so-called 'global value chains' often led by multinational companies today drive most world trade. Small advanced economies such as the Netherlands are the most integrated in to global value chains, which account for over 75 per cent of exports, while large developing economies such as Brazil and India, where they account for only 35 per cent of exports, are among the least integrated. Exporters of primary products in Africa or Latin America tend to be less integrated as they are typically at the start of the global value chain, while manufacturing exporters in East Asia tend to be more integrated as they not only export intermediates but also import them.

One result of increased trade in intermediates is that trade is more volatile than GDP. This is because the demand for manufactures, especially durable goods, is much more affected by the business cycle than the

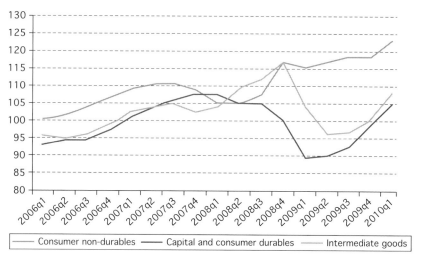

**Figure 2.4**  Composition of trade volumes. Trade volume index, Q1 2008 = 100 (IMF).

demand for services, and durable goods rely heavily on trade in inter-mediates, so they play a larger role in trade, as traditionally measured in gross terms, than in GDP: in the United States, for example, durables accounted for more than 60 per cent of trade in goods in 2008, compared to 24 per cent of GDP. The Great Recession provided a dramatic illustration of the volatility of trade. Global exports declined by 14 per cent in volume terms between the third quarter of 2008 and first quarter of 2009, while world GDP declined by about 3 per cent over the same period.[7] Trade in capital and durable goods was hit particularly hard; according to an International Monetary Fund (IMF) study, during the worst of the crisis, it fell about ten times faster than trade in consumer non-durables as, amid a global credit crunch and loss of confidence, consumers postponed any purchases that could be delayed. In addition, due to countries' specialisation in different stages of production, shocks in one country could forcefully translate into shocks to stages undertaken in another, magnifying the disruption (Figure 2.4).

Though such trade volatility does not necessarily translate into equiva-lent changes in domestic value added, it is none the less highly disruptive. With trade in intermediates growing, economies are becoming more

[7] Baldwin (2009).

intertwined, implying greater vulnerability to shocks emanating from abroad. At the same time, increased reliance on foreign demand and supply is making economies less vulnerable to domestic shocks.

Trade in intermediates means that the cost of protection is higher than is generally understood, and rising. As economists have long known, the effective rate of protection – the tariff as a share of domestic value added – is higher than the nominal tariff. Consider, for example, a T-shirt produced in the United States. Assume it trades at US$10 and uses US$5 worth of imported fabric. The domestic value added is therefore US$5. Now, if the United States imposes a tariff of 50 per cent on T-shirts, the price (US$10) of an imported T-shirt will rise to US$15, giving domestic industry a 100 per cent price advantage.[8] According to a recent report, the average effective rate of protection of domestic value added in China is much higher than suggested by looking at the tariff on gross imports because China's imports of intermediate products represent a particularly large share of its GDP.

By the same token, levying a 50 per cent tariff on the fabric imports would increase the costs for T-shirt producers by 50 per cent of their value added – effectively taxing exports as well as production for the domestic market. Because imports increasingly feed into exports, an import tariff on parts and raw materials has a big impact on exports. Tariffs on intermediates may also discourage inward bound FDI and encourage outward bound instead.[9] The danger of higher protection is particularly pronounced for smaller economies where the share of intermediate imports in a country's overall exports is large. With these considerations in mind, Canada, for example, has recently announced its intention to eliminate all its tariffs on imported inputs and raw materials (Figure 2.5).

In addition, higher trade barriers may be particularly disruptive to intra-regional trade, as countries tend to import intermediate inputs from other countries in their region, partly reflecting production networks' high sensitivity to time constraints, trade and transportation costs. EU countries tend to import intermediates from other EU members, as North American Free Trade Association (NAFTA) countries tend to do from other NAFTA countries.

In a world where production is becoming more integrated and a rising share of trade is in intermediate products, many of the points made above about the costs of protectionism apply with equal force to

---

[8] Dadush and Ali (2011).    [9] Ibid.

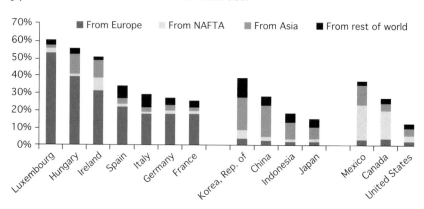

**Figure 2.5**  Import content of exports with partner countries (OECD Input-Output database). NAFTA = North American Free Trade Agreement.

inefficient logistics or burdensome customs procedures. Such 'trade costs' are estimated to be between two and five times higher than tariff-related costs. Although reducing trade costs requires investments and complex institutional reforms, while cutting tariffs can be done at the stroke of a pen, the size of trade costs calls for much greater attention to trade facilitation, both in domestic reforms and international negotiations.

An especially important implication of rising trade in intermediates and its mirror image, the declining domestic value added of trade, is to highlight the importance of services. As already mentioned, statistics on gross exports and imports greatly understate the contribution of services to world trade since services represent a large part of the domestic value added of exports of goods and exports of services are less reliant on imported intermediates than are exports of manufactures (Figure 2.6).

One implication is that global trade policies are less liberal than is generally understood. Thus, while applied tariffs have declined by about two-thirds from the mid 1980s to less than 10 per cent today, barriers to trade in services remain high. According to Borchert *et al.* (2012), barriers are relatively low in telecommunications and relatively high in transportation and professional services. Since services constitute a much higher share of world trade than previously understood, and the share of services in global GDP is steadily rising with incomes (it represents over 85 per cent of GDP in the United States, for example), the importance of negotiations in trade in services is clear. Moreover, barriers to trade in services are generally much lower in advanced than in developing countries, which brings us to the second big force transforming world trade.

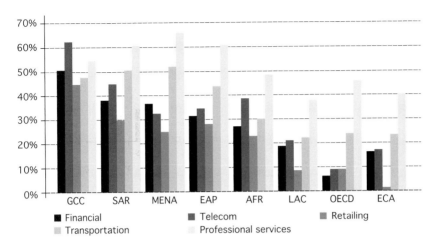

**Figure 2.6**   Index of services trade restrictiveness, by sector and region, 2008 to 2010, 103 countries included. The services trade restriction index (STRI) at the regional level is calculated as a simple average of individual country's STRI's. The STRI in the cross-border air passenger transportation subsector comes from the QUASAR database of WTO (2007). Regional abbreviations: AFR – sub-Saharan Africa, ECA – Europe and Central Africa, EAP – East Asia and Pacific, GCC – Gulf Cooperation Council, LAC – Latin America and Caribbean, MENA – Middle East and North Africa, OECD – High income OECD, SAR – South Asia (Borchert *et al.* (2012)).

## Role of developing countries

The rising economic weight of developing countries is a well-documented feature of the current era, and plausible long-term projections suggest that its impact on world trade will continue to be far reaching. The causes of the delayed development of a large mass of humanity and its relatively recent rapid catch-up have been widely discussed, including in Dadush and Shaw (2011) and are beyond the scope of this chapter. The process of convergence is driven essentially by learning the adoption of technologies invented long ago, rapid growth of the labour force in developing countries and large investments in human and physical capital.

In terms of its effects on world trade, three trends help characterise the convergence phenomenon: the diversification of developing country exports into a wide range of manufactures that greatly increases the potential size of the markets they address; the emergence of a large middle and rich class in developing countries as increasingly important customers; and the increased integration of developing country exports into global financial markets and investment flows that both facilitate and stimulate their trade.

Taken together with reduced barriers to trade and falling communications and transport costs, the implications of these trends are profound: advanced countries are discovering large new markets; the historical reliance of developing countries on markets in industrial countries is declining; China is poised to eclipse Germany and the United States on the global stage in the coming years; and all countries are facing numerous new sources of competition.

For these reasons, the ongoing transformation of world trade presents new challenges and opportunities for countries at every level of development and, because the rise of developing countries is driven by fundamental forces, the next generation is likely to see a marked accentuation of these shifts. As wages, capital/labour ratios and education levels in the most successful developing countries become closer to those in the advanced countries, existing patterns of comparative advantage will be redrawn. Developing Asia's comparative advantage in labour-intensive manufactures will weaken as wages there rise, potentially opening the door for lower-wage countries in Africa and commodity exporters in Latin America to advance exports of such goods. This process will depend, however, on sustained efforts to improve the business climate in the poorest and most commodity-dependent countries.

At the same time, today's advanced countries will at once be exposed to increased competition in their traditional preserve and simultaneously uncover vast new markets for sophisticated consumer products and industrial machinery. But if advanced countries hope to benefit from these new markets in a sustained way, they will have to retain the edge in innovation and product differentiation, as well as in the predictability and efficiency of their business environments.

Domestic reform measures designed to make business environments in developing economies more attractive will be essential to, but not sufficient for, deriving the benefits of the transformation. A more effective set of international trade rules must also be designed to make trade more open and predictable.

Developing countries already play a large role in world trade. Their relative weight grew enormously over the ten years preceding the Great Recession, reflecting China's meteoric rise as an exporter, surging oil prices, and increasing exports from the Middle East and North Africa (MENA), Eastern Europe and Central Asia. Since the recession struck, with its epicentre in the advanced countries, these trends have accelerated.

By 2012, developing economies accounted for 62 per cent of world merchandise exports (excluding intra-EU trade), up from roughly half in 2006. Nearly half of this growth was driven by the 'Big Five' developing countries Brazil, China, India, Indonesia and Russia (BRIIC), whose share of world merchandise exports rose from 17.7 to 22.2 per cent. China accounted for a significant portion of this growth – its share of world exports increased from 10.5 to 13.8 per cent.

On the other hand, India, which, as another large and rapidly growing economy, is often compared to China, advanced at a much slower pace. Its share of goods exports remained very low (little more than 1 per cent) in 2006, though its share in commercial services exports advanced from 0.6 to 2.5 per cent over the same period. In recent years, Indian exports did slightly better, despite a marked faltering of economic growth. By 2012, goods exports had expanded to 2 per cent of total world exports, while service exports exceeded 3 per cent of the world total (Figure 2.7).

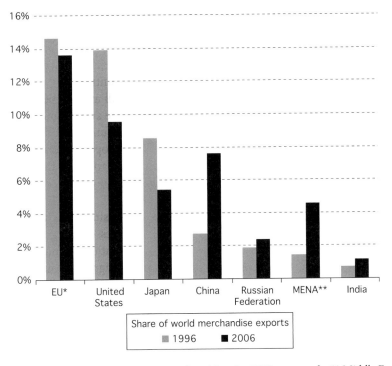

**Figure 2.7** Geographical composition of world trade: * EU extra-trade; ** Middle East and North Africa (UN Comtrade).

As oil prices rose, oil exporters also experienced large increases in their shares of world exports. MENA's share increased from 1.4 to 4.5 per cent, while the share of Sub-Saharan Africa rose from 0.7 to 1.6 per cent. Having transitioned into market economies, the Eastern European and Central Asian countries also saw large increases in export shares, matched by even larger increases in imports and rising current account deficits.

By contrast, the export share of most industrialised countries fell, with the US share decreasing from 13.9 to 9.5 per cent. Japan's decline was particularly stark; its share fell from 8.6 per cent in 1996 to 5.4 per cent, less than China's share alone, in 2006. Developing countries' merchandise exports expanded twice as fast as the average for high-income countries in 2007 and 2008, and fell by less in 2009.

The importance of developing countries as an export market has grown as well, reflecting increased foreign exchange availability, a rapidly growing middle class and a great appetite for the quality and diversity provided by imported goods. EU exports to China more than quadrupled from 1996 to 2006, while its exports to Russia, Sub-Saharan Africa, Eastern Europe and Central Asia more than tripled. The United States also increased its exports to developing countries, from 31 per cent of its total exports in 1996 to 38 per cent in 2006. On the other hand, over the decade, exports from the European Union to Japan were unchanged at about 2 per cent of total exports, while exports to other industrialised countries fell from 9 to 7 per cent.

### Manufactured goods exports

Historically, countries that have moved up the ladder of development have diversified from primary commodities to manufactured goods, which offer better prospects for export earnings growth and provide greater price stability.

Following the historical pattern, today's developing countries have increased their presence in manufactured goods exports. China's manufactured goods exports surpassed those of both Japan and the United States in 2006, as China's share of global manufactured goods exports increased from 3.2 per cent in 1996 to 9.8 per cent in 2006. Other developing countries have also increased their manufactured goods exports, with the share of manufactured goods in Sub-Saharan Africa's total exports rising from 7.1 to 18.7 per cent. In addition, manufactured goods have played an increasing role in South–South trade, accounting for 37 per cent of total South–South trade in 2005, up from 31 per cent in 1995. Since the recession struck, these patterns have become even more pronounced.

Between 2006 and 2012, developing countries' share of manufactured goods exports rose from 30.2 to 38.8 per cent. The BRIIC economies drove over three-quarters of this growth; their share of manufactured goods exports increased from about 20 to 27 per cent of world exports. China accounted for over 90 per cent of this surge, its share of manufactured goods exports rising from 15.5 to 21.8 per cent. Outside the BRIICs, developing economies did not fare as well, either just managing to hold their share or, in the case of Sub-Saharan Africa and Latin America and the Caribbean, actually losing share.

Exports of manufactured goods may have increased even more and export diversification progressed even further had exports of minerals not surged as substantially as they did. Largely as a result of higher prices, but also because of new natural resource discoveries and increased efficiency in production, developing countries significantly increased exports of mineral fuels and chemicals. Sub-Saharan Africa's mineral fuels exports rose from US$14.5 billion to US$80.9 billion between 1996 and 2006. In 2006, MENA's mineral fuels exports reached US$360 billion, nearly ten times their US$36.9 billion level in 1996.

*Financial integration*

Much like the advance of trade, the financial integration of developing countries progressed impressively over the decade preceding the crisis, and the two processes reinforced one another.

Amid robust global growth and a favourable financing environment, private capital inflows to developing countries surged. Net international private capital inflows to developing countries averaged US$489 billion in 2005–2007, up from US$151 billion in 1995–1997. As a share of developing country GDP, they increased from 2.8 to 4.1 per cent. The crisis appears to have represented only a brief interruption in capital flows to developing countries. Between 2010 and 2012, net international private capital inflows to developing countries averaged US$1.2 trillion, or roughly 9 per cent of developing country GDP.

Improved macroeconomic policies making investments in developing countries more sustainable have helped reassure foreign investors. During the euphoria that preceded the crisis, average spreads on emerging market sovereign bonds had narrowed to record lows. In 2002, only one in five countries in the JPMorgan Emerging Market Bond

Index had bond spreads below 200 basis points; by April 2007 the proportion had risen to three in four. Bond spreads surged during the crisis, reaching 900 basis points across emerging markets, but remained well below the levels reached during previous crises. (In the throes of the Asian financial crisis, to provide a comparison, bond spreads in emerging markets averaged close to 1500 basis points.) Following a small spike related to uncertainty in Cyprus, bond spreads trailed down to about 300 basis points in the first quarter of 2013.

Countries with more open trade also attract higher levels of FDI as a percentage of their GDP. Trade openness encourages capital inflows because it allows investors to take advantage of outsourcing opportunities by making importing inputs easier and because it is associated with improved efficiency.

As incomes in developing countries rise, they tend to become more attractive destinations for capital for many reasons, including increased market size, stability and creditworthiness. The growing attractiveness of developing countries may also be attributed in part to higher prices of energy and other natural resources.

Over time, however, the per capita income level threshold associated with the ability to attract FDI has fallen. The per capita income associated with FDI flows of at least 1 per cent of GDP in 2005–2007 (1.7 per cent of US GDP per capita) is less than that in 1995–1997 (3.1 per cent of US GDP per capita). In 2005–2007 GDP per capita was below the level needed to achieve FDI inflows of 1 per cent of GDP in approximately thirty-six developing countries. Based on pre-crisis trend growth rates, twenty-three of these countries will cross the threshold by 2020, and an additional seven will do so by 2030.

Increased trade and financial integration have been associated with larger current account surpluses and deficits, indicating an increased ability to borrow abroad in the former case, or invest abroad in the latter. In surplus developing countries, current account balances as a share of GDP rose from an average of 4.5 per cent in 1995–1997 to 10.6 per cent in 2005–2007; they widened a more modest 0.8 percentage points in deficit developing countries, reaching 8.1 per cent in 2005–2007. In addition, more countries have been able to run sustained current account deficits – that is, to borrow abroad over long periods. In 2010–2012, as the global financial crisis ebbed, current account balances as a share of GDP averaged 7.2 per cent in surplus developing countries; in deficit developing countries, they averaged 8.5 per cent.

Developing countries have also become a significant source of foreign capital for other developing countries. South–South FDI has increased sharply over the past two decades, from US$3.7 billion in 1990 to over US$73.8 billion in 2007. Reflecting regional integration, intra-regional South–South investment in Latin America and South-east Asia accounted for 93.7 per cent and 77 per cent of total South–South FDI in each region in 2007. In 2009, the latest year for which data are available, South–South FDI dipped from its high of US$187 billion the previous year, but remained robust at US$149 billion.

Given fundamental macroeconomic improvements and favourable GDP and trade projections, private capital flows to developing countries are also likely to continue rising. Even assuming that FDI grows at the same rate as GDP, and not faster, as it has in recent history, developing countries' share of net FDI inflows will almost triple from 25 per cent in 2005–2007 to 66 per cent in 2050.

## *Emerging global middle and rich (GMR) class*

As noted by the World Bank and others, the rapid economic growth of developing countries will lead to the emergence of a new GMR class, defined as those with annual incomes of at least US$4,000 in 2005 purchasing power parity (PPP). This class will be able to demand more overall and increase the demand for advanced goods and services in particular, rapidly expanding the markets for internationally traded products, such as automobiles and consumer durables. People in this class are also likely to demand more and better education, health and international tourism services.

Our estimates show that the GMR population in the developing G-20 economies – Argentina, Brazil, China, Indonesia, India, Mexico, Russia, South Africa and Turkey – is likely to grow from 739 million in 2009 to 1.3 billion in 2030, reaching 1.9 billion in 2050. By 2030, the GMR population in developing countries will have overtaken that in advanced countries, up from 24 per cent today; by 2050, about 60 per cent of the total GMR population will reside in developing countries. However, the purchasing power of the GMR class in advanced countries will be about 60 per cent more than the average income of the GMR class in developing G-20 countries in 2050 (Figure 2.8).

In China, the GMR class will grow from about 120 million in 2009 to 780 million in 2030 and 1.1 billion in 2050, and a significant portion of

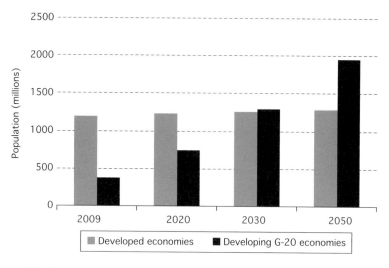

**Figure 2.8**   Size of the global middle and rich (GMR) class (author's projections).

the Chinese population will have transitioned to the 'rich' class (i.e. earning above US$17,000) by 2050.

Other developing countries will contribute to the increase in the GMR class. China and India, which together accounted for approximately 42 per cent of the developing G-20 countries' GMR class in 2009, will account for about 70 per cent by 2050. In Indonesia, approximately 70 million additional people will enter the GMR class by 2050, and an additional 40 million will do so in Russia.

As a result, the class will account for an increasing share of the total population of the G-20 developing countries, reaching 48 per cent by 2050, up from 11 per cent in 2009 and 33 per cent in 2030. Even in Brazil, where income inequality is particularly high, the share of the GMR class in the country's total population will reach 65 per cent in 2050, up from 33 per cent in 2009.

National data on passenger cars in circulation suggest that the size and growth rate of the middle class in developing countries may be underestimated. The passenger car index developed by the Carnegie Endowment for International Peace (Dadush and Ali, 2012), which uses the ability to purchase a car as a certain critical threshold of purchasing power, suggests that the global middle class is as much as 50 per cent larger, and growing three times faster, than suggested by conventional income-based methods. In particular, the middle class is roughly twice

Table 2.1 *Size of the global middle and rich (GMR) class population (millions)*

|  | 2009 | 2020 | 2030 | 2050 |
|---|---|---|---|---|
| **Developed economies** | 1,193 | 1,225 | 1,254 | 1,284 |
| **Developing G-20 economies** | 368 | 740 | 1,295 | 1,958 |
| China | 118 | 375 | 779 | 1,092 |
| Brazil | 66 | 80 | 110 | 170 |
| Russian Federation | 57 | 82 | 93 | 98 |
| India | 37 | 69 | 121 | 273 |
| Mexico | 37 | 51 | 72 | 111 |
| Turkey | 17 | 29 | 46 | 70 |
| Indonesia | 11 | 20 | 33 | 81 |
| Argentina | 17 | 21 | 28 | 40 |
| South Africa | 9 | 13 | 14 | 23 |
| **Large African economies** | | | | |
| Nigeria | 4 | 6 | 10 | 22 |
| Kenya | 4 | 7 | 10 | 26 |
| Ethiopia | 3 | 6 | 11 | 34 |
| Ghana | 1 | 3 | 5 | 18 |

*Source:* author's projection.

as large as current estimates in India, Mexico, Russia, South Africa and Turkey, and over four times as large as the current estimate in Indonesia (Table 2.1).

## How might world trade look in 2050?

Will these trends in the rising importance of developing countries as both exporters and export markets continue? Barring geopolitical or climate-induced catastrophes and assuming that the world does not retreat into protectionism, the share of world trade held by developing countries could – under plausible growth assumptions which reflect the slowing that occurs as economies mature – more than double over the next forty years, reaching nearly 70 per cent by 2050. In addition, developing countries' dependence on developed country markets will weaken. Reflecting high growth rates and the rise of the middle class, emerging economies will come to dominate international trade.

According to GDP projections made in Carnegie's *The World Order in 2050* brief, the weight of global economic activity is shifting substantially from advanced countries towards emerging economies. The economy of the G-20 is expected to grow at an average annual rate of 3.5 per cent, rising from US$38.3 trillion in 2009 to US$160 trillion in 2050 in real dollar terms. Over 60 per cent of this US$121 trillion expansion will come from six developing economies: the 'Big Five' and Mexico. US dollar GDP in these six economies will grow at an average rate of 6 per cent per year, while GDP in the G-7 will grow by less than 2.1 per cent annually. China and India will grow more slowly than in recent years by a still impressive 5.6 and 5.9 per cent, respectively, annually over the period 2009–2050.[10]

Based on these GDP projections, and consistent with the current trend, developing countries' share of world exports will increase from 30 per cent in 2006 to 69 per cent in 2050. China's share will increase from 7.6 to 24 per cent, while India's will reach 6.2 per cent, up from just 1.2 per cent. Conversely, the industrialised countries' share will decline, with that of the United States decreasing from 9.5 to 7 per cent and that of Japan falling dramatically from 5.4 to just 2.4 per cent.

Developing countries' role as an export market will significantly increase as well. Based on a conservative GDP elasticity of trade of 1.3, China's imports from the United States and the European Union will account for 3.1 per cent of world trade in 2050, representing more than a twofold increase in importance since 2006. In terms of US and EU exports, which are projected to grow more slowly than world trade, China's importance will increase more than fourfold. In addition, while a large share (49 per cent) of EU exports will be intra-regional, China will emerge as its second largest export destination. Latin America will be the United States' largest export market, followed by China, accounting for 27 per cent of the country's total exports. Because US and EU exports appeal to the middle class, even these numbers probably underestimate the rise in exports from advanced countries to China and other developing giants.

Developing countries will also become an increasingly important export market for one another. This will be the case for lower-income countries in Africa in particular, and as a result their dependence on the developed country market will weaken. A booming China and India indicate strong demand not only for primary products, but also for niche manufactures and services, as well as industrial inputs and equipment from other developing countries. With countries in the South at different

---

[10] Complete GDP projections are available in the annex to Dadush and Shaw (2011).

stages of diversification and specialisation, and growing rapidly, their production and consumption patterns are becoming increasingly diverse, promoting proportionally more trade in the South.

In 2006, the United States and the European Union were the two largest markets for China's exports. The European Union was also a leading export market for India and Sub-Saharan Africa, accounting for 22.3 and 30.7 per cent of their total exports, respectively. By contrast, in 2050, China will be the largest export destination for India, accounting for 26.4 per cent of its total imports, up from 6.9 per cent in 2006, and the second largest export market for Sub-Saharan Africa, importing 24.7 per cent of the region's total exports, up from 4.8 per cent in 2006. MENA and the Asia Pacific will also be major trading partners for India, accounting for 19 and 15.7 per cent of its total exports respectively. Africa's export dependence on developed economies will fall, with only 27 per cent going to the United States and the European Union in 2050, down from 54 per cent in 2006. Instead, intra-African trade will account for 25 per cent of the region's total exports; this could increase further if infrastructure and trade logistics constraints are addressed (Table 2.2).

For both advanced and developing countries, trade with developing countries will overwhelmingly dominate bilateral trade. In 2006, bilateral trade between advanced countries was most significant, with bilateral trade between the United States and other industrialised countries accounting for 10.4 per cent of world trade. Reflecting the trade integration in Asia, China will be the world's leading trade partner in 2050, and total trade between China and the Asia Pacific developing countries will account for 9 per cent of world trade, up from less than 2 per cent in 2006. Trade between China and India will reach US$2 trillion, or 3.7 per cent of world trade, in 2050, from just 0.3 per cent in 2006. The bilateral trade of the United States, the European Union and other industrialised countries with China will account for a larger per cent of world trade than their bilateral trade with any other country or region (Table 2.3).

Even in an environment of slower growth, the message that the weight of developing countries in world trade will rise sharply is likely to retain its validity. Lower growth may result from the materialisation of various risks, including increased protectionism, geopolitical strife, recurrence of financial crises and the effects of climate change. Under a lower-growth scenario, found in Dadush and Shaw (2011), average annual growth rates – relative to the baseline case – are expected to be from 0.5 to 0.9 per cent lower in advanced economies, 1.5 to 1.6 per cent lower in China and India, 1.1 to 1.5 per cent lower in other emerging economies and

Table 2.2 *Top five export destinations for China, the European Union, India, Sub-Saharan Africa and the United States, 2006–2050*

| | 2006 | | 2050 | |
|---|---|---|---|---|
| Partner country | % of total exports | Partner country | | % of total exports |
| **China** | | | | |
| United States | 25.9 | United States | | 17.4 |
| European Union | 23.1 | Asia Pacific[b] | | 16.4 |
| Other industrialised[a] | 13.4 | European Union | | 16.3 |
| Japan | 11.6 | Other industrialised | | 10.1 |
| Asia Pacific[b] | 7.2 | India | | 7.9 |
| **United States** | | | | |
| Other industrialised[a] | 34.1 | Latin America | | 26.6 |
| European Union | 21.7 | China | | 23.7 |
| Latin America[c] | 19.8 | Other industrialised | | 18.5 |
| Japan | 6.0 | European Union | | 11.0 |
| China | 5.6 | Asia Pacific | | 5.9 |
| **European Union** | | | | |
| European Union | 67.5 | European Union | | 49.2 |
| United States | 7.8 | China | | 11.2 |
| Other industrialised[a] | 6.8 | Eastern Europe and Central Asia | | 7.3 |
| Eastern Europe and Central Asia | 4.4 | MENA | | 5.8 |
| MENA | 3.4 | United States | | 5.5 |
| **India** | | | | |
| European Union | 22.3 | China | | 26.4 |
| MENA | 17.9 | MENA | | 18.9 |
| United States | 15.8 | Asia Pacific | | 15.7 |
| Other industrialised[a] | 11.0 | European Union | | 10.1 |
| Asia Pacific[b] | 10.6 | Sub-Saharan Africa | | 9.5 |
| **Sub-Saharan Africa** | | | | |
| European Union | 30.7 | Sub-Saharan Africa | | 24.7 |
| United States | 23.3 | China | | 20.5 |
| Sub-Saharan Africa | 16.2 | European Union | | 15.6 |
| Other industrialised | 8.7 | India | | 13.0 |
| Japan | 4.8 | United States | | 11.3 |

*Notes:* [a] 'Other industrialised' refers to Australia, Canada, Iceland, Israel, Republic of Korea, New Zealand, Norway, Singapore and Switzerland. [b] Asia Pacific developing economies. [c] Latin America excluding Brazil.
*Source:* UN Comtrade, author's projections.

Table 2.3 *Top trading pairs*[a] *in world trade*

| 2006 | | 2050 | |
|---|---|---|---|
| Trading pairs | % of world trade | Trading pairs | % of world trade |
| United States–Other industrialised | 10.4 | China–Asia Pacific developing | 9.0 |
| European Union–Other industrialised[b] | 8.4 | China–Other industrialised | 6.3 |
| European Union–United States | 7.4 | China–United States | 6.2 |
| United States–Latin America[c] | 6.6 | China–European Union | 5.6 |
| European Union–Eastern Europe | 4.4 | United States–Latin America | 4.3 |
| European Union–China | 3.5 | China–India | 3.7 |
| Intra-EU[d] | 28.2 | | 6.3 |

*Notes:* [a] Intra-EU trade is excluded. [b] 'Other industrialised' refers to Australia, Canada, Republic of Korea, Singapore and Switzerland. [c] Latin America excluding Brazil. [d] World trade including intra-EU trade.
*Source:* UN Comtrade.

1.1 to 1.7 per cent lower in non-G-20 economies in Sub-Saharan Africa. Under this scenario, the share of developing countries in world exports will be nearly 60 per cent, 9 per cent lower than their share under baseline projections. Export shares of advanced countries will be slightly higher under this low-growth scenario, but not large enough to displace China as the world's leading exporter. China's exports will account for about 22 per cent of world exports in 2050, followed by the European Union's 18 per cent.

## A brief reflection on policy

The rapid embedding of trade in domestic as well as international production and distribution chains, taken together with the remarkable rise of developing countries as the drivers of growth in international trade, carry important policy implications, some of which have already been highlighted. Many countries, developing as well as advanced, have become so integrated with the world trading system that major back-tracking appears unlikely. In these nations, large investments in both physical and human capital have been made on the presumption that trade remains open, and production structures have adapted, so that the political economy of protectionism has become much less palatable: the interests of exporters and of importers have increased weight relative to that of import-competing sectors, some of which have greatly declined in absolute as well as relative terms.

While the projections presented above point to significant opportunities – from shifts in comparative advantage to a large expansion of world trade to deepening financial integration – policy must be reformed on both the national and international levels if the full potential on any of these fronts is to be realised.

The extent to which comparative advantage will shift in manufactured goods and developing countries will serve as markets for one another will depend largely on domestic reforms in developing countries. These reforms are particularly important in lower-wage countries in Asia, Africa and their competitors in other regions. To bolster exports, the quality and predictability of their business climate must be improved. While such improvements are important for all sectors, they are absolutely essential for stimulating investment in manufacturing, where deficiencies cannot be offset by abundant or unique resource endowments. If done gradually and with supportive measures, reducing the high import protection that is still prevalent in many sectors would also foster efficiency, exposing firms to international competition and easing their access to imported inputs. By making trade less expensive, reducing customs and logistical impediments would have similar effects. Forging new South–South links in trade and finance through regional agreements and institutions – which can share information, promote common regulations and support cross-border projects – would also help harness the expanding complementarities in South–South trade.

At the same time, the success of developing countries in manufactures will force rich countries to accelerate the pace at which they innovate and differentiate, as well as requiring them to make their business environment more flexible and predictable. Several advanced countries have a comparative advantage in the provision of rapidly growing business services, which they will need to exploit as traditional manufacturing declines. Private investments in specialised skills and research and development are likely to increase in importance, and governments can support the trend in various ways.

While the projections suggest that a large expansion in world trade, as well as marked increases in efficiency, innovation and, ultimately, human welfare, are likely in the coming forty years, an open, rules-based system appropriate for this new world economy is still work in progress, as shown by the floundering Doha process. In particular, incorporating the diverse interests of developing countries in trade rules and liberalisation agreements is crucial – but the need to achieve consensus among the WTO's large membership cannot be allowed to dilute agreements to the lowest common denominator. Far-reaching reforms of the WTO are needed to make the process of multilateral negotiations more flexible and responsive to individual countries and regional groups or 'clubs' interested in making progress in specific areas. Disciplines must be strengthened to ensure that the progress of world trade is not hampered, or worse reversed, in the middle of another crisis.

As with trade, increased financial integration of developing countries will also present new opportunities. In Africa, for example, where the crisis has made prospects for aid flows even more uncertain, the potential for private capital inflows remains relatively untapped. However, increased financial integration will also present new challenges for macroeconomic and regulatory policy. On the one hand, it needs to ensure that capital is used effectively and is less sensitive to artificial distortions or market euphoria; on the other, it must establish safeguards against sudden stops or reversals of capital flows.

Prudent levels of internal and external debt, sound banking regulations, exchange rate flexibility and monetary policy geared at keeping inflation under control will all help in this regard. Furthermore, capital account regulations that guard against over-reliance on short-term capital inflows and instead highlight FDI and other long-term, resilient sources of capital can play an important role.

In sum, a number of needed trade-related policy measures stand out at each of the three levels of global governance:

- At the national level, the need is to reduce barriers in services as well as goods and to adopt reforms and investments that facilitate trade. These reforms are especially important in developing countries where barriers are highest, especially in services, and where trade logistics are less efficient.
- Correspondingly, at the global level, reforms that reduce market barriers in developing countries as well as those facing them, such as in agriculture and garments, are crucial. The WTO accession process has

already played a significant role in this regard even as the Doha Round talks faltered – and more accessions are in the works. At the same time, the need to develop better multilateral disciplines in services, FDI and trade facilitation has taken on even greater importance.

- At the regional level, where trade agreements have proliferated and now cover over 50 per cent of world trade, many opportunities exist to promote reforms in developing countries, to increase their market access and to push out the frontier in areas of increased global significance such as investment, trade facilitation and services. The new mega-regionals, such as TPP and TTIP, may, if successful, achieve gains in all these areas and extend them to countries accounting for over 60 per cent of world GDP. Unfortunately, however, they currently exclude the large developing countries most in need of reforms and which are likely to dominate world trade in the future.

There is little doubt that the trends highlighted above portend a steadily increasing role for trade and foreign investment as central planks of prosperity throughout the world. There is also little reason why reforms at both the global and regional level cannot work synergistically with autonomous national reforms to open trade even further and make a retreat into protectionism even less politically feasible than it is today. But equally, there is a long way to go before the legal system of national, regional and global institutions satisfactorily ensures that markets are fully and durably contestable.

## Acknowledgements

This chapter extends and updates 'The Transformation of World Trade', a Carnegie paper authored by Uri Dadush and Shimelse Ali in 2010. Research assistance by Zaahira Wyne and Mustapha Sekkate is gratefully acknowledged.

## References

Baldwin, R. (2009). 'The great trade collapse: causes, consequences and prospects', Centre for Economic Policy Research. Retrieved from www.voxeu.org/epubs/cepr-reports/collapse-global-trade-murky-protectionism-and-crisis-recommendations-g20.

Borchert, I., B. Gootiiz and A. Mattoo (2012). 'Policy barriers to international trade in services: evidence from a new database', Washington, DC, The World Bank, Policy Research Working Paper Series 6109.

Dadush, U. and S. Ali (2011). 'Trade in intermediates and economic policy', VOX Research-based market analysis and commentary from leading economists. Retrieved from www.voxeu.org/article/rise-trade-intermediates-policy-implications.

Dadush, U. and S. Ali (2012). 'In search of the global middle class: a new index', Washington, DC, Carnegie Endowment for International Peace. Retrieved from http://carnegieendowment.org/files/middle_class.pdf.

Dadush, U. and W. Shaw (2011). *Juggernaut: How Emerging Markets Are Reshaping Globalization*. Washington, DC, Carnegie Endowment for International Peace.

Nordås, H. K. (2003). 'Fragmented production: regionalization of trade?' Organisation for Economic Co-operation and Development (OECD), August. Retrieved from http://papers.ssrn.com/sol3/papers.cfm?abstract_id=925789.

OECD, WTO and World Bank Group (2014). 'Global value chains: challenges, opportunities and implications for policy'. Retrieved from www.oecd.org/tad/gvc_report_g20_july_2014.pdf.

O'Rourke, L. (2009). 'Annual report 2009', *Laing O'Rourke Annual Review History*. Retrieved from www.laingorourke.com.

Subramanian, A. and M. Kessler (2013). 'The hyperglobalization of trade and its future?', Washington, DC, Peterson Institute for International Economics, Working Paper Series 13–17.

3

# The WTO and the global economy: contemporary challenges and possible responses

BERNARD M. HOEKMAN

ABSTRACT

*The high economic growth rates that have been achieved by many countries in Asia have led to a contemporary world economy that is multipolar. This has had repercussions for the WTO, as well as for other multilateral organisations. The deadlock in the WTO's Doha Round has led the United States and the European Union increasingly to turn their attention towards the negotiation of preferential trade agreements, including so-called 'mega-regional' partnerships. This chapter discusses some of the implications for – and possible responses by – the economies that have the greatest stake in a well-functioning multilateral trading system. These economies may find themselves caught in the midst of disagreements between the major trading nations, with few prospects of participating in the mega-regionals. The chapter argues that these economies – including those that have acceded to the WTO since its creation – need to take a more proactive leadership role in the WTO to enhance the transparency of what is done in the 'megaregionals' and to facilitate the pursuit of rule-making initiatives in the WTO on a plurilateral basis.*

The global trade regime embodied in the General Agreement on Tariffs and Trade (GATT)/WTO has provided an important framework for countries to agree to trade policy disciplines and commitments, as well as a mechanism through which these can be enforced. After the limited membership of low-income countries in the GATT in 1948 – twelve of the original twenty-three signatories were developing economies – in the

The analyses in the chapters in this book were finalised at the end of December 2014. Since then the Republic of Seychelles acceded to the World Trade Organization (WTO) on 26 April 2015. This expanded total WTO membership from 160 to 161. Please see the editors' note.

1960s there was a substantial expansion of developing country membership. With the creation of the WTO, membership continued to expand steadily, standing at 161 currently, up from 128 in 1995.[1] Twenty-three countries are in the process of negotiating accession.

Developing country engagement in the WTO has been based on the premise of 'more favourable' or 'special and differential treatment' (S&D). This takes several forms. One is acceptance by the WTO membership of higher trade barriers in developing nations and 'less than full reciprocity' in multilateral trade negotiations. Another is a promise by high-income countries to provide preferential access to their markets for exports from developing countries – through the Generalised System of Preferences (GSP) or through better than GSP treatment – duty-free, quota-free (DFQF) access for the least-developed countries (LDCs). A third dimension involves exceptions and exemptions from specific disciplines. For example, countries with a per capita income of less than US$1,000 are permitted to use export subsidies. In general, developing countries also have longer time periods in which to implement negotiated disciplines.

The first round of multilateral trade negotiations launched under WTO auspices in Doha, Qatar, in 2001 was called the Doha Development Agenda (DDA). The inclusion of the word 'development' reflected the rising influence of developing countries in the WTO and their perception that more needed to be done to address an apparent 'development deficit'. After the creation of the WTO in 1995, it had come to seem to many developing countries that the implementation of WTO agreements might not be a priority from a development perspective, that a number of WTO disciplines constrained the ability to use national policies to promote development, and that more needed to be done to recognise and address the capacity constraints that limited the ability of many countries to benefit from existing market access opportunities. Key objectives included making S&D provisions more effective and operational; improving preferential (non-reciprocal) access to major markets; increasing financial assistance to improve trade capacity; and 'rebalancing' the rules and disciplines of the WTO by addressing instances of 'reverse S&D', as existing provisions in the WTO permitted high-income countries to use policies that had detrimental impacts on developing

---

[1] The Accession Protocol of Yemen was approved on 4 December 2013 at the Ninth WTO Ministerial Conference; see WTO document (WT/MIN(13)/24 and WT/L/905). Yemen deposited its Instrument of Ratification on 26 May 2014 and became the 160th member of the WTO on 26 June 2014.

country exports. Examples included tariff escalation, agricultural subsidy policies and barriers to the cross-border movement of natural persons providing services.

Progress was made in achieving results on the preferential market access and the aid elements of this agenda. Milestones that resulted from this effort included the Integrated Framework for Trade-related Assistance for Least-Developed Countries, created at the Singapore Ministerial Meeting in 1997; improvements in preferential access to markets (such as the EU Everything But Arms programme and the US African Growth and Opportunity Act), and the launch of the DFQF market access initiative for LDCs and the Aid for Trade initiative at the 2005 WTO Ministerial Meeting in Hong Kong, China. Further progress was made at the Bali Ministerial Meeting in December 2013 with the adoption of an agreement on trade facilitation. Indeed, the Agreement on Trade Facilitation is particularly innovative in recognising and constructively addressing the great diversity that exists across the WTO membership in terms of capacity to adopt good practice in the areas of customs clearance, transit and border management. But to date no progress has been made in redefining the core rules of the WTO or agreeing on a set of new reciprocal market access commitments and policy disciplines affecting trade in agricultural products, manufactures or services.

There has been much discussion and analysis of the factors that have led to the deadlock in the DDA. Among the more compelling arguments are that the perceived cost of non-agreement is low and the potential upside from agreeing on a deal spanning the issues that remain on the table is limited. There are different flavours to these arguments, including that the negotiating set is too small and that the issues that are on the table are not very relevant for international business today. Wolfe (2013), among others, stresses changes in the structure of the world economy, and in particular the explosive growth of China, as a key factor that has made the DDA agenda, as conceived in 2001 and restructured in 2003, increasingly less relevant as time has passed.

A fundamental source of the breakdown in the talks was the difference in what the Organisation for Economic Co-operation and Development (OECD) member countries, in particular the United States, wanted to obtain from the large emerging markets, especially Brazil, China and India (BCI), and what these countries were willing to offer and looking for in return. A key factor has been that the issues that have been the focus of negotiation in the DDA are not significant enough to allow a deal to be struck. India is a *demandeur* on services, but seeks to maintain the ability to restrict agricultural imports and to support domestic farmers. Brazil is a *demandeur* on further reform of agricultural policies in OECD countries, including bio-fuels, but wants to continue to have the flexibility to raise the level of protection for national industries. For much of the DDA, China took the position that it had already made major commitments as part of its 2001 WTO accession. To some extent India took a similar line, arguing (quite reasonably) that credit should be given for the unilateral trade liberalisation that the country had implemented during the 2000s.

For most large firms – whether from BCI or the OECD – agriculture does not matter, while non-agricultural market access (NAMA) is 'nice to have' but not critical given that average tariffs in major markets are now low and firms appear to perceive the probability of governments raising tariffs again to be small (as a result of vertical specialisation, cross-hauling of foreign direct investment (FDI), etc. – that is, the increasing prevalence and use of global value chains). While there remain high peak tariffs for some products in many countries, these are not widespread enough to mobilise a large enough constituency of firms to devote serious effort to lobby for a deal. Issues that could have done so – such as the prospect of significant liberalisation of services trade – were never the focus of serious negotiations during the first decade of the DDA talks.

This does not imply that the potential economic gains from implementing what was on the table are trivial – they have conservatively been estimated to be on the order of US$160 billion for the merchandise trade part of the DDA alone (Laborde, Martin and van der Mensbrugghe, 2011), not taking into account the benefits of potential tighter disciplines on issues like fishery subsidies, trade facilitation or services (Hoekman, Martin and Mattoo, 2010). What it does imply is that the potential gains are distributed in a way that they do not generate enough (political) interest to allow a deal to be concluded and that generates the best alternative to a negotiated agreement (BATNA) – the threat point – is perceived not to be too bad. It is noteworthy in this connection that the Agreement on Trade Facilitation that was agreed in Bali offers the prospect of significant welfare gains for all WTO members and for the overwhelming majority of firms and consumers in each WTO member by reducing the costs of trade. In contrast to the liberalisation of agricultural trade or trade in manufactures, as a result of which certain groups and industries lose rents, while some countries gain much more than others depending on patterns of comparative advantage, trade facilitation is something that benefits everyone (World Economic Forum, 2013).

The DDA deadlock has led the United States and the European Union to turn their attention towards the negotiation of preferential trade agreements (PTAs) – the Trans-Pacific Partnership (TPP) and the Trans-atlantic Trade and Investment Partnership (TTIP) being key examples. Time will tell to what extent these efforts to establish 'mega-regional' trade and investment agreements will succeed in going significantly beyond what is covered by the WTO. But it is clear that the world has changed as far as trade cooperation is concerned, with the majors 'going regional' and not looking to the WTO as the forum for the negotiation of new trade policy-related disciplines. These developments raise numerous questions relative to the possible consequences for developing countries – both the major emerging economies (BCI) that are on one side of the deadlock with the major OECD nations, and the mass of developing countries that are either excluded altogether or are bit players in the mega-regionals. The WTO as a multilateral institution is particularly important to small countries that do not have market power. A breakdown in the ability of the WTO to extend the reach of disciplines to new policy areas that generate negative spillovers may have the most detrimental effect on the 100-plus countries that are observers of the recent trend towards mega-regionals.

This chapter is organised as follows. The first section gives a bird's-eye view of several salient stylised facts that provide background and context. The second section discusses the implications of these trends and changes in the trade environment for developing countries in the WTO, distinguishing between the subset of countries that no longer make S&D the central plank of their engagement in the WTO and those that continue to do so. The third section argues that the current disagree-ments between the elephants (BCI, the European Union and the United States) create both an incentive and the opportunity for smaller countries to take a more proactive leadership role in the WTO and use available mechanisms to help them safeguard their interests and prepare the ground for cooperation in areas that are not (yet) on the multilateral trade agenda. The fourth section concludes.

## Some stylised facts and trends

### Global trade expansion

One of the distinctive features of the post-Second World War period has been the steady and sustained increase in international commerce, which, with the exception of a few episodes when the world went into recession (most notably in 2008), has grown more rapidly than output year in, year out. The extent to which world trade has grown since the 1950s is dramatic, especially when put in historical perspective. The volume of trade increased twenty-seven-fold between 1950 and 2008, three times more than the growth in global gross domestic product (GDP). The value of global trade in goods and services passed the US$20 trillion mark in 2011 (WTO, 2012) or 59 per cent of global GDP, up from 39 per cent of GDP in 1990.[2]

The basic drivers were a steep fall in trade costs, the result of techno-logical change and the pursuit of policy changes, especially the adoption of outward-(export-)oriented policies. Technological changes have been both hard and soft and include advances in information and communi-cations, which have led to a sharp drop in the costs of international telecommunications, and the adoption of containerisation and other improvements in logistics that have led to a sharp fall in unit transport costs. Average tariffs were previously in the 20–30 per cent range in 1950 (WTO, 2007), complemented by a plethora of non-tariff barriers that were often more binding (including quantitative restrictions and exchange controls). Today the average uniform tariff equivalent in OECD countries for merchandise trade is only 4 per cent, mostly reflect-ing protection of agriculture, and the average level of import protection around the world has dropped to the 5 to 10 per cent range (Kee *et al.*, 2009). Average most-favoured-nation (MFN) tariffs have come down a lot since the mid 1990s, and effective tariffs for firms are often much lower than MFN rates as a result of free trade agreements. China undertook a massive trade and investment liberalisation programme pre- and post-accession, with applied tariffs declining to less than 7 per cent today; all tariffs are bound in the WTO at 9.8 per cent on average and numerous service industries have been opened to foreign competi-tion (Sally and Sen, 2011). Similarly, the average applied MFN tariff in India is now around 6 per cent.

An ever-increasing share of world trade comprises intermediate inputs, reflecting the ability of firms to splinter the production process of goods and services into ever-finer parts and to locate different activ-ities (tasks) in different countries so as to minimise the total costs of production. This process has been supported by cross-border movement

[2] Trade openness ratios were calculated from the World Bank Global Economic Prospects database.

of capital and know-how. The global value of the stock of FDI rose more than six-fold between 1990 and 2008, substantially faster than the growth in trade, which increased 'only' 3.5 times over the same period. Much of this FDI was associated with services, driven in part by decisions by governments around the world to privatise state-owned utilities (such as telecommunications). A network of over 3,500 bilateral investment agreements (BITs) helped to provide a framework to support these FDI flows.

Much, if not most, of the policy reforms – and of course the technical innovations – that drove the increase in trade and increasing specialisation had little to do with the GATT/WTO but were the result of decisions and actions taken autonomously at the national level. The multilateral trading system provided a supporting framework and reduced uncertainty for traders, but it was not a direct driver of the explosion in trade.

### Rise of China and other emerging markets

The share of manufactures in the total exports of developing countries has increased from just 30 per cent in 1980 to over 70 per cent today, with a substantial proportion of this comprising intra-industry trade – the exchange of similar, differentiated products. Since the 1990s, intra-industry trade ratios for high-growth developing and transition economies have risen to 50 per cent or higher. Much of this trade is intra-regional – e.g. about half of all East Asian exports of manufactures go to other East Asian economies, often as part of a supply chain. Often, these tasks and activities involve business, intermediation and knowledge services (research and development, design, engineering, etc.). Much of the value of the goods that is recorded when products cross borders comprises the value of imported parts and components, but the countries that have been most successful at moving into the production of manufactured goods by integrating into international supply chains are also increasing the amount of value added that is generated in their countries. China and other emerging market developing countries have been generating an increasing share of global manufacturing value added – this tripled from around US$1 trillion in the early 2000s to almost US$3 trillion in 2012 (Timmer *et al.*, 2013). The rate of growth for China – which accounts for over half of this total – accelerated after 2001, the year China joined the WTO (and the DDA was launched).

In 2010, China was the world's largest single-country exporter in gross value terms, with a 10.4 per cent share of global merchandise exports

(WTO, 2011). The United States remains the world's largest importer, but China has the second slot. Brazil and India are nowhere near China, while India's imports of merchandise are less than those of Belgium. If the EU-28 is considered as a bloc (and netting out intra-EU trade), it is the largest exporter (15 per cent), followed by China (13 per cent) and the United States (11 per cent). These three entities are also the largest importers, accounting for 45 per cent of global merchandise imports. Brazil and India are much smaller players in merchandise trade, ranking 22nd and 20th respectively. They are surpassed by countries such as Mexico on both the export and import side. Thus, as is often pointed out, when it comes to trade, China is the dominant force among the developing countries.[3] Overall, including trade in both goods and services, China exports five times more than India. Much of China's trade growth has occurred in the last decade. In 2000, as it was entering the WTO, China accounted for 3.7 per cent of global trade. This increased by 6.7 percentage points in the following decade.

This very rapid growth is sometimes argued to be a major factor explaining the difficulty in concluding the DDA in that 'fear of China' is leading countries to become less willing to commit to further liberalisation via the WTO on an MFN basis. Arguments that the inability to conclude the DDA is in (large) part due to the rise of China and a desire by countries not to make it easier for Chinese goods to come in are not particularly compelling. The same is true for the related argument that OECD countries are already so open that they have little left to put on the table to 'buy' further trade reform by China, and that this is a 'last chance' to negotiate with China. The WTO offers various instruments such as anti-dumping (AD)/countervailing duties (CVD) and safeguards that countries can use to restrict Chinese imports if these cause or threaten injury to domestic producers. Indeed, as noted below, many countries are doing so. The fact that once China is granted market economy status it will become harder to use such instruments is not persuasive as there remains significant scope to impose temporary trade barriers using standard WTO-legal instruments. Similarly, there is still much to 'trade' in terms of policy commitments if attention turns to policies affecting access to natural resources and services markets. What is needed is agreement to expand the set of issues that are on the table.

---

[3] India is a much bigger player in trade in services, ranking fifth for both exports and imports (China is third after the European Union and the United States).

### Diverging performance across countries

There is substantial variation across countries in trade growth and
diversification. Sub-Saharan African countries in particular remain heavily dependent on natural resources and agricultural products. And
although there has been a sea change in trade policy everywhere, the
poorest countries often tend to have higher barriers and trade costs, in
part because a lack of 'connectivity', reflecting weaknesses in infrastructure. To date most of Africa has not seen the shift towards intra-industry
trade, vertical specialisation and participation in international supply
chains that has been a driver of trade growth in East Asia, Mexico,
Turkey, or Central and Eastern Europe. Although barriers to trade have
fallen everywhere, average trade costs are much higher for low-income
countries than richer ones. In the last fifteen years trade costs have fallen
much more in richer nations (Figure 3.1). This has a number of implications. One is that it reduces the payoffs to preferential access programmes:
DFQF access will be offset in part by actions by other countries that
reduce trade costs for everyone.[4] Another is that it is unclear how much
international trade cooperation can do to help low-income countries
address their trade cost agendas – this is mostly a matter for domestic
policy and public investment.

### Servicification and digitisation

Although technology is permitting greater 'dematerialisation' of trade,
the share of services in global trade has been remarkably constant
since the 1980s – varying between 20 and 25 per cent. What has
changed is the composition of this trade, with private business services
growing in importance and the travel and transport share declining.
The value of world trade in services has been expanding rapidly but so
has trade in goods – as a result the overall ratio has not changed much,
although the increasing share of services in GDP as countries grow
richer is accompanied by an increasing share of the value of all
products reflecting services inputs. While there is significant discrimination against foreign suppliers of services in some services sectors – e.g.
professional services providers – the observed explosion of global trade
has been possible in part because of the liberalisation of services

---

[4] In addition, the greater the number of free trade agreements that high-income countries
conclude, the less the value of DFQF.

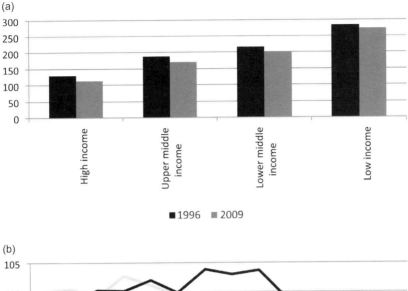

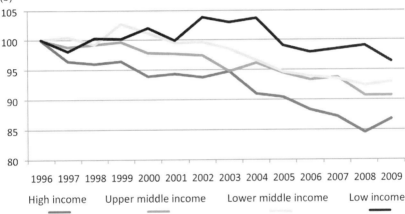

**Figure 3.1**  Average trade costs for manufactured exports by country income group, 1996–2009. Bars (a) indicate average trade costs as percentage *ad valorem* equivalents for the ten largest importing partner nations for each country in the sample; (b) trend over time is an index with 1996 = 100 (Arvis *et al.*, 2013).

markets in many parts of the world. Examples include the deregulation of air and road transport; the abolition of anti-trust exemption for maritime liner transport; the privatisation of ports and port services; the divesture and breakup of state-owned telecommunications monopolies; and so forth. The types of services that are increasingly being provided cross border through the Internet (itself the result of a variety of services policy reforms and technological advances in the information communication technology area) are not subject to restrictive trade policies in most countries. The 'market access' agenda in this area increasingly revolves around regulation, for example, requirements pertaining to privacy and cross-border transfers of data, matters that are not covered by the WTO.

### Changes in agricultural policies and demand for natural resources

Historically, agriculture has tended to be taxed in developing countries, often in part as an element of industrialisation strategies. In recent decades, the policy stance in many countries has become much more neutral (Anderson, 2009). Although exports of agricultural products remain of great importance for many low-income countries, and the policies of rich countries in support of the sector create negative spillovers for many of them, higher prices of food resulting from climate change and the expanding size of the global middle class can be expected to generate greater supply, and have been beneficial for farmers and rural communities. Supply responses in low-income countries to higher prices will depend in large part on domestic policies and the level of trade costs. An implication for the WTO is that the traditional agricultural negotiating agenda is becoming less relevant. Issues such as access to natural resources and food have become more of a concern, including the use of export restrictions by net exporters.

### Changing political economy of trade policy

The process of vertical specialisation and fragmentation of production, in conjunction with extensive flows of FDI into developing countries, has greatly attenuated the incentives to use trade policy to protect specific industries as this is more likely to hurt than help. Being able to compete in a specific niche or activity requires that firms are able to integrate into the relevant value or production chains. Significant levels of import protection would impede their ability to do so. The 2008 financial crisis and subsequent global recession illustrated the change in the incentives to use traditional import protection instruments. Gawande *et al.* (2014) show that the intensity of vertical specialisation helps explain observed trade policy responses to the crisis as well as the level of trade protection pre-crisis. The major emerging economies did not utilise the 'policy space' they have – given tariff bindings that are generally far above applied rates (with the exception of China) – as a result of the incentives created by participation in supply chain trade. These incentive constraints were complemented by those created by trade agreements. Countries that are members of deep free trade agreements, such as Mexico (North American Free Trade Association (NAFTA)) and Turkey (a customs union with the European Union), or that bound their tariffs at applied levels in the WTO (first and foremost China) were much more constrained than other countries.

The increasing vertical specialisation of production and trade helps to explain the increasing use (and relative share) of measures that restrict exports of natural resources that are upstream inputs into global value chains. This acts as a subsidy, making domestic processors and the chains they connect to more competitive.[5] While the increase in supply chain trade affects the incentives to use alternative trade policy instruments, these continue to provide a basis for the negotiation of international disciplines to internalise the associated spillovers. An implication is that the focus of rule-making efforts needs to be on a broader set of policies.

## *Developing country participation in the WTO*

Developing countries have become very active players in the WTO. This is true not just for the DDA, but also in terms of the use of dispute settlement procedures and instruments of contingent protection that are permitted by the WTO. Examples include the G-20 group of developing countries that was created in the run-up to the Cancún Ministerial Meeting in 2003 and the formation of coalitions such as the Africa Group and the LDC group. Developing nations were defendants in only 8 per cent of all the cases brought during the GATT years; in the post-1995 WTO period this figure rose to 35 per cent. Developing countries accounted for about one-third of all complaints during the period 1995–2012. They increasingly use WTO procedures against each other – over 40 per cent of all complaints have been directed at other developing countries. BCI account for over one-third of all cases brought by developing countries, but smaller middle-income states such as Argentina, Chile,

---

[5] A number of major exporters have also imposed measures to restrict the exports of agricultural products, mostly food staples, in an effort to lower domestic prices for consumers.

Mexico and Thailand have also been very active.[6] Developing countries are also increasingly active users of contingent protection, using instruments such as anti-dumping to target exports from other developing countries. China has become the main target for such actions, but the instrument is also used to check imports originating in other developing economies. In Brazil and China, anti-dumping covers around 2 per cent of total imports; in India – now the world's most active user – the figure is 4 per cent (Bown, 2011).

### PTAs – the outside option

Although the current focus of attention is on the 'mega-regional' PTA negotiations that involve the United States (TPP, TTIP, Trade in Services Agreement (TISA)), a number of high-income and developing countries are also very active in negotiating PTAs. Brazil is an outlier among major emerging economies in that it has not done much beyond Mercosur, but China and India as well as many other countries have negotiated a large number of PTAs. But the extant evidence suggests that PTAs to date have not been a substitute for progress at the multilateral level for BCI in the sense that they are not doing on a bilateral or regional basis what they are not willing to do at the WTO level. The exception is China and East Asia (Chia, 2010; Sally and Sen, 2011). In part, this reflects the intensity of regional trade. Regional trade is much more important for China than for Brazil or India, accounting for over 30 per cent of both exports and imports of goods. Gao (2009) argues that China's strategy is to connect to countries that are themselves part of a PTA network, are often natural resource exporters and that political objectives are important (e.g. obtaining market economy status).

Most PTAs negotiated since the mid-1990s go beyond the WTO in terms of coverage. One measure of this additionality is the sectoral coverage of services. Figure 3.2, taken from Van der Marel and Miroudot

---

[6]  Noteworthy examples are use of the Dispute Settlement Understanding (DSU) by Brazil and India to attack preference programmes that benefit poorer/smaller developing countries. Examples include a 1998 decision by Brazil to contest the EU GSP scheme as inconsistent with the Enabling Clause (which requires that preferences be 'generalized, non-reciprocal and nondiscriminatory'). This led to a six-year waiver being negotiated for EU preferences for African, Caribbean and Pacific (ACP) countries in Doha in 2001, and the launch of the negotiations between the European Union and the ACP to establish reciprocal economic partnership agreements (EPAs). Other examples are the 2003 cases brought by India against the EU GSP+ programme and by Brazil against EU export subsidies for sugar.

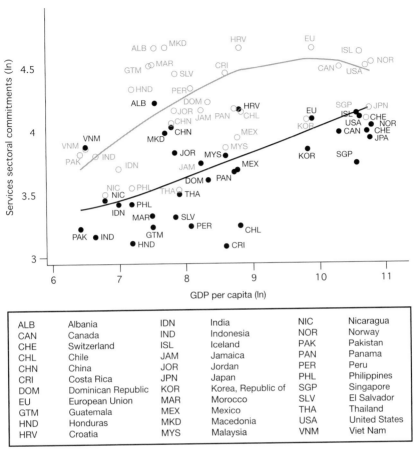

Figure 3.2  Sectoral coverage: GATS vs. PTA averages. Dark dots are average number of sectors in GATS commitments; hollow dots are the average number of sectors subject to commitments in PTAs of each country listed (Van der Marel and Miroudot (2014)).

(2014), illustrates this by plotting the average number of sectors subject to commitments in PTAs against each PTA member's commitments in the General Agreement on Trade in Services (GATS). However, the substantive disciplines (rules) that are included in many PTAs are similar to those in the GATS, i.e. the depth of the associated commitments often does not go much beyond what PTA members committed to under the WTO (Fink and Jansen, 2009). In areas where there are no WTO disciplines, there often tend not to be rules in PTAs either – examples are safeguard provisions and rules on subsidies and domestic regulation (Horn *et al.*, 2010). Two important exceptions are investment and public procurement, policy areas that are not covered by general WTO disciplines.

## Consequences for developing countries in the WTO

Grossly simplifying, developing countries have pursued two very different approaches in the WTO. One set of countries has actively pursued a 'global integration' strategy, liberalising trade, seeking inward FDI and promoting participation by local firms in international supply networks. Examples include the Pacific Alliance countries (Chile, Colombia, Peru and Mexico), Costa Rica, Turkey and the countries participating in the TPP. Another (larger) group of developing countries have put greater stress on the historical S&D strategy, calling for non-reciprocal market access concessions from industrialised nations, limiting the extent of any commitments they might make and seeking greater 'policy space' to restrict trade. As far as the largest emerging economies are concerned, China is clearly in the 'global integration' camp, whereas Brazil and India have tended to be less focused on leveraging foreign trade opportunities to support economic growth and development.

An implication of the trends just summarised and the DDA deadlock is that the returns to continued pursuit of S&D will be limited at best because there is nothing to seek exceptions from and no scope to argue for more favourable treatment. The DDA deadlock also means no progress on market access and new rules in areas that are of importance to developing countries.[7] This not to deny that the strategy of raising development concerns has not had payoffs – in some respects it has led to issues that were of most concern to the poorest developing countries in the late 1990s/early 2000s having been addressed at least in part in the WTO.[8] As mentioned in the introduction, there was a concerted push

---

[7] Examples are tariff escalation or the elimination of support for cotton production in OECD nations. As the latter have made it clear that any deal on agricultural policies or NAMA will need to be balanced by market access concessions offered by BCI, there is little that small developing nations such as the Cotton-4 (Benin, Burkina Faso, Chad and Mali) can do beyond advocacy. A deal is in the hands of the large WTO members: the European Union, United States, Brazil, India and China in particular. Small developing countries are price-takers in international negotiations on market access and agricultural support programmes.

[8] This is also true with respect to other concerns regarding the operation of WTO processes, e.g. internal transparency and access to information and consultations. See Hoekman (2012).

during the DDA to make preferential market access programmes more meaningful by expanding their product coverage and relaxing the 'conditionality' that applied, especially with respect to rules of origin. This push led to the Hong Kong Ministerial Meeting Declaration calling for at least 97 per cent of LDC exports to developed country markets to benefit from DFQF access. Many OECD countries (the United States being the notable exception) have now completely opened their markets for merchandise imports from LDCs, which also increasingly benefit from DFQF access for many of their exports to BCI as well.[9] In addition, concerns about limited supply capacity (lack of competitiveness) were translated into a major effort to increase development assistance for trade-related projects. This led to the launch of the Aid for Trade initiative at the 2005 Hong Kong Ministerial Meeting and the creation of the Enhanced Integrated Framework (EIF) for trade-related technical assistance for the LDCs. Aid for Trade has become a mechanism to engage development agencies (bilateral and multilateral) more in the trade integration agenda and helps to raise the profile of trade issues in the process of determining priorities for investment and policy reform at the country level. These achievements address part of the 'development deficit' in the design of the WTO.[10]

The challenge for the majority of countries that are not part of the current 'mega-regional' negotiations is to identify actions that can be taken to reduce potential downsides and/or to also benefit from these initiatives. This is an important challenge not just for all the countries in Africa, the Middle East, Central and South Asia and those parts of Latin America that are not part of the TPP. It is also important for the East

[9] While the success of the LDCs and other African countries in improving and defending preferential access to major export markets post-2001 is a significant achievement, it also had a downside: it created tensions between developing countries (DFQF only extends to the LDCs and not to other countries that may be very similar in terms of per capita income and other development indicators), and gave rise to incentives to resist the preference erosion that would result if the DDA was to reduce the applied MFN tariffs of preference-granting countries. This negative dynamic is illustrated most notably in the resistance by the United States to extending DFQF treatment to Asian LDCs (Bangladesh, Cambodia, Lao PDR), which is driven in part by concern that doing so would erode the value of the preferential market access provided to eligible African countries under the African Growth and Opportunity Act.

[10] Note that both imply differentiation across developing countries: the focus is on the poorest and poorer developing countries. BCI do not benefit from deeper forms of preferential access and are only eligible for Aid for Trade on whatever terms and conditions are applied by donors and development agencies.

Asian countries that are not part of the TPP – not just China but also six of the Association of South-East Asian Nations (ASEAN) member countries, including Indonesia, the Philippines and Thailand. And it applies to all developing countries when it comes to the TTIP.

One potential response to the shift by the United States to mega-regionals is to pursue PTAs in turn – which of course is already (and has been) happening. This can help generate greater trade with a set of countries that are growing more rapidly than the European Union and United States and where traditional barriers to trade are substantially higher. If such PTAs result in meaningful preferential liberalisation, the associated trade diversion could become an incentive for a renewed effort to conclude a multilateral deal, which might also become more feasible than it is today by eroding the power of the interest groups in major emerging economies that currently resist market opening on a MFN basis. The Regional Comprehensive Economic Partnership (RCEP) is a possible example of this strategy, involving both China and India.[11] However, to date PTAs involving BCI have tended to be shallow, with substantial exceptions and exclusions to safeguard 'sensitive' products and industries and no disciplines on the use of industrial policy-related instruments.

Classic trade diversion costs generated by preferential removal of tariffs in agreements that involve the United States are likely to be limited because average tariffs in most of the countries participating in the TPP and TTIP are low.[12] However, in some sectors tariffs are still significant – e.g. textiles and clothing – and thus there will be negative effects for developing countries that are excluded from an agreement such as TPP as insiders are given preferential access to the US market. There is also potential for *de facto* discrimination resulting from measures that have the effect of reducing the market-segmenting effects of differences in regulatory policies. Much will depend on whether third country firms will be able to benefit from access to the larger market created by the PTA if they are able to demonstrate compliance with the relevant regulatory standards. In practice it may be difficult to exclude third country firms

---

[11] At the time of writing, the RCEP involves sixteen countries: the ten ASEAN members (Brunei, Cambodia, Indonesia, Lao PDR, Malaysia, Myanmar, the Philippines, Singapore, Thailand and Viet Nam) and six countries with which ASEAN has a free trade agreement (Australia, China, India, Japan, Republic of Korea and New Zealand).

[12] In part such additional costs will be low because the United States already has PTAs with most of the other TPP countries.

from benefiting from initiatives that lower the fixed costs associated with enforcement of regulation in member countries.[13]

Given their proclaimed goal of being high of quality, 'twenty-first-century' agreements that address the regulatory causes of market segmentation and reduce the cost-raising effects of differences in prevailing domestic policies, another response is to focus resources on understanding what members of these PTAs actually do and to learn from the initiatives that are pursued. Achieving the objectives that the countries participating in the new PTAs have set themselves will not be straightforward by any stretch of the imagination. There will be much to be learned from the experience obtained as a result of implementing these PTAs. The WTO can be used for this purpose. Doing so is fully consistent with its transparency mandate(s), but making it happen will require concerted action by non-members of the PTAs to give the WTO a mandate to provide such 'services' (Hoekman, 2014).

Yet another response to the proliferation of PTAs and the WTO deadlock on rule-making is to consider what can be done to reduce the incentive to use the PTA route for countries that want to go beyond existing WTO disciplines, and to multilateralise specific features of the PTAs that are effective in reducing regulatory trade costs. As discussed further below, the WTO allows for so-called plurilateral agreements among a subset of its membership that apply only to signatories. Insofar as the increased recourse to PTAs is not driven by traditional market access and third market competition issues – tariffs, quotas, (export) subsidies, etc. – there is no prima facie reason for countries to go down the PTA track if they want to cooperate in a given area that is not covered by the WTO. Much of the 'twenty-first-century' trade agenda revolves around regulation where the issue is not necessarily the pursuit of deliberate discrimination. This suggests there should be greater flexibility and willingness by the WTO membership to encourage countries to pursue cooperation on regulatory matters *inside* the WTO rather than accepting that PTAs must be the default option. Doing so will not only help reduce the fragmentation of the trading system, but provide a vehicle for all WTO members to benefit from the initiatives and experimentation that will be pursued in the context of the mega-regionals (and other PTAs).

---

[13] The literature investigating the effects of regional harmonisation of standards has found that this may benefit excluded countries, but that this is conditional on their capacity to satisfy the norms and mechanisms that are adopted by a PTA. See e.g. Chen and Mattoo (2008) and Shepherd (2007).

## Embracing diversity: complementing law-making efforts with more jaw-jaw

The WTO is geared towards the negotiation of enforceable commitments. This is its primary strength: binding disciplines reduce uncertainty for traders who know that the dispute settlement mechanism can be used to ensure that governments live up to what they sign on to. But a precondition for the negotiation process to work is that a subject generates cross-border spillovers (affects the terms of trade) and that countries have a reasonable sense of what the orders of magnitude are of the net benefits of any specific proposed deal. The WTO tends to take a 'silo approach', addressing policy areas in isolation. In practice, given that regulation and domestic policies are increasingly the source of market segmentation and a determinant of the profits that accrue to domestic vs. foreign firms and factors of production, some degree of positive integration (agreement on common rules or mutual recognition) may be needed to achieve joint increases in economic welfare (e.g. Antras and Staiger, 2012). Determining what would produce such increases is not straightforward – it certainly may not suffice to focus on just one policy instrument. Figuring out what matters most, and what policy areas should be on the table jointly, is something that will take substantial preparatory work. Moreover, in some areas it simply may not be possible or appropriate to negotiate binding rules and the best that may be feasible is to increase transparency and the information that countries have about the aim and effects of policies. This is the case in particular when it comes to behind-the-border regulatory policies as cooperation will be required by the regulatory agencies that are charged with their design and implementation.

From a competitiveness and economic development perspective, bringing down trade costs is today the priority for many countries. Much of the associated policy agenda will involve autonomous, unilateral reforms and investments by national and local governments. As these actions will benefit the large mass of firms and consumers in the countries concerned, the political economy rationale for exchanging reform commitments in a trade agreement is weaker than it is for tariffs – especially insofar as the associated policies (or lack thereof) that give rise to the real trade costs do not generate rents that accrue to specific vested interests. However, there will be situations where such rents exist and trade costs will give rise to negative spillovers for trading partners as well as local firms and households. Thus there remains an incentive for countries to cooperate.

The rise of supply chain trade and international production makes it imperative that a more holistic approach is taken towards international cooperation to reduce trade costs. Hoekman (2014) argues that an implication of the increasing prevalence of global value chains and vertical specialisation of firms is that governments need to be much more cognisant of how policies in very different areas collectively affect supply chain trade opportunities and investments. The standard approach that is embedded in the structure of the WTO, and the approach that has been taken in the DDA, is to negotiate in specific silos: tariffs for manufactured goods, agricultural support, services, etc. But the cost, quality and variety of available services in an economy are a critical determinant of the competitiveness of farm products and manufactured goods. Similarly, access to a wide variety of goods is a critical input into the production of services and the competitiveness of services suppliers. The same applies to agriculture. This suggests that a supply chain informed approach to negotiating market access commitments and new rules could help ensure that the policies that matter most from a trade perspective are discussed, in the process making the WTO negotiating process more relevant for businesses.

Many aspects of the 'trade cost' policy reform agenda are on the WTO table, including trade facilitation, rule-making on non-tariff measures (NTMs) and increasing access to services markets. All are important determinants of the competitiveness of firms. Making progress in international cooperation to reduce the negative impacts on trade that are created by policies in these areas is a complex, multi-dimensional challenge. As noted in Hoekman and Mattoo (2013), part and parcel of such an approach is that it needs to take regulatory concerns and constraints seriously. Mechanisms that bring together sectoral regulators, trade officials and stakeholders to assess current policies and identify beneficial reforms are likely to be a precondition for reducing trade barriers in sectors that are regulated. Such mechanisms are a feature of some of the deeper PTAs that have been negotiated in recent years and there is much that might be transferred or adopted in the WTO context along similar lines.

A feature of some PTAs that distinguishes them from the WTO is the incorporation of non-binding (non-enforceable) 'soft law' forms of cooperation. Often these take the form of provisions to provide technical and other forms of assistance, and the establishment of mechanisms for the exchange of information, interactions between business associations, investors and civil society groups, and non-economic forms of cooperation (e.g. student or cultural exchanges). PTAs often also create a variety of official bodies that are tasked with implementation of the agreement in specific areas and that can act as mechanisms through which the regulators and other officials from the participating countries establish working relationships. One lesson from successful North–South PTAs is that the prospects for PTAs to enhance the welfare of developing country signatories are improved if the focus extends beyond market access and government-to-government interaction. Including complementary measures that aim at improving the domestic regulatory environment, bolstering related institutions, the provision of technical and financial assistance and active engagement by the private sector in surveillance and enforcement of the PTA are equally if not more important (Hoekman, 2011).

Much of the agenda on the new vintage PTAs concerns the trade-impeding effects of regulation and regulatory policies – various forms of NTMs. Examples are product regulation (to achieve health, safety or security objectives), licensing requirements, certification and conformity assessment procedures, data reporting standards, border management procedures, the quality of transport and communications infrastructure and the degree of competition that prevails in services markets. Frequently, one cause of excess cost is a multiplicity of regulatory norms and related enforcement requirements that are pursued independently by many different government agencies. Many of these regulatory policies often apply equally to local and foreign firms and products, but they generally increase trade costs more for foreign than for domestic suppliers simply because regulations differ across countries or because foreign firms are subject to a multiplicity of requirements that are redundant (duplicative). More important, however, is that regulatory policies can raise costs across the board – for domestic and foreign firms – and thus the price of goods and services for buyers, whether firms or households.

Such measures cannot simply be abolished as presumably they fulfil specific social or economic purposes that are not discriminatory in intent, even if the effect is to restrict trade. Addressing the trade effects of regulation requires first an understanding at the national level of the effects of prevailing policies and the likely impacts of alternative possible reforms. Many such reforms will not require actions by other governments (trading partners), but international agreements on the rules of the game may help either to mobilise the needed attention to an issue or to overcome resistance by vested interests to welfare-enhancing reform.

Indeed, international cooperation can help countries identify what would be beneficial reforms. But this is likely to require not so much reciprocal exchanges of policy commitments – the standard modality of trade negotiations – as agreement on processes that centre attention on building an understanding of the potential gains from reforms.

This implies that PTAs are a learning opportunity – not just for the countries that are members, but for those that are not. The proliferation of PTAs offers the WTO membership as a whole an opportunity to learn from the many experiments and approaches that are being pursued. PTAs are in some sense laboratories. The experiments that are successful in specific PTAs may be transferable. Over time, WTO members may come to embed some of the processes and approaches that have proved successful in a PTA context into the WTO. A precondition for such learning is transparency: WTO members need to have information on what is being done in the PTA context. Rather than attempting to determine this individually, this is much better done by the WTO Secretariat and by the signatories to PTAs providing information and sharing their experiences with the broader WTO membership, with discussions supplemented by external analysis of the impacts of specific processes or approaches that have been taken in PTAs.

An important contribution the WTO could make in this regard is to go beyond simply reporting on the provisions of any given PTA, as is done today by the Transparency Review Mechanism. Collecting and analysing information on the factors affecting implementation of PTA disciplines would allow a much better understanding of what is actually being done in the PTA context. As mentioned, this will require collaboration with the business community. Data on implementation and its impacts are critical inputs into any assessment of progress made in addressing the barriers and helping WTO members to understand better why measures are effective or why they are not effective. A constraint in this connection is that business may be hesitant to make the relevant data publicly available for fear of adverse reactions by government agencies or worries about revealing useful information to competitors. Conversely, governments may discount information provided by business because of perceptions that firms will seek to remove any policies that raise their costs even if the underlying measures are implemented efficiently by the administrative bodies responsible for enforcement of policy. The WTO Secretariat could become a trusted intermediary, acting as the depository of data provided by business and ensuring that this is relevant and appropriate in measuring and assessing the impacts of implementation of specific measures agreed by the signatories to a PTA.[14]

In addition to doing more to learn from PTAs, a good case can be made that WTO members should consider a greater focus on the conclusion of plurilateral agreements under the auspices of the WTO. This can take two forms. The first are so-called critical mass agreements, where a smaller group of countries agree on certain rules of the game that apply only to signatories, with the benefits extended to all WTO members, whether they join or not. Examples are the negotiations to liberalise trade in environmental goods that were launched in July 2014, the 1997 Information Technology Agreement (ITA) and the ongoing talks to conclude an ITA-2 with broader product coverage. A precondition for such agreements is that a critical mass of countries participate that together cover most of the trade in the products concerned, thereby allowing free-riding by the majority of the WTO membership. These critical mass initiatives illustrate that despite the DDA deadlock there is continuing appetite among WTO members to use trade agreements to liberalise international commerce.

Critical mass agreements by their nature require the participation of the large players and thus do not offer the mass of the WTO membership an instrument to shift the focus of the United States and the European Union away from PTAs as a vehicle to agree to rules of the game in areas that are not covered by the WTO. One reason why PTAs are used is because cooperation on regulatory matters cannot automatically be extended to any country – many preconditions may need to be in place for regulatory agreements to be feasible. Agreement on cooperation on regulatory matters among 161 WTO members will in most cases be difficult, if not impossible. But PTAs are not the only game in town when it comes to negotiating policy commitments among a 'club'. The WTO offers another mechanism for members to do so: conclusion of a plurilateral agreement under Article II.3 of the Marrakesh Agreement Establishing the World Trade Organization (Lawrence, 2006). This provision permits sub-sets of the WTO membership to agree to new disciplines applying to signatories only. In contrast to a PTA, which must cover substantially all trade in goods (Article XXIV GATT), and/or have substantial sectoral coverage of services (Article V GATS), plurilateral

---

[14] Such a role is played by other international organisations for other types of data – e.g. the International Chamber of Commerce (ICC) for data on trade finance and the World Bank for firm- and household-level data.

agreements can be issue specific. At present there are two plurilateral agreements in force in the WTO, the Agreement on Government Procurement (GPA) and the Agreement on Civil Aviation.

Hoekman and Mavroidis (2013) argue that greater effort should be given to fostering more club formation under the umbrella of the WTO in the shape of plurilateral agreements. Reasons for this include the fact that plurilateral agreements are Pareto sanctioned in the sense that no WTO member is made worse off, as their content must be approved by the WTO membership as a whole. PTAs are reviewed by the WTO, but there is no sanctioning of their content or assessment of whether they comply with WTO rules (see Mavroidis, 2012). The review is limited to supply of information, which stops at the moment a PTA has been reviewed. There is no obligation to continue to supply information to the WTO after that. In contrast, plurilateral agreements will involve regular reporting on activities. The plethora of PTAs results in significant dispersion in rules and approaches and thus transactions costs and trade diversion – Jagdish Bhagwati's famous spaghetti bowl analogy. PTAs are also mostly closed to accession by new members. Plurilateral agreements in contrast are required to be open. Last but not least, PTAs often have their own dispute settlement procedures, so the WTO is in the dark as to what happens after its initial review. Dispute settlement, of course, is the most frequent form of 'contract completion', and as a result the WTO misses out on important information. In contrast, plurilateral agreements use the WTO Dispute Settlement Mechanism.

An important impediment to negotiating new plurilateral agreements is the requirement that any plurilateral agreement be approved by the whole WTO membership: plurilateral agreements require consensus. This means that countries that have no interest in joining can none the less block approval of a new proposed plurilateral agreement. The prospects of achieving the required consensus can be enhanced through a process of agreeing on a code of conduct for plurilateral agreements (World Economic Forum, 2010). This could include that membership in plurilateral agreements is voluntary; that the subject is a core trade-related issue; that those participating in negotiations should have the means, or be provided with the means as part of the agreement, to implement the outcomes; that the issue under negotiation should enjoy substantial support from the WTO membership; and that the 'subsidiarity' principle should apply in order to minimise the intrusion of 'club rules' on national autonomy (see World Economic Forum, 2010).

Plurilateral agreements would of course benefit from having the participation of the major traders. But there is no impediment against smaller countries taking the lead and seeking to conclude such agreements on subjects that are of interest to them but that are not covered by existing WTO rules. There are many possible areas in which plurilateral agreements can help governments experiment and learn without implicating the whole WTO membership. To give just one example: some governments may want to create a mechanism to harmonise approaches to product classification and to share data on advance rulings by customs agencies. The point is that there is no need to pursue cooperation on new issues through a PTA.

Economic growth rates in much of the developing world have largely been the result of autonomous reforms pursued by the governments of these countries. The GATT/WTO has played only a limited direct role in the 'rise of the rest', although the principles of openness, predictability and transparency that underpin the trading system were very beneficial in supporting the growth in global trade that has occurred. The role of – and approaches by – developing countries in the WTO have changed substantially. The poorest countries have continued to push for S&D, but in a way that has been more effective than in the GATT years. Relative to the mid 1980s, preferential access programmes for LDCs are more meaningful in that there are fewer product exclusions and more liberal rules of origin in the major OECD markets. More generally, the growth in the size of export industries in many developing nations and their increasing integration into global value chains has meant that the WTO regime has become more relevant to these countries. One reflection of this is the recourse to the WTO dispute settlement mechanism to defend market access benefits and the willingness by the more advanced (and thus 'less-preferred') developing country governments to put pressure on high-income countries to abide by the WTO rules.

The changes that have occurred in the structure of the world economy as a result of policy reforms and technological advances – reflected in production fragmentation and the geographic splintering of value chains – have resulted in strong incentives for countries to lower trade costs and much reduced incentives to protect domestic markets. One consequence has been that many developing countries have become much more active in negotiating and implementing preferential and regional trade agreements and pursuing cooperation with neighbours and other trading partners to reduce trade costs. Indeed, for many governments, the primary focus of trade-related policy initiatives is unilateral and regional/preferential, not the WTO. Insofar as the primary focus of regional cooperation is on actions that reduce trade costs and lower barriers for all traders, the rise of regionalism may be 'multilateralising'.[15] The fact that the large emerging economies have not been active (or successful) in negotiating deep PTAs with each other or the largest OECD nations, suggests that the WTO will remain an important vehicle to engage in and address trade issues. PTAs can and do drive reforms in areas not covered by the WTO – e.g. investment – but we have yet to see any major developing country conclude a deep PTA with another large nation, developed or developing. This situation may change, as there are ongoing negotiations between the European Union and India, and between the European Union and Mercosur, but it is striking that recent initiatives like the TPP and the discussions on a TISA do not include BCI.

Although BCI have not taken a leadership role in pushing for a stronger rules-based trading system, the lack of progress in Doha should not be taken to imply a lack of interest in and commitment to the WTO. WTO negotiations are now more complex and slower to conclude because developing countries have interests that they want to defend and objectives they want to achieve. PTAs may well be more effective mechanisms to address certain issues, especially of a regulatory nature or involving the liberalisation of politically sensitive areas such as the movement of people. But to date they have not been instruments that address subjects that feature prominently on the DDA agenda, e.g. agricultural policies, and that are important to BCI and other developing countries.

Insofar as the mega-regional and other new vintage PTAs generate new approaches towards dealing with the market segmenting of the effects of, or differences in, regulatory policies, they can help all countries to identify approaches that can usefully be emulated. Most countries are not part of the 'megaregionals' but have a strong interest in understanding what these PTAs will end up doing or achieving. Using the WTO infrastructure to document, analyse and assess the approaches that are implemented by PTAs to reduce barriers would help ensure both transparency and potentially inform a process of learning about what works and what does not. A PTA 'learning' initiative could help identify specific features of cooperation in PTAs that can and should be multilateralised.

---

[15] See the contributions of Baldwin and Low (2009) for further discussion and analysis.

Plurilateral agreements offer a vehicle for such multilateralisation, given the likelihood that many WTO members will not be ready to adopt the disciplines and mechanisms in question at any given point in time. They allow for gradual expansion of membership as countries deem that it is in their interest to participate. Enabling even limited progress on specific areas of rule-making should be welcomed. Many of the issues that are on the table in the new vintage PTAs are regulatory in nature. In such areas it is understandable that countries are inclined to pursue small-numbers agreements and arrangements – establishing the trust needed for regulatory cooperation and convergence requires time and recurring bilateral interaction. But it seems perverse to insist – as is implied by the explicit rejection by Brazil and India of suggestions to pursue additional plurilateral agreements in the WTO – that if countries want to cooperate on regulatory matters that affect trade and investment, they must negotiate a PTA or do so outside the ambit of the WTO. Given the negotiating deadlock that currently prevails in the WTO, movement in the proposed directions will require leadership by the large mass of the WTO membership that is largely a bystander in the deadlock in the WTO and the move towards mega-regionals.

Countries that have gone through accession to the WTO are well placed to take such a leadership role. A corollary of the accession process – which as discussed at great length and in detail in the many chapters that are included in this volume, is a very demanding one – is that the end result is that the countries that acceded to the WTO after 1995 have an efficient trade regime and a clear trade policy framework that is aligned to the nation's overall economic development strategy. Recently acceded countries may have a much better ability to identify trade policy-related issues where international cooperation could benefit growth prospects than countries that have never been through the accession process. They are also more likely to have put in place the institutional framework and domestic coordinating bodies and mechanisms that are needed to sustain engagement on such issues. Perhaps most important, having gone through the very demanding accession process, these are countries with a 'revealed preference' for – and commitment to – the continued health and development of a rules-based multilateral trading system.

## References

Anderson, K. (ed.) (2009). *Distortions to Agricultural Incentives: A Global Perspective, 1955–2007*. Washington DC, Palgrave-Macmillan and World Bank.

Antras, P. and R. Staiger (2012). 'Offshoring and the role of trade agreements', *American Economic Review*, 102(7): 3140–3183.

Arvis, J. F., Y. Duval, B. Shepherd and C. Utoktham (2013). 'Trade costs in the developing world: 1995–2010', Washington DC, World Bank, Policy Research Working Paper 6309.

Baldwin, R. and P. Low (eds.) (2009). *Multilateralizing Regionalism*. Cambridge University Press.

Bown, C. (ed.) (2011). *The Great Recession and Import Protection: The Role of Temporary Trade Barriers*. Washington DC, CEPR and World Bank.

Chen, M. and A. Mattoo (2008). 'Regionalism in standards: good or bad for trade?', *Canadian Journal of Economics*, 41(3): 838–863.

Chia, S. (2010). 'Regional trade policy cooperation and architecture in East Asia', Tokyo, Asian Development Bank Institute, ADBI Working Paper 191.

Fink, C. and M. Jansen (2009). 'Services provisions in regional trade agreements: stumbling or building blocks for multilateral liberalization?', in R. Baldwin and P. Low (eds.), *Multilateralizing Regionalism*. Cambridge University Press.

Gao, H. (2009). 'China's strategy for free trade agreements: political battle in the name of trade'. Retrieved from http://ink.library.smu.edu.sg/sol_research/971.

Gawande, K., B. Hoekman and Y. Cui (2014). 'Determinants of trade policy responses to the 2008 financial crisis', *World Bank Economic Review*, 28(3).

Hoekman, B. (2011). 'North–South preferential trade agreements', in J. Chauffour and J. Maur (eds.), *Preferential Trade Agreements and Development: A Handbook*. Washington DC, World Bank.

(2012). 'WTO reform: a synthesis and assessment of recent proposals', in A. Narlikar, M. Daunton and R. Stern (eds.), *The Oxford Handbook on the World Trade Organization*. Oxford University Press.

(2014). *Supply Chains, Mega-Regionals and Multilateralism: A Road Map for the WTO*. London, CEPR Press.

Hoekman, B. and A. Mattoo (2013). 'Liberalizing trade in services: lessons from regional and WTO negotiations', *International Negotiation*, 18(1): 131–151.

Hoekman, B. and P.C. Mavroidis (2013). 'WTO à la carte or WTO menu du jour: assessing the case for plurilateral agreements', Fiesole, Italy, European University Institute, Robert Schuman Centre for Advanced Studies, Working Paper 2013/58.

Hoekman, B., W. Martin and A. Mattoo (2010). 'Conclude Doha: it matters!', *World Trade Review*, 9(3): 505–530.

Horn, H., P. Mavroidis and A. Sapir (2010). 'Beyond the WTO? An anatomy of EU and US preferential trade agreements', *World Economy*, 33(11): 1565–1588.

Kee, H., A. Nicita and M. Olarreaga (2009). 'Estimating trade restrictiveness indices', *Economic Journal* 119(534): 172–199.

Laborde, D., W. Martin and D. van der Mensbrugghe (2011). 'Implications of the Doha market access proposals for developing countries', Washington DC, World Bank, Policy Research Working Paper 5679.

Lawrence, R. (2006). 'Rulemaking amidst growing diversity: a "club of clubs" approach to WTO reform and new issue selection', *Journal of International Economic Law*, 9(4): 823–835.

Mavroidis, P. C. (2012). *Trade in Goods*. Oxford University Press.

Sally, R. and R. Sen (2011). 'Trade policies in South-East Asia in the wider Asian perspective', *World Economy*, 34(4): 568–601.

Shepherd, B. (2007). 'Product standards, harmonization, and trade: evidence from the extensive margin', Washington DC, World Bank, Policy Research Working Paper 4390.

Timmer, M., A. Erumban, B. Los, R. Stehrer and G. de Vries (2013). 'Slicing up global value chains', GGDC Research Memorandum 135. Retrieved from www.ggdc.net/publications/memorandum/gd135.pdf.

Van der Marel, E. and S. Miroudot (2014). 'The economics and political economy of going beyond the GATS', *Review of International Organizations*, 9(2): 205–239.

Wolfe, R. (2013). 'First diagnose, then treat: what ails the Doha Round?', Fiesole, Italy, European University Institute, Robert Schuman Centre for Advanced Studies, Working Paper 2013/85.

World Economic Forum (2010). 'A Plurilateral "Club-of-Clubs" Approach to World Trade Organization Reform and New Issues'. Geneva, Global Agenda Council on the Global Trade System and FDI.

World Economic Forum (with Bain & Co. and World Bank) (2013). *Enabling Trade: Valuing Growth Opportunities*. Geneva, WEF.

WTO (2007). *Six Decades of Multilateral Trade Cooperation: World Trade Report 2007*. Geneva, WTO.

   (2011) *International Trade Statistics*. Geneva, WTO.

   (2012). *International Trade Statistics*. Geneva, WTO.

# 4

# The structural reform implications
of WTO accession

MONA HADDAD, CLAIRE H. HOLLWEG AND
ALBERTO PORTUGAL-PEREZ

## ABSTRACT

*This chapter looks at the relationship between the WTO accession process and structural reforms in developing countries. It finds that developing economies that are in the process of acceding to the WTO commit to more policy reforms (proxied by prior actions in the context of the World Bank's development policy lending) than developing countries that are already members of the WTO or that have not applied to become members. It also finds that, for almost all developing economies acceding to the WTO, the country risk, measured by a composite indicator of political, financial and economic risk called the International Country Risk Guide, and the policy and institutional indicator, measured by the World Bank Country Policy and Institutional Assessment, significantly improve when a country achieves WTO membership compared with at the beginning of the WTO accession process.*

Developing countries have been growing faster than advanced economies since the mid 2000s. This sustained growth has been supported by external factors, such as the expansion of global value chains, lower transportation and communication costs, buoyed global trade and easy financing conditions. But domestic factors – such as structural reforms that promote market forces, better policy-making, stronger institutions and greater trade and financial openness – have also played an important role. These reforms have increased the productivity of developing countries and allowed them to take advantage of global trade opportunities.

The analyses in the chapters in this book were finalised at the end of December 2014. Since then the Republic of Seychelles acceded to the World Trade Organization (WTO) on 26 April 2015. This expanded total WTO membership from 160 to 161. Please see the editors' note.

Today their trade is growing faster than that of developed countries. The share of developing countries' trade in global trade rose from 10 per cent in the mid 1990s to more than 30 per cent by 2012.

The structural reforms undertaken by developing countries over the past two decades have varied depending on their level of income. In low-income countries, structural reforms have focused on reducing trade barriers, rolling back distortionary agricultural subsidies and price controls, reforming the banking sector and improving basic education and the institutions needed for market-based economic activity. In lower-middle-income countries, maintaining the productivity growth required reforms in the banking and agricultural sectors, reducing barriers to foreign investment, as well as increasing competition in product markets, improving the quality of secondary and tertiary education and alleviating infrastructure bottlenecks. In upper-middle-income countries, productivity enhancements came from deepening capital markets, developing more competitive and flexible product and labour markets, fostering a more skilled labour force and investing in research and development and new technologies (Christiansen, Schindler and Tressel, 2009).

## Structural reforms and WTO accession

As developing countries pursued macroeconomic stability and structural reforms, they also sought WTO accession if they were not members already. WTO accession can be used as an important tool for development. It can be a mechanism to intensify and accelerate domestic structural reforms beyond simple trade policy. Applying for WTO membership signals the readiness of a government to undertake deep reforms regardless of that membership. When countries decide to join the WTO, they are already thinking about a reform process that is wider than the WTO itself. WTO membership enables countries to adhere to multilateral rules, thus reducing the potential for policy reversal and raising confidence among investors. Typically, WTO accession is part of the structural reform package and not its cause. But governments that are acceding to the WTO accelerate and deepen their structural reforms compared with those that are not going through an accession process or are already members of the WTO. While the final outcome of accession brings much benefit, the accession process itself, which takes about ten years, on average, is also important. It is during that phase that many reforms are actually implemented.

The link between the WTO accession process and the structural reforms undertaken by acceding governments depends on the types of government that have recently acceded to the WTO or are in the process of accession. These fall into three categories. The first includes Eastern European and former Soviet Union economies, which constituted the bulk of new WTO members in the 1990s. These countries were shifting from a communist regime to a more market-oriented economy and used the WTO to help them in that process. Some of them were also applying for European Union (EU) membership and had to undergo broader and deeper structural reforms. The second includes low-income and least-developed countries (LDCs) that wanted to accelerate reforms, such as Cabo Verde, Cambodia, Lao PDR and Nepal. Six LDCs have acceded since the establishment of the WTO, and another nine are in the process of acceding (comprising over one-third of the accessions in progress). The third category includes large and influential countries which have a big impact on other countries and whose accession was often politically tainted, such as China, Russia and Saudi Arabia.

Currently, there are twenty-two countries in the ongoing process of WTO accession, eleven of which had working parties established in the 1990s (or earlier as in the case of Algeria). The accessions of Belarus and Uzbekistan, for example, have been ongoing for twenty years, their working parties having been established in 1993 and 1994 respectively, while the Azerbaijan and Kazakhstan applications were received over fifteen years ago. In this group of countries, WTO accession still seems out of reach and not squarely at the heart of their reform processes.

## The accession process as an impetus for reforms

The WTO, with its 161 members, plays a significant role in safeguarding countries' commitments to globalisation. However, the membership process is long and demanding. Candidates for accession are typically required by WTO members to undertake a wide range of reforms during the period over which accession is negotiated, before membership is granted. During the accession process, a working party is established that involves WTO members showing an interest in the membership application, with which the candidate makes commitments regarding market access and in other reform areas. In addition, candidates commit to further reform within a defined time-frame after formally becoming WTO members. Policy reforms mandated in the WTO accession agreements can be extensive and politically difficult, but are legally binding as long as the country remains a member of the WTO.

The accession process is long, but it gives time for acceding governments to adjust their policies and institutions before membership is granted. Since the establishment of the WTO in January 1995, the timeline of the accession process has lengthened (Evenett and Primo Braga, 2005). On average, it takes 9.7 years for a country to accede to the WTO from the moment it submits an application (Table 4.1). The average length of time taken since working party establishment for the first five acceding governments after 1995 to negotiate their WTO entry was 5.4 years, in comparison with the last five accessions which took, on average, 15.5 years. This latter group includes Russia, whose accession process lasted 19.2 years – the longest accession yet – while it took around 15 years, more or less, for China, Lao PDR, Nepal and Vanuatu to achieve WTO membership. This asymmetry can be explained in large part by the increasingly demanding and complex accession process, with recently acceding governments having been asked to commit to more significant reforms than were asked of those that joined earlier. This is even more the case when considered against those countries that joined under the General Agreement on Tariffs and Trade (GATT), which were allowed to retain high bound tariff rates after membership, for example (Tang and Wei, 2006).

WTO accession signals readiness for reforms and commitment to globalisation. WTO accession is often part of broader structural reforms that lead to growth. Rather than the WTO being the initiator of reforms, many of the reforms may have been autonomous policy initiatives that could have been implemented unilaterally regardless of WTO membership. WTO application may also signal the readiness of a government to undertake deep institutional reforms, and countries that are prepared and willing to implement substantial policy reform may self-select to apply for WTO accession. Many of the benefits of WTO accession come from countries' own internal structural reforms, with an impact on export development, domestic market enhancement, investment in infrastructure and human capital, and domestic and social reform measures.

Reforms accompanying WTO accession can be wide reaching, affecting a wide range of policies and institutions. Accession Packages focus on commitments to liberalise trade, but during accession countries will undertake or commit to other structural reforms that extend well beyond tariff policy and touch on areas such as fiscal, monetary and regulatory policies. Such reforms are designed, at least in part, for

Table 4.1 *Completed WTO accessions as of January 2014*

| No. | Article XII member | Date of application | Date of membership | Total time of accession process |
|---|---|---|---|---|
| 1 | Albania | 11/1992 | 09/2000 | 7 years 10 months |
| 2 | Armenia, Republic of | 11/1993 | 02/2003 | 9 years 3 months |
| 3 | Bulgaria | 09/1986 | 12/1996 | 10 years 3 months |
| 5 | Cambodia[a] | 11/1999 | 07/2008 | 8 years 8 months |
| 4 | Cabo Verde[a] | 12/1994 | 10/2004 | 9 years 10 months |
| 6 | China | 07/1986 | 12/2001 | 15 years 5 months |
| 7 | Croatia | 09/1993 | 11/2000 | 7 years 2 months |
| 8 | Ecuador | 09/1992 | 01/1996 | 3 years 4 months |
| 9 | Estonia | 03/1994 | 11/1999 | 5 years 8 months |
| 10 | Georgia | 07/1996 | 06/2000 | 4 years 1 months |
| 11 | Jordan | 01/1994 | 04/2000 | 6 years 4 months |
| 12 | Kyrgyz Republic | 02/1996 | 12/1998 | 2 years 10 months |
| 13 | Lao PDR[a] | 07/1997 | 02/2013 | 15 years 7 months |
| 14 | Latvia | 11/1993 | 02/1999 | 5 years 3 months |
| 15 | Lithuania | 01/1994 | 05/2001 | 7 years 5 months |
| 16 | Moldova, Republic of | 11/1993 | 07/2001 | 7 years 4 months |
| 17 | Mongolia | 07/1991 | 01/1997 | 5 years 6 months |
| 18 | Montenegro | 12/2004 | 04/2012 | 7 years 4 months |
| 19 | Nepal[a] | 05/1989 | 04/2004 | 14 years 11 months |
| 20 | Oman | 04/1996 | 11/2000 | 4 years 7 months |
| 21 | Panama | 08/1991 | 09/1997 | 5 years 1 months |
| 22 | Russian Federation | 06/1993 | 08/2012 | 19 years 2 months |
| 23 | Samoa[a] | 04/1998 | 05/2012 | 14 years 1 months |
| 24 | Saudi Arabia, Kingdom of | 06/1993 | 12/2005 | 12 years 6 months |
| 25 | Chinese Taipei | 01/1992 | 01/2002 | 10 years |
| 26 | Tajikistan | 05/2001 | 03/2013 | 11 years 10 months |
| 27 | Former Yugoslav Republic of Macedonia | 12/1994 | 04/2003 | 8 years 3 months |
| 28 | Tonga | 06/1995 | 07/2007 | 12 years 1 months |
| 29 | Ukraine | 11/1993 | 05/2008 | 14 years 6 months |
| 30 | Vanuatu[a] | 07/1995 | 08/2012 | 17 years 1 months |
| 31 | Viet Nam | 01/1995 | 01/2007 | 12 years |
| 32 | Yemen[a] | 04/2000 | 06/2014 | 14 years 2 months |

*Notes:* [a] Least-developed country (LDC). Cabo Verde acceded to the WTO as an LDC. It graduated from LDC status on 20 December 2007. The WTO was established in January 1995. Some countries in this table began the process of acceding to the GATT 1947 before WTO accession processes were available.
*Source:* Based on 'Protocols of Accessions for New Members since 1995, including Commitments in Goods and Services' (www.wto.org/english/thewto_e/acc_e/completeacc_e.htm, and authors' calculations), WTO Accessions Annual Report 2014.

applicants to align their domestic institutions and policies with internationally recognised standards under WTO disciplines in preparation for a more open trading environment. The reform process also allows countries to align their trade and domestic policies to best practices such as the principles of non-discrimination and transparency. Applying international best practices helps to create an enabling environment for business and trade in the country. Moreover, WTO accession encourages governments and the private sector to look at the overall competitiveness of the domestic economy and to remove the sources of inefficiencies in the business climate.

In addition to being a conduit for structural reforms, WTO accession enables governments to lock in reforms and to be less subject to the influence of interest groups. WTO membership can act as a hand-tying manoeuvre for governments to lock in reforms that may be politically difficult to implement otherwise. For example, Ferrantino (2006) argues that the primary external anchor for China's reforms has been its WTO accession. China's lengthy and complex WTO accession process, extending from 1986 to 2001, covered a very substantial portion of the history of China's economic reforms. The trajectory of China's reforms, in specific areas such as services and intellectual property as well as the massive unilateral tariff reduction undertaken by China during the early 1990s (which were also accompanied by special policies related to foreign direct investment (FDI) and economic zones), was conditioned by the external anchoring effect of repeated engagement with the WTO working party, including bilateral engagement with large members such as the European Union, Japan and the United States. Ferrantino (2006) suggested that WTO commitments were portrayed as a tool that Beijing could use to obtain consistency and uniformity from increasingly independent provincial and local governments.

One of the key reasons why WTO accession is important for development is the political economy dimension, as this may be a key step for carrying out structural reforms in a country. Lobbying and political economy considerations often allow special interests to strongly influence policy so that reforms are slow. The external pressure of WTO membership can encourage governments to practise sound economic policy-making and avoid the temptation for policy reversal. This was evident during the global financial crisis when, by and large, protectionism was kept under control – an outcome attributed to the commitment of countries to a multilateral system and the discipline embodied in the WTO.

But the view that WTO accession produces pro-growth reforms has not been universally shared. For instance, Rose (2004) does not find evidence that the WTO/GATT had a more significant impact on the trade flows and openness of members than those of non-members. Yet the sample also included countries that had joined the GATT before the WTO was established at the Uruguay Round conclusion, and early GATT members did not have the stringent requirements on policy reform that later WTO candidates have been facing. Indeed, Subramanian and Wei (2007) document that new (i.e. post-Uruguay Round) WTO members tend to be systematically more open than old developing country members of the GATT. They find that new developing country members of the WTO trade about 30 per cent more, on average, than old developing country members.

## Development impact of WTO accession

WTO accession can be an effective lever to promote not only trade liberalisation but also substantive domestic regulatory reform that extends beyond the border, helping countries move to a more open and market-oriented model of economic development. A country's negotiations on bilateral market access with the countries on its WTO working party on accession include measures that go beyond tariff policy, such as customs administration, technical barriers to trade and sanitary and phytosanitary measures. They also include liberalisation of the foreign investment regime (in particular regulations relating to the services sector); privatisation, including the dissolution of state monopolies; taxation; government procurement; price controls; foreign exchange regimes; transparency in trade regulations and trade-related governance matters.

### Export development

WTO membership facilitates an acceding government's access to foreign markets and encourages the development of its exports. Border measures to enhance market access – be they tariffs, non-tariff barriers, the foreign exchange system or customs procedures – are the most fundamental structural reforms undertaken during the WTO negotiation commitments and directly affect the flow of exports and imports. The link between reforms at the border and export development is developed through various channels.

The first point to note is that accession guarantees that exporters receive most-favoured-nation (MFN) treatment from WTO members for goods, services and trade-related intellectual property. By binding national tariffs, committing to eliminate quotas on imports and reforming other border measures, acceding governments in return receive greater, more secure and less discriminatory market access abroad for their exports. Even if a country had negotiated MFN status with its significant trading partners without WTO membership, those preferences and market access conditions could be changed by the importing country. Members also have access to the Dispute Settlement Body of the WTO where they can take action against another government believed to be violating an agreement or commitment made in the WTO. For example, countries may gain improved treatment of exporters through anti-dumping cases. Thus WTO membership provides exporters with more security and predictability.

Indeed, there is a trend for exports to grow faster, starting a few years prior to WTO membership and continuing thereafter. Without attempting to capture anything more than correlation, Figure 4.1(a) and (b) presents this stylised fact using a graphical event study analysis (to account for countries becoming members in different years). Figure 4.1(a) plots the average export level of a (constant) sample of thirteen countries (Albania, Armenia, Bulgaria, Cambodia, China, Ecuador, Jordan, Lithuania, Former Yugoslav Republic of Macedonia, Moldova, Mongolia, Nepal and Panama) that have acceded to the WTO since 1995 (solid line), centring the data so that the year of membership is 0, the year prior to membership is -1, etc. It plots the nine years before membership (the average length of countries' accession processes) and five years after. Figure 4.1(b) excludes China, but a similar pattern appears. Looking at the evolution of countries' exports around WTO accession, there is a clear break in the trend about two years prior to accession. On average, acceding governments' exports have grown at an increased rate for at least the five years post-WTO accession.

While China's exports have since outperformed the world average, for other countries WTO accession is associated with convergence with the world average export performance. Figure 4.1 takes into account that world exports have also been growing over time, by plotting countries' exports as if they had evolved according to the world average export growth rate over the past thirty years (dotted line). When including China in Figure 4.1(a), countries' actual exports increased at a much faster rate than if they were trending at the world average. But excluding

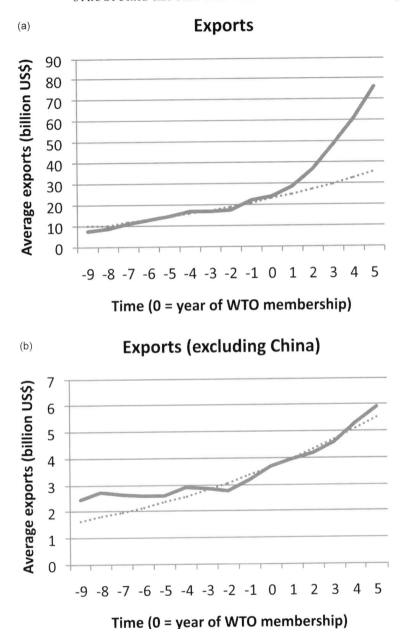

**Figure 4.1**  Export levels around date of WTO accession (a) including China and (b) excluding China. Solid line = actual progression, dotted line = progression according to world average rate over the past 30 years. The Kingdom of Saudi Arabia, Tonga and Viet Nam which were acceding in 2008–9, are excluded so as to not capture the global fall in world exports and imports during the financial crisis of those years. Taken from World Bank World Development Indicators.

China, WTO-acceding governments' exports grew at the average world rate beginning about two years prior to accession, whereas before that their export growth was below average.

Second, export development is enhanced by a country's own reduction of import restrictions, by which it gains greater access to key imported inputs and technology. Many countries are being asked to commit to tariff rates below WTO mandates. For example, acceding LDCs are asked to bind 95 per cent of non-agricultural products at an average rate of 35 per cent and all agricultural tariff lines at an average rate of 50 per cent, but Lao PDR bound non-agricultural and agricultural rates at 18.7 per cent and 19.3 per cent respectively. On the basis of recent accession experience, other developing country applicants have bound their agricultural tariffs at an average rate well below 20 per cent and below 10 per cent for non-agricultural goods (Evenett and Primo Braga, 2005). Countries also make commitments to eliminate quantitative import restrictions (including prohibitions, quotas and licensing), non-tariff barriers (anti-dumping, countervailing duties and safeguard restrictions) or customs procedures such as customs valuation, that all act to lower import prices. Ukraine, for example, committed to using the Harmonised Commodity Description and Coding Systems of the World Customs Organization to classify goods for customs purposes. With the rise of global value chains, it is becoming more the case that a country's imports are not of finished products for consumption but of intermediate inputs used for domestic production that is ultimately exported. A fall in the price of imports benefits not only consumers, who then have access to cheaper goods, but also exporters who import intermediate inputs.

WTO accession is also correlated with higher import growth rates – above those experienced prior to accession but also above world averages. Taking a similar approach to that in Figure 4.1, Figure 4.2(a) plots the average imports for a (constant) sample of thirteen countries that have acceded to the WTO since 1995 (solid line), centring the data around the year of accession. Again it takes into account that world imports have also been growing over time by plotting countries' imports as if they had evolved according to the world average import growth rate over the past thirty years (dotted line). Figure 4.2(b) excludes China, but in both samples import growth picked up in the year of WTO accession and remained above world import growth for at least five years thereafter.

Third, greater trade openness is believed to foster productivity improvement, which makes producers better able to compete on world markets for their exports. Tariff reduction should lead to improved

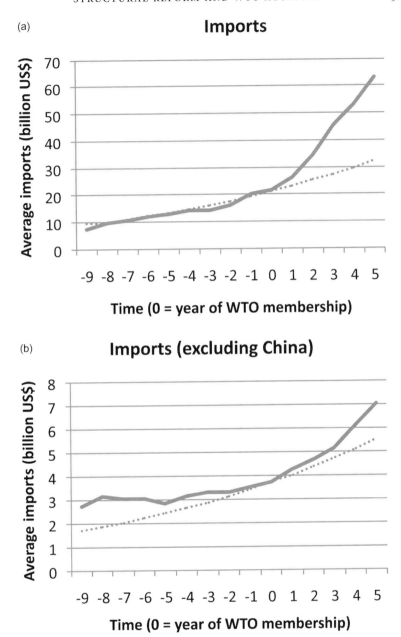

**Figure 4.2** Import levels around date of WTO membership (a) including China and (b) excluding China. Solid line = actual progression; dotted line = progression according to world average rate over the past 30 years. The Kingdom of Saudi Arabia, Tonga and Viet Nam are excluded so as to not capture the global fall in world exports and imports during the financial crisis of 2008–9. Taken from World Bank World Development Indicators.

allocation of resources, as resources will be induced to shift to sectors with the strongest comparative advantage. Tariff reductions also facilitate producers' imports of products that contain new and diverse technologies from more advanced economies, thereby helping developing countries to develop and modernise. While the most productive firms self-select to become exporters, exporting may itself make additional productivity gains through enhanced learning when firms interact with the rest of the world.

### Domestic market enhancement

Many of the measures that WTO-acceding governments are asked to implement during the accession process lead to the enhanced competitiveness of their domestic market. This includes reforms to the investment regime, including FDI and services, which increase opportunities for the private sector; fiscal policies such as taxation; privatisation, to encourage competition; and transparency and governance, to combat corruption.

The first point to note is that WTO commitments typically reduce barriers to investment in the domestic market and set the stage to attract more FDI, particularly in the services sectors. Acceding governments are requested to provide a summary of their investment policies in their memorandum upon application for accession, as well as other types of policy that restrict investment. Liberalising the investment regime often comes from concessions such as removing bans on investment in certain sectors, increasing foreign ownership percentages, eliminating investment approval procedures, removing conditions imposed on investment such as technology transfer or trade-balancing requirements, and granting the right of investors to repatriate profits. Such commitments encourage multinational service providers to increase FDI to supply the domestic market in areas such as telecommunications, banking, insurance, transportation and other business services, resulting in a more competitive environment in these sectors. Domestic businesses gain improved access to the services of multinational service providers, which should reduce the cost of doing business and increase the productivity of domestic firms using these services.

There is evidence of a dramatic shift in foreign investment into acceding governments that is associated with WTO membership – even more dramatic than that observed for exports and imports. Figure 4.3(a) explores the evolution of net FDI inflows, plotting the average level around the year of accession for a (constant) sample of ten countries (Armenia, Cambodia, China, Ecuador, Jordan, Oman, Panama, Saudi

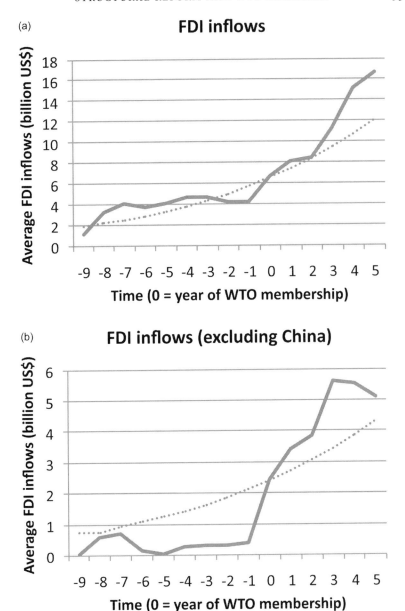

Figure 4.3    FDI inflows around date of WTO membership (a) including China and (b) excluding China. Solid line = actual progression; dotted line = progression of evolved according to world average rate over the past 30 years. Taken from World Bank World Development Indicators.

Arabia, Tonga and Viet Nam). On average, FDI into acceding govern-ments increases, beginning in the year prior to WTO membership and continuing to grow strongly thereafter. This is particularly pronounced once China is excluded from the sample (although the levels of invest-ment drop significantly), as shown in Figure 4.3(b). Again, there is evidence of improvements in countries' FDI performance above what would have evolved according to the world average FDI trends over the past thirty years (dotted line). Tang and Wei (2009) find that WTO/ GATT accessions are often associated with significant increases in growth and investment that last for about five years, but the effects work only for those countries that have to undertake substantial reforms.

One of the most significant parts of China's WTO Accession Package was its commitment to liberalise most segments of the services sector, including banking, insurance, telecommunications and professional services. Concessions were made to abolish permits for investment and eliminate most restrictions on foreign entry and ownership, as well as most forms of discrimination against foreign firms (Mattoo, 2001). Restrictions on FDI were also removed in some industries, including light manufacturing and electronics. Walmsley, Hertel and Ianchovi-china (2006) find that investment and capital stocks increased substan-tially as a result of China's accession. Looking specifically at insurance services, prices have fallen while the wages of skilled workers in the insurance sector have grown, and there has also been growth in domestic insurance companies due to better access to foreign capital as foreign investors have sought to obtain local partners. Jensen, Rutherford and Tarr (2003) estimate that liberalisation of the barriers to FDI in the services sector will be the most important source of gains for Russia from its WTO accession, representing 70 per cent of the total gains. Labour in the business services sectors is expected to gain from FDI even if capital owners in these sectors lose.

Second, WTO accession can trigger privatisation and demonopolisa-tion of state trading enterprises, plus the reduction and eventual removal of all forms of discriminatory government assistance to those enterprises (such as preferential credit). Many acceding governments pursued market-based reforms during their WTO accession, in particular transi-tion economies, including China, Lao PDR and the post-Soviet states. For such countries, WTO membership was a means to signal their commit-ment to becoming more market-based economies and to facilitate the reform process. Lao PDR reformed its state trading enterprises in agri-culture as part of its WTO accession. Albania also vigorously pursued a programme to establish a market economy and to become a full participant in the international community, and the area of privatisation was the most important of the country's economic reforms. More than 75 per cent of national wealth had been privatised by the time of accession, including 96 per cent of agricultural land, 100 per cent of services, 100 per cent of agricultural mechanics and 100 per cent of road transport.

Third, negotiations may also cover fiscal reforms such as government budget and taxation. There are no specific provisions in the General Agreement on Trade in Services (GATS) on taxation, and the aspects of taxation covered by the rules in the GATT only consider the application of internal taxes to imports and exports. While not required to do so, countries are often asked to remove export taxes. Cambodia, for example, maintained export taxes on certain unprocessed raw materials so as to encourage local processing. But as an acceding government has to rebalance its revenue sources from external to domestic taxes, reforms during accession may also involve an overhaul of the domestic tax system. While Cambodia was reducing its import duties, excise taxes were being increased to ensure that the tax reform would be revenue neutral.

Fourth, WTO accession creates new rules in the country, and thus requires the establishment of institutions and policies that are critical for the enforcement of those rules. Institutional reforms are particularly important in countries with low governance and high corruption levels. This may involve, for example, enhanced transparency of regulations and policies, promoting the rule of law, the evolution of an independent judicial system and reforms to reduce incentives for rent-seeking behaviour (Bacchetta and Drabek, 2004). Azerbaijan, for example, is currently working to simplify bureaucratic procedures as part of its accession commitments, improving the efficiency of government agencies' activities and the transparency of the economy (Jafarova, 2013). Bacchetta and Drabek (2002) find that three of the five transition economies that acceded to the WTO between 1995 and 2000 saw their corruption indices improve during their negotiation process. These countries (Bulgaria, Estonia, Kyrgyz Republic, Latvia and Mongolia) committed to publishing laws and other legal instruments related to trade, making them accessible to traders prior to implementation. In Estonia, this also extended to the practices of other government institutions, including the central bank. Parts of China's commitments included publishing previously undisclosed laws and regulations and establishing formal procedures to resolve disputes in court (Kolesnikova, 2013).

Corruption and lack of transparency have large costs for economic development as they undermine well-functioning markets. Cross-country comparisons find evidence that higher levels of corruption are correlated with slower growth and lower levels of per capita income (Kaufmann *et al.,* 1999). Controlling for other economic factors, Drabek and Payne (2002) find a statistically significant, positive and causal relationship between governance and FDI inflows. Tang and Wei (2009) also find that policy commitments associated with WTO accessions were helpful, especially for countries with poor governance.

## *Secondary effects: domestic social reform measures*

WTO accession and liberalisation of a country's trade regime will inevitably lead to changes in the relative prices of domestic goods and services. This, in turn, creates incentives for resources such as capital and labour to move into expanding sectors that are now more profitable and efficient. There will also be increased competitive pressures on industries that had, prior to liberalisation, been protected by import restrictions. This process of resource reallocation is not without costs, calling for domestic social reform measures to address sectors in which displacement costs have emerged.

While it is generally understood that in the long run there are gains from trade liberalisation, such as higher wages and employment, during the transition period workers in certain sectors may suffer. Employment will expand into sectors that export most intensively and other sectors will inevitably contract. Workers in the contracting sectors will suffer losses from transitional unemployment and are likely to incur expenses related to retraining or relocation. Rutherford and Tarr (2005) expected that the protected manufacturing sectors of the Russian Federation would contract after WTO accession while export-intensive manufacturing sectors would experience the largest expansion. Following reforms to the investment regime, most services sectors receiving FDI in Russia would expand employment, driven by multinationals employing a majority of local labour.

Research undertaken by the World Bank shows that the magnitude of labour adjustment costs can be very large, especially in developing countries (Hollweg *et al.,* 2014). In examining the labour adjustment costs of trade reforms, workers, rather than firms, bear the brunt of adjustment. Costs incurred by workers – lost earnings being the main preoccupation – far outweigh firms' costs, including lost profits due to an overextended payroll or depreciation due to unliquidated capital. Frictions in the labour market that prevent workers from moving between sectors of the economy also act to reduce the gains to trade.

To the extent that restructuring improves allocation of the resources that enhance productivity and growth, the aim of domestic social reform measures should be to alleviate these short-term adjustment costs without preventing the restructuring. For this purpose, governments usually negotiate to phase out import restrictions for certain products. Governments also use safety nets, while the source of friction will determine the best policy to reduce the cost. For costs related to geographical relocation, for instance, compensation for moving expenses could be provided to workers showing proof of relocation, with the level of compensation potentially tied to the destination market. If workers are risk averse about moving because they lack information about other job markets, job search assistance and/or labour exchanges could reduce difficulties in accessing information and increase the probability of their finding a job. If job search is costly, transitional income support – such as unemployment benefits with a job search requirement – could facilitate the search process, particularly in single-earner households. In the case of skills mismatch, workers may wish to acquire new skills adapted to market demand, but training programmes need to be carefully designed, targeted and incentivised (Hollweg *et al.*, 2014).

## Mapping the structural reform efforts of acceding governments

To map the structural reforms that acceding governments undertake, Tables 4.2(a) and (b) use the sample of World Bank Development Policy Operations (DPOs) which typically support countries' structural reforms. DPOs are one type of lending to countries by the World Bank and act as a budgetary support mechanism. DPO loans are disbursed only after countries undertake certain agreed-upon prior actions ('development policy actions'), which are typically policy and regulatory measures (as opposed to investment loans which fund investments such as roads, schools, etc.). These actions are used to map structural reforms during the accession process, with the caveat that prior actions are only illustrative of the broader structural reforms a government may be undertaking (see Table 4.2(a) for the mapping of governments that acceded to the WTO, and Table 4.2(b) for those that are currently acceding).

Under each theme, prior actions can encompass a range of different activities. For example, trade and integration can include policies that

Table 4.2(a) *Development policy actions of countries that have acceded to the WTO*

| | Armenia, Republic of | Bulgaria | Cabo Verde | Cambodia | China | Croatia | Ecuador | Georgia | Jordan | Kyrgyz Republic | Lao PDR | Latvia | Lithuania | Former Yugoslav Republic of Macedonia | Moldova | Mongolia | Montenegro | Nepal | Panama | Russian Federation | Samoa | Tajikistan | Ukraine | Viet Nam |
|---|---|---|---|---|---|---|---|---|---|---|---|---|---|---|---|---|---|---|---|---|---|---|---|---|
| **Economic management** | | | | | | | | | | | | | | | | | | | | | | | | |
| Debt management and fiscal sustainability | X | X | X | X | | X | X | X | | | | X | X | | | | | | X | X | | | X | X |
| Economic statistics, modelling and forecasting | | | | | | | | | | | | | X | | | | | | | | | | | |
| Macroeconomic management | X | X | X | X | | X | X | X | X | X | X | X | X | X | X | X | | X | X | X | | | X | X |
| **Public sector governance** | | | | | | | | | | | | | | | | | | | | | | | | |
| Administrative and civil service reform | X | X | X | X | | X | X | X | X | X | X | X | X | X | | | | X | X | X | X | X | X | X |
| Decentralisation | | | | | | | | | | | | X | | | | | | | | X | X | X | X | |
| Public expenditure, financial management and procurement | X | X | X | X | | X | X | X | X | X | X | X | X | X | X | X | | X | X | X | X | X | X | X |
| Tax policy and administration | X | X | X | X | | | X | X | X | X | X | X | | | | | | X | X | X | X | X | X | X |

Managing for development results

E-government

**Rule of law**

Judicial and other dispute resolution mechanisms

Legal institutions for a market economy

Personal and property rights

**Financial and private sector development**

Corporate governance

Infrastructure services for private sector development

Regulation and competition policy

Micro, small and medium enterprise support

International financial standards and systems

State-owned enterprise restructuring and privatisation

E-services

99

Table 4.2(a) (cont.)

| | Armenia, Republic of | Bulgaria | Cabo Verde | Cambodia | China | Croatia | Ecuador | Georgia | Jordan | Kyrgyz Republic | Lao PDR | Latvia | Lithuania | Former Yugoslav Republic of Macedonia | Moldova | Mongolia | Montenegro | Nepal | Panama | Russian Federation | Samoa | Tajikistan | Ukraine | Viet Nam |
|---|---|---|---|---|---|---|---|---|---|---|---|---|---|---|---|---|---|---|---|---|---|---|---|---|
| Financial consumer protection and financial literacy | | | | | | | | | | | | | | | | | | | | | | | | |
| **Trade and integration** | | | | | | | | | | | | | | | | | | | | | | | | |
| Export development and competitiveness | X | X | | | | | | X | X | | | X | | X | X | | | X | X | X | | X | X | X |
| International financial architecture | | | | | | X | | | | | | | | | | | | | | | | | | |
| Regional integration | | | | | | | | | | | X | X | | | | | | | | X | | | X | |
| Technology diffusion | | | | | X | | | | | | | | | | | | | | | | | | | |
| Trade facilitation and market access | X | X | X | | | | | X | X | | X | X | | X | X | | | X | X | X | | X | X | X |

*Note:* X indicates a prior action undertaken during the period of WTO accession.
*Source:* World Bank Development Policy Actions Database.

Table 4.2(b) Development policy actions of governments currently acceding to the WTO

| | Afghanistan | Algeria | Azerbaijan | Belarus | Bhutan | Bosnia and Herzegovina | Comoros | Ethiopia | Iraq | Kazakhstan | Lebanese Republic | Liberia, Republic of | Sao Tomé and Principe | Serbia | Seychelles | Uzbekistan | Yemen |
|---|---|---|---|---|---|---|---|---|---|---|---|---|---|---|---|---|---|
| **Economic management** | | | | | | | | | | | | | | | | | |
| Debt management and fiscal sustainability | | X | | | | | | | | X | | | X | X | | | |
| Economic statistics, modelling and forecasting | | | | X | | | | X | | | | | X | | | | |
| Macroeconomic management | X | | X | X | X | X | | X | X | X | | | | | | X | |
| **Public sector governance** | | | | | | | | | | | | | | | | | |
| Administrative and civil service reform | X | X | | | X | X | X | X | X | X | X | X | X | X | X | | X |
| Decentralization | | | | | | | | X | | | | | | | | | |
| Public expenditure, financial management and procurement | X | X | X | | X | X | X | X | X | X | X | X | X | X | X | | X |
| Tax policy and administration | X | X | X | X | | X | | | | X | | X | X | | | X | X |
| Managing for development results | | | | | | | | | | | | | X | | | | |
| E-government | | | | | | | | | | | | | | | | | |
| **Rule of law** | | | | | | | | | | | | | | | | | |
| Judicial and other dispute resolution mechanisms | X | | | | | | | | | X | | | | | | | |
| Legal institutions for a market economy | | | X | | | | | | | | | | | X | X | | |
| Personal and property rights | | X | | | | | | X | | | | | | | | | |
| **Financial and private sector development** | | | | | | | | | | | | | | | | | |
| Corporate governance | | X | | | | | | X | X | | | | | X | | | |
| Infrastructure services for private sector development | | X | | | | | | X | X | | | | | | | | |
| Regulation and competition policy | X | X | X | | | | | X | | | X | X | X | X | X | X | X |
| Micro, small and medium enterprise support | | | | | | | | | | | | | | | X | X | X |

101

Table 4.2(b) (cont.)

| | Afghanistan | Algeria | Azerbaijan | Belarus | Bhutan | Bosnia and Herzegovina | Comoros | Ethiopia | Iraq | Kazakhstan | Lebanese Republic | Liberia, Republic of | Sao Tomé and Principe | Serbia | Seychelles | Uzbekistan | Yemen |
|---|---|---|---|---|---|---|---|---|---|---|---|---|---|---|---|---|---|
| International financial standards and systems | X | X | | | | | X | X | X | X | | | | | X | | X |
| State-owned enterprise restructuring and privatisation | X | X | X | X | | | X | X | X | X | X | | | X | X | X | X |
| E-services | | | | | | | | | | | | | | | | | |
| Financial consumer protection and financial literacy | | | | | | | | | | | | | | | | | |
| **Trade and integration** | | | | | | | | | | | | | | | | | |
| Export development and competitiveness | | | | X | | | | | | | | | | | | X | |
| International financial architecture | | | | | | | | | | | | | | | | | |
| Regional integration | | | | | | | | | | | | | | | | | |
| Technology diffusion | | | | | | | | | | | | | | | | | |
| Trade facilitation and market access | | X | | X | | | | X | | | | X | | | | X | |

*Note:* X indicates a prior action undertaken since the start of WTO accession.

*Source:* World Bank Development Policy Actions Database. Prior actions of DPOs are policy and institutional actions that are deemed critical to achieving the objectives of the development policy lending. Prior actions are grouped under eleven themes that reflect the major objectives of the reform measures supported by the operation. Five themes are directly related to structural reforms that countries usually undertake during their WTO accession process: economic management, public sector governance, rule of law, financial and private sector development, and trade and integration. Between 1980 and 2012, these five themes accounted for over two-thirds of all prior actions.

promote export development, competitiveness, trade facilitation and market access. Public sector governance, to which the majority of the DPO prior actions relate (40 per cent of actions between 2009 and 2012), covers areas such as administrative and civil services reform; accountability and anti-corruption; tax policy and administration; and public expenditure, financial management and procurement. Financial and private sector development are also important for DPO prior actions (22 per cent of actions between 2009 and 2012), including actions relating to infrastructure services for private sector development, regulation and competition policy and state-owned enterprise restructuring and privatisation.

The first point to note is that acceding governments undertake a greater number of reforms during their accession process. The number of DPOs and the number of DPO prior actions of acceding governments, as a proxy for structural reforms undertaken, increase in the years leading up to WTO membership. For the (constant) sample of countries that have acceded to the WTO since 1995, Figure 4.4(a) plots the total number of DPOs and prior actions (4.4(b)) in each of the nine years leading up to WTO membership. Because countries become members in different years, the data are centred so that the year of accession is 0, the year prior to accession is -1, etc. There is a strong and increasing trend in the number of DPOs and prior actions that peaks about two years before WTO membership.

Second, acceding governments take on significantly more reforms than those that have not yet acceded to the WTO. Throughout the 1990s, the average number of prior actions undertaken by acceding governments was substantially higher than that undertaken by countries that were already WTO members; today the number is about the same (Figure 4.5). The large number of prior actions by acceding governments in the mid 1990s might be due to the fact that the bulk of those countries were Eastern European countries that had large structural reform programmes under way as they moved towards becoming market economies. Since the 2000s, for those governments acceding to the WTO, the average number of prior actions per country has been falling. This might be due to the fact that the bulk of those countries are LDCs, with access to special and differential treatment. Countries that are neither WTO members nor seeking accession typically have no DPOs, so are likely to have few structural ongoing reforms.

Third, acceding governments commit to more structural reforms than do WTO members or non-acceding governments; the number of reforms

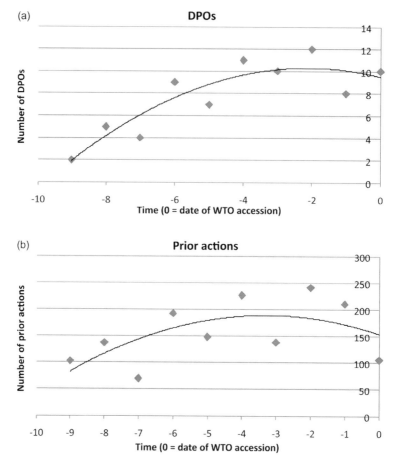

**Figure 4.4**   (a) DPOs and (b) prior actions around date of WTO accession for all countries that have acceded to the WTO since 1995 with available data (unavailable for Chinese Taipei, Oman, Saudi Arabia and Vanuatu). Total number of DPOs and prior actions for all countries that have acceded to the WTO since 1995 are plotted in each of the nine years prior to their accession. Time is equal to 0 in the year of WTO accession, -1 the year prior to WTO accession, etc. Taken from World Bank Development Policy Actions Database.

is highest prior to accession, and falls afterwards. For the group of countries that have acceded to the WTO since 1995, the average number of prior actions per DPO under the five themes of interest was only nine for DPOs disbursed after WTO accession (Figure 4.6). In contrast, the average was twenty-one during the WTO accession process (from

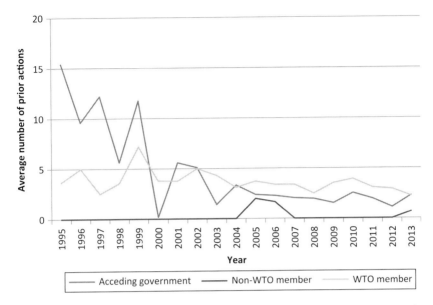

**Figure 4.5** Average number of prior actions for WTO members, non-members and acceding governments with available data. Non-WTO member countries in the Development Policy Actions Database include Marshall Islands, Somalia and Timor-Leste. Acceding governments include those that were in the process of acceding from 1995 until they become a WTO member and those that are still acceding today. Taken from World Bank Development Policy Actions Database.

working party establishment to accession) and twenty prior to working party establishment. This fall in numbers might reflect a 'reform or accession fatigue', given the intensity of the accession process. Including countries that are still in the process of negotiating WTO accession, the average number of prior actions per DPO for acceding governments (eighteen) is higher than that for WTO members (fourteen), and much higher than that for non-WTO members (six).

Fourth, acceding governments that request development policy lending from the World Bank are selective in their reforms. For all acceding governments in a particular year, of the prior actions under the five relevant themes, public sector governance is overwhelmingly targeted, particularly since 2004 (Figure 4.7). Financial and private sector development, while also an important area of reform, has become less important since 2004. As with most other countries requesting DPOs, the accompanying policy and institutional reform measures do not significantly

(a)  **Average number of prior actions per DPO**

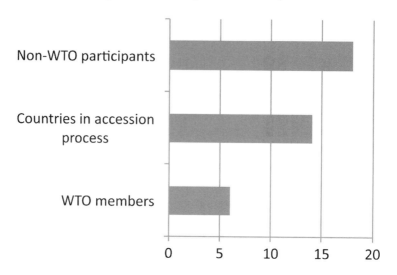

(b)  **Average number of prior actions per DPO for countries that completed accession**

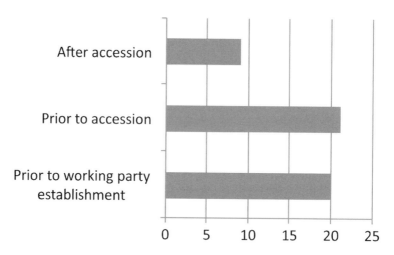

**Figure 4.6**  Number of prior actions implemented, by countries' accession status: (a) accession in progress; (b) after accession. Taken from World Bank Development Policy Actions Database.

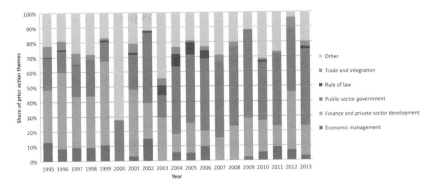

**Figure 4.7**    Share of prior action themes for governments acceding to the WTO that have available data. Acceding governments include those that were in the process of acceding since 1995 until they become a WTO member and those that are still acceding today. Taken from World Bank Development Policy Actions Database.

cover trade and integration. This might be because these measures are directly addressed within the WTO negotiations, while the broader structural reforms are supported by other aid agencies.

## Impact of WTO accession on country policy and institutions

As the WTO accession process usually feeds into a broader structural reform agenda for developing countries, does it lead to improved policies and institutions? This is analysed next, through the evolution of two proxies for policy and institutional quality: (i) the International Country Risk Guide (ICRG) rating constructed by Political Risk Services;[1] and (ii) the Country Policy and Institutional Assessment (CPIA) constructed by the World Bank.

The ICRG score encompasses twenty-two variables in three subcategories of risk: political, financial and economic. A separate index is created for each of the subcategories on a monthly basis. The political risk index is based on 100 points, financial risk on 50 points and economic risk on 50 points. The sum of the three indicators is divided by two to obtain a composite country risk index that ranges from 0 to 100, with low values suggesting poorly performing institutions. In contrast to most institutional measures that are purely cross-sectional or

---

[1] See www.prsgroup.com.

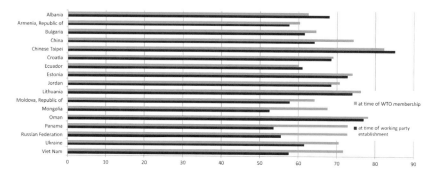

**Figure 4.8**   ICRG composite score at the beginning of WTO accession negotiations and at the time WTO membership was reached.
The following countries did not have available ICRG scores going back to the month of working party establishment, so the most recent available ICRG data were used (month and year in brackets): the Republic of Armenia (December 1998), Croatia (June 1999), Estonia (November 1998), Lithuania (December 1998), the Republic of Moldova (December 1998), Ukraine (December 1998). Taken from PRS Group, Political Risk Services, ICRG; World Bank CPIA.

exhibit limited time variability, the ICRG indicator exhibits substantial within-country variation on a monthly basis. The ICRG indicator has been used as a proxy for policy and institutional quality in other work not related to the WTO, such as that of Papaioannou (2009) and Catrinescu *et al.* (2009).

Policy and institutional quality, as proxied by the ICRG score, improved for acceding governments in the period between their early negotiations and WTO membership, with the exception of Albania, Ecuador and Chinese Taipei. Figure 4.8 shows the ICRG composite scores in the month of the establishment of the accession working party, and the rating in the month WTO membership was reached, for countries with available ICRG data (as detailed in Table 4.1). Albania's accession coincides with a period of war in the Balkans, whereas Ecuador's accession coincides with a period of political instability. Panama, Russia, Mongolia, Viet Nam and China (in that order) experienced the highest increases in the indicator.

As some of the countries did not have ICRG scores going back to the month of the working party establishment, the earliest available ICRG data were used in this analysis in order to keep the maximum number of countries in the sample. In these countries (the Republic of Armenia, Croatia, Estonia, Lithuania, the Republic of Moldova and Ukraine), the improvement in policy and institutional quality is still positive but may be underestimated. Indeed, as the earliest available ICRG score does not go back to the month of the working party establishment, it is very likely that it already considers some institutional improvement that occurred since the working party establishment.

The CPIA rates countries against a set of sixteen criteria grouped into four clusters: economic management (macroeconomic management, fiscal policy and debt policy); structural policies (trade, financial sector and business regulatory environment); policies for social inclusion and equity (gender equality, equity of public resource use, building human resources, social protection and labour, and policies of institutions for environmental sustainability); and public sector management and institutions (property rights and rule-based governance; quality of budgetary and financial management; efficiency of revenue mobilisation; quality of public administration; and transparency, accountability and corruption in the public sector). These criteria are chosen to capture key factors in the quality of each country's current policies and institutions that foster pro-poor growth and poverty alleviation. CPIA ratings are constructed on a 1–6 scale on a yearly basis, with low values suggesting poorly performing economic policy and institutions.[2]

The CPIA data have more extensive coverage of WTO members than do ICRG data. Available CPIA data for most countries go back only until 1995 or 1996. Again, to keep the maximum number of countries in the sample, the earliest CPIA score available was used for the Republic of Armenia, China, Ecuador, Estonia, Jordan, Lithuania, the Republic of Moldova, Mongolia, Panama, Russia and Ukraine, corresponding to the year after actual working party establishment (again with a risk of underestimating the results). Figure 4.9 depicts CPIA scores in the year of the working party establishment compared with those at the time of WTO membership.

Figure 4.9 indicates that, except for Albania, Ecuador, Estonia, Jordan and Panama, which joined the WTO in 2000 or earlier, CPIA scores have increased at the time of WTO accession compared with the year the working party was established. Lithuania, Russia, Tonga, Samoa, Vanuatu and Nepal (in that order) experienced the highest increases in the CPIA. In addition, as countries in Figure 4.9 are listed in

---

[2] Prior to the CPIA redefinition that took place in 1998, CPIA indicators were outlined on a 1–5 scale. In order to use CPIA indicators for 1997 or previous years, the indicators were rescaled by exploiting the relative change in a country's score between 1997 and 1998.

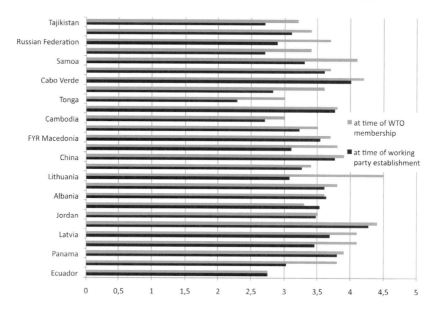

**Figure 4.9**    CPIA overall score for countries having joined the WTO, at the beginning of WTO accession negotiations and at WTO accession. Countries ranked in chronological order with more recent members listed first. The following countries did not have available CPIA scores going back to the year of working party establishment, so the oldest available CPIA data were used (year in brackets): the Republic of Armenia (1995), China (1995), Ecuador (1996), Estonia (1996), Jordan (1996), Lithuania (1996), the Republic of Moldova (1996), Mongolia (1995), Panama (1996), Russia (1996), Ukraine (1996). Taken from PRS Group, Political Risk Services, ICRG; World Bank CPIA.

chronological order of WTO membership, with more recent members listed first, it is clear that more recent members tend to have a relatively higher increase in CPIA scores. Criteria for membership in terms of institutional infrastructure and policy may have become more stringent over time and recently acceding governments may have been asked to commit to more significant reforms than were asked of those that joined the WTO earlier. Tang and Wei (2006) made a similar point when describing how countries which had joined under the GATT before the Uruguay Round were allowed to retain high bound tariff rates after membership, unlike those joining the WTO.

The extent of policy and institutional improvement has been different across countries. Of course, countries have heterogeneous policy and

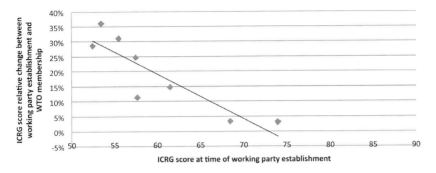

**Figure 4.10** ICRG change between the beginning of WTO accession negotiations and WTO accession (World Bank CPIA).

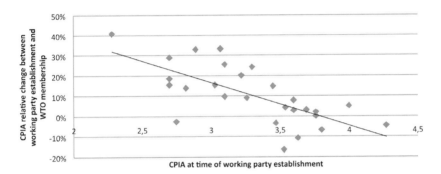

**Figure 4.11** CPIA change between the beginning of WTO accession negotiations and WTO accession (World Bank CPIA).

institutional performance when becoming WTO members, as measured by the ICRG indicator and the CPIA. Figure 4.10 shows the ICRG in the month of working party establishment, or the earliest data available, against the relative increase in the score from the month the working party was established to the month WTO membership was achieved. Figure 4.11 provides a similar picture for a larger sample of countries with CPIA data available.

The extent of policy and institutional improvement has been greater for lower performing countries as measured at the time the WTO accession process began to be negotiated. For all eight countries with ICRG data available, the lower the performance at the beginning of negotiations, the higher the relative increase. Countries with low policy and institutional quality early in the process of WTO negotiations seem to have improved more, relatively, by the time WTO membership was concluded. The correlation between the CPIA score at the time of working party establishment (or the earliest score available) and the relative increase in the CPIA is also negative. Indeed, policy and institutional performance has tended to improve more, proportionally, during the WTO accession period for countries with lower initial performance.[3]

Looking in greater depth at seven specific policy and institutional indicators related to structural adjustment, similar results can be seen of improved performance after WTO accession. Many of the criteria of the CPIA are closely related to reforms that countries undertake during a phase of structural adjustment which might include WTO accession. Figures 4.12(a)–(g) provide more detail on how seven of the sixteen individual criteria have changed between the time of working party establishment and accession and the time when WTO membership was achieved. CPIA scores range from 1 (low performance) to 6 (high performance). Figures 4.12(a)–(g) replicate the previous figures but for each of these components separately, plotting the criterion's index value in the year of working party establishment against the relative increase in the score from the year the working party was established to the year WTO membership was achieved.

Within economic management, monetary and exchange rate policies and fiscal policy are used. The first component captures whether the monetary and exchange rate policy framework is consistent with economic stability and sustained medium-term growth. Scores are assigned based on the extent to which the monetary and exchange rate policy framework: (i) maintains short- and medium-term internal and external balances and is consistent with price stability objects; and (ii) offers flexibility to deal with internal and external shocks. The fiscal policy component captures the quality of the fiscal policy in its stabilisation (achieving macroeconomic policy objectives in conjunction with coherent monetary and exchange rate policies, such as smoothing business cycle fluctuations and accommodation shocks) and allocation (appropriate provision of public goods) functions.

---

[3] It is important to note, however, that no control was introduced for the endogeneity of the relationship, as countries that are prepared to undertake policy and institutional reforms are likely to self-select for WTO accession. In addition, no control was introduced for countries that have not acceded to the WTO or that were members prior to 1995, in order that the extent to which these variables may be trending over time could be seen.

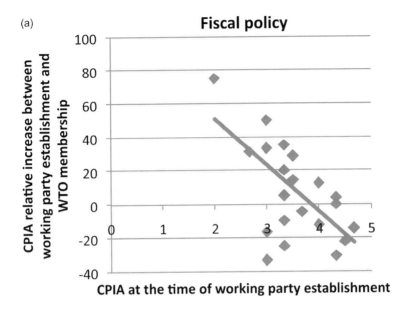

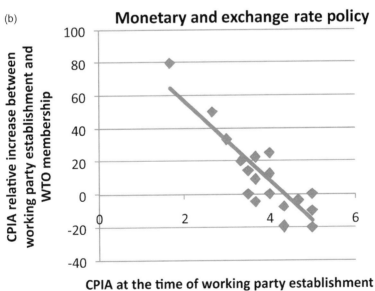

**Figures 4.12(a)–(b)** CPIA sub-component change between the beginning of WTO accession negotiations and WTO accession. The oldest available CPIA data were used for countries that did not have available CPIA scores going back to the year of working party establishment. The criteria of the CPIA have undergone multiple revisions since 1995. To measure the change in each of the criteria over the years, the most relevant categories were chosen, but it is acknowledged that they are not directly comparable over the year (World Bank CPIA).

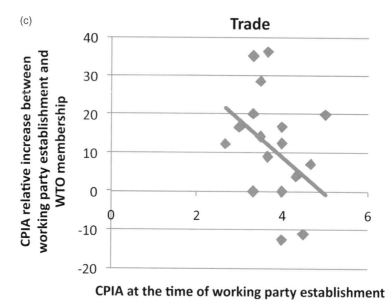

**Figures 4.12(c)–(e)**   CPIA sub-component change between the beginning of WTO accession negotiations and WTO accession. The oldest available CPIA data were used for countries that did not have available CPIA scores going back to the year of working party establishment. The criteria of the CPIA have undergone multiple revisions since 1995. To measure the change in each of the criteria over the years, the most relevant categories were chosen, but it is acknowledged that they are not directly comparable over the years. A relevant category for business regulatory environment was only available after 1997 (World Bank CPIA).

 

The structural reform policy cluster also consists of three relevant criteria: trade, financial sector and business regulatory environment. The trade criterion captures how the policy framework fosters global integration in goods and services. The first focus is on the impact of trade taxes, the degree of transparency and predictability of the trade regime, the role of non-tariff barriers and non-tariff measures and the degree of restrictiveness of the policies covering trade in services. The second focus is on trade facilitation, assessing the predictability and transparency of the trade facilitation framework, the degree of reliance of border agencies on risk management and modern technologies to expedite trade while performing their duties and the restrictiveness of the regulations affecting logistic service providers.

(d)

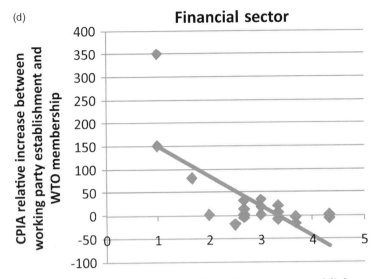

(e)

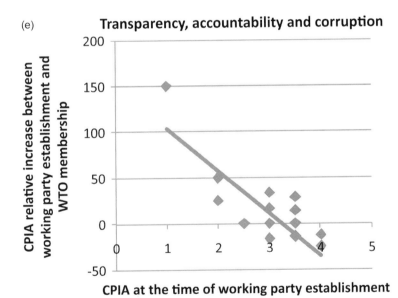

Figures 4.12(c)–(e) (cont.)

(f)

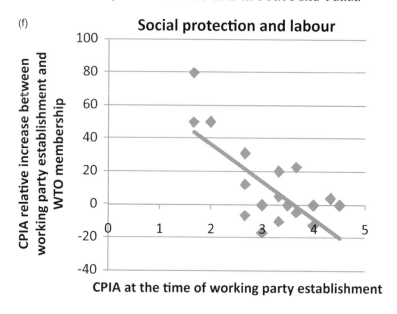

**CPIA at the time of working party establishment**

(g)

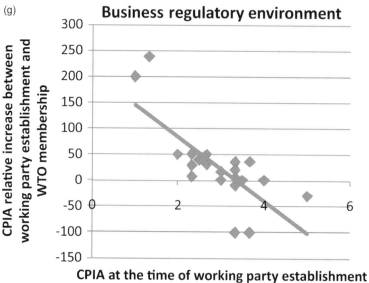

**CPIA at the time of working party establishment**

**Figures 4.12(f)–(g)**   CPIA subcomponent change between the beginning of WTO accession negotiations and WTO accession. The oldest available CPIA data were used for countries that did not have available CPIA scores going back to the year of working party establishment. The criteria of the CPIA have undergone multiple revisions since 1995. To measure the change in each of the criteria over the years, the most relevant categories were chosen, but it is acknowledged that they are not directly comparable over the years. A relevant category for transparency, accountability and corruption was only available after 1998 (World Bank CPIA).

The financial sector component assesses the policies and regulations that affect financial sector development, including: (i) financial stability; (ii) the sector's efficiency, depth and resource mobilisation strength; and (iii) access to financial services. Considerations when scoring this criterion include bank exit and entry policies, contracting and enforcement, credit reporting, accounting and auditing, corporate government, interest rate policies and direct lending. Also taken into account are the funding methods of the financial sector, the degree of adherence to international principles and different factors that are conductive to improved access to financial services.

The business regulatory environment criterion captures the extent to which the legal, regulatory and policy environment helps or hinders private business in investing, creating jobs and becoming more productive. Emphasis is on direct regulations, including: (i) regulations affecting entry, exit and competition; (ii) regulations of ongoing business operations; and (iii) regulations of factor markets. Scores are assigned for each, taking into account how cumbersome and excessive are bans or licensing practices. Similarly, countries with extensive labour market controls and rigidity of labour regulations, or private land ownership restrictions or costly property registration, receive lower scores.

Transparency, accountability and corruption in the public sector is one criterion of the public sector management and institutions component of the CPIA that can also be expected to improve during WTO accession. Many transition economies see WTO accession as facilitating both political and economic reform processes within their countries, and political indicators can be expected to improve in addition to macroeconomic and structural indicators. This criterion captures the extent to which the executive, legislators and other high-level officials can be held accountable for their use of funds, administrative decisions, etc. It covers four dimensions: (i) the accountability of the executive and other top officials for effective oversight of institutions; (ii) access of civil society to timely and reliable information on public affairs and public policies; (iii) state capture by narrow vested interests; and (iv) integrity in the management of public resources.

Finally, this analysis examines social protection and labour policies, which comprise one criterion of the social inclusion and equity cluster, to determine the extent to which enabling policies are also pursued during WTO accession. The criterion considers policies that are associated with risk prevention (by supporting savings and risk-pooling through social insurance), protection (through redistributive social safety net programmes) and promotion (of human capital development and income generation). Two of the five subcomponents are relevant for programmes that can assist the short-term costs associated with market liberalisation. These include social safety net programmes, and labour market programmes and policies aiming to promote employment creation and productivity growth while protecting core labour standards and ensuring adequate working conditions.

The first point to note is that institutional performance, along with fiscal policy and monetary and exchange rate policy, has tended to improve more, proportionally, during the WTO accession period in countries with lower initial performance (Figures 4.12(a)–(b)). For example, the scores take into consideration whether the central bank is following policy goals and publishing targets throughout the year, and whether the government's fiscal policy stance remains supportive of growth, including the level of government spending and where that spending is targeted. While there were improvements in most countries, some countries registered negative trends in these components (which were not observed in examination of the overall CPIA index).

Second, in trade, and the financial sector and business environment, improvements in the CPIA score were largely positive. Figures 12(c)–(e) plot these three criteria. Between the time of working party establishment and the time of WTO accession, the trade score increased by 40 per cent for some countries, and there were almost no backward steps among countries. In addition, there was no longer strong evidence that countries that started off relatively worse improved more. This is consistent with the argument that, for some countries, the benefits stemmed more from internally oriented reforms. For one recently acceding government, for example, WTO accession helped the trade process become more transparent and predictable, and this was reflected in a higher CPIA score in the trade component. The improvement was driven in part by market access and national treatment commitments for trade in services. Customs reform, resulting from the nationwide deployment of the automated customs processing system, the application of risk-based inspections across the network and reforms to the customs processing path, was also noted. Financial sector stability is also a concern of the CPIA for some post-WTO accession countries, in particular the ability of the central bank to supervise the banking system. For example, growth in consumption-financed loans from commercial banks and the inability of government to slow down bank lending due to a substandard regulatory framework and weak enforcement was an issue of concern. Inadequate risk management practices lowered the financial sector score for another recently acceding government.

Third, for transparency, accountability and corruption, and social protection and labour, the scores improved for some countries and worsened for others. Figures 4.12(f)–(g) plot these two criteria. This negative relationship appears to be especially strong for the transparency, accountability and corruption criterion of the CPIA. Countries' scores on this criterion are based on the extent to which different conditions are met, such as checks and balances, transparent decision-making, defined boundaries between public and private sectors, and the use of public funds. For one country that recently acceded to the WTO, one issue of concern was transparency, as checks and balances on executive powers remained weak and accountability institutions were highly susceptible to executive influence. Furthermore, social accountability mechanisms such as the media do not operate freely there, in that they do not openly criticise or challenge the executive authorities. Large improvements by countries were also seen in the social protection and labour criteria between the time of working party establishment and that of WTO accession, in which countries' scores are based on the quality of the strategies and programmes that the government has adopted. The focus in the past few CPIAs has been on the ability of governments to coordinate social programmes designed to support their country through difficult economic situations. Some have demonstrated this during the global financial crisis by leveraging social assistance benefits, such as unemployment benefits and active labour market policies, including subsidies to the private sector for employment and on-the-job training initiatives.

Many developing countries have completed laborious WTO accession processes in which they undertook significant structural reforms. Recently, acceding governments have been asked to commit to more significant reforms than were asked of those that joined earlier, and the time taken to complete the WTO accession process has been increasing. These reforms have been wide reaching, extending beyond trade liberalisation and affecting a wide range of policies and institutions.

Structural reforms undertaken during WTO accession can have important implications for different aspects of countries' development. Most fundamental is the development of exports. Other reforms aimed at domestic market enhancement can improve important components of the national business environment which, in turn, may bring payoffs in the long run, such as expanded investment and stimulus to growth. Domestic social reform measures such as government safety nets may be necessary to cushion possible negative impacts of accession, as there is a need to alleviate adjustment costs following liberalisation.

Overall, membership in the WTO is positively related to structural policy measures and institutional improvement. For almost all governments acceding to the WTO, structural policy measures and institutions improve significantly during the period of negotiations. Furthermore, there is evidence that the improvement in the quality of structural policy measures and institutions tends to be proportionally higher for countries with a lower starting point at the early stage of the accession process.

## Acknowledgements

The authors are grateful to Michael Ferrantino and Sebastián Sáez for helpful comments and to Patrick Ibay for capable research assistance, and they take responsibility for any remaining errors. The findings, interpretations and conclusions expressed are entirely those of the authors. They do not represent the view of the World Bank, its Executive Directors, or the countries they represent.

## References

Bacchetta, M. and Z. Drabek (2002). 'Effects of WTO Accession on Policy-Making in Sovereign States: Preliminary lessons from the recent experience of transition countries', Geneva, World Trade Organization, WTO Working Paper DERD-2002–02

  (2004). 'Tracing the effects of WTO accession on policy-making in sovereign states: preliminary lessons from the recent experience of transition countries', *World Economy*, 27(7): 1083–1125.

Catrinescu, N., M. Leon-Ledesma, M. Piracha and B. Quillin (2009). 'Remittances, institutions, and economic growth', *World Development*, 37(1): 81–92.

Christiansen, L., M. Schindler and T. Tressel (2009). 'Growth and structural reforms: a new assessment', Washington DC, International Monetary Fund, IMF Working Paper 09/284.

Drabek, Z. and W. Payne (2002). 'The impact of transparency on foreign direct investment', *Journal of Economic Integration*, 17(4): 777–810.

Evenett, S. and C. Primo Braga (2005). 'WTO accession: lessons from experience', Washington DC, World Bank, Trade Note 22.

Ferrantino, M. (2006). 'Policy anchors: do free trade agreements serve as vehicles for developing country policy reform?', Washington DC, US International Trade Commission Office of Economics, Working Paper 2006–04-A.

Hollweg, C. H., D. Lederman, D. Rojas and E. R. Bulmer (2014). *Sticky Feet: How Labor Market Frictions Shape the Impact of International Trade on Labor Market Outcomes*. Washington DC, World Bank.

Jafarova, A. (2013). 'Azerbaijan's WTO membership key step for economic reforms', *AzerNews*, 19 December.

Jensen, J., T. Rutherford and D. Tarr (2003). *Economy-Wide and Sector Effects of Russia's Accession to the WTO*. Washington DC, World Bank.

Kaufmann, D., A. Kraay and P. Zoido-Lobatón (1999). 'Governance matters', Washington DC, World Bank, Policy Research Department Working Paper 2196.

Kolesnikova, I. (2013). *WTO Accession and Economic Development: Experience of Newly Acceded Countries and Implications for Belarus*. Warsaw, Center for Social and Economic Research.

Mattoo, A. (2001). 'China's accession to the WTO: the services dimension', *Journal of International Economic Law*, 6(2): 299–339.

Papaioannou, E. (2009). 'What drives international financial flows? Politics, institutions and other determinants', *Journal of Development Economics*, 88(2): 269–281.

Rose, A. (2004). 'Do we really know that the WTO increases trade?', *American Economic Review*, 94(1): 98–114.

Rutherford, T. and D. Tarr (2005). 'Russia's WTO accession: what are the macroeconomic, sector, labor market and household effects?', in G. B. Navaretti (ed.), *Handbook of Trade Policy and WTO Accession for Development in Russia and the CIS*. Washington DC, World Bank.

Subramanian, A. and S.-J. Wei (2007). 'The WTO promotes trade, strongly but unevenly', *Journal of International Economics*, 72(1): 151–175.

Tang, M.-K. and S.-J. Wei (2006). *Does WTO Accession Raise Income? When External Commitments Create Value*. Washington DC, Research Department, International Monetary Fund.

——— (2009). 'The value of making commitments externally: evidence from WTO accessions', *Journal of International Economics*, 78(2): 216–229.

Walmsley, T. L., T. W. Hertel and E. Ianchovichina (2006). 'Assessing the Impact of WTO Accession on China's Investment', *Pacific Economic Review*. http://onlinelibrary.wiley.com/doi/10.1111/j.1468-0106.2006.00318.x/abstract.

# 5

# The macroeconomic implications of WTO accession

## ALEXEI KIREYEV

### ABSTRACT

*This chapter proposes a holistic framework by which acceding governments may evaluate the macroeconomic impact of joining the WTO. Because both acceding governments and WTO members are interested in preserving their own systemic stability and the stability of the multilateral trading system, evaluation of the Accession Package can be achieved by examining its impact on the domestic and external stability of the acceding country. The chapter concludes that, in the long run, the impact should be positive, and should be driven by better resource allocation as the acceding economy opens to international trade, makes deep structural reforms and aligns its institutions and policies with internationally recognised standards. However, in the short term, implementation of WTO commitments may lead to substantial adjustment costs in the public and private sectors. Overall, the design and implementation of WTO accession commitments is a matter of public policy that should aim to promote systemic stability and accelerate domestic reform, while addressing transitional costs.*

Accession to the WTO is an outcome of negotiations. The applicant government engages in bilateral negotiations with interested WTO members on concessions and specific commitments on market access for goods and services. The results of these bilateral negotiations are consolidated into the final Accession Package. New members enjoy the privileges that the incumbent members give to them and the security that the trading rules provide. In return, acceding countries make commitments to abide by WTO rules and to open their markets. Such commitments have different dimensions – legal, institutional and economic – and usually focus mainly on general rules and individual products and sectors. However, while not explicit, there are also substantial macroeconomic dimensions to the WTO accession commitments, which are the focus of this chapter.

The macroeconomic implications of WTO accession can be viewed through the prism of systemic stability. Obviously, no acceding country would accept commitments that would destabilise its own economic system but, rather, would try to leverage WTO negotiations towards reaching its own domestic goals while using the opportunities opened by WTO membership. On the other hand, it is in the interest of the WTO as a whole to preserve the stability of the multilateral trading system by contributing to maintaining the stability of its members.

Systemic stability is most effectively achieved when each country adopts policies that promote its own balance of payments and domestic stability. Balance of payments stability refers to a balance of payments position that does not, and is not likely to, give rise to disruptive exchange rate movements and is achieved by promoting domestic stability. Domestic stability refers to orderly economic growth with reasonable price stability, with due regard to the circumstances of the relevant member, and orderly underlying economic and financial conditions and a monetary system that does not tend to produce erratic disruptions (IMF, 2012).

## What is known about the macroeconomics of accession?

### The macroeconomic components of accession

Accession to the WTO is a trade agreement between the acceding country and other WTO members. Trade agreements aim at limiting unilateral policies that restrict trade and prevent countries from reaping the full benefits of an unobstructed resource reallocation based on a liberalised trade regime (WTO, 2009). Free trade is not required. Article XII of the 1994 Marrakesh Agreement Establishing the World Trade Organization states that 'any State or separate customs territory possessing full autonomy in the conduct of its external commercial relations and of the other matters provided for in this Agreement and the Multilateral Trade Agreements may accede to this Agreement, on terms to be agreed between it and the WTO' (WTO, 1999). Only two rules of accession are clearly established: the single undertaking (i.e. the acceding country must comply with all rules of WTO agreements) and the obligation of the acceding country to accept specific commitments as specified in its schedules of commitments. In most other respects, WTO accessions are guided mainly by unwritten rules derived from precedents.

From the macroeconomic perspective, Accession Packages usually include two groups of measures. The first directly affects trade and includes commitments on market access for goods (import tariffs and quantitative restrictions) and services (financial and other) and trade-related fiscal measures, mainly related to export duties, internal taxes, and fees and other charges. The second group of commitments covers non-trade areas of the economy, which nevertheless may have a substantial impact on trade. Commitments in the most important non-trade areas include commitments regarding different types of subsidies (agriculture, domestic support, export, industrial), price controls, state monopolies, trade-related investment measures and intellectual property rights, and privatisation and transparency. Based on a review of key accession commitments of ten recently acceded countries (2007–2013), the main commitments that are critical from the macroeconomic standpoint can be summarised as per Table 5.1.

Accession Packages focus on the commitments to liberalise trade. All acceding countries are expected to bind their import tariffs. These bindings can be at a level that is higher, equal to or lower than the applied tariffs. If the bound-level tariff is higher than the applied tariff, then accession does not lead to tariff reductions, as the acceding country may have liberalised trade unilaterally and faster than required by its accession commitments. If the bound tariff is equal to the applied tariff, there is still no liberalisation. It is only when the bound tariff is lower than the applied rate that the acceding country effectively liberalises imports and may experience the macroeconomic impact of its WTO membership. Some downward pressure on the applied rates may be felt even if the bound rates are higher than the applied rates.

Binding the tariffs can take a variety of forms. In some cases (Lao PDR, Samoa, Tajikistan), countries have bound their tariffs at a level that is higher than the applied tariffs. Some acceded countries have agreed to tariff reductions on some, mainly industrial, products that should be applied either immediately after accession or phased in over a transition period. This period can vary by country – one year (Tonga), three years (Vanuatu), five years (Ukraine), ten years (Cabo Verde, Montenegro) – and schedules may vary by product. In other cases, substantial applied tariff reductions are required, because the bound tariff is lower than the applied tariff. In Russia, for example, tariffs should be reduced from the applied rate of 10 per cent in 2011 to an average bound rate of 7.8 per cent. A third of tariff cuts should be implemented on the date of accession and the longest implementation

Table 5.1 *Recent WTO accessions: macroeconomically relevant commitments*

| Country | | | Viet Nam | Tonga | Ukraine | Cabo Verde | Montenegro | Samoa | Russian Federation | Vanuatu | Lao PDR | Tajikistan |
|---|---|---|---|---|---|---|---|---|---|---|---|---|
| Year of accession | | | 2007 | 2007 | 2008 | 2008 | 2012 | 2012 | 2012 | 2012 | 2013 | 2013 |
| Market access | Goods | Import tariffs | X | X | X | X | X | X | X | X | X | X |
| | | Quantitative restrictions | X | | | | X | X | X | | | |
| | Services | Financial | X | | X | | X | X | X | X | X | X |
| | | Other | X | X | X | X | X | X | X | X | X | X |
| Export duties | | | X | | X | | X | | X | | X | |
| Internal taxes | | | | | | | X | | X | | X | |
| Fees and charges | | | | X | | | X | X | X | | X | |
| Subsidies | Agricultural | | X | | X | X | X | X | X | | | |
| | Domestic support | | | | X | X | | X | X | X | | |
| | Export | | X | | X | X | X | X | X | | X | |
| | Industrial | | | X | | | X | X | X | | | X |
| Price controls | | | | | | | X | X | X | | X | X |
| TRIMs | | | | | | | | | X | X | X | X |
| TRIPs | | | | | | | | X | X | X | X | X |
| Privatisation | | | | | | | X | X | X | | | |
| Transparency | | | | | | | X | X | X | X | X | X |

*Note:* TRIMs = trade-related investment measures; TRIPs = trade-related aspects of intellectual property rights.

*Source:* WTO Accessions Gateway (www.wto.org/english/thewto_e/acc_e/acc_e.htm).

period is eight years. In Vanuatu, applied tariffs should be reduced for ninety-eight tariff lines.

Quantitative restrictions on imports in acceding countries are usually eliminated, which should, in principle, increase imports. Their commitments cover such non-tax measures as quotas, licences, bans, permits, prior authorisation and other qualitative requirements not justified under the WTO provisions. As a result of accession negotiations, such measures in most cases should be eliminated and not reintroduced (Montenegro, Russia). A tariff quota (lower in-quota import duties and higher out-of-quota duties) is a measure combining the features of tariff and quantitative restrictions. They are usually allowed (in Russia for beef, pork, poultry and some whey products; in Viet Nam for eggs, tobacco, sugar and salt; in Ukraine for raw cane sugar), at least for some time, in the expectation that they will be eliminated after a period of up to three years following accession.

Accession commitments on services also have important macroeconomic dimensions, in particular for promoting inward foreign direct investment (FDI) and enhancing the financial sector. Most acceding countries make commitments to improve conditions for service delivery through foreign commercial presence, that is, allowing an office, branch or subsidiary in the country, which often implies FDI. They also usually commit to enhancing market access in financial services (banking, insurance, accounting) that directly affect the performance of the national financial sector. Other service areas critical for macroeconomic performance include transportation, communication, research and development and business services. In Viet Nam, some service areas (e.g. accountancy) were opened for foreign ownership immediately upon accession. In other cases, limits to foreign ownership have been established (in telecommunications in Viet Nam, and overall foreign participation in the banking system in Russia); conditions on a gradual phasing out of restrictions on foreign ownership are included in the accession commitments (express delivery courier services in Viet Nam, telecommunication and insurance services in Russia) or restrictions are imposed on foreign ownership to promote small local businesses (Vanuatu).

Other trade-related accession commitments affect different taxes levied on tradable goods, other than import duties. Some acceded countries have export duties which perform mainly fiscal functions. Accession Packages include commitments not to apply or reintroduce export duties (Montenegro), to eliminate them with some exceptions (300 items in the case of Tajikistan), to reduce them only on specific items (ferrous and non-ferrous metals in Viet Nam), to reduce and bind them in line with a detailed schedule (oil seeds, live cattle, hides, ferrous and non-ferrous scrap in Ukraine) and to bind them at a certain level (for over 700 tariff lines in the case of Russia). Commitments on internal taxes require that the value-added tax (VAT), excise and other taxes applied to imported products be the same as those applied to similar domestically produced products, in line with the WTO principle on national treatment (Lao PDR, Montenegro). Other fees and charges on imports, in addition to ordinary customs duties, are usually bound at zero from the date of accession (Lao PDR, Montenegro, Samoa) or not applied at all (Ukraine). In some cases, accession commitments require the elimination of tax exemptions. For example, in Russia, the VAT exemption applied to certain domestic agricultural products should have been eliminated upon accession.

Subsidies are usually heavily regulated by accession commitments, and their reduction or elimination may have substantial macroeconomic implications. Allowed agricultural subsidies can be fixed by the schedule of commitments to a certain amount (Lao PDR, Russia). For example, in Russia, total trade-distorting agricultural support should not have exceeded US$9 billion in 2012 and will be gradually reduced to US$4.4 billion by 2018. Other agricultural subsidies can be bound at zero (Russia, Samoa). Export subsidies either do not exist (Cabo Verde) or are usually banned upon accession (Lao PDR, Samoa, Ukraine, Viet Nam), as are import-substitution subsidies (Montenegro). Domestic support that has minimal impact on trade is usually allowed, mainly for environmental purposes, forest management and water conservation (Cabo Verde, Ukraine, Viet Nam). However, trade-distorting domestic support provided to farmers that has a direct impact on prices or quantities is usually limited by an annual ceiling (US$613 million in Ukraine, US$246 million in Viet Nam). Industrial subsidies prohibited under WTO rules are either eliminated from the date of accession (Tonga) or modified so that any subsidy provided would not be contingent on exportation or on the use of domestic over imported goods (Russia).

Accession Packages usually include a commitment to follow WTO rules on price control. The basic rule is that any regulation of internal prices must provide national treatment for imported goods. If the authorities continue to apply price controls, this should be done in a WTO-consistent manner, in particular on the products of natural monopolies (Lao PDR, Montenegro, Tajikistan). For example, in Russia, after accession to the WTO, price controls continue to be applied on certain products and services, including natural gas, raw diamonds, vodka, water supply services, gas transportation, baby food, medical goods, public transport and railway transportation. However, these price controls should not be used to protect domestic products, and the list of goods subject to price control should be published. Pricing of energy should be based on normal commercial considerations, recovery costs and profit. Prices for other products should be liberalised.

Most acceding countries commit to comply with the WTO trade-related investment rules immediately upon accession, which may have substantial impact on specific industries. Such commitments generally prohibit including in investment agreements a local-component requirement forcing foreign enterprises to use domestic products, a trade-balancing requirement capping the enterprise's imports to the amount of goods it exports and any foreign exchange restrictions on the sales of foreign exchange to pay for the imports of investment goods. Lao PDR, Russia, Tajikistan and some other recently acceded countries have committed to abiding by these rules. In Russia, for example, all WTO-inconsistent investment measures, including preferential tariffs or tariff exemptions applied to the automobile investment programmes, should be eliminated by 2018.

Other areas of WTO accession commitments may also have important macroeconomic implications as they affect the structure of the economy and the business climate. Commitments on privatisation usually include annual reporting to WTO members on developments in the ongoing privatisation programme (Montenegro, Russia, Samoa, Tajikistan). Commitments on TRIPs include enforcement of the corresponding WTO agreement (Russia, Samoa). There are also numerous commitments on transparency, related mainly to the timely publication of all trade-related laws, licensing and other procedures, and notifications of trade-related measures to the WTO. In some cases (Russia, Tajikistan), acceded countries are required to publish all legislation affecting trade in goods, services or intellectual property rights before their adoption, and to provide a reasonable period of time for WTO members to comment.

Finally, Accession Packages usually include extended commitments in related areas that under certain circumstances may also have macroeconomic implications. These include commitments related to the functioning of preferential trade arrangements, anti-dumping, countervailing and safeguard measures, monopolies, technical barriers to trade, customs valuation, licensing procedures, information technology, standards, competition and other areas.

WTO accession negotiations have an ability to influence policy-making – they have traction. Aside from the specific commitments, there may also be a policy credibility effect associated with WTO commitments, as highlighted in the theoretical literature (e.g. Maggi and Rodriguez-Clare, 1998) and in the empirical literature (e.g. Tang and Wei, 2009). Countries make commitments which they will have to follow for the length of their WTO membership. This is longer than the commitments under the programmes supported by any other international institution, including the International Monetary Fund (IMF) and the World Bank.

## Empirical evidence

The literature on the impact of WTO accession remains scarce and has focused on only a few areas. Most trade-related research touches on this issue in the context of the impact of the multilateral trading system on the volumes of bilateral trade, growth, fiscal revenue, individual industries and overall governance. On a general level, the most comprehensive treatment of the linkages between macroeconomics and trade can be found in the *World Trade Report* devoted to coherence (WTO, 2004), which includes the monetary model of the balance of payments, as well as a detailed discussion of options for fiscal, monetary and exchange rate policy response to external disequilibrium. Later *World Trade Reports* (WTO, 2007; 2009) complement this discussion by providing an overview of economic theories on the rationale for trade agreements, commitments versus flexibility and other macroeconomic reasons for trade policy cooperation between countries.

There are no conclusive results on the impact of WTO membership on trade volumes. On the one hand, using a large dataset and a variety of econometric techniques, Rose (2004a; 2004b; 2005a; 2005b) estimated the effect of multilateral trade agreements on international trade and found little evidence that countries joining or belonging to the WTO have different trade patterns from those of outsiders. On the other hand, Subramanian and Wei (2007) claim that there is robust evidence that the WTO has had a powerful, positive but uneven impact on trade. WTO membership has been associated with a large increase in imports, mainly by industrial countries and developing countries that joined the WTO after the Uruguay Round, but not for other developing countries. The impact across sectors has been asymmetric. Goldstein, Tomz and Rivers (2007), by adding to formal members other participants (colonies, newly independent states, provisional members), found that WTO membership helped increase trade. Country-by-country estimates of the impact on trade volumes from accessions are equally inconclusive because national experiences are very different (Evenett and Gage, 2005). The question of whether accession to the WTO unambiguously correlates with increasing trade remains very much open.

The impact on growth from WTO membership has been found to be generally positive. Tang and Wei (2009), focusing on developing countries, found that accession to the WTO tends to raise the income of acceded countries, as higher growth and investment generally last for about five years after accession. This conclusion was valid only for those acceded countries that had undertaken substantial reforms as a result of the post-1994 rule requiring acceding countries to negotiate their terms. Li and Wu (2004) conducted a study of accessions to the General Agreement on Tariffs and Trade (GATT)/WTO of seventy-four countries in the period 1968–1998 and found that only high-income economies experienced significantly faster growth after accession. This conclusion implies that openness by itself is not sufficient to promote growth and that it needs to be combined with proper economic institutions. The reasons for the positive impact of WTO accession on growth are not entirely clear. It can be explained by the long-lasting nature of accession commitments, which are legally binding as long as the country remains a WTO member.

The fiscal implications of WTO accession may be substantial. Ebrill, Stotsky and Gropp (1999) show that the revenue implications of trade liberalisation are uncertain and depend on the country's initial conditions and the reform strategy, especially if its tariff structures are complex and highly restrictive. Baunsgaard and Keen (2010), using a panel of 111 countries over twenty-five years, showed that not all countries managed to offset reductions in trade tax revenue by increasing their domestic tax revenue. While high-income countries have clearly recovered revenue losses, for middle-income countries recovery has been about 45–60 per cent. Recovery has been extremely weak in low-income countries, which depend most on trade tax revenue. They have recovered no more than 30 per cent. Exploring the impact of accession on fiscal revenue, Drabek and Bacchetta (2004) found that tariff reduction should not have caused any significant problems in transition economies because their customs revenue had never been a substantial part of government revenue. Although tariff revenue declined as a share of imports in countries that joined the WTO, this decline cannot be entirely attributed to accession commitments but, rather, to signing liberalisation agreements within Europe. Regarding the impact on expenditure, Drabek and Woo (2010) and Laird (2009) underscore that WTO accession can lead to significant budgetary and other adjustment costs, in particular in the short term, as acceded countries need to finance the reforms of their trade institutions to align them with WTO requirements.

Offsetting trade tax revenue lost as a result of accession with domestic revenue was found to be difficult, in particular in low-income countries. In Sub-Saharan Africa, for instance, trade taxes still account for one-quarter of all tax revenue, and the impact of the lost revenue on the budget can be severe. The standard policy recommendation for revenue recovery is to combine tariff reduction with increases in consumption taxes (IMF, 2011a). For example, import tariff cuts on excisable products can be offset by a comparable increase in excise taxes. This would preserve the efficiency gains from trade liberalisation, and include domestic production in addition to imports in the tax base and reduce consumer prices (Keen and Lighthart, 2002). If the informal sector is substantial, then an appropriate withholding tax can be applied to imports to improve compliance (Keen, 2008). Because VAT is already high in many developing countries, an increase in VAT rates is generally not recommended as it may worsen compliance; but broadening of the VAT base *is* recommended and there is a lot to be done in this area in most countries. Moreover, countries with a VAT have not been particularly successful in replacing lost trade tax revenue (Baunsgaard and Keen, 2010). Case studies (IMF, 2005) suggest that the successful offsetting of revenue losses has been associated with increases in a range of domestic taxes, including the income tax.

WTO accession, by binding a government's policies, generally helps promote better governance. Tang and Wei (2009) have found that the beneficial effects of policy commitments taken during WTO accession negotiations seem more pronounced among countries with poor governance. Maggi and Rodriguez-Clare (1998) show that, by committing to free trade and signing free trade agreements, governments may credibly distance themselves from domestic lobbies. However, Ferrantino (2009), using a number of governance indices, finds little impact of WTO accession on governance and the overall policy environment.

The impact of WTO accession is usually positive for the welfare of the country as a whole but uneven across individual sectors. To assess the overall impact, studies adopt the general equilibrium approach, and most of them have focused on China and Russia as the largest recently acceded countries. One example of the general equilibrium approach (Kharitonov and Walmsley, 2004), based on a Global Trade Analysis Project (GTAP) model, found that the welfare impact of accession will be positive but quite small. At the same time, there can be substantial structural shifts as the services sector expands and most other sectors contract, in particular in the short term. In China, Wang (2001) used a recursive dynamic, seventeen-region, twenty-five-sector computable general equilibrium model and found substantial benefits in terms of trade volume and welfare growth for China and the rest of the world. There have also been numerous studies for individual countries (e.g. ITC, 2012), focusing mainly on gains and losses in individual sectors.

Finally, trade policy has been found to be intermittently tied to macroeconomic policies. The fundamental linkages between national saving and investment, on the one hand, and the current account in the balance of payments, on the other, are well known from economic theory. They have been discussed in the WTO in the context of coherence in the international policy-making between the WTO, IMF and World Bank on a number of occasions (WTO, 2004). According to Drabek and Bacchetta (2004), 'these linkages have been well understood by the original GATT negotiators'. Nevertheless, the effects of the WTO discipline on macroeconomic policies remains, perhaps, the 'least familiar' and 'most understated' in the whole debate about the WTO, including in the assessment of the consequences of WTO accession. And this is where this chapter's discussion starts.

## Macroeconomic framework for impact evaluation

### Accounting framework

One way to look at the macroeconomic implications of WTO accession is through the prism of the System of National Accounts (SNA). The SNA provides an internationally recognised accounting framework, which allows the compilation and presentation of macroeconomic data in a consistent manner (Bart and Hemphill, 2000). Economic agents in any economy can be subdivided into five sectors: households, enterprises, financial intermediaries, the government and the rest of the world. They are all linked by accounting identities. In a simplified form these linkages can be presented as follows (Figure 5.1).

In any economy, there is supply of resources and demand for resources or their use. Supply of resources consists of its own output, $Y$, and

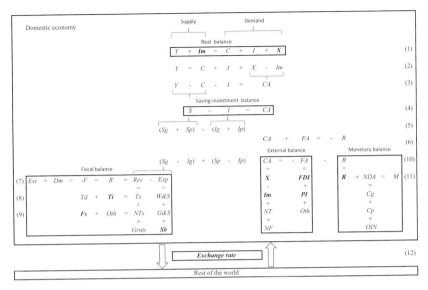

**Figure 5.1**    WTO accession: accounting framework for impact evaluation (author's analysis).

imports, *Im*. These resources are used for consumption, *C*, investment, *I*, and exports, *X* (1). According to the expenditure approach, income generated by the output is equal to the sum of its final uses (2). Additional income for the country includes net factor income and net transfers, which can be added to both sides of the identity but are omitted here to simplify the presentation. Income not consumed equals saving, *S*, and the difference between exports and imports equals the current account, *CA*, in the balance of payments (3). Therefore, *ex post*, the gap between saving and investment is equivalent to the current account balance (4). In other words, the current account deficit is driven by investment exceeding saving and should be financed from abroad. The current account surplus reflects saving exceeding investment and can be used to finance investment abroad. The saving–investment balance, which is equal to the current account, is the fundamental identity of international macroeconomics.

The outcome of the saving and investment balance depends on the performance of the public and private sectors. In Figure 5.1, on the left-hand side of the saving–investment balance, national saving can be presented as a sum of government saving, *Sg*, and private saving, *Sp*, and national investment as a sum of government investment, *Ig*, and private investment, $Ip$ (5). On the right-hand side of the saving–investment balance, the current account itself is part of the balance of payments identity. It says that the current account balance, $CA$, plus the financial account balance, $FA$, should equal the change in international reserves, $R$, of the country (6). In other words, any disequilibrium between saving and investment in either the public or private sector would be reflected in the flows in the financial account or reserves. Assume for simplicity that the private sector always adjusts to the equilibrium, its saving–investment balance is zero, that is, $Sp - Ip = 0$, and the saving–investment balance of the government sector is the only determinant of the current account.

The saving–investment balance of the public sector broadly reflects the government's budget position. The level of government saving, $Sg$, depends on the fiscal balance, $B$, which is the difference between revenue, $Rev$, and expenses, $Exp$, and is financed, $-F$, either from external sources, $Ext$, or domestic sources, $Dm$ (7). Revenue consists of tax revenue, $Tx$, non-tax revenue, $NTx$, and grants, $Grnts$. Expenses include only final consumption expenditure by the general government, that is, usually payments of wages and salaries, $W\&S$, procurements of goods and services, $G\&S$, and subsidies, $Sb$. In turn, tax revenue consists of domestic taxes, $Td$, and taxes on international trade and transactions, $Ti$ (8). Non-tax revenue includes fees and charges, $Fs$, and other revenue, $Oth$ (9).

The current account is a crucial component of the balance of payments and the external balance. Depending on the balance between domestic saving and investment, the current account can be in deficit or surplus. In the case of a deficit, it is financed by inflows in the financial account, $FA$, and/or drawing down international reserves, $R$ (10). This is a budget constraint for the economy, because the deficit can persist only as long as financial inflows are maintained and the reserve level remains appropriate. In a current account surplus, the country finances the rest of the world by outflows in the financial account and/or accumulates reserves. The current account balance is usually determined mainly by the balance on trade in goods and services, $X - Im$. In addition, the net factor income, $NF$, and net transfers, $NT$, may be important for the current account in certain countries. The flows in the financial account can be, $FDI$, portfolio investment, $PI$, and other flows, $Oth$, which consist mainly of public and private loans.

The saving–investment balance has an important impact on monetary accounts. Assuming international reserves equal net foreign assets (NFA), $NF$, of the central bank and there are no changes in the NFA of commercial banks, then change in reserves, $R$, generated by the balance of payments outcome together with the changes in net domestic assets, $NDA$, lead to changes in broad money, $M$ (11). Changes in the $NDA$ can be driven by net credit to the government, $Cg$, credit to the private sector, $Cp$, and other items net, $OIN$. The monetary sector identity shows the distinction between money of external origin, NFA ($NF$), reserves, and domestic origin, $NDA$, domestic credit. Unless sterilised, any accumulation of international reserves would translate into an increase in the supply of broad money for a given level of domestic credit. Because in equilibrium money supply always equals money demand, rapid accumulation of reserves may lead to a spike in inflation. Conversely, any expansion in domestic credit at a given level of reserves can have similar consequences.

Finally, the saving–investment balance of any country is closely linked to the level of the exchange rate of its currency. The exchange rate level broadly reflects the balance between supply and demand for currency between residents of the domestic economy and the rest of the world. This balance of supply and demand for currency may be an outcome of: (i) current account transactions as exporters sell their foreign currency earnings and importers buy foreign currency to pay for imports; (ii) financial account transactions as residents demand foreign currency to invest abroad and non-residents need local currency to invest domestically; and (iii) transactions with international reserves as the central bank buys and sells foreign currency to achieve its policy objectives. As a result, flows under all three key accounts of the balance of payments – the current account, the financial account and international reserves account – have an impact on the level of the exchange rate (12).

How do the macroeconomic features of WTO accession enter into this simple framework? On a purely accounting level, commitments taken by countries in the process of accession directly affect their saving–investment balance. The impulse may originate in any of the four sectors from the variables shown in bold italic in Figure 5.1. In the real sector, WTO accession commitments directly influence the volumes of imports and exports, generally by liberalising the former and often changing the conditions for the latter. In the fiscal sector, the impulse would originate on both the revenue and expenditure sides. On the revenue side, the level of taxes on international trade and other fees and charges related to imported goods and services will be affected the most because in many cases the acceding country has to reduce import duties. The impact on the expenditure side will be mainly through the revision of government subsidies and the need to cover any costs of institutional restructuring associated with WTO membership. In the external sector, the impulse should be expected from FDI and portfolio investments as acceding countries liberalise modes of service delivery through foreign commercial presence and accepting WTO trade-related investment rules. Finally, in the monetary sector, the impulse may originate from the level of reserves if the government has to finance costs of its WTO accession by using domestic credit in excess of the increase of broad money warranted by the evolution of the nominal gross domestic product (GDP).

## Behavioural framework[1]

Commitments made by countries as part of their WTO Accession Packages can have an impact on behavioural macroeconomic relationships. The economic theory points out numerous fundamental factors that can affect each variable in the saving–investment identity (4) and shift saving, investment and the current account. Following the ongoing IMF research on the Pilot External Balance Assessment Methodology (IMF, 2013), these factors can be presented in a generic form as follows:[2]

$$S(Z_S) - I(Z_I) = CA(Y, Z_S, Z_I, Z_{CA}, Z_{FA}, R)$$

where $Y$ is the domestic output gap, $R$ the change in international reserves, $FA$ the balance on the financial account, and $Z$ is all factors affecting saving, $Z_S$, investment, $Z_I$, the current account, $Z_{CA}$, and the financial account, $Z_{FA}$. The real effective exchange rate $REER$, which implicitly affects both the current and financial accounts, is intentionally omitted from the list of fundamental factors, because the $CA$ and the $REER$ are both endogenous and simultaneously determined as a function of other variables. Most factors influencing the $CA$ would also influence the $REER$. Therefore, the analysis of the fundamental factors underlying the $REER$ would be broadly symmetrical.

---

[1] This section draws on the ongoing IMF research (IMF, 2013).

[2] In this identity, variables appearing on the right-hand side do not necessarily appear on the left-hand side. The identity will hold in equilibrium, so technically any adjustment in a right-hand side variable will be reflected in the left-hand side variables, thereby making the left-hand side variables a function of the right-hand side variables. As this relationship is not direct, but is only captured through an equilibrium adjustment mechanism, there is no need to include all variables on both sides of the equation. In other words, all factors included in brackets can be seen as factors that affect the variables of interest.

The sources for the external imbalance can be domestic and external. On the domestic side, any factors affecting national saving and investment would have an impact on the $CA$. In particular, these are: saving/consumption shifters, $Z_S$, such as the current and expected per capita income, population growth, aging speed, dependency ratio, fiscal balance (revenue and expenditure, including social expenditure) and changes in savings patterns; and investment shifters, $Z_I$, such as the current and expected per capita income, the investment climate and the relative price of capital, competitiveness and productivity. On the external side, there are several exogenous factors that would have an impact on the $CA$, independently of the domestic saving and investment decisions. These are: the $CA$ shifters, $Z_{CA}$, which may include the terms of trade, commodity prices including oil and international interest rates; and the financial account shifters, $Z_{FA}$, such as global risk aversion and share of the country's currency in the world total stock of international reserves.

Assessment of the macroeconomic implications of WTO accession using this behavioural framework can consist of two stages. At the first stage, the $CA$ of the acceding country could be evaluated for consistency with the underlying fundamentals and the $CA$ gap, if any, could be identified as a difference between the actual $CA$ and the estimated $CA$ norm. At the second stage, the impact of accession commitments on the estimated $CA$ gap could be evaluated. Because this $CA$ gap is itself a sum of several policy gaps (related to fiscal, social, capital controls, reserve accumulation, financial and monetary policies), the impact of accession commitments on each of these gaps can be estimated. The goal would be to find out whether the configuration of the Accession Package would bring the actual $CA$ of the acceded country closer to the norm and therefore induce greater external stability in the long run or, to the contrary, whether such commitments would increase the $CA$ gap and inflict additional instability.

At the first stage, the fundamentals underlying the $CA$ in the acceding country can be identified using the latest vintage of the IMF External Balance Assessment (EBA) current account model. This would allow the $CA$ norm for the acceding country to be established. The model regresses the current account/GDP ratios of forty-nine advanced and emerging-market countries accounting for about 90 per cent of world GDP in 1986–2010 on a set of fundamental explanatory variables that should determine the $CA$ according to economic theory. Almost all explanatory variables are measured on a relative basis; for example, for the fiscal balance it is the difference between a country's own fiscal balance and the world's average fiscal balance. The identified fundamentals of the CA can be subdivided into several groups: non-policy variables (income, productivity, demographics) and financial, cyclical and policy variables. The latter can be influenced by the government's policies (Table 5.2). Most coefficients are significant and have the expected sign. Running separate saving and investment regressions, using the same specification as for the CA, suggests that most fundamentals affect the CA mainly through the saving channel. The investment channel is important but only for the output gap and the expected GDP growth.

The list of fundamentals includes variables that cannot be directly affected by public policies. They are related to productivity, income and demographics, and most are highly statistically significant. For example, a 1 per cent increase in relative productivity is associated with 0.06 per cent improvement in the CA in countries with no capital controls but has virtually no effect in countries with capital controls. Or, conversely, capital tends to flow to countries with lower productivity and income levels, but the scale of inflows depends on financial openness. An increase in the growth forecast by 1 percentage point is associated with a worsening of the CA by almost 0.5 of a percentage point, because countries that grow faster invest more and therefore tend to have lower CA balances. Countries with a relatively high net foreign assets NFA position tend to have higher CA balances. The relative coefficient is very small and not significant if an interaction dummy for countries with their NFA position below 60 per cent of GDP is added. The oil and gas trade balances are strongly and positively associated with the CA as countries with substantial energy resources tend to run CA surpluses. Countries where the population is aging more rapidly are richer and are more likely to have a current account surplus, because a 1 percentage point increase in the aging speed is associated with a CA improvement of 0.6 per cent of GDP. Financial centres tend to have a CA balance about 3 per cent of GDP higher than other countries. Finally, a reduction of institutional and political risks by one standard deviation is associated with a weaker CA by about 1 percentage point of GDP as financial inflows increase.

Financial variables are all significant CA fundamentals. The share of a country's own currency in world reserves shows the potential to finance its CA by issuing internationally accepted own currency. For every 10 per cent increase in global reserve held in its currency, the current account balance of that country declines by 0.45 of a percentage point. Indicators of global market conditions and risk aversion suggest that an

Table 5.2 *Current account: the fundamentals (estimation period: 1986–2010; pooled GLS estimates); dependent variable:* CA/GDP

| | |
|---|---|
| ***Non-policy variables*** | |
| Relative output per worker × Capital account openness (lagged one period) | 0.065 *** |
| Output per worker relative to top three economies | 0.007 |
| GDP growth, forecast in five years | −0.471 *** |
| Net foreign assets/GDP (lagged one period) | 0.016 ** |
| Net foreign assets/GDP × (dum=1 if NFA/GDP < −60 per cent), (lagged one period) | −0.012 |
| Oil and gas trade balance × Resource temporariness/GDP (if > 10 per cent) | 0.615 *** |
| Financial centre dummy (1 if country is a financial centre) | 0.033 *** |
| Ageing speed (relative to world average) | 0.156 *** |
| Dependency ratio (relative to world average) | −0.030 |
| Population growth (relative to world average) | −0.629 |
| Safer institutional/Political environment index | −0.109 *** |
| ***Financial variables*** | |
| Own currency's share in world reserves | −0.045 *** |
| Risk aversion index × (1-capital control index)(lagged one period) | 0.068 *** |
| Risk aversion index × (1-capital control index) × (currency's share in world reserves) | −0.136 |
| Private credit/GDP | −0.260 *** |
| ***Cyclical variables*** | |
| Output gap | −0.400 *** |
| Terms of trade gap × Openness | 0.230 *** |
| ***Policy variables*** | |
| Cyclically adjusted fiscal balance (instrumented) | 0.324 *** |
| Public health spending/GDP (lagged one period) | −0.551 *** |
| Changes in reserves/GDP × Capital control (instrumented) | 0.346 ** |
| Constant | −0.014 *** |
| Observations | 1080 |
| Number of countries | 49 |
| Root MSE | 0.033 |

*Note:* **significant at 5 per cent; ***significant at 1 per cent.
*Source:* IMF (2013).

increase in the corresponding index by 10 percentage points is associated with an improvement in the CA. In non-reserve currency countries with open capital accounts, this improvement leads to corresponding capital outflows of about 0.7 per cent of GDP. The private credit-to-GDP ratio is used as a proxy for financial policies.

Cyclical variables include the output gap and the commodity terms of trade and are also important CA fundamentals. The output gap captures business cycle effects and temporary demand shocks; for example, a positive demand shock would cause output to rise above potential and the current account balance to decline. The cyclically lower output is associated with high saving and lower investment: an increase in the relative output gap by 1 percentage point is associated with a decline of the CA by about 0.4 per cent of GDP. As expected, an improvement in the country's commodity terms of trade is associated with CA improvement.

Finally, the model includes policy variables, which capture those CA fundamentals that can be directly influenced by measures of public policies. Such policy instruments include the cyclically adjusted fiscal balance, social protection spending and foreign exchange market capital controls (included as an interaction term). The results indicate that stronger fiscal positions, lower levels of social protection, faster reserves accumulation and higher degrees of capital controls are associated with higher CA balances. For example, an increase in the fiscal balance by 1 percentage point of GDP is associated with an improvement of the CA by about 0.3 of a percentage point of GDP. Because social protection reduces the need for precautionary saving, an increase in public health spending/GDP by 1 percentage point of GDP is associated with a reduction of the CA by about 0.6 per cent of GDP. Under imperfect capital mobility, foreign exchange intervention (changes in foreign exchange reserves) should affect the exchange rate and by implication the CA: an increase in reserve accumulation of 2 percentage points of GDP is associated with a CA that is higher by 0.3 of a percentage point of GDP. Capital controls enter the CA fundamentals as interaction terms with both the reserves level and the level of development. Inclusion of the private credit-to-GDP ratio among policy fundamentals is an attempt to reflect the failure of public policies to prevent excessive financing that causes demand booms, weakens the CA and leads to real appreciation. An increase in the ratio of 10 percentage points is associated with a weakening of the CA by 0.3 of a percentage point.

The current CA norm for most acceding countries can be estimated based on these fundamentals. For that, the estimated coefficient should be run by the time series of the relevant macroeconomic variables for the acceding country. If the estimated *CA* norm is close to the actually observed *CA* level, the acceding country may be in external equilibrium. In this case, it is desirable that WTO accession commitments have a macroeconomically neutral impact so as not to disturb the equilibrium. However, most probably the actual *CA* of the acceding country would diverge from the estimated *CA* norm and the country would experience external imbalance. In this case, WTO accession commitments could be designed to help the country's *CA* to adjust to the balanced position in the long run.

If the acceding country is found in external disequilibrium, at the second (normative) stage, the contribution to the *CA* gap of the policy variables should be identified. The *CA* measured in per cent of GDP can be estimated as:

$$CA = \alpha + Z'\beta + P'\gamma$$

where $Z$ is the vector of non-policy variables affecting the *CA*, and $P$ is the vector comprising all policy variables. If $P^*$ is the vector of desirable values of policy variables, then simply adding and subtracting $P^{*\prime}\gamma$ from the right-hand side of the equation would obtain:

$$CA = \alpha + Z'\beta + P^{*\prime}\gamma + (P - P^*)\gamma$$

The first term $(\alpha + Z'\beta + P^{*\prime}\gamma)$ is the *CA* norm, that is, the *CA* level implied by fundamentals. This means that all policies are at their desirable levels, and all other variables at their actual levels. The second term $(P - P^*)\gamma$ represents the contribution of the policy gaps to the deviations of the actual *CA* from the norm. These policy gap contributions are measured as the product of each of the estimated coefficients on the respective policy variables.

To compare the observed level of policy variables to their desirable values or policy benchmarks, the latter should be specified. This requires specification of the appropriate level $P^*$ for all policy fundamentals that contribute to the *CA* gap and are under the control of the authorities: the fiscal balance, capital controls, social spending, reserve accumulation, financial policies and monetary policy. The level of these fundamentals should be appropriate for a given acceding country over the long-term horizon under the assumption that the economy will be at full employment.

Substantial judgement is needed to identify the appropriate level of the policy benchmarks $P^*$ for each acceding country. For fiscal policy, it may be the desired level of the fiscal balance targeted for the medium term. For social protection, the benchmark can be derived from a regression of public health spending as a share of GDP on a country's per capita GDP, the age dependency ratio and income inequality. The benchmark related to desirable financial policies (private credit/GDP) can be selected for the acceding country if there are signs of overheating owing to inappropriate financial policies. For capital controls, the benchmark is either the cross-country average level of the capital controls index (0.17 in 2011, out of a range from 0 to 1) or a country's actual level, whichever is smaller. For the change in international reserves benchmark, an assumption can be made that for most countries the observed change in the past year was appropriate. However, for a country having reserves exceeding the level suggested by the IMF's reserve adequacy matrix, the appropriate change in reserves can be specified as zero. Finally, regarding the monetary policy benchmark, if the current policy stance were judged inconsistent with inflation, the monetary policy gap can be defined as the interest rate differential.

The sum of differences $P - P^*$ between the observed levels and the benchmarks for all policy fundamentals equals the overall $CA$ gap. The contributions of each policy gap to the $CA$ are estimated taking the relevant regression coefficients estimated at the first stage and multiplying them by the corresponding policy gaps. These contributions, together with the regression residual, are then summed up to form a country's total $CA$ gap. Assume that the acceding country has a fiscal deficit of –7 per cent of GDP but the benchmark level is –1 per cent of GDP. Therefore, the fiscal gap is –6 per cent of GDP. The contribution of the fiscal gap to the overall $CA$ balance is estimated (Figure 5.1) as 0.32 times the gap between the actual fiscal balance minus the benchmark fiscal balance. The total $CA$ gap will be the regression residual (0 per cent) plus (–6 per cent) × 0.32 = 1.92 per cent of GDP. If the country has an actual $CA$ deficit of 2 per cent of GDP it is almost entirely due to deviations of fiscal policy from its recommended position.

Once the contribution of each policy variable to the overall $CA$ gap is identified, WTO accession commitments may be designed to contribute to helping the country to close the gap. Although accession commitments are not designed to redress macroeconomic imbalances, at a minimum they should be conducive to external stability. For example, if the $CA$ gap is due mainly to expansionary fiscal policies and high fiscal deficits, the WTO accession commitment could put more emphasis on the need to preserve tax revenue eroded by tariff reduction and reduce subsidies to improve the fiscal balance. If the gap is explained mainly by suboptimal capital controls, WTO accession commitments may put additional emphasis on the liberalisation of commercial presence and observance of trade-related investment rules. If there are signs of inadequate financial policies, additional commitments in trade in financial services may be justified. Obviously, in all cases the numerical results on the fundamental determinants of the $CA$ should be treated with caution. Substantial judgement is still required to inform and guide policy decisions.

## Sectoral impact of accession

### Real effects

Trade liberalisation as a result of WTO accession should have an impact on the real sector. Accession to the WTO may improve access for the exports of the acceded country to international markets. Although incumbent WTO members are not obliged to reduce their import duties in the process of the accession negotiations, they will not be able to apply discriminatory tariffs against the acceded country once it becomes a member. This adds predictability, security and transparency to the acceded country in access to the markets of its trading partners. Moreover, acquiring WTO membership allows a country to participate in the upcoming rounds of multilateral trade negotiations and share their benefits. Therefore, it is reasonable to assume that exports, which are part of aggregate demand, may increase with WTO accession (Table 5.3). Trade openness, along with other macroeconomic conditions, has usually been found to be important for growth (WTO, 2004).

A possible increase in investment, which is also part of domestic demand, would be another driver of growth as a result of WTO accession. Government investment is generally a policy instrument used to promote public goals. If a WTO accession frees additional fiscal space, for example by eliminating subsidies, the government will have more resources for investment that should promote growth. Private sector investment may also increase as WTO accession improves the confidence of private producers regarding their future access to external markets. They may also feel more confident regarding the availability of external financing as their country starts to abide by internationally accepted trade-related investment rules and opens for foreign commercial presence. Greater predictability in tax policies – as most import tariffs will be bound upon accession – can also encourage private investment.

Table 5.3 *Real effect of WTO accession*

| Supply | Impact | Demand | Impact |
|---|---|---|---|
| GDP | | GDP | |
| Primary sector | +/– | Gross domestic expenditure | + |
| Secondary sector | +/– | Consumption | + |
| Tertiary sector | +/– | Private | +/– |
| Public administration | +/– | Public | + |
| | | Gross fixed investment | + |
| | | Public | +/– |
| | | Private | + |
| | | Change in stocks | |
| | | Resource gap | +/– |
| | | Exports of G&NFS* | + |
| | | Imports of G&NFS* | – |

*Note:* *G&NFS = goods and non-factor services.
*Source:* Adapted from United Nations (2008).

Consumption may also increase as a result of WTO accession and contribute to the aggregate demand. Government consumption can be driven mainly by policy considerations related to the need to finance adjustment to WTO requirements. Private consumption will benefit from the change in relative prices, as imported goods should become cheaper. Additional favourable effects on private consumption will result from the greater predictability of the tax regime, anchored expectations and greater credibility of government's policies which are framed into long-term WTO commitments.

Because the real effects of WTO accession operate mainly through the demand side, the supply side may impose serious constraints, mainly related to adjustment costs in the private sector. If certain local industries were not sufficiently competitive by international standards, market opening achieved by removing protective import duties and subsidies could depress their production and exports. In the long run, trade liberalisation should bring better resource allocation to the economy of the acceded country and increase its overall efficiency. However, in the short term such massive resource reallocation from uncompetitive to more competitive sectors can lead to substantial adjustment costs. Experience of recent accessions suggests that agriculture, food process-ing, automotive industries, civil aircraft and pharmaceuticals are the most vulnerable sectors. Neither capital nor labour will be able to adjust immediately to the new production structure dictated by market openness. Whole sectors may be disrupted, with a serious adverse impact on growth. Public policies have an important role in mitigating the adjustment costs in the private sector by providing investment incentives and social support, and retraining the labour force.

## Fiscal effects

Commitments undertaken as part of the Accession Package may affect the fiscal balance of the acceding country. As shown above, the fiscal balance is directly linked to the saving–investment balance of the public sector and therefore has a major impact on external and balance of payments stability. Any changes in government revenue and consumption resulting from accession will translate into changes in the level of government saving, which, for a given level of public investment and an unchanged private sector saving–investment balance, would shift the current account of the acceding country. The direction of the shift will largely depend on whether the acceding commitments improve the overall fiscal balance or lead to its deterioration. The outcome depends on their relative impact on specific revenue and expenditure lines, primarily those shown in italics in Table 5.4.

WTO accession commitments to liberalise imports will definitely affect the revenue line 'Customs and other import duties'. This line covers revenue collected on goods entering the acceded country or services delivered by non-residents to residents. This revenue line includes duties levied under the customs tariff schedule, including surcharges, consular fees, tonnage charges, statistical taxes and fiscal duties. The impact depends on whether the acceding country has to reduce its applied duties to the bound level, the elasticity of import volumes to changes in the duty rate, the relative importance of customs revenue in overall revenue and whether the acceding country has made the commitment to replace quotas with customs duties. WTO accession commitments may lead to a drop in customs revenue, but only if the acceded government has to reduce applied import duties, if import volumes do not increase after this reduction, if no quotas were replaced with import duties and if it has to remove import surcharges. On balance, available empirical evidence suggests that the impact of accession on customs revenue has been negligible, at least in transition economies, and has not caused any major budgetary problems, probably because the liberalisation took place before accession to the WTO (Drabek and Bacchetta, 2004).

Table 5.4 *Fiscal effects of WTO accession*

| Revenue | Impact | Expenses | Impact |
|---|---|---|---|
| **Taxes** | | **Current expenditure** | |
| On income, profits and capital gains | | *Compensation of employees* | + |
| On payroll and workforce | | *Use of goods and services* | + |
| On property | | | |
| On goods and services | | | |
| *General (VAT, sales, turnover)* | – | Subsidies | |
| *Excise* | – | *To public corporations* | – |
| Profit of fiscal monopolies | | *To private enterprises* | – |
| Specific services | | Interest | |
| Use of goods | | On external debt | |
| On international trade and transactions | | On domestic debt | |
| *Customs and other import duties, o/w* | +/– | Social benefits | |
| | | Other | |
| *Taxes on exports* | – | | |
| *Profit of export and import monopolies* | +/– | **Capital expenditure** | |
| | | *Externally financed* | + |
| *Exchange profits and taxes* | + | *Domestically financed* | + |
| *Other duties and charges* | – | **Fiscal balance (net lending/ borrowing)** | +/– |
| **Social contributions** | | | |
| **Grants** | | **Financing** | –/+ |
| *From foreign governments* | + | | |
| *From international organisations* | + | Domestic | |
| From other government units | | Bank | |
| **Other revenue** | | Central bank | |
| Property income | | Commercial banks | |
| Interest | | Non-bank | |
| Sales of goods and services | | External | |
| Fines, penalties | | *Drawing* | + |
| | | Repayments | |

*Source:* Adapted from IMF (2001).

Obviously, the magnitude of both positive and negative impacts will depend on the share of import duties in overall revenue, and will be more pronounced in those acceding countries that rely heavily on revenue from import tariffs.

In fact, customs revenue in acceded countries may increase. If 'tariffi-cation' (the conversion of non-tariff barriers into tariffs) is part of the Accession Package, this will raise revenue by transforming the rents previously captured by quota holders into government revenue. The reduction of other non-tariff barriers will normally generate more imports and expand the tax base, thus bringing additional revenue because the liberalised imports are typically subject to tariff. Eliminating tariff exemptions on imports, including imported inputs, would reduce the effective protection and improve resource allocation, and could also generate additional revenue. In addition, the modernisation of customs administration induced by WTO accession commitments (streamlining customs inspections, applying WTO valuation procedures, addressing governance problems) would ease impediments to imports and expand their volume, which, if properly taxed, would increase revenue. Finally, if accession takes away the revenue function of customs (i.e. the tariff), an economy is then forced to focus on domestic taxation to finance the budget. This can be seen as an opportunity to modernise the tax system from a highly distortionary and rent-seeking tariff-based system to a much less distorting and more growth-friendly tax system (VAT, excises, etc.). In fact, VAT introduction was motivated in many countries by a shift from tariffs to domestic taxes, which drove the modernisation of the whole tax administration, and which had an indirect impact on non-VAT revenue collection (e.g. corporate tax revenue).

Taxes on exports in the acceded country may decline. This category includes all levies on goods transported out of the country or services delivered by residents to non-residents. Although WTO rules do not set out obligations to bind export tariffs, a number of acceding countries have been asked to undertake special commitments in this area. The scope and nature of these commitments vary widely – from complete elimination of export duties, at one end, to applying them 'in accordance with WTO rules', on the other. Although some acceding countries have been allowed to preserve at least some existing export duties, no coun-tries have been allowed to increase duties (Qin, 2012). In principle, export taxes should be used only temporarily to absorb windfall profits from exceptionally favourable shifts in the terms of trade.

The fiscal impact from WTO accession commitments related to state trading enterprises is ambiguous. State trading enterprises can be governmental or non-governmental enterprises, including marketing boards that deal with goods for export or import. All acceding countries have to commit to the general WTO principle that such enterprises in their import or export decisions act in accordance with the general principle of nondiscrimination and are guided only by commercial considerations. They are also expected not to apply quantitative restrictions, to preserve the value of tariff concessions and to function transparently. Profits of state trading enterprises remitted to government are considered tax revenue. For example, in Tajikistan, state trading enterprises are required to make purchases and sales which are not for the government's own use in accordance with commercial considerations. Also, foreign companies should be afforded adequate opportunity to compete for participation in their purchases or sales.

Exchange profits and taxes may, potentially, increase after the country accedes to the WTO. Trade liberalisation should increase trade and therefore the turnover of foreign exchange. If the authorities tax sales to importers or purchases of foreign exchange from exporters, this revenue item in the budget should increase. Also, as WTO accessions help to liberalise the movement of natural persons, remittances may increase. If purchase of foreign exchange to be remitted or receipts of inward remittances are taxed, this should contribute to the fiscal revenue of the acceded country, although the increase may not be significant.

Acceding countries generally commit not to use other duties and charges, including import surcharges. Other duties and charges should be consolidated into the tariff structure, so that the nominal tariffs reflect the true protection level. The use of import surcharges is often justified by the need to address fiscal or balance of payments disequilibrium quickly. By raising the domestic price of imports, import surcharges switch demand to domestic goods and improve the current account, at least in the short term. By raising revenue the surcharge is expected to improve the fiscal balance, the overall saving–investment balances and the external position. However, with a flexible exchange rate, import surcharges are redundant because lower demand for imports causes an excess supply of foreign exchange, leading to an appreciation of the domestic currency, which would offset the initial impact of the surcharge. Under fixed exchange rates, an import surcharge may initially cause domestic demand to contract and reduce imports. However, the surcharge is an implicit tax on exports that will, over time, undermine any impact on the current account. Empirical studies indicate that the fiscal impact of import surcharges on fiscal revenue has been substantially below the anticipated 0.2 to 1 per cent of GDP in five countries that have used import surcharges recently (Argentina, Bulgaria, Hungary, Poland, the Slovak Republic).

The impact of WTO accession commitments on internal taxes will most probably be negative but small. For all acceded countries, WTO rules require that internal taxes not be used to protect domestic production and that imported goods cannot be subject to internal taxes in excess of those applied to like domestic products. Therefore, acceding countries which did not provide national treatment to imported goods will have to reduce their internal taxes on imported goods, which will lead to revenue losses, mainly in VAT and excise collection. On the other hand, in a few cases accession commitments require the elimination of tax exemptions afforded to domestically produced goods to increase their international competitiveness, in particular on agricultural and food items. If such exemptions are significant, their elimination will help to increase revenue.

On the expenditure side, subsidies are the main line that can be affected by WTO accession. In the process of accession negotiations, the acceding country needs to present information on its subsidies. All subsidies are then divided into agricultural and non-agricultural, as different rules apply to each (the Agreement on Agriculture and the Agreement on Subsidies and Countervailing Measures respectively). The amount of each subsidy is then calculated: for agricultural subsidies as an aggregate measurement of support (AMS) and for non-agricultural subsidies as a simple product-, enterprise- or industry-specific table of subsidies. The subsidies classified as agricultural are subdivided into 'green box' (allowed subsidies), 'amber box' (allowed subsidies but subject to reduction) and 'blue box' (direct payments to farmers under production-limiting agreements, not subject to reductions). The subsidies classified as non-agricultural are subdivided into prohibited (export subsidies and import substitution subsidies); allowable, but actionable (challengeable by other members through the dispute settlement mechanism or through bilateral countervailance); and allowable non-actionable subsidies (Table 5.5).

Direct budgetary savings from the elimination of subsidies may be significant and depend on the amount of such subsidies and the reduction schedule agreed on during the accession negotiations. Based on subsidy classification, members ask the acceding country to undertake commitments so that its legislation and practices are 'in conformity with the WTO rules'. From the macroeconomic perspective, this means that the acceding country will have to eliminate export subsidies and import substitution subsidies upon accession and reduce the 'amber box' subsidies in accordance with a negotiated schedule. On non-agricultural goods, the acceding country can enjoy substantial budgetary savings by

Table 5.5 *WTO rules on subsidies at a glance*

| Agricultural subsidies | Coverage | Non-agricultural subsidies |
|---|---|---|
| HS* Chapters 1–24, less fish and fish products plus selected other products | | Specific subsidies only; a financial contribution by a government or any public body, which confers a benefit. |
| Allowed subsidies not subject to reduction | Green box | Allowable, non-specific and non-actionable subsidies |
| Domestic support subsidies subject to reduction | Amber box | Allowable but actionable subsidies |
| Direct payments under production-limiting programmes, not subject to reduction | Blue box | Does not exist |
| Does not exist | Red box | Prohibited subsidies: export subsidies and import substitution subsidies |

*Note:* *HS = Harmonised System.
*Source:* Adapted from WTO (1999).

removing export subsidies and import-substitution subsidies, which are prohibited under WTO rules, with some limited exceptions for least-developed countries (LDCs) and small economies. Other non-agricultural subsidies are allowed. On agricultural subsidies, fiscal savings can be low and materialise only in the medium term, as all types of agricultural subsidies are allowed under WTO rules. However, some of them, as a result of accession negotiations, can be subject to reduction or even bound at zero, usually after a transition period.

Implementation of WTO accession commitments may lead to substantial budgetary costs. In most cases, the acceded country has to introduce deep institutional and legislative reform to bring its trade regime into conformity with WTO rules. Implementation of many WTO agreements and legal procedures is technically complex, in particular, the Agreement on Sanitary and Phytosanitary Measures, the Agreement on Technical Barriers to Trade, the Agreement on Trade-Related Aspects of Intellectual Property Rights and some other agreements. It requires extensive training of personnel, procurement of new equipment and technology, the redrafting of domestic regulation and the corresponding institutional changes, including strengthening enforcement capacity. The specific expenditure items that can be affected by the need to finance these implementation costs may include wages and salaries, because the authorities need to hire and train additional staff, procure goods and services to purchase equipment and invest in rebuilding trade infrastructure. Investment can be financed domestically and externally. Some recently acceded countries already receive the support of external donors for the adjustment period. In such cases, the source of financing can be either loans, shown as a financing item in the budget, or grants, including from international institutions, included in revenue.

Overall, the fiscal implications of WTO accession seem ambiguous. The impact on the fiscal balance and the saving–investment balance of the government will largely depend on the relative impact of revenue and expenditure items affected by WTO accession commitments. On average, tax revenue will most probably remain unchanged or decline, but modestly and mainly in the year of the most intense implementation of WTO import liberalisation commitments. Transition periods should help smooth out this negative impact, and an increase in the taxable base with growth of trade will help offset some losses. At the same time, expenditure increases may be substantial, mainly driven by the implementation costs of the accession commitments. Reduction in subsidies will most probably not be enough to offset these costs, because export subsidies are rare in acceding countries, while the reduction of agricultural subsidies is usually phased in over the medium term. Therefore, adequate financing, from multilateral and bilateral sources, may be needed to cover a temporary increase in the fiscal deficit associated with the implementation of WTO commitments.

### Monetary effects

The monetary implications of WTO accession depend on a number of macroeconomic and institutional factors. Chief among them are the level of economic activity induced by the accession to the WTO in the real sector of the acceded country; changes in its reserves, which are the outcome of the balance of payments; and the country's exchange-rate regime and policies on capital mobility.

Changes in broad-money demand depend largely on real activity, inflation and factors affecting velocity. Assume that WTO accession will accelerate GDP growth by promoting export demand and enhancing investment. Lower tariffs on imported goods should, in principle, help

Table 5.6 *Monetary effects of WTO accession (monetary accounts)*

| Assets | Impact | Liabilities | Impact |
|---|---|---|---|
| **Net foreign assets** | | **Broad money** | +/- |
| Central bank | +/- | Narrow money | |
| Commercial banks | | Currency in circulation | |
| **Net domestic assets** | | Demand deposits | |
| Domestic credit | | Quasi-money | |
| Net claims on | + | Time and savings | |
| government | | deposits | |
| Claims on other sectors | – | Foreign currency | |
| Other items net | | deposits | |

*Source:* Adapted from IMF (2000).

reduce the external component of domestic inflation. Other things being equal, with higher GDP but lower inflation, nominal money demand may remain unchanged and thus unaffected by the implementation of WTO accession commitments. This money demand would have to be met from domestic and external sources (Table 5.6). If a particular WTO accession leads to an increase in the fiscal deficit, most probably credit from the banking system to the government will expand. If at the same time this accession worsened the current account, the central bank would most probably have to sell some of its international reserves, while still leaving substantial credit resources for the private sector. However, if with unchanged NFA of commercial banks international reserves of the central bank increase, some crowding out of the private sector is possible.

If WTO accession liberalises capital inflows, this can have an impact on the authorities' ability to conduct monetary policy. The impact would depend on the exchange rate regime maintained by the acceding country. Under a fixed exchange rate regime, the more the country liberalises capital flows, the less autonomy in monetary policy it would leave itself. Although independent monetary policy is not possible with a fixed exchange rate, in principle it can be used in the short to medium term. With no capital mobility and expansionary monetary policy aimed at promoting growth, the country will be losing international reserves, but this loss will be driven by increased imports. Because imports may react to increased income with a lag of several months to years, the central bank may have some scope for a discretionary monetary policy during this period. However, if capital mobility is expanded as a result of accession, the spillovers will be short-term capital flight, which would contract money supply and render monetary policy completely ineffi-cient, even in the short term.

If the acceded country maintains a flexible rate regime, liberalisation of capital flows will not have any impact on monetary policy. It would remain an efficient instrument for macroeconomic adjustment under any policy on capital mobility. All adjustment would be carried out through the exchange rate. With no capital mobility, an expansionary monetary policy will lead to the exchange rate depreciation driven by increased imports. With high capital mobility, this depreciation will be triggered by short-term capital outflows. In both cases, however, the depreciation would induce additional exports and lead the economy to a higher level of income.

### Balance of payments effects

Commitments made in the WTO accession process should help preserve the acceding country's balance of payments stability. An assessment of balance of payments stability requires a close look at key flows under each balance of payments rubric, including $CA$, capital and reserve flows; developments in the stocks of reserves and other assets and liabilities, including the accumulation of balance sheet mismatches; and institu-tional, legal and other controls imposed on these flows and stocks.

Depending on the scope of the accession commitments, their direct impact may be expected on most balance of payments flows (Table 5.7). The impact on the current account should be expected mainly from the general merchandise balance and the balance of trade in services, as trade in goods and services is liberalised as a result of accession. Shifts in both can be in favour of or against the acceded country. In particular, exports of goods may increase as a result of better access opportunities to foreign markets opened by WTO accession. But they may also decline if the export base is eroded by reduced protection from more efficient imports, eliminated export subsidies, reduced domestic support and unfavourable shifts in relative prices. Imports will most probably increase once acces-sion commitments to liberalise them are implemented. However, they may also be constrained by collapsing domestic demand if the overall impact of the Accession Package on GDP is negative and the adjustment costs in key sectors are disproportionately high.

The overall balance on trade in services would most probably worsen following accession but improve in selected services. Because the

Table 5.7 *Balance of payments effects of WTO accession (balance of payments accounts)*

| 1. Current account | Impact | 2. Capital account | Impact |
|---|---|---|---|
| **Goods and services** | | Gross acquisitions/ | |
| **Goods** | | disposals of non- | |
| General merchandise | +/− | produced non- | |
| Net exports of goods | | financial assets | |
| under merchanting | | Capital transfers | + |
| Non-monetary gold | | | |
| **Services** | | **3. Financial account** | |
| Manufacturing services | − | | |
| Maintenance and repair | − | Direct investment | + |
| services | | Portfolio investment | + |
| Transport | +/− | Financial derivatives | |
| Travel | +/− | Other investment | |
| Construction | − | Other equity | |
| Insurance and pension | − | Currency and deposits | |
| services | | Loans | |
| Financial services | +/− | Insurance, pension and | |
| Charges for the use of | +/− | standardised | |
| intellectual property | | guarantee schemes | |
| Telecommunications, | +/− | Trade credit and | +/− |
| computer and | | advances | |
| information services | | Other accounts | |
| Other business services | − | Special Drawing Rights | |
| Personal, cultural and | − | | |
| recreational services | | **4. Reserve assets** | |
| Government goods and | | | |
| services | | Monetary gold | |
| **Primary income** | | Special Drawing Rights | |
| Compensation of employees | − | Reserve position in the IMF | |
| Investment income | − | Other reserve assets | +/− |
| Other primary income | | | |
| **Secondary income** | | | |
| General government | | | |
| Financial corporations, | + | | |
| non-financial | | | |
| corporations, households | | | |
| Adjustment for change in | | | |
| pension entitlements | | | |

*Source:* Adapted from IMF (2011b).

incumbent countries are not expected to take additional commitments on market access in accession negotiations, and rarely do so, the negotiations mainly target the market opening of the acceding country. Specific commitments on services in recent accessions have been extensive and usually span all 10–11 core services sectors and about 70–130 subsectors, depending on the country. In some service areas, acceding countries chose to accept temporary or permanent obligations not applicable to other WTO members. Because these commitments generally include increased foreign participation and rights of establishment in different service sectors oriented mainly to the internal market of the acceded country, export of services will most probably not be affected, while imports may substantially increase. However, in services sectors with a strong export potential (transport, travel, financial and information technology) a substantial increase in exports can be expected in the medium term, once best managerial and other international practices are introduced in the acceded country.

The balance on the primary and secondary income accounts would be affected mainly through the lines related to dividends and interest transfers on direct and portfolio investment. Inward investment and therefore outward transfers of dividends and interest may increase substantially as foreign corporations gain better access to the local market and acquire the rights to a commercial presence and equity participation in local industries. If the acceding country makes specific commitments on the presence of natural persons as a mode of service supply, outflows under the balance of payments line of compensation of employees can also increase.

The impact of accession on the capital and the financial accounts will most probably be positive. The acceded country may expect to receive current and capital grants and loans from international institutions and bilateral donors to help finance the adjustment costs associated with entering into WTO membership. Increased inflow of direct and portfolio investment would be induced by the liberalisation commitments in key industrial and service sectors. The overall impact on the balance of payments, and therefore on the reserve position of the acceded country, seems ambiguous and would largely depend on the outcome on the current account and the availability of external financing.

Implementation of WTO accession commitments may affect the balance of payments through the REER. Under a fixed exchange rate regime, this channel would operate through changes in relative prices. On the one hand, the reduction of import duties should reduce prices of imported commodities and therefore domestic inflation. On the other hand, the commitments to remove price controls, to price energy products based on normal commercial considerations, and not to discriminate between domestic and imported goods in transportation charges, may mean price increases in a number of important sectors, in particular in acceding countries with extensive price controls. If, as the result of accession, there is a spike in inflation exceeding the inflation rate in key partner countries, the REER will appreciate. This would lead to an overall deterioration in external price competitiveness, reduce exports, increase imports and perhaps worsen the overall balance of payments position.

If the acceding country maintains a flexible exchange rate regime, the impact on the REER will be mainly through the nominal exchange rate. If the application of accession commitments leads to a temporary, unsustainable current account deficit, the nominal exchange rate will automatically depreciate. This would make domestic goods cheaper in terms of foreign goods and would help restore the balance by promoting exports and constraining imports. Under full capital mobility, no further adjustment in the financial account or relative prices would be needed. In addition, depreciation of the nominal exchange rate will change the price of tradable versus non-tradable goods, which will affect consumption, shift it to domestically produced goods, encourage their production and larger investment in them, and prop up growth.

## Conclusion

WTO accessions lead to greater openness of economies and therefore to a better allocation of resources, which improves economic efficiency in the long run. The scope of this positive impact will depend on the macroeconomic content of the negotiated Accession Package, the economic structure of the acceding country and the length of transition periods. All of this will differ from country to country. Most probably the impact will be felt across all macroeconomic sectors. While WTO accession will have positive aggregate effects, it may also create winners and losers as overall efficiency gains are usually accompanied by standard income distribution effects. In the short term, application of WTO accession commitments can result in substantial costs for the public and the private sectors. These short-term effects will most probably be offset by substantial efficiency gains in the long run.

WTO accession creates a unique opportunity to accelerate domestic structural reforms. Such reforms will be driven by the need to adapt the

existing institutional structure of the acceded country to the internationally recognised standards. The reforms will most probably go beyond
trade and trade policies and may require, for example, a substantial
overhaul of the tax system, as the acceded country has to rebalance its
revenue sources from external to domestic taxes, and improvement in the
procedures for international capital mobility, the business climate and
governance. Also, WTO accession will encourage governments and the
private sector to take a hard look at the overall competitiveness of the
domestic economy, to remove sources of inefficiencies, and to promote
the most promising sectors that will ultimately drive growth and employment creation.

Preserving systemic stability after accession is in the core interest of
the acceding country and other WTO members as macroeconomic
stability is important for trade. Both external and domestic imbalances
reflect macroeconomic policies and conditions. The macroeconomic
components of WTO Accession Packages cannot by themselves address
these imbalances because they are not designed for this purpose. However, by locking countries into a negotiated set of policies for the length
of their WTO membership, such commitments can play an important
complementary role to fiscal, monetary, exchange rate and structural
policies in reducing systemic imbalances. At the very least, the design
of the accession commitments should not aggravate the existing imbalances from the outset.

The impact of accession should be assessed within a holistic macroeconomic framework. This framework could consist of a simple accounting framework anchored on the saving–investment balance and a
behavioural framework for the current account fundamentals. The
former would allow assessment of the impact of WTO accession commitments for consistency of sectoral developments with the overarching
goal of preserving systemic stability. The latter would allow assessment of
the current account for consistency with fundamentals and identification
of policy areas that can be influenced by accession commitments, in
addition to other policies, to improve systemic stability.

Public policies have an important role to play in closing the policy gaps
and helping countries to cope with the adjustment costs of accession. The
appropriate public policy response includes measures of fiscal, monetary,
exchange rate and structural policies. Usually, fiscal and structural policies are better suited to promoting domestic stability, and monetary and
exchange rate policies to promoting balance of payments stability. Public
policies should provide support to the sectors and population groups

affected by the adjustment induced by WTO membership, help reform the institutional structure and rebalance the tax system from external to domestic taxes to preserve fiscal revenue. Overall, implementation of WTO accession commitments is a matter of public policies that should support promoting systemic stability.

## References

Bart, R. and Hemphill, W. (2000). *Financial Programming and Policy: The Case of Turkey*. Washington DC, International Monetary Fund.

Baunsgaard, T. and M. Keen (2010). 'Tax revenue and (or?) trade liberalization', *Journal of Public Economics*, 94(9–10): 563–577.

Drabek, Z. and M. Bacchetta (2004). 'Tracing the effects of WTO accession on policy-making in sovereign states: preliminary lessons from the recent experience of transition countries', *World Economy*, 27(7): 1083–1125.

Drabek, Z. and W. Woo (2010). 'Who should join the WTO and Why? A cost–benefit analysis of WTO membership', in Z. Drabek (ed.), *Is the World Trade Organization Attractive Enough for Emerging Economies?* New York, Palgrave Macmillan.

Ebrill, L., J. Stotsky and R. Gropp (1999). 'Revenue implications of trade liberalization', Washington DC, International Monetary Fund, IMF Occasional Paper 180.

Evenett, S. and J. Gage (2005). *Evaluating WTO Accessions*. Oxford University Press.

Ferrantino, M. (2009). 'Policy anchors: do free trade agreements and WTO accessions serve as vehicles for developing-country policy reform?', in Z. Drabek (ed.), *Is the World Trade Organization Attractive Enough for Emerging Economies?* New York, Palgrave Macmillan.

Goldstein, J., M. Tomz and M. Rivers (2007). 'Do we really know that the WTO increases trade?' *American Economic Review*, 97(5): 2005–2018.

International Monetary Fund (IMF) (2000). *Monetary and Financial Statistics Manual*. Retrieved from www.imf.org/external/pubs/ft/mfs/manual.

   (2001). *Government Finance Statistics Manual*. Retrieved from www.imf.org/external/pubs/ft/gfs/manual.

   (2005). 'Dealing with the Revenue Consequences of Trade Reform', IMF Policy Paper. Retrieved from www.imf.org/external/np/pp/eng/2005/021505.htm.

   (2011a). 'Revenue Mobilization in Developing Countries', IMF Policy Paper. Retrieved from www.imf.org/external/pp/longres.aspx?id=4537.

   (2011b). *Balance of Payments and International Investment Position Manual*. Retrieved from www.imf.org/external/pubs/ft/bop/2007/bopman6.htm.

   (2012). 'Guidance Note for Surveillance under Article IV Consultations', 10 October. Retrieved from www.imf.org/external/np/exr/facts/refsurv.htm.

(2013). 'External Balance Assessment (EBA): Technical Background of the Pilot Methodology', 25 June. Retrieved from http://www.imf.org/external/np/res/eba.

International Trade Center (ITC) (2012). *Russia's Accession to the WTO: Major Commitments, Possible Implications*. Retrieved from www.intracen.org.

Keen, M. (2008). 'VAT, tariffs, and withholding: border taxes and informality in developing countries', *Journal of Public Economics*, 92(10–11): 1892–1906.

Keen, M. and J. Lighthart (2002). 'Coordinating tariff reduction and domestic tax reform', *Journal of International Economics*, 56(2): 489–507.

Kharitonov, V. and T. Walmsley (2004). 'Impact of Russia's WTO Accession on the Structure of the Russian Economy', Mimeo. Retrieved from www.gtap.agecon.purdue.edu/resources/res_display.asp?RecordID=1566.

Laird, S. (2009). 'Cost of implementation of WTO agreements', in Z. Drabek (ed.), *Is the World Trade Organization Attractive Enough for Emerging Economies?* New York, Palgrave Macmillan.

Li, D. D. and C. C. Wu (2004). 'GATT/WTO accession and productivity', in T. Itō and A. K. Rose (eds.), *Growth and Productivity in East Asia*. NBER–East Asia Seminar on Economics, vol. 13. University of Chicago Press.

Maggi, G. and A. Rodriguez-Clare (1998), 'The value of trade agreements in the presence of political pressures', *Journal of Political Economy*, 106(3): 574–601.

Qin, J. (2012). 'Reforming WTO disciplines on export duties: sovereignty over natural resources, economic development and environmental protection', *Journal of World Trade*, 46(5): 1147–1190.

Rose, A. K. (2004a). 'Do we really know that the WTO increases trade?' *American Economic Review*, 94(1): 98–114.

(2004b). 'Do WTO members have more liberal trade policy?' *Journal of International Economics*, 63(2): 209–235.

(2005a). 'Does the WTO make trade more stable?' *Open Economies Review*, 16(1): 7–22.

(2005b). 'Which international institutions promote international trade?' *Review of International Economics*, 13(4): 682–698.

Subramanian, A. and S.-J. Wei (2007). 'The WTO promotes trade, strongly but unevenly', *Journal of International Economics*, 72(1): 151–175.

Tang, M.-K. and S.-J. Wei (2006). 'Is Bitter Medicine Good For You? The Economic Consequences of WTO/GATT Accessions', Mimeo. Retrieved from www.imf.org/external/np/res/seminars/2006/trade04.

(2009). 'The value of making commitments externally: evidence from WTO accessions', *Journal of International Economics*, 78(2): 216–229.

United Nations (2008). *System of National Accounts*. Retrieved from http://unstats.un.org/unsd/nationalaccount/sna2008.asp.

Wang, Z. (2001). 'The impact of China's WTO accession on trade and economic relations across the Taiwan Strait', *Economics of Transition*, 9(3): 743–785.

World Trade Organization (WTO) (1999). *The Results of the Uruguay Round of Multilateral Trade Negotiations: Legal Texts.* Cambridge University Press.

(2004). *World Trade Report 2004: Exploring the Linkage between the Domestic Policy Environment and International Trade.* Geneva, WTO.

(2007). *World Trade Report 2007: Six Decades of Multilateral Trade Cooperation: What Have We Learnt?* Geneva, WTO.

(2009). *World Trade Report 2009: Trade Policy Commitments and Contingency Measures.* Geneva, WTO.

# 6

# The future of Asia: unleashing the power of trade and governance

EMIL P. BOLONGAITA AND MAIKA OSHIKAWA

## ABSTRACT

*Half a century ago, the future of Asia looked quite bleak. Civil and regional conflict ravaged many parts of the region. China was still closed to the world, and in the throes of its Cultural Revolution. India and Pakistan were recovering from wars, Indonesia and the Philippines were under authoritarian rule, and several Central Asian countries were mere shadow states of the former Soviet Union. Since then, Asia has surprised the world: Japan and the rest of East Asia have rapidly become industrialised, and successive years of high growth have been attained by other Asian countries, notably China, India and several countries in the Association of Southeast Asian Nations. This growth has been driven in great part by rapidly expanding trade, with the liberalisation of China in the late 1970s and of India in the 1990s, greater integration among North-east and South-east Asian countries, and the collapse of the Soviet Union.*

Asia's trade-driven growth has benefited greatly from the development reforms promoted by the WTO. By the middle of the twenty-first century, Asia is projected to account for more than 50 per cent of global trade. With the support of regional institutions, the WTO is vital to the future of Asia. As its weight in the global economy increases inexorably, Asia will find the WTO essential to alleviating the frictions that come with progress and change. Without the WTO as a pillar for free and fair trade, it is difficult to imagine how the tensions and uncertainties that are to be expected as part of the dynamic and driven pace of Asia can be peacefully and properly managed.

Asia's growth is in great part driven by regional trade integration and by its growing links with global supply chains. Asia's intraregional trade expanded considerably from about 30 per cent in the early 1970s to almost 55 per cent in 2012. Economic interdependence within East Asia

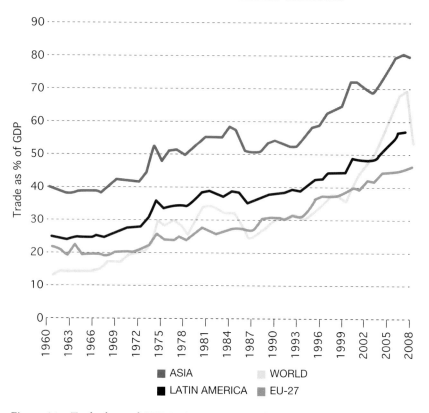

**Figure 6.1**    Trade share of GDP in Asia: 1960–2008 (IMF, 2011).

and South-east Asia has grown the most, while growth in South Asia and Central Asia remains quite slow, and in the Pacific it is actually declining. The development of supply chains and production networks, driven by low trade barriers, open capital markets and high levels of investment, has been a key factor in the robust growth of East Asia and South-east Asia. This is reflected in Asia's higher volume of trade in intermediate goods, which represented two-thirds of its merchandise trade in 2009, in comparison with the world average of almost 60 per cent. The period of increased intraregional trade has mirrored an expansion of Asia's share in world merchandise trade, growing from around 13 per cent in 1960 to over 30 per cent in 2011 (ADB, 2012).

In effect, Asia's growth during the past half-century has been nothing short of phenomenal. No region in the world has managed to achieve so much in terms of economic development. No region in the world offers as much promise in terms of prosperity as does Asia in the next half-century. But will the promise be fulfilled?

## Asia's governance deficit

While Asia's growth has been phenomenal, it is also paradoxical. Asia has achieved much in terms of economic development despite the fact that its governance environment has, in many areas, remained far below that of other regions.[1] Governance in much of Asia has stagnated, if not declined. The World Bank's governance indicators suggest that, while government effectiveness and regulatory capacity have improved substantially among Asia's top seven economies compared with the rest of Asia, there is little progress in terms of political stability, voice and accountability, rule of law and control of corruption. 'Disappointingly', the Asian Development Bank (ADB) reports, 'even the Asia-7 does not fare too well viz. the rest of the world on any of the governance dimensions' (ADB, 2012).[2]

The substantial divergence between Asia's robust growth and its weak governance performance gives rise to questions concerning the sustainability of the Asian trajectory. The uncertainty is made more acute because of the fact that Asia faces serious governance issues across many sectors. And of the different sectors suffering high governance risks, none is perhaps more serious than the financial sector, as are the implications this poses for commerce and trade.[3]

---

[1] There are many definitions of governance. For the purposes of this chapter, the definition used by the World Bank suffices: governance is 'the traditions and institutions by which authority in a country is exercised for the common good. This includes (i) the process by which those in authority are selected, monitored and replaced, (ii) the capacity of the government to effectively manage its resources and implement sound policies, and (iii) the respect of citizens and the state for the institutions that govern economic and social interactions among them'. See http://go.worldbank.org/MKOGR258V0.

[2] The top six economies in the ADB's categorisation, with per capita income over US $12,196, are: Brunei Darussalam; Hong Kong, China; Republic of Korea; Macao, China; Singapore; and Chinese Taipei. If the two economies of China and India were included, the collective governance ratings of the group would fall further downwards.

[3] A serious risk that will not be addressed in this chapter is the eruption of interstate conflict between Asian countries. While Asia has enjoyed relative stability in recent decades, and the region has grown on the back of this relative peace, the reality is that Asia has had more conflicts than any other region in the world since the Second World War. Fortunately for Asia, these conflicts have not hindered its drive to development because the conflicts have been contained. But flashpoints remain across South Asia, South-east Asia and Central Asia.

The remarkable growth of many Asian countries has changed the financial landscape of the region in positive and negative ways. But the negative ways have intensified far more than the region's capacity to contain them. In Asia, sophisticated trading centres coexist with informal banking systems and cash-based economies. Consequently, growing Asian companies are constrained by the relatively underdeveloped financial sector. Small and medium-sized enterprises (SMEs) are perceived as too risky by the traditional banks and liquidity and the provision of credit by the capital markets are limited (ADB, 2012). Those that can do so prefer to tap European and North American financial services.

Even as Asia increases its financial clout in the global arena, corruption, money laundering and other financial crimes are increasing and becoming more sophisticated. Competition among countries to offer stronger banking secrecy has worsened the problems. As companies from countries with poor governance expand around the region, concerns are raised about corruption risks as these companies tend to do business as they would in their home countries. In some countries, such as China, India and Myanmar, money laundering is connected to the trafficking of humans and of drugs such as opium and heroin through the Golden Triangle and Golden Crescent. These countries, as well as Indonesia and the Philippines, are also faced with terrorist financing as a source of laundered money (United States Department of State, 2013).

## Governance and the middle-income trap

Unless Asia is able to address its governance deficits, the region is unlikely to overcome the dreaded 'middle-income trap'. This trap refers to the institutional constraints on Asia's affluent development, when its export-oriented growth and integration into the global economy will have reached natural limits, e.g. where the costs of production of its exports have risen to levels that make them uncompetitive with those of low-wage countries. At the same time, they will also not be competitive with advanced economies that are producing more sophisticated products and services (Kharas, 2013). The ADB plainly states: 'Governance and institutional capacity form the Achilles heel of most Asian economies. If recent adverse trends in the quality of institutions and corruption continue unchecked, the region's ability to realize the Asian century will be jeopardized' (ADB, 2012).

The likelihood of getting caught in the middle-income trap is worsened by the prospect of increased protectionism in the advanced economies, as governments of these countries 'feel increasingly threatened by the success of Asia and begin retreating into fortresses' (Mahbubani, 2008). Protectionism has been on the rise among Western countries, costing developing countries far more than they receive in foreign aid. This is unfortunate, and ironic, given that Asia's rise has been driven in great part by the determined efforts of the West, led by the United States, to foster free trade since the end of the Second World War.

Nevertheless, there is no doubt that Asia is turning into a middle-income region. During the period 2001–2010, per capita income in Asia grew at about 10 per cent annually. External debt decreased to 14.5 per cent of GDP and the region became the largest net lender to developed countries and is now generating about 45 per cent of the increase in the world's capital stock. It is estimated that during the period 2030–2050, the region will hold 70 per cent of net additions to the world's capital stock (ADB, 2012).

It should also be noted that even if Asia does not escape the so-called middle-income trap, it is estimated that it will still lead the global economy in terms of GDP by 2050 (Figure 6.2). The region's growing economic mass carries inexorably increasing weight. But if the leading countries in Asia do manage to overcome the region's governance deficits and escape the middle-income trap, the financial dominance of the region will arguably be far more formidable (ADB, 2012).

Notably, China is shaping much of Asia's trajectory. It has become the world's biggest saver and, in 2012, its central bank, the People's Bank of China, accumulated the world's largest stock of foreign currency reserves (US$3.3 trillion). The country is using its strong financial position to diversify its foreign assets worldwide. For example, China has become the biggest provider of loans to Latin America, exceeding those of the World Bank and the Inter-American Development Bank (Dobbs, Leung and Lund, 2013).

## WTO accession and its impact on growth

Since the establishment of the WTO in 1995, the share of Asia's merchandise trade in world trade has grown from 25 per cent to 32 per cent in 2012 (WTO, 2013a).[4] This period coincides with a sizable number of Asian countries joining the multilateral trading system through an

---

[4] It should be noted that the WTO definition of Asia does not include countries in the Commonwealth of Independent States (CIS). The ADB, however, counts five of the nine CIS countries as Asia (namely Azerbaijan, Kazakhstan, Kyrgyz Republic, Tajikistan and Uzbekistan).

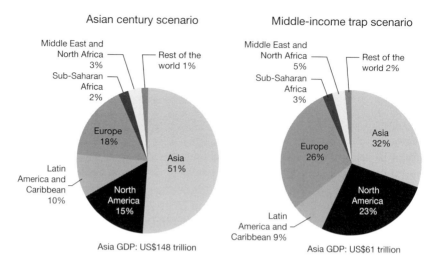

**Figure 6.2** 'Asian century' and 'middle-income trap' scenarios (ADB, 2012).

accession process as provided in Article XII of the 1994 Marrakesh Agreement Establishing the World Trade Organization. A most notable example is China's accession to the WTO in 2001. Its share in world trade doubled from around 5 per cent to 11 per cent in ten years, enabling it to become the world's top merchandise trader in 2013. Along with China, thirteen other Asian countries joined the WTO, the majority of which were transition economies. The WTO accessions of these countries played a critical role in the transition and nascent transformation of centrally planned economies to market-oriented ones, which had initially started with China's opening under Deng Xiaoping in the early 1980s and was followed by the collapse of the Soviet Union in 1991.

In addition to China, the other Asian economies that acceded are post-Soviet countries (Armenia, Georgia, Kyrgyz Republic and Tajikistan), two least-developed countries (LDCs) from the Association of Southeast Asian Nations (ASEAN) (Cambodia, Lao PDR), Mongolia and Nepal (Table 6.1). An accession process for these transition economies has taken an average of ten years to complete as it involves domestic reforms to set the foundation for a market-based economy. In addition, six remaining countries from the region (Afghanistan, Azerbaijan, Bhutan, Iran, Kazakhstan and Uzbekistan) are all associated with the transition from centrally planned to market-oriented economies, with most of them having been in the accession process for over fifteen years (Table 6.4).

Table 6.1 *Economic performance and legislative reforms of WTO Article XII members*

| Member | Year of application | Year of membership | Between accession year and 2012 (%) | | | |
|---|---|---|---|---|---|---|
| | | | Average GDP growth rate | Average merchandise trade growth rate | Average commercial services trade growth rate | Legislative/ regulatory quantum |
| Armenia Rep. of* | 1993 | 2003 | 7.2 | 15.9 | 18.5 | 112 |
| Cambodia* | 1994 | 2004 | 8.0 | 17.7 | 17.8 | 85 |
| China* | 1986 | 2001 | 10.2 | 20.0 | 18.2 | 2300 |
| Georgia* | 1996 | 2000 | 6.0 | 23.4 | 18.6 | 106 |
| Kyrgyz Republic* | 1996 | 1998 | 3.9 | 5.1 | 20.9 | 155 |
| Lao PDR* | 1997 | 2013 | NA | NA | NA | 170 |
| Mongolia* | 1991 | 1997 | 6.7 | 20.4 | 22.9 | 33 |
| Nepal* | 1989 | 2004 | 4.5 | 12.6 | 13.7 | 47 |
| Samoa | 1998 | 2012 | 2.9 | 2.3 | NA | 111 |
| Chinese Taipei | 1992 | 2002 | NA | 9.5 | 7.4 | 167 |
| Tajikistan* | 2001 | 2013 | NA | NA | NA | 141 |
| Tonga | 1995 | 2007 | 1.2 | 10.1 | 14.2 | 84 |
| Vanuatu | 1995 | 2012 | 2.3 | -5.4 | 7.8 | 170 |
| Viet Nam* | 1995 | 2007 | 6.0 | 19.0 | 14.4 | 139 |

*Note:* *Transition economy. NA = not applicable.
*Sources:* WTO Statistics Database; World Bank Database; WTO Secretariat.

For current and future Article XII members, the impact of their accession processes and results in improving their national governance arrangements cannot be overstated. In many ways, the WTO and its agreements have been used as external tools to augment the argument of national reformers for raising domestic standards and practices to international levels. The prospective benefits of accession, in the experience of the acceding governments, have been a powerfully compelling argument for bearing the high costs of change. Without the promise of the greater trade and investment that could be secured through membership, and the consequent improvements in the quality of life for all, it is unlikely that opposition from entrenched interests could have been overcome. For acceding governments, WTO membership represented a credible, hard-won 'label' of approval by the international community for their market-oriented economic reforms. For investors, the WTO has been a synonym for a set of values representing growth and competitiveness; openness and integration; and non-discrimination, rule of law and transparency.

Looking at the economic performance of Article XII members, those from Asia have indeed done well after their accession to the WTO (Table 6.1). Their average annual GDP growth rates after accession and until 2012 range from over 10 per cent in China, 8 per cent in Cambodia and 6.7 per cent in Mongolia to 6 per cent in Viet Nam. Some of the post-Soviet economies have also achieved relatively high rates of growth, such as 7.2 per cent in Armenia and 6.7 per cent in Georgia. With regard to trade performance, several Asian Article XII members have registered impressive growth after accession, with average annual growth rates around 15 to 20 per cent for trade in both goods and services (Armenia, Cambodia, China, Georgia, Mongolia and Viet Nam). Their trade performance stands out even among Article XII members as a whole, with faster growth than the original WTO members. For the period between 1995 and 2012, the average annual growth rates in trade in goods and services of Article XII members were 14.1 per cent and 11.9 per cent respectively, while those of global trade in goods and services were 8.3 per cent and 8 per cent, respectively (WTO, 2013b).[5]

The credibility of economic reforms that Article XII members have undertaken as part of their accession processes is derived from their 'commitments' – both market access and rules-related – as inscribed in

---

[5] The numbers are based on thirty-one Article XII members in 2013.

the Accession Protocols and working party reports that form integral parts of the WTO agreements. The commitments are not only regularly monitored by WTO bodies, but also subject to its powerful Dispute Settlement Mechanism if any member feels that any such commitments are not being respected. Another element of accession credibility is the process of legislation-based domestic reforms through the enactment of WTO-consistent legislation. Table 6.1 indicates that the accession of China to the WTO involved the enactment and amendment of more than 2,300 laws, decrees and departmental regulations at the central government level, which set the foundation for its market-oriented, post-socialist economy to take off. Even for smaller transition economies, the number of legal and regulatory changes ranged from 112 for Armenia, 139 for Viet Nam, 155 for Kyrgyz Republic and 141 for Tajikistan, to 170 for Lao PDR.

The degree of market opening and integration that had to be accomplished by Article XII members is reflected in the depth of market access commitments in the areas of trade in goods and services. In the area of goods (Table 6.2), all the Article XII members have tariff binding coverage of 100 per cent or near 100 per cent, while many of the original developing members from Asia had far less coverage, including some below 50 per cent. The commitment and discipline to openness is also evident in the gaps or differences between the bound and applied rates, or so-called 'water', which are far tighter for Article XII members than for the original members from the region, which in general have more liberal commitments (Table 6.3). In the area of services, the number of commitments by Article XII members is greater than those of the original members, providing greater predictability and transparency in their market access regimes, which are subject to the multilateral principles of non-discrimination and transparency. Furthermore, Asia accounts for five of the eight successfully concluded LDC accessions since the establishment of the WTO. Tables 6.2 and 6.3 show that Asian members' market access commitments, while retaining a comfortable level of policy space, demonstrate far more progressive levels of openness than in the original LDC members. It is perhaps no wonder that some of these members are ahead of their peers in graduating from their LDC status.[6]

---

[6] Samoa graduated from LDC status in 2014, while Vanuatu is scheduled to do so in 2018; in addition, Cabo Verde graduated in 2008.

Table 6.2 *Commitments made by Article XII members*

| Member | Accession working party report: number of commitment paragraphs | Market access commitments on goods | | | | Market access commitments on services: number of services subsectors |
| | | Binding coverage | Average final bound rate (%) (latest available average MFN* applied rate (%)) | | | |
| | | | All products | Agricultural products | Non-agricultural products | |
|---|---|---|---|---|---|---|
| Armenia, Republic of | 39 | 100 | 8.5 (3.5) | 14.7 (7.0) | 7.6 (3.0) | 106 |
| Cambodia** | 29 | 100 | 19.1 (10.9) | 28.1 (15.2) | 17.7 (10.3) | 94 |
| China | 144 | 100 | 10.0 (9.6) | 15.8 (15.6) | 9.2 (8.7) | 93 |
| Georgia | 29 | 100 | 7.4 (1.5) | 13.1 (6.7) | 6.5 (0.6) | 125 |
| Kyrgyz Republic | 29 | 100 | 7.5 (4.6) | 12.6 (7.4) | 6.7 (4.2) | 136 |
| Lao PDR** | 26 | 100 | 18.8 (NA) | 19.3 (NA) | 18.7 (NA) | 79 |
| Mongolia | 19 | 100 | 17.5 (5.0) | 18.9 (5.1) | 17.3 (5.0) | 37 |
| Nepal** | 25 | 99.4 | 26.0 (12.3) | 41.5 (13.9) | 23.7 (12.0) | 77 |

| | | | | | | |
|---|---|---|---|---|---|---|
| Samoa* | 37 | 100 | 21.1 (11.4) | 25.8 (14.5) | 20.4 (10.8) | 80 |
| Chinese Taipei | 63 | 100 | 6.3 (6.1) | 17.3 (16.4) | 4.7 (4.5) | 119 |
| Tajikistan | 40 | 100 | 8.1 (7.8) | 11.4 (10.8) | 7.6 (7.3) | 111 |
| Tonga | 29 | 100 | 17.6 (12.0) | 19.2 (11.5) | 17.3 (12.1) | NA |
| Vanuatu** | 30 | 99.9 | 39.7 (9.1) | 43.6 (17.5) | 39.1 (7.8) | 69 |
| Viet Nam | 70 | 100 | 11.4 (9.5) | 18.5 (16.1) | 10.4 (8.4) | 105 |
| Average of Article XII members | 40.5 | | | | | |

*Notes:* *MFN = most-favoured-nation. **LDC (Samoa graduated from LDC status in 2014); NA = not applicable.
*Source:* WTO Secretariat.

Table 6.3 *Market access commitments by original WTO members*

| | Market access commitments on goods | | | | Market access commitments on services: number of services subsectors |
|---|---|---|---|---|---|
| | | Latest available average MFN* applied rate (%) | | | |
| Member | Binding coverage | All products | Agricultural products | Non-agricultural products | |
| Australia | 97.1 | 10.0 (2.7) | 3.5 (1.2) | 11.0 (2.9) | 103 |
| Bangladesh* | 15.5 | 169.2 (14.4) | 192.0 (17.2) | 37.3 (14.0) | 9 |
| Brunei Darussalam | 95.3 | 25.3 (2.5) | 30.7 (0.1) | 24.5 (2.9) | 22 |
| Fiji | 51.3 | 41.5 (12.0) | 46.0 (23.9) | 40.0 (10.2) | 1 |
| Hong Kong, China | 45.6 | 0.0 (0.0) | 0.0 (0.0) | 0 (0.0) | 68 |
| India | 73.8 | 48.7 (12.6) | 113.1 (31.4) | 34.6 (9.8) | 37 |
| Indonesia | 96.3 | 37.1 (7.0) | 47.0 (8.1) | 35.6 (6.9) | 45 |
| Japan | 99.7 | 5.3 (5.3) | 22.8 (23.3) | 2.6 (2.6) | 112 |
| Korea, Republic of | 94.6 | 16.6 (12.1) | 56.1 (48.6) | 10.2 (6.6) | 98 |
| Macao, China | 27.9 | 0.0 (0.0) | 0.0 (0) | 0.0 (0.0) | 25 |
| Malaysia | 84.3 | 23.0 (6.5) | 66.8 (10.8) | 14.9 (5.8) | 73 |
| Maldives | 97.1 | 36.9 (20.5) | 47.9 (18.3) | 35.1 (20.8) | 5 |
| Myanmar* | 17.6 | 83.4 (5.5) | 103.4 (8.9) | 23.0 (5.0) | |
| New Zealand | 100.0 | 10.1 (2.0) | 6.0 (1.4) | 10.7 (2.1) | 90 |
| Pakistan | 98.7 | 59.9 (13.9) | 95.6 (17.0) | 54.6 (13.4) | 45 |
| Papua New Guinea | 100 | 32.1 (5.1) | 45.8 (14.8) | 30.0 (3.6) | |
| Philippines | 67.0 | 25.7 (6.1) | 35.1 (8.7) | 23.4 (5.7) | 51 |

Table 6.3 (*cont.*)

| Member | Market access commitments on goods | | | | Market access commitments on services: number of services subsectors |
| | Latest available average MFN* applied rate (%) | | | | |
| | Binding coverage | All products | Agricultural products | Non-agricultural products | |
|---|---|---|---|---|---|
| Singapore | 69.7 | 10.3 | 26.9 | 6.4 | 67 |
| | | (0.0) | (0.2) | (0.0) | |
| Solomon Islands* | 100 | 78.7 | 73.7 | 79.4 | |
| | | (10.1) | (16.0) | (9.2) | |
| Sri Lanka | 38.1 | 30.2 | 50.0 | 19.7 | 27 |
| | | (10.2) | (26.3) | (7.8) | |
| Thailand | 75.0 | 28.0 | 39.9 | 25.5 | 75 |
| | | (9.8) | (22.0) | (8.0) | |
| Average of original LDC members | 53.6 | 65.2 | 79.9 | 45.4 | 20 |

*Note:* *LDC. The Maldives graduated from LDC status in 2010.
*Source:* WTO Secretariat.

The rules-enhancing aspect of an accession process is reflected in the number of 'specific commitments' undertaken by Article XII members. These specific commitments often go further and deeper than those made by the original WTO members (see Chapter 1). In the case of China, there were 144 specific commitments; there were 70 for Viet Nam, 63 for Chinese Taipei and 40 for Tajikistan (Table 6.2). In the area of transparency, according to the WTO, specific commitments undertaken by the thirty-three Article XII members have gone beyond the re-affirmation of existing notification obligations under a particular agreement and, in many cases, have included the provision of information regarding the programme for privatisation of state-owned enterprises and the publication of information on trade before implementation and enforcement (WTO, 2013b). In China's accession, an additional commitment was made to provide information on a range of areas to thirteen WTO bodies on an annual basis during the first ten years of membership.

## WTO accession and its impact on governance

WTO accession has also contributed significantly to improving governance. Accession negotiation is a long-term process, a transparency-enhancing exercise through information sharing on trade policy and practices. As part of the negotiation, each acceding government is requested to provide baseline data, by submitting negotiating inputs, based on completing checklists and questionnaire templates. These templates are structured in accordance with established WTO notification formats. Moreover, during their negotiations, acceding governments are routinely asked to adhere to certain WTO practices of transparency, including: (i) the notification of the planned measure/legislation in a timely manner; (ii) sharing copies of the draft legislation/measure, upon request; (iii) the provision of reasonable time for members to review and comment on the planned measure/legislation; and (iv) the provision of explanation, and/or adjustments, as necessary, on the results of comments made by members on the planned measure/legislation.

Consequently, the commitments and obligations undertaken by those countries that joined the WTO through their Article XII accession negotiations since 1995 have systematically strengthened the governance and transparency of the multilateral trading system. After years of transparency building in accession negotiations, Article XII members have become promoters of greater transparency in the WTO. Collectively, Article XII members have achieved a higher level of transparency than did the original WTO members. Figure 6.3 shows the average number of notifications made between 2008 and 2013 by: (i) original members; (ii) Article XII members; and (iii) all WTO members. It shows that Article XII members had a consistently higher notification rate. On average, an Article XII member submitted between five and eleven more notifications annually compared with an original member. This trend can be attributed to the fact that: (i) the WTO accession process requires Article XII members to put in place appropriate mechanisms for submitting notifications upon accession; and (ii) the specific transparency commitments, negotiated during the Article XII accession process, have reconfirmed and strengthened existing notification requirements under the Marrakesh Agreement.

In this context, the contribution of the accession process to the economic transformation and improved governance of Article XII members suggests that it has great potential for the countries that are still in the process of accession. They are mainly from Central Asia

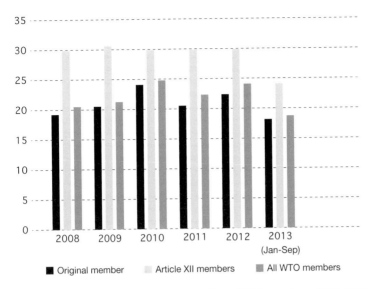

**Figure 6.3**  Average notifications made annually by WTO members, 2008–2013, including original members and Article XII members (WTO, 2013b).

(including three former Soviet republics), and many of them have already been negotiating WTO membership for more than fifteen years (Table 6.4). The length of the accession process reflects the degree of complexity of the challenges faced by these countries, whose changes are linked to geopolitical issues arising from the shift in global economic dynamics and weight to Asia. Fundamentally, the accession-based domestic reforms have provided an instrument for these countries to make the transition from centrally planned to market-based regimes, and from closed political environments to regimes of greater transparency, trade openness and connectivity with the rules-based global economy.

## The rise of Asia's SMEs

The benefits of Asia's integration into the global economy under the auspices of the WTO have been due in large part to the growing role of its SMEs and their increasing participation in international trade. A strong SME sector has been the driver of the region's fast-growing economies, notably China. SMEs' contribution to China's exports in the period from

Table 6.4 *Asian countries in accession to the WTO*

| Acceding government | Application date | Establishment of working party | Chair | State of play |
|---|---|---|---|---|
| Afghanistan | November 2004 | December 2004 | HE Mr Roderick van Schreven (Netherlands) | Near conclusion Draft Accession Package circulated 3 March 2014 |
| Azerbaijan | June 1997 | July 1997 | HE Mr Walter Lewalter (Germany) | Mid-stage |
| Bhutan | September 1999 | October 1999 | HE Mr Thomas Hajnoczi (Austria) | Dormant No substantive inputs since 2008 |
| Iran | July 1996 | May 2005 | Pending | Initial stage |
| Kazakhstan | January 1996 | February 1996 | HE Mr Vesa Himanen (Finland) | Advanced stage Priority for conclusion in 2014 |
| Uzbekistan | December 1994 | December 1994 | HE Mr Seokyoung Choi (Korea, Rep. of) | Dormant No substantive inputs since 2005 |

*Note:* Turkmenistan has indicated its interest in possible application for WTO membership in the near future.
*Source:* WTO Secretariat.

Table 6.5 *Contribution of SMEs to trade, 2001–2009*

|  | Exports in GDP (%)[a] | SMEs in exports (%) |
|---|---|---|
| **East Asia** | | |
| Japan | 15.1 | 53.8 |
| China | 31.4 | 69.2 |
| Korea, Republic of | 56.0 | 39.0 |
| **South-east Asia** | | |
| Brunei Darussalam | 81.3 | |
| Cambodia | 54.1 | |
| Indonesia | 26.4 | 20.0 |
| Lao PDR | 38.0 | |
| Malaysia | 91.6 | 96.0 |
| Myanmar | - | |
| Philippines | 32.0 | |
| Singapore | 207.2 | 16.0 |
| Thailand | 76.9 | 30.6 |
| Viet Nam | 87.0 | 20.0 |

*Notes:* [a]For 2011 (World Bank).
*Source:* United Nations Economic and Social Commission for Asia and the Pacific (2011).

its accession in 2001 until 2009 is over 69 per cent. But, in comparison with the industrialised economies of East Asia, there is still significant room for improvement in the trade participation of SMEs in other regions, particularly South-east Asia (Wignaraja, 2012). Here, SMEs account for more than 90 per cent of all enterprises, employ 50 to 97 per cent of the workforce, and contribute 6 to 85 per cent of total domestic economic output in their countries (Lim and Kimura, 2009). However, SMEs' contribution to South-east Asia's international trade remains limited. Their average export share in South-east Asia is 14.3 per cent but the figures vary significantly across countries (Table 6.5).

SMEs, however, face serious external constraints. The business operating environment and governance conditions of most Asian economies are poor to fair. As SMEs start to engage more international players, the operating environment becomes more critical to forging business linkages and attracting foreign investors and partners. Bureaucratic obstacles, such as burdensome regulations and vague rules, can hamper SMEs' effectiveness over their life cycle (World Bank,

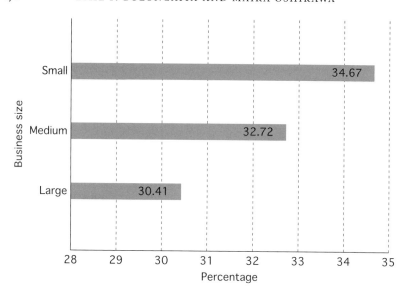

**Figure 6.4** Perception of corruption as a business obstacle, by size of firm (UNIDO, 2007).

2014).[7] Quite simply, a weak business operating environment will impose inefficiencies and curtail market competitiveness, not just for SMEs but for all market players.

Perhaps the most problematic obstacle in the governance and business operating environment for SMEs is corruption. One survey found that SMEs are more likely to be constrained by corruption than are large firms (UNIDO, 2007) (Figure 6.4).

It has been found that SMEs pay a higher percentage of their annual revenue in bribes to public officials and that they make additional payments to get things done more frequently than do large companies. Limited financial resources and the inability to exert strong influence over public officials (e.g. lack of bargaining power) make it very difficult for SMEs to avoid engaging in corrupt practices. Among the costs of corruption are higher operating expenses, lost contracts and limited access to public procurement (UNIDO, 2007).

---

[7] The World Bank's 'ease of doing business' analysis assesses different phases of a firm's operations and looks at eleven areas: starting a business, employing workers, dealing with construction permits, getting electricity, registering property, getting credit, protecting investors, enforcing contracts, resolving insolvency, paying taxes and trading across borders.

SMEs also face tariff and non-tariff trade barriers that are more onerous for them than to large enterprises. While tariffs have decreased over recent decades, they can still be a hindrance for SMEs from developing countries exporting to other developing rather than developed countries. SMEs also face non-tariff barriers in the form of domestic regulations and customs procedures. For example, the imposition of special product requirements or serious requirements for testing or certification is an impediment to firms that wish to export. SMEs also have to contend with weak enforcement of policies to protect their intellectual property (OECD, 2006).

## Financial crimes and their risks to trade

Compounding the costs of corruption is the underdevelopment of the financial sector in Asia that further constrains trade, the growth of SMEs and improvement of governance. Nowhere is this more evident, perhaps, than in the growing problem of money laundering and its systems that shield 'dirty money'. The weakness of legal and regulatory regimes to counter money laundering creates incentives for the various predicate crimes that fuel money laundering.

## Enhancing governance, trade and finance in Asia

To realise the Asian century and overcome the middle-income trap, Asia needs to plug its governance deficits. It needs to improve institutional quality, especially in the financial sector, to further empower SMEs to gain the technology and capital to participate in global value chains. The future of Asia rests on meeting the macro-requirements of good governance, including enhancing financial sector integrity, along with the micro-needs of SMEs. No less important, it requires the strengthening of global governance, notably WTO governance measures that protect the integrity of trade.

### *Applying technology in the public and private sector*

Technology can be catalytic in reducing opportunities for corruption as well as enhancing financial inclusion for SMEs. This can be done, for example, by introducing electronic payments in the payment system of governments. This would be a tremendous opportunity for cash-based economies in Asia. Take India, for example. While the introduction of electronic payments in the Indian public sector has been estimated to entail a one-off cost of about US$13.5–15.8 billion, the savings in terms of reduced inefficiencies and waste will be approximately US$22.5 billion a year. The Indian government could see the return of its investment within a year (Tilman *et al.*, 2011).

Notably, banking and financial institutions in Asia will be better prepared to detect fraud and corruption if they have in place business intelligence tools to analyse large volumes of data in a short period of time. Many organisations are gathering data but are unable to make the best use of it with regard to detecting corruption and money laundering. Investment in more advanced technology to analyse data could significantly increase the capacities of companies to detect fraud and corruption and curb its consequences (EY, 2013).

## Expanding transparency and disclosure requirements

Financial institutions should have the obligation to report who their real owners are. A centralised records office of corporate organisations that provides information about beneficial owners could be a game changer. Intermediaries and professional service providers (such as insurance agents, lawyers, accountants, real estate professionals, currency exchange staff, notaries and credit institutions) of those companies could also be required to identify and report the ultimate owners of the corporate customers with which they have established relationships. This will help prevent intermediaries from becoming involved in money laundering either by conspiring with launderers or by being cheated by them, because criminals can take advantage of professional confidentiality obligations (World Economic Forum, 2012).

The requirement for public servants to disclose information about their assets and sources of income is also an effective mechanism to detect and prevent illicit enrichment and other forms of corruption. It is important to extend this asset declaration to the relatives of public servants since many of them use their spouses or sons to hide ill-gotten wealth. In addition, this mechanism serves as an anticorruption tool for civil society and the media to monitor and apply pressure for accountability. Lastly, the enforcement of laws requires having in place an independent anti-corruption agency with strong capacities to identify, investigate and prosecute corrupt practices. Likewise, the introduction of technology in the collection and reporting of data could accelerate the detection of corruption (Martini, 2013).

## Enhancing global governance

At the global level, the WTO is increasingly becoming a key player in the enhancement of good governance through transparency and predictable rules.[8] Under various provisions and mechanisms in the WTO agreements, members have both general and specific obligations on transparency. Deepening this adherence to transparency is an invaluable instrument for maintaining and fostering a predictable trading environment for all stakeholders and fending off protectionist pressures. Among various instruments, mechanisms and platforms that exist to counter corruption at the global level, the WTO is increasingly considered a comparatively successful forum for the expression and development of good governance values (Ala'i, 2008a).

Transparency is generally established through three interrelated, mutually reinforcing instruments and mechanisms available in the WTO: (i) general and specific provisions on transparency, including Article X of the 1994 General Agreement on Tariffs and Trade (GATT) and corresponding provisions throughout the agreements; (ii) specific notification obligations contained in the agreements; and (iii) monitoring and surveillance mechanisms, including the Trade Policy Review Mechanism (TPRM), the transparency mechanisms for regional and preferential trade agreements, and the Trade Monitoring Mechanism. These transparency provisions and mechanisms together have made the formulation and decision-making of trade policies and regulations more predictable and have strengthened accountability.

Article X of the GATT 1994 contains the core transparency provisions relating to trade in goods. It governs the publication and administration of trade regulations and stipulates two key principles: (i) transparency in trade policy and regulations; and (ii) uniform application of these policies and regulations. The transparency provisions stipulated in GATT Article X are reaffirmed throughout the WTO agreements, such as in the Agreement on Implementation of Article VII of GATT, Agreement on Rules of Origin, and Agreement on Safeguards, as well as GATT Article III and Article 63.1 of the Agreement on Trade-Related Aspects of Intellectual Property. Increasingly, Article X has been referred to in WTO dispute settlement and taken into account by the panels and the Appellate Body. Since 1995, there have been over twenty cases referring

---

[8] According to the WTO glossary, transparency refers to the 'degree to which trade policies and practices, and the process by which they are established, are open and predictable'.

to Article X of GATT (Ala'i, 2008a). As a result, the governance provisions of the WTO, namely those addressing transparency and due process, are increasingly central to WTO disputes (Ala'i, 2008b).

In addition to the general transparency provisions contained in GATT Article X and other agreements, detailed notification requirements are prescribed in the individual WTO agreements. Timely notification is recognised as one of the key principles of the multilateral trading system, as reflected in the 1979 GATT Understanding Regarding Notification, Consultation, Dispute Settlement and Surveillance, and the 1994 WTO Decision on Notification Procedures.[9] Most WTO agreements contain a one-off notification provision/requirement, that is, notifications that require to be submitted only once, as well as provisions that stipulate regular/periodic or ad hoc notification obligations. The scope and content of these notifications vary from agreement to agreement. For instance, under the Agreement on Implementation of Article VI of the GATT 1994 (anti-dumping), each member must notify its competent authorities to initiate and conduct investigations, and its domestic procedures governing the initiation and conduct of such investigations (Article 16.5; one-off notification), all ad hoc preliminary or final anti-dumping actions taken without delay and reports of anti-dumping actions semi-annually (Article 16.4; every six months), and laws, regulations and administrative procedures relevant to anti-dumping (Article 18.5; once and whenever there are changes). On average, a member submits over twenty notifications per year.

Finally, to complement the above transparency provisions, the WTO has several horizontal mechanisms for monitoring and surveillance. The TPRM is the first of such mechanisms that was first provisionally introduced in 1988 before its formal incorporation into Annex 3 of the WTO agreements, with a view to conducting periodic reviews of members' trade policies and practices, based on comprehensive reports prepared by the Secretariat and the member under review. TPRs operate as 'peer reviews' by other WTO members. They encourage governments to adhere to WTO rules and disciplines and fulfil their commitments (Table 6.6). The four largest traders – China, the European Union, Japan and the United States – are examined once every two years; the next sixteen members, in terms of their share of world trade, are reviewed every four years and the remaining members every six years. As eleven of

---

[9] The 1979 Understanding is contained in WTO documents; L/4907; and Basic Instrument Selected Document 26S/210.

Table 6.6 *Trade policy reviews of Asian countries, 1995–2014*

| | |
|---|---|
| Armenia, Republic of* 2010 | Maldives 2003, 2009 |
| Australia 1998, 2002, 2007, 2011 | Mongolia* 2005, 2014 |
| Bangladesh 2000, 2006, 2012 | Myanmar 2014 |
| Brunei Darussalam 2001, 2008 | Nepal* 2012 |
| Cambodia* 2011 | New Zealand 1996, 2003, 2009 |
| China* 2006, 2008, 2010, 2012, 2014 | Pakistan 1995, 2002, 2008 |
| Fiji 1997, 2009 | Papua New Guinea 1999, 2010 |
| Georgia* 2009 | Philippines 1999, 2005, 2012 |
| Hong Kong, China 1998, 2002, 2006, 2010, 2014 | Singapore 1995, 2000, 2004, 2008, 2012 |
| India 1998, 2002, 2007, 2011 | Solomon Islands 1998, 2009 |
| Indonesia 1998, 2003, 2007, 2013 | Sri Lanka 1995, 2004, 2010 |
| Japan 1995, 1998, 2000, 2002, 2005, 2007, 2009, 2011, 2013 | Chinese Taipei* 2006, 2010, 2014 |
| | Thailand 1995, 1999, 2003, 2007, 2011 |
| Korea, Republic of 1996, 2000, 2004, 2008, 2012 | Tonga* 2014 |
| | Viet Nam* 2013 |
| Kyrgyz Republic* 2006, 2013 | |
| Macao, China 2001, 2007, 2013 | |
| Malaysia 1997, 2001, 2006, 2010, 2014 | |

*Note:* *Article XII members.
*Source:* WTO Secretariat.

the top twenty world traders come from Asia – Australia, China, Chinese Taipei, India, Indonesia, Japan, Hong Kong, China, the Republic of Korea, Malaysia, Singapore, Thailand – their relative progress is a major determinant of Asia's continuing growth.

Moreover, the WTO's surveillance and monitoring function was further enhanced by the introduction of the Regional Trade Agreements (RTA) Transparency Mechanism in 2006.[10] This provides for early announcement of any RTA and its notification to the WTO.[11] At the Committee on RTAs, WTO members consider the notified RTAs on the

---

[10] The decision on the establishment of the RTA Transparency Mechanism is an early harvest of the Doha Development Agenda (DDA) negotiations and has been implemented on a provisional basis.

[11] The Committee on Regional Trade Agreements will consider RTAs falling under Article XXIV of the GATT and Article V of the General Agreement on Trade in Services (GATS).

basis of a factual presentation by the WTO Secretariat. The number of RTAs has been increasing since the early 1990s. Asia has been the driving force of this phenomenon in recent years. As of 31 January 2014, some 583 notifications of RTAs (counting goods, services and accessions separately) had been submitted to the GATT/WTO and, of these, 377 were in force. Of the 258 RTAs notified to the WTO, 45 per cent involve at least one party from Asia. Moreover, in 2010, a similar transparency mechanism was established to review and monitor unilateral preferential trade agreements (PTAs) based on notifications. Finally, following the global financial crisis of 2008 which led to concerns of a possible rise in protectionist pressures, the WTO introduced trade monitoring reports to enhance transparency of trade policy developments around the world. There are two series of such reports, published twice a year, including: (i) WTO-wide reports on trade-related developments covering all WTO members and observers;[12] and (ii) joint reports with the Organisation for Economic Co-operation and Development (OECD) and the United Nations Conference on Trade and Development (UNCTAD) on trade and investment measures taken by G-20 economies.[13]

## Shaping Asia's future

This chapter has discussed key factors that have been driving Asia's phenomenal growth during the past half-century. It has focused on how Asian countries' efforts at integrating themselves within the global economy through WTO accession have facilitated, if not compelled, the implementation of institutional and economic reforms. Notably, it has discussed how SMEs are a critical component of the sustainability of trade-driven growth. With an eye on the future, it has emphasised how governance deficits present the biggest challenge to overcoming the middle-income trap that looms large for the region's fast-growing economies. In this regard, the work of the WTO and its agreements enshrining transparency and its mechanisms for monitoring and reviews contribute significantly to addressing these governance deficits.

In the coming years, Asian countries could enhance the closing of their governance gaps by deepening their engagement in the multilateral rules-based trading system, even as they boost regional institutions and

---

[12] The last report, 'Overview of Developments in the International Trading Environment, Annual Report by the Director-General', contained in WTO document WT/TPR/OV/17, was issued in November 2014 (WTO, 2014).

[13] The last 'Report on G20 Trade and Investment Measures' was issued in December 2013.

initiatives that can provide peer-to-peer support. At the same time, Asia must demonstrate leadership in the drive to strengthen institutions that level the playing field internationally and domestically. The story of the tremendous trajectory of trade in Asia is in many ways a story of leadership in regional cooperation and integration. Without the leadership of the West at the end of the Second World War in pushing a free trade agenda and bearing the costs that this entailed, global trade would not have risen dramatically, from just 7 per cent of world GDP in 1940 to 56 per cent in 2010.

There is little doubt that improving governance at the global, regional and national levels will bring tremendous economic benefits. The World Bank estimates that reduced corruption and improved transparency would lower trade costs and thereby increase trade significantly. It is estimated that, with increased transparency and lower levels of corruption, trade in the Asia-Pacific region would increase by 11 per cent on average and US$406 billion would be added to global output. For some countries where governance constraints on trade are more considerable than elsewhere, the upside for reforms could be as high as a 20 per cent increase in their GDP (Abe and Wilson, 2008).

In the years ahead, the WTO will play an enormous role in enhancing global governance as it continuously consolidates a rules-based, transparent and non-discriminatory multilateral trading system.

## Acknowledgement

Leila Deles and Antonella Guidoccio contributed to writing this chapter.

## References

Abe, K. and J. Wilson (2008). 'Governance, corruption, and trade in the Asia Pacific Region', Washington DC, World Bank, Policy Research Paper 4731.

Ala'i, P. (2008a). 'The WTO and the anti-corruption movement', *Loyola University Chicago International Law Review*, **6**(1): 259–278.

(2008b). 'From the periphery to the center? The evolving WTO jurisprudence on transparency and good governance', *Journal of International Economic Law*, **11**(4): 779–802.

Asian Development Bank (ADB) (2012). *Asia 2050: Realizing the Asian Century*. Manila, ADB.

Dobbs, R., N. Leung and S. Lund (2013). 'China's rising stature in global finance', *McKinsey Quarterly*, July. Retrieved from www.mckinsey.com/insights/win ning_in_emerging_markets/chinas_rising_stature_in_global_finance.

EY (2013). *Building a More Ethical Business Environment: Asia-Pacific Fraud Survey 2013*. EYGM.

International Monetary Fund (IMF) (2011). *Direction of Trade Statistics Yearbook*. New York, International Monetary Fund.

Kharas, H. (2013). 'Developing Asia and the middle-income trap', *East Asia Forum* 5(2), 5 August. Retrieved from www.eastasiaforum.org/2013/08/05/develop ing-asia-and-the-middle-income-trap/.

Lim, H. and F. Kimura (2009). 'The Internationalisation of SMEs in Regional and Global Value Chains'. Paper presented at the Fifth LAEB Annual Meeting, Singapore, 15 July. Retrieved from www10.iadb.org/intal/intalcdi/PE/2012/11143a05.pdf.

Mahbubani, K. (2008). *The New Asian Hemisphere: The Irresistible Shift of Global Power to the East*. New York, Public Affairs.

Martini, M. (2013). 'Asset declaration regimes in selected Asian countries', *U4 Expert Answer*, 381. Retrieved from www.u4.no/publications/asset-declar ation-regimes-in-selected-asian-countries/.

Organisation for Economic Co-operation and Development (OECD) (2006). *The Role of Trade Barriers in SME Internationalisation*. Retrieved from www.oecd. org/trade/ntm/37872326.pdf.

Tilman, E., L. Rajiv, S. Supriyo, T. Naveen and Z. Adil (2011). 'E-payments in India: setting the stage for financial inclusion', *McKinsey on Payments*, June: 37–38.

United Nations Industrial Development Organization (UNIDO) (2007). *Corruption Prevention to Foster Small and Medium-Sized Enterprise Development*, vol. 1. Retrieved from www.unodc.org/documents/corruption/Publications/2012/UNIDO-UNODC_Publication_on_Small_Business_Development_and_Corruption_Vol1.pdf

United States Department of State (2013). *International Narcotics Control Strategy Report, Volume II: Money Laundering and Financial Crimes*. Retrieved from www.state.gov/j/inl/rls/nrcrpt/2013/vol2/.

Wignaraja, G. (2012). 'Engaging small and medium enterprises in production networks: firm-level analysis of five ASEAN economies', Tokyo, Asian Development Bank Institute, ADBI Working Paper 361. Retrieved from www.adbi. org/working-paper/2012/06/01/5076.engaging.small.medium.enterprises.

World Bank (2014). *Doing Business 2014: Understanding Regulations for Small and Medium-Size Enterprises*. Washington DC, World Bank.

World Economic Forum Global Agenda Council on Organised Crime (2012). *Organized Crime Enablers*. Geneva, World Economic Forum.

World Trade Organization (WTO) (2013a). *International Trade Statistics 2012*. Geneva, World Trade Organization.

(2013b). *Director-General's 2013 Annual Report on Accessions*. WT/ACC/21; WT/GC/155; WT/MIN(13)/6.

(2014). 'Overview of Developments in the International Trading Environment, Annual Report by the Director General'. WT/TPR/OV/17.

# 7

# Eurasian Economic Union integration: timetable, priorities and challenges

ANDREY SLEPNEV

## ABSTRACT

*This chapter focuses on the objectives of the Eurasian Economic Union (EAEU) of the Republic of Armenia, the Republic of Belarus, the Republic of Kazakhstan, Kyrgyz Republic and the Russian Federation within the multilateral trading system. The EAEU has become one of the largest trading blocs in the world, with a land area of more than 20 million square kilometres and a population of more than 176 million people.*

*This chapter analyses the history of Eurasian integration and presents its current status, as well as the prospects of the Eurasian Economic Union for 2015.*

## Eurasian integration: current standing

The process of integration in Eurasia began over two decades ago, almost immediately after the collapse of the Soviet Union. At that time, countries in the region were looking for new opportunities to renew their economic, industrial and trading ties, having faced a serious systemic crisis and growing social and political tensions.

Deep interdependence and advanced cooperative ties in the production and trade spheres, together with common cultural and language backgrounds, constituted a foundation for economic integration in Eurasia, which has developed progressively from the Commonwealth of Independent States (CIS) and the CIS Free Trade Area,[1] to the Eurasian Economic Community (EurAsEC),[2] to the Customs Union (CU) and the

---

[1] Simultaneously, the system of bilateral agreements between CIS countries has been transformed into the CIS Free Trade Agreement (adopted in 2011).

[2] Belarus, Kazakhstan, Kyrgyz Republic, Russia and Tajikistan.

Single Economic Space (SES), to the EAEU (Armenia, Belarus, Kazakhstan, Kyrgyz Republic and Russia).

Today's EAEU provides an opportunity to acquire the experience of cooperating in open markets and enhancing administrative practices on the basis of WTO principles and norms.

In 2010, when the CU was established, its main elements – a single customs territory, common customs tariff and customs code – had been put in place. This led to immediate effects on internal CU trade. One of these was an increase in the mutual trade turnover of 33 per cent in 2011 as compared to 2010, and of 7.5 per cent in 2012 as compared to 2011.

The EAEU member states form a common market of goods, services, capital and labour, with total area of more than 20 million square kilometres (the largest in the world), a population of more than 176 million people, an aggregate nominal gross national product (GNP) of US$2,157.4 billion, and a foreign trade volume amounting to US$868.5 billion in 2014.[3]

In 2012, when the SES was established, the growth of mutual trade between the CU member states exceeded the growth rate of their foreign trade.

The positive effects within the SES were largely based on the following:

- ongoing work on eliminating any existing technical, economic, administrative and legal barriers;
- harmonisation of technical requirements and standards;
- promotion of agreed agricultural and industrial policies in the CU/SES member states;
- free movement of labour;
- close work of regulatory bodies and business communities aimed at focusing the pan-CU regulatory efforts on key economic challenges;
- optimisation of the tariff policy in correspondence with the needs of the CU/SES member state economies (without contravening international obligations).

The Treaty on the Eurasian Economic Union and its thirty-three annexes were signed on 29 May 2014 in Astana, Kazakhstan, by the presidents of Belarus, Kazakhstan and Russia. The Treaty was ratified by the national Parliaments of the three above-mentioned member states and came into force on 1 January 2015.

The Treaty on the Accession of the Republic of Armenia to the Eurasian Economic Union was signed on 10 October 2014 and entered into force on 2 January 2015.

---

[3] Statistical data are given for the three member states of the CU/SES (the Republic of Belarus, the Republic of Kazakhstan and the Russian Federation) as of 2014.

The Treaty on the Accession of the Kyrgyz Republic to the Eurasian Economic Union was signed on 23 December 2014 and will enter into force simultaneously with the respective protocols that are now at the final negotiation phase.

The EAEU constitutes an advanced stage of integration of some ex-Soviet countries. The President of Kazakhstan, Nursultan Nazarbayev (the author of the idea of Eurasian integration) has estimated the value of integration development at US$900 billion by 2030.

## Institutional structure of the EAEU: authorities of the EAEU

### Supreme Eurasian Economic Council

The Supreme Eurasian Economic Council, consisting of heads of states, is the supreme body of the EAEU. Sessions of the Supreme Eurasian Economic Council are held at least once a year, except when there are urgent matters to discuss. The Council deals with questions of principle and governs the strategic directions and prospects of the integration development.

### Eurasian Intergovernmental Council

Sessions of the Eurasian Intergovernmental Council, which consists of heads of governments, are held at least twice a year, except when there are urgent matters. The Eurasian Intergovernmental Council is working on the realisation of the Treaty on the Eurasian Economic Union, as well as international treaties and decisions of the Supreme Council.

### Eurasian Economic Commission

In order to implement supranational functions regarding CU issues, to ensure proper coordination of intergovernmental dialogue and to monitor the implementation of the international treaties of the CU, the Commission of the Customs Union was created in 2009.

By the end of 2011, the Commission of the Customs Union had adopted over 900 decisions. The competences of this body at that period of time are described in the Report of the Working Party on the Accession of the Russian Federation to the WTO.[4]

---

[4] See WTO document WT/ACC/RUS/70 (WT/MIN(11)/2) of 17 November 2011.

In 2012, the Commission of the Customs Union was replaced by the Eurasian Economic Commission (Commission), which is now the single permanent regulatory body of the EAEU.

The Commission is a collegiate body; its structure, powers, rules and procedures are determined in the Annex 1 to the Treaty on the Eurasian Economic Union. It consists of a council and of a board.

The Commission's work is based on the principles of guaranteeing benefit to all CU member states, as well as equal rights and respect for the national interests of the parties, transparency, publicity, impartiality and economic validity in the decision-making process.

The Council of the Commission is responsible for the general regulation of the integration processes within the EAEU, as well as for general management of the Commission's activity.

The Board of the Commission is its executive body. It develops proposals to promote integration within the EAEU by developing its regulations within the key competencies of the Commission, including trade policy. Most regulatory decisions in the EAEU are adopted by the Council and the Board of the Commission.

In the trade regulation sphere, the Commission's competency covers most of the issues regulated by the WTO, such as tariff and non-tariff regulation, customs administration, technical regulation, sanitary and phytosanitary measures, establishing trade regimes in relation to third parties, foreign and mutual trade statistics, etc.

## Court of the Eurasian Economic Union

The Court of the Eurasian Economic Union (before January 2015 it was the Court of the Eurasian Economic Community) has the role of court of appeal for EAEU member states. It has been functioning since 1 January 2012.

The Court has jurisdiction over cases on compliance of regulations issued by the bodies of the EAEU with the international agreements that constitute the EAEU legal framework, as well as cases challenging decisions or acts of the bodies of the EAEU.

The Court may also interpret the above-mentioned treaties or decisions adopted within the EAEU and settle disputes between the Commission and the member states, or between the member states in connection with the fulfilment of their obligations undertaken within the EAEU.

## Trade policy in the EAEU

The EAEU has common policies and laws in many trade-related areas. These areas include:

- establishing trade regimes with third parties;
- tariff regulation;
- non-tariff regulation;
- trade remedies;
- trade facilitation procedures and unified application of liberalisation measures.

At the same time, in many areas of WTO mandate, it is the EAEU member states which are fully responsible for implementing the laws and regulations. There are some issues in respect of which members share competency with the Commission or have exceptional authority, e.g. in trade in services or subsidies.

Regarding the relationship with the WTO, it is necessary to mention that, in November 2011, the three presidents proclaimed their commitment to ensure the accession of all three economies to the WTO.

Currently, Russia is the only CU member state that is a member of the WTO. Kazakhstan and Belarus are at different stages of negotiations and we are looking forward to their accession to the WTO.

The legal framework of the CU was elaborated with due account for the WTO rules and best practices in the field of trade regulation. This approach extended the scope of application of the multilateral rules and strengthened their role through implementation of the WTO rules within EAEU member states that are not yet WTO members.

In order to ensure the fulfilment of commitments undertaken by the CU member states during the WTO accession process, the Treaty on the Functioning of the CU within the Framework of the Multilateral Trade System was adopted in May 2011.

Thus, in fact, all these member states comply with the WTO rules in the spheres delegated to the supranational level, which comprises most important issues of regulation of external trade, as described above.

Currently, the Common Customs Tariff of the EAEU is updated on a regular basis in accordance with Russia's tariff commitments in the WTO.

In 2012 the reduction of import duty rates affected nearly 1,000 tariff lines of the Common Customs Tariff; in 2013, it was nearly 5,100; and in 2014, 4,800.

The weighted average import duty rate of the Common Customs Tariff fell from 9.3 per cent in 2011 to 7.02 per cent in 2013.

In the field of non-tariff regulation, certain instruments have been introduced to optimise the conditions for foreign trade transactions for businesses, such as a single list of goods subject to restrictions on import or export by the member states within trade between the EAEU and third countries; and the regulation on the application of restrictions.

Trade remedies as an instrument of foreign trade regulation are also applied by the Commission in full correspondence with WTO regulations.

Despite all the differences, both regulatory and economic, that previously existed, the member states have succeeded in creating a trade regulation system based on WTO rules that respects the interests of all the member states and ensures proper protection of domestic producers from damaging imports and the unfair competition of foreign manufacturers.

Member states have delegated to the Commission their competency to conduct countervailing anti-dumping and safeguard investigations and apply justified trade remedies.

The Commission's Department for Internal Market Defence has submitted to Russia more than a dozen draft notifications on safeguard measures, drafted semi-annual reports and *ad hoc* notifications of anti-dumping measures, which have been published on the official website and made available to WTO members.

In the field of technical regulation, active work is being done under Chapter 10 of the Treaty on the Eurasian Economic Union. As of April 2015, thirty-five technical regulations of the EAEU have been adopted (thirty-four have entered into force).

A new edition of the Provision on the Procedure of Development, Adoption, Amendment and Cancellation of the Customs Union Technical Regulation was also adopted. This Provision provides for a shortening of the period and simplification of development procedures; it provides for the participation of representatives of industry and business, as well as experts, from member states and third countries in the drafting process. This is fully in line with the WTO Agreement on Technical Barriers to Trade.

As for ensuring the transparency of the process of drafting, adopting, modifying or cancelling CU technical regulations, the above-mentioned regulation requires that the Commission make the first draft of a technical regulation and related documents publicly available on the

Commission's official website. It also sets forth detailed terms and procedures related to public discussion and dealing with feedback commentaries and proposals received during consultations and public discussion. It should also be noted that the developer of the relevant draft technical regulation must include every comment or proposal in the summary of comments and specify whether it has been accepted or not, stating reasons for rejection.

The new edition provides no options for 'procedural' delays in the adoption of technical regulations.

A Common Register of Certification Bodies and Test Laboratories (Centres), created on the basis of proposals from the national accreditation bodies of the parties, is maintained.

The competency of the Commission in the field of sanitary and phytosanitary (SPS) measures application consists of the development and approval of common SPS requirements while national authorities of the member states are responsible for their enforcement.

The Commission contributes to fulfilling Russia's WTO commitments in the field of SPS measures, which are contained in the Protocol of Accession of the Russian Federation to the WTO, in particular:

- to ensure compliance with the international standards, recommendations and regulations, including those of the World Organisation for Animal Health (OIE), proper amendments were made to the common veterinary requirements and the common forms of veterinary certificates; and
- to ensure transparency of the process of adoption of regulations in the field of SPS measures by the Commission, public consultations of draft decisions in this field are displayed on the Commission's official website.

### International cooperation of the Eurasian Economic Commission

Cooperation with key EAEU trade partners and international organisations has a vital practical role in terms of sharing experience and applying international standards to promote Eurasian integration.

In this regard, the Commission develops cooperation with United Nations institutions. As of today several memoranda of cooperation and understanding between the Eurasian Economic Commission and United Nations Economic Commission for Europe (UNECE), the United Nations Conference on Trade and Development (UNCTAD), the

International Organization for Migration (IOM), the International Electrotechnical Commission (IEC), the Food and Agriculture Organization of the United Nations (FAO), the Economic and Social Commission for Asia and the Pacific (ESCAP) and the OIE have been signed.

Following the Commission–UNECE Second Conference on Trade Facilitation and Single Window which took place in Moscow in April 2013, the parties worked out recommendations enabling them to develop the EAEU single window system.

The Commission is attentive to the development of bilateral relationships between the EAEU and its key trade partners, such as CIS countries, the European Union and China.

Alongside the liberalisation of trade within the framework of the EAEU, its member states participate in other integration processes in Eurasia. In 2012, the Commonwealth of Independent States Free Trade Area Agreement entered into force.

As of June 2014, the Republic of Armenia, the Republic of Belarus, the Republic of Kazakhstan, the Russian Federation, Kyrgyz Republic, the Republic of Moldova, Ukraine and Uzbekistan ratified this Agreement. Tajikistan has not yet completed the ratification due to intergovernmental procedures.

As the acceleration of global trends towards the creation of large cross-regional free trade areas has become a decisive factor in global trade and economic cooperation, the Commission has been paying special attention to the regional processes that are actively ongoing all over the world.

The EAEU actively participates in the processes of establishing free trade areas.

In 2013, negotiations on a free trade agreement with Viet Nam were launched. According to preliminary estimates, such an agreement, if concluded, could increase the trade turnover between the member states and Viet Nam by up to US$12 billion by 2020. Today free trade agreements have become an effective mechanism to promote bilateral trade, economic and investment interaction. Trade blocs formed so far will considerably expand trade between their members through elimination of tariff and non-tariff barriers, harmonisation of technical regulations, phytosanitary measures, customs procedures, etc.

Moreover, approaches to integration processes are changing now. Nowadays a fundamentally new model of integration is developing – the 'new regionalism'.

At present, according to experts' estimations, the share of trade carried out under free trade regimes is 15 to 20 per cent of global trade. The figure is expected to rise to 60 to 80 per cent in the coming five to seven years as new free trade zones emerge.

This issue requires thorough consideration and discussion within the WTO in order to guarantee such fundamental WTO principles as the most-favoured-nation principle and to ensure non-discriminatory access for WTO members to external markets.

## From CU/SES to the EAEU

In accordance with the Declaration on the Eurasian Economic Integration, dated 18 November 2011, the next stage in Eurasian integration was the establishment of the Eurasian Economic Union. The EAEU has enjoyed an international legal personality since January 2015.

According to the Article 28 of the Treaty on the EAEU, the internal market includes an economic space that provides for the free movement of goods, persons, services and capital.

### Common market of goods

Within the framework of the functioning of the internal market, member states do not apply mutual import and export customs duties (or any other equivalent duties, taxes or charges), non-tariff measures, or safeguard, anti-dumping or countervailing measures, except in cases determined in the Treaty.

### Common market of services

According to the Treaty, member states are responsible for forming and providing the functioning of the common market for services in most sectors. Thereby the suppliers of services are given the following opportunities:

- the supply of services without the additional formation of a legal entity – it means that a company from one member state does not have to create a subsidiary when it carries out activities on the territory of other member states;
- the supply of services with the permission of its own state, i.e. permission issued in one member state will be applied also on the territory of the other member states;
- mutual recognition of the qualifications of services suppliers.

It should be noted that the establishment of single market for services should be carried out by the gradual reduction of existing exemptions and restrictions and harmonisation of the legislation.


## Common labour market

The Treaty on the Eurasian Economic Union provides for elimination of any labour quotas for citizens of the member states of the EAEU.

Equal free medical assistance (in urgent and emergency forms) has to be provided for citizens on the whole territory of the EAEU.

It should be noted that the *de facto* labour market of the EAEU member states is already integrated, while all reconsiderations made after 1 January 2015 are technical in their nature and are not expected to occasion serious changes for foreign citizens entering employment.


## Potential enlargement of the EAEU

Successes achieved by the existing member states have made accession to the EAEU attractive for other countries in the region, particularly for the traditional trade partners of the member states in the CIS area, Armenia and Kyrgyz Republic.

It is expected that the main economic effect of the accession of Armenia and Kyrgyz Republic to the EAEU will contribute both to an increase in GDP and foreign trade or extended investment cooperation, and to the development of internal distribution networks.

After three years since Russia's accession to the WTO, we are looking hopefully toward the accessions of Belarus and Kazakhstan. We believe that the EAEU should have the following short-term objectives within the WTO multilateral trading system:

- monitoring the existing and newly developed EAEU legal and regulatory framework for compliance with the WTO Agreement, including fulfilment of Russia's commitments to WTO members;
- participating in the negotiations on the agenda of the Doha Round within the competence of the Eurasian Economic Commission;
- contributing to the acceleration of the accessions of Kazakhstan and Belarus to the WTO.

We take into account that the enlargement of the EAEU, especially the accession of WTO members to the EAEU, will potentially affect many aspects of the EAEU current trade policy and relations with new member states.

This will require substantial efforts on the part of the Commission in the near future. But the process of unification of the trade policy regime in the member states, supported by liberal commitments adopted as a result of Russia's accession to the WTO, is very significant and corresponds to the interests of WTO members.

The Commission attaches great importance to the negotiations of the Doha Round, and appreciates the work of WTO members to prepare the complicated, compromise, but very important decisions of the Bali Ministerial Conference.

The Commission participated in the Ninth Ministerial Conference of the WTO as part of the delegation of Russia, and we are of the view that an early agreement on the Doha Development Agenda, as a whole, would make an important contribution to the increase of confidence in the multilateral trading system, and enable WTO members and acceding countries to look at its future with optimism.

We are confident that the successful accomplishment of negotiations regarding matters on the agenda of the Ninth Ministerial Conference will make a consequential contribution to strengthening the multilateral trading system, and will also give the new political impetus that is so necessary for advancing the negotiations of the Doha Round, in general.

We especially want to emphasise the importance of the decision on trade facilitation matters, as the Trade Facilitation Agreement aims to make a contribution to optimising trade processes, simplifying the operations of importers and exporters, and customs clearance for commercial freight.

Broadly, the Commission highly appreciates the endeavours of the WTO in trade liberalisation, eliminating administrative barriers and assisting governments acceding to the WTO.

In this regard we are hopeful that the accession of Kazakhstan to the WTO will be achieved in 2015. We also hope that the negotiations on the accession of the Republic of Belarus, which are still in progress, will come to a rapid conclusion.

We encourage WTO members to make the accessions of Kazakhstan and Belarus priority tasks for the WTO for the near future, as the results of these accessions will be mutually beneficial for all interested parties.

# 8

# WTO accessions: what does the academic literature say?

ALEXEI KIREYEV AND MUSTAPHA SEKKATE

## ABSTRACT

*This chapter takes stock of the recent academic literature on accessions. It focuses only on the analytical work published since 2000 in books, academic journals and working papers by key WTO scholars across the world. These contributions are related to the procedural, legal, economic and institutional aspects of WTO accessions, and to the proposals for their reform. Country-specific studies, research on the impact of accessions on individual industries and reports on accessions by national and international institutions are not included.*

Revisiting the literature on WTO accessions accumulated since the start of the twenty-first century is a daunting exercise. The literature is vast and includes both in-depth theoretical analyses and empirical studies. It covers the legal, economic and institutional aspects of accessions, and includes numerous country- and sector-specific cases. A simple search for 'WTO accessions 2000–2014' in Google Scholar, which indexes scholarly literature, returns about 33,000 academic contributions across an array of publishing formats and disciplines.

Two relatively recent publications on accessions stand out clearly from this extensive list. First, *A Handbook on Accession to the WTO* (Williams, 2008), prepared by the WTO Secretariat, presents a broad overview of key aspects of accessions and provides the general reader with a basis for informed discussion and analysis of the WTO's membership process. It places accession in the context of the WTO, sets out the basic provisions governing accession and the standard procedures and terms of accession and brings together key documents used in the accession process. Second, the two-volume *The WTO and Accession Countries* (Primo Braga and Cattaneo, 2009), with contributions by some of the authors included in this review, explores the intertwined economic, legal and political dimensions of accessions. It also includes country cases and sector-specific issues in agriculture, services and intellectual property. Both publications remain valuable reference sources for scholars and practitioners grappling with the increasing complexity of WTO accession.

The academic literature broadly converges on the overall assessment of the accession process. The rationale of WTO accession includes better integration into the world economy by securing permanent and unconditional most-favoured-nation (MFN) status and protection against arbitrary protectionist measures by major trading partners. Negotiating costs are reduced by negotiating multilaterally rather than bilaterally or regionally, participating in international trade rule-making and accessing an impartial and binding dispute settlement mechanism. The accession process itself is unanimously viewed in the literature as very complex and lengthy, a fact explained mainly by the complexity of the multilateral trading system itself, unevenness in the capacity of the applicants to implement the needed reforms and the demanding and multi-layered negotiating machinery. The applicant country clearly plays the central role in the accession process and needs to demonstrate sustained commitment to accession. The incumbent members, on the other hand, have an inherent interest in obtaining concessions from acceding governments and leveraging their negotiating capacity accordingly. However, in the end, accession decisions should be made unanimously by the membership, introducing systemic balance between the interests of the incumbent and acceding governments.

The discussion of legal aspects of accessions in academic literature presents a mixed picture. Most authors agree that there is a single body of WTO accession law, which should be viewed dynamically, with specific legal rules inferred from the international legal system, the 1994 Marrakesh Agreement Establishing the World Trade Organization ('WTO Agreement'), Accession Protocols and WTO case law. However, on the issue of the legal fairness of WTO accessions, views diverge substantially. A large body of academic literature explores the legitimacy of the existing practice whereby incumbent WTO members prescribe obligations for acceding governments that exceed the requirements of the WTO Agreement. These authors come to the conclusion that accessions lack substantive fairness, which contributes to the WTO's legitimacy crisis. Other authors, however, argue that the fundamental question is whether accession practices strengthen or weaken the multilateral system. They claim that greater commitments by acceding governments complement the existing rules, help to close loopholes and contribute to ongoing reforms of the multilateral trading rules. On balance, a number of practical suggestions on upgrading the existing accession rules are gradually emerging from this rich discussion.

The economics of accession has been studied in academic literature mainly through the prism of cost–benefit analysis. With some exceptions, scholars have found that joining the WTO brings substantial benefits to the acceded economy. Membership of the WTO contributes to an increase in trade volumes, faster growth, institution building and better governance in the acceded economy. The impact on the fiscal balance has been found to be generally ambiguous and dependent on the acceding economy's pre-existing revenue and expenditure compositions, the depth of tariff and subsidy reduction and the elasticity of trade volumes to higher openness. At the same time, there is broad agreement that the direct and indirect costs of accession may be substantial. In the short term, such costs may outweigh the immediate benefits, but in the long run, better resource allocation should help re-establish the balance. Overall, the implementation of accession commitments is seen as catalytic for a broad range of domestic policy reforms.

The literature offers a number of guide posts for reform of the accession process. These range from simply updating the catalogue of all existing accession rules that deviate from WTO rules, and including them in the official WTO analytical index for ease of reference, to developing a comprehensive WTO agreement on accessions that would become an integral part of WTO law. The references to accessions in the existing WTO law, and in particular the concept of accessions on 'terms to be agreed', should be clarified, and the process of accession negotiations could be streamlined. Sceptics, however, observe that, as the incumbent members have little to gain from such reforms, progress in this area may be slow.

## Accession process

What is the rationale for joining the WTO? Why are applicant countries willing to submit to the stringent, far-reaching and asymmetrical requirements of the WTO accession process? According to Cattaneo and Primo Braga (2009), for the acceding government the rationale for joining the WTO includes acquiring permanent and unconditional MFN status, protection against arbitrary measures imposed by trading partners, reduction in the costs of trade negotiations, participation in international

trade rule-making and access to an impartial and binding dispute settlement mechanism. At the same time, membership of the WTO leads to
more efficient and credible trade policies in the acceded economies and
anchors their domestic regulatory and administrative reforms. Davis and
Wilf (2011) note that geopolitical interests, and similarities in foreign
policies and democratic development to the incumbent countries, often
dominate purely economic and market considerations of countries' decisions to apply for WTO membership. Neumayer (2013) views the benefits of accession in terms of increased trade, reduced trade volatility and
greater predictability and improved market access. Joining the WTO also
allows acceding governments to pursue and lock in trade policy reforms
under the banner of complying with international agreements. In a world
in which most countries participate in multilateral preferential trade
agreements (PTAs), outsiders may see few alternatives to joining as well.
Some countries decide to join even if there is an absolute welfare loss,
because the cost of remaining outside may be even higher and rising with
an increasing number of members in the WTO. Drabek and Woo (2010)
suggest that some countries may regard WTO accession as the lesser of
two evils for 'fear of being left behind', despite the costly and asymmetrical admission process.

The WTO accession process is often seen as overly complex. Evenett
and Primo Braga (2006) raise concerns that the process is unusually
so and that there is uncertainty about the price of WTO accession.
Cattaneo and Primo Braga (2009) call for more solidarity in guiding the
acceding governments through the complexities of accession, which
would ultimately contribute to making the multilateral trading system
truly inclusive and sustainable. Milthorp (2009) argues that the accession process is complex because WTO agreements are complex.
Accession consists of government-to-government negotiation conducted at two mutually interactive levels. Negotiations are conducted
in parallel on a multilateral level between the acceding government
and the collective WTO membership, and on a bilateral level between
the acceding government and individual members. For accession
negotiations to reach the endgame, negotiators must engage in both
international and domestic diplomacy to create a balanced package
acceptable to WTO members and domestic stakeholders. At times,
the complexity of accession can be viewed as an obstacle to the universality of WTO membership. Osakwe (2011) argues that the very nature
of the accession process is complex because accession commitments
are interlocked with domestic reforms and the rules of the multilateral

trading system. This is the nature of the WTO, which should be viewed as its strength, not as a weakness.

Answering the pertinent question raised by practitioners and academics – why accessions take so long – led to the use of the endurance model and survival analysis. Jones (2009) shows that the time elapsed from WTO application to accession has increased with the number of completed accessions, suggesting that WTO members have learned over time to bargain for more demanding concessions from applicants. Regarding the terms of accession, the number of rules has increased and the level of bound tariffs has fallen, as the number of completed accessions has increased. Jones and Gai (2013) think that several factors account for a lengthy and often difficult accession negotiation experience. On the one hand, WTO incumbents have superior bargaining positions, follow a highly legalistic approach to accessions, and put increasing demands for concessions on new members. The applicant countries, on the other hand, differ in their capacity to implement institutional reforms and are often overwhelmed by the demands of the negotiations. Additional factors that lengthen accession negotiations include governance problems in acceding economies, the gap between their trade regime and the state needed to complete WTO accession, higher pre-application tariff levels and a higher incidence of anti-dumping cases and their political regime. Wong and Yu (2008) also find that the accession process is likely to be shorter for an applicant whose political regime is more democratic. It is possible that democratic countries, which tend to participate more in international organisations, may expect from the applicant country comparable standards before approving its accession to the WTO.

The applicant country clearly plays the central role in the accession process. Milthorp (2009) argues that the most arduous negotiations fall upon the government of the acceding economy because it must develop a focused yet flexible negotiating mandate, implement economic reforms that may cause short-term hardship to some previously protected sectors and ensure that negotiations progress steadily – all to retain political support for ratification. Detailed preparations by the acceding government are vital, as is a skilled negotiator, with resources, political authority and a good team. Negotiators need to know their domestic constraints. This is critical to securing an end result that the acceding government is happy to accept, and to defending the terms of accession later during the ratification process. Acceding governments also need to keep WTO members' attention on their accession by maintaining a consistent pace of liberalising reform in the context of the negotiations. Kavass (2007) reviews the procedures and obstacles facing applicant countries and concludes that accession is entirely dependent on the applicant country's commitment to the process. The burden of understanding the complexities of accession rests with the applicant country. Aside from becoming convinced about the potential benefits of WTO membership, the country needs to learn that there are no shortcuts to accession and that the process is bound to involve many years of very demanding work. Once the applicant country understands the work involved, the accession process begins to move forward.

WTO accessions obviously look different from the point of view of incumbent members. Lacey (2007) thinks that WTO accessions offer members a unique opportunity to leverage issues against the applicant country to a degree they will probably not be able to achieve again. This dynamic is not likely to change anytime soon as members are interested in maintaining the status quo. Once bilateral deals have been completed with the few major members, accession negotiations tend to become easier, with less important players. Pelc (2011) argues that accession terms are driven by the domestic export interests of existing members. As a result, relatively greater liberalisation is imposed on those entrants that have more valuable market access to offer upon accession: the more a country has to offer, the more it is required to give. Although institutional norms lead members to exercise restraint *vis-à-vis* the poorest countries, the richest countries have the greatest bargaining expertise and thus obtain better terms. Middle-income countries end up with the most stringent terms, and have to make the greatest relative adjustments to their trade regimes.

Clearly, not all existing members participate equally in accession negotiations. Based on an empirical analysis of accession working parties, Neumayer (2013) finds that existing WTO members selected themselves into the working party to have the option to strategically delay membership by the applicant and extract concessions from it. Existing members select themselves to become working party members, in two cases: if their bilateral trade with the applicant country represents a large share of their gross domestic product (GDP), unless they already have a PTA with the applicant; or if they are structurally similar to the applicant country and compete with it in terms of export products and market structure. If existing members have PTAs with a third large country in common with the applicant, they are less likely to enter the working party. All these determinants of the self-selection of existing members into the working parties were found to be statistically significant.

Accessions to the WTO should be approved unanimously by the membership, which requires establishing a delicate balance between the interests of incumbent and acceding governments. Powerful states often accept unanimity voting on accession, even though this enables weak states to blackmail powerful states into providing costly side payments. Although such a choice is usually attributed to efforts to bolster the legitimacy of international institutions, Schneider and Urpelainen (2012) show that the choice of unanimity also has a strategic component, as unanimous accession rules can profit powerful states by creating uncertainty about the minimum level of reform that enables accession. If accession is valuable enough and the acceding government is uncertain about the decision of weaker countries on whether to support or reject its accession, the acceding government will play it safe by implementing ambitious reforms that improve the efficacy of the WTO. The unanimity rule enhances legitimacy while allowing powerful states to induce significant reforms by applicants to the benefit of current members.

## Legal aspects of accession

The legal provisions of accession have been thoroughly reviewed because accessions are unique among international institutions. Parenti (2000) points out that accessions to the WTO can be compared to 'catching a moving train' as WTO rules and membership expand in the course of a country's accession. Accessions should be viewed dynamically, in conjunction with specific legal rules that can be inferred either directly from the WTO or indirectly from the international legal system. The WTO accession regime is unique among international organisations in that it permits the conclusion of Accession Protocols to alter the rights and obligations of its members under the underlying treaties of the WTO, all without going through the formal procedures for amendment. The WTO, unlike other international organisations, may require its acceded governments to accept more stringent rules of conduct than those binding on its original members. The scope and content of such rules are country specific, depending on the result of accession negotiations. The country-specific rules are set out in the Protocol of Accession concluded between the acceding government and the WTO. Cumulatively, accession rules form a significant part of WTO law, and some have given rise to major disputes, generating WTO case law on accession. This raises important questions about the legality of WTO practices.

Although a single body of WTO accession law does not exist, some authors have tried to map out its basic topology. Charnovitz (2007) observes that, overall, studies of WTO accessions have been impeded by the lack of a framework for distinguishing the various types of accession commitments and how they relate to general WTO law. Detailed accession commitments that go well beyond current WTO rules have been made on many domestic policy issues and trade policies. The success in incorporating these new norms into the WTO and making them enforceable leads to the question of whether these new norms should become obligations for all WTO members, not just obligations for acceding members. The standard protocol states that accession agreements 'shall be an integral part of the WTO Agreement'. That appears to solve the problem of enforceability because if one agreement is an integral part of the WTO then it should be enforceable in the same way as any other part of the WTO. However, because an Accession Protocol is not a WTO amendment, there is some tension between Article XII of the WTO Agreement and the provisions in Accession Protocols that impose obligations on all WTO members or on WTO bodies.

Accession Protocols effectively modify WTO multilateral trade agreements, but the legal basis for their doing so remains unclear. Qin (2015) believes that the normatively differential treatment of acceded members derogates from the WTO principle of non-discrimination, but does so without proper justification. Confusion over the legal nature of Accession Protocols and the lack of a clear rationale for the country-specific rules have led to problematic jurisprudence, creating uncertainty about the rights and obligations of acceded members *vis-à-vis* other members of the WTO. Legally, WTO Accession Protocols can be characterised as the subsequent practice of an international organisation modifying its underlying treaties. The lack of reasoning and transparency in the accession rules is the main legitimacy problem.

Whether WTO accessions have been 'fair' has been a question of major academic and practical interest for many years. Cattaneo and Primo Braga (2009) observe that, because the scope of WTO discipline largely exceeds that of the General Agreement on Tariffs and Trade (GATT), which is applied to existing members, the level of commitments required for new entrants is usually substantially higher than in the early years of the GATT. The incumbent members often see accession negotiations as an opportunity to prescribe obligations exceeding existing requirements of WTO agreements – the so-called 'WTO-plus' obligations and 'WTO-minus' rights, that is, forgoing rights available to other WTO members. The ultimate test of the fairness and adequacy of the terms of accession is the capacity of acceding governments to implement their commitments fully. On purely legal grounds, Bienen and Mihretu (2010) also claim that the accession process to the WTO lacks procedural fairness because acceding governments have been treated differently from their peer WTO founding members. This has had a negative effect on both acceding governments and the WTO. Charnovitz (2007) points out that, by assigning to each new WTO member a unique set of WTO obligations, the WTO undermines the rule of law in two ways – first, by treating some members more favourably than others and, second, by fragmenting the coherence of WTO law. Although in principle the scope of WTO law can be broadened into new areas, it seems odd to conduct such experiments only on the newest members. WTO-minus provisions also delineate the obligations of incumbent members towards the acceding member and water down the normal disciplines.

A very specific aspect of accessions – granting special and differential treatment to acceding developing economies – has been extensively debated in the context of fairness in WTO accessions. Developing country members of the WTO benefit from special and differential treatment, a flexible application of WTO principles and rules according to their developmental needs and capacities. However, this treatment is not granted to acceding countries – almost all of which today are developing countries. Bienen and Mihretu (2010) argue that these acceding economies receive 'inverse' special and differential treatment and are compelled to offer more far-reaching liberalisation commitments than WTO members themselves. Neither the procedure nor the outcomes of accession negotiations take fairness, or substantive fairness, fully into account.

Discussions on the legality of WTO accession practice do not prejudice the question of the legitimacy of the practice. The legitimacy of the differentiated terms must be derived from the procedural and substantive fairness of WTO practice. Qin (2015) points out that, despite the growing number of accession rules, the WTO has not catalogued and indexed them, and nor has it acknowledged that these rules constitute another category of MFN derogation in WTO law. The lack of transparency and articulated reasoning in the accession rules contravenes the basic norms of procedural fairness. Substantively, it is difficult to justify why acceding members, most of which are developing countries, should be required to adhere to more stringent legal standards than the original members. What has enabled this troublesome practice to arise is the absence in the WTO Agreement of the requirement for equal or consistent treatment between the acceded and original members of the WTO, a lacuna in sharp contrast with the membership provisions of other major international organisations. In the view of Bienen and Mihretu (2010), the lack of fairness in accession contributes to the WTO's growing 'legitimacy crisis'.

The fundamental question regarding accessions is whether they strengthen the multilateral trading system or weaken it. Osakwe (2011) argues that higher-level commitments have been decidedly positive, tightening loopholes and modernising existing multilateral rules in areas that lack clarity. In fact, existing WTO rules provide for departures from non-discrimination, but only with agreement by members about whether the terms of accession apply to other members. While the non-discrimination principle and provisions are constant, accession terms vary. This is not contradictory because dispute settlement remains the final arbiter on whether the principle of non-discrimination has been violated, and WTO jurisprudence demonstrates that non-discrimination has been consistently upheld with rulings against discrimination. Overall, WTO-plus commitments have tended to strengthen the rules and engender trade liberalisation and reform.

Taking stock of the current debate on legal aspects of WTO accession, Qin (2015) reaches the following conclusions: (i) it was not the original intention of the parties to the WTO Agreement to allow accession terms to modify the underlying trade agreements as the WTO Agreement 'does not distinguish in any way' between the original and acceded members; (ii) when an accession agreement prescribes additional and different terms from the provisions of the WTO Agreement, it effectively amends the WTO Agreement in its application to the acceded member, but does so without a proper legal basis; (iii) WTO Accession Protocols can be viewed as a 'subsequent agreement' or 'subsequent practice' that modifies WTO agreements, thus recognising the independent authority of an international organisation over its members; and (iv) while the external legality of WTO accession practice can be established under public international law, its legality under the institutional law of the WTO remains questionable. As a practical matter, however, the act of the WTO authority is unlikely to be challenged.

## Economics of accession

Most research discusses the economics of accession through the prism of its impact on the volumes of trade after accession. Rose (2005) estimates the effect of multilateral trade agreements on international trade and finds little evidence that countries joining or belonging to the WTO have different trade patterns from those of outsiders. This negative finding arises from a tendency to overlook the role of non-member participants. The GATT created rights and obligations not only for contracting parties but also for colonies, newly independent states and provisional members. Evenett and Gage (2005) suggest that the impact on trade from WTO accession will probably most differ by country, and Evenett and Primo Braga (2006) find that country-by-country estimates of the impact of WTO accession on imports and exports indeed vary. Once Goldstein *et al.* (2007) account for all GATT participants, their analysis shows that participation – either as a formal member or as a non-member participant – substantially increases trade. In the same vein, Subramanian and Wei (2007) find that there is robust evidence that the WTO has had a powerful, positive but uneven impact on trade. WTO membership has been associated with a large increase in imports, mainly for industrial countries and developing countries that joined the WTO after the Uruguay Round but not for other developing countries. Osakwe (2011) shows that the trade of all recently acceded members increased significantly as they began to implement their accession-related reforms, some of these prior to accession, others upon accession and some through agreed phased transition. Allee and Scalera (2012) explain the differentiated impact of WTO membership on trade volumes by the level of trade liberalisation commitments accepted by countries in the process of accession negotiations. Countries facing greater scrutiny from the WTO usually engage in greater trade liberalisation and usually experience more increase in trade volume upon joining than those who face little scrutiny and engage in little, if any, liberalisation.

Evidence shows that income in acceded governments usually increases, in particular in the first few years after accession. Li and Wu (2004) find that only high-income economies experienced significantly faster growth after accession. Tang and Wei (2009) show that higher growth and investment generally last for about five years after accession, but only in those acceded economies that have undertaken substantial reforms. However, trade openness brought about by WTO membership itself is not sufficient to promote growth and needs to be combined with proper economic institutions. In the same vein, they find that accession tends to raise income, but only for those countries that were subject to rigorous accession procedures. Policy commitments associated with accession were helpful, especially for countries with poor governance.

The impact of accession on the government's budget may be ambiguous as accession commitments may lead to revenue increases or shortfalls, and to expenditure savings or the need for additional spending. Ebrill *et al.* (1999) show that the revenue implications of trade liberalisation are uncertain and depend on countries' initial conditions and reform strategy, especially if their tariff structures are complex and highly restrictive. Primo Braga and Cattaneo (2009) suggest the calculations of accession costs and benefits should also include revenue forgone when the transaction value replaces the minimum prices for customs valuation, increased revenue owing to the termination of rebates and duty exemptions in line with the WTO Agreement on Subsidies and Countervailing Measures, and expenditure to repay technical assistance loans from development partners. Using transitional economies as an example, Drabek and Bacchetta (2004) find that tariff reduction did not cause any significant problems because customs revenue in those economies had never been a substantial part of government revenue.

The costs of WTO accession can also be relatively high. Kavass (2007), Drabek and Woo (2010) and Laird (2009) raise the issue of the costs of accession, which may be substantial, in particular in the short term, as acceded governments need to finance the reforms of their trade institutions to align them with WTO requirements. Adjustment to WTO accession requirements is always a source of economic, social and political stress, as the adjustments directly affect people's income and living conditions. In terms of indirect costs, Cattaneo and Primo Braga (2009) also draw attention to the substantial resource reallocations that can be expected in the private sector, because not all traditional sectors will be competitive internationally without substantial tariff protection. Reallocation of capital and labour to more competitive sectors may lead to social costs and pressure on the government's budget. Although accession rules usually include exemptions from certain commitments, transition periods and substantial technical assistance, in many cases such flexibilities may still not be sufficient. Wong and Yu (2008) point to yet another cost in terms of the potentially lengthy negotiation process, as the costs will increase with the length of the accession process and require additional resources. Prediction of the accession period could give the potential applicant a reference in its cost–benefit analysis of accession. With the rising costs of accession, more solidarity is needed in supporting WTO-related activities by acceding governments, including technical assistance at all stages of the accession process, from early negotiations to implementation.

## Accession and domestic reforms

Accession to the WTO has generally been found to be conducive to a broad range of domestic reforms. Domestic reforms in the context of accession to the WTO have led to systemic transformation of the economies of acceding governments through more efficient and credible trade policies, resulting in an improved business climate for domestic producers and foreign investors. Drabek and Bacchetta (2004) view adherence to the rules-based multilateral trading system as a credible anchor for domestic regulatory and administrative reforms. Osakwe (2011) shows that the accession process has been used by individual recently acceded members as an important instrument for domestic policy reforms and has allowed them to advance a broader domestic modernisation agenda spanning well beyond trade. Responding to a combination of national development priorities and complying with multilateral trading rules and pursuing reforms in line with their accession commitments, many acceded governments have achieved substantial progress in their domestic reform agenda, better trade performance and stronger resilience to exogenous shocks.

Accession to the WTO generally has had a positive impact on acceded economies in terms of improved governance. Drabek and Bacchetta (2004) point out that WTO accession goes hand in hand with higher institutional quality and efficiency, and reduces rent-seeking behaviour and corruption. Tang and Wei (2009) find that the beneficial effects of policy commitments made during WTO accession negotiations seem more pronounced among countries with initially poor governance. This result suggests that WTO commitments are a partial substitute for quality of governance, perhaps justifying the lengthier negotiations. But can longer negotiations help achieve better governance? The effect of lengthier bargaining is likely to reach a point of diminishing economic returns. Improved governance capacity – for example, through technical assistance and foreign aid – would make shorter negotiations possible, without sacrificing the benefits of WTO discipline. Maggi and Rodriguez-Clare (1998) show that, by committing to free trade, governments may credibly distance themselves from domestic lobbies. However, Ferrantino (2009), using a number of governance indices, finds little impact of WTO accession on governance and the overall policy environment. Using incidences of tariff evasion as an indicator for the evolution of governance, Javorcik and Narciso (2013) find that WTO accession helped limit tariff evasion because the implementation of WTO rules limited the discretion of customs officials in assessing the unit values of goods.

The impact on the quality of institutions in accessed countries has been positive, although at times uneven. Basu (2008), using a composite measure of domestic economic institutions, finds that WTO accession has a positive and significant impact on the institutions in acceded economies. Hence, the WTO accession mechanism could be seen as a package deal that provides countries with the opportunity to make credible commitments by inducing deeper economic policy changes and improving institutions. Basu *et al.* (2009) also find that the expanding scope of trade policy commitments places an additional strain on institution building, especially in developing countries. The problem is the insufficiency of the mechanisms in the accession process itself, which does not sufficiently account for differing levels of institutional capacity in acceding economies. This may place a heavier burden of policy implementation and institutional reform on countries with limited human, administrative and financial resources, such as least-developed countries (LDCs).

## Reform prospects of the accession process

What, if anything, should be done to reform the WTO accession process? Some researchers have called for a WTO agreement on accessions, which would spell out the binding procedural rules and substantive requirements that can be expected from applicant countries. At the same time, Bienen and Mihretu (2010) argue that, on the one hand, introducing a WTO agreement on accessions would appear beneficial, bringing the institution closer to the WTO's objective of providing a rule-based multilateral trade system; but on the other hand, to the extent that the possibility of extracting concessions from applicants and delaying their accession provides existing members with the necessary leverage, major reforms – which take away this option – may prove counterproductive to the WTO's overall objective of further and deeper trade liberalisation. Neumayer (2013), however, notes that reform of the WTO's accession procedures is a moot point, as non-members have no say on the reforms of the WTO accession process, while those benefiting from the status quo (existing members) have nothing to gain from such reforms.

Several ways are proposed to achieve improvement on the legal side of the WTO accession process. Qin (2015) suggests that, at a minimum, the WTO Secretariat should catalogue all the accession rules that expand or deviate from the provisions of WTO agreements and include these rules in the official WTO analytical index. Substantively, the effect of unprincipled rule-making can be mitigated through treaty interpretation, which is the responsibility of the WTO judiciary. Such an approach should take into account the historical and political contexts of WTO accession negotiations, and aim to arrive at conclusions in line with the declared principles and objectives of the WTO.

To overcome the legitimacy concerns regarding fairness in the WTO accession process, the literature offers several approaches. Bienen and Mihretu (2010), for example, suggest: (i) strengthening procedural fairness by establishing criteria for the accession 'terms to be agreed' and elevating the rules on accession into a WTO agreement on accession, which would become part of the WTO rules; (ii) introducing a panel of experts to examine the WTO compatibility of the applicant's trade regime instead of the self-interested working party system; (iii) refraining from asking acceding governments to commit to more than the commitments of comparable WTO members; (iv) establishing criteria by comparison with similar economies for assessing the level of commitments that could be expected from the acceding government; and (v) addressing sectoral reforms, especially in services, outside the WTO, unless they are clearly related to trade. Acceding governments should be expected to assume mandatory obligations. Other liberalising measures should not be required if acceding governments show resistance to them and if members with a comparable development status have not undertaken comparable commitments.

Finally, a number of steps are proposed to accelerate accession. Tang and Wei (2009) suggest that the incumbent WTO members improve the accession process by introducing more flexibility in transition periods, linking progress towards compliance goals with corresponding WTO market access benefits, limiting the demand for substantial concessions from applicants until later stages and improving the coordination of aid to finance internal reforms. Some of these provisions are already in place, formally or informally, for LDC applicants. However, a formal implementation of these reforms and their extension to applicants with incomes above the LDC level could contribute to achieving universal membership. Otherwise, for many applicant countries with limited governmental resources, the accession process will remain slow.

Accessions should be evaluated on the outcomes, not on the process. Indeed, the academic literature correctly presents accession to the WTO as a complex, dynamic, iterative process with intertwined political, institutional, economic and legal dimensions. This inherent complexity makes accession naturally vulnerable because not all parts of this sophisticated social machinery can fit together perfectly at all times. Nevertheless, accession outcomes reflect an acceptable compromise for all, with results that not only safeguard the benefits of the multilateral trading system but also help take it forward. Even when trade negotiations stall, accession negotiations continue and contribute to rule-making, eliminating legal ambiguities and, overall, upgrading the multilateral trading system. The academic evidence supports strong developmental outcomes of accession.

The analytical research agenda on accessions remains vast. For practitioners, in particular WTO negotiators, strong analytical underpinning of positions in accession negotiations would help improve their leverage and gain additional policy traction for the approval of Accession Packages at home. For academics, accession is a fertile ground for research, which allows digging deep into any of the individual areas of expertise of the accession process itself, or analysing it as a multidisciplinary object from a bird's-eye view. Academics are in a position to approach WTO accessions with a breadth and depth of analysis, and have space to identify not only today's challenges, but also those of tomorrow. Therefore, a regular stocktaking of the literature on accessions is called for to benefit both acceding and incumbent WTO members.

Finally, accessions will reform with the reform of the WTO itself. Perfectly in line with the post-Bali work programme, the academic literature clearly points to the key principles of such reforms: transparency; inclusiveness and preservation of key principles of the multilateral trading system, including non-discrimination; integration of developing economies and LDCs more fully into the multilateral trading system; provision of technical assistance; and the creation of conditions for the acceleration of trade negotiations, including on accessions. All these reforms are vital for WTO members, their growth and development, and the defining test of whether the multilateral system works. Further academic scrutiny of accessions is essential to ensure that the WTO passes this test.

## References

Allee, T. L. and J. E. Scalera (2012). 'The divergent effects of joining international organizations: trade gains and the rigors of WTO accession', *International Organization*, 66(2): 243–276.

Basu, S. R. (2008). 'Does WTO accession affect domestic economic policies and institutions?', Geneva, Graduate Institute for International Studies, HEI Working Paper 03/2008.

Basu, S. R., V. Ognivtsev and M. Shirotori (2009). 'Building trade-relating institutions and WTO accession', Geneva, United Nations Conference on Trade and Development, Policy Issues in International Trade and Commodities Study Series 41.

Bienen, D. and M. Mihretu (2010). 'The principle of fairness and WTO accession: an appraisal and assessment of consequences', London, London School of Economics and Political Science, Society of International Economic Law Working Paper 2010/29.

Cattaneo, O. and C. A. Primo Braga (2009). 'Everything you always wanted to know about WTO accession (but were afraid to ask)', Washington DC, World Bank, Policy Research Working Paper 5116.

Charnovitz, S. (2007). 'Mapping the law of WTO accession', Washington DC, George Washington University, GWU Legal Studies Research Paper 237.

Davis, C. and M. Wilf (2011). 'Joining the Club: Accession to the GATT/WTO', paper presented at the American Political Science Association (APSA) Annual Meeting, Seattle, 24 August.

Drabek, Z. and M. Bacchetta (2004). 'Tracing the effects of WTO accession on policy-making in sovereign states: preliminary lessons from the recent experience of transition countries', World Economy, 27(7): 1083–1125.

Drabek, Z. and W. Woo (2010). 'Who should join the WTO and why? A cost–benefit analysis of WTO membership', in Z. Drabek (ed.), Is the World Trade Organization Attractive Enough for Emerging Economies? New York, Palgrave Macmillan.

Ebrill, L., J. Stotsky and R. Gropp (1999). 'Revenue implications of trade liberalization', Washington DC, International Monetary Fund, IMF Occasional Paper 180.

Evenett, S. and J. Gage (2005). Evaluating WTO Accessions: The Effect of WTO Accession on National Trade Flows. Oxford University Press.

Evenett, S. J. and C. A. Primo Braga (2006). 'WTO accession: moving the goalposts?', in R. Newfarmer (ed.), Trade, Doha, and Development: A Window into the Issues. Washington DC, World Bank.

Ferrantino, M. (2009). 'Policy anchors: do free trade agreements and WTO accessions serve as vehicles for developing-country policy reform?', in Z. Drabek (ed.), Is the World Trade Organization Attractive Enough for Emerging Economies? New York, Palgrave Macmillan.

Goldstein, J., M. Tomz and M. Rivers (2007). 'Do we really know that the WTO increases trade?' American Economic Review, 97(5): 2005–2018.

Javorcik, B. S. and G. Narciso (2013). 'Accession to the World Trade Organization and tariff evasion', London, Centre for Economic Policy Research, CEPR Discussion Paper 9592.

Jones, K. (2009). 'The political economy of WTO accession: the unfinished business of universal membership', World Trade Review, 18: 279–314.

Jones, K. and Y. Gai (2013). 'Joining the WTO: Why does it take so long?', *Open Economies Review*, 24(4): 695–716.

Kavass, I. (2007). 'WTO accession: procedure, requirements and costs', *Journal of World Trade*, 41: 453–474.

Lacey, S. (2007). 'WTO accession from the perspective of WTO members: the view from the other side of the table', in J. Streatfield and S. Lacey (eds.), *New Reflections on International Trade: Essays on Agriculture, WTO Accession and Systemic Issues*. London, Cameron May.

Laird, S. (2009). 'Cost of implementation of WTO agreements', in Z. Drabek (ed.), *Is the World Trade Organization Attractive Enough for Emerging Economies?* New York, Palgrave Macmillan.

Li, D. D. and C. C. Wu (2004). 'GATT/WTO accession and productivity', in T. Itō and A. K. Rose (eds.), *Growth and Productivity in East Asia*, vol. 13. NBER–East Asia Seminar on Economics, University of Chicago Press.

Maggi, G. and A. Rodriguez-Clare (1998). 'The value of trade agreements in the presence of political pressures', *Journal of Political Economy*, 106(3): 574–601.

Milthorp, P. (2009). 'WTO accessions: the story so far', *The Hague Journal of Diplomacy*, 4: 103–112.

Neumayer, E. (2013). 'Strategic delaying and concessions extraction in accession negotiations to the World Trade Organization: an analysis of working party membership', *World Trade Review*, 12(4): 669–692.

Osakwe, C. (2011). 'Developing countries and GATT/WTO rules: dynamic transformations in trade policy behavior and performance', *Minnesota Journal of International Law*, 20(2): 365–436.

Parenti, A. (2000). 'Accession to the World Trade Organization: a legal analysis', *Legal Issues of Economic Integration*, 27(2): 141–157.

Pelc, K. J. (2011). 'Why do some countries get better WTO accession terms than others?', *International Organization*, 65(4): 639–672.

Primo Braga, C. A. and O. Cattaneo (eds.) (2009). *The WTO and Accession Countries*. Cheltenham, Edward Elgar.

Qin, J. (2015). 'The conundrum of WTO Accession Protocols: in search of legality and legitimacy', *Virginia Journal of International Law*. In press.

Rose, A. (2005). 'Which international institutions promote international trade?' *Review of International Economics*, 13(4): 682–698.

Schneider, C. and J. Urpelainen (2012). 'Accession rules for international institutions: a legitimacy-efficacy trade-off?', *Journal of Conflict Resolution*, 56(2): 290–312.

Subramanian, A. and S.-J. Wei (2007). 'The WTO promotes trade, strongly but unevenly', *Journal of International Economics*, 72(1): 151–175.

Tang, M.-K. and S.-J. Wei (2009). 'The value of making commitments externally: evidence from WTO accessions', *Journal of International Economics*, 78(2): 216–229.

Williams, P. J. (2008). *A Handbook on Accession to the WTO*. Cambridge University Press.

Wong, K.-F. and M. Yu (2008). 'Democracy and the GATT/WTO accession duration', retrieved from http://ssrn.com/abstract=982032.

# PART II

## Overview: systemic outcomes from accessions

# 9

# Contributions and lessons from WTO accessions: the present and future of the rules-based multilateral trading system

CHIEDU OSAKWE

## ABSTRACT

*WTO accession still holds a magnetic attraction for non-members. Why is this so, in spite of the challenges faced by the organisation, conclusions by analysts of deadlock in the Doha Development Agenda, assessments that trade policy action has shifted elsewhere to preferential trade arrangements (bilateral and regional trade agreements, including more recently, 'mega-regionals') and repeated forecasts about the WTO's 'irrelevance' and 'unravelling'? Systemically, what have WTO accessions contributed to the rules-based trading system through their processes, procedures, best practices and results? What effects have accession negotiations had on domestic reforms in Article XII members? Are there broader lessons for the WTO? This chapter demonstrates that, after the coming into force of the WTO in 1995, results from WTO accession negotiations served to update trade rules continuously (including influencing WTO jurisprudence), enlarged market access opportunities, provided acceding governments with a critical multilateral instrument for legislation-based domestic reforms, and supported geopolitical and geo-economic transformations from centrally planned to market-based economies, the rule of law and good governance. The changes associated with these results were evident from the 1989 fall of the Berlin Wall and the 1991 collapse of the Soviet Union. The evidence strongly suggests that the accession process and its results have established a legal framework for international cooperation, contributed to the global economic*

The analyses in the chapters in this book were finalised at the end of December 2014. Since then the Republic of Seychelles acceded to the World Trade Organization (WTO) on 26 April 2015. This expanded total WTO membership from 160 to 161. Please see the editors' note.

*transformation of command to market economies and provided a plat-form for Article XII members to implement their development and modernisation priorities. Overall, the legal, economic and trade policy impact from the deposited Accession Protocols and the process of acces-sion negotiations* per se *have not only reinforced existing rules and raised the systemic bar, with associated catalytic effect for domestic reforms, but have also staked out the parameters for the future of the rules-based trading system, including a future WTO work programme.*

The rules governing the multilateral trading system were last updated comprehensively in 1994 with the results from the Uruguay Round of Multilateral Trade Negotiations. In 2001, the Doha Round was launched based on the rationale of achieving a further clarification, review, reform and update of the rules from previous multilateral trade negotiations and expanding market access to support global economic growth and recovery.[1] From 2005, a systemic message stressed in WTO *argumentaires* was that concluding the Doha Round negotiations would serve to 'update' organ-isational rules (Supachai[2] and Lamy,[3] 2005; Azevêdo, 2013[4]). Since the failure of the 2008 WTO Mini-Ministerial Meeting to narrow the gaps and establish the basis for concluding the Doha Round negotiations, pursuant to the principle of a single undertaking,[5] questions have been raised in the trade policy community on the future of the rules-based multilateral trading system. Specifically, these questions have revolved around the reputation of the WTO as a serious forum for market access

---

[1] Doha Ministerial Declaration adopted at MC4, 14 November 2001.

[2] Speeches by former WTO Director-General Supachai Panitchpakdi retrieved at www.wto.org/english/news_e/spsp_e/spsp_e.htm.

[3] Speeches by former WTO Director-General Pascal Lamy retrieved at www.wto.org/english/news_e/sppl_e/sppl_e.htm.

[4] Speeches by current WTO Director-General Roberto Azevêdo retrieved at www.wto.org/english/thewto_e/dg_e/dg_e.htm.

[5] In this chapter, the concept of the 'single undertaking' is used in two different ways: the 'Political Single Undertaking' in General Agreement on Tariffs and Trade (GATT)/WTO negotiations, on the one hand, is distinguished from the 'Legal Single Undertaking', on the other hand. The former refers to the practice in negotiations according to which negoti-ations are not completed until every aspect of the mandated negotiations are completed, whereas the latter refers to the jurisprudential conclusion that all provisions of the WTO are cumulative and simultaneously applicable; a non-static concept that may include different rights and obligations for different members. Appreciation is expressed to Gabrielle Marceau, Senior Counsellor in the WTO Legal Affairs Division for clarifying this distinction (Marceau, 2002; Marceau and Trachtman, 2014; and e-mail exchange on 27 August 2014).

expansion, its capacity for rule-making and regulating the commercial transactions of its members. Questions have been asked about the credibility and the relevance of the WTO.

Some positions have been ominous. There have been suggestions about the long-term drift and decline of the WTO. In this context, some scholars have pointed to the danger in the erosion of 'WTO-centricity' (Baldwin 2008; 2013). In 2013, while the success of the Ninth WTO Ministerial Conference in Bali, Indonesia, was acknowledged, it was argued that the conference had only provided breathing space and respite to reflect on the future of the WTO for the 'exploration of options for the renovation of the multilateral trading system over the longer term'. The negotiating authority of the WTO had to be 're-asserted' (Harbinson, 2013). This argument suggested either a lost or surrendered primacy. Even with account taken of the WTO Bali Ministerial, it was also argued that the WTO would remain on the 'back burner' for a while because governments had invested most of their energy in a slew of preferential trade agreements (PTAs) (Harbinson, 2013). It was affirmed that efforts at liberalising and negotiating new rules had shifted; action had increasingly moved elsewhere (Hoekman, 2014). On the associated question of a WTO work programme, some noted that it was not clear that much thinking had been undertaken by WTO members on this subject before the Bali Ministerial Conference (Evenett and Jara, 2013).

Since Bali, although there have been delays, progress has been registered. On 27 November 2014, the General Council of the WTO adopted the Protocol Amending the Marrakesh Agreement so as to insert the Trade Facilitation Agreement into Annex 1A of the WTO Agreement.[6] The adopted Decision also opened the Protocol for acceptance. Although the adoption of the Protocol was significant, several of the critics maintain their positions and have not been quieted.

The argued positions of the critics are only correct in part. The canvas is broader and the painting, however, requires completion. For instance, as argued by WTO Director-General Roberto Azevêdo, although there has been a lot of talk about regional and bilateral agreements, and these were initiatives to be welcomed, the multilateral trading system has never been the only option for international trade negotiations. The trading system had always co-existed with and benefited from other initiatives,

---

[6] See WTO document WT/PCTF/W/28.

bilateral or regional, which had never been mutually exclusive alternatives (Azevêdo, 2014).

The rules-based multilateral trading system has never been monolithic. It has always acknowledged and accommodated variable trading arrangements in support of trade opening. Article XXIV of the GATT 1994 and Article II.3 of the Marrakesh Agreement Establishing the World Trade Organization (WTO Agreement) were drafted to provide such legal accommodation for a variable geometry. This co-existence has accounted for demonstrable progress. In the WTO, it has been manifested in multilateral negotiations in the regular work of the WTO, with substantial and positive systemic results, as opposed to multilateral negotiations in launched trade rounds, such as in the Doha Development Agenda negotiations.

Although WTO rules had been last updated, comprehensively, in 1994, in the GATT, with the results from the Uruguay Round of Multilateral Trade Negotiations, updates to the rules continued through multilateral and plurilateral negotiations in the regular work of the WTO. In 1996, the Plurilateral Information Technology Agreement (ITA) was concluded and came into effect. ITA expansion is a work in progress. In 1997, the Multilateral Agreement on Basic Telecommunications and the Financial Services Agreement were concluded and came into effect. In 2005, the WTO amended the Trade-Related Aspects of Intellectual Property Rights (TRIPs) Agreement through multilateral decision-making. In April 2014, the Protocol Amending the Agreement on Government Procurement (GPA) entered into force.

Beyond these sector-specific agreements, multilateral negotiations have been non-stop in the WTO since 1995, pursuant to Article XII of the WTO Agreement. These have resulted in thirty-three Accession Protocols, so far. Accession Protocols are international treaty obligations deposited with the WTO. They form part of the WTO Legal Single Undertaking. The negotiating process *per se* and the resulting Accession Protocols have had wide-ranging systemic multilateral and domestic effects. Specifically, they have updated multilateral trade rules; liberalised trade with consequent new trade opportunities; provided acceding governments with a critical instrument for domestic reforms; and fostered broader international cooperation with evident contributions to global economic transformations following the 1989 fall of the Berlin Wall and the 1991 collapse of the Soviet Union. In the range of its effects, as will be demonstrated in this chapter, the four areas of impact from WTO accessions complement and several areas exceed the negotiating agenda and envisaged impact from alternative PTA negotiating scenarios under way, including in the mega-PTAs.

## Accession mandate

For non-original members of the WTO, accession is based on mandated negotiations, pursuant to Article XII of the WTO Agreement, which provides that:

1 Any State or separate customs territory possessing full autonomy in the conduct of its external commercial relations and of the other matters provided for in this Agreement and the Multilateral Trade Agreements may accede to this Agreement on terms to be agreed between it and the WTO. Such accession shall apply to this Agreement and the Multilateral Trade Agreements annexed thereto.

2 Decisions on accession shall be taken by the Ministerial Conference. The Ministerial Conference shall approve the agreement on the terms of accession by a two-thirds majority of the Members of the WTO.

3 Accession to a Plurilateral Trade Agreement shall be governed by the provisions of that Agreement.

The terms and conditions for new members of the WTO have been neither formulaic nor identical; nor are they expected to be. Even original members of the WTO do not have identical terms and conditions of membership. It bears emphasising that, although all WTO members are subject to the same principles, rules and disciplines, specific terms and conditions vary for individual membership. Among other things, the variations reflect tariff concessions and commitments in goods schedules and specific commitments in services schedules with appropriate most-favoured-nation (MFN) exemptions on the latter.

Hence, the same governing mandate, negotiating guidelines for least-developed countries (LDCs)[7] and accumulated practices from WTO accessions have yielded a range of accession-specific commitments. It is argued that, taken together, the pattern of commitments has served to safeguard, reinforce and advance the rules-based multilateral trading system.

This chapter is divided as follows. The first section covers: (i) systemic impact and the effects of rules and influence on jurisprudence; (ii) domestic

---

[7] Negotiating guidelines were agreed by the WTO in 2002 (WTO document WT/L/508 of 10 December 2002) for LDCs and reinforced on 25 July 2012 in Addendum 1 by the General Council. The purpose of these guidelines is to facilitate LDC accessions and not to modify WTO rules and disciplines.

reforms beyond the systemic impact; and (iii) systemic impact related to market access. The next section discusses the 'nature of the beast' – accession negotiations and global order, managing complexity and best practices. This is followed by a discussion on accession-specific best practices and organising to cope with complexity, followed by a conclusion.

## Systemic impact of WTO accessions – beyond the trading system

Pursuant to Article XII of the WTO Agreement, thirty-three governments have negotiated WTO membership since 1995. Of these, thirty-two are (sovereign) countries[8] and one is a separate customs territory.[9] These members[10] currently account for 20 per cent of WTO membership, underlining the systemic significance of their specific obligations and the overall impact from WTO accessions. The uniqueness of WTO accession negotiations and results are that they link the specific obligations of Article XII members to WTO rules, market access, domestic reforms and broader international cooperation. The results from WTO accessions have been wide-ranging with significant systemic effects, as represented in Figure 9.1.

Results in these areas have clarified, reinforced and extended multilateral rules in several respects, expanded market access opportunities, provided an instrument to acceding governments for sustained long-term, legislation-based domestic reforms, and contributed to stabilising, to a large extent, global economic transformation, and to a legal framework for international cooperation among members in their trade relations.

### *Systemic impact: rules effects and influence on jurisprudence*

Article XII members are bound by the rules and disciplines that existed at the coming into force of the WTO in 1995. These are the 'WTO Agreement', the Ministerial Declarations and Decisions, and the Understanding on Commitments in Financial Services, which together embody the legal results – final act – of the Uruguay Round negotiations.

---

[8]  Albania; Republic of Armenia; Bulgaria; Cambodia; Cabo Verde; China; Croatia; Ecuador; Estonia; the former Yugoslav Republic of Macedonia; Georgia; Jordan; Kyrgyz Republic; Lao PDR; Latvia; Lithuania; Moldova; Mongolia; Montenegro; Nepal; Oman; Panama; Russia; Samoa; Saudi Arabia; Seychelles; Tajikistan; Tonga; Ukraine; Vanuatu; Viet Nam; and Yemen.

[9]  Chinese Taipei.       [10]  These 'members' are referred to as 'Article XII members'.

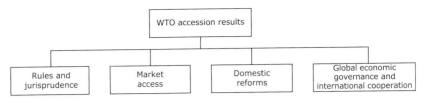

**Figure 9.1**   Systemic impact of WTO accessions – beyond the trading system.

Article XII members are also bound by the negotiated terms and conditions of their WTO membership, as embodied in the accession-specific obligations they accepted. These 'specific commitments' are to be read in conjunction with the WTO Agreement; hence, the Legal Single Undertaking. On multilateral rules, thirty-three Article XII members accepted such accession-specific commitments; these latter total 1,361, of which 175 by seven LDCs (see Annex 9.1 of this chapter).

There are several distinguishing features of accession-specific obligations in relationship to the GATT/WTO accession architecture that should be highlighted. First, these specific commitments range across thirty-six core sub-sections of the accession working party reports of Article XII members, where accession-specific obligations have been accepted.[11] Second, the pattern of commitments demonstrates direct relationships with the rules and disciplines of the WTO. Third, specific commitments have either reconfirmed existing rules, clarified or made them more precise and, in specific instances, 'enhanced' the rules through WTO plus commitments. Fourth, in part, the uniqueness of the specific obligations by Article XII members, codified in their terms and conditions of membership, is reflected in the formal linkage between the treaty dialogue in accession working party reports, the specific obligations also in working party reports, and the tariff concessions and commitments in goods schedules and specific commitments in services schedules. These are tightly interwoven. They are formally listed and codified in paragraph 2 of the standard WTO Protocol of Accession. The organic unity of the WTO Accession Package is unique *per se*. Fifth, even more, in negotiating accession-specific obligations, members had in mind 'gaps and loopholes', ambiguities, including those formulated constructively, including in the terms and conditions of original members, because more precise formulation would have made acceptance impossible at the time of the

---

[11]  Seven additional necessary, but non-core standard areas, are nevertheless reflected in the frequency chart (see Figure 9.2).

negotiations. The correction of these ambiguities in the original rules is evident in the question and answer (Q&A) dialogue in working party reports (the methodology for accession treaty-making). Members sought to close these through greater precision and shutting the interstices in the system. Finally, the architecture of the WTO Accession Package, built on the standard Accession Protocol from 1947, was further strengthened. The 1947 Accession Protocol baseline was extended and modernised. The application of this process in the practices of WTO accession for post-1995 acceding governments culminated in the organic unity of the terms and conditions of their membership Accession Package, which had never been applied to any original member. It should be underlined that the treaty dialogue and the background negotiating history of these accession-specific obligations are indispensable in seeking to determine the intentions of members and the directions they pursued as they sought to strengthen the rules, disciplines and template of the WTO, via negotiations with Article XII members. This is why, among other things, the results from WTO accessions have served to renew the organisation.

Taken together, accession-specific commitments and references to them in WTO dispute settlement proceedings have combined to elaborate GATT/WTO rules and disciplines. They have reinforced and safeguarded the rules-based multilateral trading system through deeper and clarified/clearer commitments.

Accession-specific obligations reveal the frequency of areas of the foreign trade regime of repeated priority importance for members, across the thirty-three completed accessions. (Figure 9.2 and Annex 9.2 are illustrative.)

The substantive core of accession-specific obligations, integral to the WTO Agreement, is summarised, in the main, in the results grid of Annex 9.1. There are nuances and specificities which are only captured and fully understood by a word-for-word reading of the 1,361 specific obligations. For example, in the thirty-three Accession Protocols so far, on the critically commercially vital topic of 'requirements on undisclosed information, including trade secrets and test data' (typically ranging across the areas of intellectual property rights protection, import licensing and publication of information on trade), although there is a Q&A dialogue between members and the thirty-three acceding governments in the working party reports, only in five[12] did binding and enforceable

---

[12] See Bulgaria: Working Party Report, para. 84; Chinese Taipei: Working Party Report, para. 199; Ukraine: Working Party Report, para. 432; Vanuatu: Working Party Report, paras. 116 and 121; and Russia: Working Party Report, paras. 1294 and 1295.

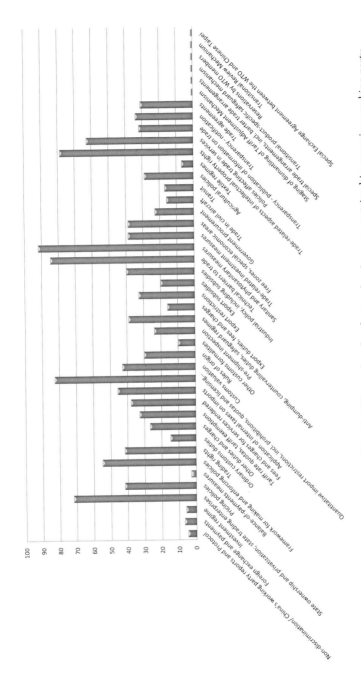

**Figure 9.2** Frequency of commitments of Article XII members by chapters/sections, as contained in accession working party reports and Accession Protocols (see Annex 9.2).

obligations result. Taking account of this caveat, the accessions results grid summary in Table 9.1, spells out how the results on the rules aspect from thirty-three accessions have not only consolidated the principles, rules and disciplines as they came into effect in 1995, but have also gone beyond to significantly advance them, through clarification, greater precision and extension.

### Domestic reforms: beyond systemic impacts

Although accession results have been hugely and uniformly positive for Article XII members, the rules-based multilateral trading system and broader international cooperation, it is challenging and complex. The explanation, in part, for this unique complexity is based on the fact that it is directly linked to a legislation-based process of WTO-consistent domestic reforms. Hence, acceding governments are obliged, in the negotiations, to enact accession-specific obligations in legislation and associated implementing regulations (government 'circulars') before they can accede, or in some cases, within duly negotiated transition periods. The scale of these laws enacted and associated implementing regulation are shown in Table 9.1. The number of legal and regulatory changes involved in the Accession Protocols of China and Russia are illustrative.

These laws and regulations have involved fundamental adjustments in the legal and regulatory framework of acceding governments. They approximate trade and economic regime change, particularly, for the economies that have made the transition from central economic planning to the market economy based on the rule of law, transparency and good governance. One obvious result, from a legal and regulatory basis, is that Article XII members accede, ready to implement their obligations and exercise the rights of membership from day one. Their membership has been on a more secure legal and regulatory foundation than for the vast majority of original members. This has been reflected in the regular operational functioning of the WTO. Accompanying the substantive process of the legal and regulatory changes are the changes that are made to the 'soft infrastructure' and adaption to new processes and ways in the conduct and management of trade policy. For instance, bills (draft laws) and regulations have to be provided in one of the official WTO languages, regardless of the official domestic language. Members comment on drafts and request adjustments for WTO-consistency. Progress in the negotiations is halted if the changes are not made. Internet trade portals

Table 9.1 *Accession-related laws and regulations by Article XII members*

| Article XII member | Date of membership | Legislative/ regulatory quantum |
|---|---|---|
| 1 Ecuador | 21 January 1996 | 70 |
| 2 Bulgaria | 1 December 1996 | 26 |
| 3 Mongolia | 29 January 1997 | 33 |
| 4 Panama | 6 September 1997 | 50 |
| 5 Kyrgyz Republic | 20 December 1998 | 155 |
| 6 Latvia | 10 February 1999 | 77 |
| 7 Estonia | 13 November 1999 | 126 |
| 8 Jordan | 11 April 2000 | 55 |
| 9 Georgia | 14 June 2000 | 106 |
| 10 Albania | 8 September 2000 | 107 |
| 11 Oman | 9 November 2000 | 90 |
| 12 Croatia | 30 November 2000 | 135 |
| 13 Lithuania | 31 May 2001 | 137 |
| 14 Moldova, Republic of | 26 July 2001 | 174 |
| 15 China | 11 December 2001 | 2,300 |
| 16 Chinese Taipei | 1 January 2002 | 167 |
| 17 Armenia, Republic of | 5 February 2003 | 112 |
| 18 The former Yugoslav Republic of Macedonia | 4 April 2003 | 133 |
| 19 Nepal | 23 April 2004 | 47 |
| 20 Cambodia | 13 October 2004 | 85 |
| 21 Saudi Arabia, Kingdom of | 11 December 2005 | 205 |
| 22 Viet Nam | 11 January 2007 | 139 |
| 23 Tonga | 27 July 2007 | 84 |
| 24 Ukraine | 16 May 2008 | 449 |
| 25 Cabo Verde | 23 July 2008 | 84 |
| 26 Montenegro | 29 April 2012 | 133 |
| 27 Samoa | 10 May 2012 | 111 |
| 28 Russian Federation | 22 August 2012 | 1166 |
| 29 Vanuatu | 24 August 2012 | 170 |
| 30 Lao People's Democratic Republic | 2 February 2013 | 170 |
| 31 Tajikistan | 2 March 2013 | 141 |
| 32 Yemen | 26 June 2014 | 69 |

are required to be established by national governments for greater ease of the international community in tracking changes in trade policy, monitoring and providing comments. These have to be understood not as difficulties or barriers to WTO accession, but changes for improved domestic economic coordination within governments, modernisation and trade integration in the new global economy, defined by global value chains.

### Systemic impact: market access

A long-standing accession maxim states that, 'at the heart of any agreement that truly qualifies as a trade agreement *qua* trade agreement, is a schedule or schedules, containing tariff concessions and/or specific commitments'; otherwise the so-called trade agreement is rhetoric. In reality, trade agreements do not exist without schedules.

After twenty years of market access negotiations, in the thirty-three deposited Accession Protocols, 504 bilateral market access agreements on goods and 244 bilateral market access agreements on services have been negotiated, signed and deposited with the WTO Director-General *ex officio*.[13] These agreements were consolidated into Schedules of Tariff Concessions and Commitments on Goods and Specific Commitments on Trade in Services, annexed to the Accession Protocols of the acceding governments and applied on an MFN basis to virtually all WTO members. Consolidated draft schedules become the final market access 'offers' by acceding governments.

Accession-related market access outcomes underline several facts which have accumulated and become self-evident since the coming into force of the WTO in 1995. Real market access openings and improved opportunities (at the border and behind the border, the latter through significant reductions in regulatory non-tariff barriers) have been largely a consequence of accession-negotiated outcomes. First, binding tariff concessions and commitments were made on virtually all agricultural and non-agricultural merchandise, hence improving certainty and predictability, while for original members only 75 per cent of those products were 'bound'. Second, the average final bound rate level (13.8 per cent) is significantly more liberal than the corresponding average level of the final bound rate of original members (45.5 per cent). Third, since 1995, the nominal trade growth performance of the thirty-three Article XII

---

[13] Register for Bilateral Market Access Agreements (WTO Secretariat).

members has been consistently and substantially stronger than that of original members; the average yearly growth rate of their commerce for the period from 1995 to 2013 was 12.4 per cent, almost double that of original members (6.7 per cent). This resulted in the increase of Article XII members' share of world trade from 7.8 per cent in 1995 to 17.6 per cent in 2013. Fourth, the reach of the rules-based multilateral trading system has been expanded to 98 per cent of world trade in 2014, from 90.9 per cent in 1995. Fifth, beyond market access, headnotes in specific schedules of Article XII members have pointed the direction, if not clarified and reinforced 'market rules' in such areas as initial negotiating rights (INRs), geographical indications (GIs), tariff rate quotas (TRQs) and the use of parity language. Finally, as described in the largely prosaic chapters on trade in services, there have been significant reductions in regulatory barriers reflected in specific commitments in services schedules, including commitments in the area of domestic regulations, an area where the WTO membership is yet to advance, concretely. Table 9.2 indicates significant coverage in the number of services sectors and sub-sectors where Article XII members have undertaken specific commitments.

## Agriculture

Agriculture has always had a special place and mention in GATT/WTO negotiations. The results from accession negotiations go further than what original members registered in 1995 and what remains unachieved in the Doha Round and previous rounds of negotiations. For the thirty-three Article XII members,[14] accession-specific obligations in domestic support for agriculture and export subsidies show the following:

- accession-specific commitments with respect to trade-distorting support – agriculture measurements of support (AMS) – are neither left indeterminate, nor unbound:
- twenty, including Seychelles (the most recent) out of thirty-three Article XII members have a zero or 'nil' total AMS commitment, which requires them to keep their annual AMS category support within *de minimis*;
- the remaining thirteen Article XII members have a precise monetary limit (final bound AMS) inscribed in their Goods Schedules, along with established 'base period' data.

---

[14]  See Annex 9.4 to this chapter.

Table 9.2 *Summary of thirty-two Article XII accession market access outcomes*

|  |  | Final bound rates (goods) (%) | | | Services |
|---|---|---|---|---|---|
|  | Binding coverage | All products | Agricultural | Non-agricultural |  |
| Original members | 74% | 45.5 | 65.4 | 34.0 |  |
| Article XII members | 99.9% | 13.8 | 20.1 | 12.9 |  |

|  |  |  |  | Goods-average final bound rate | | | |
|---|---|---|---|---|---|---|---|
| Number | Member | Date of membership | Binding coverage | All products | Agricultural products | Non-agricultural products | Number of services sub-sectors |
| 1 | Albania | 8 September 2000 | 100 | 7.0 | 9.5 | 6.6 | 108 |
| 2 | Armenia, Republic of | 5 February 2003 | 100 | 8.5 | 14.7 | 7.6 | 106 |
| 3 | Bulgaria | 1 December 1996 | 100 | 24.5 | 35.6 | 23.0 | 80 |
| 4 | Cambodia[a] | 13 October 2004 | 100 | 19.1 | 28.0 | 17.7 | 94 |
| 5 | Cabo Verde[a] | 23 July 2008 | 100.0 | 15.8 | 19.3 | 15.2 | 103 |
| 6 | China | 11 December 2001 | 100 | 10.0 | 15.7 | 9.2 | 93 |
| 7 | Chinese Taipei | 1 January 2002 | 100 | 6.3 | 16.9 | 4.7 | 119 |
| 8 | Croatia | 30 November 2000 | 100 | 6.1 | 10.4 | 5.5 | 127 |
| 9 | Ecuador | 21 January 1996 | 100 | 21.7 | 25.7 | 21.2 | 66 |
| 10 | Estonia | 13 November 1999 | 100 | 8.6 | 17.5 | 7.3 | 103 |
| 11 | The former Yugoslav Republic of Macedonia | 4 April 2003 | 100 | 7.1 | 12.9 | 6.3 | 116 |

| | | | | | | |
|---|---|---|---|---|---|---|
| 12 | Georgia | 14 June 2000 | 100 | 7.4 | 13.0 | 6.5 | 125 |
| 13 | Jordan | 11 April 2000 | 100 | 16.3 | 23.6 | 15.2 | 110 |
| 14 | Kyrgyz Republic | 20 December 1998 | 100 | 7.5 | 12.8 | 6.7 | 136 |
| 15 | Lao People's Democratic Republic[a] | 2 February 2013 | 100 | 18.8 | 19.3 | 18.7 | 79 |
| 16 | Latvia | 10 February 1999 | 100 | 12.7 | 34.6 | 9.4 | 121 |
| 17 | Lithuania | 31 May 2001 | 100 | 9.3 | 15.2 | 8.4 | 110 |
| 18 | Moldova, Republic of | 26 July 2001 | 100 | 7.0 | 14.0 | 5.9 | 147 |
| 19 | Mongolia | 29 January 1997 | 100 | 17.5 | 18.9 | 17.3 | 37 |
| 20 | Montenegro | 29 April 2012 | 100 | 5.1 | 10.8 | 4.3 | 132 |
| 21 | Nepal[a] | 23 April 2004 | 99.4 | 26.0 | 41.4 | 23.7 | 77 |
| 22 | Oman | 9 November 2000 | 100 | 13.7 | 27.6 | 11.6 | 97 |
| 23 | Panama | 6 September 1997 | 100 | 23.4 | 27.6 | 22.7 | 70 |
| 24 | Russian Federation | 22 August 2012 | 100 | 7.8 | 10.8 | 7.3 | 122 |
| 25 | Samoa[a] | 10 May 2012 | 100 | 21.1 | 25.8 | 20.4 | 80 |
| 26 | Saudi Arabia, Kingdom of | 11 December 2005 | 100 | 11.1 | 15.4 | 10.5 | 120 |
| 27 | Tajikistan | 2 March 2013 | 100 | 8.0 | 10.4 | 7.6 | 111 |
| 28 | Tonga | 27 July 2007 | 100.0 | 17.6 | 19.2 | 17.3 | 90 |
| 29 | Ukraine | 16 May 2008 | 100 | 5.8 | 11.0 | 5.0 | 137 |
| 30 | Vanuatu[a] | 24 August 2012 | 100 | 39.7 | 43.6 | 39.1 | 69 |
| 31 | Viet Nam | 11 January 2007 | 100 | 11.4 | 18.5 | 10.4 | 105 |
| 32 | Yemen[a] | 26 June 2014 | 100 | 21.1 | 24.9 | 20.5 | 78 |

*Note:* [a]Members which acceded as LDCs.

233

- Final total AMS, as elaborated in agriculture supporting tables, are bound in Part IV of the Goods Schedules.
- Final bound total AMS in the thirty-three Goods Schedules, annexed to the Accession Protocols, have never exceeded 10 per cent of the value of production in the base years.
- *De minimis* allocation has never exceeded 10 per cent for developing economies and LDCs; and 5 per cent for the twelve that acceded as developed (Albania, Bulgaria, Chinese Taipei, Croatia, Estonia, the former Yugoslav Republic of Macedonia, Georgia, Kyrgyz Republic, Lithuania, Moldova, Montenegro and Russia).
- Export subsidies have been bound at zero for all thirty-three, with the exception of Bulgaria that later, after WTO accession, acceded to the European Union.

Agriculture in accession negotiations is an area where the Secretariat has had a firm understanding of the drive by the membership. Agriculture plurilaterals are chaired by the Secretariat. It is useful to highlight relevant aspects of accession treaty dialogue and associated practices that have been evident in agriculture plurilaterals.[15]

First, negotiations have been strictly within the framework (rules and disciplines) of the Agreement on Agriculture. Second, the results so far have reflected an undiminished commitment to the market reform process in agriculture. Third, the practice, reflected in Accession Proto-cols, has ensured 'specific binding and enforceable commitments' (in market access, domestic support and export competition). Fourth, Article XII members were (and acceding governments are being) steered away from non-product-specific support (DS9) to 'green box'-type (DS1) support, although this has to be demonstrated and neither asserted nor taken as a given. Fifth, regardless of the accommodation provided by members in a working party, notification and updates, including in agriculture supporting tables, are immutable requirements. Finally, although food security programmes have been reflected and accommodated in agriculture supporting tables, they are required to be scheduled with clarity on crop specificity, and accession working party reports reflect treaty dialogue on the conditions for the release of public stock-holdings for food security purposes. Blank cheques are not provided.

---

[15] The author chaired agriculture plurilaterals in the accession negotiations of Lao PDR, Russia, Samoa and Seychelles and plurilaterals in ongoing accessions.

## The 'nature of the beast' – accession negotiations and global order: managing complexity and best practices

In retrospect, after twenty years, it is evident that 'original' membership of the WTO was relatively easy. In 1994, to become an original member of the WTO on 1 January 1995, a country or a separate customs territory was required to agree or sign up to the results of the Uruguay Round of multilateral trade negotiations, i.e. the WTO Agreement, and submit, for 'technical verification', draft schedules of tariff concessions and commitments on goods and specific commitments for trade in services, that were, for the most part, not negotiated.

Membership of the GATT 1947, prior to WTO membership in 1995, was easier still, pursuant to GATT 1947 Article XXXIII and XXVI:5(c). GATT membership could be secured through successorship, sponsorship and/or grandfathering (Osakwe, 2011). Members under the GATT/WTO enjoyed the ease and privilege of original membership. Two interrelated questions have been frequently asked and repeated. The first one is whether original membership should have been so lenient and non-rigorous, in a rules-based multilateral trading system, with a negotiation-driven reform rationale[16] and a Dispute Settlement Understanding with enforceable conclusions, post-1995. Conversely, the other question, asked by non-original members, post-1995 (Article XII members), has been why their applications for membership could not have been automatically accepted without the long-drawn-out years of accession negotiations and painful WTO-consistent adjustments required prior to WTO *de jure* membership status. These questions are now largely academic, leaving aside the merits of the questions.

Post-1995, states and separate customs territories have negotiated the terms and conditions of their membership with incumbent members, pursuant to Article XII of the WTO Agreement.

The WTO accession process, post-1995 and pursuant to Article XII of the WTO Agreement, is unique, complex, challenging and plagued with sensitivities. Why is this so? It is unique when compared to the accession procedures of comparable international organisations such as the United Nations, the World Bank, the International Monetary Fund (IMF) and the Organisation for Economic Co-operation and Development (OECD).

---

[16] The WTO was created to provide a common institutional framework for the conduct of trade relations among its members (WTO Agreement Article II.1) and a permanent forum for 'negotiations' (WTO Agreement, Article III.2).

European Union enlargement procedures and negotiations are probably closest, but even the European Union requires candidate countries in its enlargement process to first accede to the WTO before proceeding with EU membership negotiations. This is to avoid subsequent questions about the WTO-consistency of the laws, regulations and market access commitments and concessions of its enlargement candidates, if they first acceded to the European Union before WTO membership.

Several factors combine to explain the unique and challenging complexity of WTO membership negotiations. Operationally, by long-standing practice, the negotiations are multi-tracked: they are domestic, bilateral, plurilateral and multilateral. The domestic challenge of the domestic negotiating track turns on several factors. First, leadership in the domestic political economy has to build consensus from the partisanship and sensitivities associated with globalisation: either to be more open, transparent and liberalising, exposing the domestic economy to competition, or to be more closed, 'protecting' state trading enterprises (STEs) and rent-seekers and providing accommodation for import substitution approaches. Second, domestic reforms for WTO membership must be legislation-based, accompanied by establishment of the institutional framework (the soft infrastructure), to support the effective implementation of WTO membership on day one of membership. The intra-governmental negotiations between departments in acceding governments are compounded with the difficulties associated with separation of powers between the executive branches of governments and legislatures. Original members were not required to fulfil these conditions upfront in order to secure membership. The domestic track of negotiations reflects these complexities, the results of which, regardless, must ensure WTO compatibility and, at the same time, respond to the priorities of acceding governments for economic growth, job creation and modernisation. In an ongoing accession, the chief negotiator admitted that 'my toughest negotiations are not with members, but domestic'. This is a frequently repeated assessment in virtually all completed and ongoing accession negotiations. It turns on the fact that accession negotiations are fundamentally about deep and long-term legislation-based domestic reforms that unambiguously commit governments to the market economy, the rule of law, good governance and global economic integration in a global economy increasingly characterised by global value chains.

In the end, however long it takes – currently ten years, on average – the tracks must align, regardless of the shunts, for the train to pull into the end terminal. Substantively, the negotiations reflect a complex mix of legislation-based domestic reforms that must pass the litmus test of WTO consistency; domestic programmes for development and modernisation; domestic debates of the pros and cons of the globalisation debate; and, finally, the twists and turns of geopolitics. Also, as the WTO continues to mature, in time, and the difficulty with further trade liberalisation has become more self-evident, the WTO is considered by its core membership as a global public good to be safeguarded, tightly and fiercely. Membership will be granted only to those that undertake specific binding obligations, and, upon membership, will defend the core values of the WTO. WTO accession negotiations are used as an opportunity in a permanent negotiating forum to push the frontiers of existing rules through clarification, precision and advancement.

With 98 per cent of the global economy covered by WTO rules and hence brought under the Dispute Settlement Understanding of the WTO, although 'universality of membership' remains the WTO's strategic priority, the core membership considers that the work of enlargement is virtually complete with the exception of a few major economies[17] still negotiating the terms and conditions of their membership.

In the take-off and evolution of accession negotiations, the process and substance are heavily influenced by the twists and turns of geopolitics and broader international cooperation. The heavy geopolitical influence in accession negotiations has been most evident in the accession negotiations of the states that emerged from the 1991 collapse of the Soviet Union and the associated transformations to achieve a (regional) geopolitical order to substitute the rule of law, good governance and pro-competitive law and regulations of a market economy for the failed command and centrally planned economies of the defunct Soviet Union. The cardinal objective of geopolitical pressures has been positively directed at safeguarding, pursuant to the legal framework of the WTO, the rules, disciplines and core values of the WTO. There are striking examples, and there are those that are less obvious. Among the most striking were the accessions of Ukraine, Russia and Tajikistan.[18] Russia's

---

[17] These include Algeria, Iran and Kazakhstan (the accession negotiations of Kazakhstan and its draft Accession Package, were finalised on 10 June 2015).

[18] The complex geopolitical effects on accession negotiations are being manifested in an unprecedented manner in the accession negotiations of Kazakhstan, because of the crisis in Ukraine, Russia's annexation of Crimea in March 2014 and the conclusion and signing of the EAEU Treaty on 29 May 2014.

accession negotiations were further complicated by its 2008 war with Georgia over South Ossetia and Abkhazia, and the 2010 formation of the Customs Union (CU) of Belarus, Kazakhstan and Russia. The conflict between Russia and Georgia was mediated by Ms Micheline Calmy-Rey, then President of the Swiss Confederation, as a 'side agreement' to the Accession Protocol of Russia. The side agreement established a mechanism for customs administration and monitoring of all trade in goods that entered or exited specific pre-defined trade corridors.[19] The CU of Belarus, Kazakhstan and Russia, like all free trade agreements (FTAs), is in part commercial and economic and, in part, strategic. As recently noted, in the context of references to other plurilateral agreements and argued positions about the fundamental strategic logic of trade, such agreements (FTAs/PTAs/mega-regionals) are as important strategically as they are economically (Froman, 2014). On 29 May, the Eurasian Economic Union (EAEU) Treaty, meant to replace the CU of Belarus, Kazakhstan and Russia, was signed. The EAEU Treaty came into effect on 1 January 2015. It has influenced the ongoing accession negotiations of Kazakhstan in substance and timing and will influence subsequent accessions of other members of the CU that are not yet WTO members and those WTO members, such as Armenia and Kyrgyz Republic, that joined the EAEU. The geopolitical influence associated with the 2010 CU and its transformation into the EAEU in 2014, combined with the 2014 regional crisis in Eurasia, with Ukraine as its epicentre, is the most striking example of the intersection of geopolitics with WTO accession negotiations. There are others at lesser levels of challenge.

On the rise and fall of geopolitical pressures and their influence, more broadly, the question is whether these are unusual, or episodic. As argued by some, in interpreting the Ukraine crisis, neither should the expectation have arisen nor the conclusion been reached that 'old-fashioned

---

[19] Paragraph 210 of the Report of the Working Party on the Accession of Russia, see WTO documents WT/ACC/RUS/70 (WT/MIN(11)/2). The author (as Director of the Accessions Division) was requested by WTO Director-General Pascal Lamy to 'represent' the WTO, 'as witness', at the Green Room signing ceremony of the Side Agreement, on 9 November 2011, between Georgia (represented by Sergi Kapanadze, Deputy Minister of Foreign Affairs; Zurab Tchiaberashvili; and Tamara Kovziridze) and Russia (Ambassador Yury Khromov, Chief Negotiator Maxim Medvedkov and Dmitry Lyakishev) and with the Government of Switzerland as mediator (represented by Peter Maurer, State Secretary of the Swiss Confederation; Ambassador Luzius Wasescha; Ambassador Heidi Grau; and Tobias Privitelli).

geopolitics' would go away; this would amount to a fundamental misreading of history and what the collapse of the Soviet Union has meant; geopolitics have always accompanied international relations (Mead, 2014).[20]

The not-so-obvious examples, which do not appear in the headlines, concerning WTO accession negotiations, are the inter-relationship between the completed accession negotiations of Armenia (now a WTO member) and the accession negotiations of Azerbaijan, which are still in progress. The Communication from Armenia, in the final stage of Armenia's WTO accession negotiations, on the as yet-to-be completed WTO accession of Azerbaijan, is illustrative. In its Communication, the Minister of Foreign Affairs of Armenia 'confirmed', among other things, that:

> [T]he Republic of Armenia will remain committed to its constructive position regarding the expansion of the WTO Membership to the entire South Caucasus region. The Republic of Armenia shall not take any direct or indirect action that would impede or slow down the accession process of the Republic of Azerbaijan to the WTO. The Republic of Armenia undertakes not to block, in the future, the decision making process concerning the accession of the Republic of Azerbaijan to the WTO. These commitments will govern any involvement of the Republic of Armenia in the work relating to the WTO accession process of the Republic of Azerbaijan.[21]

Several uncompleted accessions are subject to considerations of broader international cooperation, notably, the accession of Iran. Its accession negotiations, within the legal framework of the WTO, have enabled a cross-section of the membership and the acceding government of Iran to exchange views and strive for an understanding on a range of questions in their bilateral and regional relationships. Rather than castigate the accession process, what should be welcomed is the legal framework provided by the WTO, as a rules-based multilateral trading system, for managing serious questions of international relations and global order.

In spite of these geopolitical influences, the WTO has coped and managed as shown by the evidence, in part because of an accession best practice of pragmatism. As stated by the WTO Director-General Azevêdo, a major benefit of the WTO is that 'the WTO has provided

---

governments with a legal framework to manage their trade relations and over-heated bilateral relations, pragmatically, within a system of trade law'.[22]

## Best practices
### Rules and practices

It has been frequently alleged that, 'there are no clear rules in the accession process' and, as a consequence, some have judged it to be inherently unfair and unbalanced (Talib, 2014;[23] Medvedkov and Lyakishev, in Chapter 21 of this volume). Others have argued an opposite view that, 'there is no blueprint for accession – and that there should not be' (Pholsena and Vilavong, Chapter 22 of this volume).

Even in a rules-based system, such as the WTO, it is self-evident that the totality of rules and custom cannot be codified. It is patently unrealistic to conclude that rules, and/or guidelines, formally codified, can cover every aspect of accession-negotiating behaviour and practices. Much has been governed by accession-specific practices, from within the framework of the GATT golden age and improvements from some of the more relatively modernised practices of the WTO as an international organisation.

### Negotiating formats

There are repeated questions about opacity versus transparency in WTO accession negotiations. Sensitive negotiations have tended to include those where geopolitical influences exist and pragmatic solutions have to be found to immutable 'red lines' of members and acceding governments. Such consultations must be confidential, so as not to jeopardise or damage the substance of the negotiations by making it impossible for plenipotentiaries to negotiate. Yet the facts also show that the balance between transparency, on the one hand, and restricted information for time-sensitive information, on the other, has been consistently and successfully managed in accession negotiations. The push has been

---

[22] WTO Director-General Roberto Azevêdo, message to the Astana International Conference on 'Kazakhstan's Role in a Globalizing World: Trade and Investments', 4 September 2014.

[23] Press conference, following the Ceremony of the Deposit of the Instrument of Acceptance of the Protocol on the WTO Accession of Yemen, by WTO Director-General Roberto Azevêdo and Dr Saadaldeen Ali Bin Talib, Trade and Industry Minister Yemen, 27 May 2014 (www.wto.org/english/news_e/news14_e/acc_yem_27may14_e.htm).

against the invocation of transparency as a mantra, and the failure to understand that under time-sensitive-specific conditions, full transparency can damage negotiations. As observed by the working party chairperson for the accession of Russia: 'This accession process would not have gotten anywhere if we were resigned to work only in big formal meetings with everyone present. The Secretariat's experience of completed accessions showed that it would not have been conducive to real negotiations'. The challenge is ever-present on the necessity to balance confidentiality on sensitive dimensions of the negotiations, on the one hand, with the equal necessity for systemic transparency and inclusiveness, on the other. This balance has been found in accession negotiations reconciling systemic necessity for transparency and inclusivity, on the one hand, and controlled information flows, on the other.

In reality, the operation of WTO accession shows that although all the rules and practices may not be formally codified, they exist as long-standing custom and accession best practices. These practices have been dynamic, tailored to the peculiarities of different economies and governance systems and adjusted over time. In the end, however, although the accession process is within a multilateral framework, it functions in an intergovernmental setting of sovereign states. There is no formula to apply in a global economy of sovereign states, albeit integrated. Tact, discretion and circumspection, with respect for the 'sovereign' are indispensable, if multilateralism is not to be damaged and fail.

Several long-standing accession best practices are worth re-identification. Although there have been instances of deviation, there has been acceptance of and adherence to these best practices:

- *Standstill trade and no rollback regime*: if you are moving forward, do not engage a reverse gear. Acceding governments set their accession negotiations back by years, if in the course of their negotiations, they take protectionist measures. Rollback measures in the course of an accession process, shunt and delay.
- *Market access negotiations*: it is the right of any WTO member to request bilateral market access negotiations. A range of practices are associated with market access negotiations, which tend to be considered as the heart of accession negotiations. These negotiations are confidential to the bilateral parties. Negotiations are initiated by a 'specific request' formally addressed to the acceding government and copied to the chairman of the working party and the WTO Secretariat. In the practice of accession negotiations, a formula or formulae have

not been used. The negotiations are by tariff line. The format of these negotiations has served the system well in the improvement of market access opportunities and in correcting disguised and explicit trade restrictions to market access and protection for domestic rent-seeking interests and lobbies. In more recent practice, working party chairpersons have set a time-frame and 'called time' on the conclusion of these negotiations. The latter has been in reaction to excesses in the exercise of the right of members to request bilateral market access negotiations and to avoid these negotiations carrying on endlessly. It is also to stop the incidents, albeit few, of any member, at any point in time, regardless of the stage of the accession, requesting bilateral market access negotiations. This 'excess' has caused long delays and in some instances has lent itself to the abuse of this infrangible right of any member to negotiate improvements in market access opportunities.

• *Consolidation and technical verification*: the chairman of the working party mandates the start and conclusion of bilateral market access negotiations. It is also an accession best practice that the right of members to market access negotiations is 'closed' after the Secretariat has consolidated and circulated to all signatory members the results of all the negotiated, concluded and signed bilateral market access agreements with the acceding government, deposited with the Director-General, as depositary. At this stage, no further requests for bilateral market access negotiations can be entertained. The WTO Secretariat undertakes the consolidation.

• *Draft bills and implementing regulations*: trade-relevant draft legislation and associated implementing regulations are subject to review and commentary by members of a working party. This practice has occasionally provoked sensitivity and resentment with some acceding governments which consider this practice as an erosion of sovereignty, in particular sovereign parliamentary autonomy. It has been explained that the 'opportunity' to comment on trade-related and specific draft laws and implementing regulations is a practice that has developed around the rules, such as the GATT 1994 Article X, the General Agreement on Trade in Services (GATS) Article III, the TRIPs Article 63, etc. Many now consider that the more integrated character of the contemporary global economy, reflected, *inter alia*, in global value chains has reinforced the rationale underpinning this best practice.

• *The 'down payment'*: even before the conclusion of bilateral negotiations, member(s) may request 'down payments' on a market access 'tariff concession' or services 'specific commitments', already committed in either a bilateral market access agreement or a consolidated schedule. The examples from the 2008 accession of Cambodia and the ongoing accession of Kazakhstan are illustrative. Why is this so? In part, this is explained as confidence building in situations of degrees of trust deficit; and the need for initial evidence-based confirmation of a binding commitment. In part, also, it relates to obtaining a market access head start by some.

- *Binding*: the principle and practice of binding predates accession negotiations. It is a WTO core value to achieve predictability of laws and regulations and security of market access. It has established the legal and policy framework to 'contain' and 'check' lobbies and pressure groups from distorting negotiated economic and trade policy.

- *Final working party*: the final meeting of the working party on any accession considers and adopts the draft Accession Packages *ad referendum*. The meeting is conducted in a process equivalent to a parliamentary process to enact a law. The draft Accession Package is first considered informally and then formalised, at the same sitting. After the formal adoption of the draft Accession Package *ad referendum*, the working party adjourns indefinitely. Out of thirty-three accessions, only in the case of the accession of Vanuatu was an accession working party reconstituted, with the Secretariat presiding. This was entailed under the specific circumstance in which Vanuatu requested the 'delay to review' its draft Accession Package in 2001 and reverted seven years later requesting adoption. The working party was reconstituted by the Chairman of the General Council, who requested that the Director-General designate a Deputy Director-General[24] to chair the review process. An Accession Package is an international treaty obligation, and is justiciable under public international law.

### Excesses and abuses

Although these have been few, rare and have now virtually disappeared, there have been excesses in accession negotiations, when acceding governments have been placed in very difficult situations, thereby provoking questions about fairness, good order and balance in the rules-based multilateral trading system, its processes and procedures. These situations were evident in the accessions of Montenegro, Lao PDR and

---

[24] Deputy Director-General Alejandro Jara, 2005 to 2013.

Yemen. A range of factors explain the problems. There are the over-zealous negotiators, starting off and seeking to launch careers by demon-strating how 'tough' and good they are to home constituencies. These are the individual negotiators who misunderstand the need for balance between an extra market access concession for a sack of cereal, a kilo of beef or a barrel of wine, on the one hand and, on the other hand, safeguarding and strengthening an irreplaceable global public good. There are also problems of personality clashes, and of the contamination of negotiations by deeply rooted historical conflicts.

To its credit, the system has responded through a combination of approaches. First, there has been the greater application of the time-tested approach of enhanced transparency. The Informal Group on Accessions has more and more systemically shone floodlights on the problems, to clarify issues objectively and seek their resolution, through reiteration of accession best practices. Second, Directors-General *ex officio* have been involved in 'behind-the-stage hard talk' with members involved and acceding governments. Third, the unique creation of the Facilitation Mechanism for the accessions of Lao PDR and Yemen was the first major systemic effort to address and resolve a blockage. Fourth, the mediation and facilitation of the Georgia/Russia bilateral question, supported by the entire membership, was a major and important devel-opment, systemically, but also confirming the neutrality of Switzerland and its universally accepted status and role as an honest broker – this time in the context of WTO accession negotiations. Finally, no less important has been systemic preemption, such as the Facilitation Mech-anism, reflected in the understanding in the Accession Package of Armenia that it would not oppose the accession of another acceding government – that of Azerbaijan.[25]

## Timing

There is a degree of uncertainty regarding the timing for completion of the accession process. There are unforeseeable twists and turns in the dynamics of a domestic-reform process, complicated by the idiosyncra-cies of personalities and the fog of geopolitical changes. Just as econo-mists have had real difficulties in predicting recessions, in the long-run cycle of economic growth and recession, neither chairpersons nor

---

[25]  See WTO document WTO/ACC/ARM/22.

Secretariat officials have been successful in calling accession completion timelines. Gambler's luck is rare in the context of accessions.

## Accession-specific best practice – organising to cope with complexity

Accession negotiations reflect domestic and regional PTAs and geopolitical complexities. At the start, proper organisation at the domestic level is indispensable, if the complexities are to be managed efficiently, expeditiously and rationally, as part of the foreign economic and trade policies of the acceding government. If the negotiating and reporting structures and clear lines of authority are not defined, it is not advisable to initiate negotiations. Because decisions to be taken at every level have far-reaching consequences for the structure, composition and direction of government, the economy and foreign economic policy, and the head of state/government must assume direct responsibility and designate a chief negotiator. The chief negotiator must have a seat in the cabinet, be accorded standing in government, be technically competent and intellectually secure, articulate and with an unmediated line of authority to the head of state/government. Strategically, the chief negotiator should develop a road map for the conduct and management of the negotiations.

Many acceding governments have started 'short', playing with obvious handicaps. For instance, accession negotiations may be initiated without the designation of chief negotiators, or negotiators who are designated without authority. Assigning the jurisdiction for negotiations to trade ministries with no cross-cutting domestic authority for economic planning and foreign policy has hardly ever worked. Foreign trade policy and WTO accession negotiations are much too important to be left to trade departments. The WTO accession negotiation is a legislation-based process of WTO-consistent domestic reforms, entailing all aspects of foreign and domestic policy and the geopolitical priorities and challenges faced by the acceding government. It combines core economic policies and the foreign and trade policies of governments. From the accumulated lessons from the first 20 years of WTO accession negotiations, the organogram 'Organising to cope with accession complexity' (Figure 9.3), is an approximation of how the negotiating teams should be structured.

An appointed chief negotiator, reporting directly to the president or prime minister, should head a team with clear responsibilities. This team should have designated focal points to cover the domestic and multilateral (external) dimensions of the negotiations. Domestically, the

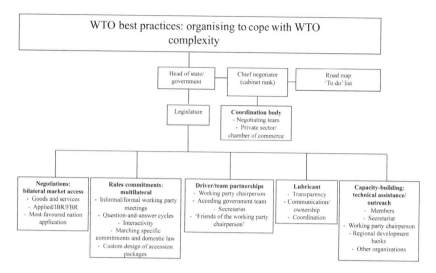

**Figure 9.3**   WTO accession best practice organising to cope with accession complexity (IBR = initial bound rate, FBR = final bound rate).

relationships should primarily be built up with legislators, inter-departmental relations, industry, the private sector and civil society, the latter for domestic buy-in. Externally, broadly, the teams and focal points should be organised to negotiate market access (goods and services); rules, laws and regulations; formation of consultative partnerships to drive the entirety of the accession together with the chairperson of the working party and the international civil servants in the WTO Secretariat and planners for capacity-building and outreach. In the structure, organisation and planning, adjustments should normally be made in the course of the negotiations. Although there are no formulae to apply, and many acceding governments stumble along for many years, it is impossible to stumble or muddle through to conclusion on any accession. The process is so designed that no matter how long it takes, acceding governments are required to get their act together before they join. The exercise is based on law, policy, trade and tariff numbers and specific commitments by the acceding government and it takes as long as it takes. *Ab initio*, structured organisation, based on trained focal points, a clear road map and the direct oversight of the head of state/government, can avoid wasted years.

To achieve rapid economic growth, an agenda for structural reform, mainstreamed into an overall plan for national development, is an indispensable requirement. Enlarged, open and competitive markets, properly regulated, within a system of enforceable multilateral trade rules have contributed hugely to global economic prosperity. WTO accession negotiations have offered a robust and tested rules-based multilateral instrument and agenda for such structural reforms. Although there is scope for improvement, the results from thirty-three completed accessions, analysed and reviewed in this book, provide strong evidence to suggest positive conclusions for growth and development. On the basis of deeper and more sustainable WTO-compliant domestic reforms, Article XII members have grown faster in trade and gross domestic product (GDP) terms than original WTO members, have demonstrated greater resilience in crisis and have been more successful in attracting investment than original members. In the scope and substantive content of the specific commitments they have undertaken in rules and market access, the net effects have consolidated GATT/WTO rules and disciplines, clarified them with greater precision and in several areas advanced the rules. The results from accessions have acted as new wine in the 'old bottles' of the membership. They have renewed the WTO, strengthened it and taken it forward. Yet, it is to be borne in mind that the positive results from trade opening materialise and are maximised with companion policies, principally a system based on an open and competitive market economy, the rule of law, good governance and intellectual property rights.

Accession negotiations are non-stop multilateral trade negotiations in the regular work of the WTO. They are distinct and separate from multilateral negotiations in launched trade rounds, such as the Doha Round. From these negotiations, important lessons have been learned and questions have been raised. Both the lessons and questions merit broader reflection and analysis by the wider membership so as to ascertain how these negotiations, which have taken place in a relatively 'constrained space',[26] could be applied to broader negotiations in the WTO, as a whole and beyond it.

The lessons and associated questions are several. First, accession negotiations confirm the huge and incalculable benefits that flow from trade opening in a rules-based system, governed by a globally accepted dispute settlement system. Coupled to this reaffirmation of the 'benefits and lessons', on the one hand, is the fact that trade negotiations are tough and complex, in technical substance and labour under the ever-present

---

[26] I have borrowed this expression from Uri Dadush, my co-editor, who has kept constant watch to guard against my conveying an excessively Panglossian view of WTO accessions.

influence of geopolitics, on the other. Hence, establishment of timelines is artificial and creates expectations that may not be met. They take time. They cannot be hurried along and political declarations at summit levels, including bilaterally, cannot substitute for technical work at the level of negotiators, word by word, line by line. A repeated lesson is that assurances of support for an accession by a WTO member head of state/government to the head of state/government of an acceding government neither substitute for nor translate into a technical agreement on texts and numbers. This technical work permanently resides with technical negotiators.

Second, based on the fundamentally significant results from accession negotiations, reviewed in this book, is whether mandates for launched standalone trade rounds continue to be necessary. The market access and rules results are comparable to, or may even exceed, the 'actual' results from any previously launched trade round or the ongoing Doha Round. It is argued that the *raison d'être* for all-encompassing launched trade rounds may have been reduced with the built-in mandates for multilateral negotiations in the regular work of the WTO, pursuant to the WTO Agreement. Several mandates stand in evidence. Article II.1 of the WTO Agreement establishes the WTO as the 'common institutional framework for the conduct of trade relations amongst its Members'. Article II.3 is a built-in mandate for plurilateral agreements. Article XII establishes an all-encompassing mandate for accession negotiations, for any state or separate customs territory, on 'terms to be agreed between it and the WTO'. GATT 1994 Article XXVIII, XXVIII *bis* and its application to customs unions (GATT 1994 Article XXIV.6) create mandates for negotiations. Taken together, in addition to decisions that could be and are taken in the work of regular bodies of the WTO, is there a continuing necessity for standalone launched rounds? Real world negotiations may have answered this question without the need for a 'formal decision'.

Third, the evidence shows that accession negotiations are at the outermost frontiers of multilateral trade liberalisation. Almost like wind vanes, they have pointed the system in the direction of wind flow. More, they have enabled the WTO to identify, if not to discover, where the real 'red lines' of members and acceding governments exist. What will countries and/or separate customs territories accept, concede and actually implement? What will they be forced to accept, concede, but then not implement? It is argued here that perhaps this is really one of the main areas of insight if not gain from accession negotiations. Because accessions are negotiated, in a range of formats and configurations that allow for honest conversations, away from headline news, they have allowed for the discovery of the possibilities and limitations in multilateral trade negotiations, beyond which there would be severe consequences and blowback.

Fourth, even in a rules-based multilateral trading system, there can never be a 'one-size-fits-all'. The operational modalities and the results from accession negotiations have provided proof of this theoretical point. A strong point from accession negotiations is that 'treaty-making' is the culmination of treaty dialogue, through a structured process of questions and answers that ranges across many years (on average ten years for each of the thirty-three completed accessions). What results is a raft of accession-specific commitments (currently 1,361) that are integral to the WTO Agreement. Does the risk exist that this situation may create different tiers of membership – in other words, different rules for different members?[27] The facts and the logic suggest that this would not be the case. It is argued that although the principles, disciplines and rules (the norms) are the same for all members, specific terms and conditions of individual members are different. It could not be otherwise. The principles, disciplines, rules and their exceptions, are accompanied with the variant conditions in the Schedules of Goods and Services of different members. Although founded and governed by the core values, the rules-based multilateral trading system from origin has never been a one-size-fits-all and should never be.

The setting of accession negotiations, in particular, and trade negotiations more broadly describes and explains why they are complex, tedious and, in several instances, uniquely challenging. It is useful to dwell on this a little more in concluding.

Trade negotiations are intertwined with changes in the relative balance of power and adjustments to the global order. The contemporary structure of the global economy is multipolar (Hoekman, 2014). Trade negotiations have reflected this multipolarity. Complex multipolarity has been accompanied and compounded by the forceful re-emergence of geopolitics.

More recently, in the past two decades, this complex polarity re-emerged with the collapse of the Soviet Union in 1991 and the rise of the emerging economies. The various efforts reconstituting and re-ordering what was previously part of the economic and political space

---

[27] See WTO document JOB/GC/55: paragraph 1.21, 'Looking Back, Moving Forward', farewell statement by former WTO Director-General Pascal Lamy, 25 July 2013.

of the defunct Soviet Union – the Commonwealth of Independent States (CIS), the CU of Armenia, Belarus, Kazakhstan, Kyrgyz Republic and Russia, or its current transition to the EAEU Treaty – injected complexity, change and challenge into trade and economic relations. Unable to adjust to fast-changing configurations in the global economy, signified by and worsened with the failures of WTO mini-ministerial meetings in 2008 and 2010, WTO members have sought deeper trade opening and hedged their bets with FTAs/PTAs and now mega-regionals. While the management of the Doha Round negotiations is yet to fully adjust to these change and challenges, these adjustments have been reflected in the real-time transactional and bargaining engagement of the process of accession negotiations. The trial and exploratory adjustment efforts to construct systemic accommodation were first made with the accession of Russia in 2011 and remain ongoing in the accession negotiations of Kazakhstan. Beyond accessions, the negotiating behaviour between members in the WTO has to exhibit greater nimbleness in adapting to a changed global trade and economic environment characterised by complex polarities in a process still in dynamic transformation from the inertia of the past. Membership negotiating behaviour is not yet in tandem with the ongoing rapid transformation. There is urgency to adapt and transform.

Over many years, WTO accession negotiations and their results have been caught up in the merits and demerits of the arguments for trade liberalisation, globalisation and, as a consequence, the question of what is good for development. Although the welfare gains from trade are globally acknowledged, they are accompanied by strong concerns and rising opposition, some embedded in the protection and rent-seeking behaviour of special interests. But several of the concerns are genuine and compel continued reflection. The fundamental logic of trade has been repeatedly argued, most recently by Froman (2014). From a non-theoretical, but practical perspective, the logic of trade inheres in the fact, among other things, that it is a force multiplier. It enables countries to build and expand their economies, enhance prosperity and create the conditions for projecting power and influence abroad (Froman, 2014). The challenges of trade opening and integration have also been analysed as a paradox. While there is acceptance that trade in the aggregate generates gains and promotes economic growth, it tends to result in winners and losers (Lawrence, 2007). While increased trade is a 'good thing', particularly between high-wage and low-wage countries, offering the latter their 'best hope of moving up the income ladder', other effects have emerged over time that are not so modest, such as the shift in jobs from high- to low-income countries, wage effects, employment effects, etc. These should not be ignored. So, companion policies need to be developed to support the adjustment of those that 'lose' (Krugman, 2007). With the paradoxes, the dilemmas and the various issues involved, several have argued for a less textbook-based approach. These champions of open markets and the benefits of integrated global market have made the point that a new case has to be made for trade because of the necessity to confront the broader issue that the growing prosperity of global economy may not be in their interests (Summers, 2008a). Recent studies, to a large extent, tend to have underscored the point of this angst connected to rising inequality (Piketty, 2014). Summers (2008b) argues that withdrawal from the global economy is 'untenable' and that reduction of the pace of integration is also 'untenable'. However, a strategy to promote a healthy globalisation is needed and advocated to reduce inequality and insecurity (equity and security).

It is in the nature of the process and substance of accession negotiations that they do not conclude, either naturally, or routinely. The delivery of an accession has to be 'midwifed'. Perhaps, an area of continued improvement in accession negotiations should be to emphasise greater sensitivity to equity and fairness questions associated with what is good for development. At the same time, it must be reiterated that a key explanation of the benefits from accessions has been based on far-reaching and sustained domestic reforms. Although development priorities have not been set out as a purpose of accession negotiations, the net results demonstrate that there have been resultant development gains.

In future, the negotiating business of the WTO and progress to be achieved will most probably be through accession-type negotiating formats. The global economic environment (for better or for worse, that is, with regard to liberalisation) will have to adjust to manage encounters between regional and mega-regional trade groupings. These latter will reflect geopolitical transformations such as in FTAs, PTAs, mega-regionals, etc. Accession results and output have contributed to the stabilisation of the system, in a rules-based multilateral trading system in which the Dispute Settlement Understanding and its effective functioning remain the foundation.

Annex 9.1 *Accession results grid*

| AI rules | Specific obligations and influence on rules and WTO jurisprudence |
|---|---|
| Foreign exchange and payments | Out of thirty-three Article XII members, five[1] undertook specific obligations on foreign exchange and payments. The results of these commitments: |
| | • Accept the obligation that the application of any measures/restrictions on foreign exchange shall be consistent with WTO provisions, and accept the elimination of prior authorisation requirements on foreign exchange and payments upon WTO accession. |
| Investment regime, as economic policy[2] | Out of thirty-three Article XII members, five members accepted specific obligations on the investment regime. (No specific WTO rules are referred to, as the WTO does not currently have an agreement on investment, *per se*.) Yet the results/effects of these commitments are as follows: |
| | • Confirm that national treatment would be applied precisely to direct taxation[3] (a commitment not undertaken by original members.) |
| | • Accept that future domestic investment laws and their implementation would be in full conformity with the WTO Agreement.[4] (This goes beyond any comparable commitments by original members.) |
| | • Accept specific obligations, linking 'specific commitments', entered in the Schedule on Specific Commitments in Services, with the investment policy regime in the working party report/protocol, and confirm that the investment regime shall be WTO-compliant.[5] (The 'organic unity' linking the working party treaty dialogue, specific commitments, listed in Accession Protocols and schedules, is a unique feature of Article XII members.) |
| State ownership and privatisation/STEs (GATT) | Thirty-three Article XII members accepted seventy-two specific obligations on state-owned enterprises (SOEs)/STEs and privatisation. The results/effects of these commitments: |
| | • Clarify the relationship between Articles XVII:1(a) and XVII:1(b) of the GATT 1994 by the distinction of |

Annex 9.1 (*cont.*)

| AI rules | Specific obligations and influence on rules and WTO jurisprudence |
| --- | --- |
| | a separate category of commitment on STEs/SOEs pursuant to operation 'in accordance with commercial considerations'.[6]<br>• Identify the criteria for commercial considerations for making purchases and sales (including price, quality, availability, marketability and transportation);[7] and the listing of the existing STEs/SOEs in working party reports.[8]<br>• Define STEs/SOEs through state ownership criteria, allowing a wider sub-set of entities to be covered by WTO rules, so a broader range of discriminatory or anti-competitive practices could be internationally regulated, and listing of the STEs.[9]<br>• Improve transparency requirements with respect to STEs/SOEs and notification of privatisation programmes by extension of the transparency rules beyond GATT Article XVII:4 provisions on notification, and further clarification thereof, for example:<br>  – ensuring that import purchasing procedures of STEs/SOEs are fully transparent;[10]<br>  – ensuring the transparency of ongoing privatisation programmes,[11] etc.<br>• Confirm and enhance the non-discrimination requirements for STEs/SOEs by setting out market-specific obligations applied to entities provided with financial or regulatory advantages, for example:<br>  – setting out a list of products subject to state trading;[12]<br>  – ensuring that no price increase in particular would result in protection with respect to imports, by STEs, beyond that allowed in the schedule of concessions and commitments on goods or that was not otherwise justified under WTO rules,[13] etc.<br>• Acceptance of specific commitments encouraging the phasing-out of STEs/SOEs.[14] |

Annex 9.1 (*cont.*)

| AI rules | Specific obligations and influence on rules and WTO jurisprudence |
|---|---|
| Pricing policies | Out of thirty-three Article XII members, twenty-nine[15] undertook specific obligations to: |
| | • Enhance transparency requirements to publish information on state price controls,[16] including publication of price-setting mechanisms and policies.[17] |
| | • Establish explicit binding and enforceable requirements for non-use of price controls to protect domestic industries or services providers, or limitation of market access commitments on goods and services.[18] |
| | • Define and list non-discrimination requirements specific to price control measures.[19] |
| | • Identify patterns for WTO-consistent price-control measures regulating tariff rates for goods and services rendered by natural monopolies (including their operation on the basis of normal commercial considerations).[20] |
| Balance-of-payments measures | Out of thirty-three Article XII members, fourteen members: |
| | • Reconfirmed adherence to GATT Article XII and the Understanding on Balance-of-Payments requirements.[21] |
| Framework for making and enforcing policies | Out of thirty-three Article XII members, twenty-six[22] undertook fifty-two commitments on their framework for making and enforcing policies. The results of these commitments: |
| | • Confirm the international status of the WTO Agreement and its precedence over national legislation.[23] |
| | • Clarify that WTO commitments shall be respected at the regional trade agreement (RTA) level.[24] |
| | • Confirm the specific obligation to apply WTO provisions uniformly throughout the entire customs territory and other territories under members' control, including in regions engaging in border trade or frontier traffic, special economic zones, and other |

Annex 9.1 (*cont.*)

| AI rules | Specific obligations and influence on rules and WTO jurisprudence |
|---|---|
| | areas where special regimes for tariffs, taxes and regulations are established.[25] |
| | • Confirm that sub-central authorities shall have no jurisdiction or autonomous authority over issues covered by WTO provisions.[26] |
| | • Confirm also that all laws, regulations and other measures of sub-central authorities comply with the WTO provisions[27] and are administered in a uniform, impartial and reasonable manner,[28] and all measures taken by sub-central authorities that are inconsistent with the WTO Agreement are eliminated or nullified.[29] |
| | • Establish the obligation that when appraised of a situation where WTO provisions are not being applied or are applied in a non-uniform manner, central authorities shall act to enforce WTO provisions without requiring affected parties to petition through courts.[30] |
| | • Confirm and elaborate the right of traders to appeal administrative rulings on matters subject to the WTO Agreement to an independent tribunal (i.e. the provision of the right to an independent review)[31] in conformity with the WTO commitments, including but not limited to Article X:3(b) of the GATT 1994, and the relevant provisions of the Agreement on Subsidies and Countervailing Measures (SCM), the Agreement on Customs Valuation, the TRIPs Agreement and the GATS.[32] |
| | • Establish the obligation for the definition of a special mechanism[33] or a tribunal responsible for prompt review of all administrative actions relating to the implementation of laws, regulations, judicial decisions and administrative rulings of general application,[34] to be established/designated and operated, and that the government authorities shall act promptly to address the situation, and inform the individual or entity of the decision or action taken in writing,[35] with an opportunity to appeal.[36] |

Annex 9.1 (*cont.*)

| AI rules | Specific obligations and influence on rules and WTO jurisprudence |
|---|---|
| | • Establish the obligation that such tribunals shall be impartial and independent of the agency entrusted with administrative enforcement and shall have no substantial interest in the outcome of the matter.[37]<br>• Confirm the adoption of all laws and legislative instruments necessary for the application of WTO commitments prior to accession.[38] Should a transition period be granted, provide that all measures inconsistent with WTO provisions shall be revised or annulled,[39] and all central government measures be fully implemented in a timely manner, or the accession commitments shall be otherwise honoured.[40]<br>• Confirm the obligation to have the WTO Agreement as the legal basis of trade with other members and to ensure consistency with WTO rules.[41] |
| Trading rights | Twenty-eight Article XII members have undertaken thirty-nine commitments related to trading rights and registration requirements for import/export operations. The results of these commitments:<br><br>• Confirm the right to trade in goods (import/export) on a non-discriminatory basis, at any level of distribution.<br>• Liberalise the scope and availability of trading rights, including through granting the right to trade to all enterprises and the elimination of the system of examination and approval of trading rights.[42]<br>• Ensure that all legislation and fees, charges and taxes levied on trading rights are in conformity with WTO obligations (particularly, Articles VIII:1(a), XI:1, III:2, III:4 of the GATT 1994).[43]<br>• Clarify that any enterprise shall be permitted to register as importer/exporter.[44]<br>• Set out that existing registration systems shall conform to WTO rules. They shall not restrict trade[45] or be more burdensome than necessary.[46]<br>• Confirm the trading right to select distributor(s).[47] |

Annex 9.1 (*cont.*)

| AI rules | Specific obligations and influence on rules and WTO jurisprudence |
|---|---|
| | • Eliminate requirements for physical presence or investment in the Article XII member.[48]<br>• Confirm that requirements for commercial registration or application for trading rights shall be for customs and fiscal purposes only.[49] |
| **Import regulations**<br>Ordinary customs duties | Out of thirty-three Article XII members, seven accepted thirteen specific obligations under the section on 'Ordinary Customs Duties' of the working party report, in addition to the tariff concessions and commitments contained in their Goods Schedules with accompanying 'headnotes'. The results of these commitments:<br><br>• Provide stability to ensure that the application of seasonal, specific, mixed and/or compound duties does not exceed the tariff bindings contained in the Goods Schedules.[50]<br>• Bind to an assessment/adjustment mechanism that requires that the *ad valorem* equivalent of the specific duty rate of a combined duty would be no higher than the alternative *ad valorem* duty rate for that tariff line in the Goods Schedule.[51]<br>• Confirm participation in the Information Technology Agreement (ITA).[52]<br>• Confirm application of customs duties on specified products.[53]<br>• Confirm application of the Generalised System of Preferences Scheme (in the member's tariff preferences for developing economies and LDCs) in conformity with the relevant provisions of the WTO Agreement.[54] |
| Other duties and charges | Out of thirty-three Article XII members, twenty-three accepted twenty-six specific obligations on 'other duties and charges'. The results/effects of these commitments:<br><br>• Confirm the elimination of any existing other duties and charges, upon accession, or within agreed |

Annex 9.1 (*cont.*)

| AI rules | Specific obligations and influence on rules and WTO jurisprudence |
|---|---|
| Tariff rate quotas (TRQs) and tariff exemptions | transition periods, and bind them at zero in their goods schedules,[55] except in two cases where the two Article XII members were allowed to keep other duties and charges in their goods schedules.[56]<br><br>Out of thirty-three Article XII members, twenty accepted thirty-four specific obligations on TRQs and tariff exemptions. The results/effects of these commitments:<br><br>• Confirm that tariff exemptions and TRQs would be applied and administered in conformity with WTO rules and regulations.<br>• Confirm specific obligations to replace TRQs for certain products with tariff only regime and, at the same time, to replace quantitative import restrictions on a number of other products by TRQs.[57]<br>• Set out the specific principles governing the TRQ scheme.[58]<br>• Elaborate the specific terms for TRQ administration.[59] |
| Application of internal taxes to imports | Thirty-three Article XII members accepted forty-six specific obligations on the application of internal taxes to imports. The results/effects of these commitments:<br><br>• Confirm application of domestic taxes, including value-added and excise taxes, in a non-discriminatory manner consistent with Articles I and III of the GATT 1994.<br>• Confirm acceptance of specific reforms to eliminate WTO-inconsistent tax regulations.[60]<br>• Equalise the tax treatment on 'like products', in particular tobacco and alcohol products.[61] |
| Quantitative import restrictions, including prohibitions and licensing systems | Thirty-three of thirty-three Article XII members accepted eighty-two specific obligations on quantitative import restrictions, including prohibitions, and licensing systems. The results/effects of these commitments: |

Annex 9.1 (*cont.*)

| AI rules | Specific obligations and influence on rules and WTO jurisprudence |
|---|---|
| | <ul><li>Establish that quantitative import restrictions, prohibitions and other non-tariff measures (such as licensing, quotas, prohibitions, bans and other restrictions having equivalent effect) that cannot be justified under the WTO Agreement, shall be eliminated, not introduced, re-introduced or applied.[62]</li><li>Confirm that the legal authority to suspend/ban/ restrict imports and exports would be applied in conformity with the WTO Agreement,[63] pursuant in particular to Articles XI, XII, XIX, XX, and XXI of the GATT 1994, and the Agreements on Agriculture, Sanitary and Phytosanitary (SPS) Measures, Import Licensing Procedures, Safeguards and Technical Barriers to Trade (TBT) and the Understanding on Balance-of-Payments Provisions.</li><li>Link, explicitly, to commitments with regard to the Agreement on TBT and the Agreement on SPS Measures.[64]</li><li>Identify the products subject to quantitative import restrictions, including prohibitions, and licensing systems, to be eliminated, phased out and/or brought into conformity with the WTO Agreement.[65]</li><li>Set transition periods for the full implementation of the relevant WTO obligations.[66]</li><li>Reiterate exemptions envisaged in Articles XX and XXI of the GATT 1994 covering, among other things, protection of public morals,[67] culture[68] and religion.[69]</li><li>Clarify that sub-central authorities have no right to formulate non-tariff measures; only the central government can issue regulations on non-tariff measures; and that these measures would be implemented or enforced only by the central government or subnational authorities with authorisation from the central government.[70]</li><li>Explain that the administration of quotas and import licences shall be consistent with the WTO</li></ul> |

Annex 9.1 (*cont.*)

| AI rules | Specific obligations and influence on rules and WTO jurisprudence |
|---|---|
| | Agreement, including Article XIII of the GATT 1994 and the Agreement on Import Licensing Procedures. The establishment of the value of imports would be based on the information collected by customs officials and the provisions of the Customs Valuation Agreement (CVA).[71] |
| | • Provide that the period of validity of import licences could be subject to extension.[72] |
| | • Confirm that any procedures or requirements relating to licensing the imports of goods, containing encryption technology, whether by the acceding government or the competent regional bodies, shall be applied on a non-discriminatory basis and in conformity with WTO rules.[73] |
| Customs valuation | All thirty-three Article XII members accepted a total of forty-four specific commitments on customs valuation. The results of these commitments: |
| | • Confirm a uniform and predictable system for the valuation of goods for customs purposes, pursuant to Article VII of the GATT 1994 and the WTO Agreement on the Implementation of Article VII of the GATT 1994 (Canadian value added/CVA), including the Interpretative Notes in Annex I, which form an integral part of the CVA. |
| | • Enhance the implementation of a predictable system for the valuation of goods either by referencing or reaffirming the obligation to apply/implement the following WTO Customs Valuation Committee Decisions: |
| | (i) Decision 3.1 On the Treatment of Interest Charges in Customs Value of Imported Goods[74] |
| | (ii) Paragraph 2 of Decision 4.1 On the Valuation of Carrier Media Bearing Software for Data Processing Equipment. |
| | • Clarify that, as an international agreement, the provisions of the WTO CVA supersede domestic law, upon accession.[75] |

Annex 9.1 (*cont.*)

| AI rules | Specific obligations and influence on rules and WTO jurisprudence |
| --- | --- |
| | • Confirm that all relevant domestic legislation is in compliance with the WTO CVA; and identify any areas of non-conformity of domestic legislation, which would need to be adapted, in order to ensure full conformity with WTO requirements, upon accession.<br>• Focus in several cases on specific provisions of the WTO CVA, such as those related to posting of bonds for prompt clearance of goods,[76] the right of appeal to an independent administrative tribunal[77] and the valuation of cinematographic films.[78] |
| Rules of origin | Out of thirty-three Article XII members, twenty-eight members accepted thirty-one specific commitments on rules of origin. The results of these commitments:<br><br>• Confirm overall conformity with the provisions and requirements of the WTO Agreement on Rules of Origin, in the application of preferential and non-preferential rules of origin, upon accession.<br>• Refer, specifically, to the provisions/requirements of Article 2(h) and Annex II, paragraph 3(d) of the Agreement,[79] including to the issuance of assessments of the origin of imports, the terms under which these would be provided and the need for these to be incorporated in domestic legislation; and the management of consistent, uniform, impartial and reasonable rules of origin.<br>• Underscore, in four instances, specifically the compliance with 'relevant WTO provisions on transparency and the provision of information about rules of origin and their application'.[80] |
| Other customs formalities | Out of thirty-three Article XII members, seven members accepted eight specific commitments on 'other customs formalities'. The results of these commitments:<br><br>• Confirm that upon accession:<br>Consularisation/notarisation by consular officers in the country of export would not be required for the import of goods.[81] |

Annex 9.1 (*cont.*)

| AI rules | Specific obligations and influence on rules and WTO jurisprudence |
|---|---|
| | A dispute settlement mechanism, as part of the customs service, would be established to address concerns raised on smuggling and any other customs administration issues, within a specific time-frame.[82] |
| | A list of specific goods, as annexed to the accession working party report, would remain subject to measures requiring declaration and/or entry/exit at designated customs checkpoints. The measures would be applied in conformity with the WTO Agreement.[83] |
| | All 'laws, regulations, decrees, decisions, judicial decisions and administrative rulings of general application connected with the importation/exportation of goods, including those related to statistical control, customs clearance, documentation, and any changes to existing legislation, measures and rulings' shall adhere to transparency requirements under the WTO Agreement by reaffirming timely publication. This information shall be published on the official website of the responsible governmental authority to promote trade and investment by making it easily accessible to member governments, traders and investors.[84] |
| | There shall be application in a 'uniform, impartial and reasonable manner of any such legislation, rulings and/or measures throughout the territory of the member, as required by the WTO Agreement.[85] |
| | A review of the existing regime on the distribution of collected duties to customs union partners within the customs union in question, will take place after a three-year transition period.[86] |
| | Classification of goods for customs purposes would be made solely in accordance with the World Customs Organization (WCO) Harmonised Commodity Description and Coding Systems.[87] |

Annex 9.1 (*cont.*)

| AI rules | Specific obligations and influence on rules and WTO jurisprudence |
|---|---|
| Preshipment inspection | Out of thirty-three Article XII members, twenty-three members accepted twenty-four specific commitments on preshipment inspection (PSI). The results/effects of these specific commitments:<br><br>• Clarify whether the acceding governments have concluded contracts with PSI service providers, and reaffirm that any existing or future PSI regimes/ programmes would fully adhere to/implement the requirements of the Agreement on Preshipment Inspection.<br>• Ensure that any existing or future PSI regimes conducted by PSI service providers, on behalf of the government, would be solely temporary, until customs authorities could carry out the activities, which were temporarily performed by PSI service providers.[88]<br>• Confirm that acceding governments have the sole responsibility in ensuring that PSI enterprises, operating on behalf of acceding governments, comply with the provisions of the WTO Agreement.[89]<br>• Reaffirm and strengthen the existing transparency requirements of the WTO Agreement, specifically Article X of the GATT 1994,[90] the Agreement on PSI and the Agreement on the Implementation of Article VII of the GATT 1994 (in particular, with regard to the publication of legislation, measures, rulings).<br>• Underscore that fees and charges for any such PSI would correspond to the service(s) provided, in conformity with Article VIII:1 of the GATT 1994.[91]<br>• Reinforce the right of appeal of decisions taken by PSI service providers, and identify the relevant legislation.[92] |
| Trade remedies | Out of thirty-three Article XII members, thirty members accepted thirty-eight specific commitments on anti-dumping, countervailing and safeguard measures. The results/effects of these commitments: |

Annex 9.1 (*cont.*)

| AI rules | Specific obligations and influence on rules and WTO jurisprudence |
|---|---|
| | • Require that anti-dumping, countervailing and safeguard measures are not applied until either: existing legislation related to anti-dumping, countervailing, and safeguard measures are brought into conformity with the requirements contained in the WTO Agreement; or WTO-consistent legislation is adopted and duly notified.[93] <br> • Reaffirm specifically, full conformity with Article VI of the GATT 1994, the Agreement on the Implementation of Article VI, the Agreement on SCM and Article XIX of the GATT 1994 and the Agreement on Safeguards.[94] <br> • Underscore and strengthen, in two cases, the application of specific provisions of the Agreement on Implementation of Article VI of the GATT 1994, including Articles 9.3, 11.2 and 11.3[95] and 9.4.[96] |
| **Export regulations**[97] <br> Export control requirements: <br><br> – quantitative export restrictions <br> – export tariffs, taxes, charges and fees applied to exports <br> – export subsidies | Out of thirty-three Article XII members, twenty-eight members[98] undertook fifty-seven specific accession commitments on export regulations, including export control requirements (export restrictions, export tariffs, taxes, charges and fees applied to exports). These commitments, in the main, were not previously undertaken by original members. These accession-specific obligations on export regulations: <br><br> • Confirm that non-tariff export regulations (bans, export quotas and export licensing requirements, taxes, fees and charges imposed on or in connection with exports, obligatory minimum export prices, etc.), shall conform and be applied consistently with the provisions of the WTO Agreement, including those contained in Articles III, VIII,[99] XI, XII, XIII, XVII, XIX, XX and XXI of the GATT 1994.[100] <br> • Enhance transparency (beyond levels and commitments by original members) by application of export restrictions based on specific annexed |

Annex 9.1 (*cont.*)

| AI rules | Specific obligations and influence on rules and WTO jurisprudence |
|---|---|
| | 'lists' and accompanied by commitment to notify and publish.[101] |
| | • Accept a commitment to eliminate export bans on specific goods.[102] |
| | • Encourage the removal of export licensing requirements.[103] |
| | • Extend the requirements of the Agreement on Import Licensing Procedures to export licensing procedures, and reaffirm that such procedures shall comply with Article XI of the GATT 1994 and other WTO requirements.[104] |
| | • Confirm that export TRQs shall be administered consistently with the WTO Agreement, in particular the GATT 1994 and the Agreement on Import Licensing Procedures.[105] |
| | • Accept a commitment to minimise the use of export taxes, post-accession.[106] |
| | • Extend the scope of commitments to elimination of all internal taxes, charges and fees applied to exports (with exemptions for listed products)[107] and specific export-related measures, including re-export approvals[108] and non-automatic export licences.[109] |
| | • Clarify that export control measures available pursuant to Article XX(i) of the GATT 1994, should they be introduced, shall not be operated to increase exports or protect domestic industries.[110] |
| | • Accept a commitment to abolish or phase out export duties[111] or reduce based on a binding schedule[112] (including through the creation of a new section – Part V – of the Goods Schedule[113]) and apply these duties in conformity with the WTO Agreement, including Article I of the GATT 1994,[114] and accept the commitment that no other measures, with equivalent effects, shall be applied on those products,[115] or identify tariff line exclusions where export duties would not be applied.[116] |
| | • Accept a commitment to foreclose on the use of export duties.[117] |

Annex 9.1 *(cont.)*

| AI rules | Specific obligations and influence on rules and WTO jurisprudence |
|---|---|
| Export subsidies[119] | • Elaborate, clarify and expand the WTO commitments on export regulations to address RTA-related questions relative to the Customs Union/Eurasian Economic Union Treaty.[118] Under this section, sixteen Article XII members[120] accepted nineteen specific commitments on export subsidies. The results of these commitments: |
| | • Confirm that prohibited subsidies, within the meaning of Article 3 of the SCM Agreement, including export subsidies, shall not be maintained or introduced.[121] • Encourage the elimination of all incentives inconsistent with the SCM Agreement.[122] • Clarify the scope of the notification requirements applied to export subsidy programmes.[123] |

**Internal policies affecting trade in goods**

| | |
|---|---|
| Industrial policy, including subsidies | Out of thirty-three Article XII members, twenty-nine members[124] accepted forty specific obligations related to industrial policy, including subsidies. The results of these commitments: |
| | • Confirm the obligation to administer subsidy programmes in accordance with the SCM Agreement,[125] to eliminate[126] subsidies inconsistent with the SCM Agreement, including within the stipulated transition period,[127] and not maintain[128] or introduce/reintroduce[129] them in future. • Clarify the scope of measures falling under the definition of a 'prohibited subsidy' in Article 3 of the SCM Agreement,[130] and the methodologies used for the establishment of the existence of a subsidy for the purposes of Articles 1.1, 1.2 of the SCM Agreement.[131] • Strengthen notification requirements with respect to subsidy programmes.[132] |
| TBTs | Out of thirty-three Article XII members, thirty[133] accepted eighty-four specific obligations on TBTs. The results/effects of these commitments: |

Annex 9.1 (*cont.*)

| AI rules | Specific obligations and influence on rules and WTO jurisprudence |
|---|---|
| | • Provide for the establishment of enquiry points and notification authorities.[134] |
| | • Confirm that technical regulations and conformity assessment procedures would be developed and applied in conformity with the provisions of the TBT Agreement, including publication prior to implementation to allow interested parties the opportunity for review and comment, as provided for in the TBT Agreement and relevant decisions and recommendations adopted by the TBT Committee.[135] |
| | • Set transition periods to comply with the TBT Agreement.[136] |
| | • Provide for the replacement of mandatory standards with voluntary standards or technical regulations.[137] |
| | • Confirm that internal mechanisms exist to inform and consult with government agencies and private sector interests on the rights and obligations under the GATT 1994 and the TBT Agreement.[138] |
| | • List products that had been subject to measures that would need to be brought into conformity with the WTO Agreement.[139] |
| | • Report the conclusion of mutual recognition agreements with conformity assessment bodies in other members.[140] |
| | • Confirm that voluntary standards contained in private sector agreements would not be enforced.[141] |
| | • Confirm that federal governmental bodies would prepare and apply all technical regulations, including those adopted by the competent bodies of the Eurasian Economic Community (EurAsEC) and the CU, in accordance with the WTO Agreement; and that the CU Agreement on Uniform Technical Regulation Principles provides for the use of international standards or relevant parts as the basis for the development of technical regulations 'except in cases where such documents did not conform with |

Annex 9.1 (*cont.*)

| AI rules | Specific obligations and influence on rules and WTO jurisprudence |
|---|---|
| | the purposes of the technical regulations of the Customs Union'.[142] |
| | • List membership in international standard-making bodies (e.g. ISO).[143] |
| | • Confirm that no multiple or duplicative conformity assessment procedures would be maintained and that no requirements would be exclusively imposed on imported products.[144] |
| SPS | Out of thirty-three Article XII members, all thirty-three members accept a record number of ninety-two SPS accession-specific obligations (that have also exercised an influence on WTO jurisprudence). The results of these specific commitments: |
| | • Confirm acceptance of binding specific obligations on SPS measures by all thirty-three Article XII members to achieve a record number of ninety-two specific commitments. |
| | • Extend the existing requirements for harmonisation of SPS measures with international standards guidelines and recommendations 'on as wide a basis as possible'[145] to an obligation to base all such measures on international standards.[146] |
| | • Enhance, significantly, transparency and notification provisions of the SPS Agreement[147] to include requirements on the precise forms and modalities for publishing proposed SPS measures[148] and/or the source for publication of draft SPS requirements.[149] |
| | • Enhance, significantly, a binding commitment that requires public comments on SPS proposals prior to the adoption of SPS measures.[150] |
| | • Regulate, precisely, specific categories of SPS measures, particularly, those in respect of goods subject to veterinary control.[151] |
| | • Confirm acceptance of accession-specific binding frameworks, additional (plus) to the basic requirements of the WTO SPS Agreement for more |

Annex 9.1 (*cont.*)

| AI rules | Specific obligations and influence on rules and WTO jurisprudence |
|---|---|
| | itemised commitments, based on Article 8 and Annex C to the SPS Agreement (Control, Inspection and Approval Procedures).[152] These commitments add specific obligations in respect of (i) import permits, (ii) transit, (iii) veterinary certificates, (iv) establishment approval, and (v) inspections. Notably, these stand out as positive example of the systemic contributions resulting from accession commitments to the regulatory development of specific categories of SPS measures within the WTO framework. |
| Trade-Related Investment Measures (TRIMs) | Out of thirty-three Article XII members, all members have taken specific obligations on TRIMs and, without exception, with specific reference to the WTO Agreement on TRIMs. The results/effects of these commitments: |

- Confirm that Article XII members shall not maintain any measures inconsistent with the TRIMs Agreement, and shall apply the TRIMs Agreement from the date of accession, in most cases, without requesting any transitional period, whereas for most original members, WTO-inconsistent TRIMs existed at membership and still exist.
- Accept the specific obligation that, in instances of WTO TRIMs-inconsistency, in specific sectors at the time of the accession, that the relevant acceding governments shall eliminate the WTO-inconsistent measures within the negotiated time-frame.[153]
- Re-confirm the requirement of the WTO non-discrimination principle and discipline with regard to TRIMs by specifically enhancing this obligation with the qualifying phrase of 'in a non-discriminatory manner'.[154]

| Government procurement | Twenty-three[155] out of thirty-three Article XII members have accepted twenty-six specific obligations on government procurement. The results/effects of these commitments have: |

Annex 9.1 (*cont.*)

| AI rules | Specific obligations and influence on rules and WTO jurisprudence |
|---|---|
|  | • Enlarged the number of parties[156] to the Plurilateral Agreement on Government Procurement (GPA), and the number of observers[157] in the GPA Committee.<br>• Confirmed that commitments to accede to the GPA are associated with candidature to join the European Union.[158]<br>• Established that government entities would conduct their procurement in a transparent and non-discriminatory manner, as provided by published laws, guidelines and procedures.[159]<br>• Clarified that procurement of goods and services, which were not purchased for governmental purposes, but with a view to commercial resale or to be used for production of goods and supply of services for commercial sale, such purchases and sales would not be considered to be government procurement.[160]<br>• Indicated that no discrimination against foreign suppliers would be introduced.[161]<br>• Evolved from 'best endeavour' language in the early post-1995 accessions to more meticulous provisions in the more recent accessions. |
| Free zones, special economic areas | Thirty-three Article XII members accepted thirty-four specific obligations on free zones and special economic areas.[162] The results/effects of these commitments:<br><br>• Confirm that free zones and special economic areas are fully subject to specific obligations in the Accession Protocols.<br>• Clarify that normal customs formalities, tariffs and taxes are applied when goods produced or imported into the free zones enter the rest of the acceding governments' economy under the special tax and tariff regime of those zones.<br>• Accept the obligation to identify, list and make precise those specific WTO agreements for which acceding governments would ensure enforcement |

Annex 9.1 (*cont.*)

| AI rules | Specific obligations and influence on rules and WTO jurisprudence |
|---|---|
| | and compliance of their WTO obligations in free zones and special economic areas.[163] This precision excluded ambiguity. |
| | • Accept the obligation to update and report to members on the actual status of their relevant legislation on free zones and special economic areas of the acceding governments to ensure compatibility of domestic laws with WTO principles and disciplines.[164] |
| | • Accept the specific commitment to list and notify WTO-inconsistent requirements (such as export performance, trade balancing, or local content requirements) that shall be banned in the free zones and special economic areas of the acceding governments.[165] |
| | • Accept the obligation for the non-discrimination principle and its application to preferential arrangements provided to foreign invested enterprises within the special economic areas.[166] This specific obligation remains unique to WTO accession obligations. |
| | • Accept the obligation to notify the WTO with statistics on trade between its special economic areas and the other parts of its customs territory on a regular basis.[167] |
| Transit | Seventeen Article XII members[168] accepted (a total number of twenty) specific obligations on 'Transit'. These commitments: |
| | • Clarify and extend the definition of goods in transit under Article V of the GATT 1994 to include energy goods.[169] |
| | • Improve and enhance, significantly, transparency requirements with respect to publication of charges and fees imposed in connection with transit and railway tariffs for transit of goods.[170] |
| | • Establish specific requirements for the transit of goods subject to veterinary control.[171] |

Annex 9.1 (*cont.*)

| AI rules | Specific obligations and influence on rules and WTO jurisprudence |
|---|---|
| | • Enhance the requirement of Article V:4 of the GATT 1994 on the reasonableness of charges imposed on traffic in transit.[172] |
| Agricultural policies | Thirty-three Article XII members, variously, accepted a range of related specific obligations[173] 'entered' in Part IV of their Goods Schedules and correlated, relevantly, in the text of their accession working party reports. The results of these commitments: |
| | • Bind at zero (i.e. with 'Nil' entry) the total agriculture measurements of support (AMS) commitment of eighteen[174] of the thirty-three Article XII members. As a consequence, the eighteen Article XII members with this obligation are required to maintain their annual AMS category support within *de minimis*. |
| | • Bind precise monetary limits (i.e. final bound AMS) together with established 'base period' data, in the goods schedules of thirteen[175] of these thirty-three Article XII members. |
| | • Bind acceptance of commitment of 'final total AMS' in Part IV of their goods schedules. |
| | • Bind commitments at 10 per cent or lower the value of production of final bound total AMS, in the base years of all thirty-three Article XII members. |
| | • Bind commitments for *de minimis* allocation at 10 per cent of value of production for thirteen developing countries[176] and seven LDCs[177] and 5 per cent for the twelve Article XII members that acceded as developed members.[178] |
| | • Bind commitment to zero export subsidies for all thirty-three Article XII members, with the exception of Bulgaria. |
| Trade in civil aircraft | Seventeen Article XII members accepted eighteen specific obligations on 'Trade in civil aircraft'. The results/effects of these commitments: |
| | • Expand the membership of the Agreement on Civil Aircraft: |

Annex 9.1 (*cont.*)

| AI rules | Specific obligations and influence on rules and WTO jurisprudence |
|---|---|
| | ten Article XII members confirmed that they would join this plurilateral Agreement upon WTO accession;[179] |
| | three Article XII members undertook duty free treatments on products 'used in civil aircraft' in their goods schedules and committed to initiate negotiations for membership of the Agreement; or join the Agreement with a defined time-frame;[180] |
| | two Article XII members undertook to initiate negotiations for membership of the Agreement with/without a time-frame for accession.[181] |
| | • Undertake commitments to revise specific measures affecting trade in civil aircraft.[182] |
| TRIPs | All thirty-three Article XII members accepted specific obligations on intellectual property rights. The results of these commitments: |
| | • Confirm that Article XII members would fully apply all the provisions of the TRIPs Agreement no later than the date of accession, without recourse to a transitional period[183] and/or, in nine instances, no later than the negotiated time-frame.[184] |
| | • Confirm that should a transition period be granted, the relevant acceding government would: (i) ensure that the MFN and national treatment provisions in the TRIPs Agreement would be implemented; (ii) confirm that any change made in its laws, regulations and practice during this period would not result in a lesser degree of consistency with the provisions of the TRIPs Agreement that existed on the date of accession; (iii) ensure that existing rates of infringement would not significantly increase and that any infringement of intellectual property rights would be addressed immediately in cooperation with assistance from affected right holders; (iv) seek all available technical assistance to ensure that capacity to fully enforce a TRIPs-consistent legal regime upon expiration of the transition periods is assured; |

Annex 9.1 (*cont.*)

| AI rules | Specific obligations and influence on rules and WTO jurisprudence |
|---|---|
| | (v) make available all legislation in draft and promulgated form to WTO members so that advice on TRIPs consistency can be obtained; and (vi) adhere to the Action Plan as found in the working party report for TRIPs Agreement implementation.[185]
• Request members to recognise the right to an additional transitional period with respect to Sections 5 and 7 of Part II of the TRIPs Agreement, until 1 January 2016, in light of paragraph 7 of the Doha Declaration on the TRIPs Agreement and Public Health.[186]
• Assure members in the case where in specific intellectual property areas there is no compatibility with the TRIPs Agreement that the relevant acceding government would implement necessary measures and amendments by the date of accession.[187]
• Reaffirm the non-discrimination provisions by confirming that acceding governments would ensure and apply national treatment and MFN to foreign right-holders regarding all intellectual property rights across the board in compliance with the TRIPs Agreement.[188]
• Inform members, in accordance with transparency obligations, of the current status, and in some instances, the objectives of relevant intellectual property legislation and confirm that the specific procedures and provisions of the new draft legislation would be compatible with the TRIPs Agreement from the date of accession.[189]
• Clarify for members the meaning of specific legal provisions as found in national intellectual property laws and provisions in order to ensure compatibility with the TRIPs Agreement[190] and, in some instances, confirm the content of specific intellectual property laws and provisions in place.[191]
• Confirm for members that all laws, administrative regulations and implementing rules would be enforced by national courts.[192] |

Annex 9.1 (*cont.*)

| AI rules | Specific obligations and influence on rules and WTO jurisprudence |
|---|---|
| | • Confirm for members the enhancement of enforcement measures and reduction of infringement efforts by relevant agencies, in number of instances, referring to special border measures.[193]<br>• Confirm specific actions which would be undertaken, in most instances, to ensure that the legal environment would be able to meet the requirements for enforcing the TRIPs Agreement.[194] |
| Policies affecting trade in services | Out of thirty-three Article XII members, ten members undertook specific obligations on Policies Affecting Trade in Services.[195] The major contribution of these commitments is in relation to GATS Article VI (Domestic Regulation). The results/effects of these commitments: |
| | • Improve, significantly, GATS Article VI (Domestic Regulation), so that licensing procedures and conditions in acceding governments are more transparent, user-friendly and impartial.[196] This result, thus, provides a degree of certainty to members that their services providers in the acceding governments would be treated fairly, predictably, and in a non-discriminatory manner.<br>• Pre-commit the Article XII members to consult with members to develop domestic regulations on a specific services activity.[197]<br>• Confirm that for the services consolidated in the Schedule of Specific Commitments, relevant regulatory authorities would be separate from, and not accountable to, any service suppliers that the authorities regulated.[198]<br>• Reinforce, concretely, members' confidence and certainty in the Article XII members' service-related domestic policy, as they specifically declare that domestic policy that is incompatible with its GATS Schedule would be brought to WTO dispute settlement.[199] |

Annex 9.1 (*cont.*)

| AI rules | Specific obligations and influence on rules and WTO jurisprudence |
|---|---|
| | • Identify, explicitly, the relevant domestic laws on certain services sectors, boosting members' confidence in legislation-based domestic reform in the acceding governments.[200] <br> • Confirm non-discriminatory treatment, when regulatory changes occur, for information access in a certain service sector, thus foreign services suppliers receive fair competitive opportunities in that service market of the Article XII member.[201] <br> • Lock in a specific time-frame allowing foreign services providers in a certain service sector.[202] <br> • Guarantee the freedom of foreign services suppliers, so that they have the right to choose their partners.[203] |
| Transparency[204] | Twenty-two Article XII members have undertaken thirty-three specific transparency commitments in the section on publication of information on trade;[205] and thirty-one Article XII members have undertaken thirty-three specific transparency commitments in the subsection on notifications.[206] <br> The results/effects of the commitments on the publication of information on trade: <br><br> • Require that all relevant laws, regulations, decrees, judicial decisions and administrative rulings and measures of general application are published in a WTO-consistent manner. <br> • Confirm full implementation of transparency requirements in the WTO Agreement requiring notification and publication, including Article X of the GATT 1994, Article III of the GATS and Article 63 of the TRIPs Agreement. <br> • Ensure that measures are published promptly/before implementation,[207] and specify, in some cases, a minimum period for review/comment prior to the implementation of any measures.[208] <br> • Identify the mode of publication, i.e. in an official journal/gazette[209] and/or a website[210] and/or in newspapers.[211] |

Annex 9.1 (*cont.*)

| AI rules | Specific obligations and influence on rules and WTO jurisprudence |
|---|---|
|  | • Require the establishment of enquiry point(s) where information can be obtained relating to measures affecting trade in goods, services, TRIPs and foreign exchange measures.[212] |
|  | • Specify, in some cases, relevant information that should be included in publications, i.e., the names of the authorities responsible for implementing a particular measure, the effective date of the measure and a list of the products and services affected, identified by appropriate tariff line and classification.[213] |
|  | • Confirm the availability of translations of relevant legislation and measures (in one or more of the official WTO languages – English, French, Spanish).[214] |
|  | • Clarify, in one specific case, that 'official letters' are not recognised as legal normative documents. If an 'official letter' provided for legal normative rules, it would be null and void and sanctions would be applied for its issuance in accordance with domestic legislation.[215] |
|  | • Require the provision of trade data to the Integrated Data Base (IDB) of the WTO, and reaffirm participation in other WTO mechanisms, such as the Trade Policy Review Mechanism and other WTO Council and Committee reviews, for the exchange of information and increased transparency.[216] |
|  | The results/effects of the commitments on notifications: |
|  | • Require the submission of all initial notifications pursuant to the WTO Agreement. |
|  | • Clarify that any laws, regulations, or other measures enacted subsequent to the entry into force of the Accession Protocol conform to the requirements of the WTO Agreement and must be notified in a WTO-consistent manner. |
|  | • Confirm, in three specific cases, that draft notifications were prepared as part of the accession |

Annex 9.1 (*cont.*)

| AI rules | Specific obligations and influence on rules and WTO jurisprudence |
|---|---|
| | process,[217] and reaffirm the formal submission of these notifications upon accession.[218]<br>• Ensure, in one case, that certain notifications are submitted during a transitional period to relevant WTO bodies.[219] |
| Trade agreements | Out of thirty-three Article XII members, twenty-nine members[220] have taken specific obligations on trade agreements. The results/effects of these commitments:<br><br>• Reinforce the provisions of the WTO, including Article XXIV of the GATT 1994, paragraph 3 of the Enabling Clause[221] and Article V of the GATS, so that the acceding governments observe these WTO provisions in their trade agreements.<br>• Enhance the scope of the transparency, so that the provisions of Article XXIV of the GATT 1994, paragraph 3 of the Enabling Clause, and Article V of the GATS for notification, consultation and other requirements concerning free trade areas and customs unions, of which Article XII members are members, shall be in force from the date of accession. |
| **AII Schedule headnotes** | Headnotes of the thirty-three Article XII members' Schedules of Concessions and Commitments (Goods Schedules) set out specific terms of the application of bound rates contained in Part I of the Schedules (MFN tariff). These terms include:<br><br>• Time-frame (staging) for tariff reduction.[222]<br>• Quantity or currency units used for non-*ad valorem* tariff.[223]<br>• Application of specific rates conditional to possible future change of tariff regimes.[224]<br>• Definition of specific products, e.g. 'high-quality beef'.[225]<br>• Establishing special terms for customs classification of specific products.[226]<br>• Fixing the same bound and applied rates for 'like or substitute products'.[227] |

Annex 9.1 (*cont.*)

| AI rules | Specific obligations and influence on rules and WTO jurisprudence |
|---|---|
| | • Establishment of terms to prevent the member concerned from using product descriptions as means or basis of the enforcement of geographical indications at the border.[228]<br>• Reconfirmation of the equal treatment of products imported by non-state and state trading enterprises.[229]<br>• Specific terms on TRQ administration.[230] |

[1]China, Viet Nam, Cabo Verde, Ukraine and Russia.

[2]Related to the sub-section on 'Trade-Related Investment Measures', under the section on 'Internal Policies Affecting Foreign Trade in Goods'.

[3]Estonia.

[4]China and Tonga.

[5]Samoa and Saudi Arabia.

[6]STEs/SOEs to operate in accordance with commercial considerations in GATT Article XVII:1. See the Appellate Body Report on *Canada – Wheat*. Twenty Article XII WTO members have undertaken a specific commitment on the application of commercial considerations for trade transactions for any enterprise whose activities were subject to Article XVII of the GATT 1994, the WTO Understanding on that Article and Article VIII of the GATS (Bulgaria, Cambodia, Cabo Verde, Estonia, Jordan, Kyrgyz Republic, Lao PDR, Moldova, Mongolia, Montenegro, Oman, Panama, Russia, Samoa, Saudi Arabia, Tajikistan, Ukraine, Vanuatu, Viet Nam, Yemen).

[7]Article XVII:1(b) of the GATT 1994.

[8]For example see WTO document WT/ACC/UKR/152: Working Party Report on the Accession of Ukraine to the WTO, 25 January 2008, paras. 41–50, 103.

[9]On the precedence of the exclusive rights and privileges criterion, see the WTO Understanding on the Interpretation of Article XVII.

[10]See WTO document WT/L/432: Protocol on the Accession of the People's Republic of China to the WTO, 23 November 2001: Section 6, para. 1.

[11]Eighteen Article XII WTO members have undertaken this commitment (Albania, Armenia, Cambodia, Cabo Verde, Croatia, Estonia, the former Yugoslav Republic of Macedonia, Georgia, Kyrgyz Republic, Latvia, Lithuania, Moldova, Montenegro, Samoa, Tajikistan, Russia, Ukraine and Viet Nam).

[12]See WTO document WT/ACC/CHN/49: Working Party Report on the Accession of the People's Republic of China to the WTO, 1 October 2001, paras. 210, 212, 213.

[13]See WTO document WT/ACC/CHN/49 of 1 October 2001: Working Party Report on the Accession of the People's Republic of China to the WTO, para. 217.

[14]Example: Estonia: see WTO document WT/ACC/EST/28, 9 April 1999: Working Party Report on the accession of Estonia to the WTO, para. 103; Oman: see WTO document WT/ACC/OMN/26 of 28 September 2000: Working Party Report on the Accession of Oman to the WTO, para. 114.

[15]Bulgaria, Kyrgyz Republic, Latvia, Georgia, Estonia, Jordan, Croatia, Albania, Oman, Lithuania, Moldova, China, Chinese Taipei, the former Yugoslav Republic of Macedonia, Armenia, Cambodia, Nepal, Tonga, Saudi Arabia, Viet Nam, Cabo Verde, Ukraine, Vanuatu, Samoa, Russia, Montenegro, Lao PDR, Tajikistan and Yemen.

[16]All twenty-nine members have accepted a commitment to publish the list of goods and services subject to price control.

[17]China: see WTO document WT/ACC/CHN/49: Working Party Report, para. 60.

[18]China: see WTO document WT/ACC/CHN/49: Working Party Report, paras. 62 and 64; Russia: see WTO document WT/ACC/RUS/70: Working Party Report, para. 133.

[19]Tonga undertook the commitment that any price controls applied to imports upon accession would also be applied to similar domestically produced goods. Tonga: see WTO document WT/ACC/TON/17: Working Party Report, para. 35. Ukraine and Russia confirmed that their state controlled rail transportation fees shall be applied on a non-discriminatory basis. Ukraine: see WTO document WT/ACC/UKR/152: Working Party Report, para. 72; Russia: see WTO document WT/ACC/RUS/70: Working Party Report, para. 115.

[20]Saudi Arabia: see WTO document WT/ACC/SAU/61: Working Party Report, para. 33; Russia: see WTO document WT/ACC/RUS/70: Working Party Report, para. 132; Tajikistan: see WTO document WT/ACC/TJK/30: Working Party Report, para. 596.

[21]Bulgaria, Georgia, Estonia, Albania, Lithuania, Moldova, Cambodia, Nepal, Tonga, Cabo Verde, Samoa, Russia, Lao PDR and Yemen.

[22]Kyrgyz Republic, Latvia, Georgia, Estonia, Jordan, Croatia, Albania, Oman, Lithuania, Moldova, China, Chinese Taipei, Armenia, Cambodia, Nepal, Tonga, Saudi Arabia, Viet Nam, Cabo Verde, Ukraine, Vanuatu, Samoa, Russia, Montenegro, Lao PDR, Tajikistan and Yemen.

[23]Estonia: Working Party Report, para. 30; Jordan: Working Party Report, para. 43; Croatia: Working Party Report, para. 41; Armenia: Working Party Report, paras. 36 and 37; Viet Nam: Working Party Report, para. 119; and Vanuatu: Working Party Report, para. 31.

[24]Russia: Working Party Report, paras. 183 and 214 and paragraphs in other sections throughout its Working Party Report.

[25]Twenty-one Article XII members accepted this commitment: Georgia: Working Party Report, para. 40; Estonia: Working Party Report, para. 30; Jordan: Working

Party Report, para. 43; Croatia: Working Party Report, para. 41; Albania: Working Party Report, para. 38; Lithuania: Working Party Report, para. 29; Moldova: Working Party Report, para. 48; China: see WTO document WT/ACC/CHN/49: Working Party Report, para. 73 and China: WT/L/432: Protocol on the Accession of the People's Republic of China, para. 2(A)1; Armenia: Working Party Report, para. 36; Tonga: Working Party Report, para. 48; Saudi Arabia: Working Party Report, para. 88; Viet Nam: Working Party Report, para. 134; Cabo Verde: Working Party Report, para. 60; Ukraine: Working Party Report, para. 84; Vanuatu: Working Party Report, para. 31; Samoa: Working Party Report, para. 58; Russia: Working Party Report, para. 214; Montenegro: Working Party Report, para. 59; Lao PDR: Working Party Report, para. 55; Tajikistan: Working Party Report, para. 76; and Yemen: Working Party Report, para. 59.

[26]Fifteen Article XII members accepted this accession-specific obligation: Latvia: Working Party Report, para. 30; Estonia: Working Party Report, para. 30; Jordan: Working Party Report, para. 43; Croatia: Working Party Report, para. 41; Albania: Working Party Report, para. 38; Lithuania: Working Party Report, para. 29; Moldova: Working Party Report, para. 48; China: Working Party Report, para. 70; Armenia: Working Party Report, para. 36; Tonga: Working Party Report, para. 48; Ukraine: Working Party Report, para. 84; Vanuatu: Working Party Report, para. 31; Samoa: Working Party Report, para. 58; Montenegro: Working Party Report, paras. 56 and 59; and Tajikistan: Working Party Report, para. 76.

[27]Kyrgyz Republic: Working Party Report, para. 26; Georgia: Working Party Report, para. 40; Estonia: Working Party Report, para. 30; China: Working Party Report, para. 70; and Moldova: Working Party Report, para. 48. Moldova specifically accepted the obligation that all fiscal, financial and budgetary activities performed by local governments shall be in compliance with Article III of the GATT 1994.

[28]China: see WTO document WT/L/432: Protocol on the Accession of the People's Republic of China, para. 2(A)2.

[29]Kyrgyz Republic: Working Party Report, para. 28; Latvia: Working Party Report, para. 30; Albania: Working Party Report, para. 38; Chinese Taipei: Working Party Report, para. 15; and Armenia: Working Party Report, para. 36.

[30]Eighteen Article XII members accepted this commitment. Georgia: Report of the Working Party, para. 40; Estonia: Working Party Report, para. 30; Jordan: Working Party Report, para. 43; Albania: Working Party Report, para. 38; Lithuania: Working Party Report, para. 29; Moldova: Working Party Report, para. 48; Armenia: Working Party Report, para. 36; Tonga: Working Party Report, para. 36; Saudi Arabia: Working Party Report, para. 88; Viet Nam: Working Party Report, para. 134; Cabo Verde: Working Party Report, para. 60; Ukraine: Working Party Report, para. 84; Vanuatu: Working Party Report, para. 31; Samoa: Working Party Report, para. 58; Montenegro: Working Party Report, para. 59; Lao PDR:

Working Party Report, para. 55; Tajikistan: Working Party Report, para. 76; and Yemen: Working Party Report, para. 59.

[31]Russia: Working Party Report, para. 215.

[32]Sixteen Article XII members accepted this specific obligation: Kyrgyz Republic: Working Party Report, para. 26; Georgia: Working Party Report, para. 35; Croatia: Working Party Report, para. 37; Oman: Working Party Report, para. 32; Armenia: Working Party Report, para. 34; Cambodia: Working Party Report, para. 36; Saudi Arabia: Working Party Report, para. 85; Viet Nam: Working Party Report, para. 135; Cabo Verde: Working Party Report, para. 66; Ukraine: Working Party Report, para. 92; Samoa: Working Party Report, para. 54; Russia: Working Party Report, para. 215; Montenegro: Working Party Report, para. 56; Lao PDR: Working Party Report, para. 52; Tajikistan: Working Party Report, para. 71; and Yemen: Working Party Report, para. 57.

[33]China: see WTO document WT/ACC/CHN/49: Working Party Report, para. 75 and China: WT/L/432: Protocol on the Accession of the People's Republic of China, paras. 2(D)1 and 2(D)2; and Russia: Working Party Report, para. 214.

[34]Nepal: Working Party Report, para. 31; and Tonga: Working Party Report, para. 43.

[35]China: see WTO document WT/ACC/CHN/49: Working Party Report, para. 75 and China: WT/L/432: Protocol on the Accession of the People's Republic of China, paras. 2(D)1 and 2(D)2; Russia: Working Party Report, para. 214.

[36]Nepal: Working Party Report, para. 31; and Tonga: Working Party Report, para. 43.

[37]China: see WTO document WT/ACC/CHN/49: Working Party Report, para. 78; Nepal: Working Party Report, para. 31; Viet Nam: Working Party Report, para. 60; Cabo Verde: Working Party Report, para. 66; and Yemen: Working Party Report, para. 57.

[38]Armenia: Working Party Report, para. 37.

[39]China: see WTO document WT/ACC/CHN/49: Working Party Report, paras. 68, 70 and 78.

[40]China: see WTO document WT/ACC/CHN/49: Working Party Report, para. 68.

[41]Russia: Working Party Report, para. 209.

[42]Example: China: see WTO document WT/ACC/CHN/49: Working Party Report, 1 October 2001; paras. 83, 84 and 86.

[43]Twenty-four Article XII members undertook respective specific commitments: Kyrgyz Republic, Latvia, Georgia, Estonia, Jordan, Croatia, Albania, Oman, Lithuania, Moldova, the former Yugoslav Republic of Macedonia, Armenia, Cambodia, Nepal, Tonga, Saudi Arabia, Viet Nam, Cabo Verde, Ukraine, Vanuatu, Samoa, Lao PDR, Tajikistan and Yemen.

[44]Example: Chinese Taipei: see WTO document WT/ACC/TPKM/18: Working Party Report on the Accession of the Separate Customs Territory of Taiwan, Penghu, Kinmen and Matsu to the WTO of 5 October 2001, para. 19.

[45]Ibid.

[46]Example: Russia: see WTO document WT/ACC/RUS/70, para. 227: Working Party Report, 17 November 2011.

[47]Example: Viet Nam: see WTO document WT/ACC/VNM/48, para. 147, 27 October 2006: Working Party Report.

[48]Example: Ukraine: see WTO document WT/ACC/UKR/152, 25 January 2008, para. 115: Working Party Report; Lao PDR: see WTO document WT/ACC/LAO/45, 1 October 2012, para. 59: Working Party Report; Tajikistan: see WTO document WT/ACC/TJK/30, 6 November 2012, para. 92: Working Party Report.

[49]Example: Tajikistan: see WTO document WT/ACC/TJK/30, 6 November 2012, para. 92: Working Party Report. Yemen: see WTO document WT/ACC/YEM/42 of 4 October 2013, para. 68: Working Party Report.

[50]Armenia: Working Party Report, para. 53; Kyrgyz Republic: Working Party Report, para. 34; Viet Nam: Working Party Report, para. 155.

[51]Russia: WT/ACC/RUS/70: Working Party Report, para. 313.

[52]China: Working Party Report, para. 92; Montenegro: Working Party Report, para. 80; Tajikistan: Working Party Report, para. 97; and Russia: Working Party Report, para. 324.

[53]China: Working Party Report, paras. 19 and 93; Russia: Working Party Report, para. 323.

[54]Russia: Working Party Report, para. 319.

[55]Albania: Working Party Report, para. 51; Armenia: Working Party Report, para. 54; Bulgaria: Working Party Report, paras. 29, 30, 32 and 33; Cambodia: Working Party Report, para. 55; China: Working Party Report, para. 96; Chinese Taipei: Working Party Report, para. 40; the former Yugoslav Republic of Macedonia: Working Party Report, para. 71; Jordan: Working Party Report, para. 58; Lao PDR: Working Party Report, para. 63; Mongolia: Working Party Report, para. 10; Montenegro: Working Party Report, para. 83; Nepal: Working Party Report, para. 42; Panama: Working Party Report, para. 16; Samoa: Working Party Report, para. 73; Tajikistan: Working Party Report, para. 100; Russia: Working Party Report, para. 369; Tonga: Working Party Report, para. 59; Ukraine: Working Party Report, para. 127; Vanuatu: Working Party Report, para. 45; Viet Nam: Working Party Report, para. 162; Yemen: Working Party Report, para. 75.

[56]Saudi Arabia: Working Party Report, para. 115; Cabo Verde: Working Party Report, para. 88.

[57]China: Working Party Report, para. 115.

[58]China: Working Party Report, para. 116; Chinese Taipei: Working Party Report, para. 37; Tajikistan: Working Party Report, para. 105; Ukraine: Working Party Report, para. 136; Viet Nam: Working Party Report, para. 174.

[59]China: Working Party Report, paras. 117, 119 and 120; Chinese Taipei: Working Party Report, para. 39; Russia: Working Party Report, paras. 351, 364 and 366; Ukraine: Working Party Report, para. 136.

[60]Armenia: Working Party Report, paras. 64 and 65; Bulgaria: Working Party Report, para. 45; Chinese Taipei: Working Party Report, paras. 50 and 55; Georgia: Working Party Report, para. 62; Kyrgyz Republic: Report of the Working Party on the Accession of the Kyrgyz Republic: para. 53; Samoa: Working Party Report, para. 85; Tajikistan: Working Party Report, para. 124; Russia: Working Party Report, paras. 417 and 424; Ukraine: Working Party Report, para. 154; Viet Nam: Working Party Report, para. 198.

[61]Armenia: Working Party Report, para. 70; Bulgaria: Working Party Report, para. 45; Ecuador: Working Party Report, para. 19; the former Yugoslav Republic of Macedonia: Working Party Report, para. 97; Georgia: Working Party Report, para. 57; Lithuania: Working Party Report, para. 66; Nepal: Working Party Report, para. 64; Vanuatu: Working Party Report, para. 55; Viet Nam: Working Party Report, para. 199.

[62]Albania: Working Party Report, para. 65; Armenia: Working Party Report, para. 87; Bulgaria: Working Party Report, para. 50; Cabo Verde: Working Party Report, para. 123; Cambodia: Working Party Report, para. 82; China: Working Party Report, paras. 122 and 136; Chinese Taipei: Working Party Report, para. 73; Croatia: Working Party Report, para. 73; Ecuador: Working Party Report, para. 34; Estonia: Working Party Report, para. 65; Georgia: Working Party Report, para. 65; Jordan: Working Party Report, para. 88; Kyrgyz Republic: Working Party Report, para. 60; Lao PDR: Working Party Report, para. 82; Latvia: Working Party Report, para. 59; Lithuania: Working Party Report, para. 71; Moldova: Working Party Report, para. 78; Mongolia: Working Party Report, para. 20; Montenegro: Working Party Report, para. 114; Nepal: Working Party Report, para. 50; Oman: Working Party Report, para. 57; Panama: Working Party Report, para. 41; Russia: Working Party Report, para. 487; Samoa: Working Party Report, para. 109; Saudi Arabia: Working Party Report, paras. 155 and 158; Tajikistan: Working Party Report, para. 137; the former Yugoslav Republic of Macedonia: Working Party Report, para. 107; Tonga: Working Party Report, para. 84; Ukraine: Working Party Report, para. 192; Vanuatu: Working Party Report, para. 63; Viet Nam: Working Party Report, para. 227; and Yemen: Working Party Report, para. 107.

[63]Albania: Working Party Report, para. 65; Armenia: Working Party Report, para. 87; Bulgaria: Working Party Report, para. 49; Cabo Verde: Working Party Report, para. 123; Cambodia: Working Party Report, para. 82; Chinese Taipei: Working Party Report, paras. 72 and 73; Croatia: Working Party Report, para. 73; Ecuador: Working Party Report, para. 38; Estonia: Working Party Report, para. 65; Georgia: Working Party Report, para. 65; Jordan: Working Party Report, para. 88; Kyrgyz Republic: Working Party Report, para. 60; Lao PDR: Working Party Report, para. 82; Latvia: Working Party Report, para. 59; Lithuania: Working Party Report, para. 71; Moldova: Working Party Report, para. 79; Mongolia: Working Party Report, para. 20; Montenegro: Working Party Report, para. 114; Nepal: Working Party Report, para. 50; Oman: Working Party Report, para. 57; Panama:

Working Party Report, para. 42; Russia: Working Party Report, para. 487; Samoa: Working Party Report, para. 109; Saudi Arabia: Working Party Report, paras. 155 and 158; Tajikistan: Working Party Report, para. 137; the former Yugoslav Republic of Macedonia: Working Party Report, para. 107; Tonga: Working Party Report, para. 84; Ukraine: Working Party Report, para. 192; Vanuatu: Working Party Report, para. 63; Viet Nam: Working Party Report, para. 227; and Yemen: Working Party Report, para. 107.

[64]Cambodia: Working Party Report, para. 77; Chinese Taipei: Working Party Report, para. 73; Mongolia: Working Party Report, para. 20; Panama: Working Party Report, para. 42; Ukraine: Working Party Report, para. 192; and Viet Nam: Working Party Report, para. 209.

[65]Albania: Working Party Report, para. 65; Armenia: Working Party Report, para. 73; Bulgaria: Working Party Report, para. 50; Cambodia: Working Party Report, para. 77; China: Working Party Report, paras. 122, 126 to 129; Chinese Taipei: Working Party Report, paras. 61, 66, 68, 69 and 71; Ecuador: Working Party Report, para. 34; Jordan: Working Party Report, para. 88; Kyrgyz Republic: Working Party Report, para. 60; Latvia: Working Party Report, para. 59; Lithuania: Working Party Report, para. 71; Montenegro: Working Party Report, para. 114; Oman: Working Party Report, para. 57; Panama: Working Party Report, para. 41; Russia: Working Party Report, paras. 472, 476, 477, 480, 481 and 486; Samoa: Working Party Report, paras. 98, 101 and 106; Saudi Arabia: Working Party Report, paras. 128, 132, 142, 153 and 158; Tajikistan: Working Party Report, para. 137; the former Yugoslav Republic of Macedonia: Working Party Report, para. 107; Tonga: Working Party Report, para. 79; Ukraine: Working Party Report, paras. 173 and 192; Viet Nam: Working Party Report, paras. 206, 208, 209, 215, 216 and 218; and Yemen: Working Party Report, para. 93.

[66]Cambodia: Working Party Report, para. 77; China: Working Party Report, para. 122; Chinese Taipei: Working Party Report, paras. 61 and 69; Ecuador: Working Party Report, para. 34; Jordan: Working Party Report, para. 88; Tonga: Working Party Report, para. 79; Samoa: Working Party Report, paras. 98, 101 and 106; Saudi Arabia: Working Party Report, para. 132; the former Yugoslav Republic of Macedonia: Working Party Report, para. 107; and Viet Nam: Working Party Report, para. 208.

[67]Saudi Arabia: Working Party Report, paras. 132 and 158.

[68]Viet Nam: Working Party Report, paras. 215 and 218.

[69]Yemen: Working Party Report, para. 93.

[70]China: Working Party Report, para. 123.

[71]Ibid.: paras. 127 to 131.

[72]Mongolia: Working Party Report, para. 21.

[73]Russia: Working Party Report, para. 472.

[74]Bulgaria: Working Party Report, para. 73; Cabo Verde: Working Party Report, para. 130; China: Working Party Report, para. 143; Estonia: Working Party Report,

para. 71; Georgia: Working Party Report, para. 69; Kyrgyz Republic: Working Party Report, para. 63; Moldova: Working Party Report, para. 90; Montenegro: Working Party Report, para. 119; Oman: Working Party Report, para. 64; Russia: Working Party Report, para. 527; Tajikistan: Working Party Report, para. 146; and Viet Nam: Working Party Report, para. 238.

[75] Albania: Working Party Report, para. 74; Bulgaria: Working Party Report, para. 73; Estonia: Working Party Report, para. 71; Kyrgyz Republic: Working Party Report, para. 63; and Moldova: Working Party Report, para. 90.

[76] Chinese Taipei: Working Party Report, para. 78; and Tajikistan: Working Party Report, para. 146.

[77] Nepal: Working Party Report, para. 53.

[78] Albania: Working Party Report, para. 75; and Croatia: Working Party Report, para. 83.

[79] Albania: Working Party Report, para. 79; Armenia: Working Party Report, para. 102; Cambodia: Working Party Report, para. 96; Cabo Verde: Working Party Report, para. 136; China: Working Party Report, para. 100; Croatia: Working Party Report, para. 88; Jordan: Working Party Report, para. 100; Lao PDR: Working Party Report, para. 94; Lithuania: Working Party Report, para. 86; Moldova: Working Party Report, para. 94; Montenegro: Working Party Report, para. 123; Nepal: Working Party Report, para. 68; Russia: Working Party Report, para. 548; Samoa: Working Party Report, para. 120; Saudi Arabia: Working Party Report, para. 167; Tajikistan: Working Party Report, para. 152; the former Yugoslav Republic of Macedonia: Working Party Report, para. 115; Tonga: Working Party Report, para. 96; Ukraine: Working Party Report, para. 213; Vanuatu: Working Party Report, para. 72; Viet Nam: Working Party Report, para. 244; and Yemen: Working Party Report, para. 122.

[80] Russia: Working Party Report, para. 548; Samoa: Working Party Report, para. 120; Tonga: Working Party Report, para. 96; and Vanuatu: Working Party Report, para. 72.

[81] Lao PDR: Working Party Report, para. 96; Samoa: Working Party Report, para. 122; and Yemen: Working Party Report, para. 125. Yemen was granted a transition period until 1 January 2017 in order to terminate the existing certification/notarisation requirement.

[82] Cambodia: Working Party Report, para. 99.

[83] Russia: Working Party Report, paras. 562 and 677.

[84] Ibid.

[85] Ibid.

[86] Saudi Arabia: Working Party Report, para. 169.

[87] Ukraine: Working Party Report, para. 216.

[88] Albania: Working Party Report, para. 81; Armenia: Working Party Report, para. 104; Cambodia: Working Party Report, para. 105; Cabo Verde: Working Party Report, para. 141; Lao PDR: Working Party Report, para. 98; Moldova:

Working Party Report, para. 96; Montenegro: Working Party Report, para. 126; Nepal: Working Party Report, para. 71; Samoa: Working Party Report, para. 124; Tajikistan: Working Party Report, para. 155; Tonga: Working Party Report, para. 98; Ukraine: Working Party Report, para. 218; Vanuatu: Working Party Report, para. 75; Viet Nam: Working Party Report, para. 250; and Yemen: Working Party Report, para. 128.

[89] Albania: Working Party Report, para. 81; Cambodia: Working Party Report, para. 105; Cabo Verde: Working Party Report, para. 141; Moldova: Working Party Report, para. 96; Samoa: Working Party Report, para. 124; Tonga: Working Party Report, para. 98; Vanuatu: Working Party Report, para. 75; Viet Nam: Working Party Report, para. 250; and Yemen: Working Party Report, para. 128.

[90] Armenia: Working Party Report, para. 104; Cambodia: Working Party Report, para. 105; Cabo Verde: Working Party Report, para. 141; Georgia: Working Party Report, para. 76; Jordan: Working Party Report, para. 103; Lao PDR: Working Party Report, para. 98; Moldova: Working Party Report, para. 96; Montenegro: Working Party Report, para. 126; Russia: Working Party Report, para. 566; Samoa: Working Party Report, para. 124; Saudi Arabia: Working Party Report, para. 174; Tajikistan: Working Party Report, para. 155; Ukraine: Working Party Report, para. 218; Viet Nam: Working Party Report, para. 250; and Yemen: Working Party Report, para. 128.

[91] Cambodia: Working Party Report, para. 105; Cabo Verde: Working Party Report, para. 141; China: Working Party Report, para. 146; Georgia: Working Party Report, para. 76; Jordan: Working Party Report, para. 103; Lao PDR: Working Party Report, para. 98; Moldova: Working Party Report, para. 96; Montenegro: Working Party Report, para. 126; Russia: Working Party Report, para. 566; Samoa: Working Party Report, para. 124; Saudi Arabia: Working Party Report, para. 174; Tajikistan: Working Party Report, para. 155; Ukraine: Working Party Report, para. 218; Viet Nam: Working Party Report, para. 250; and Yemen: Working Party Report, para. 128.

[92] Albania: Working Party Report, para. 81; Armenia: Working Party Report, para. 104; Cabo Verde: Working Party Report, para. 141; Georgia: Working Party Report, para. 76; Lao PDR: Working Party Report, para. 98; Montenegro: Working Party Report, para. 126; Nepal: Working Party Report, para. 71; Russia: Working Party Report, para. 566; Tajikistan: Working Party Report, para. 155; Tonga: Working Party Report, para. 98; Ukraine: Working Party Report, para. 218; Vanuatu: Working Party Report, para. 75; Viet Nam: Working Party Report, para. 250; and Yemen: Working Party Report, para. 128.

[93] Albania: Working Party Report, paras. 84 and 86; Armenia: Working Party Report, para. 106; Bulgaria: Working Party Report, para. 55; Cambodia: Working Party Report, para. 108; Cabo Verde: Working Party Report, para. 144; China: Working Party Report, paras. 144, 152, 154 and China: the Protocol on the Accession of the People's Republic of China: WT/L/432: Section I.15; Chinese

Taipei: Working Party Report, paras. 86 and 89; Croatia: Working Party Report, para. 99; Ecuador: Working Party Report, para. 57; Estonia: Working Party Report, para. 78; Georgia: Working Party Report, para. 78; Jordan: Working Party Report, para. 107; Kyrgyz Republic: Working Party Report, para. 70; Lao PDR: Working Party Report, para. 99; Latvia: Working Party Report, para. 66; Lithuania: Working Party Report, para. 91; Moldova: Working Party Report, para. 98; Montenegro: Working Party Report, para. 129; Nepal: Working Party Report, para. 75; Oman: Working Party Report, para. 73; Russia: Working Party Report, paras. 591, 613 and 620; Samoa: Working Party Report, para. 127; Saudi Arabia: Working Party Report, para. 178; Tajikistan: Working Party Report, para. 165; the former Yugoslav Republic of Macedonia: Working Party Report, para. 122; Tonga: Working Party Report, para. 100; Ukraine: Working Party Report, para. 227; Vanuatu: Working Party Report, para. 77; Viet Nam: Working Party Report, para. 253; and Yemen: Working Party Report, para. 130.

[94]Three Article XII WTO members (that were in transition from centrally planned to market economies) negotiated transition periods, during their accession negotiations. These were: China: the Protocol on the Accession of the People's Republic of China: WT/L/432: Section I.15; Tajikistan: Working Party Report, para. 164; and Viet Nam: Working Party Report, para. 255. During the transition periods, nonmarket economy (NME) provisions apply and allow for the application/use of alternative methodologies in: determining price comparability under Article VI of the GATT 1994 and the Anti-dumping Agreement; and identifying and measuring the subsidy benefit under the Agreement on SCM. These transition periods expire once the concerned Article XII WTO member establishes, pursuant to the domestic law of the importing WTO member, that it is a full market economy; and at the end of the negotiated transition period. In addition, if, pursuant to the domestic law of the importing WTO member, market economy conditions are established in a particular industry/sector, NME provisions shall no longer apply to that specific industry/sector.

[95]China: Working Party Report, para. 152.

[96]Russia: Working Party Report, para. 613.

[97]Accession-specific obligations/commitments on Export Regulations are dispersed across different chapters and sections of Accession Packages. This 'dispersal problem' arose over the years, as members considered, reconsidered and grappled with the question of how and where best to embed these obligations. The objective of members was to tighten the system and plug loopholes for circumvention. The grid summary regroups these accession-specific obligations, coherently, from different chapters and sections of working party reports.

[98]Albania, Armenia, Bulgaria, Cambodia, China, Croatia, Estonia, Georgia, Jordan, Kyrgyz Republic, Lao PDR, Latvia, Lithuania, Moldova, Mongolia, Montenegro, Nepal, Oman, Panama, Russia, Samoa, Saudi Arabia, Tajikistan, Tonga, Ukraine, Vanuatu, Viet Nam and Yemen.

[99] For example, Nepal accepted a specific obligation that its 'export service fee' shall be consistent with Article VIII of the GATT 1994.

[100] Twenty-three Article XII members accepted accession-specific commitments of this kind: Albania: Working Party Report, para. 90; Bulgaria: Working Party Report, para. 49; Georgia: Working Party Report, para. 86; Estonia: Working Party Report, para. 83; Jordan: Working Party Report, para. 116; China: Protocol on the Accession of the People's Republic of China to the WTO: WT/L/432, para. 11; Croatia: Working Party Report, para. 105; Oman: Working Party Report, para. 77; Lithuania: Working Party Report, para. 97; Moldova: Working Party Report, para. 101; Armenia: Working Party Report, para. 112; Cambodia: Working Party Report, para. 115; Nepal: Working Party Report, para. 84; Tonga: Working Party Report, para. 106; Saudi Arabia: Working Party Report, para. 182; Viet Nam: Working Party Report, paras. 260 and 269; Vanuatu: Working Party Report, para. 79; Samoa: Working Party Report, para. 134; Russia: Working Party Report, para. 677; Montenegro: Working Party Report, para. 135; Lao PDR: Working Party Report, para. 105; Tajikistan: Working Party Report, para. 181; and Yemen: Working Party Report, para. 135.

[101] China: Working Party Report, paras. 157 and 165; Saudi Arabia: Working Party Report, para. 179; Russia: Working Party Report, para. 677.

[102] Saudi Arabia: Working Party Report, para. 181; Ukraine: Working Party Report, para. 255.

[103] Mongolia: Working Party Report, para. 24.

[104] Kyrgyz Republic: Working Party Report, para. 79; China: Working Party Report, para. 162; Ukraine: Working Party Report, para. 255; and Russia: Working Party Report, para. 669.

[105] Russia: Working Party Report, para. 638.

[106] Bulgaria: Working Party Report, para. 39; Estonia: Working Party Report, para. 80; and Georgia: Working Party Report, para. 82.

[107] China: see WTO document WT/L/432: Protocol on the Accession of the People's Republic of China, para. 11.3; and Tajikistan: Working Party Report, para. 169.

[108] Saudi Arabia: Working Party Report, para. 183.

[109] Montenegro: Working Party Report, para. 135.

[110] Russia: Working Party Report, para. 668.

[111] Latvia: Working Party Report, para. 69; Mongolia: Working Party Report, para. 24; and Tajikistan: Working Party Report, para. 169.

[112] For example: China: Protocol on the Accession of the People's Republic of China: Annex 6; Ukraine: Working Party Report, para. 240; Viet Nam: Working Party Report, para. 260.

[113] Russia bound its export duties on products listed in Part V of its Schedule of Concessions and Commitments on Goods (CLXV).

[114]Russia: Working Party Report, para. 638.

[115]Russia: Working Party Report, para. 638; and Ukraine: Working Party Report, para. 240.

[116]For example, Saudi Arabia accepted a specific obligation not to impose export duties on iron and scrap. Saudi Arabia: Working Party Report, para. 184.

[117]Montenegro: Working Party Report, para. 132; and Tajikistan: Working Party Report, para. 169.

[118]For example, Russia accepted a specific obligation to eliminate and not introduce WTO-inconsistent export restrictions both at the national level and at the level of the Customs Union of Russia, Belarus and Kazakhstan. Russia: Working Party Report, para. 668.

[119]Accession *acquis* and associated obligations by the thirty-three Article XII members on export subsidies on agricultural products, specifically, are entered in the 'Agricultural Policies' section of this grid.

[120]Kyrgyz Republic, Albania, Armenia, Cambodia, China, Chinese Taipei, Croatia, Estonia, Georgia, Jordan, Lithuania, Moldova, Oman, Saudi Arabia, the former Yugoslav Republic of Macedonia and Ukraine.

[121]Thirteen Article XII members accepted this specific commitment: Georgia: Working Party Report, para. 89; Estonia: Working Party Report, para. 85; Jordan: Working Party Report, para. 126; Croatia: Working Party Report, para. 108; Albania: Working Party Report, para. 92; Oman: Working Party Report, para. 81; Lithuania: Working Party Report, para. 102; Moldova: Working Party Report, para. 105; Chinese Taipei: Working Party Report, para. 97; the former Yugoslav Republic of Macedonia: Working Party Report, para. 132; Armenia: Working Party Report, para. 115; Saudi Arabia: Working Party Report, para. 186; and Ukraine: Working Party Report, para. 259.

[122]Kyrgyz Republic: Working Party Report, para. 84; and China: Working Party Report, paras. 167 and 168.

[123]Jordan: Working Party Report, para. 126; and Cambodia: Working Party Report, para. 120.

[124]Albania, Armenia, Cabo Verde, Cambodia, China, Chinese Taipei, Croatia, Estonia, Georgia, Jordan, Lao PDR, Latvia, Lithuania, Moldova, Mongolia, Montenegro, Nepal, Oman, Panama, Russia, Samoa, Saudi Arabia, Tajikistan, the former Yugoslav Republic of Macedonia, Tonga, Ukraine, Vanuatu, Viet Nam and Yemen.

[125]Twenty-three Article XII members accepted this accession commitment: Albania, Armenia, Cabo Verde, Cambodia, Croatia, Estonia, Georgia, Jordan, Lao PDR, Latvia, Lithuania, Moldova, Nepal, Oman, Russia, Samoa, Saudi Arabia, Tajikistan, the former Yugoslav Republic of Macedonia, Tonga, Vanuatu, Viet Nam and Yemen.

[126]China: Working Party Report, para. 174; Nepal: Working Party Report, para. 88; Panama: Working Party Report, para. 63; Russia: Working Party Report, para. 698;

Ukraine: Working Party Report, para. 276; and Viet Nam: Working Party Report, paras. 286 and 288.

[127]For example, Mongolia committed to eliminate incentives that constituted a prohibited subsidy within the meaning of Article 3 of the SCM Agreement by 1 December 2002: Mongolia: Working Party Report, para. 23; Cabo Verde: Working Party Report, para. 163 (by 1 January 2015); and Viet Nam: Working Party Report, para. 288 (within five years from the date of its WTO accession).

[128]Croatia: Working Party Report, para. 111; Montenegro: Working Party Report, para. 142; Samoa: Working Party Report, para. 141; Tajikistan: Working Party Report, para. 191; the former Yugoslav Republic of Macedonia: Working Party Report, para. 135; and Tonga: Working Party Report, para. 115.

[129]Chinese Taipei: Working Party Report, para. 106; Lithuania: Working Party Report, para. 104; and Yemen: Working Party Report, para. 148.

[130]For example: Chinese Taipei: Working Party Report, paras. 106 and 113; Mongolia: Working Party Report, para. 23; and Ukraine: Working Party Report, para. 276.

[131]Tajikistan: Working Party Report, para. 190; and Ukraine: Working Party Report, para. 275.

[132]Twenty-seven Article XII members accepted this accession commitment: Albania, Armenia, Cambodia, Chinese Taipei, Croatia, Estonia, Georgia, Jordan, Lao PDR, Latvia, Lithuania, Moldova, Mongolia, Montenegro, Nepal, Oman, Panama, Russia, Samoa, Saudi Arabia, Tajikistan, the former Yugoslav Republic of Macedonia, Tonga, Ukraine, Vanuatu, Viet Nam and Yemen.

[133]Albania: Working Party Report, para. 104; Armenia: Working Party Report, paras. 135 and 136; Bulgaria: Working Party Report, para. 64; Cabo Verde: Working Party Report, para. 171; Cambodia: Working Party Report, para. 131; China: Working Party Report, paras. 177, 178, 180, 182, 184, 185, 187, 190, 191, 192, 193, 194, 195, 196 and 197; Chinese Taipei: Working Party Report, paras. 121, 127 and 126 *bis*; Croatia: Working Party Report, para. 22; Estonia: Working Party Report, para. 98; Georgia: Working Party Report, paras. 99 and 100; Jordan: Working Party Report, paras. 137 and 140; Kyrgyz Republic: Working Party Report, para. 94; Lao PDR: Working Party Report, para. 125; Latvia: Working Party Report, para. 88; Lithuania: Working Party Report, para. 113; Moldova: Working Party Report, para. 124; Montenegro: Working Party Report, para. 154; Nepal: Working Party Report, para. 98; Oman: Working Party Report, paras. 96 and 97; Panama: Working Party Report, para. 47; Russia: Working Party Report, paras. 712, 714, 715, 719, 728, 738, 739, 744, 745, 756, 761, 765, 772, 773, 784, 785, 787, 789, 798, 799, 803, 804 and 813; Samoa: Working Party Report, para. 145; Saudi Arabia: Working Party Report, paras. 197, 201, 203 and 205; Tajikistan: Working Party Report, paras. 194, 199, 207 and 209; the former Yugoslav Republic of Macedonia: Working Party Report, para. 145; Tonga: Working Party Report, para. 119; Ukraine: Working Party Report, paras. 280, 285,

299, 300, 301, 302 and 303; Vanuatu: Working Party Report, para. 89; Viet Nam: Working Party Report, para. 303; and Yemen: Working Party Report, para. 165.

[134]Cabo Verde: Working Party Report, para. 171; China: Working Party Report, para. 177; Russia: Working Party Report, para. 761; Samoa: Working Party Report, para. 145; and Tonga: Working Party Report, para. 119.

[135]Cabo Verde: Working Party Report, para. 171; China: Working Party Report, para. 178; Samoa: Working Party Report, para. 145; Tonga: Working Party Report, para. 119; Vanuatu: Working Party Report, para. 186; and Russia: Working Party Report, para. 114.

[136]Cambodia: Working Party Report, para. 131; Georgia: Working Party Report, para. 99; Jordan: Working Party Report, para. 137; Lao PDR: Working Party Report, para. 125; Nepal: Working Party Report, para. 98; Russia: Working Party Report, para. 738; Ukraine: Working Party Report, paras. 299 and 300; and Yemen: Working Party Report, para. 165.

[137]Jordan: Working Party Report, para. 137; Moldova: Working Party Report, para. 124; and Oman: Working Party Report, para. 96.

[138]China: Working Party Report, para. 178; and Russia: Working Party Report, para. 712.

[139]China: Working Party Report, paras. 190 and 196; Chinese Taipei: Working Party Report, para. 126 *bis*; Georgia: Working Party Report, para. 99; Oman: Working Party Report, para. 96; Russia: Working Party Report, paras. 738, 739, 744, 772 and 789; Saudi Arabia: Working Party Report, para. 201; and Ukraine: Working Party Report, paras. 285 and 299.

[140]Armenia: Working Party Report, para. 135; Tajikistan: Working Party Report, para. 207; Ukraine: Working Party Report, para. 302; and Russia: Working Party Report, para. 784.

[141]Cabo Verde: Working Party Report, para. 171.

[142]Russia: Working Party Report, paras. 715 and 719.

[143]China: Working Party Report, paras. 180 and 187.

[144]Ibid., para. 192.

[145]WTO SPS Agreement, Article 3.1.

[146]Jordan accepted the specific obligation that no stricter rules than those laid out by international organisations would be applied (Working Party Report: see WTO document WT/ACC/JOR/33, para. 151, 3 December 1999). Ukraine accepted the specific obligation to base all its SPS measures on the Codex Alimentarius, OIE and IPPC standards, guidelines and recommendations in accordance with the requirements of the WTO SPS Agreement: Working Party Report: see WTO document WT/ACC/UKR/152, para. 326, 25 January 2008.

[147]Saudi Arabia accepted a specific obligation in respect of notification – both to the WTO and all WTO members – of proposed SPS measures and notification of all actions relating to SPS issues: Working Party Report: see WTO document WT/ACC/SAU/61, para. 216, 1 November 2005.

[148]Tonga accepted a specific obligation to specify the manner for publishing any proposed SPS measures (Working Party Report: see WTO document WT/ACC/TON/17, para. 126, 2 December 2005).

[149]Saudi Arabia: Working Party Report: see WTO document WT/ACC/SAU/61, para. 125, 1 November 2005.

[150]Ukraine accepted a specific obligation in respect of any proposed limits on MRLs: Working Party Report: see WTO document WT/ACC/UKR/152: para. 320, 25 January 2008.

[151]The bloc of commitments contains specific obligations in respect of (i) import permits; (ii) transit; (iii) veterinary certificates; (iv) establishment approval; and (v) inspections. See Russia: Working Party Report (see WTO document WT/ACC/RUS/70, paras. 870, 875, 876, 880, 885, 890, 893, 895, 901, 904, 908, 923, 926, 927, 928, 932, 935, and 936).

[152]'Additional' SPS commitments of Russia were necessary and required because of the establishment of the Customs Union between Russia, Belarus and Kazakhstan.

[153]Two years for China, five years for Ecuador and six years for Russia. The specific sector of exemption for the immediate elimination of WTO-inconsistent measures was automotive for China and Russia. For Russia, see WTO documents WP/ACC/RUS/70; WT/MIN(11)/2: Working Party Report, paras. 1089 and 1090. Ecuador did not specify the sector.

[154]For example, Montenegro, Tajikistan and Ukraine.

[155]Albania: Working Party Report, para. 123; Armenia: Working Party Report, para. 153; Bulgaria: Working Party Report, para. 80; China: Working Party Report, paras. 339 and 341; Croatia: Working Party Report, para. 156; Estonia: Working Party Report, para. 107; Georgia: Working Party Report, para. 117; Jordan: Working Party Report, para. 170; Kyrgyz Republic: Working Party Report, para. 120; Latvia: Working Party Report, para. 100; Lithuania: Working Party Report, para. 140; Moldova: Working Party Report, para. 150; Mongolia: Working Party Report, para. 59; Montenegro: Working Party Report, para. 182; Oman: Working Party Report, para. 121; Panama: Working Party Report, para. 68; Russia: Working Party Report, paras. 1137, 1143 and 1144; Saudi Arabia: Working Party Report, para. 231; Chinese Taipei: Working Party Report, para. 166; Tajikistan: Working Party Report, para. 244; the former Yugoslav Republic of Macedonia: Working Party Report, para. 177; Ukraine: Working Party Report, para. 358; and Vanuatu: Working Party Report, para. 108.

[156]Seven Article XII members have acceded to the GPA, after joining the WTO: Armenia, Bulgaria, Chinese Taipei, Croatia, Estonia, Latvia and Lithuania. Nine out of the ten members that are currently in the process of acceding to the GPA are Article XII members: Albania, China, Georgia, Jordan, Kyrgyz Republic, Moldova, Montenegro, Oman and Ukraine. Five other Article XII members

have provisions regarding GPA Accession in their respective Protocols of Accession: the former Yugoslav Republic of Macedonia, Mongolia, Russia, Tajikistan and Saudi Arabia.

[157]Fifteen Article XII members are observers to the GPA Committee: Albania, China, Georgia, Jordan, Kyrgyz Republic, Moldova, Mongolia, Montenegro, Oman, Panama, Russia, Saudi Arabia, the former Yugoslav Republic of Macedonia, Ukraine and Viet Nam.

[158]Five out of the seven Article XII members that have acceded to the GPA are EU member states: Bulgaria, Croatia, Estonia, Latvia and Lithuania. Montenegro is currently pursuing its accession to the GPA (see WTO document GPA/121, para. 3.14).

[159]China: Working Party Report, para. 339; and Russia: Working Party Report, paras. 1143 and 1144.

[160]Russia: Working Party Report, para. 1137.

[161]Vanuatu: Working Party Report, para. 108.

[162]Bulgaria, Chinese Taipei and Estonia have *not* taken on specific obligations on 'free zones, Special Economic Area'.

[163]For example, the specific WTO Agreements noted in this regard are TRIPs (in the working party reports of Armenia, Georgia, Jordan, Lithuania, Montenegro, Oman, Panama, Samoa, Saudi Arabia and Ukraine); TRIMs (Armenia, Georgia, Montenegro, Oman, Samoa, Saudi Arabia, Tajikistan and Ukraine); and subsidies (in the working party reports of Armenia, Georgia, Montenegro, Oman, Samoa, Saudi Arabia, Tajikistan and Ukraine).

[164]For example: Cambodia, the former Yugoslav Republic of Macedonia and Viet Nam.

[165]For example: the former Yugoslav Republic of Macedonia, Montenegro, Samoa, Russia, Tajikistan, Ukraine and Viet Nam.

[166]For example: China: Working Party Report: see WTO document WT/ACC/CHN/49, para. 228.

[167]For example: China.

[168]Latvia, Georgia, Estonia, Croatia, Lithuania, Armenia, Cambodia, Saudi Arabia, Viet Nam, Cabo Verde, Ukraine, Vanuatu, Samoa, Russia, Montenegro, Lao PDR and Tajikistan.

[169]Four Article XII members accepted accession-specific obligations in respect of any measures governing transit of goods (including energy): Ukraine, Russia, Montenegro and Tajikistan.

[170]Russia: Working Party Report, see WTO document WT/ACC/RUS/70, paras. 117 and 1161, 17 November 2011.

[171]Russia accepted the specific obligation that measures relating to the transit of goods subject to veterinary control would be applied in compliance with the OIE Code and the SPS Agreement. Working Party Report: see WTO document WT/ACC/RUS/70, para. 885, 17 November 2011.

[172]Russia accepted the specific obligation to provide information on the revenue collected from customs fees and charges imposed on traffic in transit, upon request: Working Party Report: see WTO document WT/ACC/RUS/70, para. 1161, 17 November 2011.

[173]For the range of the obligations accepted by all thirty-three Article XII members, see Annex 9.3 at the end of this chapter.

[174]Ecuador, Mongolia, Panama, Kyrgyz Republic, Latvia, Estonia, Georgia, Albania, Oman, Armenia, Nepal, Cambodia, Tonga, Cabo Verde, Samoa, Vanuatu, Lao PDR and Yemen.

[175]Bulgaria, Jordan, Croatia, Lithuania, Moldova, Chinese Taipei, the former Yugoslav Republic of Macedonia, Saudi Arabia, Viet Nam, Ukraine, Montenegro, Russia and Tajikistan.

[176]Ecuador, Mongolia, Panama, Latvia, Jordan, Oman, China, Armenia, Saudi Arabia, Viet Nam, Tonga, Ukraine and Tajikistan.

[177]Nepal, Cambodia, Cabo Verde (now graduated), Samoa, Vanuatu, Lao PDR and Yemen.

[178]Albania, Bulgaria, Chinese Taipei, Croatia, Estonia, the former Yugoslav Republic of Macedonia, Georgia, Kyrgyz Republic, Lithuania, Moldova, Montenegro and Russia.

[179]Albania: Working Party Report, para. 154; Chinese Taipei: WT/ACC/TPKM/18: Working Party Report, para. 223 and Chinese Taipei: WT/L/433: Protocol of Accession of the Separate Customs Territory of Taiwan, Penghu, Kinmen and Matsu: para. I.5; Croatia: Working Party Report, para. 168; Estonia: Working Party Report, para. 116; the former Yugoslav Republic of Macedonia: Working Party Report, para. 180; Georgia: Working Party Report, para. 125; Latvia: Working Party Report, para. 110; Lithuania: Working Party Report, para. 157; Montenegro: Working Party Report, para. 193; and Tajikistan: Working Party Report, para. 258.

[180]Armenia: Working Party Report, para. 213; Moldova: Working Party Report, para. 153; and Ukraine: Working Party Report, para. 360.

[181]Kyrgyz Republic: Working Party Report, para. 122; and Oman: Working Party Report, para. 128.

[182]China: see WTO document WT/ACC/CHN/49: Working Party Report, para. 240; and Russia: Working Party Report, para. 1200.

[183]Mongolia confirmed that its laws in the field of intellectual property rights 'were already in conformity with the provisions of the TRIPs Agreement'. Russia committed to apply fully the provisions of the TRIPs Agreement 'including provisions for enforcement'.

[184]Transition periods for the implementation of intellectual property commitments were accorded to nine Article XII members: Ecuador (0.5 years); Nepal (2.7 years); Cambodia (2.2 years); Tonga (0.9 years); Cabo Verde (4.4 years); Samoa (1.1 years); Vanuatu (0.25 years); Lao PDR (3.8 years); and Yemen (2.5 years).

[185]These commitments to be undertaken during the transition period were made by Cambodia; Cabo Verde; Lao PDR; Nepal; Samoa; Vanuatu; Tonga and Yemen. Cambodia, Tonga and Vanuatu additionally made a commitment not to grant patents, trademarks or copyrights, or marketing approvals for pharmaceuticals or agricultural chemicals inconsistent with the provisions of the TRIPs Agreement during the transition period. Vanuatu and Tonga also undertook a commitment to protect unfair commercial use of undisclosed test or other data during its transition period. Tonga would also implement the provisions of Article 70.8 and 70.9 to provide 'pipeline' protection and exclusive marketing rights during the transition period. Lao PDR also committed to adopt draft implementing legislation shared with members without any substantial amendments.

[186]The reference to the Doha Declaration on the TRIPs Agreement and Public Health (2001) is found in the reports of the working party on the accessions of Nepal, Cambodia (confirmed later), Cabo Verde, Samoa, Lao PDR and Yemen. This is an additional transition period until 1 January 2016 for the protection of pharmaceutical patents and undisclosed test data protection. (Lao PDR confirmed that it would avail itself of special and differential treatment for LDCs under the TRIPs Agreement and various Ministerial Conference Declarations, including the Hong Kong Ministerial Declaration (para. 47), TRIPs Council Decision (IP/C/40) and the Eighth Ministerial Conference Decisions.)

[187]Armenia, China, Chinese Taipei, Russia, the former Yugoslav Republic of Macedonia, Ukraine and Yemen.

[188]China, Chinese Taipei, Russia, the former Yugoslav Republic of Macedonia and Yemen.

[189]China, Chinese Taipei, Russia, the former Yugoslav Republic of Macedonia and Viet Nam.

[190]China with respect to 'reasonable evidence', Russia with respect to the term 'exclusive rights' and Yemen also confirmed that Article 33(b) of the Patent Law was limited to practices determined after judicial or administrative procedures to be anti-competitive, in compliance with Article 31 of the TRIPs Agreement and that Article 33(b) would continue to be interpreted in this manner.

[191]China, Russia, Ukraine and Yemen.

[192]China.

[193]China, Russia, Ukraine and Lao PDR.

[194]For example, China accepted the obligation to lower monetary thresholds in order to pursue criminal action to deter future piracy and counterfeiting; Chinese Taipei accepted the obligation to destroy all contraband smuggled or counterfeit imports of alcohol and tobacco products seized, taking into account the practices of WTO members and also to take additional efforts to prevent such illegal imports; Russia accepted the obligation to sustain actions against the operation of websites with servers located in its territory that promote illegal distribution of content protected by copyright or related rights; Ukraine accepted the obligation to

abolish the customs fees charged to right-holders for lodging applications by the date of WTO accession; Viet Nam accepted the obligation to issue appropriate legal instruments mandating that all government agencies use only legitimate computer software and not infringe the copyright of such software.

[195]In total, 63 specific obligations were accepted by Croatia (1), China (12), Montenegro (4), Russia (11), Chinese Taipei (1), Saudi Arabia (4), Ukraine (8), Vanuatu (1), Viet Nam (17), and Tajikistan (4).

[196]For example, China, Montenegro, Russia, Ukraine, Viet Nam and Tajikistan.

[197]For example, China on 'sales away from a fixed location': China: Working Party Report, para. 310.

[198]For example, China, Russia and Viet Nam. In the case of Russia, the relevant commitment language only covers 'not accountable to', not mentioning 'be separate from'.

[199]For example, China.

[200]For example, Montenegro, Russia, Saudi Arabia, Vanuatu and Viet Nam.

[201]For example, Ukraine for the insurance sector.

[202]For example, Ukraine for direct branching for foreign insurance companies.

[203]For example, Tajikistan.

[204]In addition to commitments undertaken in the dedicated transparency chapter of accession working party reports, accession-specific commitments on transparency have also been undertaken in other chapters/sections of accession working party reports. These commitments reaffirm existing transparency and notification obligations pursuant to the provisions of particular WTO Agreements and, in some cases, reinforce them or explicitly link them to GATT Article X provisions.

[205]Of these, five Article XII members (namely, Lao PDR, Montenegro, Tajikistan, Ukraine and Vanuatu) were granted transitional periods for one part of their overall commitment by receiving a 'grace period' for the establishment/designation of either an official journal or website.

[206]Of these, five Article XII members were granted transitional arrangements to implement general WTO notification requirements. Jordan, Lao PDR, Ukraine and Yemen undertook the specific obligation to submit all remaining initial notifications no later than six months from the date of accession. Russia undertook the specific obligation for a set of initial notifications, as identified in Table 38 of its Working Party Report, ninety days from the date of accession. Table 38 of the Working Party Report of Russia covers the following areas: customs valuation; subsidies and countervailing measures; trade-related investment measures (TRIMs); import licensing; and rules of origin.

[207]In some of these specific commitments, an exception is included in cases of emergency or security, or in cases where publication would impede law enforcement.

[208]Armenia: Working Party Report, para. 215; Cabo Verde: Working Party Report, para. 262; Montenegro: Working Party Report, para. 273; Russia: Working Party Report, para. 1427; Samoa: Working Party Report, para. 243; Saudi Arabia: Working Party Report, para. 305; Chinese Taipei: Working Party Report, paras. 217 and 219; Tajikistan: Working Party Report, para. 343; Tonga: Working Party Report, para. 180; Ukraine: Working Party Report, para. 499; Vanuatu: Working Party Report, para. 134; and Viet Nam: Working Party Report, para. 518.

[209]Armenia: Working Party Report, para. 215; Bulgaria: Working Party Report, para. 40; Cambodia: Working Party Report, para. 217; Cabo Verde: Working Party Report, para. 262; China: Working Party Report, para. 332; Lao PDR: Working Party Report, para. 243; Montenegro: Working Party Report, para. 273; Nepal: Working Party Report, para. 147; Oman: Working Party Report, para. 150; Panama: Working Party Report, para. 115; Samoa: Working Party Report, para. 243; Saudi Arabia: Working Party Report, para. 305; Tajikistan: Working Party Report, para. 343; Tonga: Working Party Report, para. 180; Ukraine: Working Party Report, para. 499; Vanuatu: Working Party Report, para. 134; and Viet Nam: Working Party Report, para. 518.

[210]Cambodia: Working Party Report, para. 217; Cabo Verde: Working Party Report, para. 262; Lao PDR: Working Party Report, para. 243; Montenegro: Working Party Report, para. 273; Russia: Working Party Report, para. 1426; Samoa: Working Party Report, para. 243; Saudi Arabia: Working Party Report, para. 305; Tajikistan: Working Party Report, para. 343; Ukraine: Working Party Report, para. 499; Viet Nam: Working Party Report, para. 518; and Vanuatu: Working Party Report, para. 134.

[211]Lao PDR: Working Party Report, para. 243; and Mongolia: Working Party Report, para. 44.

[212]China: Working Party Report, para. 336; Chinese Taipei: Working Party Report, para. 217; Moldova: Working Party Report, para. 235; and Russia: Working Party Report, para. 1426.

[213]Cabo Verde: Working Party Report, para. 262; China: Working Party Report, paras. 331–332 and 336; Lao PDR: Working Party Report, para. 243; Montenegro: Working Party Report, para. 273; Nepal: Working Party Report, para. 147; Samoa: Working Party Report, para. 243; Saudi Arabia: Working Party Report, para. 305; Tajikistan: Working Party Report, para. 343; Tonga: Working Party Report, para. 180; Ukraine: Working Party Report, para. 499; Vanuatu: Working Party Report, para. 134; and Viet Nam: Working Party Report, para. 518.

[214]China: no later than ninety days upon implementation and enforcement of a measure: China: Working Party Report, para. 334; Chinese Taipei: no later than ninety days upon enactment and issuance of a measure: Working Party Report, para. 217.

[215]Viet Nam: Working Party Report, para. 517.

[216]Russia: Working Party Report, para. 1413.

[217]As part of the WTO accession process, draft notifications have been requested on STEs; industrial subsidies; customs valuation; SPS; TBT; export subsidies; and agricultural policies. These requests are not necessarily dealt with and referred to the Transparency Chapter of accession working party reports. Rather, these can be found in the specific chapter covering the relevant area.

[218]China: see WTO document WT/L/432: Protocol on the Accession of the People's Republic of China, Annex 5A; Mongolia: Working Party Report, para. 60; Panama: Working Party Report, para. 113.

[219]China: Working Party Report, para. 322 and China: Protocol on the Accession of the People's Republic of China: I.18.1 and Annex 1A.

[220]Except China, Chinese Taipei and Yemen.

[221]Some cases only, for example, Cabo Verde, Ecuador, Lao PDR, Mongolia, Nepal and Panama.

[222]For example, the 'final bound rate' of duty, if differing from the 'bound rate at date of accession', will be implemented according to the date specified in the 'implementation' column. The implementation column indicates the date, referring to 1 January of the year indicated when the final bound rate will be achieved.

[223]For example, 'In this schedule the following symbols are used with the meanings respectively indicated below: €: euro; $: United States dollar'.

[224]For example, 'In the case of elimination of the tariff rate quota for fresh and chilled beef (HS 0201), a flat bound rate of 27.5% shall apply.'

[225]Headnotes 6 and 7 of Part I Section 1-A of the Goods Schedule (CLXV) of Russia.

[226]For example, 'coffee in berries, coffee beans, coffee beans not skinner and any other kind of coffee beans are included in HS 09011100'.

[227]For example, member X 'shall maintain its applied rates for crude sunflower oil (HS 1512 11) at a level no higher than the lowest of the bound level for low erucic acid rape or colza oil and its fractions, crude (HS 1514 11)'.

[228]Headnotes 4-f) of Part I Section 1-A of the Goods Schedule of Russia: 'Product descriptions for tariff lines in HS 0406, by and of themselves, shall not give rise to the enforcement of geographical indications at the border. This is without prejudice to the enforcement of any current or future geographical indications corresponding to such descriptions legally recognised by Russia. If Russia should recognise legally geographical indications corresponding to any of the product descriptions in tariff lines in HS 0406, the tariff rates applied to such products which do not conform to the geographical indication's specifications shall not be affected.'

[229]Headnotes 3 of Part I Section 1-A of the Goods Schedule of the People's Republic of China.

[230]Ibid.

Annex 9.2 *Number of 'specific commitment paragraphs' in the working party reports/Accession Protocols of thirty-two Article XII members*[1]

| | Member | Date of membership | Number of commitment paragraphs |
|---|---|---|---|
| 1 | Russian Federation | 22 August 2012 | 163 |
| 2 | China | 11 December 2001 | 144 (+ 24 in Accession Protocol) |
| 3 | Viet Nam | 11 January 2007 | 70 |
| 4 | Ukraine | 16 May 2008 | 63 |
| 5 | Chinese Taipei | 1 January 2002 | 63 (+ 2 in Accession Protocol) |
| 6 | Saudi Arabia, Kingdom of | 11 December 2005 | 59 |
| 7 | Tajikistan | 2 March 2013 | 40 |
| 8 | Armenia, Republic of | 5 February 2003 | 39 |
| 9 | Samoa* | 10 May 2012 | 37 |
| 10 | Montenegro | 29 April 2012 | 35 |
| 11 | Vanuatu* | 24 August 2012 | 30 |
| 12 | Kyrgyz Republic | 20 December 1998 | 29 |
| 13 | Tonga | 27 July 2007 | 29 |
| 14 | Jordan | 11 April 2000 | 29 |
| 15 | Albania | 8 September 2000 | 29 |
| 16 | Cambodia* | 13 October 2004 | 29 |
| 17 | Georgia | 14 June 2000 | 29 |
| 18 | Lithuania | 31 May 2001 | 28 |
| 19 | Moldova | 26 July 2001 | 28 |
| 20 | Yemen* | 26 June 2014 | 28 |
| 21 | Panama | 6 September 1997 | 24 |
| 22 | Bulgaria | 1 December 1996 | 27 |
| 23 | Croatia | 30 November 2000 | 27 |
| 24 | Cabo Verde | 23 July 2008 | 26 |
| 25 | Lao People's Democratic Republic* | 2 February 2013 | 26 |
| 26 | Oman | 9 November 2000 | 26 |
| 27 | Nepal* | 23 April 2004 | 25 |
| 28 | Estonia | 13 November 1999 | 24 |
| 29 | The former Yugoslav Republic of Macedonia | 4 April 2003 | 24 |
| 30 | Latvia | 10 February 1999 | 22 |

Annex 9.2 (*cont.*)

| | Member | Date of membership | Number of commitment paragraphs |
|---|---|---|---|
| 31 | Ecuador | 21 January 1996 | 21 (+ 1 in Accession Protocol) |
| 32 | Mongolia | 26 June 1997 | 17 (+ 1 in Accession Protocol) |
| **33** | Total LDCs' commitments | | **175** |
| **34** | Working party report total specific commitments | | **1,290** |
| **35** | Grand total of working party report specific commitments and protocol-specific commitments | | **1,321** |

*Notes:* *LDCs. Note that Cabo Verde acceded as an LDC and graduated in December 2007; and Samoa graduated in January 2014.

[1] Annex 9.2 reflects the total number of all specific commitment paragraphs, as contained in the thirty-two accession working party reports. These specific commitment paragraphs, cross-referenced in the 'Conclusions Paragraph' of the thirty-two accession working party reports, are referenced in paragraph 2 of the standard Accession Protocols.

Annex 9.3 *Frequency of commitments of Article XII members by working party report chapter/sub-chapter*

| Working party reports/protocol sections | Frequency of specific commitments | Article XII members |
|---|---|---|
| Non-discrimination/China's Working Party Report and Protocol | 5 | 1/32 |
| Foreign exchange and payments | 7 | 6/32 |
| Investment regime | 6 | 6/32 |
| State ownership and privatisation; STEs | 72 | 32/32 |
| Pricing policies | 42 | 31/32 |

Annex 9.3 (*cont.*)

| Working party reports/protocol sections | Frequency of specific commitments | Article XII members |
|---|---|---|
| Balance-of-payments measures | 3 | 3/32 |
| Framework for making and enforcing policies | 55 | 27/32 |
| Trading rights | 42 | 28/32 |
| Ordinary customs duties | 15 | 9/32 |
| Other duties and charges | 27 | 24/32 |
| TRQs, tariff exemptions | 33 | 19/32 |
| Fees and charges for services rendered | 38 | 31/32 |
| Application of internal taxes on imports | 46 | 32/32 |
| Quantitative import restrictions, including prohibitions, quotas and licensing systems | 83 | 32/32 |
| Customs valuation | 43 | 32/32 |
| Rules of origin | 30 | 27/32 |
| Other customs formalities | 10 | 8/32 |
| PSI | 24 | 23/32 |
| Anti-dumping, countervailing duties and safeguard regimes | 39 | 30/32 |
| Export duties, fees and charges | 16 | 15/32 |
| Export restrictions | 33 | 25/32 |
| Export subsidies | 20 | 18/32 |
| Industrial policy, including subsidies | 40 | 28/32 |
| TBTs | 85 | 30/32 |
| SPSs measures | 92 | 30/32 |
| TRIMs | 39 | 32/32 |
| Free zones, special economic areas | 39 | 30/32 |
| Government procurement | 23 | 22/32 |
| Trade in civil aircraft | 16 | 16/32 |
| Transit | 17 | 17/32 |
| Agricultural policies | 29 | 15/32 |
| Textile regimes | 7 | 6/32 |
| TRIPs | 79 | 32/32 |
| Policies affecting trade in services | 63 | 10/32 |
| Transparency – publication of information on trade | 32 | 21/32 |
| Transparency – notification | 34 | 31/32 |
| Trade agreements | 31 | 29/32 |
| Staging of dismantling of tariff adjustment mechanism | 1 | 1/32 |

Annex 9.3 (*cont.*)

| Working party reports/protocol sections | Frequency of specific commitments | Article XII members |
|---|---|---|
| Special trade arrangements, including barter trade arrangements | 1 | 1/32 |
| Transitional product-specific safeguard mechanism | 1 | 1/32 |
| Reservations by WTO members | 1 | 1/32 |
| Transitional review mechanism | 1 | 1/32 |
| Special exchange agreement between the WTO and Chinese Taipei | 1 | 1/32 |
| Grand total of all specific obligations contained in thirty-two accession working party reports and Accession Protocols | 1,321 | |

The table in Annex 9.3 reflects the frequency of accessions-specific commitments by chapters/sections (areas of the foreign trade regime), as contained in the thirty-two accession working party reports as well as the thirty-two Accession Protocols.

Specifically, the figures in Annex 9.2 reflect the accounting methodology used in the totalling of the specific commitments.

The specific commitment paragraphs of the thirty-three Article XII members, as contained in their accession working party reports, total 1,290 specific commitment paragraphs.

Three accession working party reports contain a single commitment paragraph for both TBT and SPS. These are: paragraph 64 of Bulgaria's Working Party Report: see WTO document WT/ACC/BGR/5; paragraph 88 of Latvia's Working Party Report: see WTO document WT/ACC/LVA/32; and paragraph 98 of Estonia's Working Party Report: see WTO document WT/ACC/EST/28. For the purpose of Annex 9.2, i.e. an account of the accurate frequency of obligations by area of the 'foreign trade regime' section, these three commitment paragraphs have been counted twice – once for TBT and once for SPS. Thus, an addition of three commitment paragraphs has to be added to the total figure of 1,290, i.e. 1,293.

Twenty-four additional specific obligations were located in China's Accession Protocol, in addition to those specific commitments located in

Annex 9.4 *Agriculture accession-specific obligations*

| Member | Accession year | Final bound total AMS | Final bound total AMS as % of value of production in the base years ** | De minimis | Export subsidy commitment |
|---|---|---|---|---|---|
| Ecuador | 1996 | 0 | | 10% | 0 |
| Bulgaria | 1996 | 520 (ECU million) | NA: value of production for the base period is not available | 5% | 44 products, final bound commitment level at 102.61 million ECU (total budgetary outlay) |
| Mongolia | 1997 | 0 | | 10% | 0 |
| Panama | 1997 | 0 | | 10% | Export subsidies bound at zero, but after phasing out at the end of 2002 |
| Kyrgyz Republic | 1998 | 0 | | 5% | 0 |
| Latvia | 1999 | 0 | | SDR 24 million until 31 December 2002, 5% thereafter | 0 |
| Estonia | 1999 | 0 | | 5% | 0 |
| Jordan | 2000 | 1.334 (JOD million) | 0.24% | 10% | 0 |
| Georgia | 2000 | 0 | | 5% | 0 |

| | Year | Value | | Rate | |
|---|---|---|---|---|---|
| Albania | 2000 | 0 | | 5% | 0 |
| Oman | 2000 | 0 | | 10% | 0 |
| Croatia | 2000 | 134 (euro million) | NA: value of production for the base period is not available | 5% | 0 |
| Lithuania | 2001 | 94.56 (US$ million) | 6.75% | 5% | 0 |
| Moldova | 2001 | 12.78 (SDR million) | 2.23% | 5% | 0 |
| China | 2001 | 0 | | 8.5% | 0 |
| Chinese Taipei | 2002 | 14,165 (NT$ million) | 5.97% | 5% | 0 |
| Armenia Republic of | 2003 | 0 | | 10% until 31 December 2008, 5% thereafter | 0 |
| The former Yugoslav Republic of Macedonia | 2003 | 16.3 (euro million) | 2.04% | 5% | 0 |
| Nepal* | 2004 | 0 | | 10% | 0 |
| Cambodia* | 2004 | 0 | | 10% | 0 |
| Saudi Arabia, Kingdom of | 2005 | 3218.28 (million Saudi riyals) | 8.83% | 10% | 0 |
| Viet Nam | 2007 | 3,961.59 (VND billion) | 3.07% | 10% | 0 |

Annex 9.4 (*cont.*)

| Member | Accession year | Final bound total AMS | Final bound total AMS as % of value of production in the base years ** | De minimis | Export subsidy commitment |
|---|---|---|---|---|---|
| Tonga | 2007 | 0 | | 10% | 0 |
| Ukraine | 2008 | 3043.4 (UAH million) | 3.37% | 5% | 0 |
| Cabo Verde * | 2008 | 0 | | 10% | 0 |
| Montenegro | 2012 | 333,278 (euro) | 0.13% | 5% | 0 |
| Samoa * | 2012 | 0 | | 10% | 0 |
| Russian Federation | 2012 | 4.4 (US$ billion) | 5.64% | 5% | 0 |
| Vanuatu * | 2012 | 0 | | 10% | 0 |
| Lao People's Democratic Republic * | 2013 | 0 | | 10% | 0 |
| Tajikistan | 2013 | 182,667 (US$ thousand) | 7.26% | 10% | 0 |
| Yemen * | - | 0 | | 10% | 0 |

*Notes:* * LDCs. Note that Cabo Verde acceded as an LDC and graduated in December 2007; and Samoa graduated in January 2014.
** Values of production were sourced from the agriculture supporting tables referenced in the Schedules of Concessions and Commitments on Goods.

China's Accession Working Party Reports. Twenty-four were added to 1,293, totalling 1,317.

Two specific obligations were located in Chinese Taipei's Accession Protocol. These are: Part I.5 of Chinese Taipei's Accession Protocol on Trade in Civil Aircrafts; and Part I.4 and Annex II of Chinese Taipei's Accession Protocol on the Special Exchange Agreement between the WTO and Chinese Taipei in accordance with paragraph 6 of Article XV of the GATT 1994. These two were added to 1,317, totalling 1,319.

One specific accession obligation was located in Ecuador's Accession Protocol (Parts I.4 and II.5 of Ecuador's Accession Protocol on staging of the dismantling of the Tariff Adjustment Mechanism). It was added to 1,319, totalling 1,320. One obligation was derived from Mongolia's Accession Protocol (Part I of Mongolia's Accession Protocol on notifications). It was added to 1,320, generating a grand total of 1,321 commitments – capturing all sections of the accession working party reports and Accession Protocols.

## Acknowledgements

The contributions of many colleagues are gratefully acknowledged. I valued very much the countless brainstorming sessions with colleagues over the years regarding how we should interpret accession negotiating processes, procedures and outcomes in relation to what many considered the missteps and fumblings in the Doha Round negotiations and the failure to draw on the vast lessons of accession negotiations, which are non-stop multilateral negotiations in regular work. I register in particular my gratitude to Alexandra Bhattacharya, Amara Okenwa, Anna Varyanik, Dayong Yu, Gabrielle Marceau, George Tebagana, Joan Apecu, Josefita Pardo de Leon, Juneyoung Lee, Lidet Kebede, Petra Beslać and Uri Dadush.

## References

Azevêdo, R. (2014). 'Bali Package – trade multilateralism in the 21st Century', *Interpress Service* (IPS), 20 January.

Baldwin, R. (2008). 'The tipping point', VoxEU.org.

(2013). 'APEC-like duties for a post-Bali WTO', in S. J. Evenett and A. Jara (eds.), *Building on Bali: A Work Programme for the WTO*. VoxEU.org e-Book.

Evenett, J. S. and A. Jara (eds.) (2013). *Building on Bali: A Work Programme for the WTO*. VoxEU.org e-Book.

Froman, M. (2014). 'The Strategic Logic of Trade'. Remarks at the Council on Foreign Relations, New York, 16 June.

Harbinson, S. (2013). 'How to reassert the WTO's negotiating authority', in S. J. Evenett and A. Jara (eds.), *Building on Bali: A Work Programme for the WTO*. VoxEU.org e-Book.

Hoekman, B. (2014). *Supply Chains, Mega-Regionals and Multilateralism: A Road Map for the WTO*. London, Centre for Economic Policy Research (CEPR) Press.

Krugman, P. (2007). 'Trouble with trade', *New York Times*, 28 December, p. A23.

Lawrence, R. (2007). 'The Globalisation Paradox: More Trade Less Inequality'. Retrieved from www.voxeu.org/article/globalisation-paradox-more-trade-less-inequality.

Marceau, G. (2002). 'A map of the World Trade Organization Law of Domestic Regulation of Goods: The Technical Barriers to Trade Agreement, the Sanitary and Phytosanitary Measures Agreement, and the General Agreement on Tariffs and Trade', *Journal of World Trade*, 36(5): 81; also revised in F. Ortino and E. U. Petersmann (eds.) (2003), *WTO Dispute Settlement Jurisprudence*. International Law Association, London, Kluwer, 275.

Marceau, G. and P. J. Trachtman (2014). 'A map of the World Trade Organization Law of Domestic Regulation of Goods: The Technical Barriers to Trade Agreement, the Sanitary and Phytosanitary Measures Agreement, and the General Agreement on Tariffs and Trade', *Journal of World Trade*, 48(2): 351–432. Retrieved from https://www.kluwerlawonline.com/abstract.php?area=Journals&id=TRAD2014013.

Mead, Walter Russell (2014). 'The return of geopolitics: the revenge of the revisionist powers'. Retrieved from www.foreignaffairs.com/articles/141211/walter-russell-mead/the-return-of-geopolitics.

Osakwe, C. (2011). 'Developing countries and GATT/WTO rules: dynamic transformations in trade policy behaviour and performance', *Minnesota Journal of International Law*, 20(2): 365–436; also republished in P. D. Steger (ed.) (2014), *World Trade Organization: Critical Perspectives on the World Economy*. London, Routledge.

Piketty, T. (2014). *Capital in the Twenty-First Century*. Cambridge, MA, Belknap Press.

Summers, L. (2008a). 'America needs to make a new case for trade', *Financial Times*, 28 April.

(2008b). 'A strategy to promote healthy globalisation', *Financial Times*, 5 May.

# 10

# WTO rule-making: WTO Accession Protocols and jurisprudence

VALERIE HUGHES

ABSTRACT

*This chapter examines rule-making in the WTO. It explains the legal provisions governing how rules are made in the WTO, and describes WTO rule-making in practice, including through the adoption of decisions by the Ministerial Conference and the General Council and by way of dispute settlement. The role of consensus and voting in WTO rule-making are discussed. The chapter also refers to different types of rules and decisions – such as ministerial declarations, authoritative interpretations, amendments and waivers – and considers their legal value and effect, as well as how different types of rules or decisions have been interpreted or applied. Finally, it also includes a look at rule-making in the context of accessions, and considers Accession Protocols and working party reports through the lens of WTO dispute settlement.*

This chapter does not purport to be a comprehensive review of decision-making in the WTO. Rather, it offers a general overview that may be useful to those involved in rule- or decision-making, be they delegates, chairpersons, secretaries to committees or other followers of the WTO. It may assist them in choosing the appropriate avenue to follow in making a rule or decision, depending upon the effect the instrument is intended to have in the WTO. It may also serve to provide guidance to those involved in crafting rules or decisions or other instruments, especially in its explanation of the importance of careful and precise legal drafting. Finally, it may alert those preparing for dispute settlement in which a particular instrument – such as a ministerial decision or an accession

The analyses in this chapter was finalised in August 2014. Since then the Republic of Seychelles acceded to the World Trade Organization (WTO) on 26 April 2015. This expanded total WTO membership from 160 to 161.

protocol or a working party report – may have been invoked to the lessons that may be drawn from the jurisprudence addressing the import of such instruments.

Rule-making lies at the heart of the WTO, as it did in the days of its predecessor, the General Agreement on Tariffs and Trade (GATT). The practices and procedures in rule-making have evolved somewhat since GATT's inception in 1947, but the general approach remains the same today. At the creation of the GATT, the fundamental approach was that international trade relations should be governed by the rule of law. This approach informed the functioning of the GATT throughout its forty-seven years, directed its transition to the WTO in 1995 and guides the WTO today.

Rule-making is effected in different ways in the WTO, and by a variety of entities. As explained below, a rule may come about as a result of a decision adopted by the Ministerial Conference or the General Council, or in panel and Appellate Body reports adopted by the Dispute Settlement Body (DSB). Some rule-making is of a formal nature, as prescribed in the Marrakesh Agreement Establishing the World Trade Organization (WTO Agreement), while other rule-making has evolved through practice, often as the needs of the moment dictated. Regardless of origin or subject, however, one feature has been constant: consensus has pride of place in WTO rule-making.

## GATT beginnings – a brief overview

The GATT had an unusual start, at least as far as international organisations are concerned. The GATT began not as an institution but as an agreement, or a set of rules. The agreement, negotiated in 1947 and signed by twenty-three states, dealt with the reciprocal reduction of tariffs on trade in goods. It was intended to form part of a package, together with a charter establishing an international trade institution to be called the International Trade Organization, or the ITO. However, the ITO did not materialise. The twenty-three GATT parties (called contracting parties) nevertheless agreed to apply the provisions of the GATT among themselves through a mechanism known as a Protocol of Provisional Application, or PPA. Under the PPA, the contracting parties agreed to apply the GATT rules provisionally as of 1 January 1948.[1] This continued

---

[1] Basic Instrument Selected Document, vol. 4, 77.

for almost fifty years, when the GATT was replaced by the WTO. Thus the GATT rules were never formally adopted by the contracting parties. But they were no less effective as a result.

As a practical matter, the GATT became more than a set of rules, and developed into a *de facto* international organisation for governing international trade relations. Although there were few provisions dealing with institutional matters – see for example Article XXV on 'Joint Action by the Contracting Parties' and Articles XXII and XXIII on dispute settlement – the contracting parties developed mechanisms over time for organising meetings, conducting business and making decisions. From the outset, decision-making was by consensus, a principle that was highly valued and staunchly protected.

The GATT membership expanded, as did the GATT rules governing multilateral trade relations. Eight successive rounds of trade liberalisation, between 1947 and 1994,[2] led to significant reductions in tariffs on industrial goods as well as to reductions in non-tariff barriers. The last round of GATT multilateral trade negotiations – the Uruguay Round – started in 1986 and included a broad mandate, expanding beyond traditional subjects to include new areas such as services and intellectual property rights. It culminated in the establishment of the WTO in 1995 and the adoption of a new set of agreements covering a broad range of disciplines.

Evident throughout was the rule of law. The GATT contracting parties valued and nurtured a rules-based system where all contracting parties were accountable to and equal before the law, and where all contracting parties participated in decision-making and pursued the fair application of the law. This has been carried forward into the WTO. For unlike a power-based system, a rules-based system provides greater certainty in relations between states and guards against arbitrariness.

## Rule-making in the WTO: the provisions

The rules-based tradition under the GATT was explicitly carried over into the WTO, and in some respects was strengthened. When adopting the Marrakesh Declaration of 15 April 1994 marking the conclusion of

[2] Chronologically these were: the Geneva Round (1947); the Annecy Round (1949); the Torquay Round (1951); the Geneva Round (1956); the Dillon Round (1960–1961); the Kennedy Round (1964–1967); the Tokyo Round (1973–1979); and finally the Uruguay Round (1986–1994).

the Uruguay Round of Multilateral Negotiations and saluting the historic achievement, ministers welcomed 'the stronger and clearer legal framework they [had] adopted for the conduct of international trade'.[3]

Unlike the GATT, the WTO was established as an international institution from the outset.[4] The WTO Agreement sets out the main institutional provisions, including on the scope[5] and status[6] of the WTO, its membership[7] as well as procedures governing accessions[8] and withdrawals,[9] the functions[10] and structure[11] of the WTO, the establishment of a Secretariat headed by a Director-General,[12] provisions on the budget and contributions,[13] procedures for amendments[14] and other matters.

## Article IX of the WTO Agreement: decision-making

### Consensus is preferred

The WTO Agreement also prescribes decision-making in the WTO. Article IX, entitled 'Decision-Making', provides importantly that '[t]he WTO shall continue the practice of decision-making by consensus followed under the GATT 1947'. Consensus is defined in a footnote as follows: 'The body concerned shall be deemed to have decided by consensus on a matter submitted for its consideration, if no Member, present at the meeting when the decision is taken, formally objects to the proposed decision'.[15]

Article IX:1 permits voting only if specifically provided for or 'where a decision cannot be arrived at by consensus'.[16] In such cases, decisions of the Ministerial Conference and the General Council, the two highest decision-making bodies of the WTO, 'shall be taken by a majority of the votes cast' unless otherwise provided. Voting is not, however, permitted for actions in the DSB, the body established to administer the rules and procedures of dispute settlement in the WTO.[17] Article IX:1 states explicitly in footnote 3 that decisions in the DSB 'shall be taken only in accordance with' Article 2.4 of the Understanding on Rules and

---

[3] www.wto.org/english/docs_e/legal_e/marrakesh_decl_e.pdf.
[4] WTO Agreement, Article I.      [5] WTO Agreement, Article II.
[6] WTO Agreement, Article VIII.      [7] WTO Agreement, Article XI.
[8] WTO Agreement, Article XII.      [9] WTO Agreement, Article XV.
[10] WTO Agreement, Article III.      [11] WTO Agreement, Article IV.
[12] WTO Agreement, Article VI.      [13] WTO Agreement, Article VII.
[14] WTO Agreement, Article X.      [15] See footnote 1 to Article IX.
[16] WTO Agreement, Article IX:1, second sentence.
[17] The DSB is composed of all WTO members and generally meets monthly.

Procedures Governing the Settlement of Disputes (generally referred to as the Dispute Settlement Understanding or the DSU). Article 2.4, in turn, requires that all DSB decisions be taken by consensus, and defines consensus in the same way as in Article IX, quoted above. Interestingly, the DSU provides for positive and negative consensus, depending on the matter being decided. Certain decisions (establishment of a panel, adoption of a panel or Appellate Body report) are taken by negative consensus, so that the action will occur unless all members are opposed to it. This renders such actions semi-automatic, because the proposal to take action naturally will not be opposed by the member making the proposal.

Decisions are taken under Article IX:1 as a matter of course in conducting WTO business, as are decisions under Article 2.4 of the DSU in administering WTO dispute settlement rules.

## Multilateral interpretations

Article IX:2 deals with a special type of decision generally referred to as an 'authoritative interpretation' or 'multilateral interpretation'. According to Article IX:2, the Ministerial Conference and the General Council 'shall have the exclusive authority to adopt interpretations' of the WTO agreements. This authority must be exercised on the basis of a recommendation by the Council overseeing the functioning of the agreement in question. For example, an authoritative interpretation of a provision in the Trade-Related Aspects of Intellectual Property Rights Agreement (TRIPs) would be made on the basis of a recommendation by the TRIPs Council. Moreover, Article XI:2 prescribes that the decision to adopt an interpretation 'shall be taken by a three-fourths majority of the Members'. Of note is that such decision is *not* to be taken on the basis of consensus. Finally, Article IX:2 makes clear that the procedure thereunder is not to be used as a means of 'undermining' the amendment provisions under Article X of the WTO Agreement. This provision guards against members trying to circumvent the lengthier and perhaps more cumbersome amendment procedure through the ostensible adoption of an interpretation.

No authoritative interpretations have ever been adopted, and nor has any council put one to the Ministerial Conference or the General Council for consideration. If one were, seeking to secure the required three-quarters majority of the members would present novel challenges given that, traditionally, voting has not been pursued in the WTO.

## Waivers

Article IX:3 provides for yet another type of decision, known as a waiver. Such decisions are adopted in 'exceptional circumstances' where the Ministerial Conference agrees to waive an obligation imposed on a member under the WTO.[18] Proposals to waive an obligation under WTO Agreements in Annexes 1A or 1B or 1C to the WTO Agreement are considered first in the respective councils and go thereafter to the Ministerial Conference (which sometimes sits as the General Council), while waiver proposals concerning the WTO Agreement itself go directly to the Ministerial Conference. Members have adopted the Understanding in Respect of Waivers of Obligations under the GATT 1994, which specifies that a request for a waiver must describe the measures which the member proposes to take, the specific policy objectives which the member seeks to pursue, and the reasons that prevent the member from achieving its policy objectives by measures consistent with its obligations under the GATT 1994.

A decision granting a waiver must state the exceptional circumstances justifying the decision. Waivers are granted only for one year and may include terms and conditions. Extensions beyond one year may be granted by the Ministerial Conference if the circumstances justifying the waiver are considered to still exist and if the terms and conditions attached to the waiver have been met.[19]

Article IX:3 specifies that three-quarters of the members must agree to adopt a waiver.[20] However, in November 1995, the General Council agreed that waiver decisions would be taken in accordance with Article IX:1 – that is, by consensus, and only if a decision cannot be reached by consensus would the matter be determined by the three-quarters vote provided for in Article IX:3.[21]

Numerous waivers[22] have been granted over the years, including the Lomé Waiver covering the EC's import regime for bananas,[23] the waiver

---

[18] Decisions to waive obligations under a plurilateral trade agreement are governed by the terms of the particular agreement. See footnote 5 to the WTO Agreement.

[19] See WTO Agreement, Article IX:4.

[20] However, consensus agreement is necessary where the waiver concerns an obligation subject to a transition period or a period of staged implementation, as well as for a request for a waiver concerning the WTO Agreement. See Article IX:3(a) and footnote 4 to the WTO Agreement.

[21] See WTO document WT/L/93, 24 November 1995.

[22] As of 30 September 2011, thirty-one waivers had been granted. See *WTO Analytical Index. Guide to WTO Law and Practice*, Cambridge University Press, 3rd edn, 2012, vol. 1, p. 47.

[23] See WTO document WT/L/186, 18 October 1996.

of obligations under the TRIPs Agreement with respect to the grant of a compulsory licence (implementing the declaration on the TRIPs Agreement and public health),[24] and the waiver decision implementing the Kimberley Process Certification Scheme for Rough Diamonds.[25]

## Article X of the WTO Agreement: Amendments

Article X of the WTO Agreement deals with amendments to the WTO. Amendments are effected through different procedures depending upon the provision(s) being amended. For example, amendments to the following provisions take effect only upon acceptance by *all* WTO members:

- Articles IX and X of the WTO Agreement;
- Articles I and II of the GATT 1994 (most-favoured-nation (MFN) and Schedules of concessions);
- Article II:1 of the General Agreement on Trade in Services (GATS) (MFN);
- Article 4 of the TRIPs Agreement (MFN).

Amendments to most WTO provisions take effect upon acceptance by two-thirds of the membership, but only for those members who have formally accepted the amendment.[26] This is because, as a general rule, international law prohibits creating obligations for states without their consent. Thus although an amendment will come into force for those members that have accepted it as soon as the two-thirds threshold has been achieved, the amendment will take effect for the remaining third of members only upon each such member accepting the amendment. The two-thirds approach is followed for amendments to provisions of the Multilateral Agreements on Trade in Goods (other than Articles I and II of the GATT 1994), the TRIPs Agreement (other than Article 4 and Article 71.2), Parts I (Scope and Definition), II (General Obligations and Disciplines, other than Article II:1) and III (Specific Commitments) of the GATS and the respective annexes, and the WTO Agreement (other

---

[24] See WTO documents: WT/L/540, 2 September 2003; WT/L/540, Corr. 1, 29 July 2005.

[25] See WTO documents: WT/L/518, 27 May 2003; WT/L/676, 19 December 2006; WT/L/876, 14 December 2012.

[26] However, if the amendment is 'of a nature that would not alter the rights and obligations of the Members, [the amendment] shall take effect for all Members upon acceptance by two thirds of the Members'. See WTO Agreement, Article X:4.

than Articles IX and X). However, amendments to Parts IV (Progressive Liberalization), V (Institutional Provisions), and VI (Final Provisions) of the GATS and the respective annexes take effect for *all* members upon acceptance by two-thirds of the members.[27]

Acceptance is effected through deposit with the Director-General of an Instrument of Acceptance, usually within a prescribed period of time.[28] The Instrument of Acceptance is a formal legal document that reflects the agreement of the member to be bound on the international plane to an international provision or agreement. In keeping with the significance of taking such a step, a member's Instrument of Acceptance must be deposited in the original (not a photocopy or e-mail) and must contain certain key information, including clearly identifying the agreement or provision being amended (such as by referring to its title and place and date of its original adoption), stating that the member concerned formally accepts the amendment and specifying the date and the place of issuance of the Instrument of Acceptance. In addition, the Instrument of Acceptance must be signed by the head of state, the head of government or the minister for foreign affairs, and it must include the name and title of the person signing the instrument.[29]

Some WTO amendments take effect without the need to file instruments of acceptance. For example, amendments to the DSU are made by consensus and take effect for all members upon approval by the Ministerial Conference.[30] In addition, decisions to approve amendments to the Trade Policy Review Mechanism take effect for all members upon approval by the Ministerial Conference.[31] To date, no amendments to the DSU or the Trade Policy Review Mechanism have been proposed.

Finally, the Ministerial Conference can decide by consensus to add a plurilateral trade agreement to Annex 4 of the WTO Agreement upon the request of the members parties to that plurilateral agreement.[32] Amendments to plurilateral trade agreements are governed by the respective agreement. To date, no plurilateral agreements have been

---

[27] WTO Agreement, Article X:5.     [28] WTO Agreement, Article X:7.

[29] See, for example, 'How to accept the Protocol Amending the TRIPs Agreement', (www.wto.org/english/tratop_e/trips_e/accept_e.htm). The United Nations follows a similar practice. See *Summary of Practice of the Secretary-General as Depositary of Multilateral Treaties*, prepared by the Treaty Section of the Office of Legal Affairs, United Nations, New York, 1999, ST/LEG/7/Rev. 1.

[30] WTO Agreement, Article X:8.     [31] Ibid.     [32] WTO Agreement, Article X:9.

proposed for addition to Annex 4, although some have been amended or terminated.[33]

Like most international agreements, amending WTO agreements can be cumbersome and time-consuming. Requiring formal acceptance from a two-thirds majority is not exceptional in current international practice, however. The two-thirds rule serves to protect any 'substantial minority group', in that in most instances the two-thirds majority is not able to impose obligations on the minority one-third.[34] Nevertheless, with an increasingly universal membership, requiring that two-thirds of the WTO membership formally accept an amendment before it comes into force may considerably delay the entry into force of an amendment, as experienced with the Protocol Amending the TRIPs Agreement.[35] The General Council adopted a decision amending the TRIPs Agreement in December 2005,[36] but the amendment has not taken effect because it has not yet been accepted by two-thirds of the membership.

## Article XII of the WTO Agreement: accessions

Article XII of the WTO Agreement governs accession and stipulates how decisions on accession are made. Any state or separate customs territory possessing full autonomy in the conduct of its external commercial relations may accede to the WTO. Article XII stipulates that decisions on accession shall be taken by the Ministerial Conference, which is to 'approve the agreement on the terms of accession by a two-thirds majority' of the WTO members. However, in a decision adopted in November 1995, the General Council determined that accession decisions would be taken in accordance with Article IX:1 – that is, by consensus, and only if a decision cannot be reached by consensus would the matter be determined by the two-thirds vote provided for in Article XII.[37]

---

[33] WTO Agreement, Article X:10. See for example, the Agreement on Trade in Civil Aircraft, which has been amended twice (AIR/65 and TCA/4). The Agreement on Government Procurement is still in force, but a revised agreement was negotiated in 2012 and came into force on 6 April 2014, the date on which acceptances of the Protocol of Amendment for two-thirds of the parties to the original agreement had been received. The International Dairy Agreement and the International Bovine Meat Agreement were terminated at the end of 1997.

[34] International Law Commission, 'Draft Articles on the Law of Treaties with Commentaries', *Yearbook of the International Law Commission*, 1966, vol. 2, p. 194.

[35] See WTO document WT/L/641, 8 December 2005.      [36] See ibid.

[37] See WTO document WT/L/93, 24 November 1995.

Thirty-three accession decisions have been adopted thus far – the most recent with respect to Yemen in December 2013.[38] Only one accession has proceeded by way of formal vote – that for Ecuador in 1995 (prior to the November 1995 decision regarding proceeding by consensus first) taken under unique circumstances. The meeting to approve the accession of Ecuador was convened on short notice and on the cusp of the summer break (31 July 1995). The Chair of the General Council, noting that Article XII required approval of the terms of accession by a two-thirds majority of members and stating that there were insufficient members present at the meeting, submitted the decision on Ecuador's accession to members for a vote by postal ballot. Members present cast their votes at the meeting, while others did so by postal ballot within thirty days thereafter.[39]

Also of note is that on 10 December 2002, the General Council adopted a Decision on guidelines for the accession of least-developed countries (LDCs) to facilitate and accelerate negotiations for the accession of LDCs through simplified and streamlined procedures. The Decision sets out guidelines for market access negotiations for goods and services, whereby members are to exercise restraint in seeking concessions and commitments from acceding LDCs. It also calls for the application of special and differential treatment to acceding LDCs as well as transitional periods for implementation of the obligations they have undertaken. It refers to making available to acceding LDCs procedures such as the good offices of the Director-General and expedited document exchange with the assistance of the Secretariat, and to providing targeted technical assistance and capacity-building to acceding LDCs on a priority basis, including with respect to the accession process.[40] These guidelines were strengthened in a follow-up decision adopted by the General Council in July 2012 in response to a Decision on accession of LDCs adopted by ministers at the Eighth WTO Ministerial Conference held in 2011. The Addendum Decision stipulates principles and benchmarks to guide market access negotiations on goods and services, including overall average bindings for goods and flexibilities for LDCs to open fewer sectors and to liberalise fewer types of transaction. The Addendum

---

[38] See WTO document WT/L/944, 12 December 2014, Seychelles became a fully fledged WTO member on 26 April 2015, thirty days after it notified its Instrument of Acceptance to the Director-General of the WTO.

[39] See WTO documents: WT/GC/M/6, 20 September 1995 and WT/ACC/ECU/5, 22 August 1995, footnote 1.

[40] See WT/L/508, 20 January 2003; WT/L/508/Add. 1, 30 July 2012.

Decision also calls for enhanced transparency in accession negotiations, affirms the application of special and differential treatment to acceding LDCs, and requires consideration of transition periods for acceding LDCs beyond those foreseen in WTO agreements. Further, the Addendum Decision calls for technical assistance framework plans as part of each LDC accession process and for progress reports on the technical assistance support provided.

Although these decisions are framed as 'guidelines', which suggests that they do not impose requirements or rules but are rather indicative of how LDC accessions should be conducted, the language found in both Decisions is more of an obligatory nature. In calling on members to take certain actions, the Decisions do not generally use the usually hortatory 'should', but regularly use the mandatory 'shall'.

## Rules of procedure

Finally, mention should be made of the Rules of Procedure for sessions of the Ministerial Conference and meetings of the General Council,[41] most of which are also followed by the various committees.[42] These rules address, among other things, how business is to be conducted, including what constitutes a quorum, raising points of order, time limits for interventions, circulating written statements and reflecting them in the minutes and the content of discussions under 'Other business'. The Rules also govern the procedure for convening meetings, development and advance circulation of agendas, member representation, representation by observers and observer status and election of officers. In addition, the Rules refer to taking decisions in accordance with, *inter alia*, Article IX of the WTO Agreement, which gives preference to consensus.[43] In a 2002 General Council decision on the procedures for the appointment

---

[41] See WTO document WT/L/161, 25 July 1996.

[42] For example, Rule 1 of the Rules of Procedure for the DSB states that 'When the General Council convenes as the DSB, it shall follow the rules of procedure for meetings of the General Council, except as provided otherwise in the Dispute Settlement Understanding (DSU) or below'. See WT/DSB/9, 16 January 1997.

[43] See WT/L/161, 25 July 1996. Rule 28 applicable to sessions of the Ministerial Conference provides as follows: 'The Ministerial Conference shall take decisions in accordance with the decision-making provisions of the WTO Agreement, in particular Article IX thereof entitled "Decision-Making".' Rule 33 applicable to the meetings of the General Council provides as follows: 'The General Council shall take decisions in accordance with the decision-making provisions of the WTO Agreement, in particular Article IX thereof entitled "Decision-Making".'

of Directors-General, reference is made to recourse to voting 'as a last resort' and that it was 'understood to be an exceptional departure from the customary practice of decision-making by consensus, and shall not establish any precedent for such recourse in respect of any future decisions in the WTO'.[44] As demonstrated above, the WTO approach to decision-making clearly favours consensus and voting has almost always been avoided.

## Rule-making in practice in the WTO

Having reviewed the various rule-making provisions, we turn next to a discussion of WTO rule-making in practice. From the outset, WTO rule-making has taken a variety of forms and has covered many different subjects. Certain types of instruments have the effect of modifying WTO law, while others may be used to interpret existing rules.

### Ministerial declarations and decisions

Ministerial declarations and ministerial decisions are regular features of WTO work. Several examples of both types are found in the recent 'Bali Package', adopted by consensus at the close of the Ninth Ministerial Conference held in Bali, Indonesia in December 2013.[45] For example, ministers adopted the Bali Ministerial Declaration, a broad-ranging instrument in which ministers take note of reports from the General Council and its subsidiary bodies, welcome the several decisions and declarations adopted during the course of the Conference, and instruct the Trade Negotiations Committee to prepare a work programme on the remaining Doha Development Agenda.

The decisions adopted at the Ninth Ministerial Conference include those falling under the regular work programme, such as the decisions on TRIPs Non-violation and Situation Complaints[46] and Aid for Trade,[47] as well as the Decision on the Accession of the Republic of Yemen.[48] These are found in Part I of the Ministerial Declaration. In Part II of the Declaration, ministers welcomed the progress made at the Conference in the Doha Development Agenda (DDA) and the adoption of the

---

[44] See WTO document WT/L/509, 20 January 2003.
[45] See WTO document WT/MIN(13)/DEC, 11 December 2013.
[46] See WTO document WT/MIN(13)/31 – WT/L/906, 11 December 2013.
[47] See WTO document WT/MIN(13)/34 – WT/L/909, 11 December 2013.
[48] See WTO document WT/MIN(13)/24 – WT/L/905, 5 December 2013.

decisions and a declaration in that regard, including the Ministerial Decision on Trade Facilitation,[49] the Ministerial Decision on Public Stockholding for Food Security Purposes,[50] the Understanding on Tariff Rate Quota Administration Provisions of Agricultural Products,[51] the Ministerial Decision on Cotton[52] and the Ministerial Declaration on Export Competition.[53]

The decisions falling under Part II of the Ministerial Declaration begin with the following words:

> The Ministerial Conference,
>> Having regard to paragraph 1 of Article IX of the Marrakesh Agreement Establishing the World Trade Organization;
>> Decides as follows:[54]

This language makes clear that Article IX is the legal basis for the decision. The declarations adopted at the Bali Ministerial do not refer to Article IX, although they were adopted by consensus and in the same manner as were the decisions.

Questions have arisen as to the legal value or effect of such decisions and declarations. In *US–Lead and Bismuth II*,[55] an early (1999–2000) dispute between the United States and the European Communities, a panel and the Appellate Body had occasion to examine the Declaration on Dispute Settlement Pursuant to the Agreement on Implementation of Article VI of the General Agreement on Tariffs and Trade 1994 (Anti-Dumping Agreement) or Part V of the Agreement on Subsidies and Countervailing Measures, which provides as follows:

> Ministers,
>> Recognize, with respect to dispute settlement pursuant to the Agreement on Implementation of Article VI of GATT 1994 or Part V of the Agreement on Subsidies and Countervailing Measures, the *need for the consistent resolution* of disputes arising from anti-dumping and countervailing duty measures [italics added].

---

[49] See WTO document WT/MIN(13)/36 – WT/L/911, 11 December 2013.
[50] See WTO document WT/MIN(13)/38 – WT/L/913, 11 December 2013.
[51] See WTO document WT/MIN(13)/39 – WT/L/914, 11 December 2013.
[52] See WTO document WT/MIN(13)/41 – WT/L/916, 11 December 2013.
[53] See WTO document WT/MIN(13)/40 – WT/L/915, 11 December 2013.
[54] Some of the instruments include additional language before the words 'Decides as follows'.
[55] See WTO document WT/DS138.

In that case, one disputing party had argued that, by virtue of the Declaration, the standard of review to be applied in dispute settlement must be the same in disputes under the SCM Agreement as in disputes under the Anti-Dumping Agreement. The panel observed that there was nothing in the Declaration to create an obligation with respect to the standard of review to be applied, and viewed the instrument as a 'mere' Declaration 'lack[ing] the mandatory authority' of a Ministerial Decision.[56] The panel contrasted the Ministerial Declaration where ministers 'simply "recognize . . . the need" for the consistent resolution of disputes' with a Ministerial Decision where ministers '"decide" that certain action shall be taken'.[57]

The Appellate Body agreed with the panel, finding that '(b)y its own terms' the Declaration does 'not impose an obligation to apply' a certain standard of review.[58] The Appellate Body explained that the 'Declaration was couched in hortatory language; it uses the words "Ministers recognize"' and it 'merely acknowledges "the need for the consistent resolution of disputes arising from anti-dumping and countervailing duty measures"'.[59] The Appellate Body further observed that the Declaration 'does not specify any specific action to be taken. In particular, it does not prescribe a standard of review to be applied.'[60] Although the panel seemed to consider that the form of instrument itself – that is, declaration versus decision – was indicative of its legal effect, the Appellate Body focused on the language of the instrument in opining on its import.

The legal value or effect of a Ministerial Decision was considered recently in the context of dispute settlement in *US–Clove Cigarettes*, a dispute between the United States and Indonesia. In that case, the complainant challenged under Article 2.12 of the Technical Barriers to Trade (TBT) Agreement the fact that the respondent had allowed only a three-month interval between publication and entry into force of the measure in question. Article 2.12 of the TBT Agreement does not set out

---

[56] Panel Report, *United States – Imposition of Countervailing Duties on Certain Hot-Rolled Lead and Bismuth Carbon Steel Products Originating in the United Kingdom*, see WTO document WT/DS138/R and Corr. 2, adopted 7 June 2000, paragraph 6.17, upheld by Appellate Body Report in WTO document Appellate Body Report, WT/DS138/AB/R, DSR 2000:VI, 2623.

[57] Ibid.

[58] Appellate Body Report, *United States – Imposition of Countervailing Duties on Certain Hot-Rolled Lead and Bismuth Carbon Steel Products Originating in the United Kingdom*, see WTO document WT/DS138/AB/R, adopted 7 June 2000, DSR 2000:V, 2595, paragraph 49.

[59] Ibid.     [60] Ibid.

a specific time period for the interval, requiring only that 'Members shall allow a reasonable interval between the publication of technical regulations and their entry into force'.[61] Nevertheless, the complainant argued that the Ministerial Decision on Implementation-Related Issues and Concerns,[62] which was adopted at the WTO Ministerial Conference held in Doha in 2001, required that there be a six-month interval between publication and entry into force. Paragraph 5.2 of the Ministerial Decision states that:

> 5.2 Subject to the conditions specified in paragraph 12 of Article 2 of the Agreement on Technical Barriers to Trade, the phrase 'reasonable interval' *shall be understood to mean* normally a period of not less than 6 months, except when this would be ineffective in fulfilling the legitimate objectives pursued [italics added].

The complainant contended that paragraph 5.2 of the Ministerial Decision constitutes a binding interpretation under Article IX:2 of the WTO Agreement, with the result that the respondent's failure to allow a six-month interval between publication and coming into force rendered the measure inconsistent with Article 2.12 of the TBT Agreement. The respondent disagreed and considered that paragraph 5.2 of the Ministerial Decision should not be applied as a rule amending Article 2.12 of the TBT Agreement.

The Appellate Body observed that paragraph 5.2 'clearly expresses a common understanding, and an acceptance of that understanding among Members with regard to the meaning of the term "reasonable interval" in Article 2.12 of the *TBT Agreement*'.[63] It opined further that paragraph 5.2 'bears specifically'[64] upon the interpretation of the term in question. On that basis, the Appellate Body concluded that paragraph 5.2 of the Ministerial Decision constituted a 'subsequent agreement' regarding the interpretation of the TBT Agreement within

---

[61] The full text of Article 2.12 reads as follows: 'Except in those urgent circumstances referred to in paragraph 10, Members shall allow a reasonable interval between the publication of technical regulations and their entry into force in order to allow time for producers in exporting Members, and particularly in developing country Members, to adapt their products or methods of production to the requirements of the importing Member.'

[62] See WTO document WT/MIN(01)/17, 20 November 2001.

[63] Appellate Body Report, *United States – Measures Affecting the Production and Sale of Clove Cigarettes*, see WTO document WT/DS406/AB/R, adopted 24 April 2012, DSR 2012: XI, p. 5751, paragraph 267.

[64] Ibid., paragraph 266.

the meaning of Article 31(3)(a) of the Vienna Convention on the Law of Treaties[65] (Vienna Convention), which meant that paragraph 5.2 could be used as a tool to interpret the meaning of the treaty provision in question, namely Article 2.12 of the TBT Agreement.[66] The Appellate Body explained that the terms of paragraph 5.2 'must be "read into" Article 2.12 for the purpose of interpreting that provision. . .'.[67] It drew attention to specific language found in the Ministerial Decision, observing that 'the understanding among Members with regard to the meaning of the term "reasonable interval" in Article 2.12 of the *TBT Agreement* is expressed by terms – *"shall be understood to mean"* – that cannot be considered as merely hortatory'.[68] In other words, the Appellate Body considered that paragraph 5.2 of the Ministerial Decision had legal effect in that it informed the legal interpretation of Article 2.12 of the TBT Agreement. The Appellate Body found for the complainant on that ground.

Soon after, in the Appellate Body Report in *US–Tuna II* issued by the Appellate Body a few months after it issued its report in *US–Clove Cigarettes*, the Appellate Body determined that the Decision of the [TBT] Committee on Principles for the Development of International Standards, Guides and Recommendations with Relation to Articles 2, 5 and Annex 3 of the Agreement[69] 'can be considered' as a subsequent agreement within the meaning of the Vienna Convention and observed that the Decision informs the interpretation and application of a provision of the TBT Agreement because it 'bears specifically' on the terms under consideration.[70] The Appellate Body drew attention to a number of factors in its reasoning. First, it pointed out that the TBT Committee comprised all WTO members and that the Decision was adopted by

[65] 1155 United Nations Treaty Series 331.

[66] Article 31 of the Vienna Convention falls under the section on 'Interpretation of Treaties' and is entitled 'General rule of interpretation'. Article 31(3)(a) provides as follows: 'There shall be taken into account together with the context any subsequent agreement between the parties regarding the interpretation of the treaty or the application of its provisions.'

[67] Appellate Body Report, *United States – Measures Affecting the Production and Sale of Clove Cigarettes*, see WTO document WT/DS406/AB/R, adopted 24 April 2012, DSR 2012: XI, p. 5751, paragraph 269. The Appellate Body made clear that reading terms into a provision for purposes of interpreting it does not mean that the terms replace or override the original terms of the provision.

[68] Ibid., paragraph 267.      [69] G/TBT/1/Rev. 10, pp. 46–48, 9 June 2011.

[70] Appellate Body Report, *United States – Measures Concerning the Importation, Marketing and Sale of Tuna and Tuna Products*, see WTO document WT/DS381/AB/R, adopted 13 June 2012, DSR 2012: IV, p. 1837, paragraph 372.

consensus.[71] It observed that a number of parties to the dispute argued that the Decision should inform the Appellate Body's interpretation of the provision in question.[72] It also noted that the title of the Decision expressly referred to specific provisions of the TBT Agreement, which included the provision it was seeking to clarify (namely, Article 2.4 of the TBT Agreement). Finally, it looked to the background of the Decision and the reasons it was developed, which included the application of the provision the Appellate Body was seeking to clarify in that appeal.[73]

These two recent Appellate Body Reports suggest that Ministerial Decisions are not vehicles that create new, legally binding rules in and of themselves. Indeed, the Appellate Body made clear in *US–Clove Cigarettes* that the terms of paragraph 5.2 of the Ministerial Decision did not 'replace or override the terms contained in Article 2.12 [of the TBT Agreement]'.[74] However, such instruments can – indeed will – assist in interpreting and applying existing rules if certain conditions are met. For the Appellate Body, the language of the instruments was highly relevant in determining their effect or legal value. In both recent cases where the legal value of Ministerial Decisions was raised, the Appellate Body concluded that the Decisions reflected a clear, common understanding among WTO members bearing specifically on the meaning of the provision in question. And in both instances, the Appellate Body paid heed to the Decisions in interpreting the WTO provisions.

### Multilateral interpretations under Article IX:2

The *US–Clove Cigarettes* dispute also raised issues about authoritative interpretations adopted under Article IX:2 of the WTO Agreement. As mentioned above, one party in the dispute maintained that paragraph 5.2 of the Ministerial Decision regarding the meaning of Article 2.12 of the TBT Agreement (quoted above) constituted an authoritative interpretation under Article IX:2 of the WTO Agreement and hence had to be followed as a binding interpretation.[75] The Appellate Body disagreed. It observed that Article IX:2 establishes 'specific requirements' that apply to

---

[71] Ibid., paragraph 371.    [72] Ibid., paragraphs 366, 367, 368, 369.
[73] Ibid., paragraph 372.
[74] Appellate Body Report, *United States – Measures Affecting the Production and Sale of Clove Cigarettes*, see WTO document WT/DS406/AB/R, adopted 24 April 2012, DSR 2012: XI, p. 5751, paragraph 269.
[75] Ibid., paragraph 244.

the adoption of multilateral interpretations, one of which is that such interpretations be taken on the basis of a recommendation by the Council overseeing the functioning of the relevant agreement (in this case, the TBT Agreement, which is overseen by the Council for Trade in Goods).[76] No such recommendation had been made in the case of paragraph 5.2, and hence no multilateral interpretation could have been adopted. Noting that Article IX:2 uses the term 'shall' exercise their authority to adopt an interpretation, on the basis of a recommendation' by the Council overseeing the functioning of that Agreement, the Appellate Body concluded that 'the terms of Article IX:2 do not suggest that compliance with [the recommendation requirement] is dispensable'.[77]

According to the Appellate Body, 'the recommendation from the relevant Council is an essential element of Article IX:2, which constitutes the legal basis upon which the Ministerial Conference or the General Council exercise their authority to adopt interpretations. . .'.[78] Thus, contrary to the Panel's opinion that 'it could be argued'[79] that the absence of this formal requirement is insufficient to deprive the paragraph of legal effect as a binding multilateral interpretation, the Appellate Body found that the failure to meet one of the requirements of Article IX:2, namely that a multilateral interpretation be based on a recommendation of the Council overseeing the relevant Agreement, was fatal to the argument that paragraph 5.2 constitutes a multilateral interpretation.[80] According to the Appellate Body, the exclusive authority to adopt multilateral interpretations 'must be exercised within the defined parameters of Article IX:2' and 'the view expressed by the Panel does not respect a specific decision-making procedure' of that provision.[81]

In making its ruling, the Appellate Body 'set forth some general considerations on the role and function of multilateral interpretations adopted pursuant to Article IX:2'.[82] It is instructive to mention some of them here. First, the Appellate Body recalled its findings in *EC–Bananas III (Article 21.5 – Ecuador II)/EC–Bananas III (Article 21.5 – US)* that

---

[76] Ibid., paragraph 251.     [77] Ibid., paragraphs 251, 254.     [78] Ibid., paragraph 254.
[79] Panel Report, *United States – Measures Affecting the Production and Sale of Clove Cigarettes*, see WTO document WT/DS406/R, adopted 24 April 2012, as modified by Appellate Body Report, see WTO document WT/DS406/AB/R, DSR 2012: XI, p. 5865, paragraph 7.575.
[80] Appellate Body Report, *United States – Measures Affecting the Production and Sale of Clove Cigarettes*, see WTO document WT/DS406/AB/R, adopted 24 April 2012, DSR 2012: XI, p. 5751, paragraph 254.
[81] Ibid., paragraph 253.     [82] Ibid., paragraph 247.

interpretations adopted pursuant to Article IX:2 are 'meant to clarify the meaning of existing obligations, not to modify their content'.[83] It also observed that the authority of the Ministerial Conference and the General Council to adopt multilateral interpretations 'is situated within defined parameters established by Article IX:2'.[84] Third, the Appellate Body explained that '[m]ultilateral interpretations adopted pursuant to Article IX:2 of the *WTO Agreement* have a pervasive legal effect. Such interpretations are binding on all Members.'[85]

These 'general considerations' assist in distinguishing multilateral interpretations from findings in adopted panel or Appellate Body reports pronouncing on the violation or otherwise of WTO provisions, which also figure in a discussion of WTO rule-making. An authoritative interpretation is a binding interpretation of a provision and is adopted by the highest WTO body on the basis of a three-fourths majority vote of the membership and a recommendation from the relevant Council. Once adopted, it is binding on all members.

A finding in a panel or Appellate Body report, by contrast, is binding only on the parties to the dispute and has no legal implications for any other member. It is true that panel and Appellate Body reports tend to have precedential value as a matter of practice, but the doctrine of *stare decisis* – whereby courts will follow and adhere to previous rulings – does not apply in the WTO dispute settlement system.[86] Moreover, panels and the Appellate Body are mandated under the DSU to 'clarify' the existing provisions of WTO agreements, rather than to 'interpret' them *per se.*[87]

The clear lesson about multilateral interpretations that may be taken from the Appellate Body's decision in *US–Clove Cigarettes* is that such

---

[83] Appellate Body Reports, *European Communities – Regime for the Importation, Sale and Distribution of Bananas – Second Recourse to Article 21.5 of the DSU by Ecuador*, see WTO document WT/DS27/AB/RW2/ECU, adopted 11 December 2008, and Corr. 1/ *European Communities – Regime for the Importation, Sale and Distribution of Bananas – Recourse to Article 21.5 of the DSU by the United States*, see WTO document WT/DS27/ AB/RW/USA and Corr. 1, adopted 22 December 2008, DSR 2008: XVIII, p. 7165, paragraph 383; Appellate Body Report, *United States – Measures Affecting the Production and Sale of Clove Cigarettes*, see WTO document WT/DS406/AB/R, adopted 24 April 2012, DSR 2012: XI, p. 5751, paragraph 249.

[84] Appellate Body Report, *United States – Measures Affecting the Production and Sale of Clove Cigarettes*, see WTO document WT/DS406/AB/R, adopted 24 April 2012, DSR 2012: XI, p. 5751, paragraph 249.

[85] Ibid., paragraph 250.

[86] *Stare decisis* is Latin for 'to stand by that which is decided'. The doctrine is applied in common law systems.

[87] See Article 3.2 of the DSU.

decisions must follow exactly the requirements set out in Article IX:2. Otherwise, the decision will probably not be considered to be a multilateral interpretation binding on all members. The Appellate Body's approach underscores the legal significance of multilateral interpretations adopted pursuant to Article IX:2. As the Appellate Body explained, 'the broad legal effect of these interpretations is precisely the reason why Article IX:2 subjects the adoption of such interpretations to clearly articulated and strict decision-making procedures'.[88] And it is presumably precisely the reason why the Appellate Body has taken a very strict view in clarifying the meaning of Article IX:2.

As noted above, the WTO has yet to adopt a multilateral interpretation pursuant to Article IX:2 of the WTO Agreement. Nor has any Council ever submitted one to the General Council or Ministerial Conference for adoption.

### Waivers under Article IX:3

As mentioned above, numerous waivers have been adopted under Article IX:3 of the WTO Agreement following the consensus procedure agreed in November 1995.[89] Nevertheless, the Appellate Body has stressed 'the exceptional nature' of waivers and has made clear that waivers must be interpreted 'with great care'.[90] This approach reflects the wording of Article IX:3, which begins 'In exceptional circumstances, the Ministerial Conference may decide to waive an obligation imposed on a Member'.

The Appellate Body has been careful to pay close heed to the language of waivers in determining their meaning; for example, the Appellate Body reversed a panel finding that the Lomé Waiver justified a deviation from Article XIII of the GATT 1994 because the scope of Article XIII is identical to that of Article I of the GATT 1994, the provision to which the waiver explicitly referred. The Appellate Body explained that it could not 'disregard the clear and plain wording of the Lomé Waiver by extending its scope to include a waiver from the obligations under

---

[88] Appellate Body Report, *United States – Measures Affecting the Production and Sale of Clove Cigarettes*, see WTO document WT/DS406/AB/R, adopted 24 April 2012, DSR 2012: XI, p. 5751, paragraph 250.

[89] More than thirty waivers have been adopted under the WTO Agreement thus far. See *WTO Analytical Index*, vol. 1, p. 47.

[90] Appellate Body Report, *European Communities – Regime for the Importation, Sale and Distribution of Bananas*, see WTO document WT/DS27/AB/R, adopted 25 September 1997, DSR 1997: II, p. 591, paragraphs 184–187.

Article XIII'.[91] The Appellate Body cautioned that 'a waiver is a specific and exceptional instrument subject to strict disciplines' and that such 'elements do not suggest that a waiver should be construed as an agreement on issues not explicitly reflected in its terms and conditions, justifying circumstances, and stated policy objectives'.[92]

The negotiating history of waivers is also important when seeking to determine their meaning. For example, in determining the import of the Lomé Waiver, the Appellate Body considered the drafting history of the Waiver and concluded that it reflected the drafters' intentions to restrict the scope of the Waiver.[93]

Finally, the Appellate Body has made clear that the purpose of a waiver is not to 'modify existing provisions . . . let alone create new law or add to or amend the obligations under a covered agreement or Schedule'.[94] Thus adoption of a waiver does not create rules; rather, it temporarily suspends the operation of an existing rule.

### Amendments under Article X

Only one amendment under Article X of the WTO Agreement has ever been adopted, and it has yet to enter into force because it has not yet been accepted by two-thirds of WTO members. In December 2005, the General Council adopted by consensus the Amendment to the TRIPs Agreement dealing with patents and public health, essentially facilitating exports, in certain circumstances, of pharmaceuticals manufactured under compulsory licences to countries with insufficient or no

---

[91] Ibid., paragraph 183.

[92] Appellate Body Reports, *European Communities – Regime for the Importation, Sale and Distribution of Bananas – Second Recourse to Article 21.5 of the DSU by Ecuador*, see WTO document WT/DS27/AB/RW2/ECU, adopted 11 December 2008, and Corr. 1/ *European Communities – Regime for the Importation, Sale and Distribution of Bananas – Recourse to Article 21.5 of the DSU by the United States*, see WTO document WT/DS27/ AB/RW/USA and Corr. 1, paragraph 381.

[93] Appellate Body Report, *European Communities – Regime for the Importation, Sale and Distribution of Bananas*, see WTO document WT/DS27/AB/R, adopted 25 September 1997, DSR 1997: II, p. 591, paragraph 186.

[94] Appellate Body Reports, *European Communities – Regime for the Importation, Sale and Distribution of Bananas – Second Recourse to Article 21.5 of the DSU by Ecuador*, see WTO document WT/DS27/AB/RW2/ECU, adopted 11 December 2008, and Corr. 1/ *European Communities – Regime for the Importation, Sale and Distribution of Bananas – Recourse to Article 21.5 of the DSU by the United States*, see WTO document WT/DS27/ AB/RW/USA and Corr. 1, adopted 22 December 2008, DSR 2008: XVIII, p. 7165, paragraph 382.

manufacturing capacities in the pharmaceutical sector. Once it comes into force, the amendment will effect a legally binding change to the TRIPs Agreement by adding a provision (Article 31bis) after Article 31 and by inserting an annex to the TRIPs Agreement after Article 73, which elaborates on Article 31bis.[95] The amendment will take effect in accordance with Article X:3 of the WTO Agreement, which means that, initially, it will bind only the two-thirds of the membership that has deposited an Instrument of Acceptance of the Protocol of Amendment. It will come into effect for other members only when the relevant member deposits its Instrument of Acceptance.[96]

A second amendment under Article X of the WTO Agreement was to be adopted by the General Council by 31 July 2014; however, this deadline was missed.[97] According to a Ministerial Decision adopted at the Ministerial Conference in Bali in December 2013, the Preparatory Committee on Trade Facilitation (which is open to all WTO members) was mandated to draw up a Protocol of Amendment to insert the entire Trade Facilitation Agreement into Annex 1A of the WTO Agreement.

The Protocol is expected to stipulate that the Protocol of Amendment will be open for acceptance until 31 July 2015 and that the Protocol of Amendment shall take effect in accordance with Article X:3. In other words, the new Trade Facilitation Agreement will come into effect once two-thirds of the membership has deposited instruments of acceptance of the Protocol, but only for those members. It will come into effect for other members as and when they deposit their respective instruments of acceptance.

The insertion of the Trade Facilitation Agreement into Annex 1A of the WTO Agreement is important for dispute settlement purposes and

---

[95]  See WTO document WT/L/641, 8 December 2005.

[96]  Prior to the adoption of the Decision, the Chair of the General Council 'place[d] on the record' a statement that she said 'represents several key shared understandings of Members regarding the amendment to be submitted for acceptance and the way in which it will be interpreted and implemented'. The statement indicated that the amendment 'should be used in good faith to protect public health and . . . not be an instrument to pursue industrial or commercial policy objectives', addressed preventing diversion from intended markets, identified several developed members who had opted out of using the scheme as importers, and identified other members who would use the system as import- ers only in emergency situations. See WTO document WT/GC/M/82, p. 6, 25, 26 and 30 August 2003. The legal effect of this statement has not yet arisen in the context of WTO dispute settlement and is unlikely to do so before the amendment comes into force.

[97]  As of the date of writing (August 2014), the implications of missing the deadline are unknown.

hence for its legal enforceability. The DSU stipulates in Article 1 that the 'rules and procedures of this Understanding shall apply to disputes brought pursuant to … the agreements listed in Appendix 1 to this Understanding'. Appendix 1 includes Annex 1A. This means that members will be able to bring claims and assert defences with respect to the provisions of the Trade Facilitation Agreement in the same way as they can with respect to any of the other WTO agreements, subject to any explicit provisions to the contrary.

## Accessions under Article XII

In joining the WTO, acceding governments agree to abide by WTO rules. The acceding member's commitments and obligations are set out in a Protocol of Accession, which becomes, by its terms, 'an integral part of the WTO Agreement'.[98] As mentioned above, accessions are governed by Article XII of the WTO Agreement. Any state or separate customs territory possessing full autonomy in the conduct of its external commercial relations may accede to the WTO agreement on terms to be agreed between it and the WTO. Article XII:2 requires that decisions on accession be taken by the Ministerial Conference, which is to approve the agreement on the terms of accession by a two-thirds majority of WTO members. However, as pointed out above, a Decision adopted by the General Council in November 1995 provides that in considering accessions, the General Council shall seek to decide on the basis of consensus, and only if that proves impossible will the two-thirds rule apply.[99] All accessions decisions made since then have been taken by consensus.

Protocols of accession and working party reports have been raised in close to 30 disputes thus far, almost 20 of which have proceeded to the panel stage.[100] The disputes that went forward were often combined together, such as when they were against the same member and

---

[98] See, for example, paragraph 2 of the Protocol on the Accession of Russia, which is typical of what is found in all Accession Protocols and which states: 'The WTO Agreement to which the Russian Federation accedes shall be the WTO Agreement, including the Explanatory Notes to that Agreement, as rectified, amended or otherwise modified by such legal instruments as may have entered into force before the date of entry into force of this Protocol. This Protocol, which shall include the commitments referred to in paragraph 1450 of the Working Party Report, *shall be an integral part of the WTO Agreement.*' See WTO document WT/L/839, 17 December 2011, p. 2 (italics added).

[99] See WTO document WT/L/93.

[100] Eleven different panels had considered twenty-eight different disputes as of August 2014.

concerned the same matter.[101] The Protocols of Accession of Armenia, China, and Viet Nam have been cited in disputes, but only those of China and Viet Nam have come under review because the dispute involving Armenia did not proceed beyond the consultations stage. Panels and the Appellate Body have been asked to clarify a number of provisions included in Accession Protocols and working party reports. Their findings, discussed below, provide useful lessons for negotiators and drafters of protocols of accession and working party reports.

Most of the disputes have involved China's Protocol of Accession.[102] The first three were challenges by Canada, the (then) European Communities and the United States in *China–Automobile Parts*, which was adjudicated by a single panel and subsequently the Appellate Body.[103] The complainants challenged China's commitments under paragraph 93 of China's Working Party Report, dealing with tariff treatment for kits for motor vehicles, as well as under paragraphs 1.2, 7.2 and 7.3 of the Accession Protocol. The Panel did not find it necessary to make findings with respect to the paragraphs in China's Accession Protocol. In considering the challenge regarding paragraph 93 of China's Working Party Report, the Panel observed that:

> All parties agree that China's commitments under its Working Party Report are enforceable in WTO dispute settlement proceedings. The Accession Protocol is an integral part of the WTO Agreement pursuant to Part I, Article 1.3 of the Accession Protocol. In turn, paragraph 342 of China's Working Party Report incorporates China's commitments under its Working Party Report, including paragraph 93, into the Accessions Protocol. Therefore, China's commitment in paragraph 93 of the Working Party Report is also an integral part of the WTO Agreement.[104]

---

[101] See Article 9 of the DSU. For example, three disputes were filed against China by the United States, the European Union and Japan, respectively, concerning China's measures related to the exportation of rare earths, tungsten and molybdenum. The three disputes were heard by a single panel. The panel produced three separate reports with common pages save for the conclusions and recommendations: see Panel Reports, *China – Measures Related to the Exportation of Rare Earths, Tungsten, and Molybdenum*, see WTO documents: WT/DS431/R, WT/DS432/R, WT/DS433/R, and Add. 1, circulated to WTO Members 26 March 2014.

[102] See WTO document WT/L/432, 23 November 2001.

[103] Panel Reports, *China – Measures Affecting Imports of Automobile Parts*, see WTO documents: WT/DS339/R, WT/DS340/R, WT/DS342/R, Add. 1 and Add. 2, adopted 12 January 2009, upheld (WT/DS339/R) and as modified (WT/DS340/R, WT/DS342/R) by Appellate Body Reports WT/DS339/AB/R, WT/DS340/AB/R, WT/DS342/AB/R, DSR 2009: I, p. 119.

[104] Ibid., paragraph 7.740 (footnotes omitted).

The Panel also decided that it would interpret China's commitment under paragraph 93 of the Working Party Report in accordance with the interpretative rules of the Vienna Convention on the Law of Treaties.[105] Article 3.2 of the DSU requires that the provisions of the WTO covered agreements be clarified 'in accordance with customary rules of interpretation of public international law', which the Appellate Body has confirmed include the rules codified in Articles 31 (General rule of interpretation) and 32 (Supplementary means of interpretation) of the Vienna Convention on the Law of Treaties.[106] The Panel reasoned that, as China's Working Party Report constitutes an integral part of the WTO agreement, it would 'accordingly'[107] interpret China's commitments in accordance with the customary rules of interpretation of public international law.

The significance of this case for the purpose of this chapter lies in the approach to the legal status of China's Accession Protocol and Working Party Report. As the Appellate Body observed, the Panel had proceeded on the basis that China's commitment under paragraph 93 is enforceable in WTO dispute settlement and that the interpretative rules codified in the Vienna Convention were applicable. The Appellate Body also noted that '[n]either of these propositions has been disputed at any point in these proceedings'.[108] The Panel and Appellate Body reports were subsequently adopted by the DSB.[109] It was clear, therefore, that commitments

---

[105] Ibid., paragraph 7.741. The Panel also determined that China's Schedule of Concessions was annexed to the GATT 1994 pursuant to paragraph II.1 of China's Accession Protocol and therefore must be interpreted in accordance with the rules codified in the Vienna Convention. See Ibid., paragraph 7.652.

[106] Appellate Body Report, *United States – Standards for Reformulated and Conventional Gasoline*, see WTO documents: WT/DS2/AB/R, adopted 20 May 1996, DSR 1996: I, p. 16. Appellate Body Report, *Japan – Taxes on Alcoholic Beverages*, WT/DS8/AB/R, WT/DS10/AB/R, WT/DS11/AB/R, adopted 1 November 1996, DSR 1996: I, p. 97.

[107] See Panel Reports, *China – Measures Affecting Imports of Automobile Parts*, WTO documents: WT/DS339/R, WT/DS340/R, WT/DS342/R, Add. 1 and Add. 2, adopted 12 January 2009, upheld (WT/DS339/R) and as modified (WT/DS340/R, WT/DS342/R) by Appellate Body Reports WT/DS339/AB/R, WT/DS340/AB/R, WT/DS342/AB/R, DSR 2009: I, p. 119, paragraph 7.741.

[108] Appellate Body Reports, *China – Measures Affecting Imports of Automobile Parts*, see WTO documents: WT/DS339/AB/R, WT/DS340/AB/R, WT/DS342/AB/R, adopted 12 January 2009, DSR 2009: I, p. 3, paragraph 214. The Appellate Body subsequently put this in its own words in *US–Tyres*, 118, referring in that case to section 16 of China's Accession Protocol: Appellate Body Report, *United States – Measures Affecting Imports of Certain Passenger Vehicle and Light Truck Tyres from China*, see WTO document WT/DS399/AB/R, adopted 5 October 2011, DSR 2011: IX, p. 4811, paragraph 118.

[109] See WTO document WT/DSB/M/262, 9 March 2009, pp. 4–5.

under working party reports incorporated into Accession Protocols, which are in turn integral parts of the WTO Agreement, are enforceable under WTO dispute settlement proceedings and may be interpreted in accordance with the customary rules of interpretation of public international law codified in the Vienna Convention on the Law of Treaties.[110]

Having established these principles, the next key issue to be adjudicated regarding Accession Protocols concerned the specific relationship of Accession Protocols with other WTO instruments. This was first considered in *China–Publications and Audiovisual Products*.[111] In that case, the United States challenged a series of Chinese measures regulating activities relating to the importation and distribution of certain publications and audiovisual entertainment products. The Panel, upheld by the Appellate Body, found among other things that China had acted inconsistently with its obligations under paragraph 5.1 of China's Accession Protocol, which deals with China's trading rights commitments. China had sought to justify its inconsistent measures by relying on Article XX(a) of the GATT 1994, which permits WTO members to justify inconsistent measures if they are necessary to protect public morals. The issue before the Appellate Body was whether China was entitled to invoke Article XX of the GATT 1994 in seeking to justify a violation of a

---

[110] This was confirmed in subsequent disputes. See, for example, Appellate Body Reports, *China – Measures Related to the Exportation of Various Raw Materials*, see WTO documents: WT/DS394/AB/R, WT/DS395/AB/R, WT/DS398/AB/R, adopted 22 February 2012, DSR 2012: VII, p. 3295, paragraph 278, where the Appellate Body observed as follows: Paragraph 1.2 of China's Accession Protocol provides that the Protocol 'shall be an integral part of the *WTO Agreement*. As such, the customary rules of interpretation of public international law, as codified in Articles 31 and 32 of the Vienna Convention on the Law of Treaties . . . are, pursuant to Article 3.2 of the DSU, applicable in this dispute'; Panel Reports, *China – Measures Related to the Exportation of Various Raw Materials*, WT/DS394/R, WT/DS395/R, WT/DS398/R, Add. 1 and Corr. 1, adopted 22 February 2012, as modified by Appellate Body Reports WT/DS394/AB/R, WT/DS395/AB/R, WT/DS398/AB/R, DSR 2012: VII, p. 3501, paragraph 7.114, where the Panel observed that: 'In this dispute, as with previous disputes concerned with China's Accession Protocol, all parties agree that China's Accession Protocol forms an integral part of the WTO Agreement. Moreover, all parties agree that WTO Members can initiate WTO dispute settlement proceedings on the basis of a claim of violation of China's Accession Protocol. Finally, all parties agree that commitments included in the related Working Party Report, and incorporated into the Accession Protocol by cross-reference, are binding and enforceable through WTO dispute settlement proceedings' (original footnote excluded).

[111] See WTO document WT/DS363.

commitment found not in the GATT 1994, but rather, in China's Accession Protocol. Article XX of the GATT 1994 reads in part as follows:

> *General Exceptions*
> Subject to the requirement that such measures are not applied in a manner which would constitute a means of arbitrary or unjustifiable discrimination between countries where the same conditions prevail, or a disguised restriction on international trade, nothing in this Agreement shall be construed to prevent the adoption or enforcement by any contracting party of measures:
> (*a*) necessary to protect public morals[.]

The Appellate Body determined that China could rely on Article XX(a) to justify a violation of its trading rights commitments referred to in Article 5.1 of the Protocol. The Appellate Body's reasoning centred on the wording of the commitment in paragraph 5.1 itself, which reads in part as follows:

> Without prejudice to China's *right to regulate trade in a manner consistent with the WTO Agreement*, China shall progressively liberalize the availability and scope of the right to trade, so that, within three years after accession, all enterprises in China shall have the right to trade in all goods throughout the customs territory of China ... Such right to trade shall be the right to import and export goods. All such goods shall be accorded national treatment under Article III of the GATT 1994, especially paragraph 4 thereof, in respect of their internal sale, offering for sale, purchase, transportation, distribution or use, including their direct access to end-users[112] [emphasis added].

The Appellate Body determined that the words in the opening phrase of paragraph 5.1 – 'in a manner consistent with the WTO Agreement' – signified that China's right to regulate trade was circumscribed by WTO disciplines as a whole. The Appellate Body reasoned that measures may be consistent with WTO disciplines in one of two ways: (i) a measure does not contravene a WTO discipline; or (ii) a measure does contravene a WTO discipline but it is justified under an applicable exception. It also determined that the phrase 'in a manner consistent with the WTO Agreement' encompassed both types of inconsistency. After finding that the measure at issue was 'clearly and intrinsically related to the objective of regulating the goods'[113] in question, the Appellate Body determined

---

[112] See WTO document WT/L/432, 23 November 2001, p. 4.

[113] Appellate Body Report, *China – Measures Affecting Trading Rights and Distribution Services for Certain Publications and Audiovisual Entertainment Products*, see WTO document WT/DS363/AB/R, adopted 19 January 2010, DSR 2010: I, p. 3, paragraph 230.

that China was entitled to invoke the exception under Article XX(a) of the GATT 1994.[114]

The availability of Article XX defences in justifying violations of commitments in China's Accession Protocol was explored further in *China–Raw Materials*,[115] where the United States, the European Union and Mexico challenged several Chinese measures on the exportation from China of certain raw materials. On this occasion, the Appellate Body determined that China was not entitled to rely on Article XX of the GATT 1994 to justify a violation of its Accession Protocol. The Appellate Body's reasoning turned on the wording of China's commitment at issue in that case.

In this dispute, the Panel had found that export duties imposed by China on certain raw materials were inconsistent with paragraph 11.3 of China's Accession Protocol, which reads as follows:

> China shall eliminate all taxes and charges applied to exports unless specifically provided for in Annex 6 of this Protocol or applied in conformity with the provisions of Article VIII of the GATT 1994.

Only one of the raw materials subject to the export duties at issue was listed in Annex 6.[116] China sought to rely on Article XX of the GATT 1994 to justify its failure to comply with paragraph 11.3.[117] Referring to wording in a note to Annex 6 that permits increasing 'presently applied' tariff levels in 'exceptional circumstances', China argued that permitting otherwise WTO-inconsistent export duties in exceptional circumstances

---

[114] The Appellate Body ultimately determined that China had not established that its provisions were necessary to protect public morals, and thus China's provisions were not justified under Article XX(a) of the GATT 1994: Ibid., paragraphs 222–223, 229–230, 336–337.

[115] See WTO documents WT/DS394, WT/DS395 and WT/DS398.

[116] A total of eighty-four products are listed in Annex 6.

[117] In this dispute, China sought to rely upon Article XX(b) and Article XX(g) to justify its export duties:

> Subject to the requirement that such measures are not applied in a manner which would constitute a means of arbitrary or unjustifiable discrimination between countries where the same conditions prevail, or a disguised restriction on international trade, nothing in this Agreement shall be construed to prevent the adoption or enforcement by any contracting party of measures:
>
> (b) necessary to protect human, animal or plant life or health;
>
> (g) relating to the conservation of exhaustible natural resources if such measures are made effective in conjunction with restrictions on domestic production or consumption.

demonstrated members' shared intent that China be permitted to have recourse – whether directly or indirectly – to the exceptional circumstances set forth in Article XX.[118] The Panel did not agree. It observed that Article XX of the GATT 1994 refers in the opening paragraph of the article to 'nothing in this Agreement', which 'suggests that the exceptions therein relate only to the GATT 1994, and not to other agreements'.[119] It also noted that the provisions of Article XX have on occasion been incorporated by cross-reference into other covered agreements, such as in the Trade-Related Investment Measures (TRIMs) Agreement, and that other WTO agreements include their own exceptions, such as the GATS for GATS violations, and the TBT and sanitary and phytosanitary (SPS) agreements for their own flexibilities.[120] It concluded that under the circumstances, 'it is reasonable to assume that, were GATT Article XX intended to apply to Paragraph 11.3 of China's Accession Protocol, language would have been inserted to suggest this relationship ... However, no such language is found in paragraph 11.3 of China's Accession Protocol.'[121]

The Appellate Body upheld the Panel's finding. The Appellate Body found it:

> difficult to see how this language [in Annex 6] could be read as indicating that China can have recourse to the provisions of Article XX of the GATT 1994 in order to justify imposition of duties on products that are *not* listed in Annex 6 ... We see nothing in the Note to Annex 6 suggesting that China could invoke Article XX of the GATT 1994 to justify the imposition of export duties that China had committed to eliminate under Paragraph 11.3 [emphasis original].[122]

---

[118] Panel Reports, *China – Measures Related to the Exportation of Various Raw Materials*, see WTO documents: WT/DS394/R, WT/DS395/R, WT/DS398/R, Add. 1 and Corr. 1, adopted 22 February 2012, as modified by Appellate Body Reports WT/DS394/AB/R, WT/DS395/AB/R, WT/DS398/AB/R, DSR 2012:VII, p. 3501, paragraph 282. A note at the end of Annex 6 provides as follows: 'China confirmed that the tariff levels included in this Annex are maximum levels which will not be exceeded. China confirmed furthermore that it would not increase the presently applied rates, except under exceptional circumstances. If such circumstances occurred, China would consult with affected members prior to increasing applied tariffs with a view to finding a mutually acceptable solution.' See WTO documents WT/L/432, 23 November 2001, p. 95.

[119] Ibid., paragraph 7.153.       [120] Ibid.       [121] Ibid., paragraph 7.154.

[122] Appellate Body Reports, *China – Measures Related to the Exportation of Various Raw Materials*, see WTO documents: WT/DS394/AB/R, WT/DS395/AB/R, WT/DS398/AB/R, adopted 22 February 2012, DSR 2012: VII, p. 3295, paragraphs 284–285.

China also sought to rely on the reference in paragraph 11.3 of the Protocol to Article VIII of the GATT 1994 to support its view that Article XX of the GATT 1994 may be invoked to justify a violation of paragraph 11.3. China reasoned that, pursuant to paragraph 11.3, export taxes and charges that are not applied in conformity with Article VIII would constitute a violation of both paragraph 11.3 and Article VIII. For China, given that Article XX may be invoked to justify a violation of Article VIII, Article XX must also be available for violations of paragraph 11.3. Otherwise, argued China, it would be deprived of a defence under Article XX simply because a complainant decided to pursue a claim about the export duties under the Protocol of Accession rather than under Article VIII of the GATT 1994. The Appellate Body disagreed with China, noting that export duties are expressly excluded from Article VIII and therefore the question of conformity with that provision would not arise in connection with export duties. Thus although Article XX of the GATT 1994 can be invoked to justify fees and charges regulated under Article VIII of the GATT 1994, it cannot be invoked to justify export duties, which are not regulated under Article VIII.[123]

The Appellate Body also recalled in this context its ruling in *China–Publications and Audiovisual Products*, which was grounded in the opening words of paragraph 5.1 of the Accession Protocol ('without prejudice to China's right to regulate trade in a manner consistent with the *WTO Agreement*'). The Appellate Body pointed out that paragraphs 11.1 and 11.2 of the Protocol of Accession both contain an obligation to ensure that certain fees and charges 'are in conformity with the GATT 1994', but that this obligation is not found in paragraph 11.3. The Appellate Body also observed that China's obligation to eliminate export duties arises exclusively from China's Accession Protocol and not from the GATT 1994, and thus it considered it 'reasonable to assume that, had there been a common intention to provide access to Article XX of the GATT 1994 in this respect, language to that effect would have been included in Paragraph 11.3 or elsewhere in China's Accession Protocol'.[124] The Appellate Body concluded that 'in the light of China's explicit commitment contained in Paragraph 11.3 to eliminate export duties and the lack of any textual reference to Article XX of the GATT

---

[123] Appellate Body Reports, *China – Measures Related to the Exportation of Various Raw Materials*, see WTO documents: WT/DS394/AB/R, WT/DS395/AB/R, WT/DS398/AB/R, adopted 22 February 2012, DSR 2012: VII, p. 3295, paragraphs 288–290.

[124] Ibid., paragraph 293.

1994 in that provision, we see no basis to find that Article XX of the GATT 1994 is applicable to export duties found to be inconsistent with Paragraph 11.3'.[125]

China again sought to invoke Article XX of the GATT 1994 to justify violations of its Accession Protocol in the dispute *China–Rare Earths*,[126] a case involving challenges by the European Union, Japan, and the United States to export duties and export quotas imposed by China on rare earths, tungsten and molybdenum. Although the panel ruled that China was entitled to invoke the defences of Article XX of the GATT 1994 to justify its export *quotas*, it found that China was not entitled to do so with respect to its export *duties*.[127] The difference in treatment related to the difference in the nature of the obligations themselves.

In *China–Rare Earths*, China's imposition of export quotas was challenged under Article XI:1 of the GATT 1994 and paragraphs 162 and 165 of China's Working Party Report. In addition, China's administration of its export quotas was challenged under paragraph 5.1 of China's Accession Protocol together with paragraphs 83 and 84 of China's Working Party Report. China's invocation of Article XX of the GATT 1994 in respect of violations of Article XI:1 of the GATT 1994 was not in question; Article XX exceptions clearly apply to a violation of obligations under Article XI:1 of the GATT 1994.[128]

The Panel found that China was entitled to invoke Article XX defences for its obligations under Article 5.1 of China's Accession Protocol and paragraphs 83 and 84 of China's Working Party Report.[129] It recalled the

---

[125] Ibid., paragraph 306.

[126] See WTO documents: WT/DS/431, WT/DS/432, WT/DS/433.

[127] One panellist dissented on this point.

[128] Although China was entitled to invoke Article XX(g), ultimately the Appellate Body found that China's export quotas for rare earths, tungsten and molybdenum were not justified under that provision. Panel Reports, *China – Measures Related to the Exportation of Rare Earths, Tungsten, and Molybdenum*, see WTO documents: WT/DS431/R, WT/DS432/R, WT/DS433/R, and Add. 1, circulated to WTO members 26 March 2014, paragraphs 7.680, 7.845, 7.970.

[129] Article 5.1 is reproduced above. Paragraph 83 addresses how, during the three years of transition, China would progressively liberalise the scope and availability of trading rights for Chinese and foreign-invested enterprises, and provides that within three years after accession, all enterprises in China would be granted the right to trade. Paragraph 84 explains how China would eliminate its system of examination and approval of trading rights within three years after accession and that, at that time, China would permit all enterprises in China and foreign enterprises and individuals to export and import all goods, subject to certain exceptions. China committed that such rights would be granted in a non-discriminatory and non-discretionary way.

findings of the Appellate Body in *China–Publications and Audiovisual Products* related to China's obligations under paragraph 5.1 (referred to above) and determined that, as did the Appellate Body in that earlier dispute, the obligations under paragraphs 83 and 84 of the Working Party Report dealt with the same subject matter as paragraph 5.1 and that the obligations thereunder should be interpreted consistently with those in paragraph 5.1. It acknowledged that paragraphs 83 and 84 do not contain the introductory language found in paragraph 5.1 ('without prejudice to China's right to regulate trade in a manner consistent with the WTO Agreement'), but considered that it did not necessarily follow therefrom that members intended to deprive China of the right to regulate trade. The Panel also observed that if it were to find that China could not invoke Article XX of the GATT 1994 with respect to violations of China's trading rights under paragraphs 83 and 84, a complainant could too easily assert claims under those paragraphs only and thereby circumvent the defence offered to trading right violations under paragraph 5.1. Finally, the Panel also followed the Appellate Body in *China–Publications and Audiovisual Products* in noting that to succeed with an Article XX defence, the measures would have to have a 'clearly discernible, objective link to the regulation of trade'.[130]

Turning from the issue of export quotas to the finding on export duties, as noted above, China committed in paragraph 11.3 of its Accession Protocol to eliminate all export duties except for those products listed in Annex 6 of the Accession Protocol, where the permissible level of export duties for certain products is capped. None of the eighty-two products at issue in *China–Rare Earths* was listed in Annex 6, and China did not dispute before the panel that its export duties were inconsistent with paragraph 11.3. However, as in *China–Raw Materials*, China sought to justify its export duties under Article XX of the GATT 1994.[131] The

---

[130] Panel Reports, *China – Measures Related to the Exportation of Rare Earths, Tungsten, and Molybdenum*, see WTO documents: WT/DS431/R, WT/DS432/R, WT/DS433/R and Add. 1, circulated to WTO members 26 March 2014, paragraphs 7.1016–7.1033; Appellate Body Report, *China – Measures Affecting Trading Rights and Distribution Services for Certain Publications and Audiovisual Entertainment Products*, WT/DS363/AB/R, adopted 19 January 2010, DSR 2010: I, p. 3, paragraph 230. Although China was entitled to invoke Article XX(g) of the GATT 1994 relating to the conservation of exhaustible natural resources, ultimately the Appellate Body found that China's administration of export quotas for rare earths, tungsten and molybdenum was not justified under that provision.

[131] China argued that its export duties were necessary to protect human, animal or plant life or health pursuant to Article XX(b) of the GATT 1994.

Panel, recalling the Appellate Body's admonition in a previous case that 'absent cogent reasons, an adjudicatory body will resolve the same legal question in the same way in a subsequent case',[132] concluded that Article XX of the GATT 1994 could not be invoked by China to seek to justify a violation of paragraph 11.3, because it found no cogent reasons for departing from the Appellate Body's previous ruling on this issue. However, the Panel did so only after carefully reviewing China's arguments, some of which had not been raised in the previous case and which were considered by the Panel to be systemic in nature and central to the dispute. The Panel explained that it wished to conduct a full exploration of the novel arguments in order to assist the Appellate Body in its review, should the matter be appealed.[133] As it turns out, this issue is currently before the Appellate Body.[134]

Of note is that the Panel emphasised that its findings with respect to the non-applicability of Article XX of the GATT 1994 to justify a violation of Accession Protocol commitments on export duties were narrow in scope, and should not be understood as implying any view on whether Article XX of the GATT 1994 was applicable to other provisions of China's Accession Protocol or other members' Accession Protocols. The Panel also underscored that the implications of its finding in this respect were limited in terms of China being able to adopt measures to protect the environment and the life and health of its population. As the Panel explained, the only implication was that China must, according to paragraph 11.3, use instruments other than export duties to achieve these goals.[135]

---

[132] Appellate Body Report, *United States – Final Anti-Dumping Measures on Stainless Steel from Mexico*, see WTO document WT/DS344/AB/R, adopted 20 May 2008, DSR 2008: II, p. 513, paragraph 160. See also, Appellate Body Report, *United States – Continued Existence and Application of Zeroing Methodology*, see WTO document WT/DS350/AB/R, adopted 19 February 2009, DSR 2009: III, p. 1291, paragraph 362, where the Appellate Body made the same point and referred to the need for security and predictability in the dispute settlement system.

[133] Panel Reports, *China – Measures Related to the Exportation of Rare Earths, Tungsten, and Molybdenum*, see WTO document: WT/DS431/R, WT/DS432/R, WT/DS433/R and Add. 1, circulated to WTO members 26 March 2014, paragraph 7.59.

[134] The Appellate Body Report was issued on 7 August 2014, following the drafting of this article. The Appellate Body essentially upheld the Panel Report on this aspect of the appeal: Appellate Body Reports, *China – Measures Related to the Exportation of Rare Earths, Tungsten, and Molybdenum*, see WTO documents: WT/DS431/AB/R, WT/DS432/AB/R, WT/DS433/AB/R (adoption pending as of this writing).

[135] Panel Reports, *China – Measures Related to the Exportation of Rare Earths, Tungsten, and Molybdenum*, see WTO documents: WT/DS431/R, WT/DS432/R, WT/DS433/R

Also of note is that one panellist appended a separate opinion in which he expressed the view that the obligations under paragraph 11.3 were subject to the general exceptions in Article XX of the GATT 1994. He considered that the question of whether Article XX may be invoked to justify a violation under paragraph 11.3 was informed by the fact that the WTO functions as a Single Undertaking.[136] For him, a coherent implementation of China's obligations required that 'provisions from an Accession Protocol prohibiting border export tariffs must be interpreted and applied together with [Articles II and XI of the GATT 1994] allowing Members to use them'.[137] He asserted that the defences provided in the GATT 1994 'are automatically available to justify any GATT-related obligations, including border tariff-related obligations – unless a contrary intention is expressed'.[138] In his view, because paragraph 11.3 forms an integral part of the GATT system of rights and obligations and because China did not explicitly give up its right to invoke Article XX of the GATT 1994, the general exception provisions were available to China to justify a violation of paragraph 11.3.[139]

China's Accession Protocol was also raised in several other disputes touching upon a variety of legal issues, and has sometimes formed the basis of a claim by China against another WTO member. For example, in *EC–Fasteners*, China alleged violations of paragraph 15 of its Protocol on the part of the European Communities in connection with China's claims against the European Communities' Basic Anti-Dumping Regulation (Council Regulation (EC) No. 384/96 of 22 December 1995, as amended).[140] Paragraph 15 governs how the Anti-Dumping Agreement and the Subsidies and Countervailing Measures Agreement shall apply in proceedings involving imports of Chinese origin into a WTO member.[141] China did not pursue this claim before the Panel and did not seek a finding that the European Communities were in violation of the Protocol.

---

and Add. 1, circulated to WTO members 26 March 2014. Panel Reports, *China – Measures Related to the Exportation of Rare Earths, Tungsten, and Molybdenum*, see WTO documents: WT/DS431/R, WT/DS432/R, WT/DS433/R and Add. 1, circulated to WTO members 26 March 2014, paragraphs 7.116–7.117.

[136] Panel Reports, *China – Measures Related to the Exportation of Rare Earths, Tungsten, and Molybdenum*, see WTO documents: WT/DS431/R, WT/DS432/R, WT/DS433/R, and Add. 1, circulated to WTO members 26 March 2014, paragraph 7.121.

[137] Ibid., paragraph 7.136.     [138] Ibid., paragraph 7.137.     [139] Ibid., paragraph 7.138.

[140] Request for Consultations, *European Communities – Definitive Anti-Dumping Measures on Certain Iron or Steel Fasteners from China*, see WTO documents: WT/DS397/1, G/L/891, G/ADP/D79/1, 4 August 2009.

[141] See WTO document WT/L/432, 23 November 2001, pp. 8–9.

Nevertheless, both China and the European Communities (as well as third parties) referred extensively to the Protocol in their arguments on appeal. The Appellate Body conducted a thorough analysis of the meaning of section 15, which informed its overall decision that paragraph 15 could not be read in the way the European Communities had suggested and hence did not permit the challenged treatment of Chinese exporters.[142] The Appellate Body was, however, not called upon to determine whether or not the European Communities had violated the Protocol.

Viet Nam has brought two challenges against the United States arguing that US measures violated Viet Nam's Protocol of Accession[143] (including the Working Party Report), as well as various provisions of the Anti-Dumping Agreement. One of the disputes is still before a Panel.[144] The other (completed) dispute concerned a number of anti-dumping measures on shrimp from Viet Nam. Viet Nam eventually did not pursue a ruling under the Protocol itself and, although the Panel examined a number of provisions of the Working Party Report, it concluded that they 'had no bearing' on its evaluation of Viet Nam's claim under the Anti-Dumping Agreement.[145] The Panel Report was not appealed.

As mentioned above, Armenia's Accession Protocol[146] has also been invoked in dispute settlement in the case *Armenia – Measures Affecting the Importation and Internal Sale of Cigarettes and Alcoholic Beverages*.[147] In that case, Ukraine alleged that Armenia's law 'On Presumptive Tax for Tobacco Products' and its law 'On Excise Tax' were in violation of Articles II and III of the GATT 1994 and of Armenia's obligations under paragraph 1.2 of Armenia's Protocol of Accession, insofar as it incorporates by reference the commitments set out in paragraph 72 of the Report of the Working Party, which provides that Armenia 'would

---

[142] Appellate Body Report, *European Communities – Definitive Anti-Dumping Measures on Certain Iron or Steel Fasteners from China*, see WTO document WT/DS397/AB/R, adopted 28 July 2011, DSR 2011: VII, p. 3995, paragraphs 283–291.

[143] See WTO document WT/L/662, 15 November 2006.

[144] *United States – Anti-Dumping Measures on Certain Frozen Warmwater Shrimp from Viet Nam*, see WTO document WT/DS 429.

[145] Panel Report, *United States – Anti-Dumping Measures on Certain Shrimp from Viet Nam*, see WTO document WT/DS404/R, adopted 2 September 2011, DSR 2011: X, p. 5301, paragraph 7.251.

[146] See WTO document WT/L/506, 17 December 2002.

[147] See WTO document WT/DS411.

apply its domestic taxes in a non-discriminatory manner consistent with Article I and III of the GATT 1994'. Ukraine also complained that the law appeared to violate paragraph 53 of the Working Party Report, which records a commitment on rates of customs duty bound in Armenia's WTO Schedule of Concessions on Goods annexed to the Protocol. Finally, Ukraine charged that the excise tax law appeared to violate paragraphs 72 and 70 of the Working Party Report, wherein Armenia had committed to implement legislation to equalise the level of excise duties applied.[148]

Ukraine requested the DSB to establish a panel to examine these matters,[149] but later withdrew its request without prejudice to its right to bring the matter back to the DSB, stating that it was in consultations with Armenia and expected that a solution would be found.[150] The dispute has not been raised again in the DSB.

This survey of cases addressing Accession Protocols and working party reports demonstrates the importance of these instruments in WTO law and WTO decision-making more generally. The DSB has thus far adopted numerous Panel and Appellate Body reports where these instruments have been legally scrutinised, and their number will no doubt continue to grow. These legal decisions underscore the critical importance of careful drafting in protocols and working party reports.

As noted above, WTO law provides that these instruments form an integral part of the WTO Agreement. As such, and in accordance with Article 3.2 of the DSU, their provisions will be clarified in accordance with 'customary rules of interpretation of public international law',[151] which the Appellate Body determined in two early cases are codified in Articles 31 (General rule of interpretation) and 32 (Supplementary means of interpretation) of the Vienna Convention on the Law of Treaties.[152] Article 31 requires WTO panels and the Appellate Body to

---

[148] Request for Consultations, *Armenia – Measures Affecting the Importation and Internal Sale of Cigarettes and Alcoholic Beverages*, WT/DS411/1, 22 July 2010, paragraphs 2, 3, 5, 7, 8.

[149] See WTO documents: WT/DS411/2, 16 September 2010; WT/DS411/2/Rev. 1, 8 October 2010.

[150] See WTO documents: WT/DSB/M/288, 15 December 2010, pp. 11–12; WT/DSB/M/289, 21 January 2011, p. 1.

[151] Article 3.2 of the DSU provides that the dispute settlement system serves to 'clarify the existing provisions of [the WTO agreements] in accordance with customary rules of interpretation of public international law'.

[152] 1155 United Nations Treaty Series 331. See also, Appellate Body Report, *United States – Standards for Reformulated and Conventional Gasoline*, see WTO documents:

interpret the provisions of these agreements 'in good faith and in accordance with the ordinary meaning to be given to the terms' of the provision under examination 'in their context and in the light of the [agreement's] object and purpose'. Article 32 provides that recourse may be had in certain situations to supplementary means of interpretation 'including the preparatory work of the "agreement" and the circumstances of its conclusion'.

The dispute settlement decisions reviewed above provide an important lesson to anyone tasked with drafting protocols of accession and working party reports: it is absolutely critical that you say what you mean, and mean what you say.

## Rules of Procedure

As noted above, the Rules of Procedure for Sessions of the Ministerial Conference and Meetings of the General Council guide the members in carrying out WTO business. The Rules have worked well to ensure the smooth operation of the various committees for close to twenty years. In addition to these formal rules, however, practices have developed to complement the formal WTO rule-making procedures. This is perhaps not surprising, given the diplomatic origins of the organisation.

One example of a practice that has complemented the formal decision-making process is the use of the Chair's statement. Under this approach, the Chair of the Ministerial Conference or of the General Council or of another WTO committee reads a statement setting out an understanding or additional information about a decision to be formally adopted by the committee. The statement has usually been the subject of consultations with several if not most members prior to its being read by the Chair at the relevant meeting. The Chair usually proposes that the decision be adopted in the light of the statement just made or that the Ministerial Conference (or General Council, or DSB, or some other body) take note of the statement, and this fact is recorded in the minutes. The Chair's statement is often circulated subsequently to the membership and/or reproduced in full in the minutes of the meeting, which are eventually uploaded on the WTO website. The purpose of a Chair's statement is usually to respond to a concern or preoccupation of one or more

WT/DS2/AB/R, adopted 20 May 1996, DSR 1996: I, p. 16. Appellate Body Report, *Japan – Taxes on Alcoholic Beverages*, WT/DS8/AB/R, WT/DS10/AB/R, WT/DS11/AB/R, adopted 1 November 1996, DSR 1996: I, p. 97.

members about the decision to be formally adopted and which cannot be explicitly addressed in the decision itself for fear of losing consensus support.

The interesting issue for the purposes of this chapter is the legal status or value of such statements in terms of rule-making. Although they are used frequently,[153] they have rarely been discussed in the context of dispute settlement and, therefore, it is difficult to provide a definitive view on their value. In one case, *US–FSC*, the Panel (upheld by the Appellate Body) relied on a Chair's statement in order to interpret an understanding adopted at the same meeting at which the statement was read out by the Chair. According to the Panel, 'it is clear that the understanding and the accompanying statement were part of a single integrated proposal, and that the statement did not represent impromptu after-the-fact remarks by the Chairman'.[154] In another dispute, *EC–Bananas III*, a statement by the Chair of the DSB about anticipated coordination of work between the Panel and the arbitrators informed the conclusion of the arbitrators about how they should proceed in their work. The arbitrators said that they were 'mindful of the DSB Chairman's statement at the meeting . . . when the DSB decided to refer this matter to us in our capacity as Arbitrators' and then reproduced in their decision an excerpt from the Chair's statement.[155]

Given the limited jurisprudence addressing WTO Chairs' statements, it is difficult to provide a definitive view on their value for WTO rule-making. The frequency with which they are used, however, suggests that the case law in this area may expand over time.

Rule-making is central to the WTO, for the institution is based on the rule of law. This is because a rules-based system ensures that WTO members enjoy equal and fair treatment in the multilateral trading system, and that might does not mean right.

---

[153] See H. M. G. Ruse-Khan, 'The Role of Chairman's Statements in the WTO', *Journal of World Trade*, 41(3): 475–534, 2007. See also footnote 96 above.

[154] Panel Report, *United States – Tax Treatment for 'Foreign Sales Corporations'*, see WTO documents: WT/DS108/R, adopted 20 March 2000, as modified by Appellate Body Report WT/DS108/AB/R, DSR 2000: IV, p. 1675, paragraph 7.69; Appellate Body Report, *United States – Tax Treatment for 'Foreign Sales Corporations'*, WT/DS108/AB/R, adopted 20 March 2000, DSR 2000: III, p. 1619, paragraphs 112, 114.

[155] Decision by the Arbitrators, *European Communities – Regime for the Importation, Sale and Distribution of Bananas – Recourse to Arbitration by the European Communities under Article 22.6 of the DSU*, see WTO document WT/DS27/ARB, 9 April 1999, DSR 1999: II, p. 725, paragraph 4.9.

There are a variety of provisions in WTO agreements governing the formation of rules, and twenty years of WTO practice has contributed to the 'how to' book on WTO rule-making. Moreover, a number of Panel and Appellate Body Reports have resulted in a wealth of guidance on the legal effect and import of different types of legal instruments. Several disputes have concerned provisions found in Accession Protocols and working party reports, and it is likely that the number will grow over time. Important lessons may be gleaned from the jurisprudence thus far, including that Accession Protocols and working party reports are enforceable in WTO dispute settlement proceedings and that they form an integral part of the WTO Agreement. Accordingly, should provisions of such instruments come under scrutiny in WTO dispute settlement, they will be clarified – as are other WTO provisions – in accordance with the customary rules of interpretation of public international law. This in turn means that Accession Protocols and working party reports must be crafted carefully so that the members' intentions are properly and accurately reflected in the terms used.

## Acknowledgement

This chapter is based on a presentation by Valerie Hughes, Director, Legal Affairs Division, to the global seminar on WTO Accessions held in Geneva on 23 September 2013.

# 11

# The evolution of the GATT/WTO Accession Protocol: legal tightening and domestic ratification

PETRA BESLAĆ AND CHIEDU OSAKWE

## ABSTRACT

*Where are the legal roots of WTO Accession Protocols? How much was carried over from the General Agreement on Tariffs and Trade standard and practice? What customary practice governs the preparation and approval of accession decisions and protocols? What is the current substantive standard and basic architecture of Accession Protocols? Are there unique provisions in Accession Protocols that have emerged in twenty years of WTO accession history? To what extent do Accession Protocols come into play in the context of WTO dispute settlement? By comparing the empirical data contained in the WTO Accession Protocols with preceding GATT Accession Protocols, this chapter offers waterfront coverage of WTO Accession Protocols from the GATT baseline. The chapter shows that, although rooted in its GATT predecessor base, and remarkably consistent over time, some unique provisions have been incorporated into the architecture of the WTO Accession Protocols since 1995. Because Accession Protocols become integral parts of WTO Agreement after they come into force, the chapter argues that the specific 'terms and conditions of accession' in WTO Accession Protocols have had a direct and salutary impact on the entirety of the WTO Agreement through its tightened safeguard and upgrade. The chapter concludes by arguing that the evidence suggests that the WTO Agreement has been expanded by the absorption of the Accession Protocols over the course of the last twenty years, and that the effect on the WTO Agreement has been significant, rather than marginal.*

The analyses in the chapters in this book were finalised at the end of December 2014. Since then the Republic of Seychelles acceded to the World Trade Organization (WTO) on 26 April 2015. This expanded total WTO membership from 160 to 161. Please see the editors' note.

Accession to the [World Trade Organization] is achieved through negotiation with other WTO Members. Pursuant to Article XII of the Marrakesh Agreement [Establishing the World Trade Organization], accessions take place 'on terms to be agreed' between the acceding Member and the WTO membership. Most accession processes take several years to complete and lead to detailed negotiated provisions. The terms of each WTO Member's accession are set out in its Accession Protocol and accompanying Working Party Report. The negotiated agreement between the WTO membership and the acceding Member results in a delicate balance of rights and obligations, which are reflected in the specific wording of each commitment set out in these documents. Ultimately, the acceding Member and the WTO membership recognize that the intensively negotiated content of an Accession Package is the 'entry fee' to the WTO system.[1]

Nineteen years following its inception, the WTO counts 161 members – 123 original members, pursuant to Article XI of the Marrakesh Agreement Establishing the World Trade Organization (WTO Agreement); five members acceded, as former General Agreement on Tariffs and Trade (GATT) 1947 contracting parties, through a fast-track procedure; and thirty-three states or separate customs territories that have negotiated their 'terms of accession' pursuant to Article XII of the WTO Agreement (hereafter referred to as 'Article XII members').[2]

Upon entry into force, the terms of accession of individual Article XII members are multilateralised and become an integral part of the WTO Agreement. Thus, their role has been to reconfirm by building on existing obligations under the WTO agreements and strengthening the rules of the WTO.[3]

---

[1] *China – Measures related to the exportation of various raw materials*, see WTO document WT/DS394/R, p. 1.

[2] These are (by date of WTO membership): Ecuador (1996); Bulgaria (1996); Mongolia (1997); Panama (1997); Kyrgyz Republic (1998); Latvia (1999); Estonia (1999); Jordan (2000); Georgia (2000); Albania (2000); Oman (2000); Croatia (2000); Lithuania (2001); Moldova (2001); China (2001); Chinese Taipei (2001); Armenia (2003); FYR of Macedonia (2003); Nepal (2004); Cambodia (2004); Saudi Arabia (2005); Viet Nam (2007); Tonga (2007); Ukraine (2008); Cabo Verde (2008); Montenegro (2012); Samoa (2012); Russian Federation (2012); Vanuatu (2012); Lao PDR (2013); Tajikistan (2013); Yemen (2014); and Seychelles (2015). Five states acceded through a fast-track procedure, under Article XII, between 1995 and 1996. These were: Qatar; Saint Kitts and Nevis; Grenada; Papua New Guinea; and the United Arab Emirates. Although they were GATT 1947 contracting parties, they only finalised their WTO schedules in 1995 and therefore acceded to the WTO instead of becoming original WTO members, pursuant to the Decision on Finalization of Negotiations on Schedules on Goods and Services of 31 January 1995.

[3] The term 'WTO Agreements' refers to the Marrakesh Agreement Establishing the World Trade Organization, the umbrella agreement, the multilateral trade agreements and the plurilateral trade agreements.

Research undertaken on Accession Protocols so far has been limited. Most research has revolved around 'WTO plus' and 'WTO minus' commitments; the legal hierarchy and the relationship of the WTO Accession Protocol *vis-à-vis* the WTO agreements; and the question of its enforceability through WTO dispute settlement. This emerging interest in Accession Protocol-related research is to a large extent due to the rising number of disputes citing Accession Protocols which have been deposited at the WTO in recent years.[4]

This chapter contributes to the existing literature on WTO Accession Protocols through a more in-depth description of the record and evolution of the standard Accession Protocol – from its GATT origins to the WTO – and shedding additional light on the contemporary standard WTO Accession Protocol.

In this chapter, we offer the following:

- a historic overview of the principal documents and developments which had an impact on the emergence and evolution of the standard WTO Accession Protocol text;
- an analysis of the Accession Protocol in the context of the WTO accession process, culminating in its approval;

---

[4] Research and papers dealing directly or indirectly with Accession Protocols include, but are not limited to: S. Charnovitz (2013), 'Mapping the Law of WTO Accession', GWU Legal Studies Research Paper No. 237; S. Charnovitz and B. Hoekman (2013), '*US–Tyres*: Upholding a WTO Accession Contract – Imposing Pain for Little Gain', *World Trade Review*, 12, pp. 273–296; C.-D. Ehlermann and L. Ehring (2005), 'Decision-Making in the World Trade Organization – Is the Consensus Practice of the World Trade Organization Adequate for Making, Revising and Implementing Rules on International Trade?', *Journal of International Economic Law*, 8(1); M. Kennedy (2013), 'The Integration of Accession Protocols into the WTO Agreement', *Journal of World Trade* 47(1), pp. 45–76; A. Lanoszka (2001), 'The World Trade Organization Accession Process – Negotiating Participation in a Globalizing Economy', *Journal of World Trade*, 35(4), pp. 576–602; Y.-S. Lee (2002), 'The Specific Safeguard Mechanism in the Protocol on China's Accession to the WTO', *Journal of World Intellectual Property*, 5(2), pp. 219–231; J. Miranda (2014), 'Interpreting Paragraph 15 of China's Protocol of Accession', *Global Trade and Customs Journal*, 9(3); F. Piérola (2010), 'The Availability of a GATT Article XX Defence with Respect to a Non-GATT Claim: Changing the Rules of the Game? – Comments on the Appellate Body Report in *China – Measures Affecting Trading Rights and Distribution Services for Certain Publications and Audiovisual Entertainment Products*', *Global Trade and Customs Journal*, 5(4); Julia Ya Quin (2014), 'The Conundrum of WTO Accession Protocols: in Search of Legality and Legitimacy', *Virginia Journal of International Law*, forthcoming; M. Tyagi (2012), 'Flesh on a Legal Fiction: Early Practice in the WTO on Accession Protocols', *Journal of International Economic Law*.

- a review of the structure and provisions of the current standard Accession Protocol;
- a compendium of provisions contained in some WTO Accession Protocols which are divergent from the standard architecture;
- a snapshot of the role of WTO Accession Protocols in WTO dispute settlement.

## Origins of the WTO Accession Protocol – from the GATT to the WTO

Original contracting parties to the GATT 1947 joined the Agreement through a simple procedure: namely, the signature of the Protocol of Provisional Application, which was open for signature until 30 June 1948 by any government signatory to the Final Act of the Second Session of the Preparatory Committee for the United Nations Conference on Trade and Employment. Thereafter, interested parties would have to accede to the GATT pursuant to the provisions set out in GATT Article XXXIII.

During the Annecy Round in 1949, the twenty-three original GATT contracting parties[5] discussed various options for possible accession procedures and 'terms of accession' for new GATT contracting parties. This discussion produced the 'Procedures Governing Negotiations for Accession', a 'Model Protocol of Accession' and the 'Annecy Protocol of Terms of Accession to the General Agreement on Tariffs and Trade'.[6] These documents have provided the blueprint for the conduct of all accession negotiations since then, including accessions pursuant to Article XII of the WTO Agreement.[7] The GATT contracting parties continued to refine the procedures for accession during successive rounds of tariff negotiations. For instance, during the 1960–1962 Dillon Round, a legal drafting group was set up by the Tariff Negotiations Committee 'to draw up the instruments in which the results of the Tariff

---

[5] Australia; Belgium; Brazil; Burma; Canada; Ceylon; Chile; China; Cuba; Czechoslovakia; France; India; Lebanon; Luxembourg; Netherlands; New Zealand; Norway; Pakistan; Southern Rhodesia; Syria; South Africa; United Kingdom; and the United States.

[6] See Annexes 11.1 and 11.2 of this chapter.

[7] Many requirements and procedures of the WTO accession process have their origins in GATT accessions, such as the 'terms of reference', the Memorandum on the Foreign Trade Regime, etc. Examples of GATT accession procedures and documents similar to WTO accessions: (i) Accession of Iceland – a request to negotiate full accession was received on 2 December 1965, see GATT document L/2521; (ii) Accession of Yugoslavia – the Memorandum on the Foreign Trade Regime (MFTR) was circulated in GATT document L/2488, on 2 November 1965. The MFTR totalled 17 pages only.

Conference should be embodied'. The report by the legal drafting group contained legal instruments, including accession decisions and protocols, and elaborated associated procedures for their approval.[8] In contrast to the detailed process that has emerged under the WTO, GATT accessions were conducted under relatively streamlined procedures.

Although the original 1948/1949 models continued to evolve substantively in accordance with evolving accession practices,[9] it is notable that the four-part structure of the protocol text, established in the early GATT Accession Protocols, has provided the basic architecture for almost all subsequent Accession Protocols, including those under the WTO.[10] The four parts of the protocol text are:

- the Preamble;
- Part I: General;
- Part II: Schedules;
- Part III: Final Provisions.

A good example of this structure can be found in the GATT Protocol of Accession of Yugoslavia of 1966.[11] GATT Accession Protocols bound the acceding government to apply the rules of the multilateral trading system and implement the commitments contained in the market access schedules negotiated during the accession process.[12] The same practice has continued under the WTO.

---

[8]  See GATT document TN.60/60 of 5 December 1961.

[9]  Examples of the evolved procedures and texts can be found in GATT documents: (i) CP.6/W/5/Rev. 1/Corr. 2 of 10 October 1951 on 'Negotiations with a government not party to the General Agreement', which provides guidance on procedures and other matters connected with the conduct of the accession negotiations, notably paragraph 6 referring to the submission of a draft Protocol of Accession and a draft decision; (ii) C/W/76 of 6 July 1964 on 'Applications for Accession', which also describes elements of the procedure for the conduct of accession negotiations; (iii) C/W/115 of 26 June 1967 containing a 'Draft Decision on Accession'; (iv) L/7317 of 2 November 1993 on 'Complementary procedures to be followed in the organization and pursuit of negotiations'; (v) C/COM/4 of 16 November 1994 on the 'Management of Accession Negotiations'.

[10] For more background on GATT Accession Protocols, see Annexes 1–3 of this chapter; see GATT document GATT/CP.6/34 of 19 October 1951, Annex A of 'Report of Working Party 4 on Arrangements for Tariff Negotiations'; Annex A of GATT document GATT/CP.6/34 of 19 October 1951, 'Report of Working Party 4 on Arrangements for Tariff Negotiations'; and *WTO Analytical Index: Guide to GATT Law and Practice*, 3rd edn, Cambridge University Press, 2012, vol. 2, p. 1021.

[11] See GATT document L/2681 of 1 August 1966 and Annex 11.3 to this chapter.

[12] References to specific accession obligations, as contained in the accession working party report, started appearing in GATT Accession Protocols in the late 1980s (e.g. Mexico's Accession Protocol, circulated in GATT document L/6036 on 14 August 1986). This

During the transitional phase from the GATT to the WTO, the authors of the WTO Agreement sought to establish standard approaches and formats for recurring procedures and decisions, building on the heritage of the GATT. Thus, in 1994 and 1995, specific transitional arrangements were put into place to facilitate WTO membership for governments that did not meet the general requirements for original membership under Article XI of the WTO Agreement.[13] The provisions adopted included paragraph 5 of the Final Act embodying the results of the Uruguay Round of Multilateral Trade Negotiations; the Decision on the Acceptance of and Accession to the Agreement Establishing the World Trade Organization; the Decision on Measures in Favour of

approach was sustained in WTO Accession Protocols. A notable difference from WTO Accession Protocols was the grandfather clause, contained in Part I(b) of the GATT Accession Protocols, which stipulated that the acceding government 'shall apply provisionally and subject to this Protocol ... Part II of the General Agreement to the fullest extent not inconsistent with its legislation existing on the date of this Protocol'. See example, GATT Protocol of Accession of Yugoslavia, in Annex 11.3 to this chapter. See GATT documents: MTN.GNG/NG7/W/71 of 2 May 1990 and MTN.GNG/NG7/W/70 of 26 February 1990 on the 'Grandfather clauses in the Protocol of Provisional Application and in Accession Protocols'.

[13] Article XI of the WTO Agreement provides for 'Original Membership' and stipulates that 'the contracting parties to the GATT 1947 ... shall become original Members of the WTO.' In accordance with Article XIV, the WTO Agreement was open for acceptance by GATT contracting parties until 1 January 1997. The WTO Agreement entered into force for 76 of the 123 original WTO members on 1 January 1995. These were: Antigua and Barbuda; Argentina; Australia; Austria; Bahrain; Bangladesh; Barbados; Belgium; Belize; Brazil; Brunei Darussalam; Canada; Chile; Costa Rica; Côte d'Ivoire; Czech Republic; Denmark; Dominica; European Communities (now the European Union); Finland; France; Gabon; Germany; Ghana; Greece; Guyana; Honduras; Hong Kong, China; Hungary; Iceland; India; Indonesia; Ireland; Italy; Japan; Kenya; Republic of Korea; Kuwait; Luxembourg; Macao, China; Malaysia; Malta; Mauritius; Mexico; Morocco; Myanmar; Namibia; Netherlands (for the Kingdom in Europe and for the Netherlands Antilles); New Zealand; Nigeria; Norway; Pakistan; Paraguay; Peru; Philippines; Portugal; Romania; Saint Lucia; Saint Vincent and the Grenadines; Senegal; Singapore; Slovak Republic; South Africa; Spain; Sri Lanka; Suriname; Swaziland; Sweden; Tanzania; Thailand; Uganda; United Kingdom; United States; Uruguay; Bolivarian Republic of Venezuela; and Zambia. The remaining 47 original members accepted the WTO Agreement after 1 January 1995: Angola; Benin; Plurinational State of Bolivia; Botswana; Burkina Faso; Burundi; Chad; Cameroon; Colombia; Congo; Democratic Republic of the Congo; Cuba; Cyprus; Central African Republic; Djibouti; Dominican Republic; Egypt; El Salvador; Fiji; Gambia; Guatemala; Guinea; Guinea Bissau; Haiti; Israel; Jamaica; Lesotho; Liechtenstein; Madagascar; Malawi; Maldives; Mali; Mauritania; Mozambique; Nicaragua; Niger; Poland; Rwanda; Sierra Leone; Slovenia; Solomon Islands; Switzerland; Togo; Trinidad and Tobago; Tunisia; Turkey; Zimbabwe (source: *WTO Analytical Index*).

Least-Developed Countries; and the Decision on the Finalization of Negotiations on Schedules on Goods and Services.[14]

At its meeting on 17 August 1995, the General Council noted that, in accordance with the Decision on the Finalization of Negotiations on Schedules on Goods and Services, a draft Protocol of Accession was being prepared for a subset of contracting parties – those which had joined the GATT in 1994, but needed additional time to finalise their negotiated WTO schedules.[15] These were Grenada, Papua New Guinea, Qatar, Saint Kitts and Nevis, and the United Arab Emirates. A WTO task force on accessions was set up to ensure Secretariat-wide coordination of all accession-related work and to prepare a draft Protocol of Accession. This work was coordinated by the WTO Legal Affairs Division.[16] The draft Protocol of Accession, prepared by the WTO Secretariat, was reviewed in a series of informal consultations with WTO members. Following informal meetings on 6 October 1995 and 16 October 1995, members reached an agreement on a 'Draft Decision' and a 'Draft Protocol of Accession' for contracting parties which joined the GATT in the course of 1994, but were unable to complete negotiations on their schedules. The resulting template retained the established four-part Protocol structure used in GATT Accession Protocols. This model would thus be used for all future WTO accessions pursuant to Article XII of the WTO Agreement.[17]

In accordance with the Decision on the Finalization of Negotiations on Schedules on Goods and Services, WTO accession working parties were not established for the five GATT contracting parties subject to the fast-track procedure. Instead, the General Council's approval of their schedules over the course of 1995–1996 was considered as WTO members' approval of the 'terms of accession' under Article XII.2 of the WTO Agreement.[18]

---

[14] See WTO document WT/L/30 adopted on 31 January 1995.

[15] See WTO document WT/GC/M/5, p. 9.

[16] The first task force meeting was held on 4 October 1995. The task force was made up of representatives of several WTO divisions, including Accessions, Legal Affairs, Market Access, Services, and Economic Research and Analysis.

[17] See Annex 11.4 of this chapter for the WTO Secretariat report and notes on informal consultations in 1995 on the Accession Protocol model. The following members participated in the informal consultations: Argentina, Australia, Brazil, Canada, Colombia, European Communities, Hong Kong, China, India, Malaysia (ASEAN), Japan, Republic of Korea, Mexico, New Zealand, Norway, Singapore, Spain, Switzerland and the United States.

[18] The General Council approved the respective draft decisions and draft protocols at its meetings on 13 December 1995, 6 February 1996, 22 February 1996 and 28 May 1996. The WTO Agreement entered into force for each acceding government, thirty days after its

In 1995, the WTO also finalised the first negotiated WTO accession under the provisions of Article XII of the WTO Agreement. During the review of the Accession Package of Ecuador at the meeting of the General Council on 31 July 1995, the Chairperson of the accession Working Party, Mr Manhusen (Sweden), stated that:

> The Appendix to the report reproduced a draft Decision and a draft Protocol of Accession of Ecuador to the Agreement Establishing the WTO. *In accordance with the practice utilized in accessions to the GATT, the Protocol of Accession incorporated the commitments undertaken by Ecuador in relation to certain specific matters negotiated in the Working Party.* Ecuador would be the first Government to become a WTO Member pursuant to Article XII of the WTO Agreement [Article XII Member] [italics added].[19]

As in the case of Ecuador, for states or separate customs territories with already established GATT accession working parties, the working parties with their respective chairpersons were carried over to the WTO, with standard terms of reference.[20]

Work on optimising established and emerging standard formats for recurring decisions and procedures, including WTO accession decisions and Accession Protocols, continued over the following decade.[21]

## WTO Accession Protocols in the context of accession negotiations

Typically, acceding governments and accession working party members direct their attention to WTO Accession Protocols only in the final stages

---

acceptance of its Accession Protocol. See WTO documents: WT/GC/M/8; WT/GC/M/9; WT/GC/M/10 and WT/GC/M/11. The adopted accession decisions and approved Accession Protocols are contained in the WTO documents: WT/L/94 and WT/L/95 (St Kitts and Nevis); WT/L/96 and WT/L/97 (Grenada); WT/L/98 and WT/L/99 (Papua New Guinea); WT/L/100 and WT/L/101 (Qatar); and WT/L/128 and WT/L/129 (United Arab Emirates).

[19] See WTO document WT/GC/M/6, p. 2.

[20] See WTO document WT/GC/M/1, p. 7 and PC/R, paragraph 35. Note: twenty WTO accessions, carried over from the GATT, have been completed. These include Albania; Armenia; Bulgaria; Cambodia; China; Croatia; Ecuador; Estonia; FYR of Macedonia; Jordan; Latvia; Lithuania; Moldova; Mongolia; Nepal; Panama; Russia; Saudi Arabia; Chinese Taipei; and Ukraine. Four accession working parties carried over from the GATT are yet to be completed. These are Algeria, Belarus, Sudan and Uzbekistan. In the period from 1 January 1995 to 30 June 2014, the General Council established twelve accession working parties that have completed their work. These are Cabo Verde; Georgia; Kyrgyz Republic; Lao PDR; Montenegro; Oman; Samoa; Tonga; Tajikistan; Vanuatu; Viet Nam; and Yemen.

[21] See, for example, WTO non-paper JOB(00)4868 of 4 September 2000.

of an accession process. Nonetheless, references to the Accession Proto-
col already appear in the early stages of the WTO accession process.
Thus, it is essential to place the Accession Protocol in the context of the
WTO accession process so as to better understand the customary pro-
cedures that relate to the preparation and approval of Accession
Protocols.

Pursuant to Article XII of the WTO Agreement, a state or separate
customs territory possessing full autonomy in the conduct of its external
commercial relations and of the matters provided for in the WTO
Agreement and the Multilateral Trade Agreements annexed thereto
may accede to the WTO 'on terms to be agreed between [such state or
separate customs territory] and the WTO'. Any state or separate customs
territory has to submit a communication to the WTO Director-General
indicating its desire to accede to the WTO under Article XII of the WTO
Agreement. This communication is circulated to all WTO members and
the General Council/Ministerial Conference considers the request.
A positive consideration results in the establishment of an accession
working party with standard terms of reference. These terms of reference
contain the first reference to the WTO Accession Protocol, stipulating
that accession working parties are 'to examine the application for accession to the WTO under Article XII and to submit to the General Council/
Ministerial Conference recommendations which may include *a draft
Protocol of Accession*' (italics added).[22]

The 'train tracks' analogy is often used to illustrate how the WTO
accession process proceeds along three parallel tracks – bilateral negotiations on market access; discussions with interested WTO Members on
specific, technical issues; and multilateral work focusing on compliance
with WTO rules (see Figure 11.1).[23]

Typically, the WTO Accession Protocol is not brought up again until
the latter stages of the WTO accession process. As soon as the text of the
draft working party report is considered technically advanced, the WTO
Secretariat incorporates the standard draft accession decision and draft
protocol text as an appendix to the draft accession working party

---

[22] Note: the standard terms of reference of WTO accession working parties originate from
the standard terms of reference of GATT accession working parties; see for instance,
GATT document L/2736 of 13 January 1967 on the GATT Working Party on the
Accession of Poland.

[23] These three tracks relate to negotiations within the setting of the accession working party.
However, as described in Chapter 9, there is a fourth 'domestic level negotiating track', of
equal, if not greater challenge for the acceding government.

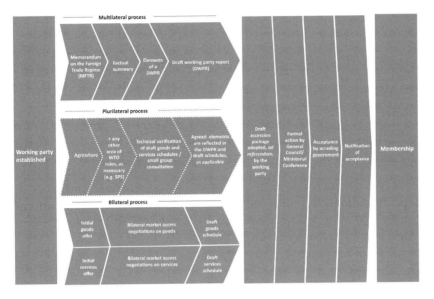

**Figure 11.1**  WTO accession process – three tracks.

report.[24] These drafts remain in square brackets, subject to agreement at the working party level.

As the accession train approaches the 'membership terminal', the train tracks converge and a draft Accession Package emerges. This package of documents consists of:

(i) the draft report of the working party;
(ii) a draft decision and a draft Accession Protocol, appended to the report;
(iii) the draft goods and services schedules presented in addenda 1 and 2.

Accession working parties conclude their mandate by adopting the draft Accession Package, including the Accession Protocol, *ad referendum*,[25] and by forwarding the 'report' of the working party to the Ministerial Conference/General Council for decision.[26] The customary procedure for formal decision by the Ministerial Conference/General Council[27]

---

[24] See Figure 11.2 for a 'Model accession working party report appendix'.

[25] Subject to final approval by the Ministerial Conference/General Council.

[26] Upon the adoption at the working party level, the WTO Secretariat re-issues the draft Accession Package in the WT/ACC document series.

[27] Prior to the approval of an Accession Protocol, and of the entire Accession Package, by the Ministerial Conference/General Council, individual WTO members can invoke

contains three main procedural steps. At the invitation of the Chairperson of the Ministerial Conference/General Council, the WTO membership:

- approves the draft Accession Protocol, as contained in the Report of the Working Party;
- adopts the draft Decision, as contained in the Report of the Working Party, in accordance with the decision-making procedures under Articles IX and XII of the WTO Agreement;
- adopts the Report of the Working Party, including the Goods Schedule (Addendum 1) and the Services Schedule (Addendum 2).

In adopting the Decision and approving the Accession Protocol, the WTO offers the acceding government the 'terms of accession'. Although voting procedures have been foreseen in Article XII.2 of the WTO Agreement, in accordance with long-standing WTO practice, the Ministerial Conference/General Council adopts reports of accession working parties, including the entire Accession Packages, by consensus.[28]

---

the non-application clause stipulated in Article XIII of the WTO Agreement, which provides that the respective WTO member will not apply the WTO Agreements to an acceding government upon membership. In WTO history to date, Article XIII has been invoked twelve times, El Salvador *vis-à-vis* China (WTO document WT/L/429), withdrawn (WTO document WT/L/926); Turkey *vis-à-vis* Armenia (WTO document WT/L/501); United States *vis-à-vis* Armenia (WTO document WT/L/505), withdrawn (WTO document WT/L/601 and Corr. 1); United States *vis-à-vis* Georgia (WTO document WT/L/318), withdrawn (WTO document WT/L/385); United States *vis-à-vis* Kyrgyz Republic (WTO document WT/L/275), withdrawn (WTO document WT/L/363); United States *vis-à-vis* Moldova (WTO document WT/L/395), withdrawn (WTO document WT/L/879); United States *vis-à-vis* Mongolia (WTO document WT/L/159), withdrawn (WTO document WT/L/306); United States *vis-à-vis* Romania (WT/L/11), withdrawn (WTO document WT/L/203); United States *vis-à-vis* Russia (WTO document WT/L/837), withdrawn (WTO document WT/L/877); United States *vis-à-vis* Tajikistan (WTO document WT/L/781); United States *vis-à-vis* Viet Nam (WTO document WT/L/661), withdrawn (WTO document WT/L/679); Russia *vis-à-vis* United States (WTO document WT/L/838), withdrawn (WTO document WT/L/878).

Before an Accession Package can be adopted by the Ministerial Conference/General Council, the acceding government needs to fully redeem its financial obligations to the WTO. To avoid accumulating financial arrears, acceding governments should make their annual contributions on a regular basis during the accession process.

[28] See WTO document WT/L/98 of 24 November 1995, 'Decision-Making Procedures under Articles IX and XII of the WTO Agreement'. Note: decision-making practice differed only once in 1995 on the accession of Ecuador, where the decision was subject to a vote by postal ballot. See WTO document WT/GC/M/6 of 20 September 1995, Minutes of General Council Meeting held on 31 July 1995, pp. 2–5.

On WTO decision-making, see also: Ehlermann, and Ehring, 'Decision-making in the World Trade Organization'.

Following the adoption of the decision, the representative of the acceding government and the WTO Director-General, *ex officio*, sign the Protocol of Accession. The WTO Legal Affairs Division prepares the Decision and the Protocol of Accession for circulation in the WT/L document series.[29]

Thereafter, domestic action may be required by the acceding government to ensure the entry into force of the protocol approved by the WTO membership. This is discussed in the next part of this chapter, which will consider the substance and scope of the current standard of the WTO Accession Protocol.

### Protocol of Accession – standard architecture

The standard template of the WTO Accession Decision and Protocol, which has emerged over the course of more than sixty years of combined GATT and WTO accession history, is reproduced in Figure 11.2.

The Decision on Accessions by the Ministerial Conference/General Council is the legal instrument through which the acceding government is formally offered the right to accede to the WTO Agreement on the terms and conditions set out in the Accession Protocol annexed to the Decision.

The structure of the Accession Protocol is based on the four standard parts inherited from GATT Accession Protocols: the Preamble; Part I: General; Part II: Schedules; and Part III: Final Provisions. The market access schedules are annexed. In the preambular paragraph, the Accession Protocol identifies the parties to the agreement and refers to the report of the working party. Parts I, II and III, as well as the annexed market access schedules, contain the specific terms and conditions of accession. Parts I to III contain a total of ten paragraphs.

Several provisions in the standard Accession Protocol warrant specific mention. Notably, paragraph 2 of Part I stipulates that the state or separate customs territory accedes to the 'WTO Agreement as rectified, amended or otherwise modified by such legal instruments as may have

---

[29] In the period from 1995 to early 2001, WTO accession decisions and protocols were circulated in the WT/ACC document series. In 2001, this conduct changed taking into account that General Council/Ministerial Conference decisions are normally circulated in the WT/L document series. Given that final decisions on accessions, including the approval of the Accession Protocol, are also undertaken at the Ministerial Conference/ General Council level, accession decisions and protocols have been issued in the WT/L document series since mid 2001 (starting with China's Accession Protocol).

| | RESTRICTED |
|---|---|
| **WORLD TRADE ORGANIZATION** | **Accessions Guidelines/2014-05** |
| | 14 July 2014 |
| (14-0000) | Page: 1/4 |
| | Original: English |

**MODEL - ACCESSION WORKING PARTY REPORT APPENDIX**

[ Draft Decision

**ACCESSION OF [...]**

*Decision of [...]*

The [Ministerial Conference][General Council],

*Having regard to* paragraph 2 of Article XII and paragraph 1 of Article IX of the Marrakesh Agreement Establishing the World Trade Organization (the "WTO Agreement"), and the Decision-Making Procedures under Articles IX and XII of the WTO Agreement agreed by the General Council (WT/L/93),

[*Conducting* the functions of the Ministerial Conference in the interval between meetings pursuant to paragraph 2 of Article IV of the WTO Agreement,]

*Taking note of* the application of [...] for accession to the WTO Agreement dated [...],

*Noting* the results of the negotiations directed toward the establishment of the terms of accession of [...] to the WTO Agreement and having prepared a Protocol on the Accession of [...],

*Decides* as follows:

1.      [...] may accede to the WTO Agreement on the terms and conditions set out in the Protocol annexed to this Decision.

Figure 11.2    Model accession working party report appendix.


entered into force before the date of entry into force of this Protocol'. Paragraph 2 also refers to all specific commitments undertaken as part of the accession process. These commitments are contained in the accession working party report and are listed in its 'Conclusions' chapter. Pursuant to paragraph 2 of the standard Accession Protocol text, as provided, 'the commitments referred to in paragraph [...] of the working party report, *shall be an integral part of the WTO Agreement*' (emphasis added). Paragraph 3 of Part I covers transitional periods for the implementation of certain obligations, as negotiated between members and the acceding government. Specifically, this paragraph stipulates that the obligations in

DRAFT PROTOCOL

ON THE ACCESSION OF [...]

Preamble

The World Trade Organization (hereinafter referred to as the "WTO"), pursuant to the approval of the [Ministerial Conference][General Council] of the WTO accorded under Article XII of the Marrakesh Agreement Establishing the World Trade Organization (hereinafter referred to as the "WTO Agreement"), and [...],

*Taking note* of the Report of the Working Party on the Accession of [...] to the WTO Agreement reproduced in document WT/ACC/[...]/[...], dated [...] (hereinafter referred to as the "Working Party Report"),

*Having regard* to the results of the negotiations on the accession of [...] to the WTO Agreement,

*Agree* as follows:

PART I - GENERAL

1.      Upon entry into force of this Protocol pursuant to paragraph 8, [...] accedes to the WTO Agreement pursuant to Article XII of that Agreement and thereby becomes a Member of the WTO.

2.      The WTO Agreement to which [...] accedes shall be the WTO Agreement, including the Explanatory Notes to that Agreement, as rectified, amended or otherwise modified by such legal instruments as may have entered into force before the date of entry into force of this Protocol. This Protocol, which shall include the commitments referred to in paragraph [...] of the Working Party Report, shall be an integral part of the WTO Agreement.

3.      Except as otherwise provided for in paragraph [...] of the Working Party Report, those obligations in the Multilateral Trade Agreements annexed to the WTO Agreement that are to be implemented over a period of time starting with the entry into force of that Agreement shall be implemented by [...] as if it had accepted that Agreement on the date of its entry into force.

4.      [...] may maintain a measure inconsistent with paragraph 1 of Article II of the Schedule of Specific Commitments annexed to the General Agreement on Trade in Services (hereinafter referred to as "GATS") provided that such a measure was recorded in the list of Article II Exemptions annexed to this Protocol and meets the conditions of the Annex to the GATS on Article II Exemptions.

PART II - SCHEDULES

5.      The Schedules reproduced in the Annex to this Protocol shall become the Schedule of Concessions and Commitments annexed to the General Agreement on Tariffs and Trade 1994 (hereinafter referred to as the "GATT 1994") and the GATS relating to [...]. The staging of the concessions and commitments listed in the Schedules shall be implemented as specified in the relevant parts of the respective Schedules.

6.      For the purpose of the reference in paragraph 6(a) of Article II of the GATT 1994 to the date of that Agreement, the applicable date in respect of the Schedule of Concessions and Commitments annexed to this Protocol shall be the date of entry into force of this Protocol.

Figure 11.2    (*cont.*)

Accessions Guidelines/2014-05

- 3 -

PART III - FINAL PROVISIONS

7.    This Protocol shall be open for acceptance, by signature or otherwise, by [...] until [...] or such later date as may be decided by the General Council.

8.    This Protocol shall enter into force on the thirtieth day following the day upon which it shall have been accepted by [...].

9.    This Protocol shall be deposited with the Director-General of the WTO. The Director-General of the WTO shall promptly furnish a certified copy of this Protocol and a notification of acceptance by [...] thereto pursuant to paragraph 7 to each Member of the WTO and to [...].

10.    This Protocol shall be registered in accordance with the provisions of Article 102 of the Charter of the United Nations.

    Done at [...] this [...] day of [...] in a single copy in the English, French and Spanish languages, each text being authentic, except that a Schedule annexed hereto may specify that it is authentic in only one of these languages, and the Working Party Report is authentic in English only.

———————

Accessions Guidelines/2014-05

- 4 -

ANNEX

SCHEDULE [...] – [...]

Authentic only in the English language.

(Circulated in document WT/ACC/[...]/../Add.1)

———————

SCHEDULE OF SPECIFIC COMMITMENTS ON SERVICES

LIST OF ARTICLE II EXEMPTIONS

Authentic only in the English language.

(Circulated in document WT/ACC/[...]/../Add.2)  ]

———————

Figure 11.2   (cont.)

the multilateral trade agreements annexed to the WTO Agreement, 'except as otherwise provided in paragraph [...] of the Working Party Report', shall be implemented as if the acceding government had accepted the WTO Agreement on the date of its entry into force.

Part II, paragraph 5 of the standard Accession Protocol provides that the market access schedules reproduced in the annex to the protocol become the Schedule of Concessions and Commitments (i.e. the goods schedule) annexed to the GATT 1994; and the Schedule of Specific Commitments (i.e. the services schedule) annexed to the General Agreement on Trade in Services (GATS).

Part III, paragraph 7 indicates the date at which the Accession Protocol shall be open for acceptance by the acceding government. This could either be by signature or by signature subject to ratification, depending on domestic constitutional procedures.[30] The period for acceptance is typically in the range of three to six months, but could also be longer. In practice, the acceding government specifies and proposes the length of time that would be required for completing the domestic procedures for the acceptance of the terms of accession. Table 11.1 provides the basic data related to Accession Protocols, including the date of approval; the document reference; the agreed period for acceptance; the actual acceptance period; the document reference of the Instrument of Acceptance; and the date of membership.

Figure 11.3 illustrates how the acceptance period has varied significantly from one acceding government to another. It also shows that the agreed period for acceptance, as specified in the Accession Protocols, may differ from the actual time it takes the acceding government to notify acceptance. For instance, in the case of Oman, although the acceding government agreed to notify acceptance within a 21-day period, the protocol was approved by the General Council and signed and accepted by Oman on the same day (i.e. 10 October 2000). In the case of China, the acceding government agreed to notify acceptance by 1 January 2002 (i.e. within 51 days).[31] However, China's acceptance of its

---

[30] On the conclusion and entry into force of treaties, see Part II of the Vienna Convention of the Law of Treaties (VCLT). Specifically, with regard to expressing the consent of a state to be bound by a treaty, with full powers, see Article 7.1 of the VCLT; and without full powers, see Article 7.2 of the VCLT. See also Articles 12 and 14 of the VCLT; and the 'Summary of Practice of the [United Nations] Secretary-General as Depositary of Multilateral Treaties', see WTO document ST/LEG/7/Rev. 1, paragraphs 6, 101, 102, 110, 121, 122, 123, 128 and 131.

[31] See WTO document WT/L/432, p. 11.

Table 11.1 Base data related to Accession Protocols – date of approval, acceptance period, Instrument of Acceptance, date of membership

| Article XII member | Date of approval of Accession Protocol, entire Accession Package, by Ministerial Conference/ General Council | Accession Protocol | Agreed date for acceptance, as contained in the Accession Protocol | Agreed period for acceptance (in calendar days) | Actual acceptance period (in calendar days) | Date of deposit of the Instrument of Acceptance | Notification of acceptance and entry into force | Date of membership |
|---|---|---|---|---|---|---|---|---|
| Ecuador | 16/08/95 | WT/ACC/ECU/6 | 31/12/95 | 137 | 128 | 22/12/95 | WT/LET/53 | 21/01/96 |
| Bulgaria | 02/10/96 | WT/ACC/BGR/7 | 30/04/97 | 210 | 30 | 01/11/96 | WT/LET/117 | 01/12/96 |
| Mongolia | 18/07/96 | WT/ACC/MNG/11 | 31/12/96 | 166 | 165 | 30/12/96 | WT/LET/130 | 29/01/97 |
| Panama | 02/10/96 | WT/ACC/PAN/21 | 30/06/97 | 271 | 309 | 07/08/97 | WT/LET/161 | 06/09/97 |
| Kyrgyz Republic | 14/10/98 | WT/ACC/KGZ/29 | 01/12/98 | 48 | 37 | 20/11/98 | WT/LET/262 | 20/12/98 |
| Latvia | 14/10/98 | WT/ACC/LVA/35 | 01/05/99 | 199 | 89 | 11/01/99 | WT/LET/281 | 10/02/99 |
| Estonia | 21/05/99 | WT/ACC/EST/30 | 31/10/99 | 163 | 146 | 14/10/99 | WT/LET/313 | 13/11/99 |
| Jordan | 17/12/99 | WT/ACC/JOR/35 | 31/03/00 | 105 | 86 | 12/03/00 | WT/LET/333 | 11/04/00 |
| Georgia | 06/10/99 | WT/ACC/GEO/33 | 01/03/00 | 147 | 222 | 15/05/00 | WT/LET/341 | 14/06/00 |
| Albania | 17/07/00 | WT/ACC/ALB/53 & Corr.1 | 31/12/00 | 167 | 23 | 09/08/00 | WT/LET/353 | 08/09/00 |

| Oman | 10/10/00 | WT/ACC/OMN/28 | 31/10/00 | 21 | 0 | 10/10/00 | WT/LET/357 | 09/11/00 |
| Croatia | 17/07/00 | WT/ACC/HRV/61 | 31/10/00 | 106 | 106 | 31/10/00 | WT/LET/359 | 30/11/00 |
| Lithuania | 08/12/00 | WT/ACC/LTU/54 | 01/05/01 | 144 | 144 | 01/05/01 | WT/LET/393 | 31/05/01 |
| Moldova | 08/05/01 | WT/ACC/MOL/40 | 01/07/01 | 54 | 49 | 26/06/01 | WT/LET/399 | 26/07/01 |
| China | 10/11/01 | WT/L/432 | 01/01/02 | 52 | 1 | 11/11/01 | WT/LET/408 | 11/12/01 |
| Chinese Taipei | 11/11/01 | WT/L/433 | 31/03/02 | 140 | 21 | 02/12/01 | WT/LET/411 | 01/01/02 |
| Armenia | 10/12/02 | WT/L/506 | 10/05/03 | 151 | 27 | 06/01/03 | WT/LET/436 | 05/02/03 |
| FYR Macedonia | 15/10/02 | WT/L/494 | 31/03/03 | 167 | 141 | 05/03/03 | WT/LET/439 | 04/04/03 |
| Nepal | 11/09/03 | WT/MIN(03)/18 | 31/03/04 | 202 | 195 | 24/03/04 | WT/LET/464 | 23/04/04 |
| Cambodia | 11/09/03 | WT/MIN(03)/19 | 31/03/04 | 202 | 368 | 13/09/04 | WT/LET/480 | 13/10/04 |
| Saudi Arabia | 11/11/05 | WT/L/627 | 31/12/05 | 50 | 50 | 11/11/05 | WT/LET/503 | 11/12/05 |
| Viet Nam | 07/11/06 | WT/L/662 | 30/06/07 | 235 | 35 | 12/12/06 | WT/LET/552 | 11/01/07 |
| Tonga | 15/12/05 | WT/L/644 | 31/07/06 | 228 | 559 | 27/06/07 | WT/LET/579 | 27/07/07 |
| Ukraine | 05/02/08 | WT/L/718 | 04/07/08 | 150 | 71 | 16/04/08 | WT/LET/616 | 16/05/08 |
| Cabo Verde | 18/12/07 | WT/L/715 | 30/06/08 | 195 | 188 | 23/06/08 | WT/LET/624 | 23/07/08 |
| Montenegro | 17/12/11 | WT/L/841 | 31/03/12 | 105 | 104 | 30/03/12 | WT/LET/849 | 29/04/12 |
| Samoa | 17/12/11 | WT/L/840 | 15/06/12 | 181 | 115 | 10/04/12 | WT/LET/850 | 10/05/12 |
| Russian Federation | 16/12/11 | WT/L/839 | 220 days | 220 | 220 | 23/07/12 | WT/LET/860 | 22/08/12 |

Table 11.1 (cont.)

| Article XII member | Date of approval of Accession Protocol, entire Accession Package, by Ministerial Conference/General Council | Accession Protocol | Agreed date for acceptance, as contained in the Accession Protocol | Agreed period for acceptance (in calendar days) | Actual acceptance period (in calendar days) | Date of deposit of the Instrument of Acceptance | Notification of acceptance and entry into force | Date of membership |
|---|---|---|---|---|---|---|---|---|
| Vanuatu* | 26/10/11 | WT/L/862 | 31/12/11 | 66 | 273 | 25/07/12 | WT/LET/861 | 24/08/12 |
| Lao PDR | 26/10/12 | WT/L/865 | 24/04/13 | 180 | 69 | 03/01/13 | WT/LET/872 | 02/02/13 |
| Tajikistan | 11/12/12 | WT/L/872 | 07/06/13 | 178 | 51 | 31/01/13 | WT/LET/878 | 02/03/13 |
| Yemen | 04/12/13 | WT/L/905 | 02/06/14 | 180 | 174 | 27/05/14 | WT/LET/943 | 26/06/14 |

*Note on Vanuatu: accession negotiations were concluded in 2001 when the working party adopted its draft Accession Package, *ad referendum*. Subsequently, the Vanuatu authorities informed the WTO Secretariat that they would need more time to consider the Accession Package before it could be forwarded to the General Council for adoption. In 2008, Vanuatu signalled its interest in resuming the accession process and asked that the draft Accession Package be updated. Under the authority of the Chairperson of the General Council, the Accession Package was technically updated by the WTO Secretariat and circulated to WTO members in the reconvened working party. The updated package was adopted on 2 May 2011, *ad referendum*, by the reconvened working party. The Accession Package was approved by the General Council at its meeting on 26 October 2011.

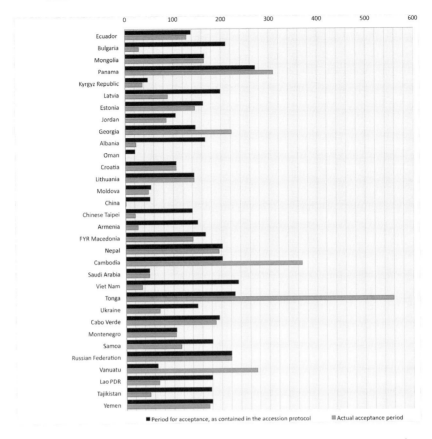

**Figure 11.3** Agreed versus actual periods of acceptance of the Accession Protocol (in calendar days).

Accession Protocol had already been announced by the Director-General on 11 November 2001, only a day following the approval of the accession protocol by the Ministerial Conference on 10 November 2001. Further examples show that Chinese Taipei took twenty-one days, while Cambodia and Tonga took over a year to complete the acceptance of their Accession Protocols. These time variations may be due to a range of factors, including, but not limited to, different constitutional procedures; translation requirements; domestic challenges; and political choices.

In the architecture of the standard Accession Protocol, paragraph 8 provides that the Accession Protocol ('terms of accession') enters into force thirty days after its 'acceptance' by the acceding government.[32] As earlier indicated, pursuant to paragraph 7 of the Protocol of Accession, acceding governments may accept the Protocol through signature or through subsequent ratification, depending on domestic constitutional procedures. The thirty-day countdown starts, therefore, from the date of acceptance by signature or, in the case of ratification, from the date of notifying the WTO of the domestic acceptance of the Protocol through deposit of an 'Instrument of Acceptance'.

In paragraph 9, the standard Accession Protocol specifies that the depositary of the Protocol of Accession, namely, the WTO Director-General, *ex officio*, issues a 'Notification of Acceptance'. The purpose of this communication is to inform the WTO membership of the entry into force of the new membership terms, specifying the date of accession.

The thirty-day period allows WTO members to prepare for the application of the WTO Agreement to the new member.

Paragraph 10 of a standard Accession Protocol stipulates that the Accession Protocol shall be registered in accordance with the provisions of Article 102 of the Charter of the United Nations.

There are provisions on the authenticity of the WTO Accession Protocol and, the entire Accession Package. Standard WTO Accession Protocols contain a provision that stipulates that they are authentic in the three WTO official languages – English, French and Spanish. The protocol further provides that the annexed schedules may specify that they are authentic in only one of the three WTO official languages. Since 2012, a further provision on languages and authenticity was added to the standard WTO Accession Protocol, namely that the report of the working party is authentic in only one of the three WTO official languages. This development can be traced back to the accession of Russia where, prior to final approval by the Ministerial Conference, errors were found in the French and Spanish translations of the agreed text of Russia's accession working party report. To proceed with the approval without undue delay, in adopting the accession working party report, the Chairperson of the Ministerial Conference stated that Russia's accession working party report was authentic in English only.[33] This provision was added to subsequent Accession Protocols, i.e., in the case of the Accession Protocols

---

[32] See Chapter IX 'Entry into Force' of the 'Summary of Practice of the [United Nations] Secretary-General as Depositary of Multilateral Treaties', see WTO document ST/LEG/7/Rev. 1, paragraph 236.
[33] See WTO document WT/MIN(11)/SR/3, paragraph 6.

of Lao PDR, Tajikistan, Yemen and Seychelles.[34] Each protocol ends with the date and the location where it was approved.

Finally, annexed to all Accession Protocols are the Schedule of Tariff Concessions and Commitments on Goods[35] and the Schedule of Specific Commitments on Services. As indicated above, pursuant to Part II paragraph 5 of the Accession Protocol, these become the Schedules of Concessions and Commitments annexed to the GATT 1994 and the Schedule of Specific Commitments annexed to the GATS.

## Divergences from the established WTO Accession Protocol model

Although the WTO Accession Protocols of the thirty-three Article XII members have all been modelled on the four-part standard carried over from GATT Accession Protocols, there have been variations from the established format (see Table 11.2). While some specific provisions remained unique and were not replicated in other Accession Protocols, others have recurred in a number of Accession Protocols, become standardised and, hence contributed to the evolution of the standard protocol.

Table 11.2 identifies that in four of the thirty-three completed WTO accessions, the standard Accession Protocol text was adapted to include specific substantive provisions unique to those accessions. These pertained to China, Ecuador, Mongolia and Chinese Taipei. Table 11.2 also shows that two new provisions have been added to the standard Accession Protocol text, and have subsequently been replicated in all Accession Protocols. These are: the GATS MFN exemption provision; and the language authenticity provision.

The most prominent variation, so far, from the standard can be found in China's Accession Protocol.[36] The Accession Protocol of China, in volume, totalled approximately 102 pages and, substantively, included specific obligations in addition to those contained in China's accession working party report. Of the 102 pages, 11 pages were Protocol text and 91 pages were dedicated to nine annexes. This model stands in sharp contrast to the standard two-page Accession Protocol, which totals approximately ten paragraphs, in addition to one annex. Following China's Accession Protocol, there was a return to the standard Protocol text in the accessions which followed.

---

[34] See WTO documents WT/L/865; WT/L/872; WT/L/905; WT/L/944.
[35] Note: Each goods schedule carries a sequential Roman numerals number. The latest goods schedule, namely, that of Yemen, has been registered as CLXIX.
[36] See WTO document WT/L/432 of 23 November 2001.

Table 11.2 *Unique provisions contained in some WTO Accession Protocols*

| Article XII Member(s) | Unique provision/variation included in some WTO Accession Protocols |
|---|---|
| Albania, Armenia, Bulgaria, Cambodia, Cabo Verde, China, Croatia, Estonia, FYR of Macedonia, Georgia, Jordan, Kyrgyz Republic, Lao PDR, Latvia, Lithuania, Moldova, Montenegro, Nepal, Oman, Panama, Russian Federation, Samoa, Kingdom of Saudi Arabia, Seychelles, Tajikistan, Chinese Taipei, Tonga, Ukraine, Vanuatu, Viet Nam, Yemen (total number: 31) | GATS most-favoured-nation (MFN) exemption(s) provision was included in WTO Accession Protocols from Bulgaria's Accession Protocol onwards.[a] |
| Ecuador | A specific provision on the staging of the dismantling of the Tariff Adjustment Mechanism was included in Ecuador's Accession Protocol[b] |
| Mongolia | A specific provision on notifications was included in Mongolia's Accession Protocol[c] |
| China | Detailed sub-sections were added under Part I of China's Accession Protocol:[d] <br> • Administration of the trade regime <br> • Non-discrimination <br> • Special trade arrangements <br> • Right to trade <br> • State trading <br> • Non-tariff measures <br> • Import and export licensing <br> • Price controls <br> • Subsidies <br> • Taxes and charges levied on imports and exports; agriculture <br> • Technical barriers to trade <br> • Sanitary and phytosanitary measures <br> • Price comparability in determining subsidies and dumping <br> • Transitional product-specific safeguard mechanism <br> • Reservations by WTO members <br> • Transitional review mechanism |

Table 11.2 (*cont.*)

| Article XII Member(s) | Unique provision/variation included in some WTO Accession Protocols |
|---|---|
| | Detailed annexes included: |
| | • Transitional Review Mechanism |
| | • Issues to be addressed by the General Council in accordance with Section 18.2 of China's Protocol of Accession |
| | • Products subject to state trading (import) |
| | • Products subject to state trading (export) |
| | • Products subject to designated trading |
| | • Non-tariff measures subject to phased elimination |
| | • Products and services subject to price controls |
| | • Notification pursuant to Article XXV of the Agreement on Subsidies and Countervailing Measures |
| | • Subsidies to be phased out |
| | • Products subject to export duty |
| | • Reservations by WTO members |
| Chinese Taipei | • Special Exchange Agreement between the WTO and Chinese Taipei;[e] |
| | • Commitment to accede to the Plurilateral Trade Agreement on Trade in Civil Aircraft[f] |
| Lao PDR; Tajikistan; Yemen | • Report of the working party is authentic in English only[g] |

*Notes:* [a]See WTO documents: WT/ACC/BGR/7; WT/ACC/PAN/21; WT/ACC/KGZ/29; WT/ACC/LVA/35; WT/ACC/EST/30; WT/ACC/JOR/35; WT/ACC/GEO/33; WT/ACC/ALB/53 & Corr.1; WT/ACC/OMN/28; WT/ACC/HRV/61; WT/ACC/LTU/54; WT/ACC/MOL/40; WT/L/432; WT/L/433; WT/L/506; WT/L/494; WT/MIN(03)/19; WT/MIN(03)/18; WT/L/627; WT/L/662; WT/L/644; WT/L/718; WT/L/715; WT/L/841; WT/L/840; WT/L/839; WT/L/862; WT/L/865; WT/L/872; WT/L/905; WT/L/944. [b]See WTO document WT/ACC/ECU/6, paragraph 4.
[c]See WTO document WT/ACC/MNG/11, paragraph 4. [d]See WTO document WT/L/432. [e]See WTO document WT/L/433, paragraph 4 and Annex II.
[f]See WTO document WT/L/433, paragraph 5. [g]See WTO document WT/L/865; WT/L/872; WT/L/905; see also the section 'Protocol of Accession – standard architecture' of this chapter for more background on this specific provision.

What explains this? In reality, China was and remains a major economy and an important player. It was unique in the sense that it was undergoing massive domestic economic transformation and reform from a centrally planned to a market economy. The scale of changes in economic operations to shift to a market economy, development of institutions and adaptation to the rule of law, were significant. The working party approached the accession of China as it has approached all other accessions namely, with the intention of safeguarding the rules-based multilateral trading system, close as many loopholes as possible and strengthen the system, through additional rules and reinforcements in the architecture of accessions.

More recently, the wording of the Accession Protocol came under scrutiny in the negotiations leading up to the conclusion of Russia's accession negotiations. While the text of the accession working party report and the accompanying Accession Protocol were still in draft form and subject to negotiation, the following specific provision was inserted in paragraph 2, of Part I of Russia's draft Accession Protocol:

> and nothing in these commitments shall be understood to derogate from the rights of the Russian Federation under the WTO Agreement as applied between the Members of the WTO by the date of accession of the Russian Federation to the WTO.[37]

The rationale by Russia for this insertion was on the right to regulate trade and trade policy. For members, two issues emerged: technical and substantive. Technically, although 'specific provisions' had previously been incorporated in the standard text of WTO Accession Protocols of Article XII members, none was comparable to this specific draft proposal. Substantively, questions arose with regard to the potential effects and implications that such a provision could have on the binding integrity and substance of the negotiated specific commitments that would be referenced in the Accession Protocol. In 2011, an exchange of views in the trilateral setting on Russia's accession negotiations was initiated, moderated by the Director of Accessions. The ensuing discussions and a dedicated e-mail exchange,[38] which remain strictly confidential, resulted in the understanding that the 2004 (draft) text, as proposed by Russia, would be incompatible with, and potentially void, the

---

[37] See WTO document WT/ACC/SPEC/RUS/25/Rev.3 of 15 October 2004 and Table 11.3.
[38] For the record, this question was resolved by Chris Wilson, lead negotiator for the United States; Peter Balas, lead negotiator for the European Union; Maxim Medvedkov, lead negotiator for the Russian Federation; and Chiedu Osakwe, Director, WTO Accessions Division. The dedicated e-mail exchanges remain strictly classified.

Table 11.3 *Variations in the draft Protocol on the Accession of the Russian Federation*

| WTO document symbol | Date of circulation | Variations in the draft Accession Protocol, as contained in the draft working party report |
|---|---|---|
| WT/ACC/SPEC/ RUS/25/Rev. 2 | 27 May 2003 | Standard WTO Accession Protocol text |
| WT/ACC/SPEC/ RUS/25/Rev. 3 | 15 October 2004 | Specific provision added to paragraph 2 of Part I of the Draft Accession Protocol, namely: 'and nothing in these commitments shall be understood to derogate from the rights of the Russian Federation under the WTO Agreement as applied between the Members of the WTO by the date of accession of the Russian Federation to the WTO.' Brackets added to the draft decision and the draft protocol |
| JOB(08)/36 | 30 April 2008 | Same protocol text, as in WT/ACC/ SPEC/RUS/25/Rev. 3 |
| JOB(08)/36/Rev 1 | 14 August 2008 | |
| WT/ACC/SPEC/ RUS/25/Rev. 4 | 4 October 2011 | Return to standard WTO Accession Protocol text |

accession-specific obligations it had accepted. The final version of Russia's accession working party report of 17 November 2011, as approved by the Eighth WTO Ministerial Conference, reverted to the standard Accession Protocol text (see Table 11.3).[39]

## WTO Accession Protocols and the Dispute Settlement Mechanism

Accession Protocols and accession working party reports have been cited in twenty-seven disputes, of which almost twenty have proceeded to the panel stage.[40] To date, panels and the Appellate Body have approached

---

[39] See WTO documents: WT/ACC/RUS/70; WT/MIN(11)/2.
[40] See WTO documents: WT/DS451; WT/DS450; WT/DS437; WT/DS433; WT/DS432; WT/DS431; WT/DS429; WT/DS419; WT/DS405; WT/DS404; WT/DS399; WT/DS398;

disputes, in which Accession Protocols have been cited, by applying the rules of interpretation codified in the VCLT, including but not limited to Articles 31, 32 and 33 of the VCLT.

WTO case law has confirmed that Accession Protocols, and accession-specific obligations referenced therein, form an integral part of the WTO Agreement, pursuant to paragraph 2 of the standard WTO Accession Protocol. Thus Accession Protocols and associated accession working party reports have been interpreted as provisions in WTO covered agreements,[41] i.e. through recourse to the VCLT. In accordance with Article 31 of the VCLT:

1. A treaty shall be interpreted in good faith in accordance with the ordinary meaning to be given to the terms of the treaty in their context and in the light of its object and purpose.
2. The context for the purpose of the interpretation of a treaty shall comprise, in addition to the text, including its preamble and annexes:
   (a) Any agreement relating to the treaty which was made between all the parties in connexion with the conclusion of the treaty;
   (b) Any instrument which was made by one or more parties in connexion with the conclusion of the treaty and accepted by the other parties as an instrument related to the treaty.
3. There shall be taken into account, together with the context:
   (a) Any subsequent agreement between the parties regarding the interpretation of the treaty or the application of its provisions;
   (b) Any subsequent practice in the application of the treaty which establishes the agreement of the parties regarding its interpretation;
   (c) Any relevant rules of international law applicable in the relations between the parties.
4. A special meaning shall be given to a term if it is established that the parties so intended.

It is argued therefore, that pursuant to Article 31 of the VCLT, in cases of dispute where Accession Protocols are cited, the intentions of the drafters would need to be determined through an analysis that would involve a determination of the 'ordinary meaning' of the terms used in the context

---

WT/DS397; WT/DS395; WT/DS394; WT/DS390; WT/DS388; WT/DS387; WT/DS379; WT/DS378; WT/DS373; WT/DS363; WT/DS359; WT/DS358; WT/DS342; WT/DS340; WT/DS339.

[41] On 'covered agreements', see Article 1.1 and Appendix 1 of the Dispute Settlement Understanding (DSU).

and in the light of the object and purpose of the WTO Agreements and the accession working party reports. On the basis of this logic, it is argued that, in interpreting measures by an Article XII member, based on provisions that may entail variations between the WTO Agreement, on the one hand, and negotiated WTO accession-specific obligations, on the other hand, the latter should 'supersede' and prevail. Furthermore, beyond the 'ordinary textual reading for meaning', panels are encouraged to make extensive use of not only the negotiating dialogue, as codified in Accession Packages, but also as contained in correspondence – the latter may provide additional clarity and make relevant intentions and purposes evident.

Disputes citing Accession Protocols, such as *China–Raw Materials*, have shown that WTO dispute settlement proceedings could be initiated based on a claim of violation of an Accession Protocol; and that the specific accession obligations, as contained in the accession working party report and as referenced in the Accession Protocol, are binding and enforceable in WTO dispute settlement. Thus, the facts point to the trend that, in the twenty-year WTO accession history, panel and Appellate Body reports have clarified the legal value and reconfirmed the enforceability of Accession Protocols and accession-specific obligations.

In this chapter, we have sought to provide a comprehensive historical account of the evolution of the WTO Accession Protocol by reconnecting it to its origins in GATT Accession Protocols. Annexes 11.1 to 11.4 of this chapter show relevant historical records dating back to 1949. We have reviewed associated customary procedures for the approval of Accession Protocols by members, their acceptance by acceding governments and their entry into force. These customary procedures also derive from GATT practices. They provide an accepted and well-established framework for finalising concluded accession negotiations. We also examined the standard text of the Accession Protocol. This basic architecture has had an invaluable advantage in providing stability in the rules-based multilateral trading system amid the complex diversity of foreign trade regimes.

The role of the Accession Protocol is critical to the accession process as it brings together the results of years of accession negotiations. This legal instrument has a direct impact on the WTO Agreement as it specifies that the obligations of the new WTO member become an integral part of the WTO Agreement. While the scope of specific accession obligations has varied, reflecting the particular dynamics of individual accession negotiations and the specificities of foreign trade regimes, it has nevertheless been accepted that the WTO Agreement is rectified, amended and modified with the entry into force of Accession Protocols of each new Article XII member.

In the recent past, panel reports and the Appellate Body (primarily on China) have triggered further debate on the relationship between WTO Accession Protocols and WTO Agreements and their legal status and enforceability in WTO dispute settlement. By treating WTO Accession Protocols as integral parts of the WTO Agreement, the reports and findings of panels and the Appellate Body have clarified and reasserted the applicability of the customary rules of treaty interpretation of protocols, as codified in the VCLT. When put to the test, WTO Accession Protocols, and associated accession-specific obligations have been found to be enforceable through WTO dispute settlement. Twenty years of WTO accession negotiating history have thus reconfirmed the role of accession obligations in strengthening and expanding the applicability and coverage of the WTO Agreement through the addition of new members.

## Acknowledgements

The authors would like to thank several colleagues for their comments, suggestions and assistance in tracing and retrieving historical background material: Stefania Bernabé, Dimitar Bratanov, Valerie Hughes, Ian Huxtable, Gabrielle Marceau, Julie Pain and János Volkai. This chapter represents the views of the authors, and is neither meant to represent the positions or opinions of the WTO, its members and the Secretariat, nor, as a whole, the 'official' position of any staff member. Errors of omission or commission are those of the authors. The discussion on the specific question 'To what extent do Accession Protocols come into play in the context of WTO dispute settlement?' in this chapter is largely referential in light of the deeper and authoritative analysis by Valerie Hughes in Chapter 10.

| GENERAL AGREEMENT ON TARIFFS AND TRADE | ACCORD GENERAL SUR LES TARIFS DOUANIERS ET LE COMMERCE | RESTRICTED LIMITED B GATT/CP.3/56 11 July 1949 ORIGINAL: ENGLISH |
|---|---|---|

Contracting Parties

Third Session

## THE ANNECY PROTOCOL OF TERMS OF ACCESSION
## TO THE GENERAL AGREEMENT ON TARIFFS AND
## TRADE

Attached hereto is the Annecy Protocol of Terms of Accession as approved by the Tariff Negotiations Committee on 11 July. This will be submitted at an early meeting of the CONTRACTING PARTIES for final approval. At that meeting the CONTRACTING PARTIES will also be asked to consider the following recommendations of the Joint Working Party on Accession which have been referred to them by the Tariff Negotiations Committee without discussion:

1) "that representatives of the contracting parties should if at all possible obtain authorization to sign the Protocol before leaving Annecy, or alternatively that they should recommend to their governments that the Protocol be signed soon thereafter instead of waiting for the final date of November 30, 1949".

2) "that the CONTRACTING PARTIES decide at the present session that the failure of any contracting party to sign the Protocol in respect of a particular acceding government by November 30, 1949, shall be deemed to be a negative vote on the decision contemplated by paragraph 11 of the Protocol and shall be so recorded".

GATT/CP.3/56
page 2

## ANNEX PROTOCOL OF TERMS OF ACCESSION

## TO THE GENERAL AGREEMENT ON TARIFFS AND TRADE

(As approved by the Tariff Negotiations Committee on 11 July 1949)

The Governments of .......................... ........... which are
the present contracting parties to the General Agreement on Tariffs and
Trade (hereinafter called "the present contracting parties" and "the
General Agreement" respectively), and the Governments of ..............
................................................. ......... (hereinafter
called "the acceding governments"),

HAVING regard to the results of the negotiations directed towards
the accession of the acceding governments to the General Agreement,

In accordance with the provisions of Article XXXIII of the
General Agreement:-

HEREBY AGREE upon the terms on which the acceding governments
may so accede, which terms are embodied in this Protocol,

AND the present contracting parties DECIDE by decisions of
two-thirds majorities, taken in the manner provided in paragraph 11
of this Protocol, upon the accession to the General Agreement of the
acceding governments.

1. (a) Subject to the provisions of this Protocol, each of the
        acceding governments shall, upon the entry into force of
        this Protocol with respect to it, apply provisionally:

        (i) Parts I and III of the General Agreement, and

        (ii) Part II of the General Agreement to the fullest
             extent not inconsistent with its legislation existing
             on the date of this Protocol.

   (b) The obligations incorporated in paragraph 1 of Article I of
       the General Agreement by reference to Article III thereof

GATT/CP.3/56
page 3

and those incorporated in paragraph 2 (b) of Article II by
reference to Article VI shall be considered as falling within
Part II of the General Agreement for the purpose of this
paragraph.

(c) For the purposes of the General Agreement, the Schedules
contained in Annex B to this Protocol shall be regarded as
Schedules to the General Agreement relating to acceding
governments.

(d) Notwithstanding the provisions of paragraph 1 of Article I
of the General Agreement, signature of this Protocol by an
acceding government shall not require the elimination of any
preferences in respect of import duties or charges which do
not exceed the levels provided for in paragraph 4 of Article
I of the General Agreement, as modified and which are in
force exclusively between Colombia on the one hand and
Ecuador and Venezuela on the other hand, and between
Uruguay and Paraguay.

2.  Upon the entry into force of this Protocol with respect to each
acceding government, that government shall become a contracting
party as defined in Article XXXII of the General Agreement.

3.  Notwithstanding the provisions of paragraph 12, the concessions
provided for in the Schedule relating to each present contracting
party and contained in Annex A to this Protocol shall not enter
into force for that contracting party unless notification of the
intention to apply these concessions has first been received by
the Secretary-General of the United Nations from that contracting
party.    Such concessions shall thereafter enter into force
for that contracting party either on the date on which this

GATT/CP.3/56
page 4

Protocol first enters into force pursuant to paragraph 12 or on
the thirtieth day following the day upon which such notification
is received by the Secretary-General, whichever is the later.
Such notification shall only be effective if received by the
Secretary-General not later than April 30, 1950.  Upon the entry
into force of such concessions the appropriate Schedule shall be
regarded as a Schedule to the General Agreement relating to that
contracting party.

4.      Any present contracting party which has given the notification
referred to in paragraph 3 or any acceding government which signs
this Protocol shall be free at any time to withhold or to withdraw
in whole or in part any concession, provided for in the appropriate
Schedule contained in Annex A or B to this Protocol, in respect
of which such contracting party or government determines that
it was initially negotiated with an acceding government which
has not signed this Protocol or a present contracting party
which has not given such notification; Provided that the present
contracting party or acceding government withholding or withdrawing in whole or in part any such concession shall give
notice to all other present contracting parties and acceding
governments within thirty days after the date of such withholding
or withdrawal and, upon request, shall consult with the contracting
parties which have a substantial interest in the product concerned;
and Provided further that, without prejudice to the provisions of
Article XXXV of the General Agreement, any concession so withheld
or withdrawn shall be applied from the thirtieth day following
the day upon which the acceding government or present contracting
party with which it was initially negotiated, signs this Protocol

GATT/CP.3/56
page 5

or gives the notification referred to in paragraph 3.

5.(a)  In each case in which Article II of the General Agreement refers to the date of that Agreement, the applicable date in respect of the Schedule annexed to this Protocol shall be the date of this Protocol.

(b)  In each case in which paragraph 6 of Article V, sub-paragraph 4 (d) of Article VII and sub-paragraph 3 (c) of Article X of the General Agreement refers to the date of that Agreement, the applicable date in respect of each acceding government shall be March 24, 1948.

(c)  In the case of the references in paragraph 11 of Article XVIII of the General Agreement to September 1, 1947 and October 10, 1947, the applicable dates in respect of each acceding government shall be May 14, 1949 and July 15, 1949, respectively.

6.  The provisions of the General Agreement to be applied by an acceding government shall be those contained in the text annexed to the Final Act of the Second Session of the Preparatory Committee of the United Nations Conference on Trade and Employment as rectified, amended, or otherwise modified on the day on which this Protocol is signed by such acceding government. Signature of this Protocol by an acceding government, to be effective, shall be accompanied by appropriate action accepting any rectification, amendment, or other modification which has been drawn up by the CONTRACTING PARTIES for submission to governments for acceptance but which has not become effective by the date of signature of this Protocol by that acceding government.

7.  Any acceding government which has signed this Protocol shall be free to withdraw its provisional application of the General

GATT/CP.3/56
page 6

Agreement and such withdrawal shall take effect on the sixtieth day following the day on which written notice of such withdrawal is received by the Secretary-General of the United Nations.

8.(a) Any acceding government which has signed this Protocol and has not given notice of withdrawal under paragraph 7, may, on or after the date on which the General Agreement enters into force pursuant to Article XXVI thereof, accede to that Agreement upon the terms of this Protocol by deposit of an instrument of accession with the Secretary-General of the United Nations. Such accession shall take effect on the day on which the General Agreement enters into force pursuant to Article XXVI, or on the thirtieth day following the day of the deposit of the instrument of accession, whichever shall be the later.

(b) Accession to the General Agreement pursuant to paragraph 8 (a) of this Protocol shall, for the purpose of paragraph 2 of Article XXXII of that Agreement, be regarded as acceptance of the Agreement pursuant to paragraph 3 of Article XXVI thereof.

9.(a) Each acceding government signing this Protocol, or depositing an instrument of accession under paragraph 8 (a), and each present contracting party giving the notification referred to in paragraph 3, does so in respect of its metropolitan territory and of the other territories for which it has international responsibility, except such separate customs territories as it shall notify to the Secretary-General of the United Nations at the time of such signature, deposit, or notification under paragraph 3.

(b) Any acceding government or present contracting party which has notified the Secretary-General, under the exception in sub-paragraph (a) of this paragraph, may at any time give notice to

GATT/CP.3/56
page 7

the Secretary-General that such signature, accession, or
notification under paragraph 3 shall be effective in respect
of any separate customs territory or territories so excepted
and such notice shall take effect on the thirtieth day following
the day on which it is received by the Secretary-General.

(c) If any of the customs territories, in respect of which an
acceding government has made the General Agreement effective,
possesses or acquires full autonomy in the conduct of its
external commercial relations and of the other matters provided
for in the General Agreement, such territory shall, upon
sponsorship through a declaration by the responsible acceding
government establishing the above-mentioned fact, be deemed to
be a contracting party.

10.(a)  This Protocol shall be open for signature at Annecy until
_____.  The original text of this Protocol
shall thereafter be deposited with the Secretary-General of
the United Nations and shall remain open for signature at the
Headquarters of the United Nations by present contracting
parties until November 30, 1949 and by acceding governments
until April 30, 1950.

(b) The Secretary-General of the United Nations shall promptly
furnish a certified copy of this Protocol, and a notification
of each signature thereto, of each deposit of an instrument of
accession under paragraph 8 (a), and of each notification or
notice under paragraphs 3, 7, 9 (a) or 9 (b), to each Member
of the United Nations and to each other government which
participated in the United Nations Conference on Trade and
Employment.

GATT/CP.3/56
page 8

(c) The Secretary-General is authorized to register this Protocol in accordance with Article 102 of the Charter of the United Nations.

11. Upon signature of this Protocol in respect of an acceding government by two-thirds of the present contracting parties, it shall constitute a decision taken under Article XXXIII of the General Agreement agreeing to the accession of that government.

12. Subject to the provisions of paragraph 3, this Protocol shall, for each acceding government in respect of which it has been signed by November 30, 1949 by two-thirds of the present contracting parties, enter into force –

(a) if it has been signed by that acceding government by November 30, 1949, on January 1, 1950, or

(b) if it has not been signed by that acceding government by November 30, 1949, on the thirtieth day following the day upon which it shall have been signed by such acceding government.

DONE at Annecy, in a single copy, in the English and French languages, both texts authentic except as otherwise specified with respect to Schedules annexed hereto, this ............... day of ......................., one thousand nine hundred and forty-nine.

A N N E X   A.

( to be inserted )

A N N E X   B.

( to be inserted )

| GENERAL AGREEMENT | ACCORD GENERAL SUR | RESTRICTED LIMITED B |
|---|---|---|
| ON TARIFFS AND | LES TARIFS DOUANIERS | GATT/CP.3/33 |
| TRADE | ET LE COMMERCE | GATT/TN.1/32 |
| | | 12 August 1949 |
| | | ORIGINAL: ENGLISH |

CONTRACTING PARTIES

Tariff Negotiations Committee

SUPPLEMENTARY REPORT OF THE JOINT WORKING PARTY

ON ACCESSION TO THE CONTRACTING PARTIES AND THE

TARIFF NEGOTIATIONS COMMITTEE

1.  **Protocol of Accession — Statement by the United States**
    **Delegation (GATT/CP.3/70)**

The Working Party, having heard further explanations by the
representative of the United States regarding the difficulties
the Annecy Protocol of Accession as at present drafted might
present to his Government, recommends to the Tariff Negotiations
Committee and the CONTRACTING PARTIES the attached draft documents:

The first is a draft of a decision of terms of accession to
be known as the Annecy Decision on Terms of Accession to the General
Agreement on Tariffs and Trade. This Decision embodies the terms
of accession in substantially the same form as those included in
the former draft protocol. Annexed to the Decision would be the
schedules of present contracting parties (Annex A), with the same
numbers as other existing schedules and with Schedule XX (United
States of America) containing a separate division for each acceding
government. There would also be annexed the schedules of the
acceding governments (Annex B). In addition to the Decision,
there would be a separate protocol for the accession of each
acceding government. This protocol would contain provisions for
the entry into force of the concessions contained in a Schedule
containing separate divisions for individual acceding governments.
The concessions of other contracting parties would enter into force
in accordance with paragraph 3 of the Decision. The separate

protocol would also contain any special provisions regarding
preferences which were previously in the Draft Protocol of Terms
of Accession. It is provided in the Decision that, upon signature
by two-thirds of the present contracting parties of the Protocol
for the accession of a particular acceding government, it (the
Decision) shall constitute a decision taken under Article XXXIII
of the General Agreement relating to the accession of that
government.

In summary, the present proposal does not differ in any
substantial degree from the scheme of the present Draft Protocol.
All contracting parties who wish to do so will be able to embody
their Annecy concessions in consolidated schedules, whereas it will
be open to any of them to have a schedule with a separate division
for each acceding government. The terms of accession embodied in
the Decision are incorporated by reference in each separate protocol.

2. Protocol embodying results of United Kingdom/Norway negotiations
   (GATT/CP/3/74).

In view of the recommendation in 1) above, the United Kingdom
and Norwegian delegations have withdrawn their proposal for a
separate protocol to embody the results of the negotiations
between the United Kingdom and Norway (GATT/CP/3/74).

3. Import restrictions on items which may be included in the
   Italian Schedule of Concessions (GATT.CP.3/81).

The Working Party considered that the objective aimed at in
the suggestion contained in GATT/CP.3/81, i.e. the insertion of
a paragraph in the Protocol of Accession or in the Italian Schedule,
could be more simply achieved by a waiver under Article XXV (5) (a)
of the General Agreement. They therefore recommend the adoption by
the CONTRACTING PARTIES of the following Decision:

   "The CONTRACTING PARTIES, on the basis of Article XXV (5) (a)
   of the General Agreement on Tariffs and Trade, decide that,
   notwithstanding anything contained in paragraph 13 of

L/2631
Page 2/3

## PROTOCOL FOR THE ACCESSION OF YUGOSLAVIA
### TO THE GENERAL AGREEMENT ON TARIFFS AND TRADE

The governments which are contracting parties to the General Agreement on Tariffs and Trade (hereinafter referred to as "contracting parties" and "the General Agreement", respectively), the European Economic Community and the Government of the Socialist Federal Republic of Yugoslavia (hereinafter referred to as "Yugoslavia"),

HAVING regard to the result of the negotiations directed towards the accession of Yugoslavia to the General Agreement,

TAKING NOTE of the request of Yugoslavia for accession dated 18 October 1965, of the discussions leading to, and in the context of, the Declaration on Relations between Contracting Parties and Yugoslavia dated 25 May 1959 and the Declaration on the Provisional Accession of Yugoslavia dated 13 November 1962 and of the report on those aspects of the terms of accession which are not directly related to the tariff negotiations,

HAVE through their representatives agreed as follows:

### Part I - General

1. Yugoslavia shall, upon entry into force of this Protocol pursuant to paragraph 6, become a contracting party to the General Agreement, as defined in Article XXXII thereof, and shall apply provisionally and subject to this Protocol:

    (a) Parts I and III of the General Agreement, and

    (b) Part II of the General Agreement - to the fullest extent not inconsistent with its legislation existing on the date of this Protocol.

The obligations incorporated in paragraph 1 of Article I by reference to Article III and those incorporated in paragraph 2(b) of Article II by reference to Article VI of the General Agreement shall be considered as falling within Part II for the purpose of this paragraph.

L/2681
Page 4

2.   (a) The provisions of the General Agreement to be applied by Yugoslavia shall, except as otherwise provided in this Protocol, be the provisions contained in the text annexed to the Final Act of the second session of the Preparatory Committee of the United Nations Conference on Trade and Employment, as rectified, amended, supplemented, or otherwise modified by such instruments as may have become at least partially effective on the day on which Yugoslavia becomes a contracting party; provided that this does not mean that Yugoslavia undertakes to apply a provision of any such instrument prior to the effectiveness of such provision pursuant to the terms of the instrument; and

(b)  in each case in which paragraph 6 of Article V, sub-paragraph 4(d) of Article VII, and sub-paragraph 3(c) of Article X of the General Agreement refer to the date of that Agreement, the applicable date in respect of Yugoslavia shall be 13 November 1962, the date of the Declaration providing for the Provisional Accession of Yugoslavia to the General Agreement.

### Part II - Schedule

3.   The schedule in the Annex shall, upon the entry into force of this Protocol, become a Schedule to the General Agreement relating to Yugoslavia.

4.   (a) In each case in which paragraph 1 of Article II of the General Agreement refers to the date of that Agreement the applicable date in respect of each product which is the subject of a concession provided for in the schedule annexed to this Protocol shall be the date of this Protocol.

(b)  For the purpose of the reference in paragraph 6(a) of Article II of the General Agreement to the date of that Agreement, the applicable date in respect of the schedule annexed to this Protocol shall be the date of this Protocol.

### Part III - Final Provisions

5.   This Protocol shall be deposited with the Director-General to the CONTRACTING PARTIES. It shall be open for signature by Yugoslavia until 31 December 1966. It shall also be open for signature by contracting parties and the European Economic Community.

6.   This Protocol shall enter into force on the thirtieth day following the day upon which it shall have been signed by Yugoslavia.

L/2581
Page 5

7.   Signature of this Protocol by Yugoslavia shall constitute final action to become a party to each of the following instruments:

(i)   Protocol Amending Part I and Articles XXIX and XXX, Geneva, 10 March 1955;

(ii)   Fifth Protocol of Rectifications and Modifications to the Texts of the Schedules, Geneva, 3 December 1955;

(iii)   Sixth Protocol of Rectifications and Modifications to the Texts of the Schedules, Geneva, 11 April 1957;

(iv)   Seventh Protocol of Rectifications and Modifications to the Texts of the Schedules, Geneva, 30 November 1957;

(v)   Protocol Relating to the Negotiations for the Establishment of New Schedule III - Brazil, Geneva, 31 December 1958;

(vi)   Eighth Protocol of Rectifications and Modifications to the Texts of the Schedules, Geneva, 18 February 1959;

(vii)   Ninth Protocol of Rectifications and Modifications to the Texts of the Schedules, Geneva, 17 August 1959; and

(viii)   Protocol Amending the General Agreement on Tariffs and Trade to Introduce a Part IV on Trade and Development, Geneva, 8 February 1965.

8.   Yugoslavia, having become a contracting party to the General Agreement pursuant to paragraph 1 of this Protocol, may accede to the General Agreement upon the applicable terms of this Protocol by deposit of an instrument of accession, with the Director-General.   Such accession shall take effect on the day on which the General Agreement enters into force pursuant to Article XXVI or on the thirtieth day following the day of the deposit of the instrument of accession, whichever is the later.   Accession to the General Agreement pursuant to this paragraph shall, for the purposes of paragraph 2 of Article XXXII of that Agreement, be regarded as acceptance of the Agreement pursuant to paragraph 4 of Article XXVI thereof.

9.   Yugoslavia may withdraw its provisional application of the General Agreement prior to its accession thereto pursuant to paragraph 8 and such withdrawal shall take effect on the sixtieth day following the day on which written notice thereof is received by the Director-General.

Council Division
16.10.95

### Protocols of Accession for the Governments Covered by the Decision
### on Finalization of Negotiations on Schedules on Goods and Services (WT/L/30)[1]

#### Informal Consultations

#### (Monday, 16 October 1995 - 3 p.m. - Room F)

1.      An informal consultation to reach agreement on a draft text for the above-mentioned Protocols in time for their consideration and approval by the General Council on 15 November was convened by Mr. Hoda.  The list of delegations invited is attached, as is also the draft text prepared by the Secretariat.

2.      The main area of disagreement concerns the date by which the acceding governments should submit the notifications that are required within specified time periods under the Multilateral Trade Agreements (paragraph 3(b) of the attached draft), where the United States has insisted on more precise language.

3.      The United States suggested draft language at the consultations which would require these notifications to be made "by 30 June 1996 or 90 days after the date on which it [the government concerned] accepts this Protocol, whichever comes earlier."  It also suggested that each Protocol be open for acceptance until "90 days after its approval by the General Council" (paragraph 6).

4.      While delegations said they did not have instructions to decide on the suggestions made by the United States, and also noted an inconsistency in the time frames in paragraphs 3(b) and 6, there appeared to be little support for the suggestions.  It was agreed that the US delegation would seek instructions to agree to the presently drafted text or, failing this, to come up with a new text to ensure consistency between paragraphs 3(b) and 6.

---

[1] These Governments are:  Grenada, Papua New Guinea, St. Kitts and Nevis, and Qatar.

PROTOCOLS/note4

- 2 -

Informal Consultations
(16 October 1995 - Room F)

Delegations invited:

Argentina
Australia
Brazil
Canada
Colombia
European Communities
Hong Kong
India
Malaysia (ASEAN)
Japan
Korea
Mexico
New Zealand
Norway
Singapore
Spain
Switzerland
United States

## ACCESSION OF [NAME OF STATE OR CUSTOMS TERRITORY]

### Draft Decision

**The General Council**

Recalling that certain contracting parties which became contracting parties to the GATT 1947 during the course of 1994 were unable to complete the negotiations on their schedules to the GATT 1994 and the General Agreement on Trade in Services (hereinafter referred to as the "GATS"),

Recalling further that the General Council decided on 31 January 1995 that these contracting parties to the GATT 1947 should be able to accede to the WTO Agreement in accordance with special procedures under which the General Council's approval of the schedules to the GATT 1994 and the GATS shall be deemed to be the approval of their terms of accession,

Noting that the negotiations on the schedules of [name] have been completed and a Protocol of Accession for [name] has been prepared,

Decides, in accordance with Article XII of the Agreement Establishing the World Trade Organization, that [name] may accede to the Agreement Establishing the World Trade Organization in the terms set out in the said Protocol.

---

## PROTOCOL OF ACCESSION OF
## [NAME OF STATE OR CUSTOMS TERRITORY]
## TO THE AGREEMENT ESTABLISHING THE WORLD TRADE ORGANIZATION

The World Trade Organization (hereinafter referred to as the "WTO"), pursuant to the approval of the General Council of the WTO accorded under Article XII of the Marrakesh Agreement Establishing the World Trade Organization (hereinafter referred to as "WTO Agreement"), and [name],

Recalling that certain contracting parties which became contracting parties to the GATT 1947 during the course of 1994 were unable to complete the negotiations on their schedules to the GATT 1994 and the General Agreement on Trade in Services (hereinafter referred to as the "GATS"),

Recalling further that the General Council decided on 31 January 1995 that these contracting parties to the GATT 1947 should be able to accede to the WTO Agreement in accordance with special procedures under which the General Council's approval of the schedules to the GATT 1994 and the GATS shall be deemed to be the approval of their terms of accession,

Noting that the negotiations on the schedules of [name] have been completed,

Agree as follows:

PROTOCOL/note3

- 2 -

### Part I - General

1.    Upon entry into force of this Protocol, [name] accedes to the WTO Agreement pursuant to Article XII of that Agreement and thereby becomes a Member of the WTO.

2.    The WTO Agreement to which [name] accedes shall be the WTO Agreement as rectified, amended or otherwise modified by such legal instruments as may have entered into force before the date of entry into force of this Protocol. This Protocol shall be an integral part of the WTO Agreement.

3.    (a)    Those obligations in the Multilateral Trade Agreements annexed to the WTO Agreement that are to be implemented over a period of time starting with the entry into force of that Agreement shall be implemented by [name] as if it had accepted that Agreement on the date of its entry into force.

[(b)    Those notifications that are to be made under the Multilateral Trade Agreements annexed to the WTO Agreement within a specified period of time starting with the date of entry into force of the WTO Agreement shall be made by [name] within that period of time starting with ▨▨▨▨▨▨▨▨ the date on which it accepts this Protocol▨▨▨▨▨▨▨.]

### Part II - Schedules

4.    The Schedules annexed to this Protocol shall become the Schedule of Concessions and Commitments annexed to the General Agreement on Tariffs and Trade 1994 (hereinafter referred to as the "GATT 1994") and the Schedule of Specific Commitments annexed to the GATS relating to [name]. The staging of concessions and commitments listed in the Schedules shall be implemented as specified in the relevant parts of the respective Schedules.

5.    For the purpose of the reference in paragraph 6(a) of Article II of the GATT 1994 to the date of that Agreement, the applicable date in respect of the Schedule of Concessions and Commitments annexed to this Protocol shall be the date of entry into force of this Protocol.

### Part III - Final Provisions

6.    This Protocol shall be open for acceptance, by signature or otherwise, by [name] until ▨▨▨▨ ▨▨▨▨▨▨▨▨▨▨▨▨▨.

7.    This Protocol shall enter into force on the thirtieth day following the day of its acceptance.

8.    This Protocol shall be deposited with the Director-General of the WTO. The Director-General of the WTO shall promptly furnish a certified copy of this Protocol and a notification of acceptance thereto pursuant to paragraph 6 to each member of the WTO and to [name].

9.    This Protocol shall be registered in accordance with the provisions of Article 102 of the Charter of the United Nations.

      Done at Geneva this ... date of ... one thousand nine hundred and ninety-five, in a single copy in the English, French and Spanish languages each text being authentic except that the Schedules annexed to this Protocol are authentic only in the [English]/[French]/[and]/[Spanish] language[s].

# PART III

Members' perspectives on accession negotiations

# WTO accessions from a member's perspective: safeguarding the rules-based system

MARK LINSCOTT AND CECILIA KLEIN

ABSTRACT

*Forms of collective action and balanced commitment through negotiations were the foundation of the General Agreement on Tariffs and Trade (GATT) and the structure for its daily work. These remain at the centrepiece of work in the WTO, in a system structured on the balance of rights and obligations. GATT contracting parties established the principles of balance and reciprocity, trade liberalisation and a system of mediation and dispute settlement for mutual resolution of GATT provisions. From this base, expansion of membership, pursuant to accession negotiations, has required a commitment to accepting GATT/WTO rules resulting from previous negotiations. WTO accession supports applicants' efforts for economic reform and integration into world markets. This is one of the most important benefits of membership. Although challenging, accession negotiations and the implementation of WTO provisions support important economic goals such as sustainable growth, the promotion of high-tech industries, attraction of foreign direct investment, raised living standards and global assertion of national trade interest.*

For over sixty-five years, nations have worked together to create a legal-diplomatic framework for international trade that can expand their market horizons beyond bilateral and regional agreements. The 1947 General Agreement on Tariffs and Trade (GATT) was the result of such an effort, intended to create an agreed structure of rules within which badly needed post-Second World War trade liberalisation could be safely

The analyses in the chapters in this book were finalised at the end of December 2014. Since then the Republic of Seychelles acceded to the World Trade Organization (WTO) on 26 April 2015. This expanded total WTO membership from 160 to 161. Please see the editors' note.

undertaken. There was hope in the 1940s that the GATT would be soon replaced with a more elaborate trade organisation, one that could stand with the World Bank and the International Monetary Fund (IMF), to support economic development and growth. However, the GATT framework of thirty-eight articles was all there was for almost fifty years. Within this simple framework of mutual commitment, the contracting parties to the GATT met periodically to elaborate principles for conducting international trade with the objective of implementing, for themselves and for future contracting parties, the benefits and obligations outlined in its text. They established the principles of balance and reciprocity in the application of trade measures. They sponsored additional multilateral efforts at trade liberalisation, i.e. 'rounds' of tariff liberalisation. They created fora for discussion between trade negotiating sessions which became accepted multilateral institutions. They established a system of mediation and dispute settlement to ensure that questions about GATT provisions could be mutually settled.

These forms of collective action and balanced commitment through negotiation were the foundation of the GATT and the structure for its day-to-day work. They remain the foundation of the WTO, which emerged from the last GATT negotiations, the Uruguay Round of Multilateral Negotiations, concluded in 1994. The Marrakesh Agreement Establishing the World Trade Organization (WTO Agreement) was implemented on 1 January 1995. Its provisions, including the additional agreements annexed to it, institutionalised and expanded the arrangements developed within the GATT structure over time (councils, committees, panels and working parties). These subsidiary WTO bodies, like their GATT counterparts before them, sustain ongoing negotiations, rule-making and dispute settlement. The day-to-day work of these bodies continues to create a strong record of ongoing rule-making, thereby solidifying and elaborating the framework of the institution.

The GATT, and the WTO Agreement that emerged from it, created a flexible framework of rules that allowed each member to promote its economic growth and development through international trade, while ensuring that each sovereign economic actor in the system could also protect its own domestic policies and market, within those same rules. To secure the long-term growth and health of that framework, the original GATT signatories established provisions for accepting new contracting parties that were equally flexible, i.e. that the terms of joining the compact would have to be negotiated with the current membership. These provisions were continued for new members of the WTO.

Accession to the GATT and later to the WTO was open both to states and to entities at the sub-state level with the status of separate customs territories capable of implementing the accession provisions. The essential factor for the eligibility of both GATT and WTO applicants is that the state or separate customs territory has to have full 'autonomy in the conduct of its external commercial relations and of the other matters provided for in this Agreement' and can negotiate terms of accession with current contracting parties or members.[1] These simple provisions were applied in the early days of the GATT as a mandate to accept new contracting parties during trade rounds based largely on acceptance of GATT provisions and the attachment of a negotiated schedule of tariff concessions to the GATT. Only over time were specific working parties established to discuss the applicants' trade regimes and formally transmit the results of the negotiations to existing contracting parties (and later, WTO members) for approval.

Based on these concepts, from the beginning, the process of expanding the membership of the international trading system through accession has always required both a commitment to accept GATT or WTO rules (the results of previous negotiations) and the establishment of trade liberalising commitments, the 'entry condition' to ensure that the new participant understood that its rights within the system depended in turn on its reciprocal obligations. And while a number of GATT contracting parties 'succeeded' to the WTO under Article XXVI:5(c) of the GATT,[2] because the GATT had previously been applied on their behalf, e.g. as colonies or other dependencies of the original or acceded contracting parties, membership of the WTO after its inception has come about through accession.

The WTO began with 128 original members, i.e. the GATT contracting parties that concluded the Uruguay Round and established the WTO in January 1995. Since that time, thirty-three additional countries and separate customs territories have negotiated accession and become WTO members, the last one being Seychelles on 26 April 2015. In each case, joining the WTO required negotiations, consisting of an extended dialogue in a working party with current members, to ensure that the applicant's trade regime would be aligned with current WTO provisions

---

[1] Article XXXIII of the GATT 1947 and Article XII of the WTO Agreement.

[2] A number of the 128 contracting parties 'succeeded' to the GATT as states for which the GATT had previously been applied on their behalf, e.g. as colonies or other dependants of the original contracting parties under Article XXVI:5(c) of the GATT.

by the time of its accession, or at least legally bound to be so by the time any phasing-in of obligations had expired. At the same time, an applicant negotiates commitments on tariffs and on services with existing members. The results of these bilateral negotiations are consolidated into the GATT and General Agreement on Trade in Services (GATS) schedules that establish a level of commitment to trade liberalisation comparable to that of other members. The applicant's schedules of tariff and services commitments and Protocol of Accession containing the commitments to WTO rules is adopted as a single package by the working party. In this way, the WTO accession process effectively validates, and collectively strengthens, WTO obligations every time a country completes the negotiations.

As a matter of policy, the United States supports WTO membership for all countries willing to incorporate WTO provisions into their trade regime and undertake trade-liberalising market access commitments. This is not just because the United States seeks an opportunity to expand trade-liberalising commitments that will benefit its exports, but also because the accession process itself reinforces the presumption that membership of the WTO has obligations as well as benefits. Members seeking an applicant's commitment to implement WTO provisions and to liberalise trade are also reminded of their own obligations in the process. The accession process re-orients a country's trade policies towards multilateral goals, e.g. it offers an instant trade relationship with all the other members, an opportunity to make collective trade rules, a broader forum for discussion and negotiations on trade issues and an agreed mechanism for resolving disputes.

Acceding to the WTO also supports the applicant's ongoing efforts towards economic reform and fuller integration into world markets. This is one of the most important benefits of accession. Economic reform is often politically and structurally difficult. In the short term, the established forms of income generation may be altered. However, for most WTO accession applicants, the long-term gains from making the changes necessary to join the WTO, e.g. simplifying customs rules, streamlining non-tariff measures, cutting tariffs and establishing a stable, transparent system of rules for importing and exporting, far outweigh the short-term difficulties. Implementing WTO provisions also supports important specific economic goals, such as achieving sustainable growth, promoting high-tech industry, attracting international investment, raising living standards and asserting national trade interests worldwide.

# 13

# WTO accessions: a market access perspective on growth – the approach of the European Union

CARLOS GIMENO VERDEJO

## ABSTRACT

*A strong multilateral trading system is vital to developing countries' long-term interests both for its rulebook and for the market access that it guarantees in all key markets. Markets are increasingly located in developing countries. Indeed, for the first time in recent history, South–South trade outweighs North–South trade, even though barriers to South–South trade are much more significant than those to developed countries' markets. Through their WTO accession, acceding economies can reap the benefits of more and better access to most world markets – that of the European Union being among the biggest.*

Market access is at the heart of European Union (EU) trade policy. Indeed, according to Article 206 of the Treaty on the Functioning of the European Union (TFEU),

> by establishing a customs union in accordance with Articles 28 to 32, the Union shall contribute, in the common interest, to the harmonious development of world trade, the progressive abolition of restrictions on international trade and on foreign direct investment (FDI), and the lowering of customs and other barriers.

Therefore, in (multilateral, plurilateral and bilateral) trade negotiations, the European Union seeks to improve and secure market access to third-country markets. This is the case in WTO accessions too.

Each accession being unique, there is no one-size-fits-all market access approach in the negotiations. As a result of the EU trade policy-making process, the European Union requests that flexibilities and targets be defined on a case-by-case basis while taking into account some general considerations.

This chapter attempts to: (i) shed some light on general considerations that play a role in the market access approaches followed by the

European Union in WTO accessions; (ii) describe the EU trade policy-making process; and (iii) identify some trends followed in the accession negotiations in the areas of trade in goods and services.

## General considerations in WTO accessions

### *An ambitious market access agenda*

Accessing markets[1] outside the European Union is crucial for jobs and growth within the European Union. An open and fair international trading system is one of the foundations of Europe's competitiveness. Addressing barriers to EU exports in other countries accounts for the bulk of the potential to improve the competitive position of EU industry. Its leading trading partners are less open than the European Union, sometimes significantly so.

The European Union therefore works to open new markets for its exporters and to improve the terms of trade around the world through its trade policy. In this regard, in line with the European Commission Communications on Global Europe[2] and on Trade, Growth and World Affairs,[3] the European Union, among other things:

- aims to reduce the barriers to the flow of goods and services in the European Union's export markets,[4] through a market access strategy designed to target and remove individual barriers in key markets. This involves negotiating the removal of tariff barriers and non-tariff barriers such as technical barriers to trade[5] and sanitary and phytosanitary measures (SPS);[6]

---

[1]  See http://ec.europa.eu/trade/policy/accessing-markets.
[2]  Communication from the Commission to the European Parliament, the Council, the European Economic and Social Committee and the Committee of the Regions, of 18 April 2007, Global Europe – a Stronger Partnership to Deliver Market Access for European Exporters (http://trade.ec.europa.eu/doclib/docs/2007/april/tradoc_134591.pdf).
[3]  Communication from the Commission to the European Parliament, the Council, the European Economic and Social Committee and the Committee of the Regions, of 9 November 2010, Trade, Growth and World Affairs – Trade Policy as a Core Component of the EU's 2020 Strategy (http://trade.ec.europa.eu/doclib/docs/2010/november/tradoc_146955.pdf).
[4]  See http://ec.europa.eu/trade/policy/accessing-markets/goods-and-services.
[5]  See http://trade.ec.europa.eu/doclib/html/150987.htm.
[6]  See http://trade.ec.europa.eu/doclib/html/150986.htm.

- wishes to access government procurement markets around the world[7] on fair terms;
- seeks to open up new opportunities for European investment and ensure predictability for EU companies to operate effectively in other markets.[8]

The Market Access Strategy pays particular attention to the needs of small and medium-sized enterprises that want to export to or invest in third countries.

Furthermore, when tariff or non-tariff barriers block the flow of primary goods into Europe or the access of European companies to markets outside Europe, Europe's competitiveness suffers. When anti-competitive practices distort or undermine resulting trade, Europe's competitiveness also suffers. Europe's market must be open to supplies of intermediary goods and raw materials for European producers of value-added products. Restricting this flow of goods raises costs for European companies, making them less competitive: the European Union needs to import to export.

Access to primary and secondary raw materials is therefore also a priority in EU trade policy. In this respect, in line with the 'raw materials initiative',[9] the European Union is promoting new rules and agreements on sustainable access to raw materials, where necessary, and ensuring compliance with international commitments at both multilateral and bilateral levels, including WTO accession negotiations, free trade agreements, regulatory dialogue and non-preferential agreements. In this context the European Commission has reinforced its work towards achieving stronger disciplines on export restrictions and improved regulation against subsidies at WTO level.

### Coherence with EU positions in the WTO

The European Union is committed to multilateralism and has acknowledged the fundamental importance of the WTO in the international trade system. Being one of the world's major global players in international trade, the European Union strongly supports the work of the WTO on multilateral rulemaking, trade liberalisation and sustainable

---

[7] See http://ec.europa.eu/trade/policy/accessing-markets/public-procurement.

[8] See http://ec.europa.eu/trade/policy/accessing-markets/investment.

[9] Communication from the Commission to the European Parliament and the Council of 4 November 2008, 'The Raw Materials Initiative — Meeting our Critical Needs for Growth and Jobs in Europe (http://eur-lex.europa.eu/LexUriServ/LexUriServ.do?uri=COM:2008: 0699:FIN:EN:PDF).

development. In this context, it has been an active player in the Doha
Development Agenda (DDA) since its launch in November 2001 in all
negotiating areas. As regards market access, the European Union has
indeed tabled and co-sponsored a good number of proposals for the
liberalisation of trade in goods and trade in services and for the establishment of disciplines in export duties.[10] Also, as regards the General
Agreement on Trade in Services (GATS) negotiations, the European
Union has submitted specific requests to its partners, either bilaterally[11]
or within the framework of collective requests.

The positions taken by the European Union in those submissions
and requests evidently serve as guidelines for market access negotiations
with acceding governments. In its requests, the European Union, not
surprisingly, will seek liberalisation commitments in line with those
proposed in the DDA and promote the use of the classification of services
sectors that it has proposed in the WTO.

The coherence with WTO positions is not only limited to the European Union 'offensive' market access agenda, though. In this respect, for
example, the European Union has a well-established position regarding
the promotion and protection of cultural diversity and, consequently,
like many other WTO members that also share the same values, does not
submit liberalisation requests in the field of audio-visual services.

### Specificities of the acceding economy and bilateral trade relations with that economy

At the time of negotiating market access, the economic level of development of an acceding economy matters. Trade is an integral part of
EU development policy[12] and, in this context, the European Commission
Communication Trade, Growth and Development[13] has clearly identified
a need for differentiation between developing countries. Against this
background, requests submitted to a big emerging economy will tend to
be more ambitious than those addressed to other developing countries,
and in particular to small and vulnerable economies and to least-developed

---

[10] See http://ec.europa.eu/trade/policy/eu-and-wto/doha-development-agenda/submissions.
[11] See http://trade.ec.europa.eu/doclib/docs/2005/january/tradoc_121197.pdf.
[12] See http://ec.europa.eu/trade/policy/countries-and-regions/development.
[13] Communication from the Commission to the European Parliament, the Council and the
European Economic and Social Committee, of 27 January 2012, Trade, Growth and
Development – Tailoring Trade and Investment Policy for Those Countries Most in
Need (http://trade.ec.europa.eu/doclib/docs/2012/january/tradoc_148992.EN.pdf).

countries (LDCs). As regards the latter, the European Union, in line with the WTO LDC accession guidelines,[14] to which it is fully committed,[15] has continuously supported and facilitated the accession of LDCs and, while preserving the integrity of WTO rules, has exercised due restraint as regards market opening and assisted LDCs in enacting and implementing new disciplines.

The economic structure of a country also matters. For example, European Union requests on the liberalisation of energy services and on the removal/reduction of export duties on energy raw materials will tend to be different for countries which are energy suppliers and for those which are not. Also, the level of ambition of European Union requests on maritime transport will naturally tend to be more modest in accession negotiations with landlocked countries.

Bilateral trade relations with the acceding government are also taken into consideration. In this respect, for example, if trade in goods between the acceding economy and the European Union is already substantially liberalised on the basis of a preferential economic integration agreement, there is little incentive to pursue ambitious requests for the reduction of most-favoured-nation (MFN) tariffs in the WTO.

### The precedents

Market access commitments undertaken by economies that have acceded to the WTO since it was established certainly provide a useful point of reference for market access negotiations with acceding governments. To calibrate the requests addressed to an acceding government, EU negotiators will normally look at, and take into consideration, the commitments that countries whose economies are similar to that of the acceding economy undertook at the time of acceding to the WTO.

## Trade policy-making in the European Union and WTO accessions

Trade policy-making in the European Union[16] is defined by Articles 207 and 218 of the TFEU. Trade negotiations are conducted by the

---

[14] Decision of the WTO General Council of 10 December 2002 (WT/L/508) and Decision of the WTO General Council of 25 July 2012 (WT/L/508/Add. 1).

[15] See report of the meeting of the General Council of 25 July 2012 (WT/GC/M/137), p. 32.

[16] See http://ec.europa.eu/trade/policy/policy-making and http://trade.ec.europa.eu/doclib/docs/2013/april/tradoc_150988.pdf.

European Commission, which negotiates with the trading partner on behalf of the European Union. During the negotiations, the European Commission works in close coordination with the European Union member states by consulting with the Trade Policy Committee, which is a working group of the Council of Ministers of the European Union in charge of discussing the full range of trade policy issues, and which keeps the European Parliament fully informed. In the end, the negotiating outcome has to be formally validated by the Council of Ministers of the European Union and, in most cases, by the European Parliament too.

In the WTO, where both the European Union and the twenty-eight EU member states are members, it is the European Commission which represents the European Union at Ministerial Conferences, the General Council and subsidiary bodies. The positions to be adopted therein on the European Union's behalf require the adoption of a decision by the Council of Ministers of the European Union in conformity with Article 218, paragraph 9, of the TFEU.

When it comes to WTO accessions, the European Commission represents the European Union in the meetings of the working parties (the multilateral track of the negotiations) and also negotiates bilaterally with the acceding government its market access commitments and other terms of its accession. Once an acceptable accession package (working party report, draft schedule of commitments on goods and draft schedule of commitments on services) for a given acceding government emerges, the European Commission submits to the Council of Ministers of the European Union a draft decision establishing the EU (favourable) position to be adopted at the WTO Ministerial Conference or the General Council that approves the accession. The European Commission will express that position on the accession approval once the decision has been formally adopted by the Council of Ministers of the European Union, a procedure which requires some time.

To secure successful outcomes in the negotiations, the European Commission has to reconcile EU member states' concerns and priorities with the positions of trading partners. Therefore, the European Commission not only has a legal obligation to consult the member states, but also has an interest in doing so. In the area of WTO accessions, the European Commission shares with them, via the Trade Policy Committee, bilateral offers or other proposals not circulated through the WTO system, and also discusses with them the positions that it intends to take in the negotiations. In this regard, besides including in the Trade Policy Committee meetings agenda items related to ad hoc accessions, the European

Commission tries to report regularly on all ongoing WTO accession negotiations. These regular reports are issued (as well as presented to and discussed with the member states) every four months. They are also presented to the European Parliament, more specifically to its Committee on International Trade (the INTA Committee), which also receives all the different documents related to accession that the European Commission transmits to the Trade Policy Committee in the Council.

The European Commission also consults with other interested groups (e.g. civil society) in the formulation of trade policy.[17]

The central role that the European Commission plays in trade negotiations is confirmed at the time of defining market access priorities in WTO accessions. Its market access database,[18] an interactive and free online service, contains valuable information on more than one hundred countries, including some WTO acceding economies, on:

. import tariffs and internal taxes;
. import formalities (e.g. customs procedures and requirements) with samples of all the necessary forms;
. the most important trade barriers faced by EU exporters abroad.

Relying on these data, on the information provided by EU delegations in the acceding economies and on the inputs submitted by EU economic operators (both those based in the European Union and those based in third countries), the Commission will carry out an assessment of the level of autonomous trade liberalisation of the acceding economy concerned and identify the key trade barriers in that market for EU business. Based on that assessment and identification, and taking into account the general considerations mentioned above, it will prepare the EU position in reaction to the acceding government's market access offers.

Member states' views on the positions that the Commission presents to them at the Trade Policy Committee will most probably already have been integrated therein. Indeed, to be more effective, in recent years the Commission has established a market access partnership with member states and European businesses. This has implied much more systematic contact and cooperation at all levels, both within the European Union and in third countries. The Commission, member states and business are working together better to establish priorities

---

[17] http://trade.ec.europa.eu/doclib/docs/2013/april/tradoc_150988.pdf.
[18] http://madb.europa.eu/madb.

for action in barrier removal, as well as linking databases and developing a network of market access specialists.

This has been particularly important on the ground in key third-country markets, where local knowledge is strongest. Commission delegations, member state embassies and European businesses operating in foreign markets are familiar with the local administrative structures and processes and usually best placed to offer initial reviews of market access problems, to identify cases requiring coordinated action with specialists in Brussels and to conduct local follow-up.

This Market Access Partnership, designed to identify and remove the specific obstacles that EU companies face in foreign markets, is made up of:

- the Market Access Advisory Committee, which brings together the European Commission, member states and business representatives once a month in Brussels to exchange information and develop strategies on how to remove barriers, which is a sort of steering committee for the Market Access Strategy;
- specific working groups[19] that examine trade barriers in specific sectors by pooling the technical expertise of representatives from the European Commission, member states and business, and meet on an ad hoc basis in Brussels;
- the market access teams managed by EU delegations in non-EU countries, involving the Commission, member states, the private sector (for example EU Chambers of Commerce) and, where appropriate, other EU stakeholders, which gather local expertise to identify and tackle trade barriers.

## Trends for EU positions in WTO accession negotiations

### Trade in goods

#### Tariffs

The European Union negotiates tariffs with all acceding WTO members. The intensity of that negotiation will differ depending on the EU access priorities in the market at stake and on the other considerations referred to above (e.g. LDC status, existence of a preferential trade agreement). With this caveat, some general trends may, however, be identified in the

---

[19] See http://trade.ec.europa.eu/doclib/html/147653.htm.

positions that the European Union takes in its reaction to tariff offers tabled by acceding governments, including:

. the request to have the broadest possible binding coverage of tariff lines;
. elimination (i.e. binding at 0) immediately after accession or, exceptionally, after a short transitional period, of 'other duties and charges';
. a more offensive stance on non-agricultural market access, with special attention being paid to products covered by the WTO Information Technology Agreement (e.g. computers, telephones and inputs and components such as semiconductors) and by the WTO Agreement on Trade in Civil Aircraft. In line with the EU position in the DDA, special attention is also given to the liberalisation of sectors such as chemicals, motor vehicles, machinery, electronics, pharmaceutical and medical devices, and agricultural and construction equipment;
. special attention to divergences between the rates proposed and those currently applied;
. special attention to tariff peaks.

## Export duties

Beyond the DDA round of negotiations, the European Union and other WTO members have developed an approach in the context of WTO accession negotiations to propose disciplines (bindings) on export duties to a range of acceding economies relevant from a raw materials supply perspective. China, Russia, Saudi Arabia, Tajikistan, Ukraine and Viet Nam have thus undertaken obligations on export duties at the time of their accession to the WTO. Among countries still negotiating their accession in 2013, those of clearest interest to the European Union in terms of raw materials supply include Afghanistan, Algeria, Azerbaijan, Belarus, Iran, Iraq and Kazakhstan.

Results obtained through this approach are described in the European Commission Activity Reports on the EU Trade Policy in Raw Materials. The Second Activity Report, issued on 30 May 2012,[20] contains the following information on specific accessions:

> Russia's WTO accession negotiations were completed end 2011. Russia undertook to reduce and/or cap the levels of applied export duties on 700-odd HS10 tariff lines of products, mainly raw materials (fish, gas

---

[20] EU Trade Policy for Raw Materials – Second Activity Report of 30 May 2012 (http://trade.ec.europa.eu/doclib/docs/2012/may/tradoc_149515.pdf).

and oil products, plastic, hides and skins, precious stones and metals, and base metals), with elimination or reduction at WTO entry or over a transition period. For certain wood products, reduced export duties will apply within a quota. This will be administered by a Commission implementing Regulation setting up a system of EU management of the Russian export TRQs [tariff rate quotas]. This system involves Member States quota authorizations and corresponding Russia export licenses.

In addition to these commitments, following intensive bilateral negotiations, a solution was agreed for export duties on raw materials not included in the above list: through an exchange of letters, Russia must undertake its best efforts not to introduce new export duties on these goods, and in any case hold prior consultations with the EU should it envisage doing so.

Discussions related to Kazakhstan's WTO accession developed over the 2010–2011 period and are still on-going. The EU determined its specific interests based on a diverse set of criteria, including current Kazakh raw materials exports to the EU and to the world, the potential of Kazakhstan as a supplier based on its known geological reserves, as well as more generally EU main import interests.

As regards the WTO accession of Tajikistan, a commitment was secured on the prohibition of export duties or taxes, except for a list of products with bound rates.[21]

## Trade in services

The European Union also negotiates services commitments and MFN exemptions with all WTO acceding governments. In this respect, the same caveat mentioned for tariffs applies *mutatis mutandis* and only very general trends may be identified in the EU positions. These would be:

- requests seeking substantial coverage of the services sector being liberalised;
- special attention to those service sectors for which the European Union has submitted liberalisation proposals under the GATS, such as some professional and some business services, postal and courier services, telecommunications services, construction services, distribution services, environmental services, financial services, tourism services, and some transport and energy services;

---

[21]  See http://ec.europa.eu/trade/policy/accessing-markets/goods-and-services/raw-materials/.

- promotion of the use of the classification of some services sectors proposed by the European Union (e.g. postal and courier, telecommunications, environmental);
- special attention to liberalisation of mode 3, in line with the EU investment agenda and in the conviction of the 'win–win' results of this liberalisation FDI attraction for the acceding economy and business opportunities for EU companies;
- special attention to the divergences between the commitments proposed and the level of autonomous liberalisation in the acceding economy;
- a constructive stance *vis-à-vis* market access and/or national treatment limitations that replicate the very few that the European Union would be maintaining on the basis of the services offers that it has tabled in the DDA.

There is no crystal ball to predict the level of market access that an acceding government has to offer to secure the successful completion of bilateral negotiations with the European Union (and with other WTO members). Some general considerations and trends described above can provide some guidance on the ingredients. Mixing them, offers will then have to be fine-tuned in the course of the negotiations. To that end the European Union, as a strong supporter of WTO accessions, will cooperate and always be open to a constructive dialogue with the acceding government.

# 14

# WTO accessions: a rules perspective on growth – the approach of the European Union

RUTA ZARNAUSKAITE

## ABSTRACT

*In today's difficult economic conditions and in the aftermath of the global financial crisis, growth is more than ever the priority of governments. Economic growth, employment, wealth, health and political stability are intrinsically linked notions, and each is essential for the others. Trade and economic integration have been credited as core means to deliver growth. The heads of the EU member states have recently reiterated the importance of free, fair and open trade for growth, and have highlighted the European Union's objective to promote, among other things, international regulatory convergence. Trade liberalisation is a major structural reform in itself, creating incentives for investments, modernisation and increased competitiveness. Moreover, in a world of increasing production interdependence as a consequence of global supply chains, achieving regulatory convergence is not a question for consideration but an imminent necessity if trade and growth are to be preserved and stimulated. The WTO offers both a beacon for economic reforms and an unprecedented forum for economic partnership.*

This chapter has four main parts. First, it addresses the issue of the systemic and institutional importance of adherence to WTO rules for the growth of different economies and emphasises how the process of accession to the WTO plays a special role in achieving this objective. The second and third parts present two types of WTO working party reports of acceding economies: sanitary and phytosanitary (SPS) measures and transparency. In order to illustrate the contribution of regulatory convergence to economic gains, several examples are provided in the area of SPS from the European Union's internal harmonisation experience and the chapter outlines the European Union's approach with regard to this area of regulation in the WTO accession negotiations. The argument is made that in order to create regulatory conditions for growth in addition to substantive convergence, it is indispensable to ensure transparency of the environment and procedures to make and implement regulations. Finally, before concluding, the discussion turns to one of the key dilemmas for every acceding economy: the need to liberalise for the sake of growth through modernisation and diversification, on the one hand, and the need to protect fragile domestic industries, on the other.

## WTO: a unique platform to anchor growth-targeting reforms

The WTO is founded on the assumption that free trade and the use of competitive advantages will enable global economic growth. When seeking economic growth, countries are better served to aim at 'sustainable' growth that can secure long-term effects. Thus, well-crafted, long-sighted policies are essential. Balanced regulations are generally better suited to bringing the expected sustainable growth, as opposed to temporary and ad hoc measures. The latter often serve self-centred protectionism, which, albeit tempting due to possible short-term gains for selected constituencies, cannot secure balanced future growth. And that is for the very reason that they are adopted at short notice in reaction to new, often transitory circumstances or changes in political leadership. More frequently they overlook broader considerations and long-term implications, which is what need to be kept in mind to achieve sustainable growth. To quote former WTO Director-General Pascal Lamy, 'we should remember that the gains [globalisation] brings could be nullified or at least mitigated if short-term pressures are allowed to override long-term interests' (WTO, 2013). From the economic operator's point of view, it is the so-called 'risk premium' that is at stake: '[W]ith a certain amount of rule stability, there can be a reduction in the risk involved in the billions of decisions made every day by millions of entrepreneurs in a market-oriented system' (Jackson, 2003).

Since the creation of the WTO in 1995, the candidates to accede to the WTO have been predominantly emerging and developing economies and least-developed countries (LDCs). That means economies with dynamically changing regulatory bases or those planned to be transformed. Therefore, in terms of boosting growth through regulatory reforms, WTO membership interests these countries for at least three reasons.

First, being nearly universal, time unlimited and subject to regular peer review (via the Trade Policy Review Body, but also through the work of other regular WTO bodies), the WTO serves as an effective international establishment in which to deposit a member's commitment to free trade and restrict the freedom of domestic politics to alter the direction of travel for the sake of short-term objectives. Moreover, the dispute settlement system of the WTO has been effectively used to enforce the obligations of members. Thus, from the internal point of view, one of the motives for a candidate to accede to the WTO is to anchor its own domestic reforms geared toward trade liberalisation, modernisation and enhanced competitiveness.

Second, from the external point of view, one of the key objectives of any economy is to improve access to export markets by removing non-tariff barriers. New export markets open new opportunities for business to sell more, to expand and to diversify destinations in order to secure sustainable demand. Since the early days of governmental trade relations, the removal of the most obvious of trade barriers to access external markets – customs tariffs – has been the first priority in trade agreements. However, it is the non-tariff barriers, be they the mandatory requirements, customs procedures or state ownership rules of a country, which constitute the major bulk of barriers in today's trade. To boost growth, transaction costs need to be minimised and new value added. Diverging regulations and, thus, standards, requirements, procedures, etc., contribute considerably to the costs of the final product.

To address this reality, at the creation of the WTO in 1995, a number of agreements, now constituting what are called the 'covered agreements' of the WTO, were added to the old General Agreement on Tariffs and Trade (GATT) to help reduce some of the main non-tariff barriers. These agreements impose basic principles and often quite specific requirements for regulations in a particular field. Since the WTO's rules have been accepted nearly universally, the level playing field created by the WTO is unique and distinct from broad-ranging and ever-expanding regional initiatives. Once a government or customs state territory joins the WTO pool, it reaps the benefits of access to the export markets of all WTO members.

Finally, and still from the external point of view, one should not overlook the value of access to imports through increased regulatory liberalisation and convergence. In the light of the conclusions from the recent joint study by the WTO and the Organisation for Economic Co-operation and Development (OECD) of trade in value added (also known as the study on global value chains) (OECD, 2013), the demonstrated growing interdependence of international production underpins the importance of the WTO's principles and mission. Countries need inputs from each other in order to advance their own economic activity. In other words, it is not only exports, but also imports that are crucial for growth and further export expansion. The report on global value chains makes it clear that access not only to cheaper imports of goods, but often also essential services, plays a vital role in diversifying production and in the adoption of the newest technologies, inspiring innovation and thus spurring sustainable growth at home. The level of regulatory convergence imposed by the WTO ensures easier access to foreign goods and services used by domestic industries.

Thus, all three prerequisites for growth – stability of internal economic regulation, predictable access to external markets and access to foreign goods and services – can be facilitated through adherence to WTO norms. The accession process represents a necessary step and an unmatched opportunity for a critical look at the regulatory regime of all future members. It allows them to assess their readiness to join the WTO community and helps set in motion the reform process for fully-fledged participation in global economic governance.

It is for these reasons that the European Union has been systematically engaged in consultations with acceding governments not only on the market access side of the accession terms but also, and with no less vigour, on the rules side. Upon the initial presentation of the regulatory regime by a candidate, a lengthy discussion commences between this candidate and members of the working party on its accession, in order to clarify the existing regime and specify the regulatory changes needed to bring it in line with the WTO rules. There are the usual suspects in the areas where the most heated and complex discussions develop, which unambiguously relate to the most persistent non-tariff barriers.

## Case study: SPS measures

Agricultural trade makes up somewhat less than 10 per cent of world trade, but by its nature remains vital for certain constituencies in each country, whether developed, least developing or least-developed country. In today's world, agricultural trade is often hampered not by high tariffs, but by SPS measures stemming from regulations and/or their implementation or lack thereof. While such measures could be used to achieve legitimate policy objectives (food safety, consumer protection, animal health, etc.), they are, arguably, sometimes used to manipulate the terms of trade and protect domestic producers from foreign competition.

This chapter will proceed to demonstrate how international harmonisation of the regulatory regime in a substantive area such as SPS measures could deliver economic gains, through the example of the European Union's internal harmonisation.

Until the mid-1960s, the member states of the then European Economic Community had a diversity of rules governing food safety and measures against animal diseases. At that time, international bodies such as the International Plant Protection Convention (IPPC) and the Codex Alimentarius, which are currently accepted as reference institutions for common standards, were just beginning their work. The work of the World Organisation for Animal Health (Office International des Epizooties (OIE)) was already well under way. Lack of harmonised requirements for animal breeding, food processing, etc., meant that the disease situation varied across European countries. Poor hygienic conditions were posing a significant threat to public health (e.g. brucellosis and tuberculosis in cattle posed a risk of transmission to humans). The spread of diseases led to great loss of livestock. Trade was increasing the risk of transmission beyond national borders. In turn, lack of harmonisation and unpredictability of risks compelled member states to implement disproportionately protectionist measures. An overall result was an artificial cap on growth potential and an impediment to free trade within the internal European Economic Community market.

Then, in the mid-1960s, a new approach was endorsed by leaders of the European Economic Community to put an end to regulatory divergences and consolidate the regulation, based on science and in line with the uniform international standards of the OIE (and later of the Codex Alimentarius and IPPC). The main goals were to improve the health situation of livestock across Europe and eliminate or reduce the frequency of diseases causing economic losses and threats to human health. Between 1964 and 1993, a body of fundamental veterinary legislation was elaborated foreseeing common safety standards, including the surveillance of major diseases, rules for the restriction and elimination of sick animals and vaccination campaigns. That created conditions, in 1993, to implement the common market, which meant virtually no intra-EU SPS barriers for trade in animal products, and standardised safety conditions for live animals.[1] As a result, the economic gains were

---

[1] The summary description of the currently applicable SPS regime of the European Union is provided for in the most recent Trade Policy Review Report by the WTO Secretariat; see WTO document WT/TPR/S/284 of 28 May 2013, paragraphs 3.105–3.128.

threefold: (i) the health situation of animal stock improved and further damage was avoided; (ii) the adoption of common rules and the principle of solidarity increased confidence and allowed businesses to expand their production capacities; and (iii) the uniform standards made the intra-EU system integrated and removed the question of whether products could travel freely and be marketed across the territory of the European Union. It enlarged the trading area of previously regionally traded products, bringing more diversity to consumers and expanding intra-EU trade possibilities. Predictability and convergence cut all the transaction costs previously associated with import procedures and other administrative burdens in the way of reaching consumers in another member state. A level playing field for operators and simplified procedures also helped to fight corruption – a further economic and institutional advantage.

It seems very likely that a similar result could be achieved among WTO members through adherence to international standards and norms as well as acceptance of aligned regulatory regimes for certification, systems' auditing, etc. The SPS Agreement was devised with a twofold objective in mind: (i) to render agricultural liberalisation effective given the notorious sensitivity of the sector; and (ii) to balance trade policy with health policy. It encourages members to adhere to existing international standards and requires them to base SPS measures on science where they choose to deviate from international norms. Approximation to the latter would enable members to come closer to each other in their regimes for food safety and protection of the life and health of humans, animals and plants. It is no less important to harmonise the administrative procedures associated with the realisation of the cited objectives, e.g. related to risk assessment, than to observe the principles of proportionality, necessity and reasonableness – not only at the stage of setting the appropriate level of protection, but also when choosing measures to achieve that level of protection.

Given the sensitivity of issues at stake, members use the WTO accession talks to assess in detail the SPS regime of the acceding government against the benchmark set by the WTO. A discussion on the existing conditions, problems and desired changes is essential for several purposes: (i) increased awareness about the functioning of the regime, essential for business operations; (ii) guidance for the acceding government on the required regulatory changes and changes in practices of implementing authorities; and, equally important, (iii) as a precondition for constructive future cooperation with WTO members and prevention of disputes on known contentious issues.

The most prominent example is the report of the working party on the accession of Russia to the WTO,[2] which dedicates nearly ninety pages (249 paragraphs, a table and annex) to the SPS regime applicable in the country along with regulatory changes requested by members in order for Russia to adhere to the WTO norms and international principles. The unparalleled level of detail could be explained by several factors, but, most notably, by the variety of persistent SPS barriers faced by a number of working party members. Also important was the quickly changing regulatory regime due to the establishment of the Customs Union of Belarus, Kazakhstan and Russia, whereby regulatory competences in the area of SPS were transferred to supranational institutions. The working party report not only describes the new regime and planned reforms, but also includes very precise commitments related to alignment to specific international norms. For example, it includes commitments to implement, from the date of accession, Codex Alimentarius guidelines related to a national regulatory food safety assurance programme regarding veterinary drugs in food-producing animals, to align to relevant Codex Alimentarius codes of practice for on-site inspections and to apply relevant international norms in the procedures for recognition of equivalence, as well as to bring the maximum residue levels of specified pesticides and maximum level of nitrates into line with international standards.[3] Furthermore, Russia committed itself to engage in negotiations with interested members on the process of amending the applicable system of veterinary requirements and certificates.[4] Also, some commitments were dedicated to tackling specific existing practices that working party members considered incompatible with WTO norms, e.g. regarding the issuance, grounds for refusal and appropriate application of permits on imports of goods subject to veterinary control,[5] concerning on-site inspections, suspension of imports based on inspections or systemic failures of the official system of control,[6] to eliminate the practice of applying veterinary requirements for goods in transit,[7] and to amend the relevant domestic act in order to bring it in line with international norms concerning importation of plants with soil attached.[8]

---

[2] See WTO documents: WT/ACC/RUS/70, WT/MIN(11)/2, 17 November 2011.
[3] See ibid., paragraphs 844, 932, 1030, 1031, 981 and 989 respectively.
[4] See ibid., paragraph 893.      [5] See ibid., paragraphs 870, 875 and 876.
[6] See ibid., paragraphs 950, 926 and 928 respectively.      [7] See ibid., paragraph 880.
[8] See ibid., paragraph 944.

## Case study: transparency[9]

Transparency requirements relate innately to the institutional set-up of any member. Predictability of the functioning of the institutional system in creating, modifying and implementing the regulatory regime are crucial for any business or investment decision and thus to the growth potential of a country. On the one hand, it has been increasingly recognised that markets will not work without appropriate institutions. On the other, the lack of transparency of national regulations functions as another non-tariff barrier.[10]

WTO agreements include a number of rules governing several key aspects of transparency obligations:[11] to publish all trade measures of general application promptly and in such a manner that all interested parties can access them (the jurisprudence of the WTO clarified that the publication is a precondition for enforcement),[12] to establish a single enquiry point for information, to notify relevant WTO bodies on the implementation of negotiated commitments or changes to the legal regime, to provide due process to and inform interested parties of essential facts in trade defence instruments' cases, to publish the exchange rate used for customs value determination, etc. In some cases, the rules impose that trade measures can be adopted only after a prior public consultation (e.g. new technical barriers to trade (TBT)

---

[9] This contribution addresses the principle of transparency as applied by WTO contracting parties and not by the WTO as an international organisation.

[10] See, for example, an elaboration of this phenomenon by Van den Bossche (2005: 467–471).

[11] The main transparency requirements can be found in Article X of the General Agreement on Tariffs and Trade (GATT) 1994, Articles III and III *bis* of the General Agreement on Trade in Services (GATS), Article 18 of the Agreement on Agriculture, Articles 6, 7 and 12 of the Agreement on Implementation of Article VI of the GATT 1994, Articles 9 and 12 of the Agreement on Implementation of Article VII of the GATT 1994, Articles 1 and 5 of the Agreement on Import Licensing Procedures, Article 5 of the Agreement on Preshipment Inspection, Articles 2, 3 and 5 of the Agreement on Rules of Origin, Articles 3 and 12 of the Agreement on Safeguards, Article 7 and Annex b of the Agreement on the Application of Sanitary and Phytosanitary Measures, Articles 22 and 25 of the Agreement on Subsidies and Countervailing Duties, Article 2 and Annex 3 of the Agreement on Technical Barriers to Trade, Article 63 of the Agreement on Trade-Related Aspects of Intellectual Property Rights, Article 6 of the Agreement on Trade-Related Investment Measures, and Articles XVII and XVIII of the Agreement on Government Procurement. With regard to some of these provisions, exceptions apply as provided for in relevant agreements.

[12] See Report of the Appellate Body in *United States – Underwear*; see WTO document WT/DS24/AB/R.

standards), or only enter into force after a reasonable interval upon their publication (e.g. SPS regulations) so that economic operators can adapt to the new requirements. Many of the above-mentioned transparency requirements are subject to general exceptions and/or exceptions related to law enforcement, other public interests or legitimate commercial interests and confidentiality. Observance of transparency requirements in the WTO is carried out through the periodic Trade Policy Review Mechanism.

The European Union attaches great importance to transparency in making regulations and to accountability to its stakeholders for policy decisions taken. Therefore, in its internal procedures the European Union has adopted an approach going beyond the WTO requirements. The Treaty on the European Union and the Treaty on the Functioning of the European Union (TFEU) include provisions regarding the principle of transparency.[13] Transparency in relation to regulatory initiatives starts very early, in the pre-legislative stage. Every five years, the European Commission publishes a five-year programme setting out the strategic objectives of that period. This programme is later specified in the Annual Policy Strategy, which is presented for consultation to the Council, European Parliament and other relevant EU institutions. Following this inter-institutional dialogue, the European Commission adopts a detailed work programme for a particular year, which lists the legislative and non-legislative measures to be introduced. Certain important policy initiatives are also sketched out in so-called green papers[14] which are subject to public consultation. In order to improve public consultations and obtain a better understanding of the needs of stakeholders, as well as to provide interested stakeholders with an active say in regulation-making, in 2001, the European Union launched the interactive policy making initiative. This is an online consultation platform allowing for improved assessment of the impact of planned policies or their absence. It has permitted the successful launch of more than 370 public consultations, available on the web portal 'Your Voice in Europe',[15] which is the single access point

---

[13] The most relevant provision of the EU treaties related to transparency are: Articles 1, 10(3), 11(2), 11(3) and 16(8) of the Treaty on the European Union, and Article 15(2) and (3) of the TFEU. The latter provision is the most elaborate and sets out such obligations to ensure transparent legislative process, publication of legal acts and access to documents. The right of access to documents is also provided for by Article 42 of the Charter of Fundamental Rights, which, since 2009, has been incorporated into the EU treaties.

[14] See http://ec.europa.eu/green-papers/index_en.htm.

[15] See more on this initiative and public consultations at http://ec.europa.eu/yourvoice/index_en.htm.

for European Commission consultations.[16] A number of legislative initiatives will require impact assessment, which is also conducted in close consultation with civil society stakeholders.[17] Finally, the legislation in the pipeline is publicly available at every stage of the legislative process on the dedicated Internet portal for stakeholders' information in all twenty-four EU official languages.[18]

Once a legal act has been adopted, it has to be published in the Official Journal of the European Union and only upon its publication can it enter into force. As for post-legislation, the more recent Communication on EU Regulatory Fitness[19] highlighted the European Commission's commitment to strengthening its various smart regulation tools (impact assessment, evaluation, stakeholder consultation) and launched the Regulatory Fitness and Performance Programme. Through this, the European Commission services have mapped the entire EU legislative stock, by each policy area, looking to identify burdens, gaps and inefficient or ineffective measures, including possibilities for simplification or repeal. The initial findings of the European Commission are publicly available and give a good idea of what it considers should be done to improve regulation in each policy area, including trade and SPS, so as to better respond to the needs of the European Union and its stakeholders.[20] This illustrates that the European Union sees transparency not as a goal in itself but as a core principle, adherence to which is essential to fulfil the European Union's public service function.

Furthermore, Regulation No. 1049/2001[21] on access to documents provides the public with a right to enquire about any document, including those relating to preparatory work for the legal acts as well as

---

[16] For further detail on the EU policy with regard to public consultations on policy initiatives, see, among others, A White Paper by the European Commission on European Governance, COM(2001) 428 final; Communication from the Commission, European Governance: Better Lawmaking, COM(2002) 275 final; and Communication from the Commission, Towards a Reinforced Culture of Consultation and Dialogue – General Principles and Minimum Standards for Consultation of Interested Parties by the Commission, COM(2002) 704 final.

[17] See more on impact assessment of the European Commission at http://ec.europa.eu/governance/impact/index_en.htm.

[18] Legislation in the pipeline can be followed at http://ec.europa.eu/prelex/apcnet.cfm?CL=en.

[19] Communication from the Commission to the European Parliament, the Council, the European Economic and Social Committee and the Committee of the Regions, EU Regulatory Fitness, COM(2012) 746 final.

[20] Commission Staff Working Document, Regulatory Fitness and Performance Programme (REFIT): Initial Results of the Mapping of the Acquis, SWD(2013) 401 final.

[21] Regulation (EC) No. 1049/2001 of the European Parliament and of the Council of 30 May 2001 regarding public access to European Parliament, Council and Commission documents.

documents emanating from the member states. This right is limited by a few defined exceptions. Finally, the European Ombudsman and the European Court of Justice supervise how the EU institutions observe the principle of transparency in their work.

To ensure transparency, the European Union, alongside its WTO partners, consistently seeks commitments from candidate partners in the WTO accession negotiations. Specific commitments often extend the standard provisions of the WTO in that they reflect the particular situation of the individual candidate and identify specific steps which the working party considers essential in order to improve the predictability and the attractiveness of the acceding economy for investment and doing business. For instance, acceding economies specify where and how their regulations and other trade measures will be published (e.g. China, Lao PDR, Russia, Samoa (transitional arrangements foreseen), Saudi Arabia, Tajikistan and Ukraine); commit to establishing a single or several dedicated enquiry points to assist with information concerning any trade measure upon an interested party's request (e.g. China, Russia); commit to publish information that is not specified in the WTO agreements as subject to mandatory publication (e.g. state-regulated railway tariffs, by Russia; names of entities and contact points in charge of implementing specific trade measures, by Saudi Arabia); commit to provide more specific information upon individual request of interested parties (e.g. on the revenue collected from a specific customs fee or charge and on the costs of providing the associated services, by Russia); or commit that their trade measures will be translated into one or more official languages of the WTO so that economic operators have easier access to them (China). Some new members also commit to consulting stakeholders on draft measures prior to their adoption (e.g. China, Russia, Samoa, Saudi Arabia, Tajikistan and Ukraine) or to publish information concerning the implementation of certain procedures otherwise not required by the WTO rules (e.g. a list of organisations/authorities in charge of regulating services activities, by China; a list of accredited certification bodies related to technical regulations, by Russia). Many of these commitments are subject to exceptions specified in the individual working party reports.

## The acceding economy's dilemma: the need to liberalise vs international competition

First of all, it is worth recalling the positive phenomenon of intra-industry trade: countries may export and import similar products but instead of facing a 'win–lose' situation competitors would end up in a 'win–win' situation. This is because of consumers' love of variety, leading to overall higher consumption, on the one hand, and economies of scale in production on each side, on the other.[22] This is to say that opening a specific segment of one market to foreign competition does not automatically lead to a reduction in domestic economic activity in that sector. Instead, it can be an important opportunity for growth. Furthermore, it means domestic supply at affordable prices for consumers, thus doubling its contribution to economic welfare by improving households' purchasing power. However, certain conditions have to be met: products have to be similar (in terms of quality, among other factors) but not perfectly substitutable, so as to permit consumer preferences to vary to a certain degree.

Yet, very often, acceding governments face a different scenario: their producers or service providers cannot compete in terms of quality or price due to lagging technologies and/or inefficient production methods. Accepting international regulatory standards, substantive or institutional, may entail high costs (new legislation, staff training, installation of new IT technologies or physical facilities, etc.). Adherence to multilateral norms in the area of SPS is a case in point. Thus, building a competitive domestic industry will require knowledge, designated financial resources and time. It is in these instances that openness to global markets is associated with job losses in sectors that are uncompetitive, and not with growth.

Hence, certain constituencies of an acceding economy call to suspend the process which, in their view, is likely to deliver immediate gains for existing WTO members but temporary or even mid-term negative effects to their economy due to the reduced competitiveness of domestic producers or service suppliers. In reality, WTO accession does not reduce companies' competitiveness but exposes those companies to international competition which will reveal their existing lack of competitiveness. Effectively, such exposure is what is often necessary to provide for incentives to modernise and increase efficiency or go out of business, leaving the market for products and services of better quality and price. The resulting social costs and anxiety are real and call for an appropriate policy response, but they should not lead to overlooking the strongly positive effects that openness and integration into world markets have on a country's overall economic performance.

This is easier said than done. In order to mitigate the expected negative effects for certain lagging sectors, the acceding government should, at the outset, accompany economic reforms with legitimate internal policies geared to help redeploy the uncompetitive production factors (by retraining, relocation, etc.) where appropriate. It is crucial to make the smooth

---

[22] See further elaboration of this phenomenon in WTO (2013: 69).

adjustments necessary in ailing industries or regions and, thus, maximise the overall benefits of economic openness. In this respect, competitiveness must begin with the right domestic policies in relation to education, elasticity of the labour market, innovation, protection of intellectual property and a number of other areas directly linked to creation of a friendly business and investment climate.

In conclusion, it can be reiterated that integration into global markets and enhanced regulatory convergence are not just options in today's world of consolidating production chains. They are necessary for the growth of every economy. The WTO encompasses a range of basic rules that, once observed, pave the way for a more level playing field and serve as a springboard for further economic approximation. The history of the European Union's domestic harmonisation offers examples of how cutting regulatory barriers, both substantive and institutional, stimulates economic activity. The WTO emulates these results on a global scale and provides a unique platform to anchor domestic reforms aimed at fully fledged participation in international economic governance. The process of accession to the WTO is an exclusive opportunity for every acceding government to obtain assistance from WTO members to evaluate their trade regime against international benchmarks and to set a regulatory reform programme in motion. However, from the very outset, economic reforms need to be carefully balanced with other domestic policy adjustments, including in the areas of education, innovation and employment, so as to respond to the sensitivities of particular constituencies.

## Acknowledgement

The author acknowledges the valuable input from colleagues Ms Catherine Chapoux and Ms Lucie Carrovée working at the European Commission in the field of health and consumer protection.

## References

Jackson, J. H. (2003). 'The impact of China's accession on the WTO', in D. Z. Cass, B. G. Williams and G. Barker (eds.), *China and the World Trading System: Entering the New Millennium*. Cambridge University Press.

Organisation for Economic Co-operation and Development (OECD) (2013). *Interconnected Economies: Benefiting from Global Value Chains: Synthesis Report*. Paris, OECD.

Van den Bossche, P. (2005). *The Law and Policy of the World Trade Organization: Text, Cases and Materials*. Cambridge University Press.

World Trade Organization (WTO) (2013). *World Trade Report 2013: Factors Shaping the Future of World Trade*. Geneva, WTO.

# 15

# WTO accession negotiations: trends and results in agriculture plurilaterals

JULIE-ANN GUIVARRA

ABSTRACT

*Thirty-three members have acceded to the WTO since it was established in 1995. In the majority of these accession negotiations, reforms to the agriculture sector have featured as a particularly sensitive issue for acceding governments. Why is this the case? What are the existing members' expectations of acceding governments in relation to agriculture? And how have acceding governments fared through this process? While agriculture trade accounts for less than 10 per cent of world merchandise trade, the agriculture sector, particularly for many developing countries, can be significant in terms of its contribution to both gross domestic product and employment.*

For many acceding governments, accession marks a time of transition and more significant reforms to the economy. The agriculture sector tends to be one where there is a slower adjustment time-frame. Support to the agriculture sector is often perceived as having an important redistributional aspect. Governments also often act to protect their domestic agriculture markets from international prices (Anderson *et al.*, 2013).

Agriculture sector reforms are not only challenging at the domestic level; the inclusion of specific rules for agricultural trade in the multilateral trading system is also a relatively recent phenomenon, with the introduction of the WTO Agreement on Agriculture (AoA) during the Uruguay Round of multilateral trade negotiations.

The AoA was an important step in international trade rules which sought to establish an effective long-term reform process for agriculture

The analyses in the chapters in this book were finalised at the end of December 2014. Since then the Republic of Seychelles acceded to the World Trade Organization (WTO) on 26 April 2015. This expanded total WTO membership from 160 to 161. Please see the editors' note.

trade which had historically been the subject of numerous distortions and had experienced little market opening, in contrast to industrial goods (Croome, 1999).

While negotiations on agriculture in accession have been difficult, as demonstrated here, acceding WTO members generally join with minimal trade-distorting forms of support.

## What are members looking to achieve during negotiations with acceding governments on agriculture?

In negotiating with acceding governments, existing WTO members are looking for their acceding partners to take on board a general commitment to the agriculture reform process as embodied in the AoA.

The preamble to the AoA contains the long-term objective 'to establish a fair and market-oriented agriculture trading system and that a reform process should be initiated through the negotiations of commitments on support and protection and through the establishment of strengthened and more operationally effective GATT rules and disciplines'.[1]

Furthermore, in establishing the Doha Development Agenda (DDA) negotiations members agreed: 'Building on the work carried out to date and without prejudging the outcome of the negotiations we commit ourselves to comprehensive negotiations aimed at: substantial improvements in market access; reductions of, with a view to phasing out, all forms of export subsidies; and substantial reductions in trade-distorting domestic support'.[2]

## What has happened in accessions to date?

Acceding governments' agriculture commitments on domestic support and export subsidies are reflected in Part IV of their goods schedule and may be supplemented through specific wording in their working party report (rules-based obligations). These commitments and obligations generally comply with the reform direction established under the AoA.

There are three categories of domestic support which are exempted from aggregate measurement of support (AMS) calculations: (i) minimally trade- and production-distorting forms of support ('green box');

[1] GATT: General Agreement on Tariffs and Trade 1994.
[2] Doha WTO Ministerial 2001: Ministerial Declaration on TRIPs and Public Health; see WTO document WT/MIN(01)/DEC/1, 20 December 2001.

(ii) investment subsidies that are generally available and input subsidies that are generally available to low-income or resource-poor producers in developing countries (under Article 6.2); and (iii) direct payments under production-limiting programmes ('blue box'). All other support measures in favour of agriculture producers are subject to negotiated commitments.

Guidance on the preparation of these domestic support and export subsidy tables is contained in WT/ACC/4. Reviewing the agriculture supporting tables ('AGST supporting tables') of the thirty-three members who have acceded since 1995[3] reveals some overall trends in agriculture trade policy reforms (Table 15.1). This work builds on previous studies (including Brink, 2003). Of the thirty-three acceding governments, sixteen can be identified as developing countries for the purposes of their agriculture commitments.

In reviewing acceding governments' AGST supporting tables and the tenor of discussions which have typically transpired during the accession working party meetings, there has been a strong disposition among the WTO membership to encourage acceding members to adopt 'green box' programmes over more trade-distorting measures.

Of the developing economies that have acceded since 1995, most have been able to use both 'green box' and Article 6.2 'input and investment subsidies' flexibilities.

Nineteen of the thirty-three acceding governments have set their final bound total AMS at zero. This commitment limits their use of trade-distorting support to the respective *de minimis* levels (generally either 5 or 10 per cent) of their total current value of production.[4]

Twelve of the thirty-three acceding governments have final bound total AMS commitments. These commitments have generally been established following the principle of 'standstill and reduction of' from a historical base total AMS, which reflects the Uruguay Round approach to limit and reduce domestic support as well. For developed countries this has generally resulted in reductions of 20 per cent from their historical base total AMS spending levels; developing countries' reductions were generally 13 per cent of the historical base total AMS levels.

In terms of the selection of the historical base total AMS, working guidance for members can be found in WT/ACC/4, which establishes

---

[3] This analysis was completed before the accession of Yemen on 26 June 2014.
[4] With the exception of China, whose *de minimis* is bound at 8.5 per cent of its value of production.

Table 15.1 *Agriculture domestic support and export subsidy commitments made by acceding governments*

| Accession year | Members | Base years for commitments | Base total AMS | Final bound rates | Reduction (%) | De minimis | Export subsidy commitment | Notes |
|---|---|---|---|---|---|---|---|---|
| 1996 | Ecuador | | 0 | | NA | 10 | 0 | Staging of AMS reductions from 1996 to 2001 |
| | Bulgaria | 1986–1988 | 2,513 (euro million) | 502 (euro million) | 79 | 5 | 43 products | |
| 1997 | Mongolia | | 0 | | NA | | 0 | |
| | Panama | 1991–1993 | 0 | | NA | 10 | 0 | Export subsidies bound at zero after phasing out at the end of 2002 |
| 1998 | Kyrgyz Republic | 1994–1996 | | | NA | 5 | 0 | |
| 1999 | Latvia | 1994–1996 | | | NA | 8 to 5 | 0 | Staged *de minimis* and bound export subsidies at zero despite spending in base years |
| 2000 | Estonia | 1995–1997 | 0 | | NA | 5 | | |
| | Jordan | 1994–1996 | 1539 (JOD 000) | 1334 (JOD 000) | 13 | 10 | 0 | |
| | Georgia | 1996–1998 | 0 | 0 | NA | 5 | 0 | |
| | Albania | 1996–1998 | 0 | 0 | NA | 5 | 0 | |

| Year | Country | Base period | | | | | | Notes |
|---|---|---|---|---|---|---|---|---|
| | Oman | 1994–1996 | 0 | 0 | NA | 10 | 0 | |
| | Croatia | 1996–1998 | 168 (euro million) | 134 (euro million) | 20 | 5 | 0 | Bound export subsidies at zero despite spending in base years |
| 2001 | Lithuania | 1995–1997 | 118 (US$ million) | 95 (US$ million) | 20 | 5 | 0 | |
| | Moldova, Republic of | 1996–1998 | 16 (SDR million) | 13 (SDR million) | 20 | 5 | 0 | Staging of AMS reductions over 2001–2004 |
| | China | 1996–1998 | 0 | 0 | NA | 8,5 | 0 | |
| 2002 | Chinese Taipei | 1990–1992 | 17,706 (TWD million) | 14,165 (TWD million) | 20 | 5 | 0 | |
| 2003 | Armenia, Republic of | 1995–1997 | 0 | 0 | NA | 10 to 5 | 0 | |
| | Former Yugoslav Republic of Macedonia | 1998–2000 | 16 (euro million) | 16 (euro million) | NA | 5 | 0 | |
| 2004 | Nepal | 1995/96–1997/98 | 0 | 0 | NA | 10 | 0 | Bound export subsidies at zero despite spending in base years |
| | Cambodia | 1998–2000 | 0 | 0 | NA | 10 | 0 | |

Table 15.1 (*cont.*)

| Accession year | Members | Base years for commitments | Base total AMS | Final bound rates | Reduction (%) | De minimis | Export subsidy commitment | Notes |
|---|---|---|---|---|---|---|---|---|
| 2005 | Saudi Arabia, Kingdom of | 2001–2003 | 3711.9 (million Saudi riyals) | 3214.28 (million Saudi riyals) | 13 | 10 | 0 | Staging of AMS reductions over 2006–2015 |
| 2007 | Viet Nam | 1999–2001 | 3,961.59 (VND billion) | 0 | NA | 10 | 0 | Bound export subsidies at zero despite spending in baseyears and Base AMS was below 10 per cent *de minimis* |
| | Tonga | 1996/97–1998/99 | 0 | 0 | NA | 10 | 0 | |
| 2008 | Ukraine | 2004–2006 | 3043.4 (UAH million) | 3043.4 (UAH million) | NA | 5 | 0 | |
| | Cabo Verde | 2003–2005 | 0 | 0 | NA | 10 | 0 | |
| 2012 | Montenegro | 2005–2007 | 333,278 (euro) | 333,278 (euro) | NA | 5 | 0 | |

| Year | Member | Base period | | | | | | Notes |
|---|---|---|---|---|---|---|---|---|
| | Samoa | 2005/06–2008/09 | 0 | 0 | NA | 10 | 0 | |
| 2012 | Russian Federation | 2006–2008 | 9 (US billion) | 4.4 (US$ billion) | 51 | 5 | 0 | Staging of AMS reductions over 2013–2018 |
| | Vanuatu | | 0 | 0 | NA | 10 | 0 | Democratic Republic |
| 2013 | Lao People's | 2001–2003 | 0 | NA | 10 | 0 | 0 | |
| | Tajikistan | 2008–2010 | 182,667 (US$ 000) | 182,667 (US$ 000) | NA | 10 | 0 | Bound export subsidies at zero despite spending in base years |

*Source:* WTO Agriculture Support Tables (AGST) for Members

that the data would be sourced 'normally using the average of the most recent three year period'. Again, practice has varied slightly depending on certain factors, including the length of negotiation of the accession.

Of course, there are also exceptions to these 'norms'. We have seen some acceding governments with variations in *de minimis* levels, exemptions from reducing their historical base total AMS and differing levels of 'reductions', and exceptions to the use of Article 6.2 flexibilities by developing countries. These exceptions from the 'norm' tend to be negotiated to reflect the particularities of an acceding member's agricultural programmes.

Another pronounced feature of the thirty-three accessions to date has been the strong commitment made by acceding governments to eliminate agricultural export subsidies. With the exception of two members, all acceding governments have committed to bind their export subsidies at the level of zero from the time of accession.

This is consistent with the AoA built reform agenda (paragraph 20) and the desire of members to have agricultural export subsidies phased out, as has been the case for other sectors as part of the DDA negotiations. While this goal is yet to be fully achieved, there have been significant reductions in the utilisation of agricultural export subsidies compared with commitment levels.

## Links between market access, domestic support and export subsidy commitments

While this chapter focuses on domestic support and export subsidy commitments, equally important is an acceding government's market access commitments. While the AoA makes a legal distinction between these 'three pillars', they are in effect a working system of protection. Tariff levels raise costs of imported products to a level of domestic intervention prices, and export subsidies provide for the disposal of surpluses to maintain domestic prices. In assessing an acceding government's agricultural policies, members of the WTO will be looking to ensure the right balance is struck across the three pillars (of market access, domestic support and export subsidies).

### Interactions between acceding governments and existing members

For members acceding to the WTO, the objectives of the Uruguay Round and the aspirations of members for continuing agriculture reform, as reflected in the Doha Declaration, are evident in the discussions which take place with existing WTO members. The discussions and specific commitments which members make are reflected in the acceding governments' working party reports and their goods schedules.

A review of the working party reports of the thirty-three members which have acceded since 1995[5] reveals issues in which members have expressed an interest in the context of agriculture policies.

Working party members are generally interested in the overall policy orientation of the acceding governments, as well as specific programmes and practices which might be considered as inconsistent with the principles of the reform agenda more generally, or specific rules and disciplines under the WTO Agreements.

Questions to acceding governments on agriculture policy cover not only the specific disciplines of the AoA, but also issues relevant to other WTO agreements, including the Agreement on Import Licensing Procedures and the 1994 GATT.

Some lines of questioning tend to be of a more systemic nature. In the cases of Georgia and the Republic of Moldova, existing members were looking for confirmation that these acceding governments were not utilising programmes such as direct payments or export credits (respectively).

However, there are many instances where questions are tailored specifically to the policies and practices of an acceding government which have been identified as having effects on other members. Countries' specific concerns are often reflected in terms of commitments in the acceding government's working party report.

For example, in the case of Ecuador, members questioned the operation of a price band mechanism which imposed variable levies on agriculture imports. The exchanges between members and the acceding government led to Ecuador agreeing to phase out this system.

Another example was the case of Russia, which acceded in 2012. In this particular case there had been lengthy discussions between Russia and existing members regarding the placement of programmes under 'product-specific' and 'non-product specific' categories of support. The placement of support in these categories has impacts for the calculation of *de minimis* and AMS levels, given that members have separate *de minimis* levels for all product-specific programmes and non-specific

---

[5] This review was completed before the accession of Yemen on 26 June 2014.

programmes. A specific solution was devised whereby 'the sum of all product-specific support does not exceed 30 per cent of the non-product specific aggregate measurement of support'. As some commentators have remarked, 'this constraint on product-specific AMS support echoes the initiatives in the Doha negotiations to set product-specific limits' (Brink et al., 2013).

Devising the appropriate commitment language involves considerable negotiation and an expression of goodwill in order to reach a mutually acceptable agreement between the acceding member and existing members.

The experience of acceding governments over the past eighteen years has also demonstrated that interest in agriculture policies extends to even the smallest of acceding governments. For example, Samoa's sugar policies and Vanuatu's operations of its coffee and copra production were discussed during their accession processes and are reflected in their working party reports.

## How have acceding governments fared?

During their negotiations many acceding governments foresaw difficulties for their agriculture sector. But the vast majority of these members have witnessed continued growth in their agriculture sectors in their post-accession period.

A recent study of the benefits to the agriculture sector from membership of the GATT/WTO found that membership increased agriculture trade by 68 per cent, compared with 31 per cent for non-agriculture trade. In addition, among export-oriented developing countries, membership of the GATT/WTO increased agriculture exports to developed-country markets by developing countries by 144 per cent and by LDCs by 93 per cent (Grant and Boys, 2010).

A snapshot of agriculture exports of three acceding governments – China (Figure 15.1), Nepal (Figure 15.2) and Viet Nam (Figure 15.3) – indicates that, while growth levels have varied, exports of agriculture products have increased since the economy's accession to the WTO.

Of course, the benefits of accession are not only for the acceding government. Recent analysis of Russia's accession to the WTO in 2012 has highlighted that some of its key developing-country trading partners have fared favourably from some of the reforms and market opening which was a direct result of Russia's accession negotiations (Kiselev and Romashkin, 2012).

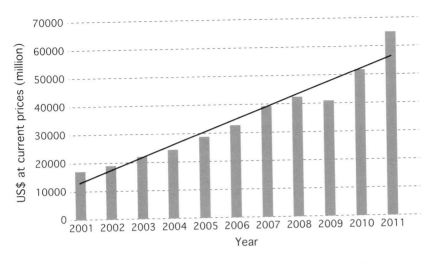

**Figure 15.1**    China's agriculture exports by value, 2001–2011 (WTO trade time series data).

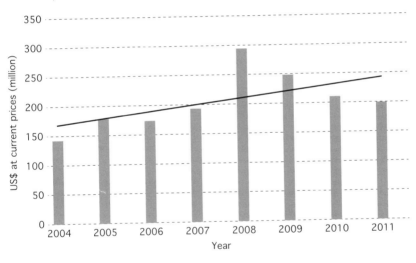

**Figure 15.2**    Nepal's agriculture exports by value, 2004–2011 (WTO trade time series data).

## What happens after WTO accession and what role do members play in continuing the agriculture reform effort?

Once an acceding government joins the WTO it has an important role to play in continuing the agriculture reform process.

Table 15.2 *Questions to newly acceding governments in the WTO CoA*

| Member | Year of accession | No. of questions in the CoA |
|---|---|---|
| Mongolia | 1997 | 1 |
| Panama | 1997 | 27 |
| Albania | 2000 | 5 |
| Moldova, Republic of | 2001 | 10 |
| Chinese Taipei | 2002 | 62 |

*Source:* WTO Agriculture Information Management System.

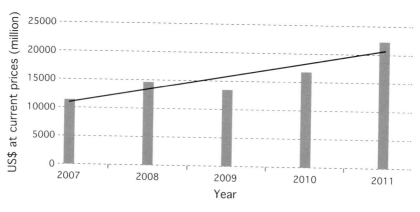

**Figure 15.3**   Viet Nam's agriculture exports by value, 2007–2011 (WTO trade time series data).

Members' specific commitments on market access, domestic support and export subsidies are routinely reviewed through the WTO Committee on Agriculture (CoA). Questioning of members' implementation of their commitments is mandated under Article 18.6 of the AoA.

Questions to newly acceded members have varied depending upon the frequency of notifications, the levels of interest members have in newly acceded members' agriculture policies, and the capacity of these newly acceded members to impact on international markets and trade. By way of example, Table 15.2 provides a snapshot of the numbers of questions posed by members to a selection of newly acceded members since their accessions.

In addition to reviews, acceding governments participate in negotiations of the 'new rules' for agriculture. Part of the mandate of the DDA negotiations which commenced in 2001 is to continue the agriculture reform process.

The direction of that reform process is reflected in the agriculture draft modalities (TN/AG/W/4/Rev. 4). These establish a series of measures aimed at reducing tariffs and domestic support and eliminating all forms of export subsidies. These modalities specifically undertook to: (i) account for the possibility of overlapping reduction commitments from both accession and the DDA; and (ii) provide for a degree of flexibility from the generally prescribed reductions, via recognition of the reform commitments implemented during the accession process. These DDA agriculture negotiations are yet to be concluded.

It is evident from this review of the commitments taken by thirty-three members that have acceded to the WTO since 1995 that these members have contributed significantly to ongoing agriculture trade reform efforts through their binding commitment levels. It is also fair to say that these new members' commitments have gone beyond the reforms undertaken by some of the other members of the WTO. The notion of the ongoing reform agenda in the agriculture negotiations is to ensure there is a fairer system for all – this means some of the existing members taking on more significant commitments in areas such as export competition.

The majority of acceding governments, in establishing their agriculture commitments under the WTO and reforming their agriculture policies, have followed a path of limiting trade-distorting support (restricting themselves to *de minimis* levels). They have also subscribed to eliminating agricultural export subsidies, which are known to be among the more trade-distorting forms of support.

While the accession negotiations are often an arduous process for the acceding government, there are clear benefits for the acceding government's agriculture sector – in terms of access to the international trading environment and protection under WTO rules. Reforms are never a simple task. However, accession negotiations often provide the tools to justify hard reforms at home.

Collectively, the work of the WTO and its members is to ensure a fairer, more predictable trading system for all. It is clear that accessions can assist in achieving this goal, particularly in the agriculture sector.

# References

Anderson, K., G. Rausser and J. Swinnen (2013). 'Political economy of public policies: insights from distortions to agriculture and food markets', Washington DC, World Bank, Policy Research Working Paper 6433.

Brink, L. (2003). 'New members of the WTO: their commitments in agriculture and provisions proposed in the Doha negotiations'. Paper presented to the International Conference on Agriculture Policy Reform and the WTO: Where Are We Heading?, Capri, Italy, June 23–26.

Brink, L., D. Orden and G. Datz (2013). 'BRIC agricultural policies through a WTO lens', *Journal of Agricultural Economics*, 64(1): 197–216.

Croome, J. (1999). *Guide to the Uruguay Round Agreements*. The Hague, Kluwer Law International.

Grant, J. H. and K. A. Boys (2010). 'Agriculture and the World Trade Organization: does membership make a difference?', Canadian Agricultural Trade Policy and Competitiveness Research Network, CATPCRN Working Paper 2010–03.

Kiselev, S. and R. Romashkin (2012). 'Possible effects of Russia's WTO accession on agriculture trade and production', Geneva, International Centre for Trade and Sustainable Development, Issue Paper 40.

# The 2001 WTO accession of China: negotiating experience – challenges, opportunities and post-accession approaches

XIANKUN LU

ABSTRACT

*China is among the Article XII members which joined the WTO after its establishment in 1995. Membership of the WTO has served as a major stabiliser and strong accelerator for China's economic take-off, although China's accession commitments were highly demanding. One of the most profound impacts brought about by China's accession has been that the country fully embraced the rules-based spirit upheld by the WTO. Concepts such as non-discrimination, transparency and the rule of law are no longer trade jargon but common words for the general public. To this end, China conducted the largest legislative reform in its history to establish a WTO-consistent legal system. China's accession brought tangible benefits to the Chinese people, quadrupling the gross domestic product per capita increasing people's income and improving people's livelihood. Household income increased from about US$800 to US$3,300, marking an annual growth of 10 per cent. More than 200 million people were successfully lifted out of poverty. As China benefited from integration into the WTO and the rules-based multilateral trading system, it has shared these benefits with other WTO members, including and in particular least-developed countries.*

The expansion of the General Agreement on Tariffs and Trade 1994 (GATT) and the WTO is remarkable. The GATT began with just

The analyses in the chapters in this book were finalised at the end of December 2014. Since then the Republic of Seychelles acceded to the World Trade Organization (WTO) on 26 April 2015. This expanded total WTO membership from 160 to 161. Please see the editors' note.

23 members in 1947 and the WTO now has 161 members. Different countries choose to be part of the rules-based multilateral trading system for different reasons. But there is one common reason behind each and every accession, and that is that it is overwhelmingly in the member's interests to accede. The privileges that other members offer, the security that the trading rules provide and, in return, the commitment by acceding governments to open markets and abide by the rules, have brought tangible benefits to their economies. At the same time, successfully concluded accessions will strengthen the rule-based multilateral trading system and enhance its representativeness.

## The WTO accession of China – contributions to China and the WTO

China is among the thirty-three Article XII members which joined the WTO after its establishment in 1995. Membership of the WTO has served as a major stabiliser and strong accelerator in China's economic take-off. During the years since China's accession, the Chinese economy and society have been developing rapidly and the benefits of opening up the economy have trickled down to the average Chinese individual. This process of China's integration into the world economy has also been a process of complementing and sharing with the rest of the world. Through more liberal international trade, greater integration of global supply chains and more efficient economic exchanges, both China and the rest of the world have secured a 'win–win' scenario.

As stated by Ambassador Yi Xiaozhun, one of the negotiators of China's accession to the WTO:

> The first question is: has China truly benefited from its accession to the WTO? Our answer is 'YES'. As you have witnessed, the past thirty-odd years [have] registered an unprecedented transformation of China's economy and society. We have embarked on a development path to drive our reform and promote our development with a consistent policy centred on opening up. Joining the WTO has constituted a milestone in this process. In 2001, despite many difficulties and challenges, domestic and abroad, China made an emphatic choice to accept the multilateral trading rules. Ever since then, our reform and opening-up process has entered into a new phase with much faster economic development.[1]

---

[1] Ambassador Yi Xiaozhun, statement at the Conference on Russia's Accession to the WTO, organised by the Higher School of Economics (HSE) and the International Centre for Trade and Sustainable Development (ICTSD), Moscow, 11 October 2012.

# WTO accession is a milestone in China's history of reform and opening up

The inception of China's reform and opening-up policy was in 1978; China embarked on a path to drive its reform and promote its development with a consistent policy centred on opening up. As commented upon by Ambassador Yi, the past thirty-odd years have registered an unprecedented transformation of China's economy and society. That period – from 1986, when China first put forward its accession application, to 2001, when China finally joined the WTO – has become a milestone in the history of China's reform and opening up. Despite numerous difficulties and challenges, the leadership of China has always remained firm in its resolve to embrace the multilateral trade rules by making extensive and in-depth commitments on all aspects of China's economy. This is absolutely a difficult, while brave, choice for a big developing country such as China, but history has rewarded it with a growth phenomenon miracle rarely witnessed before. Since 2001, China's reform and opening-up process have entered a new era of continuously locking in reforms and pursuing further transformation.

# China has faithfully implemented its commitments since its accession to the WTO

It is widely recognised that the commitments made by China to accede to the WTO were highly demanding. Many of the commitments not only went beyond the commitments made by other acceding developing governments, but also surpassed the level, both in terms of market access and regulatory disciplines, of many existing members, including some developed ones. There were questions around the world about whether China could or would honour its commitments. These questions have been well answered by China's performance since its accession.

China has kept its word on all aspects by gradually lowering tariffs, abolishing import quotas and other restrictions, offering free access to foreign trade operations, and substantially opening up for foreign investment. To take but a few examples: China's overall bound tariff has been cut from 15.3 per cent to 9.8 per cent, far lower than the average of other developing countries, with the average tariff on agriculture even lower than in some major developed countries; China has opened up over one hundred service sub-sectors, including banking, insurance and telecommunications, at a level similar to those in developed countries; China has also striven to bring its trade regime into conformity with WTO rules by scrubbing over 3,000 laws, decrees and regulations at the central level and almost 200,000 at the regional level.

In a word, as Professor John Jackson[2] has put it, no country has made as many huge efforts to join the WTO and fulfil its commitments as China has done. Former WTO Director-General Pascal Lamy rated China's performance in fulfilling its accession commitments as 'A-plus'.

## Accession to the WTO made significant contributions to the economic and social development of China

### *China's overall economy has been substantially upgraded*

In the period 2001–2011, China's gross domestic product (GDP) growth rate averaged 10.5 per cent annually, pushing its ranking up from the sixth- to the second-largest economy in the world. In 2012, China's GDP growth was maintained at 7.8 per cent despite international economic difficulties.

On trade in goods, China has grown from the sixth- to the second-largest trading country in the world. In 2012, its overall trade volume stood at US$3.87 trillion, of which exports were US$2.05 trillion and imports US$1.82 trillion, ranking first and second in the world respectively. On trade in services, China's exports and imports stood at US$191 billion and US$281 billion respectively in 2012, ranking the country as the fifth-largest exporter and third-largest importer of services in the world. On investment, China's utilised foreign direct investment (FDI) stood at US$111.7 billion in 2012, ranking second in the world. China is now among the few developing countries that successfully participate in global value chains.

It is worth mentioning that China's industries have successfully weathered the fierce international competition brought by WTO accession, especially in agriculture and automobiles, two sectors deemed most vulnerable at the time of accession.

---

[2] Mr John Jackson, Professor of Law in Georgetown. See link http://en.wikipedia.org/wiki/John_Jackson_(law_professor).

*China's mind-set has been shifted towards being reform oriented,*
*and its legal system streamlined towards being rules based*

The most profound impact brought about by China's accession is that the country has now fully embraced the rules-based spirit upheld by the WTO. Concepts such as non-discrimination, transparency and the rule of law are no longer trade jargon but common words for the general public. It is by this shift in the mind-set of the Chinese people, from the top leaders to the population at the grassroots level, that China has successfully deepened its market-oriented reform, enhanced a more foreseeable trade regime and fostered a more investment-friendly environment. It is by the guidance of this spirit that China has conducted the largest legislative reform in history to establish a WTO-consistent legal system. And that process has become more continuous with its own merits than the mere delivery of China's accession commitment. For example, in recent years China systematically revised its foreign investment law, unifying income tax levied on domestic and foreign-invested enterprises. In 2011, the government of China revised the Catalogue for the Guidance of Foreign Investment Industries, opening more sectors to foreign investment. China has also implemented an anti-monopoly law and strengthened its intellectual property protection system.

*China's accession brought tangible benefits to the Chinese people*

From 2001 to 2011, China's GDP per capita quadrupled, greatly increasing people's income and improving their livelihood. China's household income increased from about US$800 to US$3,300, marking an annual growth of 10 per cent. More than 200 million people were successfully lifted out of poverty and started a decent life. And each year, 10.4 per cent more rural people have been urbanised.

At the same time, the government of China has implemented a series of measures in the sectors of education, employment, income distribution, social security and medical care so as to improve people's livelihoods and realise inclusive growth. It is the government's strong belief that every citizen should benefit from the opening up and economic development. The 'four big items' (i.e. the marriage 'must-haves'), have changed from 'sewing machine, bicycle, radio and wristwatch' in the 1970s to 'good job, nice car, big apartment and ample savings' nowadays.

*A pool of well-trained talent for WTO participation*
*is carefully nurtured*

Ever since its accession process was initiated, China has paid particular attention to training people with talent in necessary knowledge and skills. The compact negotiating team (fewer than twenty in the coordinating Ministry of Commerce, MOFCOM), well trained by the accession negotiation, was gradually expanded into a regiment (e.g. fifty in the WTO Department of MOFCOM) in various ministries. This pool of talent has played a key role in implementing China's commitments, as well as participating in various WTO activities, particularly the Doha Development Agenda (DDA).

Meanwhile, China has organised large-scale training courses for officials at all levels of government, including ministers and provincial governors. Mass campaigns have also been initiated through media and university contests to help people from all walks of life better understand the WTO, China's commitments and potential opportunities, and also the challenges it faces. For several years after accession, 'WTO' was one of the ten most-used words in China. These efforts to forge consensus and coherence in the whole country have served as the greatest guarantee to overcoming difficulties and responding to the challenges arising out of WTO accession, particularly considering that China has had to make significant reforms within a relatively short time.

## China's twelve-year membership of the WTO represents twelve years of benefit sharing with the rest of the world

### China offers huge market opportunities to its partners

During the past decade, China has grown from being the sixth- to the second-largest importer in the world. Its imports have increased by 4.7 times, not only greatly diversifying domestic consumption, but also creating enormous employment opportunities for people in other countries.

In each recent year, since then, China has imported about US$300 billion worth of energy, mineral and agricultural products; about US$430 billion worth of machinery, electronics, high-tech, steel and non-ferrous products; nearly US$400 billion worth of intermediate goods for manufacturing; and over US$150 billion worth of services such as tourism, transportation and financial services. China's import of goods amounted to US$1.7 trillion, accounting for 9.5 per cent of the world's total imports in 2012. In 2011, China was ranked the number one trading partner for 124 countries and the number one export market for 77 countries, both developed and developing.

In these ten years, China attracted a total of over US$700 billion of FDI contributed by 347,000 new foreign-funded enterprises operating in 29 categories of manufacturing sectors and 100 services sectors in China. Of the 'Fortune 500', 480 have invested or started operations in China. Foreign companies have established over 1,400 research and development centres in China. For many of them, China has always been their most rewarding investment destination. China's outward investment grew from less than US$1 billion ten years ago to over US$77 billion in 2012, and is anticipated to maintain a rapid increase in the years to come. With that, two-way investment will become more balanced.

After the outbreak of the global financial crisis, China substantially increased its financial contributions to international financial institutions and extended a helping hand to other developing countries. China has also increased bond purchases from developed countries and played its part in assisting the economic and social development of relevant countries and stabilising the international economic and financial situation.

### China strives to achieve common development with other developing countries, especially the least-developed countries (LDCs)

As the biggest developing country in the world, China, while trying to achieve its own developmental objectives, has been committed to sharing benefits with other developing countries so as to achieve the objective of common development. Despite the various challenges it faces, China has actively participated in and contributed to the WTO Aid for Trade initiative in infrastructure, public construction, social welfare facilities, agriculture, healthcare and education, among other sectors. China is also the only developing country that has donated to establish a WTO country-specific programme for LDCs, i.e. China's LDCs and Accessions Intern Programme.

China has also tried its best to expand imports from other developing countries, particularly LDCs. Since 2000, China's imports from LDCs increased by 24 per cent annually. Since 2008, China has consistently been the largest export destination of LDCs, absorbing roughly 26 per cent of their total exports each year. In addition, China was the first developing country to announce that it would provide duty-free and quota-free market access to products of 97 per cent of tariff lines from the LDCs with which it has diplomatic ties, until 2015.

> *Along with other WTO members, China unswervingly supports*
> *the multilateral trading system and the DDA*

As repeatedly often stated by China's new leadership

> [T]he multilateral trading system, with the WTO at its core, is the basis for trade liberalisation and facilitation, which could not be replaced by any regional trade arrangement. An open, fair and transparent multilateral trading system is in the interests of every country in the world ... China, a firm supporter of the multilateral trading system, shall as always be a responsible WTO member and actively participate in the development of the multilateral trading system.[3]

Such a firm commitment is manifested by China's active and constructive engagements in all activities of the WTO, particularly the DDA negotiations. China has been strongly and consistently advocating that a comprehensive and balanced outcome of the DDA will bring significant benefits to the whole world, particularly to developing countries through the realisation of its development mandate. To that end, China has been fully engaging in DDA negotiations. On top of its extensive and comprehensive accession commitments, China has committed to making significant contributions in all aspects of the DDA. For example, simulation based on existing negotiation results shows that, in this Round, China's non-agricultural market access (NAMA) and agriculture tariffs will be further reduced by 30 per cent on its applied rates, and ten more service sectors will be opened. It is a pity that the impasse in the negotiations before the Bali Ministerial Conference in 2013 rendered it impossible for China to deliver on those commitments.

Fortunately, the success of Bali has opened a narrow window of opportunity to conclude the negotiations in due course. It is China's sincere hope that members will not only honour their commitments made at the Bali Ministerial Conference, particularly on trade facilitation,

---

[3] President HE Mr Xi Jinping, September 2013 when he met WTO Direstor-General in Russia. See China Foreign Affairs report www.fmprc.gov.cn/mfa_eng/wjb_663304/zzjg_663340/dozys_664276/gjlb_664280/3220_664352/3222_664356/t1074376.shtml.

but also strive to formulate a clearly defined post-Bali work programme on the remaining issues of the DDA. That would serve to guide the WTO ship out of the difficult water with icebergs in which it now finds itself, towards the destination of DDA success. And rest assured that China will be the most determined and hardworking member of the crew of that ship.

# 17

# The 2001 WTO accession of the Separate Customs Territory of Taiwan, Penghu, Kinmen and Matsu: negotiating experience – challenges, opportunities and approaches post-accession

THOMAS PEN-CHUNG TUNG

## ABSTRACT

*The economy of Chinese Taipei has always been highly dependent on trade. Nevertheless, its WTO accession negotiations were demanding – although the results have been significant and beneficial – involving a total of eleven formal meetings and five informal meetings for the working party, and approximately 200 bilateral meetings between Chinese Taipei and thirty different WTO members. The gradual opening of Chinese Taipei's market exposed domestic industries to global competition, necessitating a process of adjustment and adaptation that has ultimately led to economic growth. For the more vulnerable industries, the challenges of market liberalisation have acted as an incentive to restructure and reinvent in order to improve competitiveness. Chinese Taipei's accession to the WTO has also been a catalyst for the globalisation and development of these industries and necessitated a process of adjustment and adaptation that has ultimately led to economic growth. The trade policies and regulations of Chinese Taipei underwent a thorough review and revision as a result of the requirements of WTO membership, and this legislative overhaul has been highly beneficial in modernising the trade regime.*

The economy of the Separate Customs Territory of Taiwan, Penghu, Kinmen and Matsu (Chinese Taipei) has always been highly dependent on trade. During the 1970s and 1980s, Chinese Taipei was developing at a remarkable pace, with exports being the engine of its economic growth. These years of unprecedented growth have made it the twentieth largest exporter and the eighteenth largest importer of goods in the world today. In the services sector, Chinese Taipei is now the world's twenty-sixth largest exporter and the thirtieth largest importer. These achievements were not easy to accomplish. Before Chinese Taipei's accession to the WTO in January 2002, its export products were frequently subjected by its major trading partners to discriminatory trade measures, often in the form of quantitative import restrictions, the elimination of the Generalised System of Preferences (GSP) treatment and anti-dumping investigations. Whenever such trade disputes occurred, Chinese Taipei lacked the effective channels to resolve them. They were the kind of trade barriers to Chinese Taipei's products that would be considered today to constitute unfair treatment and to seriously diminish Chinese Taipei's economic interests.

The Tokyo Round of the General Agreement on Tariffs and Trade (GATT) negotiations from 1973 to 1979 proceeded smoothly, reducing tariffs on goods and eliminating non-tariff barriers (NTBs) between the participants. In addition, multilateral agreements were reached on subsidies, countervailing measures, technical barriers to trade, import licensing procedures, customs valuation and anti-dumping. Plurilateral codes were signed on bovine meat, dairy products, government procurement and trade in civil aircraft. In view of the global trend towards economic liberalisation, Chinese Taipei sensed the need for a growing urgency to join the GATT if it was to maintain its export momentum and avoid trade protectionism. At the same time, Chinese Taipei also had the intention of liberalising its economic and trade regimes, and of conforming to international standards. Therefore, the Bureau of Foreign Trade (BOFT), led by Director-General Vincent Siew, began research on GATT regulations and the various agreements reached in the Tokyo Round. BOFT also studied the feasibility of Chinese Taipei's joining the GATT, and examined the potential economic benefits and the possible impact of Chinese Taipei's membership. The findings clearly indicated that joining the GATT was both feasible and necessary.

When the Uruguay Round began in 1986, the scope of the negotiations was extended beyond trade in goods to include services, intellectual property rights, dispute settlement and many other issues as well. It was also decided at that point that a new body, the WTO, would be established on 1 January 1995 to provide a stable foundation for institutionalising and enhancing the legal framework of international trade. Aware of such developments and progress, Chinese Taipei felt that the need to join the GATT/WTO was becoming even greater. Consensus on the principle of joining was soon reached among the government agencies of Chinese Taipei, which facilitated the preparatory work for its application.

In May 1988, the task force on joining the GATT was set up, focusing on technical issues concerning Chinese Taipei's accession. In December of that same year, the strategic committee on joining the GATT was also established to resolve the policy issues. Those two teams aimed to coordinate various agencies on issues that would be discussed during the accession negotiations, including the responses from domestic industries and the adjustments that would be required. This organisational framework not only played a key role in Chinese Taipei's GATT accession process but also served as an important decision-making and communication platform for participation in international economic and trade affairs.

## Submission of Chinese Taipei's application (January 1990)

At an early stage Chinese Taipei conducted a detailed internal evaluation and officials were sent to the capitals of various GATT members to elicit their support. They were charged with making the case that Chinese Taipei's accession to the GATT would both benefit their countries and enable Chinese Taipei to contribute more to the global trading system. Minister of Economic Affairs, Vincent Siew, and Deputy Minister, Chiang Pin-kung, also made frequent trips for the same purpose. The subsequent years of preparatory and lobbying work ultimately resulted in Chinese Taipei gaining the support of the majority of signatories for its application. On 1 January 1990, Steve Ruey-Long Chen, Director of the Economic Division of Chinese Taipei's Representative Office in Switzerland, formally submitted its application to the GATT Secretariat. Pursuant to GATT Article XXXIII, Chinese Taipei sought to accede to the GATT as the 'Separate Customs Territory of Taiwan, Penghu, Kinmen and Matsu'. Attached directly to the application delivered to the Secretariat was the Memorandum on Chinese Taipei's Foreign Trade Regime, as well as other relevant information on economic and trade laws, in order to demonstrate its determination to join the GATT and to accelerate the review process of the GATT accession working group.

## Application review process (September 1992 to September 2001)

On 29 September 1992, the GATT Council formally accepted Chinese Taipei's application for accession and decided to establish a working party, to be chaired by Martin R. Morland, Ambassador of the United Kingdom to the GATT/WTO in Geneva at the time. Subsequently, after the WTO was established on 1 January 1995, this GATT working party was replaced by a WTO working party on 31 January 1995, which consisted of fifty-five members and duly continued to review Chinese Taipei's application based on Article XII of the Marrakesh Agreement Establishing the World Trade Organization.

From the first working party meeting, which took place on 6 November 1992, to the last working party meeting on 18 September 2001, at which Chinese Taipei's application to accede to the WTO was finally approved, a total of eleven formal meetings and five informal meetings were held. At the tenth working party meeting on 12 May 1999, when Chinese Taipei's delegation was led by the then Deputy Minister of Economic Affairs, Yi-fu Lin, the initial review of the draft working party report on Chinese Taipei's WTO accession was completed. At the eleventh and final working party meeting on 18 September 2001, with Deputy Minister of Economic Affairs, Steve Ruey-Long Chen, leading the Chinese Taipei delegation, the working party completed the work of adopting the various accession documents, such as the Protocol of Accession, the working party report, the consolidated tariff schedules and the schedule of specific commitments for trade in services. During the course of each working party meeting, Chinese Taipei delegations were required to provide detailed answers to questions raised by WTO members regarding its trade regime and regulatory measures. Interdepartmental coordination meetings were convened immediately following each working party meeting to draft corresponding statements and amendments to the relevant regulations.

The working party meetings ensured that WTO members gained a comprehensive understanding of Chinese Taipei's foreign trade regime. They were also an opportunity for government agencies to thoroughly review the trade regulations and measures, and to make amendments accordingly. These meetings had a profound influence on the liberalisation of trade for Chinese Taipei, laying a solid foundation for the internationalisation and institutionalisation of the economic and trade regime, as well as for Chinese Taipei's continuing participation in the WTO and free trade agreement negotiations.

In order to legislate for the new trade rules associated with Chinese Taipei's accession to the WTO, Vincent Siew, in June 1997, during his term as parliamentary legislator, set up the Legislative Planning Task Force on WTO Accession in the Legislative Yuan, while the Executive

Yuan's own counterpart 'the Inter-departmental Task Force for Communicating with the Legislative Yuan on WTO Accession' was being formed at the same time. Communication and coordination between the Executive Yuan and the Legislative Yuan was thus maintained in order to ensure that domestic consensus was reached during the review process and new trade measures could therefore be implemented without dispute.

## Formal accession (January 2002)

In all, nearly two hundred bilateral meetings were held between Chinese Taipei and thirty different WTO members, reaching agreements on tariff reductions for trade in goods, the removal of NTBs and the opening of the services market.

On 11 November 2001, the Fourth WTO Ministerial Meeting, held in Doha, Qatar, approved Chinese Taipei's WTO accession. The Protocol of Accession was signed by Lin Hsin-I, Minister of Economic Affairs, the next day. Chinese Taipei formally became the WTO's 144th member on 1 January 2002.

## Accession commitments and the impact on Chinese Taipei's industries

During its accession process, Chinese Taipei encountered many difficulties and setbacks regarding the liberalisation of its agricultural, industrial and services markets. Fortunately, it was able to overcome these difficulties and achieve its goal. Chinese Taipei made numerous concessions and commitments, which proved very helpful in the reorganisation of the industries as well as the development of related sub-sectors. The government adopted a number of industry restructuring and relief measures to assist affected sectors in making the necessary adjustments.

### Agriculture

Prior to joining the WTO, Chinese Taipei had adopted import controls and area restrictions on certain agricultural products which were inconsistent with WTO rules. During the negotiations, WTO members strongly urged Chinese Taipei to reduce tariffs significantly and open its markets. In order to complete the accession while maintaining sustainable development, Chinese Taipei adopted the following strategies for the negotiations: (i) in keeping with its level of economic development, the level of tariff reduction on agricultural products should range between those of Japan and the Republic of Korea; (ii) in vying for comparable status with other WTO members, Chinese Taipei applied the adjustment modality of the Agriculture Agreement of the GATT Uruguay Round; and (iii) Chinese Taipei retained a certain degree of flexibility for sensitive products such as rice, liquid milk, poultry, offal and peanuts, thus avoiding major impacts on domestic production. The government also provided farmer groups with regular updates on its position during the negotiations.

Some WTO members argued that since the Agreement on Agriculture had entered into force in 1995 and the date of Chinese Taipei's accession had not yet been decided, Chinese Taipei could not directly apply for any reduction formulae of the Agreement on Agriculture. Discussions with WTO members focused on issues such as which agricultural products would be eligible for tariff quotas, which markets should be opened up and what the actual quotas would be. In addition, Chinese Taipei intended to join the WTO as a developing country, whereas the United States strongly contended that it should be considered a developed country. The United States also argued that Chinese Taipei should remove restrictive import measures on specific agricultural products and should substantially reduce tariffs on all agricultural products (highest rate of 20 per cent; minimum reduction of 50 per cent). Other members provided tariff reduction request lists for their agricultural products as well. The negotiation became a long drawn-out process as each member issued stringent demands. Even though rice was the most sensitive agricultural item, Chinese Taipei had to remove the ban on imported rice when the Agriculture Agreement was concluded during the Uruguay Round. Chinese Taipei sought to adopt the Korean model of quantitative restriction in response, but the proposal was rejected by other members. After dozens of negotiating sessions, the members finally agreed that Chinese Taipei should adopt Japan's model of quantitative restriction.

### Accession commitments

Prior to Chinese Taipei's accession to the WTO, forty-one agricultural products were subject to import controls or area restrictions. Following Chinese Taipei's membership of the WTO in 2002, eighteen of these products could be freely imported and twenty-two were subject to tariff quotas, with special safeguards applying to fourteen of this latter group. Special quantitative restrictions were applied to the remaining product, rice, which were later replaced by the tariff rate quota (TRQ) system. Excluding rice, in 2002, the average tariff for the other forty products was reduced from 20.02 per cent to 14.01 per cent, and this average was further reduced to 12.56 per cent in 2008, midway between that of Japan (10.3 per cent) and the Republic of Korea (15.8 per cent).

## Economic impact

- Total production: annual agricultural production in 2002 was valued at around US$11.92 billion. Since then, this has gradually increased, reaching about US$14.31 billion in 2012.
- Trade: agricultural exports continued to grow after accession to the WTO, from US$3.03 billion in 2001 to US$5.09 billion in 2012, an increase of 68 per cent. In 2012, Chinese Taipei's agricultural imports reached US$14.67 billion, an increase of 114 per cent compared to 2001. The agricultural trade deficit was US$9.58 billion in 2012, an increase of 150 per cent compared to 2001.
- Employment and average productivity: between 2001 and 2012, the number of people employed in agriculture fell from 706,000 to 544,000, and agricultural workers as a percentage of Chinese Taipei's total labour force declined from 7.5 per cent to 5 per cent. However, average productivity per capita rose from approximately US$17,152 in 2001 to US$26,768 in 2011, at an average annual rate of 5.8 per cent.

To cope with the impact of Chinese Taipei's WTO accession on agriculture and to further improve the sector, the Fund for Redressing Damage Caused by Agricultural Imports was established, with an initial funding of around US$3.48 billion. By the end of 2013, expenditure from the fund had reached US$4.17 billion. The government also adopted several measures designed to accelerate adjustments to the structure of agricultural production.

### Manufacturing sector

Chinese Taipei's accession commitments with regard to manufactured goods included the following:

- Average tariff rate: the average tariff rate for manufactured goods was reduced from 6.3 per cent in 2000 to 5.78 per cent in the first year of membership. Tariffs were further lowered in 2003, falling to an average of 4.15 per cent in 2011. Overall, since accession, tariffs on manufactured goods have been cut by 31.17 per cent.

- Tariff structure: the percentage of tariff-free imported goods increased from 17 per cent in 2001 to 33 per cent in 2011. The percentage of imported goods with tariffs at 10 per cent and under increased from 84 per cent to 92 per cent during the same period.

- Information communication technology products: prior to accession, Chinese Taipei had already begun to reduce tariffs on various products in accordance with the Information Technology Agreement (ITA) signed in March 1997. By 2000, tariffs had been reduced, in four stages, to zero for products including data processors, semiconductors, electronic components and semiconductor manufacturing equipment, as well as telephones and wireless fax machines. Tariffs on fifteen other products, including switches, were eliminated in 2002.

- In accordance with Chinese Taipei's commitments, tariffs on pharmaceuticals, paper products, iron and steel, construction equipment, agricultural machinery, medical equipment, furniture and toys were reduced to zero by 1 January 2004. With regard to chemical products, tariff ceilings were set in accordance with the Chemical Tariff Harmonization Agreement. The bound rates for chemical products were implemented after Chinese Taipei's accession, and all tariffs were eliminated by 1 January 2006.

- Textiles: following Chinese Taipei's accession, silk, yarn and greige were subject to bound rates of 1.5 per cent, 4 per cent and 7.5 per cent respectively. Prior to Chinese Taipei's accession, the majority of apparel had been subject to a tariff of 12.5 per cent. Following accession, tariffs on most kinds of apparel were reduced to 12 per cent, while for a small proportion of products they were gradually lowered to 10.5 per cent.

- Automobile industry: automobiles and trucks were originally subject to area restrictions, which were changed to TRQ measures following Chinese Taipei's accession, so as to allow gradually more imports. This TRQ system was eventually abolished on 1 January 2011. Prior to Chinese Taipei's accession, tariff rates for automobiles and trucks had been between 30 per cent and 42 per cent. Under the TRQ system, the in-quota tariff was reduced from 29 per cent in 2002 to 17.5 per cent in 2010, while the tariff beyond the quota was reduced from 60 per cent in 2002 to 17.5 per cent in 2010. After the TRQ system was abolished, the tariff remained at 17.5 per cent. In addition, for automobiles and motorcycles, Chinese Taipei eliminated local production requirements, area restrictions and prohibitive export subsidies. Following Chinese Taipei's accession, within six months and two years respectively, imports of motorcycles above 150cc and diesel automobiles started to be permitted.

The liberalisation of the automobile sector had a significant impact on Chinese Taipei's domestic industry, thus negotiations for this particular sector proved to be the most difficult.

- Before Chinese Taipei's accession, its automobile market liberalisation policies were inconsistent with the WTO most-favoured-nation (MFN) principle. Chinese Taipei only allowed automobile imports from the United States and Europe, restricting imports from all other sources except the Republic of Korea, which was given a quota of 8,500 units. It was a significant challenge, therefore, to balance the development of the domestic industry and the interests of major automobile exporting countries during accession negotiations.
- Chinese Taipei's internal assessment suggested that accession to the WTO would have the greatest impact on Chinese Taipei's automobile industry. It was feared that, once Chinese Taipei's market was opened up, price-competitive automobiles from Japan, Europe and North America would become dominant. Therefore, discussions between Chinese Taipei's government and the domestic automobile industry were arduous. During the negotiation process, Chinese Taipei's government repeatedly consulted with the local industry, and eventually a consensus was forged with regard to Chinese Taipei's position in the negotiations. Through the TRQ system and tariff reductions, the automobile market was opened up, and domestic companies were given the opportunity to adjust their operations, so as to deal with the impact of market liberalisation. In recent years, Chinese Taipei's companies have made considerable investments in research and development and developed differentiated products that meet consumer demand. Currently, its automobile manufacturing capabilities rival those of developed nations, and locally manufactured automobiles reached a market share of 70 per cent in 2013.

## Import licensing

Import licensing was one of the major issues brought up by WTO members in the working party on Chinese Taipei's WTO accession and

**Figure 1** Ecuador. Mr Patricio Izurieta Mora Bowen, Sub-Secretary of the Ministry of Foreign Affairs of Ecuador, signs, subject to ratification, Ecuador's Protocol of Accession to the WTO in 1995 in Geneva. Ecuador became the 129th WTO member on 21 January 1996.

**Figure 2** Mongolia. Mr Tsevegmidiin Tsogt, Minister for Trade and Industry of Mongolia, signs, subject to ratification, Mongolia's Protocol of Accession to the WTO in 1996 in Geneva. Mongolia became the 131st WTO member on 29 January 1997.

**Figure 3** Bulgaria. Mr Atanas Paparizov, Minister for Trade and Foreign Economic Cooperation of Bulgaria, signs, subject to ratification, Bulgaria's Protocol of Accession to the WTO in 1996 in Geneva. Bulgaria became the 130th WTO member on 1 December 1996.

**Figure 4** Panama. Ms Nitzia R. de Villarreal, Minister for Trade and Industry of Panama, signs, subject to ratification, Panama's Protocol of Accession to the WTO in 1996 in Geneva. Panama became the 132nd WTO member on 6 September 1997.

Figure 5 Kyrgyz Republic. Mr Omuraliev Esengul Kasymovich, Head of the Interdepartmental Commission on WTO Negotiations of the Kyrgyz Republic, signs, subject to ratification, the Kyrgyz Republic's Protocol of Accession to the WTO in 1998 in Geneva. The Kyrgyz Republic became the 133rd WTO member on 20 December 1998.

Figure 6 Latvia. Mr Valdis Birkavs, Minister for Foreign Affairs of Latvia, signs, subject to ratification, Latvia's Protocol of Accession to the WTO in 1998 in Geneva. Latvia became the 134th WTO member on 10 February 1999.

**Figure 7** Estonia. Mr Toomas Hendrik Ilvis, Minister of Foreign Affairs of Estonia, signs, subject to ratification, Estonia's Protocol of Accession to the WTO in 1999 in Geneva. Estonia became the 135th WTO member on 13 November 1999.

**Figure 8** Georgia. Mr Vazha Lordkipanidze, State Minister of Georgia, signs, subject to ratification, Georgia's Protocol of Accession to the WTO in 1999 in Geneva. Georgia became the 137th WTO member on 14 June 2000.

**Figure 9** Jordan. Mr Mohammed Halaiqah, Secretary General of the Ministry of Industry and Trade of Jordan, signs, subject to ratification, Jordan's Protocol on the Accession to the WTO in December 1999 in Geneva, Switzerland. Jordan became the 136th WTO member on 11 April 2000.

**Figure 10** Albania. Signing Ceremony for Albania's Protocol of Accession to the WTO in 2000 in Geneva. Ms Ermelinda Meksi, Minister of Economic Cooperation and Trade of Albania (third from the left), signed, subject to ratification, Albania's Accession Protocol. Albania became the 138th WTO member on 8 September 2000.

**Figure 11** Croatia. Mr Goranko Fižulić, Minister of Economy of Croatia, signs, subject to ratification, Croatia's Protocol of Accession to the WTO in 2000 in Geneva. Croatia became the 140th WTO member on 30 November 2000.

**Figure 12** Oman. Signing Ceremony for Oman's Protocol of Accession to the WTO in 2000 in Geneva. Mr Maqbool Ali Sultan, Minister of Commerce and Industry of Oman (fifth from the left), signed Oman's Accession Protocol. Oman became the 139th WTO member on 9 November 2000.

**Figure 13** Lithuania. Mr Valdas Adamkus, President of Lithuania, signs, subject to ratification, Lithuania's Protocol of Accession to the WTO in 2000 in Geneva. Lithuania became the 141st WTO member on 31 May 2001.

**Figure 14** Moldova. Mr Vasile Tarlev, Prime Minister of Moldova, signs, subject to ratification, Moldova's Protocol of Accession to the WTO in 2001 in Geneva. Moldova became the 142nd WTO member on 26 July 2001.

**Figure 15** China. Mr Shi Guangshen, Minister of Foreign Trade and Economic Cooperation of China, signs, subject to ratification, China's Protocol of Accession to the WTO at the Fourth Ministerial Conference in Doha in 2001. China became the 143rd WTO member on 11 December 2001.

**Figure 16** Chinese Taipei. Mr Lin Hsin-I, Minister of Economic Affairs of Chinese Taipei, signs, subject to ratification, Chinese Taipei's Protocol of Accession to the WTO at the Fourth Ministerial Conference in Doha in 2001. Chinese Taipei became the 144th WTO member on 1 January 2002.

**Figure 17** FYR of Macedonia. Mr Besnik Fetai, Minister of the Economy of the Former Yugoslav Republic (FYR) of Macedonia, signs, subject to ratification, the Protocol of Accession to the WTO in 2002 in Geneva. FYR Macedonia became the 146th WTO member on 4 April 2003.

**Figure 18** Armenia. Mr Karen Chshmaritian, Minister of Trade and Economic Development of Armenia, signs, subject to ratification, Armenia's Protocol of Accession to the WTO in 2002 in Geneva. Behind him is Prime Minister Margaryan. Armenia became the 145th WTO member on 5 February 2003.

**Figure 19** Nepal. Signing Ceremony for Nepal's Protocol of Accession to the WTO at the Fifth Ministerial Conference in Cancún in 2003. Mr Hari Bahadur Basnet, Minister of Industry, Commerce and Supplies of Nepal (on the right), signed, subject to ratification, Nepal's Accession Protocol. Nepal became the 147th WTO member on 23 April 2004.

**Figure 20** Cambodia. Mr Cham Prasidh, Minister of Commerce of Cambodia, signs, subject to ratification, Cambodia's Protocol of Accession to the WTO at the Fifth WTO Ministerial Conference in Cancún in 2003. Cambodia became the 148th WTO member on 13 October 2004.

**Figure 21** Saudi Arabia. Mr Hashim A. Yamani, Minister of Commerce and Industry of Saudi Arabia, signs Saudi Arabia's Protocol of Accession to the WTO in 2005 in Geneva. Saudi Arabia became the 149th WTO member on 11 December 2005.

**Figure 22** Tonga. Mr Feleti Sevele, Minister for Labour, Commerce and Industries of Tonga, signs, subject to ratification, Tonga's Protocol of Accession to the WTO at the Sixth Ministerial Conference in Hong Kong in 2005. Tonga became the 151st WTO member on 27 July 2007.

**Figure 23** Viet Nam. Mr Truong Dinh Tuyen, Minister of Trade of Viet Nam, signs, subject to ratification, Viet Nam's Protocol of Accession to the WTO in 2006 in Geneva. Viet Nam became the 150th WTO member on 11 January 2007.

**Figure 24** Cabo Verde. Mr José Brito, Minister of Economy, Growth and Competitiveness of Cabo Verde, signs, subject to ratification, Cabo Verde's Protocol of Accession to the WTO in 2007 in Geneva. Cabo Verde became the 153rd WTO member on 23 July 2008.

**Figure 25** Ukraine. Mr Victor Yushchenko, President of Ukraine, signs, subject to ratification, Ukraine's Protocol of Accession to the WTO in 2008 in Geneva. Ukraine became the 152nd WTO member on 16 May 2008.

**Figure 26** Vanuatu. Mr Ham Lini Vanuaroroa, Deputy Prime Minister and Minister of Trade, Commerce, Industry and Tourism of Vanuatu, signs, subject to ratification, Vanuatu's Protocol of Accession to the WTO in 2011 in Geneva. Vanuatu became the 157th WTO member on 24 August 2012.

Figure 27 Montenegro. Mr Igor Lukšić, Prime Minister of Montenegro, signs, subject to ratification, Montenegro's Protocol of Accession to the WTO at the Eighth Ministerial Conference in Geneva in 2011. Montenegro became the 154th WTO member on 29 April 2012.

Figure 28 Samoa. Mr Fonotoe Nuafesili Pierre Lauofo, Deputy Prime Minister of Samoa, signs, subject to ratification, Samoa's Protocol of Accession to the WTO at the Eighth WTO Ministerial Conference in Geneva in 2011. Samoa became the 155th WTO member on 10 May 2012.

Figure 29 Russian Federation. Signing Ceremony for Russia's Protocol of Accession to the WTO at the Eighth Ministerial Conference in Geneva in 2011. Ms Elvira Nabiullina, Minister for Economic Development of the Russian Federation (fourth from the left), signed, subject to ratification, Russia's Accession Protocol. Mr Igor Shuvalov, Deputy Prime Minister of the Russian Federation (fifth from the left), was also present. Russia became the 156th WTO member on 22 August 2012.

Figure 30 Lao People's Democratic Republic. Signing Ceremony for the Accession Protocol of the Lao People's Democratic Republic in 2012 in Geneva. Mr Nam Viyaketh, Minister of Industry and Commerce of Lao PDR (fifth from the left), signed, subject to ratification, Lao PDR's Accession Protocol. Mr Thongloun Sisoulith, Deputy Prime Minister of Lao PDR (sixth from the left) was also present. Lao PDR became the 158th WTO member on 2 February 2013.

**Figure 31** Tajikistan. Mr Emomali Rahmon, President of Tajikistan, signs, subject to ratification, Tajikistan's Protocol of Accession to the WTO in 2012 in Geneva. Tajikistan became the 159th WTO member on 2 March 2013.

**Figure 32** Yemen. Mr Saadaldeen Talib, Minister of Trade and Industry of Yemen, signs, subject to ratification, Yemen's Protocol of Accession to the WTO at the Ninth Ministerial Conference in Bali in 2013. Yemen became the 160th WTO member on 26 June 2014.

**Figure 33** Seychelles. Signing Ceremony for Seychelles' Protocol of Accession in 2014 in Geneva. Mr Pierre Laporte, Minister of Finance, Trade and Investment of Seychelles (left), signed, subject to ratification, Seychelles' Accession Protocol. Seychelles' formal WTO membership is pending domestic ratification.

during bilateral accession negotiations. Most members expressed concern about whether Chinese Taipei's economic and trade regime was in line with WTO standards. In particular, they requested that all non-tariff measures inconsistent with WTO practices should be eliminated before or at the time of Chinese Taipei's accession, especially area restrictions and non-tariff measures, such as import controls and supplementary document requirements instituted to protect certain agricultural and industrial products. Members also requested that Chinese Taipei's import licensing procedures conform to the WTO Import Licensing Agreement (ILA).

In response to such requests, Chinese Taipei promulgated the new Foreign Trade Act, which was implemented on 5 February 1993 and no longer required all goods to be pre-approved for importation. Under this law, most goods are no longer subject to import restrictions, unless otherwise stipulated in the Foreign Trade Act or other relevant regulations. On 1 July 1994, Chinese Taipei formally implemented the negative list for import and export administration, eliminated import and export licensing requirements and simplified licensing documentation and procedures for imports and exports. On 1 December 1999, an electronic online licensing application system was implemented that made the process paperless and more streamlined.

Up until the end of December 2001, shortly before Chinese Taipei's accession, Chinese Taipei's import goods classification table had included 10,344 items, of which 382 (3.7 per cent) were restricted for importation, 252 were import controlled and 130 could be imported conditional upon approval. The remaining 9,962 items (96.3 per cent) could be imported without restriction. After Chinese Taipei's accession in January 2002, it continued to eliminate import restriction measures, and to liberalise imports or shift to the TRQ system as per WTO standards and its accession commitments. Fast forwarding to 2013, only seventy items remain restricted for importation, with fifteen requiring import licences and only eighty-five TRQs remained.

In addition, Chinese Taipei has declared a commitment to cease adopting and to start eliminating import area and quantitative restriction measures that are inconsistent with WTO standards. Chinese Taipei has also stopped imposing import restrictions using customs procedures, product safety or sanitary and phytosanitary (SPS) measures, or any other hidden trade barriers. Chinese Taipei has committed, furthermore, to comply with import licensing requirements and quantitative restrictions under the Agreement on Agriculture and the ILA, as well as TRQ implementation under GATT 1994. other instruments.

*Services sector*

## Negotiation process

Since releasing the first draft of its schedule of specific commitments and list of MFN exemptions in July 1994, Chinese Taipei has conducted over sixty rounds of bilateral services negotiations with twelve WTO members. The negotiations were finally concluded in June 1999 and the specific schedule of commitments was finalised on 30 July of the same year, during the third informal working party meeting.

The main market access requests from major members were as follows: (i) United States: professional services (legal services), financial services (banking, insurance, and securities), communication services (basic telecommunication services and interconnection fees between cellular service providers and Chunghwa Telecom) and medical services; (ii) European Union: financial services, maritime and land freight services, basic telecommunication services, legal services, port dredging services and automotive finance leasing services; (iii) Japan: legal services, courier services, financial services, maritime services and construction services; (iv) Canada: legal services, banking (private banking) services, insurance (mutual insurance) services, securities services and temporary stays of business persons and others; and (v) Australia: legal services, architectural services, broadcasting and television commercial services, placement and supply services of personnel, financial services, maritime services, acquisition of real estate and other matters.

The first draft of Chinese Taipei's schedule of specific commitments was very much a reflection of its level of liberalisation at the time. After completing various rounds of bilateral negotiations with members, Chinese Taipei incorporated many new market-opening commitments. Its final schedule of commitments covered a wide range of services sectors: (i) horizontal commitments (securities investment, entry and temporary stay of natural persons, and land acquisition rights and interests; and (ii) sector-specific commitments (eleven services including business services; communication services; construction and related engineering services; distribution services; education services; environmental services; financial services; health-related and social services; tourism and travel-related services; recreational, cultural and sporting services; and transport services).

## Services negotiations impact on Chinese Taipei's services industry

Approximately 70 per cent of Chinese Taipei's gross domestic product (GDP) is derived from the services sector, making it vital to economic growth. In addition to supporting Chinese Taipei's manufacturing and agriculture sectors, the services sector meets consumers' demand for high-quality and diversified services. A large proportion of the liberalisation of the services market has involved foreign investment in Chinese Taipei and the establishment of a commercial presence to provide services. Such liberalisation has understandably put pressure on domestic industries, some of which even had their management replaced by foreign companies. However, Chinese Taipei's domestic services industry has not been affected to the point of atrophy, nor has it suffered a decrease in employment opportunities, production value or earnings, and no negative impact on the economy at large has been observed at all. From a long-term perspective, the liberalisation of services markets shows evidence of stimulating the overall growth of the services sector and economy, bringing in new ideas and technologies, increasing service quality, lowering costs and increasing the competitiveness of Chinese Taipei's domestic services industries. Furthermore, as a result of the international marketing channels and networks brought to Chinese Taipei by foreign enterprises, domestic businesses can now bring their goods and services to the global market. These advantages are evident from the current competitiveness of the retail and financial services sectors, which have benefited from years of market liberalisation.

## Difficulties encountered during negotiations

Services negotiations covered a wide range of issues that are under the regulation of various different agencies. The Executive Yuan's Council for Economic Planning and Development (CEPD) (now the National Development Council) was in charge of coordinating the negotiation positions of different agencies on various issues. To coordinate the issues, the CEPD had to discuss the negotiation baselines and simulate responses to possible negotiation scenarios with each of the relevant agencies before negotiations with the other members could commence. Often, the efforts put into negotiating effectively internally far exceeded the efforts required to negotiate externally.

### Protection of intellectual property rights

Before Chinese Taipei's accession to the WTO, it was unable to participate in the Trade-Related Aspects of Intellectual Property Rights (TRIPs) negotiations. Chinese Taipei's domestic intellectual property (IP) rights laws and regulations were not entirely consistent with the TRIPs standards. And because of this legislative inadequacy, Chinese Taipei was faced with intense pressure from the United States, the European Union and Japan during the accession negotiations. For example, the United States was concerned, for a long time, about protection of copyrights and pharmaceutical patents, while the European Union took issue over geographical indications and pharmaceuticals.

In the early days, Chinese Taipei's IP rights were regulated by various agencies, and the government lacked resources to enforce protection against counterfeiting. Chinese Taipei's laws and regulations also required comprehensive amendments in accordance with the parts of provisions of the Paris Convention and the Berne Convention incorporated into the TRIPs Agreement before Chinese Taipei's accession to the WTO.

In the early 1990s, Chinese Taipei began overhauling its Patent Act, Trademark Act and Copyright Act in response to requests made during the accession negotiations to bring its laws and regulations into conformity with the TRIPs provisions. To encourage further development of its high-tech industries, Chinese Taipei also enacted the Integrated Circuit Layout Protection Act, the Trade Secrets Act and the Optical Disk Act. In addition, it established the Taiwan Intellectual Property Office (TIPO) in 1999, bringing regulatory jurisdiction on patents, trademarks and copyright under the same roof, thereby enhancing its effectiveness.

After joining the WTO in January 2002, Chinese Taipei participated in the TRIPs Council, often jointly co-sponsoring papers proposed by members with similar positions, and using the Council as a platform for dealing with international IP rights issues. Its cooperation with the United States, the European Union, Japan and other countries was also strengthened. Chinese Taipei set up the IP Rights Protection Police Task Force in 2003, and instituted the Intellectual Property Court in 2008. This has strengthened Chinese Taipei's ability to fight IP rights infringement, and given it a sound litigation system.

Through Chinese Taipei's participation in the WTO, it has largely improved its IP rights legislation system, aligning it with TRIPs standards. After over ten years of development, Chinese Taipei's robust IP rights protection regime has proven beneficial in upgrading its economy into one built on knowledge-based goods and services.

### Difficulties and challenges faced during the accession process

During the early stages of its bid to join the WTO, Chinese Taipei faced numerous challenges and complications.

In November 1992, in the course of the first meeting of the working party on Chinese Taipei's accession to the WTO, it submitted its application as a developing member. As the GATT Uruguay Round of negotiations reached its peak, however, many countries began to advocate the setting of higher standards and entry thresholds for prospective WTO members. As a consequence, Chinese Taipei was forced to make substantial concessions during the working party's review of its case and in bilateral negotiations with various WTO members.

Because Chinese Taipei had previously been excluded from the international trading system for a relatively long period of time, many of its government departments lacked sufficient knowledge and experience in dealing with WTO norms and operations. Similarly, many of its domestic industries were given very little time to adjust to the changes necessitated by its entry into the WTO. All these factors added significant extra challenges to Chinese Taipei's pursuit of WTO membership in what was already a complicated and difficult process.

Although Chinese Taipei had considerable appeal for many WTO members due to the massive potential of its import market and investment opportunities, its bid to join the WTO also faced significant hurdles because many domestic regulations and measures at the time did not fully comply with international standards. When the working party reviewed its foreign trade regime, WTO members submitted over four hundred questions and points of concern. Only after a lengthy process of clarification and thorough study was Chinese Taipei able to win their approval.

In order to fulfil WTO membership requirements, Chinese Taipei amended thirty-five pieces of legislation encompassing a wide range of areas, including imports, exports, tariffs, customs, commodity and business taxes, banking and securities, professional services, telecommunication services, aviation, maritime and land transportation, standards and inspections, patents, trademarks and copyrights, publication and film, livestock and food, SPS measures, state-owned enterprises, government procurement and industrial parks. Many of those amendments directly affected the core issues and fundamental layers of Chinese Taipei's economic system. A great deal of time and effort were devoted to the process, but it also helped to draw the attention of the Chinese Taipei public sector to international trade issues.

Chinese Taipei's bid to join the WTO required it to engage in bilateral negotiations with thirty members, with such a magnitude and range of negotiations that it proved to be a considerable challenge. Members made numerous requests, concerning the liberalisation of the agricultural, industrial and professional services markets, which were difficult to meet. Furthermore, different countries often had conflicting stances on certain trade issues (such as beef, fruit and automobiles), placing Chinese Taipei in an awkward position. During this time, Chinese Taipei participated in nearly two hundred negotiating sessions. Not only did negotiators have to work hard to reach consensus with Chinese Taipei's prospective trading partners, they also needed to stay in close contact with the numerous government agencies involved in the process, in order to continuously review, study and revise Chinese Taipei's negotiation positions and bottom lines.

As a consequence of delays in the reviewing of Chinese Taipei's WTO bid and the prolonged negotiation schedule, some trading partners requested a 'down payment' of certain goods and industries, so they could benefit from the concessions promised by Chinese Taipei as soon as possible. After careful consideration, these requests were agreed to so as to accelerate entry into the WTO, but some domestic industries suffered from the time limitations for adjusting to changes.

To protect some of its less competitive industries, particularly with regard to certain sensitive agricultural products, Chinese Taipei tried to push for a longer transition period to accommodate these industries. Pressure from certain WTO members, however, ultimately meant that Chinese Taipei was only able to extend the transition period for tariff reductions, tariff quotas and special safeguard measures on a very few items.

After twelve years of hard work, Chinese Taipei finally succeeded in becoming a member of the WTO on 1 January 2002. Since then, it has formulated economic and trade policies in line with WTO multilateral trading standards, which has helped to radically liberalise and globalise Chinese Taipei's trade regime. Furthermore, Chinese Taipei's exported goods and services are now able to compete on a level playing field with those of other countries. In the event of international trade disputes, effective resolutions can be sought for Chinese Taipei under the WTO dispute settlement process. To date, Chinese Taipei has submitted three cases to the WTO dispute settlement body as a complainant and has won a dispute with the European Union over the implementation of the ITA. Chinese Taipei has also participated in eighty-one other dispute cases as a third party, demonstrating its firm support for the multilateral trading system.

The gradual opening of Chinese Taipei's market has exposed its domestic industries to global competition, necessitating a process of adjustment and adaptation that has ultimately led to economic growth. For the more vulnerable industries, the challenges of market liberalisation have acted as an incentive to restructure and reinvent in order to improve their competitiveness. Chinese Taipei's accession to the WTO has also been a catalyst for the globalisation and development of its industries.

Chinese Taipei's trade policies and regulations have undergone a thorough review and revision as a result of the requirements of WTO membership. This legislative overhaul has been highly beneficial in modernising the trade regime. Furthermore, the strong team of administrators and negotiators that navigated the process of Chinese Taipei's accession to the WTO, and the experience they accrued along the way, will continue to serve as a valuable asset in future economic reforms and participation in the multilateral and plurilateral trade negotiations of the WTO.

As a developing country and the coordinator of the recently acceded members Chinese Taipei will, in the future, continue to support the WTO's multilateral trade negotiations – including the post-Bali work programme – and to participate in the Trade in Services Agreement and the expansion of the ITA as well as the negotiations on trade in environmental goods. Chinese Taipei looks forward to collaborating with other WTO members in the further liberalisation of international trade.

## Acknowledgements

The author acknowledges the outstanding contributions to accession negotiations by the chief negotiators: Pin-Kung Chiang, Ke-Sheng Sheu, Yi-Fu Lin and Steve Ruey-Long Chen.

# 18

# The 2004 WTO accession of Cambodia: negotiating priorities and experience – growth and integration eleven years later

CHAM PRASIDH

ABSTRACT

*Cambodia was the first least-developed country to complete negoti-
ations to become a member of the WTO. Its negotiations took place
in the context of the Decision on LDC accessions taken by the WTO
General Council in December 2002, in which WTO members agreed
that they would be bound by certain restraints in dealing with LDCs
seeking to join the WTO. Given the constraints that, as an LDC, it
faced when entering the negotiations, Cambodia recognised that
joining the WTO could play an important part in accelerating its
growth and development. This chapter describes Cambodia's approach
to the accession negotiations: its negotiating strategy, the negotiations
themselves and their outcome and Cambodia's post-accession activities.
The foundation of all international trading arrangements is the WTO,
its concepts and its rules, most of which are carried over into preferential trading arrangements. Being a member of the WTO provides a
member's traders with the transparent and predictable trading environment that they need to prosper. It can truly be said that being a
WTO member is one of the main pillars of Cambodia's successful
economic performance.*

Cambodia applied to become a member of the WTO in October 1994.
It completed its WTO accession negotiations in May 2003, making it the
first of the least-developed countries (LDCs) to complete negotiations
to become a member of the WTO. Cambodia shares with Nepal the

distinction of being an LDC pioneer in exploring what was then the uncharted territory of LDC accession.[1]

Cambodia's accession negotiations followed the broad outlines that are familiar to all those who have participated in the accession process. Negotiations proceeded simultaneously in four areas: WTO members' examination of Cambodia's trade regime; bilateral negotiations with members on tariff bindings on goods; bilateral negotiations with members on market access for services; and the examination of state support for agriculture.

Cambodia's negotiations took place in the context of the Decision on LDC accessions taken by the WTO General Council in December 2002.[2] In this, members agreed that they would be bound by certain restraints in dealing with LDCs seeking to join the WTO. In particular, they agreed that they would: (i) not seek sharp reductions in tariff levels; (ii) require concessions in relatively few services sectors; and (iii) allow an LDC to join the WTO before all its laws and regulations were in full compliance with WTO rules, provided that the LDC presented a detailed work plan for achieving compliance in the years immediately following accession, and committed itself to fully executing that programme.

This chapter reviews the main features of Cambodia's experience with WTO accession, and briefly describes the government's WTO-related post-accession activities and the role that accession has played in shaping Cambodia's trade and development in the years that have followed accession.

## Cambodia's approach to the accession negotiations

### Trade, development and employment

From the outset, Cambodia recognised that joining the WTO could play an important part in accelerating its growth and development. In order to maximise these benefits (and minimise any potential disadvantages) it was necessary to devise a negotiation strategy that fitted Cambodia's needs and that would lead to the kind of outcome it desired.

---

[1] Cambodia's and Nepal's WTO accession negotiations occurred at roughly the same time. Cambodia's negotiations were completed before Nepal's, but Nepal ratified its WTO accession agreement before Cambodia and became the first LDC to join the WTO.

[2] See WTO document WT/L/508.

In formulating this strategy, Cambodia started with the fundamental realities that characterise it.

Cambodia is a small country with a relatively small population (some 14 million), a large proportion of whom are impoverished. At the same time, Cambodia's population has been expanding rapidly. The number of young people entering the job market was growing rapidly at the time the strategy was being formulated, and it was expected that it would continue to grow at a rapid pace in the years ahead. Expanding employment opportunities was thus a major challenge facing Cambodia. Given the lack of purchasing power in the domestic economy, the rapid creation of new jobs could only be achieved by producing for other, larger markets. In other words, Cambodia's growth and development had to be outward oriented, with exports playing a key role in creating employment and reducing poverty.

A second Cambodian reality is that the necessary increase in exports and employment could occur only if there was a rapid expansion of investment. Because adequate savings, skills and technology are not always available within Cambodia, foreign investment has an important role to play in bringing about the necessary expansion. Foreign direct investment (FDI) has an especially critical role to play in expanding exports, since foreign firms best know foreign markets, and possess the technology, managerial experience and marketing channels that are needed to engage successfully in exporting.

This emphasis on exports and FDI must not, however, imply any neglect of the important role of small and medium-sized enterprises (SMEs) in Cambodia's development. These enterprises produce almost exclusively for the domestic market. They account for a very important share of Cambodian employment (although still a small share of the growth in employment) and are an important breeding ground for the development of indigenous entrepreneurship.

The third fundamental reality of Cambodia is that it is a rural society and economy, with most Cambodians depending directly or indirectly on agriculture for their livelihood. Cambodia is competitive or potentially competitive across a fairly wide range of agricultural sectors. The government recognised, however, that the development of its agriculture would be a long and complex process that needed to be backstopped by a trade policy providing reasonable protection to domestic producers from agricultural imports, while ensuring that competitive Cambodian agriculture had access to markets abroad.

In addition to these fundamental realities regarding Cambodia's own situation, an important reality of the international trading regime had to be taken into account. In accordance with the WTO Agreement on Textiles and Clothing, the special regime governing trade in garments was scheduled to come to an end on 1 January 2005. This regime allowed countries to apply quantitative restrictions on imports of clothing. Accordingly, the garment exports of almost all countries had been subject to quotas in major world markets, in particular the United States. Cambodia's garment exports had also been subject to quotas. On 1 January 2005, however, WTO members were obliged to eliminate quotas on clothing imports from other WTO members. As of that date, access to world markets would be unrestrained for WTO members. If Cambodia were not a member on that date, countries would be free to continue to impose quotas on Cambodia's exports, and would undoubtedly do so. Thus, failure to join the WTO by 1 January 2005 would put Cambodia's garment industry at a significant disadvantage relative to its competitors.

## Formulating an accession strategy

The considerations outlined above allowed the WTO accession negotiating team to formulate some broad guidelines for Cambodia's negotiations with WTO members. These were designed to ensure that Cambodia's negotiating strategy at the WTO was fully consistent with its view of the important role that international trade had played, and would continue to play, in its economic development. The six main building blocks around which Cambodia's strategy was constructed were as follows.

### Timing

Cambodia targeted a rapid accession to the WTO. The need for a rapid accession was driven mainly by the 1 January 2005 deadline facing its garment industry (see above). But Cambodia also believed that it was in its own interests to achieve quickly the assured access to all export markets that is guaranteed by WTO membership. Moreover, it believed that the December 2002 Decision on the accession of LDCs (outlined above) made rapid accession feasible. In that Decision, the General Council agreed that members (i) would not seek sharp reductions in tariff levels; (ii) would require concessions in relatively few services sectors; and (iii) would allow an LDC to join the WTO before all its laws and regulations were in full compliance with WTO rules, provided that the LDC presented a detailed work plan for achieving compliance in the years immediately following accession, and committed itself to fully executing that programme. Cambodia understood that it would need to draft and adopt a large number of laws so as to create a trade regime that was consistent with WTO rules. But it also knew that the Decision would allow it to do part of this after accession. Furthermore, Cambodia had not developed any domestic industries that were dependent for their survival on high tariff protection. Allowing time for domestic industry to adjust to any tariff reductions that might be required by accession was thus not a consideration.

In short, Cambodia saw a number of reasons for going forward rapidly, and no arguments in favour of a slower accession.

## Tariff concessions

Shortly before negotiations with the WTO began, Cambodia had undertaken a reform of its tariffs on imports of goods. This reform had reduced the number of tariff 'bands' from twelve to four – after the reform, all goods were charged a duty of either 0, 7, 15 or 35 per cent. In the process, Cambodia eliminated some higher tariff rates that had previously been applied. It was persuaded that these reductions and simplifications had met its needs and also contributed to the overall liberalisation of world trade. Cambodia was also mindful of the need to keep some protection in place for its SMEs and agriculture. Finally, tariffs contributed an important share of Cambodia's budget revenue. For all these reasons, Cambodia was determined during the WTO negotiations to avoid any commitment to reduce tariffs further.

## Export orientation

In order to be competitive on world markets, an export industry needs to have access to raw materials and intermediate inputs at world market prices. Cambodia had always recognised this and, under the Law on Investment, had provided export industries with duty-free access to imported capital and intermediate goods and raw materials. The way in which Cambodia did this, however, was not fully compatible with WTO rules. Nevertheless, Cambodia understood that maintaining these privileges was essential to its garment industry, and to its future ability to attract other export-oriented industries. Cambodia was thus determined to maintain its capacity to offer such advantages.

## Improving the investment climate and fostering FDI

As mentioned above, Cambodia understood that increased exports and jobs would depend on increased investment, in particular FDI.

It understood, therefore, the central importance of using accession to the WTO as a means to increase the attractiveness of Cambodia as a place to invest. WTO membership offers three main ways to do this.

First, WTO membership provides certain assurances for investors wishing to produce in Cambodia for export to other markets. This is because Cambodian exporters can be certain that their goods will be charged a rate of duty in the importing country that is no higher than the rate charged by the importing country on identical or similar goods coming from other exporting countries. Moreover, because most WTO members have 'bound' (i.e. set legal ceilings on) most of their tariff lines, a Cambodian exporter would know the maximum legal duty that could be charged on its export good in any WTO member country. Furthermore, Cambodian exporters could be certain that their exports would not be subject to quotas or any kind of quantitative restraint in their export markets. For all of these reasons, WTO membership reduces the uncertainty facing an investor that wants to produce in Cambodia for export to other markets. (For investors wishing to export to markets where Cambodian exports enjoy tariff preferences, the preferential arrangements are also an important source of certainty.)

Second, WTO membership would require an intensified effort by Cambodia to put in place the legal framework required by business. The government of Cambodia had for some time been actively engaged in developing and submitting to the National Assembly the laws necessary for a modern, liberal and business-friendly legal environment. A member of the WTO must have laws that embody WTO rules concerning international trade and activities related to trade. The Cambodian accession negotiating team understood from the outset that this would be necessary, and welcomed the requirement as a way of ordering and accelerating the government's efforts to create a proper legal framework for business that fully reflected international norms.

Third, Cambodia understood from the outset that its attractiveness to investors depended on the availability of the infrastructure required by businesses. This infrastructure includes services such as telecommunications, transportation, banking, accounting and auditing. The investment environment is also enhanced by the availability of an educated and trained labour force. Cambodia saw the WTO accession negotiations on services as an opportunity to encourage foreign investment in key services infrastructure, and therefore an opportunity to enhance its overall environment for business. Likewise, foreign participation in adult education and training would help develop the skilled workforce that is necessary to attract skill-based industries and allow for increased wages.

For these reasons, Cambodia understood that the negotiations on services could advance its overall strategy of improving the business environment. It was aware that the 2002 Decision on accession of LDCs called for WTO members to limit the scope of negotiations on services. However, rather than seeking to limit its commitments to the bare minimum referred to in the Decision, Cambodia preferred to address services issues on a case-by-case basis, and when it was convinced that committing to liberalisation in a particular services sector would help it move toward its broader development objectives, it was prepared to engage in negotiations and take on commitments.

### Retaining policy options and flexibility on agriculture

Market access (see the section on 'Timing' above) and improvements in the investment environment benefit agriculture as well as manufacturing and services. Since Cambodia is a competitive or potentially competitive agricultural producer across a broad range of agricultural products, WTO rules that would reduce the support provided by other countries to their less efficient producers would ultimately be to the benefit of Cambodia. As mentioned above, however, Cambodia understood that it needed to maintain minimum, but adequate, tariff protection of agricultural products, and retain the right to provide support to domestic producers that genuinely assisted them in becoming more competitive. Achieving these ends was an important element of Cambodia's accession strategy.

### Securing LDC benefits with regard to public health

At its Ministerial Conference in Doha in 2001, the WTO adopted a Declaration[3] granting LDCs certain special privileges as regards WTO requirements for the protection of patents on pharmaceutical products. The objective of the Declaration, and subsequent implementing decisions, was to allow LDCs to have access to cheap drug products, including the right to import cheap pharmaceuticals. This provision is particularly important for Cambodia, as it faces difficult public health issues as regards HIV/AIDS, tuberculosis, malaria and other major diseases. At the same time, it is dependent on imports of drugs to fight these diseases, and the financial resources available to it are limited. It is

---

[3] Doha Declaration on the Trade-Related Aspects of Intellectual Property Rights (TRIPs) Agreement and Public Health, adopted on 14 November 2001.

therefore of great importance that Cambodia should have access to medicines at the lowest possible prices. Ensuring that the WTO Declaration applied fully to Cambodia was thus an important objective of its accession negotiations.

These were the main considerations that guided Cambodia throughout its negotiations with WTO members.

## The negotiations

### Setting the process in motion

Cambodia first applied for membership of the WTO in 1994. It was not until 1997, however, that it was in a position to undertake the very complex tasks required to set the process of accession in motion.

The first step in the accession process is for the candidate to prepare a memorandum on its foreign trade regime, designed to inform the members of the WTO of all the laws, regulations and government decisions and policies affecting trade in its economy. The memorandum must be drawn up following an outline established by the WTO, and cover all the items included in the outline. The main topics that need to be covered by the memorandum include:

- monetary and fiscal policy;
- state ownership and privatisation policies;
- pricing and competition policies;
- rules regarding the right to trade;
- customs procedures, in particular customs valuation procedures;
- the application of internal taxes to imports;
- quantitative import restrictions, quotas and import licensing;
- preshipment inspection;
- anti-dumping, countervailing duties and safeguards;
- export regulation;
- product standards and technical regulations;
- sanitary and phytosanitary (SPS) regulations;
- investment measures related to trade;
- state trading;
- free zones and special economic zones;
- government procurement;
- agricultural policies;
- the protection of intellectual property;
- policies affecting trade in services.

The government of Cambodia was aware that the complex tasks of preparing such a memorandum and managing the negotiations that would follow required new and special governmental machinery. It instructed the Ministry of Commerce to act as the focal point for activities related to WTO accession. In addition, in September 1997, the government established an Inter-ministerial Coordinating Committee on WTO accession that was chaired by the Minister of Commerce. This Committee was made up of fifteen members at the policy level and three officials at the working level from each of the twenty-three ministries and agencies involved in WTO activities. Its role was to: (i) coordinate policy issues related to WTO accession; (ii) elaborate guidelines to implement WTO agreements; (iii) prepare the necessary documentation; (iv) define the government's priorities related to foreign trade policies; (v) ensure coordination between ministries; and (vi) report to the Prime Minister on issues related to WTO accession.

With this machinery in place, the government's WTO team proceeded to begin work on the memorandum on the trade regime. A first draft was completed in 1999 and, after extensive internal review, the final draft was submitted to the WTO in 2000. The memorandum consisted of over one hundred pages describing Cambodia's trade regime, together with many statistical tables. It was submitted to the members of the working party on Cambodia's accession, which reviewed it and, following usual WTO practice, submitted some seventy-five follow-up questions designed to further clarify aspects of Cambodia's trade regime. Cambodia provided answers to those questions, thus setting the stage for the first meeting of the working party, and the onset of negotiations.

## The Geneva process

The first meeting of the working party on the accession of Cambodia to the WTO was held in May 2001, and, like all subsequent meetings, took place at the WTO's headquarters in Geneva. Before this meeting took place, Cambodia was fortunate in being able to arrange for technical assistance to be provided by the United Nations Conference on Trade and Development (UNCTAD). UNCTAD experts have long experience in WTO accessions, and were able to brief the Cambodian negotiating team on the way in which negotiations were usually conducted, thus helping the team better understand what to expect. They also helped the Cambodian team to put the accession process in a development perspective. UNCTAD continued to assist until the end of the negotiations, which was a benefit for Cambodia.

The first meeting consisted of an examination of Cambodia's Memorandum on the Foreign Trade Regime, and of the answers that Cambodia had provided to members' questions. As is always the case in all accessions, this examination gave rise to requests for additional information. At the end of this meeting Cambodia was requested to provide replies to standard detailed questionnaires that the WTO Secretariat had drawn up in the areas of services, import licensing, intellectual property protection, support to agriculture, technical barriers to trade (TBT) and SPS regulations. Cambodia was also requested to prepare offers of the concessions it would be prepared to make on import tariffs and services.

During the months following this first meeting, Cambodia's WTO team addressed these tasks.

In drawing up the tariff offer, Cambodia had to take account of the fact that members required an acceding country to 'bind' all of its tariff lines. This meant that Cambodia would have to propose a 'bound' rate for each of its 6,823 tariff lines. This binding, in turn, would determine the maximum tariff rate that could be applied to each item. As a WTO member, Cambodia would remain free to set tariffs at levels equal to or lower than the bound rate, but would not, except in exceptional circumstances, be able to charge duties that exceeded the bound rate.

Cambodia's strategy in drawing up this initial offer was to set bound rates well above current applied rates, i.e. well above the tariff rates actually in use. As mentioned above, Cambodia's objective in the negotiation was to avoid any commitment to reduce applied tariff rates, and the negotiating team needed ample space to respond to requests to lower Cambodia's bindings while keeping that objective intact.

Formulating Cambodia's initial offer on services was more complex. A first task was to decide which services sectors to include in the offer. Unlike the case of goods, members do not require commitments in all services sectors. In fact, in the case of LDCs, members had agreed that they would require commitments on 'relatively few' services sectors (see above). Still, the WTO classifier for services contains twelve broad headings and 155 service sectors and sub-sectors, and Cambodia needed to choose between them in making its initial offer. Furthermore, the WTO has identified four different ways in which any given service can be imported. These include cross-border supply (e.g. ordering a set of architectural drawings from a Thai architect and having him mail the drawings to Phnom Penh, thus importing architectural services);

consumption abroad (for example, sailing a Mekong ferry boat to a Vietnamese shipyard for repairs, so that when the ferry returns to Cambodia it imports repair services); commercial presence (e.g. allowing a foreign architectural firm that intends to employ only Cambodian architects to establish itself in Cambodia, thus importing the archi-tectural services of the firm); and the presence of natural persons (e.g. allowing the foreign architectural firm established in Cambodia to also employ foreign architects, thus importing the services of those individuals). Finally, for each of the service sectors or sub-sectors that Cambodia chose to include, it was required to indicate, for each of the four ways the service could be imported, the degree of market access that would be allowed, and the extent to which it would regulate foreign service providers in the same way as it regulated Cambodian suppliers in that service sector ('national treatment'). As would become clear in the subsequent negotiations, members usually sought commitments to full market access and full national treatment.

Once all these materials had been prepared and approved by the government, they were sent to the WTO and the stage was set for the second working party meeting, which took place in early 2002 and established the format that would be used in all the subsequent meetings that were held in 2002 and 2003. In fact, three separate types of activity took place every time the negotiating team went to Geneva.

First, there was the working party proper. All WTO members that wished to do so attended this meeting. The purpose of the meeting was to continue the examination of Cambodia's trade laws and regulations, and to allow members to see the extent to which these laws were consistent with WTO rules. The discussion in the working party also helped the Cambodian negotiators to understand more fully the steps that still had to be taken to bring Cambodian laws and regulations into compliance with WTO rules. Throughout this period, the government was making maximum efforts to draft and have passed by the National Assembly those laws required of a WTO member. For example, the drafting of a new customs law and a new civil code was completed during this period, and the National Assembly adopted laws on trademarks and copyright. As the discussion in the working party progressed into 2003, the negotiat-ing team was able to judge the extent to which these internal efforts would allow Cambodia to be in compliance at the time it joined the WTO, and where it would need more time to put in place the necessary laws.

Second, in the days just before and after each meeting of the working party, Cambodia met with some members individually. These bilateral meetings were scheduled at the request of the individual member, and allowed the member to make requests for changes in Cambodia's initial offers with regard to tariff bindings and access to services markets. These requests usually took the form of asking for a lower bound tariff rate on products of particular trading interest to the member country, or asking for additional service sectors to be added to the services offer. Cambodia had to examine each of these requests and determine whether it could be accommodated within Cambodia's overall strategy for the negotiations.

During the course of the accession process Cambodia met bilaterally with nine WTO members (Australia, Canada, European Communities, India, Japan, the Republic of Korea, Panama, Chinese Taipei and the United States). At the end of this process, all the changes to Cambodia's initial offers agreed with these members were brought together in a consolidated schedule of commitments on tariffs and a consolidated schedule of commitments on services. These two schedules became part of Cambodia's Accession Protocol, and thus form part of Cambodia's legal obligations as a WTO member.

Third, during the week of each working party meeting Cambodia met a small number of interested members to explore Cambodia's programmes that benefit agriculture. These plurilateral meetings had the purpose of allowing members to understand whether any of these programmes were of a sort that distort international trade. While WTO rules do not limit the overall support that a government may provide to its agricultural sector, they do impose limits on specific forms of support that distort trade. It was thus important to Cambodia and to members to have a common understanding of which Cambodian programmes, if any, would fall into the category subject to limits.

## Outcome of the negotiations

At the final meeting of the working party in July 2003, the members agreed on the terms and conditions according to which Cambodia could join the WTO. These terms and conditions were the result of the negotiations described above. Their main characteristics are summarised as follows.

### Import tariffs on goods

Cambodia bound all of its tariff lines. The agreed levels of the binding were in all cases equal to or higher than the level of tariffs that were actually applied by Cambodia in 2003. Thus, no actual reductions in tariffs were required as a consequence of WTO membership. The overall average bound duty rate was 19.9 per cent. This compares with the average rate of duty actually applied by Cambodia in 2003 of 16.5 per cent. As regards agricultural products, Cambodia's average bound rate of duty was 29.4 per cent, as compared with the average rates actually applied in 2003 of 19.4 per cent. For manufactured goods, the average bound rate was 18.4 per cent, and the rate applied in 2003 was 16.0 per cent.

### Imports of services

Cambodia undertook market access commitments in at least one sub-sector under each of eleven different services headings: business services, communications services, construction and related engineering services, distribution services, education services, environmental services, financial services, health-related services, tourism and travel services, recreational services and transport services.

The commitments undertaken by Cambodia in these sectors have the following characteristics.

First, following Cambodia's strategy for services, as described above, the government centred its negotiations on areas that would contribute most to improving those services required by businesses, thus improving the environment for investment. For example, Cambodia has committed to allowing foreign firms to operate in the areas of legal services (with some exceptions), accounting, auditing, bookkeeping, banking, management consulting, telecommunications and transport.

Second, following this strategy further, Cambodia undertook commitments in areas that would help Cambodians develop the skills needed for a modern, competitive economy. Thus, it committed to allowing foreign firms to provide higher education and adult education services.

Finally, Cambodia undertook commitments in areas that it considered would contribute to improvements in healthcare and in the provision of sanitary, refuse and sewerage services. Cambodia believed that these would all contribute to improvements in public health.

A number of other considerations entered into Cambodia's decisions to agree or not agree to requests. First, Cambodia felt particularly comfortable in taking on commitments in sectors where it had long had an open policy regarding foreign participation and where that policy had served it well. This is the case, for example, in banking, tourism and courier services. Cambodia also felt particularly comfortable in opening up some sectors where it knew Cambodians could compete successfully with foreigners, for example in guide services. Where, however, Cambodia saw an advantage for itself in reserving part of a market for Cambodian SMEs, it did so. For example, Cambodia committed to opening up the hotel market only for hotels of three stars or higher, and committed to allowing the foreign supply of retailing services only for a small number of specific items or for very large supermarkets or department stores.

Overall, Cambodia considers that it came out of the negotiations on services with a set of commitments that fully reflected its strategy and that would contribute to the future development of Cambodia.

### Support to agriculture

The examination by WTO members of Cambodia's support for agriculture revealed that Cambodia did not provide such support in ways that distorted international trade. Cambodia was thus not required to commit to reducing such support. Under existing WTO rules, Cambodia remained free to provide assistance that distorted trade up to a limit equal to 10 per cent of the value of its agricultural output (in the case of support measures of a general character) and 10 per cent of the value of each crop (in the case of measures applied only to that crop). Furthermore, Cambodia remained free to provide unlimited support to its agriculture sector in ways that did not distort trade. These features, taken together, provided ample leeway for any support policies that a future government might wish to implement.

Cambodia did undertake a commitment not to subsidise agricultural exports. It has never considered providing such subsidies, and the government did not (and does not) believe that it would be sound policy. Certainly there are current features of the Cambodian economy that reduce the competitiveness of its agricultural exporters – for example, high internal transport costs as a result of poor feeder roads and various informal charges for road use. But policy and Cambodia's scarce resources need to be directed at eliminating these underlying problems, rather than attempting to use export subsidies to offset their costs to exporters, which could in any case only be a temporary expedient.

## Complying with WTO trade rules

Cambodia's Protocol of Accession contains, by reference, twenty-nine separate and sometimes detailed statements describing the way in which Cambodia will fulfil its commitment to abide by WTO rules. At the time of accession, the government and the National Assembly had already been actively engaged in preparing and passing the legislation needed to bring Cambodia into compliance with those rules. However, at the time Cambodia's accession negotiations were concluded that task had not been completed, and the twenty-nine statements reflect the fact that in some areas Cambodian legislative reform was still 'work in progress'.

Each of the twenty-nine statements dealt with a specific policy area covered by WTO rules. In seventeen of the twenty-nine areas, Cambodia's present laws and regulations were found to be either in full compliance with WTO rules, or could be made compliant by governmental decision before the date of accession. In these areas Cambodia's commitment was simply to apply the rules from the date of accession onwards. The topics in question include:

- pricing policies;
- customs charges other than normal customs duties;
- tariff exemptions;
- fees to cover the costs of customs procedures;
- domestic taxes;
- quotas, licensing and other non-tariff barriers (except for pesticides and fertiliser, see below);
- preshipment inspection;
- export restrictions;
- industrial subsidies;
- trade-related investment measures;
- state trading;
- free zones and special economic zones;
- transit trade;
- agricultural export subsidies;
- trade in textiles;
- publication of information on trade;
- free trade agreements.

This left twelve areas in which Cambodia was not in compliance with WTO rules.

In three of the twelve areas, legislation bringing Cambodia into full compliance with WTO rules was being considered by the National Assembly. In four other areas of central importance to the WTO regime, Cambodia had made considerable progress in bringing its laws and regulations into compliance with WTO rules. However, because of the complexity of these issues, it was obvious that Cambodia could not complete the actions required, quickly, to achieve full compliance. Recognising this, WTO members agreed to Cambodia's request that the special arrangements for LDCs (referred to earlier) should apply to these areas. This meant that Cambodia's accession could go forward, even though Cambodia would not be in a position to apply these rules as soon as it joined the WTO, or shortly thereafter.

As required by the special arrangements for LDCs, Cambodia worked out action plans in each of the four areas, and took on a commitment to execute these plans. The action plans spelled out the specific steps that Cambodia would take to bring itself into full conformity with the rules, and the time-frame for these steps. Cambodia's action plan on customs valuation was to be fully implemented by 1 January 2009; its action plans on TBT and on TRIPs by 1 January 2007; and its action plan on SPS measures by 1 January 2008.

These deadlines for bringing Cambodia into full WTO compliance in the four areas were not realistic, in particular given the small amount of technical assistance that was available in the years immediately following accession. None of the deadlines was met. Cambodia has nonetheless made good progress in implementing the action plans, as was acknowledged by members during its trade policy review (TPR).

A special comment is required regarding Cambodia's commitments in the area of protection of intellectual property. Questions have been raised as to whether these commitments would allow Cambodia to benefit fully from the Doha Declaration on the TRIPs Agreement and Public Health. As mentioned earlier, ensuring that Cambodia could benefit from the Declaration was one of the government's major objectives in the negotiation.

Cambodia believes that this objective was fully achieved. Some observers have commented on two sentences in Cambodia's commitment paragraphs that deal with the use of test data in patent applications. It is true that these two sentences, when read in isolation, could suggest some restriction on Cambodia's ability to benefit from the Doha Declaration. However, it should be noted that Cambodia's own Law on Patents contains provisions allowing it to fully apply the Doha Declaration. This law was available to members of the WTO well before the conclusion of the negotiations, and there was no comment by members on the provisions dealing with the Doha Declaration. Furthermore, in inviting Cambodia to join the WTO at the Cancún Ministerial Meeting, the members of the working party declared that 'the terms of this accession did not preclude access of Cambodia and LDCs to the benefits under the Doha Declaration on the TRIPs Agreement and Public Health'. Members have thus made their intent very clear, and Cambodia understands the two sentences in question in this context, and has developed its policies accordingly.

The remaining areas in which Cambodia undertook commitments cover a variety of topics. Cambodia undertook to provide information to WTO members on its privatisation programme, to set up a mechanism to accept and act on complaints from traders and governments about customs practices and to allow any registered business to be the importer of record of pharmaceuticals and veterinary medicines. Cambodia also took on a commitment not to use anti-dumping, countervailing or safeguard measures until it had passed WTO-compliant laws governing its actions in these areas.

All in all, the outcome as regards Cambodia's conformity with WTO rules was positive. This was because of Cambodia's work before and during the accession process, a large part of the government's trade regime was judged by members to be in conformity with WTO rules. In the areas in which conformity had not yet been achieved, Cambodia secured the flexibility necessary to complete the job. Of course, this left it with important tasks to address in the post-accession period, as described below.

## Post-accession activities

### The WTO work programme

Cambodia was invited to join the WTO at the Ministerial Conference in Cancún, Mexico, in September 2003. The government immediately began putting together a work programme of legislative and regulatory actions that were required by Cambodia's accession. These actions included, of course, all measures needed to bring the government into full compliance with its legal obligations as a WTO member, including measures specified in its Protocol of Accession. Cambodia also understood, however, that if it were to benefit fully from WTO membership, it would need to accelerate its overall programme of legislative reform, which included laws and regulations that were not related to the WTO (such as bankruptcy law, for example). Improving the overall legal environment for business was an important ingredient in encouraging the investment which would be triggered by WTO accession.

In early 2004, the government formally adopted its WTO work programme. The programme included a list of laws to be developed and adopted (e.g. on geographical indications and on standards). It also included regulatory actions (e.g. developing regulations governing engineering and architectural services) and administrative actions (e.g. providing an internal appeals mechanism for decisions taken by the General Directorate of Customs and Excise). In the years immediately following accession, additional items were added to the work programme, as the need for them became evident. At one point, the work programme consisted of around one hundred individual actions.

In order to ensure proper coordination of post-accession WTO-related activities, the Interministerial Coordinating Committee on WTO Accession was renamed the Inter-ministerial Coordinating Committee on Cambodia's WTO Commitments and given a fresh mandate to coordinate all governmental activities related to the WTO. In this capacity it periodically reviewed progress in executing the work programme, and coordinated Cambodia's preparations for its first TPR.

## Cambodia's first TPR

Cambodia's first TPR was held in November 2011. Among other things, this review allowed WTO members to take stock of the progress Cambodia had made in fulfilling its accession commitments. Of the roughly one hundred items in Cambodia's work programme, thirty-one dealt with WTO legal commitments. Cambodia was able to report to WTO members that for nineteen of these items the necessary laws or regulations had been adopted and implemented, and that it was very close to completing action on most of the remaining twelve items. In summing up at the end of its meeting, the Chair of the TPR body stated that 'Members appreciated Cambodia's continued commitment to fully implementing the agreements on Customs Valuation, TRIPs, TBT and SPS and acknowledged the steps taken by Cambodia to promote good governance through judicial and legal reforms and create a more transparent and predictable business environment to help attract investment'. Cambodia takes this to be recognition by members of the significant success to date of its efforts at legal reform. Of course, more remains to be done, as the Chair also mentioned in summing up.

During the period 2004–2008, Cambodia experienced double-digit growth in gross domestic product (GDP), a rapid expansion of employment and significant reduction in poverty levels. The global financial crisis of 2009–2010 briefly interrupted these trends, but in the years following the crisis Cambodia has returned to a high-growth path.

This strong economic performance is due entirely to Cambodia's success to date in integrating into the international and regional economies: exports and export-related investment have led the way in generating jobs and income.

Garment exports were the driving force behind this export growth. Since Cambodia became a WTO member before the expiration of the WTO Agreement on Textiles and Clothing in January 2005, Cambodia's garment exports were not subject to quantitative restraints after that date. As mentioned earlier, this was an important objective in Cambodia's negotiating strategy. As regards garments, therefore, WTO membership led to a direct and important boost to exports.

This does not mean, however, that membership automatically leads to trade-led development. An LDC that joins WTO needs immediately to identify the further steps that need to be taken to realise the full potential provided by membership. Post-accession policies in areas such as commercial legislation, supply-side development, export and investment promotion, trade facilitation and labour market development – to mention just a few – will ultimately determine the extent to which WTO membership triggers an acceleration of growth and development. Cambodia continues to develop and pursue policies in these areas. In doing so, Cambodia will increase further the already large benefits it has enjoyed from becoming a WTO member.

# 19

# The 2008 WTO accession of Ukraine: negotiating experience – challenges, opportunities and post-accession approaches

VALERIY PYATNITSKIY AND SVITLANA ZAITSEVA

ABSTRACT

*Ukraine embarked on its road to WTO accession in 1992, a year after it had declared its independence. Fourteen years of intense work, steep learning, persistence, political will and flexibility were to follow. Ukraine faced many immediate challenges and tasks in strengthening its independence and creating and establishing the national institutions required by an independent state, moving away from a centralised economy and reinforcing foreign policy. Ukraine had to totally eliminate its post-Soviet legacy. A new system of national government and administration had to be established. Democracy, the rule of law and a free market became the guiding principles for political, social and economic life. WTO accession implied increased competition, which turned out to be quite painful for some companies. However, the negative scenarios foreseen by some researchers did not occur; in fact, the accession offered the national economy new incentives for structural and long-lasting change. However, WTO membership is not simply a recipe for future happiness. While it stimulates trade and business environments, members must still work within the multilateral system to keep up to date.*

The task of designing and implementing an independent foreign policy was especially challenging as Ukraine was largely unknown in the world, perceived only as part of the wider Commonwealth of Independent States (CIS) and often confused with Russia. National trade policy *per se* was effectively absent and had to be adapted from existing policies which coincided with Ukraine's interest at the time. So trade policy needed to be formulated in a way that clearly identified the national economic interests of the new Ukraine while interacting with the rest of the world to allow Ukraine to build new relations and partnerships, promoting future progress and development.

From an economic point of view, Ukraine was a major part of the massive and highly inefficient Soviet economy. The collapse of the Soviet Union resulted in disruption of economic ties which were replaced by rather primitive free trade agreements (FTAs) between the CIS economies. In the case of Ukraine, this led to a 50 per cent decrease in gross domestic product (GDP) and hyperinflation, which in 1993–1994 reached more than 2,000 per cent.

In the 1990s, Ukraine had to drastically change and build a self-reliant and entrepreneurship-based economy. One must remember that in the 1990s Ukrainian business was eager and active in this objective, but was still rather weak and unable to clearly identify its needs and articulate a vision as regards trade and new markets.

## Accession to the WTO

Ukraine's process of accession to the General Agreement on Tariffs and Trade 1994 (GATT)/WTO started on 30 November 1993 with an official letter sent to the GATT Secretariat. The Working Party on the Accession of Ukraine to the WTO was established on 17 December 1993. Initially the working party consisted of forty-four members, including the European Union and later this grew to fifty-two members.

The next procedural step was presentation to the members of the working party of Ukraine's Memorandum on its Foreign Trade Regime.

Ukraine had three working party chairs during its accession: Mr A. Stoler, Deputy Permanent Representative of the United States to the WTO (1994–2000); Mr S. Marchi, Ambassador of Canada (2000–2006); and Mr M. Matus, Ambassador of Chile (2006–2008).

Ukraine highly appreciated their role in the accession, although it was not always smooth going, and was often challenging, not only for the government of Ukraine and its Parliament, but also for the chairs. Ukraine is grateful to them all for their leadership and many years of experience in the multilateral trading system which they readily shared with the Ukrainian negotiators.

Of special value to Ukraine was their diplomacy advice and high personal standards of professionalism, which allowed them to efficiently coordinate work of all the parties concerned. Each of them was sincerely dedicated to Ukraine's accession over the years and their strong belief in its success had a highly motivating effect on Ukraine's negotiators.

Experts from the Accessions Division of the WTO Secretariat undertook much work with the mass of required documentation over the fourteen years. The Ukrainian negotiating team enjoyed good and efficient cooperation with the Secretariat. All those who worked on Ukraine's accession deserve praise; the Secretariat excelled in reviewing Ukraine's documents, circulating documents in a timely manner and processing the hundreds of pages comprising Ukraine's Accession Package.

Accession 'homework' consisted of meetings in Geneva and in the working party members' many capitals, and numerous formal and informal meetings, in multilateral, plurilateral and bilateral rounds, in order to:

- agree upon a schedule of concessions on goods and specific commitments on services;
- draft the working party report and work out acceptable formulae of commitments;
- conduct numerous bilateral negotiations with fifty-two working party members (Argentina, Armenia, Australia, Bulgaria, Canada, China, Colombia, Croatia, Cuba, Czech Republic, the Dominican Republic, Ecuador, Egypt, El Salvador, Estonia, European Communities, Georgia, Guatemala, Honduras, Hungary, Iceland, India, Indonesia, Israel, Japan, Republic of Korea, Kyrgyz Republic, Latvia, Lithuania, Malaysia, Mexico, Moldova, Mongolia, Morocco, New Zealand, Norway, Panama, Paraguay, Peru, Poland, Romania, Slovak Republic, Slovenia, Sri Lanka, Switzerland, Chinese Taipei, Thailand, Turkey, United States, Uruguay and Viet Nam);
- align national legislation with the principles and rules of the WTO.

It took seventeen working party meetings and numerous technical consultations with the Accessions Division before the final working party meeting on 25 January 2008, at which the working party members agreed the final draft Accession Package of Ukraine.

During all these years, the Ukrainian Parliament (*Verkhovna Rada* of Ukraine) ensured legislative changes. For example, between 2005 and 2007 alone, the Parliament adopted nearly fifty laws to advance the accession process and, more importantly, also implement substantial internal reform. The relevant areas included intellectual property, export duties on agriculture products, banks and insurance, the regime for import of transport vehicles, taxation, veterinary medicine, considerable redrafting of customs legislation, licensing and changed to the new

Harmonised System (HS 2002). Changes included regulation of genetically modified organisms.

On 5 February 2008, at the General Council meeting, the Protocol on the Accession of Ukraine (WT/L/718) was signed. This comprised 1,170 pages of Ukraine's solid and reliable contribution within the WTO.

On 10 April 2008, the *Verkhovna Rada* ratified the Accession Package and on 16 April 2008, the Ministry of Foreign Affairs informed the Director-General of the finalisation of internal procedure on Ukraine's membership in the WTO. Thus, on 16 May 2008, Ukraine became the 158th member of the WTO.

### General overview of accession commitments

*Market access for goods*

Ukraine bound 100 per cent of its tariffs. For Ukraine, this concession was never in question.

Ukraine's final average tariff bindings were 11.16 per cent for agricultural products and 5 per cent for industrial goods (Figure 19.1).

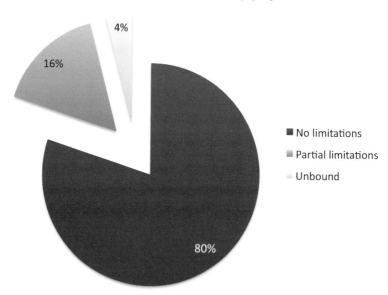

**Figure 19.1**   Final average import tariffs pre- and post-accession to WTO (www.wto.org).

# Consumption abroad

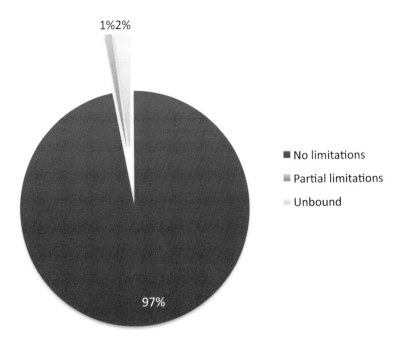

# Commercial presence

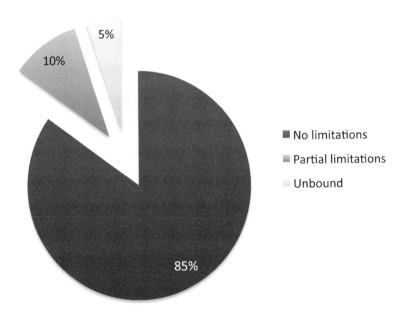

Figure 19.1 (*cont.*)

As outlined in the schedule, Ukraine has its bound duties capped at rates ranging between zero, 30 per cent (sunflower oil) and 50 per cent (sugar) and has only one tariff rate quota (TRQ) (raw cane sugar). Some bindings involved reductions, phasing out over the period up to 2013.

Other products with tariff ceilings of 25 per cent include certain radio-broadcast receivers, catgut and certain conveyor/transmission belts.

Product categories with lower tariffs that were initially or eventually eliminated (via sectoral agreements) include civil aircraft, construction equipment, distilled spirits, certain types of fish, pharmaceuticals, certain chemicals and petroleum oils, medical equipment, wood, pulp and paper, certain yarns and fabrics, certain base metals, steel, information technology products (under the Information Technology Agreement), furniture and toys.

Ukraine agreed not to apply any 'other duties and charges' beyond its ordinary customs duties.

In agriculture, Ukraine agreed not to subsidise exports and not to use special safeguards. Ukraine agreed limits to domestic support provided to farmers at UAH 3.04 billion (US$270 million, as of 1 May 2014) as well as *de minimis* of 5 per cent of the value of domestic agricultural production.

Like all WTO members, Ukraine has no spending limits on domestic support programmes that have no or minimal impact on trade, provided these programmes meet the criteria laid down in the Agreement on Agriculture.

Ukraine has a TRQ on raw cane sugar (267,500 tons). This quota is now administered on a first-come, first-served basis. Over the years this TRQ has never been filled, and from 2011 to 2013 no one applied for it.

## Market access for services

Ukraine made specific commitments in eleven 'core' service sectors – including business services, communication services, construction and related engineering services, distribution, education and environmental services, financial services (insurance and banking), health and social services, tourism and travel, recreational, cultural and sporting services, and transport services – as well as in other areas including beauty, hairdressing, spa and massage services (Figure 19.2).

The services sector was underdeveloped over the Soviet period and Ukraine counted on the services market opening under the WTO as a driver for reform.

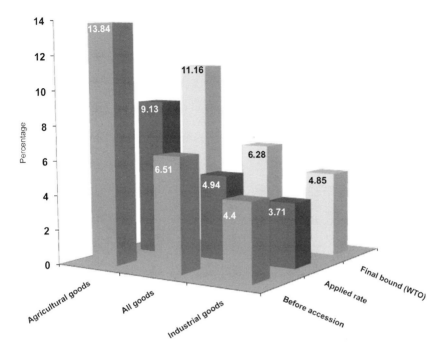

Figure 19.2    Commitments in services

## Other commitments contained in the working party report

- Privatisation: Ukraine provides regular information to the members on the developments in its privatisation programme and on other issues related to its economic reforms.
- State-owned enterprises (SOEs): Ukraine's laws governing the trading activities of SOEs fully conform to WTO provisions. All SOEs operate on a commercial basis. Ukraine regularly notifies and provides information on the activities of these companies to the WTO.
- Pricing policies: price controls are applied in accordance with WTO principles and take account of the interests of exporting members. Ukraine does not apply mandatory minimum prices on imported products. All rail transportation fees are applied on a non-discriminatory basis. Ukraine publishes a list of goods and services for which prices are determined by the government.
- Policy-making and enforcement framework: Ukraine uniformly implements WTO provisions and the Protocol of Accession on its whole

territory. Ukraine provides for the right to appeal administrative rulings on WTO matters to an independent tribunal.

- Trading rights (the right to import and export): registration fees for medicines, pesticides and agricultural chemicals, as well as licensing fees for the import and export of alcoholic beverages and tobacco products, are in compliance with WTO requirements and have been brought to the level of the cost of services provided.
- Individuals and companies wishing to import/export need only register with the relevant authorities and are not required to have physical presence or investments in Ukraine.
- Fees and charges for services rendered: Ukraine applies fees according to WTO principles and information regarding these fees is provided to WTO members upon request.
- Internal taxes (VAT and excise tax): domestic taxes are applied in a non-discriminatory manner to imports from WTO members and to domestically produced goods.
- Quantitative import restrictions, import licensing: Ukraine has eliminated and does not introduce, re-introduce or apply quantitative restrictions on imports or other non-tariff measures that cannot be justified under the Marrakesh Agreement Establishing the World Trade Organization (WTO Agreement).
- Ukraine implements its import licensing procedures in conformity with the WTO Agreement.
- Customs valuation: there was full implementation of the Customs Valuation Agreement upon accession. Ukraine made amendments to its Customs Code in 2013, improving certain articles and provisions after consultations with businesses and international trade partners.
- Rules of Origin: there was full implementation of the Rules of Origin Agreement upon accession.
- Anti-dumping, countervailing duties and safeguard regimes: Ukraine's trade remedies legislation is applied in conformity with WTO rules.
- Export duties: Ukraine reduced its export duties on oilseeds, live cattle, animal skins, ferrous and nonferrous metal waste and scrap. Ukraine does not apply any obligatory minimum export prices.
- Export restrictions: measures, including export licensing requirements, are only applied in conformity with WTO rules.
- Industrial policy, subsidies: Ukraine has eliminated all export and import-substitution subsidies.

- Technical barriers to trade (TBT) and sanitary and phytosanitary measures (SPS): Ukraine complies with the TBT Agreement and gives priority to international standards over regional and other national ones.
- All national and regional standards are voluntary, except those referred to in technical regulations intended to protect national security interests, prevent deceptive practices, and protect the life and health of people, animals or plants, as well as to protect the environment.
- Ukraine has reduced the number of products subject to mandatory third-party certification.
- Ukraine complies with the SPS Agreement.
- Agreement on trade-related investment measures (TRIMs): Ukraine does not maintain any measures inconsistent with the TRIMs Agreement.
- Free zones: such zones are administered in compliance with WTO provisions.
- Government procurement: Ukraine has become an observer to the plurilateral Government Procurement Agreement (GPA) and started negotiations to become a party to this agreement.
- Agreement on Trade-Related Aspects of Intellectual Property Rights (TRIPs): there has been full implementation of the TRIPs Agreement.
- Regional trade agreements: Ukraine submits notifications and copies of its free trade areas and customs union agreements to the WTO.

## Post-accession experience

What did Ukraine expect to receive as the result of accession? There was anticipation of the following:

- predictable and guaranteed access to markets of all the WTO members;
- integration into the international system of the free market economy and thus wider opportunities for trade and businesses;
- access to rule-based trade and the possibility of using a full range of instruments to be able to design and implement trade policy in a more systemic and coherent way, internally and internationally;
- sustainability of national trade policy-making;
- implementation and enforcement of trade rights;
- guaranteed access to the WTO Dispute Settlement Mechanism;
- the ability to conduct market access negotiations with other acceding governments to diversify trade;
- improved climate for foreign direct investment (FDI);

- wider choice of quality goods and services for consumers;
- possibilities of realising trade and economic interests through creation of or participation in preferential and regional agreements;
- strong linkages with international agencies and professional networking inside the WTO.

Seven years after accession, what does Ukraine have as a WTO member? Practically all the above-mentioned benefits and more. Some of Ukraine's post-accession experience is worth noting.

## Changes in the trade regime after accession to the WTO (2007–2013)

Ukraine's accession coincided with the 2008 global financial crisis, so there was a double challenge for its economy and trade – first, to adjust to market opening right after accession and, second, to mitigate and sustain the economy during the crisis.

The period 2008–2009 was characterised by negative effects in the national economy: a slowdown of production and investment with the backdrop of peculiarities of the national structure of the economy, which very much relied on external conditions of trade and depended on the structure of exports.

The years 2010–2012 demonstrated some growth, which was also stimulated by growth in external markets. Unfinished structural and institutional reform and social and labour force adjustment, and a lack of financial resources, did lead to bad repercussions for national growth and development.

Revived investment in 2011–2012 was due to the European Football Championship EURO 2012, the final part of which was conducted in Ukraine. At the same time, further deterioration in the international economy affected the national economy.

Thus, immediately after accession, Ukraine's economy in the period 2008–2013 found itself influenced by the global crisis with its sharp negative impact on economy and trade.

### Foreign trade in goods and services

Trade after accession was defined mostly by the global trading conditions. The high level of dollarisation and external debt of Ukraine led to a sharp drop in the hryvnia–dollar exchange rate at the beginning of the 2008–2009 crisis. This resulted in decreased national consumption and diversion of some exports to internal consumption, which was yet another important factor of influence on the trade of Ukraine.

Problems in the banking sector were further complicating circumstances for the financing of export and import operations.

As a result, the export of goods and services from Ukraine dropped by 22 per cent in volume in 2009, and imports by 39 per cent (Figures 19.3 and 19.4). There were decreases in prices of steel, oil and other commodities, and exports and imports of goods and services (in dollar equivalent) further decreased by 37 per cent and 44 per cent, respectively.

In 2010, exports and imports of goods and services grew by 4.5 per cent and 11.1 per cent, respectively, though external demand for Ukrainian exports remained substantially lower than before the crisis – but inflation in the economies of Ukraine's trade partners minimised competitive advantages. An increase in the export and import of goods and services in dollar equivalent by 28 per cent and 30 per cent, respectively, mainly reflected the gradual alignment to world prices at pre-crisis levels.

In 2011, the export of goods and services in dollar equivalent exceeded the level of 2008; imports came closer to this level because prices in 2011 exceeded the level before the crisis by more than 20 per cent. This reflects the increase in world prices for non-energy raw commodities

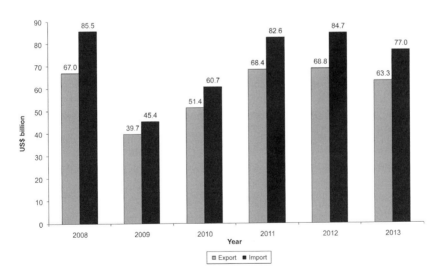

**Figure 19.3**   Trade in goods, 2008–2013 (Ministry of Economic Development and Trade of Ukraine).

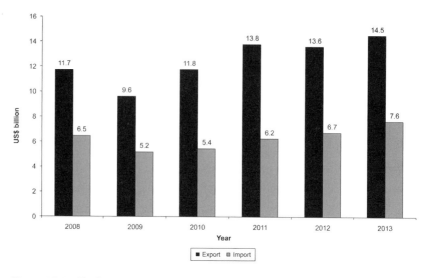

**Figure 19.4**   Trade in services, 2008–2013 (Ministry of Economic Development and Trade of Ukraine).

by 22 per cent and the high price of imported gas from Russia. At the same time, the volume of imports remained substantially lower than that before the crisis, since external demand for major Ukrainian exports had not reached the 2008 level.

In 2012, exports and imports of goods and services were at their highest levels. Record grain crops and intensified output and processing of other agricultural products contributed to export, which in turn compensated for a drop in production.

In 2013, a decrease in exports and imports of goods occurred because of the crisis in the national economy, caused by falling industrial production, issues in public finance, the worsening of conditions of trade with Russia and the evolution of a negative political situation within the country.

Overall, foreign trade performance for the period 2008–2013 (Figures 19.3–19.6) is a reflection of mainly economic fluctuations in Ukraine, caused by the crisis, and the global economic slump and its slow recovery.

In this context, finalisation and formal accession of Ukraine to the WTO just a few months before a full-scale global crisis had relatively low impact on imports, since a considerable portion of market access commitments were in fact implemented by Ukraine before its accession, i.e. before 2008.

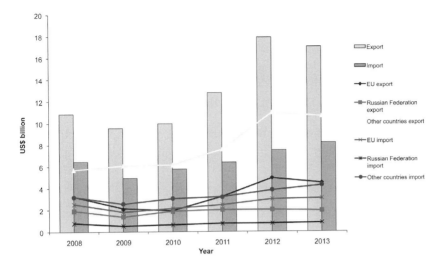

**Figure 19.5**  Trade in agricultural products, 2008–2013 (Ministry of Economic Development and Trade of Ukraine).

Trade in agricultural products in the period 2008–2013 is shown in Figure 19.5. Agriculture began its dynamic development from 2000, due to the favourable combination of improved international conditions and internal factors. In the period 2008–2013, cultivation was successful due to the natural fertility of land in Ukraine and good opportunities to export agricultural products.

Renewed agricultural production combined with strong global demand and WTO membership explain the increase in exporting capacity, e.g. the cancellation of export duties on sunflower seeds and grain, and lowering of import duties on some products of interest.

Thus, Ukraine managed to use this advantage and export increased crops of grain and oil seeds in both 2008–2009 and 2011–2012.

Rapid growth of the poultry breeding sector resulted in large increases in the export of poultry meat and its sub-products.

Since 2010, Ukraine has experienced substantial development in the production and export of dairy products and meat, as well as the export of vegetable fats. This was possible due to the considerably improved competitiveness of these national products.

Competition also increased within Ukraine after accession to the WTO due to a substantial cut in tariff protection and replacement of specific duties *ad valorem*. Nevertheless, Ukraine did not register a huge increase in the import of agricultural goods, which might have been expected. The share of agricultural imports in the domestic market is only some 5–7 per cent.

The largest imports are meat products, for which import duties were lowered substantially; for example, import duties on pork were reduced by 75 per cent and on poultry meat from between 50 per cent and over 90 per cent, depending on the type of product. These two groups of products account for about 90 per cent of all meat imports in Ukraine. The increased share of this import is explained by large demand within the country and it did not cause any contraction of domestic production.

Imports of fresh vegetables and fruit also grew after 2008, doubling and tripling, respectively, in a single year. There are two reasons for this growth: (i) lack of modern storage facilities for domestically grown vegetable and fruits; and (ii) lower import duties on vegetables and fruits not grown in Ukraine, making them more affordable for Ukrainian consumers.

Post-accession, Ukraine's balance of trade in agricultural products is positive. Farmers and agro-processors obtained access to modern and high-standard machines due to lowered duties on these tariff lines and thus were able to equip their production with modern and efficient machines and mechanisms.

It can be concluded that agrarian companies and farmers benefited from WTO accession; they are today a growth sector and are ready to enter new markets. Liberalisation of trade made this possible and led to increases in exports of grain, oilseeds, poultry meat and some other products, while growth of imports remains modest.

Industry has always played an important part in Ukraine's economy. The leading sectors are metallurgy, machine building, extractive industry and chemical production.

Trade in industrial products 2008–2013 is shown in Figure 19.6. Ukraine's trade in industrial products is dependent upon world price fluctuations and the structure of industrial capacities – a legacy of the post-Soviet period – which requires technical modernisation.

The economic crisis caused a serious drop in the export and import of industrial products in 2009 – by 50 per cent compared with 2008 – and, as a consequence, affected production as well.

The share of industrial production in GDP is approximately 40 per cent, although 60 per cent of this is the raw material component, with high technological products accounting for only 15 per cent.

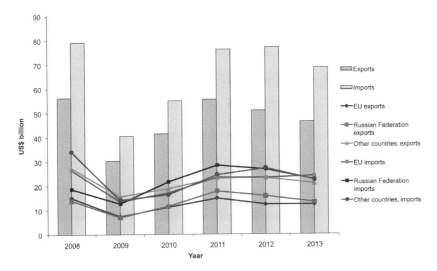

**Figure 19.6** Trade in industrial products, 2008–2013 (Ministry of Economic Development and Trade of Ukraine).

Ukraine's major industrial exports are ferrous metals and their products (32–33 per cent), machine building (17–18 per cent), minerals (15–16 per cent) and chemical products (9–10 per cent).

Ukraine's major imports are mineral products and fuels (36–37 per cent), machine building (24–25 per cent) and chemicals (15–16 per cent).

In general, Ukraine has had a negative balance of trade in industrial products since accession to the WTO, but this has not worsened since the pre-accession period.

As a result of accession, Ukraine has been able to modernise many industry sectors as enterprises are able to access modern, high-quality, durable machinery and equipment due to lowered import duties on machinery.

However, not all companies and enterprises have benefited from accession, as trade liberalisation and an increase in prices of raw materials have become a real challenge.

## Negotiation with applicant countries

In accordance with its WTO membership rights, Ukraine has joined virtually all working parties of acceding governments from May 2008.

This was a deliberate strategic approach to support its trade and economic policies and interests in the further liberalisation of trade, enhance predictability and create new market opportunities for business.

Most of Ukraine's trade is most-favoured-nation (MFN) based. Taking into consideration its considerable liberalisation of multilateral trade during its own accession, Ukraine has a long-term interest in building liberalised and predictable MFN market access.

Therefore, Ukraine has a clear position in accession negotiations with prospective new members. It supports:

- universality of the WTO;
- accessions on ambitious terms and conditions;
- flexibility for developing countries and least-developed countries (LDCs) with a country-specific approach.

Ukraine believes and pursues the principle *clara pacta, boni amici*. This is being realised through requests for concessions and the legal formulae of commitment paragraphs.

Normally, this provides a solid foundation of legal certainty for trade, so much sought for in the WTO, provided that a government respects its obligations after it becomes a member.

Ukraine and other recently acceded WTO members have made a major contribution to the multilateral trading system. However, there are occasional instances where members have neglected their obligations after acceding to the WTO. Such failures of compliance with the WTO's basic rules, when and if they occur, are inexcusable and should not happen. Members' non-compliance with commitments is naturally a cause for concern among WTO members, including Ukraine. Such non-compliance can erode the value of the multilateral trading system at a time of tension over protectionist measures and the unfinished Doha Development Agenda.

As a working party member, Ukraine seeks further market opening and deeper liberalisation of market access to ensure new market opportunities for growing businesses, which have comparative advantage and are not afraid of competition.

Ukraine expressly stated in various WTO meetings that it 'supports the universal character of the WTO and welcomes accession of new members. Accession is the first but very significant step and contribution to the system in the form of concessions.'

From 2011 to 2013, Ukraine signed bilateral protocols with Lao PDR, Montenegro, Samoa and Yemen. While finalising Montenegro's accession to the WTO, the parties also concluded an FTA.

During Yemen's accession, Ukraine experienced for the first time how facilitators can be used to assist in bilateral negotiations. Three eminent ambassadors agreed to be facilitators: HE Ambassador Smidt (Denmark), Chairman of the Sub-Committee for Least-Developed Countries; Mr Röben (Germany), Chairman of the Working Party on the Accession of Yemen to the WTO; and HE Ambassador Yi (China), Chairman of the Working Party on the Accession of Lao PDR to the WTO.

This experience did not start entirely smoothly as it was initiated by the Secretariat and Yemen without consultation with Ukraine. Prior to engaging in such facilitation, all sides should have been consulted as, without such consultation, it implies the direct interference of a third party in a confidential bilateral process. Accessions fall under Article XII of the WTO Agreement, with the clear provision, 'on terms to be agreed between it and the WTO'. Article XII neither allows for the presence of any external player in the process of accession, nor outlines the powers of such a third party in the process of accession. Ukraine has drawn attention to this fact in its statements and stressed that 'No third party may suggest instructions to parties in bilateral negotiations. It must be a sovereign decision by sovereign governments.'

If such facilitation measures are to be further used in future accessions, members should express their attitude to this, clearly accepting it and defining terms of reference. Facilitation exercises should by no means be perceived by the acceding government as a way of cutting corners.

## Technical assistance

Another important area during accession is technical assistance. The Ukrainian accession experience showed that technical assistance is of paramount importance to the acceding government and its negotiating team.

In Ukraine's case, this activity was supported by donors through both long- and short-term projects, as well as ad hoc expertise and technical assistance from the WTO Secretariat.

Ukraine's negotiating team is very grateful to all the experts from different countries who helped the government and Parliament not only to advance accession for its own sake, but who assisted in reconsidering old stereotypes (which were absolutely predominant, especially during the 1990s) and taught the Ukrainian team to think globally while being accurate and patient in details, and while building a new framework of trade policy, law and practice.

Such technical assistance has the best possible impact when it is being provided on a long-term basis by trade policy experts with good knowledge of the country, national economy, culture, policy and decisionmaking peculiarities – both strengths and weaknesses. Accessions often stall internally because at the national level it is impossible to correctly and quickly identify problems and the scope of work to be done, and to resolve the problems to advance the accession.

Acceding governments today have at their disposal the accession commitments database (ACDB), a unique tool comprising experience of Article XII members' accessions and their 'specific commitments'. During its accession Ukraine had to scrutinise all previous working party reports to explore possible formulae which could be a starting point for a commitment acceptable to all parties concerned. This does not mean that commitment language from one working party report will fit all other cases. 'One-size-fits-all' is not the rule for the WTO, and Ukraine, together with other members, worked hard to find the appropriate wording for specific obligations. Ukraine had the experience of wording which had been agreed upon being absolutely unacceptable to some members in the room, and the whole process having to start all over again.

Accession of LDCs is a very specific case in the accession work of the WTO. Special attention and technical assistance is dedicated to these countries due to their vulnerability and need for special flexibilities from the members of their working party.

The initiative on establishing guidelines for LDCs' accession, adopted by members in 2012, set certain benchmarks on goods and services. In Ukraine's view this will inevitably have both positive and negative effects.

On the negative side, this could have a demotivating effect, i.e. low or diluted international ambition as regards trade liberalisation and market opening. Less attention may be dedicated to internal reform and improvements. In one of its statements Ukraine indicated that:

> If one regards [accession] as a formalistic challenge it may become a weary and meaningless exercise, if one regards it as a window of opportunity, it becomes an engine of internal reform and growth. Ukraine, like many Members, has gone through it . . . and paid its membership fee. . . On the other hand, disguised free riding, groundless overexpectations or, which is even worse, a third party's zealous patronage or lobbyism, cannot be tolerated in accession processes. It is Members' obligation to ensure the WTO is strengthened by new Members with viable implementation capacity and value added to market opening and liberalized market access.

On the other hand, its positive side is actually in ensuring a greater level of transparency in accessions and enhanced technical assistance 'to complete their accession process, implement their commitments and to integrate them into the multilateral trading system'.

Ukraine sincerely hopes the guidelines will help LDCs prepare for responsible membership, and that all commitments agreed upon with the working party members will be respected and fully implemented.

Ukraine recognises and appreciates the readiness of most LDCs to undertake 100 per cent binding – this is a valued concession. Nevertheless, the level of bindings also matters and falls exclusively under the jurisdiction of the WTO.

At accession, Ukraine did not request the status of developing country, calculating that the members of its working party would be able to take into consideration its special condition as a transition economy. Nevertheless, Ukraine was requested to liberalise at the maximum possible level without due regard to its post-Soviet type of economy and trade.

## Ukraine and WTO dispute settlement

The WTO's procedure for resolving trade conflicts under the Dispute Settlement Understanding (DSU) is vital for enforcing the rules and therefore for ensuring that trade flows smoothly.

When trade does not proceed entirely smoothly and a member encounters problems, the process of questions and answers begins. When the objective of the measure in question and its justification remains unclear, it becomes an irritant, then, if not resolved, it transforms into a trade concern. Further on, if the measure is not improved or removed, it takes on a more tense form, i.e. a trade dispute arises and requires invocation of a special mechanism to settle it.

A dispute arises when a member has grounds to believe that another member is violating an agreement or a commitment that it had made in the WTO and is not taking steps to bring it into compliance with the WTO norm and thus ensure that trade flows smoothly.

Ultimate responsibility for settling disputes lies with members, through the Dispute Settlement Body (DSB). Disputes at the WTO are often highly complex, and can last for several years, with appeals, counter-appeals and assessments of compliance with rulings.

Nevertheless, Ukraine is a user of the DSU and deploys this mechanism for economic purposes and its systemic interest in protecting its trade rights and market access. Ukraine's history of using the DSU is not long, but the country believes that combining two tracks – litigation and negotiation – is a good and sustainable way of protecting interests with due respect of the rights and interests of other members. Following are the cases in which Ukraine is either complainant or respondent.

### Armenia — Measures Affecting the Importation and Internal Sale of Cigarettes and Alcoholic Beverages (DS411)

The dispute was about taxes and duties on cigarettes and alcohol, violating Articles II and III of the GATT 1994. In addition, Ukraine highlighted Armenia's violation of the special commitment paragraph of Armenia's Accession Protocol/working party report. This was discrimination against Ukrainian goods. Ukraine and Armenia solved the problem in consultations without recourse to the DSB, though the panel in the case was established.

Recognizing the need to comply with the international commitments in trade, the Armenian government, supported by its Parliament, passed a legislative amendment setting a new regime of taxation for imported fuel, tobacco and alcohol. Now imports fall under the regular non-discriminatory internal taxes and duties from January 2014.

The model of negotiation/consultation in resolution of a trade concern was used by Ukraine in a similar case with Georgia, but without recourse to the DSU. So Ukraine has positive experience of using consultations as a good way to settle disputes between members.

### Moldova — Measures Affecting the Importation and Internal Sale of Goods (Environmental Charge) (DS421)

The dispute filed by Ukraine concerns discrimination against Ukrainian imports due to the so-called 'environmental' fee imposed by Moldova.

In 2011, Ukraine requested consultations with Moldova regarding the latter's Law on Charge for Contamination of Environment, which imposes two types of charges on imported products only: (i) a charge on imported products, the use of which contaminates the environment, at 0.5–5.00 per cent of the customs value of imported products; and (ii) a charge on plastic or 'tetra-pak' packages that contain products (except for dairy produce) at maximum dosage level 0.80–3.00 per package.

Ukraine alleges that like domestic products are not subject to the first type of charge, while packages containing domestically produced like products are not subject to the second type of charge. Ukraine alleges that Moldova is in violation of Articles III:I, III:2 and III:4 of the GATT 1994.

The DSB established a panel for this case, but the panel composition stage is not yet active since Moldova asked to suspend it and drafted amended legislation to be passed by the Parliament to remove discrimination and fully comply with the WTO.

### Australia — Certain Measures Concerning Trademarks and Other Plain Packaging Requirements Applicable to Tobacco Products and Packaging *(DS 434)*

Ukraine has requested WTO dispute consultations with Australia in relation to Australia's tobacco plain packaging measure. Consultations were held in April 2012 in Geneva but failed to resolve the case.

At the request of Ukraine, a dispute settlement panel was established by the DSB at its meeting in September 2012. Thirty-five WTO members have indicated that they will join the dispute as third parties: Argentina, Brazil, Canada, Chile, China, Cuba, the Dominican Republic, Ecuador, Egypt, the European Union, Guatemala, Honduras, India, Indonesia, Japan, the Republic of Korea, Malawi, Malaysia, Mexico, Moldova, New Zealand, Nicaragua, Nigeria, Norway, Oman, Peru, the Philippines, Singapore, Chinese Taipei, Thailand, Turkey, the United States, Uruguay, Zambia and Zimbabwe.

Similar cases were registered at the DSB by Cuba, the Dominican Republic, Honduras and Indonesia. Ukraine requested the Director-General to establish a panel for its case, and five co-complainants and Australia joined this request, so the Director-General will establish a joint panel to regard the case.

### Ukraine — Taxes on Distilled Spirits *(DS423)*

In 2011, Moldova requested consultations with Ukraine alleging that the latter's excise tax discriminates against imported Moldovan distilled spirits (HS 22.08).

The Ukrainian Tax Code makes a distinction between cognac and brandy, with the latter being taxed at a rate more than twice as high as that for cognac. Only spirits produced in France or in Ukraine may be called cognac, a requirement that results in higher taxes for other foreign products. Moldova claims that this distinction is artificial and that the products should be treated alike with the same tax rate.

Moldova specifically claims that the 2008 amendments made to Law No. 178 of 1996 infringe Article III:2, first sentence, of the GATT 1994 by applying a tax rate to domestic products that is lower than that applied on certain similar imported distilled spirits from Moldova. Moldova further claimed that because such amendments also imposed a lower tax rate on domestic products than on certain other directly competitive or substitutable distilled spirits imported from Moldova, so as to afford protection to the domestic production, it thus violated Article III:2, second sentence, of the GATT 1994. Ukraine has introduced an amendment to its Tax Code improving the excise tax system of distilled spirits from 2014.

## Ukraine — Definitive Safeguard Measures on Certain Passenger Cars (DS 468)

In 2013, Japan requested consultations with Ukraine regarding safeguard measures imposed by Ukraine on certain passenger cars. Japan challenged Ukraine's decision taken in April 2012 to apply safeguard measures to the import of cars.

Japan maintains that Ukraine failed to notify the measure to the WTO, leaving no time for consultations with members. It also claims that Ukraine failed to justify the imposition of the measures and violated some procedural aspects. Ukraine has duly entered into consultations with Japan and provided additional clarification and answers to questions from Japan. Nevertheless, Japan requested that a panel be established for the case and, on 26 March 2014, the DSB established the panel. In the meantime, Ukraine, in line with its national law and international commitment, has liberalised the measure, and accordingly published and notified its decision to the WTO. Japan expressed satisfaction and now the Japanese legal team is considering the next steps.

## Transparency

The WTO has a number of mechanisms which cannot be overestimated, e.g. the Trade Policy Review Mechanism and notifications. By virtue of membership, Ukraine has access to both of them.

Ukraine is a strong supporter of transparency in the WTO and recognises notifications as its most viable instrument of ensuring it.

One of the important benefits of the WTO membership is free and regular access to the widest range of trade information and draft governmental measures of the members, which have direct impact on industries. The venue to discuss these measures is the WTO committees, where any member can freely express its government's position toward this or that measure (law, decree, regulation, order, etc.) of another member, which may have real repercussions for business. Ukraine uses this opportunity to the extent it finds it necessary and justified.

Timely and free access to official sources of trade-related information through the WTO's Central Registry of Notifications (CRN) and committees is crucial for both governments and industries.

Ukraine had established its enquiry point and notification authority long before accession to the WTO. Ukraine diligently submits regular and ad hoc notifications to the WTO and manages to maintain a minimum level of outstanding notifications (currently seven, which is among the lowest levels of outstanding notifications among the members).

Enquiry point staff of the WTO Division of the Ministry of Economic Development and Trade of Ukraine dedicate an important part of their time to travelling around the country to participate in different information dissemination activities organised for regional and local businesses to promote the WTO and rule-based trade for export-oriented companies. Special emphasis is laid on the enquiry point's function of providing access to trade-related information and replies to enquiries from businesses and local administrations.

Ukraine has a highly qualified 'notification team' who would be happy to share experience and help in strengthening transparency and assist acceding governments in institution-building and the transfer of knowhow.

Ukraine participates in current discussions and submits proposals on further improvement to some aspects of transparency and the format of notifications.

Ukraine is very much concerned about some members' non-compliance with the transparency obligations. Ukraine's working party experience suggests that, in accessions, while working out specific commitments, adherence to transparency and its operationalisation should be given enhanced attention.

## Challenges facing Ukraine today

WTO accession implies increased competition, which turned out to be quite painful for some companies in Ukraine. But tariff reduction overall had a positive effect. Increased competition triggered an increase in the productivity of Ukraine's companies. For the companies, especially in the processing industry, the impact of WTO accession was twofold: their products obtained better market access to new markets, and their products became more competitive in these markets.

Ukrainian researchers indicate that the negative scenario did not occur; the national economy received a new impulse for structural and long-lasting change. Legislative reform also had a positive effect on business – the conditions of doing business improved considerably due to the fact that many outdated laws and regulations were overhauled and new, improved laws were adopted in order to comply with WTO norms.

But WTO membership does not issue a recipe for a future happy life. It stimulates and modernises the trade and business environment, but any member has to work in the multilateral system to keep up to date and write new rules of the game for the coming years.

The government of Ukraine, like most governments around the world today, has to meet many challenges, which arise from time to time because of the growing interdependence and complexity of trade nowadays. Some of these are of a complex character, dictated by a mixture of internal and external factors, for example:

- implementation of coherent growth-oriented trade policy, both defensive and offensive, as an integral part of national economic development strategy;
- the raising of business-sector awareness of new market opportunities and challenges;
- establishment of a sustainable dialogue between business and government on a national strategy of expansion of trade and counteracting protectionism;
- establishment of individual export development strategies by enterprises (a task especially hard for small- and medium-sized enterprises (SMEs));
- support of national producers in their adjustment to greater openness of trade due to WTO membership and newly signed FTAs.

Trade can and must generate new jobs and be a driver for SME development and export-orientation efforts in particular, which is of immense importance for Ukraine.

Trade expansion should envisage strong regional strategies and integration policies based on best rules and practices and sophisticated enforcement instruments.

The government of Ukraine is now trying to play a leading role in ensuring an all-inclusive approach to strengthening business, i.e. ensuring government dialogue and making it a condition *sine qua non* for trade policy-making.

Even though the government, for its part, is trying to do its best to promote transparency in trade policy and measures, and encourages business associations and interest groups to engage in the dialogue, objectively there are at least two main stumbling blocks: (i) diverse interests, which businesses sometimes find difficulty in understanding; and (ii) lack of experience in 'how it all works' (though the legal teams of many companies do have good understanding of the multilateral system, its legal tools and the rights of Ukraine as a WTO member).

Businesses and industries are not always willing to be proactive in policy-making and thus share responsibility with the government, often the reason being the latter's inability to clearly identify and articulate needs and a strategic vision of markets.

So the need today is evidently to strengthen mechanisms for consultation among key sets of stakeholders: government, business, civil society and research institutions.

Another important area of work, which is being undertaken by the government of Ukraine in order to develop and realise efficient economic policy, is regular monitoring and assessment of accessions to the WTO and the results of Ukraine's membership, using the most modern instruments of economic analysis. This will allow Ukraine to make regular adjustments and fine-tuning to its trade policy and integration into the global economy.

Economic modelling done by Ukrainian researchers has shown that labour efficiency grew in all processing industries due to trade liberalisation, which means the increased competitiveness of Ukrainian products in foreign markets. Direct influence of WTO accession as estimated by managers of enterprises in Ukraine is positive to neutral today, in contrast to the negative expectation expressed during accession.

It should also be noted that WTO accession provided the opportunity for both Ukraine and its trade partners to negotiate and conclude FTAs with the European Free Trade Association (EFTA) and Montenegro, and an especially deep and comprehensive FTA with the European Union, which is an ambitious trade agreement of a new generation. One of the first responsible tasks of the government of Ukraine and business is to implement it and establish solid rule-based partnerships with the European Union.

Ukraine does not conclude FTAs for the sake of listing a preferential agreement as a benchmark of successful trade diplomacy, but in order to ensure legal certainty and potential for job creation, support SMEs, enhance regional and trans-border commercial and people ties, and ensure sustainability of trade as an engine for growth.

On the other hand, Ukraine relies on its WTO partners and is committed to staying engaged with them in finding answers to the challenges of complex global trade today.

# 20

# The year 2012: WTO accession of Montenegro – why did we apply to join? Priorities and results

GORAN ŠĆEPANOVIĆ AND DANIJELA GAČEVIĆ

## ABSTRACT

*Montenegro's path to becoming a member of the WTO began in 1966, when the Socialist Federal Republic of Yugoslavia became party to the General Agreement on Tariffs and Trade (GATT). However, pursuant to the constitution of the Federal Republic of Yugoslavia (FRY) in 1992, its application to continue as part of the GATT was not accepted. In 2000, the FRY re-started the process of accession to the WTO, aware that WTO membership would increase its competitiveness in the international market, with the acquisition of the so-called 'WTO label'. In 2004, Montenegro decided to continue the accession process as an independent customs territory. This chapter describes the process of Montenegro's accession up to and beyond its becoming a member of the WTO in 2012. With the country's membership in the WTO, an entirely new chapter begins in comparison to the period prior to accession negotiations. Post-accession, the interest of each member is to be involved as much as possible in the activities of the WTO, and to seek the scope to influence the decisions and rules that will be applied in the future.*

## Basic data on trade

According to the World Bank,[1] Montenegro is an upper-middle-income country with enormous growth potential.

In the period 2005–2012, the Montenegrin economy recorded a different level of gross domestic product (GDP) from previous years. Thus,

---

The analyses in the chapters in this book were finalised at the end of December 2014. Since then the Republic of Seychelles acceded to the World Trade Organization (WTO) on 26 April 2015. This expanded total WTO membership from 160 to 161. Please see the editors' note.
[1] www.worldbank.org/en/country/montenegro as of 27 November 2013.

Table 20.1 *GDP per capita 2005–2012 (euro)*

|  | 2005 | 2006 | 2007 | 2008 | 2009 | 2010 | 2011 | 2012 |
|---|---|---|---|---|---|---|---|---|
| GDP per capita | 2,912 | 3,443 | 4,280 | 4,908 | 4,720 | 5,006 | 5,211 | 5,063 |

*Source:* MONSTAT.

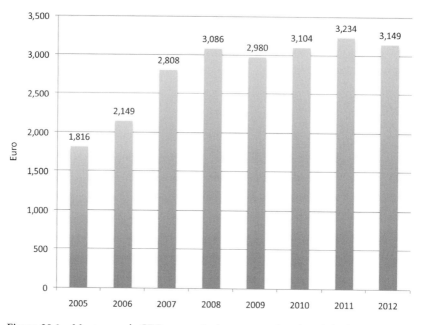

**Figure 20.1**    Montenegro's GDP per capita in current prices (euro) (MONSTAT).

according to data from MONSTAT,[2] in the period 2005–2008, significant rates of real GDP growth in the range of 4.2 to 10.7 per cent were achieved, although in 2009, the GDP growth rate was negative and amounted to 5.7 per cent. During 2010 and 2011, real growth rates were positive at 2.5 per cent and 3.2 per cent respectively. In 2012 a decrease of 2.5 per cent was recorded (Table 20.1).

Observed by year, the GDP trend in the period 2005–2012 is shown in Figures 20.1 and 20.2.

---

[2] Statistical Office of Montenegro.

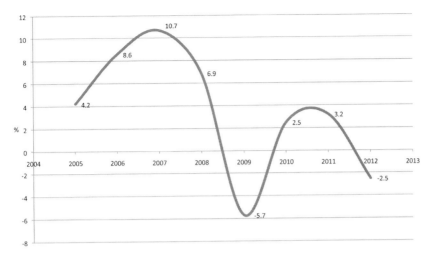

**Figure 20.2** Real growth rates of selected countries (%) (MONSTAT).

When it comes to foreign trade in goods, Montenegro traditionally records a trade deficit, and the coverage of imports by exports is at the level of around 20 per cent. Its most important trade partners are the European Union and Central European Free Trade Agreement (CEFTA) economies.[3] With those economies, free trade agreements (FTAs) are in force (Table 20.2). European Union and CEFTA economies account for over 80 per cent of imports, and over 90 per cent of exports. In addition to these, trade by preferential regime in the form of FTAs also takes place with EFTA[4] countries and Russia, Turkey and Ukraine.[5]

---

[3] On 19 December 2006, Albania, Bosnia and Herzegovina, Croatia, the former Yugoslav Republic of Macedonia, Moldova, Montenegro, Serbia and the United Nations Interim Administration Mission in Kosovo (UNMIK) on behalf of Kosovo, in accordance with United Nations Security Council Resolution 1244, signed an agreement to amend and enlarge the Central European Free Trade Agreement (CEFTA) 2006. With Croatia's joining the European Union, its membership of CEFTA ceased.

[4] The European Free Trade Association (EFTA) is an intergovernmental organisation set up for the free trade and economic integration to the benefit of its four members: Iceland, Liechtenstein, Norway and Switzerland.

[5] The subject of the FTA with Ukraine is goods and services. Other FTAs mentioned apply only to the area of goods.

Table 20.2 *Trade balance in Montenegro 2007–2012 (in thousand euro)*

| Year | Imports | Exports | Trade balance | Coverage of import by export (%) |
|------|---------|---------|---------------|----------------------------------|
| 2007 | 2,073,093 | 454,739 | −1,618,354 | 21.94 |
| 2008 | 2,529,741 | 416,165 | −2,113,576 | 16.45 |
| 2009 | 1,654,170 | 277,011 | −1,377,159 | 16.75 |
| 2010 | 1,657,329 | 330,367 | −1,326,963 | 19.93 |
| 2011 | 1,823,337 | 454,381 | −1,368,956 | 24.92 |
| 2012 | 1,820,461 | 366,891 | −1,453,570 | 20.15 |

*Source:* MONSTAT.

Montenegro is a net exporter of services. The highest incomes in trade in services are achieved from tourism (Table 20.3).

## Regional relations

On 29 June 2012, Montenegro opened accession negotiations for membership of the European Union. EU membership is a strategic goal of Montenegro.

Relations between Montenegro and the European Union in the Stabilisation and Association Process (SAP) were established in July 2001. At the Thessaloniki Summit in 2003, the European perspective of the western Balkan countries was confirmed, and in July of the same year, Enhanced Permanent Dialogue was established as a form of regular consultation between Montenegro and the European Union.

Montenegro and the European Union signed the Stabilisation and Association Agreement (SAA) on 15 October 2007, by which the legal framework for mutual cooperation and the gradual convergence of Montenegro to the European standards was established. The SAA entered into force on 1 May 2010, after ratification by all members. From 17 December 2010, Montenegro has had the status of candidate for EU membership.

The European Commission was very supportive of the process of WTO accession negotiations. Negotiations for membership of the WTO were the subject of the Subcommittee for Trade, Industry, Customs, Taxes and Cooperation with other EU Candidate Countries and after the opening of negotiations for EU membership, relations between Montenegro and the WTO were the subject of Chapter 30 – External Relations.

Table 20.3 Trade in services 2005–2012 (in thousand euro)

| | 2005 | 2006 | 2007 | 2008 | 2009 | 2010 | 2011 | 2012 |
|---|---|---|---|---|---|---|---|---|
| **Services** | **173,422** | **166,188** | **395,022** | **371,172** | **400,561** | **464,282** | **589,262** | **612,253** |
| **Transport** | **5,745** | **−23,085** | **−28,320** | **−44,524** | **−2,587** | **20,819** | **31,630** | **41,563** |
| Credit | 63,670 | 56,831 | 72,013 | 92,000 | 99,050 | 130,145 | 150,463 | 166,369 |
| Debit | 57,925 | 79,916 | 100,333 | 136,524 | 101,637 | 109,326 | 118,832 | 124,806 |
| **Travel – tourism** | **211,920** | **251,111** | **432,612** | **511,177** | **490,416** | **517,218** | **591,357** | **612,656** |
| Credit | 222,193 | 271,427 | 459,544 | 540,681 | 525,712 | 552,102 | 619,493 | 643,184 |
| Debit | 10,273 | 20,316 | 26,932 | 29,504 | 35,295 | 34,884 | 28,136 | 30,528 |
| **Construction services** | **−37,271** | **−49,800** | **13,130** | **−14,481** | **−13,748** | **−17,135** | **10,793** | **−1,476** |
| Credit | 2,469 | 27,130 | 48,967 | 50,625 | 27,695 | 26,783 | 32,271 | 34,329 |
| Debit | 39,740 | 76,930 | 35,837 | 65,106 | 41,444 | 43,918 | 21,479 | 35,805 |
| **Other business services** | **−2,970** | **−10,040** | **−11,192** | **−54,064** | **−44,629** | **−30,922** | **−22,886** | **−18,202** |
| Credit | 4,974 | 28,414 | 46,574 | 39,935 | 29,078 | 39,709 | 48,750 | 94,312 |
| Debit | 7,944 | 38,454 | 57,766 | 94,000 | 73,707 | 70,631 | 71,635 | 112,514 |
| **Other services** | **−4,002** | **−1,998** | **−11,209** | **−26,935** | **−28,891** | **−25,698** | **−21,633** | **−22,289** |
| Credit | 36,460 | 34,234 | 45,872 | 52,797 | 49,980 | 52,306 | 55,073 | 59,374 |
| Debit | 40,462 | 36,232 | 57,082 | 79,733 | 78,871 | 78,004 | 76,706 | 81,663 |

Source: Central Bank of Montenegro

In terms of EU integration, negotiations for Montenegro's membership of the WTO were significant from the aspect of commitments assumed by Montenegro in the negotiations, particularly in the area of market access for goods and services. By becoming a member of the European Union, and in order to harmonise the Montenegrin list of concessions in its goods schedule and list of specific commitments in services with EU documents, the European Union will negotiate amendments to these lists.

## Why did Montenegro decide to join the WTO?

WTO membership is different from membership of any other international organisation, as it implies an examination of each acceding member's legislation and negotiations, and the candidate government is expected to grant a significant level of concessions. The terms of accession and level of concessions are specific for each economy. Article XII of the Marrakesh Agreement Establishing the World Trade Organization (WTO Agreement), which is the legal basis for the accession process, simply says that the terms shall be agreed between the candidate country and other WTO members.

In exchange for concessions and reforms made during the negotiations, the future member receives guarantees that its exporters will be treated in the markets of other members according to clearly established rules. Membership is also a positive signal for investors as it shows that the country abides by the pre-agreed rules. All these were the motives for submitting Montenegro's application for membership.

## Accession background

The Socialist Federal Republic of Yugoslavia (SFRY)[6] became party to the General Agreement on Tariffs and Trade (GATT) in 1966. SFRY actively participated in the Uruguay Round of multilateral negotiations as well as in the work of committees and working groups. After the constitution of the Federal Republic of Yugoslavia (FRY), it submitted to the GATT an application expressing the wish for legal status within the GATT as a

---

[6] The SFRY was established in 1945. It was a socialist state, which included the territories of today's independent states of Bosnia and Herzegovina, Croatia, the Former Yugoslav Republic of Macedonia, Montenegro, Serbia and Slovenia.

continuation of that of the SFRY. The application was not accepted and the FRY was excluded from the GATT in June 1993.

In December 2000, the federal government of FRY decided to re-start the process of accession to the WTO. The application for accession was submitted in early 2001. The application was approved and a working party was established. The Ambassador of the Czech Republic at the WTO was appointed to be the chairman of the working party.

FRY submitted its Memorandum on the Foreign Trade Regime in 2002. Members submitted a series of questions and the preparation of answers indicated that a number of differences existed in the economic systems of Montenegro and Serbia. The countries decided to continue the accession process as independent customs territories. After this decision, Serbia and Montenegro submitted two separate Letters of Application to accede to the WTO in December 2004.

Montenegro's accession process was completed in December 2011, and Montenegro has been a member of the WTO since April 2012.

### Forming a team for negotiations

Accession to the WTO was one of the foreign policy priorities for Montenegro, especially because of the possibility of accession to markets of other members according to strictly determined conditions and in compliance with internationally accepted standards.

The government formed a Commission for Coordination of the Accession Process in August 2003. Representatives of the then Ministry of International Economic Relations and European Integration, the Office of the Deputy Prime Minister for Economic Policy and Economic Development, the Ministry of Agriculture, Forestry and Water Management, the Ministry of the Economy, the Ministry of Transport and Maritime Affairs, the Ministry of Environmental Protection and Physical Planning, the Ministry of Justice, the Ministry of Tourism and the Secretariat for Legislation and Customs Administration were appointed to be members of the Commission. In the period up to the completion of the accession process, the government was reconstructed several times and therefore the composition of the commission changed.

Following the submission of Montenegro's application for accession (December 2004), Professor Dr Gordana Djurovic, who was then Minister for International Economic Relations and European Integration, was appointed as chief negotiator in February 2005. She served as chief negotiator at the WTO until February 2010. In the period

2006–2009, Professor Djurovic was Deputy Prime Minister for European Integration, and then Minister for European Integration.

In the period from February 2010 until February 2011, Dr Igor Luksic, who was then Deputy Prime Minister for International Economic Cooperation, Structural Reforms and the Improvement of the Business Environment, served as chief negotiator. From February 2011, the chief negotiator at the WTO was Dr Vladimir Kavaric, Minister of the Economy.

The Department for Multilateral Trade Cooperation was in charge of preparation of negotiations and coordination on 'a daily basis'. It was originally part of the Ministry of International Economic Relations and European Integration, and after one of the reconstructions of the government, it became an integral part of the Ministry of Economy. This department was in charge of technical preparation of the negotiations, including preparation of documents, analyses, communication with representatives of institutions responsible for specific areas of negotiation, communication with the WTO Secretariat and the mission of Montenegro in Geneva, and also communication at the technical level with representatives of the WTO members interested in the accession of Montenegro.

An important part of the team was the mission in Geneva, and a permanent representative of Montenegro to the WTO was appointed in February 2005. In this way, direct communication with WTO members and the Secretariat was established.

All institutions were included in the accession process, depending on the area that was the subject of negotiations, and new institutions were also established.

In addition to government institutions, entrepreneurs were included in the process. Round tables were organised in cooperation with associations of entrepreneurs, so that they could present their requirements and expectations, become familiar with the progress of the process, as well as with the standards that would need to be applied after joining. This was particularly important, because in addition to consumers, entrepreneurs bear the ultimate effects of any economic integration, including an economy's membership of the WTO.

There was also cooperation with universities and non-governmental organisations (NGOs). In addition, the Montenegrin public was regularly informed on the status in negotiations.

During the accession process, Montenegro had the support of the European Commission. For example, in 2010, the Ministry of Economy published a book, funded by the European Commission, containing translations of the WTO Agreements into the Montenegrin language, in order to assist Montenegrin institutions.

Experts from the United States Agency for International Development (USAID), the IDEAS Centre in Geneva and GIZ[7] also provided significant assistance in all stages of the process.

Establishing a quality coordination mechanism is very important to both the accession itself and later, after joining. It is necessary to have clearly defined institutions and individuals responsible for specific issues, by which the entire process becomes more efficient.

## Basic characteristics of negotiations

During the accession negotiations of Montenegro, the working party held eight meetings.[8] Bilateral negotiations were concluded with eleven members.[9]

The negotiations were demanding for Montenegrin institutions, especially if one bears in mind that until 2006 Montenegro was part of the State Union of Serbia and Montenegro and that the seat of joint institutions was in Serbia (Belgrade). Therefore, on the one hand, as a very young country Montenegro had, and still has, limited administrative capacities in relation to what needs to be done and, on the other hand, WTO members have high expectations of and make high demands on members.

### Multilateral negotiations

The lack of administrative capacity was particularly noticeable during the multilateral negotiations; it had already become clear during the preparation of answers to the first questions of members, submitted in response to the Memorandum on the Foreign Trade Regime. That first set of questions with answers, including the annexes, were almost 200 pages long and contained questions about various areas of foreign trade.

---

[7] Deutsche Gesellschaft für Internationale Zusammenarbeit.

[8] 4 October 2005, 5 July 2006, 27 February 2007, 19 July 2007, 28 February 2008, 19 July 2008, 7 November 2008 and 5 December 2011.

[9] Brazil, Canada, China, El Salvador, European Union, Honduras, Japan, Norway, Switzerland, Ukraine and United States.

Analysis of the foreign trade regime showed that in areas such as technical barriers to trade (TBT), sanitary and phytosanitary (SPS) measures and intellectual property, it was necessary to pass and review the entire legal framework, as these areas were governed by the laws inherited from the State Union. Therefore, in accordance with the recommendations of WTO members, for TBT, among others, the following laws were adopted: the Law on Technical Requirements for Products and Conformity Assessment, the Law on Standardisation, the Law on Metrology, the Law on Accreditation and the Law on General Product Safety, as well as a number of bylaws.

Regarding SPS measures, among others the following laws were adopted: the Law on Seed Material of Agricultural Plants, the Law on Planting Material, the Law on Plant Health Protection, the Law on Pesticides, the Law on Fertilisers, the Law on Plant Varieties Protection, the Law on Food Safety, the Veterinary Law and the Law on Genetically Modified Organisms, including bylaws.

In the area of intellectual property, the following laws were adopted: the Law on Trademarks, Copyright and Related Rights Act, the Law on Designation of Origin, Geographical Indications and Indications of Traditional Specialities Guaranteed for Agricultural Food Products, the Law on Indications of Geographical Origin, the Law on Protection of Industrial Design, the Law on the Protection of Topographies of Integrated Circuits, the Law on the Protection of Undisclosed Information, the Patent Law and the Law on Enforcement of the Legislation that Regulates Protection of Intellectual Property Rights, with a series of bylaws.

For the aforementioned areas, the accession process also resulted in the establishment of entirely new institutions such as the Bureau of Metrology, the Institute for Standardisation, the Accreditation Body and the Intellectual Property Office.

In addition to these most obvious examples where it was necessary to define the legal framework and harmonise it with the relevant WTO agreements, there were other examples of measures that were not in line with the WTO rules. Specifically, in Montenegro there were about 380 state or 'social' companies. By the beginning of the accession process, a significant number of these companies had been privatised, and Montenegro was obliged to inform members about the dynamics of privatisation and the reform of the trade and economic system. The number of products that were subject to price control was significantly reduced, so that by the end of the process only the prices of certain medications, oil, oil products and electricity remained under government jurisdiction.

In the area of trading rights, the most important issue was the possibility of importing or exporting without establishing companies in Montenegro, and the Customs Law was amended to this end. Regarding fees and charges for services rendered, some were charged depending on the value of imported goods, and these were abolished, and re-established in order to comply with the relevant rules. Regarding internal taxes on imports, different rates applied to similar products, and these were also amended. The number of products for which import licences were issued was significantly reduced, and in the end, 240 tariff positions were subject to import licences.

For the purpose of creating a legal basis for the use of trade remedies, the Law on Foreign Trade and the Decree for Implementation of the Foreign Trade Law were amended. Montenegro also abolished the export duties that applied to exports of iron and rawhide. The requirement for use of domestic content in the tobacco production was also abolished. The Law on Free Zones was amended in order to comply with the principle of national treatment.

In order to better regulate the area of trade in services, Montenegro amended 133 regulations, such as the Law on Cinematography, the Law on Postal Services, the Law on Property Relations, the Law on Legal Services, the Law on Telecommunications, the Law on Banks, the Law on Insurance and the Law on Employment and the Work of Aliens.

Bilateral negotiations demanded different negotiating experience, in relation to specific tariff lines, i.e. service sectors/sub-sectors. Negotiation on specific positions implied detailed preparations, with detailed information from the political to the trade relations that Montenegro had with bilateral partners on the other side of the table. Prior to the commencement of bilateral negotiations with interested members through the WTO Secretariat, initial and then three revised offers for goods and services were distributed. In December 2008, the documents were consolidated for the first time, and on the basis of this negotiations with Ukraine commenced. The documents were consolidated for the second time in November 2011.

The first bilateral negotiations on market access for goods and services were concluded with the European Union in April 2008, in Brussels, which confirmed the support for the efforts of Montenegro by this important bilateral partner. The first bilateral meeting with the European Union was held in October 2005.

A bilateral agreement with China was concluded in September 2008, and negotiations commenced in February of the same year. The negotiations were conducted in the area of market access for goods. In addition, emphasis was placed on China's Protocol of Accession, and reaching an agreement on this was essentially a condition for the conclusion of the bilateral agreement.

After the agreement with China, there was a bilateral agreement with Switzerland, which was concluded in November 2008. Negotiations with Switzerland commenced in July 2007, and market access for goods and market access for services were negotiated with this country. The final stage was marked by requirements for lowering the import duty rates for cheeses and chocolate, as well as the opening of the banking, insurance and legal services sector.

A bilateral agreement with Brazil was concluded in November 2008, and negotiations commenced in July of the same year. Although at that point it seemed to Montenegro that Brazil's request to open negotiations had come relatively late, an agreement was quickly reached and marked by liberalisation of rates for certain types of beef. Brazil did not have requirements regarding market access for services.

Negotiations with Norway commenced in February 2008, and were concluded in November of the same year. The final stage of negotiations was marked by requirements for opening the market for fish and fishery products, as well as maritime transport and insurance.

Negotiations with Canada lasted for a relatively long time, from October 2005 to December 2008. These negotiations included opening the market for goods and services, and in the final stage, special emphasis was placed on seed potatoes, whisky, maple syrup and houses made of wood. Market access for services was the subject of negotiations with Canada.

Bilateral negotiations with Japan were conducted in the area of market access for industrial products and services, and an agreement was signed in December 2008. The negotiations commenced in July 2007. Japan was most interested in opening the market for cars and computers.

The last bilateral agreement prior to the first consolidation of documents was concluded with the United States. This agreement was formally signed in January 2009, and negotiations were concluded in the areas of goods and services. The negotiations were conducted from October 2005, virtually from the beginning of the accession process, and the requirements were mainly concerned with matters of principle. In the final stage, when it was expected that the process of accession of Montenegro was at the very end, the requirements became more specific, and the United States expressed particular interest in chicken and pork, fish and fishery products, as well as acceptance of sectoral initiatives.[10]

Although it was expected that accession negotiations would be concluded in December 2008 and the Secretariat had consolidated all accession documents and published them on the WTO members' website, the admission of Montenegro was postponed. Ukraine, at that time the youngest WTO member, after only a few months of membership, submitted a request to open bilateral negotiations in the final stage of the process.

## Bilateral negotiations with Ukraine

The negotiations with Ukraine were a special stage in Montenegro's accession process. This example once again proved one of the basic principles of all negotiations: that nothing is agreed until everything is agreed. During the period December 2008 to November 2011, ten bilateral meetings were held with this country, and negotiations were conducted in both goods and services.

The whole situation was difficult for Montenegro. Up to December 2008, enormous efforts and great progress had been made, and the working party had already assessed that Montenegro's legislation had been harmonised with the WTO rules. All bilateral agreements had been concluded, so the opening of new negotiations meant a step back, especially after the publication of consolidated documents on the members' website. In this regard, the negotiating position of Montenegro was significantly weakened because negotiations were opened after the publication of consolidated documents. This approach is generally not the practice, as the results are kept confidential until all negotiations are concluded. However, as the WTO rules did not define this situation clearly, it was decided to move forward with the process and the first meeting with Ukraine was held in December 2008.

The requirements were extensive. They referred to market access for agricultural and non-agricultural market access products as well as services. On the other hand, the volume of trade in goods between the

---

[10] The concept and practice of sectoral initiatives in trade negotiations was based on the GATT. It revolves around the notion of greater efficiency and trade opening commitments for improved welfare by grouping items rather than through item by item negotiations. For more elaboration, see *Dictionary of Trade Policy Terms*, by Walter Goode (2007).

two countries was negligible, and a difference existed even in the manner of viewing the negotiations, because for Montenegro, the negotiations for joining the WTO were in the final stage, while viewed from the side of Ukraine, that was not the case.

From the very beginning, and keeping in mind the scope and level of requirements, the priority in the negotiations was not clearly visible, i.e. which positions were of particular interest to the economy of Ukraine. Acceptance of these requirements, especially given the most-favoured-nation (MFN) principle, was questionable for Montenegro, particularly from the point of view of future development and relationships with the region. Therefore, from the first meeting, the conclusion of an FTA with Ukraine had been proposed. In that way, Montenegro would have been in a position to significantly open the market for Ukrainian products, in exchange for a waiver of certain requirements in bilateral negotiations in the context of the WTO. At that point, this approach was not acceptable to the representatives of Ukraine, but later their position on this issue was revised.

The negotiations were completed in November 2011, after almost three years. The bilateral agreement in the context of Montenegro's accession to the WTO and the FTA with Ukraine[11] were signed at the same time, on 18 November in Kiev. In the final stage of negotiations with Ukraine, significant assistance was provided to Montenegro by the WTO Secretariat's Accessions Division.

During the period when the negotiations with Ukraine were in progress, El Salvador and Honduras also requested the opening of negotiations. In some ways, this further discouraged Montenegro, but it all ended relatively simply. Both countries submitted requirements only in the area of market access for goods. The bilateral agreement with Honduras was signed in September 2009 and with El Salvador in October of the same year.

### Final stage

All bilateral negotiations were finally completed by November 2011. The meeting of the working party, which turned out to be the last one, was scheduled for the beginning of December 2011, so Montenegro had very little time to work with the Secretariat to consolidate the documents.

---

[11]  The FTA Agreement entered into force on 1 January 2013.

As the final report for Montenegro's accession before November 2011 had been redrafted for the last time in December 2008, and multilateral negotiations were 'idle', in addition to the consolidation of the results of bilateral negotiations, it was necessary to redraft the final report in accordance with the new situation. In this regard, additional questions from members emerged, while the deadlines for preparation of answers, as already mentioned, were very short.

Following extraordinary efforts and cooperation and coordination with all Montenegrin institutions, but also with the WTO Secretariat, after holding a number of formal and informal meetings, Montenegro was able to fulfil all its obligations in a timely manner.

The last meeting of the working party was held on 5 December 2011, and the working party adopted *ad referendum* the Montenegrin Accession Package of documents and determined that it had met the mandate given to it by the General Council.

The next step was the approval of accession by the Ministerial Conference. The Eighth Ministerial Conference was held on 15–17 December 2011. The accession of Montenegro was on the agenda for 17 December, and the Protocol of Accession was signed by then Director-General Pascal Lamy and Dr Igor Luksic, who was then the Prime Minister of Montenegro.

In accordance with its constitutional arrangement, for the purpose of implementation of the protocol, Montenegro was obliged to ratify it and submit the Instrument of Ratification by the date defined by the protocol. The instrument was submitted to the WTO Director-General, and Montenegro became a member thirty days after submission. In this regard, the Law on Ratification of the Protocol on the Accession of Montenegro to the WTO was prepared. The Law was published in the Official Gazette of Montenegro – International Agreements, No. 3/2012 of 8 March 2012.

The Instrument of Ratification was submitted on 30 March 2012, and Montenegro became the 154th member of the WTO on 29 April 2012.

## Summary of assumed commitments

### Rules

The area of rules is the subject of multilateral negotiations and the working party reports and it is very demanding, keeping in mind that in most cases the candidates must carry out substantial reforms in order to comply with the relevant WTO agreements, depending on market conditions in the country.

A similar situation existed in Montenegro. As already mentioned, it was necessary to amend existing laws and bylaws and to adopt new ones. The areas of customs policy, fees for services rendered, TBT, SPS measures, trade in services, protection of intellectual property rights and many others were challenging. Amendments to regulations were carried out gradually, in accordance with the recommendations of the working party and legislation action plan, and new institutions were established.

During the accession negotiations, Montenegro committed to implement fully the provisions of the WTO agreements from the date of accession. In order to comply with the principle of transparency, one of the fundamental principles that underpins the WTO, it was necessary to establish an Official Gazette no later than April 2014, where all legislation relating to foreign trade would be published.

In addition, some of the most significant commitments assumed were as follows:

- implementation of price control measures in accordance with the WTO rules;
- assumption of a series of commitments relating to market access;
- joining the Agreement on Information Technology;
- initiation of negotiations for membership in the Agreement on Government Procurement;
- signature of the Agreement on Civil Aircraft;
- abolition of export subsidies for agricultural products;
- implementation of all provisions of the Trade-Related Aspects of Intellectual Property Rights (TRIPs) Agreement without a transition period.

The Report of the Working Party on the Accession of Montenegro contains thirty-five binding paragraphs.[12]

## Market access for goods

Although the market access negotiations were conducted only with the members that had shown interest in this, they were very complicated. Montenegro concluded bilateral agreements on market access for goods with eleven partners.

---

[12] See paragraph 281 of the Report of the Working Party.

The negotiations resulted in the definition of binding rates for all tariff lines of the customs tariff. Analysed at six digits, the average Federal Board of Revenue (FBR) tariff amounts to 5.1 per cent. FBR are in the range of 0–50 per cent and all are expressed *ad valorem*. For agricultural products, the average FBR is 10.8 per cent and 4.3 per cent for industrial products. Applied rates will be reduced gradually during the transition period of ten years, which is until 2022.

Some members also requested initial negotiating rights (INRs). These rights were granted to Canada, El Salvador, Honduras, Norway, Switzerland, Ukraine and the United States.

Other fees and charges are limited to the level of 0 per cent.

### Market access for services

Montenegro has traditionally been a net exporter of services. Aware of the fact that the requirements for potential members of the WTO are growing from year to year, efforts were made to ensure that the list of specific commitments in services was, on the one hand, liberal enough to meet the requirements of members and, on the other hand, in line with Montenegrin legislation.

When making the list of specific commitments, the first issue was that Montenegrin legislation did not impose any restrictions on investment transactions that affected the provision of services, the total value of transactions in services and property, the total number of service activities, the total amount of services or the total number of natural persons that may be employed in a particular service sector. The number of suppliers of services was not subject to any limitations; exceptionally, foreigners were not allowed to establish service companies engaged in the manufacture or trade in arms and military equipment, and also not in certain 'prohibited zones'.

In the area of market access for services, Montenegro signed seven bilateral agreements.[13] The commitments were assumed in eleven key sectors covering services such as business services, including accounting/auditing/bookkeeping, architectural services, medical/dental services, veterinary, computer and related services, research and development services, communication services (including telecommunication services), construction and related engineering services, distribution services, educational

---

[13] Canada, European Union, Japan, Norway, Switzerland, Ukraine, United States.

and environmental services, financial services (insurance and banking), health services, tourism and travel, recreational, cultural and sporting services and transport services.

Regarding procedures for issuing licences, Montenegro has committed that it will not pose a barrier to market access. In this regard, the commitment to publish in the Official Gazette the list of all institutions that in any way regulate the activities of service provision has been assumed.

## Post-accession activity

Upon accession to the WTO, Montenegro commenced with the implementation of commitments assumed during the negotiations.

Therefore, observer status in the Agreement on Government Procurement was obtained and negotiations commenced with the aim of signing of the Agreement. Montenegro joined the Agreement on Trade in Civil Aircraft,[14] as well as the Ministerial Declaration on Trade in Information Technology Products (ITA).[15] Related to ITA products, Montenegro joined the initiative for additional liberalisation of this sector, ratified the Protocol on Amendments to the TRIPs Agreement, and started to submit notifications.

With the country's membership in the WTO, an entirely new chapter begins for Montenegro. It is in the interest of each member to get involved as much as possible in the activities of the WTO, because in this way it has the possibility of influencing the decisions and rules that will be applied in the future. Engaging in these activities is demanding, especially for small countries with limited administrative capacity. So far, Montenegro has appointed a Permanent Representative – Ambassador Extraordinary and Plenipotentiary to the WTO, with the view that this is a good basis for the positioning of Montenegro within the WTO.

## Benefits

The WTO is the only international organisation dealing with the rules of trade and improvements at the global level. Also, it is the only organisation with the mechanism of sanctions for members that do not apply assumed commitments. So without WTO membership, we

[14]   10 November 2012.       [15]   24 October 2012.

cannot speak of international integration of Montenegro. WTO membership is currently 161.

In order to become a member, the candidate government is expected to harmonise its legislation with WTO rules, but also to assume commitments in the area of market access for goods and services. During this process, it is necessary that all activities are consistent with the national interests in order to better take advantage of opportunities and privileges obtained by other members on the basis of the MFN principle.

Montenegro has been a member of the WTO since 29 April 2012. Enough time has not yet passed to note the concrete benefits from membership, particularly if one takes into account that it has coincided with a period of economic crisis, which has had a significant impact on Montenegro. Also, at this moment there are no final data on trade in goods and trade in services for the period since 2012, so it is extremely difficult to carry out any further analysis. However, compared to December 2004, when the process of accession commenced, an overall increase in economic activity can be seen, particularly taking into account that adjustment to the WTO rules proceeded slowly, and that it was during this period of adjustment that a significant number of laws and bylaws were amended.

On the other hand, the largest part of foreign trade is conducted under preferential conditions, taking into account that Montenegro has signed FTAs with the most important trade partners. These agreements and the WTO membership are two compatible and complementary activities for Montenegro. Indeed, the majority of provisions of FTAs are based on the WTO agreements.

Montenegro strongly believes that WTO membership will increase its competitiveness in the international market, and that the so-called 'WTO label', as the Director-General of the WTO named it after the last meeting of the working party, together with all the other integration processes in progress, will contribute to the overall development of Montenegro.

# 21

# The 2012 WTO accession of Russia: negotiating experience – challenges, opportunities and post-accession approaches

MAXIM MEDVEDKOV AND DMITRY LYAKISHEV

ABSTRACT

*The working party on the accession of Russia was the biggest and longest in WTO accession history. A big power that decides to join an international organisation, even if this is the WTO, cannot avoid political burdens. No big country can stay apart from world politics. The WTO accession process is tough, demanding and complex, with no clear rules. This raises questions about length, fairness and lack of procedural clarity. Yet it is risky to stay outside the rules-based multilateral trading system. To navigate the WTO accession process, upfront, it is critical to define a negotiating strategy and plan the end-game well in advance – a process that requires mobilisation of all negotiating resources, concentration and focus. Domestically, the challenge for the acceding government is to state a clear rationale for accession, demonstrate that there will be real benefits from accession or at a minimum, that there will be no negative consequences, and define red lines to be defended. Negotiating positions should be aligned with requirements for domestic reform. Strong and consistent political will and leadership with support from the parliamentary majority are necessary to conclude any accession negotiations. WTO accession may, in itself, play neither a negative nor a positive role for domestic economic developments, but by becoming a member, a country will obtain benefits in the medium and long term, through the creation of better terms for its trade within the WTO itself. In this chapter, Russia's practical experience of its accession negotiation, the obstacles encountered, its assessment*

The analyses in the chapters in this book were finalised at the end of December 2014. Since then the Republic of Seychelles acceded to the World Trade Organization (WTO) on 26 April 2015. This expanded total WTO membership from 160 to 161. Please see the editors' note.

*of the benefits of accession, including lessons learned during the process, are described.*

## Getting started

### *Arranging the working party: a group of supporters rather than a line of customers?*

An accession working party is established by the WTO General Council, but this decision does not identify its participants.

Any member may join the working party at any time of the accession process. This is important to know, since there could be situations where a member joins the working party at the last minute – for example, if its own accession has been just completed – and asks to enter market access negotiations when you are close to completing your own process. Be aware of such situations. Look around at any important stage of your accession and speak with those who can potentially enter the game at the last minute. You cannot prevent this move, formally, but certainly you can prepare yourself for such a turn.

Most of those who join your working party will participate in all its meetings. That is why it is always advantageous to invite your friends to your working party, as they will not be too demanding, but can support you in difficult times. It is good if such friends come from the same region – with the same type of economy and with the same type of problems.

It is also good if you manage to complete your bilateral market access negotiations with those friends within a limited period of time. This allows you to report domestically about your first victories.

The results of these negotiations may be reflected on one page, just stating the fact of their completion.

Other members can be divided into two groups. One – the smaller – will be most active, having a genuine interest in all or almost all the elements of your accession and negotiating all the elements of your deal. This is the most important group of members, and your task is not only to cooperate with this group on all of their requests, but also to build a clear strategy for the process on that basis, using arrangements with that group as an accelerator for this process.

Another, bigger group, will concentrate its efforts on a few elements, and some of them on one or two topics from your package, and will be less active in other areas or not active at all. This bigger group is equally important to your process. Your task is to get the votes of all working party members since decisions on accession are normally taken on the basis of consensus. Concluding your negotiations with members of this bigger group gets you votes for your accession.

### Joining the family: how to make 161 cousins happy

You may have the impression that some members are more demanding than others, and feel yourself a hostage in a game without rules. There are in fact no clear rules in the accession process, and each working party operates within the framework of the traditions and habits it creates by itself. However, do not try to divide members into friends and enemies. They are neither friends nor enemies – they are simply doing their job in a way they believe is optimal for success. And in any situation avoid the thought that you are somebody's hostage. Vice versa, you may simply reverse the situation and present it in an opposite way: before accession is completed, and before your country becomes a WTO member, no country is able to use the benefits from your accession either for the system itself or for specific countries or their economic operators. Therefore, everybody in the working party should be interested in fair results of negotiations being completed within a reasonable period of time.

Certainly one should not divide members. If you behave correctly and are friendly, negotiators will be able to deliver your responses to their capital and explain to their government and stakeholders what you can do for them, what you cannot do and why.

Development of the WTO has brought to life a very specific group of members: so-called 'recently acceded members' (RAMs).[1] However, most RAMs, still remembering their own accession sufferings, are sympathetic to new entrants.

### Scheduling the working party

The scheduling of working party activity is an extremely important element of the process. It depends on many elements, including the state of play of your legislative process connected to the adoption of laws necessary to comply with your commitments, the situation in your bilateral market access negotiations and many other things, which are

---

[1] Authors' note: 'Article XII Members' is now the widely used terminology that describes and has replaced the description of those members previously referred to as 'RAMs'.

mostly peculiar to each accession. An example of this would be the internal political calendar, the election cycle or the reform of governmental service. At some point, the accession of Russia virtually stopped because of parliamentary and presidential election campaigns, followed by restructuring of the government, and then by presidential elections in a couple of its major trading partners (and the respective restructuring of their governments) which took place after the situation stabilised. Things got back on track after many months of idleness. Why? Because we were unable to deliver the domestic laws required for Russia's accession, and after that period was over, our partners were simply busy with their own domestic affairs.

You should always be willing to speed up the process and to have working party meetings on a monthly basis. You should think carefully, however, about whether this is a good approach. Each working party meeting requires careful preparation not only by you, but also by its members. The working party should prepare by taking decisions and reading your accession 'book' (that is, the draft working party report) chapter by chapter. If there is no fuel for the working party engine, if there is nothing to decide, if members of the working party have different views with respect to the same subject – do not press your chairperson and the Secretariat to schedule an urgent working party meeting. You will waste your time, but what is at least equally important is that working party members will waste their time, and disappointment with the process and your position in the accession will only increase.

It is also important to maintain a balance between the multilateral process and bilateral market access negotiations. Neither of these two main directions of working party activity should be considered as a priority or supersede the other. However, neither the legislative work nor the bilateral negotiations should be left behind. There will for sure be responsible and experienced people in your working party who will help you to keep this balance.

### Personality of the working party chairperson

The working party chairperson is the key to the whole process – thus his/her personal and professional merits matter a lot. There are many criteria which should be met when identifying your chairperson. In particular, we thought it would be good to have a person with experience of the work of the WTO itself, respected within the WTO community and with a personal interest in achieving real results, physically available in Geneva and representing a WTO member with which we will always have stable relations irrespective of what is happening on the world scene. The chairperson's professionalism and neutrality are key to the success of the enterprise and that is why it makes sense to find an appropriate candidate and persuade members that he/she would be equally good for them.

### Internal work: elaborating and approving negotiating positions

Accession negotiations depend on the unilateral concessions of an acceding government. Accordingly, from the beginning of the process most domestic stakeholders consider the WTO as an enemy, not a partner, and accession of the country to the WTO as an evil. The challenge for the government is to prove that there are real benefits of accession before the accession takes place and those benefits become evident. Obtaining evidence of benefits is more likely when the balance of the concessions and benefits you receive from membership is clearly positive.

The dilemma for accession negotiators and their bosses is the same as for any trade negotiator in any area.

### How to secure transparency of the process without either damaging your negotiating strategy, or, in particular, promoting free riders?

Obviously, there is little or no sense in developing a wide commercial deal without involving all key stakeholders, since this future deal should serve their interests and not create problems for them. To address this issue we created a permanent platform for discussions of all major elements of our Accession Package involving not only responsible agencies but also businesses in all key economic sectors. This platform was active until the end of the process, and everybody could participate in development of respective positions and get the results of negotiations in advance. In our case, these results were available eight years before accession took place, which was (we thought) more than enough time to take them into account while making commercial and investment decisions. This approach worked only to certain extent – it appeared that the big pause in our accession negotiations from 2005 to 2010 created the impression that the accession process would never end. Meanwhile, most of the managers who participated in the accession dialogue, had left their posts by accession time, and some of their companies behaved as if no information about accession terms had ever been made available to them. But this was the exception rather than the rule.

Explanations of WTO rules and future commitments to the public, including regional governments, are another important part of the transparency exercise. For carrying out awareness-raising activities, international experts – the WTO, the International Trade Centre (ITC), the United Nations Conference on Trade and Development (UNCTAD), etc. – may be quite helpful. But both those people and your own experts should be prepared to talk to your stakeholders in simple language, for most WTO-related topics are quite difficult for non-professionals to understand. Just try yourself to explain in simple words the difference between most-favoured-nation (MFN) and non-discrimination... In a few years we organised hundreds of conferences and seminars in more than sixty-five (out of ninety-two) regions of Russia about the WTO and accession. Most of the regions adopted special programmes of adjustment for their regional economies and legislation to WTO rules and conditions, as well as educational programmes for local high schools. It was not an easy exercise – however, at the end of the day, everybody who wanted to know about the WTO had the opportunity to learn.

### How to isolate accession as an 'economic' exercise from domestic politics?

Any trade deal has domestic political implications, but accession, especially of a big economy, may create problems for the whole process, or at least for those political forces who are leading it in the acceding government. The strong political will of the domestic leadership, and support of the majority in Parliament, are naturally necessary for the completion of the exercise. In order to achieve this, one should persuade the locomotives of the economy that it is good for them to work under WTO rules, and that even in worst-case scenarios the consequences will not be negative. The concept, which was finally supported by all major stakeholders, was based on the assumption that WTO accession would by itself play neither a negative nor a positive role for domestic economic developments, and that, by being a member, a country would obtain benefits in the medium and long term, through the creation of better terms for its trade within the WTO itself.

To arrive at this conclusion, we undertook several studies and conducted public opinion tests. Crucially important is that such studies should be undertaken by domestic (not foreign) entities, independent of the government. Better still – not funded by the government. At the end of the day, what you need is a neutral professional assumption of how your economy would behave and function under different scenarios of accession. We were in possession of about ten studies, some of them made by WTO opponents. When we compared results, and they were very close to each other, most concerns disappeared.

Business, parliamentarians and civil society are normally suspicious about what is happening in Geneva; that does not always mean, however, that they wish to be involved in the process. Sometimes they just want to be aware what is happening. Thus, they deserve as much information as possible, provided it does not harm negotiations. The task of negotiators is to channel this information duly, dealing with the media, business associations and parliamentary groups. Talking openly and pragmatically (in commercial terms) normally makes people understand that the 'anti-WTO' campaign is just politically driven twaddle.

### Organising an effective process of domestic legislative adjustment

The difference between accession negotiations and other trade negotiations is that in accession you do not develop those rules of trade which you need yourself. Unlike in other trade deals, accession presumes that you impose on yourself rules developed by others, and controlled by others, which always generates questions – why should I do this? Are they smarter than me? Yes, probably they are, that is what we have had to explain to many domestic legal drafters, referring to the fact that 'their rules' are based on the consensus of more than 150 countries, and that consensus was reaffirmed in 1994. Most of our laws were adjusted to WTO standards from seven to ten years before accession, and in almost all cases nobody wanted to abolish or to change them – this fact by itself demonstrates they are based on sound and sustainable logic.

One of the few advantages of a long-lasting accession process is that WTO-compatible legislation is enacted several years before accession takes place, which eases the 'accession shock'. Upon accession the legislative framework does not change dramatically overnight and market participants have time to get used to the WTO-like domestic regime well before accession. Moreover, it is the case that, even before the country accedes to the WTO, its domestic businesses benefits from a more transparent, rules-based and business-friendly legal environment.

An important issue is to accumulate enough expertise among legislators, so that the finished products of this legislative work are indeed WTO compatible.

The aim of awareness-raising work with the legislators is not just garnering support to support the negotiations. To a certain extent this work eases the ratification process.

Accession may last for years or even decades. Within this period of time the acceding government is expected to have in place a standstill trade regime. Any restrictions in foreign trade introduced meanwhile are considered as a retreat, and raise suspicions that the attitude of the government towards the WTO is not serious enough.

That is the rule, tradition and informal requirement. And our recommendation is to implement it, for simple reasons: the consequences of your accession will influence your economy less and provoke less opposition, if by the date accession takes place formally you have not changed the universe of your trade regulations and cancelled implementation of recently introduced measures. At the same time your negotiating partners will believe you are entering the WTO with open eyes and with a stable trade regime which is in line with their expectations.

Any rule may have exceptions, and that exception we were forced to invoke during Russia's accession. Because of substantial delays in negotiations we had a feeling that standstill was being used by some of our trading partners as an additional argument not to speed up and to complete the process itself. It was difficult to explain why we should follow standstill rules and implement WTO provisions ad hoc without receiving the benefits of the system. Another systemic problem was caused by the nature of the economic reforms underway, which demanded from time to time temporary measures not always in line with what was required in Geneva. That is why the decision was made to adopt the necessary laws but to implement them from the date of accession only. The same approach was used with respect to several trade measures, which were adopted on a temporary basis and ceased to exist by the date of accession.

As general rule, one may advise that an economy aspiring to enter the WTO should be prepared for years of a 'frozen' trade regime. If the government thinks that the economy is not strong enough to bear this, it may be better to delay accession until better times.

A firm political approach to the liberalisation of the trade regime and integration into the world economy, if declared at the beginning of accession, will make things easier for all. Exemptions are possible, but only if they are really forced by delays in accession, limited and strictly temporary.

It is also important that your working party is well aware of your legislative activities. A so-called 'legislative action plan', although not being a formal requirement in the accession process, is very much welcomed by members. It assures them that the acceding government is serious in its intentions. Internally, the legislative action plan is also important: it shows the 'finish line' of the process to the legislators.

It is better to wrap up the legislative action plan and immediately accede otherwise members will start looking into the implementation of new laws. Regulators normally need some time to adapt themselves to the new regulations. Meanwhile, your domestic legislative process will be moving and any fresh piece of legislation will be subject to examination and, quite probably, be criticised by the members. These are the specifics of a big economy with regard to the regional aspect. It is crucial to go directly to the regions and talk to local people.

## Accession: terms, conditions and process – specifics of a big acceding economy

At the initial stage of the accession process, both the members and the acceding government are sometimes too optimistic about the terms and staging of the process. It would be wrong to believe any promises from your partners' side: they may give them sincerely, but they are not able to foresee all the difficulties and barriers ahead. If somebody tells you that your country will join the WTO in several years or even months – just don't believe it.

### General framework of accession negotiations: 'WTO-pluses' and 'WTO-minuses'

There are no standard conditions for an economy's accession to the WTO (except for some benchmarks and ceilings for least-developed countries, as agreed by the members recently). Members have a rich fantasy of inventing a new 'non-standard', so-called WTO-plus conditions for each newly acceding government. Sometimes it is really difficult to evaluate the consistency of the commitment proposed to you with the obligation of the WTO agreement, because you are also competing with the best trade lawyers from major trading powers, and even importing text letter by letter and comma by comma from the WTO Agreement into your working party report does not always guarantee you full cover.

We are absolutely persuaded that WTO-plus commitments are bad not only for the acceding government, but also for the WTO itself. The value of the WTO for the trading system is based on several pillars, one of them being the equality of all members and the multilateral character of their rights and obligations. The major problem is whether your additional commitment under WTO-plus rules coexists with your standard WTO right not to implement it under certain circumstances, for example, if necessary, to protect public health. Despite our firm view that WTO-plus commitments in no way limit new members' rights under WTO agreements, we were very reluctant to take on obligations of this kind. Nevertheless, some of them were included in our Protocol of Accession, and automatically made us a firm supporter of full implementation of the Doha mandate with respect to agricultural export subsidies. Russia was persuaded in its accession to prohibit all agricultural export subsidies upon accession. It was explained to Russia that all members would do the same under Doha Development Agenda (DDA) commitments, and that Russia, like all other recently acceding governments, would merely do this a little bit earlier. Fine. But after we agreed to this, it became apparent that the Doha Round is in bad shape, and our concession to members may continue its temporary status for years to come.

At the same time, the acceding government is also free to suggest 'individual' exceptions taking into account the specifics of its economic and trade situation. Many acceding governments negotiated transitional periods for implementing some of their commitments. The maximum transitional period for Russia will be completed in 2020. Exceptions are possible if your aim is not to make of your country one big exception from all rules. To be granted exceptions, you should explain in detail why they are really needed, for example, what economic programme is under way and why its termination in advance is impossible, as well as explaining the background for the duration of the requested exception.

Attempts to make any other economy's 'accession commitments' a sample for yours are not grounded – they can be used only as a source of ideas and commitment language. If you read Accession Protocols of the last thirty years, you will see how the same concepts and language are developed from accession to accession, going more and more beyond WTO rules but clearly meeting the request of another party. We spent a few years explaining to one of our negotiating partners that we were unable to accept commitments with respect to joint ventures since in

Russia there are no joint ventures of the kind addressed in the proposed commitment. Treat such requests seriously. You will hear thousands of arguments, the strongest one being, for example, that if you do not have 'joint ventures in Russia, the commitment will simply not apply'. Do not agree to something you do not understand in terms of substance, implications or the possibility of incorporation into domestic regulatory structure.

We do not have any specific experiences useful for acceding governments with respect to market access negotiations. Often these negotiations reminded us of the conversations between buyers and sellers in street markets, where an agreement is often reached without knowledge of each respective final position and the logic of its development. Often we were requested to bind some duty at zero, as a first negotiating request, which generated frustration and sometimes panic with respect to the possibility of reaching an effective compromise in the foreseeable future. WTO members in general are not unreasonable. Fundamentally they are not interested in ruining any sector of your economy through decreasing levels of tariff protection, simply because they want to sell in your market, and for that you need money, and to generate money you need to produce something yourself. Of course, sometimes your negotiating partners may be too insistent – and you may simply postpone your deal if the requirement goes beyond your ability to compromise.

What is really important is to keep your negotiating position in line with the requirements of domestic reforms. In Russia, plans for the development of all key industrial sectors were adopted in the middle of the negotiations, and concessions we were prepared to make were weighed against indicators in that plan. In most cases this approach was successful, and initial reductions of import tariffs after accession have not produced any particular problems for those industries.

It is important to avoid interconnection between the level of concession you make and the speed of the accession process. If you quickly satisfy all demands, be sure that new demands will emerge. One of our bosses wanted to shorten the accession period and requested the team to draft our services offer in a way which would immediately and unconditionally be accepted by all WTO members. This piece of internal draftsmanship was drafted on about twenty pages and provided for full national treatment and no market access limitation with respect to any service sector in Russia. Presenting it to the boss, we explained that even full market access would not guarantee completion of negotiations. Members would pocket it and request something more, which was normally not scheduled in the WTO, like 'freedom to construct pipelines and transit gas' or 'freedom for foreign entities to explore natural resources'. That draft never left the boss's cabinet. However, the subsequent history of other accessions has proved that our forecasts were not too pessimistic.

Lesson: the acceding government should be prepared for more discriminatory conditions of WTO membership than the 'old' members and even 'new' members who have acceded earlier. This is a serious systemic problem for the WTO which declares itself to be a club with equal rights and obligations for all members. The gap between the two classes of members is widening with every new accession. Recent activity in the Dispute Settlement Body (DSB) confirms that 'non-standard' commitments of new members are taken into consideration as their additional legal burden as compared with old members. However, as long as the WTO does not tackle this problem, this English public school style hierarchy is the truth of life. The only thing which an acceding government can do is to minimise the set of 'WTO-plus' commitments and compensate for it with some 'WTO-minus' incentives.

## 'Red lines' in the negotiating position

Certainly any country in trade negotiations has to establish its own red lines with respect to how far this country is prepared to compromise during the accession process. We think this is absolutely necessary in order not to concentrate on things which are unimportant for you. Your negotiating partner will never leave you without concessions – except in cases where he is not interested at all in your concessions because, for example, you have a free trade area and a request for a reduction of your tariff will not create any benefit for him. The level of such concessions depends on many elements, including how your concession may be sold by negotiating partners domestically. One member requested us to substantially reduce duty on refrigerators. That was impossible for us because of a domestic industry request to grant permanent tariff protection. We knew that there was no production of refrigerators in the country in question, but there were plans for the establishment of such production. The argument which we used in order to persuade the partner to withdraw the request was connected with the costs of freight of potential refrigerators to Russia if exported. These costs were almost prohibitive. Hence, our concession was not necessary for our partner, and he would not have been able to sell it domestically.

So we had to find something different for this member – but also to protect what was needed at home.

Russia has had rather few red lines, one of them relevant for domestic prices for energy. Some of our partners insisted on our commitment to regulate prices of energy in the same way as for other products. Implementation of this request could lead to substantial deterioration of energy production and supply, problems of security of supply. We informed our partners that their request was not acceptable and stated that we would simply stop Russia's accession if the request was not withdrawn. We found a compromise on a different basis, after our partners withdrew their request.

Lesson: it is worth spending time – several months – before the start of negotiations, defining your 'red lines'. This will save you much more time afterwards. Your 'red lines' should be few but clear. You should be ready to defend all of them. If you give up on one of them you will lose them all.

### Hunting an elephant: specifics of a big country's accession

The specifics of a big acceding government are connected solely with the fact that it is big. A bigger territory often means bigger markets. The geography of a big country implies many neighbours which historically have trade relations with you. If those neighbours are WTO members, they will certainly join the working party, since they are interested in expanding trade and sometimes they would like to be helpful in the accession process. Russia's customs territory is one-sixth of the customs territory of all WTO members. It has a common border with eleven WTO members, and only two of them have not entered into market access negotiations with Russia. Big countries are often rich in resources, so they often receive requests connected with access to resources. Big territories make some services sectors, like transportation, excessively lucrative, and to provide these services big countries need more aircraft, lorries and other transportation equipment duties which are exhaustively negotiated. So there is no need to attract the interest of the membership in a big country's accession – for smaller economies sometimes that is a problem.

Therefore, the acceding government of a big country should prepare for an intensive negotiation with broad involvement of the membership (and accumulate the necessary negotiating resources) while smaller economies may concentrate on tackling negotiations with a few main stakeholders.

There are only a few big countries still outside the WTO that would like to join. Our message to them is simple: if you are big, expectations with respect to your accessions are bigger, and you should be prepared to face problems which have nothing to do with the WTO itself but which influence the pace and sometimes the substance of your accession.

Big countries may have other types of specific problems. WTO commitments should be applied uniformly throughout all of your territory. WTO rules give little flexibility for implementation of regional measures – hence in order to implement some regional policies one should apply instruments which are outside the WTO, or negotiate specific solutions. Russia has in particular agreed on certain specific measures for its two geographically detached regions – Kaliningrad and Magadan – as well as for territories where indigenous people live.

Russia's working party was the biggest in WTO history, and its accession process was one of the longest, partly because of Russia's size.

## Impact of politics

A big power that decides to join an international organisation, even if this is the WTO, cannot avoid political burdens.

No big country can stay apart from big world politics – and the implications of its politics sometimes irritate other players. Some of them may try to use the accession process to make the acceding government adjust its policies. Those attempts normally have no chance of success but can disturb and delay accession.

Russia is a participant at the G-8 and G-20, as well at all major economic and political institutions of the current world. These provided additional parameters for Russia's WTO accession. The accession was driven not only by economic but also by political arguments. Sometimes these arguments played in different directions, and often they resulted in the suspension of negotiations.

A big power has more ways and means to overcome difficulties of a political nature. It seems unavoidable that presidents and prime ministers discuss the accession of their countries to the WTO with their counterparts. You should not overload them. But sometimes this helps.

The best way, however, is to divide political issues from trade issues by all ways and means. If you are able to satisfy the commercial interests of your partner, and clearly demonstrate that in spite of all political tensions, the accession of your country to the WTO will bring real commercial benefit to your partner's businesses, business will be on your side when influencing domestic political decision-making.

It is also worth noting that a member which cannot explain to other members why it is still preventing your accession when commercial issues are addressed will never get their support. Being an outsider in the WTO is risky.

Lesson: acceding governments should take a firm position insisting that the WTO accession should not be affected by non-trade issues. Russia's experience proves that this approach finds broad support among members.

## Planning the 'endgame'

At some point, when everybody feels tired and disappointed with endless negotiations, suddenly things start moving and you see (or pretend to see) the light at the end of the tunnel. That is the time for the definitive 'endgame', where there are no longer two teams (acceding government and members) but a single group of like-minded people who have one goal – to finalise that boring process.

The trickiest challenge is to feel the right moment for starting the 'endgame' (not too early and not too late). Otherwise there will be a false start with no gain.

When the endgame is launched, you need to mobilise all available resources – both in your country and in Geneva.

Declaring the conclusion of an accession by a certain date seems to be a wrong approach, although it seems that this is inevitable (that is, by the way also true for other negotiating activities in the WTO), but it is much better if you (and the members) declare that date only when you feel it is feasible.

Endgames need enormous efforts and concentration. It is the time of most important deals, of resolving issues which seemed to be insoluble for years. But even when the deals are made and the results of negotiations go to official documents, it is not the time to relax. You will have to perform scrutinised legal checking and 'scrubbing' of every page of the accession documents. The 'human factor' may be more harmful for the quality of your accession than all the efforts of your counterparts' negotiating team, and even technical mistakes and omissions may later cost your country a lot of money.

## What comes next?

### Accession does not end in Geneva

Friends from one delegation of an important member frequently told us that completion of the accession only means that you will get more hard work, and get it very soon! This is absolutely true. You will have no more than a couple of hours after the final General Council meeting to relax. The next day you will have to be prepared to do hundreds of things at the same time, starting from finalising the translation of the Accession Protocol into your official language and preparing the Accession Package for ratification in Parliament, explaining to industry, which has forgotten all the lessons learned previously, what this or that commitment means and how duties will be changed (staged implementation) over the next seven years. All this takes several months of your life, and in between you should take many steps to organise inter-agency cooperation on WTO issues, release of notifications which you committed to file or creating a system of control of draft legal acts with respect to their conformity with your commitments.

Most acceding governments declare that accession to the WTO is not a goal but an instrument; however, not all of them are ready to use this instrument in the first months of membership – the syndrome of 'a lost year' is quite common. Now you are admitted to all WTO meetings and negotiations: how to make full use of your presence, what line to take and how to react to other initiatives – understanding of all of this certainly takes months.

If you have the resources, you may prepare well in advance. We have not heard of any such newly acceding members yet.

The 'honeymoon' between an RAM and other members does not last long. Quite soon after accession, a new member is required to carry its responsibilities in full – and not all RAMs are ready for this.

Big economies are for evident reasons under heavier attack. Again, a big country's market is attractive; many members want to obtain immediate benefit from its accession concessions; any attempts by its government to delay or circumvent WTO commitments are strictly controlled.

Thus, the post-accession period requires remobilisation of all resources. In this regard, strong representation in Geneva is very important. In fact, pre-accession representation has to be structurally transformed. Previous tasks (managing observership and supporting other accession negotiations) are no longer relevant. Your people in

Geneva should be ready to become real frontmen of the new member on all fronts of the WTO activities, and they should be led by a full-fledged representative to the WTO.

Lesson: the post-accession period should be modelled and prepared before accession takes place, i.e. along with 'endgame' negotiations and ratification procedures. Domestically, it would be relevant to charge other authorities and institutions with this task, rather than those responsible for negotiations and ratification. However, it is easy to give this advice. But neither Russia nor many other RAMs have managed to duly fulfil this preparatory work in advance of their accessions.

WTO membership is an important complement to the general social and economic policy of any market-oriented economy. The accession process affects many aspects of economic regulation of an acceding government even before accession takes place. Some of these impacts are quite positive. The result of continuity, lengthy accession negotiations and the gradualism of the accession process is that the accession itself does not bring painful shocks to the economy.

Accession procedures are too lengthy, unclear and unfair. This is a systemic risk for the integrity and sustainability of the WTO. The membership should do something about this. In any case, the equality of basic legal rights and obligations (of course, with exceptions to such issues as individually agreed levels of market openness, specific provisions for developing countries and least-developed countries) should be reconfirmed.

WTO accession is not a goal but a tool. This slogan is self-evident – but what about practical implementation? Elaboration of general recommendations, of post-accession policies and activities for new members (in addition to numerous recommendations about how to get into the WTO), would be useful.

# 22

# The 2013 WTO accession of Lao PDR: specific commitments and the integration of least-developed countries into the global economy

KHEMMANI PHOLSENA AND BUAVANH VILAVONG

ABSTRACT

*When Lao PDR applied for membership of the WTO in 1997, it used the WTO accession process as a tool to implement its decision to establish a market economy and fully integrate into the world economy. Although at the outset market access was not considered to be the principal benefit to be derived from WTO accession, Lao PDR was aware that WTO membership would give its economy additional security and predictability. WTO accession negotiations allowed Lao PDR to apply international best practices and to align its trade policy with the principles of non-discrimination and transparency. Adaptation to international trade requirements is a longer-term challenge, and post-accession challenges remain, but the benefits are significant and worthwhile.*

This chapter is aimed at identifying the lessons learned for accession negotiations in the future, based on the experience of the Lao People's Democratic Republic (Lao PDR). The ultimate purpose is to contribute to strengthening the WTO system, in particular for the accession of least-developed countries (LDCs). The key questions addressed are as follows:

. Why did Lao PDR apply for WTO accession and what priorities did we set as a country?
. Domestically, how were the negotiations organised and what challenges were faced?
. What lessons did we learn?
. What specific benefits have emerged and are emerging from our WTO accession?

Lao PDR applied for membership of the WTO in 1997, the same year it joined the Association of the Southeast Asian Nations (ASEAN). The working party on the accession of Lao PDR was established in February 1998. The General Council approved the country's Accession Package in October 2012 and Lao PDR officially became the 158th member of the WTO on 2 February 2013, after its Instrument of Acceptance was ratified and deposited with the WTO Director-General. Throughout the fifteen years of preparation and negotiations, Lao PDR enacted over ninety laws and regulations both new and amended to bring them in line with WTO rules. These laws cover a wide range of areas including trading rights, import licensing, customs valuation, investment, sanitary and phytosanitary (SPS) measures, technical barriers to trade (TBT), services and intellectual property rights. As an LDC, Lao PDR's application was covered by the guidelines for accelerating LDC accessions.

Lao PDR used the WTO accession process as a very useful tool to implement its decision to establish a market economy and to fully integrate into the world economy so as to have a competitive national economy that can take full advantage of the benefits of the world market. The WTO accession process allowed Lao PDR to apply international best practices and to align its trade policy with the principles of non-discrimination and transparency, which will help to create an enabling environment for business and trade in the country.

The evidence showed that opening up the Lao PDR internal market to external competition would contribute to stimulating both import-competing and export-oriented industries to adjust. However, adaptation to the international trade requirements is a longer-term challenge. A post-accession challenge remains and both the public and private sectors need further internal preparation to overcome these.

## Commitments made by Lao PDR

The working party of Lao PDR to the WTO met ten times.[1] Sixty-six working party members were involved in examining the trade policy regime of Lao PDR and in negotiating its terms of accession.[2] Lao PDR

---

[1] 28 October 2004, 30 November 2006, 15 November 2007, 4 July 2008, 14 July 2009, 24 September 2010, 29 June 2011, 16 March 2012, 12 July 2012 and 28 September 2012.

[2] They are: Australia, Bangladesh, Brazil, Brunei Darussalam, Cambodia, Canada, China, Dominican Republic, the European Union, Haiti, Honduras, Hong Kong (China), India, Indonesia, Japan, Kingdom of Saudi Arabia, Republic of Korea, Lesotho, Malaysia,

held bilateral negotiations on market access with nine members: Australia, Canada, China, the European Union, Japan, the Republic of Korea, Chinese Taipei, Ukraine and the United States.

Commitments that Lao PDR negotiated and agreed with WTO members covered two areas: rule-making and market access, and associated domestic reforms.

Rule-making commitments are the results of multilateral negotiations in the working party during which Lao PDR committed to adhere to all WTO general principles, disciplines and its specific agreements, as provided for in its working party report. The report contains a description of Lao PDR's foreign trade regime and wide-ranging commitments on laws and measures to be brought into compliance with WTO requirements.

The working party report of Lao PDR consists of 247 paragraphs, of which 26 are specific commitment texts. Most commitments are to be implemented upon accession while some benefit from, or are subject to, transition periods (see Box 22.1).

## Objectives, priorities and constraints in the market access negotiations

### Bilateral market access negotiations

Lao PDR engaged in market access negotiations on trade in goods and trade in services with nine interested members: Australia, Canada, China, Chinese Taipei, the European Union, Japan, the Republic of Korea, Ukraine and the United States. Some other members (the Dominican Republic, Honduras, India and Switzerland) initiated bilateral consultations with Lao PDR, but either did not pursue these or later withdrew their requests.

The schedules of concessions covered market access concessions/commitments in goods and services and are part of the membership package of Lao PDR. These commitments are a combination of the offers that Lao PDR made, with additional tariff concessions and specific commitments agreed in bilateral negotiations with the nine interested members, which through the schedules applied most-favoured-nation (MFN) treatment to all WTO members.

Mongolia, Myanmar, Nepal, New Zealand, Nigeria, Pakistan, Panama, Paraguay, the Philippines, Qatar, Singapore, Switzerland, Chinese Taipei, Tanzania, Thailand, Ukraine, United States, Viet Nam and Zambia. The European Union is counted both as a single entity and as its individual member states.

BOX 22.1  KEY RULES-MAKING COMMITMENTS OF LAO PDR

## Implementation from the date of accession

- State enterprises: to import or export under commercial terms.
- Price controls: to be consistent with WTO rules on trade in goods, agricultural products and services and the list of products under price control to be published in the local publication, Official Gazette or official websites.
- Financial, monetary and settlement policy: to comply with the relevant provisions of the International Monetary Fund (IMF).
- Trade-related investment measures: to comply with WTO rules.
- Tariff bindings: to apply only ordinary customs duties, with no additional duties and charges.
- Taxes and other charges: on imports to comply with WTO agreements including national treatment and the most-favoured-nation (MFN) principle.
- Import licensing: to comply with the Agreement on Import Licensing Procedures. No quantitative restrictions such as licensing, quotas, prohibitions, bans and other restrictions are allowed; except for balance-of-payments purposes and in compliance with WTO rules.
- Customs valuation: to apply transaction and other valuation methods instead of minimum prices.
- Right to appeal: individuals and enterprises have the right to legal appeal on government administrative actions covered by WTO rules.
- Local authorities: to comply with WTO obligations throughout the customs territory, including special economic zones and other zones that receive preferences on customs, taxes and regulations.
- Other rules: such as rules of origin, preshipment inspection, export measures including prohibitions, subsidies, transit trade, and preferential trade will also be implemented upon accession.

## Phase-in obligations

- Trading rights: the right to import and export regardless of and including commercial presence for most products to be applied from membership date. A phased-in implementation for some products within two years after accession has been granted for some sensitive products.
- Anti-dumping and countervailing measures: to be imposed only after the development and adoption of fundamental laws complying with WTO rules.
- Safeguards: to be developed fully in compliance with WTO rules within five years of accession.
- TBT (product standards and labelling): to fully comply with the TBT Agreement by 1 January 2015.

BOX 22.1 (*cont.*)

- SPS measures (food safety and animal and plant health): to fully comply with the SPS Agreement by 1 January 2015.
- Intellectual property: to fully comply with the Trade-Related Aspects of Intellectual Property Rights (TRIPs) Agreement by 1 January 2017.
- Trade in services: to ensure that legislation governing trade in services is in line with commitments specified in the services schedule from the date of accession and up to seven-year transition, in some cases.
- Transparency: to submit initial notifications as required within six months after accession. All relevant laws, regulations and other measures as required are to be notified in an Official Gazette, to be set up within three years.

The commitments – tariff concessions – on trade in goods of Lao PDR encompass 10,694 tariff lines (in Harmonisation System 2002) with average bound rates of 19.3 per cent for agricultural goods and 18.7 per cent for industrial goods, compared with applied tariffs of 18.4 per cent and 10.0 per cent respectively. Most tariff commitments took effect from the date of accession, while some were staged for reduction over a five- to ten-year transition period. Given its LDC status and because of sound and rational arguments during the various rounds of bilateral negotiations, Lao PDR opted out of joining the sectoral initiatives, which were designed to cut tariffs to 0 per cent, as requested by some WTO members, but which Lao PDR did not consider to be in its interest at this stage in its trade development.

In the services negotiations, Lao PDR opened up (i.e. undertook commitments in) ten service sectors, specified in 79 sub-sectors (out of a total 161 sub-sectors). The sectors in which specific commitments were undertaken included professional, computer, research and development, telecommunications, construction, distribution, private education, environmental, financial, private health, tourism and air transport. However, more than 80 sub-sectors were not liberalised, including some professional services (doctors, nurses, veterinarians), postal services, tourism services (tour guides), audio-visual services, transport (road, train, waterways, maritime, pipeline), other financial services (related to securities) and recreational services. Most of the opening that Lao PDR undertook in the services sectors was partial, i.e. there were sub-sectors or activities that were not committed such as the wholesale and retail sale of vehicles and parts in distribution as well as privately supplied services in the education and health sectors.

## Actual and expected benefits from WTO membership

At the outset, market access was not considered to be a chief benefit for Lao PDR from WTO accession. The country enjoyed MFN access for its exports to most markets even before joining the WTO. Lao PDR benefited from preferential access, notably under the Generalised System of Preferences (GSP) in exporting to most developed countries and some developing countries. However, Lao PDR was aware that without WTO membership, those preferences and market access conditions could be changed by the importing country without any defence for Lao PDR. WTO membership would thus give Lao PDR security and predictability by ensuring that its goods, services and trade-related intellectual property would continue to receive MFN treatment from WTO members in the future. This was important for investors in Lao PDR's economy.

The main objectives of Lao PDR in seeking membership in the WTO were the following:

- Membership of the WTO would allow Lao PDR to be part of the multilateral trading system on a sound legal footing. This meant, on the one hand, that the country would enjoy a number of rights as a WTO member, while, on the other hand, it would also respect WTO obligations like other members.
- Accession to the WTO was considered as an efficient tool for the transformation of Lao PDR's economy into a market-oriented economy. Accession to the WTO is, and would continue to be, an anchor for internal reform in Lao PDR. WTO membership would provide a platform for the government of Lao PDR to sustain the restructuring of its economic sectors based on its comparative advantage in order to improve efficiency in resource allocation and distribution. This was and remains the central benefit of WTO entry along with the broader movement towards the regional integration agenda of Lao PDR.
- Greater transparency through WTO accession and increased predictability and coherence in the economic framework are conditions that have emerged from the domestic reforms required and undertaken to ensure compliance with WTO principles. These reforms have assisted in attracting and increasing the quality of investment needed. A number of WTO agreements require Lao PDR to increase transparency on regulations, such as through establishing enquiry points and publishing trade-related regulations. Newly instituted measures affecting trade also need to be notified to trading partners and published for traders to adjust their practices accordingly. Economic

framework conditions based on legal rights and obligations, more efficient transaction processes and transparent regulations are helping Lao PDR to become a stronger and more competitive trading nation and are assisting Lao PDR to achieve greater success in attracting foreign investment, which the country needs to ensure sustainable long-term development.

- A clear and expected benefit is the right to be an integral part of the trading community, based on agreed rules which are transparent and predictable. Other countries wishing to restrict imports from Lao PDR, e.g. on the grounds of food safety, cannot do so arbitrarily but have to apply internationally agreed standards or provide scientific evidence of risk. Lao PDR has 'legal rights' that can be invoked in accordance with WTO membership. WTO dispute settlement is a very effective mechanism to defend the rights of a trading nation. Lao PDR can use this to address unfair trade measures against it. The MFN principle, which ensures equal treatment for all members of the WTO, whether big or small, compensates for small economies' lack of political power in trade disputes with richer partners – even though the mechanism has been proved to be costly and challenging in terms of the capability for effective litigation.

- WTO membership gave Lao PDR a seat at the 'table' of multilateral trade negotiations. As a small country, Lao PDR does not have much leverage in negotiating trade deals bilaterally with trading partners. But in the WTO, Lao PDR has aligned its positions with negotiating groups such as ASEAN, LDCs and recently acceded members (Article XII members) to make its voice heard. As an LDC, Lao PDR may benefit from special and differential treatment under various WTO agreements, including under the Trade Facilitation negotiations, which have progressed farther than other areas in the Doha Development Agenda.

## Remaining challenges

WTO accession is not an end in itself. It is a tool for domestic reforms, designed to assist a country to adjust its internal system to the best practices in the world trade community. At the same time, accession *per se* is not the end of the reform process, just the beginning. The true benefits should materialise if Lao PDR takes the results of the accession negotiations seriously and implements the obligations which have been agreed accordingly. While most basic laws and regulations of Lao

PDR are currently in line with international obligations, further efforts are required for full implementation. Post-WTO preparations and implementation should start immediately. An enterprise survey jointly conducted by the Small and Medium Enterprise Promotion and Development Office (SMEPDO) and the Lao National Chamber of Commerce and Industry (LNCCI) in 2009 revealed that only half of the enterprises in Lao PDR were aware of the WTO and ASEAN. The proportion was even lower for smaller and micro-sized categories. It is crucial for the business community to understand the post-WTO environment and to understand how it should prepare itself. This also highlights the importance of information dissemination to wider stake-holders, including government ministries and departments and the provinces. Only if people are aware of their rights and obligations will laws and regulations be fully enforced. This will in turn help avoid the breach of commitments.

As part of its Accession Package, Lao PDR bound its tariffs for all agricultural and industrial products. A grace period was granted for products that are sensitive for domestic production or which have effects for government revenue. In the medium to long term, alternative measures that are legal under the WTO need to be put into place to address possible unforeseen difficult situations resulting from an import surge. These measures include the use of safeguards and anti-dumping or countervailing duties on import goods that are deemed to be dumped or subsidised.

In addition, WTO membership provides export opportunities, but those opportunities need to be realised and maximised. The true benefits of WTO membership will only occur if the country can overcome its supply constraints. This is a chief challenge for Lao PDR's successful integration into the region and the world economy. This is why Lao PDR will have to vigorously create opportunities to present its WTO Accession Package to the trade and investment communities, such as through trade and investment conferences, working with the WTO and the Asian Development Bank (ADB) to achieve this purpose.

## Lessons learned for LDC accession

Clearly WTO accession is a difficult and long-lasting exercise: the time and the resources required should not be underestimated. However, efforts are rewarded and therefore worthwhile. We are reluctant to dispense 'lessons': each country has its own political and economic framework conditions. One principle both the WTO and the world community is learning is that 'one shoe size doesn't fit all'.

Yet, below are some lessons learned from our experience of having been involved in the WTO accession preparation and negotiations of Lao PDR from the very beginning of the process. The 'lessons' we provide here are based on Lao PDR's situation and experience. Any acceding government will have to adapt any 'advice' to its own socio-economic and political settings. There is no blueprint for accession – and there should not be.

- Without the political will internally to undertake the required reforms, accession negotiations are likely to be very difficult. Reforms cannot be imposed from the outside. If you are in the fortunate situation – as Lao PDR was – that the accession requirements were considered as a tool for internal reforms rather than a requirement for becoming a WTO member, the accession process is very useful.
- Acceding governments should ensure that they are properly prepared from the beginning of the accession phase. First, they need to identify areas of non-compliance, e.g. non-tariff trade barriers, as well as various regulations and procedures. These should be amended and instituted in line with WTO requirements. Second, good coordination also needs to be put in place. There are coordination needs within the government (intra-ministry and executive with legislative branches), between the public and private sectors, and between the government and trading partners. Third, acceding governments need to have proper consultation mechanisms both within the government and with interested private sector parties. Lastly, complementary actions are also required, including macroeconomic reforms, adjustment assistance and training in particular, to cushion the possible impacts in the post-accession phase.
- Coordination and consultation offer a number of benefits for acceding governments. First, they greatly expand the knowledge base, which allows the negotiating team to create and implement trade agreements that maximise gains and minimise negative impacts. This mechanism also serves as an early warning system for political and technical problems. It also promotes a balance of views with the most interested parties involved in process. Very often these consultations provide the negotiating team with the necessary arguments in the negotiating process. Another benefit is to educate all interested parties, which thereby increases comfort with both the process and substance of the

accession negotiations. The coordination and consultation also help develop policy consensus among various stakeholders. Lastly, this provides time for the legislature as well as the private sector to consider the best paths for implementation and adjustment, which will help ease the implementation process.

- Do not underestimate the time it takes to negotiate an accession. The accession process is necessarily long and tedious. First you have to establish a political consensus that reform is necessary and good for your country: this takes time. Then you have to develop the content of the reform and translate it into laws and regulations: this takes technical knowledge and time both to define what you want and to consult with the various stakeholders. Then you have to negotiate the reforms with those who oppose them internally. Any reform means change and there is always opposition to change. Moreover, with each reform, there are winners and losers even if overall the country benefits from the reform. One has to consult with them and adapt your position so as to secure the largest possible support for the reform. This takes time and resources. Then you have to convince your partners in the WTO that the reform you propose is fully in line with WTO obligations. There again, you need time to develop your arguments and to defend them with WTO members. You might need to take into account their objections to some of your proposals and then negotiate their acceptance internally again. This takes time and resources.

- Always remember that WTO accession negotiations are not negotiations about which WTO obligations you will accept and those you will reject. You are joining a club and you have to accept the obligations that are inherent in membership. If one of your policies clearly violates WTO principles, you have to change your policy. Do not fight battles you cannot win. Remember, each WTO member can refuse your joining the organisation. This means that you have to convince and negotiate with any member that opposes aspects of your policies.

- Do not underestimate your opportunities to negotiate. The WTO defines principles. Each country is free to translate those principles according to its own requirements. Your job thus is not to challenge the principles of the WTO (or to refuse them), but to convince your partners that the way you propose to apply those principles to your situation is fully in line with the WTO principles. As you cannot impose your opinion on WTO members, you have to convince them about the policy application and your honesty. This requires good preparation of your arguments, a good and honest dialogue with your partners and a lot of patience. Many WTO members insist on specific applications of principles (even specific wording in your laws). The reason is often a certain mistrust that the acceding government is only 'pretending' to make reforms, but actually does not intend to apply them according to WTO requirements. The good news is that most member countries are responsive to your arguments provided you use WTO language and not protectionist arguments. Our experience has shown that the very hard positions on issues taken by some WTO members were resolved easily once you had convinced your partners that your position was based on real issues within your country and that you were serious in wanting to apply full WTO obligations. Your ability to convince your partners that you are fully committed to implementing the WTO obligation could be the most important element in the negotiations.

. Do not hesitate to defend yourself vigorously against requests which you consider to be inappropriate given your situation. Avoid attacking the request itself, but show your partner why this request – given your situation as an LDC – is not reasonable. All WTO members have agreed to the guidelines for the accession negotiations for LDCs. Do insist on their implementation by showing that forcing you to take on commitments that you cannot implement is not in the interest of the WTO. You are entitled to flexibility as an LDC and you should make sure that it is granted to you, if you need it.

. While insisting on the LDC flexibility, do not refuse WTO commitments, but show that – at this moment – you are not able to comply with them. Ask for implementation periods that take into account your capability to implement the obligations. Showing your partners all the steps you have to take to implement an obligation and proposing specific intermediate steps which can be monitored, will help you to convince your partners that you will implement the obligation in due course and that you are not asking for a transition period simply to avoid taking on the required commitments. Lao PDR managed, in this way, to obtain the flexibility it needed to be able to ensure full and credible implementation of various WTO obligations (see our negotiated transition periods above).

. Last but not least, arm yourself with a lot of patience and diplomatic skills. Even if you consider a request by a member to be totally unacceptable and unjustified, even if you have to respond to the same question many times, never lose your composure and remain cooperative. Remember, one country can stop you from becoming a member. You therefore have to induce a cooperative mood in this partner.

There is also one systemic issue that you might want to address. Lao PDR's accession process has shown us that the WTO is an excellent tool for telling us what the international best practices are and what we have to do to fully integrate into the world economy. It is thus an excellent guide for reform. However, the WTO is less useful as an instrument to help us to define the priorities for reform and their phasing. As the WTO accession process is driven by the requests of the WTO members rather than the development needs of the acceding governments, it is up to the acceding government to re-establish development priorities, pacing and sequencing of reforms. This is often a difficult process.

### Tapping into technical assistance

Given the constraints in government funding and domestic investment, international cooperation and assistance from donors can play a key role. Lao PDR has benefited from the support of international organisations and bilateral donors which can provide a good example for other accessions. Notable assistance provided to the country during its accession phase included a multi-donor trust fund, Trade Development Facility (TDF) and the Enhanced Integrated Framework (EIF). There is also ongoing assistance from such organisations as the Advisory Centre on WTO Law (ACWL), ADB, the IDEAS Centre, the International Labour Organization (ILO), the International Trade Centre (ITC), the United Nations Conference on Trade and Development (UNCTAD), the United Nations Industrial Development Organization (UNIDO), the United Nations Development Programme (UNDP), the United Nations Office for Project Services (UNOPS) and the World Bank. Bilateral donors included Australia, China, Canada, European Union, Germany, Ireland, New Zealand, Switzerland, Viet Nam and United States.

Lao PDR's experience with technical assistance has been the following:

- Assistance is available, provided the acceding government knows how to formulate its requests. However, the time required until a project is approved and the operational deployment of the assistance should not be underestimated.

- Donor agencies have a tendency to offer you the assistance they believe you need rather than what you actually need. Moreover, donors have financing guidelines which often do not allow them to finance what is most needed in the country.
- Technical assistance has to be managed. Donor support should be used effectively. Experts have a tendency to give you what they know, not what you need. Unless you specify the requirements you want a service to fulfil, the experts will develop the most perfect system in an abstract way, but one that is not adapted to your needs. Experts may usefully review your laws and provide you with their comments. However, they should not be used to make the laws which need to be embedded in your economic and political reality.
- Technical assistance should be used to fill the technical gap that is not available locally and not to implement a project in a way that places the burden on key government agencies.
- Assistance in the WTO accession context should be continuous and provided by experts who follow the process over a longer period of time. If, for each activity, you get a new expert, you are likely to waste time educating the expert about the realities of your country.

Accession to the WTO is a difficult and lengthy process. LDCs should bear in mind that the time and the resources required to complete the process should not be underestimated. With proper preparation and careful negotiations, the government of Lao PDR obtained a good deal by joining the WTO. Lao PDR took fifteen years to build national consensus to execute reforms in line with its national development agenda and complete the accession process. Its success is chiefly attributed to strong political will as well as good coordination and an effective consultation mechanism. The country also has the privilege of benefiting from various sources of technical assistance. However, WTO accession is not the end in itself. Post-accession challenges remain for Lao PDR. But it is believed that the country will overcome these challenges, and will eventually take full advantage of the opportunities that have emerged.

# 23

# The 2013 WTO accession of Tajikistan: experience of a landlocked economy in a changing regional economic configuration

SAIDRAHMON NAZRIEV

## ABSTRACT

*Tajikistan was part of the Great Silk Road, a system of caravan routes connecting Eurasian countries between the second century BC and the fifteenth century AD. The development of trade throughout Central Asia encouraged the people of this region to adapt to the demands and requirements of consumers thousands of kilometres away, both in western Europe and in China. Tajikistan's principal rationale for seeking WTO membership was to gain access to new markets and secure the General Agreement on Tariffs and Trade/WTO right of freedom of transit, reinserting Tajikistan into trading routes, comparable to its location in the historic Great Silk Road system. By becoming a member of the WTO in 2013, Tajikistan is opening up new markets for its goods, just as it did several centuries ago. Tajikistan sought WTO membership to sustain domestic reforms. Domestic reforms entailed enactment, repeal and/or amendment of approximately one hundred laws and regulations. In the experience of Tajikistan, successful negotiating factors included,* inter alia, *a technically competent negotiation team, support from WTO members, strategically defined negotiating objectives, accompanied by a strategy for cooperation. Post-accession considerations should be part of an accession strategy. This chapter outlines Tajikistan's road to the WTO.*

Territorial restrictions, lack of access to the seas, remoteness and isolation from world markets, and consequent high transit and transport costs remain an essential barrier to the social and economic development of Tajikistan. Countries without access to the sea are usually among the poorest countries of the world, with a low level of development. Sixteen out of thirty landlocked countries are least-developed countries (LDCs).

The high costs of transporting goods which landlocked countries must cover are much more significant barriers to trade than import tariffs applicable to such goods entering their markets. Emerging economies and landlocked countries pay three times more in transport costs than in applicable import tariffs. According to research conducted by Venables and Limão (2001),[1] expenses for 1,000 kilometres of shipping by sea reach about US$190, while the same distance by land would cost US $1,380, which is 7.3 times higher than the cost of transportation by sea.

The political situation in the south, civil war in the recent past and complex relations with neighbouring countries are additional factors directly affecting the development of the country. Precisely because of its complicated geographical position and the political situation in Central Asia, the leadership of the country actively initiated economic reforms with the aim of market liberalisation and compliance with international standards. Diversification of import and export routes has helped the country to ensure a certain independence and stability of imports and exports.

For an economy like Tajikistan, which depends on the stable transit of goods, acceding to an alliance of governments that adopts and complies with universally recognised rules, and that resolves infringement of these rules within the Dispute Settlement Mechanism, has become very important.

The sharp increase of costs for energy resources in the last ten years, which has affected the cost of transportation of cargo by land, motivates countries with a complex geographical position to adopt measures to ensure the competitiveness of their goods. Implementing reforms and recognition of international trade norms should play a role in the efforts of different institutions of the country to improve the investment climate in the country.

Tajikistan is a landlocked, mountainous country in Central Asia with a territory of 143,100 square kilometres. In the west, north-west and north-east, Tajikistan shares borders with Uzbekistan (910 kilometres) and Kyrgyz Republic (630 kilometres); in the east, with China (430 kilometres); and in the south with Afghanistan (1,030 kilometres). Mountains and plateau occupy 93 per cent of the total territory. The population of the country, as of 1 January 2013, stood at 7.8 million.

---

[1] 'Infrastructure, geographical disadvantage, transport costs, and trade', Nuno Limão and Anthony J. Venables, *The World Bank Economic Review* (2001), vol. 15(3), pp. 451–479.

Tajikistan is an agrarian-industrial economy. Its comparative advantage is related to agriculture: there are significant water resources, favourable climatic conditions for growing grain and animal husbandry and an abundance of cheap labour. The share of agriculture is significant in the gross domestic product (GDP) of the country.

Aluminium accounts for more than half of its export income. The shares of hydropower, cotton, fruits, vegetable oil and textiles are also high. These products are exported mostly to China, Iran, the Netherlands, Russia, Turkey and Uzbekistan.

Tajikistan imports electricity, oil products, aluminium dioxide, cars, machinery and foodstuffs. Its main import partners are China, Iran, Kazakhstan, Russia, Turkey and Uzbekistan.

The economic development of Tajikistan has been advanced through continuous reforms of the economy, diversification, increased competitiveness, improvement of the quality of the management of the economy, institutional and structural transformations in the country, and improvement of the financial and banking system.

The strategy for the economic development of the country is based on documents such as the 'National Strategy for the Development of the Republic of Tajikistan' for the period until 2015 and the 'Strategy for the Improvement of the Level of Welfare of the Population of the Country' for the period from 2013 to 2015 (third stage), which should ensure a systematic process of long-term development of the country in accordance with the Millennium Development Goals.

The realisation of the programme goals, originating from these documents, has ensured steady economic growth in the last ten years. The GDP of the country for this period increased more than twofold, and in 2012 it reached US$18.04 billion by purchasing power parity, with an annual growth rate of 7.5 per cent. The inflation rate has decreased from 17 per cent in 2003 to 5.8 per cent in 2012, nearly three times lower.

In the last ten years, the government of Tajikistan has taken important decisions to enhance the role of the mining industry in the economy of the country. The main direction of growth and development of the sector is the attraction of foreign investment to undertaking joint ventures, focused on the manufacturing of final products.

Many foreign companies participate in major investment projects related to the development of mining, exploration and production of mineral resources. The output of the country's mining industry, particularly extraction and processing of minerals, precious and semi-precious stones, are among the key elements of the country's export income, which supports the budget of the country.

## Tajikistan's road to the WTO

Tajikistan's accession to the WTO started in 2001 when the government of Tajikistan submitted its application to the WTO Secretariat requesting accession. Having considered the application of Tajikistan, the General Council decided to establish a working party on Tajikistan's accession to the WTO. Consequently, Tajikistan acquired WTO observer status.

The working party comprised thirty WTO members, although the twenty-eight EU member states are considered as one WTO member. At the time when Tajikistan acceded, the European Union had twenty-seven members.

The negotiation process started with the first working party meeting on Tajikistan's accession to the WTO. Overall, nine working party meetings for this accession took place. The accession process was particularly expedited in 2012 when four out of the nine working party meetings took place. The multilateral negotiation process was completed on 26 October 2012, at the ninth working party meeting, where it adopted the draft working party report *ad referendum* and submitted it to the WTO General Council for final approval.

The Accession Package for Tajikistan to the WTO was approved by the General Council on 10 December 2012. The Protocol of Accession of Tajikistan to the WTO was signed by the President of Tajikistan, HE Emomaly Rahmon, and the then WTO Director-General Pascal Lamy.

The Protocol of Accession was subsequently ratified by the Parliament of Tajikistan on 9 January 2013 and Notification of the Instrument of Ratification of Tajikistan's Protocol of Accession was deposited with the WTO Secretariat on 31 January 2013. Tajikistan became the 159th WTO member on 2 March 2013.

Negotiations between Tajikistan and WTO members were conducted on two tracks: multilateral and bilateral market access for goods and services. The multilateral negotiations had a format of working party meetings where WTO members were able to examine the foreign trade regime of Tajikistan.

On the bilateral level, Tajikistan negotiated with interested WTO members on market access for goods and services. Bilateral negotiations were based on initial market access offers on goods and services presented by Tajikistan. Tajikistan concluded bilateral market access negotiations for goods with thirteen WTO members and six WTO members on services. Appropriate bilateral protocols were signed.

In the process of the accession of Tajikistan, more than one hundred laws and regulations were either enacted, amended or replaced. The new laws adopted included the Law on Foreign Trade Activity, the Law on Safety of Food Products, the Law on Cryptography, the Law on Plant Protection and the Law on Conformity Assessment. The new Tax Code of Tajikistan has come into effect. Amendments have been introduced to the customs code and the civil and procedural codes of Tajikistan. In addition, Tajikistan ratified the Convention on the Recognition and Enforcement of Foreign Arbitral Awards (the New York Convention) and the Convention for the Protection of New Varieties of Plants (the UPOV Convention).

It should be noted that the negotiating team of Tajikistan based its negotiating strategy, among other things, on the critical importance of the agricultural sector for the national economy. A number of plurilateral meetings took place to discuss and negotiate the level of support for this sector. As a result, Tajikistan managed to maintain agricultural support at the level of 8 per cent of GDP.

Furthermore, in the course of bilateral negotiations, Tajikistan succeeded in protecting its national interests. As a result, the final average bound rate is 8.0 per cent. The final average bound rate is higher than that of other recently acceded WTO members, most notably Montenegro (5.1 per cent), Ukraine (5.8 per cent), Croatia (6.1 per cent), Albania (7.0 per cent), Moldova (7.0 per cent), Former Yugoslav Republic of Macedonia (7.1 per cent), Georgia (7.4 per cent), Kyrgyz Republic (7.5 per cent) and Russia (7.8 per cent). The average currently applied rate stands at 7.3 per cent (Figure 23.1 and Table 23.1).

The final average bound rate for agricultural products is 10.4 per cent. Tajikistan managed to maintain tariff peaks for a number of sensitive (strategic) products: un-denatured ethyl alcohol (80 per cent, but not less than US$2.50 per litre), alcoholic drinks (18 to 23 per cent), dried fruits (15 per cent), natural honey (20 per cent), certain fresh and prepared vegetables (20 to 23 per cent) and raw silk and cotton (20 per cent).

For non-agricultural products, the average final bound rate is 7.6 per cent. Tariff peaks were maintained for sensitive products of interest to Tajikistan, such as for textiles (20 per cent), clothing (17 per cent), footwear (20 to 30 per cent), carpets (30 per cent), aluminium products (10 per cent), construction materials (15 per cent), certain chemicals (20 per cent) and mattresses (20 per cent).

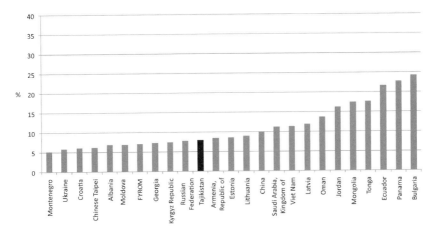

**Figure 23.1**   Article XII non-LDC members and Tajikistan: average final bound rates: all products.

Negotiations on market access on services resulted in the acceptance of specific commitments in eleven sectors and 111 sub-sectors (see Figure 23.2 and Table 23.2).

Based on the experience from the WTO accession negotiating process, a range of key factors was identified as accounting for the successful completion of the negotiation process and accession of Tajikistan.

First, the political decision of the government of Tajikistan was to complete the accession process in order to integrate the economy of the country into the global economy, taking into account national interests subject to intensive negotiations.

Second, the government of Tajikistan developed an action plan, accompanied by the approval of a relevant road map to accelerate the process of its accession to the WTO.

Third, in order to achieve the outlined goals, a two-level inter-ministerial commission was established:

- The first level included the heads of key ministries, who were obliged to identify strategic directions, approve the negotiating position, provide the single strategy for the operation of Tajikistan to engage with the WTO, make decisions on the introduction of changes and amendments to the current foreign trade regime, eliminate existing discriminating barriers, and identify the position of Tajikistan with respect to market access for goods and services.

Table 23.1 *Comparison of tariff concessions with selected members*

| Government | Date of membership | All products | Agricultural products | Non-agricultural products |
|---|---|---|---|---|
| Montenegro | 29 April 2012 | 5.1 | 10.8 | 4.3 |
| Ukraine | 16 May 2008 | 5.8 | 11.0 | 5.0 |
| Croatia | 30 November 2000 | 6.1 | 10.4 | 5.5 |
| Albania | 8 September 2000 | 7.0 | 9.5 | 6.6 |
| Moldova | 26 July 2001 | 7.0 | 14.0 | 5.9 |
| Former Yugoslav Republic of Macedonia | 4 April 2003 | 7.1 | 12.9 | 6.3 |
| Georgia | 14 June 2000 | 7.4 | 13.0 | 6.5 |
| Kyrgyz Republic | 20 December 1998 | 7.5 | 12.8 | 6.7 |
| Russian Federation | 22 August 2012 | 7.8 | 10.8 | 7.3 |
| **Tajikistan** | **2 March 2013** | **8.0** | **10.4** | **7.6** |
| Armenia, Republic of | 5 February 2003 | 8.5 | 14.7 | 7.6 |
| China | 11 December 2001 | 10.0 | 15.7 | 9.2 |
| Viet Nam | 11 January 2007 | 11.4 | 18.5 | 10.4 |

- The second level consisted of an expert group for conducting bilateral and multilateral negotiations, as well as consultations with the partner countries, reviewing issues and comments from WTO members, and preparing appropriate replies accompanied by the development of possible positions of Tajikistan with respect to the results of negotiations with WTO members.

Fourth, success in the negotiations mostly depended on the personal qualities and the competence of the national negotiating team. There was a great desire to achieve maximum results. In particular, members of the Tajik negotiation team were required to have a good knowledge of the

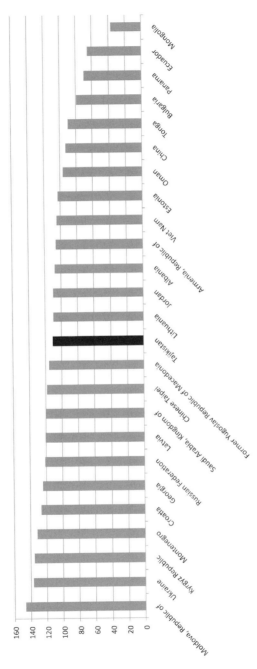

**Figure 23.2** Article XII non-LDC members and Tajikistan: number of services: subsectors with General Agreement on Trade in Services (GATS) commitments.

Table 23.2 *Comparison of services commitments with selected members*

| Government | Date of membership | Number of services sub-sectors |
|---|---|---|
| Moldova, Republic of | 26 July 2001 | 147 |
| Ukraine | 16 May 2008 | 137 |
| Kyrgyz Republic | 20 December 1998 | 136 |
| Montenegro | 29 April 2012 | 132 |
| Croatia | 30 November 2000 | 127 |
| Georgia | 14 June 2000 | 125 |
| Russian Federation | 22 August 2012 | 122 |
| Former Yugoslav Republic of Macedonia | 4 April 2003 | 116 |
| **Tajikistan** | **2 March 2013** | **111** |
| Albania | 8 September 2000 | 108 |
| Armenia, Republic of | 5 February 2003 | 106 |
| Viet Nam | 11 January 2007 | 105 |
| China | 11 December 2001 | 93 |

history of the General Agreement on Tariffs and Trade (GATT), the GATS, the Trade-Related Aspects of Intellectual Property Rights (TRIPs), the Uruguay Round of Multilateral Trade Negotiations and the Marrakesh Agreement Establishing the World Trade Organisation. Knowledge of the rules of the GATT and the WTO were required, as well as a thorough understanding of the disadvantages of protectionism and the advantages of free trade, and continuation of attempts to settle unresolved problems and discussions among WTO members. Most importantly, members of the negotiating team had to be familiar with the social and economic development features of their country, the serious problems the country faced, its development needs and the difficulties of adapting to the market economy.

Fifth, successful completion of the negotiations also depended on a 'mobile' negotiating team. When warranted by the circumstances, the members of the Tajik negotiating team visited WTO member countries, held meetings with the representatives of the embassies of these countries in Tajikistan and requested embassies of Tajikistan in other countries to conduct negotiations.

Sixth, a hugely important role was played by the direct support received from particular donor countries, such as Switzerland, the United

States and the European Union. They provided financial and technical assistance, international experts, advisors and consultants during the entire process of the accession of Tajikistan to the WTO. The strong support and great experience of these countries in international trade and the efficient cooperation with the governmental authorities of these countries played an important role in the outcome of negotiations on its accession to the WTO.

And seventh, an important successful strategy in the experience of Tajikistan was to design an optimal strategy of cooperation for the delegation of the country in the process of negotiations with WTO members and the WTO Secretariat. The negotiating team of the Secretariat established personal and working relations with representatives of WTO members and the WTO Secretariat. This network and relationship were important elements in the successful completion of the accession process.

Post-accession, because of the probability of increased competition after accession to the WTO, the government of Tajikistan has paid close attention to the adaptation of the national economy to new conditions of competition on the global scene. As a consequence, it is developing a programme on the adaptation of the national economy to WTO conditions. The content of this programme, designed to promote and defend the national interests of the country, will include activities aimed at further reforms and improvement of legislation and specific measures for the development of sensitive sectors of the industry of the country, such as the textile industry, mining industry, agricultural production, production of products of first necessity and other sectors which are competitive in the global market.

It should be noted that the government of Tajikistan is taking all measures to improve and develop the economy of the country by using available opportunities from WTO membership and by participation in the adoption of international rules and norms. Post-accession, Tajikistan has been conducting meetings with all WTO members. It is constantly searching for reliable trade partners and new markets for national products. Tajikistan will exercise its rights and obligations through the effective use of the WTO Dispute Settlement Understanding. As a land-locked country, it will exercise its right as a WTO member to guarantee its right to the free and non-discriminatory transit of goods through the territories of other WTO members.

# 24

# The 2014 WTO accession of Yemen: accession negotiations as an instrument for domestic reform, national security and international cooperation

SAADALDEEN ALI BIN TALIB

ABSTRACT

*In 2011, a popular revolution occurred in Yemen, leading to the formation of the government which brought the accession process to its conclusion in 2014, following years of long and complex negotiations. From the beginning, Yemen's accession process was envisaged not as an end in itself, but as a means to achieve other, more imperative, objectives, including poverty reduction, decreasing levels of chronic unemployment and raising levels of sustained development to meet the needs of a rapidly growing population. This chapter gives an account of the accession process, focusing on the positive effects of Yemen's accession to the WTO, both as a catalyst for long sought-after domestic reform and as a useful and convenient path to reach higher levels of reform for which the accession process acted as a spur. The aspiration was to create a competitive business environment that would lead to efficient resource allocation and ultimately boost output and productivity as well as increasing the well-being of the populace and reaping the benefits of WTO membership. Joining the WTO does not mark the end of the reform process. There is work post-accession to establish and strengthen different institutions to exercise the benefits of WTO membership for Yemen.*

When I was invited to contribute to this important book project, Yemen had just completed an accession negotiation journey that had lasted more than thirteen years, to reach the eleventh and final working party meeting on 26 September 2013. Later in the year, on 4 December 2013 at the Ninth WTO Ministerial Conference in Bali, Indonesia, the WTO adopted Yemen's Protocol of Accession and related documents. Subsequently, Yemen completed its domestic ratification process and, as

Minister for Trade and Industry, I deposited Yemen's Instrument of Acceptance of the protocol on the accession of Yemen with WTO Director-General Roberto Azevêdo on 27 May 2014. On 26 June 2014, Yemen became the 160th member of the WTO. Thus, I thought it quite apposite to participate in this noble endeavour and share some thoughts from the perspective of the Yemen accession experience.

At the outset, I must recognise that the Yemen accession – as was the case of other accessions – was the product of the hard work of many distinguished persons at the helm of the process, as well as of other officials and national stakeholders within and outside the government, who worked in harmony to create an effective national accession machine. In the case of Yemen, several former ministers of the Ministry of Industry and Trade capably contributed to this national endeavour. My participation in this national undertaking came mostly during its last two – rather difficult – years. Many of the results achieved were spread over several years of accession negotiations.

In this unassuming contribution, my focus will be on the positive effect of the accession process to the WTO as a catalyst for Yemen's long sought-after domestic reform – past, present and future. From an early stage, Yemen's accession to the WTO was utilised, as in the case of most, if not all, accessions, to advance trade and domestic economic reform. It is a rather useful and convenient path to reach higher levels of reform that might not easily be achieved otherwise, i.e. had the accession process not been present, or acted as a spur. Therefore, one clear lesson in Yemen's case was to employ the accession process to introduce and solidify domestic reforms that could face many obstacles in a non-WTO-accession era. That is why I fully concur with the statement made by the current WTO Director-General Roberto Azevêdo when he launched the first global seminar on WTO accessions on 23 September 2013: 'The process of acceding to the WTO helps to underpin domestic reforms essential for the promotion of economic growth and development.' This accurately describes the experience of Yemen, despite some scepticism that the positive impact on reducing poverty as a fundamental goal in Yemen's case may only be realised in the medium to long term.

The year 2011 was exceptional in the Arab region, including in Yemen. The Arab Spring had finally arrived to that part of the world, where political reform had been badly needed for decades. Yemen was no exception and a popular revolution toppled the old regime. A new national unity government was formed on 7 December 2011, when

I joined as Minister of Industry and Trade responsible for the completion of Yemen's accession to the WTO. One of my priorities was to see this process concluded after thirteen years of long and complex negotiations. Fortunately, Yemen will become a new member of the WTO during 2014, which Yemenis consider the new beginning of a brighter future.

On the other hand, Yemen's accession to the WTO coincides with the successful results harvested through the comprehensive National Dialogue Conference that ended its almost ten-month long and serious debates on 25 January 2014. High hopes have been building in Yemen en route to developing a 'New Yemen' of law and order. Accession to the WTO could not have come at a better time. My sincere hope and trust is that WTO membership will ease Yemen's problems faster than some might anticipate.

## Initial stage

Yemen's decision to accede to the WTO was properly taken by the government in early 1998 and was cemented by the House of Representatives (Parliament) with its adoption of a new government programme beginning in June 1998, when the intention of acceding to the WTO was formally introduced and endorsed by the two branches of government as a future objective. Hence, it can be confirmed that both the executive and legislature bodies took the decision collectively to achieve that target. On the other hand, it was clear from day one that accession to the WTO was not an end in itself, but rather a means to achieve other more imperative objectives, including poverty reduction, the reduction and elimination of chronic unemployment and achieving higher levels of sustained development to meet the needs of a rapidly growing population. The continuation of the domestic reform process, which was started a few years earlier, was envisaged through accession to the WTO as the best direction to follow.

Yemen was aware that in order to fully integrate into the multilateral trading system, the country had to be a member of the new institution overseeing it, i.e. the WTO. Consequently, in April 1999, Yemen applied for WTO observer status with a view to becoming a full member. Without much delay, a year later in the same month the government presented its request for full membership, and this was accepted by the WTO General Council on 17 July 2000. A working party was then established in accordance with the standard terms of reference under Article XII of the Marrakesh Agreement Establishing the World Trade

Organization (WTO Agreement). Yemen was privileged to have an able working party chairperson, Hartmut Röben, who wisely guided the working party process for its entire duration from 30 November 2004 when the first working party meeting was convened.

At the time of the inception of the WTO in 1995, Yemen embarked on a comprehensive reform process that was officially given the title of 'Economic, Financial and Administrative Reform Programme'. In international jargon, this was equivalent to the Enhanced Structural Adjustment Facility[1] that was initiated with the assistance of the International Monetary Fund (IMF) and the World Bank, as well as Yemen's key development partners. This programme was developed after some very injurious political developments that had earlier led to civil war from April to July 1994. Hence, the new reform programme was quite timely in overcoming the aftermath of that sad episode in Yemen's recent history, as well as its economic mismanagement for several decades in both the formerly separate North and South of Yemen, which were united as the Republic of Yemen in May 1990. Thus, Yemen was fortunate to have both tracks proceeding hand in hand. It was also no surprise that this concurrence happened, as domestic reform is a necessary requirement for a successful accession to the WTO.

Luckily, foreign trade reform and Yemen's accession were at the forefront of such an undertaking. One of the earliest steps taken, in the period between 1995 and 1998, even before the application for WTO membership, was the amendment of Yemen's Foreign Trade Law, governing international trade and economic relationships. Several provisions were introduced to ensure the way forward on the path to liberalising the Yemeni foreign trade regime. The import licensing system that had dominated the scene for years, as a means of arbitrary control of volume and quantity of imports, was abolished. The reforms of several monetary and fiscal policies were implemented, including enhancing the independence of the Central Bank of Yemen and a commitment to the obligation of Article VIII of the Articles of Agreement of the IMF. Many other laws were also amended or enacted pertaining to banks, financial exchange, supervision and monitoring of insurance companies and agents, commercial law, etc. Meanwhile, these legislative reform steps led to accelerating the serious consideration of accession to the newly established WTO.

---

[1] Initially a stand-alone programme and later supplemented by the IMF facility, see www.imf.org/external/np/pfp/1999/yemen.

## The accession process in the context of domestic reforms

The beauty of accession to the WTO under Article XII of the WTO Agreement is that it can be portrayed as a physician's job that assists the patient to overcome different ills. The first scan/image that was presented to Yemen's working party members was the usual Memorandum of the Foreign Trade Regime (MFTR) in accordance with a WTO Secretariat note (WT/ACC/1). This snapshot described the situation of Yemen at the initial stage of the accession process, which members consider to be a 'fact-finding' phase. It also showed the degree of compliance of Yemen's trade regime with the WTO Agreement. Later, hundreds of questions followed the submission of the MFTR and Yemen responded to each. The question-and-answer phase is a constant exercise between working party members and the acceding government, as was the case with Yemen. It only ends when members are satisfied with the answers received and the relevant commitment language is registered in the draft working party report, which develops from an earlier document, 'Elements of points raised', during working party meetings to a full draft report by the end of the negotiation process.

Throughout the working party process, eleven formal meetings were held and two informal stocktaking meetings were convened. Yemen's most active year of accession was 2010, when four meetings, both formal and informal, were conducted, and six bilateral market access agreements were signed. By the end of the year, nine bilateral market access agreements on goods and seven bilateral market access agreements on services had been signed. The following year, Yemen was considered as a priority least-developed country (LDC) accession, as the end of the accession tunnel was quite near. Only a few multilateral issues and one goods bilateral market access agreement were outstanding. However, that task took three difficult years to complete!

The reform process continued at a faster pace during the accession process both unilaterally and based on WTO members' requests to align Yemen's foreign trade regime with WTO law. Most notably, Yemen introduced far-reaching reforms to its tariff regime in 2005, i.e. amid the accession process, when import tariffs were streamlined into four general bands and applied tariffs were reduced based on the independent assessment of the government with the assistance of the IMF and the World Bank. Though this step was economically correct, unfortunately Yemen was not rewarded or credited for such ambitious steps while negotiating its accession to the WTO. As a result, some WTO members tried to 'push' tariff-binding level 'ceilings' to a minimum. In particular, bilateral negotiations with one member, which made 'unreasonable' demands on goods market access, were prolonged for longer than necessary and thus delayed the completion of Yemen's accession process for several months.

A comprehensive legislative action plan was initiated from an early stage of the accession process. It enclosed a wide range of law-making reforms – approximately twenty-six pieces of legislation – in order to confirm compliance with WTO agreements as well as the other additional commitments that Yemen undertook during the course of accession negotiations. Upon accession, Yemen committed to endeavouring to meet its legislative promise of full observance of WTO law. Yemen, as an LDC, considered it necessary to benefit from the special and differential treatment availed to LDCs, including those that had earlier acceded to the WTO. Therefore, Yemen attempted to shelter some critical areas with such special and differential treatment. In particular, the need for some transitional periods to implement certain WTO agreements was of paramount priority. At the end of the negotiations, some transitional arrangements were agreed with members within different timeframes up to January 2017.

## Specific reform commitments

In pursuit of the requirements for transparency and the objective of predictability in Yemen's foreign trade policy, the WTO accession process was an excellent means to enhance the priorities in Yemen's domestic reforms. This process catalysed reforms in a manner that would have been extremely difficult to achieve had Yemen not been engaged in WTO accession negotiations, pursuant to Article XII of the Marrakesh Agreement. The outcome of accession negotiations was a fairly balanced and a forward-looking trade policy that will be entirely reshaped during the membership phase. Negotiated results achieved were comparable to the results of other recently acceded LDCs. This comes as no surprise, as those accessions were conducted in accordance with the guidelines on LDC accession, as prescribed by General Council Decision WT/L/508 of 10 December 2002. Despite some vagueness in the language of the guidelines, Yemen attempted to make the best of the flexibility available to acceding LDCs. By the time the second decision in favour of LDC accession was enacted, on 25 July 2012 (Decision WT/L/508/Add. 1), Yemen had almost finalised all negotiations. Only one outstanding bilateral market access agreement was outstanding, although its outlines were already established at that time. The outstanding negotiation was finalised one year later.

The government of Yemen fully recognises the linkage between trade, growth and competitiveness. Equally, the role of trade liberalisation as a medium for enhanced economic growth has been documented throughout the years. Therefore, Yemen made several significant systemic commitments (twenty-eight in total) not only for the sake of compliance with the WTO Agreement, but equally to complement its domestic reform process. The latter will certainly continue in the future at its own pace and as needed to further support and sustain the country's development efforts.

During its accession negotiations, Yemen undertook several multilateral commitments on different issues, including accepting ambitious requests by some WTO members. The aspiration was to create a competitive business environment that would lead to an efficient resource allocation and ultimately boost output and productivity as well as increasing the well-being of the populace. In the background of the accession negotiations project was the strengthening of domestic reforms and paving the way to reap the benefits of WTO membership. To this end, Yemen committed, among other things, to:

- applying the Agreement on Trade-Related Investment Measures (TRIMs) from the date of accession;
- complying with the WTO Agreement on Rules of Origin from the date of accession;
- applying anti-dumping duties, countervailing duties and safeguard measures in full conformity with WTO provisions;
- binding agricultural export subsidies at zero from the date of accession;
- ceasing grant to all subsidies contingent upon the use of domestic over imported goods;
- bringing fees and charges in connection with importation or exportation into compliance with Articles VIII and X of the General Agreement on Tariffs and Trade (GATT) 1994;
- granting trading rights to WTO members for any product allowed to be imported into Yemen by 31 December 2014;
- granting individuals and companies the right to legally appeal against government administrative actions covered by WTO rules;
- implementing the Customs Valuation Agreement by 31 December 2016;
- implementing the Agreement on Technical Barriers to Trade starting from 31 December 2016;

- applying the Agreement on Trade Related Aspects of Intellectual Property Rights (TRIPs) no later than 31 December 2016;
- implementing the provisions of the WTO Agreement on the Application of Sanitary and Phytosanitary Measures no later than 31 December 2016;
- terminating the requirement for certificates of origin and invoices of imports into Yemen or the endorsement or notarisation by Yemeni consulates abroad by no later than 1 January 2017;
- binding other duties and charges (ODCs) at zero no later than four years from the date of accession.

Yemen contributed meaningfully to market access for WTO members, both for trade in goods and trade in services. Concessions and commitments on goods reached the optimum possible binding levels that gave both comfort and predictability to trade with Yemen. The 100 per cent tariff lines binding coverage and ambitious concessions and commitments levels agreed were quite remarkable for an LDC emerging from political turmoil and needing the goodwill and cooperation of the global community. The latter was especially anticipated from the 'Friends of Yemen', a group that was formed to assist with the stabilisation of Yemen's internal situation as well as to provide a helping hand to move Yemen smoothly towards a stable and promising future.

In its market access schedules, Yemen has bound all imported goods at rational levels with an overall average binding tariff rate for all goods at 21.1 per cent, agricultural products at 24.9 per cent and non-agricultural products at 20.5 per cent. Services specific commitments are liberal, with ample economic opportunities for investors, covering seventy-eight sub-sectors. Several key services sectors were liberalised. Consequently, market access concessions and commitments have made Yemen's market more attractive for trade and investment. What remains is for interested members to reach out for further trade and investment relations with Yemen, as the country is truly, in principle and by the fact of its WTO specific obligations, open for business.

## Governance

One major outcome of Yemen's accession to the WTO is enhancing the good governance of its foreign trade regime as well as all other aspects of government. In the interim, reducing market-distorting practices will eliminate aspects of corruption. Membership of the WTO, for Yemen, is more than simply accepting international trade rules and living by them, but rather more about promoting transparency and good governance. Living by law and order has always been one of Yemenis' long-sought-after goals. I believe that such aspirations will be more attainable, especially in the new Federate Yemeni State, based on six provinces that can compete in delivering the best government for the people.

International standards implementation, including the WTO Agreement and related commitments, will make Yemen's membership conducive to attaining higher aspirations. At the Ministry of Industry and Trade, we plan to put into operation good governance principles through the establishment of a special WTO-related structure with a special website that will enable both local and international interested trade players to learn more about Yemen's trade policies and its market. This plan will be implemented immediately upon the relocation of the Ministry of Trade and Industry to its original premises, as it is currently housed at a temporary location.

I am confident that WTO membership will improve the country's ability to address different challenges as well as its integration into the global economy. At the macro level, WTO membership will add credibility to government policies and, optimistically, should attract honest and good traders and investors to do business with Yemen, including in the transfer of technology and knowledge. At a micro level, the small- and medium-sized local businesses that characterise Yemen's economy should benefit from networking with regional and global counterparts. I hope that local businesses will integrate into fast-growing global value chains' networks of production and services provision.

Joining the WTO does not mark the end of the reform process; it is, rather, a new beginning for continued and more focused reform. Signing Yemen's Protocol of Accession in Bali in 2013 is quite different from putting it into practice. Yemen's diverse commitments to the WTO as part of that accord need to be followed up and implemented accordingly. Now is the time to fully abide by WTO law, as do all other WTO members. On the other hand, trade liberalisation cannot by itself fix all of Yemen's economic difficulties. Trade policy reform cannot succeed by itself unless complemented by other similarly sound economic policies.

Another key challenge is to diversify the Yemeni economy, and shift it from its dependence on resource extraction into a higher-technology-based economy, within its limited manufacturing and services spheres. Yemen, above all, needs to cash in on its unique geographical location on international trade routes and reap the benefit of its position as a 'launch-pad joint point' between Asia and Africa. Moreover, millions of Yemenis are living all over the world, in diaspora. Many still maintain strong ties to their motherland within different provinces of Yemen, my own family included. Hence, a more effective network with the Yemen diaspora is crucial in building the new Yemen as well as utilising its large population and workforce both inside and outside its territories. Likewise, domestic enabling measures are indispensable to strengthen the rule of law, improving and building additional infrastructure, including the key financial, telecommunications and transportation services and, above all, attracting desperately required foreign direct investment (FDI) for Yemen's rapid economic growth.

The new Yemen that is emerging from the ashes of the 2011 conflict has to deal with many challenges and opportunities. I am optimistic that the results from the comprehensive national dialogue and in particular the new Constitution will lay a solid path for a more prosperous Yemen. In a nutshell, I believe that Yemen needs to seize the prospect of WTO membership to both implement WTO law and build a fair and competitive economy. In line with WTO law, I envisage that the future policies and actions of the government of Yemen will be streamlined, to solve problems, ease any difficulty for doing business in the country and overcome any bottlenecks that impede the smooth flow of trade and FDI. Getting the house of Yemen in order is central for Yemen's future stability and continued economic growth.

During the accession negotiation process, significant internal reforms were implemented with a view to bringing domestic legislation into conformity with the principles, rules and regulations of the WTO. The bulk of national legislation was brought into compliance with WTO law. This part of the reform was concluded during the active phase of negotiations, including amending and introducing a number of laws related to a variety of economic activities.

Yemen's WTO accession commitments – as for other governments that acceded pursuant to Article XII of the WTO Agreement – are wide ranging and complex. Accession may present both advantages and disadvantages for different economic entities in Yemen. Maximisation of rewards and minimisation of weaknesses are crucial to navigating WTO membership safely. This can only be secured through a carefully thought out WTO compliance trade policy, formation of appropriate institutional structures and facilitating key national stakeholders and wider societal participation in dealing with WTO-related issues.

A second type of reform is related to strengthening and establishing different institutions in order to efficiently utilise WTO membership. This part, unfortunately, is not yet fully developed. Therefore, it will be highly important to construct it to facilitate Yemen becoming a good WTO law-abiding member, safeguarding Yemen's interests, as well as reducing any possible negative consequences. However, the creation of a well-designed structure will require technical and financial assistance, post-accession, and in particular the cooperation of Yemen's development partners. Establishing national bodies should also take into account a public–private partnership to facilitate the representation of the interests of the whole country as well as various business entities. This also relates to the application of the trade dispute settlement mechanism under the WTO, although it is unlikely that Yemen – as an LDC – will fully apply such procedures. All the same, preparations for similar scenarios are also an educational tool to improve knowledge and practice of WTO law. Therefore, domestic reforms will require the continued concentration and realisation of Yemen's new status as a WTO member, as well as the establishment and intensification of different institutional functions in order to harvest the positive results of Yemen's membership in the WTO.

On 26 June 2014, Yemen became the 160th member of the WTO. This has heralded a new beginning for Yemen. The delegation of Yemen to the WTO will be proactive, safeguarding and strengthening the system, reaping the benefits of WTO membership. Yemen calls on its trading partners at the WTO and the Secretariat to provide it with post-accession support as we move ahead together as members in one organisation – the rules-based multilateral trading system.

# PART IV

## Working party chairpersons' perspectives on accession negotiations

# 25

# Facilitating accessions: the role of the working party chairperson

CLYDE KULL

## ABSTRACT

*What is the role of the chairperson of a working party? What instruments can he or she use to manage the complexities of the WTO accession process? Typically, WTO accession negotiations are time consuming because of extensive domestic legislative and institutional reforms, which need to be aligned with economic development strategies. These reforms focus on the tough questions of eliminating trade barriers, improving governance, tackling corruption and enforcing the rule of law through WTO-consistent legislation. Formally, the function of the chairperson is to preside over working party meetings. In practice, the chairperson works as part of a team with the WTO Secretariat, led by the Accessions Division, in seeking to identify the balance of interests and what the market can bear, and hence leading the working party to develop a common view of its purpose and shared responsibility.*

The successful conclusion of WTO accession negotiations should not be taken for granted. These negotiations typically involve extensive and often time-consuming domestic legislative and institutional reforms, which need to be aligned to economic development strategies. The reforms include improving governance, tackling corruption and enforcing the rule of law. The resulting Accession Packages, therefore, represent a delicate balance that has been meticulously crafted over many years on the basis of careful analysis, hard negotiation and detailed technical work.

The chairperson works as part of a team with the WTO Secretariat Accessions Division team led by the Director of the Accessions Division, the Secretary of the working party and relevant WTO Secretariat divisions.

Formally, the function of the chairperson is to preside over the working party meetings. In reality, there is much more. The chairperson, for instance, can be instrumental in mediating between the WTO Secretariat, member states and acceding government authorities, testing the political willingness to move forward, passing messages and facilitating the clarification of positions. The chairperson's aim should be to identify and balance the interests, release the potential energies of all parties and lead the working party to develop a common view of its purposes and shared responsibility. The chairperson should play the role of a stimulator. A good understanding of the psychology of negotiations and the ability to build confidence and trust between all parties are necessary prerequisites for the work of the chairperson.

The chairperson could be compared to an operator behind the 360-degree radar screen with an overview not only of the trade and legal regimes, but also of the recent and current political and economic policies of the applicant country and its regional and international links and challenges. It is the task both of the chairperson and of the Accessions Division to spot whether or not there has been progress, in legislative reforms, and to propose to the working party the necessary next steps.

For instance, on the multilateral front, before the questions and replies form the final draft working party report, the examination of the applicant country's trade and economic policies pass through different stages. In order to move to the next stage, substantial qualitative progress has to be made. There are, however, no exact and set criteria to measure the progress and it is very much left to the chairperson and the Secretariat to test and assess the readiness to move, for example, from a stage of a 'Factual summary of points raised' document to an 'Elements of a Draft Working Party Report' document.

An important, if not necessary, part of the chairperson's functions, is to visit the acceding government. Direct contacts and meetings with the leadership of the country, its parliamentarians, different government ministries and departments, representatives of the international (donor) organisations, diplomatic corps, media and non-governmental organisations (NGOs) provide prime opportunities to 'feel the pulse', gauge the 'political will' and assess 'reform commitment'. These 'readings' provide clarity regarding the necessary steps to be taken in the legislative process as well as in bilateral negotiations. They contribute to an independent overview of the main elements of the Accession Package, ascertain the support of the legislator and offer reassurances to policy-makers who have invested political capital in the accession process. Knowledge of the locally spoken language is not a must but, as experience shows, is of great advantage.[1]

The successful conclusion of the accession process depends very much on the policy and negotiating attention of the key members of the working party. In order to establish a more direct technical relationship and drive the process forward, the chairperson may set up a smaller open-ended informal group, the 'friends of the chair'.

Looking back, Tajikistan's WTO accession process was relatively smooth, albeit longer than initially envisaged – certainly from the Tajik side. But it was also the story of the bumps and setbacks that occur when a small, landlocked country, one of the poorest in the world, with a challenging geopolitical location and a devastating civil war in its recent history, sets its sights on joining the global multilateral trade framework. The endgame did not lack a certain element of drama related to the same geopolitics. I have selected subjects and moments which seem to me usefully representative, and attempted to link them with the broader narrative of the role of the chairperson.

Tajikistan became the 159th WTO member on 2 March 2013 after the working party adopted the draft Accession Package on 26 October 2012 and the General Council formally approved the Accession Package on 10 December 2012.

Tajikistan's package of accession documents was the result of over ten years of complex negotiations during which the working party held nine formal meetings, as well as a number of meetings which helped advance the negotiations.

Tajikistan's accession to the multilateral trading system began in 2001, when a WTO working party was established to examine Tajikistan's request for accession. My personal involvement in the process began in October 2003 when I inherited the chairman's mantle from my predecessor Tomasz Jodko. In March 2004 I chaired the first meeting of the working party. This meeting marked the start of the substantive part of the negotiations.

Tajikistan tabled initial offers for market access negotiations in goods and services in March 2004, and revised offers just prior to the second meeting of the working party in April 2005.

---

[1] Ambassador Clyde Kull, an Estonian, also speaks fluent Russian. This greatly facilitated the accession negotiations of Tajikistan, for which he was chairman of the accession working party.

In April 2005, I paid my first visit to Dushanbe. The principal purpose of the visit was to conduct meetings at the highest political level as well as to prepare the Tajik delegation for the second meeting of the working party in Geneva.

The programme included meetings with the Prime Minister and the Minister for Economy and Trade. In addition, I met separately with the ambassadors of Germany and the United States and representatives of international financial institutions in Dushanbe.

The overall conclusion was that although Tajikistan's leadership was strongly committed to joining the WTO, the remoteness of the country, its low level of economic development and limited knowledge of the WTO posed considerable challenges to the accession process. I recommended that the authorities actively communicate to all stakeholders the preparations necessary for acceding to the WTO as a way of reassuring the majority of the country's population of the benefits of membership.

I stressed the importance of Tajikistan establishing a mission in Geneva to look after its interests in the course of the accession process and beyond. This project was dependent on the support of bilateral donors, notably the Swiss government.

Although Tajikistan's annual gross domestic product (GDP) was then a mere US$200 per capita, Tajikistan was not recognised as a least-developed country (LDC) by the United Nations. Tajikistan was accordingly not eligible to benefit directly from the guidelines for LDC accession adopted by the General Council in December 2002.[2] The Accessions Division had nevertheless taken several steps to facilitate this accession, including the introduction of a 'Factual summary of points raised' at an early stage in the process to guide the fact-finding and subsequent negotiations on Tajikistan's adherence to WTO rules and principles.

By the end of 2007, however, there had been virtually no further progress and the accession had been dormant since the third meeting of the working party in October 2006. No new input had been submitted for over a year and the pace of legislative reforms had slowed.

Changes and transitions in the government (a new minister and lead negotiator) temporarily slowed down the accession process.

---

[2] The Guidelines on LDC Accessions were strengthened and enhanced with the introduction of benchmarks for market access negotiations on goods and services in 2012 by the General Council (see WTO document WT/L/508/Add.1).

At the Commonwealth of Independent States (CIS) heads of state meeting held in Dushanbe in October 2007, the Eurasian Economic Community (EAEC) agreed to establish a customs and economic union, comprising Belarus, Kazakhstan and Russia. Tajikistan, notably, was not invited to join this grouping.

Tajikistan risked being left behind in the regional context once Russia and Ukraine acceded to the WTO. This served perhaps as a 'reality check'. In November 2007, the Tajiks indicated that they were still keen to advance their negotiations and that the process would be pursued independently (i.e. without being linked to the accession of Russia). There was a reorganisation of government structures with priority accorded to the WTO accession of Tajikistan.

In January 2008, together with the Director of the Accession Division,[3] I was invited to visit Dushanbe. The visit was timely and important to reactivate the process and gave an opportunity to build the political momentum and support needed to advance the accession dossier.

The accession was at this point at an intermediate stage. Twenty-nine members of the WTO were members of and participated in the working party. Bilateral market access negotiations were under way with interested members on the basis of the revised offers of June 2006. The goods offer proposed tariff bindings of 15.9 per cent for agricultural products and 9 per cent for non-agricultural products – most-favoured-nation (MFN) applied rates averaging 9.8 and 6.9 per cent respectively. In services, Tajikistan had offered access to ten service sectors (health services excluded) and to 75 sub-sectors (out of about 161).

On the multilateral front, areas where further work was needed included foreign exchange controls, the licensing regime, customs valuation, export restrictions, internal taxes, sanitary and phytosanitary (SPS) measures, the Technical Barriers to Trade Agreement (TBT) and Trade-Related Aspects of Intellectual Property Rights (TRIPs). Legislative reforms undertaken in 2004 to 2006 (including a new customs code, tax code, intellectual property laws, etc.) needed to be followed up with renewed urgency. Members had not shown any flexibility on Tajikistan's requests for transitions (e.g. to phase out export restrictions such as the mandatory prepayment requirements or auctions at the Tajik Commodity Exchange). Hard work at the technical level and some

---

[3] Arif Hussain was director of the Accessions Division from January 1995 to December 2008.

hard decisions at the political level would, therefore, be needed as the negotiations advanced.

Substantive technical assistance had been provided to Tajikistan by bilateral donors, for example, from the Swiss government (through the IDEAS Centre) and by the US Agency for International Development (USAID). Multilateral assistance was also provided by the Asian Development Bank, the World Bank, the International Monetary Fund (IMF) and the WTO. There were altogether thirty-nine WTO technical assistance activities between 2005 and 2007.

It took another year and a half before the fourth working party eventually took place in September 2009. It was preceded by the confusion surrounding the Russian accession after an announcement by the Russian authorities that they would withdraw their individual accession applications and negotiate as part of the Customs Union of the EAEC. The Tajik leadership assessed this situation as an opportunity to accelerate its accession. The elements of a draft working party report adopted at the fourth working party marked a significant advance in multilateral work on the WTO accession of Tajikistan.

The process continued gathering momentum in 2010 and by the end of 2011 had reached full speed. In particular, the solid progress on the domestic legislative front contributed greatly to the acceleration of the work during this period. It is remarkable that, since 2005, Tajikistan has adopted over one hundred pieces of new legislation, although the enactment and amendment of domestic legislation and associated implementing regulation are distinctive features of the WTO accession process.

One of the notable key elements at the endgame stage was the political will of the country's leadership to conclude the accession process on a priority basis for geopolitical considerations. The imminent WTO accession of Russia had added a new sense of urgency to the process that was now considered as a matter of national sovereignty and independence. WTO membership became an important item on Tajikistan's foreign policy agenda.

The tense relations in the region, particularly water and transit conflicts with neighbouring Uzbekistan and the cutting off of gas supplies to Tajikistan in January 2012, further exacerbated the fragile security conditions in Central Asia.

There was a clear domestic policy conviction that WTO membership would anchor Tajikistan to a wider international framework. As an instrument for regulating relations with neighbours, WTO membership would enable Tajikistan to deal with and reverse trade restrictions imposed by its neighbours and secure its autonomy and security, including in terms of energy and access to markets. As a landlocked country, Tajikistan would benefit from the WTO rules and the right to 'freedom of transit'.

The seventh working party meeting in March 2012 and my subsequent visit as the chairperson of the working party to Tajikistan in May 2012 confirmed that the conclusion of Tajikistan's accession was a realistic prospect for 2012. Several key elements had come together at this concluding stage of the process: the political will to conclude the accession process on a priority basis; the provision by Tajikistan's lawmakers of the necessary support to the government by adopting the remaining package of WTO laws on a priority basis; at the technical level, the experience and good organisation of the team, which was led by a dynamic minister. On the bilateral front, Tajikistan presented an ambitious strategy for concluding the remaining dozen or so bilateral market negotiations by the end of July 2012. During my meetings with the President, the Speaker of the Parliament and the ministerial team, I confirmed that Tajikistan's accession had been identified by members as a priority. WTO members had shown plenty of goodwill and there was now 'a window of opportunity' which should not be missed.

The main immediate steps were identified: Tajikistan's priority should be to conclude its outstanding bilateral market access agreements, as Tajikistan preferred to avoid the opening of bilateral negotiations with new WTO members. The advice was that in this concluding stage, direct and regular contact should be maintained with members at the level of the capitals. The direct involvement at the ministerial level would prove to be useful in resolving the remaining sticking points. Embassies and diplomatic representatives would also play an active role. Tajikistan should continue to reassure WTO members, through its foreign policy statements, that it remained committed to WTO membership in the nearest future.

As we approached the endgame, I used a 'Friends of the Chair' format to drive the process forward and galvanise the attention of WTO members.

As the accession approached its concluding stages, more resources were dedicated to the team. The Geneva mission needed to be reinforced. The endgame of any accession process is always a very demanding process and can be very resource intensive.

The accelerated pace suggested that the objective could be achieved in the same calendar year. The result of consultations with members was a strategy to wrap up the accession by the end of the year and to begin to construct the key components of the draft accession before late summer, so as to limit the possibility of 'reopening'.

To this end, the eighth working party in July 2012 mandated the Secretariat to 'undertake a fast-track consolidation of the Goods and Services Schedules' and to report to the chairperson of the working party on this exercise by 31 July 2012.

Meanwhile, the last remaining bilateral market access negotiations were concluded by 31 July 2012.

According to standard accession practice, the draft goods and services schedule was circulated by the Secretariat to all working party members on 20 August 2012. In accordance with practice, the verification exercise was limited to those members which had negotiated and signed bilateral market access goods and services agreements with Tajikistan and had deposited these duly concluded agreements with the WTO Secretariat, the Director-General being the depositary. Within the four-week time-frame, signatory members engaged with the delegation of Tajikistan and submitted agreed results to the Secretariat. On this basis, a revised/updated draft goods and services schedule was circulated on 28 September 2012.

With all the necessary steps concluded, the final working party meeting on the accession of Tajikistan was convened on 9 October 2012 with the aim of considering and adopting the draft Accession Package of Tajikistan *ad referendum.*

The events, however, took another turn. It turned out that Tajikistan's apprehensions, that the conclusion of its accession negotiations could be delayed, had been well founded.

Russia, which had officially become a member of the WTO on 22 August 2012, had joined the Informal Group of Accessions family, and, following its request, was registered as a member of the working party on the accession of Tajikistan (as well as for Kazakhstan and Belarus). At the first Informal Group of Accessions meeting, in which Russia participated at the end of September 2012, it asked for the draft goods schedule of Tajikistan from the Secretariat, which had been circulated on 20 August 2012.

On the eve of the final working party meeting on 9 October 2012, the Tajik delegation informed the Secretariat and the chairperson of the working party that the week before, when the presidents of Tajikistan and Russia had met, the Russian President had requested that Tajikistan suspend its accession on the grounds that the negotiated package was bad for

Tajikistan. An informal letter to this effect from the Russian Trade Minister was subsequently received.

The Tajik delegation confirmed that the instructions from the Tajik President were clear: the draft Accession Package that had been proposed to WTO members in the working party for adoption *ad referendum* reflected the interests of the government of Tajikistan and its citizens, and was commensurate with the country's development, financial and trade needs. Tajikistan would invite members to consider and adopt the package *ad referendum*.

At the working party meeting on the accession of Tajikistan on 9 October 2012, Russia was not able to join the consensus to adopt the draft Accession Package *ad referendum*. It stated that it required more time to examine the draft Accession Package for Tajikistan – a country with which it had close economic relations and with which it shared common membership of the CIS and the EAEC. The systemic reaction from members was very strong. There was unanimity (the only exception being Russia) that the draft Accession Package should be adopted *ad referendum*.

I concluded by expressing regret regarding the position of Russia, of which I had taken note. I stated that the draft Accession Package of Tajikistan represented the culmination of ten years of negotiations that I had chaired. The required time frames for members' consideration of draft Accession Package(s) had been observed, including for Russia.

While taking note of the Russian position, I invited the working party to note that 'the draft Accession Package for Tajikistan had stabilised; and, was not subject to re-opening'. I noted that, because the WTO was consensus-driven, the draft package could not be adopted *ad referendum* at this meeting. I also reminded members that the objective was for a formal decision by the General Council at its December session. The Russian delegation reiterated that its request for additional time was not in conflict with the December General Council target. The working party, therefore, took note that there was no disagreement with the conclusion by the working party chairperson.

Although the draft Accession Package of Tajikistan was adopted *ad referendum* at the resumed meeting of the working party on 26 October 2012 without objections from any delegation, the behind-the-scenes pressure on Tajikistan to reconsider its application continued until the very last meeting of the General Council in December. Russia's main argument was that the WTO membership commitments made by Tajikistan would be incompatible with its possible future membership of the Customs Union of the EAEC, and that Tajikistan at this stage was not considering its membership of the Customs Union.

The Russian negotiators provided an extensive analysis of Tajikistan's WTO commitments and pointed to potential clashes between these commitments and future customs union membership. The areas included trade remedies (because of Tajikistan's non-market economy status), Tajikistan's participation in the Government Procurement Agreement, state trading enterprises, pricing policy, appeal procedures, customs valuation, trading rights, subsidies, import licensing, tariff bindings (which are more liberal than the common tariffs of the Customs Union) and developing country status.

The main objective was to invite Tajikistan to reconsider its package of WTO commitments, the argument being that they went beyond standard WTO obligations and that they would be problematic in the light of future customs union membership.

During those days in November 2012, with the Accession Division, as chairman of the working party, I spent considerable time consulting the delegation of Tajikistan, reviewing analysis accompanied with advice regarding Russian claims and their compatibility with Tajik WTO commitments.

There was a firm conclusion that Tajikistan's terms of WTO membership were normal and fair and would facilitate the modernisation of the country. Tajikistan's Accession Package corresponded to its development level. A period of adaptation had been agreed for the staged implementation of Tajikistan's tariff concessions (up to 2018).

It is important to note that the inconsistency between the WTO regulation and customs union membership stems from the nature of the customs union.

In 2009, Belarus, Kazakhstan and Russia created the customs union without Tajikistan. Thus any perceived damage was rather the result of the decision to go ahead without Tajikistan.

Similarly, Russia indicated possible damage due to the fact that in the future it would not be possible for Tajikistan to continue with heavily subsidised common projects with certain Russian industries, and due to the loss of expected profits from such situations.

In conclusion, I would like to pay tribute to the continuous efforts, positive approach and spirit of compromise shown all around, particularly in the critical final stages. This goes to the members, to then WTO Director-General Pascal Lamy, to Secretariat colleagues in various divisions who assisted the delegation of Tajikistan and, of course, to the

Accessions Division, which led the effort. In particular, I would like to pay tribute to Tajikistan's team of devoted and committed negotiators under the leadership of Minister Rahimzoda and his chief negotiator, Vice-Minister Nazriev. The entire team was exemplary in its performance, working diligently and effectively – often around the clock – both in Dushanbe and in Geneva.

It has been a privilege and honour for me to have been associated with this enterprise.

# 26

# A podium perspective: experiences and challenges of chairing a working party

STEFÁN H. JÓHANNESSON

## ABSTRACT

*What is the perspective from the podium? What are the challenges that face the chairperson of an accession working party? The role of a chairperson of an accession working party is tough and challenging, and the functions of a chairperson can only be successfully exercised if he or she has the trust and confidence of parties involved. This role is best understood as that of a referee, assisted by the Secretariat. The accession of the Russian Federation demonstrated that, 'the real work in WTO accession negotiations is done "beyond the gavel". If the chair could only work with the gavel, the accession process would get nowhere.' Critical to any progress in the complexity of accession negotiations is political will and the ability to compromise, as geopolitics may add a thick layer of complexity to the process. The reality of accession negotiations is that all participants have to be accommodated.*

In this chapter, I present a podium perspective that describes the role of the working party chairman[1] from the experience of the WTO accession negotiations of Russia. This was a unique accession in every respect. My chairmanship of the accession of Russia reflected the management of the trade integration of a major player in the global arena. There were systemic sensitivities for the safeguard of the rules-based multilateral trading system accompanied by geopolitical considerations.

Being offered the opportunity to be the third (and fortunately last) chairman of the WTO working party on the accession of Russia was an unexpected and, quite honestly, double-edged compliment. With

---

[1] I use the term 'chairman' out of economy, not political correctness. Naturally the term is intended to be gender neutral and a synonym for the more cumbersome 'chairperson' throughout this chapter.

hindsight, I accepted the invitation too readily, not realising that the project would outlast my time in Geneva, and follow me all the way home. But my seven years in the chair turned out to be professionally rewarding, and offered an opportunity to engage in complex international diplomacy between major and minor players that otherwise might have passed me by.

What I realise now is that the chairman's role in managing an accession negotiation is best understood as that of a referee. The chairman has to make sure that the rules of the game are observed. That person supervises the process, mediates it, if required, and in doing so carries the weight of ensuring the credibility of the whole exercise. For the chairman to be able to carry out his duties with efficiency and confidence, it is essential that he has the trust and confidence of the members and the acceding government. Trust and confidence allow him to steer the process better. Trust is hard won and easily lost.

The chairman has to be alert and sensitive to the concerns of existing members and the acceding government. With the help of the Secretariat, he must stay in close contact with all the interested members to ensure that the flow of information between him, the Secretariat, members and the acceding government is unimpeded.

Although it may diminish my role, it is important to note the essential role of the WTO Secretariat. Throughout my tenure as chairman, I depended on its technical, political and legal advice and expertise. Along with the acceding government the Secretariat bears the brunt of the work. Therefore, the relationship between the chair and the Secretariat is another key element that has to be in order, based on mutual trust and confidence. Needless to say, the same applies between the Secretariat, the membership and the acceding government.

## A long and winding road

Russia's application for membership in the General Agreement on Tariffs and Trade (GATT) in 1993 was transformed into an application to the WTO with its foundation in 1995. One might wonder why it took eighteen years to conclude the accession negotiations. The reasons are multiple and perhaps not so hard to understand. Here are the range of factors that explain why.

First, the accession was hugely complicated. Russia is the largest country in the world, spanning nine time zones, and the world's ninth most populous nation. Also one should keep in mind that most WTO members, even small ones, have difficulty keeping everyone at home in line with the WTO rulebook.

Second, Russia is not just physically big – it is a major economy, in the middle of a transformation from a centrally planned economy into a more market-oriented one, accounting for about 2 per cent of world trade. It was an anomaly that such an important economy had remained outside the global rules-based system for so long.

Third, with the inclusion of Russia, over 97 per cent of world trade is covered by the rules of the WTO, consolidating its universality and further securing its *raison d'être* as a truly global rules-based trading system.

Fourth, although Russia has been a superpower for a long time, its membership was historic, in the sense that it was the last member of the G-20, the Security Council and the BRICS (Brazil, Russia, India, China and South Africa) countries to take a seat with its partners in the WTO. Russia, in other words, is now an equal player among world economies.

Finally, as in some other accessions before it, geopolitical issues added another layer of complexity to the process.

It is understandable and logical that such an important player as Russia would generate more than the usual interest among members – as shown by the record number of members who participated very actively in the process.

## The third man

When I took the gavel in 2003 the negotiations had already lasted ten years and outlasted two chairmen. The atmosphere was relatively good. President Vladimir Putin, who assumed power in 2000, had stated that WTO accession was a priority for Russia. Members and Russia were cautiously optimistic. A certain momentum could be felt. The third revision of the working party report was in its final stages and its circulation in October 2004 marked a new milestone in our work. We all hoped that with commitment, hard work and determination the accession negotiations could be concluded within a couple of years.

However, with Russia being a major player on the world scene, I soon got a better sense of how external factors, not strictly WTO related, and geopolitics would have an influence, directly or indirectly, on the negotiations. And I realised that this was not going to be a simple task. The Secretariat and I needed to be constantly aware of developments and changing moods, and often had to deal with frustrations and even anger from different sides of the table. All of those involved had to be creative, flexible, determined and patient to keep the process on track in our common endeavour to make Russia's membership a reality. The lion's share of our work was conducted beyond the gavel, which enabled us to better deal with the many hurdles that came up along the way.

Consultations under my chairmanship had to be organised in different configurations, between different members and Russia. Furthermore, the Secretariat chaired countless meetings on different technical issues such as agriculture, sanitary and phytosanitary (SPS) matters, customs, tariff schedules, etc. The accession process would not have got anywhere if we had resigned ourselves to working only in big formal meetings with everyone present. The Secretariat's experience of completed accessions showed that it would not have been conducive to real negotiations and I dare to add that this was even more true in the case of Russia, with so many interested members active in the negotiations, including the friends of Russia, who wanted the accession completed as soon as possible.

Every step taken had to be carefully prepared through consultations and contacts with members and the Russian team. We always had to make sure that we had a critical mass of texts and issues to deal with to justify a new round of negotiations, more so with negotiators flying in from half way around the globe for meetings. One of the greatest challenges in this often highly charged environment and complex process was to balance effectiveness, on the one hand, with adequate transparency and inclusiveness, on the other.

There are constant questions regarding the speed of concluding any WTO accession. When will it be completed? In the case of Russia, the speed of the process was certainly not only determined by the ability of the Russian government to deliver on commitments made, the level of technical preparation by the Russian administration before each round of talks, progress in compromises made between Russia and members, but was also greatly influenced by external geopolitical factors.

## Building momentum

At the start of my chairmanship, Russia, the United States and the European Union had publicly committed, in 2004, to advancing the accession of Russia. Accordingly, members and Russia agreed to an ambitious agenda to work towards that objective. The stage was set for possible solid progress. Everyone was cognisant of the fact that very substantial progress was needed if the public statements from all sides were to be credible.

We made significant progress in the next three years. Important milestones were achieved with the conclusion in 2004 of a bilateral agreement with the European Union and in 2006 with the United States.

To accelerate negotiations, our working procedure was to invite Russia to develop draft texts to fill gaps in individual sections of the draft working party report and to approve them in consultation with key members of the working party, in particular the United States and the European Union (in the 'trilateral' arrangement), prior to submitting the entire draft report to them. The strategy involved the chairman holding focused and quick consultations at several levels of transparency, depending on the interest of individual members in specific subjects. Here too the Secretariat's wisdom and reputation were key.

Memories tend to fade with time and become rosier. But I should not gloss over some of the problems that hampered developments of texts and consultations. There were often strong differences of viewpoints between the members involved and the Russian team on fundamental points of WTO law and principle. Some important examples were in the areas of customs (valuation and formalities), agricultural and industrial subsidies, state trading, SPS measures, intellectual property (Trade-Related Aspects of Intellectual Property Rights Agreement (TRIPs), import licensing, fees and charges and free zones. These strong differences were not helpful to the accession negotiations – and many members felt that they reflected an unwillingness on the part of Russia to obtain the necessary mandate. Much of the Russian reluctance to undertake specific commitments was due to its argued position to be 'at par' with founding members of the WTO – a difficult point since Russia was not a founding member, but a 'latecomer'. It was also sometimes hard for Russian negotiators to 'admit to' certain problems, as the official position in Moscow was, in some instances, not to recognise that these problems existed, or that associated obligations could not be accepted because they existed in the terms and conditions of other (original) WTO members.

## Growing tensions

The completion of the bilateral agreements with the European Union and later the United States were definitely positive developments. However, tensions between neighbouring countries such as Georgia, Moldova, Poland and Russia grew. Following a Russian ban on Georgian wine and mineral water, Georgia's list of grievances with Russia reached a tipping point and we ran into difficulties with the continuation of the process. In autumn 2006, after once again complaining to the WTO Director-General, Georgia indicated that it would block formal meetings of the working party. I received legal advice from the Secretariat that other members had done this in earlier accessions and that, therefore, it was possible for Georgia to do so. Although some members were of a contrary view, we were able to accommodate Georgia's concerns by convening only informal consultations of the working party, which enabled us to get on with our work. It meant that from then on the entire phase of work was beyond the gavel. Not a single formal meeting was held until the very end of the process in October of 2011, which (with Georgia's assent) approved the working party report and submitted it to the WTO Ministerial Conference which was held in December of that year.

In this increasingly tense atmosphere I held consultations in April 2008 on the circulation of a new consolidated draft of the working party report. It was high time to consolidate all the different texts we had been working on into a new document so as to register the progress made from the last version of the draft report from October 2004 and simplify the continuation of our work. Georgia, which was seeking to include language in the report that would reflect its concerns, resisted the formal publication and circulation of a revised working party report. I therefore had urgently to consult Russia, Georgia and members as to how we should address this problem. After rather tense discussions it was agreed that the Secretariat would circulate the document as an informal document entitled 'consolidation of draft texts', rather than as the 'draft Report of the Working Party on the Accession of Russia to the WTO (Revision 4)'. This was a pragmatic solution and demonstrated that while Georgia had unresolved issues with Russia it was willing to be constructive and to take the concerns and interests of other members into account and allow the substantive work to continue.

In the middle of that process, open conflict between Russia and Georgia erupted in August 2008. This led to a serious deterioration in relations between Moscow and Tbilisi, and adversely affected the emerging spirit of pragmatism and trust in Geneva. North Atlantic Treaty Organisation (NATO) expansion to the east and the American announcement of anti-ballistic missile plans in eastern Europe did not help. Furthermore, relations between the European Union and its member states had also come under some strain with some of the new eastern EU member states involved. The EU Commission was also dissatisfied with what it perceived as a lack of commitment by the Russian side to implement some previously agreed reforms, although it was also critical of Georgia's position. The US side made it clear that while it supported an early conclusion of Russia's WTO accession, this was not at any price.

Throughout the process it was very important to maintain good contacts with the government of Georgia and keep it abreast of developments and what our intentions were. Accordingly, I met regularly with senior officials from Tbilisi. On the side also, the Secretariat privately managed a parallel process with Georgia and Russia to try and settle the border issue – work ultimately completed by the Swiss in 2011.

## Russian withdrawal?

In 2008 we were facing a complicated picture in the accession process and further delays were caused not only by the conflict with Georgia, but also by a new layer of complications that was added with Russia's increased efforts to establish a customs union with Kazakhstan and Belarus.

Out of the blue, then Prime Minister Vladimir Putin announced in June 2009 that Russia was withdrawing its individual WTO application in favour of a joint bid with two other acceding economies, namely Kazakhstan and Belarus, to join the WTO as a customs union. This took the entire membership by surprise and caused a lot of confusion. Again our efforts to secure an early conclusion of the accession talks were put at risk. Everyone was puzzled and needed urgent clarification. The Secretariat advised me that it would be legally impossible for the Customs Union to accede to the WTO.[2]

---

[2] All EU member states are individual members of the WTO, and acceded to the WTO either as founding members or through their individual negotiation process pursuant to Article XII of the Marrakesh Agreement Establishing the World Trade Organization. The European Union did not join the WTO under Article XII, but through its individual states' memberships. In essence, the European Union membership of the WTO is solely an administrative tool for decision-taking purposes. Article XII does not permit Customs Unions to accede (only 'states' or 'separate customs territories'. In addition, any customs territory must possess 'full autonomy in the conduct of its external commercial relations and of the other matters provided for in this Agreement'). The Customs Union of Belarus, Kazakhstan and Russia also did not meet this requirement (it dealt only with goods at the time).

No Customs Union had ever negotiated WTO accession as a single entity and many people, including then WTO Director-General Pascal Lamy, saw the move as signalling a weakening of Russia's desire to join.

The Russian government immediately confronted problems with this notion of a joint accession of the three countries as a Customs Union. This delayed the process further, as it was effectively suspended until we could have clarity on the Russian proposal.

After thorough discussions with Maxim Medvedkov, Russia's WTO chief negotiator, and his team, I held a series of consultations with members in October 2009. Members agreed to my recommendation to restart and continue the Russian accession process. Maxim Medvedkov confirmed Russia's readiness to resume accession work in its individual, stand-alone format, confirmed the integrity of all bilateral market access agreements on goods and services, already signed, and presented a table, detailing the sections in the draft working party report to be amended, to include relevant and specific information on the Customs Union.

Members indicated their readiness to re-engage in the accession process upon submission of substantive inputs from Russia.

## The endgame

In June of 2010, US President Barack Obama and Russian President Medvedev committed themselves to overcoming the obstacles facing Russia in its accession process. Thereafter, the political stars started to align in favour of the completion of the accession. Massive US resources and political pressure then piled on. We all felt the expectation on us to deliver the end of the process.

But progress remained slow in key areas such as agriculture, export restrictions and SPS measures. Export duties on timber were also contentious – and dated back to the 2004 European Union deal. In the informal working party meeting held in September 2010, we made some progress although members were still worried that Russia was not delivering on its commitments. We held further meetings in October and December. At the December 2010 meeting I asked the Georgians and the Russians to restart dialogue to determine how a territorial dispute would affect the country's accession prospects. This was backed up by several European member states. This request was also meant as a signal that the working party was serious about accelerating its work. We were all getting nervous that we were running out of time as we were setting our minds to finalising the negotiations in time for the Ministerial Conference in

December 2011. Parallel to the multilateral informal process, the Secretariat continued plurilateral consultations on contentious issues such as agriculture and SPS rules.

Finally, we were entering the endgame. But issues between Georgia and Russia with regard to the two regions of Abkhazia and South Ossetia continued to lag – and always retained the potential to block the whole process. Georgia came under considerable pressure from members. It was agreed that Switzerland would take on the task of mediating an agreement between Georgia and Russia. Subcontracting that work beyond the gavel to the Swiss took the pressure somewhat off the accession process and allowed the members to focus their efforts on the negotiations. The Secretariat and I did our best to create the circumstances and organise our work so that we could be ready to cement whatever progress could be made and move the accession forward.

We were, therefore, all greatly relieved when Georgia and Russia found an agreed solution with mediation by Switzerland. This agreement paved the way for the completion of work and a formal meeting of the working party to be convened in November 2011. This allowed the working party to formally adopt the working party report and transmit it to the Ministerial Conference in December 2011, which formally agreed to Russia's membership, thereby concluding eighteen years of accession talks. While not a record length for an accession, it was certainly a marathon.

I believe that all of us are the better for it. Russia has taken its rightful place at the top table. Thus, we have all gained, although geopolitics continues as have always been the case to exercise influence over trading relations.

A range of lessons was evident. The starkest I learned were as follows.

The accession of Russia was very complicated. At least 80 per cent of the work, and 20 per cent of the time, was done beyond the gavel from 2006 to 2011. The work beyond the gavel was where the real work was done – and in fact if the chair could only work with the gavel, the accession process would get nowhere. Critical to any progress is political will. It is essential. After all, negotiations are an exercise in compromise – by both sides. Good preparations for negotiating rounds are essential. Negotiators must secure a realistic negotiating mandate from their bosses. The timely delivery of quality texts is essential for solid progress – but of and in itself is not enough. Geopolitics added a thick layer of complexity to the process whether people liked it or not. All participants had to be accommodated. While we all tried to expect the unexpected, when it happened, patience, tolerance, flexibility, creativity, determination and a dash of good humour are essential. In the end there is only so much that the chair and the Secretariat can do to massage the process forward. It boils down to the political will of interested members and the acceding government; these are the elements that, at the end of the day, determine success or failure.

# 27

# Are there different rules for least-developed countries in a rule-based system?

STEFFEN SMIDT

## ABSTRACT

*In July 2012, the WTO General Council agreed on a set of new and improved guidelines to facilitate and accelerate negotiations on the accession to the WTO of least-developed countries (LDCs). The process of acceding to the WTO is complex, time-consuming and resource-intensive for candidate countries, and for LDCs, which have limited institutional and administrative capacity, in particular. The WTO accession process is very much a political process, and requires countries to undertake far-reaching domestic reforms in order to be in a position to implement WTO rules from day one of membership, as well as to benefit from MFN market access from WTO members and vice versa. The prolonged accession process is designed to enable acceding LDCs (and others) to acquire the knowledge and expertise to negotiate not only the terms and conditions for their membership, but also to function as viable members of the rules-based system. This chapter examines the enhanced guidelines and asks whether the WTO needs to improve the procedures for the benefit of LDCs and of the WTO. It examines how the WTO accession process and procedures, as well as the scope of the reforms it requires, compare to EU considerations in the process of its enlargement, and argues that, while the enhanced LDC accession guidelines have made an important contribution, some additional steps may need to be contemplated in the future. However, before a further enhancement is contemplated, it must be understood that the accession process, and the substance of WTO accession negotiations, in all serious institutions, are based on a partnership. This is a fundamental lesson from all successfully completed accessions and enlargement processes. The process is neither unilateral nor automatic.*

Least-developed countries (LDCs) and others, not original WTO members, which acceded to the WTO after 1995, were not WTO-compliant and did not meet the standards and requirements of membership when they applied for membership. However, the WTO and its members have recognised the particular challenges for LDCs. Special mechanisms for assisting LDCs in their efforts to develop the necessary capacities have been established. A set of guidelines was adopted in 2002 to facilitate the accession of LDCs.[1] One essential feature of these guidelines was an invitation for members to exercise 'restraint' when negotiating commitments from LDCs on access to their markets.

The implementation of the 2002 guidelines did not meet the expectations of LDCs, in practice. Therefore, in 2011, at the Eighth WTO Ministerial Conference, it was decided that the guidelines should be further 'strengthened, streamlined and operationalized'.

The new set of guidelines introduces 'benchmarks' for the commitments on access of goods and services that the LDC will have to offer members on an MFN basis upon accession. The main purpose of these benchmarks is to provide members with assurance of reasonable access conditions to the market of the acceding LDC, and to provide LDCs with the necessary flexibility and policy space after accession.

Overall, the new set of guidelines has strengthened the hands of the acceding LDCs in their negotiations with members on the conditions for access to their markets. These negotiations are conducted bilaterally, i.e. between the acceding government and members which want to obtain specific access opportunities for their exporters to the market of the new member.

As a consequence of the new guidelines, the acceding LDCs will obtain more leeway in their negotiations. They will have to bind all agricultural tariff lines at an average level of 50 per cent. This benchmark has to be compared with recent practice, where acceding LDCs have had to bind at an average of 32 per cent.

Similarly, in the area of non-agricultural market access, acceding LDCs have the option of binding 95 per cent of their tariff lines at an average rate of 35 per cent, which means flexibility on tariff policy on the outstanding 5 per cent of tariff lines. This benchmark has to be compared with the previous situations for acceding LDCs where less than full

---

[1] See WTO document WT/L/508 and its Addendum 1, 30 July 2012: Accession of least-developed countries, Decision of 25 July 2012.

binding was hardly allowed. In addition, Article XII LDCs (i.e. recently acceding LDCs) had to bind their non-agricultural tariff lines at an average of 23 per cent, substantially less favourably than the benchmark figure of 35 per cent.

Market access for services is not quantifiable in a manner comparable to access for goods. Consequently, the new guidelines introduce some notional quantitative benchmarks coupled with some qualitative elements. The guidelines stipulate that LDCs shall not be required to commit to market openings in service sectors and sub-sectors beyond those that have been committed by existing LDC members (and no LDC has committed to market opening in more than 117 out of 163 sub-sectors).

In addition to benchmarks on market access, the new guidelines also introduced transparency in the accession process. The accession working party that accompanies each negotiation and approves the final draft Accession Package now has a greater role in reviewing the outcome of bilateral market access negotiations. The guidelines also provide scope for a discussion of difficulties encountered during the negotiations in the Sub-Committee on LDCs. And as a final element of transparency, the guidelines codify the practices according to which the Chairperson of the Sub-Committee as well as the chairpersons of LDC accessions working parties can 'facilitate' the conclusion of negotiations, including through bilateral access negotiations, if need be.

The final elements in the new guidelines are provisions for technical assistance and capacity-building to help acceding LDCs to complete accession negotiations and respect commitments upon membership.

The new guidelines are intended to create greater clarity and predictability in the accession negotiations of LDCs. They are designed to facilitate and accelerate those negotiations as foreseen in the original guidelines. It will soon be possible to verify whether these objectives have been met. The new guidelines will now be applied both by members and by acceding LDCs. It is hoped that these guidelines will lead to the intended simplification of the negotiations for the benefit of all parties and for the institution.

It is worthwhile contemplating some additional steps for the future, in order to improve some of the more complicated aspects of the negotiations. These thoughts are inspired not only by my experience on WTO accession negotiations, but also by my experience on the enlargement negotiations in the European Union, for which, in the early 1990s, I was the Director-General at the European Commission.

## European Union experience

The EU enlargement process is based on an elaborate and detailed set of rules. The starting points are specific conditions that 'candidate countries' have to meet in order to qualify for EU accession. The final overall outcome has to be accepted by the European Parliament and subsequently reflected in an 'accession treaty' that has to be ratified by the candidate country and by all member states of the European Union, in accordance with their respective constitutional rules. Given the extensive nature of the cooperation within the European Union, the enlargement process entails many features that are specifically designed to ensure that candidates are able and willing to live up to (adhere and implement) the rules and principles of the European Union – the so-called *acquis communautaire* – and define a framework for the negotiations for how the conditions are met, including through any transition period a candidate may need to fully implement specific rules.

Already in the light of the fact that EU cooperation covers many policy areas, only some features of the EU enlargement process are relevant when compared with the WTO accession process. Some of the features are, nevertheless, in my view relevant to a reflection on how the WTO accession process could be improved in order to better meet its objectives.

The first of these features is the 'collective' nature of the EU enlargement negotiations. The negotiations are both formally and in reality taking place between each individual candidate, on one side of the table and, on the other side of the table, all existing EU member states. The details are prepared in discussions between the European Commission and the candidate country. However, the various steps are on a regular basis reviewed and discussed in the negotiation fora with all members and the candidate country. The implication of this feature is, among other factors, that each and every requirement with which a candidate is confronted has been discussed and agreed in advance between the member states.

A second feature is the different levels on which EU enlargement negotiations take place. All details are discussed between specialists at the technical level and are dealt with in negotiation fora where the members and the candidate are represented at the administrative level. But regular member states and the candidate country also meet at the political level, where ministers discuss the outstanding issues. And the substance of agreements in the various fields is concluded by the ministers at the political level. One implication of this is that ministers from the candidate countries themselves are in a position to report to colleagues at home on issues raised in the negotiations and to handle difficulties that require political decisions in order to proceed.

A third feature is the fact that EU enlargement negotiations are divided into negotiating 'chapters' that reflect various policy areas in internal EU cooperation. Each chapter is opened and concluded separately. This provides possibilities for organising the negotiations specifically for each policy area and for 'control' in the negotiations. But another important implication is the opportunity for the candidate to use this feature as a means to stimulate domestic discussions and register progress in the process.

One of the biggest difficulties for the acceding LDCs are the challenges involved in handling the bilateral negotiations for market access in goods and services. The guidelines, and in particular the benchmarks and the provision on 'transparency', will, it is hoped, facilitate the process for acceding LDCs. One feature on transparency is the guidelines' codification of the practice according to which the Chairperson of the Sub-Committee and other chairpersons can 'facilitate the conclusion of the negotiations', as mentioned above. However, experience has shown the limits of this feature. The facilitators have no other power than the value of persuasion, conviction and patience.

Another feature is the provision by which the working party can provide a forum for members and acceding LDCs, collectively, to review bilateral access negotiations. This option could be used when an LDC encountered difficulties in bilateral negotiations and wanted to discuss those difficulties with members other than the individual government concerned.

The idea could be formulated as a question. Is it worthwhile asking whether members should assume some responsibility for market access negotiations collectively, at least when the issues involved raise serious problems for the acceding LDC, and in particular when questions are raised as to whether or not the benchmarks have been applied in a reasonable manner? In such cases, a discussion in 'the plenary', i.e. in the relevant working party, could not only provide transparency, but also the opportunity for members to consider any recommendation they may want to make to stimulate a reasonable outcome of the negotiations.

The outcomes of the bilateral negotiations are in any case 'multilateralised' at the end of the accession negotiations. With developments over time, characterised by the vast increase of the WTO membership and the corresponding extension of WTO rules, is it not worth contemplating, also, to what extent members can 'multilateralise' the responsibility for the specific concessions that an acceding LDC will have to undertake in controversial areas concerning market access for goods and services?

Another aspect to do with the way in which the institution handles the accession negotiations with an LDC that seems worthwhile considering, is how responsible ministers among existing members could play a more active role in the process. For the acceding LDC, probably, the most challenging feature is the necessary restructuring of economic and administrative capacities necessary to enable the country both to adhere to the commitments and rules of the WTO, and to participate properly in the work of the institution. It is a vast undertaking for most acceding LDCs and several ministers are normally heavily involved in the national restructuring process. Advice is provided by the WTO Secretariat. Ministers from member states may participate in providing advice on a bilateral basis in many cases. But, in essence, the process both in providing advice and in the negotiations is primarily an expert-driven technical process by civil servants, both bilaterally and in the collective reflections in the relevant working party. Ministers from member states are only involved collectively at the very end of the process, for example when the final decision is taken in the context of a Ministerial Conference.

Yet, the accession process is very much a political process, in particular for acceding LDCs. It seems, therefore, worthwhile to consider ways in which members' involvement could be reflected at the political level, and primarily in a collective format. Such political debates could help the acceding government in its own internal debate. It could also help to provide inspiration for solutions to specific problems during the negotiations.

There are not many opportunities for ministers to meet in the daily work of the WTO. But it seems at least worthwhile to consider the possibility of bringing ongoing accession negotiations up during the Ministerial Conferences. The purpose would be to review progress made in the negotiations, but also to consider how ministers could contribute to finding solutions to problems encountered during the negotiations.

Accession negotiations will always be time consuming and problematic, in particular for acceding LDCs. It is hoped that the new guidelines will help to alleviate some of the burdens for the newcomers. Given the importance for the acceding governments and for the institution of integrating the newcomer into the work of the WTO, there should be scope for additional steps like those mentioned, which could be taken without changing existing guidelines or rules.

# 28

# Managing the challenge of acceding post-conflict states

JOAKIM REITER

ABSTRACT

*This chapter posits that leaving WTO accession in the hands of trade experts or commercial specialists within the acceding government can be unwise. Accession to the WTO goes far beyond the remit of the trade, commerce and/or foreign ministry, and even beyond the responsibilities of the minister. In order to conclude an accession, what is required of the acceding government will involve many, if not most, ministries, call upon governmental agencies and other authorities and may very well include both regional and municipal levels of government. The acceding government must expect to make hard policy choices. Poorer developing countries are likely to come across particular challenges and solutions. Given the demanding nature of this process, it is important that the acceding government is entirely convinced, before embarking upon the process, that it has the right motivations and expectations in wishing to become a member of the WTO.*

Why join the WTO? This is the key question about which acceding governments need to have a clear idea and to which they need to respond in no uncertain way. It not only determines why the government has applied for membership; the manner in which a government responds to this question may also greatly affect the speed and degree of its success in the accession process. It is, in addition, likely to be indicative of the relative success of the government, or separate customs territory, in the WTO, when it has become a member.

The analyses in the chapters in this book were finalised at the end of December 2014. Since then the Republic of Seychelles acceded to the World Trade Organization (WTO) on 26 April 2015. This expanded total WTO membership from 160 to 161. Please see the editors' note.

So the question cannot and should not be taken lightly. And it is, arguably, all the more pertinent for poor, vulnerable, small and/or politically fragile countries. Such countries represent the majority of the current applicants for WTO membership.[1] They all face many profound developmental and transitional challenges. Of course, being poor is an enormous challenge in itself, especially for least-developed countries (LDCs). But some, if not most, of these acceding governments are also severely constrained by their lack of productive, physical and human capital and have even emerged from devastating wars, making their development challenge seem almost insurmountable.

Under these circumstances, with capacity already stretched to meet the most immediate and basic needs of their populations, why on earth would such countries, in sometimes extremely precarious economic and political situations, wish to embark on WTO accession? What will the accession process entail for them? How should they go about it? And what is, or should be, the roles of WTO members, the chairperson of the working party and the Secretariat in the process?

In this chapter, I will seek to address each of these questions. While keeping in mind the LDCs currently in the process of acceding to the WTO, the arguments put forward here are of general application. I will begin by dispelling some common misunderstandings about the accession process itself.

## What WTO accession is, and – equally important – what it is not

Perhaps the easiest way to describe the WTO accession process is to lay out what it is not, or at least what accession should not be in order for it to be successful. In a nutshell, five points should be underlined in this regard:

- WTO accession is not like joining other international organisations.
- WTO accession is not about courteous diplomatic relations or about enhancing a country's foreign policy standing or prestige.
- WTO accession is not about what the world should do for the acceding government.

---

[1] The accessions in progress, as of October/November 2014, were: Afghanistan, Algeria, Andorra, Azerbaijan, Bahamas, Belarus, Bhutan, Bosnia and Herzegovina, Comoros, Equatorial Guinea, Ethiopia, Iran, Iraq, Kazakhstan, Lebanese Republic, Liberia, Libya, Sao Tomé and Principe, Serbia, Seychelles, Sudan, Syrian Arab Republic and Uzbekistan.

- WTO accession is not about trade policy.
- WTO accession is not about negotiations.

### WTO accession is not like joining other international organisations

For most international organisations, very few preconditions need to be met before an applicant country can become a member. Also, if it is not automatic, decisions on new members are taken by voting. So the main hurdle, if any, is to garner sufficient support to ensure a positive voting outcome.

In contrast, joining the WTO presupposes compliance with WTO rules and regulations. Only when this, which can be a strenuous and long process, is ensured will the country seeking accession be subject to a decision on prospective membership. In theory, of course, voting also exists in the WTO. In practice, however, consensus is required. The combined effect of stringent entry conditions and veto power by individual members implies that no government wishing to accede to the WTO should expect shortcuts. Existing members will act as gatekeepers to ensure that the relevant conditions, and certainly those they care most about, are met before giving their approval. Merely getting support from a majority of members will not make a difference.

### WTO accession is not a matter of courteous diplomatic relations or about enhancing a country's foreign policy standing or prestige

Because WTO accession is not about securing support from a majority of existing members, diplomacy – in the sense of advocacy for the acceding government and building alliances for a positive decision – is secondary, at most. In fact, in all circumstances, it is no substitute for ensuring, at the technical, policy and political levels, compliance with WTO rules.

For this reason, motivations and/or strategies for WTO accession, solely or primarily deriving from foreign policy considerations – for example to improve a country's international reputation, standing or prestige – will also not be enough. Of course, it is probably true that WTO membership is in itself a quality stamp of relevance to investors and traders, thereby strengthening a country's 'brand' as a trading nation and investment destination. However, this is the result of the country having earned the quality stamp in the first place, not something that can be obtained through skilful diplomatic manoeuvring. In the end, there is no escape from doing one's homework. This is not to say that diplomacy is entirely irrelevant. For poor developing countries, it is useful to try to mobilise the necessary technical assistance and capacity-building from donors throughout the process. Moreover, diplomacy can matter for a final decision, especially in cases where one or very few existing members hold the end-process hostage, for example, over demands placed on the acceding government that go beyond WTO rules (the so-called WTO-plus). Such shrewd political games, however, only truly enter into play at the accession's final stage, if and when virtually all of the other conditions for accession have already been met.

### WTO accession is not about what the world should do for the acceding government

WTO accession is not about what the world should do for the acceding government but, instead, what the country, or separate customs territory must do for itself. In meeting the preconditions for WTO accession, the acceding government must undertake very comprehensive reforms. In most instances, this implies substantially transforming a (large) set of policies, laws and regulations. In embarking on the accession process, therefore, a country will do well to reflect seriously upon whether it is willing to, and capable of, change, sometimes fundamentally. The outside world of trade and trade policy will not change as a result of the accession. But the retention of the status quo in the acceding government – either for the lack of will or the incapacity to make the necessary reforms – will mean no prospect of accession.

Linked to this is the question of what guarantees an acceding government will have that WTO membership will translate into more trade and investment in order to, in turn, promote growth, development and jobs. This is a logical preoccupation, especially at the political level, but also one that is based on a misconception of the role of trade policy in general and accessions in particular. Admittedly, based on past experience, governments that have acceded to the WTO tend to perform better in international commerce. It is equally true that more open economies have tended to perform better than more closed ones, all other things being equal. Multilateral trade rules and the alignment of domestic regulations to these rules are fundamentally about creating a better trading and investment environment as a means of stimulating growth, development and jobs. Whether these improvements in the environment actually translate into tangible outcomes is another matter altogether. For the most part, it is not governments that trade with each other, but their private sectors. There can be no guarantees on the extent to which the private sector will be able to exploit new market opportunities. What remains largely undisputed, however, is that there is far less likelihood of increased trade and investment if trade and related policies are discriminatory, unpredictable, opaque, expensive and/or burdensome. In fact, the risk is of reduced trade and economic contraction. Through its rules, regular work, and negotiating function, the WTO plays an important role in promoting the shift away from, as well as avoiding future slippages towards, such damaging policies and practices.

## WTO accession is not about trade policy

Leaving WTO accession in the hands of trade experts, or commercial specialists, in the acceding government, is a terrible idea. WTO accession goes far beyond the remit of the trade, commerce and/or foreign ministry, even the responsibilities of the minister himself. It will cut across many, if not most, ministries, touch upon the responsibilities of other governmental agencies and other authorities, and may very well include regional and municipal levels of government.

This implies at least two crucial things in order for a country to be successful in its accession process.

First, the objective of WTO accession has to be unequivocally endorsed, from the very top of the government, as a key, if not overriding, priority. It is also preferable that the endorsement enjoys explicit bipartisan support (across political divides) from the legislature. And that clear-cut endorsement should exist from the start of the process. An expression of political will is insufficient. Instead, the endorsement must involve an instruction to all government ministries, authorities and other bodies to make accession happen.

Second, all ministries and agencies have to be directly involved in the preparation and execution of the accession process. While the trade or foreign ministry normally functions as coordinator of the process, thereby helping to simplify communication and cooperation with third countries, the chairperson and the Secretariat, it is not normally in a position to do the substantive work. Instead, the bulk of the real work will unavoidably have to take place in the relevant line ministries. Their commitment to, and prioritisation of, the endeavour is therefore critical. Also, stakeholders should, in the best of circumstances, be closely associated with the process. Because of the breadth and depth of the endeavour – requiring the screening of many laws and regulations from the point of view of WTO-compatibility and amending a (potentially large) set of them – the risk of domestic backlash is real. A clear political endorsement at the highest level, combined with the proper involvement of all relevant ministries and consultations with stakeholders, will facilitate the handling of domestic tensions arising from differences in interests and/or policies when the accession process enters its more difficult phases (which it unavoidably will). It will certainly help reduce the risk of any domestic backlash translating into setbacks to the accession process itself.

## WTO accession is not about negotiations

There is a natural tendency to portray the accession process like any other negotiation. From this perspective, the acceding government is seen to negotiate its terms of accession, be it with regard to the multilateral process of ensuring the alignment of domestic rules and regulations to WTO rules, or in the context of the bilateral process of request and offer to establish the country's market access commitments in goods and services.

But such simplistic descriptions overlook two very fundamental pieces of the puzzle. First, the road of accession is, even from the point of view of negotiations, a one-way street. Second, all negotiating roads lead to similar destinations.

This is certainly the case for the multilateral part of the accession process: what is actually 'negotiated' here (if one can describe it like that) is *whether, how* and *when* the acceding government has fulfilled the undisputed requirement of complying with WTO rules. On the first issue of *whether*, the answer provided by the acceding government will have to be affirmative in order for any accession to move forward. So, there is no leeway in this regard. On the second issue of *how*, again, it is first and foremost the responsibility of the acceding government to show, in a convincing manner, that the steps it has taken meet what members consider to be necessary to ensure compliance. So the acceding government may have some leeway, at the margin, but it will be heavily constrained. And any sense of filibustering by the acceding government only risks triggering tougher scrutiny by members. Finally, on the third issue of *when*, in a few key areas and especially for least-developed countries, there may be some room for the acceding government to convince members there are justifiable reasons for transitional periods. But such transitional periods for compliance with WTO rules will have to be time bound and very limited in scope. Since the accession process in itself usually takes many years, allowing the acceding government to gradually adjust its policies in line with WTO rules, members tend to be very reluctant about proposals for transitional periods post-accession.

The bilateral part of the accession process admittedly allows for a greater degree of negotiation, in the sense that the end result is less clearly defined *ex ante*. But, even here, the negotiations are not at all reciprocal in nature, as the acceding government will not be in a position to ask for concessions from existing WTO members. This, in turn, severely limits leverage by the acceding government. Persuasion, on the basis of being able to make credible arguments for why fewer concessions or less extensive concessions are justified in some areas, is arguably just as important as negotiating skills in this process. In fact, based on past experience, and in particular for small and vulnerable countries, it can be directly counterproductive in this context to try to overplay one's negotiating hand, in terms of either building in a lot of 'water' (that is, asking for a much higher level of protection than currently applied) in the market access offers or by suggesting far more sensitivities than can be convincingly argued. In the best-case scenario, playing such negotiating games will merely slow down the process of getting to an agreement on the country's market access commitments. In the worst case, it could call into question the legitimacy of the real sensitivities of the acceding government.

### Entering WTO accession with eyes wide open

WTO accession is unique among the membership procedures of other global bodies. For that reason, misconceptions and misunderstandings of the process by the acceding government are not uncommon. So, how should one describe it? And how should countries that are considering joining the WTO approach the process?

Fundamentally, the WTO is a rules-based club, albeit with nearly universal membership. As such, the underlying purpose of the accession process is to ensure a sufficient degree of like-mindedness from new members. Some may argue that like-mindedness should be achieved both at the normative/ideational level and at the practical policy level. While this may be the ideal situation, the fact of the matter is that some WTO members, including recently acceded (Article XII) members, far from fully subscribe to the established objectives of the WTO, such as for example 'being desirous to contributing … to the substantial reduction of tariffs and other barriers to trade and to the elimination of discriminatory treatment in international trade relations'. Regardless of the preamble to the Marrakesh Agreement Establishing the World Trade Organization, there seems to be no universal support among existing WTO members for more free trade. None the less, the rules-based nature of the WTO regime ensures a certain degree of like-mindedness in terms of members' policies. Existing members are held accountable, ultimately through WTO legal adjudication (dispute settlement), in case of non-compliance with WTO rules. By the same token, the acceding government will certainly have to comply with the 'club's rules' in order to become a member.

Moreover, WTO rules (i.e. the rulebook of the club) are substantial and comprehensive, affecting many important aspects of the manner in which governments organise their economies and the activities in which they engage. Practically speaking, this implies that the acceding government will have to screen a large part of its current laws, regulations and even administrative practices to ensure compliance with WTO rules in the process of accession. Any inconsistencies will have to be rectified.

Thereby, at its core, WTO accession is a matter of significant government and governance reforms. The good news is that such reforms have the potential to boost the economy, in turn fostering development and creating jobs. The bad news, not least in the interim, is that the reform process is resource intensive and the transformation is likely to be painful, especially for some stakeholders. Perhaps the simplest way to put it is that WTO accession works in the same way for the economy of the acceding government as a cold shower works for the human body: while unpleasant for a short while, and requiring a degree of stamina to endure, it certainly wakes you up and kickstarts your circulation. For this reason and notwithstanding the willingness of acceding governments to go through with accession, it is important to enter into the process with eyes wide open, to be mentally prepared and to brace oneself for it.

## The particular challenges, and solutions, for poorer acceding economies

WTO accession is foremost a process whereby the acceding economy transforms itself to comply with WTO rules and to meet any additional requirements by members. The process, therefore, is inherently more challenging for developing countries and for LDCs in particular. These countries, which constitute the majority of the current applicants for

WTO membership, often have small, vulnerable and undiversified economies and are resource constrained, with inefficient public institutions and/or, in some cases, even potentially unstable political systems. All of these factors increase the risk of failure in the accession process.

For this reason, WTO members decided on specific guidelines for the accession of LDCs.[2] The objective of these guidelines is indeed worthy. LDCs, by virtue of their weaker economic and financial situations, face significant challenges in fulfilling the preconditions for accession. Indeed, some of the preconditions for accession, requested by existing members, have increased progressively since the creation of the WTO. In fact, the market access commitments by more recently acceded (Article XII) members, including LDCs, have tended to go further than the commitments undertaken by existing developing members with the same or even higher levels of development. This is clearly improper, not to say unjustified. The guidelines, rightly, try to bring a greater degree of consistency to what members can ask of the poorest acceding governments.

This being said, the guidelines are certainly neither a panacea nor a quick fix. They are only exactly that, i.e. guidelines. While they provide a general direction, members are not bound by them in a strict legal sense. Similarly, while the overall level of ambition for market access commitments is defined, particularly for goods, this does not affect the specific demands on individual sectors or product groups that members may want to pursue. Perhaps most importantly, the guidelines do not – indeed should not – offer any shortcuts with regard to compliance with WTO rules. They stop short of recognising that acceding LDCs have the right to use existing provisions for special and differential treatment under WTO rules, as well as to request transitional periods which members should favourably consider, on a case-by-case basis. So WTO rules will, in the end, have to be complied with by all. This is by far the most important, but also most strenuous, part of the accession process from a reform and domestic resource perspective.

While the guidelines are at best a partial solution (mainly offering some possible relief regarding the market access commitments by LDCs), Aid for Trade is a key avenue to facilitate the accession of LDCs and other developing countries. Since accession is resource intensive and many acceding governments lack capacity, technical assistance and capacity-building can alleviate one of the main hurdles in accession.

---

[2] See WTO document WT/L/508 and its Addendum 1.

Particularly for the reforms required to align domestic regulations with WTO rules, such assistance can be crucial.

Of course, building capacity takes time and no acceding government can expect to have all, or even most, of the needed human capital and capacity in place before the process moves forward. After all, a substantial part of the work will be learning by doing. Also, donors cannot and should not take the 'lead', politically and policy-wise, from the acceding government. The responsibility for accession, no matter what, rests solely with the acceding government. That being said, for many countries, and especially LDCs, trade-related capacity-building is necessary for the successful completion of their accession and realisation of its full potential. Together with the guidelines (designed to counter excessive demands on market access), it provides a better starting point for those countries that are genuinely motivated to forge ahead with trade-related reforms. It will never be a substitute for real commitment and resolve, but it offers some solutions to the particular problems faced by poorer and more vulnerable acceding economies.

### Partners versus counterparts in the process: the chairperson, the Secretariat and the membership

The WTO is member driven and, ultimately, so are its accessions. Consequently, it is the members – not the Secretariat or the chairperson – that need to be convinced of a country's readiness to become a WTO member.

While existing members are commonly portrayed as counterparts to the acceding government during the accession process, and primarily play that role in the bilateral market access deliberations, they are also partners. Besides being potential donors and developmental partners, they can offer ample advice on how to interpret and implement relevant WTO provisions. They certainly have opinions about 'best practices', but additionally they represent important variations on the ways in which a country can comply with WTO rules. Acceding governments should strive to benefit as much as possible from members' wealth of experience, as well as their policy choices and lessons, in this regard. A basic premise to ensure this, and to advance better mutual understanding in the process, is for the acceding government to provide a maximum level of transparency. For sure, draft laws and regulations must be shared with WTO members, for their possible input, before adoption. Informally, it is advisable to engage bilaterally with some of the more interested members to continuously discuss what changes to regulations are envisaged, how the regulations could be amended, and when.

Also, acceding governments should try to consider current members' specific demands for increased market access not only from a defensive point of view (as concessions), but also as indications of possible new trade opportunities. This is particularly true for requests in services, where trade and investments are often more directly linked. Similarly, a number of key services sectors have the potential to improve the functioning of the business and trading environment more generally. Making 'concessions' in such sectors can actually help the acceding government or separate customs territory to stimulate its own economic activity, including its exports in goods and services. Examples of such services sectors are logistics, transportation, distribution, as well as financial services, insurance, and information and communications technology, to name a few. In a similar vein, depending on the acceding government's industrial structure, responding favourably to market access requests for intermediate goods, machines, tools, transportation equipment, etc., can offer the potential to improve the competitiveness of downstream producers domestically and/or exporters of final products. Whether the acceding government is in a position to accept such requests in the end, also considering its often competing domestic interests and priorities, is of course another matter. At the very least, the process of accession allows a country to seriously reflect on what longer-term trade policies it wants to pursue and what economic benefits, or drawbacks, these choices could entail.

As for the WTO Secretariat, in many ways, it is the closest partner of the acceding government. While carefully guarding its objectivity and impartiality, it stands ready to advise the acceding government, provide technical assistance and offer other support. Not least for poorer acceding governments, working closely with the Secretariat is key.

The chairperson, working closely with the WTO Secretariat is, simplistically put, between the acceding governments and the members. The chairperson is designated by members to oversee the process from its start to finish. However, since the chairperson is designated by members, an important part of the role is to represent the collective expectations of members and the institution in relation to the acceding government. At the same time, in the case of LDCs aspiring to WTO membership, the chairperson can and should be used more informally as a sounding board by the acceding government in planning and executing the process of accession. This requires that the acceding government collaborate closely with the chairperson, including by ensuring that the chairperson is kept fully abreast of any internal developments with regard to domestic accession preparations. Finally, there may even be situations where the chairperson needs to engage with individual WTO members to try to resolve complications, particularly when these are likely to pose a threat of deadlock in the process. The LDC accession guidelines have further strengthened this aspect of the chairmanship by explicitly allowing for the possibility of the chairperson acting as a facilitator (mediator) under certain circumstances. While this option has only been used in a few instances to date, it more broadly illustrates the increased emphasis on the chairperson shepherding the process and, if need be, acting as honest broker.

This chapter has attempted to respond, from a more principled perspective, to the questions of what WTO accession is (and, equally important, what it is not); what it entails and how acceding governments should approach the endeavour; what particular challenges – and solutions – may exist for poorer developing countries; and what roles the members, the Secretariat and the chairperson play in the process.

The key message conveyed is the importance of a country being entirely convinced of the benefits of WTO accession, having the right motivations and expectations, before embarking on the process. This will determine the speed and degree of success of the accession, as well as potentially the relative success of an economy as member of WTO once it has acceded.

The bottom line is that WTO accession is – at its core – about domestic reform. This reform is likely to be comprehensive and substantial, and in turn give rise to structural adjustments, thereby requiring unwavering political commitment and significant investment in time and effort by the acceding government. The latter can be particularly challenging for poor, small and/or vulnerable countries. Almost by definition, these acceding governments have limited resources. Part of the solution, it is being argued here, will have to come from ensuring adequate Aid for Trade, in terms of technical assistance and capacity-building. With greater supervision of members' market access demands through the most recent LDC accession guidelines, but equally important, close collaboration with members, the Secretariat and the chairperson in their respective roles, poorer acceding governments can, it is hoped, overcome some of the challenges they face. However, none of these measures is a substitute for the necessary actions, reflecting hard policy choices, to be taken domestically by the acceding government itself.

# PART V

Salient features in WTO Accession Protocols

# 29

# Market access goods negotiations: salience, results and meaning

JÜRGEN RICHTERING, ERIC NG SHING,
MUSTAPHA SEKKATE AND DAYONG YU

## ABSTRACT

*Trade negotiations and the exchange of concessions on trade in goods have been the cornerstone of the multilateral trading system. This chapter examines the salient features, results and meaning of the schedules of tariff concessions and commitments on goods of Article XII members: what they mean and what they have contributed. We find that the bilateral market access of Article XII members has shaped the landscape of tariff commitments that provide transparency and predictability to today's merchandise trade relationships. We also found that the large number of post-2001 accessions coincided with an extended period of global growth, particularly among the major emerging economies, fostered by the stability of trade regimes. When we compared Article XII members with General Agreement on Tariffs and Trade (GATT) members on bound tariffs, we found that the comparable bound tariff rates were higher for GATT members, and that a number of original members retained unbound tariff lines for non-agricultural products. Overall, results from the concluded accessions have produced more liberal tariff concessions than those of original WTO members, expanding the market access for WTO members' exports. The lower barriers to trade in these Article XII members' markets have improved economic efficiency, increased competition and led to better resource reallocation.*

The analysis in this chapter was finalised at the end of 2013. Since then the Republic of Yemen and Republic of Seychelles acceded to the World Trade Organization (WTO) respectively on 26 June 2014 and 26 April 2015. This expanded total WTO membership from 159 to 161. Please see the editors' note.

The negotiations and the exchange of concessions on trade in goods have been the cornerstone of the multilateral trading system. The schedules of concessions and commitments of the original contracting parties to the General Agreement on Tariffs and Trade (GATT), the subsequent rounds of negotiations and the bilateral market access negotiation of new WTO members have shaped the landscape of tariff commitments that provide transparency and predictability to today's merchandise trade relationships. It is interesting to note that the large number of post-2001 accessions coincided with an extended period of global growth, particularly among the major emerging economies, fostered by the stability of trade regimes.

This chapter highlights some of the salient features of the outcomes of the market access negotiation on goods of thirty-one of the members that joined the WTO after the Uruguay Round, pursuant to Article XII of the Marrakesh Agreement Establishing the WTO (the WTO Agreement) (Article XII members) and identifies the patterns and distinctive features which characterise these accessions. The specific focus is on Part I, Section I-A (agricultural products tariffs) and Section II (other products tariffs) of the schedules. A careful analysis of these accessions may also be a good reference for future accessions, although it should be emphasised that each accession is subject to its own dynamics and constraints, which makes it impossible to predict or anticipate the exact final outcome. The chapter also highlights some practical guidelines for tackling the technical side of the negotiations on goods, based on the authors' practical experience of providing technical support to acceding governments in their negotiations.

Prior to and also during the Uruguay Round, accessions[1] of developing countries were mostly not subject to extensive bilateral negotiations in contrast to the accessions in the post-Uruguay Round period. The predominance of ceiling duties in many developing countries that joined before or during the Uruguay Round and the relatively high average rates of tariff protection are distinctive features of these earlier accessions, although Article XII of the WTO Agreement is virtually the same as the GATT Article XXXIII.

While quite a range of very diverse states and separate customs territories have joined the WTO since 1995, there are nevertheless two major political and economic developments which introduced their own special dynamics. These are: (i) the dissolution of the Soviet Union and Yugoslavia, which led to the creation of a large number of independent

---

[1] GATT accession via GATT Article XXXIII.

states and the political and economic opening up of Eastern Europe; and (ii) the enlargement of the European Community, succeeded in 2009 by the European Union. These two special economic and political circumstances seem to have influenced the Accession Protocols of a good number of accessions since 1995.

## Schedules of acceding members

### Diversity of final bound rates

Table 29.1 shows the averages of final bound duties along with the recent most-favoured-nation (MFN) applied duties. The bound duties vary quite substantially with a maximum of close to 40 per cent for Vanuatu and a minimum of just 5 per cent for Montenegro. The specific outcomes in terms of final bound duties are the results of specific negotiations, which may be affected by various factors, such as the acceding government's individual economic situation, members' commercial interests and the dynamics of the global economy. Nevertheless, certain patterns linked to politico-economic situations seem to emerge. As can be seen in Table 29.2, members that are among the least-developed countries (LDCs), or were classified as such at the time of their accession, show higher bound averages than do other members. Among the other members, the bound duty averages of the governments that are part of the Commonwealth of Independent States (CIS) and/or the European geographical region have much lower bound duty averages than do the other non-LDC Article XII members.

Figure 29.1 depicts the outcomes of the accession negotiations for the thirty-one members that have joined the WTO between 1995 and 2013. Apart from some of the pre-2000 accessions, when negotiations seemed to have been less demanding in terms of market access, the three-group categorisation seems to explain a lot of the variance, found in the final bound duty averages. In the case of Eastern Europe, countries pending and/or anticipated membership of the European Economic Community, and later on the European Union, probably explains the positions and predispositions of negotiators. For LDCs, the outcome of their negotiations sets them apart from the other Article XII members, although there is some overlap with Tonga and Mongolia (countries with rather special economic circumstances).

If we look at applied rates, shown in Figure 29.2, together with the final bound rates, the difference among Article XII members is less striking,

Table 29.1 *Final bound duties and current MFN applied duties*

| Article XII members | Code | Date of membership | Average final bound duty (%) | | | Average MFN applied duty (2011) (%) | | |
|---|---|---|---|---|---|---|---|---|
| | | | All goods | AG | NAMA | All goods | Agriculture | NAMA |
| Ecuador | ECU | 21 January 1996 | 21.7 | 25.7 | 21.2 | 10.1 | 18.3 | 8.8 |
| Bulgaria⋆ | BGR | 1 December 1996 | 25.0 | 35.4 | 23.6 | 5.3 | 13.9 | 4.0 |
| Mongolia | MNG | 29 January 1997 | 17.5 | 18.9 | 17.3 | 5.0 | 5.1 | 5.0 |
| Panama | PAN | 6 September 1997 | 22.8 | 27.6 | 22.1 | 6.9 | 12.4 | 6.0 |
| Kyrgyz Republic | KGZ | 20 December 1998 | 7.5 | 12.7 | 6.7 | 4.6 | 7.5 | 4.2 |
| Latvia⋆ | LVA | 10 February 1999 | 12.7 | 34.6 | 9.4 | 5.3 | 13.9 | 4.0 |
| Estonia⋆ | EST | 13 November 1999 | 8.6 | 17.5 | 7.3 | 5.3 | 13.9 | 4.0 |
| Jordan | JOR | 11 April 2000 | 16.3 | 23.6 | 15.2 | 10.9 | 17.8 | 9.8 |
| Georgia | GEO | 14 June 2000 | 7.4 | 13.2 | 6.5 | 1.5 | 7.2 | 0.7 |
| Albania | ALB | 8 September 2000 | 7.0 | 9.5 | 6.6 | 5.0 | 8.0 | 4.6 |
| Oman | OMN | 9 November 2000 | 13.7 | 27.7 | 11.6 | 4.7 | 5.7 | 4.6 |
| Croatia | HRV | 30 November 2000 | 6.3 | 11.5 | 5.5 | 4.9 | 10.7 | 4.0 |
| Lithuania⋆ | LTU | 31 May 2001 | 9.3 | 15.2 | 8.4 | 5.3 | 13.9 | 4.0 |
| Moldova Republic of | MDA | 26 July 2001 | 7.0 | 14.1 | 5.9 | 4.6 | 10.5 | 3.7 |
| China | CHN | 11 December 2001 | 10.0 | 15.7 | 9.2 | 9.6 | 15.6 | 8.7 |
| Chinese Taipei | CHT | 1 January 2002 | 6.4 | 17.5 | 4.7 | 6.1 | 16.6 | 4.5 |
| Armenia Republic of | ARM | 2 January 2003 | 8.5 | 14.7 | 7.6 | 3.5 | 7.0 | 3.0 |
| Former Yugoslav Republic of Macedonia | MKD | 4 April 2003 | 7.2 | 13.1 | 6.3 | 7.0 | 13.5 | 6.0 |
| Nepal⋆⋆ | NPL | 23 April 2004 | 26.0 | 41.5 | 23.7 | 12.3 | 14.5 | 12.0 |
| Cambodia⋆⋆ | KHM | 13 October 2004 | 19.1 | 28.1 | 17.7 | 10.9 | 15.2 | 10.3 |

| | | | | | | | | |
|---|---|---|---|---|---|---|---|---|
| Saudi Arabia Kingdom of | SAU | 11 December 2005 | 11.4 | 17.3 | 10.5 | 4.9 | 4.8 | 4.9 |
| Viet Nam | VNM | 11 January 2007 | 11.5 | 18.5 | 10.4 | 9.5 | 16.2 | 8.4 |
| Tonga | TON | 27 July 2007 | 17.6 | 19.2 | 17.3 | 11.7 | 11.7 | 11.7 |
| Ukraine | UKR | 16 May 2008 | 5.8 | 11.0 | 5.0 | 4.5 | 9.5 | 3.7 |
| Cabo Verde** | CPV | 23 July 2008 | 15.8 | 19.3 | 15.2 | 10.2 | 12.2 | 9.9 |
| Montenegro | MNE | 29 April 2012 | 5.1 | 10.8 | 4.3 | 4.9 | 10.9 | 4.0 |
| Samoa** | SAM | 10 May 2012 | 21.1 | 25.8 | 20.4 | 11.4 | 14.5 | 10.8 |
| Russian Federation | RUS | 22 August 2012 | 7.7 | 11.5 | 7.2 | 9.4 | 14.3 | 8.7 |
| Vanuatu** | VUT | 24 August 2012 | 39.7 | 43.7 | 39.1 | 9.1 | 17.5 | 7.8 |
| Lao PDR** | LAO | 2 February 2013 | 18.8 | 19.3 | 18.7 | | | |
| Tajikistan | TJK | 2 March 2013 | 7.9 | 10.1 | 7.6 | 7.8 | 11.2 | 7.3 |
| **Memo items** | | | | | | | | |
| Article XII members | | | 13.6 | 20.1 | 12.6 | 7.1 | 12.1 | 6.3 |
| of which LDCs | | | 23.4 | 29.6 | 22.5 | 10.8 | 14.8 | 10.2 |
| of which non-LDCs | | | 11.3 | 17.9 | 10.3 | 6.3 | 11.6 | 5.5 |
| GATT–WTO members | | | 45.5 | 65.4 | 34.0 | 9.5 | 16.1 | 8.5 |
| of which LDCs | | | 65.2 | 79.9 | 45.4 | 11.7 | 15.0 | 11.2 |
| of which non-LDCs | | | 37.9 | 59.8 | 29.6 | 8.7 | 16.4 | 7.5 |
| of which developed | | | 10.4 | 40.3 | 5.8 | 4.7 | 18.3 | 2.5 |
| of which developing | | | 41.6 | 62.5 | 32.8 | 9.3 | 16.2 | 8.2 |

*Notes:*

* EU member: EU MFN applied duty is shown. ** Acceded as an LDC.

For some members, 2012 applied tariffs were used when the 2011 tariff was not notified.

*Source:* WTO, ITC and UNCTAD (2012); WTO, ITC and UNCTAD (2013). For the underlying tariff data, see https://tao.wto.org and http://tdf.wto.org.

Table 29.2 *Final bound rates (%) by geopolitical groups*

| | All accessions | | | After taking out early accessions | | |
|---|---|---|---|---|---|---|
| | Median | Average | Range | Average | Range | Early accessions |
| EE+CIS* | 7.5 | 8.9 | 5.1–25.0 | 7.3 | 5.1–9.3 | Bulgaria, Lithuania |
| Other | 15.0 | 14.2 | 6.4–22.8 | 13.0 | 6.4–17.6 | Ecuador, Panama |
| LDCs | 20.0 | 23.4 | 15.8–39.7 | 20.2 | 15.8–26.0 | Vanuatu** |

*Notes:* *Eastern Europe and the CIS. **The working party on the accession of Vanuatu to the WTO formally approved on 29 October 2001 a Protocol of Accession which is substantially identical to the final one approved in 2012.

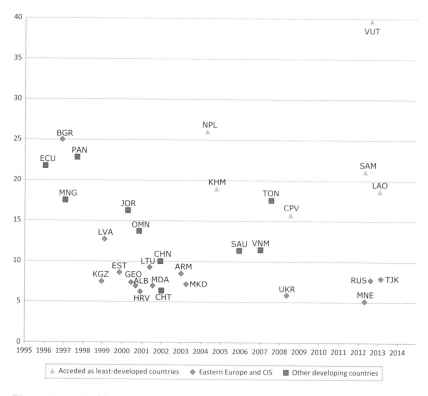

**Figure 29.1**    Final bound rates (%) by accession date (for key see Table 29.1).

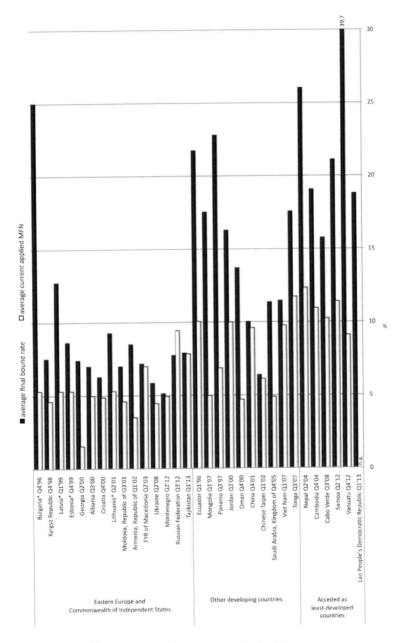

**Figure 29.2** Final bound rates (%) vs. current applied MFN.

except for the LDCs, which seem to have higher applied averages, and in most cases some binding overhang exists for most Article XII members.

Comparing Article XII members with GATT members, one can see much higher bound averages for LDCs and other developing economies. Table 29.1 shows that the comparable bound rates are two to three times higher for GATT members and, in addition, a good number of them retained unbound tariff lines for non-agricultural products. The MFN applied rates, however, show hardly any difference, which indicates that both groups of members, on average, follow similar applied policy regimes. This implies that Article XII members have much less policy space in terms of binding overhang.

Making the WTO attractive for LDCs – only about half of them were WTO members at the beginning of the Doha Development Agenda (DDA) negotiations – was a growing concern for the WTO membership. In the Decision of the General Council of 10 December 2002, WTO members agreed to facilitate and accelerate the negotiations for the accessions of LDCs to the WTO through simplified and streamlined accession procedures, with a view to concluding these negotiations as quickly as possible.[2] Ten years later, six LDCs had joined the WTO on terms that were significantly less stringent than those of other members acceding in the same period but still much more demanding in terms of market access than those of GATT LDC members. The General Council in its decision of 25 July 2012 agreed to adopt some principles and benchmarks which should guide future LDC market access negotiations. The implementation and impact of these guidelines still need to be tested in future LDC accessions.[3]

Apart from the MFN duties, which showed some diversity, other additional market access elements were treated nearly uniformly across all accessions and in a way which also set them apart from many original

---

[2] See WTO document WT/L/508: 'WTO Members shall exercise restraint in seeking concessions and commitments on trade in goods and services from acceding LDCs, taking into account the levels of concessions and commitments undertaken by existing WTO LDC Members.'

[3] See WTO document WT/L/508/Add. 1, paragraph 5: 'acceding LDCs shall bind all of their agricultural tariff lines at an overall average rate of 50 per cent', and in paragraph 7 (i): 'Acceding LDCs shall bind 95 per cent of their non-agricultural tariff lines at an overall average rate of 35 per cent', and 7 (ii): 'Acceding LDCs that choose to undertake comprehensive bindings of NAMA [non-agricultural market access] tariff lines may do so and be afforded proportionately higher overall average rates … In such cases the acceding LDC shall be entitled to transition periods of up to 10 years for up to 10 per cent of their tariff lines.'

WTO members and members that had joined earlier. First, tariff bindings covered all products – not only agricultural products in line with the outcome of the Uruguay Round but also non-agricultural products.[4] The recent recommendations on LDC accessions, however, provide flexibility to acceding governments to keep a limited number of tariff lines unbound, but the actual application of these new benchmarks has not yet been tested. Secondly, no other duties and charges (ODCs) were accepted, i.e. they were bound at zero for the sake of transparency and simplicity.[5]

### Easing the impact of tariff reductions: the use of extended implementation periods

Justifying tariff reductions resulting from WTO accession to domestic constituencies is not always easy because the gains of improved and ensured export market access for WTO members are less often visible from an immediately commercial perspective than the competition and potential fiscal revenue loss from less highly taxed imports. Therefore, extended implementation periods have been used by all acceding governments but rarely in any extensive manner. In fact, more than three-quarters of all Article XII members implemented more than half of their commitments upon their accession date. The fairly frequent use of immediate implementation could be seen as a reflection that final bound duties were often negotiated to be at or above currently or projected applied rates. It should not be forgotten that these applied rates will often have already been on a downward trend in anticipation of, and as preparation for, the expected accession requirements. The accession was then being used to enshrine already achieved market opening into bound commitments for most products. While this may apply to the majority of tariff lines, a small and possibly important part of merchandise trade has been subject to much longer implementation periods. Ten-year or longer implementation periods have in fact been negotiated for twelve of the thirty-one acceding members, in one case covering more than 1,200 tariff lines (Table 29.3).

---

[4] There were very few exceptions. Nepal, for example, negotiated unbound lines with members.

[5] There were very few exceptions: Cabo Verde (ECOWAS (Economic Community of West African States) duty 0.25 per cent) and Saudi Arabia with twenty-two tariff lines (prohibited products); and Nepal and the former Yugoslav Republic of Macedonia with phasing out in a specified period.

Table 29.3 *Article XII members' implementation periods, initial negotiating rights (INRs) and distinct duties*

| Member | Number of tariff lines | Implementation | | INRs | | Distinct bound duties | |
| --- | --- | --- | --- | --- | --- | --- | --- |
| | | Max years | Immediate (%) | Tariff lines with INRs (%) | Distinct INRs | Number | Ad valorem |
| Ecuador | 5,763 | 11 | 97.9 | 16.9 | 8 | 18 | 18 |
| Bulgaria | 10,603 | 14 | 64.5 | 10.2 | 7 | 125 | 50 |
| Mongolia | 5,562 | 8 | 83.7 | 11.3 | 6 | 12 | 12 |
| Panama | 8,411 | 14 | 18.4 | 36.4 | 10 | 46 | 46 |
| Kyrgyz Republic | 6,981 | 7 | 44.0 | 94.2 | 11 | 18 | 11 |
| Latvia | 5,292 | 9 | 83.4 | 91.1 | 5 | 23 | 21 |
| Estonia | 10,746 | 6 | 91.9 | 90.0 | 7 | 35 | 35 |
| Jordan | 6,765 | 10 | 69.6 | 45.6 | 11 | 20 | 15 |
| Georgia | 5,981 | 6 | 53.1 | 80.2 | 14 | 24 | 18 |
| Albania | 10,584 | 9 | 63.6 | 100.0 | 14 | 8 | 8 |
| Oman | 5,563 | 9 | 69.3 | 59.3 | 9 | 14 | 14 |
| Croatia | 7,404 | 7 | 78.2 | 58.4 | 19 | 246 | 38 |
| Lithuania | 6,291 | 8 | 94.4 | 64.9 | 7 | 45 | 27 |
| Moldova Republic of | 5,987 | 4 | 64.0 | 59.8 | 14 | 34 | 14 |
| China | 7,158 | 9 | 46.3 | 100.0 | 39 | 54 | 54 |
| Chinese Taipei | 8,646 | 9 | 54.8 | 73.8 | 28 | 151 | 90 |
| Armenia Republic of | 5,838 | 4 | 98.1 | 52.3 | 10 | 8 | 8 |
| Former Yugoslav Republic of Macedonia | 10,567 | 9 | 79.4 | 88.7 | 8 | 133 | 31 |

| | | | | | | | |
|---|---|---|---|---|---|---|---|
| Nepal* | 5,353 | 10 | 8.3 | 54.4 | 7 | 13 | 13 |
| Cambodia* | 6,823 | 10 | 99.4 | 21.8 | 7 | 23 | 23 |
| Saudi Arabia Kingdom of | 7,559 | 10 | 92.6 | 36.5 | 23 | 24 | 16 |
| Viet Nam | 10,444 | 12 | 59.5 | 49.4 | 18 | 50 | 48 |
| Tonga | 5,389 | 1 | 67.7 | 46.1 | 4 | 3 | 2 |
| Ukraine | 10,900 | 5 | 97.1 | 85.0 | 41 | 53 | 45 |
| Cabo Verde* | 5,792 | 10 | 38.9 | 20.1 | 2 | 12 | 12 |
| Montenegro | 10,039 | 10 | 87.0 | 67.9 | 7 | 78 | 78 |
| Samoa* | 5,318 | 10 | 99.5 | 36.0 | 6 | 22 | 17 |
| Russian Federation | 11,567 | 8 | 39.2 | 97.6 | 47 | 234 | 32 |
| Vanuatu* | 5,059 | 3 | 99.1 | 18.9 | 6 | 16 | 16 |
| Lao PDR* | 10,690 | 10 | 99.6 | 26.4 | 4 | 17 | 17 |
| Tajikistan | 10,103 | 7 | 46.4 | 42.6 | 6 | 29 | 20 |

*Note:*
* Acceded as an LDC.

*Source:* Compilations based on members' accession schedules.

## *The complexity of tariff structure and the use of non-ad valorem duties*

One aspect of transparency in members' schedules is the number of distinct duty levels among the final bound duties. While Tonga's schedule contains only three different distinct duty levels, most other economies use between ten and fifty different duty levels (Table 29.3). The extreme cases with more than one hundred distinct duty levels are the result of more extensive use of non-ad valorem duties (NAVs), i.e. duties that are not expressed only as a percentage of the customs value but as monetary value per physical unit or a combination of the two.

The use of ad valorem duties, which are more transparent in their price effects on imported goods, has been one of the elements that was proposed and pursued in the context of the DDA negotiations for non-agricultural products. NAVs usually imply higher ad valorem equivalent duties for lower priced items than for high-value items because the duty is calculated on a per-unit basis.[6] This could be seen as a systemic bias against lower unit value imports which are more likely to have their origin in developing members. It should not be forgotten, though, that NAVs lose their protective impact to the extent that inflation reduces the effective protection.[7]

About half of the Article XII members do not have any NAVs and about three-quarters do not have any NAVs for non-agricultural goods. These shares are similar to those found for GATT members.

Members have accepted NAVs in their bilateral negotiations and these have then found their way into the consolidated accession schedules. However, in most cases they have been limited to some specific product groups, and it has also been common practice to request the ad valorem equivalents in order to have a better idea of their protective impact in the negotiation process. The areas where NAVs have been used most frequently are Harmonised System (HS) chapters 02 (meat) and 22 (alcohol), followed by 24 (tobacco) and other agricultural products. In non-agricultural sectors NAVs have rarely been used.

---

[6] In the case of mixed duties (e.g. 5 per cent or US$2/kg, whichever is higher) and compound duties (e.g. 5 per cent plus US$2/kg) the bias against lower priced items comes from the specific part (US$2/kg) of the duty.

[7] Some members have used currencies other than their own to insure themselves against domestic inflationary pressures.

*INRs*

INRs reflect most directly the involvement of WTO members in the accession process of acceding governments. For some members, INRs are their only request in the accession negotiations; they emphasise the importance given to selected products which are of particular export interest to them. The number of INR-holding members gives a lower bound estimate of the members having negotiated on specific trade interests with the respective acceding member. Compared with GATT members, Article XII members have significantly higher coverage of tariff lines subject to INRs. This reflects the increased interest of members in accession negotiations.

It is not surprising that the larger acceding economies have attracted more negotiating interest than the smaller ones. Anticipated EU membership also drew interest in terms of tariff lines covered by INRs, while early Article XII accessions and LDCs saw fewer members and/or lesser tariff line coverage. While existing or future trade interests were supposed to be the driving force for requesting INRs for specific products, one can also see a number of cases where existing trade links at the time of the accession did not exist and some cases where it would appear unlikely that there would ever be any future real commercial trade interest. More widespread requests for INRs may also reflect systemic interests, i.e. to pre-empt and be party to possible post-accession renegotiations.

The United States and the European Union have traditionally been most active in requesting INRs, if one looks at the average number of tariff lines for which INRs have been requested. Nevertheless, some of the recently acceded Article XII members have joined the circle in actively requesting INRs; the most striking example is Ukraine, which has requested a very high number of INRs in three recently concluded accessions.

Figure 29.3 shows the use of INRs as a percentage share of all tariff lines covered over time. If one leaves aside the early accessions, the three groups again follow roughly similar patterns, although the picture is fuzzier than that observed for the final bound rates (Figure 29.1). The LDC group is, however, clearly distinguishable as having been less subject to requests for INRs than the other Article XII members.

*Sectoral commitments*

In the Uruguay Round, some members agreed to undertake reciprocal tariff reductions and tariff eliminations in a number of clearly defined sectors. These sectoral negotiations are known as 'zero for zero'

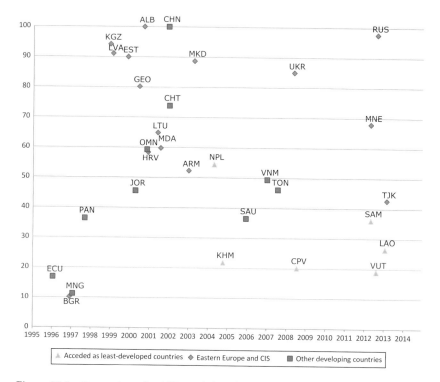

**Figure 29.3**  Proportion of tariff lines (%) with initial negotiating rights by accession date

agreements because participants agreed to duty free bound levels for those products in their schedules. They cover agricultural equipment, beer, construction equipment, distilled spirits (brown), furniture, medical equipment, paper, pharmaceuticals, steel and toys.[8] The agreement on chemicals, on the other hand, is usually referred to as a 'harmonisation' agreement because participants included in their schedules the same levels (0, 5.5 and 6.5 per cent) for different groups of chemical products. A separate plurilateral agreement on products for use in civil aircraft was annexed to the final Marrakesh Declaration and shortly afterwards it was followed by the ITA which was proposed at the Singapore Ministerial Conference and entered into force in 1997.

---

[8]  The coverage in terms of the count of HS 2007 subheadings (fully or partially covered) is as follows: agricultural equipment (26), beer (1), construction equipment (54), distilled spirits (brown) (3), furniture (20), medical equipment (39), paper (145), pharmaceuticals (261), steel (193) and toys (8); chemical harmonisation (888), civil aviation (261 subheadings mostly in partial coverage), Information Technology Agreement (ITA) (132). The exact subheading count depends on the HS version; and some subheadings are covered by more than one sector.

Most LDCs did not undertake any commitments matching the so-called 'zero for zero' or 'harmonisation' initiatives. Most of the other acceding members, however, undertook, as a result of their accession negotiations, commitments to join all or some of the zero-for-zero or harmonisation sectoral tariff initiatives of the Uruguay Round described in the preceding paragraph. With the exception of Tonga and the LDCs, all accessions concluded between 2000 and 2013 included a commitment to join the ITA formally or *de facto*.

Members have put a considerable amount of pressure on acceding governments to join a number of sectoral agreements. Creating a level playing field in an entire sector is clearly an important step in the globalisation and efficient allocation of worldwide production sites.

A much-studied example is the ITA, which has seen phenomenal growth over the last fifteen years thanks to the efficient globalised allocation of global value chains. It would be interesting to study how other sectoral agreements have contributed to global economic growth and welfare.

## Technical issues related to the goods negotiations

For acceding members, managing the market access negotiations on goods based on a list of 5,000 to 10,000 product items, keeping them consistent with the HS coding system, negotiating all or selected items on this list with a good number of WTO members (ten to sixty) over a number of years and, last but not least, keeping track of their own positions, regional commitments and other commitments already made (signed bilaterals) clearly amounts to a daunting task (even for some of the biggest economies). Any flaws or inconsistencies in this process may result in misunderstandings and ambiguities. Often, these may only be resolved by accepting the most market-opening option or undertaking renegotiations before the accession can be concluded.

To facilitate the process, focusing purely on the technical aspects, the WTO Secretariat has been providing technical support to acceding governments in their accession negotiations. Apart from offering information and guidance on the procedural aspects and background information on WTO members' schedules, the main focus has been to ensure consistency with the HS coding system, which is not always well understood, and to clarify the scope of sectoral commitments, which are frequently requested as part of the market access negotiations. Assistance starts with a review of the initial offer for HS consistency and, in some instances, guidance is provided to resolve HS classification divergences between specific bilateral requests and offers.

In the later phase of the accession process when all bilateral market access negotiations are concluded, the WTO Secretariat takes responsibility for preparing the draft schedule of concessions and commitments, which will become the legal instrument of accession after its adoption by the WTO membership. The purpose of this technical process is to consolidate the results contained in individual bilateral market access agreements into a single list of tariff concessions. Technically, the process requires multilateralising the most liberal tariff concession for each tariff line, resolving potential inconsistencies between different bilateral agreements and converting the final result of consolidation into the standard format of WTO schedules.

Utmost confidentiality in dealing with members and acceding governments alike has been the foundation for the trust which has allowed practical and focused technical assistance. Trust in the Secretariat's technical expertise in doing the consolidation work has also alleviated members' technical verification tasks. This, in turn, has led to speedier conclusions than would have been possible otherwise.

It is good practice for the acceding government to always keep track of all bilaterals, even in their preliminary versions, and to carry out draft consolidations of all offers after each single revision. An additional recommendation would be to integrate implications from headnotes/footnotes with language parity[9] directly into the preliminary draft consolidations so that the acceding government has a clear picture of where it stands. Furthermore, as was mentioned above, special care should be taken when using NAVs. It is preferable to always use the same type of NAV in all bilaterals. These recommendations may not be easily implemented, especially for some economies, but the WTO Secretariat is ready to offer its assistance at any point in the process.

There is one complication that may arise with the use of NAVs in the accession negotiations. Different duty formulations in different bilaterals result in complex duty structures in the consolidation if the duties in question are not quantitatively comparable. Since the consolidation of the bilaterals has to show the lowest duty, a comparison needs to be undertaken which allows identifying the lowest duty irrespective of the unit values of future trade flows, which may vary between traders and over time. In order to reflect all bilaterals, complex duty structures may have to be adopted. For example, a duty of 5 per cent recorded in one

---

[9] For example: 'The acceding government agrees to maintain its bound and applied rates, including other duties and charges, for HS 1205 (rape or colza (canola) seeds, whether or not broken) at a level no higher than for HS 1201 (soya beans, whether or not broken).'

bilateral is not directly comparable with a specific duty of €2/kg recorded in another bilateral for the same product. To preserve all members' rights, a consolidation will result in the following duty: 5 per cent but not higher than €2/kg. This is just a simple example and more complex cases have been found in past consolidation exercises. One possible alternative, which has been used in at least one accession, consists of using historic unit values to select the lowest duty based on its ad valorem equivalent.[10]

Acceding governments are encouraged to table their initial goods offer in the HS version that is used in their currently applied national tariff nomenclature, keeping in mind that their national nomenclature should normally be in line with the most recent HS version. All bilateral goods agreements should be signed in the same HS version and using the same national tariff line breakdown. Having commitments in different versions of tariff nomenclature is not advisable as it complicates the tracking of individual commitments. It also complicates the task of consolidation and verification in the final phase of the accession process. Should the HS version have changed in the course of the accession negotiations, it may be necessary to transpose the final consolidation of all bilateral agreements into the most recent HS version. The consolidation and its transposition will be reviewed and approved by the WTO members.

An increasing number of acceding states and customs territories are now members of one or more regional free trade agreements (FTAs). In some cases they take the form of a customs union and then imply a common external tariff (CET) with few or no product exceptions. In order not to undercut the CET, acceding governments would likely consider the CET tariff rates as their own 'red lines' in their bilateral negotiations, to maintain the viability of the customs union. This, however, would seriously reduce their negotiation margin and complicate the accession negotiations. If an acceding government enters an FTA with a CET while in the process of negotiating its own accession to the WTO, renegotiations before or after the conclusion of the accession are required to align the bound rates to the CET or the CET to the bound rates, or to negotiate exceptions to the CET. This is a real political dilemma, and strategic priorities need to be set to best underpin the longer-term trade policy and economic development objectives.

Market access negotiations are a key element of the WTO accession process. The results of the concluded accessions have been a set of more

---

[10] In one specific case, the member committed to a special mechanism to adjust the NAV on an annual basis to ensure that these NAVs did not exceed the ad valorem equivalents calculated on the basis of the trade statistic of the previous year.

liberal tariff concessions made by thirty-one Article XII members than those by the original WTO members. These tariff concessions, in particular by the larger economies, such as China and Russia, have greatly expanded the market access for WTO members' exports, in terms of lowering the cost of trade and increasing predictability. On the other hand, the lower barriers on trade in these Article XII members' markets have improved economic efficiency, increased competition and led to better resource reallocation.

The last four issues of the Director-General's annual report on accessions[11] have reported that Article XII members had grown faster and recovered quicker from the crisis, and that their economies were stronger and more resilient. These members were performing more robustly as regards foreign direct investment (FDI) attraction because of improved market access conditions and WTO-consistent trade and investment regimes. And global economic growth has without doubt been fostered by the enlarged WTO membership, and with it the more widespread application of its regulatory framework.

The characteristics of the tariff concessions resulting from already concluded accession negotiations provide useful insights for future tariff negotiations. The special status of LDCs has largely been recognised and has also further been emphasised in 2012 benchmarks supplementing the 2002 LDC accession guidelines. It has also emerged that politico-economic factors may have influenced the outcomes of accession negotiations for governments in Eastern Europe and the CIS and led to final bound rates significantly lower than those of other developing economies.

In addition, full binding coverage, elimination of ODCs, simplification of tariff formulations and concessions on sectorals have been characteristic features of the accessions to the WTO since 1996. Governments seeking to engage in WTO accession negotiations are encouraged to have a close look at this track record to guide them in their preparations for the negotiating process and to assist them in better understanding the WTO system.

## References

World Trade Organization (WTO), International Trade Center (ITC) and United Nations Conference on Trade and Development (UNCTAD) (2012). *World Tariff Profiles 2012: Applied MFN Tariffs*. Geneva, WTO, ITC and UNCTAD. (2013). *World Tariff Profiles 2013: Applied MFN Tariffs*. Geneva, WTO, ITC and UNCTAD.

---

[11] See WTO documents WT/ACC/14, 15 and 19.

# 30

# Services market opening: salience, results and meaning

ANTONIA CARZANIGA, AIK HOE LIM
AND JUNEYOUNG LEE

## ABSTRACT

*This chapter is structured around three questions. What advances have been made on services market opening? What have been the specific market access commitments of least-developed countries (LDCs)? And what is the progress made with domestic regulation disciplines? This chapter examines the extent to which the services-specific commitments and domestic regulatory disciplines of Article XII members differ from those undertaken by original WTO members at similar levels of development. Although no single indicator exists that can be used to make this comparison, given the textual nature of specific commitments, as opposed to the numerical properties of tariffs, several other possible parameters exist, which could be used alone or in combination to assess such departures. The evidence and patterns in Article XII members' services market access commitments and regulatory state-of-play and advances are examined. The trends and patterns in the depth and sectoral coverage of commitments are identified. The results from accession negotiations on the rules are reviewed with particular focus on how they compare to the envisaged disciplines on domestic regulation under the General Agreement on Trade in Services Article VI:4. Finally, the performance of Article XII LDC members in their WTO accession services negotiations is reviewed. Overall, the evidence indicates that Article XII members' services bindings go further than those of original WTO members.*

The analyses in the chapters in this book were finalised at the end of December 2014. Since then the Republic of Seychelles acceded to the World Trade Organization (WTO) on 26 April 2015. This expanded total WTO membership from 160 to 161. Please see the editors' note.

## What advances have been made on market opening commitments?

The General Agreement on Trade in Services (GATS) applies to a very wide range of measures and adopts a broad definition of trade in services.[1] It covers four different ways through which services may be supplied internationally. The 'trade barriers' it disciplines often concern measures that governments have adopted 'behind the border'.[2]

As a counterweight to its wide scope, the GATS is a flexible agreement. It does not require that services trade be universally liberalised. Rather, it is built on the notion of 'progressive liberalisation'.[3] This means that members choose the degree of services market opening they are prepared to guarantee legally, and that they are meant to improve it progressively, over time, through successive rounds of negotiations. In practice, members select the sectors in which to undertake market opening commitments, the modes of supply through which they wish to liberalise trade and the overall extent of this liberalisation. Members' selections are registered in documents called 'schedules of specific commitments'.

An interesting question is whether, and to what extent, the specific commitments of Article XII members differ from those undertaken by original WTO members at similar levels of development. Unfortunately, given the textual nature of specific commitments, as opposed to the numerical properties of tariffs, there is no single indicator that can be used to make this comparison. However, several other possible parameters exist, which may be used alone, or in combination, to assess such departures.

The first such parameter is the sectoral coverage of specific commitments. Although no sectoral classification system is mandatory, the GATS schedules have been constructed virtually universally on the basis of the WTO Secretariat services sectoral classification list,[4] which divides

---

[1] Trade in services is defined as comprising four 'modes of supply'. In addition to the 'traditional' notion of the 'cross-border' supply of a service (mode 1), trade may occur through 'consumption abroad' (mode 2), whereby the consumer is supplied a service in the territory of another member, or through the movement of the supplier abroad, either to establish a 'commercial presence' (mode 3) or as a 'natural person' (mode 4).

[2] Measures that the GATS indirectly considers as trade barriers are 'market access' restrictions, which are six types of essentially quota-type limitations, and 'national treatment' limitations, which are measures that provide for less favourable treatment for similar foreign services and service suppliers.

[3] See Article XIX:1.

[4] See WTO document MTN.GNS/W/120, dated 10 July 1991. This classification is generally referred to as 'W/120' after the document symbol it carries.

Table 30.1 *Average number of sub-sectors committed, by level of development*

| WTO members | Average number of sub-sectors committed |
|---|---|
| All members | 55 |
| Developed | 94 |
| Developing and LDCs | 47 |
| *(excluding Article XII members)* | *31* |
| Developing only, no LDCs | 53 |
| *(excluding Article XII members)* | *36* |
| LDCs | 29 |
| *(excluding Article XII members)* | *20* |
| Article XII members | 103 |

*Note:* Average for developed economies does not count individual GATS schedules of members acceding to the EU after 1995. The European Union twelve member states are counted as one member.

services into twelve large sectors that are further subdivided into around 161 sub-sectors.

Out of these 161 services sub-sectors, which are the 'universe' from which members may undertake specific commitments, the number of bindings contributed by Article XII members is striking and significant. As Table 30.1 illustrates, compared to a member-wide average of 55 sub-sectors committed, acceding countries have attained nearly twice as many. In addition, their specific commitments surpass, on average, even those assumed by the most economically advanced members. This is particularly remarkable when one considers that all the economies that have acceded to the WTO are either developing countries or LDCs. And even when compared to the specific commitments scheduled by members at comparable levels of development, acceding governments have listed more than three times as many sub-sectors.

A second useful indicator is the sectoral pattern of schedules. This enables an assessment of whether any notable differences exist between the schedules of original members and those of acceding governments in the terms of those service sectors where they have chosen to undertake legally binding specific commitments. Across all members, there exists a clear ranking of sectors. The service sector that has attracted the highest number of commitments is, by far, tourism. This is followed by infrastructural

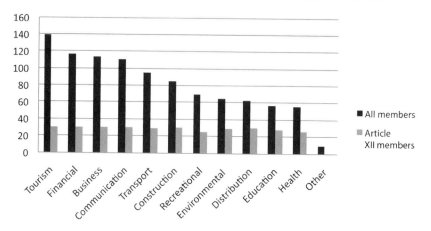

**Figure 30.1**   Sectoral distribution of commitments (the European Union twelve member states are counted as one member).

services, namely financial, business, communication and transport services, ranked in that order. At the bottom of the scale, apart from the residual category of 'other services not classified elsewhere', are the health and education sectors, where public involvement tends to be heaviest. Figure 30.1 illustrates this situation.

However Figure 30.1 also exemplifies that, when it comes to Article XII members, the situation is a lot more uniform. Within this group, all sectors have drawn exactly the same number of specific commitments except for environment, transport, education, health and recreational services, which have not been inscribed in the schedules of between one and five Article XII members. Only 'other services' stands out, as Ukraine alone has included this category in its schedule. Otherwise, virtually all acceding governments have undertaken bindings in all the sectors, at the aggregate level, with only 'other services' being left out. It has to be acknowledged, however, that this is an aggregate measurement, implying that a commitment in one tiny sub-sector is sufficient to qualify the member concerned as having bound the entire sector concerned. Regardless, this 'distortion' applies to all members indiscriminately, and in actual practice a look through members' schedules suggests that it is more likely to affect original WTO members than acceding governments, thus potentially 'overestimating' the extent of the bindings subscribed to by the former group.

A third angle from which to assess the specific commitments undertaken is the extent of the liberalisation bound. This exercise requires very detailed and time-consuming analysis, which is beyond the scope of this publication. However, by proxy and approximation, we have chosen to rely on a count of the instances in which 'none' and 'unbound' appear in schedules, assessed against the number of sub-sectors committed.

In the GATS scheduling parlance, 'none' implies that a given sub-sector has been fully bound, with regard to either market access or national treatment, for the relevant mode of supply. At the opposite end of the spectrum lies the term 'unbound', which indicates that the member concerned retains full discretion with regard to the trade restrictions that it is permitted to apply. Inbetween are commitments which, while guaranteeing some degree of liberalisation, also entitle the member concerned to impose the restrictions it has specified in its schedule. Such commitments are usually termed 'partial commitments'. Simply put, the more 'nones' found in schedules, proportionate to the number of sub-sectors inscribed therein, the higher the degree of liberalisation guaranteed by the member in question.

In counting the instances of 'none' and 'unbound' inscribed in schedules, a number of assumptions have been used. First, every 'none' has been read as referring to a full commitment and every 'unbound' as equating to no binding having been scheduled. In reality, several instances exist where both 'none' and 'unbound' have been qualified by exceptions, thereby rendering the commitments in question partial in nature (i.e. neither completely open nor completely restrictive). Second, when considering the number of sub-sectors included in a schedule, it has been assumed that each sub-sector is accompanied by its own specific entries for the four modes of supply, under both market access and national treatment.[5] Actual schedules, however, often regroup several sub-sectors when it comes to inscribing the level of market access and national treatment granted. What this means is that, although a member having committed five sub-sectors in its schedule is assumed to have inscribed a total of $5 \times 8 = 40$ entries, in practice the actual total is likely to be smaller.

In spite of these approximations, a count of the instances of 'none' and 'unbound' in schedules usefully corroborates previous findings about the overall higher level of liberalisation committed to by acceded members compared to 'original' members. On average, original WTO members have inscribed 'none' 140 times in their schedules, whereas they have

---

[5] Each sub-sector is assumed to be associated with a total of eight inscriptions, i.e. four entries (one for each mode) for market access, and another four for national treatment.

Table 30.2 *Average share (%) of full, partial and no commitments, by group of members*

|  | Full commitments ('none') | Partial commitments | No commitments ('unbound') |
|---|---|---|---|
| **Original members** | 40 | 30 | 30 |
| **Acceded members** | 40 | 40 | 20 |

inscribed 'unbound' in around one hundred instances. These figures need to be assessed against an average of 42 sub-sectors committed, implying that partial commitments have been inscribed in around one hundred cases.

Acceded members, instead, on average have inscribed 'none' more than 350 times, nearly twice as many instances as original WTO members, although against a much higher number of sub-sectors committed on average (103). While it is true that they have also scheduled 'unbound' more frequently than original members (over 150 times), these figures jointly result in a rough estimate of over 320 instances of partial commitments. As illustrated in Table 30.2, in relative terms, therefore, their specific commitments provide for greater openings than those of original members.

In reality, there is a high degree of variation in the amount of liberalisation bound under 'partial commitments', and clearly the analysis undertaken masks those differences. Although a completely truthful assessment of the degree of liberalisation bound could only be undertaken by examining each individual specific commitment in a member's schedule, our analysis does, in spite of all its caveats, provide a sufficiently solid basis to conclude that acceding governments' specific commitments do provide, overall, for a higher degree of liberalisation than those undertaken by original WTO members.

## What advances have been made specifically by Article XII LDC members?

The following part in this chapter specifically focuses its analysis on the LDC Article XII members. Since the establishment of the WTO in 1995, seven LDCs have successfully concluded their WTO accession negotiations. They are Cambodia, Cabo Verde, Lao PDR, Nepal,

Samoa, Vanuatu, and Yemen. The specific analysis here of Article XII LDCs members is twofold, presenting: (i) the horizontal commitments; and (ii) sector-specific commitments, following the GATS schedule format.

### *Trends in horizontal commitments of Article XII LDC members*

In the horizontal commitment section of the services schedules of Article XII LDC members, five limitations are generally encountered, as follows:

1 training opportunities/skills transfer;
2 juridical form; conditions for ownership, management, operation, and scope of activities of investment;
3 land ownership;
4 movement of natural persons (mode 4); and
5 subsidies, investment incentives and other state support measures.

Training opportunities or skills transfer provided by foreign investors to the acceding governments' suppliers are particularly important to LDCs in relation to their capacity constraints. Four out of the seven Article XII LDCs inscribed skills transfer requirements in the horizontal commitments section. The trend first emerged in the Cambodian schedule and has since been followed by Cabo Verde, Lao PDR and Samoa. The wording used by Cambodia and Lao PDR implies an obligation, while Cabo Verde and Samoa use a wording of lighter obligation (i.e. 'may require'). Cambodia's horizontal market access commitments under mode 3 clearly reflect a policy goal to promote Cambodia's training opportunities and skills transfer. By virtue of Cambodia's horizontal commitments, foreign investors are under an obligation to provide 'adequate' training, including promotion to senior positions for their Cambodian staff. Following this notion, Lao PDR inscribed its commitment that foreign investors 'shall' provide adequate training opportunities to Lao PDR nationals. Similarly, Cabo Verde and Samoa inscribed that foreign firms 'may be required' to train and upgrade the technical and management skills of local employees. This feature of inscribing training opportunities in the services schedules of Article XII LDCs is in recognition of the capacity constraints of the countries concerned, coupled with the aim of building domestic capacity through a process of hosting foreign investment. The positioning of this training opportunity requirement in the horizontal commitments section also shows that it is important and central to the entire services economy of Article XII LDC members.

Frequently inscribed in schedules are also measures on the juridical form required for a foreign service provider to establish a commercial presence and the conditions for establishment, ownership, management, operation and scope of investment activities. For example, Nepal, under its market access commitments, committed not to make the conditions more restrictive than at the time of its accession, for ownership, operation, juridical form and scope of activity as set out in a licence or other form of approval establishing or authorising the operation and supply of services by an existing foreign service supplier. Another example is Cambodia, which noted that the rights acquired under the requirements for juridical form are 'set out' in a licence or other form of approval. In the case of Cambodia, the scope of this commitment includes management by foreign service suppliers, whereas Nepal does not list management in its commitment, thus not committing itself in the area of foreign service suppliers' management.

Apart from juridical form, land ownership is an important consideration for service providers, especially for services requiring the establishment of commercial presence under mode 3. Generally, investors may lease but not own land. In this regard, Cambodia, Lao PDR, Samoa, Vanuatu and Yemen have placed specific restrictions on land ownership for non-natural or juridical persons. Cambodia, Vanuatu and Yemen are silent on the length of the lease, while Laos and Samoa have stipulated specific time-frames of seventy-five years and twenty to thirty years, respectively, for leases.[6] The lease terms provide clarity and predictability for investors. They also reflect the domestic policy direction towards investment: whether the Article XII LDC seeks to attract long-term, mid-term or short-term investment.

In relation to movement of natural persons (mode 4), all Article XII LDCs have committed to an exclusive list of categories for temporary entry and stay of foreign natural persons. They further set out the conditions under which those categories of persons may stay within their territories. These commitments generally reflect the need to attract skilled workers, consequently strengthening Article XII LDCs' policy of attracting high-quality foreign direct investment.

---

[6] In the case of Samoa, the time-frame is renewable. Furthermore, the two different time-frames are based on the different types of land usage, whether for industrial purposes or for a hotel.

With respect to subsidies, investment incentives and other state sup-port measures, while Lao PDR[7] and Samoa made no commitments for subsidies, investment incentives and other state support measures, Nepal inscribed in its schedule that it offered incentives and subsidies only to enterprises wholly owned by Nepalese nationals. Cabo Verde restricted subsidies only to nationals, as well as juridical persons established within its territory. Cambodia required any service provider desirous of taking advantage of state incentives under its domestic investment law to provide training opportunities to nationals in exchange.

Apart from these five common trends distilled from the seven Article XII LDC members, a distinguishing feature is found in relation to Nepal's additional commitments. These relate to the environment and repatri-ation of foreign capital. Nepal has offered predictability to investors by stipulating that within thirty days from the date of application, investors would be provided with approvals for their investments by the relevant departments. However, maintaining the balance of providing predictabil-ity for potential investors and protection of the environment, Nepal inscribed an exception in relation to the environment. This exception provided that where an environmental assessment was required, the department could exceed the thirty days in granting approval. It may also withhold approval where the investment fails to meet Nepalese environmental standards.

In addition, in its additional commitments, Nepal listed specific classes of foreign capital investment that may be repatriated outside Nepal. These include receipts from sales of the investors' share of equity, dividends or profits from an equity investment, receipts as payments of principal or interest on foreign loans and amounts received under an agreement to transfer technology approved by the Nepalese Department of Industries or the Department of Cottage and Small Industries.

### Trends in specific commitments of Article XII LDC members

The identification of Article XII LDC members' trends in their horizontal commitments is simpler than the more complex task of identifying the patterns from their sector-specific commitments. The identification of trends and assessments that follow are based on the dual parameters of market access improvements.

---

[7] It indicated that eligibility for these may be limited to particular regions, categories or persons or enterprises.

At a 'disaggregated' level, in the W/120 services sectoral classification list there are 161 sub-sectors. For the purpose of identifying trends in specific commitments of Article XII LDC members, the authors have constructed an LDC services table grid (Table 30.3) on the basis of a more 'aggregated' break-down (i.e. 55 sub-sectors in total). This grid factually summarises, numerically, the specific commitments undertaken by Article XII LDC members, reflecting their respective accession specific commitments, as in its deposited services schedules.

Numerically and sequentially, over the past ten years, starting with Nepal and ending with Yemen, Article XII LDC members have committed to between twenty-seven and thirty-five sub-sectors at the services sub-sectoral level.[8] So, for example, in Table 30.3, Nepal, in business services, committed five sub-sectors out of six.

Moreover, all seven Article XII LDC members with the exception of Samoa, utilised the flexible nature of the services schedules by inscribing transition periods for various services sectors where more time for progressive liberalisation was needed.

Some sectoral analysis is presented in Table 30.4 to illustrate how some Article XII LDC members have formulated their services schedules. None the less, it should be reiterated that commitments do not necessarily mean full liberalisation. Commitments are often inscribed with limitations (for example, a joint venture with a local partner, or limited foreign equity participation).

Several observations could be made of the specific commitments undertaken by Article XII LDC members.

First, commitments are generally valued by foreign services suppliers for the legal certainty which they offer. Market access and national treatment conditions inscribed in schedules are binding and cannot be modified without renegotiation and agreement reached with affected members on any necessary compensation. As with other WTO members, schedules of Article XII LDC members can complement other policies and initiatives aimed at creating attractive conditions for foreign direct investment. Given that Article XII LDC members generally have broader and deeper commitments than original WTO members, they are likely to have taken on bindings that are close to or at the level of their applied

---

[8] Note that the methodology for counting sectors committed in a services schedule generally varies enormously in a different range of research papers. As indicated earlier, this part of the chapter adopts the counting methodology based on the more aggregated sub-sectors.

Table 30.3 *Services sub-sectoral commitments by Article XII LDC members*

| Article XII LDC members | Business services (6)* | Communication services (5) | Construction and Related Engineering Services (5) | Distribution services (5) | Educational services (5) | Environmental services (4) | Financial services (3) | Health Related and Social Services (4) | Tourism and travel related activities (4) | Recreational cultural and sporting activities (5) | Transport services (9) | Other services not included elsewhere | TNS | TNSS (55) |
|---|---|---|---|---|---|---|---|---|---|---|---|---|---|---|
| Nepal (23 April 2004) | 5 | 2 | 2 | 4 | 3 | 3 | 3 | 1 | 2 | 1 | 3 | 0 | 11 | 29 |
| Cambodia (13 October 2004) | 4 | 2 | 5 | 5 | 3 | 4 | 2 | 1 | 3 | 1 | 4 | 0 | 11 | 34 |
| Cabo Verde (3 July 2008) | 6 | 3 | 5 | 3 | 4 | 4 | 2 | 0 | 3 | 2 | 3 | 0 | 10 | 35 |
| Samoa (10 May 2012) | 4 | 3 | 2 | 2 | 5 | 4 | 2 | 0 | 2 | 1 | 2 | 0 | 10 | 27 |
| Vanuatu (24 August 2012) | 3 | 3 | 2 | 4 | 5 | 3 | 2 | 2 | 2 | 0 | 1 | 0 | 10 | 27 |
| Lao, PDR (2 February 2013) | 4 | 2 | 5 | 3 | 5 | 4 | 2 | 1 | 3 | 0 | 1 | 0 | 10 | 30 |
| Yemen (26 June 2014) | 3 | 3 | 4 | 2 | 2 | 4 | 2 | 1 | 2 | 1 | 3 | 0 | 11 | 27 |

*Notes:* In parenthesis is the number of sub-sectors failing under the relevant sector; TNS = total number of sectors; TNSS = total number of sub-sectors.

Table 30.4 *Sectoral analysis of some Article XII LDC members'*
*commitments*

- Only Cabo Verde made commitments under all the sub-sectors under the business services sector.
- Cambodia, Cabo Verde and Lao PDR made commitments on all the sub-sectors under the construction and related engineering services sector.
- Only Cambodia made commitments under all the sub-sectors under the distribution services sector.
- Lao PDR, Samoa and Vanuatu made commitments on all the sub-sectors under the educational services sector.
- Cambodia, Cabo Verde, Lao PDR and Samoa made commitments on all the sub-sectors under the environmental services sector.
- Only Nepal made commitments on all the sub-sectors under the financial services sector.

regime. Should that be the case, their commitments could be said to offer even greater predictability.

Second, many LDCs, in comparison to other more developed countries, are at a relatively early stage of economic reform and institution building. The commitments undertaken, since they are an integral part of the GATS, are enforceable under the WTO Dispute Settlement Understanding – and offer a legal framework for determining the rights and obligations of foreign services suppliers which may sometimes not yet exist in domestic courts.

Third, these commitments were often taken alongside a process of domestic and regulatory reform. While improving market access for foreign services and service suppliers such reforms also incorporate domestic developmental needs or concerns with requirements for the transfer of technology and skills, coupled with national treatment limitations on subsidies and land ownership.

It is still too early to evaluate the impact of these commitments. Yet it has been observed that a number of Article XII LDCs that ratified their Protocol of Accession at the time of this research have made significant improvements in their economic performance. Cabo Verde and Samoa have graduated from the LDC category while Vanuatu will soon follow. Arguably, there are many contributory factors apart from services liberalisation, but for the reasons mentioned above, specific commitments are important in a strategy to attract foreign direct investment in areas of need.

## What advances have been made on domestic regulation disciplines?

Under GATS Article VI:4, WTO members have the mandate to negotiate disciplines to ensure that regulatory requirements and procedures (for example, licensing, qualifications and technical standards) do not constitute unnecessary barriers to trade in services. Article VI:4 indicates that the disciplines are intended to ensure that domestic regulations are, *inter alia*:

(a) based on objective and transparent criteria, such as competence and the ability to supply the service;
(b) no more burdensome than necessary to ensure the quality of the service; and
(c) in the case of licensing procedures, not in themselves a restriction on the supply of the service.

Based on this mandate, members were tasked with developing generally applicable disciplines (i.e. horizontal disciplines), disciplines as appropriate for individual sectors or groups thereof, and the development of general disciplines for professional services. In 1995, a working party on professional services (WPPS) was created and it produced two results in the accountancy sector: the elaboration of voluntary *Guidelines for Mutual Recognition Agreements or Arrangements in the Accountancy Sector*; and the WTO 1998 *Disciplines on Domestic Regulation in the Accountancy Sector* (accountancy disciplines). Further negotiations on domestic regulation disciplines eventually became part of the Doha Development Agenda, which has not yet been concluded.

Given this background, a striking feature of the services accession commitments has been the depth and range of domestic regulation-type disciplines which a number of acceding governments have undertaken. Out of thirty-three Article XII members, ten members have undertaken specific obligations on policies affecting trade in services.[9] See the summary of obligations in Table 30.5.

Broadly speaking, there are two types of obligation which have been undertaken:

---

[9] In total, 63 specific obligations have been committed to by Croatia (1), China (12), Montenegro (4), Russia (11), Chinese Taipei (1), Saudi Arabia (4), Ukraine (8), Vanuatu (1), Viet Nam (17) and Tajikistan (4),

Table 30.5 *Paragraphs with 'horizontal' domestic regulation-type obligations*

| | China | Chinese Taipei | Croatia | Montenegro | Saudi Arabia |
|---|---|---|---|---|---|
| **Transparency** | | | | | |
| Publication of list of regulatory authorities | Paragraph 307 | | | Paragraph 266 | |
| Publication of licensing conditions, procedures and specification of time-frames for review/ decision | Paragraph 308(b) | | | Paragraph 264(i) and (ii) | |
| Responses to enquiries by service suppliers | | | | | |
| Publication of and prior comment on draft regulation | Paragraph 308(a) (but no prior comment) | | | Paragraph 265 (incl. purpose, reasonable time between publication and implementation) | |
| **Licensing and qualification** | | | | | |
| Necessity test – licensing procedures and conditions no more trade-restrictive than necessary – not independent barriers to market access: not restrictions in themselves; not unjustified | Paragraph 308 | | | Paragraph 264 | |
| Independence of regulators | Paragraph 309 | | | | |
| Submission of applications at any time (without invitation) | Paragraph 308(c) | | | Paragraph 264(i) and (ii) | |

| Tajikistan | Russian Federation | Ukraine | Viet Nam |
|---|---|---|---|
| Paragraph 336 | Paragraph 1404 | Paragraph 490 | Paragraph 506 |
| Paragraph 335.ii | Paragraph 1404 (only acts of general application) | Paragraph 489(i) and (ii) Paragraph 490 (laws of general application) | Paragraph 507(b) |
| Paragraph 335(i) Paragraph 337 (incl. purpose, reasonable time between publication and implementation) | Paragraph 1405(a) | Paragraph 491 (incl. purpose, reasonable time between publication and implementation) | Paragraph 507(a) and (b) Paragraph 508 (incl. purpose, reasonable time between publication and implementation) |
| Paragraph 335 | Paragraph 1405 | Paragraph 489 | Paragraph 507 |
| Paragraph338 | | | Paragraph 508 |
| Paragraph 335(iii) | | Paragraph 489(iii) | |

Table 30.5 (*cont.*)

| | China | Chinese Taipei | Croatia | Montenegro | Saudi Arabia |
|---|---|---|---|---|---|
| Treatment of incomplete applications/ identification of missing information/ opportunity to resubmit | Paragraph 308(e) and (g) | | | Paragraph 264(v) | |
| Verification and assessment of qualifications (acceptance of authenticated copies) | | | | | |
| Time-frame for processing of applications/ decisions taken promptly/within period specified | Paragraph 308(b) and (f) | | | Paragraph 264(ii) and (vi) | |
| Permission to supply service after registration | Paragraph 308(h) | | | | |
| Fees commensurate with administrative costs | Paragraph 308(d) | | | Paragraph 264(iv) | |
| Licensing examinations (professionals) at reasonable intervals | Paragraph 308(i) | | | Paragraph 264(viii) | |
| Information on status of application/decision/ reasons for rejection | Paragraph 308(g) and (h) | | | Paragraph 264(vii) | |

| Tajikistan | Russian Federation | Ukraine | Viet Nam |
|---|---|---|---|
| Paragraph 335(vi) | Paragraph 1405(d)<br>Paragraph 1405(g) | Paragraph 489(v)<br>and (vi) | Paragraph 507(e) |
| | Paragraph 1405(b) | | |
| Paragraph 335(iv) | Paragraph 1405(c)<br>(fees not in<br>themselves a<br>restriction) | Paragraph 489(iv) | Paragraph 507(d)<br>(fees not in<br>themselves a<br>restriction) |
| Paragraph 335(vi) | Paragraph 1405(i)<br>(not for financial<br>svs) | Paragraph 489(vii) | Paragraph 507(i) |
| Paragraph 335(vi) | Paragraph 1405(d)<br>Paragraph 1405(e)<br>(financial svs)<br>Paragraph 1405(f)<br>Paragraph 1405(h) | Paragraph 489(v)<br>and (vi) | Paragraph 507(e)<br>and (f) |

(a) 'horizontal' obligations which apply to all services sectors included in the acceding government's schedule of specific commitments and address issues similar to those currently under GATS Article VI:4 negotiations;

(b) sector-specific obligations which address particular regulatory issues.

### 'Horizontal' domestic-regulation type obligations

These specific obligations go further than the existing provisions of GATS Article VI (domestic regulation) as they require acceding governments to undertake additional commitments to ensure that their licensing procedures and conditions are transparent, reasonable, impartial and no more burdensome than necessary.[10] This result thus provides a degree of certainty to members that their services suppliers will be treated fairly, predictably, and in a non-discriminatory manner. To illustrate, Table 30.5 provides a summary of the key domestic regulation-type obligations that acceding governments have undertaken.

Not all of the key issues, which have been the subject of much discussion in the domestic regulation negotiations, have been addressed in Accession Protocols. There are, for instance, no specific obligations on qualification requirements and procedures. Nor are there any provisions on establishing a single window for receiving applications or on aligning technical standards with international standards. Rather the focus has been on improving the transparency of regulations, and on disciplining the use of licensing procedures and conditions. Key among these obligations is the so-called 'necessity test', a potentially powerful discipline which would allow WTO members to challenge other members on whether a less burdensome and trade-restrictive measure could have been used to achieve that particular regulatory objective.

GATS Article VI:4 indicates that the disciplines should aim to ensure that measures of domestic regulation do not constitute unnecessary barriers to trade in services. Similar language can be found in TBT Agreement Article 2.2 and SPS Agreement Article 5.6. The 'necessity tests' under these agreements focus on whether a legitimate objective chosen by a WTO member could equally be achieved by means of a reasonably available alternative that is less trade restrictive. Governments should thus assess, when adopting regulations, whether they could use an

---

[10] For example, China, Montenegro, Russia, Ukraine, Viet Nam and Tajikistan.

alternative measure that would be equally able to achieve the policy objective chosen, but which would be less trade restrictive.

Using 'necessity' tests similar to those found in the TBT or SPS agreements in disciplines on domestic regulation have been a highly contentious issue in the GATS negotiations. For some members, such requirements are viewed with concern as they fear that their autonomy to choose certain policy objectives may be excessively restricted. On the other hand, proponents of the principle of such a test argue that the disciplines would be significantly devalued if they did not contain a means to address unnecessarily burdensome requirements or disguised trade restrictions. It is worth noting that WTO dispute panel and Appellate Body decisions have consistently focused on the necessity of the measure used to achieve the specified objective and not the necessity of the objective *per se*.[11]

The other area where the specific obligations have made headway has been on ensuring greater transparency of the regulatory environment (Table 30.6). Efforts have also been made to bring about greater certainty in the implementation of regulations and procedures. Service suppliers typically expect that rules (e.g. assessment criteria for an application) and procedures (e.g. deadlines for submission and time-frames for processing applications) will not be modified with a view to treating applicants unfairly. If regulations need to be modified, due process would generally require that applicants should have a reasonable time period to adjust to amended criteria or procedures. Similarly, there has been considerable attention given to the criteria for setting fees in the domestic regulation negotiations. All of these issues appear to have been addressed in the obligations undertaken by a number of acceding governments. Interestingly, there do not appear to be any obligations requiring acceding governments to simplify their licensing procedures, an issue of considerable discussion in the GATS domestic regulation negotiations. However, this may be because such issues would already be covered by the 'necessity' provision discussed earlier.

### Sector-specific regulatory disciplines

In heavily regulated sectors, such as financial services and telecommunication services, a good number of specific obligations have been undertaken to underpin the liberalisation of the market. These serve to:

---

[11] See 'Necessity Tests' in the WTO: Note by the Secretariat, see WTO document S/WPDR/W/27/Add.1, 18 January 2011.

Table 30.6 *Typical domestic regulation-type disciplines found in acceding governments' specific obligations*

| | |
|---|---|
| **Transparency** | |
| Regulatory authorities | Publish list of all organisations responsible for authorising, approving or regulating service activities for each service sector, including those organisations with delegated authority |
| Licensing conditions, procedures and time-frames | Publish licensing conditions, procedures and time-frames for review and decision; ensure that authorities keep to specified time-frames |
| Advance publication and prior comment | Publish laws, regulations, licensing procedures, conditions and implementing measures of general application, including their purpose, prior to coming into effect and allow for prior comment; ensure reasonable time between publication of the final regulation or other implementing measure and its effective date |
| **Licensing procedures and conditions** | |
| Necessity test | Ensure that licensing procedures and conditions would not act as barriers (or independent barriers) to market access and be more trade restrictive than necessary and not restrictions in themselves |
| Independence of regulator | Regulatory authorities to be separate from and not accountable to any service supplier which they regulate[a] |
| Submission of applications | Licensing applications can be submitted without invitation |
| Status and treatment of complete/incomplete applications | Inform applicant whether the application was considered complete, and in the case of incomplete applications, identify the additional information required to complete the application and provide an opportunity to rectify deficiencies; if an application was terminated or denied, inform the applicant in writing and without delay of the reasons for such action and allow re-submission |
| Time-frame for processing applications | Process and take decision within the period specified or if no time period, without undue delay |

Table 30.6 (*cont.*)

| | |
|---|---|
| Ability to supply service after licensing | The licence or approval would enable the applicant to start the commercial operations upon registration of the company and/or fulfilment of other similar administrative requirements |
| Fees commensurate with administrative costs | Any fees charged, which are not deemed to include fees determined through auction or a tendering process, to be commensurate with the administrative cost of processing an application |
| Licensing examinations at reasonable intervals | In case examinations are held for the licensing of professionals, such examinations are to be scheduled at reasonable intervals |

[a]In the case of Russia, the relevant commitment language only covers 'not accountable to', not mentioning 'be separate from'.

*Source*: based on the review of the 63 specific obligations which have been committed to by Croatia (1), China (12), Montenegro (4), Russia (11), Chinese Taipei (1), Saudi Arabia (4), Ukraine (8), Vanuatu (1), Viet Nam (17), and Tajikistan (4).

– pre-commit the acceding government to consult with members to develop domestic regulations on a specific services activity;[12]
– build members' trust in the acceding government's service-related domestic policy, as the acceding government specifically declares that a certain domestic policy that is incompatible with its GATS schedule would be brought to the WTO Dispute Settlement Panel;[13]
– identify, explicitly, the relevant domestic laws on certain services sectors, boosting members' confidence in legislation-based domestic reform in the acceding governments;[14]
– ensure non-discriminatory treatment, when regulatory changes occur, for information access in a certain service sector, so that foreign services suppliers receive fair competitive opportunities in the service market of the acceding government;[15]

---

[12] For example, China on 'sales away from a fixed location' (paragraph 310).
[13] For example, China.
[14] For example, Montenegro, Russia, Saudi Arabia, Vanuatu and Viet Nam.
[15] For example, Ukraine for the insurance sector.

- establish regulatory frameworks which would be consistent with internationally recognised standards and principles;[16]
- guarantee that regulatory bodies would be independent from any service suppliers governed by them and that foreign service suppliers would have the right to choose their partners.[17]

To what extent can the experience from accessions be used to develop the GATS disciplines on domestic regulation? There are no easy answers. Certain peculiarities of the accession process have to be taken into account. First, the acceding governments are usually under considerable pressure to meet the requirements established by existing WTO members. Their ability to 'push back' demands can be said to be relatively weak. Second, most of these obligations have been undertaken by transition economies which were already in the process of ambitious regulatory reforms, or were using their WTO accession to give that project greater political weight. It is not clear that such a dynamic situation would necessarily exist for the whole WTO membership.

That being said, there are also a number of interesting considerations. For one, it would seem that certain issues can be approached from a horizontal perspective, while others have been left at the sectoral level. In general, horizontal obligations were typically those which were concerned with transparency and in reducing discretion and arbitrariness in licensing processes and conditions. Sector-specific obligations, on the other hand, have tended to be aimed at ensuring that the regulatory environment does not skew competitive opportunities. Arguably, some of these issues could also be addressed through national treatment commitments as their main aim would appear to be to curb the modification of conditions of competition in favour of national service suppliers.

Services trade agreements in the twenty-first century will increasingly have to grapple with regulatory issues. This is driven by two main factors. First, as a result of autonomous liberalisation by many countries, formal barriers preventing the access of foreign suppliers to the domestic market have been significantly reduced. As such barriers come down, it is increasingly evident that what matters in services trade is not just access barriers but the overall contestability of the market and the conduciveness of the regulatory environment to business. Second, today's economic system is characterised by global value chains in both goods and services

---

[16] For example, Ukraine for direct branching for foreign insurance companies.
[17] For example, Tajikistan.

with suppliers linked across many countries. Regulatory divergence hampers the efficient functioning of such production, which depends on the fast and seamless flow of intermediate services and products across borders. So, while the Accession Packages may not give the full answer on how to address these issues, they do provide some food for thought.

Acceding governments' specific commitments do provide, overall, for a higher degree of liberalisation than those undertaken by original WTO members. This is borne out by the wider range of sub-sectors committed and the relatively high number of full bindings without market access or national treatment limitations. Acceding members have also taken on board many more regulatory commitments which go beyond the existing GATS obligations on domestic regulation, including the specific obligation to ensure that regulations are no more burdensome than necessary. It is striking that Article XII LDCs have also made far-reaching commitments.

# 31

# WTO accession and the private sector: the nexus of rules and market opportunities

RAJESH AGGARWAL AND CHARLOTTA FALENIUS

## ABSTRACT

*A country's bid for WTO membership can promote a feeling of challenge and uncertainty among members of the private sector as the long-established methods of conducting business are susceptible to undergoing considerable change. In order to overcome the potential resistance to this change, acceding governments have responded to the concerns of their businesses by adopting strategies to raise awareness of the long-term benefits of reform during the negotiating period. In this chapter we document some of the benefits related to trade and investment for Article XII members that have undertaken awareness raising strategies and necessary reforms during their accession processes. This chapter underlines that accession commitments, which are critical to bringing about domestic policy and regulatory reforms, need to be implemented in the right spirit to develop business competitiveness in the long run.*

WTO accession offers predictability of new market opportunities to acceding governments while requiring the implementation of a number of rules and agreements. This process can conjure up fears in the private sector as it may anticipate increased competition, a shift away from established systems of doing business and threats, especially to long-standing vested interests. After all, membership entails a range of legally binding policy changes and commitments requiring considerable efforts from acceding governments. As the private sector encounters short-term challenges stemming from more competition, acceding governments have responded by allaying the apprehensions of their businesses by raising awareness of the long-term benefits of reform well in advance during the negotiation period and making provisions for assisting businesses to operate within the new paradigm.

WTO members cover more than 97 per cent of world trade. Hence, integration into this nearly universal community acts as a strong incentive for membership. The true benefits of WTO accession have, however, been subject to numerous debates in the academic world relating to the costs and benefits of accession. As illustrated by recent cases, with sufficient preparation, including a carefully drafted plan, awareness-raising for stakeholders and preparation for adjustment, the long-term benefits and improved business environment with increased predictability of market access and binding rules outweigh the short-term costs of the negotiation process and the reforms that follow.

## Involving stakeholders in the accession process

Starting with the submission of the application, the establishment of the working party and ending with the acceptance of the country's report, protocol and lists of commitments at the WTO General Council or the Ministerial Conference, the accession process requires considerable resources and time from the acceding government. The lengthy process, involving scrutiny from other members, takes several years; the shortest negotiation finished in just under three years, while the longest took more than eighteen years to complete.

Once the decision to join the WTO is made, the candidate government will need to adopt a clear accession plan and promote the idea to relevant constituencies. With a view to selecting the best mix of national and international practices to guide the negotiations, the private sector and civil society should be directly involved in the negotiations for WTO accession. For example, in the case of Cambodia, national consensus was considered a key element with the launch of broad awareness-raising campaigns about the WTO and related agreements as well as the business implications of accession (Siphana, 2004). Likewise, Chinese chief negotiator Mr Long Yongtu has stated that in order to lead successful negotiations countries must 'mobilise domestic support'. Creating the basis for a successful accession, during the negotiation process Chinese officials visited companies and representatives from the private sector in cities and provinces in order to shed light on what was being negotiated and the potential benefits of accession (Yongtu, 2011).

By including the private sector in the policy process early enough during the accession phase, the effectiveness of reforming government policies is often improved through the private sector's first-hand knowledge of interests and potential challenges related to the implementation commitments. Throughout the accession process, by committing to WTO rules and necessary reform, the acceding governments and their private sectors have the opportunity to benefit from a stable business environment and integrate into global supply chains.

## The trade effect of WTO accession and domestic reform

WTO accession alone, without adequate domestic reform, including institutional and supply-side capacity as well as commitments to opening markets, cannot increase growth or benefit the business community in the long term. In order to ensure that sustainable development and economic growth are attained through the accession process, it is necessary to increase market access as well as to strengthen developing countries' supply-side capacity by involving the private sector (Drabek and Bachetta, 2004; Sauvé, 2005).

There seems to be a clear correlation between the degree of reform undertaken during the accession negotiations and the positive trade effects (Subramanian and Wei, 2007; Tang and Wei, 2009) to which examples of acceded developing economies such as China speak. Membership of the WTO and related reforms send a strong signal to the global community of an enhanced governance framework, conducive to investment opportunities and trade.

For developing countries, the positive impact of WTO membership on trade seems to come largely from the members that joined the WTO after 1994 and were thus required to undergo more rigorous accession negotiations than those that joined before. The developing countries that joined during the first decades of the General Agreement on Tariffs and Trade (GATT), benefiting from GATT Article XXVI:5, were not required by other members to reform their economies and have generally not experienced the same positive trade effects as those that joined the organisation after 1994. These results were obtained even when controlling for selection bias in the acceded transition economies. In fact, it has been reported that the effects of policy commitments are even stronger in poor governance countries (Tang and Wei, 2009). These findings underline the importance of liberalisation combined with adequate reform.

Some studies have, however, questioned the effect on trade, claiming that countries within the WTO do not have significantly different trade patterns from countries that are not members, and that change in trade policy does not correlate to WTO membership (Rose, 2004, 2007). Further studies have, however, pointed out that, while presenting a well-researched argument, these observations have not accounted for a number of variables such as the far-reaching obligations the WTO trading system imposes even for non-members or bilateral heterogeneity between the countries studied (Tomz et al., 2007; Eicher and Henn, 2011). A more comprehensive assessment shows that the WTO has promoted world trade significantly, by as much as 120 per cent, but the distribution of this effect has been uneven due to the uneven commitments taken. While developing country imports have reportedly experienced little change, their exporters have significantly benefited from WTO accession (Subramanian and Wei, 2007).

### Short-term costs and long-term benefits of reform

Following liberalisation commitments made during accession, acceding governments' businesses are likely to experience structural changes when confronted with increased import competition. The accession commitments, which in some cases go beyond the GATT/WTO agreements, include short-term costs that the affected domestic stakeholders should be aware of. Changes in the terms of trade result in resources being reallocated, with some stakeholders benefiting and others losing (Cattaneo and Primo Braga, 2009). Accession also affects the revenue of both government and households. For example, after China's accession, it was found that nearly 90 per cent of urban households gained from WTO accession while a significant number of rural households experienced minor losses in the short run (Chen and Ravallion, 2004).

A more immediate cost for accession is presented in the bureaucratic challenge of implementing commitments and agreements. For example, for Cambodia the cost of implementation of the Customs Valuation Agreement has been estimated at more than US$4 million (Sauvé, 2005). The financial repercussions of policy reform and the implementation of commitments need to be adequately taken into consideration during the negotiation process, with sufficient adjustment provisions and relevant assistance.

While incurring short-term costs, WTO membership, through reform, provides significant long-term benefits for the economy concerned. Accession guarantees stability from reversal on the market-oriented reform agenda with legally binding commitments which may initially have encountered resistance during the negotiation phase (Tang and Wei, 2009). Reassuring the business community, the accession process may act as an external stimulus to the domestic reform agenda, ensuring that reforms are 'locked in'. For example, during China's negotiations, the accession process was said to have exerted a 'healthy and positive pressure [on] Chinese industry', which would otherwise not have become competitive internationally (Yongtu, 2011).

Through WTO accession, export-oriented sectors are likely to experience benefits from trade liberalisation, with imported materials becoming cheaper and more readily available. By adopting WTO rules and agreements, developing coherent trade policies and gaining access to the impartial WTO dispute settlement mechanism, economies also achieve a more attractive investment climate with enhanced predictability and stability. The relationship between trade and investment has clear implications for competitiveness, economic development and job creation. Moreover, a higher level of participation in global value chains and increased domestic value added from trade are generally encountered in countries with higher rates of foreign direct investment (FDI) relative to the size of their economy (UNCTAD, 2013).

## Positive membership experiences from developing countries

### Enhanced trade and inward foreign investment

The literature on the country-specific effects of WTO accession has focused on China or Russia, largely because of its effects on their substantial trade. China's example, no doubt, underlines the trade-promoting effects of WTO accession. China became a member of the WTO in December 2001, bringing its laws and regulations into line with WTO regulations and reforming its economy with a view to creating a friendly business environment. The reforms have resulted in considerable growth in imports and exports as well as FDI (Zhao and Wang, 2009; Xiaomei, 2009). While there were short-term concerns about issues such as social stability and the implementation schedule, in the wake of accession macroeconomic shocks were avoided and the reforms produced a more predictable investment climate, promoting China's trade expansion. In the first eight years of membership, China's total trade value expanded fivefold and economic relations with its major trading partner, the United States, were stabilised (Zhao and Wang, 2009). Figure 31.2 indicates the evolution of China's exports on transformed goods after WTO accession.

Although the accession of least-developed countries (LDCs) has received less attention than that of the larger developing economies, they represent equally interesting case studies of the trade effects of WTO membership and related domestic reform. For example, Cambodia (with WTO Article XII accession) has undergone significant reforms anchored in the WTO accession process and presents a positive trade effect. This gives credit to the findings reporting a link between reform and economic gains.

Cambodia applied for WTO membership in 1994 and completed its terms of accession in 2003 as the first LDC member. The country used the WTO accession process to pursue trade liberalisation and far-reaching reforms with the government involving all the relevant stakeholders, in particular the private sector (Siphana, 2004). Cambodia's exports have grown in absolute terms in the post-accession period and there is also evidence of product and market diversification of exports. The accession process also induced improvements in the country's investment climate directly linked to FDI, as Figure 31.1 illustrates.

WTO accession has also had generally a significant positive effect on Viet Nam's imports and the provision of FDI (see Figure 31.1), indirectly

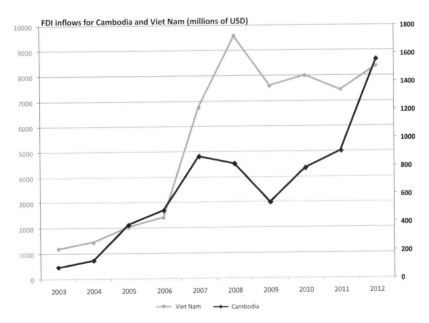

**Figure 31.1**   FDI inflows for Cambodia and Viet Nam (International Trade Centre (ITC), Geneva; the figure was constructed with data from the United Nations Conference on Trade and Development (UNCTAD) World Investment Reports (2005, 2013)).

encouraging the country's exports (Hanh, 2011). Viet Nam applied for membership of the WTO in 1995 and became a member in January 2007. Through the accession process, Viet Nam benefited from a pronounced surge in investments between 2006 and 2008, continuing beyond the financial crisis.

The above-mentioned cases illustrate that the private sector in recently acceded economies benefits from enhanced inward investment. Through committing to reform, economies have moved towards better governance, which has been found to be a critical element in attracting investment and increasing countries' productivity (Evenett and Primo Braga, 2005; ITC, 2013).

### Integration into global value chains

WTO membership seems to offer a path for integration into global production chains, which are currently changing the nature of economic globalisation. Products are no longer entirely manufactured and assembled in a single country, but also include the activity of several countries from where the intermediates are exported. Trade within global value chains can be difficult to assess. The share of exports a country has in transformed goods, however, presents one indicator of involvement in global value chains.

Figures 31.2 and 31.3 show the change in transformed export goods of China and Viet Nam. With a highly interconnected economy China, having joined the WTO in 2001, displays a marginal increase in the share of transformed goods in the following years, whereas Viet Nam, following its accession to the WTO in 2007, has experienced a clear increase in the share of transformed exports, indicating a potential move up the global value chain.

As products cross borders multiple times during the transformation process, the negative effects of trade barriers are enhanced by the existence of global value chains. The regulatory reforms and liberalisation that follow WTO accession can help remove these barriers, thereby integrating countries more effectively into the world economy.

The private sector in Article XII members has benefited, as is evident from the increased trade and inward investment that have followed WTO membership in various countries. With acceding governments reporting a more stable and predictable business environment, secure business transactions and enhanced investment opportunities, WTO membership seems to offer a path for integration into the world economy. The benefits accrue to enterprises in these countries if they are able

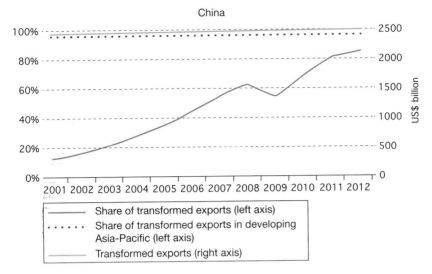

**Figure 31.2** Evolution of exports of transformed goods for China (based on International Trade Center (ITC), trade map data).

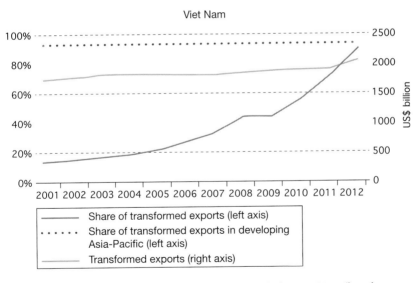

**Figure 31.3** Evolution of exports of transformed goods for Viet Nam (based on International Trade Center (ITC), trade map data).

to seize new opportunities to foster linkages with the value chains of foreign investors which are likely to emerge following improvements in the business and investment climate.

The widely adopted export-oriented approach which WTO accession promotes functions efficiently when other fundamental conditions at the core of growth policies are in place. More importantly, the accession process is not only a means to an end, but also a crucial part in developing the competitiveness of acceding economies through domestic reform and dialogue between the public and private sectors in achieving national consensus. The WTO negotiation process plays a key role as an opportunity to engage in domestic policy and regulatory reform and to reserve sufficient resources for potential structural adjustment following liberalisation.

## References

Cattaneo, O. and C. Primo Braga (2009). 'Everything you always wanted to know about WTO accession', Washington DC, The World Bank Group, Policy Research Working Paper No. 5116.

Chen, S. and M. Ravallion (2004). 'Welfare impacts of China's accession to the WTO', in D. Bhattasali, S. Li and W. Martin (eds.), *China and the WTO: Accession, Policy Reform, and Poverty Reduction Strategies*. Washington DC, World Bank, pp. 261–282.

Drabek, Z. and M. Bachetta (2004). 'Tracing the effects of WTO accession on policy-making in sovereign states: preliminary lessons from the recent experience of transition countries', *The World Economy*, 27(7): 1083–1124.

Eicher, T. and C. Henn (2011). 'In search of WTO trade effects: preferential trade agreements promote trade strongly, but unevenly', *Journal of International Economics*, 83(2): 137–153.

Evenett, S. J. and C. Primo Braga (2005). *WTO Accession: Lessons from Experience.* Washington DC, The World Bank Group.

Hanh, P. T. H. (2011). 'Does WTO accession matter for the dynamics of foreign direct investment and trade?', *Economics of Transition*, 19(2): 255–285.

International Trade Center (ITC) (2013). *Acceding to the WTO: Law and Practice.* Geneva, ITC.

Rose, A. (2004). 'Do we really know that the WTO increases trade?', *American Economic Review*, 94(1): 98–114.

(2007). 'Do we really know that the WTO increases trade? Reply', *American Economic Review*, 97(5): 2019–2026.

Sauvé, P. (2005). 'Economic impact and social adjustment costs of accession to the World Trade Organization', *Asia-Pacific Trade and Investment Review*, 1(1): 27–49.

Siphana, S. (2004). 'Experiences from Cambodia', in *Accession to the WTO: Country Experiences and Technical Assistance*. Eschborn, GTZ.

Subramanian, A. and S.-J. Wei (2007). 'The WTO promotes trade, strongly but unevenly', *Journal of International Economics*, 72(1): 151–175.

Tang, M.-K. and S.-J. Wei (2009). 'The value of making commitments externally: evidence from WTO accessions', *Journal of International Economics*, 78(2): 216–229.

Tomz, M., J. L. Goldstein and D. Rivers (2007). 'Do we really know that the WTO increases trade?', *American Economic Review*, 97(5): 2005–2018.

UNCTAD (2005). *World Investment Report: Transnational Corporations and the Internationalization of R&D*. Geneva, United Nations Conference on Trade and Development.

   (2013). *World Investment Report: Global Value Chains: Investment and Trade for Development*. Geneva, United Nations Conference on Trade and Development.

Xiaomei, E. (2009). 'WTO accession and sustainable development: challenges and policy responses', *Journal of World Trade*, 43(3): 541–569.

Yongtu, L. (2011). 'China's role in the new global order', speech given to the Open Forum at the World Trade Organization, Geneva.

Zhao, L. and Y. Wang (2009). 'China's pattern of trade and growth after WTO accession: lessons for other developing countries', *Journal of Chinese Economic and Foreign Trade Studies*, 2(3): 178–210.

# 32

# WTO accession and accession to the Agreement on Government Procurement: what is the relationship? Why should WTO acceding governments also consider GPA accession?

ROBERT D. ANDERSON AND ANNA CAROLINE MÜLLER

## ABSTRACT

*The WTO Agreement on Government Procurement (GPA) is unique in its duality as an international trade agreement that promotes and preserves market opening and as an instrument for the promotion of good governance. The recent successful renegotiation of the GPA has enhanced its coverage so that it now provides access to markets valued at US$1.7 trillion annually. In addition, the text of the GPA has been effectively modernised, making it more relevant, economically, and simplifying its implementation. Although not a substitute for domestic procurement reforms, it is a catalytic and reinforcing factor for reforms that enhance transparency and competition internally – thereby yielding important gains for governments and citizens in terms of value for money in national procurement activities. Participation in the GPA can also promote inward foreign direct investment by signalling a country's commitment to good governance and the fair treatment of all players under national legislation. The review in this chapter of the evidence from WTO and GPA accessions indicates that the WTO accession negotiations of Article XII members are often used to leverage increased GPA accessions. Specifically, of the members that have acceded to the WTO pursuant to Article XII of the Marrakesh Agreement Establishing the WTO (WTO Agreement), twenty-two have undertaken GPA-related commitments, and seven subsequently joined the GPA. Out*

The analyses in the chapters in this book were finalised at the end of December 2014. Since then the Republic of Seychelles acceded to the World Trade Organization (WTO) on 26 April 2015. This expanded total WTO membership from 160 to 161. Please see the editors' note.

*of the ten WTO members that are currently seeking accession to the GPA, nine undertook commitments related to GPA accession at the time of their WTO accessions, pursuant to Article XII of the WTO Agreement. The chapter concludes that, even though WTO accession and GPA accession are formally separate steps, the basic policy decision as to whether to join the GPA is often made long before GPA accession negotiations are started, at the time of WTO accession. This chapter provides countries and other WTO members considering taking on accession commitments with a strengthened understanding of the relevant benefits and costs.*

Increasingly, governments that join the WTO are encouraged to make commitments, at the time of their accession, to also seek to join, eventually, the WTO Agreement on Government Procurement (GPA).[1] GPA accession may seem, to some, 'a bridge too far' – an 'add-on' to the WTO accession process that requires significant policy reforms and institution-building processes. Some WTO accession candidates resist pressures to make GPA accession commitments, citing the formally 'optional' nature of the GPA in the WTO and its asserted lack of relevance to developing economies. Others make commitments but approach the actual GPA accession process with caution.

Accession to the GPA is, to be sure, a significant step with regard to which WTO accession candidates have a legitimate interest in receiving detailed information and in undertaking a careful evaluation of potential benefits and costs. Membership of the GPA entails an increased degree of transparency and exposure to international competition in a sector of the domestic economy that, in many cases, has traditionally been closed to trade and/or used to promote local suppliers. It requires the adaptation of relevant laws and institutions to the rules embedded in the GPA. In part for these reasons, until now, the GPA has been of interest principally to developed countries.

Yet, there are good reasons for even developing and transitional economies acceding to the WTO to consider accession to the GPA, and to pursue such accession enthusiastically. To begin with, GPA accession potentially provides access to markets valued at approximately US$1.7 trillion annually.[2] Furthermore, while not a substitute for domestic

---

[1] See, for details of countries having such commitments, Tables 32.1 and 32.2.

[2] See, for background, Anderson, Müller *et al.* (2012). The estimate of US$1.7 trillion includes, in addition to the coverage considered in this publication, an estimated US $80–100 billion that was added to the market access commitments under the GPA as a result of its recent renegotiation, which is discussed below.

reforms, it can catalyse and reinforce reforms that enhance transparency and competition internally, thereby yielding important gains in terms of value for money in national procurement activities. This can be an important benefit, for example, in countries seeking to improve national infrastructure endowments. GPA accession can also encourage inward foreign direct investment (FDI), by signalling an economy's commitment to good governance and the fair treatment of all players under relevant national legislation.

Accession to the GPA also entails challenges and potential costs. These may include costs relating to the adaptation of national legislation and procurement systems in addition to potential impacts on local suppliers. Yet, as will be discussed in this chapter, there are reasons for believing that such costs/challenges may be modest in relation to the potential gains, at least in many cases.

This chapter delves into the relationship between WTO and GPA accession, and the benefits and costs for acceding governments also seeking GPA accession. In addition to clarifying the basic nature of the GPA and the processes involved in acceding to it, it aims to elaborate on the complementarities involved in WTO and GPA accession.

## Basic aspects of the GPA

This section outlines the basics of the procurement sector in general and the GPA specifically. First, it describes why government procurement and good public procurement policies are important for economic progress and the development of any country. It then provides information on how the GPA contributes to the adoption of sound procurement policies based on the principles of non-discrimination, transparency and competition in participating economies.

### The procurement sector: what it is, why it matters and how international trade disciplines can help to ensure better outcomes

Government procurement refers generally to the purchasing of goods, services and construction services, or any combination thereof, by, or on behalf of, governmental bodies in fulfilment of their public service responsibilities. Government procurement is of considerable economic significance at both the domestic and international levels, accounting, for example, for 15–20 per cent of gross domestic product (GDP), on average, across the Organisation for Economic Co-operation and Development (OECD) economies and potentially an even greater proportion of economic activity in some developing countries.[3] At the domestic level, government procurement enables governments to deliver both developmentally significant public infrastructure such as highway systems, ports, airports, hospitals and sewerage systems and socially vital public services such as health care and education. In the past decade, the global importance of the government procurement sector as a whole has been reinforced by: (i) increased emphasis on government spending and infrastructure investment during and in the aftermath of the global economic crisis; and (ii) the huge and expanding infrastructure needs of the emerging economies, including not only China, India and other Asian economies, but also Eastern European transition economies and the emerging markets of Latin America and Africa.

Government procurement systems that are efficient, transparent and competitive can contribute substantially to the achievement of value for money and to the efficient utilisation of taxpayers' funds. Practical experience and the relevant economic literature establish a direct relationship between the extent of competition in government procurement markets and the achievement of best value for money in related activities. Furthermore, with public procurement accounting for the proportion of GDP noted above, every 1 per cent saving on public procurement expenditures achieved through more transparent and competitive procurement processes releases resources of up to 0.2 per cent of GDP that can be put to alternative uses.

International trade liberalisation is an important tool to improve the functioning of government procurement markets.[4] In addition to providing access to foreign markets for national suppliers, a key benefit of such liberalisation lies in the enhanced competition in the domestic market that external liberalisation creates. International liberalisation of government procurement markets can also provide access to technology that may not otherwise be available in the domestic market and, as already noted, encourage inward FDI. While, to be sure, these effects also create benefits for foreign market participants, a substantial part of the gains arising from international liberalisation will accrue directly to the countries undergoing liberalisation.

---

[3] See OECD (2002).    [4] See also Anderson, Kovacic and Müller (2011).

## The GPA: its nature, aims and disciplines

The GPA promotes the mutual opening of government procurement markets by the participating member governments, and is an instrument that can potentially deliver both market access and good governance benefits for participating countries. As a result of several rounds of negotiations, the GPA parties have opened procurement activities worth an estimated US$1.7 trillion annually to international competition (i.e. to suppliers from GPA parties offering goods, services or construction services).

The GPA is a plurilateral agreement, meaning that it comprises only a subset of the full membership of the WTO. Currently, the GPA binds forty-three WTO members which formally constitute fifteen 'parties' (the European Union and its twenty-eight member states are counted as a single party).[5] On 6 April 2014, a revised version of the GPA entered into force when two-thirds of the parties accepted the Protocol of Amendment that had been adopted on 30 March 2012.

The GPA is composed of two principal parts: the text of the GPA and the parties' market access commitments which are set out in detailed schedules known as the 'Appendix I Annexes'. The text of the GPA establishes rules requiring that open, fair and transparent conditions of competition be ensured in government procurement. Box 32.1 provides additional information on the contents of the GPA.

It should be emphasised that the GPA's rules do not automatically apply to all the procurement activities of each party. Rather, the coverage schedules play a critical role in determining whether a procurement activity is covered by the GPA or not. Only those procurement activities that are carried out by covered entities purchasing listed goods, services or construction services of a value exceeding specified thresholds are covered by the GPA. These important details are specified in each party's market access schedules (the Appendix I Annexes). As we shall see below, the negotiation of these schedules is an important aspect of the GPA accession process.

## Recent renegotiation of the GPA and its coming into force

As mentioned above, a revised version of the GPA recently entered into force. This version, which includes a modernised and streamlined text as

---

[5] The fifteen parties are Armenia; Canada; Chinese Taipei; the European Union with its twenty-eight member states; Hong Kong, China; Iceland; Israel; Japan; the Republic of Korea; Liechtenstein; the Netherlands with respect to Aruba; Norway; Singapore; Switzerland; and the United States.

BOX 32.1 MAIN ELEMENTS OF THE WTO GPA

The WTO GPA, signed by most of the world's industrialised economies at the conclusion of the Uruguay Round of multilateral trade negotiations in 1994, provides an international legal framework for the liberalisation and governance of public procurement markets. The GPA embodies the following main elements:

- general rules guaranteeing national treatment, non-discrimination and transparency with respect to each party's 'covered procurement markets'. Additional specific requirements regarding the transparency of procurement-related information (e.g. relevant statutes and regulations; evaluation criteria and contract awards);
- detailed schedules ('Appendix I Annexes') setting out the range of each party's procurements covered by the GPA. These specify covered entities, thresholds, covered services, specific exclusions, etc. The GPA also incorporates built-in procedures for modification of parties' coverage in response to relevant developments (e.g. the privatisation of covered entities);
- minimum standards (based on international best practices and incorporating significant flexibility) on aspects of the procurement process, to ensure transparent and open conditions of competition, including provisions on:
  - tendering procedures;
  - qualification of suppliers;
  - time limits, documentation, opening of tenders and contract award procedures;
- provisions relating to the establishment of independent domestic review procedures and application of the WTO dispute settlement mechanism ('enforcement tools');
- provisions regarding accession to the GPA and the availability of 'transitional measures' for developing countries that join the GPA;
- a 'built-in agenda' for improvement of the GPA, extension of its coverage and elimination of remaining discriminatory measures applied by parties.

well as enhanced market access commitments, was the outcome of a renegotiation process that lasted over a decade and was concluded in December 2011, with the formal adoption of the outcome of the negotiations in March 2012.[6] Instruments of acceptance, often based on the completion of domestic ratification procedures, had to be submitted by two-thirds of the GPA parties in order for the revised GPA to enter into force thirty days later. This requirement was fulfilled on 7 February 2014,

---

[6] See GPA/113 of 2 April 2012.

with the tenth Instrument of Acceptance of the GPA being deposited by Israel. The revised GPA consequently entered into force on 6 April 2014 for those parties that had accepted it, and for others subsequently.[7]

The GPA renegotiation was, first and foremost, an international trade negotiation; as such, the expansion of access to the parties' procurement markets by their respective suppliers was central to the process and to the agreement reached. The package of additions to market access adopted in the conclusion has been valued by the WTO Secretariat as being worth in the range of US$80–100 billion annually.[8]

The second element of the renegotiation, in the revised GPA text, is based on the same principles and contains the same main elements as the existing GPA. It none the less improves on the existing text in multiple significant ways. For example, the revised text reflects significant changes to the wording of the various provisions of the GPA to streamline them and make the text easier to understand. It updates the GPA to take into account developments in current government procurement practice, notably the use of electronic tools.

The revised text also incorporates additional flexibility for parties' procurement authorities, for example, in the form of shorter notice periods when electronic tools are used. Shorter time periods have also been allowed for procuring goods and services of types that are available on the commercial marketplace.[9] In an important additional change, the transitional measures ('special and differential treatment') that are available to developing countries that accede to the GPA have been clarified and improved.[10]

Another significant element of the revised GPA text consists in a specific new requirement for participating governments and their relevant procuring entities to conduct their procurements in ways that avoid conflicts of interest and prevent corrupt practices. This provision is unique in the context of WTO treaty obligations.[11] The significance of this new provision is reinforced by new language, in the preamble to the GPA, recognising its significance for good governance and the fight against corruption. Together, these elements signal a belief on the part of the parties that the GPA, while first and foremost

---

[7] For information on the date of entry into force of/accession to the Agreement for individual parties, see www.wto.org/english/tratop_e/gproc_e/memobs_e.htm.

[8] See, for relevant details, Anderson (2012).

[9] See, for detailed analysis, Arrowsmith (2011).    [10] See, for elaboration, Müller (2011).

[11] See Arrowsmith (2011); see also Anderson, Schooner and Swan (2012).

an international trade agreement, is directly relevant to the global struggle for good governance.[12]

## GPA accession and the WTO accession process

All WTO members are eligible to accede to the GPA, regardless of whether they have a commitment to do so or not. At present, ten WTO members are in the process of acceding. These are China, New Zealand, Montenegro, Albania, Georgia, Jordan, Kyrgyz Republic, Moldova, Oman and Ukraine. Five other WTO members have undertaken commitments, in their WTO Accession Protocols, to initiate accession to the GPA. They are the former Yugoslav Republic of Macedonia, Mongolia, Russia, Saudi Arabia and Tajikistan.

### The GPA accession process

The GPA accession process starts with the submission of an application for accession and has two main aspects: negotiations between the acceding member and parties to the GPA on the former's coverage offer; and verification that the acceding member's procurement legislation is consistent with the GPA's requirements – for example, regarding transparency, procedural fairness for suppliers and domestic review. The first element involves the circulation of market access ('Appendix I') offers by accession candidates, which are subject to comments and requests by parties and subsequent revision until a mutually agreeable equilibrium is reached. The second element is addressed through the provision of replies to a so-called 'Checklist of issues for provision of information relating to accession to the agreement', the scrutiny of such information by parties and related exchanges both orally in the committee and in written form between the accession candidate and the parties.

Pursuant to Article V of the revised GPA, special and differential treatment for developing countries in the form of transitional measures such as offsets, price preference programmes, initially higher thresholds and phasing-in of entities can be negotiated by a developing acceding economy in the accession process, subject to the agreement of the other

---

[12] See Anderson (2010).

parties and the acceding member's development needs. Provision has also been made for delaying the application of any specific obligation contained in the GPA, other than the requirement to provide equivalent treatment to the goods, services and suppliers of all other parties, for a period of five years following accession to the GPA for least-developed countries (LDCs), or up to three years for other developing economies. These periods can be extended by the decision of the Committee on Government Procurement, upon request of the country concerned.[13]

Once the terms of accession have been agreed between the GPA parties and the acceding WTO member, the committee adopts a decision inviting the member to accede to the GPA. The decision specifies the agreed terms and provides a time-frame for the acceding member to deposit its instrument of accession with the WTO Director-General (typically three to six months).

## Links to the WTO accession process

For most WTO members, participation in the GPA is entirely optional, as they have no pre-existing commitment to join it. In such cases, the decision to seek accession is one that can be taken squarely on its own merits, based on an assessment of the potential benefits and costs in the light of each member's circumstances.

Procedurally, accession to the GPA can only occur after a government has acceded to the WTO as a whole, and GPA accession negotiations are dealt with separately from WTO accession. However, increasingly, acceding WTO governments take on commitments, at the time of their accession, to join the GPA eventually, when they become WTO members. As shown in Table 32.1, out of the ten WTO members that are currently seeking accession to the GPA, nine undertook commitments related to GPA accession at the time of their WTO accessions, pursuant to Article XII of the Marrakesh Agreement Establishing the World Trade Organization (WTO Agreement).

Five other Article XII WTO members that have not yet initiated their accession to the GPA have also undertaken commitments to eventually do so. Table 32.2 provides an overview of those WTO members and their commitments.

---

[13]  See, for elaboration, Müller (2011).

Table 32.1 *WTO members in the process of acceding to the GPA and their WTO accession commitments – overview*

| WTO member | Application | GPA accession commitment | State of play |
|---|---|---|---|
| Albania | 2 October 2001 (GPA/57) | See WTO document WT/ACC/ALB/51, dated 13 July 2000, paragraph 123 | Pending |
| China | 7 January 2008 (GPA/ACC/CHN/1) | See WTO documents: WT/ACC/CHN/49, dated 1 October 2001 and WT/MIN(01)/3, dated 10 November 2001, paragraphs 340 and 341 | Active |
| Georgia | 17 October 2002 (GPA/71) | See WTO documents: WT/ACC/GEO/31, dated 31 August 1999, paragraph 117 | Pending |
| Jordan | 19 July 2000 (GPA/38) | See WTO documents: WT/ACC/JOR/33, WT/MIN(99)/9, dated 3 December 1999, paragraph 170 | Pending |
| Kyrgyz Republic | 19 May 1999 (GPA/SPEC/4) | See WTO document WT/ACC/KGZ/26, dated 31 July 1998, paragraph 120 | Pending |
| Moldova | 8 January 2002 (GPA/63) | See WTO document WT/ACC/MOL/37, dated 11 January 2001, paragraph 150 | Active |
| Montenegro | 4 October 2013 (GPA/120) | See WTO document WT/ACC/CGR/38, dated 5 December 2011, paragraph 182 | Active, close to finalisation |
| New Zealand | 1 October 2012 (GPA/115) | – | Active, close to finalisation |
| Oman | 12 July 2001 (GPA/W/141) | See WTO document WT/ACC/OMN/26, dated 28 September 2000, paragraph 121 | Pending |
| Ukraine | 9 February 2011 (GPA/107 & GPA/ACC/UKR/1) | See WTO document WT/ACC/UKR/152, dated 25 January 2008, paragraph 358 | Active |

Table 32.2 *Other WTO members with commitments to accede to the GPA*

| WTO member | Date of WTO accession | GPA accession commitment |
|---|---|---|
| Former Yugoslav Republic of Macedonia | 4 April 2003 | See WTO document WT/ACC/807/27, dated 26 September 2002, paragraph 177 |
| Mongolia | 29 January 1997 | See WTO document WT/ACC/MNG/9, dated 27 June 1996, paragraph 59. |
| Russia | 22 August 2012 | See WTO document WT/ACC/RUS/70, dated 17 November 2011, paragraph 1143 |
| Saudi Arabia | 11 December 2005 | See WTO document WT/ACC/SAU/61, dated 1 November 2005, paragraph 231 |
| Tajikistan | 2 March 2013 | See WTO document WT/ACC/TJK/30, dated 6 November 2012, paragraph 244 |

Reviewing the thirty-three WTO members that have acceded to the WTO pursuant to Article XII of the WTO Agreement, i.e. since the creation of the WTO in 1995, it is notable that of these, twenty-two (or 69 per cent) have undertaken GPA-related commitments, and seven (or 22 per cent) have subsequently completed accession to the GPA (some of them by way of becoming a member of the European Union). Out of the ten (or 31 per cent) that have not done so, three (or 9 per cent) have indicated that they are ready to contemplate GPA accession at a later stage, and seven (22 per cent) have indicated a lack of interest in the GPA or not addressed the issue (Figure 32.1).

This suggests that even though WTO accession and GPA accession are formally separate steps, for countries wishing to become members of the WTO, the basic policy decision as to whether the country in question intends to join the GPA (or not) is often made long before GPA accession negotiations are started, at the time of WTO accession. This highlights the need for wider dissemination of information on the significance of international trade disciplines in the government procurement sector, and a methodology for enabling countries to better access the potential benefits and costs of GPA accession. The following sections respond to these concerns.

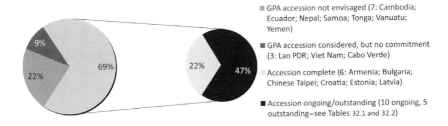

Figure 32.1 Overview of GPA-related commitments by new WTO members.

## Potential benefits and costs of GPA accession

Each acceding WTO member must ultimately assess the potential bene-fits and costs for itself. To assist in this process, Box 32.2 sets out a list of potential benefits and costs that can be relevant together with factors that can impact on their magnitude. Aspects of these costs are discussed further below.[14]

### Market access dimension

A first important dimension of the pros and cons of GPA accession consists in market access considerations. How much market access will the acceding government have to provide to other GPA parties? And, most importantly: how much market access will it gain?

The available data on the extent of the GPA parties' market access commitments are less robust and systematic than would be ideal. None the less, the data that are available provide important insights. To begin with, the total value of existing market access opportuni-ties under the GPA has been estimated at around US$1.6 trillion in 2008.[15] According to statistical reports submitted by GPA parties, the European Union and the United States provided approximately 75 per cent of the total value of existing market access opportunities under the GPA, i.e., US$1.2 trillion.[16] Furthermore, as a result of the conclu-sion of the GPA coverage negotiations reached in March 2012, new

---

[14] See, for a more detailed treatment, Anderson, Müller *et al.* (2012), from which this section of the chapter draws.

[15] See United States, Office of the United States Trade Representative (undated).

[16] Anderson, Müller *et al.* (2012).

---

BOX 32.2 POTENTIAL BENEFITS AND COSTS FROM GPA ACCESSION
AND FACTORS IMPACTING ON THEIR MAGNITUDE: A CHECKLIST

| B. Potential costs | Relevant factors |
|---|---|
| 1. Export market gains and a safeguard against protectionist or 'buy national' measures introduced by other GPA parties, based on legal guarantees of rights to participate in other GPA parties' procurement markets | GPA accession opens up possibilities for export market gains; the actual gains to be achieved also depend on the underlying competitiveness of the acceding party<br><br>The value of legal guarantees of market access rights may itself be increasing with the apparent trend towards 'buy national' or other potentially access-limiting measures |
| 2. Enhanced efficiency/value for money in the acceding party's own procurement markets, through:<br>• strengthening of competition<br>• improved governance/deterrence of corruption<br>• locking in of internal reforms and greater coherence across internal regions/sub-central governments | Possibly the most important set of benefits for some acceding parties (those with limited internal competition/particular governance challenges)<br><br>Some evidence that these gains may exceed 20 per cent of the value of covered procurements, depending on related circumstances<br><br>Generally, achievement of these benefits also depends on necessary internal reforms and institution-building (but GPA accession can be a catalyst for these) |
| 3. Other benefits:<br>• ability to influence the terms of other GPA accessions<br>• ability to influence the future evolution of the GPA | Potentially a significant consideration for WTO members with interests in the procurement markets of future accession candidates (e.g. other major emerging economies, beyond China)<br><br>Built-in possibilities for review of the GPA |
| **B. Potential costs** | |
| 1. Negotiating costs, including necessary internal studies and consultation | Likely to be small as compared to potential benefits, but still a factor, especially for small delegations<br><br>Some possibilities for assistance, e.g. from governance-focused organisations |

BOX 32.2 (*cont.*)

| B. Potential costs | Relevant factors |
|---|---|
| 2. Costs of necessary legislative/ institutional adaptations | Relevant costs may already have been incurred (i.e. necessary adaptations already made), e.g. due to participation in bilateral or regional agreements incorporating GPA-type provisions, or at the suggestion of development-lending organisations |
| 3. Impact on local industry/workers | Strong likelihood that foreign suppliers, when they win a contract, will subcontract to local firms/ workers |
| | Possible spillover benefits from foreign market entry (e.g. technology transfer) |
| | Possibility of transitional measures/ negotiated exclusions from coverage to limit exposure of sensitive sectors |

*Source:* Anderson, Müller *et al.* (2012).

additional market access opportunities worth between US$80 and 100 billion have now become available with the entry into force of the revised GPA.

Research carried out by the Secretariat confirms that the goods and services whose procurement is covered by the GPA span a very wide range of sectors of potential interest to developing and transition economy in addition to developed country suppliers. A few of many examples would include sectors such as construction services; pharmaceutical products, health services and other procurements by health-related entities; computer and related services; telecommunication services; chemical products; fuels and petroleum products; machinery and associated products; transport equipment; textiles, clothing and footwear; plastic and rubber products; metal and associated products; mineral products; and wood products.[17]

---

[17] Ibid.

*Complementarity of market access for WTO members' businesses
under the GPA with other WTO agreements*

While the market access highlighted above is an important factor in itself, the GPA and the market access provided thereunder also reinforce and are complementary to the market access provided under other WTO agreements.

Market access provided under the General Agreement on Tariffs and Trade (GATT) and the General Agreement on Trade in Services (GATS) has, for example, a very significant impact on suppliers' ability to compete in government procurement markets if and to the extent that the goods or services supplied to the government are sourced internationally. In other words, international suppliers need to take into account two different types of regulations when importing goods or services for the supply of the government: their ability to apply for contracts and offer internationally sourced goods and services will depend on government procurement regulations, i.e. the GPA, while their competitiveness in such goods and services will, to a large extent, depend on the general market access rules for these.

The interface between coverage commitments under the GATS and the GPA, as the two agreements which allow for limitations in the scope of application of their rules through coverage schedules, illustrates this point well. Possible interactions between coverage commitments under the GPA and GATS are illustrated in Table 32.3. On the one hand, rights of establishment for foreign service providers that are provided under the GATS can have an important bearing on how procurement contracts covered by the GPA are performed and, therefore, on the ability of a foreign service provider to compete effectively for such contracts. At the limit, GPA commitments may be relatively meaningless without some degree of corresponding GATS commitments. On the other hand, access to procurement markets (governed by the GPA) can have an important bearing on the scale of operations and therefore the competitiveness of individual suppliers generally. Often, in fact, the largest services contracts will be with government entities; if a foreign supplier is excluded from these, this will affect its commercial presence in the market, independent of relevant GATS disciplines. GPA coverage thus adds commercial value and viability to services commitments in the GATS, and the other way around.[18]

---

[18] See Anderson and Müller (2008).

Table 32.3 *Illustration of the interaction between GPA and GATS commitments*

| GPA service commitments? | GATS commitments? | Commercial result |
| --- | --- | --- |
| Yes | Modes 1 and 2 only | Limited ability to compete in procurement markets, notwithstanding that relevant service is covered |
| Yes | All modes | Full ability to compete in procurement markets of interest |
| No | Modes 1 and 2 only | Negative effects of exclusion from procurement markets are reinforced by limited GATS commitments |
| No | All modes | Notwithstanding GATS rights in respect of all modes, commercial utility may be affected by exclusion from procurement markets |

*Source:* Anderson and Müller (2008).

### Structural factors enhancing the importance of the GPA as a bulwark of the global economy

The market access guarantees that are available on joining the GPA are becoming more valuable over time. As the previous paragraphs have demonstrated, among the parties to the GPA, determined efforts have been undertaken to achieve both export market and internal benefits through the progressive strengthening of the GPA, the expansion of its coverage among the existing parties and the expansion of its membership.

At the same time, however, a parallel, potentially disturbing trend is in evidence: a trend towards the consideration or introduction of measures potentially limiting access to procurement markets in circumstances where this is not precluded by the GPA or other international agreements. The Global Trade Alert, an academic institute that monitors policy developments affecting global trade, has found that as many as 213 measures actually or potentially affecting trade in public procurement markets have been implemented since it commenced monitoring such measures in the middle of the global economic crisis.[19]

---

[19] See the website of the Global Trade Alert (www.globaltradealert.org).

This provides a powerful argument for countries interested in protecting their suppliers' access to offshore markets to consider participation in relevant agreements, even where they have not, in the past, elected to do so. In particular, it suggests that, whereas in the past the suppliers of countries not participating in the GPA of similar preferential agreements may have enjoyed a degree of access to some GPA parties' procurement markets on a tacit or informal basis, this is less likely to be true in the future. On the contrary, the costs of non-participation in the GPA appear to be rising.

### Significance of GPA membership in promoting good governance

The GPA is unique in that it is both an international trade agreement and an instrument of governance. That being so, it is relevant to issues that are at the forefront of current thinking and research on economic development, which identifies governance mechanisms (i.e. appropriate laws and institutions) as being an essential underpinning of development and of the welfare of citizens.[20]

The specific channels through which the GPA promotes good governance and deters corruption include, at a minimum: (i) its many provisions relating to transparency and fair treatment of individual suppliers; (ii) its domestic review provisions, which require all parties to put in place mechanisms to ensure the independent, objective review of supplier complaints; and (iii) a new provision in the revised GPA text that imposes a specific requirement on GPA parties to avoid conflicts of interest and corrupt practices, as discussed below.

Good governance, in turn, brings other benefits. These may include, for example, reduced leakages from the public treasury from corrupt practices, enhanced trust in government and the promotion of inbound FDI as suppliers become confident of receiving fair and equitable treatment under relevant national laws.

### Enhancing competition in procurement markets: the necessity of market opening for augmenting national competitiveness and welfare improvement

The GPA promotes competition, and therefore increased efficiency and value for money in public procurement activities, in at least three main

---

[20] See, for example, for background Rodrik (2012).

ways. First, it fosters and provides a vehicle for the progressive opening of parties' markets to international competition through legally enforceable provisions on non-discrimination which apply to procurements that are 'covered' by the GPA. Second, the various provisions of the GPA relating to the provision of information to potential suppliers, contract awards, qualification of suppliers and other elements of the procurement process provide a framework to ensure transparency and non-discriminatory conditions of competition between suppliers. Third, the GPA's provisions relating to the establishment of domestic review procedures and (though much less frequently used), access to the WTO's dispute settlement mechanism provide important tools to enforce parties' commitments regarding fair and non-discriminatory conditions of competition and to address related abuses.

Case histories and examples that illustrate the gains from the promotion of competition in government procurement regimes are fewer and less well documented than would be ideal.[21] None the less, such examples as are available suggest that the gains can be substantial. A number of such examples, taken from an OECD survey, are collected in Box 32.3 giving examples of cost savings in developing countries based on the implementation of more transparent and competitive procurement systems. The examples referred to therein indicate that savings to public treasuries of between 17 and 43 per cent have been achieved in some developing countries through the implementation of more transparent and competitive government procurement regimes.

In a broadly similar vein, an independent external study for the European Commission found that increased competition and transparency resulting from implementation of the public procurement directives of the European Communities in the period between 1993 and 2002 generated cost savings of between a little less than €5 billion and almost €25 billion.[22]

A further important corroborating source of information regarding the benefits of competition which is sometimes overlooked is provided by evidence of *higher* costs to public treasuries that arise when competition is suppressed, for example, through collusive tendering. For the present it may be noted that collusion in public procurement markets has been conservatively estimated to raise prices on the order of 20 per cent or

---

[21] See Evenett and Hoekman (2004).
[22] Europe Economics, Evaluation of Public Procurement Directives, Markt/2004/10/D, September 2006.

---

BOX 32.3 EXAMPLES OF COST SAVINGS IN DEVELOPING COUNTRIES
BASED ON THE IMPLEMENTATION OF MORE TRANSPARENT AND
COMPETITIVE PROCUREMENT SYSTEMS

A 2003 OECD study of the benefits of transparent and competitive procurement processes refers to the following examples of benefits achieved:

- in Bangladesh, a substantial reduction in electricity prices due to the introduction of transparent and competitive procurement procedures;
- a saving of 47 per cent in the procurement of certain military goods in Colombia through the improvement of transparency and procurement procedures;
- a 43 per cent saving in the cost of purchasing medicines in Guatemala, due to the introduction of more transparent and competitive procurement procedures and the elimination of any tender specifications that favour a particular tender;
- a substantial reduction in the budget for expenditures on pharmaceuticals in Nicaragua, due to the establishment of a transparent procurement agency accompanied by the effective implementation of an essential drug list;
- in Pakistan, a saving of more than Rs 187 million (US$3.1 million) for the Karachi Water and Sewerage Board through the introduction of an open and transparent bidding process.

*Source:* OECD (2003).

---

more above competitive levels. The benefit of introducing competition where it has not previously existed may be expected to be of a comparable magnitude.[23]

## Costs and challenges related to GPA accession

To be sure, GPA accession inevitably entails costs or challenges in addition to benefits of the types noted above. As shown in Box 32.2, these are likely to be of three major kinds: first, the direct costs of preparing an offer and negotiating with the existing parties; second, institutional costs relating to the implementation of the GPA's requirements regarding, for example, the transparency of procurement procedures, the implementation of an independent domestic review ('bid challenge') system, and so forth; and third, costs relating to the adjustment of domestic firms to competition from foreign entities based in

---

[23] See Anderson, Kovacic and Müller (2011).

other GPA parties, including possible employment and other effects. Without discounting the reality of these costs or challenges and the importance of considering them, there are reasons for believing that they may, at least in many cases, be modest in relation to the resulting benefits. Some of these considerations are set out below.[24]

To begin with, regarding the first element (negotiating costs and challenges), these are an undeniable aspect of participation in the WTO. Without discounting their importance or reality, it should be noted that supportive governance institutes and other intergovernmental organisations can play a very useful role in facilitating a government's preparations for accession. For example, SIGMA, a governance institute affiliated to the OECD and the European Union, played an important role in preparatory work related to the accession of Armenia. More recently, the European Bank for Reconstruction and Development (EBRD) has played a very useful role in supporting work on the GPA accessions of economies in its catchment area, for example Moldova, Montenegro and Ukraine. Important assistance with regard to capacity-building is, of course, also available from the WTO Secretariat and, in several cases, the other GPA parties.

Regarding the second element of costs/challenges (institutional adjustment or implementation costs), these can also be significant. It is important, however, to note that a large number of WTO members and observers have already implemented, or are in the process of implementing, reforms to their national legislation and procurement policies which, in many cases, substantially enhance their readiness for GPA accession. This may be the result either of unilateral reforms, of initiatives promoted by multilateral lending institutions, or of participation in relevant preferential agreements.[25] The point is that, to this extent, the costs of legislative or institutional adaptations that are necessary for GPA accession may already have been incurred, or may be desirable or inevitable for reasons that are independent of GPA accession *per se*. To that extent, they should not be counted as costs of the GPA accession process.

Furthermore, as mentioned above, in Article V of the revised GPA, additional flexibilities and transitional measures have been provided for developing economies that accede to it. As a result, developing economies do not have to face the entire cost of legislative and institutional

---

[24] See, for elaboration, Anderson, Müller *et al.* (2012).
[25] See, regarding the latter aspect, Anderson, Müller *et al.* (2011).

adaptation immediately upon accession, but can implement any GPA-compliant reform process step by step over a longer, but pre-defined period of time.

Concerning the third aspect of costs (firm adjustment and economy-wide effects), this, too, is an important issue that undoubtedly merits careful consideration by potential GPA accession candidates, taking good account of their particular circumstances and potential vulnerabilities. Nevertheless, the following points are relevant.

To begin with, we would note that it is a mistake to equate the simple fact that, under a non-discriminatory procurement regime, some contracts may be won by offshore suppliers, on the one hand, with a loss of employment equal to the value of such contracts, on the other hand. Even where a contract is nominally 'won' by a foreign supplier, there may well be important benefits for the local economy. Such benefits may be of two types: first, in many cases, foreign contractors will find it convenient to enter into subcontracts with local firms to fulfil aspects of the contract, particularly labour-intensive aspects. Second, the participation of foreign firms in the market (whether with or without the involvement of local subcontractors) can result in a transfer of technology to the host country that will ultimately strengthen the competitiveness of locally based firms.

In addition, and as has been noted separately by Anderson and Osei-Lah, there are other reasons for believing that participation by foreign suppliers in national procurement markets is unlikely to displace the role of local firms. For example, in many developing country markets, foreign firms are likely to target mainly segments of relevant procurement markets that local firms are unlikely to be in a position to supply, and vice versa.[26]

Moreover, it should be recalled that a degree of foreign penetration is often occurring already, independently of the GPA, whether due to the requirements of development assistance providers, autonomous liberalisation and/or the necessity to seek out foreign suppliers to meet specific needs. For these reasons, and given the relatively high thresholds that typically apply under the GPA and the flexibilities that are potentially available to developing countries under the revised text, GPA accession is likely to pose less of a threat to local employment in developing countries than is sometimes pictured.

---

[26] Anderson and Osei-Lah (2011).

# Accession to the GPA by select transition (Article XII member) economies: some examples

The following sections provide information on the accessions to the GPA of three recent WTO accession 'graduates': Armenia, which completed its accession in 2012; Montenegro, which is very close to becoming a full GPA party; and Ukraine, which is actively negotiating accession. All three acceded to the WTO pursuant to Article XII of the WTO Agreement, i.e. since 1995. They undertook specific commitments in their WTO Accession Protocols to accede to the GPA. Their experience is of interest in that it points to the relative ease with which transition economies can potentially accede to the GPA if they are prepared to work hard (as these countries have done) and respond effectively to the interests of the existing GPA parties.

One other GPA accession which clearly is taking longer to conclude than many had hoped is that of China.[27] We continue to believe that China's accession to the GPA, when it occurs, and subject to the appropriate terms, will be of immense benefit to both China and the GPA parties. The time that it is taking may be less surprising if one considers the size and complexity of the Chinese economy and its procurement system, and the extent of institutional change that is involved in its accession to the GPA.[28]

## Armenia

Armenia applied for GPA accession on 4 September 2009. Related discussions took place in 2009 and 2010. These discussions addressed both Armenia's coverage offer as well as its legislation. In addition, Armenia provided additional documentation with regard to its accession. Parties expressed their appreciation to Armenia for the strength of its commitment, the high quality of its documentation and the substance of its offer.

In November 2010, Armenia circulated its final offer and revised draft Law on Procurement, together with the terms agreed with regard to the coming into force of the GPA for it in the form of a draft Committee decision. In the course of its meeting on 7 December 2010, the Committee adopted a Decision inviting Armenia to accede to the GPA on terms that had been agreed.[29] Under that Decision, Armenia was required to

---

[27] See, for related discussion, Annual Report of the Committee on Government Procurement to the General Council (GPA/122 of 15 October 2013).
[28] Anderson, Schooner and Swan (2012).    [29] GPA/105, dated 7 December 2010.

adopt and bring into force legislation in conformity with the provisions of the GPA as required by its Article XXIV:5(a), and to submit to the Committee the legislation in question, together with information regarding its entry into force.

In a formal meeting on 9 March 2010, the Committee on Government Procurement confirmed that Armenia had met the terms and conditions for its accession, specifically with respect to its national legislation, and that it could, therefore, proceed to deposit its instrument of accession to the GPA.[30] On 16 August 2011, Armenia deposited its instrument of accession with the Director-General of the WTO.[31] Pursuant to paragraph 2 of Article XXIV of the GPA, it entered into force for Armenia on 15 September 2011. The Committee considered Armenia's accession to be a very significant development that had clearly shown the relevance of the GPA for transition economies.

## Montenegro

Montenegro submitted its application for accession and its replies to the checklist of issues, together with additional documentation on its legislative framework, on 4 October 2013. It then followed up on these initial steps with the circulation of an initial offer in early November 2013 and a first revised offer with detailed explanatory notes a few weeks later, taking into account comments received by parties. Based on further discussions, Montenegro circulated its second revised offer on 18 June 2014. In the Committee's informal sessions on 25 June 2014, it was already evident that no party had major outstanding concerns with the proposed terms of accession of Montenegro.

Montenegro's final offer, which received enthusiastic support from all the GPA parties, was circulated on 18 July 2014. On 29 October 2014, the Committee adopted a formal decision inviting Montengro to accede to the GPA on the terms agreed. Montenegro reported having completed its internal ratification procedures and is very close to submitting its Instrument of Accession.

## Ukraine

Ukraine submitted its application for GPA accession on 8 February 2011. Its replies to the checklist of issues and initial offer were circulated on

---

[30]  GPA/M/43, dated 22 March 2011.     [31]  GPA/109, dated 13 September 2011.

2 August 2011 and 13 December 2012 respectively. Substantive discussions of the initial offer were held in 2013. In the course of those discussions, parties expressed their appreciation to Ukraine for its initial offer, which they considered as a good basis for further negotiations. Several issues that had been identified by parties for further discussion were adressed in Ukraine's further revised offers, submitted on 7 March 2014 and 27 April 2015. After having circulated its revised procurement legislation on 20 May 2015, Ukraine submitted a draft final offer on 27 May 2015. In a meeting of the Committee of 3 June 2015, this offer won the provisional support of all GPA parties, and it is expected that a decision inviting Ukraine to accede to the GPA will be adopted as soon as GPA parties have completed their internal procedures enabling them to express their formal consent to such a decision.

## Conclusions

As outlined in this chapter, the GPA provides a framework for the progressive liberalisation of international trade in relation to government procurement markets and the promotion of transparency and procedural fairness in procurement activities that is of increasing interest to countries worldwide. The entry into force of the revised GPA on 6 April 2014 – following a ten-year renegotiation process – effectively modernised the GPA, making it both easier to implement and more relevant to today's global economy.

Increasingly, governments that join the WTO are encouraged to make commitments, at the time of their accession, to also seek to join, eventually, the GPA. In the past, some countries have received these requests with a degree of trepidation. Yet, as has been discussed in this chapter, there are good reasons for developing and transition economies acceding to the WTO to consider accession to the GPA, and to pursue such accession with enthusiasm. GPA accession provides access to markets valued at approximately US\$1.7 trillion annually. Furthermore, as we have shown, important complementarities exist between GPA accession on the one hand and, on the other hand, the commercial value and usefulness to participating economies' suppliers of commitments and disciplines under other elements of the WTO agreements.

Also, while not a substitute for domestic reforms, accession to the GPA can catalyse and reinforce reforms that enhance transparency and competition internally, thereby yielding important gains in terms of value for money in national procurement activities. GPA accession can also encourage inward FDI, by signalling a government's commitment to good governance and the fair treatment of all players under relevant national legislation.

To be sure, accession to the GPA also entails challenges and potential costs. As has been discussed in this chapter, these include first, the direct costs of preparing an offer and negotiating with the existing parties; second, the costs of relevant legislative and institutional adaptations; and third, costs relating to the adjustment of domestic firms to competition from foreign entities based in other GPA parties, including possible employment and other effects. Again, though, without discounting the need to consider these costs, there are reasons for believing that they may be modest in relation to the resulting benefits, at least in many cases. A principal reason is that, in many cases, WTO members or observers contemplating accession to the GPA will already have incurred many of the relevant costs, whether these relate to legislative and institutional adaptations or the implications of market opening for local suppliers.

Overall, as we have seen, over time, important trends are at work in global procurement markets which are enhancing the value of GPA participation. GPA parties have made determined efforts to achieve both export market and internal benefits through the progressive strengthening of the GPA; the expansion of its coverage among the existing parties; and the expansion of the GPA's membership. At the same time, a parallel, potentially disturbing trend is in evidence: a trend toward the consideration or introduction of measures potentially limiting access to procurement markets in circumstances where this is not precluded by the GPA or other international agreements. Parties to the GPA will enjoy treaty-established rights that protect them from such measures; those outside will not, except where such rights are secured by other (preferential) agreements. They will also not enjoy the reinforcement that comes from participation in the pre-eminent global agreement that promotes trade, competition, transparency and value for money in national procurement activities. Nor will they enjoy the 'stamp of approval' that GPA membership provides, with its potential benefits, for example in encouraging FDI. In this light, GPA accession may come to be seen not so much as an onerous requirement, but an opportunity that acceding WTO governments and Article XII members would not want to miss.

Seychelles undertook, in its GPA Accession Protocol, to initiate negotiations to accede to the WTO Agreement on Government Procurement within one year from the date of its accession (WT/ACC/SYC/64, para. 322). In addition, since the writing of this chapter, Tajikistan and Australia have submitted their respective requests for accession to the GPA (GPA/127 of 12 February 2015 and GPA/129 of 2 June 2015).

## Acknowledgement

The views expressed are the personal responsibility of the authors and should not be attributed to the WTO or its Secretariat.

## References

Anderson, R. D. (2010). 'The WTO Agreement on Government Procurement (GPA): an emerging tool of global integration and good governance', *Law in Transition*, Autumn, pp. 1/8–8/8, at p. 5/8. Retrieved from www.ebrd.com/downloads/research/news/lit102.pdf.

(2012). 'The conclusion of the renegotiation of the WTO Agreement on Government Procurement: what it means for the Agreement and for the world economy', *Public Procurement Law Review*, 21:83.

Anderson, R. D. and A. C. Müller (2008). 'Market access for government procurement of services: comparing recent PTAs with achievements', in M. Roy and J. Marchetti (eds.), *Services Trade Liberalization: Preferential Trade Agreements vs. the GATS*. Cambridge University Press.

Anderson, R. D. and K. Osei-Lah (2011). 'Forging a more global procurement market: issues concerning accessions to the Agreement on Government Procurement', in S. Arrowsmith and R. D. Anderson (eds.), *The WTO Regime on Government Procurement: Challenge and Reform*. Cambridge University Press.

Anderson, R. D., W. E. Kovacic and A. C. Müller (2011). 'Ensuring integrity and competition in public procurement markets: a dual challenge for good governance', in S. Arrowsmith and R. D. Anderson (eds.), *The WTO Regime on Government Procurement: Challenge and Reform*. Cambridge University Press.

Anderson, R. D., A. C. Müller, K. Osei-Lah, J. Pardo de León and P. Pelletier (2011). 'Government procurement provisions in regional trade agreements: a stepping stone to GPA accession?' in S. Arrowsmith and R. D. Anderson (eds.), *The WTO Regime on Government Procurement: Challenge and Reform*. Cambridge University Press.

Anderson, R. D., A. C. Müller, K. Osei-Lah and P. Pelletier (2012). 'Assessing the value of future accessions to the WTO Agreement on Government Procurement (GPA): some new data sources, provisional estimates, and an evaluative framework for individual WTO members considering accession', *Public Procurement Law Review*, 21(4).

Anderson, R. D., S. L. Schooner and C. D. Swan (2012). 'The WTO's Revised Government Procurement Agreement: an important milestone toward greater market access and transparency in global public procurement markets', Washington DC, George Washington University, GWU Legal Studies Research Paper no. 2012–7.

Arrowsmith, S. (2011). 'The revised Agreement on Government Procurement: changes to the procedural rules and other transparency provisions', in S. Arrowsmith and R. D. Anderson (eds.), *The WTO Regime on Government Procurement: Challenge and Reform*. Cambridge University Press.

Europe Economics, *Evaluation of Public Procurement Directives*, Markt/2004/10/ D, September 2006. Retrieved from http://ec.europa.eu/internal_market/pub licprocurement/docs/final_report_en.pdf.

Evenett, S. J. and B. Hoekman (2004). *International Co-operation and the Reform of Public Procurement Policies*. Retrieved from http://papers.ssrn.com/sol3/ papers.cfm?abstract_id=821424.

Müller, A. C. (2011). 'Special and differential treatment and other special measures for developing countries under the Agreement on Government Procure- ment: the current text and new provisions', in S. Arrowsmith and R. D. Anderson (eds.), *The WTO Regime on Government Procurement: Challenge and Reform*. Cambridge University Press.

OECD (2002). 'The size of government procurement'. Retrieved from www.oecd. org/document/63/0,3343,en_2649_34487_1845951_1_1_1_1,00.html.

   (2003). *Transparency in Government Procurement: The Benefits of Efficient Governance* (TD/TC/WP/(2002)31/Rev2/14 April 2003). OECD Publica- tions, France. http://www.oecd.org/trade.

Rodrik, D. (2012). *The Globalization Paradox: Democracy and the Future of the World Economy*. New York, W. W. Norton & Company, Inc.

United States, Office of the United States Trade Representative (undated). 'The WTO Government Procurement Agreement: a tremendous opportunity for China'. Retrieved from http://shenyang.usembassy-china.org.cn/wto-gpa. html.

# 33

# Energy-related rules in Accession Protocols: where are they?

JUNEYOUNG LEE, AMARA OKENWA, GEORGE
TEBAGANA AND PRAJWAL BARAL

## ABSTRACT

*Energy issues have not been systematically discussed by WTO members in the multilateral trading system. This is owing to the fact that there is no rule on energy* per se *in WTO agreements. Yet all tradable energy goods and services are covered by the General Agreement on Tariffs and Trade 1994 and the General Agreement on Trade in Services respectively. With energy security and climate change high on the global agenda, there is increasing interest in how to deal with energy-related issues during WTO accession negotiations, particularly given that several energy-producing countries, energy-transit countries and energy-consuming countries are currently in accession negotiations. Following the examples of earlier accessions, the ongoing negotiation dossiers would need to negotiate energy-related specific obligations in their terms of accession. This chapter identifies five key themes relating to energy in the WTO Accession Protocols of the Article XII members and explains the rationale of how these topics relate to trade in energy based on the existing WTO rules. Further, it categorizes similar energy patterns and trends for Article XII members. Finally, the chapter draws lessons for future WTO rule-making by arguing that these 'updated' rules on energy, found in Article XII members' Accession Protocols, will have the potential to guide the envisaged regular work of the WTO on future rule-making on trade in energy, thereby contributing to international energy cooperation in the context of the rules-based multilateral trading system.*

The analyses in the chapters in this book were finalised at the end of December 2014. Since then the Republic of Seychelles acceded to the World Trade Organization (WTO) on 26 April 2015. This expanded total WTO membership from 160 to 161. Please see the editors' note.

The importance of energy in the world economy is evident from the fact that it is a fundamental input to almost all economic activities.[1] It also constitutes a considerable percentage of the world's aggregate gross domestic product (GDP). For instance, in the period 2009–2010, Africa, the Middle East and the Commonwealth of Independent States (CIS) all had resource shares in total exports in excess of 70 per cent, while North America, Europe and Asia all had 20 per cent or less. South and Central America were in between, at 47 per cent.[2]

Energy will continue to play an important role in the world economy. In 2012, the International Energy Forum (IEF) projected that energy needs would rise by nearly one-third by 2035. Most of this growth and increased demand for energy is expected to come from emerging economies. Energy demand will barely rise in OECD (Organisation for Economic Co-operation and Development) countries, although there is a pronounced shift away from oil and coal (and, in some countries, nuclear energy) toward natural gas and renewables.[3]

Energy also entails a national security element for both consuming/importing and producing/exporting countries, because the price volatility of energy has a proportional impact on several import and export commodities of these countries.[4] The importance of oil in maintaining international security is often given as an example. The availability and affordability of oil has been responsible both for economic recessions in the past and political instability in both the oil-importing and oil-exporting countries along with the entire international community.[5]

Despite its importance (and its projected future role) for governments, there is no single codified rule in energy that can regulate the treatment of energy on an international level. For example, energy rules can be found in the Energy Charter Treaty[6] and the Statute of the Organization of the Petroleum Exporting Countries (OPEC).[7] However, these two frameworks cannot have a multilateral application because of limited membership and hence, leading to their fragmentation.[8] At the same

---

[1] WTO (2013).    [2] WTO (2010).    [3] IEF (2012).    [4] WTO (2013).
[5] Desta (2004).
[6] It covers all aspects of commercial energy activities including trade, transit, investment and energy efficiency.
[7] Under Article 2 of the OPEC Statute, OPEC's mission is to coordinate the policies of the oil-producing countries. The goal is to secure a steady income for the member states and to secure supply of oil to the consumers.
[8] The Energy Charter Treaty has been signed or acceded to by fifty-one countries and the European Union, while OPEC has only twelve members (as of March 2014).

time, these energy issues have not been systematically discussed at the multilateral level, especially in the WTO.

Applying the General Agreement on Tariffs and Trade (GATT) rules on energy has not been very smooth. Some energy goods have a peculiar character which makes it difficult to apply WTO disciplines to them. For example, characterising electricity as a 'good' has been a subject of a WTO panel interpretation. The Appellate Body explained in the *Canada - Feed-in Tariff* case[9] that 'Electricity has a number of specific properties compared to other goods ... A critical physical characteristic of electricity is that it is intangible and, with certain limited exceptions, cannot be effectively stored.'[10] Therefore, questions such as 'when is the product (e.g. electricity, or other energy goods like nuclear energy) deemed to be in transit?' remain problematic. This status quo points to the need for more energy-specific rules.

The lack of multilateral rules in trade in energy can be explained by two important factors. First, international trade rules under the WTO have generally dealt with market access (through elimination of import barriers) for imports from other countries with less emphasis on eliminating export barriers.[11] It is no surprise, therefore, that since its inception in 1995, the Dispute Settlement Body has considered only a handful of disputes on the issue of export restrictions compared to disputes surrounding import restrictions.[12] Yet, in energy trade, restrictions are more pertinent to export barriers.

Secondly, most energy-producing countries were not GATT contracting parties until the 1980s,[13] and some of the major players in the energy sector (for instance China, Russia, Saudi Arabia and most Middle East energy producers/exporters) were largely outside the WTO even until the beginning of this century. This meant there was no unified voice on the need for agreements specifically governing energy.

---

[9] WTO Dispute Panel Reports, *Canada - Certain Measures Affecting the Renewable Energy Generation Sector*; see WTO documents: WT/DS412/R, and *Canada - Measures Relating to the Feed-In Tariff Program*, WT/DS426/R (19 December 2012). These reports were appealed.

[10] Paragraph 7.11.    [11] Selivanova (2010).

[12] The first dispute concerning quantitative export restrictions under Article XI of the GATT was the case of the *European Commission and Argentina - Hides and Leather*; see WTO document WT/DS155/10 (31 August 2001). The second dispute (concerning *China Rare Minerals* – see WTO document WT/DS394/AB/R) was only initiated in 2013. A panel has been established but was yet to hear the dispute as of March 2014.

[13] By the 1980s, of all the major energy producers, only the United States was a GATT contracting party.

However, the last decade has witnessed the accession of a number of key energy players to the WTO. The WTO has successfully concluded the accessions of China, Ecuador, Russia, Saudi Arabia, Tajikistan, Ukraine and Yemen, bringing important world energy players under the purview of the WTO's multilateral trade rules. Several other leading energy producers/exporters (such as Algeria, Iran, Iraq and Kazakhstan) are currently negotiating their Accession Protocols.

As a result, the key energy players that acceded to the WTO after 1995 will be bound by a series of new rules and commitments which they have undertaken during the WTO accession negotiations. The commitments will affect their trade-related policies and, more specifically, the way they deal with their energy resources. Suffice to say that new and broader commitments than those originally undertaken by GATT contracting parties have been undertaken by these new members. Largely following the examples of earlier accessions thus far, the currently ongoing negotiation dossiers may also need to negotiate energy-related specific obligations in their terms of accession.

This chapter identifies five key themes relating to energy in the WTO Accession Protocols of the thirty-three Article XII members (including Yemen)[14] and explains the rationales of why these topics relate to trade in energy based on the existing WTO rules. Furthermore, it categorises similar patterns and trends in energy-related commitments for the thirty-two Article XII members. Finally, the chapter draws lessons for the future of the WTO to the extent of arguing that these 'updated' rules on energy found in Article XII members' Accession Protocols will have the potential to guide the envisaged regular work of the WTO on future trade in energy. Therefore, WTO accession commitments on energy will contribute to international energy cooperation in the context of the multilateral trading system.

### Rationale for energy-related commitments in WTO accession negotiations

Although renewable energy technologies have occupied the central stage in today's global discussions on global warming and climate change,

---

[14] Yemen's Accession Protocol was adopted by the Ninth Ministerial Conference in Bali, Indonesia, in December 2013. Yemen deposited with the WTO Director-General its Instrument of Acceptance of Yemen's Protocol of Accession to the WTO on 27 May 2014, and became a WTO member *de jure* on 26 June 2014.

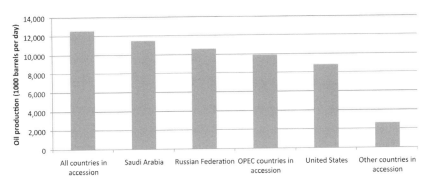

**Figure 33.1**   Oil production, 2012.

fossil fuels have dominated the energy-related commitments, if any, of the acceded countries so far. The scope of energy-related discussions in this chapter, thus, will be limited to fossil fuels, although they may provide relevant benchmarks for future accession negotiations when these are called upon to consider non-fossil fuel energy goods and services.

Since 1995, thirty-three governments have successfully negotiated the terms and conditions of their WTO accessions. The kinds of energy-related commitments the Article XII members have made since the establishment of the WTO can have impacts on the other acceding governments, and guide future commitments, thus potentially forming the basis of an energy-related rule-making process within the multilateral trading system.

The overall importance of these acceding governments in terms of determining the energy regime within the rule-based trading system can be emphasised by a closer analysis of the total world energy market share they command. Figure 33.1[15] shows that oil production (including crude oil, shale oil, oil sands and natural gas liquids) in 2012 had a striking balance between three of the major oil producers (Russia, Saudi Arabia and the United States) and the WTO acceding OPEC (Algeria, Iran, Iraq and Libya) and non-OPEC (Azerbaijan, Kazakhstan and Uzbekistan) countries.[16] The combined oil production of four WTO acceding OPEC countries was 11.4 per cent, greater than that of the United States (9.6 per cent) and close to that of Russia (12.8 per cent) and Saudi Arabia (13.3 per cent). If the oil production from both OPEC and non-OPEC WTO

---

[15]  BP (2013).
[16]  Only those countries whose production is at least 0.1 per cent of the 2012 total have been considered.

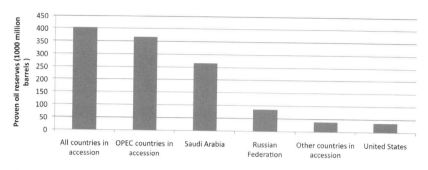

**Figure 33.2** Proven oil reserves of the oil-producing countries, 2012.

acceding governments is combined, it stands at 14.6 per cent, greater than any of the three major oil producers in 2012.

The picture is even more striking if we look at the proven oil reserves of these countries. Figure 33.2[17] shows that the combined oil reserves of the countries currently in the course of the accession process stands at 24.2 per cent, which is almost twelve times as the share of the United States (2.1 per cent), five times that of Russia (5.2 per cent) and larger than that of Saudi Arabia (15.9 per cent). The combined share of WTO-acceding OPEC countries is itself much greater (22 per cent of world total) than that of either of the top oil-producing countries. It should be noted here that the proven reserves are generally taken to be those quantities that geological and engineering information indicate with reasonable certainty can be recovered in the future from known reservoirs under existing economics and operating conditions.[18]

Moving beyond oil, if we look at the proven natural gas reserves of the same countries in Figure 33.3,[19] there is a similar finding. The combined proven natural gas reserves of oil-producing countries, currently in the accession process, stands at 24.9 per cent, which is much greater than the shares of the United States (4.5 per cent), Russia (17.6 per cent) and Saudi Arabia (4.4 per cent).

The stock-taking of energy-related commitments of the Article XII members and analysis of their possible implications for commitments that can be undertaken by the currently acceding governments, as well on the overall energy-related rule-making process within the WTO framework, looks pertinent if we consider Figure 33.4.[20] This clearly presents a balanced picture of oil production distribution between the original

[17] BP (2013).    [18] BP (2013).    [19] BP (2013).    [20] BP (2013).

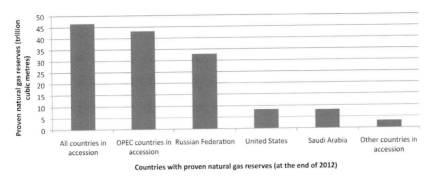

Figure 33.3    Proven natural gas reserves of the oil-producing countries, 2012.

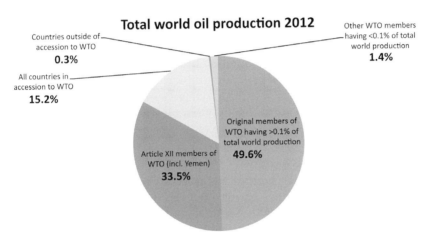

Figure 33.4    Oil-producing countries, 2012.

WTO members, Article XII members (including Yemen) and those that are currently acceding.[21] Although Saudi Arabia (13.3 per cent of world total), Russia (12.8 per cent of world total) and China (5 per cent of world total) comprise the bulk of oil production by Article XII members, the energy-related commitments made by other Article XII members, namely Ecuador, Oman and Viet Nam, cannot be overlooked, because all these commitments could form the basis of future commitments by currently acceding governments and a broader energy framework within the WTO regime.

---

[21]  Only those countries whose production is at least 0.1 per cent of the 2012 total have been considered.

## Selected themes and energy-related commitments

In light of above background, it is pertinent to look into energy-related commitments undertaken by Article XII members, as these are likely to be the basis for ongoing and future accession negotiations involving energy. The following five themes will be considered and analysed in terms of energy-related commitments, if any, and their implications for both ongoing and future accessions, as well as the broader energy-related rule-making process within the WTO's multilateral trading system. The rationale behind picking up these five themes and detailed discussion is presented below.

### Transit

### Freedom of transit

The choice of mode of transportation for energy depends on the nature of the energy product/goods under consideration. Unlike other goods, energy products, such as oil and gas, require special means of transportation, often through an important set of infrastructures, such as pipelines.[22] Typically, the transportation route involves three types of country, namely the originating/producing/exporting country, the transit country and the destination/importing country.[23]

Energy transportation is faced with several challenges, the major one being to find a cost-effective transit route. Transportation from exporting countries through transit countries requires enormous investment in infrastructure. It has been estimated that approximately US$26 trillion will need to be invested in energy infrastructure to meet global energy demand by 2030.[24] Therefore, exporting countries must find cost-effective routes to mitigate transport costs. This is where transit states play a prominent role. They need to cooperate with exporting states to guarantee that a more convenient and cost-effective route is available to the exporter. The absence/denial of transit rights by a transit country will usually force the exporting country to revert to a more expensive and/or insecure route.

In order to mitigate transit problems faced by exporting countries, the GATT Article V:2 guarantees freedom of transit for the goods of an exporting member through the territory of each member via the routes most convenient for international transit, for traffic in transit to or from

---

[22] Sidley Austin LLP (2012).     [23] Ugaz (2011).     [24] IEF (2010).

the territory of other members.[25] It provides further that traffic in transit (i) cannot be subject to any unnecessary delays or restrictions; and (ii) is to be exempt from customs duties and from all transit duties except those for transportation or the costs of services rendered.[26]

While the exact scope of 'freedom' is not defined in GATT Article V, the WTO Dispute Panel in the *Colombia – Ports of Entry* case[27] noted that it means the 'unrestricted use of something'. Therefore, freedom of transit requires extending unrestricted access through the most convenient routes for the passage of goods.

Despite the guarantees in GATT Article V, the freedom of transit envisaged may not suitably apply to transportation of certain types of energy goods. For example, one wonders at what stage of trade 'electricity' should be deemed to be in transit. Whereas other goods can be transported on already existing transport infrastructures, the transit of electricity may necessitate the exporting country constructing transit infrastructures (like grids or transmission lines) in the territory of the transit state. It remains to be agreed whether freedom of transit entails the right by the exporting country to construct transit infrastructures in the territory of the transit state. Bringing this question into the context of the WTO, WTO membership is an issue as some of these transit countries are still outside the WTO and hence not subject to WTO rules.

### Status of commitments for freedom of transit for energy

Out of the thirty-three Article XII members since 1995, nine (namely, China, Ecuador, Kyrgyz Republic, Oman, Russia, Saudi Arabia, Tajikistan, Ukraine and Yemen) have proven oil reserves.[28] The energy-related commitments these members have undertaken during their accession negotiations would make a significant contribution to the development of energy-specific rules for trade in energy in the WTO.

Specific commitments related to freedom of transit for energy were first undertaken in the WTO by Ukraine in 2008 (thirteen years after the birth of the WTO). During the thirteen years, twenty-three new governments had acceded to the WTO, but none had made energy-related commitments regarding freedom of transit. Out of the twenty-three

---

[25]  Article V:2, GATT 1994.    [26]  Ibid.
[27]  WTO Panel Report, *Colombia – Indicative Prices and Restrictions on Ports of Entry*, WTO doc. See WTO document WT/DS366/R, paragraph 7.456 (27 April 2009).
[28]  *The World Fact Book* (2013).

members, only five, namely China, Ecuador, Oman, Saudi Arabia and Tajikistan, are oil-exporting countries. One may wonder why, in the thirteen years following the birth of the WTO, acceding governments never made specific commitments for freedom of transit for energy goods. As discussed earlier, the need for specific energy-related rules in the WTO has gained considerable prominence in recent times. Some energy-related issues were introduced in the current round of trade negotiations.

When the Doha mandate was negotiated in 2001, some issues with relevance to trade in energy goods, particularly trade facilitation, were given prominence.[29] The Doha Round Trade Facilitation negotiating mandate[30] was defined as clarifying and improving the relevant aspects of GATT 1994: Article V, among others, 'with a view to further expediting the movement, release and clearance of goods, including goods in transit'.[31] As a result from the Doha Development Agenda negotiations, the Agreement on Trade Facilitation sought to improve and clarify the text of Article V GATT.[32] While the agreement has yet to be operationalised,[33] the specific commitments on freedom of transit that have been undertaken by some Article XII members are likely to clarify and reinforce this GATT provision.

Through specific binding commitments to guarantee freedom of transit for energy, enhanced legal certainty may be developed. These commitments may provide a benchmark for acceding governments which are currently negotiating their Accession Protocols (or those which will soon apply for accession) to make commitments on freedom of transit for energy goods. The trend (from 2008) appears to suggest that energy-related commitments may always be an issue for consideration during accession negotiations for new governments.

---

[29] Paragraph 27 of the Doha WTO Ministerial Declaration; see WTO document WT/MIN (01)/DEC/1 (adopted on 14 November 2001).

[30] Annex D of the WTO Doha Work Programme; see WTO document WT/L/579, Decision adopted by the General Council on 1 August 2004.

[31] Ibid.

[32] See Annex to the WTO Ministerial Decision of 7 December 2013 (Agreement on Trade Facilitation); see WTO document WT/MIN(13)/36, WT/L/911 (adopted 11 December 2013).

[33] A Preparatory Committee on Trade Facilitation was established by the Ninth Ministerial Conference to, among other things 'ensure the expeditious entry into force of the Agreement'. See the Annex (Agreement on Trade Facilitation) to the WTO Ministerial Decision of 7 December 2013, WT/MIN(13)/36, WT/L/911 (11 December 2013).

While negotiations in the Doha Round are ongoing, we can envisage a situation where energy-related rules could be concurrently negotiated and adopted during accession negotiations. Members have been able to agree with acceding governments for them (the acceding governments) to make commitments regarding freedom of transit for energy goods, thence reinforcing the negotiating and rule-making mandate of the WTO.

It is important to note that following the initial energy-specific commitments in transit in energy by Ukraine in 2008,[34] other energy-producing countries which acceded subsequently (Montenegro in 2012,[35] Russia in 2012[36] and Tajikistan in 2013)[37] all made specific energy-related commitments relative to freedom of transit. Suffice it to say that all the commitments are couched in similar standard language. They are all made in positive confirmatory terms. They are all related to replies to requests by members to the acceding government to guarantee freedom of transit for goods.

Thus the 'representative of (Montenegro, the Russian Federation, Tajikistan or Ukraine) confirmed that ... would apply all its laws, regulations and other measures governing transit of goods (including energy) ... in conformity with the provisions of Article V of the GATT 1994 and other relevant provisions of the WTO Agreement'.[38]

Regarding the date of commencement of the commitments undertaken, three of the countries (Russia, Tajikistan and Ukraine) did not expressly state the effective date. However, in the case of Montenegro, it was expressly stated in the Protocol of Accession that these commitments would take effect upon accession to the WTO.

On the mode of transit, save for Russia (whose Accession Protocol specifically states that freedom shall be guaranteed in all modes of transit, including air and rail) none of the other members' protocols specified the mode of transportation. It follows that freedom is available in all modes of transit for energy goods. Additionally, in the case of Russia, the fact that the list of transit modes is an inclusive one means that the guaranteed freedom of transit is applicable to all modes of transport, including

---

[34] Working Party Report WT/ACC/UKR/152, paragraph 367.
[35] See WTO document WT/ACC/CGR/38, paragraph 185.
[36] See WTO document WT/ACC/RUS/70, paragraph 1161.
[37] See WTO document WT/ACC/TJK/30, paragraph 248.
[38] See Working Party Reports: WT/ACC/CGR/38 (paragraph 185), WT/ACC/RUS/70 (paragraph 1161), WT/ACC/TJK/30 (paragraph 248) and WT/ACC/UKR/152 (paragraph 367).

those which are not mentioned (and which are peculiar to energy goods, for instance transmission lines for electricity, and pipelines for oil and gas). GATT Article V:1 states *inter alia* that 'Goods ... and also vessels and other means of transport shall be deemed to be in transit'.

The other feature of the energy-related commitments for freedom of transit is the confirmation by the governments of Montenegro, Russia, Tajikistan and Ukraine during their accessions that 'other laws and measures governing transit of goods' would be brought into compliance with Article V and other provisions of the GATT and principles of the WTO. It appears that even if there is a change in the WTO rules concerning freedom of transit for energy in the future, the laws and policies of these governments will also be amended to bring them into conformity (with the GATT 1994).

Since the initial energy-related commitment guaranteeing freedom of transit was made (by Ukraine in 2008), there has been a growing trend for (energy-producing) governments, namely Montenegro, Russia and Tajikistan, to make energy-related commitments (for freedom of transit) during their accession negotiations. These commitments go beyond those which were made by the original members. It appears that a trend/ practice is being entrenched which may be emulated by future accession working parties. However, the other Article XII members (none of which are energy producers) which acceded after 2008 (namely Lao PDR in 2013, Samoa in 2012 and Vanuatu in 2012) did not make specific commitments for freedom of transit for energy goods.

## Energy-related quantitative export restrictions

None of the thirty-three Article XII members made any specific commitments not to impose quantitative export restrictions specific to trade in energy goods. Yet there are reaffirmations of the original rules/commitments not to impose quantitative export restrictions pursuant to the GATT Article XI for all goods. These rules, normatively, equally apply to energy. The major restrictions on trade in energy goods relate to production quotas. There are more controls in energy in terms of production quotas (especially imposed on OPEC member states).[39] WTO rules discipline production quotas. As long as the energy resources are not produced, it appears that they remain outside the ambit of the

---

[39] Article 2B of the OPEC Statute 2012 mandates OPEC to devise ways and means of stabilising prices in the international oil market to eliminate unnecessary fluctuations.

WTO.[40] No dispute has been initiated before the WTO Dispute Settlement Body to challenge production quotas for energy.

There is recognition of permanent sovereign rights over natural resources.[41] While emphasising this right, the WTO Panel in the case of *China concerning Measures Related to the Exportation of Rare Earths, Tungsten, and Molybdenum*[42] observed that 'it is entirely in that Member's discretion whether its conservation measures should "decrease the absolute quantity" of materials extracted or "control the speed" of such extraction'.[43] Such goods will only fall within the ambit of the GATT Article XI once extracted and ready for export. In that case, a member cannot control its exports on purely market considerations. In the United States case of *Softwood Lumber IV*,[44] the Appellate Body Report observed that once natural resource products have entered the market and are available for sale, they are subject to GATT disciplines in the same way as any other product. This being so, no WTO member has, under WTO law, the right to dictate or control the allocation or distribution of rare earth resources to achieve an economic objective. WTO members' right to adopt conservation programmes is not a right to control the international markets in which extracted products are bought and sold.

## State ownership and privatisation, state trading entities

In the past, major facilities in the energy sector, notably the transmission and distribution chains, were owned and run by large vertically integrated state-owned monopolies. These suppliers in most cases occupied a dominant position in the domestic market. The dominant position impeded or discriminated against new entrants. Where competition existed, it was skewed by the presence and operations of the state-owned enterprises (SOEs) as well as government interventions on behalf of the

---

[40] Desta (2010).

[41] UN General Assembly resolution 1803 (XVII) on the Permanent Sovereignty over Natural Resources of 14 December 1962.

[42] WTO Panel Reports, *China – Measures Related to the Exportation of Rare Earths, Tungsten, and Molybdenum*; see WTO documents: WT/DS431/R, WT/DS432/R, WT/DS433/R as of 26 March 2014, paragraph 7.266.

[43] Ibid.

[44] Appellate Body Report, *United States – Final Countervailing Duty Determination with Respect to Certain Softwood Lumber from Canada*; see WTO document WT/DS257/AB/R, adopted 17 February 2004, DSR 2004: II, p. 571.

SOEs both domestically and within the multilateral trading system.[45] The agreements covered under Article XVII of the GATT 1994 provide disciplines for state trading enterprises (STEs) within the multilateral trading system.

However, STEs (used interchangeably with SOEs) are not defined under the GATT 1994. The WTO accession standard working party report format has a designated section named 'State Owned Enterprises, State Trading Enterprises and Privatisation', in which Article XII members have accepted commitments in relation to Article XVII of the GATT. With respect to disputes brought before the WTO, it is possible that sensitive distinctions may be drawn between SOEs and STEs disciplined under Article XVII of the GATT 1994. Nevertheless, these clear distinctions are not the purpose of this chapter. Rather, it interprets the results from accessions in relation to the specific commitments made by Article XII members in their working party reports.

Accordingly, STEs have been defined as 'commercial entities' owned and operated by the state; they are authorised to conduct trade and may have a bearing on international trade. SOEs are typically characterised by targeted government policies and support. Often they have a monopoly or near monopoly on a specific sector, or on the import or export of a good. The examples of these 'commercial entities' include marketing boards.[46] Whether in part or in full, the major definitive element is some form of state control. In the case of *Korea – Various Measures on Beef* dispute,[47] the panel decided that 30 per cent ownership was deemed sufficient control.

The challenge for global trade is that SOEs do not readily allow for the efficiency gains of trade. Targeted government policies and sometimes financial support may have trade distorting and trade diversionary effects. SOEs may also put market economies within the global trading system at a competitive disadvantage.

The turn of the century has also seen several centrally planned economies transform and become more open. Most of these economies are converging towards becoming market economies. However, the process requires major structural reforms which tend to be resisted by domestic and often powerful beneficiaries in the country. In this regard, WTO accessions have been valuable in helping Article XII members,

---

[45] See WTO document S/C/W/311 WTO Secretariat Background Note on Energy Services, 12 January 2010 (paragraph 79).
[46] Goode (2007), p. 401.    [47] Paragraph 786.

specifically those Article XII members from previously centrally planned economies such as China, Russia and Ukraine, to implement and lock in difficult structural reforms with regard to the activities of their SOEs. The reforms, especially for the inefficient SOEs, are intended to break their market monopoly, facilitate privatisation and promote the entry of new market players.

In spite of the privatisation trend, many countries still maintain their SOEs in some sectors. SOEs still play an important role in driving government policy objectives and creating welfare in many countries. In this regard, SOE accession commitments on notification requirements, transparency and applying ordinary commercial considerations have been valuable in ensuring that there is an effective legal and regulatory framework for governing SOEs in countries that operate the state-capitalist model and minimising distortions to the multilateral trading system.

## Energy-specific SOE, STE and privatisation commitments for Article XII members

Out of the thirty-three Article XII members (Yemen included), all have made specific commitments of a general nature on SOEs or STEs. Here, commitments of a general nature were those commitments in relation to conformity with Article XVII of the GATT 1994, operating within ordinary commercial considerations, notification and transparency of all SOEs within the territories of Article XII members.

These seemingly simple commitments on notification, transparency and the undertaking to act within ordinary commercial considerations are huge milestones, especially those commitments emanating from some of the major players in the global energy markets like China, Russia and Saudi Arabia.

These commitments signal a shift in the operations of the global energy market from being largely dominated by SOEs which are subject to influence by the government policies of major players, to setting the stage for a more open global energy market. The commitments on notification are important for ensuring transparency while the undertaking to operate within ordinary commercial considerations guarantees predictability. The value to the global energy market covered by the multilateral trading system is tremendous as these measures help to create more stability with regard to prices and distribution in the world energy markets.

Four Article XII members – China,[48] Chinese Taipei,[49] Nepal[50] and Samoa[51] – made direct specific commitments in relation to energy, specifically mentioning oil companies or the term 'crude oil'. Interestingly, there were no common patterns in the four commitment paragraphs. For example, Nepal in its commitment paragraph undertook to notify and provide information on the activities of the Nepal Oil Corporation in accordance with Article XVII of the GATT 1994, whereas China, in response to concerns expressed by some members over its crude oil controls, confirmed in its specific commitment paragraph that imports allocated to non-state traders of crude and processed oil would be carried over to the next year if they were not fully utilised. China also committed to publishing related quotas and licences on a quarterly basis.

Five Article XII members – Bulgaria,[52] the former Yugoslav Republic of Macedonia,[53] Kyrgyz Republic,[54] Saudi Arabia[55] and Ukraine[56] – in

---

[48] Paragraph 212: China Working Party Report, see WTO document WT/ACC/CHN/49 + Corr. 1 – WT/MIN(01)/3.

[49] Paragraph 147: Chinese Taipei Working Party Report, see WTO document WT/ACC/TPKM/18 – WT/MIN(01)/4.

[50] Paragraph 111: Nepal Working Party Report, see WTO document WT/ACC/NPL/16.

[51] Paragraph 40: Samoa Working Party Report, see WTO document WT/ACC/SAM/30 – WT/MIN(11)/1.

[52] Paragraph 69 Bulgaria Working Party Report, see WTO document WT/ACC/BGR/5 + Corr. 1. This paragraph made reference to Document WT/ACC/BGR/3 which contains a list of 670 companies, including oil companies such as Avis.

[53] Paragraph 160 FYR Macedonia Working Party Report, see WTO document WT/ACC/807. This referenced paragraph 156, which reads thus: 'Responding to a specific question, he said that an agreement with a foreign oil-trading company did not contain any elements falling within the scope of Article XVII of the GATT 1994. He confirmed that upon the expiration of the licensing requirements listed in Tables 5(b) and 7(a), the importation and exportation of petroleum and fuel products will be open to all and will not be restricted by governmental agreements with foreign oil-trading companies.'

[54] Paragraph 113 Kyrgyz Republic Working Party Report, see WTO document WT/ACC/KGZ/26 + Corr. 1. This paragraph made reference to paragraph 107 which reads thus: 'At present, the Government had examined the following enterprises: Kyrgyz Energy Holding Company (electric power and thermal energy); Kyrgyzgas (natural and liquefied natural gas); Kyrgyzjilkommunsojuz (thermal energy, water pipe water and sewage).'

[55] Paragraph 52 Saudi Arabia Working Party Report, see WTO document WT/ACC/SAU/61. This paragraph made reference to paragraph 44 which listed the following energy-related companies: Saudi Arabian Basic Industries Corporation (SABIC) (downstream petrochemical products); Saudi Electricity Company (SEC) (electrical power utilities and Electricity Corporation); Saudi Arabian Oil Company (Saudi Aramco) (exploitation of crude oil and natural gas, including their derivative products).

[56] Paragraph 53 Ukraine Working Party Report, see WTO document WT/ACC/UKR/152. This referenced paragraphs 41–50 and 103 (note that the specific commitments made under 053 apply to them). Specific to our purposes, paragraph 45 provided for Table 3

their specific commitment paragraphs made reference to secondary sources such as other paragraphs, annexes and documents which refer to SOEs or STE in the energy sector. For example, Ukraine in its specific commitment paragraph made reference to some paragraphs of the working party report, including paragraph 43, which listed the closed joint-stock company UkrGasEnergo,[57] which had a monopoly on natural gas imports from Russia and Central Asia for distribution to private industrial users in the Ukraine as an STE within the meaning of the understanding on the interpretation of Article XVII of the GATT 1994.

Even without strict disciplines prohibiting SOEs, in any way; regulating the activities of SOEs touches on competition and these may be early steps for energy competition governance and disciplines within the WTO. This is also instructive for future accessions; other major oil- and energy-related acceding governments such as Algeria,[58] Azerbaijan,[59] Iraq[60] and Kazakhstan,[61] may within the course of negotiating the terms and conditions of their accession make energy-specific commitments or in the very least commitments of a general nature with regard to their SOEs upon accession.

which listed SOEs within the meaning of the GATT Article XVIII to include the national joint-stock company Naftogas of Ukraine and its subsidiaries. Also paragraph 43 listed the closed joint-stock company UkrGasEnergo (a 50–50 joint venture between Naftogas of Ukraine and RosUkrEnergo – which had a monopoly on natural gas imports from Russia and Central Asia for distribution to private industrial users in Ukraine (Naftogas of Ukraine had previously been the monopoly supplier of natural gas to Ukraine) as an STE within the meaning of the understanding on the interpretation of Article XVII of the GATT 1994.

[57] This is comprised of a 50–50 joint venture between Naftogas of Ukraine and RosUkrEnergo.

[58] According to the CIA *World Fact Book*, Algeria ranks fifteenth in the world for crude oil production, sixteenth for crude oil exports, sixteenth for proved crude oil reserves and tenth for proven natural gas reserves (retrieved 18 March 2014 from www.cia.gov/library/publications/the-world-factbook/geos/ag.html).

[59] According to the CIA *World Fact Book*, Azerbaijan ranks twenty-fifth in the world for crude oil production, seventeenth for crude oil exports, twentieth for proven crude oil reserves and twenty-eighth for natural gas reserves (retrieved 18 March 2014 from www.cia.gov/library/publications/the-world-factbook/geos/aj.html).

[60] According to the CIA *World Fact Book*, Iraq ranks eighth in the world for crude oil production, fourth for crude oil exports, fifth for proven crude oil reserves and eleventh for proven natural gas reserves (retrieved 18 March 2014 from www.cia.gov/library/publications/the-world-factbook/geos/iz.html).

[61] According to the CIA *World Fact Book*, Kazakhstan ranks eighteenth in the world for crude oil production, twelfth for crude oil exports, eleventh for proven crude oil reserves and fourteenth for proven natural gas reserves (retrieved 18 March 2014 from www.cia.gov/library/publications/the-world-factbook/geos/kz.html).

## Pricing policies

By definition, pricing policy determines the wholesale and retail prices of goods and services produced. It is an important component of the economic policy of a country, and is one of the themes under which WTO members negotiate the terms and conditions of membership with acceding governments. Price control by the government or state trading entities resulting in 'dual pricing' (also called 'double pricing' or 'two-tier pricing'[62] or differential pricing) is especially significant when pricing policy is discussed in relation to energy goods and services. This is because the price of energy goods and services determines the cost of commodities produced by energy-intensive industries along the entire domestic supply chain. This, in turn, results in a competitive advantage for domestic products against their counterparts from other countries.

Since price control in energy goods and services is usually done through the government or STEs of the members by charging domestic producers/consumers lower prices than the export or world prices, or by providing domestic entities with subsidies of general nature, pricing policy is often studied in conjunction with STEs.

Thirty-one Article XII members have made specific commitments in pricing policies (the exception was Mongolia). Those commitments relate to conformity with Article III:9 of the GATT 1994 and notification and transparency. Among these thirty-one Article XII members, four (Chinese Taipei, Russia, Saudi Arabia and Tajikistan) have made specific commitments related to energy.

Although Article III:9 of the GATT 1994 imposes no substantive obligation on price control measures and does not provide that the prices should be based on normal commercial considerations, it is important to note that the recently acceded Article XII members (Chinese Taipei in 2002, Saudi Arabia in 2005, Russia in 2012 and Tajikistan in 2013) have undertaken obligations in addition to those that bind WTO original members. For example, Saudi Arabia made a specific commitment that 'producers/distributors of NGLs [natural gas liquids] in Saudi Arabia would operate, within the relevant regulatory framework, on the basis of normal commercial considerations, based on the full recovery of costs and a reasonable profit'.[63] Similar is the specific obligation taken by

---

[62] Selivanova (2008: 6).

[63] World Trade Organization, Working Party Report, see WTO document WT/ACC/SAU/61, paragraph 33.

Russia that: 'the representative of the Russian Federation stated that upon accession, producers/distributors of natural gas in the Russian Federation would operate, within the relevant regulatory framework, on the basis of normal commercial considerations, based on recovery of costs and profit'.[64]

Despite significant achievements in accommodating some of the major energy exporters within the ambit of the WTO's multilateral trading system, it cannot be fully justified that the accession negotiations have eliminated the price controls and dual pricing of energy goods and services. For example, Saudi Arabia, in its specific commitment in paragraph 37 of its Accession Protocol has mentioned that goods and services listed in Annex A[65] were currently subject to state price or profit control. These include goods such as fuel oil, gasoline, liquefied petroleum gas, diesel, crude oil (used as fuel), etc., and services such as energy transportation services including pipeline transportation services, electricity consumption for houses and commercial purposes on a monthly basis, etc. Similarly, Russia, in its specific commitment in paragraph 133 of its Accession Protocol, has mentioned that it would apply price controls to products and services contained in Tables 7, 8 and 9[66] from

[64] World Trade Organization, Working Party Report, see WTO document WT/ACC/RUS/70, paragraph 132.

[65] Annex A-1: Goods subject to price regulation: fuel oil, gasoline, diesel, kerosene, liquefied petroleum gas (LPG) (cooking gas), natural gas liquids (propane, butane, natural gasoline), asphalt, natural gas (ethane and methane), crude oil (used as fuel). Annex A-3: Government price regulation in services sectors: energy transportation services, including pipeline transportation services, port-bulk cargo (including bulk handled at the cement silos, grains, oils or similar; excluding crude oil, gas and liquefied petroleum products) and (a) electricity consumption for houses & commercial purposes from 1 – 4000 kilowatt per hour on a monthly basis; (b) electricity consumption for houses & commercial purposes from 4001 – 6000 kilowatt per hour on a monthly basis; (c) electricity consumption for houses & commercial purposes from 6001 and more kilowatt per hour on a monthly basis.

[66] Table 7 – List of goods and services for internal consumption for which prices are regulated by the government of the Russian Federation and federal executive bodies: natural gas (excluding as sold to the population); accompanying oil gas and stripped dry gas (excluding the gas sold by the producers not affiliated with the open joint-stock company Gazprom; joint-stock companies Yakutgazprom, Norilskgazprom, Kamchatgazprom, and Rosneft-Sakhalinmorneftegaz and excluding gas sold to population and building cooperative societies); liquefied gas for household needs (excluding gas sold to the population); gas transportation services through truck pipelines; nuclear fuel cycle products; electric power and heat power generated by the entities supplying the electricity energy on the wholesale market; electricity energy network transmission services; operational dispatch control services and other services provided on the electric energy

the date of accession. These include natural gas, gas transportation services, heat power transmission services, nuclear fuel cycle products, etc. Similar is the case with other Article XII members (Albania, Armenia, Bulgaria, Estonia, Kyrgyz Republic, Lithuania, Panama) that have listed some 'energy goods and services' as an exception to 'goods and services not subject to price controls'.

It must, however, be noted that the notification and transparency commitment undertaken by these members has strengthened the transparency and predictability of prices of energy goods and services. For example, although Annex 4 of China's Accession Protocol still lists both gas and electricity subject to price controls, it has made a specific commitment that 'it would publish in the official journal the list of goods and services subject to state pricing and changes thereto, together with price-setting mechanisms and policies'.[67] Since major energy exporters are still negotiating their accession terms and conditions, it could be argued that the commitments made so far by Article XII members have created momentum for both incentives and pressure on currently acceding governments to accept specific commitments for their energy markets, as part of the multilateral trading system, to either reduce or eliminate dual pricing and, at a minimum, to accept the commitments accepted by other Article XII members. To what extent dual pricing is reduced will be subject to future negotiations between acceding governments and members.

(power) markets at the tariffs (prices) regulated by the Federal Service for Tariffs according to the list approved by the Government of the Russian Federation (services of the commercial operator, services for securing the system stability, technological joining the networks); transportation services of crude oil and oil products through trunk pipelines. Table 8 – List of goods and services for internal consumption for which prices are regulated by sub-federal executive bodies: gas distributed to the population, as well as distributed to housing operating, organisations managing tenement buildings, building cooperative societies, householders' societies for the population household needs; heat power transmission services; heat power produced by power plants carrying out production by the means of electric power and heat power combined generation; technological connection to electricity networks and/or standardised tariff rates defining the amount of these payments for territorial network organisations; solid fuel, furnace fuel for household use and kerosene distributed to the population, managing organisations, householders' societies, housing, housing construction or other special-purpose consumers' cooperatives created with the purpose of satisfying the population's needs in accommodation.

[67] World Trade Organization, Working Party Report, see WTO document WT/ACC/CHN/49, paragraph 60.

## Energy services

There is no descriptive list or definition of the term 'energy services' under the GATS. Nor do the WTO services schedules format contained in W/120 or the United Nations Central Product Classification (UNCPC) codes contain a dedicated energy services sector. At the Council for Trade in Services, there are proposals from some members[68] for an energy services sector classification under the GATS. There are several sections of the W/120 relating to energy services that are scattered under different sections, such as business services, construction, distribution and transport services, which may have a bearing on energy-related activities or services. There are presently three sub-sectors that explicitly refer to 'energy': 'Services incidental to mining' (CPC 883, 5115) and 'Services incidental to energy distribution' (CPC 887), which are found in the business services chapter; and 'Pipeline transportation' (CPC 713) which is found in the transport services chapter.[69] In view of this, most of the analysis below will be made in the light of these three sub-sectors.

From the outset, WTO members have taken up energy specific commitments in their services schedules. However, Table 33.1 shows that, comparatively, more Article XII members have taken up energy-specific services commitments than original WTO members.

### Services incidental to mining (CPC 883, 5115)

This is the area of energy services with the largest number of commitments by members: 21 per cent of original members made specific services commitments under this heading whereas in contrast 65.6 per cent of Article XII members made such commitments. For the Article XII members, as with original members, for services incidental to mining, the scope of the commitments varied. Some members amplified while others narrowed down the scope of their commitments. For example, Oman amplified its commitment by adding 'including oil field drilling', whereas Viet Nam in its commitments expressly listed some activities not covered by the scope of its commitments made under services incidental to mining.[70]

---

[68] The list includes the US (S/CSS/W/24), EC (S/CSS/W/60), Japan (S/CSS/W/42 Suppl.3), Cuba (S/CSS/W/114) and Venezuela (S/CSS/W/69, Addendum 1 & 2).

[69] S/C/W/311 WTO Secretariat Background Note on Energy Services, 12 January 2010.

[70] 'Services Incidental to Mining (CPC 883) 1. The commitments specified here are not understood to cover the following activities: supply of equipment, materials and

Table 33.1 *Total number of commitments vs. accession commitments*

|  | Total number of commitments of all members (161 countries) | Commitments of original members (128 countries) | Commitments of Article XII members (33 countries) |
|---|---|---|---|
| Services incidental to mining | 48 | 27 | 21 |
| Services incidental to energy distribution | 20 | 8 | 12 |
| Pipeline transportation | 14 | 3 | 11 |

This was the sub-sector with the largest number of commitments. Twenty-one out of thirty-three Article XII members made commitments hereunder. The commitments undertaken by members under limitation to market access and national treatment were very similar. Summarily, under mode 1 only three members – Bulgaria, Ecuador and Lao PDR – made no commitments. All the thirty-three Article XII members made commitments under mode 2. Thirty-one Article XII members made commitments under mode 3. Also, the nature of commitments under mode 3 varied as some Article XII members placed limitations on foreign equity participation on the nature of the commercial presence required. Prior to the accession of Nepal in 2004, no Article XII member placed any limitations on foreign capital participation or the nature of commercial presence under mode 3 in relation to mining services. However, since the accession of Nepal, such language has been included in the schedules of Russia, Viet Nam and Tajikistan.

*Services incidental to energy distribution (CPC 887)*

Twelve out of thirty-three Article XII members made commitments hereunder. Comparatively, 6.3 per cent of original members made specific services commitments under this heading whereas, in contrast,

chemicals, supply base services, offshore/marine support vessels, accommodation and catering, helicopter services. 2. The commitments specified here are made without prejudice to the rights of the Government of Viet Nam to set out the necessary regulations and procedures to regulate the oil and gas related activities carried out within the territory or jurisdiction of Viet Nam in full conformity with the rights and obligations of Viet Nam under the GATS.'

37.5 per cent of Article XII members made such commitments. Apart from the Kyrgyz Republic, which only made commitments on mode 3, most Article XII members made commitments under modes 1, 2 and 3. Regarding mode 4, no Article XII member made commitments except as indicated in the horizontal section.

## Pipeline transportation (CPC 713)

Eleven out of thirty-three Article XII members made commitments hereunder. Comparatively, 2.3 per cent of original members made specific services commitments under this heading whereas, in contrast, 34.4 per cent of Article XII members made such commitments. Trends show that commitments made by Article XII members under this section have evolved from pipeline transportation (CPC 713), more specifically the transportation of fuels (CPC 7131).[71] This was first listed by Moldova in 2001. Thereafter, other Article XII members who made commitments under this section have also narrowed down the scope of their commitments to transportation of fuels (CPC 7131).

Under the four modes of service, apart from Montenegro which made no commitment for the liberalisation of any of the four modes, and Tajikistan, which was unbound for mode 1, the Article XII members undertaking obligations under this section did so on very liberal terms under modes 1, 2 and 3. None made any commitment for openness under mode 4 except as indicated in the horizontal section.

Montenegro and Ukraine made additional commitments on transparency and non-discrimination for transportation of fuels (CPC 7131). The additional commitments on transparency were in relation to how measures affecting access to and trade in services of pipeline transportation were formulated, adopted and applied, while the additional commitment on non-discrimination relates to treatment of access to and use of pipeline networks under its jurisdiction, with regard to the origin, destination or ownership of product transported, without imposing any unjustified delays, restrictions or charges, as well as without discriminatory pricing based on differences in origin, destination or ownership. The inclusion of additional commitments shows clearly that WTO accession has been helpful in creating some of the much needed rules for energy transit services governance within the multilateral trading system.

---

[71] This started with Moldova which acceded on 26 July 2001.

These may also act as a precursor, if the WTO membership decides to negotiate and further expand the scope by bringing energy services specifically under the coverage of GATS disciplines. Ukraine upon its accession in 2008 was the first Article XII member to make additional commitments on transparency and non-discrimination for transportation of fuels (CPC 7131). Following this trend, Montenegro upon its accession in 2012 undertook identical additional commitments to Ukraine. There is a geopolitical dimension to this trend; Ukraine and Montenegro are strategically positioned as transit countries within the Eurasian region. They are both part of the Black Sea Economic Cooperation Organization.[72] Ukraine has been a major energy transit country for energy from Russia to the European Union, particularly for gas.[73] The European Union, seeking to facilitate energy trade within the region and reduce reliance on the Turkish straits, has been seeking to develop energy infrastructure such as pipeline projects in the wider Black Sea region, including Montenegro.[74]

A similar trend with regard to additional commitments for transportation of fuels (CPC 7131) could be followed by other acceding governments in the Balkan peninsula such as Bosnia and Herzegovina and Serbia.[75] Belarus is another acceding member strategically located as a transit country which may make similar additional commitments for transportation of fuels (CPC 7131).

Apart from the three sub-sectors discussed above, China made energy-specific services commitments which do not fall within the three sub-sectors. It made commitments related to onshore and offshore oil field services geological, geophysical and other scientific prospecting services (CPC 86751). For these services, China made full commitments on modes 1 and 2, partial commitments in relation to mode 3, and mode 4 was unbound except as indicated in the horizontal schedules.

In conclusion, there is an increasing level of commitment of energy services as seen in the services schedules of Article XII members. Geopolitical nuances, especially in the Eurasian region, may also imply

---

[72] Other members of the Black Sea Economic Cooperation Organization include Albania, Azerbaijan, Bulgaria, Georgia, Greece, Moldova, Romania, Russia, Serbia and Turkey.

[73] http://ec.europa.eu/energy/international/bilateral_cooperation/ukraine_en.htm.

[74] European Communities Communication from the Commission to the Council and the European Parliament Black Sea Synergy – A New Regional Cooperation Initiative, COM (2007) 160 final, Brussels, 11 April 2007 (retrieved 18 March 2014 from http://ec.europa.eu/world/enp/pdf/com07_160_en.pdf).

[75] Serbia is a member of the Black Sea Economic Cooperation Organization.

that WTO members may require acceding governments in that region to make similar energy-related services commitments. These commitments facilitate transparency, non-discrimination, predictability and may even be useful for fostering peace and cooperation within the region.

The Article XII members, in their Accession Protocols, have made different kinds of energy-related commitments in order to be part of the WTO. Nevertheless, not all of them have accepted the same kind of commitments, it being difficult, in consequence, to identify the pattern which acceding governments follow.

It should be emphasised that during accession negotiations, members and the acceding government/s are free to agree on to terms and commitments which go beyond those that were undertaken by original members. The GATT Article XII which governs accessions provides for wider flexibility to the working party and the acceding government/s during accession negotiations. The provision does not define or limit what substance or commitments should be demanded by members or agreed upon by acceding governments. Members, therefore, are free to bring any issue to the negotiating table provided it contributes to achieving the overall objective of the WTO. However, it appears from the Accession Protocols that energy issues are not discussed in the case of countries which are not energy producers. Although accession-specific commitments give a clear direction, the extent of binding on non-energy producers is unclear if in future they also discover tradable energy resources within their territories. The issue that remains to be examined is how non-energy producing countries (which are in most cases net importers of energy) which have not undertaken specific energy-related commitments will be affected by the specific energy-related rules. To a large extent, panel and Appellate Body conclusions and findings and emergent WTO dispute settlement jurisprudence will have a huge role to play. Obviously, accession-specific obligations by approximately 20 per cent of the WTO membership cannot be discounted.

The chapter concludes that through these additional energy-related commitments made by Article XII members, new and clear rules on freedom of transit, pricing policy, SOEs and energy services, which will guide trade in energy, are definitely evolving. World energy markets are being unlocked. Restrictive trading practices are being frozen. State monopolies are being unbundled for open and regulated market competition.

The outcome of energy-related commitments in the WTO accession negotiations becomes more striking when compared to the level of ambition in ongoing[76] discussions on energy in the Transatlantic Trade and Investment Partnership (TTIP). Putting aside the differing views of the European Union and the United States regarding the feasibility of a stand-alone chapter on energy in their mega-regional TTIP, the level of ambition in the proposals for regulating trade in energy is not on a par with and falls below the results from the specific commitments already achieved in the Accession Protocols.[77] These latter are as original as they are multilateral.

These facts are particularly demonstrated in two areas: the freedom of transit of energy, and the dual-pricing policy.

Furthermore, both of the TTIP negotiating parties have already made known that their negotiating objectives to exclude obligations of a binding nature (encompassing only common principles), and also exclude any changes to domestic laws and regulations. Legally, such a non-binding rule lags behind energy-specific 'binding' obligations that have been committed to by four Article XII members (Montenegro, Russia, Tajikistan and Ukraine) during their WTO accession negotiations, particularly for ensuring the freedom of transit of energy.

On dual-pricing policies, which the TTIP may aim to prohibit, this topic has already been streamlined and clarified by four Article XII members (Chinese Taipei, Russia, Saudi Arabia and Tajikistan) during their WTO accession negotiations.

These two areas of specific obligations existed before the TTIP negotiations, initiated in July 2013. Furthermore, in terms of the scope of these WTO accession obligations, these accession-specific commitments apply most-favoured-nation (MFN) status, compared to the TTIP. The outcome of the WTO accessions negotiations benefits much more than a group of specific participants in any possible mega-regional agreement. Thus, the implication of WTO accessions negotiations for international cooperation, in a geopolitically sensitive area, such as energy, is greater than mega-regional commitments, at this stage.

It remains to be seen whether the standards set by already acceded energy-producing-exporting members will act as a guide for future working party negotiations. Will members during these working parties demand more substantive market access commitments in the energy sector? Verbal commitments such as that by the Bahamas

---

[76] As of June 2014.

[77] *Inside US Trade* (2014). 'EU pursues strong energy chapter in TTIP, along the lines of leaked paper', 3 June.

(currently in the process of accession)[78] in a recent speech by Prime Minister Christie, to reform the energy sector and liberalise electricity market for boosting the economic growth, is a positive signal.

## List of cases

1  Appellate Body Report, *United States – Final Countervailing Duty Determination with Respect to Certain Softwood Lumber from Canada*; see WTO document WT/DS257/AB/R (adopted 17 February 2004).

2  WTO Dispute Panel Reports, *Canada – Certain Measures Affecting the Renewable Energy Generation Sector*; see WTO documents WT/DS412/R; and *Canada – Measures Relating to the Feed-In Tariff Program*, WT/DS426/R (19 December 2012).

3  WTO Panel Reports *China – Measures Related to the Exportation of Rare Earths, Tungsten, and Molybdenum*; see WTO documents WT/DS431/R, WT/DS432/R, WT/DS433/R (26 March 2014).

4  WTO Panel Report, *Colombia – Indicative Prices and Restrictions on Ports of Entry*; see WTO document WT/DS366/R, paragraph 7.456 (27 April 2009).

5  WTO Panel Report *EC and Argentina – Hides and Leather*; see WTO document WT/DS155/10 (31 August 2001).

6  WTO Panel Report, *Korea – Measures Affecting Imports of Fresh, Chilled and Frozen Beef*; see WTO documents WT/DS161/R, WT/DS169/R (adopted 10 January 2001), as modified by Appellate Body Report WT/DS161/AB/R, WT/DS169/AB/R, DSR 2001: I, p. 59.

## References

British Petroleum (BP) (2013). *BP Statistical Review of World Energy.* Retrieved 9 March 2014 from www.bp.com/content/dam/bp/pdf/statistical-review/statistical_review_of_world_energy_2013.pdf.

Desta, M. G. (2004). *OPEC and the WTO: Petroleum as a Fuel for Cooperation in International Relations.* Retrieved 2 April 2014 from www.mafhoum.com/press7/185E17.htm.

[78] *The Freeport News* (2014), 'Parliament reforming the energy sector of the Bahamas'. Retrieved 25 March from http://freeport.nassauguardian.net/Politics/Parliament/Reforming-the-energy-sector-of-The-Bahamas.

(2010). 'To what extent are WTO rules relevant to trade in natural resources?' WTO Publications. Retrieved from www.wto.org/english/res_e/publica tions_e/wtr10_forum_e/wtr10_desta_e.htm.

Goode, W. (2007). *Dictionary of Trade Policy Terms*. Cambridge University Press.

International Energy Forum (IEF) (2010). *The Maturing Producer-Consumer Dialogue*. Twelfth IEF Ministerial background paper, International Energy Forum, Cancun, Mexico, 30–31 March. Retrieved from www.ief.org/ _resources/files/events/12th-ief-ministerial-cancun-mexico/ief-background-paper.pdf.

(2012). *World Energy Outlook 2012*. Retrieved from www.worldenergyoutlook. org/media/weowebsite/2012/exsum/German.pdf.

OPEC (Organization of the Petroleum Exporting Countries) (2012). OPEC Statute 2012. Retrieved from www.opec.org/opec_web/static_files_project/media/ downloads/publications/OPEC_Statute.pdf.

'Parliament reforming the energy sector of the Bahamas' (2014). *The Freeport News*. Retrieved 25 March 2014 from http://freeport.nassauguardian.net/ Politics/Parliament/Reforming-the-energy-sector-of-The-Bahamas.

Selivanova, J. (2008). Energy Dual Pricing in WTO Law – Analysis and prospects in the context of Russia's accession to the WTO. London, Cameron May Ltd.

(2010). *Challenges for Multilateral Energy Trade Regulation: WTO and Energy Charter*. Paper presented at the 2nd Biennial Global Conference the University of Barcelona and its IELPO Programme, 8–10 July; also in Society of International Economic Law, Working Paper No. 2010/20. Retrieved from http://papers.ssrn.com/sol3/JELJOUR_Results.cfm?form_name=journal browse&journal_id=1588914.

Sidley Austin LLP (2012). 'Russia and the World Trade Organization: Consequences of Accession for the Russian Fuel and Energy Complex and Other Industries of Russian Economy'. Background Paper for Roundtable Moscow, 29 March. Retrieved from http://rosenergo.gov.ru/upload/english.pdf.

Ugaz, P. (2011). 'Prospects for a transit regime on energy in the WTO Agenda', *Internacional Ano*, XVIII(29): 247–298.

*World Fact Book* (2013). Retrieved 27 February 2014 from www.cia.gov/library/ publications/the-world-factbook/fields/2244.html.

World Trade Organization (WTO) (2010). 'Trade in natural resources', *World Trade Report*.

(2013). 'Factors shaping the future of world trade', *World Trade Report*. Retrieved from http://wto.org/english/res_e/booksp_e/world_trade_report13_e.pdf.

# 34

# Domestic framework for making and enforcing policies

JOSEFITA PARDO DE LEÓN AND RAFAT AL-AKHALI

## ABSTRACT

*A core objective of accession results is to establish a legal foundation for the conduct and management of trade policy based on the rule of law. Implementation of accession commitments hinges on the existence of an effective domestic framework for making and enforcing policies. Customarily, this is described in the third chapter of working party reports. Twenty-eight of the members that acceded pursuant to procedures in Article XII of the Marrakesh Agreement Establishing the World Trade Organization (WTO Agreement), have undertaken a total of fifty-five accession-specific commitments in this regard. The uniquely definable pattern that has emerged from WTO Accession Protocols confirms the uniform applicability of the WTO Agreement throughout and across the entirety of the customs territory of the new member, the exclusive authority of central governments to implement and enforce WTO rules, the strengthening of due process and the rule of law, and the precedence of ratified international treaties over domestic legislation, in many instances. These commitments are integral to the WTO Agreement and are enforceable under the WTO Dispute Settlement Understanding. Although normative and standard, they confirm the long-standing accession practice that a range of original members have not confirmed and from which several deviate. This chapter studies the specific accession-specific commitments in the domestic framework for making and enforcing policies. It also investigates the relationship between Accession Protocols and domestic legal systems and asks whether original members undertook similar obligations.*

The analyses in the chapters in this book were finalised at the end of December 2014. Since then the Republic of Seychelles acceded to the World Trade Organization (WTO) on 26 April 2015. This expanded total WTO membership from 160 to 161. Please see the editors' note.

729

## The WTO Agreement and the Domestic Framework for Making and Enforcing Policies

Accession commitments are to be implemented, in most cases, upon accession.[1] In practice, implementation takes place through the amendment and/or enactment of legal instruments, which are, in turn, applied and enforced by designated authorities. Article XVI:4 of the Agreement Establishing the World Trade Organization WTO Agreement provides that 'Each Member shall ensure the conformity of its laws, regulations and administrative procedures with its obligations as provided in the annexed Agreements'.

Nevertheless, the WTO Agreement does not provide instruction as to the architecture necessary to comply with Article XVI:4. Hence, each member enjoys the sovereign right to design its domestic institutions and processes. Different agreements establish the standard on how this should be effected. For instance, the last sentence of Article 1 of the Agreement on Trade-Related Intellectual Property Rights (TRIPs Agreement) explicitly establishes that 'Members shall be free to determine the appropriate method of implementing the provisions of this Agreement within their own legal system and practice'.

The Agreement on the Implementation of Article VI (Anti-dumping Agreement) of the General Agreement on Tariffs and Trade (GATT) 1994 provides a transparency obligation, in its Article 16.5, to notify to the Anti-dumping Committee '(a) which of its authorities are competent to initiate and conduct investigations . . . and (b) its domestic procedures governing the initiation and conduct of such investigations'.

In the Agreement on Technical Barriers to Trade (TBT Agreement), Articles 10.1 and 10.3 provide that: 'Each Member shall ensure that an enquiry point exists which is able to answer all reasonable enquiries from other Members and interested parties in other Members as well as to provide the relevant documents'.

The above-mentioned provisions contained in the TRIPs, Anti-dumping and TBT Agreements suggest that members have a degree of freedom to design their own institutional infrastructure. The councils and committees responsible for the administration of the agreements serve as the platform for discussions on implementation. Furthermore, members undertake periodic peer reviews of their trade policies under

---

[1] Some Article XII members negotiated an implementation period for certain WTO obligations; see Table 9.1.

the Trade Policy Review Mechanism.[2] And, last but not least, members can use the Dispute Settlement Understanding to address non-compliance with the WTO Agreement.[3]

From the perspective of WTO accession, acceding governments need to demonstrate the existence of an effective domestic framework for making and enforcing policies. This is particularly important in the case of economies in transition and those countries evolving towards a more open and democratic political system, which are still developing their institutional infrastructure.

The first three reports of accession working parties (Ecuador[4], Mongolia[5] and Bulgaria[6]) did not have a section describing the domestic framework for making and enforcing policies. The Report of the Working Party on the Accession of Panama[7] had only one descriptive paragraph under this section.

The subsequent twenty-eight reports by working parties contain comprehensive sections. Over the years, the treaty dialogue has become more detailed, as members endeavour to better understand the architecture for decision-making and enforcement of each acceding government and propose enforceable accession-specific obligations for the effective operation of this infrastructure. Hence, the treaty dialogue has evolved from a self-contained, one-paragraph account of the executive, legislative and judicial powers[8] to a detailed explanation of political systems and of the division of authority between central and subcentral governments, as well as information regarding the precedence of international treaties and ratification procedures.[9]

Twenty-eight of the thirty-three members that acceded through the procedures in Article XII of the WTO Agreement (Article XII members) undertook specific commitments under the section on the domestic framework for making and enforcing policies. These are the result of multilateral negotiations with members and complex internal processes involving domestic stakeholders. The section has been traditionally

---

[2] Articles A to G of the Trade Policy Review Mechanism.
[3] Article 1 of the Understanding on Rules and Procedures Governing the Settlement of Disputes.
[4] See WTO document WT/L/77, dated 14 July 1995.
[5] See WTO document WT/ACC/MNG/9, dated 27 June 1996.
[6] See WTO document WT/ACC/BGR/5, dated 20 September 1996.
[7] See WTO document WT/ACC/PAN/19, dated 20 September 1996.
[8] See WTO document paragraph 11, WT/ACC/PAN/19.
[9] For example, paragraphs 65 to 76 of WT/ACC/TJK/30.

divided into two sub-sections: (i) 'powers of the executive, legislative and judiciary'; and (ii) 'authority of sub-central governments'.

## Powers of executive, legislative and judicial branches of government

The sub-section on powers of the executive, legislative and judicial branches of government starts with a description of the political system and the balance of power between the executive, legislative and judicial branches of the acceding government.

In this context, members seek information on how the executive branch is constituted (i.e. whether through elections, direct appointments or other means), as well as on the entities with authority to implement and enforce the WTO Agreement.

The legislative branch plays a key role in amending and/or enacting WTO-related legislation. Therefore, members are also interested in understanding its composition and structure. A review of the empirical evidence demonstrates that 80 per cent of acceding governments have had to amend and/or enact legislation to implement the TRIPs Agreement, disciplines regarding trade remedies and customs valuation.[10] This underpins the value of having a well-functioning legislature with the capacity to consult, draft and enact in a timely manner.

The relationship of the domestic legal framework, including the Constitution, on the one hand, to the WTO Agreement,[11] on the other hand, has been extensively discussed in working parties. Five Article XII members[12] undertook specific commitments stating that ratified international treaties had precedence over their domestic legislation. Two of these Article XII members[13] also made commitments describing their respective domestic ratification procedures. In requiring such detail, members have obtained assurance that the WTO Agreement will have legal standing in the respective jurisdiction.

---

[10] See WTO document paragraph 78, WT/ACC/19.

[11] In most jurisdictions, the Constitution gives precedence to international treaties over domestic law. In such cases, domestic laws that are not compliant with the WTO Agreement would not need to be individually amended, as the respective WTO rules would supersede them. In jurisdictions where international treaties do not have precedence, non-compliant domestic laws will need to be identified and specifically amended to be brought into conformity (e.g. the United States).

[12] Armenia (paragraphs 36 and 37); Estonia (paragraph 30); Jordan (paragraph 40); Vanuatu (paragraph 31); and Viet Nam (paragraph 119).

[13] Armenia (paragraph 37); and Viet Nam (paragraph 119).

Some Article XII members have accepted specific commitments with regard to: (i) disclosing draft amendments to the list of prohibited or conditional investment sectors;[14] (ii) promulgating all regulations in a timely manner so as to fully implement commitments within the relevant timelines;[15] and (iii) creating a mechanism under which individuals and enterprises may bring to the attention of the national authorities cases of non-uniform application of WTO rules.[16]

More recently, Russia undertook commitments under the domestic framework for making and enforcing policies: (i) to create a mechanism for publication of draft laws, before their adoption; (ii) to provide a reasonable period of time to receive comments by members or interested persons; and (iii) that no legal act would enter into force prior to publication.[17] It also undertook that the WTO Agreement would be the legal basis for the new member's trade relations with existing members.[18]

The commitments described in the two previous paragraphs highlight the transparency principle, as provided, for instance, in Article X:2 of the GATT 1994. The Appellate Body, in *United States – Restrictions on Imports of Cotton and Man-Made Fibre Underwear*, provided an elaboration in this regard, particularly useful in accessions:

> Article X:2 may be seen to embody a principle of fundamental importance – that of promoting full disclosure of governmental acts affecting Members and private persons and enterprises, whether of domestic or foreign nationality. The relevant policy principle is widely known as the principle of transparency and has obviously due process dimensions. The essential implication is that Members and other persons affected, or likely to be affected, by governmental measures imposing restraints, requirements and other burdens, should have a reasonable opportunity to acquire authentic information about such measures and accordingly to protect and adjust their activities or alternatively to seek modification of such measures.[19]

Accession treaty dialogue also describes and reviews the structure and functioning of the judicial branch, which covers the hierarchy of the domestic court system, right of appeal, procedures regarding commercial cases, availability of commercial arbitration and information on membership in international arbitration conventions (e.g. the New York Convention on the Enforcement of Foreign Arbitral Awards).

[14] Viet Nam (paragraph 117).    [15] China (paragraph 68).    [16] China (paragraph 75).
[17] Russia (paragraph 183).    [18] Russia (paragraph 209).
[19] See WTO document, page 21 of WT/DS24/AB/R.

Due process and the appellate process are fundamental. Twenty-six of the thirty-three reports of working parties record discussions on the right to appeal against administrative decisions. Article X:3(b) of the GATT 1947 is the cornerstone of due process in the multilateral trading system. This provision has evolved[20] and has been enshrined in several facets of the WTO Agreement.[21] Important guidance with regard to the application of Article X:3(b) of the GATT 1994 has been developed through dispute settlement. For example, the panel on the *EC – Selected Customs Matters* stated that:

> [A] due process theme underlies Article X of the GATT 1994. In the Panel's view, this theme suggests that an aim of the review provided for under Article X:3(b) of the GATT 1994 is to ensure that a trader who has been adversely affected by a decision of an administrative agency has the ability to have that adverse decision reviewed.[22]

In the same case, the Appellate Body noted that:

> [W]e are of the view that Article X:3(b) of the GATT 1994 requires a WTO Member to establish and maintain independent mechanisms for prompt review and correction of administrative action in the area of customs administration.[23]

Several Article XII members have accepted commitments regarding the establishment of a system of appeal;[24] the right for independent[25] or judicial review;[26] and a system of commercial courts.[27] These commitments safeguard and strengthen due process and the rule of law, not only in these jurisdictions but in the multilateral trading system as a whole. The acceptance of accession-specific obligations in this area, enforceable under the DSU, has been critical in the integration of transition economies into the rules-based multilateral trading system. They have exercised

---

[20] Ala'i (2011).

[21] Article X:3(b) of the GATT 1994; Article VI:2 of the General Agreement on Trade in Services (GATS); and Articles 41 and 42 of the TRIPs Agreement.

[22] See WTO document, paragraph 7.536 of WT/DS315/R.

[23] See WTO document, paragraph 303 of WT/DS315/AB/R.

[24] Armenia (paragraph 34); Cambodia (paragraph 36); Cabo Verde (paragraph 66); Croatia (paragraph 37); Georgia (paragraph 35); Kyrgyz Republic (paragraph 26); Montenegro (paragraph 56); Nepal (paragraph 31); Oman (paragraph 32); Samoa (paragraph 54); Saudi Arabia (paragraph 85); Tajikistan (paragraph 71); Ukraine (paragraph 92); Vanuatu (paragraph 28); and Yemen (paragraph 57).

[25] Russia (paragraph 215) and Tonga (paragraph 43).

[26] China (paragraphs 78 and 79); Lao PDR (paragraph 52); and Viet Nam (paragraph 135).

[27] Cambodia (paragraph 36).

a potent influence in the liberalisation and outward orientation of previously centrally planned non-market oriented economies.

It should be noted that Cambodia (which acceded on 13 October 2003) undertook commitments to establish an appeal system by December 2004 and a commercial court system by 1 January 2005.[28] The most recent state of play in the implementation of its commitments was included in the trade policy review.[29]

### Authority of sub-central governments

The requirement on the authority of central and sub-central governments is pursuant to Article XXIV:12 of the GATT 1994, which provides that: 'Each contracting party shall take such reasonable measures as may be available to it to ensure observance of the provisions of this Agreement by the regional and local governments and authorities within its territories'.

With regard to trade in services, Article I:3(a) of the GATS provides that: '(a) "measures by Members" means measures taken by: (i) central, regional or local governments and authorities; and (ii) non-governmental bodies in the exercise of powers delegated by central, regional or local governments or authorities'.

The distribution of authority between central governments, on the one hand, and subcentral governments, on the other, is another core feature of the treaty dialogue. The discussions are systemic, resting on the bedrock of how bills are drafted, enacted into law, transparency provisions and their applicability across the territory of the acceding government. In the question-and-answer process, members have sought to understand the latitude and associated scope of authority, including 'interference', of local authorities with regard to the implementation of the WTO Agreement. This is an area where the obligations accepted by Article XII members have strengthened the original rules and ensured that they are systemically iron clad.

Accession results show that eighteen Article XII members have undertaken commitments stating that subcentral or local government entities have no autonomous authority regarding subsidies, taxation, trade policy or any other measures covered by WTO provisions.[30]

---

[28] Ibid.  [29] See WTO document, paragraphs 6 to 10, WT/TPR/S/253/Rev. 1.

[30] Albania (paragraph 38); Armenia (paragraph 36); China (paragraph 70); Croatia (paragraph 41); Estonia (paragraph 30); Jordan (paragraph 43); Kyrgyz Republic (paragraph 28); Lao PDR (paragraph 55); Latvia (paragraph 30); Lithuania (paragraph 29); Moldova

Furthermore, Kyrgyz Republic[31] undertook that central authorities would be solely responsible for establishing foreign trade policy and that the central government would implement the provisions of the WTO that were relevant to subcentral governments.

Regarding enforcement of the WTO Agreement, twenty-two Article XII members committed that central government authorities would eliminate or nullify measures taken by sub-central or local authorities that were inconsistent with WTO provisions, and enforce these provisions without requiring the affected parties to petition through the courts or requiring formal legal proceedings.[32]

Furthermore, thirty Article XII members accepted specific obligations that the provisions of the WTO Agreement would be applied uniformly throughout their customs territories, including regions engaging in border trade and frontier traffic, special economic zones and other areas where special regimes for tariffs, taxes and regulations were established and at all levels of government.[33]

## Beyond the 'domestic' framework for making and enforcing policies

The formation of the Customs Union of Russia, Kazakhstan and Belarus took place in parallel with the last stages of the Russian accession, in 2010–2011. Members required detailed information on the Customs Union[34] and its influence on the Russian trade regime. Of particular interest was the fact that the Treaty on the Functioning of the Customs

---

(paragraph 48); Montenegro (paragraph 59); Samoa (paragraph 58); Seychelles (paragraph 96); Tajikistan (paragraph 76); Tonga (paragraph 48); Ukraine (paragraph 84); Vanuatu (paragraph 31).

[31] Kyrgyz Republic (paragraph 28).

[32] Armenia (paragraph 36); China (paragraphs 68 and 70); Chinese Taipei (paragraph 15); Croatia (paragraph 41); Estonia (paragraph 30); Georgia (paragraph 40); Jordan (paragraph 40); Kyrgyz Republic (paragraph 28); Lao PDR (paragraph 55); Latvia (paragraph 30); Lithuania (paragraph 29); Moldova (paragraph 48); Montenegro (paragraph 59); Russia (paragraph 214); Samoa (paragraph 58); Saudi Arabia (paragraph 88); Seychelles (paragraph 96); Tajikistan (paragraph 76); Tonga (paragraph 48); Ukraine (paragraph 84); Vanuatu (paragraph 31); Viet Nam (paragraph 134); Yemen (paragraph 59).

[33] Albania (paragraph 38); China (paragraph 73); Croatia (paragraph 41); Estonia (paragraph 30); Georgia (paragraph 40); Jordan (paragraph 40); Lao PDR (paragraph 55); Lithuania (paragraph 29); Moldova (paragraph 48); Montenegro (paragraph 59); Russia (paragraph 214); Samoa (paragraph 58); Saudi Arabia (paragraph 88); Seychelles (paragraph 96); Tajikistan (paragraph 76); Tonga (paragraph 48); Ukraine (paragraph 84); Vanuatu (paragraph 31); Viet Nam (paragraph 134); Yemen (paragraph 59).

[34] Russia (paragraphs 154 to 188).

Union in the Framework of the Multilateral Trading System provides that obligations in WTO Accession Protocols would become an integral part of the Customs Union, and that the Treaty was directly applicable in all the jurisdictions of parties to the Customs Union.[35] The Customs Union is a work in progress as part of the ongoing process of Eurasian economic integration.

## Obligations of original members

In contrast to Article XII members, original WTO members were not required to provide upfront information on their domestic framework for making and enforcing policies. Their only commitment was to implement the WTO Agreement.

Since 1995, discussions on implementation have taken place in the councils and committees responsible for the administration of the agreements annexed to the WTO Agreement. These discussions took into account the transition periods that were negotiated during the Uruguay Round, as well as legislation notified to the relevant bodies. Furthermore, in trade policy reviews, members ask questions and offer substantive comments. These contribute to improving the transparency and understanding of the institutions and measures of the member under review. This is a critical pillar of the rules-based multilateral trading system. Yet experience has demonstrated the reliance of members on the Dispute Settlement Mechanism, which is the most effective mechanism for addressing non-compliance with the WTO Agreement.

At the end of the Uruguay Round, the majority of original members undertook a range of domestic procedures to ratify the WTO Agreement. The approach by the United States was unique and notable. The United States implemented the WTO Agreement through detailed legislation and administrative actions, as provided for in the Uruguay Round Agreements Act of 1994 (URAA), which was signed into law in December 1994;[36] its statement on administrative action (SAA)[37] provides that: '[i]f there is any conflict between US law and

---

[35] Russian Federation (paragraphs 185 and 186).

[36] See Leebron (1997) and Reams and Schultz (1995).

[37] The SAA was submitted together with the URAA to the US Congress. Section 102(d) provides that the SAA 'shall be regarded as an authoritative expression by the United States concerning the interpretation and application of the Uruguay Round Agreements and this Act in any judicial proceeding in which a question arises concerning such interpretation or application'.

any of the Uruguay Round agreements, section 102(a) of the implementing bill makes clear that US law will take precedence'.

Article XII accession commitments[38] have ensured the precedence
of the WTO Agreement over and above conflicting domestic laws and
regulations, including for those Article XII members that are parties to
a customs union.[39] The effect is that the *acquis* of these members has
tightened the implementation of their commitments and reinforced the
integrity of the rules-based system. Their commitments have enabled
the system to maintain progress and strength, particularly with regard to
the integration of new members from non-market, centrally planned
economies. Reconciled with the obligations of original members, what
is demonstrable and has been argued is that the rules-based multilateral
trading system is sensitive to the sovereign right of members to determine the manner in which the WTO Agreement should be implemented.

The analysis in the first part of this chapter shows that Article XII
members have accepted precise commitments with regard to their
domestic framework for making and enforcing policies. Commitment
language has been tailored on a case-by-case basis. Nevertheless, it
should be taken into consideration that, when the Uruguay Round was
concluded in 1994, negotiators did not have actual experience on the
implementation of such a far-reaching agreement. Since then, members
have acquired experience and *savoir faire* on the domestic 'mechanics'
of implementation. As a result, members have realised the need for a
solid framework for trade-related decision-making and enforcement.
Naturally, this is reflected in detailed commitments, aimed at ensuring
that successive government administrations are bound to operate
under the same rules-based system. This evolution towards more specific rule-making does not apply only to accessions. The complexity
of issues under discussion and negotiation in the WTO has increased
over the years, for example, in the claims and arguments presented in
dispute settlement cases, discussions and decisions in regular councils
and committees and the Doha Round.

The WTO Agreement fosters due process and the rule of law. The specific
commitments under the section on a domestic framework for making and
enforcing policies have an overarching influence on the successful implementation of the obligations undertaken by acceding governments.

---

[38] Armenia (paragraphs 36 and 37); Estonia (paragraph 30); Jordan (paragraph 40); Vanuatu (paragraph 31); Viet Nam (paragraph 119).
[39] Russian Federation (paragraphs 185 and 186).

Since 1995, the importance of this section has increased, as members draw lessons from approximately twenty years of implementing the WTO Agreement. The commitments undertaken lock in the establishment and operation of the institutions, and strengthen due process and the rule of law. The emerging pattern shows that these commitments explicitly provide for the uniform application of the WTO Agreement throughout the customs territory, and for the exclusive authority of central governments on implementation and enforcement.

Furthermore, commitments confirming the right to appeal against administrative decisions not only mirror the provisions in the GATT 1994 (and other agreements covering trade in goods), the GATS and the TRIPs Agreement, but they also take account of developments in jurisprudence. Article XII members that undertook to establish an appeal system took a major step towards ensuring due process and strengthening the rule of law. As a result, policy-makers and government officials need to act accountably, accept challenges and questioning from the public, and learn to listen to and interact with domestic constituencies.[40]

An important contribution of the section on a domestic framework for making and enforcing policies is clarity with regard to the relation between the WTO Agreement and the domestic legal systems of Article XII members. The direct applicability of the WTO Agreement, in most jurisdictions, enhances certainty and predictability.

While it might seem that Article XII members have accepted commitments beyond those undertaken by original members, a careful analysis reveals that they actually reflect existing provisions in the WTO Agreement. However, it should be recognised that the precision of commitment language has increased. Therefore, it could be perceived as 'stricter' and more prescriptive. This is the result of the combination of accumulated experience on implementation, dispute settlement jurisprudence and the specific situation and needs of the acceding governments.

The rules-based multilateral trading system is in constant evolution as a result of decisions in regular councils and committees, dispute settlement and negotiations. WTO accessions are at the forefront of its regular work and are influenced by developments in other areas. The reports of working parties demonstrate this fact. Regular analysis to understand this evolution is necessary to ensure that the rules-based multilateral trading system continues to function smoothly and predictably.

---

[40] See Aaronson and Rodwan (2011).

# References

Aaronson, S. and A. M. Rodwan (2011). 'Does the WTO help member states clean up?' Washington DC, Institute for International Economic Policy, George Washington University, Working Paper 2011–13.

Ala'i, P. (2011). 'Transparency and the expansion of the WTO mandate', *American University International Law Review*, 26(4): 1009–1029.

Leebron, D. W. (1997). 'Implementation of the Uruguay Round results in the United States', in J. H. Jackson and A. O. Sykes (eds.), *Implementing the Uruguay Round*. Oxford University Press, Chapter 6.

Reams Jr, B. D. and J. S. Schultz (eds.) (1995). *Uruguay Round Agreements Act: A Legislative History of Public Law No. 103–465*. Buffalo, NY, Institute for International Legal Information, W.S. Hein & Co.

# 35

# Export duty commitments: the treaty dialogue and the pattern of commitments

CHIEDU OSAKWE, DAYONG YU AND PETRA BESLAĆ

## ABSTRACT

*This chapter focuses, pursuant to Article XII accession-specific commitments, on the evolving disciplines on export duties, distinguished from the broader setting of export restrictions. From a rules angle, export duties were not subject to disciplines, in contrast to import duties that have, classically, been bound in schedules of concessions and commitments on goods since GATT 1947. Pursuant to Article XI:1 of the General Agreement on Tariffs and Trade (GATT) 1994 (rules for 'quantitative restrictions'), prohibitions or restrictions on imports and exports, such as bans, quotas and restrictive licences, are generally prohibited, except for duties, taxes or other charges. In economic operations, export duties with price discrimination effects between domestic and foreign producers have resulted in efficiency losses and anti-competitiveness, and have undermined economic welfare. In accession negotiations, the establishment of disciplines and improvement in economic welfare has framed the treaty dialogue. This dialogue has made evident a range of issues that are systemic and that have involved questions on international economic cooperation, revolving around the broader use of export restrictions and their overlap with export duties. This chapter reviews the substance of the treaty dialogue on export duties and identifies the extent and pattern of specific obligations on export duties in the Article XII Accession Protocols deposited thus far. The analysis shows that fifteen Article XII members have accepted accession-specific obligations on the application of export duties. These obligations range across 'abiding' by the provisions of the WTO Agreement; 'binding and/or fixing' applied export duty rates; and,*

The analyses in the chapters in this book were finalised at the end of December 2014. Since then the Republic of Seychelles acceded to the World Trade Organization (WTO) on 26 April 2015. This expanded total WTO membership from 160 to 161. Please see the editors' note.

*'reducing', 'eliminating' or 'foreclosing' on the use of such duties. Of precedential value is the modification of the classical 1947 architecture of the GATT Goods Schedule to create a Part V on Export Duties in the context of the WTO accession commitments of Russia in its Goods Schedule. This chapter argues that accession-specific commitments have deepened and extended original WTO rules governing export duties as an instrument of trade policy. The overall systemic effect has been positive, namely to constrain, reduce, eliminate and/or bind, hence contributing to clarity and predictability of the rules with pro-competitive effects, enhancement of market access opportunities and improvements in economic welfare. The chapter argues that WTO accession-specific obligations for export duties have set the multilateral standard for disciplines in this area. Nevertheless, it is worrying that even as the disciplines on export duties are being formulated and strengthened via Article XII members, the facts suggest the higher use of such export duties by original members over the period from 2003 to 2009.*

Export duties (taxes) are neither illegal nor prohibited in General Agreement on Tariffs and Trade (GATT)/WTO rules and over time they have been used by a range of members. They have both price and trade effects. Overall, analysis demonstrates that export duties have distortive effects on trade, leading to efficiency losses, encouraging production and consumption distortions and resource misallocation. While they may have transient short-run gains, export duties are unhealthy for global economic welfare and anti-competitive, favouring domestic producers and enterprises over foreign ones.[1]

Although export duties have been prohibited in several free trade agreements[2] and some bilateral trade agreements,[3] the specific obligations in WTO Accession Protocols represent the best efforts, so far, multilaterally, to substantively discipline the use of export duties.

---

[1] For a review of the role, applications and economic effects of export duties in the area of primary commodities (export tax, commodity prices and export volumes), see Piermartini (2004) and Jeonghoi (2010).

[2] Export duties are prohibited among the parties in the European Union, the North American Free Trade Association (NAFTA), the Caribbean Community (CARICOM), MERCOSUR (Common Market of the South: Argentina, Brazil, Paraguay, Uruguay and Venezuela) and the Australia–New Zealand Closer Economic Relations Trade Agreement (ANZCERTA).

[3] These include, *inter alia*, Canada–Chile, Canada–Costa Rica, European Union–Mexico and Japan–Singapore.

## Export-duty-specific obligations in WTO Accession Protocols

- Fifteen Article XII members undertook specific commitments on the application of export duties: Bulgaria, China, Croatia, Estonia, Georgia, Latvia, Mongolia, Montenegro, Nepal, Saudi Arabia, Tajikistan, Russia, Tonga, Ukraine and Viet Nam (see Annex 35.1 to this chapter).
- Relevant specific commitment paragraphs are contained, normally, in working party reports and referenced in paragraph 2 of the standard Accession Protocols. In the case of China, however, these specific obligations were contained in its Accession Protocol. For Russia, its commitments on export duties included the 'fixing' of the export duty rates in Part V of the Schedule of Concessions and Commitments on Goods of the Black Sea Economic Cooperation Organization.
- Six Article XII members – Bulgaria, Croatia, Estonia, Georgia, Nepal and Tonga – either generally 'reaffirmed' that they would 'abide' by the provisions of the WTO Agreement, regarding the application of export duties, or that they would 'minimize the use of' export duties.
- Eight Article XII members (China, Latvia, Mongolia, Saudi Arabia, Russia, Tajikistan, Ukraine and Viet Nam) specifically committed to either eliminating, reducing, binding, or fixing export duties, of which:
  - two Article XII members (China and Tajikistan) used 'negative lists' to define the scope of the application of export duties, to confirm that they would not apply any export duties on the products not listed;
  - six Article XII members (Latvia, Mongolia, Saudi Arabia, Russia, Ukraine and Viet Nam) adopted a 'positive list' approach, committing to eliminate, reduce, bind or fix export duties *only* on the products listed.
- One Article XII member (Montenegro) foreclosed the future use of export duties.
- One Article XII member (Ukraine) referred to 'the exceptions of the GATT 1994' in its export duties commitments.

Fifteen, or 46.8 per cent of WTO Article XII members (or 9.4 per cent of the total WTO membership of 161, at this time) have accepted binding specific commitments on export duties. These specific accession commitments on export duties have expanded the current disciplines.[4] The

---

[4] In the standard architecture of WTO Accession Protocols, paragraph 2 (Part I – General) provides that, 'The WTO Agreement to which X accedes shall be the WTO Agreement, including the Explanatory Notes to that Agreement, as rectified, amended or otherwise modified by such legal instruments as may have entered into force before the date of entry

factual substance of these specific commitments suggests several observations. First, these commitments have deepened and extended the
current WTO rules that govern export duties as an instrument of trade
policy. Export duties have emerged as a critical area where existing rules
are being clarified, made more precise and updated. Second, a review of
the totality of these specific commitments indicates a pattern and a level
of ambition that members have sought for a discipline and the rules for
export duties. On the basis of the underlying treaty dialogue in working
party reports and informal exchanges, the consistent aim of members has
been to constrain, reduce, eliminate and/or bind. Third, in working
parties, members have sought to achieve the systemic objectives of clarity
and predictability. Fourth, a constant argument from the economic
theory and evidence is the argument by members that export duties
undermine competition and restrict trade, and should, therefore, be
either bound/fixed and constrained or reduced or eliminated. Finally,
procedurally, the modalities of either positive or negative lists have been
used to establish enforceable binding commitments in Accession Protocols. In the case of Russia, the classical Schedule of Concessions and
Commitments on Goods was redesigned with the creation of a 'new'
Part V (CLXV). This established a precedent.

Acceding government(s) made an effort to nullify the pattern of
binding specific commitments in their negotiations with members,
through (direct and indirect) linkage(s) to GATT Article XX conditional exceptions, so as to trump, *inter alia*, their export duty
commitments. These efforts by the acceding governments were
opposed by members in working parties. The recent example, in
2011 in the course of the negotiations in the framework of the working
party on the accession of the Russian Federation is illustrative and
instructive. In 2008, a revised version of the draft Working Party Report
on the Accession of the Russian Federation was circulated in WTO

---

into force of this Protocol. This Protocol, which shall include the commitments referred to
in paragraph X of the Working Party Report, shall be an integral part of the WTO
Agreement'. While this provision and associated commitments are argued by several as
being binding and applicable, exclusively, to the Article XII members that accepted them,
it has also been argued by several others that WTO Accession Protocols are agreed and
adopted multilaterally by members in working parties, *ad referendum*, and thereafter, after
thirty days, decided by consensus by the entire membership either in the General Council
and/or Ministerial Conferences. These latter argue that, as a consequence, the specific
obligations in Accession Protocols point to the future directions and the standards for
rules in the rules-based multilateral trading system desired by WTO members.

document JOB(08)/36/Rev. 1.[5] The Draft Protocol on the Accession of the Russian Federation,[6] annexed to this 2008 JOB document, paragraph 2, provided, *inter alia* as follows:

> [T]his Protocol, which shall include the commitments referred to in paragraph ... of the Working Party Report, shall be an integral part of the WTO Agreement [, *and nothing in these commitments shall be understood to derogate from the rights of the Russian Federation under the WTO Agreement as applied between the Members of the WTO by the date of accession of the Russian Federation to the WTO*] [emphasis added].

Members of the working party expressed serious concern about the language in the JOB document. In 2011 (three years later), in the year of the conclusion and adoption of the Report of the Working Party on the Accession of the Russian Federation, in a three-way exchange of e-mails between the Director of the Accessions Division, several members and Russia, the position of members was infrangible that the formulation had to be eliminated before proceeding with the preparation of the draft Accession Package of the Russian Federation. The logic of the position of members was that the formulation would effectively undermine the binding integrity of the specific commitments accepted by Russia. The 'offending' formulation was eliminated.

More broadly, on export duties, the treaty dialogue in the actual negotiations (in accession working parties), reflected only in part in the records, revolves around WTO principles and disciplines of reducing barriers to trade, levelling the conditions for competition, adherence to transparency obligations and ensuring predictability through bindings. In the negotiating dialogue on export duties, but not limited to them, there have been linkages – direct and indirect – to the question of the 'right to regulate trade', as illustrated in the aforementioned language in the draft Working Party Report (WTO document JOB(08)/36/Rev. 1) of Russia.

Furthermore, these discussions on export duties, formally, in the treaty dialogue and, informally, overlapped with wider discussions, echoing classical debates about 'national policy objectives' that frequently underpin the policy use of export restrictions. These had thematic echoes to several questions, including 'ownership over natural resources', on the one hand, versus 'access to raw materials', on the other; global

---

[5] See WTO document JOB(08)/36/Rev. 1: Accession of the Russian Federation. Consolidation of texts registered since the circulation of Revision 3 of the Draft Working Party Report (WT/ACC/SPEC/RUS/25/Rev. 3), 14 August 2008.

[6] See WTO document, page 426 of JOB(08)/36/Rev. 1.

competitiveness of downstream industries in an integrated global economy and rules-based multilateral trading system; fiscal receipts considerations; environmental protection and conservation of natural resources,
pursuant to the conditional exceptions in GATT 1994 Article XX; food
security in agriculture; tackling the problem of tariff escalation to address
terms of trade questions; etc.[7]

### Existing rules applicable to export duties

The main provision of the WTO Agreement pertaining to export measures
is Article XI:1 of the GATT 1994:

> No prohibitions or restrictions other than duties, taxes or other charges,
> whether made effective through quotas, import or export licences or other
> measures, shall be instituted or maintained by any contracting party on
> the importation of any product of the territory of any other contracting
> party or on the exportation or sale for export of any product destined for
> the territory of any other contracting party.

This provision stipulates the general elimination of all trade-restrictive
measures on importation and exportation of goods,[8] except for 'duties,
taxes or other charges'. In other words, 'duties, taxes or other charges' are
the only measures covered by GATT 1994 Article XI.

On import duties, Article II of the GATT 1994 established clear rules.
It obliges WTO members to exempt the products described in their
Schedule of Concessions and Commitments (hereafter Goods Schedule)
from ordinary customs duties and other duties or charges in excess of
those set forth in the goods schedule.[9] The tariff bindings on imports
provide a substantial degree of market security and predictability for

---

[7] For a general discussion of several of these questions as they have emerged theoretically in
economic literature, with examples, see Jeonghoi (2010).

[8] Unless such measures can be justified by exceptions allowed by the WTO Agreement,
namely provisions contained under Articles XI:2(a), XX and XXI of the GATT 1994, and
Article 12 of the Agreement on Agriculture (AoA).

[9] Article II:1(b) of the GATT 1994: 'The products described in Part I of the Schedule
relating to any contracting party, which are the products of territories of other contracting
parties, shall, on their *importation* into the territory to which the Schedule relates, and
subject to the terms, conditions or qualifications set forth in that Schedule, be exempt from
ordinary customs duties in excess of those set forth and provided therein. Such products
shall also be exempt from all other duties or charges of any kind imposed on or in
connection with the *importation* in excess of those imposed on the date of this Agreement
or those directly and mandatorily required to be imposed thereafter by legislation in force
in the importing territory on that date.'

traders and investors and represent one of the key pillars of the multilateral trading system.

On export 'duties, taxes or other charges' (hereafter export duties), in contrast, the WTO Agreement does not stipulate a general requirement for binding, as it does for imports, pursuant to Article II of the GATT 1994. The main provisions of the GATT 1994 applicable to export duties are: Article I[10] (application of export duties on a most-favoured-nation basis), Article X[11] (transparency) and Article XXVIII *bis*[12] (preparedness to negotiate reduction on export duties).

Member(s), but mainly Article XII members have undertaken, *inter alia*, binding specific commitments on export duties in their Accession Protocols/working party reports and/or goods schedules, which form integral parts of the WTO Agreement. These commitments include the following:

---

[10] Article I:1 of the GATT 1994: 'With respect to customs duties and charges of any kind imposed on or in connection with importation or *exportation* [emphasis added] or imposed on the international transfer of payments for imports or *exports*, [emphasis added] and with respect to the method of levying such duties and charges, and with respect to all rules and formalities in connection with importation and *exportation*, [emphasis added] and with respect to all matters referred to in paragraphs 2 and 4 of Article III, any advantage, favour, privilege or immunity granted by any contracting party to any product originating in or destined for any other country shall be accorded immediately and unconditionally to the like product originating in or destined for the territories of all other contracting parties.'

[11] Article X:1 of the GATT 1994: 'Laws, regulations, judicial decisions and administrative rulings of general application, made effective by any contracting party, pertaining to the classification or the valuation of products for customs purposes, or to rates of duty, taxes or other charges, or to requirements, restrictions or prohibitions on imports or *exports* or on the transfer of payments therefore, or affecting their sale, distribution, transportation, insurance, warehousing inspection, exhibition, processing, mixing or other use, shall be published promptly in such a manner as to enable governments and traders to become acquainted with them. Agreements affecting international trade policy which are in force between the government or a governmental agency of any contracting party and the government or governmental agency of any other contracting party shall also be published. The provisions of this paragraph shall not require any contracting party to disclose confidential information which would impede law enforcement or otherwise be contrary to the public interest or would prejudice the legitimate commercial interests of particular enterprises, public or private.'

[12] Article XXVIII *bis*:1 of the GATT 1994: 'The contracting parties recognize that customs duties often constitute serious obstacles to trade; thus negotiations on a reciprocal and mutually advantageous basis, directed to the substantial reduction of the general level of tariffs and other charges on imports and *exports* and in particular to the reduction of such high tariffs as discourage the importation even of minimum quantities, and conducted with due regard to the objectives of this Agreement and the varying needs of individual contracting parties, are of great importance to the expansion of international trade. The contracting parties may therefore sponsor such negotiations from time to time.'

- Australia: in Part I Section (II) of its Uruguay Round Schedule of Concessions and Commitments, Australia undertook the commitment that: '[t]here shall be no export duty on' 15 specific tariff lines.[13]
- Russia: as a negotiated result of the accession negotiations of Russia, a new Part V was added to the longstanding classical architecture of the Goods Schedule. In this section of the Russian Goods Schedule (CLXV), export duties of Russia are 'fixed' and bound on 704 tariff lines, of which 544 are subject to reduction commitments.[14]
- Fifteen Article XII members (including Russia)[15] have undertaken specific commitments to abide by the provisions of the WTO Agreement, or to eliminate, reduce and/or bind export duties in their working party reports/Accession Protocols.[16]

## Article XII accession specific obligations on export duties

In the process of Article XII accession negotiations, members requested acceding governments to provide full information on all levied export duties and sought the elimination of export duties that may distort trade, undermine competitiveness and reduce members' access to supplies of basic materials. Resulting from the negotiations, acceding governments have undertaken binding specific commitments to bind, reduce or eliminate export duties.

Of the thirty-three Article XII members, fifteen have undertaken specific commitments on export duties, taxes, fees or charges (Table 35.1). A total of twenty-seven specific commitments on export duties, undertaken by these fifteen Article XII members, have been identified in their respective working party reports/Accession Protocols.

Seven broad categories of these specific commitments are evident, according to the nature and scope of the commitments (Table 35.1). The categories range from general confirmation of compliance with WTO rules (categories 1 and 2) to binding specific commitments on non-application (foreclosing the use) of any export duties (category 7).

---

[13] HS Code: 2601.11.00, 2614.00.00, 2615.10.00, 2701.11.00, 2701.12.00, 2701.19.00, 2701.20.00, 2702.10.00, 2702.20.00, 2703.00.00, 2704.00.00, 7403.11.00, 7501.20.00, 7502.10.00 and 7801.99.00.

[14] See the next section for details.

[15] Bulgaria, China, Croatia, Estonia, Georgia, Latvia, Mongolia, Montenegro, Nepal, Saudi Arabia, Tajikistan, Russia, Tonga, Ukraine and Viet Nam.

[16] See the next section for details.

Table 35.1 *Scope of specific commitments on export duties by Article XII members*

| Type of commitment | Bulgaria | China | Croatia | Estonia | Georgia | Latvia | Mongolia | Montenegro | Nepal | Saudi Arabia, Kingdom of | Tajikistan | Russian Federation | Tonga | Ukraine | Viet Nam |
|---|---|---|---|---|---|---|---|---|---|---|---|---|---|---|---|
| 1 Commitments on transparency (publishing the application of export duties in the official journals/gazettes; notification to the WTO) | Y | Y | Y | Y | Y | Y | | | | | Y | | | Y | |
| 2 General reaffirmation to abide by existing WTO rules | Y | | Y | Y | Y | | | | Y | | | Y | Y | | Y |
| 3 Commitments to 'minimise the use' of export duties (taxes) | Y | | | Y | Y | | | | | | | | | | |
| 4 Commitments to eliminate, reduce and/or bind export duties on specific product ('positive list') | | | | | | Y | Y | | | Y | | | | Y | Y |
| 5 Commitments in the goods schedules on binding and reducing of export duties | | | | | | | | | | | | Y | | | |
| 6 Commitments on the elimination of all export duties, unless specifically provided in the list annexed to the working party reports/ Accession Protocols or applied in conformity with the provisions of Article VIII of the GATT 1994 ('negative list') | | Y | | | | | | | | | Y | | | | |
| 7 Commitments on non-application or non-reintroduction of export duties, from the date of accession | | | | | | | | Y | | | | | | | |

## Transparency obligation

In category 1, Article XII members confirm their obligation to ensure transparency with regard to the application of export duties. Six members (Bulgaria, Croatia, Estonia, Georgia, Latvia and Ukraine) undertook a commitment to publish any application of export duties in official journals/gazettes. In the case of Tajikistan, the specific commitment obliges the government to notify (the application of) export duties to the WTO 'on the day of their publication and in any case at least thirty days before any such changes enter into force'.

## Commitment to WTO-compliance and reference to specific articles

In category 2 specific commitments, Article XII members reaffirm that (any) export duties will be applied in accordance with the provisions of the WTO Agreement. It is noteworthy that the majority of such commitments do not refer to specific Articles of the WTO Agreement, except in the cases of Nepal ('in particular with Article VIII of the GATT 1994'), Russia ('in particular with Article I of the GATT 1994') and Tonga ('in particular with Articles VIII:1(a), XI:1 and III:2 and 4 of the GATT 1994').

## Commitment to minimise export duty use

In addition to the specific export duties commitments with regard to publication and compliance with WTO provisions (i.e. categories 1 and 2), Bulgaria, Estonia and Georgia also committed that they would 'minimise the use of export taxes' upon accession to the WTO. These commitments were not further elaborated, i.e. by including clearly defined requirements with regard to the elimination, binding or reduction of export duties. These specific commitments, undertaken by these three Article XII members, have been classified/categorised in category 3.

## Commitments to bind, reduce and/or eliminate with 'positive lists'

Category 4 covers specific commitments to bind, reduce and eliminate export duties for specific products. These specific commitments included 'positive lists' of products, which were subject to elimination, reduction or binding. These lists were included in the commitment paragraphs or annexed to the working party reports, specifically:

- Latvia committed to abolish export duties on certain wood products, metal waste and scrap (thirty-six tariff lines listed in Annex 3) within a clearly defined time-frame (by 1 January 2000), but to retain export duties on antiques (also listed in Annex 3 with export duties under both the most-favoured-nation and free trade regime).

- Mongolia committed to replace the prohibition on the export of raw cashmere with an export duty at the ad valorem rate of not more than 30 per cent by 1 October 1996, and this export duty would be 'phased out and eliminated within ten years of the date of Mongolia's accession to the WTO'.

- Saudi Arabia confirmed that it 'would not impose export duties on iron and steel scrap'.

- Ukraine confirmed that 'export duties were applied only to the goods listed in Table 20(a). Ukraine would reduce export duties in accordance with the binding schedule contained in Table 20(b) and would 'not increase export duties, nor apply other measures having an equivalent effect, unless justified under the exceptions of the GATT 1994'. Table 20(a) includes twenty-three items defined at HS four- and six-digit or national tariff line level; Table 20(b) includes sixty-five items defined at HS four- and six-digit or national tariff line level.

- Viet Nam confirmed that 'with regard to export duties on ferrous and non-ferrous scrap metals, . . . Viet Nam would reduce export duties in accordance with Table 17, and that Table 17 included all export duties that Viet Nam applied to ferrous and non-ferrous scrap metal'. Table 17 included twenty lines at HS four-digit or eight-digit national tariff levels.

It should be noted that, in the specific commitment paragraphs on export duties of Latvia, Saudi Arabia, Ukraine and Viet Nam, these Article XII members also confirmed the full scope of export duties that existed/ applied at the time when these specific commitments were made. Notably, there was no specific reference made with regard to the application/non-application of export duties in the future, for products not subject to export duties at the time when the specific commitment was undertaken.

## 'Fixing' and/or 'reducing' export duties: a new Part V in the Goods Schedule

The binding specific commitment by Russia for binding and reducing export duties was in essence the same as the commitments classified in category 4. The reason for classifying the specific commitment undertaken by Russia separately, i.e. in category 5, is due to the fact that, for the first time, these specific commitments were incorporated as Part V in the redesigned Schedule of Concessions and Commitments on Goods, rather than in the working party report/accession protocol, as had been the case of the specific commitments classified in category 4. The creation of Part V in the Goods Schedule of Russia was of systemic significance. It set a precedent to mainstream export duties into the goods schedule, which previously only contained concessions and commitments on import duties.[17]

The accession-specific export duty commitments undertaken by Russia under Part V were also unique from a technical point of view. The commitments on the 704 tariff lines included bindings of export duties in specific or mixed duty specifications; non-linear implementation periods; level of bindings conditional on product (oil) prices; and export tariff rate quotas. Part V also included a headnote stating:

> [t]he Russian Federation undertakes not to increase export duties, or to reduce or to eliminate them, in accordance with the following schedule, and not to re-introduce or increase them beyond the levels indicated in this schedule, except in accordance with the provisions of the GATT 1994.

## Commitments made with negative lists

Similar accession commitments undertaken by China and Tajikistan have been classified in category 6. China committed that it 'shall eliminate all taxes and charges applied to exports unless specifically provided for in Annex 6 of this Protocol or applied in conformity with the provisions of Article VIII of the GATT 1994'. Similarly, Tajikistan confirmed that it 'shall not introduce and shall eliminate all duties, taxes, fees and charges applied to exports, unless specifically provided for in

---

[17] Except for the case of Australia, which was not, in any event, in a separate section of the goods schedule, expressly designed for export duties.

Table 9 of this Protocol or applied in conformity with the provisions of Article VIII of the GATT 1994'.

The commitments of China and the commitments of Tajikistan were based on a 'negative list' approach. In other words, the lists provided the product scope within which export duties could be applied. For any products which were not in the list, no export duties could be applied. There were eighty-four tariff lines on China's list (Annex 6 of WT/ACC/CHN/49) with predefined maximum levels, which would 'not be exceeded' in the application of export duties. Tajikistan's list (Table 9 of WT/ACC/TJK/30) included 313 tariff lines at either the HS six-digit level or eight-digit national tariff line level. Among these, 257 lines were flagged as 'unbound', and 56 lines had 'maximal applicable export duties rates' – in the form of ad valorem, specific, or mixed duties, or defined by formulae.

### Foreclosing the use of export duties

Finally, the specific commitment undertaken by Montenegro has been classified as category 7. The commitment stipulates that 'from the date of accession, Montenegro would neither apply nor reintroduce any export duty'. The wording of this commitment represents the strictest discipline on export duties to date in all Article XII accessions, as it completely prohibits the right to apply export duties, from the date of accession.

### Location of specific commitments in Accession Packages

The specific commitments on export duties have been located in accession working party reports, listed in Accession Protocols, except in the case of China, where the specific commitments on export duties were incorporated in China's Accession Protocol. In the case of Russia, in addition to the commitments in the Working Party Report, a new Part V was created in its Schedule of Concessions and Commitments on Goods.

### Modalities for export duties commitments: positive and/or negative lists

Specific commitments by Latvia, Mongolia, Saudi Arabia, Russia, Ukraine and Viet Nam were made on the basis of 'positive lists'; i.e., listing products, which were subject to binding, reduction and/or elim- ination. Notably, none of these specific commitments specifically addressed the application/non-application of products not included in the lists.

The specific commitments of China and Tajikistan were based on 'negative lists'; these lists provided the product scope within which export duties could be applied. Consequently, no export duties should/could be applied to products, which had not been included in the lists.

The strictest commitment (without recourse to any positive or nega- tive list approach) was undertaken by Montenegro, whose negotiations were concluded in 2011, with Montenegro becoming a member in 2012. Montenegro committed not to apply and hence foreclosed on any export duties from the date of accession.

## Export duties commitments are included in a member's goods schedule

For the first time ever in the history of Article XII WTO accessions, in the accession of Russia, the specific commitments on export duties were bound in a newly created Part V of the Schedule of Concessions and Commitments of Russia. This was a first, and is of systemic significance setting a precedent for all forthcoming WTO Article XII accession negotiations.

All other commitments on elimination/reduction of specific export duties made by China, Latvia, Mongolia, Saudi Arabia, Tajikistan, Ukraine and Viet Nam were contained in the working party reports and/or the Accession Protocols.

## Availability of GATT exceptions

'GATT exceptions' were only specifically referred to in the specific commitments undertaken by Ukraine, stating:

> He [the representative of Ukraine] also confirmed that as regards these products, Ukraine would not increase export duties, or apply other measures having an equivalent effect, *unless justified under the exceptions of the GATT 1994* [emphasis added by authors].

Annex 35.1 *Accession commitments of Article XII members on export duties*

| Article XII member | Date of membership | Reference | Commitment text | Category |
|---|---|---|---|---|
| Bulgaria | 01/12/1996 | Working Party Report paragraph 39 | The representative of Bulgaria stated that his government applied export taxes for the relief of critical shortages of foodstuffs or in cases of critical short supply for the domestic industry, and that after accession, *any such taxes would be applied in accordance with the provisions of the WTO Agreement.* He noted that, at the current time, Bulgaria applied the export taxes only to the goods and services listed in Annex 2 to the Report. Bulgaria would, after accession, *minimise its use of* such taxes and confirmed that any changes in the application of such measures, their level, scope or justification, would be *published in the State Gazette.* The Working Party took note of these commitments. | 1, 2, 3 |
| China | 11/12/2001 | Accession Protocol Article 11.3 | China shall *eliminate all taxes and charges applied to* exports unless specifically provided for in Annex 6 of this Protocol or applied in conformity with the provisions of Article VIII of the GATT 1994. | 6 |
| Croatia | 30/11/2000 | Working Party Report paragraph 101 | The representative of Croatia confirmed that after accession to the WTO, Croatia *would apply export duties only in accordance with the provisions of the WTO Agreement and published in the Official Gazette* 'Narodne Novine'. Changes in the application of such | 1, 2 |

Annex 35.1 (*cont.*)

| Article XII member | Date of membership | Reference | Commitment text | Category |
|---|---|---|---|---|
| | | | measures, their level and scope would also be published in the Official Gazette, 'Narodne Novine'. The Working Party took note of this commitment. | |
| Estonia | 13/11/1999 | Working Party Report paragraph 80 | The representative of Estonia confirmed that after accession to the WTO, Estonia would *minimise the use of export taxes and any such taxes applied would be in accordance with the provisions of the WTO Agreement and published in the Official Journal 'Riigi Teataja'* (State Gazette). Changes in the application of such measures, their level, scope, or justification, would also be published in the Official Journal, 'Riigi Teataja' (State Gazette). The Working Party took note of these commitments. | 1, 2, 3 |
| Georgia | 14/06/2000 | Working Party Report paragraph 82 | The representative of Georgia confirmed that after accession to the WTO, Georgia intended to *minimise the use* of export taxes and any such taxes applied would be in *accordance with the provisions of the WTO Agreement and published in the Official Journal.* Changes in the application of such measures, their level, scope or justification, would also be published in the Official Journal. The Working Party took note of these commitments. | 1, 2, 3 |

| | | | | |
|---|---|---|---|---|
| Latvia | 10/02/1999 | Working Party Report paragraph 69 | The representative of Latvia confirmed that present export tariff rates related only to the goods listed in Annex 3 Export Duty Tariffs. All customs tariff changes were *published in the Official Journal of the Republic of Latvia – the newspaper Latvijas Vēstnesis*. Latvia would *abolish all export duties listed in Annex 3* by 1 January 2000 with the exception of the duty on antiques. The timetable for elimination of export duties would be similar for regional trade agreement partners and partners to which most-favoured-nation treatment was applied as indicated in Annex 3. The Working Party took note of these commitments. | 1, 4 |
| Mongolia | 29/01/1997 | Working Party Report paragraph 24 | The representative of Mongolia also stated that his government would maintain the prohibition on the export of raw cashmere only until 1 October 1996, when an export duty at the rate of not more than 30 per cent ad valorem would be introduced. That export duty would be phased out and *eliminated within ten years of the date of Mongolia's accession to the WTO*. The representative of Mongolia also stated that export licensing requirements for ferrous and non-ferrous metals would be removed by 1 January 1997. The Working Party took note of these commitments. | 4 |

Annex 35.1 (*cont.*)

| Article XII member | Date of membership | Reference | Commitment text | Category |
|---|---|---|---|---|
| Montenegro | 29/04/2012 | Working Party Report paragraph 132 | The representative of Montenegro confirmed that, from the date of accession, Montenegro *would not apply or reintroduce any export duty*. The Working Party took note of this commitment. | 7 |
| Nepal | 23/04/2004 | Working Party Report paragraph 79 | The representative of Nepal said that from the date of accession Nepal would charge an export service fee representing the approximate cost of the services rendered, and would apply this and other fees and charges for services rendered to exports *in accordance with WTO Agreements, in particular with Article VIII of the GATT 1994*. In this regard, the current charge of 0.5 per cent would be at a flat rate expressed in NRs (Nepalese rupees) to ensure that it did not exceed the approximate cost of the export services rendered. The Working Party took note of these commitments. | 2 |
| Saudi Arabia, Kingdom of | 11/12/2005 | Working Party Report paragraph 184 | Some members of the Working Party requested information on export duties applied by Saudi Arabia. Those members noted that the export duties applied by Saudi Arabia appeared to be imposed only for revenue purposes and would have trade-distorting effects. In response, the representative of Saudi Arabia stated that Article XI of the GATT 1994 expressly permitted the | 4 |

758

| | | | | 1, 6 |
|---|---|---|---|---|

imposition of export duties, and did not restrict the right to impose such duties. Export duties applied only to untanned hides and skins, falling under HS Nos. 4101, 4102 and 4103. The rate of export duty was SAR 2000/ton (roughly 20 per cent). The representative of Saudi Arabia confirmed that Saudi Arabia *would not impose export duties on iron and steel scrap.* The Working Party took note of this commitment.

| Tajikistan | 02/03/2013 | Working Party Report paragraph 169 |

The representative of Tajikistan confirmed that *Tajikistan shall not introduce and shall eliminate all duties, taxes, fees and charges applied to exports, unless specifically provided for in Table 9 of this Protocol or applied in conformity with the provisions of Article VIII of the GATT 1994. Tajikistan shall notify to the WTO any changes of its duties, taxes, fees and charges applied to exports on the day of their publication and in any case at least thirty days before any such changes enter into force.* The Working Party took note of these commitments.

2, 5

| Russian Federation | 22/08/2012 | Working Party Report paragraph 638 |

The representative of the Russian Federation confirmed that the Russian Federation *would implement, from the date of accession, its tariff concessions and commitments contained in Part V of the Schedule of Concessions and Commitments on Goods of the Russian Federation. Accordingly, products described*

Annex 35.1 (*cont.*)

| Article XII member | Date of membership | Reference | Commitment text | Category |
|---|---|---|---|---|
| | | | in Part V of that Schedule would, subject to the terms, conditions or qualifications set forth in that Part of the Schedule, be exempt from export duties in excess of those set forth and provided therein. The representative of the Russian Federation further confirmed that the Russian Federation would not apply other measures having an equivalent effect to export duties on those products. He confirmed that, from the date of accession, the Russian Federation would apply export duties *in conformity with the WTO Agreement, in particular with Article I of the GATT 1994.* Accordingly, with respect to export duties and charges of any kind imposed on, or in connection with exportation, any advantage, favour, privilege or immunity granted by the Russian Federation to any product destined for any other country shall be accorded immediately and unconditionally to the like product destined for the territories of all other WTO members. The representative of the Russian Federation confirmed that the Russian Federation would, from the date of accession to the WTO, administer export tariff | |

| | | | |
|---|---|---|---|
| | | rate quotas (TRQs) in a manner that is consistent with the WTO Agreement and in particular the GATT 1994 and the WTO Agreement on Import Licensing Procedures. The Working Party took note of these commitments. | |
| Tonga | 27/07/2007 | Working Party Report paragraph 102 | The representative of Tonga confirmed that from the date of accession, Tonga *would apply all fees and charges for services rendered to exports in accordance with WTO Agreements*, in particular Articles VIII:1(a), XI:1 and III:2 and 4 of the GATT 1994. The Working Party took note of this commitment. | 2 |
| Ukraine | 16/05/2008 | Working Party Report paragraph 240 | The representative of Ukraine confirmed that at present export duties were applied only to the goods listed in Table 20(a), and further confirmed that Ukraine *would reduce export duties in accordance with the binding schedule contained in Table 20(b)* and that as regards these products, Ukraine would not increase export duties, nor apply any other measures having an equivalent effect, unless justified under the exceptions of the GATT 1994. The representative further confirmed that the current duties and any changes in their application *would be published in the Official Gazette* that from the date of accession, Ukraine will not apply any obligatory minimum export prices. The Working Party took note of these commitments. The Working Party | 1, 4 |

Annex 35.1 (*cont.*)

| Article XII member | Date of membership | Reference | Commitment text | Category |
|---|---|---|---|---|
| | | | agreed that these commitments do not constitute a reinterpretation of GATT 1994, nor affect the rights and obligations of other members in respect of provisions on the application of export duties, that are measures in accordance with GATT 1994. | |
| Viet Nam | 11/01/2007 | Working Party Report paragraph 260 | The representative of Viet Nam confirmed that Viet Nam would apply export duties, export fees and charges, as well as internal regulations and taxes applied on or in connection with exportation *in conformity with the GATT 1994*. With regard to export duties on ferrous and non-ferrous scrap metals, it was confirmed that Viet Nam *would reduce export duties in accordance with Table 17*, and that Table 17 included all export duties that Viet Nam applied to ferrous and non-ferrous scrap metal. The Working Party took note of these commitments. | 2, 4 |

# References

Jeonghoi, K. (2010). 'Recent trends in export restrictions', Paris, Organisation for Economic Co-operation and Development, OECD Trade Policy Papers No. 101.

Piermartini, R. (2004). 'The role of export taxes in the field of primary commodities', Geneva, WTO, WTO Discussion Paper.

# 36

# Disciplining state trading practices: lessons from WTO accession negotiations

DIMITAR BRATANOV

## ABSTRACT

*This chapter addresses a number of concerns associated with state trading. What are the applicable WTO rules in this area and have they kept up with the evolving nature of production methods and the changing landscape of state trading enterprises (STEs)? How have state trading practices been approached in WTO accession negotiations? How many WTO members acceding under the provisions of Article XII of the Marrakesh Agreement Establishing the World Trade Organization (WTO Agreement) have accepted specific obligations aimed at disciplining the operations of STEs? What specific patterns have emerged across these commitments and how have they evolved over time? Have the commitments resulting from WTO accession negotiations offered a more effective and forward-looking approach to disciplining STE activities? What is the systemic relevance of STE-related accession commitments and what lessons can be drawn about possible future multilateral disciplines in this area? What has been the contribution of accession commitments relating to transparency in privatisation programmes? STE disciplines have been in the rulebook of the multilateral trading system since 1947, but have not kept track with the evolving nature of state trading operations. State trading plays a significant role in the economies of the majority of Article XII members. The applicability of existing WTO rules in this area has therefore been put to practice in their accession negotiations. The commitments resulting from accession negotiations have produced more comprehensive and forward-looking disciplines, which arguably capture modern-day state trading operations more adequately. Specifically,*

The analyses in the chapters in this book were finalised at the end of December 2014. Since then the Republic of Seychelles acceded to the World Trade Organization (WTO) on 26 April 2015. This expanded total WTO membership from 160 to 161. Please see the editors' note.

*STE-related accession commitments have evolved over time to extend the scope of obligations to the purchases and sales of both goods and services, contribute further definitional clarity to the term 'state trading enterprise' and address the transparency deficit in this area. In addition to steering the operations of acceding governments' STEs towards conformity with WTO principles, the evolution of these commitments is of systemic relevance to the multilateral trading system, as it points to the possible direction of future disciplines in this area. While not pre-judging the future development of multilateral provisions on state trading, it is argued that Article XII members, which today account for one-fifth of the WTO membership, are well placed to influence the direction of future discussions in the area of STEs.*

A significant number of state-owned enterprises (SOEs) are active internationally. A recent Organisation for Economic Co-operation and Development (OECD) study[1] of the two thousand largest global public companies identifies 204 firms in which the state has a majority stake. These companies originate from some thirty-seven different countries and the value of their sales is equivalent to almost 6 per cent of world gross domestic product (GDP). Three Article XII WTO members[2] emerge among the top ten economies with the highest share of state involvement in their countries' leading international businesses: China, Russia and Saudi Arabia. State ownership is also an important consideration in many former centrally planned economies, as well as in developing countries seeking to find the optimal policy mix for sustained economic growth. Most Article XII members belong to one of these two categories.

Arguably, there are valid reasons, both strategic and commercial, to maintain state control in certain economic sectors. The discussions in WTO accession negotiations offer a comprehensive range of illustrative examples. For many governments, state intervention is an essential

---

[1] See Kowalski *et al.* (2013).

[2] Thirty-three members have negotiated their accession to the WTO under the provisions of Article XII of the Marrakesh Agreement Establishing the World Trade Organization (WTO Agreement). These are (by date of WTO membership): Ecuador (1996); Bulgaria (1996); Mongolia (1997); Panama (1997); Kyrgyz Republic (1998); Latvia (1999); Estonia (1999); Jordan (2000); Georgia (2000); Albania (2000); Oman (2000); Croatia (2000); Lithuania (2001); Moldova (2001); China (2001); Chinese Taipei (2001); Armenia (2003); former Yugoslav Republic of Macedonia (2003); Nepal (2004); Cambodia (2004); Saudi Arabia (2005); Viet Nam (2007); Tonga (2007); Ukraine (2008); Cabo Verde (2008); Montenegro (2012); Samoa (2012); Russian Federation (2012); Vanuatu (2012); Lao PDR (2013); Tajikistan (2013); Yemen (2014); Seychelles (2015).

instrument for attaining development objectives or addressing national security concerns.[3] State influence is also considerable in the agricultural sector.[4] For their part, resource-rich economies typically assign a significant role to the state in the management of natural resources through the exercise of discretionary powers over the exploitation and distribution of natural wealth.[5] In countries that have undergone transition from centrally planned to market economies, a high degree of state ownership remains as one of the legacies of the planned economy system. In some cases, key privatisation programmes have not been completed, leaving significant sectors of the economy under state control. The discussions in some of the early WTO accession processes are particularly instructive in this regard.[6]

National administrations use different criteria for defining what constitutes an SOE – a minority stake, a majority stake or 100 per cent state ownership. The legal form of enterprise also varies, ranging from non-listed statutory corporations, with distinct legal status, to publicly traded limited liability companies or joint-stock companies. From the perspective of international trade however, what matters is not the share of state participation in a company's capital, but the influence that the state exercises – through formal or informal channels – on the trade-related operations of a company. Accordingly, the regulatory framework of the multilateral trading system has not been designed to impose particular obligations with respect to property ownership.

The incidence of state ownership is considerable in many economic sectors which are internationally traded.[7] It is a matter of concern, therefore, that traders benefiting from privileges granted by the state may circumvent the WTO's non-discrimination principles and members' market access commitments through their decisions regarding purchases or sales. In particular, such decisions may lead to discrimination between

---

[3] For a recent example, see report of the working party on the accession on Lao PDR, paragraph 31; see WTO document WT/ACC/LAO/45. See also report of the working party on the accession of Viet Nam, paragraph 53; see WTO document WT/ACC/VNM/48.

[4] See report of the working party on the accession of Ukraine, paragraphs 47–49; see WTO document WT/ACC/UKR/152.

[5] See report of the working party on the accession of Yemen, paragraphs 38–40; see WTO document WT/ACC/YEM/42.

[6] See report of the working party on the accession of Bulgaria, paragraph 24; see WTO document WT/ACC/BGR/5.

[7] See Kowalski *et al.* (2013), paragraph 95.

trading partners or between domestic and imported goods. Exclusive import privileges may be used to influence the level of imports and undermine market access commitments. On the export side, governments may be tempted to secure a dominant share of the world market by granting exclusive export rights and influencing export competition. Much of the potential for contravening WTO obligations stems from the possibility that decision-making, when not based on market principles, is non-transparent and may result in discrimination.[8] Over time, the WTO has developed a set of dedicated multilateral disciplines to address these concerns.

With respect to trade in goods, the multilateral trading system foresees specific rules designed to discipline the activities of economic operators benefiting from special or exclusive privileges granted by the government in connection with their trading activities. In WTO jargon, these entities are referred to as state trading enterprises (STEs), as covered under Article XVII of the General Agreement on Tariffs and Trade (GATT). It is important to note that an STE can take distinct institutional forms and that the concept does not presuppose the degree of direct government involvement. Thus, a private enterprise benefiting from a privilege not generally available to other market operators could also be considered to constitute an STE. A separate set of provisions applies in the area of services where the relevant WTO disciplines are covered under Article VIII of the General Agreement on Trade in Services (GATS) with respect to 'monopolies and exclusive service suppliers'. These provisions pertain to all legal monopolies which have been authorised or established formally or in effect.[9] The degree of state ownership, as such, is again not relevant to this definition.

GATT Article XVII recognises the importance of negotiations between members aimed at minimising the scope for trade distortions inherent in the operations of STEs. Other than streamlining transparency provisions, however, the Uruguay Round has not produced additional substantive disciplines on STEs. The core provisions have thus remained unchanged since they were first introduced in the GATT rulebook in 1947. In the

---

[8] See Hoekman and Trachtman (2008).
[9] Natural monopolies, which exist without government facilitation, fall outside the scope of these provisions. Natural monopolies arise when there are high costs associated with the establishment and maintenance of the supply infrastructure, such as in the energy distribution and railway sectors. For a comparison of the provisions of GATS Article VIII dealing with monopolies (services) and GATT Article XVII dealing with STEs (goods) see Mattoo (1997).

area of trade in services, as discussed below, the relevant GATS disciplines are more limited in scope and do not readily integrate with those of the GATT. As a result, the existing multilateral framework of rules remains fragmented and in some ways inadequate when it comes to disciplining the trading operations of modern enterprises in which both goods and services contribute as inputs in international production value chains.

With the WTO accession of a number of major economies in which state trading plays a significant role, there has been a general interest in clarifying existing rules and enhancing the relevant transparency provisions, yet no substantive progress has been achieved in this area under the Doha Development Agenda. In the meantime, the accession process has provided a testing ground for developing possible approaches to dealing with practical concerns related to state trading.

This chapter explores how the results of WTO accession negotiations in the area of state trading are of systemic relevance to the multilateral trading system. In particular, it is argued that accession commitment language has evolved over time to, first, compensate for some of the lack of definitional clarity regarding the term 'state trading enterprise'; second, establish a more effective obligation extending to both goods and services; and third, address the transparency deficit in this area. While commitment language has also touched upon other dimensions of the discussion – including the possible channels through which the state exerts influence on traders – a uniform commitment pattern has not emerged in such areas. This chapter notes the role played by accession commitments relating to transparency in privatisation programmes in contributing additional transparency and in supporting autonomous domestic market reforms. In addition, it is argued that, as a consequence of the groundwork laid during the WTO accession process, Article XII members are well placed to play an active role in the development of future WTO disciplines on state trading.

This chapter will first outline the relevant WTO legal provisions and case law before reviewing state trading in the context of WTO accession. It then offers some thoughts on the development of the next generation of rules in the area of state trading; and the role of Article XII members in this process.

## Legal provisions

The multilateral trading system presupposes that economic operators act according to market principles, rather than on the basis of state directives. GATT Article XVII and the Understanding on the Interpretation of Article XVII of the GATT 1994 seek to discipline the operations of enterprises which influence international trade, but may not be acting in accordance with economic considerations as a result of their institutional proximity to the state. GATS Article VIII lays down disciplines on the operations of state-sanctioned monopolies and exclusive services suppliers. Other WTO provisions are also relevant to state trading, including the interpretative note to GATT Articles XI, XII, XIII, XIV and XVIII; GATT Articles II:4, III and XI; Article 4.2 of the Agreement on Agriculture; and the Agreement on Subsidies and Countervailing Measures.[10]

GATT Article XVII does not provide a clear definition of what constitutes a 'state trading enterprise'. Paragraph 1 of the article refers to two types of entity: (i) 'state enterprise', which is most likely analogous to the term SOE; and (ii) 'any enterprise' granted exclusive or special privileges by the state for trade-related purchases or sales. Some specific illustrations mentioned elsewhere in the text provide additional guidance on the types of entities covered by the article – notably 'import monopolies' (Article XVII:4(b)) and 'marketing boards' (note ad Article XVII:1). As in other areas of the GATT, procurement for governmental use is excluded from the coverage of the article (Article XVII:2).

The principal legal obligation in GATT Article XVII is the respect of non-discrimination. WTO case law has confirmed that non-discrimination in this context refers to at least most-favoured-nation (MFN) treatment.[11] There is less agreement on whether, in addition to MFN, national treatment is also covered under state trading rules.[12]

[10] Under the GATT, the Interpretative Note to Articles XI, XII, XIII, XIV and XVIII dealing with quantitative restrictions stipulates that throughout these articles, references to quantitative restrictions include restrictions made effective through state trading operations. Concerning a specific type of STE – an import monopoly operating in the area of trade in goods – GATT Article II:4 provides that any such enterprise listed in a member's tariff schedule cannot operate so as to afford protection in excess of the level 'provided for in that Schedule'. According to Article 4.2 of the Agreement on Agriculture, members should not maintain, with certain exceptions, non-tariff measures 'of the kind which have been required to be converted into ordinary customary duties', i.e. the non-tariff measures made subject to tariffication during the Uruguay Round. The footnote to Article 4.2 specifies that this includes non-tariff measures maintained through STEs. The Agreement on Subsidies and Countervailing Measures is also relevant. While a particular 'privilege', in the sense of GATT Article XVII, may be consistent with STE obligations, the subsidy would also need to comply with disciplines under the Subsidies Agreement (which are limited to trade in goods).

[11] See Mavroidis, (2007), p. 316.

[12] The Panel Report on *Korea – Various Measures on Beef* states that non-discrimination 'includes at least the provisions of Articles I and III of GATT' (paragraph 753). This

Article XVII further provides that to act in accordance with the non-discrimination principle, STEs need to make purchases or sales solely in accordance with 'commercial considerations' and to afford the enterprises of other members 'adequate opportunity ... to compete' for participation in such purchases or sales.

WTO jurisprudence has shed additional light on the meaning of the term 'commercial considerations'. In particular, the Panel in *Canada – Wheat Exports and Grain Imports* found that sales below market price, and sales which did not generate profit for the enterprise, were not necessarily inconsistent with 'commercial considerations'. In addition, STEs should not be expected to refrain from using their privileges on the grounds that this might put private companies at a disadvantage. 'Commercial considerations' are thus understood to include a range of possible motivations, defined by the type of business and the economic rationales relevant to the particular market.[13] In other words, the obligations under GATT Article XVII have not been interpreted to impose competition law-type disciplines on STEs.[14] The case findings have also provided additional insights on the obligation concerning the 'adequate opportunity ... to compete'. Specifically, in relation to the sale of products, the enterprises to be accorded adequate opportunities are identified as those interested in buying these products, not the enterprises competing for sales of the same product.[15]

Given that the opaque nature of STE operations creates a potential for contravening WTO obligations, the transparency provisions included in paragraph 4 of GATT Article XVII are of great relevance. These provisions require WTO members to notify products imported into or exported from their territories by the enterprises in question. The Understanding on the Interpretation of GATT Article XVII was drafted during the Uruguay Round to provide additional guidance, including a 'working definition' of enterprises subject to notification. Effectively, the Understanding narrows down the scope of the notification obligation to enterprises that have been granted exclusive or special rights and

---

finding was not appealed. For a discussion on the alternative view, see Jackson, Davey and Sykes (1995), p. 1144.

[13] Appellate Body Report, *Canada – Wheat Exports and Grain Imports*, paragraph 140 (see WTO document WT/DS276/AB/R).

[14] Appellate Body Report, paragraph 145. See also Mavroidis (2007), p. 317, on the interpretation of 'commercial considerations' in *Canada – Wheat Exports and Grain Imports*.

[15] Appellate Body Report, paragraph 157.

privileges through which they influence the level and direction of imports and exports.[16] The document also spells out that STEs may be 'governmental or non-governmental' entities. In recognition of the importance of enhanced transparency in this area, the Understanding sets up a working party with a mandate to review the notifications submitted by members on behalf of the Council for Trade in Goods.

State ownership plays a significant role in economically important services sectors, which also account for a considerable share of trade in services.[17] While there is no direct equivalent to the provisions of GATT Article XVII in the area of services, Article VIII of the GATS sets out obligations with respect to the operations of 'monopolies' and 'exclusive services suppliers'. These provisions call on members to respect the basic non-discrimination principle and lay down notification procedures.[18] In this way, they are to some extent symmetrical to the state trading disciplines under the GATT. However, on the GATS side, the provisions only apply to the supply of services, or 'sales', by the monopoly and not to its purchases. The scope of application of the GATS provisions is also limited to the specific commitments undertaken by sector and by mode of supply recorded in each member's schedule of specific commitments on services (including with respect to national treatment). As a result, the scope for disciplining state trading activities under the GATS is narrower.

There is broad agreement in the literature on the need to clarify or strengthen the WTO provisions dealing with state trading, including GATT Article XVII and GATS Article VIII.[19] The interplay between the rules in the areas of goods and services has not yet been tackled. In particular, the purchases of goods and services by services suppliers do not fall under existing disciplines. The purchases of services by goods producers are also not covered under current rules. An integrated set of

---

[16] 'Governmental and non-governmental enterprises, including marketing boards, which have been granted exclusive or special rights or privileges, including statutory or constitutional powers, in the exercise of which they influence through their purchases or sales the level or direction of imports or exports'; Understanding on the Interpretation of Article XVII of the General Agreement on Tariffs and Trade 1994, paragraph 1.

[17] See Kowalski et al. (2013), paragraphs 64–65. Relevant sectors, accounting for over 40 per cent of world services trade, include civil engineering; architectural and engineering services; transportation services (including land transport and transport via pipelines); air transport; and financial services (except insurance and pension funding).

[18] The notification requirement applies only to monopoly rights granted for the supply of a service covered by the specific commitments listed in the schedule.

[19] For a discussion of the perceived inadequacies of the WTO provisions, see Petersmann (1998) and Mattoo (1997).

disciplines is required to capture the practical realities of modern production methods in which goods and services are interlinked in value chains contributing to final output. A revised set of disciplines should also address the scope of coverage of the provisions with a view to clarifying and expanding them, e.g. a precise definition of the categories of enterprises concerned. It has also been recognised that more could be done to promote transparency.

The streamlining of both of these key WTO provisions has not featured prominently on the negotiating agenda of the WTO. In what follows, it is argued that the WTO accession process has established an effective avenue for advancing the discussions in this area and addressing some of the perceived gaps.

## State trading: perspectives from accession negotiations

### State trading in GATT accessions

State trading has been a recurring theme in accession negotiations since the days of the WTO's predecessor, the GATT. Working party discussions in this area would typically concern centrally planned economies seeking to become contracting parties. In recognition of the challenges involved in applying GATT rules to a non-market system, planned economies accepted the inclusion of special membership obligations in their reports requiring them to progressively increase imports from other GATT contracting parties. These commitments stipulated minimum rates of import growth as part of their terms of accession.[20] In addition to being impractical, these provisions failed to address concerns relating to the potential for the state trading country to discriminate among suppliers, in violation of the MFN principle.[21]

By the time the WTO was established in 1995, there had been a significant shift in the perception of the state's role in the economy. The solutions found in addressing concerns related to the state trading practices of countries seeking to join the GATT would no longer be viable. In fact, under the WTO's Article XII accession process, all applicants have had systems based on market mechanisms, or have been in the

---

[20] See protocol for the accession of Poland to the GATT, Annex B, in document L/2851 of 19 September 1967 and protocol for the accession of Romania, Annex B, in document L/3601 of 21 October 1971.

[21] See Jackson *et al.* (1995), p. 1151.

process of transforming their economies by adopting market economy principles. A reference to this change in approach would be included in the accession documentation of the first completed WTO accession of a transition economy.[22]

## State trading in WTO Article XII accessions

Accession working party reports are organised under broad headings,[23] which are divided into sections dealing with specific areas of WTO rules. The opening sections, under the heading 'Economic Policies', provide a description of the general economic and policy framework relevant for the understanding of an acceding government's foreign trade regime. The discussion in these sections places the acceding government's policies in the overall context of WTO rules and deals with issues relating to both trade in goods and trade in services. The role of the state in the economy has typically been discussed in this part of the text under the section entitled 'State Ownership and Privatisation'. The narrower discussion relating to STE rules has traditionally been taken up in the section of the report dedicated to trade in goods, under the title 'State Trading Entities'. Over time, both aspects of the discussion have been merged into a single section – dealing with state ownership, privatisation and STEs – under the 'Economic Policies' heading. Issues relating specifically to monopolies and exclusive services suppliers, as per the provisions of GATS Article VIII, have been discussed under the 'Policies Affecting Trade in Services' heading of the report.

In general, discussions relating to state trading practices have consisted of a number of key elements: collection of factual information on the incidence of state ownership in the economy; description of past and ongoing privatisation programmes; identification of specific STEs, if applicable; and specific accession commitments – i.e. legal obligations

---

[22] 'Members believed that for accession to the Agreement Establishing the WTO the relationship between the Bulgarian State and its trade and industry had to be clear. The representative of Bulgaria affirmed his government's intention to ensure the transparency of its national trade policies and practices ... This was not to be regarded as a basis for the imposition of specific obligations under the Agreements or as the basis for the adoption of new special policy commitments. Bulgaria could not take commitments exceeding the regular membership obligations' – report of the working party on the accession of Bulgaria (document WT/ACC/BGR/5 of 20 September 1996), paragraph 24.

[23] Introduction; economic policies; framework for making and enforcing policies; policies affecting trade in goods; trade-related intellectual property regime; policies affecting trade in services; transparency; trade agreements; and conclusions.

undertaken by the acceding government, which become an integral part of the WTO Agreement upon accession. The accession commitments of Article XII members fall into three broad categories: (i) a commitment to conduct state trading activities in compliance with WTO rules; (ii) a commitment to provide relevant notifications on the operation of STEs in accordance with applicable WTO provisions; and (iii) a commitment to ensure transparency, through regular notification, on privatisation programmes and other issues related to ongoing economic reforms. Where appropriate, supplementary commitments – either of a more general nature or relating to specific enterprises – have also been agreed on a case-by-case basis. All commitments have either been divided up between the 'State Ownership and Privatisation' and 'State Trading Entities' sections, or in more recent accession reports, contained in the consolidated section dealing with state ownership, privatisation and STEs.

### The specific commitments: state trading operations

The incidence of state trading practices in the economies of Article XII members is significant. Through the progressive refinement of the commitment language included in accession working party reports, WTO members have sought to ensure that enterprises carry out purchases and sales on commercial grounds and in a non-discriminatory fashion. Four main stages in the evolution of the commitment language can be identified. These substantive 'shifts' have coincided with the conclusion of the accession negotiations of three major Article XII economies – China (2001), Saudi Arabia (2005) and Russia (2012).

In the early years of Article XII negotiations (1995–2000), the structure and content of commitment language developed rapidly and contained significant variations, reflecting the fact that both members and acceding governments needed time to familiarise themselves with the new WTO framework of multilateral rules. The following basic template emerged around 1998:

> The representative of . . . confirmed that his/her Government would apply its laws and regulations governing the *trading activities of any state-owned enterprises* and *other enterprises with special or exclusive privileges* in full conformity with the provisions of the WTO Agreement, in particular Article XVII of GATT 1994 and the Understanding on that Article and Article VIII of the GATS [regarding state trading, in particular abiding by the provisions for *notification*, *non-discrimination*, and the application of *commercial considerations* for trade transactions] [emphasis added].

This early template was not particularly detailed. Nevertheless, it arguably introduced additional clarity to the ambiguity inherent in the STE definition provided by GATT Article XVII. In particular, the phrase 'trading activities of state-owned enterprises' conveys additional specificity than the more indeterminate formulation, 'state enterprise', found in the GATT. Another notable feature of this early commitment language is the attempt to create a bridge between the related, but distinct, provisions of the GATT and the GATS. As noted previously, the key disciplines of GATS Article VIII extend to notification and non-discrimination in the operations of state-sanctioned monopolies. By introducing terminology found in GATT Article XVII – 'enterprises with special or exclusive privileges' – in the operational sentence referencing both the GATT and the GATS, the drafters conceivably sought to create a link between the provisions on trade in goods and those on trade in services. In addition, some commitment paragraphs from this period specify that the key provisions are understood to include 'notification', 'non-discrimination' and the 'application of commercial considerations'.[24] The last of these three notions is not found in the GATS.

While this early template places elements drawn from the GATT into a broader context encompassing the GATS, the resulting commitment language leaves scope for interpretation as regards the application of GATT STE disciplines to enterprises falling under the provisions of GATS Article VIII. Interestingly, in two of the earlier accessions from this period, the link between the GATS and the GATT has been rendered much more explicit by developing the commitment language as follows:

> would abide by the provisions for *notification, non-discrimination,* and the *application of commercial considerations* for trade transactions for *any enterprise* whose activities were subject to Article XVII of the GATT 1994, the WTO Understanding on that Article, and *Article VIII of the GATS* [emphasis added].

Possibly as a result of negotiation dynamics, this additional commitment language was not retained in the template for later accessions. Nevertheless, even at this early stage of Article XII accessions, it placed a marker for the direction in which commitment language in this area would evolve.

---

[24] Bulgaria (see WTO document WT/ACC/BGR/5), paragraph 69; Kyrgyz Republic (see WTO document WT/ACC/KGZ/26), paragraph 113; Estonia (see WTO document WT/ACC/EST/28), paragraph 103; Jordan (WTO document WT/ACC/JOR/33), paragraph 161; Oman (see WTO document WT/ACC/OMN/26), paragraph 114.

The next significant development in the commitment language on state trading can be traced back to the accession of China, which was concluded in 2001. Although the precise wording of the text remains unique when compared to subsequent commitments in the area, it contains some key elements that would be taken up in later accessions. The core commitment reads as follows:

> China would ensure that all state-owned and *state-invested enterprises* would make *purchases and sales based solely on commercial consider-ations, e.g. price, quality, marketability and availability,* and that the enterprises of other WTO Members would have *an adequate opportunity to compete* for *sales to* and *purchases from* these enterprises on non-discriminatory terms and conditions. In addition, the Government of China *would not influence, directly or indirectly, commercial decisions* on the part of state-owned or state-invested enterprises, *including on the quantity, value or country of origin of any goods purchased or sold,* except in a manner consistent with the WTO Agreement[25] [emphasis added].

This paragraph departs significantly from earlier approaches in a number of ways. It reproduces key elements of GATT Article XVII, restating that purchases and sales should be 'based solely on commercial consider-ations' and enumerating examples of such considerations, as well as recalling that foreign enterprises should be afforded 'an adequate oppor-tunity to compete'. In particular, it builds on the existing wording of GATT Article XVII by explicitly stating that the opportunity to compete should be for 'sales to' and 'purchases from' the state-controlled enter-prises in question. This formulation is analogous to the interpretation of the Appellate Body in *Canada – Wheat Exports and Grain Imports,* which argued (in 2004) that adequate opportunities should be afforded to foreign enterprises interested in purchasing products from the STE in question, rather than competing with the STE for sales of the same product.[26] The commitment builds further on the GATT language by including the term 'state invested', in addition to 'state owned'. Finally, the second part of the paragraph establishes a supplementary obligation – not derived from the GATT – which reinforces the commitment by

---

[25] Report of the working party on the accession of China, paragraph 46 (see WTO document WT/ACC/CHN/49 of 1 October 2001).

[26] The language in GATT Article XVII appears to be less precise as it stipulates that STEs are to 'afford the enterprises of other Members adequate opportunity' to 'compete for participation in such purchases or sales'. The Appellate Body found that the phrase refers to the opportunity to become an STE's counterpart, but not to replace the STE as a participant in the transaction.

stipulating that the government undertakes not to 'influence, directly or indirectly, commercial decisions . . . including on the quantity, value or country of origin of any goods purchased or sold'. This additional language is aimed at identifying the various channels through which influence could be exerted. It is also notable that, unlike the approach taken in earlier accessions, China's commitment contains no reference to the relevant provisions of the GATT or the GATS. However, the inclusion of the commitment language in the opening part of the report, under the broad heading 'Economic Policies' (rather than under 'Policies Affecting Trade in Goods'), implies that the obligation is understood to extend to both trade in goods and trade in services.[27]

A number of accessions completed after the conclusion of China's negotiations reverted to the use of the 'old template' commitment language and re-established the two distinct STE-related sections of the report. It was not until Saudi Arabia's accession in 2005 that a new comprehensive template emerged. The new wording was accepted by seven[28] Article XII members, thus establishing the *de facto* minimum standard in accession negotiations from 2005 to 2011. Based on the China model, the new text consolidated the updated approach to commitment language on state trading as follows:

> The representative of . . . confirmed that, from the date of accession, enterprises that are state-owned, *state-controlled,*[29] *and enterprises with special or exclusive privileges,* would make purchases of goods *and services,* which are not for government use, and sales in international trade in accordance with commercial considerations, including price, quality, availability,

---

[27] The terminology 'enterprises with special and exclusive privileges' has not been retained in China's commitment paragraph, or elsewhere in the working party report. This reflects the particular dynamics of the negotiating process. In the case of China, prior to accession, trading rights were controlled by SOEs, while both domestic and foreign enterprises faced trading rights restrictions.

[28] Saudi Arabia (see WTO document WT/ACC/SAU/61, paragraph 44), Ukraine (see WTO document WT/ACC/UKR/152, paragraph 53), Cabo Verde (see WTO document WT/ACC/CPV/30, paragraph 45), Montenegro (see WTO document WT/ACC/CGR/38, paragraph 36), Samoa (see WTO document WT/ACC/SAM/30, paragraph 40), Vanuatu (see WTO document WT/ACC/VUT/17, paragraph 23), Yemen (see WTO document WT/ACC/YEM/42, paragraph 42). It should be noted that, although Yemen's accession negotiations were concluded in 2014, the process had been virtually completed, but dormant, since 2011.

[29] The term 'state-invested' has been used instead of 'state-controlled' in two accession working party reports from this period – Cabo Verde (see WTO document WT/ACC/CPV/30 of 6 December 2008, paragraph 37) and Vanuatu (see WTO document WT/ACC/VTU/17 of 11 May 2011, paragraph 23). 'State-controlled' has continued to be the default terminology in subsequent accessions.

marketability and transportation,[30] and would afford enterprises of WTO
Members adequate opportunity, *in conformity with customary practice*,
to complete for such purchases or sales [emphasis added].

The text builds on the language of China's commitment by expanding
the range of enterprises covered under the obligation to those which are
'state-controlled' and 'with special and exclusive privileges'. The text is
also explicit in that the commitment would apply to both goods and
services. Additional wording from GATT Article XVII has again been
incorporated in the commitment language to recall that 'conformity with
customary practice' should be one of the considerations in affording
foreign firms an adequate opportunity to compete. Several countries have
also accepted the supplementary obligation contained in the second part
of China's commitment, identifying the various channels through which
the state could exert influence.[31]

The most recent update of the core commitment language on state
trading was introduced with the adoption of the Accession Package of the
Russian Federation in 2011. This latest template has since been replicated
in three[32] recently concluded accessions and is also set to be incorporated
in the results of one[33] advanced ongoing accession process. The text
resembles the previous template and reads as follows:

> The representative of . . . confirmed that, from the date of accession,
> enterprises that are state-owned, state-controlled, and other enterprises
> with special or exclusive privileges, would make purchases ~~of goods and
> services~~, which are not intended for governmental use, and sales in
> international trade in accordance with commercial considerations,
> including price, quality, availability, marketability, *transportation and
> other conditions of purchase or sale*,[34] and would afford enterprises of

---

[30] The term 'transportation', derived from the wording of GATT Article XVII, has not been included in four accession working party reports from this period (Viet Nam, Cabo Verde, Vanuatu and Yemen), but has featured in all subsequent accessions.

[31] Viet Nam, Cabo Verde, Vanuatu and Yemen. As in the case of China, the additional text reads: 'In addition . . . would not influence, directly or indirectly, commercial decisions on the part of the state-owned, state-controlled and other enterprises with special or exclusive privileges, including on the quantity, value or country of origin of any goods purchased or sold, except in a manner consistent with the WTO Agreement'.

[32] Lao PDR (see WTO document WT/ACC/LAO/45, paragraph 35), Tajikistan (see WTO document WT/ACC/TJK/30, paragraph 51) and Seychelles (see WTO document WT/ACC/SYC/64, paragraph 76).

[33] Afghanistan.

[34] The term 'other conditions of purchase or sale', derived from the wording of the GATT XVII, was not included in the commitment of Russia but has featured in all other subsequent accessions.

WTO Members adequate opportunity, in conformity with customary *business* practice, to complete for *participation in* such purchases or sales [strikethrough and emphasis added].

This text builds on the earlier template in two significant ways. First, it continues to flesh out the commitment language by incorporating several additional terms from the wording of GATT Article XVII – specifically, 'transportation', 'other conditions of purchase or sale', 'business' and 'participation in'. Second, it leaves out the explicit reference to 'goods and services', in recognition of the fact that this reference has become redundant with the consolidation of the discussion on state trading under the broad heading 'Economic Policies'. Thus, the pattern initiated with the accession of China – i.e. borrowing the language of GATT Article XVII and applying it to enterprises supplying both goods and services – has arguably been distilled to its essential elements. Mindful of the expanded scope of the provision, negotiators have included additional language – uniquely in the case of Russia – emphasising that the obligations relating to state trading are without prejudice to the limitations recorded in the Russian schedule of specific commitments on services and the general rights and obligations under the GATS. It may also be noted that one[35] accession commitment from this most recent period has retained the supplementary obligation identifying the various channels through which the state could exert influence (i.e. second part of the 'China template').

While not constituting a general pattern, the limiting of state trading practices has been raised in a number of accession commitments. The intention to eliminate state trading altogether has been documented in two cases.[36] In three other instances, Article XII members have undertaken commitments to limit the scope of state trading. In particular, China undertook a series of commitments to phase out state trading in accordance with specific provisions set out in an annex to its working party report and accession protocol.[37] Chinese Taipei undertook to

---

[35] Lao PDR (WT/ACC/LAO/45, paragraph 35).

[36] Estonia, paragraph 103 (see WTO document WT/ACC/EST/28) and Oman, paragraph 114 (see WTO document WT/ACC/OMN/26).

[37] Prior to accession, foreign-invested enterprises in China obtained only limited trading rights based on their approved scope of business. Domestic enterprises also faced a number of trading rights restrictions. According to its accession commitments, China has agreed to progressively liberalise the scope and availability of the right to trade. The previous system, controlled by SOEs, would be gradually transformed so that SOEs, as well as domestic and foreign private businesses, could all participate. Thereafter, except as

eliminate any special or monopoly privileges granted to its import/
distribution monopoly on tobacco and alcohol.[38] For its part, Cambodia
committed not to grant new privileges in terms of GATT Article XVII
to its STEs.

In some cases, WTO members have considered that the degree
of influence of the state on the economy of an acceding country made
supplementary commitments necessary. These commitments have
been adapted to address particular concerns and have not been of
systemic relevance in establishing general patterns across all Article XII
accessions.[39]

## The specific commitments: transparency and notifications

In addition to non-discrimination, the second basic principle of state
trading rules has been transparency. Specifically, regular notifications are
required to ensure that the operations of enterprises remain transparent
and that the applicable substantive disciplines are enforced. STE notifications are based on a standard questionnaire, which was originally
established in the 1960s and subsequently revised in 1998 and in
2003.[40] The required information includes the enumeration of all STEs,
the reason and purpose for their introduction and maintenance, a
description of their operation and relevant statistical information. The
questionnaire is part of the set of initial documents that each acceding
government submits to the working party to initiate the examination
of its foreign trade regime. Most acceding governments will also need
to update this information over the course of the accession process.[41]
In addition, enterprises of particular concern to WTO members may be
enumerated in the descriptive parts of the report.[42] While non-binding in

otherwise provided in China's Protocol of Accession, all enterprises would be permitted
to trade in all goods throughout the customs territory of China. In the meantime, China
has reserved the right to exclusive state trading for a number of products – including
cereals, tobacco, fuels and minerals – which would not be subject to progressive
liberalisation.

[38] See WTO document WT/ACC/TPKM/18, paragraphs 149 and 158.

[39] E.g. operation of state-owned banks in the case of Russia (see WTO document WT/ACC/
RUS/70, paragraph 1392).

[40] The most recent version of the questionnaire is contained in document G/STR/3/Rev. 1 of
14 November 2003.

[41] See, for instance, WTO document WT/ACC/VNM/14 and Revision 1.

[42] See, for instance, Saudi Arabia, paragraph 44 (see WTO document WT/ACC/SAU/61)
and Russian Federation, paragraph 88 (see WTO document WT/ACC/RUS/70).

itself, the identification of state trading operations in the descriptive paragraphs constitutes a valuable inventory, which may inform future work, as discussed later in this section.

In addition to providing information on the incidence and operation of STEs, Article XII members have undertaken specific commitments concerning the notification of such enterprises. In this context, it may be recalled that the Understanding on the Interpretation of GATT Article XVII has effectively narrowed down the scope of the notification obligation to enterprises that have been granted exclusive or special rights and privileges through which they influence the level and direction of imports and exports.

The specific commitments undertaken by Article XII members could be classified in four broad categories (see Table 36.1). Most acceding governments have either made commitments to notify enterprises falling within the scope of GATT Article XVII (eleven governments) or within the scope of the Understanding on that article (seven governments). Given that the definition of notifiable enterprises under the Understanding is narrower, it could be argued that the scope of the notification commitment is broader for acceding governments for the former category. Another group of accession commitments contains a reference to notification requirements in the context of the general obligation to conform to the provisions of GATT Article XVII, its Understanding, and GATS Article VIII. This type of commitment was agreed in six of the earlier (pre-2003) accessions. The last type of commitment focuses on the notification of specific enterprises identified directly, or through cross-reference, in the commitment paragraph. With the exception of the former Yugoslav Republic of Macedonia and Chinese Taipei,[43] acceding governments in this group have not undertaken specific commitments to conform to the notification provisions of GATT Article XVII. Instead, their commitment paragraphs contain a general reference to compliance with WTO rules on state trading. Finally, in four cases, no specific reference to STE notifications has been registered in the commitment paragraph. Nevertheless, in all these cases, state trading practices have been discussed in the descriptive parts of the text and/or have been notified during the accession process.

---

[43] The former Yugoslav Republic of Macedonia (FYROM) has made a commitment to notify under GATT Article XVII, but the commitment paragraph also cross-references a specific list of enterprises that are to be notified. Chinese Taipei makes an explicit commitment to fill in the STE questionnaire (see document G/STR/3) upon accession.

Table 36.1 *STE notification commitments of Article XII members*

| Type of commitment | Article XII member | Specific commitment |
|---|---|---|
| 1 Notification of enterprises within the scope of GATT Article XVII | Albania, Croatia, Georgia, FYR Macedonia, Latvia, Tonga, Vanuatu | Notify any enterprise falling within the scope of Article XVII |
|  | Kyrgyz Republic, Mongolia, Panama, Saudi Arabia | Notify enterprises falling within the scope of GATT Article XVII *upon accession* |
| 2 Notification of enterprises within the scope of GATT Article XVII and/or the Understanding on that article | Montenegro, Russian Federation | Notify enterprises falling within the scope of the Understanding on GATT Article XVII *upon accession* |
|  | Cabo Verde, Yemen | *Upon accession*, notify and provide information on the activities of all state-owned, [state-controlled] [state-invested], and other enterprises with special and exclusive privileges in accordance with GATT Article XVII and the Understanding on that article |
|  | Lao PDR | *Upon accession,* notify the imports and exports of products by all state-owned, state-controlled, and other enterprises with special and exclusive privileges in accordance with GATT Article XVII and the Understanding on that article |
|  | China | As part of notification under the GATT and the Understanding on the Interpretation of GATT Article XVII, to also provide full information on the pricing mechanisms of STEs *for exported goods* |
|  | Ukraine | Notify any enterprise falling within the scope of the Understanding on GATT Article XVII *within one year of accession* |

Table 36.1 (*cont.*)

| Type of commitment | Article XII member | Specific commitment |
|---|---|---|
| 3 Conformity with GATT Article XVII and GATS Article VIII notification requirements | Bulgaria, Cambodia, Estonia, Jordan, Moldova, Oman | Conformity with GATT Article XVII, the Understanding on GATT Article XVII, and GATS Article VIII, with respect to notification requirements |
| 4 Notification of specific enterprises enumerated in the commitment paragraph | Ecuador, FYR Macedonia, Nepal, Samoa, Chinese Taipei | Notification of specific enterprises and reference to compliance with WTO rules on state trading |
| 5 No specific reference to STE notifications in the commitment language | Armenia, Lithuania, Tajikistan, Viet Nam | No specific reference to STE notification in the commitment language |

The overall contribution of the accession process in this area cannot be fully assessed, however, without an overview of the post-accession behaviour of Article XII members. In many ways, the accession process is an exercise in transparency, which prepares acceding governments for assuming their future WTO membership obligations. As soon as they become WTO members, governments are required to submit notifications to the working party on STEs every two years, for collective review.[44] This review consists of questions raised by interested WTO

---

[44] See document G/STR/8 of 8 June 2012, 'Recommendation on the Frequency of Notifications'. 'New and full' notifications, i.e. a complete set of answers to the standard questionnaire, are due every two years. Prior to 2004, new and full notifications were due every three years with updating notifications in the intervening years. This was changed to a biennial obligation to ease the burden on members and encourage compliance with notification obligations.

members and responses provided by the notifying member. Notifications must be made even if no STEs exist.[45] To address non-compliance, the Understanding on the Interpretation of GATT Article XVII has also added the possibility for members to counter-notify STEs that have not been duly notified. Despite the existence of well-established procedures, however, notification obligations have been consistently neglected by WTO members, as repeatedly noted by the chairperson of the working party.[46]

Table 36.2 provides an overview of the notifications submitted by Article XII members in the period 2000–2010. This period provides a representative sample of the notification behaviour of governments that have come through the accession process. Blanks indicate that the required notification has not been submitted. Shaded boxes indicate that notifications were not due either because the acceding government was still negotiating accession or had joined the European Union. For comparison purposes, Table 36.2 also provides information on the number of notifications made by all WTO members over the same period.

Table 36.2 reveals that the majority of the twenty-five Article XII members under consideration have made at least one notification over this period. Thirteen Article XII members have submitted 'nil notifications', indicating that they have not identified any STEs operating on their territories. In seven cases, all required notifications have been submitted. Conversely, six Article XII members – mostly least-developed countries and low-income economies – have not met any of their notification obligations during the period. When compared to the reporting behaviour of WTO members as a whole, the notification rate of Article XII members has been consistently higher over the period (see Figure 36.1). Article XII members have thus contributed to enhancing transparency and strengthening the credibility of the collective review mechanism.

Despite that, with less than half of Article XII members making notifications in 2008 and 2010, it is clear that the compliance record

---

[45] See, for example, document G/STR/N/15/GEO.

[46] For instance, in October 2013, the Chairperson noted that 'many Members remained in arrears in terms of completing their notification obligations' and that 'there was a need to improve the notification record' (see minutes of the meeting of the working party on STEs held on 7 October 2013 in document G/STR/M/25).

Table 36.2 *Post-accession notification behaviour of Article XII members*[a]

| | 2000 | 2001 | 2002 | 2003 | 2004 | 2006 | 2008 | 2010 |
|---|---|---|---|---|---|---|---|---|
| Ecuador | N | N | N | N | N | N | N | N |
| Bulgaria[§] | | N | N | | N | | | |
| Mongolia | N | N | | | | | | |
| Panama | N | N | N | N | N | N | N | N |
| Kyrgyz Republic | | | | | | | | |
| Latvia[§] | N | N | N | N | | | | |
| Estonia[§] | | N | N | N | | | | |
| Jordan | X | X | X | X | | | | |
| Georgia | | N | N | N | N | N | N | N |
| Albania | | | | | N | N | N | |
| Oman | | X | | X | | | | |
| Croatia | | | N | N | N | N | N | N |
| Lithuania[§] | | X | | | | | | |
| Moldova | | N | N | N | N | N | N | N |
| China | | X | X | X | | | | |
| Chinese Taipei | | | X | X | X | X | X | X |
| Armenia | | | | | N | N | N | N |
| FYR Macedonia | | | | | N | | | |
| Nepal | | | | | | | | |
| Cambodia | | | | | | | | |
| Saudi Arabia | | | | | | N | N | N |
| Viet Nam | | | | | | | | |
| Tonga | | | | | | | | |
| Ukraine | | | | | | | X | X |
| Cabo Verde | | | | | | | | |
| Article XII members subject to notification requirements | 12 | 15 | 16 | 18 | 17 | 18 | 21 | 21 |
| No. of notifications made by Article XII members | 5 | 11 | 10 | 11 | 10 | 9 | 10 | 8 |

Table 36.2 (*cont.*)

|  | 2000 | 2001 | 2002 | 2003 | 2004 | 2006 | 2008 | 2010 |
|---|---|---|---|---|---|---|---|---|
| Notification rate of Article XII members (%) | 41.7 | 73.3 | 62.5 | 61.1 | 58.8 | 50.0 | 47.6 | 38.1 |
| Notification rate of all WTO members (%) | 41.6 | 50.0 | 42.6 | 38.2 | 41.5 | 39.5 | 40.5 | 35.7 |
| No. of notifying members/no. of members | 52/125 | 64/128 | 55/129 | 50/131 | 51/123 | 49/124 | 51/126 | 45/126 |

*Notes:* ᵃAdapted from document G/STR/10 of 14 October 2013. Prior to 2004, new or updated notifications were due every year. As of 2004, the periodicity has been changed to two years. With respect to the count of WTO members, the European Union and its twenty-eight member states provide one notification for each notification period. However, the member states that joined the European Union on 1 May 2004 and on 1 January 2007 (including four Article XII members) are considered separately in order to provide information on the period preceding the European Union enlargements. X indicates that a notification has been received by the WTO. N indicates that a nil notification has been made. § indicates that the country is currently a member of the European Union. Blank box indicates that no notification has been received by the WTO.

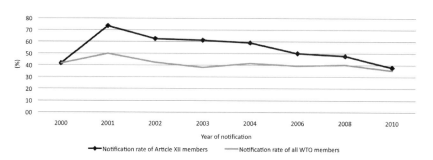

**Figure 36.1**   STE notification rates, 2000–2010.

can be further improved. Two recent examples illustrate how the fact-finding work carried out during the accession process may make a positive impact in this regard. Specifically, members have made repeated enquiries about the status of Russia's notification of Gazprom as an STE.[47] Their request has been based on information provided during the accession process, identifying Gazprom as an STE. While Russia has not undertaken a legally binding specific commitment in its accession working party report, the reassurances contained in the descriptive text[48] have given members sufficient grounds to press for a specific STE notification. As part of the broader trend to encourage members to abide by notification obligations, a counter-notification – the first of its kind in the area of STEs – was made against China in August 2014. Of the 153 enterprises listed in the counter-notification, 109 had already been enumerated in China's 2003 notification, which in turn has been based on the enterprises identified in the accession negotiations.[49] Thus, the identification of state trading practices during the accession process establishes a valuable inventory, which promotes further transparency in the post-accession stage.

## The specific commitments: privatisation

Many acceding governments have approached the WTO accession process as an instrument for reinforcing and consolidating necessary domestic economic reforms. For the majority of Article XII members, substantive privatisation programmes have been carried out in parallel to their accession negotiations as part of their transition to market economy regimes. Twenty-two[50] Article XII members have undertaken specific commitments in this area. The standard commitment has been:

> The representative of ... confirmed that his/her Government would ensure the transparency of its on-going privatization programme. He stated that his/her Government would provide [annual][periodic] reports to WTO Members on developments in its privatization programme as long as the programme would be in existence. [He also stated that his/her government would provide annual reports on other issues related to economic reforms as relevant to its obligations under the WTO.]

[47] See minutes of the meetings of the working parties on STEs held on 30 October 2012 and 7 October 2013 (documents G/STR/M/24 and 25).
[48] See WTO document WT/ACC/RUS/70, paragraph 88.
[49] See WTO document WT/ACC/CHN/49, Annex 2.
[50] Bulgaria, Mongolia, Kyrgyz Republic, Latvia, Estonia, Georgia, Albania, Croatia, Lithuania, Moldova, Chinese Taipei, Armenia, FYR Macedonia, Cambodia, Saudi Arabia, Viet Nam, Ukraine, Cabo Verde, Montenegro, Samoa, Russia and Tajikistan.

The commitment language has remained remarkably consistent over the years. No acceding government has undertaken a commitment to scale down the degree of state ownership in the economy. Instead, WTO members have sought to ensure that the privatisation process is conducted in a transparent manner. Most commitments provide for reports to be submitted on an annual basis, for the duration of the privatisation programme. Case-specific variations have also been negotiated. For two[51] Article XII members, the periodicity of reports has been greater than one year, while in three[52] cases the periodicity has not been defined. Unlike most commitments resulting from accession negotiations, it is notable that these obligations do not refer to an existing WTO rule, given the absence of multilaterally agreed disciplines in this area.

## Summary observations

A number of specific observations emerge from the overview of the results of WTO accession negotiations in the area of state trading:

- State trading has come under scrutiny in all WTO accession processes. In general, specific commitments have been undertaken in three broad areas – non-discrimination in the operations of STEs; notification of STEs; and transparency in ongoing privatisation programmes. Supplementary commitments, addressing specific concerns, have also been undertaken, but have not developed into a standard pattern across all accession processes.
- The commitment language relating to non-discrimination in STE operations has evolved significantly. The explicit reference to GATT Article XVII has gradually been left out. In the meantime, commitments have followed increasingly closely the wording of this article, by restating its principal provisions. This accession practice underscores the continuing relevance of this GATT provision to disciplining the operations of STEs in the multilateral context.
- Conversely, accession commitments have not drawn on the specific wording of GATS Article VIII and, in recent commitments, the reference to this article has been removed. The limitations of GATS Article VIII in terms of scope (state-sanctioned monopolistic service

---

[51] Bulgaria (eighteen months) and Mongolia (two years).
[52] Cambodia, Ukraine and Tajikistan.

suppliers[53]) and specific disciplines (non-discriminatory behaviour in the sale of services and limited notification requirements) have put into question its effectiveness in providing effective disciplines that would be relevant to the operations of modern-day STEs.

- Rather, the practice has emerged of applying the language drawn from GATT Article XVII to enterprises supplying both goods and/or services. The probable implication of the adoption of this consolidated approach is the expansion of the coverage of accession commitments to: (i) the purchases of services by goods producers; and (ii) the purchases of goods and services by services suppliers. This approach addresses the implicit limitations associated with applying two discrete sets of rules under the GATT and the GATS. As distinct provisions, these articles are arguably limited in the way they would apply to the full spectrum of purchase/sale operations of enterprises. This is particularly relevant given the practical realities of modern integrated production methods.

- Over time, the accession commitment language has also introduced a degree of additional clarity and specificity with respect to the categories of enterprises covered under the STE definition, by building on the formulations found in GATT Article XVII (e.g. 'state owned' and 'state-controlled' enterprises).

- Given the lack of transparency and shortage of comprehensive data on state trading, the fact-finding aspect of accession negotiations has helped fill some of the existing information gaps in the STE landscape. Specifically, enterprises of particular concern have been identified during the accession process, making post-accession compliance with notification obligations more effective. In addition, the acceptance by acceding governments of specific accession commitments on STE notifications has further strengthened the systemic emphasis on transparency.

- No specific commitments have been made by acceding governments concerning the extent of state ownership, in recognition of the existence of different views on the role of government involvement in the economy. Nevertheless, emphasis has been placed on ensuring that, in economies undergoing structural reform, privatisation is conducted

---

[53] Mattoo (1997) argues that changing market structures and the evolving nature of ownership patterns have meant that traditional service monopolies (e.g. national telecommunication operators) are gradually disappearing, thus reducing the relevance of GATS Article VIII.

in a transparent manner. From the perspective of WTO members, notification commitments in this area contribute to shedding additional light on enterprises which may behave as STEs given their historical links to the state. From the perspective of acceding governments, these commitments can help anchor ongoing economic reforms by lending additional credibility to the domestic actions of reform-minded governments.

### Development of future WTO disciplines on state trading and the role of Article XII members

The development of STE disciplines is currently on the agenda of the ongoing 'mega-regional' initiatives, including the Trans-Pacific Partnership (TPP) and the Transatlantic Trade and Investment Partnership (TTIP). While STE provisions have been a feature of free trade agreements in the past,[54] these new initiatives seek to set updated yardsticks for global trade rules by creating disciplines which can ensure that STEs compete against private firms on a commercial basis. In a recent statement in relation to the TTIP, the European Trade Commissioner noted that while the WTO provides 'many of the rules we need', there are still gaps 'for issues like how to treat state-owned enterprises'.[55] In addition to the overriding objective of creating a new legal framework, which could eventually be incorporated into multilateral trade rules, the participants in these regional initiatives seek to address specific trade-related concerns. For instance, under the TPP, the United States has expressed an interest in strengthening STE rules with a view to disciplining the behaviour of SOEs operating in China, in the event of China joining the TPP.[56] As for the TTIP, the European Union considers the development of STE disciplines to be of particular relevance for companies active in the raw materials and energy sector.[57]

Apart from the possible new yardsticks that may emerge from the 'mega-regional' initiatives, the development of disciplines relevant to the operation of STEs is also on the current work agenda of the WTO.

---

[54] See Solano and Sennekamp (2006). Of the eighty-six free trade agreements notified to the WTO between 2001 and 2005, the majority (fifty-five) contain provisions referring to specific treatment reserved for state enterprises and state monopolies, with a focus on non-discrimination provisions.
[55] De Gucht (2014).      [56] *Inside US Trade*, 28 February 2014.
[57] European Commission (2013).

The voice of Article XII members, which today represent one-fifth of the WTO membership, is likely to play a role in shaping the development of new rules in this area. While the outstanding issues in the Doha Development Agenda are interlinked, agriculture continues to play a key role in determining the prospects for the WTO's 'post-Bali' agenda. State trading has emerged as an essential piece of this puzzle. In particular, the development of disciplines on agricultural exporting STEs is under consideration in the 'export competition' pillar of the agriculture negotiations where WTO members have been working towards the 'parallel elimination of all forms of export subsidies and disciplines on all export measures with equivalent effect'.[58] At the Ninth WTO Ministerial Conference in Bali in December 2013, members reaffirmed this objective, emphasising the need to enhance transparency in order to support the WTO reform process.[59] More specifically, to be in a position to discuss the development of new rules on export competition, WTO members are examining developments in this area on the basis of all available information, including a specifically designed questionnaire. A part of this questionnaire is dedicated to information on agricultural exporting STEs.

It is notable that Article XII members have been active participants in this process. Of the forty members that have provided responses to the questionnaire, ten are Article XII members. In addition, of the twenty members that have identified agricultural exporting STEs, five are Article XII members.[60] While it would be premature to speculate on possible outcomes, it is likely that the disciplines emerging from these discussions would be influenced by the results of completed WTO accession negotiations and, in particular, the views and positions of Article XII members. The reasons are twofold. Article XII members have developed a thorough understanding of state trading practices in their economies during the WTO accession process and are, therefore, well equipped for the debate.

---

[58] See WTO document WT/MIN(05)/DEC of 22 December 2005. The Ministerial Declaration further elaborates that 'as a means of ensuring that trade-distorting practices of STEs are eliminated, disciplines relating to exporting STEs will extend to the future use of monopoly powers so that such powers cannot be exercised in any way that would circumvent the direct disciplines on STEs on export subsidies, government financing and the underwriting of losses'.

[59] At the Ninth WTO Ministerial Conference, ministers adopted a Declaration on Export Competition (see WTO document WT/MIN/(13)/40).

[60] See document G/AG/W/125 of 2 June 2014. Article XII members account for about half of the seventy-seven agricultural exporting STEs identified by the WTO Secretariat.

At the same time, having undertaken comprehensive accession commitments which arguably address concerns in this area more effectively than existing WTO rules, they may seek to level the playing field by using, as benchmarks, their own accession commitments.

It is recognised that the WTO accession process – with its emphasis on a detailed and transparent examination of national foreign trade regimes, coupled with the negotiation of legally binding commitments – asks difficult questions of acceding governments. From a systemic point of view, however, questions have also been asked of the WTO accession process itself, in particular, whether the addition of new WTO members has contributed to strengthening the multilateral trading system and whether the process has been able to prepare new members for effective participation in the WTO. State trading – an area in which accession commitment language has evolved significantly over time – presents an instructive case study.

Over the last twenty years, economic policy has been characterised by the progressive dismantling of state monopolies and the gradual divestment of state assets. While, as a consequence, direct state control over the operations of enterprises has gradually diminished, governments continue to exert indirect influence and to pursue strategic objectives through the granting of exclusive or special privileges. In the meantime, enterprises have adopted internationalised methods of production based on value chains of intermediate inputs of goods and services. In this complex global trading environment, the potential for contravening WTO obligations through state trading operations is considerable and calls into question the adequacy of existing WTO provisions. In particular, the integrated structure of modern STEs may not be readily captured by the distinct disciplines of the GATT (Article XVII) and the GATS (Article VIII).

Accession negotiations have developed a comprehensive and forward-looking approach to the subject. The basic template for the accession commitments undertaken by Article XII members has been drawn from the provisions of GATT Article XVII. These provisions are aimed at encouraging entrepreneurial decision-making by the state and companies benefiting from exclusive rights. Accession commitments have gone further, however, by building on this basic template in a number of ways. First, by extending the scope of obligations to the purchases and sales of both goods and services, the results of accession negotiations have arguably produced stronger and more effective disciplines, which are more attuned to the operations of modern STEs. Second, accession negotiations have highlighted the need for additional precision in this area of WTO rules by contributing further definitional clarity to the term 'state trading enterprise'. Third, the provision of detailed descriptive information on STEs during the accession process, combined with specific commitments to provide STE notifications after accession, have enhanced systemic transparency and have rendered post-accession notification work more effective.

Concerning the incidence of state ownership *per se*, from a systemic point of view accession commitments on privatisation may be placed within the broader context of transparency – where these undertakings have contributed to strengthening the related transparency disciplines on STEs. From the perspective of acceding governments, these commitments may also provide valuable additional support for locking in autonomous domestic reforms. It should be noted that these undertakings have invariably been without prejudice to the sovereign decision to embark on economic reforms involving the divestment of state assets.

Accession negotiations could be seen as a barometer of the direction in which multilateral disciplines in this area may yet evolve. Ongoing work on state trading under the Doha Development Agenda has focused on an important but limited aspect of their operations – the exporting practices of STEs in the agricultural sector. At the same time, the results of accession negotiations point to possible ways to address some of the remaining concerns associated with modern-day state trading practices. Article XII members have become active participants in the work of the WTO, as evidenced by their notification record in this area and their involvement in ongoing work under the export competition pillar of the Doha Development Agenda. As such, they are well placed to influence further work in the development of more comprehensive disciplines pertaining to the operations of STEs.

## Acknowledgements

The author would like to thank Petra Beslać, Chiedu Osakwe and Pietro Poretti for their suggestions and ideas, and Adalsteinn Leifsson for his support. This chapter represents the personal opinions of the author, they do not represent the view of EFTA or its members. Any errors are the responsibility of the author.

# References

De Gucht, K. (2014). *What We Need to Make the TTIP Work?* German Economy
    Ministry Conference on the Transatlantic Trade and Investment Partner-
    ship, Berlin, 5 May.

European Commission (2013). Initial European Union Position Paper on Raw
    Materials and Energy. Retrieved from http://trade.ec.europa.eu/doclib/docs/
    2013/july/tradoc_151624.pdf.

Hoekman, B. and J. P. Trachtman (2008). 'Canada–Wheat: discrimination,
    non-commercial considerations, and the right to regulate through state
    trading enterprises', *World Trade Review*, 7: 45–66.

Jackson, J. H., W. J. Davey and A. O. Sykes, Jr. (1995). *Legal Problems of Inter-
    national Economic Relations*. West Group; 3 Sub-edition.

Kowalski, P. *et al.* (2013). 'State-owned enterprises: trade effects and policy impli-
    cations', Paris, OECD, Trade Policy Paper No. 147.

Mattoo, A. (1997). 'Dealing with monopolies and state enterprises: WTO rules
    for goods and services', WTO, WTO Staff Working Paper (TISD-98–1).

Mavroidis, P. (2007). *Trade in Goods*. Oxford University Press, USA.

Petersmann, E.-U. (1998). 'GATT law on state-trading enterprises: critical evalu-
    ation of Article XVII and proposals for reform', in T. Cottier and P. C.
    Mavroidis (eds.), *State Trading in the Twenty-First Century*. Ann Arbor,
    University of Michigan Press.

Solano, O. and A. Sennekamp (2006). 'Competitions provisions in regional trade
    agreements', Paris, Organisation for Economic Co-operation and Develop-
    ment, OECD Trade Policy Paper No. 31.

# 37

# Intellectual property rights protection: the plus/minus debate from a least-developed country perspective – sense and nonsense

ALEXANDRA BHATTACHARYA AND JOAN LAKER APECU

## ABSTRACT

*This chapter asks whether distinctions exist between the original WTO least-developed country (LDC) members and the Article XII LDCs in respect of their obligations under the WTO Trade-Related Aspects of Intellectual Property Rights (TRIPs) Agreement. The chapter examines the evidence from the protocols of accession of the seven Article XII LDCs in the context of the associated treaty dialogue in their working party reports. It finds that distinctions exist and that the commitments accepted by Article XII LDCs, in some respects, go beyond the original requirements of the TRIPs Agreements and therefore also go beyond the TRIPs obligations of original LDC members. The chapter investigates these WTO TRIPs 'plus' commitments and assesses their merits in relation to the sovereign determined domestic reform priorities of the Article XII members and possible implications for the rules-based multilateral trading system. It is argued that the TRIPs Agreement is a minimum standards agreement, consisting of both principles and substantive obligations, with built-in flexibilities and considerable scope for interpretation and national implementation of its provisions. WTO members may deviate from these minimum standards to the extent that they benefit from longer or shorter periods of transitional relief, which may vary according to an LDC member's status as either an original member or Article XII member. Accession-specific commitments and associated treaty dialogue also show that there is implementation 'flexibility' on the basis of pre-determined action plans. The chapter finds that, in those instances where Article XII LDCs members have undertaken legally binding commitments to implement WTO-plus obligations, the substantive minimum standards of protection of the TRIPs Agreement have been increased. These WTO-plus binding commitments have been used to 'lock in' domestic institutional and structural reforms, based on domestic development priorities to encourage innovation and attraction of foreign direct investment, and they have served a domestic reform purpose to encourage innovation, induce foreign direct investment and strengthen the TRIPs Agreement by increasing substantive minimum standards.*

The WTO Agreement on Trade-Related Aspects of Intellectual Property Rights (TRIPs Agreement) is the most comprehensive multilateral agreement on intellectual property (IP) rights, containing all aspects of IP rules, and also substantive obligations rules for enforcement and dispute settlement. The TRIPs Agreement in Article 66 includes special provisions (with respect to transition periods and the transfer of technology) for least-developed countries (LDCs) in view of their specific situation. With the accession of seven LDCs[1] under Article XII of the 1994 Marrakesh Agreement Establishing the World Trade Organization (WTO Agreement), a distinction seems to have arisen between WTO LDC members in the context of their TRIPs Agreement obligations.

The primary basis for this distinction between the twenty-nine original WTO LDC members and the seven Article XII LDC members is the specific negotiated commitments included in the accession working party reports and protocols of the Article XII LDC members. These negotiated IP commitments undertaken by Article XII LDC members are garnering special attention. Specifically, discussion has focused on whether the commitments go beyond the requirements of the TRIPs Agreement and therefore also beyond the TRIPs Agreement obligations of the original LDC members who did not have to 'negotiate' WTO entry. In other words, are these IP commitments in addition to ('plus') the obligations of the TRIPs Agreement and to those of original LDC members? Another discussion relates to the consequences or merits of these accession commitments and their implications for both the multilateral trading system and the acceding country.

In this chapter, an assessment is undertaken of the IP rights protection commitments of the seven Article XII LDC members and evaluated against the requirements of both the TRIPs Agreement and the TRIPs

---

[1] The seven Article XII LDC members and their dates of accession to the WTO are: Nepal (23 April 2004), Cambodia (13 October 2004), Cabo Verde (23 July 2008), Samoa (10 May 2012), Vanuatu (24 August 2012), Lao PDR (2 February 2013) and Yemen (26 June 2014).

Agreement obligations of original members.[2] The chapter also examines whether there is 'sense' or purpose to this trend in LDC accessions in both a multilateral and national context.

The chapter points to the conclusion that 'plus' IP rights protection commitments are indeed undertaken by Article XII LDCs in the context of systemic issues such as transition periods and also in specific substantive IP areas. Additionally, currently original LDC members are not obliged to implement the TRIPs Agreement in full (except Articles 3, 4 and 5) due to the TRIPs Council Decision (see WTO document IP/C/ 64) which extended the transition period to 1 July 2021. The chapter argues, however, that these legally binding commitments undertaken by Article XII LDCs result in both the reinforcement and expansion of the WTO multilateral IP rules and also, at national level, the 'locking in' of domestic legal, institutional and structural reforms in the area of IP which contribute to the encouragement of domestic innovation and foreign domestic investments. The chapter emphasises that these results are shaped by key elements in the LDC WTO accession process: the provision of needs-based technical assistance/capacity building and the predetermined action plans found in the accession working party reports.

## Assessment of TRIPs Agreement obligations

From the outset, it is pertinent to underline that the very notion of accession provides a criterion of difference between original LDC members and those acceding under Article XII. The working party reports and the Accession Protocols contain factual information of the acceding countries' IP regimes and the legal commitments undertaken upon accession, including implementation timelines or action plans.[3]

---

[2] A caveat is in order when undertaking these assessments. Higher substantive IP laws cannot always be attributed to accession commitments, especially if higher standards were in force prior to accession negotiations. For example, Samoa has provided for seventy-five years of protection for copyright, which is beyond the fifty-year requirement in the TRIPs Agreement. This law has been in place since 1998, prior to the initiation of its WTO accession negotiations. The difficulty of assessing the pre-WTO accession negotiation stage makes the need for a post-transition period assessment more imperative for an accurate comparative assessment. It is also necessary to note that the actual level of implementation rather than substantive obligations will provide a more useful parameter for comparison.

[3] The legal status of commitment paragraphs has been confirmed by the Dispute Settlement Body (DSB) case *China – Measures Related to the Exportation of Various Raw Materials*. The dispute panel, in a finding not appealed by any party to the dispute, confirmed that

On the other hand, original LDC members did not individually 'negotiate' specific legal commitments during the Uruguay Round with regard to the TRIPs Agreement but automatically ratified it with all its substantive provisions upon the establishment of the WTO. Thus, Article XII LDC members have an inherent and fundamental difference from original members with regard to the TRIPs Agreement which stems from their specific accession commitments and action plans geared towards achieving full TRIPs compliance at a certain date.

In undertaking a comparative exercise among the seven WTO LDC members with regard to their IP obligations within the context of the TRIPs Agreement, it is useful to recall that the TRIPs Agreement is a minimum standards agreement consisting of both principles and substantive obligations. In this context, there is considerable room for interpretation and national implementation of the provisions. This results in the 'fluidity' of the comparative exercise.

*Principles*

The TRIPs Agreement includes the two basic principles of national treatment and most-favoured-nation (MFN) found in Articles 3, 4 and 5 which are to be applied as a general standard by all WTO members irrespective of whether they are original or Article XII members, and their level of development. It is important to note that no transition period applies with respect to these two principles, which are to be implemented by both original and Article XII LDC members immediately upon joining the WTO. Furthermore, recognition of certain fundamental objectives and principles, such as the 'promotion of technological innovation' in Article 7 and the legitimacy of public interest exceptions as found in Article 8 also apply for all members with no scope for deviation. These principles have been said to confirm 'a horizontal flexibility which affects the understanding of all individual TRIPs obligations'.[4] It is also understood that these principles may be influenced by external norms which may inform or have an impact on the interpretation of

---

terms of Accession Protocols are integral parts of the WTO Agreement and are enforceable in dispute settlement. All parties also agreed that commitments included in the related working party report, and incorporated into the accession protocol by cross-reference, are binding and enforceable through WTO dispute settlement proceedings.

[4] Cottier, T. and M. Foltea (2011). 'Global governance in intellectual property protection: Does the decision-making forum matter?', Bern, Swiss National Centre of Competence in Research, NCCR Trade Working Paper No. 2011/45.

conflicting TRIPs provisions. The Appellate Body confirmed in its decision in *United States – Standards for Reformulated and Conventional Gasoline*[5] that WTO law as a specific rule system cannot be understood in 'clinical isolation from public international law'. Overall, these principles are applicable to all LDC members and no reference has been made to their exclusion in any accession working party report to date.

## Substantive obligations

The normative standards espoused by the TRIPs Agreement through substantive obligations are minimum thresholds which include built-in flexibilities. WTO members may deviate from these minimum standards to the extent that they benefit from longer or shorter periods of transitional relief which vary with a member's status as either 'developing' or an LDC. This differs from the principles of MFN and national treatment which all WTO members regardless of their status must immediately implement.

Article 1(1) of the TRIPs Agreement states that members are free to determine the appropriate method of implementing the provisions of the Agreement within their own legal system and practice. In other words, under this so-called implementation 'flexibility', WTO members can exploit creative solutions to transpose into national law and practice those concepts that the TRIPs Agreement simply enunciates but does not define. Examples include concepts such as novelty and inventiveness as found in Article 27(1), or situations of extreme urgency for the purposes of issuing compulsory licences in Article 31(b). The exhaustion of IP rights as stated in Article 6 has also left considerable discretion to members to determine their own regimes.

Both Article XII and original LDC members are able to utilise this 'implementation' flexibility as it is built into the TRIPs Agreement. However, during the accession process, it is seen that acceding LDCs may additionally be requested to provide copies of IP legislation for assessment by the working party.[6]

---

[5] See WTO document WT/DS24/AB/R.
[6] For example, the working party reports of Cambodia (see WTO document WT/ACC/KHM/21, paragraph 205) and Lao PDR (see WTO document WT/ACC/LAO/45, paragraph 226) state that all legislation in draft and promulgated form would be made available to the WTO members so that advice on TRIPs consistency could be obtained. A similar text is also found for Nepal, Cabo Verde and Samoa and Yemen.

As mentioned, the TRIPs Agreement is merely a minimum standards agreement and, in this context, WTO members are permitted to implement more stringent IP standards than are found in the TRIPs Agreement if so required. Specifically, Article 1(1) of the TRIPs Agreement states that 'Members may, but shall not be obliged to, implement in their law more extensive protection than is required by this Agreement, provided that such protection does not contravene the provisions of this Agreement'. For example, in the area of patents in Part II, Section 5, obligations include all the uniform minimum standards of protection with permissible limitations on scope of protection such as the possibility of excluding diagnostic, therapeutic and surgical methods for the treatment of humans or animals. In the case of trademarks, the Agreement includes all the minimum standards contained in the Paris Convention and also establishes a universally valid legal definition of a trademark in Article 15(1). A definitional article is not found for copyright or patents. Thus, it can be construed that there are more standardised obligations with respect to trademarks than for, for instance, copyright or patents.

Overall, this flexibility in the TRIPs Agreement as to the substantive standards of protection allows WTO LDC members to nuance IP laws according to their own requirements. Hence, Article XII LDCs have in some instances undertaken legally binding commitments to implement 'plus' obligations in some substantive IP areas. In other words, for these members, the substantive minimum standards of protection of the TRIPs Agreement have been increased.

Another flexibility found in the TRIPs Agreement is in the area of permissible exceptions to the substantive provisions. Article 17 states that 'Members may provide limited exceptions to the rights conferred by a trademark, such as fair use of descriptive terms, provided that such exceptions take account of the legitimate interests of the owner of the trademark and of third parties'. In the context of the protection of industrial designs in Article 26(2), members may provide that designs are not new or original if they do not significantly differ from known designs or combinations of known design features. Article 9.2 of the TRIPs Agreement also states that protection is to be denied to 'ideas, procedures, and methods of operation or mathematical concepts as such' which can also be interpreted as setting a form of 'maximum standard'. Similarly, Article 27.3 allows for exclusion from patent protection of diagnostic, therapeutic and surgical methods for the treatment of humans and animals, as well as plants and animals other than microorganisms. This research has not found instances where permissible exceptions of the TRIPs Agreement have not been available for Article XII LDCs. Rather, the focus has been on extending substantive standards of protection.

With regard to enforcement, the TRIPs Agreement (in Part III): (i) identifies the mechanisms that members are obliged to adopt in order to make enforcement rights available to IP owners; and (ii) prohibits members from adopting stricter measures against defendants than those that are established. Nevertheless, members can resort to their own legal system and practices to implement enforcement obligations. For example, WTO members are free to maintain their own judicial system. They also can use enforcement measures to implement flexibilities as to the standards of protection. It is seen that Article XII LDCs may have restricted flexibility in this area as in the case of Lao PDR with regard to Article 58 on *ex officio* action by customs officials.[7] Additionally, it seems that one way of an acceding country guaranteeing that it will have unhindered flexibility in this area would imply the country establishing national IP enforcement structures prior to the commencement of the accession negotiation process and the Article XII LDC will have to 'ensure that any infringement of IP rights would be addressed immediately in cooperation with the assistance from affected right holders'.[8]

In conclusion, specific standards espoused by some TRIPs Agreement provisions may be difficult to ascertain due to substantial flexibilities in the text, particularly with regard to substantive obligations, and there is substantial room for interpretation. The 'standard' with regard to principles is more constant as it is applicable to all WTO members, both Article XII and original LDCs. With regard to substantive TRIPs Agreement obligations, as will be detailed below, it is seen that Article XII LDC members may have 'plus' obligations in some particular cases.

---

[7] Paragraph 226 of the working party report of Lao PDR (see WTO document WT/ACC/LAO/45) states that 'Lao PDR, would no later than the end of that transition period, authorise consistent with Article 58 of the TRIPs Agreement competent authorities to act upon their own initiative and to suspend the release of goods in respect of which they had acquired prima facie evidence that an intellectual property right is being infringed by counterfeit trademark goods or pirated copyright goods'. Additionally, the action plan for TRIPs implementation (Table 20(B)) included in Lao PDR's working party report includes the authorisation of *ex officio* action in compliance with TRIPs Article 58 within the timeframe of 2012–2016.

[8] This commitment is found in the working party reports of all seven Article XII LDCs: Cabo Verde, Cambodia, Lao PDR, Nepal, Samoa, Vanuatu and Yemen.

## IP commitments of seven recently acceded WTO LDC members in relation to the TRIPs Agreement

This section will assess the TRIPs commitments of Article XII LDC members and include a twofold evaluation. The first assessment component will be whether the Article XII LDC members have undertaken commitments that go beyond the provisions of the TRIPs Agreement and are therefore 'plus' to both the TRIPs Agreement and the IP obligations of original LDC members. Secondly, and simultaneously, there will be a comparison of IP commitments among the seven acceding LDCs themselves.

For ease of comparison, this analysis of the IP commitments focuses on two areas: (i) broader systemic issues such as transition periods for full implementation of the TRIPs Agreement, transition periods for protection of pharmaceutical patents and undisclosed test data protection; and (ii) more specific substantive IP provisions such as accession to other treaties, plant variety protection, exclusivity for test data and *ex officio* action by customs officials.

### *Systemic issues*

### Transition periods for full implementation of the TRIPs Agreement (except Articles 3, 4 and 5)

The issue of transition periods for the full implementation of the TRIPs Agreement for LDCs is one of the key systemic issues not only for the WTO accession process but for all WTO LDC members.

The TRIPs Agreement in its preamble recognises 'the special needs of the least-developed country Members in respect of maximum flexibility in the domestic implementation of laws and regulations in order to enable them to create a sound and viable technological base'. Additionally, provisions on transitional arrangements are found in Part VI (Articles 65–67) of the TRIPs Agreement. In particular, Article 66.1 stipulates that, in view of the special needs and requirements of LDCs, their economic, financial and administrative constraints and their need for flexibility to create a viable technological base, LDC members would not have to apply the TRIPs Agreement obligations for ten years, that is, until 1 January 2006 (with the exception of Articles 3, 4 and 5).

This transition period for LDCs has subsequently been extended by two 'duly motivated requests'. In 2005, the TRIPs Council Decision (IP/C/40) extended the transition period for implementing the TRIPs

Agreement (except Articles 3, 4 and 5) to July 2013. The TRIPs Council, in another decision (IP/C/64) in 2013, extended the transition period to 1 July 2021, which means that the original WTO LDC members do not have to implement the TRIPs Agreement in full until that date.

On the other hand, Article XII LDCs have individually negotiated transition periods for implementing the TRIPs Agreement. The length of the transition periods for full implementation of the TRIPs Agreement as found in the working party reports for Cabo Verde, Cambodia, Lao PDR, Nepal, Samoa, Vanuatu and Yemen are 4.4 years, 2.2 years, 3.8 years, 2.7 years, 1.1 years, 0.25 years and 2.5 years respectively.[9] It is observed that the average transition period for the seven LDC Article XII members is 2.4 years, which is far less than the ten years first accorded in the TRIPs Agreement for original LDC members to fully implement the Agreement. Additionally, these individual and negotiated transition periods are significantly shorter than the total length of the transition period of 24.5 years which has been accorded to original LDCs in the TRIPs Agreement through Article 66.1 and the two TRIPs Council Decisions (with 1 January 1996 as the effective date of the Agreement and 1 July 2021 as the end of the transition period). In essence, this could imply that Article XII LDC members are expected to bring their intellectual property rights (IPR) regime into conformity with the TRIPs Agreement and any additional IP commitments within a shorter period of time.

Furthermore, in contrast to the obligations of 'original' LDC members, Article XII members must undertake a number of additional commitments during their transition periods for implementing the TRIPs Agreement. These commitments include:

- Not granting patents, trademarks or copyrights, or marketing approvals for pharmaceuticals or agricultural chemicals inconsistent with the provisions of the TRIPs Agreement. This commitment, for example, is found in the working party reports of Cambodia (see WTO document WT/ACC/KHM/21, paragraph 204) and Vanuatu (see WTO document WT/ACC/VUT/17, paragraph 120).
- Ensuring that existing rates of infringement would not significantly increase and that any infringement of IP rights would be addressed

---

[9] The respective dates for full implementation of the TRIPs Agreement are Cabo Verde, 1 January 2013; Cambodia, 1 January 2007; Lao PDR, 31 December 2016; Nepal, 1 January 2007; Samoa, 1 July 2013; and Vanuatu, 1 December 2012.

immediately in cooperation with the assistance of affected right holders. This commitment was also made by all seven acceding LDC members.[10]

- A substantive IP commitment made by Cambodia to be implemented during its transition period was to protect against unfair commercial use of undisclosed test or other data for a period of at least five years from the date on which Cambodia granted marketing approval to the person who produced the data.[11] However, the right of Cambodia to avail itself of the flexibilities and transition period as afforded under the Doha Declaration on the TRIPs Agreement and Public Health (2001) was later confirmed during the Cancún Ministerial by a statement made by former WTO Deputy Director-General Rufus Yerxa. The commitment to protect unfair commercial use of undisclosed test or other data during its transition period does, however, exist for Vanuatu, whose working party report does not include a reference to the Doha Declaration on the TRIPs Agreement and Public Health.[12]

- The obligation to seek out all available technical assistance to ensure that the capacity to fully enforce a TRIPs-consistent legal regime upon expiration of the transition periods is found in the working party reports of all the Article XII LDC members in their respective IP commitment paragraphs.

- The obligation to ensure that all legislation will be made available to WTO members in draft and promulgated forms to WTO members so that advice on TRIPs consistency can be obtained.[13]

For systemic reasons more clarity is required regarding the implications of the recent TRIPs Council Decision (IP/C/64) on the LDC TRIPs Agreement transition period of Article XII members. All of the seven Article XII LDC members, as shown above, have made legal commitments to implement the TRIPs Agreement in full prior to July 2021.

---

[10] Cabo Verde (see WTO document WT/ACC/CPV/30, paragraph 245), Cambodia (see WTO document WT/ACC/KHM/21, paragraph 205), Lao PDR (see WTO document WT/ACC/LAO/45, paragraph 226), Nepal (see WTO document WT/ACC/NPL/16, paragraph 137), Samoa (see WTO document WT/ACC/SAM/30, paragraph 222), Vanuatu (see WTO document WT/ACC/VUT/17, paragraph 121).

[11] See WTO document WT/ACC/KHM/21, paragraph 205.

[12] See WTO document WT/ACC/VUT/17, paragraph 121.

[13] This commitment has been made by Cabo Verde (see WTO document WT/ACC/CPV/30, paragraph 245), Cambodia (see WTO document WT/ACC/KHM/21, paragraph 205), Lao PDR (see WTO document WT/ACC/LAO/45, paragraph 226), Nepal (see WTO document WT/ACC/NPL/16, paragraph 137) and Samoa (see WTO document WT/ACC/SAM/30, paragraph 222).

Furthermore, language in the TRIPs Agreement commitment para-graphs of LDC working party reports does not explicitly mention the right of the acceding LDC to avail itself of subsequent or future special and differential treatment (S&D) provisions such as the TRIPs Council Decisions on LDC transition periods for TRIPs implementation.

In terms of recourse to S&D provisions, the IP commitment language in the working party reports of Cabo Verde, Cambodia, Nepal, Samoa, Vanuatu and Yemen does not refer to the right to use any S&D provisions which may be provided by subsequent WTO legal instruments such as TRIPs Council Decisions which extended the transition period for full implementation of the TRIPs Agreement.

On the other hand, the IP commitment paragraph of Lao PDR's working party report (see WTO document WT/ACC/LAO/45, paragraph 227) states that Lao PDR would avail itself of S&D treatment for LDCs under the TRIPs Agreement and various Ministerial Conference Declarations including the Hong Kong Ministerial Declaration (paragraph 47), the TRIPs Council Decision (see WTO document IP/C/40) and the Eighth Ministerial Conference Decisions. The working party reports of five Article XII LDCs (Cabo Verde, Nepal, Samoa, Lao PDR and Yemen) contain language reaffirming these rights through references to the Doha Declaration on the TRIPs Agreement and Public Health (2001). How-ever, despite Lao PDR stating that it intends to make use of all the S&D provisions available under the TRIPs Agreement, including the TRIPs Council Decision of 2005, it is not clear whether Lao PDR automatically has access to all future and subsequent S&D provisions which would include the more recent TRIPs Council Decision (see WTO document IP/C/64) which extended the transition period to 1 July 2021. Addition-ally, if Lao PDR does indeed have the right to make use of all future S&D provisions with regard to transition periods, could this render its acces-sion commitment to fully implement the TRIPs Agreement no later than 31 December 2016 non-compliant with the latest TRIPs Council Deci-sion (see WTO document IP/C/64) on LDC transition periods for TRIPs implementation? This question warrants further analysis and future research, particularly within the context of the hierarchy of norms within the WTO accession process.[14]

---

[14] The DSB case *Indonesia – Certain Measures Affecting the Automobile Industry* has reaffirmed that members must comply with all of the WTO provisions, which must be interpreted harmoniously and applied cumulatively and simultaneously. Thus, the WTO

## The Doha Declaration on TRIPs and Public Health (2001) and LDC Article XII member accession commitments

Another systemic issue which arises relates to the right to use the flexibilities and transition periods for the protection of pharmaceutical patents and undisclosed test data protection as provided for in the Doha Declaration on the TRIPs Agreement and Public Health (2001).

The working party reports of five Article XII LDCs (Cabo Verde, Nepal, Samoa, Lao PDR and Yemen) contain language reaffirming these rights through references to the Doha Declaration on the TRIPs Agreement and Public Health (2001).[15] As previously mentioned, the right of Cambodia to avail itself of the flexibilities and transition period was confirmed during the Cancún Ministerial by a statement made by then WTO Deputy Director-General Yerxa.[16] The inclusion of specific language on the Doha Declaration would mean that those members would have until 1 January 2016 to implement patent protection for pharmaceutical products and undisclosed information with regard to pharmaceutical patents.

The exception to this is Vanuatu's working party report which does not include a reference to the Doha Declaration on the TRIPs Agreement and Public Health (2001). This could imply that Vanuatu has until 1 December 2012 to implement the TRIPs Agreement in full, including patent protection for pharmaceuticals and undisclosed test data protection.

## National and MFN treatment

As previously mentioned, the application of national treatment and MFN treatment to foreign nationals (Articles 3, 4 and 5 of the TRIPs

---

treaty is in fact a 'single agreement' which has established an 'organised legal order'. Indeed, accessions are fast becoming one of the most active areas not only within the WTO but also in the creation of WTO law and jurisprudence via accession commitments made in working party reports.

[15] Cabo Verde (see WTO document WT/ACC/CPV/30, paragraphs 244 and 246); Nepal (see WTO document WT/ACC/NPL/16, paragraph 129); Samoa (see WTO document WT/ACC/SAM/30, paragraphs 185, 207, 211 and 221) and Lao PDR (see WTO document WT/ACC/LAO/45, paragraph 227 and Tables 20(A) and 20(B)).

[16] The accession of Cambodia illustrated the doubts and uncertainty regarding whether Article XII automatically obtained S&D treatment (particularly in the context of transition periods). Cambodia's right to the flexibility was therefore confirmed during the Cancún Ministerial when Deputy Director-General Rufus Yerxa, speaking on behalf of the chairperson of Cambodia's working party, stated 'The results achieved in the case of Cambodia speak for themselves, and in this context I should also add that the terms of this accession do not preclude access to the benefits under the Doha Declaration on the TRIPs Agreement and Public Health to Cambodia as a least-developed country'.

Agreement) is to be granted immediately (i.e. from 1 January 1996) by original LDCs, with no scope for a transition period. Similarly, all seven Article XII LDCs have the obligation to implement Articles 3, 4 and 5 of the TRIPs Agreement without recourse to transition periods. For example, in the case of Cambodia, the working party report in paragraph 174 explicitly states that 'The representative of Cambodia said that national and MFN treatment was granted to all foreign nationals under the existing IP legislation, and all draft legislation continued to integrate the same principles'. Similarly, the working party report of Samoa in paragraph 188 stated that 'Samoa's intellectual property legislation (both current and new) complied with the MFN and National Treatment principles'. It can thus be concluded that no discernible differences exist in the application of MFN and national treatment between original and Article XII LDC members.

### 'No roll back' clauses

The 2005 TRIPs Council Decision (see WTO document IP/C/40) on the extension of the transition period under Article 66.1 included an obligation for LDCs to uphold or maintain any existing level of IP during their transition period. This is also known as the 'no roll back' clause. In other words, this clause does not allow members to use the transition period to reduce the level of IP protection in a way which would result in a lesser degree of consistency with the requirements of the TRIPs Agreement. Interestingly, since the post 2005–13 period, all seven LDC working party reports have included a similar 'no roll back' provision. For example, the working party report of Nepal in paragraph 136 states that 'Nepal will also ensure that any change made in its laws, regulations and practice during this period will not result in a lesser degree of consistency with the provisions of the TRIPs Agreement'. Cambodia's working party report in paragraph 204 also states that it will ensure that 'any change made in its laws, regulations and practice during this period will not result in a lesser degree of consistency with the provisions of the TRIPs Agreement tha[n] existed on the date of accession'.

However, the most recent TRIPs Council Decision (see WTO document IP/C/64) in June 2013 which extended the transition period for LDCs to 2021 does contain such a 'roll back' provision. Thus, currently this provision is only applicable for the seven Article XII LDC members and not for original LDC members. As a case in point, Yemen, the latest LDC to accede on 26 June 2014 (after the 2013 TRIPs Council Decision) committed to maintain 'a no roll back' clause[17] which yet again points to appreciable differences with respect to systemic issues between Article XII and original LDC members.

## Specific substantive IP provisions

### Accession to other treaties

In their accession negotiations on IP matters, some LDC Article XII members have undertaken specific commitments to accede to additional IP treaties such as the WIPO Copyright Treaty (WCT) and WIPO Performances and Phonograms Treaty (WPPT).

In terms of the 'plus or minus' debate, the obligation to join additional IP treaties which impose additional substantial obligations with respect to IP protection can be termed as being 'TRIPs-plus' as this is not an obligation found in the TRIPs Agreement and thus also beyond the obligation of original WTO members. For example, Vanuatu in paragraph 116 of its working party report 'recognised that membership of the Paris, Berne, Geneva, Brussels, UPOV[18] and WIPO Conventions would facilitate compliance with the TRIPs Agreement and would accede to these treaties by no later than 1 December 2012'. This was also included in its TRIPs action plan (Table 6). Similarly, Nepal in paragraph 122 of its action plan for TRIPs Agreement implementation (Table 10) in its working party report states that 'Nepal would join the Berne Convention, by December 2005, and join the Rome Convention and the Treaty on Intellectual Property by 2006'.

There are also references in other working party reports to the accession to other IP treaties with less binding language. For example, in Lao PDR's working party report in paragraph 182, there is no accession commitment with regard to this issue but a statement that the government 'would nevertheless study the implications of acceding to the various Agreements'. Samoa's working party report in paragraph 187 also states that the '[g]overnment was seeking more information on the Geneva Phonogram Convention, the WIPO Copyright Treaty, the WIPO Performance and Phonogram Treaty and the 1961 Rome Convention'. In a similar format, Cabo Verde in paragraph 206 of its working party report also did not explicitly commit to accede to other IP treaties

---

[17] See WTO document, paragraph 261 of WT/ACC/YEM/42.
[18] International Union for the Protection of New Varieties of Plants.

(WIPO Copyright Treaty, the WIPO Performances and Phonograms Treaty and the Geneva Phonograms Convention) and indicated that it would consider these matters further. The working party report of Yemen, also similarly, states that Yemen 'would examine the feasibility of acceding to them, in particular the WIPO Copyright Treaty and the WIPO Performances and Phonograms Treaty'.

### Plant variety protection and accession to the International Union for the Protection of New Varieties of Plants (UPOV)

The TRIPs Agreement provided members the flexibility to protect plant varieties under an effective *sui generis* system, patents or a combination of both (Article 27.3(b)). As per the TRIPs Agreement there is no obligation to become a member of the UPOV, which entails binding obligations such as those contained in the 1991 Act of the UPOV convention.

In the case of five Article XII LDC members (Samoa and Yemen being exceptions), there have been references to both the consideration of membership of UPOV and legal commitments to join it by the end of a certain period. For example, Nepal in its working party report in paragraph 122 noted the possibility of joining UPOV 1991 in the future. This was also similarly indicated by Cabo Verde in paragraph 206 of its working party report which stated that it would 'take a position on accession to the International Union for the Protection of Plant Varieties (UPOV) ... at a later stage'. Lao PDR in paragraph 182 of its working party report, in a similar vein, said that 'the Government would nevertheless study the implications of acceding to the various Agreements'.

Interestingly, Cambodia's working party report in paragraph 172 stated that the '[g]overnment was also considering membership in the International Convention for the Protection of New Varieties of Plants (UPOV), and a new law was being drafted to this end with the assistance of UPOV'. However, Cambodia's action plan for TRIPs implementation (Table 12) includes a time-frame for implementation which states that the membership to UPOV would be completed no later than 1 January 2006 and therefore is a legal commitment. Similarly, Vanuatu made a commitment to join the UPOV by the end of its transition period (no later than 1 December 2012).

The commitments made by Vanuatu and by Cambodia to join UPOV may be termed substantively as 'plus' and 'higher' than those of original LDC members and of the requirements of the TRIPs Agreement. However, it is not clear whether the accession to UPOV was part of the long-term national IP policy of the two countries where the value in joining was seen as voluntary, or whether these countries accepted the UPOV membership as part of their accession negotiations. As of 10 June 2014 (date of the latest information available from UPOV), all of the seven acceded LDC members were yet to join the UPOV.

### Ex officio *action by customs officials*

Article 58 of the TRIPs Agreement outlines the conditions for situations when members require competent authorities such as customs officials to act upon their own initiative (also known as *ex officio* action) and to suspend the release of what they believe to be IP-infringing goods. This is not a mandatory provision in the meaning that *ex officio* action by competent authorities is an obligation under the TRIPs Agreement. Rather, Article 58 outlines certain conditions if and when a member decides to implement such action.

In the case of Article XII LDCs, Lao PDR has committed to this enforcement procedure in paragraph 226 of its working party report which states that 'Lao PDR, would no later than the end of that transition period, authorise consistent with Article 58 of the TRIPs Agreement competent authorities to act upon their own initiative and to suspend the release of goods in respect of which they had acquired prima facie evidence that an intellectual property right is being infringed by counterfeit trademark goods or pirated copyright goods'. Therefore, according to both this commitment paragraph and also the action plan (Table 20(B)) included in the working party report, Lao PDR is obliged to implement this commitment within the period 2012–2013. This commitment made by Lao PDR can be seen to be 'plus' or exceeding the requirements of both the TRIPs Agreement and those made by original LDC members.

However, references to *ex officio* action by customs officials are also found in the working party reports of Cabo Verde (paragraph 239), Cambodia (paragraph 200), Samoa (paragraph 214) and Yemen (paragraph 255) under the section 'Special Border Measures', although with less binding language. These working party reports indicate that national legislation implementing Article 58 of the TRIPs Agreement and more generally on *ex officio* action by customs officials would be implemented or was already in place.

### WTO accessions and domestic reforms in IP

The previous sections illustrated, while bearing in mind the fluidity of the comparative exercise, that, in some instances, Article XII LDCs have undertaken IP accession commitments which can be seen as 'plus' to the requirements of the TRIPs Agreement and to those currently required by original LDCs. However, this assessment must be undertaken against the broader backdrop of the WTO accession process and its intrinsic linkage to the domestic legal, institutional and administrative reform process.

The implementation of the TRIPs Agreement by an LDC requires not only legislative changes but also structural reforms in the administration of IP rights, creation of institutions, enforcement and human resource training. IP domestic reforms undertaken by LDCs during the accession process exemplify how WTO accession facilitates domestic reforms in the area of IP while ensuring a structured and technical assistance-based process based on individual country needs.

Domestic legislative reforms undertaken by LDCs in the area of IP during the accession process can be assessed through WTO accession documentation such as TRIPs action plans which are found within the working party reports and also in separate WTO accession documents. Action plans are blueprints for both members and the acceding country to ensure that the regime of the acceding country is brought into compliance with specific provisions of the TRIPs Agreement as soon as possible. They set out details of the steps that remain to be taken to achieve the objective of full implementation of the TRIPs Agreement and the timetable for each step. Additionally, they guide the acceding LDC through its national IP reform process and also identify areas where technical assistance and capacity building may be required during the transition period. For example, Nepal's working party report in paragraph 135 states that the 'plan would constitute an understanding between Nepal and the Working Party on how Nepal would use the transition period, and form a blueprint for technical assistance making compliance possible within the timeframe contemplated'. An action plan for the implementation of the TRIPs Agreement in the form of a table is found in all seven working party reports and in most cases there is also additional documentation such as checklists on TRIPs implementation. This additional documentation depends on the individual accession process. There is no uniform requirement. Therefore, TRIPs action plans, as part of the WTO accession process, fulfil the task of aiding LDCs in ensuring that the domestic reform process is ongoing during the transition period with the end objective of full implementation. On a broader level, these legislative domestic reforms instigated by the WTO accession process induce investor confidence in the regulatory and legal IP regime while also providing a conducive environment for opportunities aimed at improving economic and social welfare.

### Action plans for the implementation of the WTO TRIPs Agreement

A general assessment of the seven Article XII LDC TRIPs Agreement implementation action plans researched in this chapter shows that the inclusion of a specific action and of the time-frame to implement it is not uniform and is very much dependent on each accession negotiation process and the individual needs of the acceding LDC. Generally, specific actions are geared towards the approval of legislation, establishment of MFN and national treatment in all areas covered by TRIPs, establishment of institutions and training of personnel.

However, as previously mentioned, this varies according to the individual accession process, with some substantive areas being subject to greater emphasis in the action plans. Additionally, the dates for the implementation of specific action are negotiated during the accession process. The TRIPs implementation action plans of six Article XII LDCs (excepting Cabo Verde) also state the date for the full implementation of the TRIPs Agreement by which date all the actions must be completed.[19]

The seven action plans reveal areas where particular emphasis was placed by members during the accession process. These are areas which the working party identified as key to ensuring the successful implementation of the TRIPs Agreement. For example, in Nepal's action plan, the establishment of IP offices (Copyright Registrar Office, Trademark Information Centre, etc.) was particularly singled out with the implementation date prior to the end of the transition period for full implementation of the TRIPs Agreement. On the other hand, Cabo Verde's action plan places emphasis on the implementation of industrial property and copyright laws and regulations with a detailed breakdown of the legislative process. Lao PDR's action plan is closely linked to technical assistance with the specific laws/actions referring to the provider of technical assistance.

Similarities within the action plans also exist where members have placed emphasis on the creation of public awareness for the protection of IP rights (Cabo Verde, Lao PDR, Nepal, Samoa and Yemen).

---

[19] The date for full implementation of the TRIPs Agreement for Cabo Verde (1 January 2013) is found in paragraph 246 of WTO document WT/ACC/CPV/30 and not in the action plan table.

Readiness to participate in regional and international IP administrative cooperation (the Pacific Islands Forum, Patent Cooperation Treaty (PCT), Madrid System for the International Registration of Marks) is found in Samoa's and Vanuatu's action plans. Other similarities include the emphasis on capacity building for key IP personnel and training of various enforcement authorities on the various substantive aspects of IP protection.

## Additional documentation

The importance of reforms in the area of IP during the accession process is also demonstrated through the additional documentation often produced during the accession process on national TRIPs Agreement implementation. Aside from an action plan table within the working party reports, Cabo Verde, Cambodia, Lao PDR, Nepal, Samoa and Yemen also had action plans as separate and more detailed documents.[20] These separate action plan documents detail the date of TRIPs-compliant legislation and also focus on other aspects of domestic reforms such as training, creation of departments, creation of manuals and computerisation of data (the implementation of these aspects is usually also linked to the provision of technical assistance). These documents are also complemented by legislative action plans which provide a timetable for enactment of legislation.[21]

Acceding LDCs have also submitted copies of their newly enacted IP legislation for assessment by the working parties. A number of accession question and reply documents reveal the emphasis placed on domestic reforms in this area, with members paying particular attention to the drafting of the IP legislation. For instance, in the case of Samoa, a document assessing the compatibility of Samoa's IP legislation with TRIPs Articles 1–61 was produced during the accession process.[22] Similarly, Cambodia's and Nepal's accession documents also included a checklist of TRIPs requirements and implementation which also assessed the compatibility of national IP legislation with the TRIPs Agreement.[23] Cambodia's and Lao PDR's working party reports also stated that they would make available all legislation in draft and promulgated form to

---

[20] See WTO documents: WT/ACC/KHM/16/Rev.1, WT/ACC/CPV/9/Rev. 3, WT/ACC/NPL/14,WT/ACC/LAO/15/Rev. 17, WT/ACC/SAM/13 and WT/ACC/YEM/8/Rev. 3.

[21] As in the case of Nepal (see WTO document WT/ACC/NPL/10/Rev. 1).

[22] See WTO document WT/ACC/SAM/11.

[23] See WTO documents WT/ACC/KHM/7/Rev. 2 and WT/ACC/NPL/7.

WTO members so that advice on TRIPs consistency could be obtained – which again highlights the emphasis on the legislative reform process for WTO accession, locked in by the end of the accession process. The submission of newly enacted legislation can be seen as a step not only in the accession process but also in achieving the long-term goal of inducing investor confidence and creating a national legal environment based on multilateral rules.

## Technical assistance and IP reform

The provision of technical assistance and capacity-building forms an integral part of the WTO accession process for LDCs. In many ways, linkages exist between the provision of technical assistance and appreciation of the differences in capacity of the acceding LDC and the domestic reforms undertaken in the area of IP during and after accession.[24]

The implementation of the TRIPs Agreement could require an overhaul of the acceding country's laws, regulations, administrative structure, infrastructure and human resources. This requires not only assistance in the form of human resource training and capacity building in order to implement and enforce IP laws, but also technical assistance for drafting laws, computerising data, formulating IP manuals and reorganising departments. In this context, the provision of technical assistance and capacity-building has been included in the working party reports of all seven acceding LDCs. In all of the seven working party reports there is a reference to the effect that the acceding LDC will seek out all available technical assistance in order to ensure that it has sufficient capacity to enforce a fully TRIPs-consistent regime upon expiry of the transition period.[25] This reference also reinforces the linkage of the transition period provided to LDCs with the provision of technical assistance and capacity-building. However, the obligation to seek out technical assistance rests with the acceding country.

---

[24] For example, as previously mentioned, the action plan for Lao PDR as found in Table 20B of the Lao PDR working party report closely links to the provision of technical assistance. It also includes details of the sources of the technical assistance provision. Similarly, Nepal's working party report states that the action plan is also a blueprint for technical assistance geared towards TRIPs implementation during the transition period.

[25] Cabo Verde (paragraph 245), Cambodia (paragraph 205), Lao PDR (paragraph 226), Nepal (paragraph 137), Samoa (paragraph 222), Vanuatu (paragraph 121) and Yemen (paragraph 262).

An overview of the technical assistance references in the working party reports and the action plans for IP shows that the greatest amount of technical assistance and capacity building will generally be needed in the areas of legislative reform and human resource training capacity building. Despite the general emphasis on these two areas, however, every action plan and the technical assistance activity attached to it is based on the individual and specific needs of the acceding country.

### Sense and nonsense debate: implications of IP protection accession commitments on multilateralism and domestic reforms

As the previous section has shown, Article XII LDC members have undertaken 'plus' commitments in the area of IP in some specific areas, both in the context of the TRIPs Agreement itself and in comparison with original LDC members. However, there is a need to assess these commitments in the context of their potential impact at both the multilateral and national levels.

It could be argued from the perspective of multilateralism that the IP commitments undertaken by the Article XII LDCs, although onerous, could contribute towards rule-making which inevitably strengthens both the multilateral trade and IP regimes. The terms of WTO Accession Protocols have been deemed to form integral parts of the WTO Agreement and as such contribute to the creation of new legal norms for the acceding country *vis-à-vis* other WTO members. Additionally, these IP commitments, which are tied to an action plan for implementation, also result in greater predictability and transparency of the multilateral rule-based system.

The 'plus' IP commitments also take into account developments in other IP fora, particularly those relating to regional and bilateral arrangements. For example, Lao PDR is also a member of the Association of South-East Asian Nations (ASEAN) and by already undertaking reforms in the area of IP is also simultaneously implementing the ASEAN Intellectual Property Rights Action Plan 2011–2015. Therefore, the commitments undertaken in the WTO accession context may also be deemed to be complementary to other processes.

On the domestic front, the WTO accession process is a vehicle of the domestic reform process in the area of IP. One of the main tools provided to acceding LDCs to implement these domestic reforms is the TRIPs action plan which attempts to ensure an effective and efficient, progressive evolution of the reform process with technical assistance and capacity building. In essence, the IP obligations, 'plus' or not, 'lock in' domestic reforms through a structured legislative and institutional reform process.

Although, with regard to transition periods and some areas of substantive IP law, it appears that Article XII LDCs have undertaken more expansive IP commitments, the provision of structured technical assistance during the transition period according to the individual needs of the Article XII LDC members remains one of the defining elements of WTO accession and remains part of the institutional arrangements of the entire process. Although original LDCs have also been requested to submit their individual priority needs for technical and financial cooperation under the 2005 TRIPs Council Decision, so far only nine LDCs have submitted their needs.[26] By integrating technical assistance into the IP implementation action plan, the accession process ensures that, by the end of the transition period, the Article XII LDC will be better placed to implement the commitments.

From an academic perspective and with respect to a potential area for further research, the assessment of the post-transition period for original LDCs (i.e. July 2021) will be critical in order to obtain a more accurate comparison between acceding and original LDC WTO members with regard to substantive provisions.

Therefore, it can be concluded that, substantively, the obligations for Article XII members in some specific subject matter might appear more stringent or 'plus' compared with the requirements of the TRIPs Agreement and the obligations on original LDC members. However, the implications of these commitments must be assessed in a broader context, bearing in mind implications at both the multilateral and domestic levels.

This chapter has attempted to show that the design of the WTO accession process, which may in some instances result in more 'plus', substantive IP obligations, nevertheless ensures that, with the provision of needs-based technical assistance and structured action plans, Article XII LDCs are able to integrate more smoothly into the multilateral

---

[26] 2013: Madagascar (see WTO document IP/C/W/584) and Togo (see WTO document IP/C/W/597); 2012: Mali (see WTO document IP/C/W/575); 2011: Senegal (see WTO document IP/C/W/555); 2010: Bangladesh (see WTO document IP/C/W/546), Rwanda (see WTO documents IP/C/W/548 and IP/C/W/548/Add. 1), Tanzania (see WTO document IP/C/W/552); 2007: Sierra Leone (see WTO documents IP/C/W/499 and IP/C/W/523), Uganda (see WTO documents IP/C/W/500 and IP/C/W/510).

trading system, which results in the strengthening of the system and the 'locking in' of their national domestic reforms in the area of IP.

In conclusion, although differences in substance with respect to IP obligations do exist between original and Article XII LDC members, it should be borne in mind that full compliance with the TRIPs Agreement at a future date, which will signify the end of the transition period, is the ultimate goal. Full implementation is therefore not an option but, rather, mandatory for both original and Article XII LDC members. Therefore, in the context of comparative analysis, the main difference between the 'two categories' of WTO LDC members with regard to the TRIPs Agreement lies in the process, mechanism and timeline for progressing towards full compliance with the Agreement.

# 38

# The future of multilateral investment rules in the WTO: contributions from WTO accession outcomes

CHIEDU OSAKWE AND JUNEYOUNG LEE

## ABSTRACT

*Foreign direct investment and trade are increasingly interlinked due to the deepening integration of trade and production networks. Today, there is an ever-increasing percentage of imports in a country's production. Responding to this increase, some countries have sought to limit the percentage of imports in their production by requiring that foreign investors use locally produced inputs, as an aspect of implementing priorities in development plans and/or strategic industrial policy. These policies and priorities have also been complicated and exacerbated by protectionism, whereby countries discriminate blatantly in order to promote local industries with policies that grant more favours to local producers and/or products and materials. All these practices impact negatively on international trade by distorting the conditions for fair competition. Although different rules have been developed at an international level to streamline these practices, currently there is no single comprehensive framework to govern them at the multilateral level. Despite this, WTO members, through accessions, have negotiated with acceding governments to refine and improve extant investment-related rules in the WTO. This chapter argues that WTO-specific outcomes, as in deposited Accession Protocols, have contributed to improving significantly the predictability of the investment regulatory laws and policies of Article XII members, reinforcing existing*

The authors acknowledge the technical contributions and comments from James Zhan, Anna Varyanik, Amara Okenwa and George Tebagana.

The analyses in the chapters in this book were finalised at the end of December 2014. Since then the Republic of Seychelles acceded to the World Trade Organization (WTO) on 26 April 2015. This expanded total WTO membership from 160 to 161. Please see the editors' note.

*investment-related rules on trade in goods and services, and enhancing the business-friendliness of WTO rules and the relationship with the private sector (including through expanded opportunities for investment), by binding, for example, their status quo policies and rules, and accession-specific obligations codified in domestic law and regulation.*

Across the global economy, in countries at all levels of development, there is strong acknowledgement of the vital importance and contribution of trade and investment to the creation of jobs and the promotion of 'strong, sustainable and balanced growth and development'.[1] Yet, there is no single comprehensive multilateral framework on investment rules at an international level, although there have been several efforts in the past to achieve such an objective. Where should efforts to develop a single multilateral set of rules start? Previous efforts to develop a single comprehensive multilateral framework have resulted in limited gains. Currently, the general rules on investment are based on and dispersed in different instruments: regional trade agreements, bilateral and multilateral investment treaties/agreements and investment disciplines from various international organisations, including the WTO, the World Bank and the Organisation for Economic Co-operation and Development (OECD).[2]

As logically argued by scholars, in the real economy, trade and investment are 'inextricably linked'.[3] As demonstrated consistently in all economies, policy-makers pursue trade and investment objectives in tandem and their relationship is virtually inseparable. The evidence is overwhelming regarding the priority attached to the trade and investment relations by governments in different settings. United Nations Conference on Trade and Development (UNCTAD) data indicate the

---

[1]  Joint Communiqué at the Fourth Meeting of the BRICS Trade Ministers, Fortaleza, 14 July 2014, paragraph 6. Retrieved from http://brics6.itamaraty.gov.br/media2/press-releases/211-the-4th-meeting-of-the-brics-trade-ministers-joint-communique-fortaleza-14-july-2014.

[2]  The Organisation for Economic Co-operation and Development (OECD) has developed a Policy Framework for Investment (PFI), which aims at mobilising private investment and maximising its development benefits. The PFI is a series of ten mutually reinforcing checklists in the ten policy domains determined by the OECD to have the strongest impact on the investment environment: investment policy, investment promotion and facilitation, trade policy, competition policy, tax policy, corporate governance, responsible business conduct, human resource development, infrastructure and financial sector development, and public governance. See OECD (2006). *Policy Framework for Investment.* Retrieved from www.oecd.org/daf/inv/36671400.pdf.

[3]  See Footer (2013).

quantum of international investment agreement regimes that point to the massive scale of such agreements globally. There are approximately three thousand in 2014.[4] These agreements exceed the coverage of WTO-specific-type investment obligations which are the focus of this chapter. However, the data underline the critical point about the policy and rule premium accorded by governments to the trade and investment relationship.

Yet, the obvious question that arises is why attempts to formulate multilaterally coherent rules in a common framework for trade and investment have foundered and achieved limited gains. In fact, some of the results have produced real world outcomes considered sub-optimal, that nobody wants. For instance, on the question of investor–state dispute settlement in the area of investment, without prejudice to different national sovereign objectives, the European Commission Trade Commissioner noted the existence of 1,400 bilateral investment treaties that currently bind the EU member states.[5] Obviously, this cannot be a desirable outcome, in a relationship where all policy-makers seek a unified objective and framework that links trade and investment in law and economics.

Despite the lack of a single comprehensive multilateral agreement on investment, progress is being made, although current data suggest it is a 'pilgrim's progress'. In this chapter, based on evidence from thirty-two Accession Protocols, we argue that acceding governments and WTO members are steadily advancing to create a raft of binding investment-related rules through negotiations in the context of WTO accessions. Acceding governments (hereafter Article XII members) have undertaken (and continue to undertake) investment-related commitments in their Accession Protocols. These accession investment-related commitments (which upon ratification of the Protocol of Accession, become an integral part of WTO rules) continue to shape the treatment of foreign investors in the territories of WTO members.

Yet, as some have argued, perhaps, the time is ripe to start discussions for a multilateral investment framework to introduce coherence to the governance of foreign direct investment (FDI), 'define clear and consistent rules, tackle barriers and distortions, and thus promote much needed, increased global investment and trade flows'.[6] The questions that arise are: should there be a starting point? What should that starting point be?

---

[4] These data disaggregate to about 2,902 bilateral investment treaties and 339 other international investment agreements.
[5] See De Gucht (2014).     [6] See Gonzalez (2013).

And at what level should ambition be pitched?[7] We do not aim to answer all these questions in this chapter. The subject is much too expansive and there is a wide range of views. Our focus is very limited. We argue in this chapter that when, and if, WTO members decide to re-engage and intensify multilateral dialogue on trade and international investments, with a view to defining multilateral rules for investment, WTO accession-specific commitments *à-propos* investments provide a coherent and substantive starting point.

In this context, we examine how investment-related commitments, when accepted by acceding governments in the context of their negotiations for their accession to the WTO, shape multilateral investment rules and principles. The rules on investment in the multilateral trading system are being strengthened via investment-related commitments in WTO accessions. These commitments have produced effects for greater predictability and a more conducive regulatory environment for attracting FDI. Evidence from FDI data[8] suggests a relationship between far-reaching WTO accession-related reforms by Article XII members that have provided concrete opportunities for investors through greater clarity, predictability and specific commitments, on the one hand, and positive investment flows, on the other. Yet the key question is whether and how such rules reinforce the existing body of investment rules and therefore contribute to efforts to develop a comprehensive framework on investment.

In the WTO, investment-related disciplines are mainly found in two instruments: the Agreement on Trade-Related Investment Measures (TRIMs) and the General Agreement on Trade in Services (GATS). The TRIMs Agreement disciplines those investment-related conditions or restrictions that are imposed on foreign investors and have the effect of distorting international trade[9] and applies to trade in goods only.[10] It relates to those conditions which violate the General Agreement on Tariffs and Trade (GATT) principles on national treatment (Article III)

---

[7]  The authors acknowledge the considered and exhaustive comments by James Zhan on a wide range of questions that have underpinned previous negotiating efforts encompassing, but not limited to, systemic questions and the management of factors related to sustainable development in the different negotiating settings: bilateral, regional and multilateral. Obviously, these are serious questions that have to be addressed by negotiators if and when they decide that the 'time is ripe'.

[8]  FDI data in this study are drawn exclusively from the UNCTAD Annual World Investment Reports, which remain the flagship reports on global FDI investment flows.

[9]  See the Preamble to the TRIMs Agreement: paragraph 4.

[10]  See Article 1, TRIMs Agreement.

and prohibition of quantitative restriction of imports and exports (Article XI).[11] The GATS provides a certain level of rules for investment in service sectors. These rules can be found in the sections for horizontal commitments, specific sectors and most-favoured-nation (MFN) exemptions. The investment-related disciplines under these two agreements are discussed further below.

## Investment-related commitments in the TRIMs

The TRIMs Agreement provides that no member shall apply a trade-related investment measure which is inconsistent with the GATT 1994.[12] The Agreement contains an illustrative list of what are considered to be inconsistent TRIMs, namely local content requirements, trade balancing requirements, foreign exchange balancing requirements and domestic sale requirements. These measures are considered to distort free trade if imposed on a foreign investor because they extinguish conditions for fair competition by giving an advantage to local producers/investors over their foreign counterparts.[13]

An examination of the protocols of accession of the thirty-three Article XII members reveals that investment-related issues have formed an integral part of WTO accession negotiations. All thirty-three Article XII members have made investment-related commitments. They have all confirmed that they will comply with the requirements of the TRIMs Agreement, albeit in different measures. In some instances, members have made commitments going beyond the TRIMs, some of which are subject to WTO litigation.[14] However, these commitments provide a broader level of legal certainty and reinforce existing members' efforts to strengthen investment rules in the context of the WTO.[15]

---

[11] See Article 2:1, TRIMs Agreement.    [12] Ibid.

[13] See the Panel Report, *Indonesia – Certain Measures Affecting the Automobile Industry* (see WTO documents WT/DS54/R, WT/DS55/R, WT/DS59/R and WT/DS64/R), adopted 23 July 1998.

[14] For example, see Panel Reports on *China – Measures Affecting Imports of Automobile Parts* (see WTO documents WT/DS339/R, WT/DS340/R and WT/DS342/R) adopted 12 January 2009, as modified by WTO Appellate Body Reports (see WTO documents WT/DS339/AB/R, WT/DS340/AB/R and WT/DS342/AB/R).

[15] For the existing members, the TRIMs Committee serves as a forum to discuss the range of members' concerns about other members' TRIMs. For example, in the June 2014 meeting, members discussed sector-specific measures (telecommunications, energy, automotive and agricultural equipment, water utilities, retail, buy national provisions, etc.) involving concerns about alleged local content requirements.

Of the thirty-three Article XII members, twenty-five did not have any WTO-inconsistent trade-related investment measures in their foreign investment regimes prior to their accession to the WTO.[16] In contrast, five Article XII members (China, Chinese Taipei, Ecuador, Russia and Yemen) had inconsistent trade-related investment measures in their foreign investment regimes prior to their WTO accession. For example, China maintained measures regarding foreign exchange balancing and trade balancing requirements, local content requirements and export performance requirements,[17] and restrictions on powers of provincial governors to grant permission to foreign investment in which categories of the automotive sector to invest. In the case of Chinese Taipei, it administered mixing requirements for coal and cement as well as local content and sourcing requirements.[18] Ecuador had TRIMs in the automotive industry. Russia maintained TRIMs in the form of preferential taxes and tax exemptions for parts used in motor vehicles.[19] Finally, Yemen had tax exemptions granted to investment projects with at least 25 per cent Yemeni equity.[20]

Five major issues emerge from a review of the investment-related commitments of the thirty-three Article XII members from the perspective of trade in goods. These are classified under the following headings: (i) application of transition periods by some Article XII members; (ii) commitments in specific sectors; (iii) deepening of the transparency principle; (iv) strengthening of the non-discrimination principle; and (v) reference to alternative dispute settlement.

### Application of transition periods by some Article XII members

On request, developing countries are allowed longer transition periods within which to implement their commitments under the TRIMs

---

[16] The members are: Albania, Armenia, Cabo Verde, Cambodia, Croatia, Estonia, Georgia, Jordan, Kyrgyz Republic, Lao PDR, Latvia, Lithuania, Moldova, Mongolia, Nepal, Oman, Panama, Samoa, Saudi Arabia, Tajikistan, the former Yugoslav Republic of Macedonia, Tonga, Ukraine, Vanuatu and Viet Nam.

[17] Paragraph 204, Report of the Working Party on the Accession of China, see WTO document WT/ACC/CHN/49.

[18] Paragraph 140, Report of the Working Party on the Accession of Chinese Taipei, see WTO document WT/ACC/TPKM/18.

[19] Paragraph 1063, Report of the Working Party on the Accession of the Russian Federation, see WTO documents WT/ACC/RUS/70 and WT/MIN(11)/2.

[20] Paragraph 26, Report of the Working Party on the Accession of Yemen, see WTO document WT/ACC/YEM/42.

Agreement.[21] The utilisation of transition periods, in respect of investment-related commitments, by Article XII members differed from country to country. These members can be classified into three groups:

- those twenty-seven Article XII members which did not apply any TRIMs prior to their accession to the WTO and therefore committed to promptly comply with the TRIMs Agreement;[22]
- those two Article XII members which applied the TRIMs in their investment regimes prior to accession to the WTO, but committed to promptly eliminate them upon accession to the WTO, without recourse to any transition periods;[23]
- those three Article XII members which applied the TRIMs prior to their accession to the WTO and asked for a transition period to eliminate them progressively after accession to the WTO.[24]

With respect to the third category, China, Ecuador and Russia requested the transition period regarding their motor vehicle production and automotive industry.

In the case of Russia, the transition period that was granted would extend up to July 2018. Russia committed to eliminate all WTO-inconsistent measures, including preferential tariff rates and tax exemptions, applied under its Auto Investment Programmes and agreements concluded under these programmes within this transition period.[25]

China committed to progressively phasing out restrictions on the powers of provincial governments to grant permits in the automotive sector within the six years following its accession. It confirmed that it agreed to raise the limit within which investments in motor vehicle manufacturing could be approved at provincial government level only: from the current level of US$30 million to US$60 million one year after accession; then to US$90 million two years after accession; and finally to

---

[21] See Article 5, TRIMs Agreement.

[22] The members are Albania, Armenia, Bulgaria, Cabo Verde, Cambodia, Croatia, Estonia, Georgia, Jordan, Kyrgyz Republic, Lao PDR, Latvia, Lithuania, Moldova, Mongolia, Montenegro, Nepal, Oman, Panama, Samoa, Saudi Arabia, Tajikistan, the former Yugoslav Republic of Macedonia, Tonga, Ukraine, Vanuatu and Viet Nam.

[23] Chinese Taipei (paragraph 140, Report of the Working Party on the Accession of Chinese Taipei, see WTO document WT/ACC/TPKM/18), and Yemen (paragraph 184, Report of the Working Party on the Accession of Yemen; see WTO document WT/ACC/YEM/42).

[24] China, Ecuador and Russia.

[25] Paragraph 1090, Report of the Working Party on the Accession of Russia (see WTO documents WT/ACC/RUS/70 and WT/MIN(11)/2).

US$150 million four years after accession.[26] Similarly, measures restricting investment in categories or models of vehicles would be removed two years after accession.[27]

Consequently, China eliminated its TRIMs within the agreed transition time-frame. For instance, in China's first Trade Policy Review, in 2006, it was observed that there had been progressive reduction and eventual elimination of China's performance requirements. Similarly, as a result of its accession to the WTO, China had carried out investment-related reforms. It had, among other things, ended preferences based on export performance and local content.[28] As a result of these reforms, there had been an improvement in competition and strong growth in private sector activities. Similarly, the Automotive Industry Development Policy of 2004, issued by the National Development and Reform Commission (NDRC), abolished requirements on foreign exchange balancing, local content and export performance.[29]

The benefits of the elimination of trade-distortive TRIMs by Article XII members can be clearly demonstrated by the resurgence of the Chinese economy following its accession to the WTO. China's immediate success in attracting FDI has been attributed in part to internal factors: the government's emphasis on opening up the economy and attracting foreign investment; and the improved legal framework and investment environment.[30] Through its WTO commitments, China reduced its trade and investment barriers. As a result of its WTO accession, China's FDI inflows significantly improved and it became the world's third largest FDI recipient after the United States and the United Kingdom. For instance, in 2004, inflows of FDI into China were US$60.6 billion; those into the United States and the United Kingdom were US$95.9 billion and US$78.4 billion, respectively.[31]

The increase in FDI inflow into China has further progressed through the years. The *2013 World Investment Report* revealed that FDI flows to China rose by nearly 8 per cent, reaching a record level of US$124 billion, enabling it to maintain its spot as top third in the globe.[32] Similarly, a

---

[26] Paragraphs 205 and 206, Report of the Working Party on the Accession of China (see WTO document WT/ACC/CHN/49).

[27] Ibid.

[28] Trade Policy Review Report of China (see WTO document WT/TPR/S/161, page 61).

[29] Transitional Review Mechanism pursuant to paragraph 18 of the Protocol of Accession of the People's Republic of China to the World Trade Organization, Report of the Chairman (see WTO document WT/G/L/708), 8 November 2004.

[30] See OECD (2006).     [31] See UNCTAD (2005).     [32] See UNCTAD (2013).

survey by UNCTAD revealed that China continued to be in the top spot as investors' preferred destination for FDI for the period 2012–2014.[33]

Article XII members are generally reported to have attracted more FDI upon their accession to the WTO. Chinese Taipei is another example. The first Trade Policy Review of Chinese Taipei in 2006 indicated that the improvement of its investment environment contributed to attracting in-bound direct investment and improving the efficiency of its economy.[34] Thus in 2012, Chinese Taipei was reported as the leading FDI receiver in Asia.[35]

It is important to note that the restructuring of the investment regimes of some of the Article XII members should have a positive trickle-down effect on their neighbouring trading partners by increasing more FDI into their territories. The *World Investment Report* has argued, for instance, that the restructuring of Russia's investment regime will have a positive effect on FDI flow on transition economies of South-eastern Europe. The report projected continued growth of FDI flows to these economies because of the WTO accession by Russia.[36] Russian accession to the WTO, it was argued, would increase investor confidence because it would guarantee transparency and predictability.[37] The report also noted that Russia's accession to the WTO has had an impact on investors' decision-making for certain projects.[38]

Russia undertook far-reaching legislation-based domestic reforms, pursuant to its WTO accession negotiations. It was estimated that, with full and effective implementation of its accession-specific obligations, there would be positive effects for the improvement of the business environment and attraction of FDI in dealing with systemically entrenched questions surrounding the rule of law, good governance and corruption. In 2014, however, in the third year of its WTO membership, the geopolitical consequences arising from the crisis in Ukraine and Crimea increased the risks for investment flow and growth. Application of sanctions against Russia and conflict in the region reduced trade and led to outflow of investments. The International Monetary Fund (IMF), in its June 2014 'health check' of the Russian economy, concluded that lingering geopolitical uncertainties were likely to affect investment and that Russia's slow pace of growth in 2013 reflected pre-existing structural problems and the fallout of geopolitical tensions with Ukraine.

---

[33] Ibid.
[34] WTO Trade Policy Review Report of Chinese Taipei (see WTO document WT/TPR/S/165).
[35] See UNCTAD (2012).    [36] See UNCTAD (2013).    [37] Ibid.    [38] Ibid.

Specifically, it was noted that, 'geopolitical uncertainties following Russia's action in Crimea have recently depressed the economy further, with a particularly negative effect on investment'.[39] These effects may linger for an indeterminate period until the geopolitical risks subside and the effective implementation of WTO accession-specific obligations is pursued to address the pre-existing structural challenges in the domestic economy.

## Commitments in specific sectors

Making investment-related commitments in certain specific sectors of their economies was identified as one of the characteristics of these commitments. Of the thirty-three Article XII members, twenty-eight[40] made investment-related commitments for all sectors of their economies

---

[39]  See IMF (2014).

[40]  These twenty-eight Article XII members include: Albania (paragraph 110 of Working Party Report, WTO document WT/ACC/ALB/51), Armenia (paragraph 144 of Working Party Report, WTO document WT/ACC/ARM/23), Bulgaria (paragraph 83, WTO document WT/ACC/BGR/5), Cabo Verde (paragraph 180 of Working Party Report, WTO document WT/ACC/CPV/30), Cambodia (paragraph 144 of Working Party Report, WTO document WT/ACC/KHM/21), Croatia (paragraph 137 of Working Party Report, WTO document WT/ACC/HRV/59), Estonia (paragraph 99 of Working Party Report, WTO document WT/ACC/EST/28), Georgia (paragraph 109 of Working Party Report, WTO document WT/ACC/GEO/31), Jordan (paragraph 153 of Working Party Report, WTO document WT/ACC/JOR/33), Kyrgyz Republic (paragraph 106 of Working Party Report, WTO document WT/ACC/KGZ/26), Lao PDR (paragraph 152 of Working Party Report, WTO document WT/ACC/LAO/45), Latvia (paragraph 90 of Working Party Report, WTO document WT/ACC/LVA/32), Lithuania (paragraph 124 of Working Party Report, WTO document WT/ACC/LTU/52), Moldova (paragraph 136 of Working Party Report, WTO document WT/ACC/MOL/37), Mongolia (paragraph 42 of Working Party Report, WTO document WT/ACC/MNG/9), Montenegro (paragraph 169, WTO documents WT/ACC/CGR/38 and WT/MIN(11)/7), Nepal (paragraph 109 of Working Party Report, WTO document WT/ACC/NPL/16), Oman (paragraph 107 of Working Party Report, WTO document WT/ACC/OMN/26), Panama (paragraph 112 of Working Party Report, WTO document WT/ACC/PAN/19), Samoa (paragraph 164 of Working Party Report, WTO document WT/ACC/SAM/30), Saudi Arabia (paragraph 226 of Working Party Report, WTO document WT/ACC/SAU/61), Tajikistan (paragraph 233 of Working Party Report, WTO document WT/ACC/TJK/30), the former Yugoslav Republic of Macedonia (paragraph 155 of Working Party Report, WTO document WT/ACC/807/27), Tonga (paragraph 130 of Working Party Report, WTO document WT/ACC/TON/17), Ukraine (paragraph 331 of Working Party Report, WTO document WT/ACC/UKR/152), Vanuatu (paragraph 102 of Working Party Report, WTO document WT/ACC/VUT/17), Viet Nam (paragraph 332 of Working Party Report, WTO document WT/ACC/VNM/48) and Yemen (paragraph 184, WTO document WT/ACC/YEM/42).

regarding compliance with the TRIMs. These members had standard commitment paragraphs in their respective protocols of accession, as in the following terms:

> The representative(s) of...[41] confirmed that they would not maintain nor introduce any measures inconsistent with the Agreement on TRIMs and they would promptly comply with the Agreement from the date of accession without recourse to any transition periods.

Their investment-related commitments were not made in respect of any particular identified type of TRIMs nor explicitly tagged on a specific sector of their economies.

However, four Article XII members, namely China,[42] Chinese Taipei,[43] Ecuador[44] and Russia[45] undertook investment-related commitments in specific sectors. The automotive industry was the most frequent sector in all these members. In addition, countries made investment-related commitments in separate sectors. For example, Chinese Taipei undertook to eliminate mixing requirements for locally produced coal and cement, while Russia accepted the elimination of preferential taxes and tax exemptions in its automotive industry.

## Deepening of the transparency principle

The transparency principle is one of the cardinal principles of the multilateral trading system. The TRIMs Agreement requires all WTO members to notify the WTO of their TRIMs if they are inconsistent with the provisions of the WTO Agreement.[46] The requirement to notify

---

[41] Ibid.

[42] See paragraph 203, Report of the Working Party on the Accession of China (see WTO document WT/ACC/CHN/49).

[43] See paragraph 140, Report of the Working Party on the Accession of Chinese Taipei (see WTO document WT/ACC/TPKM/18).

[44] See paragraph 76, Report of the Working Party on the Accession of Ecuador (see WTO document WT/L/77).

[45] Russia confirmed that the amount of any requirement to purchase or use domestically produced parts and components would not exceed 25 per cent of the ex-factory price of the automobiles annually. With regard to the manufacture of components under Auto Investment Program No. 2, the amount of any requirement to purchase or use domestically produced parts and components would not exceed 25 per cent of the total aggregate value of inputs of the manufacturer of car components annually (see paragraph 1090, Report of the Working Party on the Accession of the Russian Federation, WTO documents WT/ACC/RUS/70 and WT/MIN(11)/2).

[46] Article 5, TRIMs Agreement.

TRIMs enables the WTO to monitor and review a member's investment policies to ensure that they are in compliance with the WTO provisions. This reinforces the transparency principle of the WTO. Transparency is a requirement that contributes to rules that are stable and consistent with WTO principles, disciplines and provisions.

By committing to comply with the notification requirement in the TRIMs Agreement, acceding governments effectively safeguard the transparency principle. For instance, Russia committed to engage in consultations with interested WTO members no later than 1 July 2016 regarding its WTO-consistent measures applied in connection with its Auto Investment Programmes. It would therefore notify WTO members of any measures planned to replace the WTO-inconsistent measures applied under the Auto Investment Programmes at least six months prior to the adoption of such new measures.[47]

Similarly, Ecuador committed to comply with the transparency and notification requirements as provided, for example, in Article 6 (transparency) of the TRIMs Agreement.[48] Ecuador executed its commitment when in 1996 it informed the WTO of its TRIMs that were published in its official journal.[49] In April 1999, Ecuador notified the Complementarity Agreement for the Automotive Sector as a TRIM inconsistent with the provisions of the TRIMs Agreement.[50]

All of these transparency commitments contribute to improvements in predictability in the investment climate, promoting and encouraging FDI inflows to the host countries.

### Strengthening the non-discrimination principle

All Article XII members confirmed that they would apply their respective investment measures on a non-discriminatory basis between municipal and foreign investors. Thus, even if a restrictive measure was allowed, it would be applied on an MFN basis. Yemen, for example, was allowed to ban investments in products prohibited on religious grounds by

---

[47] Paragraph 1090, Report of the Working Party on the Accession of the Russian Federation, see WTO documents WT/ACC/RUS/70 and WT/MIN(11)/2.

[48] Paragraph 75, Report of the Working Party on the Accession of Ecuador (see WTO document WT/L/77).

[49] See WTO document G/TRIMS/N/2/Rev. 6, 16 July 1999.

[50] See WTO document G/TRIMS/N/1/ECU/1, 2 April 1996.

Shari'a law. But the ban would be applied on an MFN basis, in other words to investors of both domestic and foreign origin.[51]

China confirmed that it would provide the same treatment to Chinese enterprises, including foreign-funded enterprises, and foreign enterprises and individuals in China.[52] Similarly, Yemen guaranteed that foreign and domestic investment would receive equal treatment with no discrimination in respect of rights, obligations, rules and procedures.[53]

### Reference to alternative dispute settlement

The WTO Dispute Settlement Understanding only applies to state-to-state disputes. However, through WTO accessions, there have been references to the right of private investors' access to impartial procedures to settle investment-related disputes with host governments.

Three Article XII members (Georgia, Kyrgyz Republic and Yemen), in their working party reports, referred to an alternative dispute settlement forum, such as the International Centre for Settlement of Investment Disputes (ICSID). Georgia noted that disputes between the state and a foreign investor could be settled in the courts of Georgia or other fora, including arbitration fora, such as the ICSID, established in accordance with the International Convention for the Settlement of Investment Disputes between the state and the nationals of another state (the ICSID Convention, signed in Washington DC on 19 March 1965).[54]

Similarly, Kyrgyz Republic laid out the possibility for an investor resorting to settlement of disputes by arbitration in accordance with Regulations of the Arbitration Court under the Chamber of Industry and Commerce of Kyrgyz Republic; the ICSID Convention, if applicable; Arbitration (Auxiliary) Regulations of the ICSID, if applicable; and Arbitration Regulations of the United Nations Commission on International Trade Law (UNCITRAL).[55]

---

[51] Paragraph 18, Report of the Working Party on the Accession of Yemen (see WTO document WT/ACC/YEM/42).

[52] Paragraph 18, Report of the Working Party on the Accession of China (see WTO document WT/ACC/CHN/49).

[53] Paragraphs 26 and 181, Report of the Working Party on the Accession of Yemen (see WTO document WT/ACC/YEM/42).

[54] Paragraph 12, Report of the Working Party on the Accession of Georgia (see WTO document WT/ACC/GEO/31).

[55] Paragraph 7, Report of the Working Party on the Accession of Kyrgyz Republic (see WTO document WT/ACC/KGZ/26).

Yemen also granted the choice of forum where disputes would be settled to investors. To settle a dispute with the Yemeni government or state, an investor could opt for arbitration under Yemeni rules and procedures or invoke the procedures of the Unified Investment Agreement for Arab Capital Investment in Arab countries, the ICSID Convention, the commercial arbitration rules and procedures of UNCITRAL or any international or bilateral agreement to which Yemen was a signatory.[56]

Concerning the cases of investor states, the references of these three Article XII members do not reach the level of 'commitment' language. However, their deliberate consideration of investor-state dispute settlement, citing their domestic laws, is noticeable and could be included in the debate in this area.

## Investment-related commitments in the GATS

In the context of the GATS, there are no specific provisions or disciplines dedicated to investments. However, investment-related rules and disciplines for investment in services can be derived from the substance of the entries in the GATS schedules. Commitments in the GATS schedules are valid as rules because the schedules are an integral part of the WTO Agreement.[57]

Investment-related rules are embedded in dispersed forms in various sections of the GATS schedules of WTO members. These rules are services commitments that may have the effect of either restricting or encouraging and streamlining FDI inflows in services. Specifically, they can be found in the following sections of the GATS schedules: (i) the horizontal commitments section; (ii) mode 3 (commercial presence) of the members' services schedules of specific commitments; and (iii) the MFN exemptions section.

The horizontal commitments section contains overarching entries that cover the entire scope of the services schedules, while the MFN exemptions section describes measures *exempted* by: (i) indicating its inconsistency with Article II of the GATS; (ii) enumerating the countries to which the measure applies, indicating the intended duration of the exemption; and (iii) stating the conditions creating the need for the

---

[56] Paragraph 22, Report of the Working Party on the Accession of Yemen (see WTO document WT/ACC/YEM/42).

[57] Article XX (3), GATS.

exemption. Finally, mode 3 is one of the four modes of services supply that is reflected in the sectoral section of the GATS schedules. Mode 3 applies to the services 'by the services supplier of one member, through commercial presence in the territory of any other member'. The underlining feature of this mode of supply is the phrase 'commercial presence'.

The connection between investment and mode 3 under the GATS is underlined in the definition of FDI. The IMF defined FDI as 'direct investment that is made to acquire a lasting interest in an enterprise operating in an economy other than that of the investor, the investor's purpose being to have an effective voice in the management of the enterprise'.[58] The phrase 'through commercial presence in the territory of any other member', which defines GATS mode 3 commitments, fits the above description of a foreign investment. This is the working premise by the authors, used in the analysis of the services schedules, of thirty-three Article XII members with a view to identifying embedded investment rules and associated commitments and hence showing how these investment-related rules have emerged in the WTO through the accession process. The analysis focuses on the 'horizontal'[59] commitments and the MFN exemptions.

A general overview of the various aspects of the investment-related services commitments shows that Article XII members have used their GATS schedules as a signalling device to investors to demonstrate economic opportunities. This is because the schedules can be designed to restrict or attract and streamline FDI inflows in specific services sectors. Also, the schedules have been used to reflect and lock in domestic reforms in specific investment-related services sectors. Finally, the services schedules of Article XII members are transparent international trade policy instruments. The commitments in the schedules are legally enforceable undertakings and can be subject to WTO dispute settlement. Therefore, they are an important and credible tool for offering guarantees to foreign investors. A detailed assessment of the investment-related entries is identified below from the selected sections in specific GATS schedules of Article XII Accession Protocols.

[58]  See IMF (1993).

[59]  A more detailed study with regard to the depth of investment rules can be derived from a further look at the mode 3 services commitments. This chapter focuses on the 'horizontal' aspect of investment-related commitments in the thirty-three Article XII members.

When focusing on the services schedules of Article XII members, save for Ecuador, Mongolia and Kyrgyz Republic, twenty-nine[60] Article XII members have made investment-related entries in their horizontal commitments and MFN exemptions sections. From an assessment of the services schedules of these twenty-nine Article XII members, six investment-related themes have emerged. These six themes, which are discussed in detail below, include: (i) juridical form relating to conditions for ownership, management, operation and scope of activities of investment; (ii) land; (iii) transition periods; (iv) subsidies, investment incentives and other state support measures; (v) additional commitments; and (vi) MFN exemptions.

### Juridical form

Out of the thirty-three Article XII members, twenty[61] have inscribed commitments setting out the parameters within which foreign service suppliers may operate in their territories. There were no major trends

---

[60] The document references for the GATS schedules of these Article XII members are as follows: Albania (see WTO document WT/ACC/ALB/51 + Corr. 1), Armenia (see WTO document WT/ACC/ARM/23), Bulgaria (see WTO document WT/ACC/BGR/5 + Corr. 1), Cabo Verde (see WTO document WT/ACC/CPV/30), Cambodia (see WTO document WT/ACC/KHM/21), China (see WTO documents WT/ACC/CHN/49 and Corr. 1 and WT/MIN(01)/3), Chinese Taipei (see WTO documents WT/ACC/TPKM/ 18 and WT/MIN(01)/4), Croatia (see WTO document WT/ACC/HRV/59), Estonia (see WTO document WT/ACC/EST/28), the former Yugoslav Republic of Macedonia (see WTO document WT/ACC/807/27), Georgia (see WTO document WT/ACC/GEO/31), Jordan (see WTO documents WT/ACC/JOR/33 and Corr. 1), Lao PDR (see WTO document WT/ACC/LAO/45), Latvia (see WT/ACC/LVA/32), Lithuania (see WTO document WT/ACC/LTU/52), Moldova (see WTO documents WT/ACC/MOL/37 and Corr. 1 and Corr. 2 and Corr. 3 and Corr. 4), Montenegro (see WTO documents WT/ ACC/CGR/38 and WT/MIN(11)/7), Nepal (see WTO document WT/ACC/NPL/16), Oman (see WTO document WT/ACC/OMN/26), Panama (see WTO documents WT/ ACC/PAN/19 and Corr. 1), Russia (see WTO documents WT/ACC/RUS/70 and WT/ MIN(11)/2), Samoa (see WTO documents WT/ACC/SAM/30 and WT/MIN(11)/1), Saudi Arabia (see WTO document WT/ACC/SAU/61), Tajikistan (see WTO document WT/ACC/TJK/30), Tonga (see WTO documents WT/ACC/TON/17 and WT/MIN(05)/ 4), Ukraine (see WTO document WT/ACC/UKR/152), Vanuatu (see WTO document WT/ACC/VUT/17), Viet Nam (see WTO document WT/ACC/VNM/48), Yemen (see WTO document WT/ACC/YEM/42/Add. 2).

[61] Albania, Bulgaria, Cambodia, China, Chinese Taipei, Croatia, the former Yugoslav Republic of Macedonia, Georgia, Jordan, Lao PDR, Montenegro, Nepal, Oman, Panama, Russia, Saudi Arabia, Tajikistan, Vanuatu, Viet Nam and Yemen.

with regard to the various parameters set by these twenty Article XII members. However, the parameters form the bulk of investment-related rules in the horizontal section of the schedules. These parameters establish conditions for the ownership, management and operation, as well as the scope of activities for investment in services. They operate as lock-in mechanisms for domestic reforms. They offer a transparent framework of investment-related rules for trade in services and overall predictability for the services investment regime which is embedded in the multilateral trading system. Specifics are discussed below.

## Form of commercial presence

Eight Article XII members[62] stipulated (in the horizontal section of their commitments schedules), the form required for a foreign service provider to establish a commercial presence within their territories. The various forms required in Article XII members varied from country to country. These are summarised in Table 38.1.

In addition to indicating the form of commercial presence required, some Article XII members have also elaborated the requirement of approvals and registration by/with the government authorities. In Bulgaria, the former Yugoslav Republic of Macedonia, Nepal, Saudi Arabia and Vanuatu, as a pre-condition for establishing commercial presence, foreign service providers are required to seek approvals from the government authorities or be registered with government offices or departments. Bulgaria,[63] Nepal[64] and Saudi Arabia[65] went further to stipulate the specific government office. Bulgaria went even further still to indicate that the purpose of the registration was for statistical and tax purposes only.

---

[62] Bulgaria, China, the former Yugoslav Republic of Macedonia, Jordan, Lao PDR, Oman, Saudi Arabia and Viet Nam.

[63] Foreign investments are registered with the Ministry of Finance for statistical and taxation purposes only.

[64] All foreign investments except for financial services require approval by the Department of Industry.

[65] Foreign service suppliers require approval from the Saudi Arabian General Investment Authority for establishing a commercial presence in Saudi Arabia according to the Foreign Investment Law of April 2000 and Article 5:3 of the Regulation of the Foreign Investment Act.

Table 38.1 *List of Article XII members with their indication of the form of commercial presence required*

| Article XII member | Required form of commercial presence |
| --- | --- |
| Bulgaria | Limited liability company or joint-stock company with at least two shareholders |
| China | Wholly foreign-owned enterprise[a] or joint-venture enterprise (the joint-venture enterprises in China are further divided into two; the equity joint ventures and the contractual joint ventures) |
| Former Yugoslav Republic of Macedonia | Registered as a sole proprietor, a trading company or a branch |
| Jordan | Investment in public utilities 'must be in the form of Public Shareholding Companies' |
| Lao People's Democratic Republic | Company incorporated in the specific legal form in accordance with laws and regulations of Lao PDR |
| Oman | Company incorporated in Oman |
| Saudi Arabia, Kingdom of | Subject to incorporation under the Companies Act either as joint-stock companies or as limited liability companies |
| Viet Nam | Business cooperation contract, joint-venture enterprise or 100 per cent foreign-invested enterprise |

Note: [a] Also referred to as foreign capital enterprises.

## Operation and management

Georgia and Panama are the only Article XII members which set out, in their commitment schedules, requirements for the operation and management for a foreign service entity within their territories. In this regard, there was no common trend. In its horizontal commitments section, Georgia set out conditions for managing a limited liability corporation and a representative office. In Georgia, at least one manager must be domiciled in Georgia. Also branch offices require a representative in the form of a natural person domiciled in Georgia and duly authorised to fully represent the company. Panama set out a minimum percentage of not less than 90 per cent for the domestic workforce and a maximum percentage of not more than 15 per cent for foreign specialised or technical personnel required for the operation of a foreign service provider within Panama.

## Limitation on foreign equity participation

Four[66] out of the thirty-three Article XII members indicated the proportion of foreign equity participation.[67] Bulgaria inscribed a mechanism for monitoring the co-ownership of its state-owned enterprises (SOEs) by indicating that where the public share in a company exceeds 30 per cent, transfer of shares in that company to a third party requires authorisation. For its part, Viet Nam put a cap on its foreign equity participation for its enterprises. It indicated that the total foreign equity capital contribution for the purchase of shares in each of its enterprises 'may not exceed 30 per cent of the enterprise's chartered capital unless otherwise provided by Viet Nam's laws or authorised by Viet Nam's competent authority'. Viet Nam further indicated that this limitation will be phased out one year after its accession except for 'capital contribution in the form of buying shares of joint-stock commercial banks, and sectors not committed in Viet Nam's schedules'.

With regard to entries capping the proportion of foreign equity participation generally, Oman limited foreign equity participation to 49 per cent.[68] It further inscribed its commitment to increase the allowable proportion of foreign equity participation to 70 per cent by 1 January 2001. In the case of China, it indicated a minimum cap of no less than 25 per cent of the registered capital of the joint venture for equity joint ventures. Bulgaria's entry is a monitoring mechanism only, while China, Oman and Viet Nam have set out specific proportions for minimum capital participation. Out of these three Article XII members that have entries setting out specific proportions for minimum capital participation, only China did not employ transition periods as a tool to decrease the proportion of its limitations at a later date.

## Minimum foreign capital participation

Four out of the thirty-three Article XII members indicated figures for minimum foreign capital participation[69] within their territories. These members are Jordan, Oman, Vanuatu and Yemen. To establish a commercial presence in these countries, a foreign service provider is required to invest a minimum capital of JD50,000 for Jordan, RO150,000 for

---

[66] Bulgaria, China, Oman and Viet Nam.    [67] GATS Article XVI, 2(f).
[68] Starting from the effective date of the relevant legislation.    [69] GATS Article XVI, 2(f).

Oman,[70] US$40,000 (VT5 million) for Vanuatu and YR50 million for Yemen. Again, there is no specific trend on how these minimum capital requirements are phrased. Oman indicated its commitment to phase out the use of the minimum capital requirement within a month from its accession. Vanuatu indicated that the sum indicated was adjustable to reflect inflation, while Yemen listed sectors not subject to its minimum capital requirements.[71]

## Good governance commitment

Four[72] out of the thirty-three Article XII members inscribed an undertaking not to make the terms of establishment and operation for foreign service suppliers in their territories more onerous than the conditions existing at the time of their accession. The identical commitments for the four members read:

> The conditions of ownership, operation and scope of activities, as set out in the respective contractual or shareholder agreement or in a license establishing or authorizing the operation or supply of services by an existing foreign service supplier, will not be made more restrictive than they exist as of the date of [. . .'s] accession to the WTO.

This specific obligation was first reflected in the services schedule of China in 2002. Thereafter, it has also been reflected in the schedules of Cambodia, Nepal and Viet Nam. This specific commitment provides predictability for intending investors. Investors can rely on the undertaking that the investment-related rules in the services schedules act as a lock-in policy tool.

## Representative offices

China, the former Yugoslav Republic of Macedonia, Oman, Russia, Tajikistan and Viet Nam made entries in relation to the establishment

---

[70] This requirement was to be in place until 31 December 2000. No such requirement will apply as from 1 January 2001.

[71] Business services; 7.B(xv) provision and transfer of financial information, and financial data processing and related software by providers of other financial services; 7.B(xvi) advisory, intermediation and other auxiliary financial services on all the activities listed in sub-paragraphs (v) to (xv), including credit reference and analysis, investment and portfolio research and advice, advice on acquisitions and on corporate restructuring strategy; 9.B travel agency and tour operator services (CPC 74710); 10.B news agency services (CPC962); and 11.H(c) maritime freight transport agency services.

[72] Cambodia, China, Nepal and Viet Nam.

of representative offices. Representative offices could be established within their territories provided that they were not for profit. In addition, Oman indicated that a commercial presence would be allowed for representative offices in Oman within one month of its WTO accession.

## Branches

Croatia, China, the former Yugoslav Republic of Macedonia and Viet Nam made entries in relation to the establishment of branches. China and Viet Nam indicated that, unless provided for in the sectoral commitments section, the limitation on establishment of branches was unbound in their territories. The former Yugoslav Republic of Macedonia indicated that branches could be registered in its territory. Croatia indicated that, while branches could operate all kinds of businesses within Croatia, they were not considered to be independent. Their rights and obligations were vested in the parent company. This provision might be valuable for the purpose of taxation or in relation to disputes before domestic courts and attaching assets.

## Other investment-related entries

Other noteworthy investment-related entries made by Article XII members in the horizontal commitments section of their services schedules include the following:

- Public utilities: Jordan, Montenegro and Russia made entries relating to investment in public utilities. Jordan indicated that investments in its public utilities were by way of concessions. Montenegro and Russia indicated that services considered to be public utilities might be subject to public monopolies or to exclusive rights granted to private operators to carry out such services.
- Repatriation of capital: Albania, Bulgaria and Nepal made entries setting out conditions for repatriation of capital and classes of capital to be repatriated.
- Privatisation: Bulgaria, Georgia, Russia and Tajikistan made entries indicating limitations for participation in privatisation for foreign service providers.
- Training requirements: Cabo Verde, Cambodia, Lao PDR and Samoa inscribed training requirements in their horizontal commitments section. These four Article XII members are/were least-developed

countries (LDCs). In their entries, Cambodia went further to indicate that in order to take advantage of its investment incentives, a foreign service provider was required to provide training opportunities for Cambodian nationals.

- Taxes: Oman and Saudi Arabia made entries in relation to taxes. Saudi Arabia indicated that apart from the Islamic practice of *Zakat* its tax measures would comply with its MFN and national treatment obligations under the GATS. Oman indicated that domestic tax rates applied for companies with foreign equity of up to 70 per cent, while higher rates applied to companies with higher foreign equity participation.

## Land

FDI in land can be a controversial issue. On the one hand, FDI in land can be perceived domestically as a 'land grab' question, which has tended to be sensitive and sometimes controversial in WTO accession negotiations. Yet it has also been perceived by several as an opportunity for development and expansion of commerce. The controversy requires striking a balance between the polarising perceptions of FDI in land. The GATS entries on land are closely linked to facilitating commerce, specifically investments under mode 3 of the GATS. For example, Bulgaria offered investment-related waivers for approval requirements related to the ownership of building and other property rights of real estate in Bulgaria by non-residents. Armenia made a distinction between foreign nationals and foreign juridical persons in relation to the ownership of land. Juridical persons by their nature would be expected to establish a commercial presence in the host country. Therefore, by indicating in its GATS schedules that foreign nationals may not own land but that foreign juridical persons may do so, one possible policy intention could be that Armenia has 'signalled' that land acquisition by 'foreign persons' in its territory would be for the purpose of attracting investments.

The investment-related entries on land in the GATS schedules of Article XII members offer transparency and predictability for services-related FDI in land. Typically, FDI in land is marked by a lack of information, uncertainty and a lack of transparency. These uncertainties may adversely affect the domestic population[73] and/or the commercial

---

[73] For example, employees.

interests of the investor(s). Therefore, the GATS entries which clarify conditions and time-frames under which land may be acquired or leased by the foreign service provider(s) are valuable transparency tools. Finally, these investment-related entries on land also contribute to the overall body of investment-related rules in the multilateral trading system.

In the horizontal commitments section, twenty-six[74] out of the thirty-two Article XII members made clear and precise entries streamlining services—related FDI in land. The entries include rules on ownership, leasing, duration and usage of the land for FDI by foreign services providers. The foreign service provider needs to comply with the rules and conditions set out in the GATS schedules of these twenty-six Article XII members in order to establish a 'physical' commercial presence. Only six Article XII members, namely Ecuador, Estonia, Kyrgyz Republic, Lithuania, Mongolia and Nepal,[75] were silent on land. The twenty-six Article XII members with land-related entries discussed either the ownership of the land, leases or a combination of both acquisition and leases.

In relation to the acquisition of land, eleven[76] out of the twenty-six Article XII members made entries indicating that foreign service providers cannot own land within their territories, whereas five Article XII members[77] set conditions under which foreign service providers can acquire land. The entries relating to the purchase of land can be grouped under two major categories. The first is agricultural land and the second

---

[74] Albania, Armenia, Bulgaria, Cabo Verde, Cambodia, China, Chinese Taipei, Croatia, the former Yugoslav Republic of Macedonia, Georgia, Jordan, Lao PDR, Latvia, Montenegro, Moldova, Oman, Panama, Russia, Samoa, Saudi Arabia, Tajikistan, Tonga, Ukraine, Vanuatu, Viet Nam and Yemen.

[75] Nepal, however, included an entry with regard to real estate, which stated that the Nepalese Civil Code prohibits citizens from selling, mortgaging, gifting or endowing or disposing of any real property to a foreign individual.

[76] Bulgaria, Cambodia, Jordan, Lao PDR, Latvia, Oman, Samoa, Tajikistan, Tonga, Vanuatu and Yemen.

[77] Croatia requires residents established and incorporated to obtain approval of the Ministry of Foreign Affairs to acquire land for the supply of services by branches. Jordan indicated that purchase by non-Jordanian firms must be related to the business and is subject to approval by the Cabinet. Montenegro indicated that apart from arable and restricted areas, foreign persons may own land subject to reciprocity. Saudi Arabia indicated that foreign establishments with the authority to carry out business in Saudi Arabia may acquire land subject to the laws and regulations governing foreign ownership of real estate. Tajikistan indicated that foreign persons (natural and juridical) may only obtain land for perpetual use of land on the condition that they establish joint venture(s) with a Tajik person.

is non-agricultural land. Six[78] Article XII members indicated that the foreign service providers cannot acquire agricultural land within their territories, while two[79] clearly indicated conditions for the acquisition of either non-agricultural land or agricultural land. Albania specified that a foreign service provider could acquire state-owned non-agricultural land to carry out its business, on the condition that the value of investment was three times higher than the value of the land.[80] Georgia noted that a foreign service provider could acquire agricultural land by joint venture.

Regarding leases, eighteen[81] out of the thirty-three Article XII members made entries relating to leases. Only Chinese Taipei indicated that agricultural lands, forests and mines in its territory could not be leased. The remaining seventeen[82] of the eighteen Article XII members indicated that foreign service providers could lease their land. Regarding the time-frame for leases, five Article XII members[83] were silent on the issue, whereas twelve[84] indicated various periods (the longest is ninety-nine years, while the shortest is twenty years).[85]

---

[78] Bulgaria, Chinese Taipei, Montenegro, Moldova, Russia and Ukraine.

[79] Albania and Georgia.

[80] Albania further indicated that the value of the non-agricultural land would be defined by the Council of Ministers.

[81] Albania, Cabo Verde, Cambodia, China, Chinese Taipei, Georgia, Jordan, Lao PDR, Latvia, Moldova, Oman, Russia, Samoa, Tajikistan, Tonga, Vanuatu, Viet Nam and Yemen.

[82] Albania, Cabo Verde, Cambodia, China, Georgia, Jordan, Lao PDR, Latvia, Moldova, Oman, Russia, Samoa, Tajikistan, Tonga, Vanuatu, Viet Nam and Yemen.

[83] Albania (non-agricultural land only), Cabo Verde, Cambodia, Vanuatu and Yemen.

[84] China, Georgia, Jordan, Lao PDR, Latvia, Moldova, Oman, Russia, Samoa, Tajikistan, Tonga and Viet Nam.

[85] The following entries were made with respect to time-frames:

- Latvia, Moldova and Tonga indicated a period of ninety-nine years.
- China indicated the following periods for different categories of leases: (i) seventy years for residential purposes; (ii) fifty years for industrial purposes; (iii) fifty years for the purpose of education, science, culture, public health and physical education; (iv) forty years for commercial, tourist and recreational purposes; and (v) fifty years for comprehensive utilisation or other purposes set out specific time-frames for different categories of leases.
- Jordan indicated that a lease of more than three years required approval.
- Georgia indicated a period of forty-nine years for agricultural land and ninety-nine years for non-agricultural land.
- Oman and Tajikistan indicated a period of fifty years. Oman went further to state that the lease was subject to renewal for land and business.
- Lao PDR indicated a period up to seventy-five years.

## Transition periods

Three Article XII members (Albania, Oman and Viet Nam) used transition periods in their horizontal commitments section. In this regard, there were no commonalities concerning the usage of the transition periods. Albania committed to eliminate its reserved right to maintain capital controls applied on a national treatment basis ten years after its accession, while Viet Nam committed to eliminating the 30 per cent foreign equity limitation for acquisition of Vietnamese enterprises[86] one year after its accession.

Oman used transition periods three times in its horizontal commitments section. However, the transition periods were relatively short, and would expire within months of its accession. These transition periods were used first, to increase the minimum cap on the proportion of foreign equity participation. Second, they were used to allow for the establishment of a commercial presence for representative offices. Finally, they were also used to phase out the minimum capital requirement for foreign service providers.

No LDC Article XII members used transition periods in their horizontal commitments section. An explanation could be that these transition periods were reflected more precisely in the sectoral commitments section of the LDCs' services schedules. All the LDCs apart from Samoa used transition periods in the sectoral commitments section of their services schedules.

## Subsidies, investment incentives and other state support measures

Seventeen[87] out of the thirty-three Article XII members made entries in relation to subsidies, investment incentives and other state support measures. The various entries can be summarised as follows:

- Russia indicated that a foreign service provider can 'rent' for a period of forty-nine years which is subject to further extension.
- Samoa indicated that the lease can subsist for thirty years, renewable once in the case of land leased or licensed for industrial purposes, or a hotel, and twenty years renewable once in the other cases.
- Viet Nam indicated that the lease can be extended for as long as the licence to operate subsists.

[86] Except for capital contributions in the form of buying shares of joint-stock commercial banks, and except for the sectors not committed in this schedule.

[87] Armenia, Cabo Verde, Cambodia, China, Croatia, the former Yugoslav Republic of Macedonia, Georgia, Jordan, Lao PDR, Lithuania, Montenegro, Russia, Samoa, Tajikistan, Tonga, Ukraine and Viet Nam.

- Thirteen[88] out of the thirty-three Article XII members indicated in their horizontal commitments section that subsidies were unbound. In addition, eight out of these eleven made specific entries with regard to their state support measures. China, Montenegro, Russia and Tajikistan listed specific sectors that were unbound for subsidies and other state support measures.

- Thirteen[89] out of the thirty-three Article XII members indicated that access to subsidies is granted to only citizens and/or legal persons within their territory.

- Eight[90] out of the thirty-three Article XII members indicated that eligibility for subsidies may be limited to particular regions.

- Cambodia and Montenegro made unique entries in relation to their subsidies, investment incentives and other state support measures. Cambodia indicated that foreign service providers desirous of taking advantage of its investment incentives were under an obligation to provide training opportunities for Cambodian nationals, while Montenegro indicated that the supply of a service or its subsidisation within the public sector was not a breach of commitment.

The above entries show that Article XII members may apply flexibilities to limit the eligibility for subsidies and other state support measures to particular sectors, regions, categories of persons, or enterprises. Also, these entries on the subsidies, investment incentives and state support measures are transparency tools that offer predictability for the investment framework within the GATS. This is because the entries circumscribe and define the terms under which state support measures may be applied by the Article XII members.

### Additional commitments

Nepal and Saudi Arabia took additional commitments in their horizontal section. The additional commitments are not similar. Saudi Arabia in its additional commitments indicated that its tax measures will be applied in

---

[88] Armenia, Cambodia, China, Georgia, Jordan, Lao PDR, Montenegro, Russia, Samoa, Tajikistan, Tonga, Ukraine and Viet Nam.

[89] Armenia, Cabo Verde, Croatia, the former Yugoslav Republic of Macedonia, Montenegro, Lao PDR, Lithuania, Nepal, Russia, Saudi Arabia, Tajikistan, Ukraine and Viet Nam.

[90] Croatia, Georgia, Lao PDR, Lithuania, Montenegro, Russia, Tajikistan and Ukraine.

a manner consistent with the MFN and national treatment principles under the GATS, except in relation to the Islamic practice of *Zakat*.[91] For its part, Nepal took additional commitments relating to the environment and repatriation of foreign capital.

Nepal in its additional commitments section stipulated that, within thirty days from the date of application, investors would be provided with approvals for their investments by the relevant departments. However, it made an exception in relation to the environment. Where an environmental assessment was required, the department could exceed the thirty days and could also withhold approval where the investment failed to meet environmental standards. Furthermore, in its additional commitments section, Nepal listed the classes of foreign capital investment that could be repatriated outside Nepal. These include receipts from sales of the investors' share of equity; dividends or profits from an equity investment; receipts as payments of principal or interests on foreign loans and amounts received under an agreement to transfer technology approved by the Nepalese Department of Industries or the Department of Cottage and Small Industries.

From the foregoing, the additional commitments operate as transparency and flexibility tools. Saudi Arabia and Nepal have used their additional commitments to incorporate flexibilities for sensitive issues, such as religious practices, environmental protection and capital controls in a transparent manner. The value for the multilateral trading system is that the additional commitments operating as a transparency tool offer predictability for trading partners. Thus, additional commitments may be used by acceding governments to protect their sensitive sectors. They continue, however, to comply with the fundamental WTO principle of transparency.

### MFN exemptions

Six[92] Article XII members made investment-related entries in their MFN exemptions section. Jordan was the first Article XII member to

---

[91] A term used in Islamic finance to refer to the obligation that an individual has to donate a certain proportion of wealth each year to charitable causes. *Zakat* is a mandatory process for Muslims in order to physically and spiritually purify their yearly earnings that are over and above what is required to provide the essential needs of a person or family.

[92] Lao PDR, Jordan, Tajikistan, Russia, Vanuatu and Viet Nam.

specify 'investment' in its MFN exemptions section. All six entries are summarised below.

Lao PDR and Tajikistan made similar entries. They both indicated that they would offer preferential treatment to services and services suppliers under bilateral investment and trade agreements entered into force prior to their WTO accession for the duration of the bilateral investment treaty. Apart from Lao PDR and Tajikistan, the other investment-related entries made by the remaining four Article XII members in their MFN exemptions section are dissimilar.

Jordan made investment-related MFN exemptions for modes 3 (commercial presence) and 4 (movement of natural persons). Under mode 3, Jordan indicated that it would extend preferential treatment indefinitely to all countries that have bilateral investment treaties with Jordan. In addition, Jordan indicated under mode 4 that in order to promote investment with the Arab region, its service fees may discriminate between Arab and non-Arab service providers. Russia indicated MFN exemptions for existing and future agreements on measures concerning investment activity and available protection which are related to mutual protection and investment promotion. Vanuatu, for its part, indicated that in order to facilitate regional integration among Melanesian countries, it would grant investment waivers to citizens and permanent residents of Melanesian Spearhead Group countries, while Viet Nam indicated that, to foster investment in the country, it would extend preferential treatment under mode 3 to all countries that have signed bilateral investment treaties with Viet Nam.

The value of the investment-related rules as embedded in the investment-specific entries in the MFN exemptions section is twofold. They operate as instruments for transparency and coordination. First these MFN exemptions entries are transparency instruments as they clearly describe the measure exempted by indicating its inconsistency with Article II of the GATS, enumerating the countries to which the measure applies, indicating the intended duration of the exemption, and stating the conditions creating the need for the exemption. Secondly, the MFN exemptions are also coordination instruments. These MFN exemptions enable members to coordinate obligations with other bilateral investment treaties with WTO obligations.

From the analysis of Article XII members' services specific commitments, this chapter finds that there are no 'formulated' trends with regard to investment-related rules. This could be explained by the structure of the services schedules and the varying FDI needs of the thirty-three

Article XII members that have acceded to the WTO. Structurally, the schedules operate as signalling devices for foreign investors.

From a review of the various investment-related commitments of Article XII members, we conclude that members use WTO accession as an instrument for domestic reforms as well as to offer broader guarantees for predictability and transparency to foreign investors. Article XII members have developed the regulatory infrastructure to attract FDI inflows in their economies through their investment-related WTO accession commitments. WTO accessions have contributed to creating sound, stable and conducive investment climates by either reinforcing the existing investment-related rules on goods and services or broadening these rules through additional commitments. The collective value of these investment-related commitments of Article XII members is that they 'jointly' (for the systemic value in the multilateral trading system) and 'individually' (for the individual country's value) operate as the rulebook on investment-related matters in the WTO. The value of rules is that they lock in the government policy, thus providing predictability for the multilateral trading system and confidence for the foreign investors.

The question that arises is whether Article XII members have benefited in their attraction of FDI with their improved services schedules, post-accession, in relation to the pre-accession baseline? This is a question that requires deeper data-based analysis that the authors do not address in this chapter. However, a rapid analysis provides interesting findings.

The available evidence on FDI strongly suggests a relationship between accession-related domestic reforms, on the one hand, and inward FDI to Article XII members, on the other. This is an area in which further and deeper research would be helpful. However, even now, a rough analysis of the empirical data of selected Article XII members indicates such a relationship. On the basis of eight selected Article XII members,[93] inward FDI flows were reviewed. Using 1995 as a baseline (pre-WTO accession), when compared to the most recent three years for which data are available (2011–2013), inward FDI stocks show calculable and positive FDI gains, which steadily increased over the three years for all eight members. While care is exercised not to remotely make a claim of causality between Article XII WTO membership, on the one hand, and

---

[93] The regional location, the development status and the timing of the accession of an Article XII member have been taken into consideration in the selection.

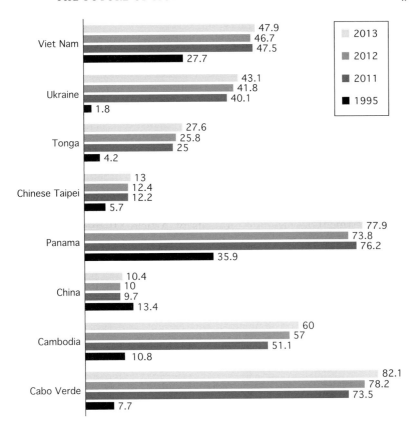

**Figure 38.1**    Inward FDI stocks as a percentage of GDP (UNCTAD, *World Investment Report* 2014).

enhanced FDI gains, on the other, the proposition is plausibly argued that the entirety of accession-specific domestic reforms, including those directly based on 'investment regimes' negotiated in the accession working party report and clarified through specific commitments in the services schedules annexed to Accession Protocols, have exercised a positive influence on attracting FDIs for Article XII members. Figure 38.1 shows the selected eight Article XII members' inward FDI growth and as a percentage of their gross domestic product (GDP), respectively. For example, Ukraine's inward FDI was 1.8 per cent of its GDP in 1995. In the third year of its accession (2011) onwards, its inward FDI stocks gradually increased from 40.1 per cent (2011) to 43.1 per cent (2013). In the case of China, although its inward FDI stocks decreased from 13.4 per cent (1995) to 10.4 per cent (2013), it should be noted that in the *2014*

*World Investment Report*, China recorded its largest ever inflows and maintained its position as the second largest recipient in the world.[94]

In conclusion, this chapter has tried to offer a comprehensive and succinct stocktaking of investment-related outcomes from the WTO accession process. We have shown that WTO accessions have advanced investment rule-making at the multilateral level, thereby suggesting that, should WTO members decide to engage in multilateral dialogue on investment with a view to defining trade-related multilateral rules for investment, WTO accession-specific commitment on investment could provide a coherent and substantive starting point. With the empirical examples drawn from the WTO Accession Protocols and working party reports, the chapter has illustrated the important impact Article XII members have had on investment rule-making, particularly in a rules-based multilateral trading system with the most powerful dispute settlement system in public international law. Overall, as we have endeavoured to show, the sum of the accession-specific obligations we have studied can be broadly grouped as: (i) binding and locking in the status quo of acceding governments; (ii) going beyond, to lock in the accession-driven liberalisation of trade in services and specific obligations to this end; and (iii) deepening the transparency obligation with enhanced implementation.

## Acknowledgement

The authors acknowledge the technical contributions and comments from James Zhan, Anna Varyanik, Amara Okenwa and George Tebagana.

## References

De Gucht, K. (2014). 'Statement by Commissioner Karel De Gucht on TTIP'. European Parliament Plenary debate, Strasbourg, 15 July, p. 3.

Footer, M. (2013). 'On the laws of attraction: examining the relationship between foreign investment and international trade' in R. Echandi and P. Sauvé (eds.), *Prospects in International Investment Law and Policy: World Trade Forum*. Cambridge University Press.

Gonzalez, A. (2013). 'The rationale for bringing investment into the WTO', in S. J. Evenett and A. Jara (eds.), *Building on Bali: A Work Programme for the WTO*. Retrieved from www.voxeu.org/content/building-bali-work-pro gramme-wto.

---

[94] See UNCTAD (2014).

IMF (1993). *Balance of Payments Manual*, 5th edition. Washington DC, International Monetary Fund.

   (2014). Retrieved from www.imf.org/external/pubs/ft/survey/so/2014/CAR 063014A.htm.

OECD (2006). *Investment Policy Reviews – China: Progress and Reform Challenges.* Retrieved from www.oecd.org/general/fdiintooecdcountriesjumps27in2005. htm.

UNCTAD (2005). *World Investment Report: Transnational Corporations and the Internationalisation of R&D.* New York and Geneva, United Nations. In 2006. UNCTAD reported that in 2005 FDI inflows to China were unchanged at some US\$ 60.3 billion. See UNCTAD (2006). *World Investment Report: FDI from Developing and Transition Economies: Implications for Development.* Geneva and New York, United Nations.

   (2012). *World Investment Report: Towards a New Generation of Investment Policies.* Geneva and New York, United Nations.

   (2013). *World Investment Report: Global Value Chains: Investment and Trade for Development.* Geneva and New York, United Nations.

   (2014). *World Investment Report.* Geneva and New York, United Nations, p. xiv.

# 39

# Sanitary and phytosanitary measures: trends in accession plurilateral negotiations

CHIEDU OSAKWE AND ANNA VARYANIK

## ABSTRACT

*Since 1947, effective levels of average tariff protection have declined, as regulatory protectionism – behind the border – has risen. To a large extent, the greater gains from continued trade opening lie in the area of pro-competitive domestic regulatory reform, codified in duly enacted legislation with associated implementing regulations. In the practice of WTO acces-sion negotiations, specific obligations have focused more on regulatory areas of the foreign trade regime. The evidence from thirty-three deposited Accession Protocols shows that there have been ninety-three specific obligations undertaken on sanitary and phytosanitary (SPS) measures. Pursuant to WTO Accession Protocols, these are now integral to the Marrakesh Agreement Establishing the World Trade Organization (WTO Agreement). The quantum of citation in WTO jurisprudence in the area of SPS is considerable: since 1995, 42 out of 494 WTO dispute settlement cases have cited the WTO Agreement on Sanitary and Phytosanitary Measures in the request for consultations. This chapter examines the evolution of accession results on SPS from 1995 to 2015, and their contributions to the enhancement of the existing WTO legal and policy framework on SPS. Specifically, this chapter focuses on the increas-ing importance of SPS regulatory issues in the foreign trade regimes of WTO members, the substance of specific SPS obligations undertaken by Article XII members and their relationship to the WTO Agreement, and the core questions that have emerged on the SPS accession treaty dialogue in the context of customs union agreements. As demonstrated in this chapter, SPS accession commitments undertaken by thirty-three Article*

The analyses in the chapters in this book were finalised at the end of December 2014. Since then the Republic of Seychelles acceded to the World Trade Organization (WTO) on 26 April 2015. This expanded total WTO membership from 160 to 161. Please see the editors' note.

*XII WTO members have exercised a significant influence on WTO juris-prudence. To a large extent, this has further clarified and strengthened WTO law.*

Recent studies show that trade protectionism remains a challenge. Protectionism has been on the rise across the world over the past several years.[1] With the increase in WTO jurisprudence, potentially trade-restrictive measures have become more sophisticated, that is, less clear. The trend suggests both tariff and non-tariff measures, of which measures aimed at protecting human, animal or plant life or health constitute a considerable part. To better counter the protean nature and pernicious trade effects of murky protectionism in this area of the foreign trade regime, the negotiating treaty dialogue in accession negotiations has been more pointed, targeted and exhaustive, culminating in a record ninety-three WTO accession commitments on sanitary and phytosanitary (SPS) measures undertaken by thirty-three Article XII WTO members.

The qualified right of WTO members to regulate trade with the aim of protecting human, animal or plant life or health is provided for in the General Agreement on Tariffs and Trade (GATT) 1994, Article XX(b), and the WTO Agreement on Sanitary and Phytosanitary Measures (SPS Agreement).[2] The preamble to the SPS Agreement explicitly provides that no WTO member 'should be prevented from adopting or enforcing measures necessary to protect human, animal or plant life or health', provided that such measures are not 'applied in a manner which would constitute a means of arbitrary or unjustifiable discrimination between countries where the same conditions prevail, or a disguised restriction on international trade'.[3] The WTO Appellate Body, in its conclusions and findings, upholds the right of WTO members to implement the trade

---

[1] From 1 May 2012 to 31 May 2013, 154 new potentially trade-restrictive measures were introduced (as compared to 123 measures introduced over eight months in September 2011 to May 2012), and only 18 such measures were rolled back during that period. Only 107 potentially trade-restrictive measures have been removed since October 2008, while 688 measures remained in place (Tenth Report on Potentially Trade-Restrictive Measures Identified in the Context of the Financial and Economic Crisis, p. 4, retrieved at http://europa.eu/rapid/press-release_IP-13-807_en.htm).

[2] Article 2.1 of the SPS Agreement provides that 'Members have the right to take sanitary and phytosanitary measures necessary for the protection of human, animal or plant life or health, provided that such measures are not inconsistent with the provisions of this Agreement'.

[3] GATT Article XX, Preamble.

measures necessary to achieve the level of SPS protection they establish.[4] Specialists in this area have also underscored this right of members.[5]

Article 1.1 of the SPS Agreement provides that it applies to all SPS measures which 'may, directly or indirectly, affect international trade'. The scope of such measures is enormously broad. In general, any measure related to the protection of human, animal or plant health can be considered as an SPS measure. The four specific objectives of these measures are identified in Annex A(1) to the SPS Agreement.[6] The measures can take many forms. According to Annex A(1), they include:

> all relevant laws, decrees, regulations, requirements and procedures ... processes and production methods; testing, inspection, certification and approval procedures; quarantine treatments including relevant requirements associated with the transport of animals or plants, or with the materials necessary for their survival during transport; provisions on relevant statistical methods, sampling procedures and methods of risk assessment; and packaging and labelling requirements directly related to food safety.

All these measures are governed by the WTO rules reflected in the SPS Agreement.

Such a broad scope, combined with the very nature of SPS measures, makes them highly potentially trade restrictive. The SPS Agreement recognises the impracticability of their firm regulation, which effectively implies a need for an exceptional regulatory flexibility of international rules in this area. In light of the special sensitivity of trade in agricultural goods and the overall trend towards elimination of tariff barriers, the increasing role played by the SPS measures as an effective market entry barrier makes them a focus of WTO members' permanent attention.

---

[4] WTO Appellate Body Report on *EC – Hormones II* (see WTO document wt/ds/320/AB/R).

[5] See J. Scott (2007), *WTO Agreement on Sanitary and Phytosanitary Measures: a Commentary*, Oxford University Press.

[6] Annex A(1) to the SPS Agreement identifies four types of SPS measures, i.e. those applied: (a) to protect animal or plant life or health within the territory of the member from risks arising from the entry, establishment or spread of pests, diseases, disease-carrying organisms or disease-causing organisms; (b) to protect human or animal life or health within the territory of the member from risks arising from additives, contaminants, toxins or disease-causing organisms in foods, beverages or feedstuffs; (c) to protect human life or health within the territory of the member from risks arising from diseases carried by animals, plants or products thereof, or from the entry, establishment or spread of pests; or (d) to prevent or limit other damage within the territory of the member from the entry, establishment or spread of pests.

Not surprisingly, the level of attention paid by WTO members to the WTO commitments of acceding governments in the SPS area has risen significantly over the years. As demonstrated below, since the establishment of the WTO in 1995, the number of SPS commitments per Article XII WTO member has increased in quantum and substance, depending on the particular market. Accession-specific SPS commitments by acceding governments have emerged as one of the most critical and significant areas in WTO accession negotiations. More recently, in the past two decades, these commitments have become more detailed, aiming at establishing a more binding and effective legal framework to contain and reduce the propensity to protectionist risks inherent in the SPS regime. The biggest challenge, so far, in SPS accession negotiations, emerged in the course of the SPS plurilateral negotiations for the accession of Russia in 2011.[7] These challenges carried over into the SPS plurilateral negotiations in the accession negotiations of Kazakhstan. In both cases, the challenge was rooted at two levels. First, in uncertain jurisdictional competence for SPS in the evolution of the 2010 Customs Union of Belarus, Kazakhstan and Russia and, thereafter, in the transformation from the Customs Union into the Eurasian Union Agreement, the latter signed on 29 May 2014. And, second, on the substance of the decisions by the Eurasian Economic Commission (the regulatory arm of the Customs Union/Eurasian Union) and the national SPS decisions of the parties, decisions and regulations, in some cases, duplicated, overlapping and in conflict.

The process of accession negotiations on SPS mirrors the overall trend in respect of WTO accessions: they have become lengthier and more complex. It is expected that members' attention to SPS will continue to grow.

## Accession negotiations on SPS

Traditionally, discussions on SPS-related issues form a part of the multilateral track of negotiations in WTO accession, in which WTO members negotiate with the acceding government collectively. The SPS discussions, now often held plurilaterally on the margins of the respective working party meetings, serve two basic purposes: (i) to increase WTO

---

[7] Chiedu Osakwe, as Director of the WTO Accessions Division, chaired the SPS plurilateral negotiations for the WTO accession negotiations for Russia and Kazakhstan. Anna Varyanik was a member of the negotiating team for the accession of Russia before joining the WTO Secretariat.

members' knowledge and improve their understanding of the SPS regime in place in the acceding government; and (ii) to elaborate a 'roadmap' for the reforms required to bring the acceding government's SPS regime into compliance with the WTO standard. The necessity for the SPS plurilateral track among the parallel multilateral and bilateral negotiations process is reflected in three areas: legislation harmonisation; information transparency requirements; and implementation supervision.

According to the fundamental provision governing WTO accessions, Article XII:1 of the Marrakesh Agreement Establishing the World Trade Organization (WTO Agreement), a state, or separate customs territory, may accede to the WTO, on terms to be agreed between it and the WTO membership.

Although this provision does not specify the precise WTO accession commitments because the domestic regimes of acceding governments vary enormously, in practice the objective is to ensure that the acceding government is WTO-compliant on day one of membership, or with agreed action plans for WTO-consistency, over a negotiated transition period.

The rule of law is a core WTO value and a major benefit for acceding governments. This core fundamental value requires WTO members to fully comply with the WTO rules: either from the first day of WTO membership, or upon the expiry of the negotiated transition period, if the acceding government – for example, a least-developed country (LDC) – is eligible for it.

Full compliance with WTO rules cannot be achieved without the domestic construction of a fully functioning WTO-consistent trade regime. To provide guidance on the reforms needing to be undertaken, WTO members scrutinise the existing SPS regime of the acceding government, or separate customs territory in the course of its WTO accession. The review of the existing SPS practices tends to encompass: (i) mandatory SPS requirements; (ii) veterinary controls; (iii) import permits; (iv) transit conditions; (v) certification; (vi) inspections; (vii) quarantine controls; (viii) protection of human health, etc. Under the guidance of WTO members, the acceding government, in coordination with the WTO Secretariat, is required to submit documents and answer questions in specific areas regarding the competent authorities for the regulation of trade in agricultural products, development of technical regulations/mandatory requirements on SPS, trade in goods subject to veterinary control, trade in goods subject to phytosanitary control, and protection of human health, etc. Other relevant critical issues can also be separately listed in submitted documents on SPS measures, such as transparency, notification and enquiry point obligations. During the review exercise, specific problems are identified, and suggestions are made on the specific areas of SPS regulation which need to be improved. The burden of adjustment of the SPS trade regime falls on the acceding government. This is a part of the entry fee which must be paid for the privilege of the WTO membership, above all to ensure the WTO-consistency of the SPS regime of the acceding government.

These discussions, and the specific SPS commitments agreed, are reflected in a specific section of the working party report devoted to SPS, forming a part of the WTO Accession Package. According to the recent five- to ten-year trend, the section is generally divided into four subsections: (i) general regulatory framework; (ii) participation in international bodies; (iii) overview of existing practices; and (iv) compliance with specific WTO rules on SPS. Revision of compliance with specific provisions of the SPS Agreement may relate to non-discrimination, harmonisation with international standards and norms, risk assessment and equivalence, etc.

The length of this negotiating exercise is mainly determined by the adjustment that an acceding government must undertake to bring its SPS regime into compliance with WTO rules and the extent of the acceding governments' willingness to meet the demands made by WTO members. The bigger and the more important the specific market is, the longer this process takes.

SPS discussions face specific challenges caused by the general complexities of SPS regulation. The measures attracting WTO members' attention may take many forms: insufficiently defined criteria for inspections; cumbersome procedures; diverging standards; duplicated requirements, etc. Such a review requires strong technical expert knowledge in sanitary and phytosanitary questions. If an acceding government is a party to a customs union agreement, the review may additionally be complicated by the issues of supranational, joint and national competences in the area and overlaps. Such a situation may require the acceding government to undertake commitments both in respect of national SPS regulation, and that of the customs union.[8] Evidence on SPS from customs unions also

---

[8] For example, Russia committed that 'all sanitary and phytosanitary measures, whether adopted by Russia or the competent bodies of the CU (Customs Union), would be based on international standards, guidelines or recommendations' (Report of the Working Party on the accession of the Russian Federation to the WTO (see WTO document WT/ACC/RUS/70 of 17 November 2011), paragraph 1009). All principal WTO accession documents are available at www.wto.org/english/thewto_e/acc_e/completeacc_e.htm.

indicates a continuing clash, on the one hand, with customs union members seeking exemptions to allow for manoeuvring scope and uncertainty, and, on the other hand, WTO members seeking precision, clarity and exclusion of uncertainty through binding and enforceable accession commitments.

Overall, the purpose of SPS negotiations can be expressed as finding the right balance between trade and health policy, i.e. minimising the negative trade impact of the SPS measures on trade, as reflected in the SPS Agreement,[9] on the one hand, and on the other hand, ensuring that the level of SPS protection reflects life and health protection, and does not constitute a means of protection of domestic industries. This aim often leads WTO members to bring up some SPS matters that may appear to be relatively unimportant in bilateral trade, but which can potentially have a great significance for preserving the multilateral trading system as a whole.

## SPS commitments of Article XII members: general overview

The main SPS commitment, which all acceding governments must undertake, is the reaffirmation to apply, unqualifiedly, the SPS Agreement. This commitment has been undertaken by all thirty-three Article XII members which have acceded to the WTO to date (Figure 39.1).[10] Effectively, the commitment implies an obligation to fully comply with the set rules established by the SPS Agreement, including those on nondiscrimination, necessity and reasonableness, proportionality, harmonisation (Article 3), equivalence (Article 4), risk assessment (Article 5), transparency (Article 7), control, inspection and approval (Article 8), etc.

---

[9] SPS Agreement, Preamble, paragraph 1: 'Reaffirming that no Member should be prevented from adopting or enforcing measures necessary to protect human, animal or plant life or health, subject to the requirement that these measures are not applied in a manner which would constitute a means of arbitrary or unjustifiable discrimination between Members where the same conditions prevail or a disguised restriction on international trade'.

[10] To date, thirty-three WTO members have acceded to the WTO pursuant to Article XII of the WTO Agreement: Albania, Armenia, Bulgaria, Cambodia, Cabo Verde, China, Croatia, Ecuador, Estonia, the Former Yugoslav Republic of Macedonia, Georgia, Jordan, Kyrgyz Republic, Lao PDR, Latvia, Lithuania, Moldova, Mongolia, Montenegro, Nepal, Oman, Panama, Russia, Samoa, Saudi Arabia, Chinese Taipei, Tajikistan, Tonga, Ukraine, Vanuatu, Viet Nam and Yemen.

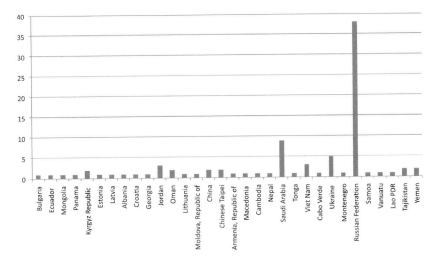

**Figure 39.1**    Number of SPS commitment paragraphs contained in working party reports of thirty-three Article XII members.

The commitment to apply the SPS Agreement can either be of a general nature or be detailed. Notably, before the accession of Panama in 1997, SPS commitments were not distinguished into a separate category of obligations. Before 2000, there had basically just been general commitments to apply the SPS Agreement (with the exception of Montenegro, which undertook such a general commitment when it acceded to the WTO in 2012). So far, the Accession Protocols of six Article XII members contain a standard general commitment to apply the SPS Agreement from the date of accession to the WTO only.[11]

---

[11]   Estonia, Report of the Working Party on the accession of Estonia to the WTO (see WTO document WT/ACC/EST/28 of 9 April 1999), paragraph 98; Latvia, Report of the Working Party on the accession of Latvia to the WTO (see WTO document WT/ACC/LVA/32 of 30 September 1998), paragraph 88; Albania, Report of the Working Party on the accession of Albania to the WTO (see WTO document WT/ACC/ALB/51 of 13 July 2000), paragraph 108; Georgia, Report of the Working Party on the accession of Georgia to the WTO (see WTO document WT/ACC/GEO/31 of 31 August 1999), paragraph 107; Montenegro, Report of the Working Party on the accession of Montenegro to the WTO (see WTO document WT/ACC/CGR/38 of 5 December 2011), paragraph 168. Ecuador gave the assurance that its SPS measures were in conformity with the provisions of the SPS Agreement (Ecuador, Report of the Working Party on the accession of Ecuador to the WTO (see WTO document WT/L/77 of 14 July 1995), paragraph 51).

However, with the increasing complexity of WTO accession negotiations in many accessions, and the challenges presented by the transition
economies, tighter legal frameworks ensuring full consistency of a particular SPS regime with the WTO rules became the standard. This can be
seen from examples of twenty Article XII non-LDC members, which
have undertaken a wide variety of SPS-related obligations. The substance
of these commitments often depended on the state of internal SPS
regulation of the acceding government at the time when the accession
negotiations took place. So far, Russia has accepted the most SPS-specific
accession commitments with its WTO membership in 2012 when it
undertook thirty-eight specific commitments.[12]

The difference between the general and detailed SPS commitments is
one of degree rather than substance. Many detailed commitments
clarify the specific provisions of the SPS Agreement with the aim of
further elaborating and enhancing a general commitment to act within
the rules of the SPS Agreement. Such specific commitments cover the
harmonisation of SPS requirements with international standards, risk
assessment, regionalisation, equivalence, non-discrimination, transparency, notification, establishment of enquiry points, proportionality,
necessity and reasonableness, etc. Eight WTO members[13] have
explicitly undertaken commitments to apply all sanitary requirements
consistently with the requirements of both the SPS Agreement and the
WTO Agreement on Import Licensing Procedures. One member

---

[12]  To compare, the average number of SPS commitment paragraphs per Article XII member
is one or two.

[13]  Mongolia, Report of the Working Party on the accession of Mongolia to the WTO (see
WTO document WT/ACC/MNG/9 of 29 June 1996), paragraph 20; Panama, Report of
the Working Party on the accession of Panama to the WTO (see WTO document
WT/ACC/PAN/19 of 20 September 1996), paragraph 51; Kyrgyz Republic, Report of
the Working Party on the accession of the Kyrgyz Republic to the WTO (see WTO
document WT/ACC/KGZ/26 of 31 July 1998), paragraph 103; Lithuania, Report of the
Working Party on the accession of Lithuania to the WTO (see WTO document WT/
ACC/LTU/52 of 7 November 2000), paragraph 122; Armenia, Report of the Working
Party on the accession of Armenia to the WTO (WTO document WT/ACC/ARM/23 of
26 November 2002), paragraph 143; former Yugoslav Republic of Macedonia, Report of
the Working Party on the accession of the Former Yugoslav Republic of Macedonia to the
WTO (see WTO document WT/ACC/807/27 of 26 September 2002), paragraph 153;
Ukraine, Report of the Working Party on the accession of Ukraine to the WTO (see
WTO document WT/ACC/UKR/152 of 25 January 2008), paragraph 327; Tajikistan,
Report of the Working Party on the accession of Tajikistan to the WTO (see WTO
document WT/ACC/TJK/30 of 6 November 2012), paragraph 231.

remarkably committed to the implementation of the SPS Agreement prior to its accession to the WTO.[14]

In addition to these general commitments, Article XII members often undertake specific commitments in respect of legislation. Usually, such explicit commitments are undertaken by countries in which the establishment of a WTO-consistent legislative framework plays a critical role. Thus, one member committed to ensuring the conformity of all its laws, regulations, decrees, requirements and procedures relating to SPS measures with the SPS Agreement.[15] The SPS commitment of another member included a broader reference to 'the relevant WTO provisions'.[16] One member undertook to reconcile inconsistencies between its domestic SPS legislation, so that all its laws, regulations, procedures and other requirements for importation were consistent with the SPS Agreement, and undertook commitments in respect of specific SPS-related legislative acts.[17]

Similarly, Article XII members undertake commitments to review their existing SPS measures: either generally, in the light of the obligations under the SPS Agreement,[18] or upon request of a WTO member identifying a specific measure.[19] For example, one member committed to bringing all its existing SPS measures into conformity with the SPS Agreement,[20] whereas another member committed to developing all its future SPS measures in accordance with the WTO Agreement.[21]

The commitment to develop SPS measures in line with the WTO rules corresponds to the requirement of Article 1.1 of the SPS Agreement that SPS measures be 'developed and applied in accordance with the provisions' of the Agreement. Effectively, this requirement confirms that the

---

[14] Moldova, Report of the Working Party on the accession of Moldova to the WTO (see WTO document WT/ACC/MOL/37 of 11 January 2001), paragraph 135.

[15] China, Report of the Working Party on the accession of the People's Republic of China to the WTO (see WTO document WT/ACC/CHN/49 of 1 October 2001), paragraph 200.

[16] Moldova, paragraph 135.

[17] Saudi Arabia, Report of the Working Party on the accession of the Kingdom of Saudi Arabia to the WTO (see WTO document WT/ACC/SAU/61 of 1 November 2005), paragraphs 208, 216.

[18] Tonga, Report of the Working Party on the accession of Tonga to the WTO (see WTO document WT/ACC/TON/17 of 2 December 2005), paragraph 126; Vanuatu, Report of the Working Party on the accession of Vanuatu to the WTO (WTO document WT/ACC/VUT/17 of 11 May 2011), paragraph 100.

[19] Saudi Arabia, paragraph 210.       [20] Ukraine, paragraph 327.

[21] Russian Federation, paragraph 1033.

relevance of the distinction between SPS measures as such and SPS measures as applied for the purposes of the SPS Agreement.[22]

Accordingly, a number of accession commitments specifically refer to the application of SPS-related legislation. For example, two members committed to applying their internal legislation in conformity with the provisions of the SPS Agreement.[23] As to the manner of administration of the specific SPS requirements, the most commonly undertaken commitment – so far, undertaken by six Article XII members[24] – refers to the sanitary and other certification requirements, which will be administered in a 'transparent and expeditious manner'. Some other specific commitments may also be undertaken in this respect.[25]

### Non-discrimination: proportionality and necessity

The principle of non-discrimination is one of the fundamental principles entrenched in the SPS Agreement and the WTO Agreement. In the SPS Agreement, it is reflected in the Preamble, Articles 2.3 and 5.5, and in Annex B to the Agreement. Generally, the principle can be defined as a prohibition of discrimination between WTO members – most-favoured-nation (MFN) treatment – and a prohibition of discrimination between domestic and imported goods and services (national treatment). Compliance with the non-discrimination requirements of the SPS Agreement have emerged as one of the main WTO members' concerns.

The principle has broadly been reflected in the SPS commitments of Article XII members. Some Article XII members have undertaken general commitments that their existing or new SPS measures would be applied on a non-discriminatory basis, providing for national treatment

---

[22] WTO Appellate Body Report on *EC – Measures Affecting the Approval and Marketing of Biotech Products* (DS291, DS292, DS293).

[23] Moldova, paragraph 135; Tajikistan, paragraph 231.

[24] Bulgaria, Report of the Working Party on the accession of Bulgaria to the WTO (see WTO document WT/ACC/BGR/5 of 20 September 1996), paragraph 64; Kyrgyz Republic, paragraph 103; former Yugoslav Republic of Macedonia, paragraph 153; Ukraine, paragraph 327; Seychelles, paragraph 297; Tajikistan, paragraph 231.

[25] Thus, Tonga committed to administer its existing requirements on imports for SPS purposes (listed in Table 10 of the Report of the Working Party) based on principles of pest risk analysis and the international standards of Codex Alimentarius, the International Plant Protection Convention (IPPC), the FAO, and the Office International des Epizooties (OIE) (Tonga, paragraph 126).

and MFN treatment to all imports.[26] Some members committed that their SPS measures would not 'arbitrarily or unjustifiably discriminate between Members where identical or similar conditions prevail',[27] in strict line with the wording of Article 2.3 of the SPS Agreement[28] and the preambular language of the GATT 1994 Article XX.

The examples illustrate that the issue of non-discrimination in SPS regulation is closely linked to the WTO SPS principles of proportionality, necessity and reasonableness.[29] Embodied in Articles 2.1 and 2.2 of the SPS Agreement,[30] the necessity requirement originates from the 1994 GATT Article XX(b), providing that a measure 'necessary to protect human, animal or plant life or health' shall be exempted from the GATT provisions, but subject to the headnote in the article.[31] The proportionality principle implies 'a legal standard against which an individual or state measures can be reviewed'.[32] Disregard of and non-compliance with these basic principles in formulating and implementing SPS measures are considered by members as arbitrary or unjustifiable level of SPS protection. As confirmed by the WTO Appellate Body in *Australia – Salmon*,

---

[26] Tonga, paragraph 126; Vanuatu, paragraph 100; Yemen, Report of the Working Party on the accession of Yemen to the WTO (see WTO document WT/ACC/YEM/42 of 4 October 2013), paragraph 178.

[27] Tajikistan, paragraph 231; Russia, paragraph 1062.

[28] The interpretation of terms 'arbitrary or unjustifiable discrimination' in Article 2.3 is provided guidance by the WTO Appellate Body's findings with respect to the ordinary meaning of 'arbitrary or unjustifiable' from the chapeau of Article XX of the GATT 1994 (see WTO Appellate Body Reports on *United States – Certain Measures Affecting Imports of Poultry from China* (DS392), *Australia – Measures Affecting Importation of Salmon* (DS18)).

[29] In the practice of WTO accessions negotiations in SPS plurilateral meetings, over which the WTO Secretariat presides, the three 'WTO SPS principles' of proportionality, necessity and reasonableness have been applied by members in reviewing the chapter on the SPS foreign trade regime in the working party reports of acceding governments and, consequently their acceptance of specific obligations in this regard.

[30] Article 2.1 of the SPS Agreement sets out the right of WTO members to 'take sanitary and phytosanitary measures necessary for the protection of human, animal or plant life or health, provided that such measures are not inconsistent with the provisions of this Agreement'.

[31] GATT Article XX(b); Jan Neumann and Elisabeth Türk, 'Necessity Revisited: Proportionality in World Trade Organization Law after Korea–Beef, EC–Asbestos and EC–Sardines', 37 *Journal of World Trade* 199, 231–33 (2003).

[32] Mads Andenas and Stephan Zleptnic, *Proportionality: WTO Law in Comparative Perspective*, 2007; p. 375; Malcolm Ross, 'Behind Proportionality: The Cultural and Constitutional Context', in *English Public Law and the Common Law of Europe* 83, 91 (Mads Andenas ed., 1998); Axel Desmedt, 'Proportionality in WTO Law', 4 *Journal of International Economic Law* 441, 441–480 (2001), at 478.

'All "arbitrary or unjustifiable distinctions" in levels of protection will lead logically to discrimination between products'.[33]

Accordingly, Article XII members may choose to commit that they will apply all SPS measures in the least trade-distortive manner,[34] and in a 'manner which would not act as a disguised restriction on trade'[35] or, specifically, 'only to the extent necessary to protect human, animal, or plant life or health and not be more trade restrictive than required to achieve the appropriate level of SPS protection'.[36]

In the case of some Arab countries, the specific concerns of WTO members referred to the lack of national treatment for the unnecessary inspection of imported meat and meat from live animals, and certain stricter SPS requirements which appeared to apply only to 'non-Arab' countries, which might constitute a violation of the MFN principle. To address the concerns, one member undertook a commitment to abide by the provisions of paragraphs 1(a), 1(e) and 1(g) of Annex C to the SPS Agreement[37] and implement the least trade-restrictive requirements possible to prevent deceptive practices vis-à-vis consumers of meat, taking into account the national treatment requirements of the GATT Article III.[38] Another member was obliged to revise its laws[39] to ensure compliance with relevant WTO obligations.

The SPS commitments of some Article XII members can be more detailed. In the case of non-discrimination, one member's commitment language refers to all SPS measures developed and applied, which must comply with the non-discrimination provisions of the SPS Agreement, including those relating to the principles of national treatment and MFN treatment.[40] When determining the appropriate level of SPS protection, this member committed to take into account the objective of minimising negative effects on trade.[41] A specific commitment has been undertaken

---

[33] WTO Appellate Body Report on *Australia – Salmon* (see WTO document WT/DS18/AB/R: paragraph 169, 20 October 1998).

[34] Jordan, Report of the Working Party on the accession of Jordan to the WTO (see WT/ACC/JOR/33 of 3 December 1999), paragraph 151.

[35] China, paragraph 199.

[36] Tajikistan, paragraph 231; Russia, paragraph 1060; Seychelles, paragraph 297.

[37] Containing the requirements with respect to any procedure to check and ensure the fulfilment of SPS measures.

[38] Jordan, paragraph 149.

[39] Such as the 'Approval of Importing Alfalfa and Vegetable Seeds from Non-Arab Countries' and 'Approval of Importing Flower and Forage Crop Seeds from Non-Arab Countries' (Saudi Arabia, paragraph 222).

[40] Russia, paragraph 1033.   [41] Russia, paragraph 1060.

in respect of the practices of veterinary control, where, as was declared by the member, official import control carried out only in accredited laboratories would ensure uniformity of treatment.[42]

The non-discrimination provisions of the SPS Agreement cover a variety of specific aspects of the SPS regulation. For example, paragraph 1(f) of Annex C to the SPS Agreement provides that 'any fees imposed for the procedures on imported products are equitable in relation to any fees charged on like domestic products or products originating in any other Member and should be no higher than the actual cost of the service'. Some Article XII members specifically committed that their fees imposed for procedures on imported products should be in compliance with this provision,[43] or confirmed the absence of any fee. For example, one member stated that no fee was charged for the inspection of seeds.[44]

Similarly, some WTO members committed to the elimination of specific WTO-inconsistent discriminatory import bans, which existed before their WTO accession. For example, one member committed that live swine that met quarantine requirements would be allowed entry.[45]

### Transparency: publication, notification, enquiry points

Transparency requirements underpin all WTO agreements. In the SPS Agreement, they are reflected in Article 7 and Annex B to the Agreement. The entirety of SPS transparency obligations can be divided to three categories of commitments: (i) to publish SPS regulations;[46] (ii) to notify SPS regulations to the WTO;[47] and (iii) to establish enquiry points responsible for the provision of answers to members' questions and the provision of relevant documents.[48]

Paragraphs 1 and 2 of Annex B provide that WTO members shall ensure that all adopted SPS regulations are published promptly in such a manner as to enable other WTO members to become acquainted with them. A reasonable interval between the publication of a SPS regulation and its entry into force must be provided in order to allow time for producers in exporting members, and particularly developing country

---

[42] Russia, paragraph 1035.    [43] Russia, paragraph 936.
[44] Saudi Arabia, paragraph 218.
[45] Chinese Taipei, Report of the Working Party on the accession of the Separate Customs Territory of Taiwan, Penghu, Kinmen and Matsu to the WTO (see WT/ACC/TPKM/18 of 5 October 2001), paragraph 135.
[46] Annex B(1), B(2) to the SPS Agreement.    [47] Article 7 of the SPS Agreement.
[48] Annex B(3), B(4) to the SPS Agreement.

members, to adapt their products and methods of production to the requirements of the importing member.[49] Whereas the commitments of some Article XII members are formulated in exact line with this wording,[50] some Article XII SPS commitments may also further clarify the regulation in this area. Thus, some members committed to the publication of SPS regulations prior to their implementation to allow interested parties the opportunity for review and comment.[51]

There have also been a number of commitments in respect of publication of specific SPS regulations. Thus, five Article XII members committed to publish the criteria for granting prior authorisation or securing the required certification for imported products,[52] one member committed to publish its minimum/maximum residue levels (MRLs),[53] and one member its import permit regime,[54] etc. Some WTO members went beyond the level of commitments on publication prescribed by the SPS Agreement, and committed to specify the manner for publishing proposed SPS measures[55] or the internet source for publication of some draft SPS requirements;[56] and committed to adopting some SPS measures pursuant to transparent procedures allowing for public comment on the respective proposals.[57]

Article 7 of the SPS Agreement requires WTO members to notify changes in their SPS measures and provide information on their SPS measures in accordance with the notification procedures established in Annex B. Only four Article XII members have undertaken commitments in this area. A number of these members agreed to provide notification of future changes to import requirements relating to SPS matters,[58] or to notify existing requirements on imports for SPS purposes to the WTO[59] or, more broadly, to notify 'all relevant laws, decrees, regulations, and administrative rulings of general application relating to SPS measures, including product coverage and relevant international standards,

---

[49] Annex B(1), B(2) to the SPS Agreement.     [50] Panama, paragraph 51.
[51] Tonga, paragraph 126; Vanuatu, paragraph 100.
[52] Bulgaria, paragraph 64; former Yugoslav Republic of Macedonia, paragraph 153; Kyrgyz Republic, paragraph 103; Ukraine, paragraph 327; Tajikistan, paragraph 231.
[53] Ukraine, paragraph 320.     [54] Russia, paragraph 876.
[55] Tonga committed to specify clearly the manner for publishing any proposed SPS measures (Tonga, paragraph 126).
[56] Saudi Arabia, paragraph 215.
[57] Ukraine undertook such a commitment in respect of any proposed limits on MRLs (Ukraine, paragraph 320).
[58] Saudi Arabia, paragraph 215.     [59] Tonga, paragraph 126; Vanuatu, paragraph 100.

guidelines and recommendations'.[60] One member went beyond these and undertook a 'WTO-plus' commitment in respect of notification – both to the WTO and all WTO members – of proposed SPS measures and notification of 'actions relating to SPS issues'.[61]

Paragraph 3 of Annex B to the SPS Agreement requires that WTO members establish enquiry points responsible for the provision of answers to all reasonable questions from interested members as well as for the provision of relevant documents. The respective commitments have been undertaken by three members.[62] In addition, two of these members made a number of commitments as to the information which should be published on the website of the enquiry point.[63]

## Consultations

The consultation requirement is reflected in Articles 4.2, 11, 12 of the SPS Agreement.

The SPS Agreement provides for consultations on the equivalence of SPS measures, consultations in the context of Articles XXII and XXIII of the GATT 1994 (dispute settlement) and the WTO Committee on SPS Measures as a regular forum for consultations. However, to ensure greater predictability and transparency in the SPS regimes of acceding governments, WTO members often seek additional accession commitments in respect of consultations. So far, four Article XII members have expressed their willingness to consult with WTO members concerning the effect of their SPS requirements on trade, with a view to resolving specific problems.[64] Two members committed to such consultations.[65] One member expressed its readiness to consult with other WTO members and committed to modify the relevant requirements to bring

---

[60] Chinese Taipei, paragraph 137.    [61] Saudi Arabia, paragraph 216.

[62] Tonga, paragraph 126; Saudi Arabia, paragraph 223; Russia, paragraph 1055.

[63] Russia committed to publish (i) a list on the website of the national enquiry point in English of the products which were permitted to be imported into its territory; (ii) the countries and establishments authorised to export to Russia and the territory of the Customs Union; and (iii) the conditions for import (Russia, paragraph 1051). Tonga committed to 'specify the Government body/bodies responsible for developing and applying such measures, and to which bodies importers and exporters could direct enquiries concerning import requirements and other relevant information' (Tonga, paragraph 126).

[64] Bulgaria, paragraph 64; Mongolia, paragraph 20; Kyrgyz Republic, paragraph 103; former Yugoslav Republic of Macedonia, paragraph 153.

[65] Ukraine, paragraph 327; Tajikistan, paragraph 231.

them into compliance with international standards, guidelines, or recommendations consistent with the SPS Agreement, if necessary, as a
result of such consultations.[66] Additional commitments have also been
taken in respect of consultations over specific issues. For example, one
member explicitly committed to consult with exporting WTO members
on the phytosanitary requirements, if requested.[67]

In the case of LDCs, the importance of such consultations has been
greater, given the transition periods provided and guidance which may
be required to proceed with the SPS reforms. Five out of the seven LDC
governments that have acceded to the WTO since 1995, with the
exception of Lao PDR, committed to consult with other WTO
members, upon their request, if these members deemed that any SPS
measures applied by these LDCs during the transition periods affected
trade negatively.[68]

## Harmonisation with international standards and risk assessment

The SPS Agreement aims to reduce and eliminate SPS barriers to trade by
fostering harmonisation of national health-related regulations with international standards, guidelines and recommendations, and basing the SPS
rules on scientific evidence. The reason for this is that the divergent SPS
rules of WTO members may lead to different levels of SPS protection
and, as a consequence, different levels of risks for life and health.
Harmonised standards ensure uniformity and predictability of SPS rules.

Many specific SPS commitments of Article XII members explicitly
refer to the international organisations establishing internationally
agreed benchmarks for SPS standards. The SPS Agreement mentions
three international organisations whose activities are relevant to its
objectives: the FAO/WHO Codex Alimentarius Commission, the OIE
and the international and regional organisations operating within the
framework of the FAO IPPC.[69] WTO members should adopt their SPS
requirements in compliance with the standards established by these
organisations. SPS measures which conform to international standards,
guidelines or recommendations will be deemed to be necessary to protect

---

[66] Russia, paragraph 904.    [67] Russia, paragraph 952.
[68] Cambodia, paragraph 142; Nepal, paragraph 107; Cabo Verde, paragraph 177; Samoa,
paragraph 162; Yemen, paragraph 180.
[69] Sixth paragraph of the Preamble, Articles 3.4 and 12.3 of the SPS Agreement.

human, animal or plant life or health, and presumed to be consistent with the relevant provisions of the SPS Agreement and the GATT 1994.[70]

Article 3.1 of the SPS Agreement requires that WTO members harmonise their SPS measures with international standards, guidelines or recommendations 'on as wide a basis as possible'.[71] The requirement that SPS measures be 'based on' international standards does not mean that SPS measures must 'conform to' such standards.[72] The SPS Agreement allows WTO members to establish protection levels exceeding international standards, if there is a 'scientific justification'[73] or if it determines that the standard does not meet its acceptable level of protection, provided that a measure is based on a proper evaluation of the actual risks involved (risk assessment requirement)[74] and is subject to a range of other conditions set out in Article 5 of the SPS Agreement, to establish substantial safety margins as a precautionary measure.

Article XII members have explicitly undertaken 'WTO-plus' obligations that are stricter than those laid out by international organisations.[75] One member committed to base all its SPS measures on the Codex Alimentarius, OIE and IPPC standards, guidelines and recommendations in accordance with the requirements of the SPS Agreement.[76]

Some Article XII WTO members accepted obligations pursuant to the general commitment that their SPS standards system should be in compliance with the SPS Agreement,[77] or that they should administer the SPS

---

[70] Article 3.2 of the SPS Agreement.      [71] Article 3.1 of the SPS Agreement.

[72] WTO Appellate Body Report on *EC – Hormones* (DS 26, DS 48).

[73] Article 3.3 of the SPS Agreement. Article 2.2 of the SPS Agreement requires SPS measures not to be 'maintained without sufficient scientific evidence', where 'sufficiency' is a 'relational concept between two elements: the scientific evidence and the measure at issue' (WTO Appellate Body Report on *Japan – Apples* (Article 21.5 – US) (DS245)). By using the term 'scientific evidence', Article 2.2 excludes in essence not only insufficiently substantiated information, but also such matters as non-demonstrated hypotheses.

[74] Article 5.1 of the SPS Agreement requires that there be a 'rational relationship' between the measure at issue and the risk assessment (WTO Appellate Body Report on *EC – Hormones* (DS26, DS48). The obligation to conduct risk assessment is not satisfied merely by a general discussion of the disease sought to be avoided by the imposition of the SPS measure; rather an evaluation of the risk must connect the possibility of adverse effects with an antecedent or cause. The definition of 'risk assessment' requires that the evaluation of the entry, establishment or spread of a disease be conducted according to the SPS measures which might be applied, not merely measures which are being currently applied (WTO Appellate Body Report on *Japan – Apples* (DS245)).

[75] Jordan, paragraph 151.      [76] Ukraine, paragraph 326.

[77] Croatia, Report of the Working Party on the accession of Croatia to the WTO (see WTO document WT/ACC/HRV/59 of 29 June 2000), paragraph 135; Saudi Arabia, paragraph 224.

requirements that exist on the date of WTO accession, based on the international standards of Codex Alimentarius, IPPC, FAO and OIE,[78] and base their future SPS measures on international standards in accordance with the SPS Agreement.[79] Article XII members with larger economies additionally committed to the development and application of international standards on SPS measures through membership and active participation in the above-mentioned organisations,[80] or specifically ensured that their SPS measures would not be maintained without sufficient scientific evidence.[81] The issue of whether the available scientific evidence is sufficient would then be inseparable from the consideration of the level of SPS protection pursued by the WTO member.[82]

In cases where the obligation to harmonise the SPS standards could not be taken from the date of WTO accession, acceding governments committed to an action plan requirement to harmonise its national standards with international ones, and report to the WTO annually on implementation progress until the SPS standards are in conformity with WTO rules.[83]

Accession-specific obligations on the appropriate level of SPS protection with regard to precautionary measures have varied. For instance, one member accepted a specific obligation to base its SPS measures on scientific principles and, where they exist, on international standards, guidelines and recommendations. Pursuant to Article 2.2 of the SPS Agreement, it accepted the obligation to maintain SPS measures without sufficient scientific evidence, except as provided for in Articles 5.7, 5.8 of the SPS Agreement (provisional adoption of SPS measures in cases where relevant scientific evidence is insufficient, pending review, within a reasonable time of additional information).[84] A specific commitment was undertaken by this member in respect of compliance with international standards in the context of subjecting some categories of goods to veterinary control, and the application of the veterinary measures applied to each category of such goods consistently with international standards or based on science and risk assessment.[85]

---

[78] Tonga, paragraph 126; Vanuatu, paragraph 100.
[79] Tajikistan, paragraph 230; Russia, paragraph 1009. Plus, Russia specifically confirmed that it would implement the Guidelines of Codex Alimentarius.
[80] Russia, paragraph 847.        [81] China, paragraph 199.
[82] WTO Appellate Body Report on *EC – Hormones II* (see WTO document WT/DS/320/AB/R, paragraph 686).
[83] Kyrgyz Republic, paragraph 100.        [84] Russia, paragraphs 1009, 1062.
[85] Russia, paragraph 1011.

Before 2003, three Article XII members had to commit specifically, in respect of notification of diseases other than those listed in former OIE Classes A and B,[86] that if a decision was taken to require such a notification, any such decision must be taken in conformity with the SPS Agreement.[87] One member committed to remove from its legislation the reference to the establishment of a national animal identification system as a consideration for risk assessment.[88]

One of the recent challenging SPS question-and-answer dialogues in accession working party reports relates to the requirements for the MRLs on antibiotics (tetracycline, etc.) and growth-promoting hormones. This question is also being extensively discussed in ongoing accession negotiations, including two WTO accessions negotiations of post-Soviet countries.[89]

So far, one member has committed to generally apply minimum/maximum residue limits based on standards set by the Codex Alimentarius, and not adopt or maintain MRLs in excess of these standards without a risk assessment.[90] The commitment of another member refers to the revision of the MRLs of nitrates in accordance with international standards, the application of MRLs on a number of pesticides[91] corresponding to international standards in conformity with the SPS Agreement and establishing these MRLs in the legislation. Both members committed to provide to interested WTO members scientific evidence and a risk assessment, on their request.[92]

## Equivalence

The SPS Agreement recognises varied ways of ensuring life and health protection in WTO members. Article 4.1 of the SPS Agreement requires

---

[86] Resolutions adopted by the International Committee of the OIE during its 72nd General Session (23–28 May 2004) instructed the OIE to establish a single OIE list of notifiable terrestrial and aquatic animal diseases to replace the former Lists A and B. OIE-listed diseases, infections and infestations in force in 2014 are available at www.oie.int/en/animal-health-in-the-world/oie-listed-diseases-2014/.

[87] Panama, paragraph 51; Kyrgyz Republic, paragraph 103; former Yugoslav Republic of Macedonia, paragraph 153.

[88] Ukraine, paragraph 318.      [89] Ukraine, paragraph 320; Russia, paragraph 844.

[90] Ukraine, paragraph 320.

[91] Russia, paragraph 981: chlorothalonil, clofentezine, cyprodinil, kresoxim-methyl, iprodione, propamocarb, pirimicarb, thiabendazole, carbendazim, famoxadone, copper compounds, and lambda cyhalothrin.

[92] Ukraine, paragraph 320; Russia, paragraph 984.

that WTO members should accept the SPS measures of other members as equivalent, even if these measures differ from their own, when the same level of protection is achieved. The acceptable level of protection should be similar for comparable risks. Importing WTO members should be provided reasonable access for inspection, testing and other relevant procedures, upon request.

Two Article XII members have undertaken specific commitments in this respect. One member specifically committed that it would ensure compliance with Article 4 of the SPS Agreement. In addition, it confirmed that its procedures for recognition and determination of equivalence would be based on relevant international standards,[93] and that its resident inspectors would be provided information and training on the application of the principle of equivalence.[94]

Another member committed that it would not require additional certification or testing or sanitary registration for products which had been certified as safe for human use and consumption by the officially appointed competent authorities of exporting members as notified to IPPC, OIE and Codex Alimentarius, and having been recognised by this member in accordance with the principles of the SPS Agreement.[95]

## Food safety

Nine Article XII members have explicitly undertaken specific commitments on the elimination of SPS barriers when ensuring food safety. Some of these commitments are interrelated to the issue of harmonisation with international food safety standards and equivalence. For example, three members committed to not requiring additional certification or sanitary registration for products which had been certified as safe for human use and consumption by recognised foreign and international

---

[93] Namely, the Decision of the SPS Committee of the WTO (G/SPS/19/Rev. 2), Guidelines on the Judgement of Equivalence of Sanitary Measures Associated with Food Inspection and Certification Systems of Codex Alimentarius (CAC/GL 53–2003), Codex Guidelines for the Development of Equivalence Agreements Regarding Food Import and Export Inspection and Certification Systems (CAC/GL 34–1999); Chapter 5.3 of the OIE Terrestrial Animal Health Code 'OIE Procedures relevant to the Agreement on the Application of Sanitary and Phytosanitary Measures of the World Trade Organization', and ISPM 24 'Guidelines for the Determination and Recognition of Equivalence of Phytosanitary Measures' (Russia, paragraph 1031).

[94] Russia, paragraph 932.     [95] Ukraine, paragraph 327.

bodies.[96] Another member committed that its legal framework on food safety would comply with the SPS Agreement.[97]

A specific issue which has arisen in this area concerns expiry dates and shelf-life measures. One member committed to base any entry restrictions based on shelf-life measures applied to raw food materials and food additives on scientific principles and relevant international standards, and to accept voluntary manufacturer-determined best-if-used-by dates.[98] Mandatory WTO-inconsistent shelf-life standards for 'shelf-stable foods' may be committed to elimination. For example, two members committed to establish regulations and procedures in line with international norms for 'highly perishable refrigerated' food products and to gradually replace remaining shelf-life requirements on these products with a scientific regulatory framework within the transition period.[99]

Additionally, one member undertook a transparency commitment in respect of draft food standards, which should be available at the officially designated website.[100] Another member committed that imported food products would be subject to testing and certification only by the sanitary or veterinary service, as appropriate.[101]

### Regime for trade in products subject to veterinary control

The majority of accession commitments related to the regime for trade in goods subject to veterinary control emerged from the accession protocol of one member.[102] For the WTO accession of this member, the establishment of a WTO-consistent SPS regulatory framework in the area of veterinary control was one of the most critical issues of the accession negotiations. To establish the framework, in addition to the accession obligations reflecting the basic requirements of the SPS Agreement, the member undertook more itemised commitments, based on Article 8 and Annex C to the SPS Agreement (control, inspection and approval

---

[96] Bulgaria, paragraph 64; Kyrgyz Republic, paragraph 103; former Yugoslav Republic of Macedonia, paragraph 153.

[97] Lao PDR, Report of the Working Party on the accession of Lao PDR to the WTO (see WTO document WT/ACC/LAO/45 of 1 October 2012), paragraph 149.

[98] Viet Nam, Report of the Working Party on the accession of Viet Nam to the WTO (see WT/ACC/VNM/48 of 27 October 2006), paragraph 316.

[99] Jordan, paragraph 145; Oman, Report of the Working Party on the accession of Oman to the WTO (see WTO document WT/ACC/OMN/26 of 28 September 2000), paragraph 103.

[100] Saudi Arabia, paragraph 215.     [101] Ukraine, paragraph 313.

[102] Russia, paragraphs 870, 875, 876, 880, 885, 890, 893, 895, 901, 904, 908, 923, 926, 927, 928, 932, 935 and 936.

procedures), some of which were 'WTO-plus'.[103] The bloc of commitments contains specific obligations in respect of import permits, transit, veterinary certificates, establishment approval and inspections. The obligations accepted by Russia in these areas serves as a good example of the contribution made by the accession commitments to the detailed regulation of specific categories of SPS measures within the WTO framework. Some commitments similar to those described below, for example those in respect of inspections, also emerge in Accession Packages of other Article XII members.[104]

With respect to import permits, where general commitments on compliance of these measures with the WTO Agreement has been undertaken,[105] the member also additionally committed that its procedures for considering applications for those permits would comply with OIE rules[106] and that import permits would not be refused based on minor documentation errors not altering the data contained in the applications. The administrative procedure for the revocation of the permit can only be initiated based on the discovery of systematic violations by the importer of the regulated cargo of administrative or criminal law and legislation in the field of veterinary medicine.[107] The member specifically stated that the reasons for suspension, cancellation or refusal of an import permit would be consistent with the SPS Agreement and international standards.

Additionally, information requirements for the purposes of applying for an import permit were to be limited to those necessary for approval and control procedures, and any requirements for control, inspection and approval of individual specimens of a product should be limited to what is reasonable and necessary, as provided for in Annex C to the SPS Agreement on control, inspections and approval procedures. If an import permit application was denied, the applicant should be informed of the reasons for the rejection within a period stipulated in the commitment

---

[103] To a large extent, some of the 'additional' SPS commitments of Russia were necessary in the light of the creation of the Customs Union between Russia, Belarus and Kazakhstan.

[104] For example, Vanuatu undertook a general commitment in respect of development and application of its control, inspection and approval procedures in conformity with the SPS Agreement (Vanuatu, paragraph 100).

[105] Russia, paragraph 876.

[106] That is, permits should not be refused on grounds not recognised by the OIE for the animal diseases concerned, and the principle of applying an SPS measure only to the extent necessary to protect human or animal life and health (Russia, paragraph 870).

[107] The violation could include the presentation of forged veterinary documents or the discovery of inconsistency between the presented documents and the regulated cargo (Russia, paragraph 875).

paragraph.[108] The member committed to define clearly the procedure under which an applicant for an import permit could appeal against the suspension, cancellation or refusal of an application, and notify it to the public. A written response should be provided to an applicant explaining the reasons for the final decision, and any further action required to obtain a permit.[109]

In respect of transit, the member committed that goods in transit would not be subject to veterinary requirements.[110] Legislative provisions, administrative regulations and other measures relating to the transit of goods subject to veterinary control would be applied in compliance with the OIE Code and the SPS Agreement.[111]

One of the central issues which was discussed during the SPS negotiations on the accession of Russia to the WTO concerned veterinary requirements (in particular, veterinary certificates). Russia was required to undertake a number of commitments to create and ensure a WTO-consistent mechanism and standards. Specifically, the negotiating purpose of members was to address the questions relating to and eliminate instances of overlapping, contradictory and uncertain jurisdiction arising from the creation and evolution of the Customs Union at the same time as the accession negotiations were being advanced to conclusion. Russia had to undertake obligations to eliminate duplicative requirements under its national competence, which in cases were at odds, overlapped or duplicated the supranational bodies of the Customs Union to which it was a party. Technically, the issues revolved, for example, around precise requirements for common versus bilateral veterinary certificates, the role of the individual Customs Union member versus the role of the Eurasian Economic Commission in negotiating veterinary certificates, the problem of different conditions in veterinary certificates of different Customs Union members, and the vital question of harmonising the plethora of veterinary measures with international standards. These questions were never fully resolved. It remained work in progress in subsequent Customs Union accessions.[112] However, some obligations were accepted by Russia

---

[108] Five days of the decision (Russia, paragraph 1051).    [109] Russia, paragraph 876.

[110] Russia, paragraph 885. The commitment relates to the territory of the Customs Union of Russia, Belarus and Kazakhstan and the relevant legislation of that Customs Union.

[111] Russia, paragraph 885. The commitment relates to the territory of Russia and the relevant legislation of the Customs Union.

[112] This exercise at clarifying duplicated conflicting and uncertain jurisdiction continued with the accession negotiations of Kazakhstan, still in progress at the writing of this chapter.

in line with the negotiating purpose of members to ensure that WTO-minus situations did not emerge. For example, on the general regulatory framework, the member confirmed that veterinary certificates would only be required for non-processed animal products, whereas for goods that had undergone treatment only a declaration of conformity or state registration certificate would be required.[113]

The member confirmed the amendments to the veterinary requirements and the certificate forms, making them WTO-consistent, to enter into force no later than the date of the WTO accession. Veterinary certificates should not require the certification of provisions that were not justified based on applicable mandatory requirements and surveillance.[114]

A separate specific issue related to bovine spongiform encephalopathy (BSE) requirements set out in bilateral certificates with other WTO members, existing at the time of the negotiations. They foresaw the testing of animals for BSE and required the absence of a genetic link with animals affected by BSE, thus not conforming to the OIE standards. The member specifically committed that these bilateral certificates[115] should conform to OIE standards.

The member stated its intention to work with interested WTO members to negotiate veterinary certificates.[116] Some periods of validity of existing bilateral certificates were prescribed.[117] Such certificates had to ensure the appropriate level of protection.[118]

---

[113] Russia, paragraph 826.

[114] Carried out within the territory of Russia or the Customs Union (Russia, paragraph 895).

[115] As well as the Customs Union common certificates (Russia, paragraph 901).

[116] Russia, paragraph 893: 'If an exporting country made a substantiated request prior to 1 January 2013 to negotiate such a veterinary export certificate'. The commitment related to the veterinary certificates that included requirements that differed from the Customs Union common form and specific Customs Union common requirements.

[117] Russia, paragraph 893: 'Bilateral veterinary export certificates initialled by one of the Customs Union Parties before 1 July 2010, as well as any subsequent amendments to such certificates agreed with the authorised body of such Customs Union Party, would remain valid for exports from the relevant country into the customs territory of the Customs Union until an export certificate was agreed with a Customs Union Party based on the agreed positions of the other Customs Union Parties. Bilateral veterinary export certificates initialled by one of the Customs Union Parties between 1 July 2010 and 1 December 2010 would remain valid for import and circulation of relevant goods, only in the territory of the Customs Union Party that initialled the certificate, until a bilateral veterinary export certificate was agreed with a Customs Union Party based on the agreed positions of the other Customs Union Parties.'

[118] Russia, paragraph 893. The commitment relates to the level of protection as determined by the Customs Union parties.

To ensure the right of the importer to the WTO-consistent 'establishment approval procedure' (the requirements for establishments to be approved for exports), the member confirmed that categories of goods would be added to the list of goods subject to veterinary control only if this was in compliance with the SPS Agreement. An establishment could be removed from the respective registry only at the request of the establishment itself or at the request of the competent authority of the third country. The member[119] could, in line with international standards or based on risk assessment, temporarily suspend imports from the establishment and/or subject imports from that establishment to intensified monitoring.

In emergency situations, understood in the sense provided for in the OIE, a temporary suspension of imports from an establishment could be applied only upon the request of the establishment or the competent authority of the third country, or based on repeated noncompliances with the SPS requirements; and based on the results of on-site inspection and not before it had given the exporting country the opportunity to propose corrective measures, except in case of serious risks of animal or human health. A preliminary report should be sent to the competent authority of the exporting country for comments before the report was finalised. Minor errors were not valid grounds for suspending imports from an establishment. In emergency situations, the decisions and procedures for the suspension of establishments should be in accordance with the SPS Agreement.[120]

At the same time, the member mentioned so-called 'extraordinary cases', where a decision could be taken to suspend a group of establishments or all establishments of a third country as a result of the detection of a serious systemic failure of the official system of control, as specified in the new regulation. However, in this case, the technical information and scientific justification of the detected risk should be provided to the competent authority of the third country. The third country should be requested to take corrective measures, within a specified timeframe for their adoption. Any suspension would not be implemented before the expiry of the specified timeframe. Notably, the member explicitly committed that such 'extraordinary' suspensions would conform to the necessity and proportionality requirements of the SPS Agreement ('be proportionate to the risk to human health or life, and not more restrictive to trade than necessary').[121]

---

[119] The Customs Union. Russia, paragraph 923.    [120] Russia, paragraph 923.
[121] Russia, paragraph 928.

In the area of inspections, the member committed that its resident inspectors would operate consistently with its obligations under the SPS Agreement and relevant national legislation and bilateral agreements. Together with a general non-discrimination commitment, the member committed to adhere to the requirements to control, inspection and approval procedures established in Annex C to the SPS Agreement and transparency requirements of the GATT Article X, Article 7 and Annex B to the SPS Agreement.[122] Additionally, with regard to its legislation on inspections, the member committed that its inspection guidelines would reflect the equivalence and harmonisation principles of the SPS Agreement, and provide instructions to inspectors to verify the compliance of establishments with relevant Codex Alimentarius codes of practices[123] and other relevant international standards. A new non-discriminatory regulation with regard to requirements for onsite inspections would be issued.[124]

Overall, given the importance of potential trade barriers, the specific commitments on inspections are not uncommon for Article XII members. In keeping with this pattern, one member undertook a commitment in respect of the inspection procedure for seeds.[125] Another member agreed to eliminate unnecessary inspections of imported meat and meat from imported animals.[126]

### Importation of products subject to quarantine control

Similarly, the separate set of commitments on phytosanitary measures first appeared in the accession protocol of the Russian Federation, as an Article XII member.[127] Specifically, to enhance the obligation to recognise the concept of pest-free areas and areas of low pest prevalence according to Article 6.2 of the SPS Agreement, the member committed

---

[122] Russia, paragraph 936.
[123] Russia, paragraph 932: 'Such as CAC/RCP 1–1969, recommended international code of practice general principles of food hygiene, the CAC/RCP 58–2005 code of hygienic practice for meat, the CAC/RCP 57–2004 code of hygienic practice for milk and milk products, the CAC/RCP 52–2003 code of practice for fish and fishery products'.
[124] Russia, paragraph 935.
[125] Saudi Arabia, paragraph 218: 'The seeds were first subject to a visual examination to check for impurities and to ensure that the phytosanitary information in the import documents was correct. Thereafter, samples of the seeds were sent to laboratories to check for aflatoxins.'
[126] Jordan, paragraph 149.    [127] Russia, paragraphs 944, 950, 952 and 955.

to carry out the recognition of pest-free areas in accordance with relevant International Standards for Phytosanitary Measures (ISPMs) on the basis of a request from the national plant protection organisation of the exporting country, and agreed to allow imports of plants with soil, based on such recognition.

One of the concerns expressed in this accession, related to the compliance of the member's routine nursery inspection requirements with the IPPC standards. The IPPC lists specific cases in which such inspections could be allowed.[128] The member committed to a detailed procedure, which included non-performance of such inspections on a regular basis and allowance of plants export for planting based on guarantees provided by the NPPO of the exporting country of a pest-free area or pest-free places of production (as set out in international standards). Inspections, carried out jointly, could only take place in cases of repeated non-compliances.[129]

The member also detailed the procedure in respect of the application of phytosanitary measures resulting in a higher level of protection than the level that would be achieved by measures harmonised with international standards, having committed to bilaterally providing information on the relevant risk assessment and the reasons for such measures, upon request.[130]

### Preferential trade agreements: customs union complications

The GATT Article XXIV provides scope for preferential trade agreements. WTO members recognise the desirability of increasing freedom of trade by closer trade integration, as reflected in the GATT Article XXIV:4, pursuant to specified conditions. The highest grade of such integration, a customs union, means the substitution for two or more customs territories by a single customs territory. The GATT Article XXIV:8(a) requires that: (i) 'duties and other restrictive regulations of commerce . . . shall be eliminated with respect to "substantially all trade" between the Customs Union's members (or at least with respect to substantially all trade in products originating in them)'; and (ii) 'substantially the same duties and other regulations of commerce shall be applied by each of the members of the union to the trade of third countries'.

---

[128] 'For example, when new trade was being established or when a problem existed' (Russia, paragraph 950).

[129] Russia, paragraph 950.    [130] Russia, paragraph 952.

Article XII of the WTO Agreement does not provide for a customs union membership of the WTO. Only states and separate customs territories having full autonomy in the conduct of their external commercial relations and of the other matters provided for in the WTO Agreement and the multilateral trade agreements can accede to the WTO. Consequently, non-WTO members that are also customs union members conduct WTO accession negotiations separately rather than collectively.

Similar to any international agreement, the creation of a customs union may take a lengthy period of time,[131] required both for taking decisions at the political level and the creation of the legal framework of the customs union.[132] A situation where all or some members of a customs union are not WTO members creates a significant challenge in the context of WTO accession negotiations, particularly in the area of non-tariff regulation, where a customs union may, simultaneously with the WTO accession negotiations of its members, undergo a process of transfer of jurisdiction in the respective field of regulation from the national level of the union's members to the 'supranational' level of the customs union.

To resolve this, acceding governments are required to undertake commitments to reconcile and exclude conflicts, overlapping and duplication with respect to the development and application of their national legislation and the legislative framework of the customs union to which they are party. Specifically in respect of SPS measures, so far, one member (Russia) had to undertake a wide range of commitments relating to its SPS regime and that of the Customs Union.[133] For example, in its transparency commitment with respect to the import permit regime applicable to goods subject to veterinary and quarantine control, it committed that the regime would be operated both under the decisions

---

[131] Thus, the process that has led to what is now the European Union has taken over sixty years (since the Treaty Establishing the European Coal and Steel Community in 1952).

[132] In the context of WTO accessions, the Customs Union of Russia, Belarus and Kazakhstan serves as a good example. The Customs Union was declared in June 2009 and came into force in January 2010, during the period when all the three Customs Union members were still in process of negotiating the terms and conditions of their WTO membership and also, at the same time, negotiating the specific terms binding them as members of the Customs Union. These two parallel negotiations posed a seriously complicating factor.

[133] Russia, paragraphs 826, 875, 876, 880, 885, 893, 895, 901, 904, 923, 926, 928, 932, 935, 936, 952, 955, 981, 984, 1009, 1011 and 1060.

of the Customs Union, and the national law of the member, and all legislative acts, both national and those of the Customs Union, would be published and available to the public.[134] This reconciliation to ensure coherence and WTO-consistency is also under way on the WTO accession negotiations of Kazakhstan.

In part, the WTO-plus commitments accepted by Russia, for example on its SPS obligations, were due in part to the replacement of two and/or more customs territories by the single customs territory of the Customs Union/EAEU[135] and to ensure that non-discriminatory treatment would override the duplication, overlap and conflict emerging from several customs territories. For example, to ensure national treatment Russia accepted a specific obligation in its accession protocol not to establish additional SPS requirements for imported products that exceeded the requirements established for domestic products and products originating from the Customs Union.[136]

The Accession Protocols of Saudi Arabia and Oman, two Article XII members, provide a similar example.[137] In the accession treaty dialogue of these two Article XII members, because concern was expressed about the potential for negative trade effects arising from replacement and substitution of customs territories, specific obligations were accepted not to restrict imports in one member of the Customs Union so as to ensure the free movement of goods between the members of the Customs Union. These members had to accept SPS-specific obligations on risk assessment and determination of the appropriate level of SPS protection, compliant with Article 5 of the SPS Agreement, which would ensure the minimisation of negative trade effects between members of the Customs Union and/or third parties.

The SPS-specific obligations of Russia, Saudi Arabia and Oman provide a template and have contributed to clarifying and making more precise the legal basis of how the rules-based multilateral trading system should address customs union-related SPS negotiations in ongoing

---

[134] Russia, paragraph 876.

[135] As part of the process of Eurasian economic integration, the members of the Customs Union of Belarus, Kazakhstan and Russia, concluded and signed the Treaty on the Eurasian Economic Union (EAEU) on 29 May 2014. The EAEU Treaty will come into effect on 1 January 2015.

[136] Russia, paragraph 955.

[137] Saudi Arabia and Oman, together with Bahrain, Kuwait, Qatar and the United Arab Emirates, are members of the Gulf Cooperation Council, which is in the process of forming a customs union.

accession negotiations and in any SPS-related disputes that may arise. The SPS-specific commitments in the protocols of these members go beyond the broad and general provisions in the SPS Agreement.

## Specific commitments of LDCs

The WTO Agreement, ministerial decisions and other relevant WTO legal instruments set out the provisions for special and differential treatment, applicable to LDCs. The guidelines on the accession of LDCs also set out approaches, benchmarks and measures to 'facilitate' the accession negotiations of acceding LDCs.[138]

There are transitional periods/arrangements foreseen under specific WTO agreements. These are designed to enable acceding LDCs to effectively implement WTO rules and their accession-specific commitments and obligations. As designed, these transitional periods are granted in accession negotiations taking, if requested and accompanied by specific implementation action plans. Special and differential treatment arrangements, such as transition periods, take account of individual development, financial and trade needs.[139] The implementation of the action plans will be supported by technical assistance and capacity-building measures for the acceding LDCs. Upon the request of an acceding LDC, WTO members may coordinate efforts to guide that LDC through the implementation process.[140]

Six of the seven LDC Article XII members have had recourse to the provision in the guidelines for a transitional period in their implementation of the SPS Agreement.[141] For those that committed to implementing the SPS Agreement progressively, action plans were negotiated and agreed, specifying details of steps to be taken in order to achieve full implementation of the SPS Agreement. Accession negotiations have repeatedly made it clear that the LDCs' accession guidelines are designed to 'facilitate' the accession negotiations of LDCs, but not to modify the WTO rules.

In order for an LDC government to have recourse to the special and differential treatment of a transition period, there should be 'the appropriate level of SPS protection allowing scope for the phased introduction

---

[138] Guidelines for Accession of Least-Developed Countries (see WTO document WT/L/508 of 20 January 2003 and its Addendum 1 of July 2012).

[139] Guidelines for Accession of Least-Developed Countries (see WTO document WT/L/508 of 20 January 2003 Addendum 1 of July 2012).

[140] Ibid.     [141] Namely, Cambodia, Nepal, Cabo Verde, Samoa, Lao PDR, Yemen.

of new SPS measures', as required by Article 10.2 of the SPS Agreement. Some LDC Article XII members additionally committed to ensuring that changes in their legislation and implementation practice during the transition period would not result in a lesser degree of consistency with the SPS Agreement than existed on the date of accession to the WTO,[142] and to give priority to notifications and the establishment of a functioning enquiry point. Requests for a transition period were combined with requests for technical assistance,[143] including that under Article 9 of the SPS Agreement.

Training, outreach and raising awareness of WTO rules also remain important in accession negotiations of LDCs. Tonga, for instance, explicitly committed to provide relevant government officials with training to ensure that, from the date of WTO accession, they were fully knowledgeable with the requirements of the SPS Agreement.[144]

The length of agreed transition periods for the implementation of aspects of WTO-consistent SPS regulation tended to be no longer than three years from the date of accession for full implementation of the SPS Agreement. Transition periods are not linked to the date of WTO accession, rather to the time required to complete the process of domestic reforms (see Table 39.1).

Transition periods are not only available to LDCs. Some non-LDC Article XII members have also negotiated transition periods in respect of some SPS commitments. For example, Jordan accepted a specific obligation that all its remaining prohibitions on the use of powdered milk by industrial users of dairy products would be abolished 'as soon as legislatively possible – upon accession, and in any event no later than within 12 months from the date of accession';[145] Ukraine undertook a commitment to amend its legislation on veterinary medicines to remove the requirements to establish a national animal ID system as a consideration for determining risk, within six months after the date of WTO accession; Seychelles undertook to ensure the implementation of the SPS Agreement by December 2015.[146]

SPS-specific obligations in accession negotiations have been designed to reconfirm and ensure certainty, transparency and predictability in the

---

[142] Cambodia, paragraph 142; Nepal, paragraph 107; Samoa, paragraph 162; Cabo Verde, paragraph 177; Yemen, paragraph 178.

[143] Cabo Verde, paragraph 177; Cambodia, paragraph 142; Nepal, paragraph 107.

[144] Tonga, paragraph 126.      [145] Jordan, paragraph 149.

[146] Ukraine, paragraph 318; Seychelles, paragraph 297.

Table 39.1 *Length of transition periods for implementation of SPS commitments for six Article XII members – LDCs*

| | LDC Article XII member | Membership date | Deadline for the transition period | Length of the transition period (days) |
|---|---|---|---|---|
| 1. | Nepal | 23 April 2004 | 1 January 2007 | 983 |
| 2. | Cambodia | 13 October 2004 | 1 January 2008 | 1,175 |
| 3. | Cabo Verde | 23 July 2008 | 1 January 2010 | 527 |
| 4. | Samoa | 10 May 2012 | 1 January 2012 | 0 |
| 5. | Lao PDR | 2 February 2013 | 1 January 2015 | 699 |
| 6. | Yemen | 26 June 2014 | 31 December 2016 | 555 |

rules-based multilateral trading system. This outcome has been pursued and attained, including through WTO-plus commitments. The assessment of risk and the determination of the appropriate levels of SPS protection have become central and paramount at a stage of protection where behind-the-border barriers to trade are more insidious, protean and in far greater use than tariff protection at the border. In this area, the results from accessions have safeguarded, strengthened and advanced the rules-based multilateral trading system.

The concerns, made evident in the question-and-answer methodology for accession treaty making, suggest that members consciously pursue WTO-plus commitments to address complex and unique questions thrown up by customs unions and acceding governments with rudimentary to non-existent systems in the areas of notification, transparency and legislation and the overriding consideration of trade opening as a source of growth for both regions and countries.

In accession plurilateral negotiating meetings, SPS considerations are the intersection point that reflect a range of other critical trade negotiations, such as market access, regional trade agreements (RTAs) and trading rights, etc. The pattern suggests that future SPS plurilateral meetings will be oriented towards more WTO-plus requirements and a greater focus on the technical issues (associated with the legislative framework; the development of technical regulations and mandatory requirements on SPS; trade in goods subject to veterinary control; establishment of approval, register and inspections; import permits; transit permits; trade in goods subject to phytosanitary control; protection of human health; compliance of the SPS regime with specific provisions of the WTO SPS

Agreement; transparency, notification and enquiry point obligations; and the principles of proportionality, necessity and reasonableness).

The deposited Accession Protocols provide the *acquis* and point to the direction of how the rules-based multilateral trading system will deal with these issues in the present and the future, including either in future negotiations or in WTO dispute settlement. Acceding governments are well advised to draw on the lessons from the completed accessions. In sum, the evidence shows that WTO rules, including on SPS, are non-negotiable and should be strengthened in the years to come, using the medium of WTO accession negotiations.

Annex 39.1 *Accessions negotiated pursuant to Article XII – SPS commitments*

| Government | Membership date | Working Party Report | SPS commitment paragraphs |
|---|---|---|---|
| 1 Ecuador | 21 January 1996 | WT/L/77 & Corr. 1 | 51 |
| 2 Bulgaria | 01 December 1996 | WT/ACC/BGR/5 & Corr. 1 | 64 |
| 3 Mongolia | 29 January 1997 | WT/ACC/MNG/9 & Corr. 1 | 20 |
| 4 Panama | 06 September 1997 | WT/ACC/PAN/19 & Corr. 1 | 51 |
| 5 Kyrgyz Republic | 20 December 1998 | WT/ACC/KGZ/26 & Corr. 1 | 100; 103 |
| 6 Latvia | 10 February 1999 | WT/ACC/LVA/32 | 88 |
| 7 Estonia | 13 November 1999 | WT/ACC/EST/28 | 98 |
| 8 Jordan | 11 April 2000 | WT/ACC/JOR/33 & Corr. 1 | 145; 149; 151 |
| 9 Georgia | 14 June 2000 | WT/ACC/GEO/31 | 107 |
| 10 Albania | 08 September 2000 | WT/ACC/ALB/51 & Corr. 1 | 108 |
| 11 Oman | 09 November 2000 | WT/ACC/OMN/26 | 103; 105 |
| 12 Croatia | 30 November 2000 | WT/ACC/HRV/59 | 135 |
| 13 Lithuania | 31 May 2001 | WT/ACC/LTU/52 | 122 |
| 14 Moldova | 26 July 2001 | WT/ACC/MOL/37 & Corr. 1–4 | 135 |
| 15 China | 11 December 2001 | WT/ACC/CHN/49 & Corr. 1 WT/MIN(01)/3 | 199; 200 |
| 16 Chinese Taipei | 01 January 2002 | WT/ACC/TPKM/18 WT/MIN(01)/4 | 135; 137 |
| 17 Armenia, Republic of | 05 February 2003 | WT/ACC/ARM/23 & Corr. 1 | 143 |

Annex 39.1 (*cont.*)

| Government | Membership date | Working Party Report | SPS commitment paragraphs |
|---|---|---|---|
| 18 Former Yugoslav Republic of Macedonia | 04 April 2003 | WT/ACC/807/27 | 153 |
| 19 Cambodia | 23 April 2004 | WT/ACC/KHM/21 | 142 |
| 20 Nepal | 13 October 2004 | WT/ACC/NPL/16 | 107 |
| 21 Saudi Arabia, Kingdom of | 11 December 2005 | WT/ACC/SAU/61 | 208; 210; 212; 215; 216; 218; 222; 223; 224 |
| 22 Viet Nam | 11 January 2007 | WT/ACC/VNM/48 | 315; 316; 328 |
| 23 Tonga | 27 July 2007 | WT/ACC/TON/17 WT/MIN(05)/4 | 126 |
| 24 Ukraine | 16 May 2008 | WT/ACC/UKR/152 | 313; 318; 320; 326; 327 |
| 25 Cabo Verde | 23 July 2008 | WT/ACC/CPV/30 | 177 |
| 26 Montenegro | 29 April 2012 | WT/ACC/CGR/38 WT/MIN(11)/7 | 168 |
| 27 Samoa | 10 May 2012 | WT/ACC/SAM/30 WT/MIN(11)/1 | 162 |
| 28 Russian Federation | 22 August 2012 | WT/ACC/RUS/70 WT/MIN(11)/2 | 826; 844; 847; 870; 875; 876; 880; 885; 890; 893; 895; 901; 904; 908; 923; 926; 927; 928; 932; 935; 936; 944; 950; 952; 955; 981; 984; 989; 1009; 1011; 1030; 1031; 1033; 1035; 1051; 1055; 1060; 1062 |
| 29 Vanuatu | 24 August 2012 | WT/ACC/VUT/17 | 100 |
| 30 Lao People's Democratic Republic | 02 February 2013 | WT/ACC/LAO/45 | 149 |
| 31 Tajikistan | 02 March 2013 | WT/ACC/TJK/30 | 230; 231 |
| 32 Yemen | 26 June 2014 | WT/ACC/YEM/42 | 178; 180 |

## Acknowledgements

The authors acknowledge the contributions to this chapter, through data gathering and checks, by Chen Itui, Researcher on Accessions in the Accessions Division in 2013.

# 40

# Strengthening transparency in the multilateral trading system: the contribution of the WTO accession process

PETRA BESLAĆ

ABSTRACT

*What specific obligations on transparency and notifications have been negotiated as part of the terms of accession to the WTO since 1995? What patterns and trends have emerged with regard to transparency and notification requirements in WTO accessions over time? What is the implementation behaviour on notification requirements of the states or separate customs territories that have negotiated their terms of accession, pursuant to Article XII of the Marrakesh Agreement Establishing the World Trade Organization and joined the WTO in the period 1995 to 2013? How does the compliance of Article XII members on notification requirements under the WTO Agreements compare to the compliance behaviour of original members? By reviewing the empirical data available from more than thirty completed WTO accessions since 1995, representing about one-fifth of the WTO membership, this chapter examines each of these questions, assessing the extent to which the negotiated accession commitments on transparency have affected the existing transparency and notification obligations under the WTO Agreements. The results of this review suggest that the specific transparency and notification obligations resulting from accession negotiations have safeguarded and reinforced existing transparency requirements embedded across all WTO Agreements. They have also resulted in positive implementation behaviour, with regard to notification requirements, by WTO members that joined the WTO between 1995 and 2013, and have thus improved the*

The analyses in the chapters in this book were finalised at the end of December 2014. Since then the Republic of Seychelles acceded to the World Trade Organization (WTO) on 26 April 2015. This expanded total WTO membership from 160 to 161. Please see the editors' note.

*compliance rate of the overall WTO membership. The number and scope of specific transparency commitments negotiated in WTO accessions underscores the importance that the WTO membership attaches to transparency, one of its founding principles.*

Transparency is a founding principle and central pillar of the multilateral trading system. Transparency obligations are embedded throughout all WTO agreements.[1] Their main role is to ensure that the trading environment remains predictable for all stakeholders in the multilateral system. They also provide an invaluable safety net against the build-up of protectionist pressures. The transparency principle is based on two fundamental requirements – the publication of relevant information on trade, and the timely notification of new trade-related measures and legislation.

To date, more than thirty states or separate customs territories – about one-fifth of the WTO current membership – have acceded to the WTO pursuant to Article XII of the Marrakesh Agreement Establishing the World Trade Organization 1994 (WTO Agreement). Specific accession commitments on notification and publication have systematically been included in all negotiated terms of accession of Article XII members, as contained in their WTO Accession Protocols.[2] These specific commitments have sought to reconfirm and strengthen existing obligations under the WTO Agreements. The WTO accession process has thus been used as an instrument for enhancing transparency and safeguarding the rules of the multilateral trading system.

This chapter provides an overview of the specific commitments on transparency undertaken by Article XII members, and examines their compliance with WTO notification obligations. It first outlines the established WTO requirements on transparency. Next, it identifies the intersection points between accession protocol commitments and WTO notification and publication obligations. It provides an overview of the specific transparency obligations that have been negotiated as part of

---

[1] The term 'WTO Agreements' refers to the Marrakesh Agreement Establishing the World Trade Organization 1994 (the umbrella agreement, also referred to as 'the WTO Agreement'), the multilateral trade agreements and the plurilateral trade agreements.

[2] Upon ratification of the Protocol of Accession, the specific commitments contained in the accession working party report referenced in paragraph 2 of the protocol become an integral part of the WTO Agreement, and the schedules reproduced in the annex of the protocol become the schedule of concessions and commitments annexed to the General Agreement on Tariffs and Trade (GATT) 1994 and the schedule of specific commitments annexed to the General Agreement on Trade in Services (GATS).

the WTO accession processes since 1995. Finally, it reviews and examines the empirical data for completed Article XII accessions with a view to assessing the compliance of Article XII members with notification obligations.[3]

The results of the review of the empirical data suggest that the specific transparency obligations which have been negotiated as part of the WTO accession process have strengthened existing transparency requirements under the WTO agreements, and can be linked to positive compliance by Article XII members with publication and notification requirements under the WTO agreements.

## WTO legal foundation, rules and procedures

The WTO glossary describes the principle of transparency as the degree to which trade policies and practices, and the process by which they are established, are open and predictable. It defines a WTO notification obligation as a transparency obligation, requiring WTO members to report trade measures to the relevant WTO body if the measures might have an effect on other members.[4]

Article X of the GATT 1994 lays out the key transparency provisions relating to trade in goods. It governs the publication and administration of trade regulations and stipulates two key principles: transparency in existing trade regulations; and uniform application of these regulations. The transparency requirements stipulated in GATT Article X are reaffirmed in all WTO agreements. Most publication requirements contained in the WTO agreements are also subject to notification obligations. In addition to these general obligations, detailed notification requirements are also prescribed in the individual WTO agreements dealing with a specific area of trade rules.[5]

---

[3] The second part of this chapter reviews data for thirty-three Article XII accessions, including the specific commitments negotiated as part of Yemen's WTO accession process. Yemen became the 160th WTO member on 26 June 2014. As empirical data regarding Yemen's compliance with WTO notification obligations does not exist, the third part of this chapter reviews data for thirty-one Article XII members. The research for this chapter was completed prior to the accession of Seychelles; see editors' note.

[4] See www.wto.org/english/thewto_e/glossary_e/glossary_e.htm.

[5] Article X:1 stipulates that laws, regulations, judicial decisions and administrative rulings of general application 'shall be published promptly in such a manner as to enable governments and traders to become acquainted with them'. Any agreements affecting international trade policy shall also be published. Article X:2 prescribes that measures affecting trade be published prior to their application ('enforcement'). Article X:3 stipulates that

The timely notification and publication of trade measures were recognised as key principles of the multilateral trading system in the GATT Understanding Regarding Notification, Consultation, Dispute Settlement and Surveillance of 28 November 1979:[6]

> Contracting parties ... undertake, to the maximum extent possible, to notify the Contracting parties of their adoption of trade measures affecting the operation of the General Agreement ... Contracting parties should endeavour to notify such measures in advance of implementation ... [In] cases, where prior notification has not been possible, such measures should be notified promptly *ex post facto.*

The 1994 WTO Decision on Notification Procedures builds on the 1979 Understanding and puts forward an indicative list of notifiable measures. This indicative list does not alter the WTO notification requirements found throughout WTO Agreements. The Decision contains five key elements:

- a general obligation to notify in accordance with the Understanding Regarding Notification, Consultation, Dispute Settlement and Surveillance of 28 November 1979;
- an objective to 'improve the operation of notification procedures under the WTO Agreement [and] thereby contribute to the transparency of members' trade policies and to the effectiveness of surveillance arrangements';
- a reference to the obligations under the WTO Agreement to publish and notify, 'including obligations assumed under the terms of specific protocols of accession, waivers, and other agreements entered into by members';
- establishment of a central registry of notifications (CRN)[7] for all notifications submitted by WTO members, which would be managed by the Secretariat;

---

laws, regulations, decisions and rulings be applied in a uniform, impartial and reasonable manner. Publication requirements are contained, for instance, in Article X of the GATT 1994, Article III of the GATS or Article 63.1 of the Trade-Related Aspects of Intellectual Property Rights (TRIPs) Agreement. Examples of detailed notification requirements can be found in Article V:7(a) of the GATS concerning preferential trade agreements, and Article III:5 of the GATS concerning third-party notification.

[6] See WTO document L/4907; BISD 26S/210.

[7] The CRN was established in 1995. It is a WTO database which records all regular notifications received by the WTO and descriptive information on each notification submitted.

. a review of notification obligations and procedures under the agreements in Annex 1A of the WTO Agreement to be undertaken by the Council for Trade in Goods.[8]

Most WTO agreements contain one-time notification requirements, i.e. notifications which are due only once, as well as provisions that stipulate regular or ad hoc notification obligations. The scope and content of these notifications vary from agreement to agreement. Transparency and notification provisions related to the schedules of concessions and commitments on goods, and the schedules of specific commitments on services, are found in the GATT 1994 and the GATS respectively. Changes to the schedules need to be duly notified in accordance with Article XXVIII of the GATT 1994 and Article XXI of the GATS.[9]

The WTO Secretariat has developed a *Technical Cooperation Handbook on Notification Requirements*[10] which, although partially outdated, remains relevant. Updated information on how to complete and fulfil the

---

[8] For intellectual property (IP) rights, see the Decision of the Council for TRIPs of 21 November 1995 on Procedures for Notification of, and Possible Establishment of a Common Register of, National Laws and Regulations under Article 63.2 (IP/C/2); see also notification-related IP Decisions in IP/C/3, IP/C/4 and IP/C/5. For services, see Guidelines for Notifications under the General Agreement on Trade in Services (GATS), adopted by the Council for Trade in Services on 1 March 1995 (see WTO document S/L/5) and the Decision on the Notification of the Establishment of Enquiry and Contact Points, adopted by the Council for Trade in Services on 28 May 1996 (see WTO document S/L/23). For notification requirements under the Trade Policy Review Mechanism, see Annex 3 to the Marrakesh Agreement.

[9] For further information on the different types of WTO notifications, see R. Wolfe (2013), 'Letting the sun shine in at the WTO: how transparency brings the trading system to life', Staff Working Paper ERSD-2013-03. Geneva: WTO, p. 10, Table 4. For additional information on the provision of data with respect to WTO goods schedules, see General Council Decision on The Supply of Information to the Integrated Data Base, adopted on 16 July 1997 (see WTO document WT/L/225). Relevant data on bound tariffs are available on the WTO website in the consolidated tariff schedules database, and some members' applied tariffs are available in the Integrated Data Base (IDB). Both of these databases are part of the Integrated Trade Intelligence Portal (I-TIP). For the provision of data with regard to WTO services schedules, see WT/S/L/80.

[10] This is part of the WT/TC/NOTIF series, which includes notification handbooks on the following areas of WTO rules: import licensing procedures; balance-of-payment provisions; tariffs and non-tariff measures; safeguards; state trading enterprises; trade-related investment measures; anti-dumping; agriculture; preshipment inspection; regional trade agreements (RTAs); subsidies and countervailing measures (SCM); rules of origin; sanitary and phytosanitary measures (SPS); technical barriers to trade (TBT); textiles and clothing; customs valuation; the Trade Policy Review Mechanism; TRIPs; and the GATS.

relevant WTO notification requirements can be found under each specific WTO Agreement, as well as in manuals, guidelines, notes or codes of
good practice,[11] which have been developed by members or mandated by
members and prepared by the Secretariat.

With regard to timelines, most notification requirements encourage
the prior notification of measures/regulations and some notification
requirements stipulate a strict time period by which a notification has
to be made. The 'prior publication and notification' principle ensures that
WTO members have sufficient time to familiarise themselves with new or
modified measures and legislation, prior to enforcement. However, in
most cases, the notification provisions contained in the WTO Agreement
or notification guidelines are worded as soft law and stipulate that
notifications need to be made 'promptly'.[12]

## WTO monitoring and surveillance

Monitoring, surveillance and review of the implementation of the transparency and notification obligations under WTO Agreements is a key
element of work in all WTO bodies. The WTO committees and councils
dealing with specific areas of trade rules provide a forum for the review of
new measures or amended legislation, as well as any other matters related
to transparency and notification obligations. In accordance with Annex
3 of the WTO Agreement, each WTO member also undergoes a periodic[13] peer review of its national trade policies and practices in a trade
policy review prepared by the WTO Secretariat and the member under
review.

Supplementary transparency tools have also been mandated by WTO
members, such as the trade monitoring reports and the Trade Monitoring Database.[14] The WTO Secretariat began producing periodic trade

---

[11] For instance, the SPS Committee developed recommended procedures for implementing
the transparency obligations under the SPS Agreement, which are available in document
G/SPS/7/Rev.3. Another example for the SPS area is the WTO Secretariat's *Procedural
Step-by-Step Manual for SPS Notification Authorities & SPS National Enquiry Points*. An
example for another area is the TBT Code of Good Practice.

[12] For example, Articles 2.11, 5.8 and 15.2, paragraph 0 of Annex 3 of the TBT Agreement;
paragraphs 1 and 2 of Annex B of the SPS Agreement.

[13] Pursuant to Annex 3.C. of the WTO Agreement, the determining factor in deciding on
the frequency of reviews, i.e. every two, four or six years, is the share of world trade in a
recent representative period.

[14] This database compiles all the data from the regular trade monitoring reports which are
prepared by the WTO Secretariat.

monitoring reports in response to the surge of protectionist measures occurring in the aftermath of the 2008 economic and financial crisis. These reports provide a comprehensive snapshot of the implementation of trade-liberalising and trade-restricting measures. The most recent monitoring report of January 2014[15] indicates that, in 2013, improved notification compliance rates were registered across all areas. None the less, there remains considerable scope for improvement, with uneven and slow progress noted across WTO bodies.

According to data retrieved from the CRN, actual effective compliance is relatively weak. Non-compliance with WTO notification requirements by WTO members may be due to a range of factors, such as domestic human resource constraints, weak domestic coordination and administrative negligence, lack of technical infrastructure and policy concerns. A number of challenges have been identified over time:

- while all notifications are channelled through the CRN, monitoring of the effective implementation of notification requirements is dispersed and decentralised – domestically between various ministries and agencies, and, in the WTO, among a number of WTO bodies;
- there is a lack of penalties for late submissions;
- while most WTO agreements prescribe a binding notification obligation, many of the specific provisions do not explicitly define detailed requirements, procedures, formats or timelines.

### WTO accession negotiations and WTO notification and publication obligations

#### *Specific commitments undertaken in Article XII accession negotiations*

In Accession Protocols, the majority of Article XII members have made specific commitments reconfirming the principal WTO notification obligations. In addition, in some accessions, specific obligations have been further elaborated to strengthen existing notification obligations.

During the accession process, accession working parties[16] provide the forum for discussing future notification obligations. The results of these

---

[15] See WTO document WT/TPR/OV/16.
[16] Accession working parties are WTO bodies established by the General Council with standard terms of reference. A list of the structure of bodies under the WTO can be found on pp. 3–4 of document WT/L/31 and pp. 4–5 of document WT/L/510.

discussions are recorded in the working party reports,[17] which are developed over successive meetings on the basis of written questions and replies exchanged between members and the acceding state or separate customs territory ('acceding government'). As each acceding government has a unique set-up for conducting its economic and trade policies, specific accession commitments are negotiated as a function of the specificities of individual legal and administrative frameworks and the particular negotiation dynamics in its accession working party.[18] Nevertheless, some patterns and trends in commitment language have emerged over time.

The transparency chapter contained in all working party reports is traditionally divided into two sub-sections: (i) publication of information on trade; and (ii) notifications. The first sub-section contains a description of the acceding government's domestic regime for the publication of legislation. In some cases, the commitment not only specifies that legislation and trade-related measures have to be published prior to their enforcement, but also identifies the method of publication (Official Gazette/journal, a newspaper or a website),[19] the level of detail that would need to be attached to such a notification, and the period the member would need to grant for consultation and comments, prior to enforcing the measure.[20] In other instances, the commitment includes a

---

[17] Each Accession Package contains five components: (i) decision; (ii) Protocol of Accession; (iii) accession working party report; (iv) services schedule; and (v) goods schedule. The Decision adopted by the General Council/Ministerial Conference formally offers to the applicant the terms of accession contained in the Protocol of Accession and its annexes. The Protocol of Accession references all specific commitments undertaken by the acceding government, which are contained in the accession working party report. It also annexes the services and goods schedules. Accession working party reports comprise seven principal chapters: economic policies; framework for making and enforcing policies; policies affecting trade in goods; trade-related intellectual property rights; policies affecting trade in services; transparency; and trade agreements.

[18] Accession working parties examine the acceding government's foreign trade regime and identify the necessary domestic reforms to ensure conformity with the WTO Agreement. All aspects of the acceding government's foreign trade regime are reviewed to ensure compliance with WTO rules.

[19] Examples: Cambodia, paragraph 217 (journal or website); Cabo Verde, paragraph 262 (official journal or website), Lao PDR, paragraph 243 (official website or newspaper); Montenegro, paragraph 273 (website).

[20] Examples: Armenia, paragraph 215 (two weeks); Bulgaria, paragraph 40 (two weeks); Cabo Verde, paragraph 262 (a reasonable period, i.e., no less than thirty days); China, Protocol I.2(C) 1 and 3 (a reasonable period); Montenegro, paragraph 273 (a reasonable period, i.e. no less than thirty days); Chinese Taipei, paragraph 219 (sixty calendar days);

specific reference to the emergency and security exceptions granted under the WTO Agreement.[21]

The second sub-section of the transparency chapter addresses notifications. Here, the emphasis in accession negotiations has been on ensuring adherence to the general notification requirements contained in the WTO Agreements and, specifically, the effective implementation of initial notification requirements from the date of accession.

A review of the working party reports of the thirty-three completed Article XII accession processes[22] shows the following:

- In twenty-two of the thirty-three completed accession processes, acceding governments have undertaken specific transparency commitments in the sub-section on publication of information on trade. In five cases, transitional periods were granted through a 'grace period' for the establishment/designation of either an official journal or website[23] (Table 40.1).
- In thirty-one of the thirty-three completed accession processes, acceding governments have undertaken specific transparency commitments in the sub-section on notifications. In five cases, transitional periods were granted to meet the general WTO notification requirements. Specifically, Jordan, Lao PDR, Ukraine and Yemen undertook to submit all remaining initial notifications no later than six months from the date of accession. Russia undertook to notify a set of initial notifications, as identified in Table 38 of its working party report,[24] ninety days from the date of accession (Table 40.1).
- In addition to commitments undertaken in the dedicated transparency chapter, specific commitments have also been undertaken in other chapters of the working party reports. These commitments reaffirm existing notification requirements under a particular WTO Agreement and, in some cases, reinforce them or explicitly link them to GATT

---

Tajikistan, paragraph 343 (a reasonable period, i.e. no less than thirty days); Viet Nam, paragraph 518 (no less than sixty days).

[21] Examples: Cabo Verde, paragraph 262; Lao PDR, paragraph 243; Montenegro, paragraph 273; Samoa, paragraph 243; Saudi Arabia, paragraph 305; Chinese Taipei, paragraph 219; Tajikistan, paragraph 343; Tonga, paragraph 180; Ukraine, paragraph 499; Vanuatu, paragraph 134; Viet Nam, paragraph 518.

[22] See footnote 3.      [23] Lao PDR, Montenegro, Tajikistan, Ukraine and Vanuatu.

[24] Table 38 of the report of the working party on the accession of Russia covers the following areas: customs valuation; SCM; trade-related investment measures (TRIMs); import licensing; rules of origin.

Table 40.1 Specific commitments contained in the transparency chapters of accession working party reports

| | Publication of information on trade | Notifications |
|---|---|---|
| Ecuador | Gray | Gray |
| Bulgaria | Gray | Gray |
| Mongolia | Gray | Gray |
| Panama | Gray | Gray |
| Kyrgyz Republic | Gray | Gray |
| Latvia | Gray | Gray |
| Estonia | Gray | Gray |
| Jordan | Gray | Gray |
| Georgia | Gray | Gray |
| Albania | Gray | Gray |
| Oman | Gray | Gray |
| Croatia | Gray | Gray |
| Lithuania | Gray | Gray |
| Moldova, Republic of | Gray | Gray |
| China | Gray | Gray |
| Chinese Taipei | Gray | Gray |
| Armenia, Republic of | Gray | Gray |
| FYR Macedonia | Gray | Gray |
| Nepal | Gray | White |
| Cambodia | Gray | Gray |
| Saudi Arabia | Gray | Gray |
| Viet Nam | Gray | Gray |
| Tonga | Gray | Gray |
| Ukraine | Gray | Gray |
| Cabo Verde | Gray | Gray |
| Montenegro | Gray | Gray |
| Samoa | Gray | Gray |
| Russian Federation | Gray | Gray |
| Vanuatu | Gray | Gray |
| Lao PDR | Gray | Gray |
| Tajikistan | Gray | Gray |
| Yemen | Gray | Gray |

*Notes:* Gray = commitment undertaken. White = no commitment undertaken. Article XII members are sorted by date of membership.

*Source:* Based on WTO Accession Commitments Database (ACDB) data.

Article X provisions.[25] Eighteen chapters containing such agreement-specific notification commitments have been identified (Table 40.2).

- Twenty-three of the thirty-three Article XII members have undertaken a specific commitment to regularly notify their privatisation programmes to WTO members in the chapter on state-owned enterprises and privatisation (Table 40.2). These specific commitments are not explicitly linked to a notification requirement under any particular WTO Agreement, but are aimed at enhancing systemic transparency.

This review reveals that only half of the pre-2008 working party reports contain specific transparency commitments related to the publication of information on trade. This has changed significantly. Since 2008, all Article XII members have undertaken a specific transparency commitment reiterating the existing publication requirement under the WTO Agreement. As a result of this recent trend, approximately two-thirds of Article XII members have undertaken a specific accession commitment on publication of information on trade (Table 40.1).

It should be noted that the detail and scope of specific accession protocol commitments may vary from one Article XII member to another. China, for example, undertook a detailed specific commitment in its Protocol of Accession (Article 18.1 and Annex 1A) to provide, during a specific period, information on a range of areas to relevant WTO bodies on an annual basis.[26] The notified information would need to be provided in addition to the general WTO notification requirements applicable to all WTO members pursuant to the WTO Agreement. More recently, Russia undertook specific obligations to provide trade data to the WTO Integrated Data Base (IDB), and to participate in other WTO mechanisms, such as the Trade Policy Review Mechanism and other WTO council and committee reviews, for the exchange of information and increased transparency.[27]

### The Article XII accession process as preparation for WTO membership

The review of notifications is an essential part of WTO activity and the responsibility of each WTO member. The accession process provides an

---

[25] Based on WTO Accession Commitments Database (ACDB) data.

[26] Council/committees on trade in goods, TRIPs, trade in services, balance-of-payments restrictions, market access (including the Information Technology Agreement (ITA)), agriculture, SPS measures, customs valuation, rules of origin, import licensing, TRIMs, safeguards, and trade in financial services.

[27] Russia, paragraph 1413.

Table 40.2 Specific commitments contained in the accession working party reports reaffirming WTO notification obligations

| Country | State-ownership and privatisation | Ordinary customs duties | Tariff rate quotas, tariff exemptions | Application of internal taxes on imports | Quantitative import restrictions, including |
|---|---|---|---|---|---|
| Ecuador | | | | | |
| Bulgaria | ▓ | | | | |
| Mongolia** | ▓ | | | | |
| Panama | | | | | |
| Kyrgyz Republic | | | | | |
| Latvia | ▓ | | | | |
| Estonia | ▓ | | | | |
| Jordan | | | | | |
| Georgia | ▓ | | | | |
| Albania | ▓ | | | | |
| Oman | | | | | |
| Croatia | ▓ | | | | |
| Lithuania | ▓ | | | | |
| Moldova, Republic of | ▓ | | | | |
| China* | | | | | |
| Chinese Taipei | ▓ | | | | ▓ |
| Armenia | ▓ | | | *** | ▓ |
| FYR Macedonia | ▓ | | | | |
| Nepal | | | | | |
| Cambodia | ▓ | | | | |
| Saudi Arabia | ▓ | | | | |
| Viet Nam | ▓ | | | | |
| Tonga | | | | | |
| Ukraine | ▓ | | ▓ | | XXX |
| Cabo Verde | | | | | |
| Montenegro | ▓ | ▓ | | | |
| Samoa | ▓ | | | | |
| Russian Federation | ▓ | | | | ▓ |
| Vanuatu | | | | | |
| Lao PDR | | | | | |
| Tajikistan | ▓ | | | | XXX |
| Yemen | ▓ | | | | |

| | | | | | | | | |
|---|---|---|---|---|---|---|---|---|
| prohibitions, quotas and licensing systems | | | | | | | | |
| Rules of origin | X | | | | | | X | |
| Pre-shipment (PSI)**** | | | | | | | | |
| Anti-dumping, countervailing duties and safeguard regimes | | | | | | | | |
| Customs tariffs, fees and charges for services rendered, application of internal taxes to exports and minimum export prices | | | | | | | | |
| Export subsidies | | | | | | | | |
| Industrial policy, including subsidies | | | | | | | | |
| Technical barriers to trade | | | | | | XX | | |
| Sanitary and phytosanitary measures | | | | | | | | |

Table 40.2 (cont.)

| | TRIMs | State trading entities | Free zones, special economic areas | Agricultural policies | Trade agreements |
|---|---|---|---|---|---|
| Ecuador | ■ | ■ | | | ■ |
| Bulgaria | | | | ■ | |
| Mongolia** | | ■ | | | |
| Panama | | ■ | | | █ |
| Kyrgyz Republic | | ■ | | | |
| Latvia | | | | | |
| Estonia | | ■ | | | |
| Jordan | | ■ | | | |
| Georgia | | ■ | | | |
| Albania | | ■ | | | |
| Oman | | ■ | | | |
| Croatia | | ■ | | | |
| Lithuania | | █ | | | |
| Moldova, Republic of | | ■ | | | ■ |
| China* | | ■ | ■ | ■ | ■ |
| Chinese Taipei | | ■ | | | |
| Armenia | | █ | | | |
| FYR Macedonia | | | | | |
| Nepal | ■ | ■ | | | ■ |
| Cambodia | | | | | ■ |
| Saudi Arabia | | ■ | | | ■ |
| Viet Nam | | █ | | | ■ |
| Tonga | | ■ | | | |
| Ukraine | | ■ | | | ■ |
| Cabo Verde | | ■ | | | ■ |
| Montenegro | | ■ | | | ■ |
| Samoa | | ■ | | | ■ |
| Russian Federation | ■ | ■ | | | |
| Vanuatu | | | | | |
| Lao PDR | | ■ | | | ■ |
| Tajikistan | | | | | ■ |
| Yemen | | ■ | | | |

*Notes:*

| | |
|---|---|
| | Commitment makes reference/reaffirms a specific notification obligation under the WTO Agreement. |
| | *Commitment with reference to transparency provision (publication/notification) of WTO Agreement but not specifically underpinning/reaffirming notification obligation contained in the provision:* |
| | Commitment makes reference to compliance with relevant article of the WTO Agreement, which contains a notification obligation; commitment itself does not specifically spell out notification obligation. |
| X | Commitment to abide by relevant WTO provisions on transparency and the provision of information about its rules of origin and their application. |
| XX | Reference made to transparency provisions under the TBT Agreement  i.e. Articles 2.1, 2.2, 5.1, 5.2, .4 and Annex 1.1 of the TBT Agreement. |
| XXX | Reference made to adherence to publication and provision of information, in conformity with WTO Agreement on Import Licensing Procedures. |
| | * This table takes account of China's specific commitments, as contained in the accession working party report.  It is important to note that further specific notification commitments in a range of areas are elaborated in China's accession protocol (WT/L/432), see  6.2, 7.2,  8.1, 9.2, 16.7, 16.8, 18.1, Annexes 5A and  1A. |
| | ** This table takes account of Mongolia's specific commitments, as contained in the accession working party report.  It is important to note that further specific notification commitments are contained in Mongolia's accession protocol (WT/ACC/MNG/11), including I.4(b). |
| | *** Notification obligation only during phase-out period, i.e. until 31 December 2008. |
| | ****Specific transparency commitment/Article X under the section on PSI. |

*Source:* Based on WTO Accession Commitments Database (ACDB) data.

invaluable training ground for preparing future WTO members for effective participation in the system.

To ensure compliance with WTO notification obligations and to benefit from WTO notifications made by other members, governments need to allocate the appropriate resources and human capacity early on. Specifically, they need to develop an effective domestic mechanism for processing relevant notification information. The existence of an internal coordination mechanism is indispensable for ensuring that relevant information is disseminated to ministries and agencies with the aim of eventually making this information easily accessible to stakeholders.

Under various provisions of the WTO Agreement, each WTO member has legal obligations relating to transparency. Over time, guidelines and manuals have been developed by members and the WTO Secretariat in various WTO fora. One of the objectives of these guidelines and manuals is to support and supplement the existing transparency obligations under the WTO Agreement, and ensure their effective implementation. These guidelines call on members to adhere to certain best practices when new or amended legislation or measures are envisaged. The following is an indicative list of those practices:

- to notify other WTO members of the planned measure/legislation, in a timely manner;
- to share copies of the draft legislation/measure with other WTO members on request;
- to allow reasonable time for WTO members to review the planned measure/legislation and submit comments in writing;
- to discuss these comments on request;
- to take account of other WTO members' comments and the results of any discussions;
- to explain to other WTO members how their comments would be taken into account;
- to provide additional information on the planned measure/legislation, if available and appropriate.

In accession negotiations, acceding governments are routinely asked to adhere to the same principles throughout the WTO accession process. The objective is to ensure predictability, provide clarity and make trade-related information easily accessible.

All Article XII members have been asked to provide baseline data, by completing checklists and questionnaires, which are based on established WTO notification formats across all areas of trade rules, including state trading enterprises (STEs), import licensing procedures, customs valuation, sanitary and phytosanitary measures (SPS), technical barriers to trade (TBT) and intellectual property rights (IPR) protection, as well as agricultural supporting tables (AGSTs).[28] Table 40.3 provides an overview of the draft notifications that have been requested from Article XII members, as part of their accession negotiations. In the majority of cases, Article XII members have undertaken to submit the prepared draft notifications to the relevant WTO bodies immediately upon accession.

Article XII members have also been requested to undertake specific commitments to establish enquiry points/notification authorities[29] where information can be obtained relating to measures affecting trade in goods, services, TRIPs and foreign exchange measures.[30] These enquiry points form an essential part of the transparency framework by providing stakeholders easy access to relevant information on trade-related measures in domestic trade legislation.

This work prepares the acceding governments for the obligations of future WTO membership. Upon WTO membership, new notifications need to be prepared and submitted, as appropriate. Drawing on the experience gained during the WTO accession process, Article XII members are well equipped to fulfil these notification requirements.

## Article XII members' compliance with WTO notification obligations

The above is an overview of the range of transparency commitments on notification and publication undertaken by Article XII members as a result of their accession negotiations. Specific commitments are incorporated in

---

[28] Examples: Mongolia, paragraph 3 (draft SPS; TBT; and customs valuation notification); China (Annex 5A); Moldova, paragraph 236 (schedule of notifications); Lao PDR, paragraph 108 (draft notification on export subsidies); Ukraine (draft notification on state trading enterprises); Panama, paragraph 113 (draft subsidies notification); Mongolia, paragraph 60 (draft subsidies notification); Latvia, paragraph 75 (draft subsidies notification); Chinese Taipei, paragraph 99 (draft subsidies notification); Ukraine, paragraphs 261 and 264 (draft subsidies notification); Montenegro, paragraph 136 (draft subsidies notification); Tajikistan, paragraph 182 (draft subsidies notification).

[29] Provisions stipulating the establishment of an enquiry point/notification authority can be found in all WTO Agreements, e.g. SPS Agreement, Annex B, paragraphs 3 and 4: enquiry point, and paragraphs 5 to 8: national notification authorities; TBT Agreement, Article 10.1; GATS Article III.4; and TRIPs Article 67.

[30] Examples: China, paragraph 336; Moldova, paragraph 235; Russia, paragraph 1426; Chinese Taipei, paragraph 217.

Table 40.3 *Overview of draft notifications which have been requested as part of the WTO accession process*

| WTO rules/legal references | WTO standard notification format | WTO accession negotiating input/notification format |
|---|---|---|
| Articles 1.4(a); 7.1; 7.3; 8.2(b), Agreement on Import Licensing Procedures | G/LIC/3[a] | Questionnaire on Import Licensing Procedures (WT/ACC/22, Annex) |
| Agreement on the Implementation of Article VII of the GATT 1994 "CVA Agreement" | VAL/5 | Checklist on Implementation and Administration of the Customs Valuation Agreement (WT/ACC/22, Annex) |
| Paragraph 1 of WTO Understanding on GATT Article XVII; paragraph 4(a) of GATT Article XVII | STR/3/ Rev. 1[b] | Questionnaire on State-Trading (WT/ACC/22, Annex) |
| Article 25.2 of the SCM Agreement; Article XVI:1 of the GATT 1994 | G/SCM/6/ Rev. 1 | Draft Subsidies Notification (WT/ACC/22/Add. 2) |
| TRIPs Agreement (specifically, TRIPs Article 63.2 and Part III of the TRIPs Agreement) | IP/C/4; IP/C/2; IP/C/5 | Information on the Implementation of the WTO TRIPs Agreement (WT/ACC/22/Add. 2) |
| WTO Agreement on Agriculture, Article 18.2 | G/AG/2 | Domestic Supporting Tables and Export Subsidies (AGSTs) (WT/ACC/22/Add. 1) |
| TBT Agreement: Articles 2.9.2; 2.10.1; 5.6.2; 5.7.1; and Article 10 | G/TBT/1/ Rev. 8 G/TBT/1/ Rev. 11 | Technical barriers to trade checklist of illustrative issues for consideration in accessions (WT/ACC/22/Add. 2) |
| SPS Agreement: Paragraphs 3 and 5[c] (or 6[d]) of Annex B | G/SPS/7/ Rev. 2 G/SPS/7/ Rev. 3 | Sanitary and phytosanitary measures checklist of illustrative issues for consideration in accessions (WT/ACC/22/Add. 2) |

*Notes:* [a]Originally circulated as L/3515 of 23 March 1971 and reproduced in L/5640/Rev. 10. [b]Originally circulated as Annex to L/1146. [c]For WTO accessions, paragraph 5 'routine notifications' are used. [d]Emergency notifications.

the terms of accession, as contained in the Accession Protocols, and become an integral part of the WTO Agreement.[31]

The accession protocol commitments in this area have been negotiated with a view to reinforcing existing transparency requirements under the WTO Agreement. To keep track of the continuously evolving trading environment, some of these commitments have further enhanced the established WTO transparency obligations. Particular emphasis has been placed on ensuring effective implementation in the post-accession stage. The WTO accession process has thus made a significant contribution to the overall WTO drive towards enhanced systemic transparency.

WTO members recognise the central role that transparency plays in a well-functioning multilateral trading system. This has come into particular focus since the 2008 global economic and financial crises brought about a rise in protectionist pressures. Efforts have thus been made towards improving the timeliness, quality and monitoring of regular, periodic and one-time only notifications.[32]

In the period 1995–2013, some 43,500 notifications and related information were entered in the CRN. Almost one-fifth of these notifications (17 per cent) have been made by Article XII members.[33] This number is particularly significant considering that many Article XII members have completed their accessions only relatively recently and, unlike original members, have not been subject to notification requirements since 1995. This broad indicator suggests that Article XII members have, on average, been more active in fulfilling their notification requirements. This general observation is substantiated by a comparison between the average number of notifications made by: (i) original members; (ii) Article XII members; and (iii) all WTO members.

Figure 40.1 reveals that between 2008 and 2013 Article XII members had a consistently higher notification rate than did original members. On average, an Article XII member submitted between six to eleven more notifications annually compared to an original member. This trend can be attributed to the fact that the WTO accession process requires

---

[31] See footnote 2.

[32] There are various types of notification, i.e., initial, regular, periodic and one-time only, as well as reverse and ad hoc notifications. Reverse notifications are not common, but can be made by members if they consider that another member should have notified a certain action/measure. Ad hoc notifications provide scope for WTO members to notify measures/actions (of an unforeseen nature), if taken.

[33] See footnote 3.

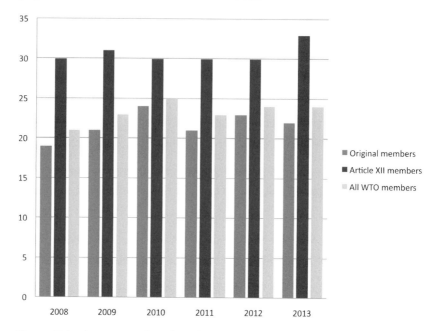

**Figure 40.1**   Average number of notifications made annually, 2008–2013. This includes original members and Article XII members. Based on WTO CRN data.

Article XII members to put in place appropriate mechanisms for submitting notifications upon accession, and the specific transparency obligations, negotiated during the Article XII accession process, have reconfirmed and strengthened existing notification requirements under the WTO Agreement.

Notwithstanding the overall positive compliance rates by Article XII members, a review of outstanding notification obligations by Article XII members indicates that compliance with transparency, and, specifically, notification obligations, can be further improved.[34] Figure 40.2 indicates that, although Article XII members have, on average, relatively few outstanding notifications, significant variations in compliance rates remain. Overall, compliance has improved in recent years, and in particular for members acceding since 2008, which coincides with the renewed emphasis on systemic transparency.

---

[34] See Figure 40.2 for outstanding notifications based on CRN data.

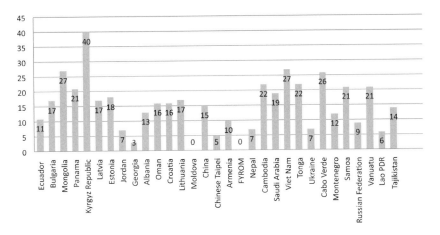

**Figure 40.2**  Outstanding notifications by Article XII members (as of March 2014).
Based on WTO CRN data.

## Conclusions

Peer monitoring and review is a core function of the WTO, which facilitates and promotes the effective implementation of all WTO Agreements. Adherence to the principle of transparency with regard to changes in legislation and trade-related measures is therefore an essential obligation for WTO members.

Like the WTO accession process itself, notification procedures and practices have evolved over time and have been refined and improved since they were first established in 1995. The WTO accession process has kept up to date with these developments through the elaboration of specific obligations on transparency which, upon accession, become an integral part of the WTO Agreement.

The specific transparency commitments negotiated as part of the WTO accession process can be linked to the positive compliance behaviour of Article XII members with publication and notification requirements under the WTO Agreement. This has a positive effect on the multilateral trading system as a whole, by promoting better overall adherence to the transparency principle across the WTO membership, and by reducing the incidence of avoidable trade disputes. The emphasis on transparency in WTO accession negotiations is a testament to the importance that WTO members attach to strengthening existing transparency obligations and improving their implementation in order to safeguard the effective functioning of the multilateral trading system.

# PART VI

Conclusion

# 41

# Accession Protocols as building blocks

CHIEDU OSAKWE AND URI DADUSH

This book provides multiple perspectives on the process and results from WTO accession negotiations. The perspectives reflected are those of economists, lawyers, academics, chief negotiators of selected original WTO members and Article XII members, chairpersons of WTO accession working parties, professionals from the multilateral institutions of the WTO, World Bank, International Monetary Fund and International Trade Centre. Analysis is combined with 'stories', enriched by anecdotes. The detailing of the facts of trade policy drudgery is accompanied by explanatory narratives that bring the situations to life. In many ways, what will strike the reader is that this is a unique book of high value that has emerged from a system that has yielded higher levels of transparency, albeit grudgingly and only when pressed.

At the outset, three key questions were established for the preparation of this book. First, how does the complex and unique process of WTO accession negotiations work, and can it be improved? Second, after two decades, what are the principal results from thirty-three completed WTO accessions, and what have been the systemic effects? Third, do the results, in process and substance, provide lessons for broader trade negotiations, such as in launched multilateral trade rounds, or in other variable configurations, such as in preferential trade agreements, regional trade agreements and the so-called mega-regionals? In addition to these core questions, the multiple perspectives in this book reveal a raft of other questions that authors have asked. For instance, some have asked whether there are indeed rules that govern accession negotiations. This question has been associated with questions about the fairness of the terms and conditions of non-original, i.e. Article XII, members. There have been questions regarding how members and acceding governments

---

The analyses in the chapters in this book were finalised at the end of December 2014. Since then the Republic of Seychelles acceded to the World Trade Organization (WTO) on 26 April 2015. This expanded total WTO membership from 160 to 161. Please see the editors' note.

engage and behave. In all, the core questions and the subset of questions have a logical relationship.

One question that virtually runs through all the chapters is why countries and/or separate customs territories want to accede. What is the rationale for countries and/or separate customs territories that overrides the tedium and misery of accession negotiations that, on average, take ten years to complete? Thirty-three have been completed. Twenty-two have accession working parties, established by the WTO General Council, at various levels of activity. Other countries, that currently have no WTO status, have signalled that they intend to apply. There is a spectrum of reasons, from the strategic, to the tactical, encompassing general and particular factors.

In all the contributions by the chief negotiators of Article XII members, WTO accession negotiations are to be used as an instrument of domestic reform, modernisation and global economic trade integration. In most accounts, but by no means all, this is the starting rationale in applying for WTO membership. There is a range of other reasons that reflect the specific conditions and reasons that drive the application for WTO membership.

Mr Long Yongtu, the chief negotiator for China's WTO accession, expressed a great-power rationale. While, clearly, domestic reforms and streamlining China's laws and national regulations were critical, China used its WTO accession to 'enhance its international status'. China was and remains a great power, a permanent member of the Security Council. It was 'unacceptable' that it was not a WTO member.[1]

For some, the objective is to address the liability and inertia of negative perceptions, to mitigate risk ratings and to effect a positive change, so as, among other things, to attract foreign direct investment. The WTO Accession Package is seen as a 'business package' for promoting trade and economic diplomacy. The associated reasoning is that belonging to a system governed by the rule of law and good governance, provides a positive boost to the business environment adding Swiss-type finishing school effects with WTO membership.

For some others, WTO accession is urgently compelling because the WTO is seen as a 'land registry' to confirm territorial integrity, autonomy and independence and to counter revanchist threats. WTO membership

---

[1] See WTO document WT/ACC/20: First China Round Table: WTO accessions best practices for least-developed countries (LDCs), Beijing, 29–31 May 2012.

is used to register a land 'title'. This has featured in the drives of the states that emerged following the fall of the Berlin Wall in 1989, the collapse of the Soviet Union in 1991, and continuing challenges to find a stable and enduring geopolitical order in the region of Eurasia.

For others, over time, urgency and ever-greater attraction, if not compulsion, to accede to the WTO are evident from the results that have emerged from WTO accessions. With China included or excluded from trade statistics, Article XII members have performed better than many, if not most original members. They have been more competitive, exhibited faster trade growth rates and been more resilient in crisis. Associated with their accession reforms are the establishment and/or reinforcement of institutional frameworks, codified in law and policy. These reflect domestic economic and development priorities and have ensured the sustainability of the reforms undertaken.

The competitiveness of these Article XII members is reviewed annually in the Director-General's Report on WTO Accessions. The 2014 report provides updated data and analysis that underscore this point.[2]

In the period from 1995 to 2013, the value of world trade in goods and services increased by 264 per cent at an average annual growth rate of 7.4 per cent. These performance metrics, though registering a positive general trend, concealed a diverse situation. Over the same period, while the share of world trade in goods and services which originated in or was destined for WTO original members' markets reduced from 90.9 per cent to 80.1 per cent, the reach of the rules-based multilateral trading system on world trade expanded from 90.9 per cent to 98 per cent. Article XII negotiations results are central for the explanation of this evolution. Over the same period, the trade growth that Article XII members registered was substantially higher at 720 per cent, reflecting an average annual growth rate of 12.4 per cent. And, even excluding the largest Article XII member by trade value (China), other Article XII members' trade grew by 418 per cent at an average annual growth rate of 9.6 per cent. In contrast, original members' trade grew by 221 per cent at an average annual growth rate of 6.7 per cent. Overall, within the multilateral trading system, Article XII members' trade growth expanded faster and consistently; enabling them to expand their share of world trade in goods and services faster by 125 per cent from 7.8 per cent in 1995, to 17.6 per cent in 2013 (Figure 41.1).

---

[2] See WTO document WT/ACC/23: Director-General's 2014 Annual Report on Accessions.

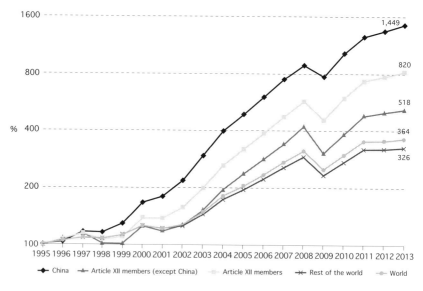

**Figure 41.1**   Value of total trade in the period from 1995 to 2013 (index, 1995 = 100).

## Accession results

Article XII members that acceded to the WTO, pursuant to Article XII of the Marrakesh Agreement Establishing the WTO (WTO Agreement) now account for approximately 20 per cent of WTO membership. Chapter 9 and its annexes detail, in summary form, the results and gains from WTO accessions. The results can be grouped into four categories.

First, there has been an impact on the rules with 1,361 specific commitments that are now integral to the WTO Agreement and form part of the 'Legal Single Undertaking' of the entirety of the rules-based multilateral trading system. The effect of the rules in some instances has been to clarify, make more precise and, in some other cases, expand the frontiers through new rule-making from WTO 'pluses' (protocol commitments that are more stringent than those of original WTO members at similar levels of economic development). This rules effect is manifested in WTO jurisprudence. As observed in Chapter 10, protocols of accession and working party reports have been raised in twenty-six disputes thus far, sixteen of which have proceeded to the panel stage.[3] Accession

---

[3] These sixteen disputes have been considered by ten different panels.

protocols are exercising a noticeable influence in WTO dispute settlement and emerging jurisprudence.

Second, WTO accessions have been an instrument for domestic reforms. WTO-consistent domestic reforms have been far-reaching and, significantly, legislation-based. Legislation is accompanied with implementing regulations for the executive branch of government. Over seven thousand (7,356) WTO-consistent laws projects of law and accompanying regulations have been enacted by thirty-three acceded governments. These are deposited at the WTO Secretariat and are registered in the 'legislative action plans' (LAPs) of the acceding government, which are developed over many years of accession negotiations. Most original members did not undertake this exercise. Continuing weaknesses are reflected in the domestic legal institutional infrastructure.

Third, there have been results and significant efforts for market access improvements that are enjoyed on a most-favoured-nation (MFN) basis, even though they were negotiated bilaterally. Twenty years of bilateral market access negotiations, in the thirty-three deposited Accession Protocols, have produced 504 bilateral market access agreements on goods and 244 bilateral market access agreements on services deposited with the Director-General as 'Depositary'. These have been consolidated, verified by relevant signatory members, and circulated as confirmed schedules of tariff concessions in goods and specific commitments on trade in services. As discussed in the technical chapters, these have provided significant improvements in market access opportunities (at the border, through lowered tariffs; and, behind the border, through significant reductions in regulatory non-tariff barriers).

On market access, for instance, binding tariff concessions and commitments were made by Article XII members on virtually all agricultural and non-agricultural merchandise, in contrast to 75 per cent binding of those products for original members. This has improved certainty and predictability. The average final bound rate level (13.8 per cent) of Article XII members is significantly more liberal than the corresponding average level of original members (at 45.5 per cent). Greater openness and liberalisation have supported the growth of Article XII members relative to original members. Since 1995, the nominal trade growth performance of the thirty-three Article XII members has been consistently and substantially stronger than that of original members. The average yearly growth rate of their commerce for the period 1995 to 2013 was 12.4 per cent, almost double that of original members (6.7 per cent). This has resulted in the increase of Article XII members' share of world trade from

7.8 per cent in 1995 to 17.6 per cent in 2013. Their more rapid growth has had positive knock-on effects for global economic growth. It is of notable significance that the reach of the rules-based multilateral trading system has been expanded to 98 per cent of world trade in 2014, from where it stood at 90.9 per cent in 1995 because of enlargement through new members.

Fourth, accession negotiations have reflected strategic factors in broader international cooperation. On the one hand, while accession negotiations have reflected the geopolitics in play at a point in time, on the other hand, accession negotiations and the legal framework of the WTO have been used, instrumentally, by members and acceding countries to manage the sensitive geopolitical dimensions of their relationship. Contrary to expectations that geopolitics will automatically produce negative effects in accession negotiations which take place within the context of the rules-based multilateral trading system, restraint, moderation and pragmatic problem-solving have been demonstrated. Why is this so? Accession-related treaty dialogue in the thousands of pages of accession working party reports and confidential negotiating conversations on the margins of formal and informal meetings suggest that there is supranational respect (not obedience) for the WTO as a global public good. There is a common will to safeguard it and not erode its authority. In part, an explanation of the length of time that elapses in accession negotiations is to ensure that the acceding government is prepared on day one of membership to function in a system based on rights and obligations. It is also to ensure that the behaviour of the acceding government is normalised to the core WTO values of non-discrimination, the rule of law, transparency and that consultative behaviour becomes the norm in which members behave to resolve problems pragmatically to achieve a *modus vivendi*. The process and substantive results of the WTO have actually contributed to enhancing the value of the WTO and its upgrade. The counter-factual question is what the situation would have been, had membership been either non-rigorous or automatic?

### What are the lessons from accessions for the WTO on the occasion of its twentieth anniversary?

Both substance and process matter; sometimes almost equally. The process of WTO accessions has contributed to its success. The negotiating formats have taken place in appropriately defined constrained spaces: bilaterally and/or plurilaterally, with final formal multilateral approval of the end product of the draft Accession Package. The accession process reconfirms an old lesson from the GATT past for the new WTO. Although a global public good, the individual negotiating stake of members differs and, as a consequence, degrees of responsibility vary. Although all members have to accept responsibilities, in a system structured on rights and obligation, major traders have the key role, as engines, to give purpose and direction. In whatever format, for any trade agreement to have a chance of success, the major economic players, reflecting the underlying shifts and periodic redistribution in trading relations and global economic power, at that moment in time, have a duty to lead and work for conclusion. Members should accept and share responsibility, proportionally. Trade negotiations that succeed in producing accessions are non-rhetorical. The temptation, in the past and present, to divide between developed and developing countries, is strenuously avoided. Accession negotiations have been largely successful in avoiding these pitfalls of contemporary negotiations.

There is no substitute for technical work, regardless of high-level political declarations, either bilaterally and/or at summits. This lesson requires better and wider dissemination. The substance of the technical aspects of trade negotiations, the application of modalities and best practices suggest the reasons that explain, in part, the result orientation from WTO accessions. For instance, formula approaches to tariff negotiations or adjustments have had virtually no track record of success in the GATT/WTO. Tariff-line-by-tariff-line negotiations remain the governing and continuing best practice. A problem-solving non-rhetorical approach to any question continues to yield positive results.

Accession negotiations have been managed technically and away from headline news. Members provide the Secretariat with the scope needed to play a relatively stronger coordinating role between members and acceding governments in the negotiations. Sensation, drama and headline news are minimised. No member is put on the spot. Accession negotiations show that attempts to marginalise or corner hegemons in the system never succeed. Even in multilateralism, major traders and economies never hoist the white flag of surrender.

The lessons from accession negotiations and a fundamentally changed global economic and trading environment suggest that, if multilateral negotiations are to improve on results, they should be mainstreamed (embedded) in the regular work of the WTO which has ample provisions for multilateral negotiations. More and more, questions are being raised about the prospects of delivery from stand-alone launched trade rounds.

The twenty-year results from WTO accession negotiations (in rules, market access, domestic reforms and international cooperation), demonstrate results that exceed the simulated gains and modelled results, based on assumptions of varying plausibility, from any one round of trade negotiations, including the ongoing Doha negotiations. Trade negotiators from the GATT past remind contemporary negotiators that the Uruguay Round was envisaged and designed to be the last of the great rounds of trade negotiations. The WTO Agreement created the WTO as a permanent negotiating forum (Article II.1 of the WTO Agreement). There is a mandate for Annex 4-type plurilateral agreements (Article II.3 of the WTO Agreement). Accession negotiations themselves, pursuant to Article XII of the WTO Agreement, are permanent, non-stop, multilateral negotiations in regular work. GATT 1994 Article XXVIII provides a mandate for tariff negotiations. And nothing prevents standing WTO bodies, as part of their regular work, from initiating negotiations, if members decide to do so. The sum of these mandates and a changed global economic environment, perhaps, suggest that the future of stand-alone comprehensive trade negotiations may be past, at this time. The contemporary situation and the facts suggest that a more realistic direction would be multilateral negotiations in the regular work of the WTO, designed to be pragmatic, problem-solving, based on shared responsibilities, reflecting shifts in the balance of trade and economic power among key trading members to safeguard, strengthen and advance the WTO as an indispensable global public good. The process of WTO accession negotiations and the substantive results provide pointers on how trade negotiations could be reorganised in the future, divorced from the paralysing, spellbinding effects of the crises and melodrama associated with launched, stand-alone trade rounds.

~

# Contributor biographies

## Editors

CHIEDU OSAKWE, from Nigeria, is Director of the WTO Accessions Division. Previous WTO positions include Special Coordinator for LDCs and Head of the Secretariat Working Group on the Integrated Framework for LDCs, Office of the Director-General (1999–2001). In this position he was Chairman of the Inter-Agency Working Group (IAWG) for the Integrated Framework. He has also held the positions of Director, Technical Cooperation Division (2001 to 2002); Director, Textiles Division (2003 to 2005), Director, Doha Development Agenda – DDA Special Duties Division, Office of the Director-General (2005 to 2008). Prior to joining the WTO Secretariat, Dr Osakwe was a Nigerian Foreign Service Officer (1979 to 1998). During this period, he served at the Permanent Mission of Nigeria to the United Nations in New York (1983 to 1986) and to the GATT/WTO (1993 to 1998). As Nigerian delegate to the WTO, he was Chairman of the Committee on Rules of Origin (1995 and 1996) and Chairman of the Committee on Pre-Shipment Inspection (1997 to 1998). He coordinated the WTO African Group in 1995. In recognition of his contributions to the Foreign Service, Nigerian President Goodluck Jonathan appointed him Ambassador *in situ* in 2010. Dr Osakwe was educated at the Universities of Ibadan and Oxford and at New York University, from where he obtained his PhD. He has published in several areas, including trade policy, the rule of law and national security. His most recent publications include: *Developing Countries and GATT/WTO Rules: Dynamic Transformations in Trade Policy Behaviour and Performance* (2011); *Are WTO Members Wrestling an Octopus? Did They Set their Sights too High?* (2005); and *Poverty Reduction and Development: The Contribution of Trade, Macroeconomic and Regulatory Policies* (2001), the tenth Joseph Mubiru Memorial Lecture, at which he was a Distinguished Speaker. He has been a contributing author to *Agreeing and Implementing the Doha Round of the WTO*

(2008), edited by H. Hohman; *Nigeria: Half a Century of Progress and Challenges* (2011), edited by C. Chiogu Ikokwu; and *Trade and Environment: Bridging the Gap* (1998), edited by A. Fijalkowski and J. Cameron. Dr Osakwe has been decorated and honoured by several governments.

URI DADUSH, from France, is Senior Associate in the International Economics Program at the Carnegie Endowment for International Peace in Washington, and President and Founder of Economic Policy International, LLC. He acts as an advisor to governments, international organisations (such as the World Bank) and private corporations on issues related to trade and macroeconomic trends and their policy implications. At Carnegie, he has authored or co-authored the following publications: *Inequality in America: Facts, Trends and International Perspective* (Brookings, 2012); *Juggernaut: How Emerging Markets Are Reshaping Globalization* (Carnegie, 2011); *Currency Wars* (Carnegie, 2011); *Paradigm Lost: The Euro in Crisis* (Carnegie, 2010); and over twenty Carnegie papers, policy briefs and journal articles. He is a contributing editor of the journal *Current History* and a member of the World Economic Forum Global Agenda Council on the Global Trade System of which he is currently the Vice-Chair. He is also a member of the Washington Trade Policy Group, a regular gathering of some twenty trade experts. Before Carnegie, he served as the Director of Trade at the World Bank, a department he founded in the run-up to the WTO Doha Ministerial Conference, and was responsible for the World Bank's relationship with the WTO. Before that he was the World Bank's Director of Economic Policy. Mr Dadush also held concurrently the position of Director of the World Bank's Economy Group, where he led the preparation of the World Bank's flagship reports on the international economy for over eleven years. Prior to joining the World Bank, Mr Dadush was President and CEO of the Economist Intelligence Unit and Business International (part of the Economist Group); Group Vice President, International, for Data Resources (now Global Insight); and a consultant for McKinsey and Co. in Europe. He is currently an advisor to AT Kearney's Global Business Council. During his Carnegie, World Bank and private sector career, Mr Dadush worked in an advisory capacity with the governments of over twenty countries. Most recently, he has been invited by the Japanese Cabinet Office to work on consultations concerning the Trans-Pacific Partnership (TPP), and by Morocco to work on consultations concerning the TPP, Trans-Atlantic Trade and Investment Partnership and the implications for developing countries.

Mr Dadush is a frequent contributor of opinion pieces in the international media, and he writes a regular column on the international economy for *L'Espresso*. He holds a BA in Economics and International Relations and an MA in Economics from the Hebrew University of Jerusalem (Israel) and a PhD in Business Economics from Harvard University, where he was a Teaching Fellow in International Trade, and also taught a tutorial on foreign direct investment. His dissertation topic was 'Interdependence in the growth process and international economic policy'.

## Contributors

RAJESH AGGARWAL, from India, is Chief of the Business and Trade Policy Section at the International Trade Centre, Geneva. For the last seven years, he has been leading a programme aimed at building the capacity of the private sector in developing countries to engage effectively in business advocacy with their governments on multilateral and regional/bilateral trade negotiations. Before joining ITC, he held a number of senior positions in the government of India for over twenty-two years, including acting as India's negotiator to the WTO covering agriculture, TRIPs and public health, rules, and trade and investment. Mr Aggarwal obtained a postgraduate degree in management from the Management Development Institute, Gurgaon, India. His publications include 'Dynamics of Agriculture Negotiations in the World Trade Organization' (2005), published in the *Journal of World Trade*.

RAFAT AL-AKHALI, from Yemen, was a researcher on accessions in the WTO Accessions Division. He was Co-Secretary to accessions of Afghanistan, Algeria and Yemen. Prior to this, Mr Al-Akhali worked in the private sector in Yemen. He is a co-founder and an executive director of a non-profit foundation focused on youth engagement in public policy in Yemen. Mr Al-Akhali holds a Bachelor of Applied Technology in Information Systems from SAIT Polytechnic (Canada), an MBA from HEC Montréal (Canada), and a Masters in Public Policy from the Blavatnik School of Government, University of Oxford (United Kingdom). Among his publications are 'The Uneven Playing Field: Political finance in post-Arab Spring countries' (2012), 'Bringing Stability to Yemen: Improving State Services to Meet People's Basic Needs' (2012), 'Fuel Subsidy Reform in Post-Revolutionary Yemen: A Participatory Approach' (2012) and 'Youth in Post-Revolution Yemen: A View from the Ground' (2011).

ROBERT D. ANDERSON, a citizen of Canada and the United States, is Counsellor and Team Leader for Government Procurement and Competition Policy at the Intellectual Property Division, WTO Secretariat. He is also Honorary Professor, School of Law, University of Nottingham (United Kingdom), and a part-time faculty member, World Trade Institute, University of Bern (Switzerland). He received his J.D. from Osgoode Hall Law School, York University (Canada) and also holds a Bachelor of Arts with Honours in Economics from the University of British Columbia (Canada). Prior to joining the WTO Secretariat in 1997, he held various positions in the Canadian Competition Bureau (Canada's national antitrust agency), the Department of Finance of the Canadian Province of Saskatchewan, and the Economic Council of Canada. He is editor of two books and author/co-author of more than fifty articles/book chapters on topics in competition policy, international government procurement policy, intellectual property and international trade policy.

JOAN LAKER APECU, from Uganda, is an economic affairs officer at the Council and Trade Negotiations Committee Division of the WTO. She is involved in servicing the WTO's four principal bodies – the Ministerial Conference, the General Council, the Trade Negotiations Committee and the Dispute Settlement Body. Previously, she served in several capacities on the Uganda Law Reform Commission, including as a Senior Legal Officer in charge of law reform and research (1999–2004), where she undertook law reform projects in several branches of the law, particularly in commercial, intellectual property and criminal justice law reform. Dr Apecu is an advocate of the High Court of Uganda. She has an academic attachment to the Permanent Mission of Uganda to the United Nations and other international organisations in Geneva, and she has been an assistant lecturer in the Faculty of Law, Uganda Christian University Mukono. Dr Apecu completed her doctoral studies in international studies with a focus on international trade law at the Graduate Institute of International and Development Studies (Switzerland). She received the 2011 Swiss Network for International Studies (SNIS) Award for the best PhD thesis in international studies for her thesis, entitled 'African Participation at the World Trade Organization – Legal and Institutional Aspects' (2010). She holds a Masters of Law Degree (LLM) in International Trade and Investment Law, from the University of Pretoria (South Africa) and the Amsterdam Law School (Netherlands), a postgraduate diploma in legal practice from the Law Development

Centre (Uganda) and a Bachelor of Laws Degree (Hons) from Makerere University (Uganda). Dr Apecu's publications include *African Participation at the World Trade Organization: Legal and Institutional Aspects* (1995–2010); *Regulating Mobile Money Services in East Africa* with a focus on Uganda; the *Law of Contract in Uganda*; and *Intellectual Property Law in Uganda*. She has also written several articles on developing countries in the multilateral trading system, law reform in Uganda, and children's and women's rights.

ROBERTO AZEVÊDO, from Brazil, has been Director-General of the WTO since 2013. He has been the Permanent Representative of Brazil to the WTO and other international economic organisations in Geneva since 2008, and also represented Brazil before other economic organisations, such as the World Intellectual Property Organisation (WIPO), the United Nations Conference for Trade and Development (UNCTAD), and the International Telecommunications Union (ITU). His last position with the Brazilian government, at the Ministry of Foreign Relations, was Vice Minister for Economic and Technological Affairs (2006 to 2008). He was Brazil's chief negotiator for the Doha Round and supervised MERCOSUR's trade negotiations with other groupings or countries outside Latin America. Prior to that, he was the Director of the Department of Economic Affairs (2005 to 2006) and Head of the Dispute Settlement Unit (2001 to 2005). He was Brazil's chief litigator in many important disputes at the WTO. He also served on and chaired a number of WTO dispute settlement panels. During his diplomatic career, Mr Azevêdo served at the embassies of Brazil in Washington (1988 to 1991) and Montevideo (1992 to 1994), as well as at the Permanent Mission of Brazil in Geneva (1997 to 2001). In Brasilia, he was also Deputy Chief of Staff for Economic Affairs to the Foreign Minister (1995 to 1996), and represented Brazil on a number of specialised international bodies, including the FAO Codex Alimentarius Commission, the International Cotton Council, the International Cotton Advisory Committee and the OECD Trade Committee. He was the leading negotiator for Brazil in the Revision of the OECD Sector Understanding on Export Credits for Civil Aircraft. Mr Azevêdo's academic background is in electrical engineering, at the University of Brasilia, and in International Relations, at the Instituto Rio Branco, the Diplomatic Academy of the Foreign Ministry. He has frequently given lectures on topics of the international economic agenda and has published numerous articles on these issues.

PRAJWAL BARAL is an independent consultant and provides services on climate finance, climate adaptation, technology transfer, international trade and sustainable investment. He has worked with the WTO, Oxfam, the CGIAR Research Program on Climate Change, Agriculture and Food Security (CCAFS), and the World Wide Fund for Nature in different capacities in Southern Asia and Europe. At the WTO, he worked in the capacity of Co-Secretary of the Working Party for the accessions of Bhutan, Liberia and Libya. He holds a BTech in Engineering from MANIT (India) and an MSc in Environmental Change and Management from the University of Oxford (United Kingdom). He is the lead author of the report *Finding the Money: A Stock Taking of Climate Change Adaptation Finance and Governance in Nepal* (Oxfam, 2014) and the co-author of *Deconstructing Local Adaptation Plans for Action (LAPA): Analysis of Nepal and Pakistan LAPA initiatives* (CCAFS Denmark, 2014). Currently, Mr Baral is providing consulting service to the World Intellectual Property Organisation (WIPO)'s Global Challenges Division for the accelerated transfer of clean technologies in developing and emerging economies.

PETRA BESLAĆ, from Germany, is a legal affairs officer at the Accessions Division of the WTO. In this position, Ms Beslać has contributed to the work on completing the WTO accessions of Lao PDR, Montenegro, Russian Federation, Samoa and Seychelles. She is currently working on the WTO accessions of Bosnia and Herzegovina, Serbia and the Syrian Arab Republic. Before joining the WTO, Ms Beslać worked for the Canadian Embassy. She holds a Master of Laws (LLM) in International and European Economic and Commercial Law from the University of Lausanne. Her LLM research focus was on EU energy law.

ALEXANDRA BHATTACHARYA, from Bangladesh, is a legal intern at the South Centre in charge of the Innovation and Access to Knowledge Programme. In 2012, she was a researcher on accessions in the Accessions Division of the WTO, where she worked as Co-Secretary of the working parties on the accessions of Afghanistan, Liberia and Iraq. She served as a teaching assistant at BRAC University (Bangladesh) in 2011, and at the International Centre for Trade and Sustainable Development (ICTSD) in 2010. Between 2008 and 2010, she was Senior Associate at Deloitte. Ms Bhattacharya has an LLB in Law from the London School of Economics and Political Science and an LLM from the University of California.

EMIL P. BOLONGAITA, from Australia, is a Distinguished Service Professor of Public Policy and Management and Deputy Director of the Carnegie Mellon University (Australia). He was Public Management Specialist in the Public Management, Financial Sector and Trade Division, South Asia Regional Department of the Asian Development Bank (ADB). Prior to joining ADB in 2010, he was a Technical Director of Management Systems International (MSI), where he led international development projects. From 2007 to 2010, he was the Director of the Enhancing Government Effectiveness Project, a USAID-funded initiative that assisted public sector reforms of select government agencies in different countries, namely Indonesia, Jordan, Morocco, Viet Nam and Yemen. He was also the Team Leader of the USAID-funded Rule of Law Effectiveness Project in the Philippines from 2004–2006. He has been an Adjunct Faculty at Carnegie Mellon University (Australia); a visiting professor at the Elliott School of International Affairs, George Washington University; Assistant Professor of Public Policy, National University of Singapore; and Assistant Professor of Development Management, Asian Institute of Management. He received his PhD in government and international studies from the University of Notre Dame. Among his publications is *Challenging Corruption in Asia: Case Studies and A Framework for Action*, World Bank, 2004 (co-edited with Vinay Bhargava).

DIMITAR BRATANOV holds dual Bulgarian/Swiss citizenship and works at the Secretary-General's Office of the European Free Trade Association (EFTA) in Geneva. Previously he worked at the Accessions Division of the WTO in Geneva (2004 to 2013). In this position, Mr Bratanov has served as Secretary of the WTO accession working parties of Afghanistan, Algeria, Belarus, Bosnia and Herzegovina, Iraq, Kazakhstan, Liberia, Sao Tomé and Principe, Seychelles, Syria and Tajikistan, and as co-Secretary for a number of other WTO accession processes. Mr Bratanov also worked for the Economic Research and Statistics Division of the WTO (2003 to 2004). He holds a Bachelor of Science (BSc) in Economics and a Master of Science (MSc) in Politics of the World Economy from the London School of Economics and Political Science (LSE).

ANTONIA CARZANIGA, from Italy, is Counsellor in the Trade in Services Division at the WTO and Secretary to the WTO Council for Trade in Services. She has undertaken many WTO technical assistance missions, including to acceding countries, focusing on services trade and the obligations and disciplines of the General Agreement on Trade in Services. Before joining the WTO Secretariat in 1998, Ms Carzaniga worked for a trade policy consultancy in London and, prior to that, for the Centre for European Policy Studies, an economic think-tank in Brussels, and for the College of Europe in Bruges. She holds an honours degree in International Economics from Bocconi University (Italy), an MA in European Economic Studies from the College of Europe (Belgium), and an MA in Regulation from the London School of Economics and Political Science, United Kingdom. Ms Carzaniga has published several papers on matters relating to trade in services, including various aspects of mode 4 (presence of natural persons) of the GATS, health services, air transport services and MFN exemptions.

HUI CHEN, from China, was researcher on accessions in the Accessions Division of the WTO. He was the Co-Secretary of the working parties on the accessions of Algeria, Kazakhstan and Serbia. He has an LLB in Law from Zhejiang University (China).

CHARLOTTA FALENIUS, from Finland, holds a MSc in Public Policy from University College London and a MSc in Global Political Economy from the University of Helsinki. An associate expert at the International Trade Centre, Ms Falenius joined the organisation in 2013 and manages technical assistance programmes for least-developed countries' WTO accessions. Prior to her current position, Ms Falenius worked for the Trade Division of the Ministry of Foreign Affairs of Finland in Helsinki and Brussels. She has also gained experience on technical assistance programmes at the European Commission's Directorate-General for Development and Cooperation – EuropeAid.

TING FANG, from China, is a former researcher on accessions in the Accessions Division of the WTO. He assisted with the coordination of the multilateral negotiation process for the accessions of Afghanistan, Algeria, the Bahamas, Kazakhstan and Seychelles. He was an intern at the International Centre for Sustainable Trade and Development (ICSTD) and a Development Instructor at Development Aid People to People in Malawi. He holds a BSc in Electrical Engineering from Guilin University of Electronic Technology (China), a NVQ-3 Certificate in Development from the College for International Co-operation and Development (United Kingdom) and an MA in Development Studies from the Graduate Institute of International and Development Studies (Switzerland).

Mr Fang is a co-author of *China's International Aid Policy and Its Implications for Global Governance* (2011).

DANIJELA GAČEVIĆ from Montenegro is a senior advisor at the Directorate for Multilateral and Regional Trade Cooperation and Foreign Economic Relations, Ministry of Economy, and has worked for the Ministry since 2007. She was a member of the Montenegrin Delegation for WTO accession negotiations, as well as in negotiations on free trade agreements with Ukraine and EFTA countries. Currently she is a member of the Montenegrin delegation for the accession negotiations to the Agreement on Government Procurement, the Protocol to the Agreement between the Government of the Federal Government of Yugoslavia and the Government of Russia on Free Trade and Free Trade Agreements with Belarus and Kazakhstan. Montenegro is also a member of the Working Group 30 – Foreign Relations for EU accession negotiations. Ms Gačević graduated after studying economy, and holds a Master's Degree in European Economic Integration from the University of Montenegro.

CARLOS GIMENO VERDEJO, from Spain, is a policy coordinator at the WTO Unit of the European Commission's Directorate-General for Trade. Before joining this department, where he also served as Head of the Trade and Economic Section of the EU Delegation in Argentina (2008 to 2012) and as negotiator for trade in services and investment (2001 to 2008), he worked for the European Commission's Directorate-General for the Internal Market (1998 to 2001) and for the European Court of Justice (1992 to 1998). Mr Gimeno Verdejo holds degrees both in law and in economics and in business management, as well as a Master in EU Law from the College of Europe.

JULIE-ANN GUIVARRA, from Australia, is Director of the Services and Trade Negotiations Section in the Department of Foreign Affairs, in the Australian government. Before that she was a counsellor of the Permanent Mission of Australia to the WTO. Ms Guivarra was the coordinator of the Cairns Group at the technical level. Prior to her posting to Geneva, Ms Guivarra held her current position, as Director in the Australian Department of Foreign Affairs and Trade (2008 to 2010). She was posted to New Delhi from 1999 to 2002. Ms Guivarra has a Bachelor of Commerce (Hons) from James Cook University (Australia) and an MA in Foreign Affairs and Trade from Monash University (Australia).

MONA HADDAD, from Lebanon, is Sector Manager of the International Trade Department, World Bank. In this capacity she manages the group responsible for supporting the development and implementation of trade-related activities at both country and regional levels. These include trade policy analysis, competitiveness, trade facilitation and standards. Prior to joining the Trade Department, Ms Haddad was the Regional Trade Coordinator for the East Asia Region, where she worked on trade issues in various countries, including China, Indonesia, Lao PDR and Viet Nam.

BERNARD M. HOEKMAN, from the Netherlands, is the Director of the research strand 'Global Economics: Multilateral Cooperation and Policy Spillovers' at the European University Institute. He has held various senior positions at the World Bank, including Director of the International Trade Department and Research Manager in the Development Research Group. He has also worked as an economist in the GATT Secretariat and held visiting appointments at Sciences Po (France). Other positions include Chairperson, Global Agenda Council on Logistics and Supply Chain Systems at the World Economic Forum. Mr Hoekman is a graduate of the Erasmus University Rotterdam and holds a PhD in economics from the University of Michigan. He is a Research Fellow of the Centre for Economic Policy Research (CEPR) (United Kingdom) and a Senior Associate of the Cairo-based Economic Research Forum for the Arab Countries, Turkey and Iran (Egypt). He has published widely on trade policy and development, the global trading system, and trade in services. His most recent co-authored book is *The Political Economy of the World Trading System* (Oxford University Press, 2009).

CLAIRE H. HOLLWEG, from the United States, is a consultant at the International Trade Department of the World Bank where she has worked since 2011. She holds an MA and a PhD in Economics from the University of Adelaide (Australia). Prior to studying economics she worked as a journalist in newspaper and radio and holds a BS in Journalism from the University of Colorado at Boulder. She also has work experience with the Government of South Australia and the Pacific Economic Cooperation Council in Singapore. Her research interests include development economics and international trade with a recent focus on trade and labour and household responses to shocks. Her most recent publication is a co-authored book entitled *Sticky Feet: How Labor Market Frictions Shape the Impact of International Trade on Jobs and Wages.*

VALERIE HUGHES, from Canada, is Director of Legal Affairs at the WTO Secretariat. She was a senior partner of the firm Gowlings Lafleur Henderson LLP and President of the Canadian Council on International Law. Prior to joining Gowlings in 2006, Ms Hughes was the Director of the Appellate Body Secretariat of the WTO (2001 to 2005), where she served as Chief Legal Counsel to the WTO Appellate Body, providing legal and administrative support. Before the WTO, she spent nineteen years with the government of Canada, during which she held various positions in the public and private international law fields, including Director and General Counsel of the Trade Law Division of the Department of Foreign Affairs and International Trade, Director and General Counsel of the General Legal Services Division of the Department of Finance, and Senior Counsel of the International Law Section of the Department of Justice. She has served as Counsel for Canada before numerous international courts and tribunals, and as Chair of the APEC Dispute Mediation Experts Group from 1998 to 1999. Ms Hughes graduated from Ottawa University (Canada) in 1979. She has a number of published works and is a regular guest lecturer at universities and speaker at international trade law conferences.

STEFÁN H. JÓHANNESSON, from Iceland, is the Secretary of State of Iceland for EU Negotiations and the chief negotiator for Iceland's accession to the European Union. From 2001 to 2005, he was Permanent Representative of Iceland to the United Nations and other international organisations in Geneva, including the European Free Trade Association (EFTA) and the WTO. From 2002 to 2011, he served as Chairman of the Working Party on the Accession of the Russian Federation to the WTO, Chairman of the WTO Negotiating Group on Market Access for Non-Agricultural Products (NAMA), Chairman of the Management Board of the WTO Pension Plan, EFTA chief negotiator and Spokesman in free trade negotiations with Lebanon, Chairman of the WTO Dispute Settlement Panel *US – Steel Safeguards*, and Chairman of the WTO Working Group on Trade and Transfer of Technology. He has served as ambassador of Iceland to Belgium, the European Union, Liechtenstein, Luxembourg and Slovenia. Mr Jóhannesson has obtained a Cand.Juris degree from the University of Iceland.

LIDET KEBEDE, from Ethiopia, was a researcher on accessions in the Accessions Division of the WTO. She was the Co-Secretary of the working party on the Accession of Afghanistan. Prior to joining the

WTO, she worked at the Regional Integration, Infrastructure and Trade Division of the United Nations Economic Commission for Africa (UNECA). She holds a BA in Economics and Management from the University Lumière Lyon 2 (France) and an MA in International Development and Governance from the University of Pierre Mendès-France (France).

ALEXEI KIREYEV, from Russia, is a senior economist at the International Monetary Fund and the former IMF representative to the WTO (2000 to 2003). He has led advanced IMF missions to member countries, provided advice on macroeconomic policies to countries with IMF-supported programmes, and reviewed IMF policy advice, financing and technical assistance. Prior to joining the IMF, he was an economic advisor to President Gorbachev, an economist at the World Bank, and a professor of international economics at universities in Russia and the United States. His degrees include a MA in Economics from the George Washington University and a PhD in Economics from Moscow State Institute of International Relations (Russia). Dr Kireyev has researched and published extensively on international economics and trade, applied macroeconomics, principles of economics, and economic problems of low-income countries. His most recent publication includes a two-volume book on *International Microeconomics and International Macroeconomics* (2013).

CECILIA KLEIN, from the United States, is Senior Director for WTO Accessions of the Office of WTO and Multilateral Affairs of the US Trade Representative. She is responsible for policy development, inter-agency coordination and negotiation with applicants for WTO accession. Prior to this, she was in charge of policy coordination for US government participation in the WTO Committee on Import Licensing Procedures (2000 to 2011) and policy coordination for US government participation in selected trade policy reviews from 1995 to 2004, as well as Director for GATT Affairs at the Office of GATT Affairs of the US Trade Representative (1985 to 1994) and Director for Western Europe and for the European Communities at the Office of Europe and Japan of the USTR (1980 to 1985). She teaches courses on the GATT, the WTO, and US policy towards the GATT/WTO at George Washington University, and lectures on the WTO at Georgetown Law School and American University. Ms Klein graduated from the Yale University. She holds a BAIA in International Affairs and an MA in Economics from the George

Washington University. Among her publications are *Joining the Global Rules-Based Economy: Challenges and Opportunities for the GCC* (2000) and *Forging a Just Global Order – Trade, Development, Political Strategy* (2005).

CLYDE KULL, from Estonia, is Deputy Permanent Representative of Estonia to the European Union. From 1991 to 2010, he also served as Political Director and Undersecretary for Political Affairs of the Ministry of Foreign Affairs of Estonia and as Ambassador of Estonia to Germany, the European Union, the Kingdom of Belgium, Netherlands and the Grand Duchy of Luxembourg, as Ambassador to the North Atlantic Treaty Organization and to the Western European Union, and as Representative of the Republic of Estonia to the Organisation for Security and Co-operation in Europe in Vienna and Permanent Representative of Estonia to the UN and other international organisations in Geneva. Mr Kull was head of the delegation at the negotiations on Estonia's accession to the WTO and chairman of the working party on accession of Tajikistan to the WTO. He graduated from the Moscow State Institute of International Relations, Faculty of International Relations (Russia).

JUNEYOUNG LEE, from the Republic of Korea, is a legal affairs officer in the Accessions Division of the WTO. At present, she is Secretary of the working parties on the accessions of the Bahamas, Bhutan, Iraq, Liberia, and Uzbekistan. Previously, she monitored and analysed regional trade agreements (RTAs) and trained government officials on issues arising from RTAs at the Trade Policies Review Division of the WTO. Prior to joining the WTO Secretariat, she worked with the United Nations Development Programme in Slovakia and the International Economic Law Institute of the Republic of Korea, among others. She holds a *Summa Cum Laude* PhD in international law from the Graduate Institute in Geneva. Her most recent publication (co-authored with Pierre Latrille) is 'Services Rules in Regional Trade Agreements: How Diverse and How Creative as Compared to the GATS Multilateral Rules'. Her forthcoming publication is *Culture and International Trade Law: From Conflict to Coordination*.

AIK HOE LIM, from Malaysia, is the Director of the WTO Trade and Environment Division. He was a Counsellor in the Trade in Services Division of the WTO and Secretary to the body responsible for negotiating domestic regulation disciplines. He has led and conducted numerous

WTO technical assistance missions, including to acceding countries, providing advice on the GATS legal framework and the drafting of services schedules. He joined the WTO in 1999 and has served as Counsellor/ Deputy Chief in the Cabinet of WTO Director-General Mike Moore (2001 to 2002), Counsellor to Director-General Dr Supachai Panitchpakdi (2002 to 2005) and Secretary/Advisor to the Director-General's Consultative Group on 'The Future of the WTO' (2003 to 2005). He also worked in the WTO External Relations Division (1999 to 2001) with responsibility for intergovernmental and parliamentary relations. Before working at the WTO, he was Senior Economic Affairs Officer of the G-15 Summit Level Group of Developing Countries and a consultant on development and labour policies for various UN agencies, including the International Labour Organisation. Mr Lim holds an MA in international economics from the University of Birmingham, a postgraduate diploma in financial economics from the SOAS, University of London and a BSc (Hons) in Land Management from the University of Reading (United Kingdom). He was a Visiting WTO Fellow to the Institute for International Trade at the University of Adelaide (2007) and is currently Adjunct Fellow of the S. Rajaratnam School of International Studies, Nanyang Technological University (Singapore). He has published several papers on trade in services, including on matters concerning regional trade agreements, education services, health services, human rights and the Trans-Pacific Partnership. He is coeditor of *WTO Domestic Regulation and Services Trade: Putting Principles into Practice* (2014).

MARK LINSCOTT, from the United States, is the Assistant US Trade Representative for WTO and multilateral affairs. He is responsible for coordinating US trade policies in the WTO, with lead responsibility in the General Council and Council on Trade in Goods and trade issues in the OECD and UNCTAD. From 2003 to 2012, he served as the Assistant US Trade Representative for Environment and Natural Resources. From 1996 to 2002, Mr Linscott worked at the US Mission to the WTO in Geneva. Between 1999 and 2002, he was one of three members appointed by the General Council to the Management Board for the WTO Staff Pension Fund. Prior to serving in Geneva, he worked in the Office of WTO and Multilateral Affairs in USTR Washington, where he concluded the Uruguay Round Government Procurement Agreement as the lead US negotiator and was responsible for preparations for the entry into force of the WTO. He started his career at the Department of Commerce, serving in Import Administration (1985 to 1988) and the Office of Multilateral

Affairs (1988 to 1992). He was accorded a Gold Medal Award for his work on the 1986 Canadian softwood lumber investigation. Mr Linscott has a BA in economics from the University of Virginia and a JD from Georgetown University Law Center.

XIANKUN LU, from China, is Chairman of the WTO's Import Licence Committee and a Counsellor, Head of Division at the Permanent Mission of China to the WTO. Before coming to Geneva, he served as a Director of Division at the Department for WTO Affairs of the Ministry of Commerce of China (2001 to 2006) and as a Deputy Director of the Division for EU and Benelux Affairs at the Department for European Affairs of the Ministry of Commerce of China (2000 to 2001). Prior to that, he worked at the Permanent Mission of China to the EU (1997 to 2000). Mr Lu holds a BA in international economics from the Shanghai Institute of Foreign Trade (China) and an LLM from the University of International Business and Economics (China).

DMITRY LYAKISHEV, from Russia, is Director of the International Cooperation Department in the Central Bank of the Russian Federation (Bank of Russia). He was a member of the Russian WTO accession team for ten years (from 2004 to 2013). Until September 2013 he led the Trade Policy Section of the Permanent Mission of the Russian Federation in Geneva. From 2002 to 2008, Mr Lyakishev worked for the Ministry of Economic Development and Trade of the Russian Federation: from 2002 to 2004 in the division responsible for trade relations with the EC, and since 2004 as head of the WTO unit in the Department for Trade Negotiations. Apart from participation in trade negotiations, he has contributed to bringing Russian legislation into compliance with WTO rules, as well as in organising WTO-related conferences, roundtables and other awareness-raising events throughout Russia. Mr Lyakishev graduated from Moscow State University in 1996. In 2002 he obtained a degree in economics (world economy and international economic relations) at the Diplomatic Academy of the Ministry of Foreign Affairs of the Russian Federation. He has contributed to several studies and manual books on trade policy and the WTO.

MAXIM MEDVEDKOV, from Russia, is Head of the Department for Trade Negotiations of the Ministry of Economic Development of the Russian Federation and is the chief negotiator of Russia at the WTO. From 2001 to 2011, he also was a chief negotiator for Russia's accession to the WTO.

Mr Medvedkov served as Deputy Minister for Economic Development and Trade of the Russian Federation (2000 to 2004) and as Director of the Centre for Trade Policy and Law in Moscow (1996 to 2000). He is a professor of the Higher School of Economics in Moscow. He also held various positions at the Ministry of Foreign Economic Relations of Russia, the Ministry of Foreign Trade of the USSR and the Trade Representation of the USSR in Switzerland. Mr Medvedkov graduated from the Moscow State Institute of International Relations. He is an author of a large number of publications on the WTO and the Russian economy.

ANNA CAROLINE MÜLLER, from Germany, is a legal affairs officer in the government procurement team of the WTO's Intellectual Property Division. She is a fully qualified lawyer admitted to the bar in Germany (*Rechtsanwältin*) and to the roll of solicitors in England and Wales. Prior to joining the WTO in June 2011, she practised law in the commercial litigation and arbitration section of Clifford Chance's Frankfurt office (2010 to 2011). In 2008–2009, she successfully completed the German bar training programme (*Oberlandesgericht Düsseldorf*) with seats in New York, USA (German Mission to the United Nations), London (Clifford Chance) and Frankfurt (Clifford Chance). She holds a law degree from Baden-Württemberg (Germany) and an LLM in Intellectual Property Law from Universität Düsseldorf (Germany), as well as a DEA (Diplôme d'Études Approfondies) in international relations from the Graduate Institute of International Studies (Switzerland). Her research is focused on international economic law, with recent publications in the field of government procurement.

SAIDRAHMON NAZRIEV, from Tajikistan, is Deputy Minister of Economic Development and Trade of Tajikistan. He was the chief negotiator for Tajikistan on its accession to the WTO. In his previous mandates, he has also held the positions of Aid to the President of Tajikistan on Economic Policy (2007 to 2009); Chief Specialist of the Executive Administration of the President of the Republic of Tajikistan – Department of Economic Reforms and Investments (2006 to 2007); Main Advisor to the Trade Representation of the Republic of Tajikistan in the Russian Federation (2003 to 2006); Head of Representation of the Ministry of Emergencies and Civil Defence, Republic of Tajikistan at the Ministry of the Russian Federation for Civil Defence, Emergencies and Elimination of Consequences of Natural Disasters (EMERCOM of Russia) (2000 to 2003); Main Advisor to the Trade Representation of the Republic of Tajikistan in the Russian Federation (1999 to 2000); Director of Rustam & Co. (1993 to 1999); Deputy Dean, Auto-Road Faculty at the Tajik Technical University (1989 to 1993); and teacher at the Tajik Technical University. Mr Nazriev conducted a postgraduate internal study at the Moscow Auto-Road Institute from 1986 to 1989. Mr Nazriev graduated from the Tajik Polytechnical Institute and the Academy of National Economy at the government of the Russian Federation.

AMARA OKENWA, from Nigeria, was a researcher on accessions in the Accessions Division of the WTO. She worked as Co-Secretary of the working parties of the accessions of Bahamas, Bhutan, Bosnia and Herzegovina and Seychelles. She provided support for meetings, and drafted and reviewed draft working party reports and other ancillary documents. Prior to working at the WTO, Ms Okenwa worked in a private law firm in Nigeria as a solicitor and litigator. She holds a BL in Law from the University of Nigeria, a postgraduate diploma certificate in international trade law and development from the Trade Policy Training Center for Africa (Tanzania) and an MSc in International Law and Economics from the World Trade Institute (Switzerland). Following a consultancy at the Deutsche Gesellschaft für Internationale Zusammenarbeit (GIZ), Nigeria, Ms Okenwa published a paper in July 2013 exploring strategic litigation options for Nigerian private sector to advance ECOWAS trade litigation.

MAIKA OSHIKAWA, from Japan, is Counsellor of the Accessions Division of the WTO, in which she is Secretary of the working party on the accessions of Belarus and Kazakhstan. Prior to joining the Accessions Division, she was Head of the Asia and Pacific Regional Desk at the Institute for Training and Technical Cooperation (ITTC) of the WTO. At the ITTC, she was responsible for managing training and technical assistance activities for thirty WTO members and observers in the Asia and Pacific region, as well as of partnership arrangements with organisations and institutions based in the region. Before joining the ITTC in 2010, she worked in several divisions at the WTO Secretariat, including the Development Division (2003 to 2010), the Technical Cooperation Division (2001 to 2002), the Office of the Director-General (2000 to 2001) and the Trade Policy Reviews Division (1998 to 2000). Ms Oshikawa obtained a MS in Development Studies from the London School of Economics, a DES in International Economics from the Graduate Institute of International Studies (Switzerland) and a BS in Foreign Services from Georgetown University.

JOSEFITA PARDO DE LEÓN, from Guatemala, has been a legal affairs officer in the Accessions Division since 2010. She serves as Secretary of the Informal Group on Accessions and Secretary of the working parties on the accessions of Algeria, Azerbaijan, Comoros, Ethiopia, Lebanon and Sao Tomé and Principe. She is also the focal point for technical assistance and LDC issues. Previously, she was a staff member of the WTO's Intellectual Property Division, Institute for Training and Technical Cooperation, Agriculture and Commodities Division and External Relations Division. Before joining the WTO Secretariat in 2004, she worked at the Ministry of Economic Affairs, the Chamber of Commerce and the Association of Exporters in Guatemala. Mrs Pardo de León holds a BA and a licence in International Relations from the Universidad Francisco Marroquín (Guatemala), and a Master's Degree in International Law and Economics from the World Trade Institute (Switzerland). She has published on government procurement provisions in regional trade agreements, EU Association Agreements in the Americas, the lock-in effects of the Free Trade Agreement between Central America, the Dominican Republic and the United States (RD-CAFTA), intellectual property and access to medicines, investment promotion and competitiveness in Guatemala, preferential rules of origin, and technical barriers to trade.

THOMAS PEN-CHUNG TUNG, from Chinese Taipei, served as Liaison Officer in the Representative Office in Geneva, Switzerland throughout Chinese Taipei's accession process during the 1990s. He also worked in Chinese Taipei, as a Secretary in the Ministry of Economic Affairs.

KHEMMANI PHOLSENA, from Lao PDR, is the Minister of Industry and Commerce of Lao PDR. She headed the Lao PDR's Enhanced Integrated Framework (EIF) Secretariat as the EIF Focal Point and the Lao Secretariat for Accession to the WTO. Previously, Ms Pholsena was Director-General of the Foreign Trade Department within the Ministry of Industry and Commerce and has been involved in foreign trade issues for more than ten years. She holds Bachelor's and Master's Degrees in international economic relations from Moscow State Institute of International Relations and a Master's Degree in public management from the National University of Singapore.

ALBERTO PORTUGAL-PEREZ, from Bolivia, is a senior economist in the International Trade Department of the World Bank and is currently working on topics related to trade policy and competitiveness in a variety of countries. He has worked on diverse assignments involving economic policy in several countries spanning Latin America, Africa, Asia, and Eastern Europe. In his previous unit at the World Bank, he worked on policy issues related to International Development Agency countries, such as debt sustainability, concessional borrowing, aid effectiveness and fragile states. He has also consulted for UNCTAD. He holds a Master's Degree in international economics from the Graduate Institute of International Studies and Development (Switzerland), and a PhD in economics from the University of Geneva. Dr Portugal-Perez is the author of many academic articles on a range of issues including trade policy, trade facilitation, regionalism, standards, investment, infrastructure, aid for trade and trade in services.

CHAM PRASIDH, from Cambodia, is the Minister for Commerce and ASEAN Economic Minister for Cambodia. He was a chief negotiator for Cambodia's accession to the WTO. He belongs to the Cambodian People's Party and was elected to represent Siem Reap Province in the National Assembly of Cambodia in 2003. He also served as Vice Chairman of the Cambodian Steering Committee for Economic Cooperation Strategy (ACMECS), Minister in charge of Greater Mekong Sub-Region Programmes, Minister in charge of Cambodia–Laos–Vietnam Development Triangle Programmes, Minister in charge of Cambodia–Laos–Thailand Development Triangle Programmes, Chairman of the Cambodia-Thai Joint Trade Committee, Chairman of the Public–Private Sector Working Group on Export Processing and Trade Facilitation, Chairman of the Inter-Ministerial Steering Committee on the Integrated Framework for Trade-Related Technical Assistance and Mainstreaming Trade Strategy for Poverty Alleviation, Chairman of the Inter-Ministerial Coordinating Committee on Intellectual Property Rights, Chairman of the Export Quotas Management Committee, Chairman of the Inter-Ministerial Coordinating Committee on Quality Control of Goods and Services, Chairman of the Committee for the Reception and Distribution of Foreign Assistance, Vice Chairman of the Council for the Development of Cambodia in charge of Foreign Direct Investments, Chairman of the Inter-Ministerial Committee for the Organization and Participation of Cambodia to International Fairs, and Vice Chairman of the Steering Committee for Private Sector Development cum Chairman of the Sub-Steering Committee on Trade Facilitation.

VALERIY PYATNITSKIY, from Ukraine, is the Ukrainian government's Commissioner for European Integration and an advisor of the Vice Prime Minister of Ukraine. He was Deputy Chairman of the Joint Parliamentary-Government Committee of Ukraine's accession to the WTO. He served as Deputy Minister for the Economy of Ukraine (2005 to 2011), Deputy Minister for the Economy and European Integration of Ukraine (2003 to 2005) and held a number of posts at the Ministry of Foreign Economic Relations and Trade of Ukraine (1996 to 1999). Mr Pyatnitskiy graduated from the Faculty of Cybernetics in Taras Shevchenko State University (Ukraine). He holds a PhD in economics from the Kyiv National University of Trade and Economics and has been a professor at both of these universities.

JOAKIM REITER, from Sweden, is Deputy Secretary-General at UNCTAD and Chairman of the Working Party on the Accession of Liberia. Previously, he was the Ambassador and Permanent Representative of Sweden to the WTO. He is also the Chairman of the Council for Trade in Services in WTO and chair of the working party on the Accession of Liberia. Ambassador Reiter was Head of the Trade Policy Unit and Minister Counsellor at the Swedish Representation to the European Union between 2008 and 2011, representing Sweden in the Trade Policy Committee of the Council, which he chaired during the Swedish presidency in 2009. Prior to that, from 2004 to 2008, Ambassador Reiter was posted to the European Commission's Directorate-General for Trade. In this capacity, he served as EU negotiator in various trade negotiations and was in charge of tariffs and trade in goods in the EU–Korea free trade agreement, as well as non-agricultural market access and rules for regional trade agreements within the Doha Development Agenda of the WTO.

JÜRGEN RICHTERING, from Germany, is Head of the Market Access Intelligence Section in the Economic Research and Statistics Division of the WTO, with responsibilities for WTO's tariff and import databases, technical advice and statistical services to senior management and member countries on tariff matters, in particular assistance to acceding governments in their goods market access negotiations. In addition, he is in charge of the recently launched Integrated Trade Intelligence Portal, a new project which integrates the WTO information systems on non-tariff measures. Prior his work at the WTO, he worked in the Asian Development Bank (1991 to 1993) and in UNCTAD (1983 to 1991 and 1994 to 1996). Mr Richtering holds an MA in economics/econometrics from the University of Münster (Germany). He has co-authored various articles on tariff simulations, trade in services statistics and WTO notifications on non-tariff measures.

GORAN ŠĆEPANOVIĆ, from Montenegro, is the Deputy Minister of the Economy for Multilateral and Regional Trade Cooperation and Foreign Economic Relations. He was a member of the Montenegrin delegation for WTO accession negotiations, as well as Chief Negotiator for Free Trade Agreements with Ukraine and EFTA countries. Currently, he is the chief negotiator for the Protocol to the Agreement between the Government of the Federal Republic of Yugoslavia and the Government of Russia on Free Trade and Free Trade Agreements with Belarus and Kazakhstan. He is also the Chief of the Working Group 30 – Foreign Relations for EU accession negotiations of Montenegro. Before joining the Ministry of Economy, Mr Šĉepanović worked for the Customs Administration of Montenegro (1994 to 2008) and headed various departments. He graduated from the University of Montenegro (Economics).

MUSTAPHA SEKKATE, from Morocco, is an economic affairs officer in the Accessions Division of the WTO, where he works as Secretary of several accession working parties. Prior to this he was a statistical officer in the Market Access Intelligence Section in the Economic Research and Statistics Division of the WTO, responsible for providing technical support and advice on goods schedules to WTO members and acceding governments. In addition, he assists the Consolidated Tariff Schedules Unit in updating members' commitments to a more recent version of the Harmonised System. Prior to joining the WTO, he worked as a business developer in the private sector (2002 to 2004). Mr Sekkate holds an MSc in International Development from the École Supérieure de Gestion et de Commerce International (France).

ERIC NG SHING, from Mauritius, is a statistical officer in the Market Access Intelligence Section in the Economic Research and Statistics Division of the WTO, responsible for providing technical support to WTO acceding governments on goods schedules and assisting the consolidated tariff schedules unit in updating members' commitments to a more recent version of the Harmonised System. Prior to his work at the WTO, he worked as a consultant to the Statistical Office of the European Communities (1995 to 2003). Mr Ng Shing holds an MA in quantitative economics and statistics from the University of Toulouse (France).

ANDREY SLEPNEV, from Russia, is Minister for Trade (Member of the Board) of the Eurasian Economic Commission. He is responsible for trade regulations, protective and anti-dumping measures, and tariff and non-tariff regulations across the Customs Union of Russia, Belarus and Kazakhstan. Before joining the Commission, he was a Deputy Minister for the Economic Development of Russia (2009 to 2011), responsible for national economic policy development and normative legal regulation of external trade and coordinated activities of the Russian negotiating team on joining the WTO and the OECD. Mr Slepnev was a Deputy Minister of Agriculture (2007 to 2009) and a Director of the Department for National Priority Projects of the Presidential Experts Directorate, supervising the national priority project 'Agriculture Development' (2005 to 2007). Before joining national administration boards, Mr Slepnev cooperated with a number of national insurance companies. He graduated from the Lobachevski State University of Nizhniy Novgorod (mathematics) and the Moscow State University (law).

STEFFEN SMIDT, from Denmark, is Permanent Representative of Denmark to the United Nations Office and other international organisations in Geneva and Chairman of the Sub-Committee on Least-Developed Countries of the WTO. From 2006 to 2010, he was Ambassador, Under-Secretary for Global Challenges, Ministry of Foreign Affairs of Denmark, Senior Advisor in the Ministry for Climate and Energy of Denmark, Representative of the Ministry of Foreign Affairs of Denmark on Climate Change Issues, Ambassador of Denmark to the OECD and UNESCO. From 1990 to 2002, he served at the European Commission as Director-General, Head of the Task Force for Enlargement, Directorate-General for Development, Directorate-General for Administration and Personnel and Directorate-General for Fisheries. Mr Smidt holds an MA in Political Science from the University of Århus (Denmark). He is Adjunct Professor at the Copenhagen Business School.

SAADALDEEN ALI BIN TALIB, from Yemen, has been Minister of Industry and Trade since December 2011. From 2007 to 2011, he was a Member of the Supreme National Authority for Combatting Corruption in Yemen. From 2005 to 2007, he was Programme Manager at the National Democratic Institute in Yemen. From 1997 to 2003, he served as a Member of Parliament, a Member of the Development and Petroleum Committee in the Parliament of Yemen, and as a Member of the Permanent Committee of the General People's Congress. Previously, Mr

Talib was a consultant for the Sembawang Corporation, a Singapore-based marine engineering company, from 1991 to 1998. Mr Talib was also a resident surgeon from 1986 to 1988, and a medical intern from 1985 to 1986, at Ain Shams University Hospital (Egypt). Mr Talib holds a Master of Surgery and a Bachelor of Medicine and Surgery (Honours) from Ain Shams University Part One (Egypt).

GEORGE TEBAGANA, from Uganda, was a researcher on accessions in the Accessions Division of the WTO. He worked on the final draft working party report of Kazakhstan and was the Co-Secretary of the working parties for the accessions of Afghanistan, Ethiopia, and Sao Tomé and Principe in the WTO. Prior to working at the WTO, Mr Tebagana served in the Government of Uganda, including the Ministry of Foreign Affairs in the capacity of Foreign Service Officer – Legal, in the Department of Multilateral Organizations and Treaties and the National Social Security Fund as Benefits Administration Officer. He represented Uganda in various international trade negotiations for the Permanent Joint Commissions with the Republic of South Sudan and the Republic of Rwanda. Mr Tebagana is an admitted attorney in Uganda. He graduated with an LLM – International Trade and Investment Law in Africa from the University of Pretoria (South Africa). His LLM research was on legal and institutional frameworks for cross-border railway development in East Africa. He also possesses a postgraduate diploma from the Law Development Centre, Kampala (Uganda), as well as a Bachelor of Laws (LLB) from Makerere University Kampala (Uganda). He is currently conducting research on trade facilitation in Africa.

ANNA VARYANIK, from Russia, is a legal affairs officer in the WTO Accessions Division and works as Secretary to the accession process of Afghanistan, Azerbaijan, Belarus, Iran, Iraq, Ethiopia and Kazakhstan. Prior to joining the WTO, she was a key member of Russia's negotiating team on its accession to the WTO, represented Russia on a number of WTO committees and bodies. She served as Dispute Settlement Officer/ Legal Advisor of the Russian Delegation. She was posted as a diplomat (lawyer) of the Trade Policy Division of the Mission of Russia to the United Nations and other international organisations in Geneva (2008 to 2013) and a leading legal expert of the Ministry of Economy and Trade of Russia (2004 to 2008). Ms Varyanik holds a BA in law from the Moscow State Law Academy and LLM in international dispute settlement from the University of Geneva.

BUAVANH VILAVONG, from Lao PDR, is the Deputy Director-General of the Department of Import and Export (DIMEX), Ministry of Industry and Commerce, based in Vientiane. Previously, he worked for the Foreign Trade Policy Department for over ten years and formed part of a core team for WTO accession negotiation. He has operational experience in the area of trade negotiations, as well as coordinating internal reforms and technical assistance to support the accession to the WTO of Lao PDR. Mr Vilavong is an economist, holding a MA from the University of Melbourne (Australia). Mr Vilavong has co-authored a number of publications, including 'The Effects of Economic Reforms on Lao Output' (2002), and 'Rules of Origin in Services: The Case of Laos' (2011), in *Lao Trade Research Digest: Volume II.*

DAYONG YU, from China, is a senior statistical officer in the Market Access Intelligence Section of the WTO's Economic Research and Statistics Division. Previously, he was Counsellor of the Accessions Division of the WTO and worked as a secretary of the working parties to facilitate acceding governments in their WTO accession process. From 2004 to 2010, he worked at the Economic Research and Statistics Division, providing technical support on non-agricultural market access and agriculture negotiations in the Doha Round. Prior to joining the WTO, he worked for the Chinese government for ten years as a specialist in tariffs, taxation, and trade and investment policies. He participated in China's WTO accession negotiations and the Doha Round multilateral trade negotiations. Mr Yu holds a Master of Science Degree in Computer Science from Jilin University (China) and a Master's Degree in International Development Policy from Duke University (United States).

SVITLANA ZAITSEVA, from Ukraine, is the Head of the WTO Division at the Ministry of Economic Development and Trade of Ukraine. She was a member of Ukraine WTO accession delegation and has more than ten years' experience in trade policy and law having worked as an expert and programme manager on a number of international projects (with the World Bank, EU, CIDA, DFAD) in support of Ukraine's WTO accession and trade policy. In 2006, she was appointed Head of the National Enquiry Point and Notification Authority of Ukraine, responsible for establishing and operationalising this government agency in Ukraine. From 2007 to 2008, she was a member of the Ukrainian negotiating team for a deep and comprehensive free trade agreement with the EU and FTA with EFTA. Currently, she is a member of the delegation of

Ukraine for trade negotiations with the CIS and other countries. From 2008 to 2011, Mrs Zaitseva worked at the Permanent Mission of Ukraine in Geneva, representing Ukraine at the WTO. She graduated from the University of Economics and Law, Kiev.

RUTA ZARNAUSKAITE, from Lithuania, is a policy officer and trade negotiator at the Directorate-General for Trade of the European Commission. From 2008 to 2011, she was the EU coordinator and negotiator in the process of the WTO accession of Russia. Her current function concerns the EU's trade policy strategy. She holds an LLM.

# INDEX